Developmental sport and
exercise psychology

Developmental Sport and Exercise Psychology: A Lifespan Perspective

DEVELOPMENTAL SPORT AND EXERCISE PSYCHOLOGY: A LIFESPAN PERSPECTIVE

Maureen R. Weiss, PhD

University of Virginia

Fitness Information Technology, Inc.
P.O. Box 4425 • Morgantown, WV 26504-4425

Library of Congress Card Catalog Number: 2003108981

ISBN: 1-885693-36-2

Copyeditor: Sandra Woods
Cover Design: 40 West Studios
Managing Editor: Geoff Fuller
Production Editor: Jamie Pein
Proofreader: Maria E. denBoer
Indexer: Maria E. denBoer
Printed by Data Reproductions

10   9   8   7   6   5   4   3   2   1

Fitness Information Technology, Inc.
P.O. Box 4425, University Avenue
Morgantown, WV 26504 USA
800.477.4348
304.599.3483 phone
304.599.3482 fax
Email: fit@fitinfotech.com
Website: www.fitinfotech.com

For…

Pookie, my honorary co-author and companion of 18 years…

My closest friends…

Who have always shown confidence in my abilities
and emotional support for my dreams

Contents

Part IV Lifespan Topics

Foreword

Developmental Sport and Exercise Psychology: A Lifespan Perspective provides an excellent and much needed resource for examining psychological principles in sport and exercise contexts from a lifespan developmental perspective. From the introductory chapter through the final chapter, it is evident that there is a paucity of literature examining psychological factors in sport and exercise psychology from a developmental perspective. However, the authors have attempted to fill a much needed gap by examining the current sport and exercise psychology literature, reviewing mainstream theories from psychology, and elaborating on how cognitive, physical, social and other developmental factors may influence behaviors in physical activity settings. Within our field the term *developmental* has often been used to refer only to changes across childhood. However, the present volume encourages researchers in the field to take a lifespan developmental approach that emphasizes changes across the entire spectrum of human behavior from infancy to advanced adulthood.

The chapters take on a similar mission in that the authors discuss relevant theories, review empirical research, suggest practical applications stemming from existing research, and recommend future directions for empirical inquiry by emphasizing a developmental theoretical approach. Because of the lack of developmentally oriented research in many of the areas, the sections on practical applications and recommendations for future research especially provide interesting and innovative ideas for the field.

The introductory chapters of the book clearly provide a background to highlight the importance of taking a lifespan developmental approach and review relevant theories that may be helpful in achieving this aim. A primary message is that behavior must be examined over time and that appropriate ages must be selected when research is conducted. The chapter on methodological issues critically examines the field and suggests that although cross-sectional studies that compare behavior amongst individuals across different ages are informative, such studies may be misleading in providing accurate information regarding developmental change. This chapter provides a strong case for performing longitudinal studies within the field of sport and exercise psychology. Unfortunately, to date, our field has fallen behind mainstream psychology in this vein; if we are to begin to understand behavior from a true developmental perspective, future research will definitely need to adopt such approaches.

The second section of the book examines developmental issues in youth and adolescence. This section covers familiar topics such as self-perceptions and motivation. However, unlike chapters on similar topics in other texts, the authors illuminate this knowledge base from a completely developmental perspective that is probably less familiar to readers. Parental influence on children in physical activity, although not extensively studied, has always been of concern, and a number of age-related issues and implications are addressed. This section of the book also highlights the lack of developmental theoretical approaches for some topics such as emotional responses and self-regulation skills. Self-regulation skills such as how individuals learn to self-monitor, manage emotions, and focus on improvement have received pointed attention in the educational psychology literature. Surprisingly, these skills, which are critical for enhancing a variety of behaviors including performance in sport and exercise settings, have barely been addressed in our field from a developmental perspective, and this chapter provides some meaningful avenues for future research.

The chapters included in the section on young, middle, and older adulthood implore researchers to adequately define terms such as *self-perceptions* and *emotions*, review and modify psychological theories for application to physical activity settings, and critically analyze psychological research on physical activity behaviors across adulthood. The authors in this section have not had volumes of developmentally based research upon which to draw their conclusions, but nonetheless provide provocative thoughts for future research.

The final section of the book covers topics that span childhood through adulthood on important topics including expertise, transitions, moral development, diversity, disabilities, and injury. Some of these topics appear in other sport and exercise psychology textbooks, but the difference here is the emphasis on a developmental lifespan approach. For example, the chapter on psychology of injury explores antecedents and outcomes of injury that may differ markedly in childhood, adolescence, and young, middle, and older adulthood. Similarly, the topic of expertise is a familiar one in the motor behavior literature but is often ignored in sport psychology texts. This topic is crucial to understanding age-related differences in cognitive development and how they translate to decision making and performance in sport. Readers will be enlightened on all the topics in this section that emphasize such developmental perspectives.

The text is designed for upper division undergraduate and graduate students. Although not entirely necessary to have a background in sport and exercise psychology, an introductory course would better prepare a student to appreciate the importance of a developmental approach. An examination of curricular offerings at many institutions, including those of the authors, indicates that many programs offer classes in motor development, youth sport, or even aging. However, very few programs offer lifespan developmental sport and exercise psychology classes that focus on cognitive, physical, emotional, and social developmental factors. It is hoped that this text will inspire more instructors, including the present authors, to incorporate such offerings in their curricula.

Penny McCullagh
California State University, Hayward

Preface

Twenty-five years ago I began my doctoral studies at Michigan State University with the expressed intent of integrating developmental psychology and kinesiology in an effort to enhance my understanding of children involved in competitive sport programs. For five years as an undergraduate and master's student I had coached youth ages 7 to 17 years in Newport Beach, California, and I was intrigued and fascinated with what I observed and experienced. There, on the volleyball court and softball field, the principles of developmental psychology were illuminated. Sport was a unique social context in which physical, social, and psychological growth and development had the potential to flourish. Children learned and improved specific sport skills and strategies; they learned to cooperate with teammates to maximize the benefits of competition; and they disagreed with and got mad at each other—from which they learned to resolve conflicts and sustain relationships. They gained confidence and improved in self-esteem as their skills matured and important adults and close peers recognized their efforts. As a result of positive experiences with caring and competent parents and coaches, these young participants sustained a "love of the game" and the joy of physical movement.

I was fortunate that I was enthusiastically encouraged to follow my vision at Michigan State. The Institute for the Study of Youth Sports had just been initiated, and as a graduate assistant I had the opportunity to become fully involved in conducting research, presenting at coach workshops, and writing educational materials. Dan Gould was an up-and-coming first-year professor and my mentor; he was always a source of inspiration, respect, and social support in every way possible. There is no doubt that my work ethic was chiseled from Dan's example and that it has allowed me to attain many academic goals. Vern Seefeldt, then the Director of the Youth Sports Institute and an expert in motor development, was generous in sharing his wisdom and challenging me to critically analyze the developmental literature. My dissertation integrated developmental and sport psychology to examine age-related differences in children's observational learning of motor skills. Surprisingly to me, it was one of the few developmentally theoretical studies in sport psychology at the time. I remember thinking that taking a developmental theoretical approach made so much sense, especially with models of developmental and educational psychology research there to guide us.

I landed another incredibly fortuitous break after graduation by securing a professorship at the University of Oregon. I was asked to direct the Children's Summer Sports Program, a program that I modified to be a developmentally appropriate sport setting for youth ages 5 to 13 years. Each summer for 15 years, I directed a staff of 30 instructors and 12 junior counselors to effectively teach motor, social, and psychological developmental principles to 300 youth participants. Developmental principles served as the cornerstone of this program. Instructors were recruited, selected, trained, and evaluated based on their "philosophy" of child development, one that put the child first and outcomes last. At the forefront of this program was the social and psychological well-being of each child, with sport participation merely the vehicle by which positive beliefs, values, and behaviors could be fostered. I consider my work with this program to be among the most significant achievements of my career. It was a long-term investment and commitment that necessitated the integration of research, teaching, and practice; and it reflected lessons I learned from my youth sport coaching experiences, my invaluable opportunities as a graduate student, and the developmental psychological literature that I have emphasized in all my writings.

Thus, this book represents a culmination of 25 years of involvement—as a coach, teacher, researcher, and administrator of youth sports. It also characterizes a long-held dream of editing a book with a developmental slant toward sport participation that may inspire graduate students and professionals to contribute to the knowledge base in developmental sport and exercise psychology. This knowledge base has grown considerably since 25 years ago but is also sorely in need of a greater quantity and quality of empirical study.

I believe it is important to remember where you came from and why you were motivated to accomplish what you set out to do in the first place. Since my college days as a youth sport coach and student of developmental psychology and kinesiology, it has been my belief that a developmental perspective is one of the most appropriate ways to understand and explain emotions, thoughts, and behaviors of youth participants in sport and physical activity contexts. This belief is stronger than ever based on the research to date in both mainstream developmental and sport psychology. Moreover, the traditional notion of developmental sport psychology characterizing infancy through adolescence has made way for a lifespan definition, one that considers continuity and change from infancy through older adulthood. This does not mean that researchers must study a topic across the entire lifespan; most developmental researchers specialize in a particular population such as children, adolescents, or middle-aged adults, but this perspective does acknowledge the processes and mechanisms of change across the entire lifespan. The chapters in this book reflect this contemporary outlook of a lifespan developmental approach.

The first section, Fundamental Concepts, consists of three chapters that overview concepts, issues, and controversies in developmental sport psychology. Topics include defining a developmental perspective, an historical review of youth sport research, directions toward a lifespan perspective, broad and specific developmental theories, a review of sport psychology research within developmental theoretical approaches, and methodological and statistical considerations when adopting a developmental approach to research questions. Key take-home messages from these chapters are that (a) we know considerably more about youth than we do about middle-aged and older adults, (b) more research is descriptive than is grounded in developmental theoretical frameworks, and (c) more longitudinal research is needed to validate what we infer from cross-sectional studies.

The second section, Youth and Adolescence, and third section, Young, Middle, and Older Adulthood, contain chapters on topics that are mirror images of one another. Companion chapters are found for self-perceptions, social influence, emotional responses, motivational processes, and self-regulation skills. Although the same topic is covered in each section, it is striking how different the knowledge base is for varying developmental time periods. In some cases, a fair amount of research has been conducted to inform us of age-related differences and similarities; in other cases minimal research has taken a developmental perspective although theory and research in educational and developmental psychology exists to guide such inquiry. Each chapter is organized to include (a) relevant theory, (b) a synthesis of empirical research, (c) practical applications that emanate from theory and research, (d) future research directions, and (e) take-home messages.

The fourth and final section, Lifespan Topics, includes areas in which authors were challenged to discuss relevant content and issues that cut across childhood, adolescence, and adulthood. Similar to the previous sections, some of these topics have a strong developmental knowledge base (e.g., development of expertise) whereas other equally important topical areas are screaming out for age-related investigations (e.g., psychology of injury, gender and cultural diversity). Still other chapters include psychosocial factors and individuals with disabilities, moral development, and transitions in and out of sport. All authors in this section were also challenged to discuss theory, research, application, and future research directions. The chapters in this section round out the various ways in which sport and physical activity have the potential to make an impact on participants' experiences and lives, and they also represent some of the topics that have often been neglected in other texts related to sport and exercise psychology.

I am indebted to the authors who accepted my invitation to contribute to this unique book. It wasn't an easy task—authors were challenged to analyze, synthesize, and criticize their areas of expertise from a developmental slant, not just review the literature as might be expected for a general text. In some cases (e.g., self regulation skills in adulthood), this posed an interesting problem—authors discovered that little developmentally oriented research existed and they were required to determine which theories might be appropriate, provide a rationale for their choice of theories, and delineate important questions to be pursued. In other cases (e.g., self-perceptions in youth), the developmental research was ample and required authors to "package" the existing data in a way that allowed for a logical synthesis and consolidation of the information. Each author did a valiant job and I am honored that so many of my close colleagues and friends joined me in this exciting yet challenging adventure. I also want to sincerely acknowledge Andy Ostrow, president of FIT, not only for his insights and vision pertaining to the book, but also for his emotional support, friendship, and flexibility. Geoff Fuller as the developmental editor for the book contributed essential organizational and technical guidance, for which I am very grateful.

I am thrilled with the realization of this anthology, but will be even more excited if in 10-20 years the chapters have had an impact in inspiring others to expand the present knowledge base in developmental sport and exercise psychology. No doubt a developmental theoretical perspective to conducting research in sport psychology will require thoughtfulness, ingenuity, and patience, but I believe that the payoff is enormous in terms of understanding and explaining sport-related thoughts, feelings, and behaviors in children through older adults. The road map to designing and implementing developmentally oriented research lies within—who among you will be inspired to navigate its course?

Maureen R. Weiss
University of Virginia

PART I
FUNDAMENTAL
CONCEPTS

CHAPTER ONE

Developmental Sport and Exercise Psychology: Research Status on Youth and Directions Toward a Lifespan Perspective

Maureen R. Weiss • Thomas D. Raedeke

Understanding *development,* whether motor, social, cognitive, or emotional, has been a central focus of inquiry in psychology for hundreds of years. How do thought processes and physical abilities change as we get older? To what extent do biological versus social environmental factors affect these changes? How are changes in the way we perceive our world and our ability to master physical tasks associated with changes in the way we feel, interact with others, and behave in achievement contexts?

Many of you, like us, have probably worked with individuals of varying ages in sport and exercise settings. We observe differences between younger and older children in how they define successful performance or determine whether they are competent in a particular activity. Similarly, it is easy to discern differences between older children and adolescents in terms of relative influence by parents and peers, as well as the importance placed on being successful in certain achievement domains. Within the adolescent years themselves we note considerable variability on a host of social, emotional, and behavioral variables. The transition from adolescence to adulthood brings with it a number of cognitive, affective, and behavioral changes related to self-imposed and societal expectations. Progression from young adulthood to middle and older adulthood prompts still different developmental issues related to physical activity, health, and quality of life. Thus, a developmental perspective necessarily means one that considers variations in and interrelationships among thoughts, emotions, and behaviors from infancy through older adulthood.

In this chapter we address what it means to take a developmental perspective in sport and exercise psychology research. We will argue that a developmental perspective is crucial for understanding and explaining varying perceptions, emotions, social factors, and achievement behaviors related to physical activity involvement across the lifespan. Despite its potential to help us better understand human behavior in physical activity contexts, most of our research has not been based on a developmental perspective. This is even more surprising given the existence of many developmentally oriented theories that could be used to develop research questions, design studies, and select age groups based on underlying developmental criteria. Thus, our overall intent is to demystify the notion of a developmental perspective and advocate its wider use in future research. Understanding age-related changes in perceptions, physical competencies, emotions, social influences, and achievement behaviors is critical in terms of developing theory, enhancing the research knowledge base, and devising applied programs to promote positive physical activity experiences for youth through older adults.

A developmental perspective considers variations in thoughts, emotions, and behaviors from infancy through older adulthood.

In light of these introductory remarks we have identified four main purposes of our chapter. First, we define what it means to adopt a developmental perspective, describe research examples in the sport psychology literature, and characterize the shift from a traditional to a lifespan developmental psychology. Second, we devote attention to youth sport research, given its prevalence in the literature, by first taking a historical perspective and then by conducting a content analysis of the last 20 years of research. Third, we address salient conceptual issues to consider in conducting future developmental research in sport and exercise psychology. Finally, we explicitly address the need to move toward a lifespan developmental perspective for guiding empirical inquiry in sport and exercise psychology.

WHAT IS A DEVELOPMENTAL PERSPECTIVE?

According to Baltes, Reese, and Nesselroade (1988), a developmental theoretical orientation seeks to describe and explain psychosocial and behavioral changes within individuals across the lifespan (i.e., intraindividual change), as well as differences and similarities in the nature of these changes among individuals (i.e., interindividual differences). The operating term in developmental theory is *change over time* such as changes in cognitive, social, and physical processes (Miller, 1989). According to Miller, the focus on change over time presents developmental theorists with three interrelated tasks: (a) to *describe changes in behavior* or psychological processes, (b) to describe changes in the *relationship among behaviors* or psychological processes, and (c) to *explain* the course of development (i.e., mechanisms or determinants of change). Baltes et al. (1988) add a fourth task required of developmental theorists: (d) to *modify* change in order to optimize development. Being able to describe and explain the course of development in a particular construct provides theorists with information about applying this knowledge to strategies or interventions that invoke positive change.

To illuminate these concepts in the physical domain, we can use Yando, Seitz, and Zigler's (1978) developmental theory of observational learning of motor and social skills as an example. According to Yando et al., attention, memory, physical capabilities, and motivational orientation are the critical factors influencing children's quantity and quality of learning through demonstration. Yando et al. *describe*, for example, maturation in attentional focus as a process moving from overexclusion to overinclusion to selective attention of modeled actions. These changes in attentional focus are intricately *related to* children's ability to remember salient aspects of the demonstration and, subsequently, the extent to which they accurately reproduce the skill. Yando et al. *explain* these changes over time in attention and their relation to memory and behavior in terms of both biological influences (i.e., cognitive and physical maturity) and social-environmental influences (i.e., social interaction and experience). Knowing that young children do not engage in selective attention or rehearsal strategies spontaneously, we can *modify* skill instruction by providing verbal labels for task components and using "show-and-tell" models to optimize children's ability to attend to, remember, and produce the modeled actions.

Developmental change can be described in both *quantitative* (i.e., amount) and *qualitative* (i.e., structural) terms (Miller, 1989). In the same example above, younger children (under age 8) have shorter attention spans and can remember fewer bits of information than do older children (age 8 or older) after observing a model demonstrate a skill. Such quantitative differences translate to faster learning and better performance on the part of older children. However, these differences also reflect variations in the way children structure, organize, and process stimuli in their environment—that is, qualitative differences in attention, memory, and motor performance. Younger children's inability to selectively attend to and spontaneously rehearse (verbally or visually) the salient aspects of a demonstration may lead to incorrect or partially correct performance. By contrast, older children are more likely to attend selectively to features of the modeled action, engage in coding and labeling memory strategies, and consequently produce superior performance coordination and technique.

It is widely believed that developmental change is a result of both nature and nurture contributions (Miller, 1989), that is, the *interaction between individual differences* (traits, cognitions, personality) *and social-environmental factors* (adult and peer influences, culture, learning experiences). The numerous theories that have been used to study children through older adults in various contexts, including physical activity, differ in their emphasis on the role of individual differences and environmental factors. Some theories emphasize cognitions and perceptions more prominently than social factors (e.g., attribution theory), whereas others highlight the social environment as key to developmental change (e.g., social learning theory). Most theories, however, acknowledge the dynamic and interactive nature of both cognitive and social processes in describing and explaining change over time in psychological and behavioral constructs (e.g., social cognitive theories of motivation, self-perception theories).

Advocating for a developmental perspective for studying children and youth in sport, Weiss and Bredemeier (1983) emphasized employing theories, designs, and methodologies that capture age-related differences in cognitions, perceptions, and behaviors in physical activity contexts. Weiss and Bredemeier suggested three means by which developmental studies could be designed: (a) select ages of participants based on specific developmental criteria (cognitive, physical, social), (b) compare age groups at key periods of development (cognitive, physical, social), and (c) follow individuals longitudinally on constructs of interest. Subsequent researchers investigated theoretical questions of age-related differences in variables of interest using these three means of designing developmental studies. In the following paragraphs we provide brief examples of studies that used each of these three means of designing developmental studies in sport psychology.

> To incorporate a developmental perspective into studies, you must employ theories, designs, and methodologies that capture age-related differences in cognitions, perceptions, and behaviors in physical activity contexts.

To illustrate the first method (i.e., select ages of participants based on specific developmental criteria), A. L. Smith (1999) designed a study to examine the influence of peer relationships on physical activity behavior among 12- to 15-year-old adolescents. This age group was deliberately chosen because one's peer group and close friends are salient sources of self-perceptions, affect, and behaviors during adolescence and because physical activity levels have been shown to decline across the adolescent years. Based on Harter's (1978, 1987) competence motivation and global self-worth theories, a model was proposed wherein peer influence (close friendship, peer acceptance) predicted physical activity behavior through the mediating effects of physical self-worth and affect. Results revealed a good fit of the model to the data for both males and females, suggesting that peer acceptance and friendship explained variations in physical self-worth, affect, and physical activity levels in middle-school-aged adolescents. Using sound developmental theory and methodology, this study provides us with information on key antecedents of physical activity motivation in an age group susceptible to declining activity levels.

The second means of examining developmental differences (i.e., compare age groups at key periods of development) is illustrated in a study by Amorose and Weiss (1998) on how various types of coach feedback serve as cues of high or low ability among children. Youths 6-8 and 12-14 years of age were selected based on Nicholls' (1989) work that suggests children falling into these age groups vary in conceptions of ability and effort. Younger children (11 years and below) view ability and effort as undifferentiated or partially differentiated (i.e., ability and effort are positively related—one is capable if one tries hard), whereas older children (above 11) have a differentiated conception of effort and ability (i.e., ability and effort are negatively related—one is more capable if one exerts less effort to succeed than others). Amorose and Weiss predicted that younger children would interpret coach praise for successful performance (i.e., hitting the baseball/softball) as an indicator of high ability and criticism following unsuccessful performance (i.e., not making contact with the baseball/softball) as an indicator of low ability. Just the opposite was predicted for the older group. Contrary to hypotheses, results revealed that both older and younger children viewed praise following success as an indicator of high ability and criticism following poor performance as a cue of low ability. However, open-ended questions revealed that older children relied more on evaluating form or technique and less on the coach's feedback to determine ability levels in comparison to the younger children. Thus it is conceivable that older youths' greater experience in sport afforded them alternative means of determining ability. Again, these results provide insight into age-related differences based on the study's grounding in developmental theory, design, and methodology.

One of the few developmentally based studies using a longitudinal design is seen in Duncan and Duncan's (1991) investigation of age-related changes in level of perceived physical competence. According to Harter's (1978) competence motivation theory, children's perceived academic competence declines over the school-age years as a result of both cognitive maturity and social-environmental influences. Duncan and Duncan were interested in knowing if declining self-perceptions extended to perceptions of physical competence. Moreover, if changes emerged were they correlated with physical maturity and chronological age? Duncan and Duncan assessed the same boys on perceptions of physical competence across grades 6, 8, and 9 (ages 11-13, 13-15, and 13-16 years, respectively). Using latent growth modeling, a statistical technique especially conducive to examining developmental differences (see Schutz & Park, 2003), results revealed that perceived physical competence increased over the three time periods and that physical maturation, but not chronological age, was associated with these changes in physical self-perceptions. The longitudinal design employed in this study provides important information on age-related differences in perceived competence based on individual differences in the rate of change on perceived competence and physical maturation.

Though developmental psychology used to mean the time period from birth through adolescence, the contemporary definition considers change from infancy through older adulthood.

The studies just described all focused upon youth populations. The phrase "developmental psychology" has *traditionally* referred to the time periods of infancy through adolescence, and this has been reflected in many developmental psychology journals and textbooks. However, development does not end at adolescence or at young or middle adulthood for that matter. The contemporary view of developmental psychology is a *lifespan* perspective, one that considers continuity and change from infancy through older adulthood (see Baltes, Lindenberger, & Staudinger, 1998). This does not mean that researchers must necessarily study a topic across the entire lifespan; indeed most developmental researchers specialize in smaller segments of the lifespan such as children, adolescents, middle age adults, or older adults (Baltes et al., 1988). This perspective does, however, acknowledge the interrelatedness of processes and mechanisms of change across the entire lifespan. In line with a lifespan developmental psychology, Chodzko-Zajko (1994) provided recommendations and examples of research designs and methodologies using middle and older adult populations in exercise contexts. He also highlighted the benefits and pitfalls of cross-sectional and longitudinal research designs and how decisions pertaining to participant selection criteria and inclusion of variables are critically related to the outcome and interpretation of research. In short, researchers interested in younger *and* older populations emphasize the need to take a developmental perspective in designing, implementing, and interpreting research.

In summary, we defined what a developmental perspective means and what its essential components are—change that can be described in quantitative and qualitative terms and explained by the interaction between individual differences and social-environmental factors. Second, we specified ways in which developmental research can be designed and implemented, and provided examples of studies in sport psychology that illustrate a developmental approach. Third, we advocated that developmental sport and exercise psychology should really be lifespan in nature. Despite the need for a lifespan developmental approach, few developmental studies on physical activity participation in adulthood exist and few developmental studies on physical activity behavior other than sport for any age group have been conducted.

Because most of our developmental research is in the youth sport area, in the following two sections we analyze and reflect upon the status of this particular knowledge base. Specifically we (a) examine youth sport research from a historical perspective and (b) describe the status (i.e., topics studied, developmental approach) of youth sport research through a content analysis of studies from 1982 to 1998.

YOUTH SPORT RESEARCH: A HISTORICAL PERSPECTIVE

An historical perspective on any research topic is important so that scholars understand the current knowledge base or "where we are now" in relation to past research or "where we have been." In developmental psychology terms, "knowing the past allows us to understand the present and to predict the future" (Baltes et al., 1988, p. 5). We start this section with an eye toward reviewing youth sport research nearly 50 years ago and taking us up to the status of research about 20 years ago.

The early research in youth sports was primarily descriptive. Skubic (1955, 1956) conducted two of the earliest systematic studies in the 1950s.[1] Both of her studies revolved around the pro's and con's of agency-sponsored organized competitive sport for boys. The first study (Skubic, 1955) was designed to answer the question "Is organized competitive youth sport too stressful?" She compared galvanic skin responses (as a measure of physiological arousal) in 9- to 15-year-old boys before and after a competitive baseball game versus their responses before and after a softball competition during physical education classes. No differences in emotional responses emerged prior to the baseball game versus the physical education class; postgame responses showed greater emotional arousal for 10-, 11-, and 13-year-olds for the physical education competition. She also compared emotional responses in baseball players prior to different levels of game importance (e.g., physical education, league, and championship games). Findings showed minimal differences in emotional responses based on level of game importance. Thus, her study contributed to advocates' position that youth sport does not place undue stress on young participants; indeed, she found that organized sport is no more stressful than participation in physical education activities.

Skubic's (1956) second study was also designed to determine whether organized competitive baseball was positive or detrimental as a socialization activity for boys aged 9 to 15 years.

She assessed players' and parents' attitudes toward organized competitive baseball experiences through the use of questionnaires. Nearly all the parents (99%) believed that organized baseball was beneficial to their sons' development, with the most frequent reasons being that it improves sportsmanship, improves cooperation, and keeps boys from being bored. The players rated developing friendships, having fun, keeping out of mischief, learning sportsmanship, and improving skills as major reasons for liking organized baseball. Importantly, this second study also reinforced the stance that the perceived benefits of playing organized baseball outweigh the potential harmful effects of playing. Based on the results of her research, suggestions for improving players' experiences included giving all players a chance to participate in games, improving effectiveness of coaches and officials, and reducing pressure from parents.

As the controversy persisted on the relative merits of organized competitive sport for youth (including girls), the 1970s marked a period in which a flurry of research activity on topics similar to those studied by Skubic (1955, 1956) emerged. Topics such as competitive stress (e.g., Scanlan & Passer, 1978, 1979), reasons for participation and dropout (e.g., Alderman & Wood, 1976; Orlick, 1973, 1974), and coaching behaviors (e.g., R. E. Smith, Smoll, & Curtis, 1979; Smoll, Smith, Curtis, & Hunt, 1978) were especially frequent. Other topics of inquiry such as sportsmanship, aggression, motivation, self-concept, and socialization were similarly driven by the interest shown in these potential sport participation effects by youth sport agencies, educators, and parents.

In response to the needs of school- and agency-sponsored sports for children and adolescents, the Youth Sports Institute at Michigan State was formally launched in 1977. The institute served as a think tank for youth sport research, coach education, and the translation of theory and research to practice. A three-phase longitudinal report of youth sport programs in Michigan was subsequently published (State of Michigan, 1976, 1978a, 1978b). This report primarily described the nature of youth participation such as frequency by age, gender, sport type, and race/ethnicity. Also reported were children's and parents' attitudes toward a number of issues such as coaches, agency policies, and sportsmanship. These early studies provided the impetus for numerous studies of participation motivation and attrition in the 1980s (see reviews of these studies by Weiss & Ferrer-Caja, 2002, and Weiss & Petlichkoff, 1989). One of the first research projects at the Youth Sports Institute was determining why children participated in swimming and why they dropped out (Gould, Feltz, Horn, & Weiss, 1982; Gould, Feltz, & Weiss, 1985). Participants cited most of the same reasons Skubic (1956) found 25 years earlier—fun, friends, and skill improvement. Lack of fun and few opportunities to improve skills were cited as reasons for attrition.

Around the same time that youth sport was rapidly becoming popular as a research topic, several theoretical papers were published that we now consider classics (Bandura, 1977; Deci, 1975; Harter, 1978; Nicholls, 1978). In graduate sport psychology courses during the late 1970s and early 1980s, professors covered all the sport psychology studies conducted to date, as well as these primary theoretical sources and other important papers in social and developmental psychology. Specifically, key theoretical papers were evaluated for their suitability to the physical domain and, if suitable, important research questions were identified that emanated from theoretical principles. Thus self-efficacy, cognitive evaluation, competence motivation, and achievement goal theories, among others, were embraced as frameworks for guiding empirical inquiry. Studies based on these and other theories appeared more frequently in the literature during the mid- to late 1980s.

In 1982 Gould published one of the first review papers on youth sport research in the *Journal of Sport Psychology*, a journal that was in its infancy at the time. He synthesized the literature to date and offered ideas for future research. One of Gould's conclusions was that the most influential research studies conducted to date possessed three common characteristics. Unfortunately only a few studies possessed one or more of these qualities. First, key studies were designed to develop or test theory, thereby extending previous descriptive studies to ones emphasizing explanation and prediction. Second, these studies asked not only theoretically based questions but also ones that were socially relevant for schools and non-school agencies. By identifying key underlying principles that could guide youth sport practices and policies, such studies reinforced Lewin's (1951) claim that there is nothing so practical as a good theory. Third, Gould suggested that those studies making the most impact were ones that were part of a series of interrelated investigations rather than isolated studies. That is, scholars conducting a programmatic line of research were able to fill in the gaps in knowledge by building upon each previous study. According to Gould's analysis, only two programmatic lines of inquiry could be identified in the 1970s. These were the work of Scanlan and Passer (1978, 1979; Passer & Scanlan, 1980) on competitive anxiety and stress, and the coaching effectiveness studies of R. E. Smith, Smoll, and colleagues (R. E. Smith et al., 1979; R. E. Smith, Smoll, & Hunt, 1977; Smoll et al., 1978).

As a result of his analysis Gould (1982) challenged youth sport researchers to consider a number of theoretical and methodological issues in future investigations. First, he implored not only that researchers test psychological theories in youth sport settings, but also that they develop sport-specific models that might explain the intricacies of individual differences and social-environmental factors in the physical domain. Second, he suggested that evaluation research methods be employed to validate the effectiveness of interventions such as coaching education programs or psychological skills training. Third, Gould encouraged the use of non-traditional analytical strategies that may complement traditional quantitative methods or may be more appropriate depending on the research question (e.g., qualitative methods). Finally, he suggested that children's sport-related experiences be considered from a multidisciplinary perspective when possible, including a host of psychological, biological, sociological, and physical factors. In sum, Gould's review and critique of youth sport research provided numerous insights for guiding future inquiry.

Weiss and Bredemeier (1983) wrote a companion piece to Gould's (1982) paper in which they focused on the need to adopt a developmental theoretical perspective for understanding children's thoughts, emotions, and behaviors in sport settings. Two aspects of the youth sport literature influenced their viewpoint at that time: (a) the predominance of atheoretical studies and (b) the application of theories that were supported primarily with adult participants (e.g., attribution theory). Thus, their position was that psychosocial phenomena in youth sport are best understood by using appropriate theoretical frameworks, most notably those that employ a developmental perspective. Weiss and Bredemeier underscored several theoretical orientations that consider developmental factors in describing and explaining children's behavior in achievement domains and thus were conducive to studying youth in physical activity contexts. These theories included Yando et al.'s (1978) developmental theory of modeling, Harter's (1978, 1981) competence motivation theory, and moral development theories (e.g., Haan, 1977; Kohlberg, 1969). In a subsequent paper Duda (1987) elaborated upon Nicholls' (1978, 1984) achievement goal perspective as a developmentally appropriate approach for understanding children's conceptions of ability and effort and, consequently, motivation in sport.

Weiss and Bredemeier (1983) conducted a content analysis of the youth sport literature from 1970 to 1981 to determine the extent to which a developmental theoretical perspective was applied (see Table 1). Of 143 empirical studies and reviews, only 15 or about 10% employed a developmental approach by selecting or comparing age groups based on underlying cognitive or physical criteria (no longitudinal studies were located). The major topics studied during this period were motivation, attributions, self-perceptions, socialization, coaching behaviors, and competitive anxiety. These topical areas were all conducive to a developmental orientation but were not usually investigated as such. In an effort to inspire more developmental research Weiss and Bredemeier specified guidelines for future inquiry on psychosocial phenomena in youth physical activity contexts. These included (a) determining the validity of applying psychological theories to study children in sport, (b) formulating hypotheses based on theoretically derived developmental criteria, and (c) designing a series of interrelated investigations to identify psychological differences among age groups and age changes in psychological constructs over time. Encouraging a developmental theoretical framework for studying youth sport issues thus integrated several aspects of Gould's (1982) earlier recommendations (e.g., theory-driven studies, programmatic line of research).

In the years following Gould's (1982) and Weiss and Bredemeier's (1983) articles, numerous studies were conducted and published in the youth sport area. Many of these studies were theory based, reflected a series of interrelated investigations, and used an array of methodologies to appropriately answer research questions. Moreover, a greater percentage of studies on youth adopted a developmental theoretical perspective to understand age-related differences on psychological constructs related to sport and physical activity participation. These studies are reviewed in the next section.

TABLE 1
Content Analysis of Youth Sport Psychology Research, 1970-1981
(Adapted from Weiss & Bredemeier, 1983. Permission granted by Human Kinetics.)

Topical area	# Empirical studies	# Review papers	# Developmental	Reference[a]
Aggression	5	3	0	
Anxiety	10	1	0	
Attitudes	7	0	1	Smoll & Schutz (1980)
Attributions	11	4	3	Bird & Williams (1980)
Coaching/teaching behaviors	10	2	0	
Cognitive strategies	3	0	1	Goebel & Harris (1980)
Competition	7	5	3	Scanlan (1982)
Expectations	7	0	0	
Modeling	7	1	1	Weiss (1981)[b]
Moral development	2	3	3	Jantz (1975)
Motivation	11	8	3	Thomas & Tennant (1978)
Self-concept/ self-confidence	17	0	0	
Social comparison	7	0	0	
Socialization	10	2	0	
Totals	114	29	15	

[a] A citation adopting a developmental approach is listed. The full citation and others appear in Weiss and Bredemeier (1983).

[b] Weiss' (1981) dissertation was subsequently published in 1983, and this is the date listed in Table 1 in Weiss and Bredemeier (1983).

A Content Analysis of Youth Sport Research From 1982 to 1998

Given the recommendations by Gould (1982) and Weiss and Bredemeier (1983) for conducting research on children and youth in sport, how have we fared over the last two decades? To answer this question, we replicated the 1970-1981 content analysis conducted by Weiss and Bredemeier. Specifically we documented the number, topic, and developmental status of youth sport psychology studies, review articles, and book chapters published between 1982 and 1998. English language resources were located using a variety of databases including PsychLit, SportDiscus, ERIC, and Medline, as well as indexes of sport-related and developmental and social psychology journals. Articles were coded by topical area and whether they employed a developmental perspective as defined by the three methodologies articulated earlier (e.g., age groups selected or compared based on underlying cognitive criteria, longitudinal design). The results of the content analysis are depicted in Table 2.

A total of 646 papers (560 empirical studies and review articles and 86 book chapters) were uncovered during the 17-year period spanning 1982-1998. This quantity is nearly five times the number of papers reported by Weiss and Bredemeier (1983) during the 12-year period of 1970 to 1981. The most frequently studied topics were motivation (participation/attrition, goal orientations, competence motivation, intrinsic motivation), self-perceptions (self-esteem, perceived competence, self-efficacy), social influences (coaches, parents), socialization (gender roles, delinquency), anxiety/stress, cognitive strategies/psychological skills, and moral development. The topic of psychological skills was notable by its absence in Weiss and Bredemeier's review, and it included stress management training, self-talk, imagery, and self-regulation skills.

In addition to coding the manuscripts by topic and developmental status we also compared the general characteristics of these studies to some of the suggestions offered by Gould (1982) and Weiss and Bredemeier (1983). Specifically we evaluated the extent to which studies or reviews were grounded in theory, conducted evaluation research, employed multidisciplinary designs, developed sport-specific models, and represented programmatic lines of research.[2] First, a majority of empirical studies were designed to test psychological theory in the physical domain (although the theories tested were not necessarily developmental ones). For example, a host of motivation theories were used as frameworks for understanding and explaining variations in cognition, affect, and behavior (e.g., cognitive evaluation, competence motivation, and achievement goal theories). This trend is likely attributable to the emergence of many mainstream psychology theories in the mid- to late-1970s along with revisions of these theories in the 1980s and 1990s. In testing psychological theory, few researchers adopted Gould's recommendations of conducting evaluation research to validate program effectiveness or using a multidisciplinary perspective (i.e., very few studies considered the combined influence of physical, social, and psychological factors). Notable exceptions of studies designed to evaluate program effectiveness include those by Gibbons and Ebbeck (Ebbeck & Gibbons, 1998; Gibbons & Ebbeck, 1997; Gibbons, Ebbeck, & Weiss, 1995) on promoting moral development in elementary-aged students and team building through physical challenges in early adolescents. Similarly, Passer's (1996) narrative on "At what age are children ready to compete?" and Iversen's (1990) synthesis of the unique individual differences and social-environmental factors related to late-maturing elite gymnasts represent some of the few papers that incorporated a multidisciplinary approach to understanding sport-related behaviors and psychosocial outcomes.

Some researchers developed sport-specific models that derived from theories in mainstream psychology. Griffin and Keogh (e.g., Crawford & Griffin, 1986; Griffin & Crawford, 1989; Griffin & Keogh, 1982; Griffin, Keogh, & Maybee, 1984; Keogh, Griffin, & Spector, 1981) developed a movement involvement cycle in which movement confidence influences participation choice, performance, and persistence. Movement confidence (i.e., self-confidence in movement situations) was defined as the interaction between a person's *perceptions of competence* in relation to task demands and expected *sensory experiences* associated with the task. For example, two children may possess high perceived swimming ability but show variations in behavior because one child's *movement sensations* are characterized by exhilaration from the feelings, smells, and sounds associated with moving in the water, whereas the other child's sensations are reflected by tension, anxiety, and fear of physical harm. Despite the developmental slant and practicality of this perspective (see Bressan & Weiss, 1982, and Weiss & Bressan, 1985,

TABLE 2
Content Analysis of Youth Sport Psychology Research, 1982-1998

Topical area[a]	# Empirical Reviews	# Book Chapters	# Developmental	Reference[b]
Aggression	5	3	0	
Anxiety/stress	36	10	4	Gould (1993)
Attitudes	18	0	1	Pellett (1994)
Attributions	12	0	1	Martinek & Griffith (1994)
Competition	9	2	5	Dickinson et al. (1983)
Emotions/Affect	12	1	2	Wankel & Kriesel (1985)
Game modifications	2	5	7	Chase et al. (1994)
Group dynamics	10	0	0	
Knowledge structures	10	4	12	Nevett & French (1997)
Modeling	14	1	9	Wiese-Bjornstal & Weiss (1992)
Moral development	24	8	12	Weinstein et al. (1995)
Motivation	112	11	17	Brodkin & Weiss (1990)
Personality	20	1	1	Keel et al. (1997)
Psychological skills	34	1	6	Orlick & McCaffrey (1991)
Readiness	0	8	8	Passer (1996)
Self-perceptions	105	4	31	Marsh (1993)
Social influence	73	8	9	Black & Weiss (1992)
Socialization	51	13	15	Coakley & White (1992)
Multiple topics	18	9	2	Brustad (1993)
Totals	560	86	142	

[a] Studies were classified under the topic that was the predominant theme of the paper. In the case of a broader approach to the paper, it was categorized as "multiple topics." The topical areas differed somewhat from those in Weiss and Bredemeier (1983) to parsimoniously classify the much larger number of studies reviewed. For example, "Coaching behaviors" is seen in Table 1 whereas "Social influence" in Table 2 includes coaching behaviors as well as parent and peer influence.

[b] A representative citation adopting a developmental theoretical approach to the topic of interest is listed. The full citation appears at the end of the References. Examples of other developmental papers in each topic can be obtained from the first author.

for applying the model in instructional settings), the movement confidence model has not been embraced in the sport psychology literature.

Chelladurai (1990) customized another sport-specific model, the multidimensional model of sport leadership, by integrating concepts of leadership behavior from organizational psychology and sport psychology. However, only a few studies have tested this model with youth (e.g., Chelladurai & Carron, 1983; Westre & Weiss, 1991). By contrast many studies have used his model as a framework for understanding coach leadership behaviors and athlete psychological responses using college-aged athletes as samples. Because the model considers member characteristics (age, gender, psychological characteristics) as variables interacting with coaching behaviors to predict psychosocial outcomes, future researchers could use this model to understand developmental differences in coaching style preferences and perceptions in sport and physical activity contexts.

Especially encouraging were the several programmatic lines of research that emerged over the last 17 years. Recall that Gould (1982) identified two programs of research at the time of his review: Scanlan and Passer's work on competitive anxiety and Smith and Smoll's coaching effectiveness studies. Our review uncovered a number of additional lines of youth sport research since Gould's review. These include research programs by (a) Horn on sources of physical competence information (see Horn, 2003; Horn & Amorose, 1998), (b) Bredemeier on moral development and aggression (see Shields & Bredemeier, 1995, 2001), (c) Duda on achievement goals (see Duda & Whitehead, 1998), (d) Scanlan on enjoyment and sport commitment (see Scanlan & Simons, 1992); (e) French and McPherson on development of expertise in sport (see French & McPherson, 2003), and (f) Weiss on observational learning and perceived physical competence (see Weiss, 1999; Weiss, Ebbeck, & Wiese-Bjornstal, 1993).

Finally . . . how did we do over the last 17 years in adopting a developmental theoretical perspective to study children and youth in sport? Of the 646 articles, reviews, and chapters published from 1982 to 1998, we counted 91 empirical studies/reviews (18% of total) and 51 book chapters (60% of total), or 22% of the total number of manuscripts, that employed a developmental perspective. Although still a marginal percentage of the total number of papers, we consider 22% to be a significant improvement over the 10% of developmental papers during the 1970-1981 time span (Weiss & Bredemeier, 1983). In this second wave of youth sport research in the 1980s and 1990s, researchers were more likely to select age groups based on cognitive or physical criteria, compare age groups at key periods of development, and assess the same participants at multiple time periods (i.e., longitudinal design) compared to past decades. We elaborate upon grounding research within a developmental theoretical perspective by presenting three representative studies that use varying designs to derive and answer a research question from a developmental perspective.

A Developmental Analysis of Children's Self-Ability Judgments in the Physical Domain (Horn & Weiss, 1991)

Horn and Weiss (1991) were influenced by Harter's (1978, 1981) work on the developmental course of perceptions of competence in specific achievement domains. Specifically, research shows an age-related decline in *level* of perceived academic competence and a concomitant increase in *accuracy* of competence judgments across the school-aged years (i.e., children's academic competence perceptions become more congruent with objective indicators of competence). One of the reasons forwarded for this phenomenon is that sources of information used to evaluate competencies shift from simple task mastery and parent feedback to peer comparison and evaluation. Horn and Weiss were curious if similar age-related trends were evident when applied to children's *physical* competence perceptions.

Horn and Weiss (1991) identified three study questions:

1. Do children become more accurate in perceived physical ability with age?

2. Are there age differences in sources of information used to judge ability?

3. Is there a relationship between accuracy of perceived competence and information sources?

Because age-related trends in perceived competence have been uncovered across the school-aged years, Horn and Weiss chose 8- to 13-year-old (third- through seventh-grade) participants to complete questionnaires on level and sources of perceived physical competence. Two individuals who instructed these youth during a 7-week sports program completed a measure of actual sport competence for each child. Thus for each study participant, assessments of level, accuracy (perceived − actual), and sources of perceived physical competence were obtained.

For the first study question, correlations between perceived and actual (i.e., teachers' ratings) competence progressively increased ($r = .21, .29, .55, .68$) for grades 3, 4, 5, and 6/7. Thus, support emerged for the concept that children become more accurate in perceived physical competence with age. Younger children (i.e., 8- to 9-year-olds) rated parental feedback as a more important physical competence information source than did 10- to 13-year-olds, who rated peer comparison and evaluation as more important. Thus the second hypothesis was supported in that sources of information used to assess physical ability change with age.

For the third study question, children were classified as accurate estimators, underestimators, or overestimators of physical competence based on discrepancy between perceived and actual competence scores. The three estimator groups were then compared on sources of physical competence information. Overestimating youth rated internal sources such as improvement, effort, and attraction toward sport significantly higher in importance than did accurate- or underestimating participants. In contrast, accurate- and underestimating youth rated peer comparison and evaluation as more important. These results support the notion that accuracy judgments are related to the use of differential sources of information.

In summary, findings uncovered age differences in *accuracy* of perceived competence and in competence information *sources*, following trends in the academic domain. Importantly, the tie between accuracy of competence judgments and sources of information suggests that changes in children's ability to reliably estimate sport ability is linked, at least in part, to children's use of information sources. Horn and Weiss' (1991) study was conceived within developmental psychological theory and designed to test developmental differences by selecting age groups that vary in cognitive criteria.

A Developmental Examination of Children's Understanding of Effort and Ability in the Physical and Academic Domains (Fry & Duda, 1997)

Fry and Duda (1997) were influenced by Nicholls' (1978, 1989) theory of achievement goals. Specifically Nicholls provided evidence supporting an age-related progression in conceptions of ability and effort on academic tasks. Specifically children under the age of about 7 years possess an undifferentiated conception of ability (i.e., children who exhibit high effort are also seen as having high ability; that is, effort and ability are strongly correlated). Children between the ages of 7 and 11 years possess a partially differentiated conception of ability (i.e., ability is viewed as different from effort, but this is not consistently applied). Children above 11-12 years hold a differentiated conception of ability (i.e., children who require high effort to complete a task are seen as having lower ability than children who require less effort; that is, effort and ability are negatively related). In turn, these conceptions are believed to influence how success is defined (i.e., goal orientations) and variations in achievement behaviors. Fry and Duda sought to replicate and extend Nicholls' developmental findings to physical achievement tasks.

The researchers selected children 5 to 13 years of age, a range that corresponds with developmental variations in conceptions of ability. Each child was presented with videotapes of two children solving math problems (academic domain) and throwing beanbags at a target (physical domain). Two scenarios were shown within each domain, one scenario in which the two children performed equally well despite one child's exerting less effort than the other, and one scenario in which the "lazier" child outscored his or her cohort. Study participants were asked to explain why both children achieved the same score despite differences in trying and how the child exerting less effort could be more successful. Children's responses were classified into categories of conceptions of ability that represented progressively more mature stages of reasoning.

Results for both the academic and physical domain scenarios were consistent with Nicholls' levels of conceptions of ability. Age and level of ability conceptions were strongly related ($r = .67$), with younger children more likely to score at lower levels (i.e., undifferentiated or partially differentiated) and older children at higher levels (i.e., differentiated). Moreover, the strong correlation ($r = .76$) found for children's ability conceptions across the two domains suggests that understanding of the concepts of ability and effort are similar for the academic and physical domains.

In summary, Fry and Duda (1997) replicated Nicholls' developmental findings concerning conceptions of effort and ability, and extended them to a physical achievement task. The study was grounded in developmental psychological theory, and children were selected based on cognitive criteria related to ability conceptions. Finding that developmental differences exist in conceptions of ability and effort in the physical domain opens the door for testing hypotheses related to ability conceptions and achievement goals.

Change in Children's Competence Beliefs and Subjective Task Values Across the Elementary School Years: A 3-year Study (Wigfield et al., 1997)

Wigfield et al. tested a number of developmental hypotheses emanating from Eccles' et al. (1983) expectancy-value theory with elementary-aged youth over a 3-year period in four activity domains: math, reading, sports, and music. Three cohorts of age groups were assessed on salient variables so that both intraindividual change and interindividual or cohort differences could be documented. Wigfield et al. hypothesized that (a) children's competence beliefs and subjective task values (i.e., attainment, utility, interest) should decline over the childhood years; (b) children's competence beliefs and subjective task values should become more stable over the childhood years; (c) the positive relationship between competence beliefs and subjective task values will strengthen across the childhood years; and (d) the relationship of children's competence beliefs with parents' and teachers' beliefs about children's competence will strengthen over the childhood years. The longitudinal design allowed for testing mean-level changes in constructs (hypothesis a) and differences in the magnitude of correlations between variables (hypotheses c and d) over time, as well as the magnitude of within-construct correlations between time periods (hypothesis b).

Support was obtained for all hypotheses dependent upon activity domain. First, children's competence beliefs did decline over the elementary school years for all activity domains, although the decline was most marked for music. Subjective task value regarding the usefulness and importance of all four activities also declined over the elementary years. However, interest value varied depending on activity domain—there was a decline in interest toward reading and music but not for sports and math. Second, the oldest children's competence beliefs and values were more stable than those of the youngest children. Third, children's competence beliefs were positively related to task value for the activity, especially interest value, and these correlations were significantly stronger for older than for younger children (except for interest toward sports). Finally, the association of children's competence beliefs with those of their parents and teachers became stronger with age, especially with their mother's competency beliefs in them.

Collectively, the results of this study provided strong support for expectancy-value theory by demonstrating developmental differences in competence beliefs and subjective task values, the two direct antecedents of achievement behavior in her model. Results also reinforced the need to consider different dimensions of subjective task value (i.e., importance, usefulness, interest) and specific activity domains (i.e., sports, music, math, reading) in studying achievement motivation, as findings varied depending on which value dimension and activity domain were analyzed. Importantly for our illustration here, the theory-driven developmental hypotheses were tested within a longitudinal research design that enabled researchers to confidently conclude that age-related differences exist on constructs of interest.

Summary

Considerable advancements in studying youth in sport have been made since the publication of Gould (1982) and Weiss and Bredemeier (1983). These include the predominance of theory testing, the customizing of psychological models to the social context of sport, and several programmatic lines of research. The percentage of studies and reviews that adopted a developmental theoretical perspective doubled, and many studies (such as the ones we outlined) provide a model for researchers seeking to extend the youth-sport knowledge base using a developmental perspective. These studies portray the potential for using developmental theory, research designs that allow examination of age-related differences, and types of methodologies necessary for testing developmental hypotheses.

CONCEPTUAL ISSUES TO CONSIDER IN FUTURE DEVELOPMENTAL RESEARCH

So far we have described the nature of early youth sport research, reviewed the developmental approach for studying children in sport, and brought us up to date with a content analysis of youth sport research from 1982 to 1998. In this section we advance several conceptual issues that we believe should be considered for advancing developmental sport psychology research. We elaborate upon three conceptual issues: (a) conceptual clarity in theory testing, (b) behavioral validation of psychological theory, and (c) embracing of underused theories. These issues extend not only to researchers studying youth in sport but also those studying young, middle, and older adults in a variety of physical activity contexts.

Conceptual Clarity in Theory Testing

There is simply no substitute for asking good research questions. If researchers do not have a conceptual framework and clearly defined constructs for guiding their research questions, they will be unable to substantively contribute to the knowledge base (Gill, 1997). Moreover, Vealey (1999) exhorts that we must ask research questions that extend beyond the "psychology of the obvious" by directing our efforts toward issues of social relevance and personal meaning for our participants. Gill's clever analogy to Alice in Wonderland illuminates the importance of conceptual clarity. Alice asks Cheshire-Puss, "Would you tell me please, which way I ought to walk from here?" Cheshire-Puss' response: "That depends a good deal on where you want to get to." When Alice says she doesn't much care where she walks, Cheshire-Puss responds, "Then, it doesn't matter which way you walk" (Gill, p. 39). Put simply, asking good questions requires that we know where we are coming from and where we want to go. With the proliferation of theories, measures, and statistical techniques, it is imperative that we first fully grasp conceptual underpinnings, define essential constructs, and then pose our research questions accordingly that will extend the knowledge base.

One way to facilitate these goals is to consult the primary theoretical sources and empirical studies testing theory-based hypotheses and not be tempted to use secondary sources as a basis for formulating questions. Today there are ample secondary sources (exhaustive reviews, book chapters) on all major topics in sport and exercise psychology, and it is convenient and easy to rely solely upon these sources for understanding theories and identifying research questions. Secondary sources provide a valuable place to start and certainly represent a first step in identifying which questions have already been asked and which ones are important to pursue. However, primary sources are critical to helping researchers form *their own interpretations* of theoretical underpinnings and empirical findings rather than being constrained by other authors' translations. To maximize conceptual clarity, then, researchers should cross-validate the accuracy of theoretical explanations and empirical findings by consulting appropriate primary sources.

A good example of conceptual clarity in theory testing is the case of the sport commitment model (Scanlan, Carpenter, Schmidt, Simons, & Keeler, 1993; Scanlan, Simons, Carpenter, Schmidt, & Keeler, 1993). Scanlan and her colleagues developed this sport-specific model based on sound conceptual reasoning and methodological protocols. They forwarded specific constructs, definitions of constructs, and associations among constructs stemming from theory and research on commitment in work and relationship contexts. However, based on the literature on participation motives and predictors of motivation in *sport*, Scanlan and colleagues customized model constructs (e.g., enjoyment, involvement opportunities) to fit the sport domain. In developing measures to appropriately assess context-specific constructs they conducted extensive pilot testing to ensure developmentally appropriate language, comprehension, and readability in children varying in age, ethnicity, and culture. Subsequently they conducted a series of studies with large and diverse youth samples to validate measures and investigate conceptually driven research questions (i.e., significance and magnitude of relationships between determinants and level of sport commitment). As a result of careful attention to conceptual clarity (i.e., defining and customizing constructs, developing valid measures), good research questions have been asked to further our understanding of sport commitment such as its dynamic nature and relationship to burnout (e.g., Carpenter & Scanlan, 1998; Raedeke, 1997).

A related issue to conceptual clarity in theory or model testing is contemporary approaches to measurement, research design, and statistical analyses (Brustad, 1998; Gill, 1997; Patterson, 1996; Schutz & Gessaroli, 1993). In recent years the number of instruments for assessing psychological constructs in physical activity settings has proliferated. However many of these measures do not consider the developmental differences that exist among children and adolescents or youth and adults in terms of the structure and content of psychological constructs such as self-perceptions, achievement motivation, and affective responses (see Brustad; Horn, 2003). Our instruments need to reflect such developmental differences, not only in terms of vocabulary and response format, but also in terms of how children, adolescents, and adults vary in the cognitive processes used to impart meaning to their experiences.

In addition, one of the pitfalls of accessible and user-friendly computer programs for crunching data representing complex designs is the possibility of asking research questions that fit a particular statistical analysis rather than asking conceptually clear questions and then choosing the mode of analysis accordingly. As both Gill (1997) and Patterson (1996) implore, the research question should drive the method and not the other way around. As such, we encourage developmental researchers to carefully couch their questions within theoretical frameworks, ask good questions that will extend the present knowledge base, and only then choose the most appropriate methodologies and statistical techniques to test hypotheses and rival explanations.

Behavioral Validation of Psychological Theory

Gill (1997) defines the content of sport psychology as the "A, B, C's" or the study of Affect, Behavior, and Cognition. However research efforts in sport psychology mostly focus upon perceptions (e.g., self-esteem, goal orientations) and emotional responses (e.g., enjoyment, anxiety), whereas behaviors such as choice, effort, persistence, participation, and performance are often neglected as key variables. Our ultimate interest and goal are to effect positive *behavior* change, and for that we need to explore correlates and determinants of physical activity-related behaviors more frequently. For example, achievement goal theory hypothesizes that individuals high in ego orientation and low in perceived competence may be at risk for maladaptive behaviors such as task avoidance, low effort, and dropout (Duda, 1987). These behaviors should be more likely within ego-involving climates. To date, however, the large majority of research on achievement goals has examined the relationship between goal orientations and cognitive and affective correlates.

Similarly, constructivist approaches to moral development (see Shields & Bredemeier, 1995) suggest that individuals lower in moral reasoning will be more likely to engage in aggressive behaviors than will those with more mature reasoning levels. This should occur especially in situations that promote "game reasoning" (e.g., team norms that condone aggression). Again, most moral development research has examined the relation between moral reasoning and self-reported *intentions* or tendencies to engage in aggressive or unfair play, not actual behaviors. Thus to contribute to theory testing and educational applications of theory, we need to include behavioral variables more frequently in our research.

A good example of testing psychological theory with consideration toward assessing thoughts, emotions, *and* behaviors is the programmatic line of research by R. E. Smith and Smoll and colleagues (see R. E. Smith & Smoll, 1996). Their coaching effectiveness studies have been premised largely in social reinforcement principles, which suggest that coaches who engage in more frequent contingent praise, instruction, and encouragement and engage in less punishment should positively influence young athletes' cognitions, affects, and behaviors. Through a series of studies, R. E. Smith and Smoll demonstrated that coaches could be trained to issue more positive and less negative behaviors. Consequently their athletes reported greater self-esteem, baseball ability, team cohesion, and enjoyment, as well as exhibited lower anxiety and dropout rates than did athletes who played for control-group coaches. R. E. Smith and Smoll assessed behavioral outcomes in both athletes (e.g., attrition) and coaches (i.e., frequency of giving praise, instruction, encouragement, and punishment). Although it is sometimes difficult to reliably assess behaviors, we urge researchers to consider assessing the A's, C's, *and* B's whenever possible.

A related issue to behavioral validation of theory is the need for more intervention studies in sport psychology. The majority of sport psychology research still employs correlational designs, whereas experimental and single-subject designs that could assess effectiveness of interventions are fewer in number. We sorely need more evidence for the efficacy of psychosocial strategies on self-perceptions, affective responses, motivation, and behaviors. Several studies have implemented theoretically driven intervention programs that include behavioral outcomes (e.g., Gibbons & Ebbeck, 1997, prosocial behaviors; Marsh & Peart, 1988, physical

The way children judge their ability changes over the elementary and middle school years.

fitness; Theeboom, De Knop, & Weiss, 1995, skill development). Although this is a good start, theory testing and educational practice will be strengthened when we are able to demonstrate more frequently the beneficial effects of physical activity interventions on participants' thoughts, emotions, and behaviors.

Interventions should also be developed and their effectiveness documented by clinical researchers and practitioners who work with children and adults individually or in groups. For instance, Danish (see Danish & Nellen, 1997) and Hellison (e.g., Hellison, Martinek, & Cutforth, 1996) have developed and implemented successful community-based programs designed to enhance life skills and self- and other-responsibility among youth. More research that quantifies the effectiveness of such interventions in accomplishing goals and objectives will bolster our knowledge about the importance and impact of these programs. In turn, we may be in a better position to make an impact on public policies.

When conducting intervention studies, it is imperative that researchers quantify the ability of interventions to effect and sustain change in self-perceptions, affective responses, and behavior by collecting multiple assessments whenever possible (e.g., Marsh, Richards, & Barnes, 1986). Conducting multiple assessments prior to, during, and especially after the intervention will help determine whether the intervention protocol has exerted immediate or longer-lasting effects. In line with documenting intervention effectiveness, researchers should also report effect sizes or other indicators of clinical significance (e.g., Weiss, McCullagh, Smith, & Berlant, 1998). An effect size goes beyond statistical significance to quantify the magnitude of change invoked by a particular intervention in comparison to a control condition. Even when statistical significance is not achieved due to small sample size or large within-subject variability (a common limitation in developmental research), calculation of effect sizes is an appropriate and informative procedure.

Embracing Underused Theories

In our content analysis of studies published between 1982 and 1998, certain theories were especially popular in youth sport research. These included cognitive evaluation (Deci & Ryan, 1985), achievement goal (Nicholls, 1989), and competence motivation (Harter, 1978) theories. These approaches are conducive to a developmental theoretical analysis, but to date, only developmental hypotheses related to achievement goal and competence motivation theories have been tested. There are several other theories or models that are developmentally appropriate and attractive for explaining and predicting behavioral variations in sport and physical activity contexts across the lifespan. More research is needed to test the applicability of these approaches to the physical domain and how they might contribute to the knowledge base in sport and exercise psychology.

Dweck and Eccles have contributed to the knowledge base in sport psychology, having been keynote speakers at NASPSPA, AAASP, and APA and having published papers that include sport as a salient achievement domain (e.g., Dweck, 1980, 1998; Eccles & Harold, 1991; Jacobs & Eccles, 1992). Both scholars have sustained continuous and impressive programmatic lines of research on achievement motivation (see Dweck, 1999; Eccles, Wigfield, & Schiefele, 1998). Moreover their theories consider a host of developmental criteria (cognitive, social, physical) and thus represent outstanding candidates for understanding and explaining children's and adolescents' sport behaviors. Yet to date Dweck's and Eccles' perspectives have received scant attention in the developmental sport psychology literature.

Dweck's (1999) notion of implicit theories of achievement points to the existence of entity or incremental conceptions of ability (i.e., intelligence) among children. In turn, these conceptions relate to achievement goals, affective responses, and behavioral patterns in response to success and failure. For example, children who view intelligence as malleable through the use of effort and self-regulated strategies (i.e., incremental view) adopt learning goals and demonstrate mastery behavior even in response to failure. In contrast, children who view intelligence as a stable or fixed trait (i.e., entity view) adopt performance goals and, in combination with low perceived competence, demonstrate learned helplessness under failure conditions. Children's worldviews about achievement in particular domains, therefore, have important implications for the types of goals adopted, self-esteem, and behavioral outcomes (e.g., choice of tasks, effort, persistence, performance).

Moreover, Mueller and Dweck (1998) showed, over a series of studies, that praise for intelligence versus praise for effort is differentially related to goal choice, attributions, enjoyment, motivation, and academic performance in 10- to 12-year-old children. Children who were praised for "being smart" following successful task completion, in comparison to children who were praised for "working hard," showed preference for a performance rather than a learning goal (i.e., a task that would allow them to continue looking smart rather than one that would help them improve). Following a failure trial, children who had been praised for intelligence attributed poor performance to lack of ability, reported lower enjoyment toward and desire to persist doing the task, and performed worse on a subsequent trial that was comparable in task difficulty to their first successful trial. Dweck's ideas pertaining to conceptions of ability, achievement goals, and subsequent cognitions, emotions, and behavior may transfer well to children's conceptions of physical ability and should be considered in future youth sport studies.

Eccles' (Eccles et al., 1983, 1998) expectancy-value model of achievement behavior has been used in a few studies investigating children's physical activity cognitions and behaviors (see Weiss & Ferrer-Caja, 2002, for a review of these studies). However, the potential of expectancy-value theory in the physical domain is just unfolding. The influence of socializers' beliefs and behaviors, the social context in which achievement behaviors occur, and developmental differences in competence beliefs and subjective task value are just a few of the many linkages in her model awaiting empirical test in the physical domain. Eccles herself has successfully shown the viability of her theory across achievement domains including math, reading, music, social interactions, and sport (e.g., Eccles & Harold, 1991; Jacobs & Eccles, 1992; Wigfield et al., 1997). We encourage researchers to consider Eccles' theory as an attractive option for testing hypotheses relating to children's achievement behaviors in sport and physical activity.

Finally, task and ego goal orientations (Nicholls, 1989) and motivational climates (Ames, 1992) have been amply studied in relation to psychological and affective responses in the physical domain. In contrast, the notion of social goals, first forwarded by Maehr and Nicholls (1980), has been neglected in explanations of sport-related motivation. This is surprising given strong evidence that individuals of all ages participate in and derive meaning from sport for reasons related to gaining approval from parents, peers, and coaches; developing and nurturing friendships; and feeling a sense of group belonging (see Weiss & Ferrer-Caja, 2002). For example, Hayashi (1996) found that social approval and social solidarity goals were important to adult exercisers of Hawaiian background in the form of ties to the peer group and in-group pride and harmony. Several researchers in the academic domain have recently urged for the inclusion of social goals in addition to task and ego goals in understanding achievement motivation (e.g., Jarvinen & Nicholls, 1996; Urdan & Maehr, 1995; Wentzel, 1998). These conceptual papers represent outstanding resources for developmental sport researchers interested in studying the contribution of achievement goals—task, ego, and social—to explaining individuals' perceptions, emotions, and behaviors in the sport context.

Toward a Lifespan Developmental Perspective for Guiding Empirical Inquiry

The frequency of employing a developmental theoretical perspective and concomitant designs and methodologies is steadily increasing in the youth sport literature. By contrast, studies of exercise adoption, maintenance, and adherence among adult populations have multiplied rapidly over the last decade, but few have employed theories or research designs based on developmental criteria. Given the documented levels of physical inactivity among adolescents through older adults (U.S. Department of Health and Human Services [USDHHS], 1996, 2000), several essential research directions can be identified from a *lifespan* developmental perspective. These include identifying critical antecedents of regular physical activity in adolescents through older adults, and understanding how physical activity during childhood and adolescence may contribute to quality of life in middle and older adulthood. Developmental sport psychologists can make a significant contribution to explaining physical activity patterns by using appropriate conceptual frameworks to develop research questions and designs that consider salient cognitive, social, physical, and cultural processes at particular developmental periods (e.g., Martin & Sinden, 2001; McPherson, 1994; Shephard, 1995; Weiss, 2000). By adopting a lifespan approach that considers the dynamic interplay of key variables at various developmental periods, we are more likely to achieve a better understanding of what factors maximize the probability of maintaining and enhancing physical activity across childhood, adolescence, and adulthood.

The content analysis we reported in this chapter demonstrates that considerable research on youth populations has taken place over the last two decades. However much of this research was conducted with youth 8-14 years old, whereas comparatively less research examined older adolescent populations (ages 14-18 years) and children younger than 8 years of age. Thus we know the most about children's sport experiences in middle childhood through early adolescence, but little about the early childhood and middle/late adolescent years (see also Horn,

2003). Thus an important direction for future research is to understand very young children's (ages 4-7) socialization through physical activity and how such experiences influence participation in later childhood years and beyond. Similarly, we know that physical activity levels decline dramatically over the teenage years (USDHHS, 1996), especially among females. It is imperative that we employ longitudinal research designs to determine developmental change in physical activity patterns during adolescence and beyond, as well as in the antecedents and consequences of physical activity (e.g., social, cognitive, and physical processes).

Middle and older adults compose other "forgotten populations" in understanding developmental issues related to psychosocial factors and physical activity behavior (see chapters in Section 3 of this volume). These chapters as well as scholarly reviews on similar topics (e.g., Chogahara, O'Brien Cousins, & Wankel, 1998; McPherson, 1994) reveal that, despite the escalation of interest in physical activity, aging, and health, the bulk of research efforts still focuses upon college-aged and young adult populations. Moreover, little of the adult-based research on such topics as self-perceptions, social influence, emotions, motivation, and self-regulation skills adopts developmental theoretical perspectives, especially longitudinal approaches. Therefore, in addition to the need for a greater quantity of studies on the determinants and outcomes of psychosocial factors and physical activity in middle and older adults, we need more studies that examine qualitative changes in each of these factors and their interrelationships over time. Understanding the unique and salient issues (cultural, social, physical, psychological) at varying adult developmental periods will allow educators and health practitioners to design the most effective interventions to maintain and enhance physical activity, well-being, and health outcomes (e.g., Martin & Sinden, 2001; McPherson, 1994; Shephard, 1995).

Conceptual and methodological issues constitute central concerns for developmental sport and exercise psychology researchers at every point in the lifespan (Baltes et al., 1988). Youth and adult researchers alike cite theoretical approaches, age-appropriate instrumentation, diverse methodologies, and intervention studies as areas meriting attention in future research. Several authors highlight the importance of adopting underused, but developmentally appropriate, theories to maximize our understanding of developmental differences in physical activity contexts (e.g., Markus' self-schema theory, see Whaley, 2003; Lazarus' cognitive-motivational-relational theory, see Crocker et al., 2003; selective optimization with compensation, see Baltes et al., 1998). Authors also address the challenge of reliably and validly assessing individuals at varying developmental levels on constructs such as self-perceptions, social influence, emotions, and motivation. Merely changing the wording and response format on a scale validated with youth will not suffice for measuring adults or vice versa because the structure and content of various constructs may differ depending on developmental level (see Baltes et al., 1988). Thus continued psychometric efforts will be needed to advance developmental research. Developmental research will also progress by considering a variety of quantitative and qualitative approaches to uncover the complex, multidimensional, and dynamic nature of constructs and their interrelationships (e.g., see Crocker et al., 2003; Gould & Chung 2003; Whaley 2003).

Finally, a common theme throughout the lifespan developmental literature is that understanding cognitive, emotional, and behavioral change must be considered within the social and cultural contexts in which these changes occur (Baltes et al., 1988). Baltes et al. (1988) succinctly put it this way, ". . . developmental psychology recognizes that the individual is changing in a changing world, and that this changing context of development can affect the nature of individual change" (p. 1). Similarly the crucial role that social context plays in physical activity involvement is highlighted in the sport and exercise psychology literature (see Brustad & Babkes, 2003; Gill, 2003). Social relationships are intertwined, dynamic, and reciprocal, meaning that individuals (youth, adolescents, adults) are influenced by, as well as influence, the social networks that define their physical activity worlds (parents, siblings, peer group, close friends, coaches, spouses, children). Such bidirectional influence is forever changing as a result of cognitive and physical maturation as well as social interactions and experiences. Thus developmental change in psychological constructs and physical activity behavior must be considered in light of the specific contexts in which interactions and experiences occur.

Conclusion

Nearly 50 years after Skubic's (1955, 1956) groundbreaking studies of youth sport participation and 20 years after the review papers by Gould (1982) and Weiss and Bredemeier (1983), we can confidently say that theory development and empirical research in youth sport have flourished. Our content analysis showed that hundreds of studies were conducted over the last two decades; and the majority tested theory, employed varied methodologies, and characterized programmatic lines of research. Although the percentage of youth studies taking a developmental perspective doubled since the last content analysis, we again advocate that researchers consider adopting a developmental approach in asking cutting-edge questions, designing studies, selecting participant criteria, and interpreting findings. Striving for conceptual clarity, behaviorally validating psychological theory, and testing underused theories are realistic and exciting goals for tackling socially relevant questions and contributing substantively to the knowledge base in sport and exercise psychology. Last, but not least, it is time we recognize that a *lifespan* developmental perspective will maximize our understanding of the psychosocial antecedents and consequences of physical activity in youth through elderly populations. Only then will we be able to solve the puzzle of maintaining or enhancing physical activity behavior, health outcomes, and quality of life in individuals of all ages.

References

Alderman, R. A., & Wood, N. L. (1976). An analysis of incentive motivation in young Canadian athletes. *Canadian Journal of Applied Sport Sciences, 1*, 169-175.

Ames, C. (1992). Achievement goals, motivational climate, and motivational processes. In G. C. Roberts (Ed.), *Motivation in sport and exercise* (pp. 161-176). Champaign, IL: Human Kinetics.

Amorose, A. J., & Weiss, M. R. (1998). Coaching feedback as a source of information about perceptions of ability: A developmental examination. *Journal of Sport & Exercise Psychology, 20*, 395-420.

Baltes, P. B., Lindenberger, U., & Staudinger, U. M. (1998). Life-span theory in developmental psychology. In W. Damon (Series Ed.) & R. M. Lerner (Volume Ed.), *Handbook of child psychology: Vol. 1. Theoretical models of human development* (5th ed., pp. 1029-1143). New York: Wiley.

Baltes, P. B., Reese, H. W., & Nesselroade, J. R. (1988). *Life-span developmental psychology: Introduction to research methods*. Hillsdale, NJ: Erlbaum.

Bandura, A. (1977). Self-efficacy: Toward a unifying theory of behavioral change. *Psychological Review, 84*, 191-215.

Bressan, E. S., & Weiss, M. R. (1982). A theory of instruction for developing competence, self-confidence and persistence in physical education. *Journal of Teaching Physical Education, 2*, 38-47.

Brustad, R. J. (1998). Developmental considerations in sport and exercise psychology measurement. In J. L. Duda (Ed.), *Advances in sport and exercise psychology measurement* (pp. 461-470). Morgantown, WV: Fitness Information Technology.

Brustad, R. J., & Babkes, M. L. (2003). Social influence on the psychological dimensions of adult physical activity involvement. In M.R. Weiss (Ed.), *Developmental sport and exercise psychology: A developmental perspective* (pp. 313-332). Morgantown, WV: Fitness Information Technology

Carpenter, P. J., & Scanlan, T. K. (1998). Changes over time in the determinants of sport commitment. *Pediatric Exercise Science, 10*, 356-365.

Chelladurai, P. (1990). Leadership in sports: A review. *International Journal of Sport Psychology, 21*, 328-354.

Chelladurai, P., & Carron, A. V. (1983). Athletic maturity and preferred leadership. *Journal of Sport Psychology, 5*, 371-380.

Chodzko-Zajko, W. J. (1994). Experimental design and research methodology in aging: Implications for research and clinical practice. *Journal of Aging and Physical Activity, 2*, 360-372.

Chogahara, M., O'Brien Cousins, S., & Wankel, L. M. (1998). Social influences on physical activity in older adults: A review. *Journal of Aging and Physical Activity, 6,* 1-17.

Crawford, M. E., & Griffin, N. S. (1986). Testing the validity of the Griffin/Keogh model for movement confidence by analyzing self-report playground involvement decisions of elementary school children. *Research Quarterly for Exercise and Sport, 57,* 67-78.

Crocker, P.R.E., Kowalski, K.C., Hoar, S.D., & McDonough, M.H. (2003). Emotion in sport across adulthood. In M.R. Weiss (Ed.), *Developmental sport and exercise psychology: A developmental perspective* (pp. 333-355). Morgantown, WV: Fitness Information Technology.

Danish, S., & Nellen, V. C. (1997). New roles for sport psychologists: Teaching life skills through sport to at-risk youth. *Quest, 49,* 100-113.

Deci, E. L. (1975). *Intrinsic motivation.* New York: Plenum.

Deci, E. L., & Ryan, R. M. (1985). *Intrinsic motivation and self-determination in human behavior.* New York: Plenum.

Duda, J. L. (1987). Toward a developmental theory of children's motivation in sport. *Journal of Sport Psychology, 9,* 130-145.

Duda, J. L., & Whitehead, J. (1998). Measurement and goal perspectives in the physical domain. In J. L. Duda (Ed.), *Advances in sport and exercise psychology measurement* (pp. 21-48). Morgantown: WV: Fitness Information Technology.

Duncan, T. E., & Duncan, S. C. (1991). A latent growth curve approach to investigating developmental dynamics and correlates of change in children's perceptions of physical competence. *Research Quarterly for Exercise and Sport, 62,* 390-396.

Dweck, C. S. (1980). Learned helplessness in sport. In C. Nadeau, W. Halliwell, K. Newell, & G. Roberts (Eds.), *Psychology of motor behavior and sport – 1979* (pp. 1-11). Champaign, IL: Human Kinetics.

Dweck, C. S. (1998, September). *Self theories and goals: Their role in motivation.* Paper presented at the annual conference for the Association for the Advancement of Applied Sport Psychology, Hyannis, MA.

Dweck, C. S. (1999). *Self-theories: Their role in motivation, personality, and development.* Philadelphia: Psychology Press.

Ebbeck, V., & Gibbons, S. L. (1998). The effect of a team building program on the self-conceptions of Grade 6 and 7 physical education students. *Journal of Sport & Exercise Psychology, 20,* 300-310.

Eccles, J., Adler, T. E., Futterman, R., Goff, S. B., Kaczala, C. M., Meece, J. L., & Midgley, C. (1983). Expectancies, values, and academic behaviors. In J. T. Spence (Ed.), *Achievement and achievement motivation* (pp. 75-146). San Francisco: W.H. Freeman.

Eccles, J. S., & Harold, R. D. (1991). Gender differences in sport involvement: Applying the Eccles' expectancy-value model. *Journal of Applied Sport Psychology, 3,* 7-35.

Eccles, J. S., Wigfield, A. W., & Schiefele, U. (1998). Motivation to succeed. In W. Damon (Series Ed.) & N. Eisenberg (Vol. Ed.), *Handbook of child psychology: Vol. 3. Social, emotional, and personality development* (5th ed., pp. 1017-1095). New York: Wiley.

French, K. E., & McPherson, S. L. (2003). Development of expertise in sport. In M. R. Weiss (Ed.). *Developmental Sport and Exercise Psychology: A Lifespan Perspective* (pp. 403-423). Morgantown, WV: Fitness Information Technology.

Fry, M. D., & Duda, J. L. (1997). A developmental examination of children's understanding of effort and ability in the physical and academic domains. *Research Quarterly for Exercise and Sport, 68,* 331-344.

Gibbons, S. L., & Ebbeck, V. (1997). The effect of different teaching strategies on the moral development of physical education students. *Journal of Teaching in Physical Education, 17,* 85-98.

Gibbons, S. L., Ebbeck, V., & Weiss, M. R. (1995). Fair play for kids: Effects on the moral development of children in physical education. *Research Quarterly for Exercise and Sport, 66,* 247-255.

Gill, D. L. (1997). Measurement, statistics, and research design issues in sport and exercise psychology. *Measurement in Physical Education and Exercise Science, 1,* 39-53.

Gill, D.L. (2003). Gender and social diversity across the lifespan. In M.R. Weiss (Ed.), *Developmental sport and exercise psychology: A lifespan perspective* (pp. 475-501). Morgantown, WV: Fitness Information Technology.

Gould, D. (1982). Sport psychology in the 1980's: Status, direction and challenge in youth sports research. *Journal of Sport Psychology, 4,* 203-218.

Gould, D., & Chung, Y. (2003). Self-regulation skills in young, middle, and older adulthood. In M.R. Weiss (Ed.), *Developmental sport and exercise psychology: A lifespan perspective* (pp. 383-402). Morgantown, WV: Fitness Information Technology.

Gould, D., Feltz, D., Horn, T., & Weiss, M. (1982). Reasons for attrition in competitive youth swimming. *Journal of Sport Behavior, 5,* 155-165.

Gould, D., Feltz, D., & Weiss, M. (1985). Motives for participating in competitive youth swimming. *International Journal of Sport Psychology, 6,* 126-140.

Griffin, N. S., & Crawford, M. E. (1989). Measurement of movement confidence with a stunt movement confidence inventory. *Journal of Sport & Exercise Psychology, 11,* 26-40.

Griffin, N. S., & Keogh, J. F. (1982). A model of movement confidence. In J. A. S. Kelso & J. E. Clark (Eds.), *The development of movement control and coordination* (pp. 213-236). New York: Wiley.

Griffin, N. S., Keogh, J. F., & Maybee, R. (1984). Performer perceptions of movement confidence. *Journal of Sport Psychology, 6*, 395-407.

Haan, N. (1977). *Coping and defending: Processes of self-environment organization.* New York: Academy Press.

Harter, S. (1978). Effectance motivation reconsidered. *Human Development, 21*, 34-64.

Harter, S. (1981). The development of competence motivation in the mastery of cognitive and physical skills: Is there still a place for joy? In G. C. Roberts & D. M. Landers (Eds.), *Psychology of motor behavior and sport – 1980* (pp. 3-29). Champaign, IL: Human Kinetics.

Harter, S. (1987). The determinants and mediational role of global self-worth in children. In N. Eisenberg (Ed.), *Contemporary topics in developmental psychology* (pp. 219-242). New York: Wiley.

Hayashi, C. T. (1996). Achievement motivation among Anglo-American and Hawaiian male physical activity participants: Individual differences and social contextual factors. *Journal of Sport & Exercise Psychology, 18*, 194-215.

Hellison, D. R., Martinek, T. J., & Cutforth, N. J. (1996). Beyond violence prevention in inner city physical activity programs. *Peace and Conflict: Journal of Peace Psychology, 2*, 321-337.

Horn, T. S. (2003). Developmental perspectives on self-perceptions in children and adolescents. In M.R. Weiss (Ed.), *Developmental sport and exercise psychology: A developmental perspective* (pp. 101-143). Morgantown, WV: Fitness Information Technology.

Horn, T. S., & Amorose, A. J. (1998). Sources of competence information. In J. L. Duda (Ed.), *Advances in sport and exercise psychology measurement* (pp. 49-64). Morgantown, WV: Fitness Information Technology.

Horn, T. S., & Weiss, M. R. (1991). A developmental analysis of children's self-ability judgments. *Pediatric Exercise Science, 3*, 312-328.

Iversen, G. E. (1990). Behind schedule: Psychosocial aspects of delayed puberty in the competitive female gymnast. *The Sport Psychologist, 4*, 155-167.

Jacobs, J. E., & Eccles, J. S. (1992). The impact of mothers' gender-role stereotypic beliefs on mothers' and children's ability perceptions. *Journal of Personality and Social Psychology, 63*, 932-944.

Jarvinen, D. W., & Nicholls, J. G. (1996). Adolescents' social goals, beliefs about the causes of social success, and satisfaction in peer relations. *Developmental Psychology, 32*, 435-441.

Keogh, J. F., Griffin, N. S., & Spector, R. (1981). Observer perceptions of movement confidence. *Research Quarterly for Exercise and Sport, 52*, 465-473.

Kohlberg, L. (1969). Stage and sequence: The cognitive-developmental approach to socialization. In D. A. Goslin (Ed.), *Handbook of socialization theory and research* (pp. 347-480). Chicago: Rand McNally.

Lewin, K. (1951). *Field theory in social science.* New York: Harper & Brothers.

Maehr, M. L., & Nicholls, J. G. (1980). Culture and achievement motivation: A second look. In N. Warren (Ed.), *Studies in cross-cultural psychology* (pp. 221-267). New York: Academic Press.

Marsh, H. W., & Peart, N. D. (1988). Competitive and cooperative physical fitness training programs for girls: Effects on physical fitness and multidimensional self-concepts. *Journal of Sport & Exercise Psychology, 10*, 390-407.

Marsh, H. W., Richards, G. E., & Barnes, J. (1986). Multidimensional self-concepts: A long-term follow-up of the effect of participation in an Outward Bound program. *Personality and Social Psychology Bulletin, 12*, 475-492.

Martin, K. A., & Sinden, A. R. (2001). Who will stay and who will go? A review of older adults' adherence to randomized controlled trials of exercise. *Journal of Aging and Physical Activity, 9*, 91-114.

McPherson, B. D. (1994). Sociocultural perspectives on aging and physical activity. *Journal of Aging and Physical Activity, 2*, 329-353.

Miller, P. H. (1989). *Theories of developmental psychology* (2nd ed.). New York: W.H. Freeman.

Mueller, C. M., & Dweck, C. S. (1998). Praise for intelligence can undermine children's motivation and performance. *Journal of Personality and Social Psychology, 75*, 33-52.

Nicholls, J. G. (1978). The development of the concepts of effort and ability, perceptions of academic attainment, and the understanding that difficult tasks require more ability. *Child Development, 49*, 800-814.

Nicholls, J. G. (1984). Achievement motivation: Conceptions of ability, subjective experience, task choice, and performance. *Psychological Review, 91*, 328-346.

Nicholls, J. G. (1989). *The competitive ethos and democratic education.* Cambridge, MA: Harvard University Press.

Orlick, T. D. (1973, January/February). Children's sport—A revolution is coming. *Canadian Association for Health, Physical Education and Recreation Journal,* 12-14.

Orlick, T. D. (1974, November/December). The athletic dropout: A high price for inefficiency. *Canadian Association for Health, Physical Education and Recreation Journal,* 21-27.

Passer, M. W. (1996). At what age are children ready to compete? Some psychological considerations. In F. L. Smoll & R. E. Smith (Eds.), *Children and youth in sport: A biopsychosocial perspective* (pp. 73-82). Madison, WI: Brown & Benchmark.

Passer, M. W., & Scanlan, T. K. (1980). The impact of game outcome on the postcompetition affect and performance evaluations of young athletes. In C. H. Nadeau, W. R. Halliwell, K. M. Newell, & G. C. Roberts (Eds.), *Psychology of sport and motor behavior—1979* (pp. 100-111). Champaign, IL: Human Kinetics.

Patterson, P. (1996). Measurement approaches to sport psychology questions. In T. M. Wood (Ed.), *Exploring the kaleidoscope: Proceedings of the 8th Measurement and Evaluation Symposium* (pp. 60-67). Corvallis, OR: Oregon State University.

Raedeke, T. D. (1997). Is athlete burnout more than just stress? A sport commitment perspective. *Journal of Sport & Exercise Psychology, 19*, 396-417.

Scanlan, T. K., Carpenter, P. J., Schmidt, G. W., Simons, J. P., & Keeler, B. (1993). An introduction to the sport commitment model. *Journal of Sport & Exercise Psychology, 15*, 1-15.

Scanlan, T. K., & Passer, M. W. (1978). Factors related to competitive stress among male youth sport participants. *Medicine and Science in Sports, 10*, 103-108.

Scanlan, T. K., & Passer, M. W. (1979). Sources of competitive stress in young female athletes. *Journal of Sport Psychology, 1*, 151-159.

Scanlan, T. K., & Simons, J. P. (1992). The construct of sport enjoyment. In G. C. Roberts (Ed.), *Motivation in sport and exercise* (pp. 199-215). Champaign, IL: Human Kinetics.

Scanlan, T. K., Simons, J. P., Carpenter, P. J., Schmidt, G. W., & Keeler, B. (1993). The sport commitment model: Measurement development for the youth-sport domain. *Journal of Sport & Exercise Psychology, 15*, 16-38.

Schutz, R. W., & Gessaroli, M. E. (1993). Use, misuse, and disuse of psychometrics in sport psychology research. In R. N. Singer, M. Murphey, & L. K. Tennant (Eds.), *Handbook of research on sport psychology* (pp. 901-917). New York: Macmillan.

Schutz, R. W. & Park, I. (2003). Some methodological considerations in developmental sport and exercise psychology. *Developmental sport and exercise psychology: A lifespan perspective* (pp. 73-100) Morgantown, WV: Fitness Information Technology.

Shephard, R. J. (1995). Physical activity, health, and well-being at different life stages. *Research Quarterly for Exercise and Sport, 66*, 298-302.

Shields, D. L. L., & Bredemeier, B. J. L. (1995). *Character development and physical activity*. Champaign, IL: Human Kinetics.

Shields, D. L. L , & Bredemeier, B. J. L. (2001). Moral development and behavior in sport. In R. N. Singer, H. A. Hausenblas, & C. J. Janelle (Eds.), *Handbook of sport psychology* (2nd ed., pp. 585-603). New York: Macmillan.

Skubic, E. (1955). Emotional responses of boys to Little League and Middle League competitive baseball. *Research Quarterly, 26*, 342-352.

Skubic, E. (1956). Studies of Little League and Middle League baseball. *Research Quarterly, 27*, 97-110.

Smith, A. L. (1999). Perceptions of peer relationships and physical activity participation in early adolescence. *Journal of Sport & Exercise Psychology, 21*, 329-350.

Smith, R. E., & Smoll, F. L. (1996). The coach as a focus of research and intervention in youth sports. In F. L. Smoll & R. E. Smith (Eds.), *Children and youth in sport: A biopsychosocial perspective* (pp. 125-141). Madison, WI: Brown & Benchmark.

Smith, R. E., Smoll, F. L., & Curtis, B. (1979). Coach effectiveness training: A cognitive behavioral approach to enhancing relationship skills in youth sport coaches. *Journal of Sport Psychology, 1*, 59-75.

Smith, R. E., Smoll, F. L., & Hunt, E. (1977). A system for the behavioral assessment of athletic coaches. *Research Quarterly, 48*, 401-407.

Smoll, F. L., Smith, R. E., Curtis, B., & Hunt, E. (1978). Toward a mediational model of coach-player relationships. *Research Quarterly, 49*, 528-541.

State of Michigan (1976). *Joint legislative study on youth sports programs, Phase I*. East Lansing: Michigan State University.

State of Michigan (1978a). *Joint legislative study on youth sports programs, Phase II*. East Lansing: Michigan State University.

State of Michigan (1978b). *Joint legislative study on youth sports programs, Phase III*. East Lansing: Michigan State University.

Theeboom, M., De Knop, P., & Weiss, M. R. (1995). Motivational climate, pyschosocial responses, and motor skill development in children's sport: A field based-intervention study. *Journal of Sport & Exercise Psychology, 17*, 294-311.

U. S. Department of Health and Human Services (1996). *Physical activity and health: A report of the Surgeon General*. Atlanta, GA: U.S. Department of Health and Human Services, Centers for Disease Control and Prevention.

U. S. Department of Health and Human Services (2000). *Healthy People 2010* (Conference Edition, in Two Volumes). Washington, D. C.

Urdan, T. C., & Maehr, M. L. (1995). Beyond a two-goal theory of motivation and achievement: A case for social goals. *Review of Educational Research, 65*, 213-243.

Vealey, R. S. (1999). The achieving personality: From anxiety to confidence in sport. In G. G. Brannigan (Ed.), *The sport scientists: Research adventures* (pp. 34-56). New York: Longman.

Weiss, M. R. (1999). A "Field of Dreams": Reflections on a career in youth sports research and practice. In J. L. Haubenstricker & D. L. Feltz (Eds.), *100 Years of Kinesiology: History, Research, and Reflections* (pp. 183-213). East Lansing, MI: Michigan State University Printing.

Weiss, M. R. (2000). Motivating kids in physical activity. *President's Council on Physical Fitness and Sports Research Digest, 3* (11), 1-8.

Weiss, M. R., & Bredemeier, B. J. (1983). Developmental sport psychology: A theoretical perspective for studying children in sport. *Journal of Sport Psychology, 5*, 216-230.

Weiss, M. R., & Bressan, E. S. (1985). Connections: Relating instructional theory to children's psychosocial development. *Journal of Physical Education, Recreation, and Dance, 56* (9), 34-36.

Weiss, M. R., Ebbeck, V., & Wiese-Bjornstal, D. M. (1993). Developmental and psychological skills related to children's observational learning of physical skills. *Pediatric Exercise Science, 5*, 301-317.

Weiss, M. R., & Ferrer-Caja, E. (2002). Motivational orientations and sport behavior. In T. S. Horn (Ed.), *Advances in sport psychology* (2nd ed., pp. 101-183). Champaign, IL: Human Kinetics.

Weiss, M. R., McCullagh, P., Smith, A. L., & Berlant, A. R. (1998). Observational learning and the fearful child: Influence of peer models on swimming skill performance and psychological responses. *Research Quarterly for Exercise and Sport*, 69, 380-394.

Weiss, M. R., & Petlichkoff, L. M. (1989). Children's motivation for participation in and withdrawal from sport: Identifying the missing links. *Pediatric Exercise Science, 1*, 195-211.

Wentzel, K. (1998). Social relationships and motivation in middle school: The role of parents, teachers, and peers. *Journal of Educational Psychology, 90*, 202-209.

Westre, K. R., & Weiss M. R. (1991). The relationship between perceived coaching behaviors and group cohesion in high school football teams. *The Sport Psychologist, 5*, 41-54.

Whaley, D.E. (2003). Seeing isn't always believing: Self-perceptions and physical activity behaviors in adults. In M.R. Weiss (Ed.), *Developmental sport and exercise psychology: A lifespan perspective* (pp. 289-311). Morgantown, WV: Fitness Information Technology.

Wigfield, A., Eccles, J. S., Suk Yoon, K., Harold, R. D., Arbreton, A. J. A., Freedman-Doan, C., & Blumenfeld, P. C. (1997). Change in children's competence beliefs and subjective task values across the elementary school years: A 3-year study. *Journal of Educational Psychology*, 89, 451-469.

Yando, R., Seitz, V., & Zigler, E. (1978). *Imitation: A developmental perspective.* New York: Wiley.

References for Developmental Papers Listed in Table 2

Black, S. J., & Weiss, M. R. (1992). The relationship among perceived coaching behaviors, perceptions of ability, and motivation in competitive age-group swimmers. *Journal of Sport & Exercise Psychology, 14*, 309–325.

Brodkin, P., & Weiss, M. R. (1990). Developmental differences in motivation for participating in competitive swimming. *Journal of Sport & Exercise Psychology*, 12, 248-263.

Brustad, R. J. (1993). Youth in sport: Psychological considerations. In R. N. Singer, M. Murphey, & L. K. Tennant (Eds.), *Handbook of research on sport psychology* (pp. 587-599). New York: Macmillan.

Chase, M. A., Ewing, M. E., Lirgg, C. D., & George, T. R. (1994). The effects of equipment modification on children's self-efficacy and basketball shooting performance. *Research Quarterly for Exercise and Sport, 65*, 159-168.

Coakley, J. J., & White, A. (1992). Making decisions: Gender and sport participation among British adolescents. *Sociology of Sport Journal, 9*, 20-35.

Dickinson, J., Sebastien, T., & Taylor, L. (1983). Competitive style and game preference. *Journal of Sport Psychology, 5*, 381-389.

Gould, D. (1993). Intensive sport participation and the prepubescent athlete: Competitive stress and burnout. In B.R. Cahill & A. J. Pearl (Eds.), *Intensive participation in children's sports* (pp. 19-38). Champaign, IL: Human Kinetics.

Keel, P. K., Fulkerson, J. A., & Leon, G. R. (1997). Disordered eating precursors in pre- and early adolescent girls and boys. *Journal of Youth and Adolescence, 26*, 203-216.

Marsh, H. W. (1993). Physical fitness self-concept: Relations of physical fitness to field and technical indicators for boys and girls aged 9-15. *Journal of Sport & Exercise Psychology, 15*, 184-206.

Martinek, T. J., & Griffith, J. B. (1994). Learned helplessness in physical education: A developmental study of causal attributions and task persistence. *Journal of Teaching in Physical Education, 13*, 108-122.

Nevett, M. E., & French, K. E. (1997). The development of sport-specific planning, rehearsal, and updating of plans during defensive youth baseball game performance. *Research Quarterly for Exercise and Sport, 68*, 203-214.

Orlick, T. D., & McCaffrey, N. (1991). Mental training with children for sport and life. *The Sport Psychologist, 5*, 322-334.

Passer, M. W. (1996). At what age are children ready to compete? Some psychological considerations. In F. L. Smoll & R. E. Smith (Eds.), *Children and youth in sport: A biopsychosocial perspective* (pp. 73-82). Madison, WI: Brown & Benchmark.

Pellett, T. L. (1994). Children's stereotypical perceptions of physical activities: A K-12 analysis. *Perceptual and Motor Skills, 79*, 1128-1130.

Wankel, L., & Kreisel, P. (1985). Factors underlying enjoyment of youth sports: Sport and age group comparisons. *Journal of Sport Psychology, 7*, 51-64.

Weinstein, M. D., Smith, M. D., & Wiesenthal, D. L. (1995). Masculinity and hockey violence. *Sex Roles, 33*, 831-847.

Wiese-Bjornstal, D. M., & Weiss, M. R. (1992). Modeling effects on children's form kinematics, performance outcome, and cognitive recognition of a sport skill: An integrated perspective. *Research Quarterly for Exercise and Sport, 63*, 67-75.

Author Note

We gratefully acknowledge Tony Amorose's assistance in compiling several of the resources needed for conducting the content analysis and for his feedback on an earlier version of the manuscript.

We would like to thank Thelma Horn for her thought-provoking and constructive feedback on an earlier draft of the paper. We also wish to acknowledge our appreciation to Diane Whaley, Windee Weiss, Cheryl Stuntz, and Susan Fretwell for their helpful feedback.

Endnotes

[1] Maureen Weiss would like to acknowledge Vera Skubic's pioneering efforts in developmental sport psychology. Weiss was attracted to the field of sport psychology through Skubic's classes and model of excellence, and was Skubic's last graduate student and teaching assistant before Skubic's retirement from the University of California at Santa Barbara in 1975. Vera Skubic passed away in March, 1999.

[2] We take a heuristic approach in describing the nature of the research studies in the content analysis rather than provide specific percentages for each type of research strategy.

CHAPTER TWO

Lifespan Development in Sport and Exercise Psychology: Theoretical Perspectives

Thelma S. Horn

REAL-WORLD SCENARIO 1

An eight-year old boy who has been taking tennis lessons since the age of 4 years begs his parents to allow him to join a very select, competitive tennis team. His parents agree, and the boy happily begins practicing at a higher level of intensity and travels regularly to weekend tournaments around the country. He is very successful and begins concentrating much of his time and attention on tennis activities (e.g., reading tennis magazines, putting up posters of his tennis heroes/heroines, training for strength and endurance, and watching tennis events on television). By the age of 14 years, however, he has lost all interest in the sport and now begs his parents to let him quit.

REAL-WORLD SCENARIO 2

Two elementary-school adult playground monitors comment to each other about the age and gender differences they consistently see in the activity level and behavior of children in Grades 1 to 6 during recess time. Specifically, most first graders are quite physically active even though the boys are mostly involved in sport-oriented activities (e.g., basketball, soccer, baseball) whereas the girls are more involved in locomotor games (e.g., hopscotch, jump rope). By sixth grade, however, the activity level has generally declined for many children. There continues to be a group of boys who are very dedicated to sport activity during recess with the remaining boys spending most of their recess time playing with Harry Potter cards, shooting marbles, and playing hand-held video games. Although there is a small group of girls who are usually physically active (e.g., playing foursquare, tag, or even basketball), the largest proportion of girls are quite sedentary—sitting around in groups talking.

Real-World Scenario 3

At a senior citizens center, an exercise class is in progress. The male and female adults in this class vary greatly in body size, shape, and composition. They also differ in regard to current health status and in physical competence. However, the exercise leader also notes considerable variation in the senior adults' exercise behavior (e.g., intensity level, endurance, and persistence) and in their reactions to the exercise activity (e.g., enjoyment, interest/disinterest, satisfaction, pride, fatigue).

Research Scenario 1

A researcher conducts an interview study for the purpose of identifying adolescents' understanding of moral behavior in general life and sport settings. The researcher finds numerous age, gender, and cultural differences in adolescents' perceptions of morality and in regard to the effect of context (general life or sport) on adolescents' assessment of moral behavior.

Research Scenario 2

A team of researchers conducts a longitudinal research project designed to study the effects of age, physical activity, and physical health on the cognitive functioning ability of middle and older adults. The results of this study do reveal age changes in cognitive functioning, but the age main effect is superseded by both birth cohort and physical activity level interaction effects.

As the stories in the five scenarios clearly illustrate, there are rather large differences between and within individuals in their behavior in particular sport and physical activity settings. As research, practicing, and applied (e.g., teachers, coaches, parents, fitness instructors) psychologists, we are interested in understanding and explaining such inter- and intraindividual variation not only in individuals' behavior but also in their cognitions, emotions, beliefs, attitudes, and values. Psychology is typically defined as the scientific study of human behavior, cognitions, emotions, and reactions whereas sport/exercise psychology is correspondingly defined as the study of the same cognitions, emotions, reactions, and behaviors in sport and physical activity contexts.

Researchers in the general psychology as well as the sport/exercise psychology fields have identified a number of factors (both individual difference as well as socioenvironmental variables) that appear to explain at least some of the variation between and within individuals in their behavior, cognitions, attitudes, emotions, and beliefs in both general and context-specific situations. One of these factors is age or, perhaps more specifically, level of maturation. As illustrated in the five vignettes described at the beginning of this chapter, children and adults at different developmental stages in their lives exhibit different behaviors, attitudes, beliefs, and perceptions. Thus, the primary focus of the subdiscipline known as developmental psychology is the study of the physical, psychological, cognitive, mental, and emotional changes that occur in individuals as a function of increasing age. Within the sport/exercise psychology field, there are also researchers interested in developmental change—especially as such change is exhibited in, or relative to, sport and physical activity contexts.

Similar to researchers in the general psychology field, researchers in the developmental psychology field often use or develop theories as a means to better understand, explain, and predict the changes that occur in individuals as a function of increasing age. The term *theory* has been rather simply defined as a set or series of statements that describe the relationship between behavior and the factors that influence it (Vasta, Haith, & Miller, 1999). From a similar perspective, Thomas (2001) writes that the term *theory* "refers to a proposal about (a) which components or variables are important for understanding a selected phenomenon— such as human development—and (b) how those components interact to account for why the phenomenon turns out as it does" (p. 28). As these definitions imply, a theory is typically developed to explain how a series of facts/findings from various research studies, case studies, or real-life observations are linked together to explain variation between individuals in their behaviors, attitudes, values, beliefs, and emotions. Often, psychologically based theories are illustrated in the form of a model—a pictorial diagram showing a set of constructs and how they are influenced by each other.

Over the last several decades, a number of psychological theories have been advanced to explain developmental change. Although there is certainly some overlap among these theories, there are also significant differences across theories in their explanation and prediction regarding developmental change. Thus, as we shall see throughout this chapter, the various theories that have been developed would provide us with quite different interpretations of the developmental and interindividual differences illustrated in the five examples provided at the beginning of this chapter.

The particular theory that we, as individual researchers and/or practitioners, choose to use in our research studies may certainly affect not only the methodologies and research approaches that we use in our research studies but also the results we obtain and the way in which we interpret our findings. As aptly stated by Thomas (2000), theories serve as lenses through which we view the changes that occur with development. Thus, the theories that we choose to use in our research work affect the type of developmental changes that we study as well as our perceptions of the importance of those changes to the process of human development.

Often, the theoretical perspectives that we choose to use in our research work are guided by the paradigm within which we work (Kuhn, 1970). The term *paradigm* refers to the overall philosophical system of ideas or worldviews that shape our perceptions of reality and thus our research traditions, methods, and discussions (see, for example, discussions by Kuhn, 1970; Lerner, 1997; Overton & Reese, 1973; Thomas, 2001). As we shall see later in this chapter, the various theoretical approaches to human development are based on very diverse worldviews. As described by Thomas (2000), some developmental theories are based on a worldview that perceives human development to be analogous to that of a machine whereas other worldviews perceive development to occur in a more dynamic or interactive way. Thomas (2000) describes these two different worldviews in the following way:

> . . . one camp of theorists pictures the growing child as a machine that reacts to things done to it by the environment; the child's behavior is primarily a product of the way the environment manipulates it. The other group pictures the child as an active, seeking organism who determines his or her own behavior by internally motivated desires. (p. 13)

Obviously, these two contrasting views or perspectives of child development would significantly affect not only the type of research questions that individual researchers ask, but also the variables they choose to measure and the way in which they interpret their results.

Although we, as individual researchers, typically work within only one paradigm and may predominantly adhere to only one or two theoretical perspectives, it is fortunate that our field (developmental psychology and developmental sport/exercise psychology) as a whole includes research work using a variety of theoretical perspectives and, to a lesser extent, a variety of paradigms. Such diversity, although often stimulating much academic controversy, ultimately does result in the advancement of knowledge regarding the processes of human development.

| Theories are developmental psychologists' attempts to incorporate observations into explanations of behavior. |

It is the purpose of this chapter to identify and review the major theoretical perspectives that have been advanced and used to examine, explain, describe, and predict changes in human behavior that occur as a function of increasing age or maturation. This chapter begins with a brief discussion of the concepts of development and developmental change, especially as these concepts are linked to the various developmental theories. In the second section, the characteristics and/or criteria that are, or can be, used to compare and contrast the various theoretical perspectives of human development are identified and discussed. Finally, the chapter concludes with an overview of the main theoretical perspectives that have been and/or are currently being used by developmental psychologists as well as developmental sport and exercise psychologists in their research quest to describe, understand, and explain age-related changes in human behavior, abilities/skills, cognitions, attitudes, beliefs, and perceptions.

Development and Developmental Change

In its most general sense, the term *development* has been defined as all the physical, cognitive, emotional, and psychological changes that humans undergo over a lifetime (Bukato & Doehler, 2001). Thus, the study of human development obviously incorporates the study of change (Overton, 1998). As Lerner (1997) notes, however, development cannot be defined as simply as "change over time." That is, development is not consonant with change (i.e., *change* and *development* are not equivalent terms). As Lerner points out, individuals experience many changes in their lives that may or may not be classified as developmental in nature. For example, during the infancy and childhood years, children's body weight typically increases rather consistently as a function of increasing age. Such body-weight changes may be classified as developmental because these changes are caused by, or at least correlated with, maturationally based and qualitative changes in body size, shape, composition, and functioning. However, during the adulthood years, individuals may consistently or suddenly gain or lose body weight as a function of changes in lifestyle (e.g., diet, exercise patterns, illness/injury). Such changes in body weight probably cannot be classified as developmental in nature.

To distinguish between changes that are developmental in nature and those that are not, Lerner (1997) suggests two additional characteristics or criteria. Specifically, developmentally based changes must (a) be systematic and organized in character and (b) have a successive character (i.e., changes seen at a later time point are, at least in part, influenced by the changes that occurred at an earlier time).

Lerner (1997) also suggests that additional qualifications to the term *development* exist, but that such qualifications or criteria are specific to particular developmental theories. For example, as we shall see later in this chapter, the biologically based theories of human development propose that another definitional characteristic of development would be that the "change" seen in an individual as a function of time serves an adaptive function (i.e., to enhance the organism's survival; Schneirla, 1957). In contrast, the cognitive-developmental theorists would suggest that changes classified as developmental in nature have to include a more sophisticated or mature level of cognitive processing. Thus, as Lerner argues, the terms *development* and *developmental change* can be generally defined as "systematic and successive changes over time" (p. 41), but more specific definitions of development are embedded within particular theoretical perspectives.

To investigate the developmental changes that occur in individuals as a function of the passage of time and/or life experiences, researchers often develop, adapt, or use a particular theoretical perspective as a framework for their research work. Given our dependence on such theoretical frameworks, it is important that we understand how the various theories differ from each other. In the next section of this chapter, a set of criteria, which outline some of the ways in which the various theories on human development differ, is presented and discussed. These criteria allow us to compare and contrast the theoretical perspectives that are discussed in the last section of this chapter.

Comparing and Contrasting the Theories on Human Development

As noted earlier, a developmental theory consists of a set of ideas, propositions, or statements that describe the processes that occur in individuals as they increase in age or level of maturation. Thus, this coordinated set of ideas or hypotheses describes developmental change and also typically provides an explanation for such observed changes across the lifespan (Vasta et al., 1999).

An examination of the various theoretical perspectives (see, for example, discussion by Thomas, 2000) suggests that they differ from each other in a number of important ways. In particular, five such differences have been identified. These five differences are outlined in Table 1 and are discussed in the following sections of this chapter.

Scope or Range of Theory

Although all of the theoretical approaches to human development focus on the changes that occur in humans across time, the scope or range of the theories does vary (see Table 1). To begin with, the various theoretical perspectives differ in regard to the chronological *age range* on which they focus. Specifically, some of the developmental theories address age-related changes only during the infancy, childhood, and adolescent years. Others are more lifespan in perspective (i.e., address developmental change across the lifespan), and a few focus specifically on an even smaller range of development (e.g., theories of infant development or theories of adolescent transition).

A second way in which developmental theories vary in regard to range or scope concerns the *domain(s) of development* on which they focus. As will be evident in the last section of this chapter, many of the theoretical approaches focus predominantly on human development in only one domain (e.g., the cognitive, social, emotional, or physical domains).

TABLE 1
Criteria for Comparing and Contrasting Theoretical Perspectives on Human Development

1. Scope or Range of Theory
   - age range of focus
   - domain(s) or subdomain(s) of interest
   - idiographic or normative focus
   - cultural bases or biases
2. Mechanisms of Developmental Change
   - nature or nurture
   - how much of each?
   - how do they interact?
3. Definition and Direction of Development
   - Is there an "end stage" to human development (i.e., a most "mature" end)?
   - What is "normal" vs. "abnormal" development?
   - What is "desirable" vs. "undesirable" developmental change?
4. Patterns of Developmental Change
   - continuous change
   - discontinuous change (stages or waves: linear or nonlinear; hierarchical or nonhierarchical)
5. Philosophical Assumptions and Investigational Methods

Furthermore, some theories even limit their scope or range to one aspect of development with-in one domain (e.g., Kohlberg's 1976, 1978 theory of moral development). There are some more recent contextually based theoretical models (e.g., Bronfenbrenner's 1993 socioecological systems model) that do consider human development within a broader framework. That is, these theoretical perspectives attempt to present or conceive of human development as a series of interacting domains, each of which interacts with, and influences, the other.

A third aspect of range or scope refers to differences between theoretical perspectives in regard to their focus on *normative or idiographic development*. Specifically, some of the theories of human development focus on the "average" or "normative" individual. Thus, these theories attempt to describe, explain, and predict developmental change by identifying commonalities in human development (i.e., what is the developmental pattern followed by "most" individuals in the study sample or across study samples?). Other theories of human development focus more specifically on identifying causes of individual differences in developmental change. This second approach assumes a more idiographic process in that such research more typically centers on the individual and the factors that produce diversity among individuals in regard to developmental change. Thus, developmental theorists who assume an idiographic approach to human development focus on intraindividual consistencies and changes in the development of a person (i.e., do the variables that comprise the individual remain the same or change throughout the individual's lifespan?). These theorists argue that the variables affecting human development may coalesce in each person in a unique way. Thus, there is a need to understand the individual and the intraindividual changes that occur over time before we can begin to understand the developmental changes that occur within a group.

A fourth way in which theories differ in scope or range is in regard to their *sociocultural bases or biases*. Although some of the theories of human development purport to be "universal" in scope (i.e., applicable to human development across all cultures, races/ethnicities, countries, and social groups), the research evidence used to develop and test the theoretical models may generally be based only on children and adults from a particular country, ethnic group, or social class. As will be seen later in this chapter, other developmental theories (e.g., contextually based theories of human development) do incorporate the notion of culture and the sociocultural environment into their theoretical formulations. Thus, these theories do tend to be more universal in scope and, perhaps, more applicable to human development across a range of cultures, countries, and groups.

Mechanisms of Developmental Change

A second major way in which developmental theories differ from each other lies in their perspective or stance regarding the nature-nurture controversy (see Table 1). Perhaps there is no issue in the field of developmental psychology that has been so long and vigorously debated as the question concerning nature versus nurture. Specifically, developmentalists have long been concerned with whether development and developmental change is the result of the individual's genetic endowment (i.e., due to inborn, biological factors) or of the kinds of experiences he or she has had (i.e., due to socioenvironmental factors). Although this question is still debated today, the particular focus has changed. As several recent developmental writers (e.g., Bukato & Doehler, 2001; Lerner, 1997; Thomas, 2000; Vasta et al., 1999) have noted, the controversy regarding nature-nurture, in its earliest form, concerned *which of the two factors* was most critical in the process of developmental change. The philosophical basis for this question assumes that nature and nurture represent two independent factors, each of which can operate in isolation of the other.

Over time, and as more research-based information was accumulated, developmental scholars generally came to believe that both factors were important contributors to human development. Thus, the question shifted to *"how much" of each* contributes to development in any particular area of behavior. One of the major points of discussion along these lines concerned the relative percentage that nature and nurture contributed to human intelligence (e.g., a 50-50 split, a 90-10, or a 70-30 split). Although this question does begin with the assumption that both factors do affect human development, it still focuses the debate on the relative, but still independent, contributions of nature and nurture.

More recent beliefs concerning this issue have shifted to discussion regarding *how these two factors interact* to affect development. Furthermore, current thinking reflects the idea that these two factors may have differential impact on development in different domains or subareas of study (i.e., genetic factors may be more critical for certain areas of development whereas environmental factors may be more critical for others). Even more complicated is the notion that the two factors may interact in different ways at different stages of development (i.e., there may be different critical periods for the effects of each factor alone as well as for the way in which these two factors interact to affect development and developmental change).

Thus, the scholarly debate and discussion regarding the nature versus nurture issue has continued over the decades even as the focus of the question changes. Furthermore, although most current developmental theorists consider themselves to be interactionists in regard to the heredity versus environment issue, there is still considerable disagreement among and between these theorists in regard to the conditions surrounding the interaction between these two factors and the degree to which each theorist actually incorporates both factors into her or his work. These distinctions will be evident later in this chapter as we examine the various theoretical approaches to human development.

Definition and Direction of Development

A third way in which developmental theories differ from each other is in regard to their definition of development and their perspective of the direction that development takes (see Table 1). In regard to the definition of development, the majority of the theories of human development specify a particular and "desirable" endpoint to the developmental process. In some cases, this endpoint may be generally defined (e.g., human development proceeds from rigidity on the part of the infant to flexibility as an adolescent as explained by Werner, 1961, or from simplicity and compartmentalization to differentiation and integration as explained by Harter, 1990). In other cases, the endpoint is specified in more specific terms. Examples of such theoretical approaches are the "stage" theories of human development (e.g., Erikson, 1959, 1963, 1968; Freud, 1938/1973; Haan, 1991; Kohlberg, 1976, 1978; Nicholls, 1984, 1989) that propose a series or sequence of stages individuals (hopefully) pass through on their way to a most "mature" level of development. The various stage-based theories do differ from each other in regard to their definition regarding the "highest" level of human development (see, for example, contrasting definitions by Kohlberg, Gilligan, and Haan concerning the highest state of moral reasoning).

Along the same lines, many of the developmental theories either directly or indirectly identify and define what constitutes "normal" versus "abnormal" development and what characterizes "desirable" versus "undesirable" developmental change. As a clear example of such theoretical differences, we can contrast the feminist and sexual identity theories of human development with that of Freud (1938/1973) and Erikson (1959, 1963, 1968). Obviously, the two contrasting theoretical groups would postulate very different definitions of "normal" and "abnormal" sexual identity development. Thus, in comparing and contrasting the theoretical approaches to human development, we need to examine not only each theory's definition of

> Most developmental theories incorporate a definition of what constitutes normal or abnormal, desirable or undesirable, developmental change.

development but also its definition of "normal" versus "abnormal" and "desirable" versus "undesirable" developmental change.

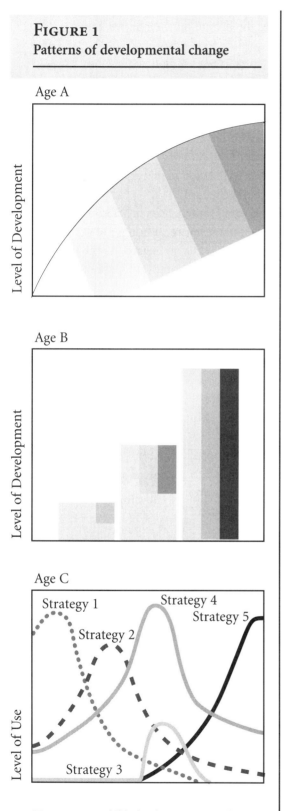

FIGURE 1
Patterns of developmental change

Note. *From Child development: A thematic approach* (4th ed.) (p. 8), by D. Bukatko and M. W. Daehler, 2001, Boston: Houghton Mifflin. Reprinted with permission.

Patterns of Developmental Change

A fourth difference between theoretical perspectives lies in their perceptions or beliefs regarding the pattern by which developmental change occurs (see Table 1). Developmentalists who adhere to a *continuity* pattern perceive development to be a continuous process in that new skills, abilities, behaviors, capacities, beliefs, and cognitions are acquired by the individual in gradual and steady increments (i.e., at a relatively uniform pace). This perspective is illustrated in Graph A (see Figure 1) and reflects a *quantitative* view of development in that the individual grows and matures through a process of "adding" new components to what already exists in the individual's repertoire (see, for example, the information-processing models of human development).

In contrast to the continuity perspective, other developmental theorists perceive development in terms of the individual's progress through a set of sequential stages, each of which represents more mature skills, abilities, behaviors, capacities, beliefs, or cognitions. Developmental change as seen from this perspective is *discontinuous* as the individual is believed to undergo rapid change and transition as she or he progresses from one stage to the next but then evidences a period of stability before entering the next stage (see Graph B in Figure 1). Furthermore, the change that an individual exhibits from one stage to the next is caused by, or is a result of, significant *qualitative* changes in how the individual thinks, perceives, feels, and behaves. Thus, the progression from one stage to the next represents a fundamental reorganization or change in the individual's repertoire of skills, abilities, and cognitions.

To illustrate the differences between the continuity and discontinuity perspectives of development, consider the growth of a tree from sapling to full size. Essentially, growth could be measured or understood to occur in a quantitative way. That is, the trunk of the tree grows larger with age; the limbs of the tree expand in size, number, and branching; and the leaves and/or fruit also increase in size and number. Thus, the difference between the sapling and the fully grown tree can be seen to occur primarily through an "adding on" process. In contrast, the growth of a frog from egg to tadpole to full adult frog could be perceived to occur in a more qualitative way. That is, the frog proceeds through recognizable stages of development, and each stage results in organizational and internal change. Thus, the adult frog is not just larger in size than the tadpole, but it can also be seen as a qualitatively different organism.

As will be seen in the next section of this chapter, the various stage-based developmental theories (e.g., Piaget, Freud, Erikson, Kohlberg, Nicholls) also differ significantly from each other in regard to individuals' progress from one stage to the next (Thomas, 2000). That is, the theories differ in regard to (a) whether and/or how the levels or stages are related to chronological age, (b) whether the stages/levels are universal (found among all individuals in all cultures) and invariant (i.e., individual's progress is sequential with no variation between individuals in their progress), (c) what the factors are that facilitate or impede individuals' progress through the stages, (d) whether an individual can regress to an earlier stage of development, and (e) the consequences of failure to progress.

In general, the stage-based theories of human development do suggest that individuals' progress from one stage to the next is discontinuous in that significant qualitative changes occur in the individual as a result of movement between successive stages. More recently, however, Siegler (1996, 1998) has proposed a modified stage interpretation of development. This perspective has been labeled an "overlapping waves" theory of development (see Graph C in Figure 1), and it suggests that individuals do progress from one stage to the next but that such progress is not so abrupt as it is portrayed in the stage theory (see Graph B in Figure 1). According to Siegler (1996, 1998), individuals at any particular developmental stage can and do use a variety of strategies or methods of responding. Which particular strategy or response the individual uses is a function of both the individual's level of maturation and the situational environment. Similar however to a stage perspective, Siegler's theory also incorporates the notion that individual strategies and responses are age linked or age related. Thus, the probability that an individual will exhibit any particular strategy or response changes (increases or decreases) with increased age or maturation. Again, the main difference between this overlapping-waves perspective and the stage model is that the overlapping-waves view of development recognizes that individuals do not abruptly move from one stage to the next but rather that the transition is more gradual and that individuals can alternate between one stage (strategy) and another for a period of developmental transition.

Philosophical Assumptions and Investigational Methods

The fifth way in which theories of human development differ significantly from each other is in regard to the philosophical origins and assumptions on which they are based (see Table 1). Such innate differences are reflected in the way in which theoretical hypotheses are formed as well as the investigative methods that are used by the developmental theorists and proponents of the theory. A good example of two theorists who differ significantly in regard to philosophical origin and investigative methods are Freud and Skinner. As Thomas (2000) notes,

> . . . Freud's main method of collecting information was to listen to neurotic adults recall incidents from their childhood and from their current dreams. Clearly the particular recollections this method evoked influenced the nature of the theory he proposed. The charge that his theory gives a gloomy, disturbed view of human development has been raised by critics who blame his choice of neurotic informants as the cause of this ostensibly pessimistic picture he paints of child growth. Likewise, his dependence on self-reports of memories and dreams as his source of data is compatible with his willingness to fashion an imaginary structure of the "mind" from which these memories and dreams are generated. In contrast, Skinner rejected introspective reports

as sources of evidence and depended instead on descriptions of child behavior as recorded by an outside observer. This dedication to observable events is compatible with Skinner's unwillingness to speculate about such hypothetical elements as an unseeable "mind" or such mental components as Freud's id, ego, and superego. (p. 49)

These two very contrasting theoretical perspectives clearly illustrate differences between the various theories in their philosophical origins and assumptions and in the investigational or research methods they choose to use in their research work.

As noted in the introductory section of this chapter, the various theories of human development differ significantly from each other because they are rooted in, or based on, very different worldviews (see discussions by Kuhn, 1970; Lerner, 1997; Overton & Reese, 1973). Thus, as illustrated in the quotation by Thomas (2000), Skinner adheres to a very mechanistic perspective of human development (i.e., the individual is analogous to a machine that changes, adapts, and develops in response to things done to it by its physical and social environment). Freud, however, assumes a more organismic perspective of human development (i.e., the individual is an active, seeking organism that interacts with its physical and social environment). Such disparate worldviews are reflected in, or embedded within, each of the theories that have been developed to explain the processes of human development.

In general, then, as the discussion in this section indicates, the various theories of human development do differ significantly from each other in a number of important ways. In the next section of this chapter, the major theories of human development are organized into broad categories or groups. These broader theoretical perspectives are then discussed and evaluated in light of the five criteria identified in Table 1 and discussed in the previous section.

THEORETICAL PERSPECTIVES ON HUMAN DEVELOPMENT

As noted earlier in this chapter, the study of human development and developmental change has a rich and varied history. Thus, it is not surprising that a very large number of theories have been advanced that purport to describe and explain the changes that occur in children, adolescents, and adults with increasing age. It would be difficult, then, to identify and discuss all individual theories. However, these individual theories have been categorized or grouped into classification systems (see, for example, Bukato & Doehler, 2001; Demetriou, Doise, & van Lieshout, 1998; Lerner, 1997; Thomas, 2000, 2001; Vasta et al., 1999).

In this chapter as well, the theories of human development are grouped into categories. These categories, which represent a hybrid of several other grouping systems, include (a) learning theory approaches, (b) cognitive-developmental approaches, (c) psychosocial/psychoanalytical approaches, (d) ethological/biological approaches, (e) contextual approaches, and (f) social movement approaches. As will be evident throughout the following sections, this categorization system reflects the differences that were identified in the previous section of this chapter (and in Table 1) and that characterize each theory's perspective on human development and the processes involved in developmental change. Thus, within each of the following sections, the primary or central propositions of each theoretical approach are explained. In addition, major developmental theorists whose work exemplifies this approach are cited. Then, links are made to research in the developmental sport and exercise psychology literature. Each section ends with an evaluation of the theories in that group using the criteria specified in Table 1. A summary of this evaluation of the various theoretical approaches is presented in Table 2.

Learning Theory Approaches

The primary or essential theoretical perspective that characterizes the developmental theories in this category is that developmental change occurs as a result of learning. Furthermore, learning occurs as a consequence of continuous interactions between the individual and the physical and social environment. Thus, the developmental changes that occur with increasing age are assumed to be acquired rather than inborn. An extreme view of this learning systems approach is illustrated in a quote by Watson (1930):

> Give me a dozen healthy infants, well-formed, and my own specified world to bring them up in and I'll guarantee to take any one at random and train him to become any type of specialist I might select—doctor, lawyer, artist, merchant-chief, and yes, even beggar-man and thief, regardless of his talents, penchants, tendencies, abilities, vocations, and race of his ancestors. (p. 104)

Most of the learning theory approaches to human development arose out of the behaviorism movement in psychology (Watson, 1913), which emphasized the objective and scientific approach to studying human behavior under different environmental conditions. Subsequent behaviorists (e.g., Baer, 1982; Bijou, 1995; Rosales-Ruiz & Baer, 1996; Schlinger, 1992; Skinner, 1974) used the principles of behavior analysis to investigate, describe, and predict developmental changes in human behavior. Such developmental changes are effected through use of classical and operant conditioning. The primary emphasis of behavior analytic theory is to describe and explain how individuals' experiences in, and interactions with, their environment results in developmental change. As such, these theories rely heavily on learning processes as explanations for the obvious changes that occur with increasing age and maturation.

Learning theory approaches maintain that developmental change occurs as a result of learning.

Another example of a learning theory approach to human development is social learning theory that focuses on, or emphasizes, learning that occurs by watching others in the social environment. One of the primary theorists in this category is Bandura (1977, 1978), who suggests that significant learning occurs as children in a society observe adults and other role models perform and are rewarded or punished for particular skills and behaviors. Thus, the process of developmental change in many areas (e.g., not only acquisition of skills but also acquisition of beliefs regarding gender roles, aggression, moral development) occurs primarily through observational learning.

More recently, Bandura (1986, 1989) has delineated the role of cognitive processes in regard to observational learning. Thus, his theory is now more frequently referred to as cognitive social learning theory. The cognitive and behavioral processes included in Bandura's developmentally based theory are attentional processes, memory processes, production processes, self-monitoring processes, and motivational processes. According to this revised perspective, a child's increasing cognitive abilities (i.e., increase in the four cognitive processes) will interact with or work with observational learning processes to effect the changes in behaviors, skills, and abilities that occur as a function of increased maturation.

Learning Theory Approaches in the Sport and Exercise Psychology Literature. Within the sport and exercise psychology literature, there has been some interest in assuming a behaviorist or behavior analytic perspective to investigate human behavior in sports context (see, for example, a recent article on this topic by Lee, 1993). However, this theoretical perspective has not typically been used to investigate developmental change in sport or exercise contexts.

In contrast, Bandura's social learning and social cognitive theories have been used by developmental researchers in sport and exercise psychology. Specifically, a number of researchers have used tenets of the social learning theoretical approach to investigate the development of

TABLE 2
Summary of the Characteristics of the Theoretical Approaches to Human Development

THEORETICAL APPROACH	SCOPE OR RANGE OF THEORY	MECHANISM(S) OF DEVELOPMENTAL CHANGE	DEFINITION AND DIRECTION OF DEVELOPMENT	PATTERNS OF DEVELOPMENTAL CHANGE	PHILOSOPHICAL ASSUMPTIONS AND RESEARCH METHODOLOGIES
Learning Theory Approaches	**Age:** Although primary emphasis is on infancy, childhood, and adolescent years, learning is assumed to occur across the lifespan. **Domain(s):** Primary emphasis on the behavioral domain, but social learning is presumed to occur in all domains. **Developmental Focus:** Normatively based. **Sociocultural Bases:** Basic mechanisms of developmental change are presumed to apply to all cultures, groups, and races/ethnicities.	Primary emphasis on nurture as the mechanism of developmental change. Some theories (e.g., Bandura's social-cognitive learning theory) include the notion that biologically-based maturation in other domains (e.g., cognitive, physical) is necessary for the child to acquire and perform more complex skills and behaviors.	Development predominantly viewed as the process of adding new skills, abilities, attitudes, and beliefs to individual's repertoire. "Desirable" and "undesirable" behaviors are determined by the sociocultural environment within which the individual lives. Acquisition of such behaviors is accomplished through reinforcement, punishment, and/or role modeling.	Continuous and predominantly mechanistic view of development and developmental change. Maturation is perceived to occur with the acquisition of a greater number of learned responses.	Predominantly positivist and experimentally based research approaches.

| Cognitive-Developmental Theoretical Approaches | **Age:** Although primary emphasis is on infancy, childhood, and adolescent years, some theorists (e.g., Harter, 1999) have expanded their work to include a lifespan perspective.

Domain(s): Although primary emphasis is on the cognitive domain, maturation in cognitive structures is presumed to affect development in other domains (e.g., social, behavioral, emotional).

Developmental Focus: Normatively based.

Sociocultural Bases: Developmental changes in cognitive structures are assumed to be universal and invariant, but the sociocultural environment is believed to affect how quickly or slowly (and whether or not) the individual proceeds through each developmental phase. | Although most theorists in this category do assume a biological basis for developmental change (e.g., reorganization of cognitive structures which mature with age), most of the research focuses on the role that the social environment plays in effecting developmental change. Thus, "nature" is tied to "nurture" by specifying chronological age ranges corresponding to each of the developmental stages. | Information-processing theorists view development as the process of accumulating progressively more cognitive skills and abilities.

Other theorists in this category perceive development in terms of stages that individuals proceed through in the development of mature attitudes, beliefs, cognitive abilities, and skills. Thus, the most mature stage within each theory is clearly identified as the "end stage" of cognitive development, and normal/abnormal, desirable/undesirable development is either stated or implied within each model. | Information-processing theorists view cognitive development to occur in a quantitative and continuous way.

Other theorists in this category (e.g., Piaget, Nicholls, Kohlberg, Haan) perceive cognitive development to be discontinuous (stage or overlapping waves pattern). | Information-processing theorists typically assume a mechanistic, positivist, and experimental research approach.

Although early work in Piagetian and the social-cognitive theoretical areas was often based on observation of and/or interviews with children of different ages, subsequent research has assumed a more positivistic, deductive, and experimental research approach. |

THEORETICAL APPROACH	SCOPE OR RANGE OF THEORY	MECHANISM(S) OF DEVELOPMENTAL CHANGE	DEFINITION AND DIRECTION OF DEVELOPMENT	PATTERNS OF DEVELOPMENTAL CHANGE	PHILOSOPHICAL ASSUMPTIONS AND RESEARCH METHODOLOGIES
Psychosocial/ Psychoanalytical Theoretical Approaches	**Age:** Although Freud focused mainly on the infancy, childhood, and adolescent years, Erikson's model is lifespan in nature. **Domain(s):** Primary emphasis on the emotional domain, but advances (or nonadvances) in the emotional domain are presumed to have significant effects on development in other domains (e.g., behavioral, cognitive, social). **Developmental Focus:** Predominantly normatively based, although Erikson does incorporate the notion of individual differences in ways to successfully resolve conflict at each stage. **Sociocultural Bases:** Developmental changes (stages of development) are presumed to be universal and invariant. But, Erikson recognized that the individual's needs at each stage can be met in very different ways in different cultures.	Interactionist perspective in that nature and nurture are presumed to interact to effect developmental change. Specifically, within each of several sequential biological (chronological) age periods, the experiences the individual has (i.e., factors within his/her social environment) determine whether or not she/he will successfully negotiate through that developmental stage.	Development is clearly defined in terms of successive and age-related stages that the individual must go through to reach maturation. Consequences of an individual's failure to progress successfully through each developmental stage are also generally clearly defined.	Discontinuous perception of developmental change (stage perspective).	Early theorists used clinical research approaches (e.g., interviews with patients, observation of behavior in therapy sessions). More recent work tends to be positivist and experimental in nature.

| Ethological/ Biological Theoretical Approaches | **Age:** Primarily limited to childhood and adolescent years. **Domain(s):** Primary emphasis on physical and behavioral domains. **Developmental Focus:** Normatively based. **Sociocultural Bases:** Mechanisms for developmental change are assumed to be universal and invariant, but physical and social environment determines which behaviors, traits, characteristics, or skills are most valuable. | Primary emphasis on "nature" as mechanism behind human development, but "nurture" (physical or social environment) determines which human behaviors, characteristics, and traits are most important. | The "successful" endpoint of human development is defined as the adaptation of the individual to the environment or the survival of the organism for reproduction. | Continuous perspective of developmental change. | Positivist and experimental research approaches. |

Summary of the Characteristics of the Theoretical Approaches to Human Development

THEORETICAL APPROACH	SCOPE OR RANGE OF THEORY	MECHANISM(S) OF DEVELOPMENTAL CHANGE	DEFINITION AND DIRECTION OF DEVELOPMENT	PATTERNS OF DEVELOPMENTAL CHANGE	PHILOSOPHICAL ASSUMPTIONS AND RESEARCH METHODOLOGIES
Contextual Theoretical Approaches	**Age:** Research based on these theoretical approaches has primarily been limited to childhood and adolescent years, but theoretical frameworks can be and have been applied to development across the lifespan. **Domain(s):** Primary emphasis on reciprocal interaction of all domains. Holistic view of developmental change. **Developmental Focus:** Primarily idiographically based, but some of the research is normatively based. **Sociocultural Bases:** Developmental changes not presumed to be universal and invariant but rather specific to cultures, groups, and even individuals.	Nature and nurture perceived to be inextricably entwined in affecting human development.	No pre-determined "end-point" for developmental change. "Normal" development defined by the entire sociocultural, socioenvironmental, physical, and sociohistorical environments within which the individual lives. Some dynamic systems theorists incorporate the notion that developmental change proceeds in the direction of more advanced, complex, or mature skills, abilities, and behaviors. But, such developmental change is presumed to be a function of the interaction of multiple systems and does not proceed in a linear pattern.	Primarily a discontinuous perspective of developmental change. However, developmental change is not perceived to be linear or hierarchical in nature. Rather, developmental change occurs as a function of the continuous and reciprocal interactions that occur between the individual and her/his environment. Thus, these theories perceive the individual to be an active agent in her/his own development.	Most of the research in these theoretical areas employs field and/or observationally based research methods. Emphasis is placed on observation within naturalistic settings and on examination of factors that are unique to the individual. Researchers (especially in the dynamic systems area), who do use more experimental and quantitative research methods, typically incorporate multiple data points and use multiple systems of analyses.

Social-Movement Based Theoretical Approaches	Age: Primary focus on infancy, childhood, and adolescent years. Domain(s): Most theories in this category focus on specific domains or sub-domains (e.g., sexual or racial identity development, self-schema). Developmental Focus: Most theories in this category are normatively based. Sociocultural Bases: Although most theories in this category were formulated within specific cultures, all contain a strong emphasis on the sociocultural environment as a major determinant of the rate, progress, and type of developmental change that occurs over time.	Primary (almost exclusive) focus on nurture as determinant of developmental change.	Most theories in this category specify an "endpoint" for developmental change and also identify and describe "normal" and "abnormal" development.	Discontinuous perspective of developmental change. Predominant emphasis on stage-like progressions.	Most theoretical approaches reflect either a post-positivist or a post-modernist perspective. Research methodologies range from a modified quantitative (deductive) to a very qualitative (inductive) approach.

particular types of attitudes, beliefs, and behaviors in children, adolescents, and young adults. Some of these studies have examined the progression in young athletes from a "play" orientation (i.e., emphasis on fairness first, followed by skill, and then winning) toward a "professional" orientation (i.e., emphasis on winning first, followed by skill, and then fairness) as a result of socializing experiences in sport contexts (e.g., Dubois, 1986; Webb, 1969). Other researchers have used social learning theory to examine children's and adolescents' tendencies to exhibit aggressive, sportspersonlike, moral, altruistic and/or prosocial behaviors in sport settings (e.g., Giebink & McKenzie, 1985; Goodger & Jackson, 1985; Mugno & Feltz, 1985; Murphy, Hutchison, & Bailey, 1983; Sharpe, Brown, & Crider, 1995; M. D. Smith, 1979; Stuart & Ebbeck, 1995; White & O'Brien, 1999). These studies have rather consistently supported the hypothesis that such attitudes and behaviors are, or can be, acquired through observational learning and reinforcement techniques (see recent review of this literature by Weiss & Smith, 2002).

Weiss and her colleagues (e.g., McCullagh, Stiehl, & Weiss, 1990; Weiss, 1983; Weiss, Ebbeck, & Wiese-Bjornstal, 1993; Weiss & Klint, 1987; Weiss, McCullagh, Smith, & Berlant, 1998) have used the theory of learning through imitation of Yando and his colleagues (Yando, Seitz, & Zigler, 1978) as well as Bandura's (1986) social cognitive theory to study observational learning in children. Employing a clear developmental perspective, these researchers have examined age-related changes in children's ability to use the performance of different types of models as well as various cognitive or mental rehearsal strategies to learn and perform basic motor tasks. The results of these studies have generally provided support for the developmental hypotheses embedded in the two social cognitive learning theories.

Evaluation of the Learning Theory Approaches. The various learning theory approaches to human development can be evaluated or analyzed using the criteria identified in the previous section of this chapter and outlined in Tables 1 and 2. Specifically, in terms of scope or range, the learning theory approaches tend to focus primarily on the infancy, childhood, and adolescent years. Although it is recognized that the process of acquiring new skills, abilities, capacities, and behaviors through a variety of learning processes (classical, operant, observational) can occur at any age, relatively little attention has been given to learning and developmental change that occurs in the middle to older adult years. This lack of research attention to adulthood is due, at least in part, to the predisposition on the part of learning theorists to believe that it is early learning experiences (i.e., learning that occurs early in life) that are most significant in shaping the individual. Watson (1928) argued, for example, that "at three years of age, the child's whole emotional life plan has been laid down, his emotional disposition set" (p. 45). Thus, many of the learning theorists endorse the notion that the brain is most malleable during the infancy and early childhood years and becomes significantly less susceptible to developmental changes in later years.

In regard to the aspects or domains on which the learning theories focus, the scope may appear to be relatively large. That is, learning theory approaches purport to apply to development across many domains—physical, emotional, social, and mental. However, as noted earlier in this section, learning theories focus predominantly on behavior (albeit in a variety of contexts) and do not really address developmental changes that may occur in cognitions, perceptions, attitudes, or beliefs. An exception to this, of course, is Bandura's (1986, 1989) social cognitive theory, which does include cognitive processes in the learning of skills, abilities, capacities, and behaviors. However, even within this theory, the primary focus is on the behaviors that result and the learning that occurs as a result of increases in individuals' cognitive abilities.

In general, the various learning theories tend to be normatively based. Thus, again, the processes that result in developmental change are assumed to be universal for all individuals even though the particular behaviors, skills, and abilities that individuals learn may differ as a result of differences in their environment, the particular social agents to which they are exposed, and the experiences they have throughout the lifespan.

In regard to the cultural bases or biases, the various learning theory approaches are not necessarily limited to any cultural setting, especially in regard to Bandura's social learning (1977, 1978) or social cognitive theory (1986, 1989), which clearly specifies that individuals will acquire the skills and abilities, competencies, and behaviors that they see performed and rewarded within their own sociocultural environment. In general, learning theorists do believe that societies differ in the behaviors that are viewed as valuable, desirable, or undesirable, but they also believe that the mechanisms of learning apply to individuals across all cultures, groups, and ability levels. Of course, relatively little developmentally based research has been conducted from the learning theory approach to investigate cross-cultural differences in skills, abilities, competencies, and behaviors.

Although the early learning theorists (e.g., Watson, Skinner) did not really recognize the role of nature (heredity) in regard to human development, most of the theorists in this category do recognize at some level that biological and genetic factors ultimately place limits on the kinds of behaviors, skills, abilities that can be learned. However, the primary focus in regard to describing and explaining the course of human development is on the role that the environment (physical and social) plays. Thus, these theoretical approaches generally fall more heavily on the side of nurture rather than nature.

In regard to the patterns of developmental change, the learning theories reflect the idea that development is continuous rather than discontinuous. That is, development and developmental change occurs in a quantifiable way as individuals acquire new skills, abilities, and capacities with increasing age. This perspective on human development is then predominantly mechanistic in nature as developmental change reflects the notion that the environment (physical and social) "acts" on the developing child to effect developmental change.

Obviously, the philosophical origins of the learning theory approaches are rooted in the theory of behaviorism, which suggests that human development can best be examined and investigated by observing, measuring, and analyzing changes in overt behaviors. Thus, the investigative methods used by learning theorists tend to be experimental in nature, and a positivist research perspective is most typically used.

In summary, then, the theories of human development that reflect a "learning" orientation and are thus categorized in this first group have generated a relatively large amount of research to show that human development and developmental change can be perceived or investigated in terms of the individual's learning through interaction with his or her physical and social environment. However, this is clearly only one way to approach the study of human development. In the next section, the more recent theoretical emphasis on cognitive processes in regard to understanding human behavior is explained.

Cognitive-Developmental Theoretical Approaches

The central construct that characterizes the cognitive-developmental theoretical approaches to human development is that development and developmental change occur as a result of changes in individuals' cognitive structures and cognitive abilities.

> Cognitive-developmental theoretical approaches to human development assert that cognitive changes in structures and cognitive abilities underlie the process of developmental change.

Perhaps the most well-known (and certainly one of the earliest) theorists in this area is Piaget (1950, 1970), whose work and writing on cognitive structures in children and adolescents initiated and stimulated a large body of developmentally based research. According to Piaget, intelligence is not something the individual has or possesses. Rather, intelligence is a process that results in the continual reorganization of knowledge into new and more complex structures. Thus, the individual's intellectual capacities undergo qualitative reorganization at different stages of development. Specifically, Piaget postulated that the child's and adolescent's cognitive structures change as a result of two complementary processes: assimilation and accommodation. Assimilation occurs as the individual, through interaction with the environment, interprets experiences and events in terms of his or her current way of understanding things (in terms of his or her existing cognitive structures). In contrast, adaptation occurs when the experiences and events that occur cause the individual's existing cognitive structure to change in order to accommodate new experiences. Thus, for Piaget, development is primarily located in cognitions and is reflected in increasing sophistication in cognitive structures and cognitive processes. Piaget proposed four stages or periods of cognitive development, with each stage representing a qualitatively different, and more sophisticated, level of thinking. The four stages include the sensorimotor (birth - age 2), the preoperational (age 2 - 6), the concrete operational (age 6 - 12), and the formal operational period (age 12 - adulthood).

Although the cognitive-developmental approach to human development is perhaps most often associated with the work of Piaget and followers of his ideas, there are certainly other theoretical perspectives. Information-processing models of human development were primarily developed in the 1960s and 1970s. These theoretical approaches are based on the assumption that human thought and action are analogous to the basic processes of computers (e.g., Bjorklund & Harnischfeger, 1990; Kail, 1986, 1991; Massaro & Cowan, 1993). Thus, human cognition and cognitive processes comprise three parts: (a) the input of information from the environment via the senses (e.g., eyes, ears, touch), (b) the processing of the inputted information by short-term and long-term memory systems, and (c) the output of processed information as exhibited via behavior (e.g., speech, social interactions, physical actions).

From a developmental perspective, information-processing approaches suggest that humans, like computers, have a limited capacity for processing information (i.e., limitations in attentional focus; the amount of information that can be processed in short-term or working memory; the speed at which information can be encoded, processed, and stored; and the efficiency with which stored memory can be retrieved and used in new situations). However, with increased age and maturation, both physical changes in the cognitive structures and in the sophistication of the strategies that individuals use to encode, process, store, and retrieve information can and should result in increasingly greater information-processing capabilities that should then result in more mature skills, abilities, and behaviors. Correspondingly, of course, maturationally related changes in the muscular and skeletal systems also contribute to the increase in the quality of the desired physical output (e.g., increased physical skill level).

Another subcategory of cognitive-developmental theories includes the social cognitively based theoretical models. The group of theoretical perspectives that fit into this subcategory continues the primary emphasis on age-related developmental changes in cognitive structures. However, this group of theories also gives prominence to social factors in terms of both causes of developmental change in cognitive structures as well as in the effects of developmental change in cognitions on social behavior. Examples of theoretical approaches in this subcategory would include the developmentally based theoretical models regarding achievement motivation (e.g., Harter, 1981, 1990, 1999; Nicholls, 1984, 1989).

Nicholls' theory (1984, 1989) proposes that individuals' behavior, cognitions, beliefs, attitudes, and affective reactions in achievement situations are largely a function of the way in which such individuals cognitively construe or define personal ability and success in achievement contexts. That is, personal ability can be norm referenced (i.e., defined in relation to how one's own performance compares to that of normative others) or self-referenced (i.e., defined in relation to personal mastery and learning). From a developmental perspective, Nicholls proposes that children's and adolescents' perceptions of personal ability, effort, task difficulty, and luck vary as a function of cognitive maturation. Thus, he and his colleagues (1984, 1989, Nicholls & Miller, 1983) have identified stages through which children and adolescents pass as they acquire increasingly more mature conceptualizations of personal ability. However, Nicholls also notes the importance of individuals' social environment in determining children's and adolescents' progress through these stages. Thus, Nicholls' theoretical model can be categorized or identified as a social cognitive developmental theory.

Although Harter's initial model of competence motivation (1981) incorporated a developmental perspective, her more recent work (as summarized in Harter, 1990, 1999) has assumed a more complete and lifespan approach to describing the developmental changes that occur in children's, adolescents' and adults' perceptions of themselves and their competencies. Such cognitively based self-perceptual beliefs across a variety of subdomains have also been linked to individuals' global self-worth and to a number of other behaviors, attitudes, beliefs, and values. Harter's recent work also clearly indicates that individuals' progress over the lifespan through these developmental cognitive stages or levels is significantly affected by individuals and events in their social environment. Again, then, Harter's developmental theory regarding individuals' self-esteem and self-perceptions can best be categorized as social cognitive in nature.

Another group of theoretical approaches that can be classified as social cognitive-developmental in nature would be the theories specifying the development of moral reasoning in children and adults (e.g., Gilligan, 1982; Haan, 1991; Kohlberg, 1976, 1978). Similar to the work of Nicholls and Harter, these more specific theories of development identify or specify stages that individuals progress through in the development of mature moral reasoning abilities. Again, however, children's and adults' progress through these stages is significantly affected by individuals, situations, and processes within their social environment.

In summary, then, the theories categorized in this section as illustrative of the cognitive-developmental approach to human development include three subcategories: (a) those that focus on cognitive development (e.g., Piaget), (b) those that focus on information processing, and (c) those that focus on the social cognitive developmental perspective. The common theme running through these theoretical approaches is the central notion that human development can be examined, described, and predicted primarily via changes that occur within individuals' cognitive structures.

Cognitive-Developmental Approaches in the Sport and Exercise Psychology Literature. The cognitive-developmental theoretical approach has been used rather extensively by developmental researchers in sport and exercise psychology. Jantz (1975), for example, used Piaget's (1970) developmental stages of morality of constraint and morality of cooperation to study the moral thinking of boys (ages 7-12) regarding rules used in the game of basketball. Similarly, Rainey, Santilli, and Fallon (1992) used Piaget's stages of cognitive development to select four groups of male baseball players who should theoretically be at different levels of cognitive development. These researchers then assessed whether these four groups of individuals differed in their conceptions of obedience to, and legitimacy of, authority. This study was based on Damon's (1983) cognitive-developmental theory regarding individuals' age-related progression through three levels of conceptions of authority.

The information-processing approach has also been used by researchers in the motor learning/motor development program area. These developmentally based studies have predominantly examined the effects of age, cognitive ability, and practice/experience on children's and adolescents' cognitive and physical performance in sport skill contexts (see, for example, Abernethy, Thomas, & Thomas, 1993; French, Spurgeon, & Nevett, 1995; Gallagher & Thomas, 1986; McPherson & Thomas, 1989).

A fairly significant amount of research has also been conducted using social cognitive developmental theoretical approaches to examine children's, adolescents', and young adults' level of moral reasoning in sport and general life contexts (see recent reviews of this research by Shields and Bredemeier, 1995, 2001, and by Weiss & Smith, 2002). This developmentally oriented research was based on the theoretical approaches proposed by Kohlberg (1976, 1978), Gilligan (1982), Haan (1991), and Rest (1986).

Harter's competence motivation theory (1981, 1990, 1999) has been used by a number of developmental researchers in sport psychology to investigate age-related changes in (a) children's and adolescents' perceptions of personal competence and/or the accuracy of their perceptions of competence (e.g., Cole et al., 2001; Duncan & Duncan, 1991; Feltz & Brown, 1984; Horn & Weiss, 1991; McKiddie & Maynard, 1997; Ulrich, 1987; Ulrich & Ulrich, 1997); (b) the sport participation motives of children, adolescents, and adults (Brodkin & Weiss, 1990); (c) the sources of information children, adolescents, and adults use to judge or evaluate their sport or physical competence (see recent review of this research by Horn & Amorose, 1998); (d) children's and adolescents' levels of intrinsic motivation (Weiss, Bredemeier, & Shewchuk, 1986); and (e) the relative influence of children's and adolescents' perceptions of competence on, and their perception of the importance of personal competence to, their level of global self-esteem (Ebbeck & Stuart, 1996).

The developmental perspectives inherent in Nicholls' (1984, 1989) achievement-goal theory have been investigated in the sport setting. Specifically, these researchers (e.g., Chaumeton & Duda, 1988; Fry, 2000a, 2000b; Fry & Duda, 1997; Watkins & Montgomery, 1989; Whitehead & Smith, 1996) have examined whether children's and adolescents' conceptions of ability and the factors that contribute to personal ability vary as a function of age-related changes in cognitive processing.

As pointed out by Weiss and Raedeke in chapter 1 of this text, there are other cognitive theoretical approaches that could be used to investigate developmental changes in individuals' cognitive reasoning relative to sport and exercise contexts. These theoretical approaches include Deci and Ryan's (1985) cognitive evaluation and self-determination theories, Dweck's (1999) notions of an entity or incremental conception of ability, and Eccles' (Eccles, Wigfield, & Schlefele, 1998) expectancy-value model of achievement behavior. Other cognitively based theoretical models (e.g., Markus' self-schema theory, 1983, and Weiner's attribution theory, 1985) could also be utilized or adapted by researchers to study lifespan developmental progressions in the sport and exercise psychology area.

Evaluation of the Cognitive-Developmental Theoretical Approaches. To evaluate the cognitive-developmental theoretical approaches, we can again use the criteria outlined in Tables 1 and 2 and discussed in the previous section of this chapter. In regard to the scope or range of the cognitive-developmental theories, the age range is most typically limited to children and adolescents. In addition to age, the scope of these theories is also limited for the most part to the examination of developmental change in the cognitive domain. However, many of the theories in this category do incorporate examination of other subdomains (e.g., affective, social, behavioral) into their research work as the theories are based on the notion that age-related changes in individuals' cognitive structures will be reflected in their attitudes, beliefs, and behaviors in other areas. In regard to the developmental focus, the theoretical approaches in this category primarily assume a normative investigational approach. That is, these theorists and researchers typically look for stages of developmental change that are based on the normal or average individual. Thus, research work is oriented toward identifying patterns of developmental change that would describe the population of study. As such, most of the theories in this category assume the prescribed developmental stages to be universal across all cultures, classes, and groups and to be invariant in regard to individuals' progress through the stages. Of course, most of these theories do incorporate the idea that the individual's sociocultural environment will exert a significant effect on his or her progress through the developmental stages.

Most of the research work on the developmental theories in this category was conducted with individuals from a limited population (i.e., individuals in the United States who are of Euro-American descent and who belong to the middle to upper-middle classes). Many of these theories purport to be universal (i.e., applicable to human development across groups, countries, and races). However, very little cross-cultural or even group research has been conducted. What cross-cultural or cross-group research has been done tends to be comparative in nature (i.e., testing whether or not individuals from different groups/countries differ in their "progress" on the identified stages of developmental change) rather than focusing on the examination of the applicability of the developmental model as a whole to groups other than the "normative" sample or population. Thus, the theoretical models in this category tend to be limited to a specific sociocultural context.

In regard to mechanisms of developmental change, the theoretical approaches described in this section do recognize the contributions of both nature and nurture in regard to human growth and development. That is, these theories do suggest that there are innate, biological, or genetic factors that regulate the changes in cognitive structures that occur with age. However, for the most part, these theories focus much of their attention on the life experiences that individuals have and that may then cause cognitive-developmental change. Piaget, for example, clearly recognized the biological bases for cognitive-developmental change but then focused most of his research on the interactions children had with their environment as the primary factor effecting change in cognitive structures. Researchers following the information-processing approach also accept or endorse the role that biological factors play in developmental change (i.e., these theories note that individuals' brains and other cognitive structures change physically with age). Again, however, much of the developmental research is focused on identifying the instructional strategies and life experiences that cause individuals to acquire better (i.e., more sophisticated) information-processing abilities.

> Cognitive-developmental theorists look for developmental change that describes the population of study.

The social cognitive developmental models focus almost exclusively on factors in the social environment (nurture) to explain, investigate, and predict developmental change. Again, although all of these developmental theories do recognize the role of biological, genetic, or inherent factors in regard to developmental change, the researchers who follow these theoretical approaches typically do not look directly at the interaction of nature versus nurture in regard to developmental change. Rather, these researchers "tie" nature and nurture together via chronological age. That is, the maturational stages that are proposed within each theory are most often associated with a particular age range, thus indicating that there are inborn (or biologically based) factors that underlie individuals' progress through the proposed stages. Most of these theories, for example, would hypothesize that the average five-year-old child would not be capable of progressing to the most mature stage because she or he lacks certain maturational capabilities or capacities. However, the inherent characteristics are only presumed to be necessary but not sufficient in regard to individuals' progress through the stages. Thus, other than associating individual stages with a specific or particular chronological age range, the theories in this category generally focus predominantly on the social-environmental factors (nurture) that effect developmental change.

In regard to the direction and definition of development, the information-processing theorists view development as the process of acquiring progressively more cognitive skills and abilities. Other theorists in this category (e.g., Piaget, Nicholls, Harter, Kohlberg) perceive development in terms of individuals' progression through a series of hierarchical stages, each of which represents a more sophisticated and mature way of thinking. Thus, the "endpoint" of development is defined or identified as the highest stage in the model. As noted earlier in this chapter, the individual theorists in this category do differ in their definition of the most mature stage (see, for example, the differing definitions of the highest level of moral reasoning offered by Kohlberg, Gilligan, and Haan). Correspondingly, these theorists also differ in their perception regarding normal/abnormal and desirable/undesirable development. However, for the most part, such differences are clearly specified in the stages of each theoretical model.

In regard to patterns of developmental change, the theoretical approaches described in this section of the chapter primarily view developmental change to occur in a stage or overlapping-waves pattern (see Figure 1). Piaget (1950, 1970, 1972) specifically identified four cognitive stages through which children progress. Similarly, the social cognitive theorists typically describe developmental change in regard to particular stages of maturation, with each stage reflecting increased maturity in cognitive processing, cognitive structures, or cognitive reasoning. Thus, the stage theorists generally perceive development to be discontinuous and primarily qualitative in nature. It is only the information-processing theorists who may see developmental change as occurring in a more quantitative and continuous way. That is, these researchers do look at age-related changes in information processing as occurring in an additive way (e.g., older, more mature children/adolescents can attend to and process more information than can younger, less mature children).

In regard to philosophical origins and investigational methods, most of the theoretical research in these areas has been conducted using quantitative techniques and assuming a positivist approach. Of course, Piaget's work in this area began with observationally based techniques, and Piaget himself primarily used an inductive approach to develop his stages of cognitive development. Many of the social cognitive models were also based on, or developed using, observation/interview techniques. However, again, most of the subsequent research using these theoretical approaches has been more deductively oriented. Thus, in general, the research basis for the theories in this section tends to be positivist and experimental in nature.

Psychosocial/Psychoanalytical Theoretical Approaches

In contrast to the cognitive-developmental theoretical approaches described in the previous section, the theories that are categorized in the psychosocial/psychoanalytical section reflect a greater focus on emotions and personality than on cognitive structures. Thus, human development is perceived, measured, and investigated in terms of changes in individuals' personality or emotional maturity. In general, psychoanalytical theories are based on the notion that human thought and action are stimulated by inherent instincts or drives. Furthermore, humans are perceived to be dynamic organisms that are continually motivated to satisfy their needs, instincts, or drives through interactions or transactions with their environment. Successful interactions with their social and physical environment at various developmental stages will result in a mature and emotionally stable adult personality.

Freud's theory perceives human behavior to be stimulated by biological instincts called libido or libidinal energy.

Perhaps the best-known theorist in this category is Freud. Freud's (1938/1973) psychosexual theory of development proposes that many aspects of an individual's personality are formed or developed through early (childhood) forms of sexuality. Freud's theory incorporates the notion that human behavior is powered or stimulated by a set of biological instincts called libido or libidinal energy. The psychological tension produced by these instincts builds and requires eventual discharge. Freud hypothesized that the locus or center of this libidinal energy changes with age. As well, the developing child learns successively more mature ways to expend this biologically induced sexual or libidinal energy. In particular, Freud identified five stages of psychosexual development: the oral stage, the anal stage, the phallic stage, the latency stage, and the genital stage. The child's progress through each stage is influenced by maturation (i.e., progress can be measured through chronological age), but Freud also believed that the environment plays a critical role in assuring that each child will progress through all stages. Children who fail to have their needs met at each stage will suffer negative consequences in terms of their personality. Thus, Freud believed that the psychological and mental health problems encountered by many adults could be traced back to their failure to have needs met at each psychosexual stage of development.

A second theorist in this category is Erikson (1959, 1963, 1968), whose theoretical work significantly extended or modified Freud's model of personality development. Erikson's psychosocial theory of human development focused less on biological and sexual sources of tension and more on psychological and psychosocial needs that should or must be met at each of several developmental stages. Thus, Erikson, like Freud, hypothesized that successful personality development is accomplished if the individual progresses successfully through the psychological demands imposed at each developmental stage. In addition, Erikson incorporated a stronger role for the individual's social environment. Specifically, Erikson hypothesized that an individual's psychological development can be fully understood only within the context of the society in which the individual lives.

In contrast to Freud, whose psychosexual developmental stages centered on the childhood and adolescent years, Erikson proposed a series of eight psychosocial stages of personality development that included the lifespan. These eight stages include (a) the oral-sensory stage (birth to 1 year) in which the infant must negotiate or resolve the trust-mistrust emotional crisis; (b) the anal-musculature stage (1 to 3 years) with its emphasis on the child's resolution of the autonomy versus shame and doubt emotional crisis; (c) the genital-locomotor stage (3 to 6 years) in which the child must cope with the initiative versus guilt emotional crisis; (d) the latency stage (6 years to puberty) in which the child must establish a sense of inferiority versus industry, especially as regards her or his participation in, or contribution to, her or his society; (e) the puberty and adolescence stage (puberty to adulthood), which Erikson hypothesized to be a critical one for developing a strong sense of personal identity (i.e., the individual must confront an emotional crisis involving identity versus identity confusion); (f) young adulthood (young adulthood) in which the young adult must resolve emotional crisis relating to intimacy versus isolation; (g) middle adulthood (middle adulthood) with its emphasis on the individual's ability to perceive personal generativity (i.e., contributing to, and producing for, the general society) versus stagnation (i.e., not making a significant contribution to society); (f) maturity (old age) in which the older adult experiences or perceives a sense of ego integrity (i.e., the feeling that one has led a full and complete life) versus a sense of despair (i.e., the feeling that one has not gained everything from life that is necessary or valuable).

For Erikson, then, successful personality development was essentially a search for identity, and the process of adapting one's self to meet the demands of the broader society. Similar to Freud, Erikson hypothesized that individuals who do not successfully negotiate their way through the demands imposed at each developmental stage may be developmentally, psychologically, and socially inhibited in regard to personality development.

Psychosocial/Psychoanalytical Approaches in the Sport and Exercise Psychology Literature. The psychosocial/psychoanalytical theoretical approaches illustrated in this section have not been used with any regularity by theory-based researchers in the developmental sport and exercise psychology area. An exception to this may be some of the research work conducted by sport psychologists interested in the effects of participation in competitive sport programs on children's/adolescents' identity (see, for example, the work of Brewer, VanRaalte, & Lindner, 1993 and Murphy, Petitpas, & Brewer, 1996). Although this work is not specifically developmentally based, the research itself is rooted in, or based on, the developmental psychology literature in regard to the development of self-perceptions in general, and self-identity in particular. Thus, the theoretical models in the psychosocial developmental literature certainly might be relevant for sport and exercise psychology researchers who are interested in this area.

Evaluation of the Psychosocial/Psychoanalytical Theoretical Approaches. Evaluating the psychosocial/psychoanalytical theoretical approaches in regard to the criteria outlined in Tables 1 and 2 reveals, first of all, that the two theories are somewhat limited in scope. Freud's psychosexual theory, for example, is limited to development during the childhood and adolescent years although he does apply the results of this development to psychological problems in adulthood. In contrast, Erikson's psychosocial model is lifespan in nature (i.e., incorporates a developmental perspective that extends from infancy to old age). As noted before, both theories are generally limited to one domain (emotional) although both also recognize the effect of the individual's search for emotional stability or identity on development in such other domains as the physical, cognitive, and social.

In regard to a normative versus an idiographic perspective of human development, Freud and Erikson predominantly focus on normative development. That is, their theoretical models assume a universalist approach to stages of personality development. In particular, Freud assumes that the stages in his psychosexual model generally applied to all humans. Erikson, in contrast, did recognize the importance of culture in determining at each stage of personality development the psychological demands or needs that the individual faced and the methods or procedures by which the individual could adapt to these demands. Thus, Erikson, although primarily a normative theorist, did incorporate an individual difference perspective into his research and writings.

In regard to the cultural bases or biases exhibited by these theoretical approaches, Freud's psychosexual theory is very much limited. That is, the research work on which his theory is based was limited to a particular population of clinically disturbed individuals, even though he assumed that the stages of personality development that he proposed were universal (i.e., would represent developmental progressions for individuals from all cultures, groups, and classes). In contrast, Erikson's theory does incorporate a more multicultural perspective in that Erikson clearly recognizes the role of the individual's sociocultural environment in determining both the obstacles the individual faces in each psychological stage and in the way in which the individual must adapt to successfully progress through that stage. Thus, Erikson's model is predicated on the notion that the particular stages in the model may be universal but that the sociocultural context will determine what "successful" development entails. Furthermore, Erikson believes that the individual's needs at each developmental stage can be successfully resolved in very different ways depending on one's sociocultural environment.

When the psychoanalytical/psychosocial theoretical approaches are evaluated in relation to their perspective on the mechanisms of developmental change, it is apparent that both Freud's and Erikson's models do incorporate to a certain extent both nature and nurture concepts. Although Freud focused considerably more than did Erikson on biological factors, both theorists did exhibit an interactionist approach to the study of human development. That is, both theorists posit the notion that there is a biological basis to personality development but that environmental factors contribute extensively and completely to the individuals' successful progress through the stages of personality development. However, much of the research work conducted to date using these developmental approaches has predominantly focused on the socioenvironmental influences (i.e., nurture).

As noted earlier, both Freud and Erikson indicate that "successful" development results in the individual's reaching the highest stage of emotional stability. As both theorists suggest, failure to negotiate the emotional issues or conflicts that arise at each developmental stage will result in the individual's failure to progress to higher levels. This "abnormal" or "undesirable" consequence occurs if or when the individual cannot move through a particular stage. Furthermore, the lower-level stage at which an individual may stay results in identifiable emotional problems that will be evident in, or even through, adulthood.

Obviously, both Freud and Erikson assume that developmental change occurs in a discontinuous or qualitative way. That is, both models propose a series of developmental stages through which individuals pass, and each stage represents a qualitatively different level (i.e., individual's personality is significantly altered or reorganized at each stage).

The philosophical origins and investigational methods used by theorists and researchers in this section are generally rooted in the clinical or psychoanalytical research tradition. Thus, much of the original work on which the theories are based were conducted via clinical interviews, especially with adults who were experiencing emotional problems or identity crises. However, Freud's theory of human development also reflects a basic science (physics) notion that energy cannot be created or destroyed but can only be transformed. Thus, Freud's beliefs concerning human drives incorporate this idea by suggesting that human instincts and drives (especially the libido) cannot be destroyed but can only be rechanneled into something more positive in regard to emotional maturity. Although both Freud's and Erikson's theories are essentially located in the psychoanalytic research tradition, subsequent work to examine the validity of the developmental stages proposed by these two theorists has often been based on normative, positivistic, and population-based research methods rather than on the inductive clinical interview procedures.

Ethological/Biological Approaches

The ethological or biological approaches to the study of human development are based primarily on an evolutionary perspective. Thus, ethological explanations for child or human development place particular emphasis on biological forces (as derived during the evolution of the species) as determinants of behavior and behavioral tendencies.

The historical roots for such approaches typically lie with the work of Darwin (1859, 1872), who believed that human and animal development was the result of evolution. The primary focus of his theory was that adaptive traits (those that improved the likelihood of survival and thus ensured a greater number of offspring for further reproduction) were more likely to be found in succeeding generations of a species. Thus, through evolutionary processes, humans inherit the biological traits and capacities that will improve their rate of survival. Over generations, then, selected biological traits and capacities will be "weeded out" because they do not enhance survival of the individual, and thus these traits and capacities cannot be reproduced in the next generation. It is only the biological traits and capacities that enhance survival that will be passed on through reproduction to the next generations.

> Sociobiological theorists suggest that social behaviors also have a biological and evolutionary basis.

Subsequent ethological theorists (e.g., Bowlby, 1969; Lorenz, 1966; Tinbergen, 1973) further explored these evolutionary approaches to human development by postulating that children (similar to animals) are predisposed to certain kinds of learning that can occur only during critical/sensitive periods of development. This form of learning, identified as imprinting, is then seen as the key to successful developmental change and adaptation.

A more recent theoretical approach that falls within this category is the sociobiological perspective. These theorists (e.g., Dekay & Buss, 1992; Scarr, 1992; Wilson, 1975) suggest that social behaviors also have a biological and evolutionary basis. Specifically, just as humans possess genes that dictate, determine, or produce particular physical characteristics (e.g., blue eyes, right-handedness), they also possess genes that produce particular social behaviors. From an evolutionary perspective, those social behaviors that enhance survival will be more apt to be passed down to subsequent generations than will those social behaviors that do not enhance survival. Thus, the genes that are responsible for producing social behaviors go through the same "natural selection" process, as do the genes responsible for producing physical characteristics or abilities. Again, then, sociobiologists approach the study of human development from a very biologically based and evolutionary perspective.

Ethological/Biological Approaches in the Sport and Exercise Psychology Literature. At this point, very little, if any, research has been conducted in the developmental sport and exercise psychology field using an ethological or biological theoretical approach. Given the social psychological tradition upon which sport and exercise psychology tends to be based, it is understandable that the ethological and biological approaches to human development have not been explored in relation to developmental sport and exercise psychology.

One area in which these theories may be applicable to the study of human behavior in sport and exercise psychology contexts is in the examination of the effects of birth order within families on children's subsequent performance, behavior, and personality. An analysis of the research in this area was recently provided by Sulloway (1996), a sociobiologist, who argues that because later-born children must find alternative ways, means, and methods of acquiring their share of the family's resources (i.e., to "survive" within the family), they may (as a function of their biological birth order) develop different personalities, behaviors, and skills than those of their first (and earlier-born) siblings. Sulloway also discusses how birth order interacts with other factors (e.g., gender, temperament, time spacing between children in families, and age) to affect each child's personality development. Although Sulloway's analysis of the research on birth order did not focus on the relationship between birth order and sport or physical activity behavior, previous researchers in our field have examined this link (e.g., Casher, 1977; Eaton, Chipperfield, & Singbeil, 1989; Landers, 1970; Yiannakis, 1976). Given, however, the myriad of other factors (individual difference and socioenvironmental) that appear to exert a stronger effect on individual's behavior in sport and physical activity contexts, birth order has typically not been investigated in our field as a significant causative influence of physical activity behavior or developmental change.

Evaluation of the Ethological/Biological Theoretical Approaches. Evaluation of these theoretical approaches relative to the criteria listed in Tables 1 and 2 shows that the ethological/biological theories are somewhat limited in scope. That is, most of the developmental work has focused on children and adolescents and has been oriented primarily to the physical and behavioral domains. The sociobiologists do focus on social issues, but their primary interests remain in the area of evolutionary biology as it affects or determines individuals' behavior in social settings. Ethological/biological theoretical approaches are also predominantly normative in nature. That is, they tend to focus on identification of the patterns of developmental change for the group (i.e., to find the most common or typical mode of change).

These theoretical approaches are purported to be universal in scope (i.e., mechanisms of developmental change are perceived to be applicable to all individuals, groups, cultures), but these theories also recognize the role of the physical and social environment within which groups live in determining which physical and social characteristics are most apt to be passed down to subsequent generations.

In regard to the mechanisms of developmental change, the ethological and biological theories appear to be based primarily on nature rather than nurture. That is, these theorists obviously perceive biology and genetics to be the primary determinant of human behavior and human development. However, theorists following these approaches also recognize nurture (i.e., the physical and social environment) in regard to its role in developmental change. Specifically, it is the physical and social environment within which individuals or groups live that determines the physical and social characteristics that are most needed for survival. Thus, ultimately the genes associated with these selected physical and social characteristics are those that are most apt to be passed down to future generations. In addition, many of the theorists in this group (particularly the ethologists) recognize the importance of the social and physical environment in determining the course of human development especially during the critical or sensitive periods of development. Thus, although the theories in this group are very biologically based, they still recognize the interactional effects of nature and nurture.

In defining what is the endpoint of developmental change and/or what is "normal" or "desirable" developmental change, the theories in this category would appear to use the concept of adaptation or survival as the defining characteristic. That is, these theories are based on the assumption that the physical and social characteristics that are most necessary for the survival of the species will be the characteristics that are most apt to be passed down to succeeding generations. Thus, optimal developmental change would be defined in terms of adaptation to the environment and the survival of the organism for reproduction.

In regard to developmental patterns, the theoretical approaches in this section primarily perceive development to occur in a continuous manner. That is, development occurs in a quantitative way as new skills, abilities, behaviors, and competencies are "added" to an existing repertoire.

Finally, it is obvious that these theories are very biologically based, and the investigational methods and research hypotheses tend to be very experimental in nature and to include behavioral bases of measurement. Thus, the philosophical assumptions and origins are positivistic and experimental.

Contextual Theoretical Approaches

The group of theoretical approaches that are illustrative of this category reflect the central notion that human development occurs within a context and, perhaps even more importantly, that the context often influences the course of that development. Furthermore, contextual models are based on the belief that individuals are active producers of their own development. That is, just as the context changes the individual, the individual also changes his or her context. Contextual models (sometimes called systems models), then, are concerned with understanding the broad range of biological, physical, and sociocultural settings and how they interact to affect, and be affected by, the course, content, and direction of human development.

One primary example of a contextually based theoretical approach to human development is Bronfenbrenner's (1977, 1979, 1993; Bronfenbrenner & Morris, 1998) ecological systems theory (more recently referred to as the bioecological model). Bronfenbrenner's model was based on his belief that much of the previous research on child development involved studying children under artificial conditions. As he argued, "much of contemporary developmental psychology is the science of the strange behavior of children in strange situations with strange adults for the briefest possible periods of time" (1977, p. 513). In contrast, Bronfenbrenner asserted that children should be studied in their own real-world settings (i.e., in ecologically valid settings). Furthermore, he suggested that the context within which human development occurs comprises, and therefore should be viewed as, a series of different levels that interact in a reciprocal manner. Thus, his ecological systems model (see Figure 2) consists of a series of interrelated layers that represent the ecological forces and systems that affect, and are affected by, the developing child. As the model in Figure 2 shows, the individual child (with his or her biological and psychological makeup) forms the center of the diagram. Immediately surrounding the child is the first level in the system. This level, identified as the microsystem, is composed of the immediate physical and social environment within which the child lives. This includes the home and members of the household, the social and educational circumstances of the child's life (e.g., daycare centers, schools) as well as the neighborhood (including both the physical characteristics as well as the people). The second layer is the mesosystem, which consists of the many interrelationships among the systems within the children's physical and social environment (e.g., the relationship between the child's home and school). The third layer is labeled as the exosystem and includes the broader social, political, religious, and economic conditions within which the child and her or his microsystem exist. The fourth layer is the macrosystem, and it represents the general beliefs, attitudes, practices, ceremonies, and customs shared by the cultural group of members of the broader society within which the child lives. Finally, Bronfenbrenner also postulates the presence and influence of the chronosystem on the course of human development. The chronosystem refers to the passage of time and thus includes the notion that the individual systems of influence (e.g., the microsystem, mesosystem, exosystem, and macrosystem) will change over time and as the result of historical events.

Bronfenbrenner's (1977, 1979, 1993) model essentially provides researchers with a conceptual framework for studying human development. It is important to understand, however, that Bronfenbrenner conceives of human development as a dynamic interactional process. Specifically, as illustrated by the model in Figure 2, the child and the environment continually influence one another in a bidirectional and transactional manner.

> Some researchers have applied a physics-based theory, the dynamic systems approach, to human development and human movement in hopes of gaining a broad understanding.

A second conceptual model is that proposed by Vygotsky (1981), a Soviet psychologist whose theory is now generally referred to as a sociohistorical theory. Although Vygotsky's primary focus is on cognitive development during the infancy, childhood, and adolescent years, his theory also emphasizes the role of culture as a major determinant of individual development. Specifically, Vygotsky suggests that children acquire much of the content of their thinking (i.e., their knowledge structures) from the culture around them. In addition, children acquire from their culture their thinking and reasoning processes (i.e., the tools of intellectual development). In combination, then, culture teaches children both *what* to think and *how* to think. The primary way by which culture affects children's cognitive development is through a dialectical process in which children learn through shared problem-solving with others (most typically adults). Thus, Vygotsky believed that language is an especially important tool because it is not only the conduit by which children get enculturated but that language is also internalized by children and thus subsequently affects the structure of their cognitions as well as the way in which they think and problem solve. Children over time begin to internalize the attitudes, norms, mores, behaviors, and cognitions that are characteristic of their culture. According to Vygotsky, then, human development can only be studied relative to the culture within which an individual lives, and the course of human development is dictated or determined by that culture.

A third theoretical perspective regarding human development that can be classified as contextual in nature is the dynamic systems perspective. The term *dynamic systems theory* does not really refer to a single theory but rather to a class of theories that explain development as the emerging organization arising from the interaction of many different processes and systems.

The dynamic systems approach was essentially developed within the science of physics (e.g., Bernstein, 1967; Haken, 1983) but has been applied to human development and human movement by several writers and researchers (e.g., Kelso, 1995; Novak, 1996; Thelen, 1995, Thelen & Smith, 1998). Similar to other contextually based theorists, dynamic systems theorists hypothesize that human development occurs as a function of the interaction of multiple systems (e.g., physical, neural, social, cognitive, social, sociocultural), but additionally the dynamic systems approach includes the notion that more advanced or complex skills, abilities, and behaviors emerge over time as a result of the interaction of the systems. Thus, development is not controlled or regulated by any one particular factor (e.g., brain, genes, child-rearing practices), but rather these systems interact and/or, at times, clash to induce the development of more mature behaviors or capacities.

The tenets of dynamic systems theory have been applied to the study of children's motor development by Thelen and her colleagues (1995; Thelen & Smith, 1998; Thelen, Ulrich, & Jensen, 1989). According to these researchers, both nature and nurture contribute to the development of motor skills during the infancy and childhood years. Specifically, Thelen suggests that as babies mature biologically and cognitively, they become more motivated to accomplish more and to gain additional motor skills (e.g., crawling, walking, reaching). When there is a task that the child is motivated to accomplish (e.g., reaching for a desired object) but does not currently possess the ability to do, that child must create or develop that ability. To do so, the child will first explore (i.e., try many different motor responses in a random way) and then select (i.e., learn which motor responses work to accomplish the desired task). Thus, according to Thelen, nature provides most of the raw material for human development, but nurture (the child's physical and social environment) determines the timing as well as the direction of development.

FIGURE 2
Bronfenbrenner's ecological model.

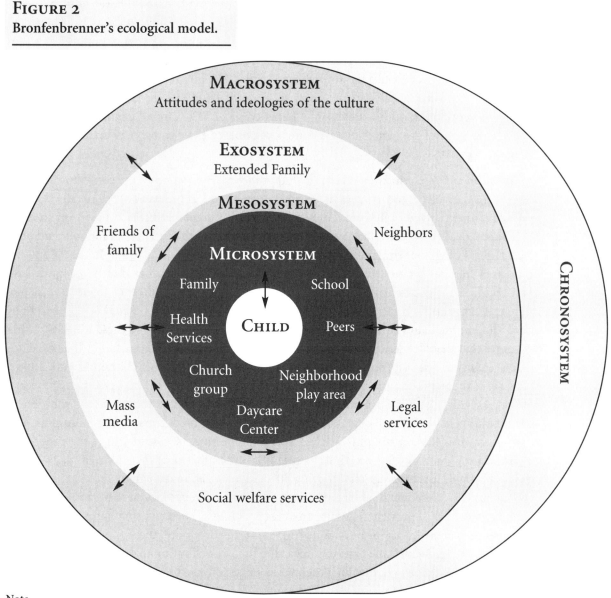

Note.
From Child development: A thematic approach (4th ed.) (p. 8), by D. Bukatko and M. W. Daehler, 2001, Boston: Houghton Mifflin. Reprinted with permission.

A second tenet of the dynamic systems view of motor development suggests that the individual child is comprised of many complex systems (e.g., skeletal, muscular, postural, sensory, perceptual, cardiovascular) (Thelen et al., 1989). Furthermore, the various body systems will interact in a variety of ways to effect maturational change in motor skill movements and patterns.

From a broader perspective, dynamics systems theory conceives of human development as the product of reorganization in behaviors, skills, cognitions, and abilities that occur as a result of the interactions of various levels of the system (physical, social, cognitive, neural, biological). Thus, development cannot really be studied by looking at, measuring, or examining only one system and the changes that occur over time within that system. Rather, the process of human development must be examined from a multiple-systems perspective.

Contextually Based Research in the Sport and Exercise Psychology Literature. As noted earlier, dynamic systems theory has been employed by motor developmental researchers (e.g., Thelen, 1995; Thelen & Smith, 1998; Thelen et al., 1989) and by motor learning/control researchers (e.g., Kelso, 1995). However, this theoretical approach has not been used to any great extent by researchers in the sport and exercise psychology field to address developmental progressions. Neither have we utilized the other contextually based theoretical approaches described in this section. However, given the increasing importance that has been given to "context" as a factor affecting human behavior as well as human development and developmental change (see, for example, arguments presented by Dzewaltowski, 1997), such theoretical approaches would be profitable to explore in our field. A framework for using Bronfenbrenner's ecological systems theory to examine children's development in sport contexts has recently been outlined by Garcia Bengoechea (2002; Garcia Bengoechea & Johnson, 2001). Thus, future research using this contextually based perspective may certainly be facilitated.

Evaluation of the Contextual Theoretical Approaches. Evaluation of the contextual theoretical approaches using the criteria listed in Tables 1 and 2 indicates, first of all, that the contextual theories are quite broad in scope. First, although the research based on most of these theoretical perspectives has been focused primarily on the infancy, childhood, and adolescent years, the theories themselves are generally lifespan in nature. In addition, the contextual theories are not limited with regard to domain, but rather clearly recognize and even emphasize the interaction of the various domains in contributing to developmental change. In contrast to other theoretical approaches, the contextually based theories tend to be more idiographic than normative in regard to developmental change as these theories clearly recognize that developmental change may not be universal in nature but rather that developmental change is prescribed or determined by the culture within which the individual lives. Thus, these theories are more likely to focus on idiographic development (i.e., interindividual differences in development as a function of different physical and sociocultural environments). Correspondingly, then, these contextual theories are not limited to particular cultures, countries, or groups. Rather, the physical and social environments within which the individual organism grows and develops are incorporated into the individual theories as a major factor affecting human development and as being affected by individual change.

Evaluation of the contextual theoretical approaches with regard to mechanisms of developmental change would indicate that these theories generally do perceive that nature and nurture are important contributors to human development. Furthermore, these theories assume that the two factors are inextricably linked in regard to their contribution to developmental change. Thus, in contrast to many of the other theoretical perspectives, the contextual theories not only consistently recognize both factors as important to developmental change but also suggest that human development cannot be assessed or examined without consideration of the reciprocal relationship that exists between nature and nurture.

In general, the contextually based theories are unique in regard to their assumption that there is no identifiable or prescribed endpoint to human development. That is, the contextually based theories do not begin with the assumption that infants, children, and adolescents exhibit "normal" progress toward some known conceptualization of mature adulthood. Rather, individuals are constantly in a state of flux or flow as they reciprocally interact with their physical and social environment. Similarly, for contextual theorists, "normal," "abnormal," "desirable," and "undesirable" development are defined by the culture within which development occurs. Again, then, there is no universal definition for these terms.

Some of the researchers who follow a dynamic systems perspective do incorporate the notion that developmental change proceeds in the direction of more complex, mature, or advanced skills, abilities, and behaviors. However, such developmental change is presumed to occur as a function of the interaction of multiple systems, and the individual is perceived to be a major and active agent in regard to her or his own development.

In regard to patterns of developmental change, the contextually based theories are predominantly discontinuous in their conceptualization of developmental change (i.e., developmental change involves qualitative reorganization or restructuring). However, the theories do vary somewhat in their notions regarding the particular pattern of change. Specifically, Vygotsky, similar to the cognitive-developmental theorists, hypothesizes stages of development. In contrast, Bronfenbrenner and the dynamic systems theorists do not really perceive developmental change to occur in identifiable or hierarchical stages. That is, although at least some of these theorists do believe that developmental change occurs and that it can be described, they also believe that such change does not proceed in identifiable stage-like transitions. Rather, developmental change is presumed to be nonlinear in nature and does not necessarily follow a smooth or hierarchical path toward some predetermined endpoint.

With the exception of Vygotsky's (1981) sociohistorical theory, most of the theoretical approaches in this category are relatively recent and originated out of dissatisfaction with traditional perspectives on human development. Specifically, the contextually based theoretical approaches primarily focus on the holistic view of human development (i.e., developmental change cannot be studied without considering all domains of development and/or without considering the social and physical context within which development occurs). Thus, the investigational methods tend to be field based and/or observationally based. When clinical interview or laboratory settings are used, investigators employ "real-world" problems to assess individuals' cognitive, affective, emotional, and behavioral responses. When quantitative or positivistic research methods are used, multiple data points are incorporated, and an attempt is made to include multiple systems within each analysis.

Social-Movement-Based Theoretical Approaches

The very eclectic group of theories included in this category reflect recent theoretical advances that originated out of social protest movements beginning in the 1960s and 1970s (e.g., antiwar protests, civil rights protests, feminist and social class protest movements) and/or as a response to academic dissatisfaction with rationalism or positivism both as a worldview and a way to understand human behavior. Thus, the theories grouped into this category are similar in that they generally represent relatively recent theoretical perspectives and are predominantly based on a postpositivist or a postmodernist worldview. In addition, these theoretical approaches are distinct from those in previous categories in that they tend to focus on socially disadvantaged groups. Thomas (2001), in his analysis of recent theoretical advances in human development, identifies and discusses four types of social-movement-based theoretical approaches. These four types correspond to four different socially disadvantaged groups. Thomas' analysis of these recent theoretical approaches is summarized in the following paragraphs.

Feminist theories have one thing in common: the premise that females in male-dominated societies will be oppressed.

The first group of theories focuses on developmental processes and progressions in *children who grow up in poverty conditions* (i.e., in lower socioeconomic environments). An example of this type of theory is Smeeding's (1995) interdisciplinary model of child well-being that incorporates macrosocial and microbehavioral perspectives to construct a macro-micro model of child development. Macro variables include the child's physical and social environment (e.g., family characteristics, community environment, social-policy environment, and social attitudes context). Micro variables include parent/family processes (e.g., adult health condition, parental behaviors, parent aspirations) and community/life processes (medical care, daycare, schooling, job training, community activities). The overall model suggests that the macro and micro systems interact in unique ways to affect children's developmental outcomes (e.g., health, self-image, cognitive achievement, interpersonal skills). Although the model can be used for studying the development of children in any social class, Smeeding's own work has focused on children growing up in poverty.

Other theoretical perspectives in this category include Garfinkel and McLanghen's (1995) microtheory concerning the impact of financial support on child development in low-income, single-parent families. Similarly, McLoyd and Wilson's (1991) stress-based model of child development in poverty-level environments constitutes another example within this category.

The second group of theories in this overall category includes theoretical perspectives regarding developmental processes in *ethnic and minority groups*. A recent example is that published by Garcia Coll and her colleagues (1996). Their integrative model for the study of developmental competencies in minority children is based on social stratification theory and emphasizes the interaction of social class, culture, ethnicity, and race in affecting and determining the development of competencies (e.g., cognitive, social, emotional, linguistic) in minority children.

From a different perspective, Helms (1990, 1995) proposes a stage-based model that describes the processes by which individuals acquire a sense of racial identity. Specifically, Helms hypothesizes a set of stages, each representing a different worldview—"cognitive templates that people use to organize (especially racial) information about themselves, other people, and institutions" (Helms, 1990, p. 19). Recognizing that the development of racial identity is very much influenced by dominant power and privilege relationships between races within any society, Helms proposes a different set of stages for each race or for each group of races that exhibit similar social and historical status within a society.

The third group of theories in this category includes those that reflect a *feminist* perspective. As both Thomas (2001) and Tong (1998) clearly point out, the broad array of feminist theories that have been proposed over the last several decades generally begin with the premise that many societies are male dominated and that females in such societies will be oppressed. However, beyond this initial premise, there are rather major differences among the feminist theorists. Thus, the groups of theories that can be labeled as feminist theories differ significantly from each other. Tong has categorized them under eleven headings: liberal, radical, Marxist, multicultural, ecological, socialist, global, psychoanalytic, gender, postmodern, and existentialist.

The fourth and last group of theories included in the broad social-movement-based theoretical approaches are those that focus on the *development of sexual orientation especially in homosexual and bisexual youth and adolescents*. Some of these theories attempt to explain how nonheterosexual orientations develop. These theories can be further classified into (a) biological explanations (i.e., homosexual tendencies due to genetics, hormonal ratios, or physiological influences prior to or shortly after birth; e.g., Hamer & Copeland, 1994); (b) sociopsychological explanations (i.e., homosexual tendencies due to learned or acquired characteristics; e.g., Freud, 1938/1973; and (c) interactionist explanations (i.e., homosexual tendencies due to interaction between body chemistry and environmental influences; e.g., Friedman, 1988).

A second subgroup of theories in this category attempt to trace the processes or ways by which homosexual and bisexual individuals come to terms with their sexual identity. Typically, these theories incorporate a "stages" approach to describe how non-heterosexually identified individuals can and do establish a positive homosexual identity. One such theory is that of Cass (1979, 1984), who proposed six stages that proceed from a low of identity confusion to a high of identity synthesis. Similar stage-based theories have been proposed by Coleman (1982), Lewis (1984), and Troiden (1988). In addition, Weinberg and his colleagues (Weinberg, Williams, & Pryor, 1988) have proposed a four-stage sequence for the development of a bisexual self-image. Most of these theories are based on extensive interviews (retrospective and longitudinal) with gay and bisexual youth and adults.

Social-Movement-Based Theoretical Approaches in the Sport and Exercise Psychology Literature. Little research has been conducted in the developmental sport and exercise psychology literature using the theoretical approaches described in this section. Certainly, however, such theoretically based research would constitute a valuable and unique addition to the developmental literature, especially as relatively little research has been conducted in the sport and exercise psychology fields on the populations of individuals who are targeted in the theoretical approaches in this section. Therefore, considerably more research is needed regarding the developmentally based experiences of gay and lesbian youth in sport as well as the ways in which children, adolescents, and adults of color are affected by their participation or experiences in sport and exercise activity.

Work based on feminist theory has been a relatively recent and certainly welcome addition to the literature in sport and exercise psychology. This work includes the research and writing of such individuals as Bredemeier (2001; Bredemeier, Carlton, Hills, & Oglesby, 1999), Krane (1994, 1997, 2001), Birrell (1988, 1989), Griffin (1992), Oglesby (2001a, 2001b), and Hall (2001). Furthermore, much of this work has been summarized and reviewed by Gill (2002) in a recent book chapter and by a series of articles contained in a special issue of *The Sport Psychologist* (2001) that was guest edited by Gill. Although much of this theoretical and empirical research work has not specifically been developmentally based, much of it is applicable to understanding the development of traditional and nontraditional ways of thinking about girls and women in sport. Thus, this work certainly does provide a strong theoretical and feminist perspective on gender issues in sport and also should form for us a good framework for conducting more specifically developmentally based research in sport and physical activity contexts.

As noted earlier, similar research is needed regarding other underrepresented populations. Along these lines, the research work of some of our colleagues in the sociology or sport sociology areas (see, for example, Brooks & Althouse, 1993; Erkut, Fields, Sing, & Marx, 1996; Lenskyj, 1991; Y. Smith, 1992) should serve as a valuable resource for developmentally based researchers in sport and exercise psychology who wish to explore the experiences of individuals from nondominant populations in physical activity contexts or to examine the influence of the social context on individuals' sport and physical activity behavior.

Evaluation of the Social-Movement-Based Theoretical Approaches. Evaluation of the social-movement-based theoretical approaches to human development using the criteria outlined in Tables 1 and 2 is particularly difficult due to the very eclectic nature of the theoretical

Recent work based on feminist theory has been a welcome addition to the literature in sport and exercise psychology.

approaches in this category. As noted at the beginning of this section, the various social-movement-based theoretical approaches have three characteristics in common. They are all relatively recent additions to the theoretical literature, and they arose out of concern for, or criticism of, the primary focus in the psychological research literature on rationalism or positivism. Furthermore, the theoretical approaches in this section also focus on socially disadvantaged groups. Despite these common characteristics, the theoretical approaches do vary significantly in worldview. That is, although most or all of the theoretical approaches do not assume a strict positivist perspective, some incorporate, or are based on, a postpositivist perspective whereas others assume a more radical postmodernist viewpoint. Thus, the various theoretical perspectives included in this category are more diverse than those within the other categories. Nevertheless, evaluating the social-movement-based theoretical approaches using the criteria in Tables 1 and 2 reveals some commonalities. Specifically, in regard to the first criterion, scope or range, the theoretical approaches tend to be limited in age range. That is, these theoretical approaches tend to focus primarily on development during childhood and adolescence. There certainly may be other social-movement-based theoretical approaches that center on developmental change in adulthood, but many, if not most, of the theories in this category are limited to the childhood and adolescent years. In addition, many of the theories in this category are limited to very specific domains or subdomains (e.g., the development of racial or sexual identity) whereas a few others tend to be more broad based (e.g., Smeeding's 1995 interdisciplinary model of child well-being). Although the theoretical approaches in this category focus on developmental processes in specific subgroups of individuals who are very much underrepresented in the mainstream developmental literature (e.g., children growing up in poverty, gay and lesbian youth, individuals of color), most of these theoretical models assume a normative approach (i.e., the researchers assume that the proposed stages or models of influence apply to all individuals in the subgroup under study), and the validation research has generally been conducted with individuals in the United States. Thus, relatively little cross-cultural research has been conducted.

In regard to the second criterion listed in Tables 1 and 2, the theoretical approaches in this category primarily assume nurture (physical and social environmental influences) to be the mechanism or cause of developmental change. Certainly, although some of the theorists in this section recognize the presence of nature (genetics or biological factors) as a contributor to developmental change, most of the focus of these theories is on the influence of both the broader and the immediate social environment as a facilitator of developmental change.

Most of the theoretical approaches in this category do propose an endpoint for human development that is typically specified either in terms of "mature" levels of knowledge, emotional stability, or beliefs or in terms of maximum well-being, competencies, or attainments. Correspondingly, desirable/normal and undesirable/abnormal development is typically clearly defined within each theory.

Generally, the theorists in this category perceive developmental change to occur in a discontinuous and qualitative way (i.e., the individual is fundamentally changed as she or he progresses from one developmental stage to the next). Furthermore, as is obvious from the previous discussion, at least some of these theories assume a "stage-like" pattern of developmental change.

As noted at the beginning of this section, most, if not all, of the theoretical approaches in this category originated either as a result of social protest movements and/or as a consequence of academic dissatisfaction with the positivist and rational view of human development. Thus, these theoretical approaches predominantly reflect either a postpositivist or a postmodernist worldview. However, in terms of philosophical assumptions and research methodologies, this still leaves significant variation within and among the theoretical approaches in this category. This wide variation is perhaps most clearly seen within the 11 subcategories of theories identified by Tong (1998) as falling within the overall feminist theoretical category. Despite such variation, however, the theoretical approaches in this section do focus on traditionally underrepresented groups of individuals within Western society, and they are essentially based on notions of power/powerlessness and oppression. Thus, continued use of these theoretical approaches by developmental researchers should contribute unique information to our research literature concerning the experiences of individuals about whom little is currently known.

CONCLUSION

As the information presented in this chapter shows, there currently exist a very large number of theories and subtheories concerning human development. These theories have already provided and can continue to provide us, as developmental sport and exercise psychology researchers, with frameworks for designing and conducting our developmentally based research studies. However, it is important for us, as individual researchers, to keep in mind that our choice of a theoretical framework will have a significant effect on the questions we form, the research methods we choose to use, the data we collect, and the way in which we interpret our results. As pointed out earlier, the theoretical perspective that we choose serves as a lens through which we view development and developmental change (Thomas, 2000).

To understand the ways in which our theoretical and worldviews affect our understanding of human behavior and human development, we can and should return to the real world and research examples provided at the beginning of this chapter. In the first real-world scenario (male tennis player whose motivation for, and interest in, competitive tennis declines significantly from age 8 to 14), researchers who adopt a learning theory approach might suggest that the 14-year-old is currently not receiving the type or amount of reinforcement (e.g., from coaches, parents, peers), role modeling, or other social experiences that he needs to remain in tennis. In contrast, the cognitive-developmental theorists might hypothesize that the maturational changes that have occurred from 8 to 14 years in the child's cognitive reasoning abilities (especially in regard to the ways in which he evaluates his personal sport ability) have interacted with the changes that have occurred over the same period in his sport/social environment (e.g., increased pressure to win, engagement in higher levels of competition) to cause decreases in his motivation, affect, and enjoyment of his sport.

In the second real-world scenario (changes that have occurred from first to sixth grade in the physical activity levels of boys and girls during school recess time), learning theorists might hypothesize that the observed age and gender changes in children's level of physical activity are a function of children's acquisition over time of gender- and age-role expectations. Older girls, in particular, exhibit declining levels of physical activity because physical competence is not considered a particularly desirable characteristic for women, and thus adolescent girls do not see societal rewards for such activity. In contrast, the ethological, biological, and sociobiological theorists might see the increases (or the maintenance) over time and age in males' level of physical activity and physical competence as an adaptive behavior in terms of obtaining physical, social, and economic status and survival in American society. Correspondingly, decreases over time and age in females' level of physical activity and physical competence might also be perceived by these theorists as an adaptive behavior as older girls in our society must begin preparing themselves for marriage and family (i.e., reproduction of the species). Finally, social-movement-based theorists would see the decreases over age and time in girls' level of physical activity and sport participation as a function of their continued oppression in a predominantly patriarchal society (i.e., at recess time, boys get first choice of all sports equipment and space because of male hegemonic societal perspectives that award males the power).

> Theorists from different schools of thought will explain the same scenario in entirely different ways.

In the third real-world scenario (interindividual variability in performance, behavior, and attitudes of senior citizens in an exercise class), the learning theorists might hypothesize that the more active and motivated senior citizens are those who have a social network (e.g., children, siblings, friends, partner, colleagues) that encourages, reinforces, and values their participation in physical activity. In contrast, the psychosocial theorists might investigate the notion that older adults who have successfully negotiated the eighth stage of Erikson's lifespan psychosocial model (developing perceptions of ego integrity rather than feelings of despair) will live healthier, happier, more energetic/active lives than will those older adults who have not successfully progressed through all stages of Erikson's lifespan model. Finally, dynamic systems researchers would proceed under the assumption that the activity levels and motor proficiencies of older adults will be a function of the continuous, complex, and reciprocal interaction of multiple body systems (e.g., neural, cognitive, cardiovascular, social, muscular). Thus, no one factor or even one system can explain interindividual variability in the behavior of individuals in an exercise class.

In the first research scenario (age, gender, and cultural differences in adolescents' understanding of moral behavior in general life and sport settings), cognitive-developmental theorists might interpret or examine these results by investigating differences in child-rearing practices that affect whether individual children progress through specified stages of moral reasoning. In contrast, researchers from the ethological/biological theoretical perspectives might suggest that over time, individuals in a particular society, culture, or subculture will develop the type of moral reasoning that will provide them with the best chance for survival in that particular society, culture, or subculture.

In the second research scenario (longitudinal research project on determinants of decrements in the cognitive functioning of older adults), information-processing theorists would assume that decrements (or nondecrements) in cognitive functioning with age are caused by changes in the individual's information-processing capabilities. Changes (or nonchanges) in such capabilities are effected by both maturation (e.g., age-related changes in the number of brain cell connectors) and life experiences (e.g., continued use of cognitive capabilities into older adulthood). In contrast, social-movement-based theorists might hypothesize that as adults in our society move into their older adulthood years, societal expectations for their cognitive functioning abilities decline. Such declining expectations serve as self-fulfilling prophecies that result in an actual decline in the cognitive functioning of older adults even though such declines have no actual basis in physiology.

As the examples in the previous paragraphs suggest, the theoretical perspectives that we, as researchers, choose to use will certainly affect our basic assumptions as well as our research questions, our methodological approaches, and the way in which we interpret our results. Thus, the information presented in this chapter concerning the various theoretical approaches should be of interest to researchers. However, although this chapter (similar to others in this text) may be primarily directed toward researchers, academicians, and professional practitioners (e.g., clinical and counseling psychologists), an understanding of the various theoretical perspectives on human development is also essential for practitioners (e.g., parents, teachers, coaches, physical activity leaders) as the particular theory (or theories) to which we adhere would clearly affect our interaction with, and our treatment of, individual children. If, for example, I am a coach who adheres to a predominantly biologically based perspective of gender and gender roles, I will assume that any differences that I see in the performance, behavior, attitudes, or beliefs of boys and girls in sport contexts are inherent (biologically based). Thus, my expectations of, and my interactions with, my male and female athletes will differ significantly. In contrast, if I, as a coach, adhere to a predominantly social learning perspective of gender differences (i.e., I believe that the gender differences I see in performance, behavior, attitudes, beliefs are due to social learning effects), I will try to facilitate my female athletes' skill level, motivation, self-confidence, and attitudes by finding appropriate role models (e.g., professional and collegiate female athletes) and by reinforcing and rewarding the behaviors, attitudes, and beliefs that I want my athletes to exhibit. Again, in contrast, if I, as a coach, adhere to a more postmodernist and radical feminist theoretical perspective, I may believe that the competitive sport context is inherently patriarchal in nature and that girls cannot truly experience joy and satisfaction or develop their sport competence in such settings. Thus, I might choose to completely redesign the sport setting to make it more relevant to the female experience (see, for example, Birrell and Richter, 1987).

Similarly, as a parent, the theoretical perspectives that I hold regarding how, why, when, and under what circumstances developmental change occurs will affect the child-rearing practices that I choose to employ. Within the social cognitive category, for example, how I as a parent "define" or perceive moral reasoning maturity will affect what behaviors, attitudes, beliefs, and cognitions that I attempt to support in my child.

As a classroom teacher, I may assume a more biologically based theoretical perspective regarding student learning and performance. If I do so, I will interpret interindividual variability in my students' academic performance, behavior, and motivation to be a function of some "fixed" or "stable" entity that resides within the child him- or herself. Thus, I may have little interest in, or motivation for, changing my pedagogical practices in an effort to change the child's performance and behavior. If I, however, as the classroom teacher, assume a more contextually based theoretical perspective regarding student learning and performance, I will assume that individual student "failures" are not permanent but that such "failure" can be remedied through changes in the contextual environment. Furthermore, I will assume that such contextual change should involve not only the child and me but also the home, the family, and the people in the child's afterschool program. Thus, in my efforts to intervene in the child's learning, I will attempt to include multiple systems and many individuals.

As the previous practitioner-based examples suggest, our interactions with individuals in multiple settings (e.g., family, education, sport, recreation) are affected or determined by our theoretical perspectives regarding human behavior and human development. It was the purpose of this chapter to identify and describe the various theoretical approaches to human development as well as to identify and discuss the ways in which these theoretical approaches differ from each other. As researchers and practitioners who have an interest in and/or a commitment to understanding development and developmental change, the various theoretical frameworks can be very useful for us in both our research and practitioner work, but we need to choose the theories we use with caution and base our choices on a complete understanding of their philosophical origins, assumptions, intent, and general worldview.

REFERENCES

Abernethy, B., Thomas, K. T., & Thomas, J. R. (1993). Strategies for improving understanding of motor expertise (or mistakes we have made and things we have learned). In J. L. Starkes & F. Allard (Eds.), *Cognitive issues in motor expertise* (pp. 317-354). Amsterdam: Elsevier.

Baer, D. M. (1982). Behavior analysis and developmental psychology: Discussant comments. *Human Development, 25,* 357-361.

Bandura. A. (1977). *Social learning theory.* Englewood Cliffs, NJ: Prentice-Hall.

Bandura, A. (1978). The self-system in reciprocal determinism. *American Psychologist, 33,* 344-358.

Bandura, A. (1986). *Social foundations of thought and action: A social cognitive theory.* Englewood Cliffs, NJ: Prentice-Hall.

Bandura, A. (1989). Social cognitive theory. In R. Vasta (Ed.), *Annals of child development: Vol. 6. Six theories of child development: Revised formulations and current issues* (pp. 1-60). Greenwich, CT: JAI Press.

Bernstein, N. (1967). *The co-ordination and regulation of movements.* Oxford, England: Pergamon Press.

Bijou, S. W. (1995). *Behavior analysis of child development.* Reno, NV: Context Press.

Birrell, S. J. (1988). Discourses on the gender/sport relationship: From women in sport to gender relations. *Exercise and Sport Sciences Reviews, 16,* 459-502.

Birrell, S. J. (1989). Racial relations theories and sport: Suggestions for a more critical analysis. *Sociology of Sport Journal, 6,* 212-227.

Birrell, S. J., & Richter, D. M. (1987). Is a diamond forever? Feminist transformations of sport. *Women's Studies International Forum, 10,* 395-409.

Bjorklund, D. F., & Harnishfeger, K. K. (1990). The resources construct in cognitive development: Diverse sources of evidence and a theory of inefficient inhibition. *Developmental Review, 10,* 48-71.

Bowlby, J. (1969). *Attachment and loss. Vol.1. Attachment.* London: Hogarth.

Bredemeier, B. L. (2001). Feminist praxis in sport psychology research. *The Sport Psychologist, 15,* 412-418.

Bredemeier, B., Carlton, E., Hills, L., & Oglesby, C. (1999). Changers and the changed: Moral aspects of coming out in physical education. *Quest, 51,* 418-431.

Brewer, B. W., VanRaalte, J. L., & Linder, D. E. (1993). Athletic identity: Hercules' muscles or Achilles heel? *International Journal of Sport Psychology, 24,* 237-254.

Brodkin, P., & Weiss, M. R. (1990). Developmental differences in motivation for participating in competitive swimming. *Journal of Sport and Exercise Psychology, 12,* 248-263.

Bronfenbrenner, U. (1977). Toward an experimental ecology of human development. *American Psychologist, 22,* 513-531.

Bronfenbrenner, U. (1979). *The ecology of human development: Experiments by nature and design.* Cambridge, MA: Harvard University Press.

Bronfenbrenner, U. (1993). The ecology of cognitive development: Research models and fugitive findings. In R. H. Wozniak & K. W. Fisher (Eds.), *Development in context: Activity and thinking in specific environments* (pp. 3-24). Hillsdale, NJ: Erlbaum.

Bronfenbrenner, U., & Morris, P. A. (1998). The ecology of developmental processes. In W. Damon (Series Ed.) & R. M. Lerner (Vol. Ed.), *Handbook of child psychology: Theoretical models of human development* (5th ed., pp. 993-1028). New York: Wiley.

Brooks, D., & Althouse, R. (1993). *Racism in college athletics: The African-American athlete's experiences.* Morgantown, WV: Fitness Information Technology.

Bukato, D., & Doehler, M. W. (2001). *Child development: A thematic approach* (4th ed.). Boston: Houghton Mifflin.

Casher, B. B. (1977). Relationship between birth order and participation in dangerous sports. *Research Quarterly for Exercise and Sport, 48,* 33-40.

Cass, V. (1979). Homosexual identity formation: A theoretical model. *Journal of Homosexuality, 4,* 219-235.

Cass, V. (1984). Homosexual identity formation: Testing a theoretical model. *Journal of Sexual Research, 20*, 143-167.

Chaumeton, N. R., & Duda, J. L. (1988). Is it how you play the game or whether you win or lose? The effect of competitive level and situation on coaching behaviors. *Journal of Sport Behavior, 11*, 157-174.

Cole, D. A., Maxwell, S. E., Martin, J. H., Pecke, L. G., Serocynski, A.D., Tram, J. M., et al. (2001). The development of multiple domains of child and adolescent self-concept: A cohort sequential longitudinal design. *Child Development, 72*, 1723-1746.

Coleman, E. (1982). Developmental stages of the coming out process. In J. C. Gonsiorek (Ed.), *Homosexuality and psychotherapy* (pp. 31-43). New York: Haworth.

Damon, W. (1983). The nature of social-cognitive change in the developing child. In W. F. Overton (Ed.), *The relationship between social and cognitive development* (pp. 103-141). Hillsdale, NJ: Erlbaum.

Darwin, C. (1859). *The origin of species by means of natural selection or the preservation of favoured races in the struggle for life*. London: J. Murray.

Darwin, C. (1872). *The expression of emotions in man and animals*. London: J. Murray.

Deci, E. L., & Ryan, R. M. (1985). *Intrinsic motivation and self-determination in human behavior*. New York: Plenum.

DeKay, W. T., & Buss, D. M. (1992). Human nature, individual differences, and the importance of context: Perspectives from an evolutionary psychology. *Current Directions in Psychobiological Science, 1*, 184-189.

Demetriou, A., Doise, W., & van Lieshout, C. (Eds.) (1998). *Life-span developmental psychology*. New York: John Wiley & Sons.

Dubois, P. E. (1986). The effect of participation in sport on the value orientations of young athletes. *Sociology of Sport Journal, 3*, 29-42.

Duncan, T. E., & Duncan, S. C. (1991). A latent growth curve approach to investigating developmental dynamics and correlates of change in children's perceptions of physical competence. *Research Quarterly for Exercise and Sport, 62*, 390-396.

Dweck, C. S. (1999). *Self-theories: Their role in motivation, personality, and development*. Philadelphia: Psychology Press.

Dzewaltowski, D. A. (1997). The ecology of physical activity and sport: Merging science and practice. *Journal of Applied Sport Psychology, 9*, 254-276.

Eaton, W. O., Chipperfield, J. G., & Singbeil, C. E. (1989). Birth order and activity level in children. *Developmental Psychology, 25*, 668-672.

Ebbeck, V., & Stuart, M. E. (1996). Predictors of self-esteem with youth basketball players. *Pediatric Exercise Science, 8*, 368-378.

Eccles, J. S., Wigfield, A. W., & Schiefele, U. (1998). Motivation to succeed. In W. Damon (Series Ed.) & N. Eisenberg (Vol. Ed.), *Handbook of child psychology* (5th ed., Vol. 3): *Social, emotional, and personality development* (pp. 1017-1095). New York: Wiley.

Erikson, E. H. (1959). Identity and the life cycle. *Psychological Issues, 1*, 50-100.

Erikson, E. H. (1963). *Childhood and society* (2nd ed.). New York: Norton.

Erikson, E. H. (1968). *Identity, youth, and crisis*. New York: Norton.

Erkut, S., Fields, J. P., Sing, R., & Marx, N. (1996). Diversity in girls' experiences: Feeling good about who you are. In B. J. Ross Leadbeater & N. Way (Eds.), *Urban girls: Resisting stereotypes, creating identities* (pp. 53-64). New York: New York University Press.

Feltz, D. L., & Brown, E. W. (1984). Perceived competence in soccer skills among youth soccer players. *Journal of Sport Psychology, 6*, 385-394.

French, K. E., Spurgeon, J. H., & Nevett, M. E. (1995). Expert-novice differences in cognitive and skill execution components of youth baseball performance. *Research Quarterly for Exercise and Sport, 66*, 194-201.

Freud, S. (1973). *An outline of psychoanalysis*. London: Hogarth. (original work published 1938).

Friedman, R. C. (1988). *Male homosexuality*. New Haven, CT: Yale University Press.

Fry, M. D. (2000a). A developmental analysis of children's and adolescents' understanding of luck and ability in the physical domain. *Journal of Sport and Exercise Psychology, 22*, 145-166.

Fry, M. D. (2000b). A developmental examination of children's understanding of task difficulty in the physical domain. *Journal of Applied Sport Psychology, 12*, 180-202.

Fry, M. D., & Duda, J. L. (1997). A developmental examination of children's understanding of effort and ability in the physical and academic domains. *Research Quarterly for Exercise and Sport, 68*, 331-344.

Gallagher, J. D., & Thomas, J. R. (1986). Developmental effects of grouping and recording on learning a movement series. *Research Quarterly for Exercise and Sport, 57*, 117-127.

Garcia Bengoechea, E. (2002). Integrating knowledge and expanding horizons in developmental sport psychology: A bioecological perspective. *Quest, 54*, 1-20.

Garcia Bengoechea, E., & Johnson, E. M. (2001). Ecological systems theory and children's development in sport: Toward a process-person-context-time research paradigm. *Avante, 7*, 20-31.

Garcia Coll, C., Lamberty, G., Jenkins, R., McAdoo, H. P., Crnic, K., Wasik, B. H., et al. (1996). An integrative model for the study of developmental competencies in minority children. *Child Development, 67*, 1891-1914.

Garfinkel, I., & McLanahan, S. (1995). The effects of child support reform on child well-being. In P. L. Chase-Lansdale & J. Brooks-Gunn (Eds.), *Escape from poverty: What makes a difference for kids* (pp. 211-138). New York: Cambridge University Press.

Giebink, M. P., & McKenzie, T. C. (1985). Teaching sportsmanship in physical education and recreation: An analysis of intervention and generalization effects. *Journal of Teaching in Physical Education, 4,* 167-177.

Gill, D. L. (2002). Gender and sport behavior. In T. S. Horn (Ed.), *Advances in sport psychology* (2nd ed., pp. 355-376), Champaign, IL: Human Kinetics.

Gilligan, C. (1982). *In a different voice: Psychology theory and women's development.* Cambridge, MA: Harvard University Press.

Goodger, M. S., & Jackson, J. J. (1985). Fair play: Coaches' attitudes towards the laws of soccer. *Journal of Sport Behavior, 8,* 34-41.

Griffin, P. (1992). Changing the game: Homophobia, sexism, and lesbians in sport. *Quest, 44,* 251-265.

Haan, N. (1991). Moral development and action from a social constructivist perspective. In W. M. Kurtines & J. L. Gewirtz (Eds.), *Handbook of moral behavior and development, Vol. 1: Theory* (pp. 251-273). Hillsdale, NJ: Erlbaum.

Haken, H. (1983). *Synergetics, an introduction: Non-equilibrium, phase transitions, and self-organization in physics, chemistry, and biology.* New York: Springer-Verlag.

Hall, R. (2001). Shaking the foundation: Women of color in sport. *The Sport Psychologist, 15,* 386-400.

Hamer, D., & Copeland, P. (1994). *The science of choice: The search for the gay gene and the biology of behavior.* New York: Simon & Schuster.

Harter, S. (1981). A model of intrinsic mastery motivation in children: Individual differences and developmental change. In W. A. Collins (Ed.), *Minnesota Symposium on Child Psychology* (Vol. 14, pp. 215-255). Hillsdale, NJ: Erlbaum.

Harter, S. (1990). Causes, correlates, and the functional role of global self-worth: A lifespan perspective. In R. J. Sternberg & J. Kolligan, Jr. (Eds.), *Competence considered* (pp. 67-97). New Haven, CT: Yale University Press.

Harter, S. (1999). *The construction of the self: A developmental perspective.* New York: Guilford Press.

Helms, J. E. (1990). *Black and white racial identity: Theory, research, and practice.* Westport, CT: Greenwood.

Helms, J. E. (1995). An update on Helms' white and people of color racial identity modes. In J. Ponterotto, J. M. Casas, L. A. Suzuki, & C. M. Alexander (Eds.), *Handbook of multicultural counseling* (pp. 181-198). Thousand Oaks, CA: Sage.

Horn, T. S., & Amorose, A. J. (1998). Sources of competence information. In J. L. Duda (Ed.), *Advances in sport and exercise psychology measurement* (pp. 49-64). Morgantown, WV: Fitness Information Technology.

Horn, T. S., & Weiss, M. R. (1991). A developmental analysis of children's self-ability judgments. *Pediatric Exercise Science, 3,* 312-328.

Jantz, R. K. (1975). Moral thinking in male elementary pupils as reflected by perception of basketball rules. *Research Quarterly, 46,* 414-421.

Kail, R. (1986). Sources of age differences in speed of processing. *Child Development, 57,* 969-987.

Kail, R. (1991). Development of processing speed in childhood and adolescence. In H. W. Reese (Ed.), *Advances in child development and behavior* (Vol. 23). San Diego, CA: Academic Press.

Kelso, J. A. S. (1995). *Dynamic patterns: The self-organization of brain and behavior.* Cambridge, MA: MIT Press.

Kohlberg, L. (1976). Moral stages and moralization: The cognitive-developmental approach. In T. Lickma (Ed.), *Moral development and behavior: Theory, research, and social issues* (pp. 31-53). New York: Holt, Rinehart, & Winston.

Kohlberg, L. (1978). Revisions in the theory and practice of moral development. *New Directions for Child Development, 2,* 83-88.

Krane, V. (1994). A feminist perspective on contemporary sport psychology research. *The Sport Psychologist, 8,* 393-410.

Krane, V. (1997). Homonegativism experienced by lesbian collegiate athletes. *Women in Sport and Physical Activity Journal, 6,* 141-163.

Krane, V. (2001). One lesbian feminist epistemology: Integrating feminist standpoint, queer theory, and feminist cultural studies. *The Sport Psychologist, 15,* 401-411.

Kuhn, T. S. (1970). *The structure of scientific revolutions* (2nd ed.). Chicago: University of Chicago Press.

Landers, D. M. (1970). Sibling-sex-status and ordinal position effects on females' sport participation and interests. *Journal of Social Psychology, 80,* 247-248.

Lee, C. (1993). Operant strategies in sport and exercise: Possibilities for theoretical development. *International Journal of Sport Psychology, 24,* 306-325.

Lenskyj, H. (1991). Combating homophobia in sport and physical education. *Sociology of Sport Journal, 8,* 61-69.

Lerner, R. M. (1997). *Concepts and theories of human development* (2nd ed.). Mahwah, NJ: Lawrence Erlbaum.

Lewis, L. A. (1984). The coming out process for lesbians: Integrating a stable identity. *Social Work, 29,* 464-469.

Lorenz, K. (1966). *On aggression.* New York: Harcourt, Brace, & World.

Markus, H. (1983). Self-knowledge: An expanded view. *Journal of Personality, 51,* 543-565.

Massaro, D. W., & Cowan, N. (1993). Information processing model: Microscopes of mind. In L. W. Porter & M. R. Rosenzweig (Eds.), *Annual Review of Psychology, 34,* 383-425.

McCullagh, P., Stiehl. K., & Weiss, M. R. (1990). Developmental modeling effects of the quantitative and qualitative aspects of motor performance acquisition. *Research Quarterly for Exercise and Sport, 61,* 344-350.

McKiddie, B., & Maynard, I.W. (1997). Perceived competence of school children in physical education. *Journal of Teaching in Physical Education, 16,* 324-339.

McLoyd, V. C., & Wilson, L. (1991). The strain of living poor: Parenting, social support, and child mental health. In A. C. Huston (Ed.), *Children in poverty: Child development and public policy* (pp. 105-135). New York: Cambridge University Press.

McPherson, S. L., & Thomas, J. R. (1989). Relation of knowledge and performance in boys' tennis: Age and expertise. *Journal of Experimental Child Psychology, 48,* 190-211.

Mugno, D. A., & Feltz, D. L. (1985). The social learning of aggression in youth football in the United States. *Canadian Journal of Applied Sport Sciences, 10,* 26-35.

Murphy, H. A., Hutchison, J. M., & Bailey, J. S. (1983). Behavioral school psychology goes outdoors: The effect of organized games on playground aggression. *Journal of Applied Behavior Analysis, 16,* 29-35.

Murphy, G. M., Petitpas, A. J., & Brewer, B. W. (1996). Identity disclosure, athletic identity, and career maturity in intercollegiate athletes. *The Sport Psychologist, 10,* 239-246.

Nicholls, J. G. (1984). Achievement motivation: Conceptions of ability, subjective experience, and task choice and performance. *Psychological Review, 91,* 328-346.

Nicholls, J. G. (1989). *The competitive ethos and democratic education.* Cambridge, MA: Harvard University Press.

Nicholls, J. G. & Miller, A. T. (1983). The differentiation of the concepts of ability and difficulty. *Child Development, 54,* 951-959.

Novak, G. (1996). *Developmental psychology: Dynamic systems and behavioral analyses.* Reno, NV: Context Press.

Oglesby, C. (2001a) To unearth the legacy. *The Sport Psychologist, 15,* 373-385.

Oglesby, C. (2001b). Intersections—women's sport leadership and feminist praxis. In S. Freeman, S. Bourque, & C. Shelton (Eds.), *Women on power: Leadership redefined* (pp. 290-310). Boston: Northeastern University Press.

Overton, W. F. (1998). Developmental psychology: Philosophy, concepts, and methodology. In W. Damon (Series Ed.) & R. M. Lerner (Vol. Ed.), *Handbook of child psychology* (5th ed.): *Theoretical models of human development* (pp. 107-188). New York: Wiley.

Overton, W. F., & Reese, H. W. (1973). Models of development: Methodological implications. In J. R. Nesselroade & H. W. Reese (Eds.), *Life-span developmental psychology: Methodological issues.* New York: Academic Press.

Piaget, J. (1950). *The psychology of intelligence.* London: Routledge & Kegan Paul.

Piaget, J. (1970). Piaget's theory. In P. R. Mussen (Ed.), *Carmichael's manual of child psychology* (Vol. 1). New York: Wiley.

Piaget, J. (1972). Intellectual evolution from adolescence to adulthood. *Human Development, 15,* 1-12.

Rainey, D. W., Santilli, N. R., & Fallon, K. (1992). Development of athletes' conceptions of sports officials' authority. *Journal of Sport and Exercise Psychology, 14,* 398-404.

Rest, J. R. (1986). *Moral development: Advances in research and theory.* New York: Praeger Press.

Rosales-Ruiz. J., & Baer, D. M. (1996). A behavior-analytic view of development. In S. W. Bijou & E. Ribes (Eds.), *New directions in behavior development.* Reno, NV: Context Press.

Scarr, S. (1992). Developmental theories for the 1990's: Developmental and individual differences. *Child Development, 63,* 1-19.

Schlinger, H.D., Jr. (1992). Theory in behavior analysis: An application to child development. *American Psychologist, 47,* 1396-1410.

Schneirla, T. C. (1957). The concept of development in comparative psychology. In D. B. Harris (Ed.), *The concept of development.* Minneapolis, MN: The University of Minnesota Press.

Sharpe, T., Brown, M., & Crider, K. (1995). The effects of sportsmanship curriculum intervention on generalized positive social behaviors of urban elementary school students. *Journal of Applied Behavioral Analysis, 28,* 401-416.

Shields, D. L. L., & Bredemeier, B. J. L. (1995). *Character development and physical activity.* Champaign, IL: Human Kinetics.

Shields, D. L. L., & Bredemeier, B. J. L. (2001). Moral development and behavior in sport. In R. N. Singer, H. A. Hausenblas, & C. J. Janelle (Eds.), *Handbook of sport psychology* (2nd ed., pp. 585-603). New York: Macmillan.

Siegler, R. S. (1996). A grand theory of development. *Monographs of the Society for Research in Child Development, 61* (1-2, Serial No. 246).

Siegler, R. S. (1998). *Children's thinking* (3rd ed.). Englewood Cliffs, NJ: Prentice-Hall.

Skinner, B.F. (1974). *About behaviorism.* New York: Knop.

Smeeding, T. M. (1995). An interdisciplinary model and data requirements for studying poor children. In P. L. Chase-Lansdale & J. Brooks-Gunn (Eds.), *Escape from poverty: What makes a difference for children* (pp. 291-298). New York: Cambridge University Press.

Smith, M. D. (1979). Towards an explanation of hockey violence: A reference approach. *Canadian Journal of Sociology, 4,* 105-124.

Smith, Y. (1992). Women of color in society and sport. *Quest, 44,* 228-250.

Stuart, M. E., & Ebbeck, V. (1995). The influence of perceived social approval on moral development in youth sport. *Pediatric Exercise Science, 7,* 270-280.

Sulloway, F.J. (1996). *Born to rebel: Birth order, family dynamics, and creative lives.* New York: Pantheon.

Thelen, E. (1995). Motor development: A new synthesis. *American Psychologist, 50,* 79-95.

Thelen, E., & Smith, L. B. (1998). Dynamic systems theories. In W. Damon (Series Ed.) & R. M. Lerner (Vol. Ed.), *Handbook of child psychology* (5th ed.) : *Vol. 1. Theoretical models of human development* (pp. 563-634). New York: Wiley.

Thelen, E., Ulrich, B., & Jensen, J. L. (1989). The developmental origins of locomotion. In M. H. Woollacott & A. Shumway-Cook (Eds.), *Development of posture and gait across the lifespan* (pp. 25-47). Columbia, SC: University of South Carolina Press.

Thomas, R. M. (2000). *Comparing theories of child development* (5th ed.). Belmont, CA: Wadsworth/Thomson Learning.

Thomas, R. M. (2001). *Recent theories of human development.* Thousand Oaks, CA: Sage.

Tinbergen, N. (1973). *The animal in its world: Explorations of an ethnologist 1932-1972.* Cambridge, MA: Harvard University Press.

Tong, R. P. (1998). *Feminist thought* (2nd ed.). Boulder, CO: Westview.

Troiden, R. R. (1988). *Gay and lesbian identity: A sociological analysis.* New York: General Hall.

Ulrich, B. D. (1987). Perceptions of physical competence, motor competence, and participation in organized sport: Their interrelationships in young children. *Research Quarterly for Exercise and Sport, 58,* 57-67.

Ulrich, B. D., & Ulrich, D. A. (1997). Young children's perceptions of their ability to perform simple play and more difficult motor skills. In J. E. Clark & J. H. Humphrey (Eds.), *Motor development: Research and reviews* (Vol. 1, pp. 24-45). Reston, VA: National Association of Sport and Physical Education.

Vasta, R., Haith, M. M. & Miller, S. A. (1999). *Child psychology: The modern science* (3rd ed.). New York: John Wiley & Sons.

Vygotsky, L.S. (1981). The genesis of higher mental functions. In J.V. Wertsch (Ed.), *The concept of activity in Soviet psychology* (pp. 144-188). New York: Sharp.

Watkins, B., & Montgomery, A.B. (1989). Conceptions of athletic excellence among children and adolescents. *Child Development, 60,* 1362-1372.

Watson, J. B. (1913). Psychology as the behaviorist views it. *Psychological Review, 20,* 158-177.

Watson, J. B. (1928). *Psychological care of infant and child.* New York: Norton.

Watson, J. B. (1930). *Behaviorism.* New York: W. W. Norton.

Webb, H. (1969). Professionalization of attitudes toward play among adolescents. In G. Kenyon (Ed.), *Aspects of contemporary sport sociology* (pp. 161-178). Chicago: The Athletic Institute.

Weinberg, M. S., Williams, C. J., & Pryor, D. W. (1988). Becoming and being "bisexual." In E. J. Haeberle & R. Gindorf (Eds.), *Bisexualities* (pp. 169-181). New York: Continuum.

Weiner, B. (1985). An attributional theory of achievement motivation and emotion. *Psychological Review, 92,* 548-573.

Weiss, M. R. (1983). Modeling and motor performance: A developmental perspective. *Research Quarterly for Exercise and Sport, 54,* 190-197.

Weiss, M. R., Bredemeier, B. J., & Shewchuk, R. M. (1986). The dynamics of perceived competence, perceived control, and motivational orientation in youth sports. In M. R. Weiss & D. Gould (Eds.), *Sport for children and youths* (pp. 89-100). Champaign, IL: Human Kinetics.

Weiss, M. R., Ebbeck, V., & Wiese-Bjornstal, D. M. (1993). Developmental and psychological skills related to children's observational learning of physical skills. *Pediatric Exercise Science, 5,* 301-317.

Weiss, M. R., & Klint, K. A. (1987). "Show and tell" in the gymnasium: An investigation of developmental differences in modeling and verbal rehearsal of motor skills. *Research Quarterly for Exercise and Sport, 58,* 234-241.

Weiss, M. R., McCullagh, P., Smith, A. L., & Berlant, A. R. (1998). Observational learning and the fearful child: Influence of peer models on swimming skill performance and psychological responses. *Research Quarterly for Exercise and Sport, 69,* 380-394.

Weiss, M. R., & Raedeke, T. D. (2003). Developmental Sport and Exercise Psychology: Research Status on Youth and Directions Toward a Lifespan Perspective. In M. R. Weiss (Ed.). *Developmental sport and exercise psychology: A lifespan perspective.* (pp. 1-26). Morgantown, WV: Fitness Information Technology.

Weiss, M. R., & Smith, A. L. (2002). Moral development in sport and physical activity: Theory, research, and intervention. In T. S. Horn (Ed.), *Advances in sport psychology* (2nd ed., pp. 243-280). Champaign, IL: Human Kinetics.

Werner, H. (1961). *Comparative psychology of mental development.* New York: Science Editions.

White, S.H., & O'Brien, J. E. (1999). What is a hero? An exploratory study of students' conceptions of heroes. *Journal of Moral Education, 28,* 81-95.

Whitehead, J., & Smith, A. G. (1996). Issues in development of a protocol to evaluate children's reasoning about ability and effort in sport. *Perceptual and Motor Skills, 83,* 355-364.

Wilson, E.O. (1975). *Sociobiology: The new synthesis.* Cambridge, MA: Harvard University Press.

Yando, R., Seitz, V., & Zigler, E. (1978). *Imitation: A developmental perspective.* New York: Wiley.

Yiannakis, A. (1976). Birth order and preference for dangerous sports among males. *Research Quarterly for Exercise and Sport, 47,* 62-68.

CHAPTER THREE

Some Methodological Considerations in Developmental Sport and Exercise Psychology

Robert W. Schutz and Ilhyeok Park

The word *some* has been included in the title of this chapter to clarify the fact that the material that follows is but a mere tip of the iceberg of the methodological issues that are pertinent to the study of developmental sport and exercise psychology. A comprehensive treatment of the major issues would include (a) research designs (for both quantitative and qualitative investigations); (b) sampling; (c) interview protocols, observational strategies, experimental designs, and survey procedures; (d) instrument development with the associated issues of validity and reliability (and numerous types of each); and (e) statistical methods—from traditional ANOVA, regression, and exploratory factor analysis, to newer techniques such as logistic regression, path analysis, meta analysis, confirmatory factor analysis, and structural equation modeling, to the less used (in this field) techniques such as log-linear analysis, item response theory, latent growth modeling (including hierarchical linear modeling), and nonlinear dynamics. Textbooks and complete issues of journals have been devoted to each of these topics, and it would be impossible to try to summarize everything in these few pages. Instead, we have opted to focus on the three topics that we feel are central to the measurement and analysis of development: (a) the statistical analysis of change, (b) the validity of the measures, and (c) the reliability of the measures. First, we make a case for the need for longitudinal studies in developmental sport and exercise psychology.

THE CASE FOR LONGITUDINAL STUDIES

In this chapter we pay special attention to the measurement and analysis of *change*. It is our position that in order to understand development, one must repeatedly observe individuals over a period of time (probably months or years for psychological phenomena). Thus, much of our focus is on measurement issues relative to longitudinal studies. Cross-sectional studies can be informative, but also very misleading. We elaborate on this statement later.

It is interesting (disturbing?) to see how few longitudinal studies have been conducted in sport and exercise psychology. Weiss (2001) expresses concern over the limited use of a developmental approach, noting that less than 10% of 500+ published studies in youth sport

The primary advantage of the longitudinal study is its ability to provide information about change.

psychology used such an approach. Even more disturbing, from our point of view, is the fact that less than 10% of those 10% used a longitudinal design. A PsycINFO search of *Journal of Sport and Exercise Psychology* articles, 1990-2000, identified only six articles that used the term *developmental*—and all six of them reported using a cross-sectional research design. A search of all issues of the *Journal of Sport and Exercise Psychology* (or *Journal of Sport Psychology* as it was originally titled) since 1979 revealed only six studies that purported to have used a longitudinal design, and only three of those continued assessments beyond one year. In contrast, in the area of personality, a recent publication (Roberts & DelVecchio, 2000) reported a meta-analysis of 152 longitudinal studies on trait consistency. Why this relative scarcity of longitudinal studies in sport and exercise psychology research? Weiss and Bredemeier (1983), in their foundational article on developmental sport psychology, largely ignore this issue, but they do recommend that we "incorporate cross-sectional and longitudinal studies to more precisely study age changes in psychological maturity over time" (p. 227). Apparently, their recommendations have gone unheeded. We acknowledge that conducting longitudinal studies is a time-consuming and costly endeavor, and probably not one that can be undertaken as a graduate student thesis or dissertation project. Nevertheless, such studies need to be done.

What are the advantages of longitudinal studies over cross-sectional studies? First and foremost, only through longitudinal studies can we make valid inferences about *change*. Cross-sectional studies permit conclusions about *differences* (but only speculations about change). For example, say we conducted a cross-sectional study in which we obtained three measures—bone density, computer skills and pro-abortion views—from four groups of women, aged in their 20s, 40s, 60s, and 80s. The results showed lower values for older women, almost a perfect negative linear trend over age, on all three measures. What can we conclude? That women lose bone density as they get older? Yes, that would be true (longitudinal studies support this). That women lose computer skills as they age? Maybe, but unlikely. We know that motor and cognitive skills do decline in many people in their 60s and 80s—but today's 60- and 80-year-old women had no computer skills when they were 20, so this may be a case of generational differences rather than change due to aging. That women become less supportive of the right to abortion as they get older? We can't tell. Maybe these 60- and 80-year old women have held those same views forever, and the differences we observe reflect a change in society's views over the last 40 or so years. A cross-sectional study just cannot distinguish between intraindividual change (change that occurs, over time, within an individual) and interindividual differences (differences between individuals that may or may not be related to the independent variable of interest, time, or age in this case). Therefore, in order to study development (a process of change), longitudinal research designs, longitudinal measurement procedures, and longitudinal statistical analyses are desirable.

An explanation regarding the sequential organization of the following three sections seems in order. It would make most sense to present the material in the order in which it is usually dealt with in any empirical research study, that is, validity, reliability, and then statistical analysis. However, in the section on reliability, we include the newer methods of reliability estimation that are based on latent growth models. The nature and form of these models is explained in the second part of the statistical analysis section, thus the need to present the statistical section before the measurement section on reliability.

Validity

A commonly used definition of validity is the degree to which a test measures what it is supposed to measure. However, a more appropriate interpretation is that validity is not a property of the test of assessment as such, but rather of the meaning of the test scores. One validates, not a test, but an interpretation of data arising from a specified procedure (Cronbach, 1971). It is a function of items, persons responding, and context of the assessment. Thus an inventory such as the CATPA (Schutz, Smoll, Carre, & Mosher, 1985), if administered to a sample of 7-year-olds, could provide a valid assessment of their reading ability but not of their attitudes towards participating in physical activity (because CATPA was not developed for such a young age group). On the other hand, if the inventory were administered to a sample of 15-year-olds, and done so in accordance with the published guidelines for its administration, and the results interpreted as indicators of these teenagers' attitudes and values towards participation in physical activity, then that most likely would be a valid use of the CATPA. Interpretations of data based on questionnaires, interview protocols, physical measures, etc. that are used on samples that may not have been representative of the population(s) on which the assessment tool was originally developed and validated cannot lead to a better understanding of the construct of interest — as the instrument is probably not providing data that is valid for the intended purposes. Additionally, data collected in a manner not in accordance with the prescribed data collection protocols is unlikely to lead to valid interpretations of the construct of interest.

The Confusion Regarding "Types" of Validity

Traditionally, validity has been construed as being a multifaceted construct consisting of numerous specific "types" of validity; however, the number of types has gradually decreased over time. Figure 1 summarizes this process. Most textbooks list at least the four types identified in publications of the American Psychological Association (APA) in the 1950s and often contain even more specific delineations that include some of the terms listed in Figure 1 under the heading "General use." The most recent reconceptualization of the concept of validity is Messick's (1995) argument that there is really only one type of validity, namely construct validity. He goes on to identify six "distinguishable aspects of construct validity": (1) content—content relevance, representativeness; (2) substantive—theoretical rationales for observed responses and processes; (3) structural—congruence of scoring structure with domain structure; (4) generalizability—interpretations generalize across populations, settings, and tasks; (5) external—convergent, discriminant, and criterion validity; and (6) consequential—validity of score interpretation as a basis for action, consequences of test use. However, others are not in full agreement with Messick's conceptualization of validity. Zimiles (1996) points out that the complexity of the concept of construct validity is such that most efforts to appraise it have serious shortcomings. He takes issue with Messick's apparent discounting of criterion-related validity, and makes a case for its re-instatement. Bornstein (1996) considers that Messick's publication to be a provocative article and argues that we should not forget about the importance of face validity.

It is obvious that validity is a complex concept and one for which there is no universally agreed upon definition or content. Thus it is not surprising that students and scholars become confused and overwhelmed when they attempt to "validate" their instrument (or their interpretation of data derived from that instrument). However, it is generally accepted that with respect to questionnaire construction and/or validation, there are three aspects of validity that must be considered: construct, criterion (which is composed of concurrent and predictive validity), and content (i.e., APA, 1985). Following are some brief definitions

> Validity is the degree to which a test measures what it is supposed to measure.

FIGURE 1
The evolution of "Types of Validity"

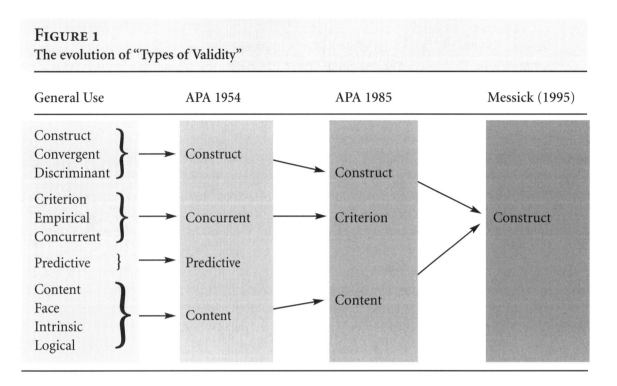

of these components of validity and suggestions for how one might evaluate the degree to which an instrument will yield valid data with respect to each aspect.

Content Validity

Content validity focuses on the content of the inventory items and its relation to the intended domain of the inventory (i.e., if an instrument *looks* like a valid measure). It is often considered to be an aspect of construct validity and is most applicable in achievement testing and selection procedures. In psychological research, content validity still must be considered, and its assessment starts with a clear and unambiguous definition of the construct (e.g., coping with anxiety) being measured. The selection of questionnaire items is then based on well-established theories of anxiety and coping, making sure that there are a sufficient number of items to represent each theoretical component of the construct (e.g., somatic and cognitive behaviors). Content validity is supported if a panel of experts agrees that (a) the items appear to represent the construct, (b) all aspects of the construct are represented by the items, and (c) if the construct has a number of subdomains (factors), then the items are assigned to the appropriate subdomains. For a comprehensive discussion on how to establish item content validity, see Dunn, Bouffard, and Rogers (1999).

Construct Validity

Construct validity focuses on the abstract construct the inventory is supposed to identify and quantify (i.e., if an instrument *acts* like a valid measure). As noted above, some authors consider construct validity to represent all aspects of validity, including content validity. Here we suggest that construct validity can be assessed by examining two aspects, (a) structural validity and (b) convergent and discriminant validity.

Structural validity. Structural, or factorial, validity is the extent to which the questionnaire is internally consistent and may be assessed with factor analysis (and sometimes with a measure of internal consistency such as Cronbach's alpha—however see Cortina (1993) for a good discussion of what alpha does and does not tell us). A factor analysis suggests the degree to which the items measure one or more dimensions of the construct. An inventory with strong structural validity of a multidimensional construct will consist of items that have high factor loadings on one and only one factor, and the factors will not be highly correlated. An issue that arises frequently in sport and exercise psychology is whether an exploratory or a confirmatory factor analysis is most appropriate. This discussion is beyond the scope of this chapter, but we are of the opinion that in most instances, the items have been constructed with an a priori expectation of what factor they represent, and thus a confirmatory factor analysis is most appropriate. See Fabrigar, Wegener, MacCallum, and Strahan (1999) for a good discussion of the role of exploratory factor analysis in psychological research and Reise, Waller, and Comrey (2000) for a comprehensive treatment of factor analysis and scale revision.

Convergent and discriminant validity. The convergent validity of an inventory refers to the extent to which there is convergence (usually quantified by a correlation coefficient) between the scores on that inventory and scores obtained from some other assessment tool that is believed to measure the same construct. For example, the inventory could be a paper-and-pencil questionnaire to assess some aspect of motivation, and the other assessment tool could be a coach's rating of the players' motivation (or some other paper-and-pencil inventory, but preferably one that has a different structure and response format). In like fashion, discriminant validity refers to the degree to which two instruments that have similar structures and response formats, but supposedly measure different constructs, do not correlate with each other. It is possible that two such inventories could be strongly correlated because both use a format (e.g., an excessive number of negatively worded items) that elicits a particular type of response or because responses to both instruments are strongly influenced by social desirability. Although it is not always possible to include both convergent and discriminant validity assessments in the same study, it is desirable to do so. Such a method is then referred to as a multitrait-multimethod approach to construct validation, and Figure 2 portrays such a design. The "high r's" are indicative of good convergent validity (same construct, different methods), and the "low r's" provide evidence of good discriminant validity (different constructs, same methods).

> If possible, include both convergent and discriminant validity assessments in your study.

Marsh (1994) suggested that many sport and exercise psychology inventories may lack adequate convergent and discriminant validity, and he encouraged researchers in this field to conduct more construct validity studies in order to test the interpretations of their measures. He used the "jingle-jangle fallacy" label often used by measurement specialists when criticizing poorly constructed psychology inventories. The jingle fallacy occurs when we (maybe falsely)

FIGURE 2
Testing for construct validity using the multirait-multimethod

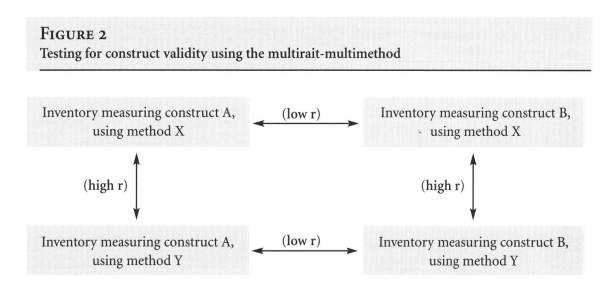

assume that scales with the same label actually reflect the same construct. Just because two or more inventories claim to measure the same thing, say, intrinsic motivation, that does not necessarily mean that they in fact do. The jangle fallacy refers to the situation in which we assume that scales with different labels really measure different constructs, when in fact they may both be indicators of a very similar psychological trait or attribute.

Criterion-Related Validity

One potential problem in developmental research is that an instrument may only be valid for a certain age range.

Criterion-related validity (hereafter just called criterion validity) focuses on the extent to which the obtained score on the inventory is related to some outcome (i.e., if an instrument predicts or is related to something else). Criterion validity is assessed by correlating the results of the inventory with the scores on some other inventory, performance, or accomplishment. For example, if aspiring physicians who score high on the MCAT eventually become better medical school graduates than those who do not score so high, then we can conclude that the MCAT has good predictive validity for success in medical school. If the results of an inventory purported to measure aggressive tendencies are strongly related to an external criterion such as penalty minutes in hockey players or bullying behavior on the playground, then we may conclude that this scale provides information that possesses criterion validity.

Concerns Over the Validity of Sport and Exercise Psychology Inventories

It is obvious that the instruments used to assess any psychological construct, behavior, or belief must yield data that are valid for the intended purposes. This is especially true in developmental research for a number of reasons. As with all research, the value, applicability, and generalizability of our results depend on valid measures. In developmental research, where we may be using the same inventory repeatedly over time, it is crucial that the same construct be measured, preferably with the same scale, at each point in time. If we administer an inventory in the first stages of the research and upon further analysis find that it lacked validity, what then? Changing to a more valid inventory seems in order, but then we cannot compare the results with the previously collected data, and thus we cannot examine development. It is obviously best to start with valid assessment tools. However, there is a potential problem in developmental research, and that occurs when an instrument may not be valid over an extended age range. This is especially so when studying children and youth. An inventory measuring self-esteem that was developed and validated on 8- to 10-year-olds may no longer yield data about self-esteem when it is administered to those same individuals when they are 14 to 16 years old, thus the need for continual validation studies whenever an instrument is to be used in a different setting or on a different population from the one on which the original validation work was performed.

Sport and exercise psychologists are well aware of the need for valid instruments, but they have frequently expressed concern that not enough attention is being given to this important component of measurement and inventory development. Duda (1998) states: "Without solid measurement, it is difficult to challenge, disconfirm, and/or extend psychological theory in sport and exercise psychology. Given the absence of meaningful, valid, and reliable assessments, our pre-assessments and post-assessments in the applied realm lack integrity and are of little value" (p. xxiii). As we have seen, this is particularly relevant in developmental research, and students and scholars are urged to be especially diligent with respect to testing the validity of their instruments when conducting longitudinal studies.

THE STATISTICAL ANALYSIS OF LONGITUDINAL DATA

The "best" way to statistically analyze change has been a topic of considerable evolution and disagreement among measurement specialists for almost 50 years. Here we will present what we consider are the traditional methods (e.g., ANOVA) and some newer, more sophisticated methods (e.g., latent growth models). For a fuller treatment of the analysis of change, see Schutz (1989) for a simple presentation of the traditional approaches and Collins and Sayer (2001) for a comprehensive coverage of more recent methods to analyze longitudinal data. However, before getting into the details of ANOVA and latent growth models, there are two important issues regarding the analysis of change that we wish to bring to the reader's attention: identifying patterns of change and difference scores.

Identifying Patterns of Change

Another disadvantage of cross-sectional studies, other than the inability to distinguish between change and differences, is that we may not be able to properly identify the *pattern of change* over time. Even with longitudinal studies, most commonly used statistical procedures can mask interesting differences (between people or between groups of people) in the pattern of change over time. For example, using standard repeated measures ANOVA models, we could easily conclude that over a 5-year period, change occurred in a linear pattern, with scores increasing about two units per year. However, it is possible that not even one subject showed a pattern of change even remotely like that. We explain this more fully with the following example.

Assume that we assessed young boys' opinions on the importance of "competition/winning" in sports (i.e., we asked questions about recording scores/times, maintaining league standings, etc.). We were interested in examining how these attitudes changed as a function of age, and to do this we measured a number of boys at each of seven ages (say, from age 6 to 12). In a real research project we would certainly use a large sample size, but for the purposes of the example here, we are keeping the data set small (N=9) so that it can be presented in its entirety. The results (Table 1) suggest that as boys grow older and become more socialized into competitive sports, they place more value on competitiveness. Interestingly, it appears as if this change occurs in a very consistent manner, a linear increase of two units per year. The standard deviations are smallest at ages 6 and 12, and largest at ages 8, 9, and 10. This implies that, initially, young boys are quite very homogeneous in their attitudes towards competition, they become more heterogeneous for a short while, and then they converge towards a common mean of 18 by age 12. We might conclude from these findings that young boys increase in competitive attitude by an average of two units per year, but that this rate of change is not constant (i.e., not the same for all boys) over the 7 years. Perhaps these differences have something to do with another variable, perhaps the age at which the boys started playing in competitive leagues.

However, to study *change* per se, rather than just differences between ages, we need to conduct a longitudinal study. It could be that the data do not really represent individual change, but rather a difference in cohort mean values. That is, perhaps the 12-year-olds had high values 6 years ago, and the

TABLE 1

Mean and Standard Deviations of Competitive Attitudes of Boys Ages 6 to 12

	Age in Years						
	6	7	8	9	10	11	12
Mean	6.0	8.0	10.0	12.0	14.0	16.0	18.0
St. Dev.	2.7	5.5	8.4	7.8	8.4	5.5	2.7

fact that today's 6-year-olds have lower values is a function of differences in how competitive sport is currently being portrayed in the schools and media (wouldn't that be nice if it were in fact true!). So, we repeat the study, but this time, we conduct it as a longitudinal study. We measure the attitudes of nine 6-year-old boys in year 1, and continue to assess them every year until age 12. Interestingly, the raw data are identical to the original data (and are presented in the Appendix, in case the reader wishes to replicate the analyses): a 2-unit change every year. An examination of the interyear correlations shows that they range from .74 to .97, with the largest coefficients representing adjacent year measures. Based upon these group statistics, we might come to the same conclusion as we did with our cross-sectional study; that is, young boys' attitudes towards competitive sport increase steadily from age 6 to 12 at a rate of two units per year, with only small interindividual differences (in strength of the attitudes and in patterns of change). However, if we look closely at the raw data in the Appendix, it can be seen that change occurs at a rate of about six units (plus or minus measurement error) per year and occurs over a 2-year period, with only random fluctuations occurring in the other 5 years. Subjects 1-3 change 12 units from ages 10 to 12 , subjects 4-6 change 12 units from ages 8 to 10, and subjects 7-9 experience their 12-unit change very early, from age 6 to 8. A fuller statistical treatment of these data is provided later in this chapter, but it should be clear at this point that a cross-sectional design would have led to considerable misunderstandings of the process of change, as would a superficial analysis of the longitudinal data.

Change Scores

Developmental research, when conducted with longitudinal designs, is, by necessity, often restricted to measurements at only two points in time. This frequently leads to the use of a difference score, $d = (X_{time\ 1} - X_{time\ 2})$, as the variable of interest and the score used in subsequent statistical analyses. The "best" way to analyze change, particularly with respect to the validity of difference scores, has been a topic of much debate in the behavioral sciences for decades (Harris, 1963), and it continues to be examined today (Zumbo, 1999). Additionally, it has been discussed in the sport and exercise science literature for over 20 years (Kane & Lazarus, 1999; Schutz; 1978, 1989, 1998). Simply put, the widely held belief has been that change scores are unreliable and therefore should not be used in any statistical analyses of change. However, Rogosa (1995) and many others have challenged these beliefs, and Rogosa lists five fallacies regarding the measurement and analysis of change. He shows that although these traditional "truths" may hold in certain conditions, there are numerous situations in which they are, in fact, fallacies. The five fallacies are (1) regression towards the mean is an unavoidable law of nature, (2) a pre-post difference score is unreliable, (3) analysis of covariance (rather than a mixed-model factorial ANOVA) is the appropriate way to analyze change, (4) measurements taken at two points in time are sufficient for the study of change, and (5) the correlation between change and the initial value is always negative. Once again, we cannot elaborate on these points in this chapter, but, very briefly, it is our opinion that (a) fallacies (1) and (5) actually do occur frequently in sport and exercise psychology research and thus are not really that fallacious for researchers in this field; (b) assuming the reliability of most psychological measures is about .70, and in a longitudinal study the pre-post correlation may be approximately .40, the reliability of a pre-post difference score would be .50 — and whether or not one considers that to be unreliable (given the measures have a reliability of only .70) is up to a researcher to decide (although we would consider it to be a somewhat unreliable measure of change); and (c) fallacies (3) and (4) are definitely fallacies, and researchers are encouraged to stay away from ANOVA and attempt to obtain measures at more than two points in time in any developmental study.

> Developmental research conducted with longitudinal designs often measures only two points in time.

Traditional Methods (ANOVA)

Example 1: Single Factor Repeated Measures ANOVA, With Trend Analysis

For this example we will use the data set briefly described previously (Appendix). The data represent scores taken once per year for 7 years. Following traditional practice, we analyzed the data using a repeated measures ANOVA, with trend analysis to examine the nature of the pattern of change over time. As expected, the results (Table 2) clearly show that the trend is linear; in fact 100% of the variability in Age is accounted for by the Linear trend (the Sum of Squares for the Age main effect is 1008, and all of this is taken up by the Linear effect), but we would be making a gross misinterpretation of the data were we to draw such conclusions — a 2-unit change per year is not typical, and in fact none of the nine boys exhibited such a pattern. How were we supposed to know this, and what characteristics of the data or analytic results might lead us to this conclusion? A closer examination of some aspects of the ANOVA table is revealing.

Previously we noted that the Linear effect accounted for a full 100% of the Age effect, but now turn your attention to the Error terms. Notice that the Quadratic component of the error term ($SxA_{quadratic}$) accounts for approximately 55% (264.2/479.7) of the error sum of squares, despite there being absolutely no Quadratic effect (the sum of squares is zero). The Quadratic error term, which is the Subjects by $Age_{quadratic}$ effect, tells us the extent to which subjects varied in their quadratic (curvilinear) pattern of change over the seven measures. Apparently there were considerable curvilinear patterns of change, but the patterns and/or degree of curvature were quite variable between subjects. That is, there are large *interindividual differences in intraindividual change* (identifying and explaining these differences is what developmental/change research is all about). In fact, they were so different that they cancelled each other out, resulting in absolutely no nonlinearity in the *mean* values over the seven ages.

TABLE 2
One-Way Repeated Measures ANOVA, With Trend Analysis, of Competitiveness, Ages 6 to 12

Source of Variation	Sum of Squares	(%)[a]	d. f.	Mean Square	F	p
Subjects (S)	1738.3		8			
Age (A)	1008.0		6	168.0	16.8	<.001
Age_{linear}	1008.0	(100%)	1	1008.0	178.1	<.001
$Age_{quadratic}$	0.0	(0%)	1	0.0	0.0	
Age_{other}	0.0	(0%)	4	0.0	0.0	
S x A (error)	479.7		48	10.0		
S x A_{linear}	45.3	(9%)	8	5.7		
S x $A_{quadratic}$	264.2	(55%)	8	33.1		
S x A_{other}	170.2	(36%)	32	5.3		
Total	3226.0		62			

[a] The percent of the Sum of Squares for the Age effect, or for the S x A effect, accounted for by its trend analysis component (linear, quadratic, and remainder).

The Linear error term, on the other hand, accounts for only 9% of the error variance, indicating that the total amount of change (increase) over the 6 years was about the same for all subjects. If we examine the data at the individual level, we can see that the boys exhibited one of the three patterns of change exhibited in Figure 3 (each of the three lines is the mean for three subjects). With only minor between-subject variability, all nine of the subjects increased their attitudes towards competition a total of 12 units over the 6 years, but all of that change was the result of a 6-unit change in each of 2 consecutive years. The only notable between-subject differences are *when* that change started.

Example 2: Mixed-Model ANOVA, With Trend Analysis

It is possible that these observed between-subject differences in when the change occurred could be accounted for by some other variable. If this were so, then that variability would be removed from the error terms, thus yielding a more powerful design — with respect to statistical power and to the ability to identify the true pattern of change. Say that this sudden six-unit per year increase in the values held for competition occurred during the first 2 years that the boy was involved in an organized league that kept team and individual statistics and gave year-end awards based on these statistics. However, some boys were introduced to this structured competition at age 6, some at age 8, and some not until age 10. This could have accounted for the observed differences in the timing of the increases. If we had hypothesized this to start with, we might have analyzed the data as a two-factor design, using an ANOVA for a Group (3) x Age (7) factorial design with repeated measures on the Age factor. The results of that analysis are presented in Table 3. There we see that most of the interindividual differences in intraindividual variability (i.e., the pattern of change over time) are now accounted for by the Group by Age effect. That is, what we thought was unexplained error variance (the Subjects by Age error term SS of 479.7 in the one-way ANOVA in Table 2), is actually almost fully accounted for by the Group by Age effect (SS=442.3), with the SS for the error variance being reduced to 37.4. Additionally, 58% (257.1/442.3) of this effect is taken up by the Group by Age$_{quadratic}$ effect, reflecting the very different quadratic shapes of Group 1 and Group 3. Figure 3 shows this quadratic pattern of change, separately by groups.

Based on this new analysis, we now reformulate our conclusions as follows. Young boys undergo a large change (an increase of approximately 6 units per year) in their values held towards competitive sports in the first 2 years of participation in organized competitive sport. Prior to such involvement, and after the 2 years have elapsed, values remain quite stable from year to year.

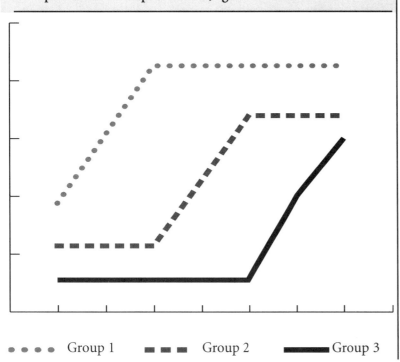

FIGURE 3
Group means for competitiveness, ages 6 to 12

• • • • Group 1   ▬ ▬ ▬ Group 2   ▬▬▬▬ Group 3

TABLE 3

Two-Way (Group by Age) Mixed-model ANOVA, With Trend Analysis, of Competitiveness, Ages 6 to 12

Source of Variation	Sum of Squares	(%)[a]	d.f.	Mean Square	F	p
				867.0	2025.0	<.001
Groups (G)	1735.7	2				
				0.43		
Subjects Within Groups (SwG)	2.6		6			
Age (A)	1008.0		6	161.6	16.8	<.001
$\quad$ Age$_{linear}$	1008.0	(100%)	1	1459.9	178.1	<.001
$\quad$ Age$_{quadratier}$	0.0	(0%)	1	0.0	0.0	
$\quad$ Age$_{other}$	0.0	(0%)	4	0.0	0.0	
G x A	442.3		12	38.9	35.5	<.001
$\quad$ G x A$_{linear}$	41.1	(9%)	2	20.6	27.8	<.001
$\quad$ G x A$_{quadratic}$	257.1	(58%)	2	128.6	108.7	<.001
$\quad$ G x A$_{other}$	144.1	(33%)	8			
SwG x A	37.4		36	1.04		
$\quad$ SwG x A$_{linear}$	4.2		6	0.7		
$\quad$ G x A$_{quadratic}$	7.1		6	1.2		
$\quad$ G x A$_{other}$	26.1		24	1.1		
Total	3226.0		62			

[a] The percent of the Sum of Squares for the Age effect, or for the G x A effect, accounted for by its trend analysis component (linear, quadratic, and remainder).

These contrived data have given us a convenient way to show the importance of analyzing data at the individual level as much as possible, but as you will have seen, we still did not really get down to the individual level for our statistical analyses. We noted, from visual inspection of individual plots, that there were differences between the boys in the pattern of change and that there appeared to be three distinct patterns. We were fortunate to have a measured variable (age of onset of competitive sport participation) that explained most of these interindividual differences in intraindividual change. Rarely is there a grouping variable that will account for this variability, and rarely are there such distinctly different patterns of change. Consequently, rarely will an ANOVA be a sufficient statistical method for analyzing data at the individual level. Latent growth modeling (e.g., see Duncan, Duncan, Strycker, Li, & Alpert, 1999) and hierarchical linear modeling (e.g., see Bryk & Raudenbush, 1992) are appropriate when we have a large (N>200) number of subjects and an adequate number (≥4) of repeated observations on each subject. We now attempt a very brief overview of one of these procedures, latent growth modeling.

> Analyze data at the individual level as much as possible.

Latent Growth Modeling

The limitations of traditional statistical methods in the analysis of change have been discussed above. An alternative method, one that takes into account the individual level of change as well as the group level of change in an analysis, is latent growth modeling (LGM). Although it contains the term *growth*, this statistical technique can be applied to any repeated measures data. However, it may be most useful when one has a prior hypothesis about the pattern of change of a variable. Based on the formative work of Rao (1958) and Tucker (1958), the LGM approach was first suggested by Meredith and Tisak (1984, 1990) within the framework of structural equation modeling (SEM) and later extended by others (e.g., McArdle, 1988; Muthen, 1997). The basic idea behind LGM is that the growth (or change) of an attribute is an unobservable latent trait. Thus, in LGM, change is described by one or more latent variables (factors).

There are several merits of LGM for the analysis of change. First, by using both the mean scores and covariances of variables, LGM takes account of individual levels of change as well as the group level of change. Second, individual change can be represented by either a straight line or a curvilinear trajectory. Third, occasions of measurement need not be equally spaced (a frequent occurrence in developmental studies). Fourth, measurement errors can be accounted for by the statistical model, and reliability estimates for the variables at each time point are available. Fifth, multiple predictors or correlates of change can be easily included in the model. Finally, as in general SEM analysis, statistical models are flexible, allowing one to extend the basic idea in several ways in order to test various hypotheses such as multivariate LGM, multigroup analysis, and cohort sequential analysis (McArdle, 1988; Meredith & Tisak, 1990; Muthen, 1997).

Although there have been some studies in which SEM was used with repeated measures data (e.g., Marsh, 1996; Schutz, 1995, 1998), the LGM method has seldom been utilized in exercise psychology research. An exception was a study by Duncan and Duncan (1991), in which they applied the LGM method to investigate the change of children's perceptions of physical competence. Although there are clear benefits of using LGM for the analysis of repeated measures data, there has been an obvious lack of studies using LGM in exercise and sport psychology. This is unfortunate, given that the LGM method first appeared more than a decade ago. However, it is also understandable, given the complexity of the method and the scarcity of easily understood papers on the topic. In the following section, we present a basic introduction to LGM and some of its extensions, with examples. However, because of limited space, we have not included all aspects of LGM. In addition, although we have tried to make this section easily understood by the intended readership, it would be helpful if readers have some knowledge about linear regression and factor analysis techniques.

The Basics of LGM

Assume that a developmental study yielded data consisting of a variable that was repeatedly measured at five occasions on the same subjects. For convenience, assume that the intervals between adjacent time points are approximately equal. Further, after reviewing a few individual scores as well as the relevant literature, the researcher hypothesized that the variable changes linearly over time at the individual level. Consequently, the researcher decided to test if each individual changes linearly over time, and used LGM to do so. Figure 4 shows the diagram for such a linear LGM. Following the general rules of SEM, boxes represent observed (measured) variables, and in Figure 4 there are five observed variables, labelled as Time1, Time2, etc. For the moment, disregard the "predictor" variable that is depicted using dotted lines. Ovals represent unobserved latent variables (factors), and here there are two latent variables, named "Intercept" and "Slope." Arrows represent the relationships among observed and latent variables. Single-headed arrows are used to show a causal relationship between variables where the variable at the tail of the arrow is hypothesized to cause (or explain) the variable at the head of the arrow. The magnitude of causal relationship between an observed variable and a latent variable is called a *path coefficient* (or *factor loading*), and it is equivalent to a B coefficient (or slope) in a linear regression analysis. Thus, in Figure 4, the Time1 through Time5 variables are dependent (endogenous) variables, whereas the intercept and slope factors are independent (exogenous) variables. The relationship between observed and latent variables can be represented by a linear equation. For example, the Time1 variable is represented as Time1 = (1) × Intercept + (0) × Slope + ε1. The double-headed arrow shows the covariances (correlations in standardized units) between two variables.

Note that all path coefficients in Figure 4 are fixed at certain values, unlike in a regression analysis or a usual SEM. Because of these fixed coefficients, the latent variables have specific meanings. The intercept factor represents a true score at the first time point (initial status), and the slope factor represents the true rate of linear change over time. Each subject has his or her own intercept and slope, and it is expected that there will be between-subject variation in the intercept and in the slope. The mean and the variance of the intercept factor are represented by α_i and ψ_{ii}, respectively. The mean and the variance of the slope factor are represented by α_s and ψ_s, respectively. The covariance between the intercept and slope factors is represented by ψ_{is}. An error (ε) represents that part of an observed variable that is not explained by the intercept and slope factors. Thus, according to Figure 4, the score of each individual at each time point can be expressed as

> Time1 = Intercept + (0) × (Slope) + e1,
> Time2 = Intercept + (1) × (Slope) + e2, and so on for Times 3, 4, and 5

LGM takes into account individual levels of change as well as the group level of change.

It becomes clear that, apart from error, which is unique at each time point, the difference between Time1 and Time2 is Slope, and the difference between Time1 and Time3 is 2 × Slope and so on, implying a linear change over time. That is, one's score at any time point is a function of one's own intercept and slope. The means and variances of the observed variables and covariances between observed variables are used as data for the statistical analysis. The means

FIGURE 4
Linear LGM

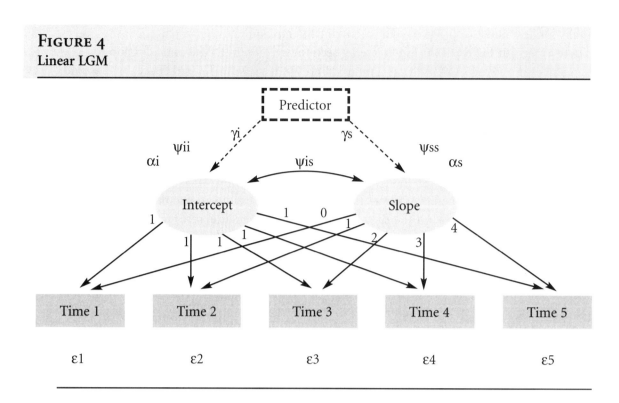

and variances of the latent variables and covariance between the two latent variables are estimated by the model. The mean and the variance of the intercept factor are the true mean and the between-subject variance of the initial time point. The mean of the slope factor is the average linear change between adjacent time points, and the variance of the slope factor is the between-subject variation of the magnitude of the linear change over time. The covariance between the two factors shows the magnitude and the direction (positive or negative) of the relationship between the score at the initial time point and the rate of the change. The variances of the errors are also estimated by the model.

This basic model can be extended in several ways. First, by adjusting some of the path coefficients of the slope factor or by adding additional change factor(s), a model can describe a curvilinear change. In Figure 4, if the last three path coefficients of the slope factor are freely estimated rather than fixed at specific values, the model can fit data that are not well identified by a quadratic, cubic, or higher-order polynomial. This type of model can be described as an "unstructured curve" model, hereafter just referred to as the "curve model". In this case, the second path coefficient should be still fixed at 1 to give a unit to the change factor. On the other hand, if one adds a third factor to a linear model (a "Quadratic" factor with path coefficients of 0, 1, 4, 9, and 16), it becomes a quadratic model that describes a quadratic change over time. Another model can be formed by adding a predictor of the intercept and change. A model testing a predictor effect on the intercept and slope is depicted in Figure 4 using a dotted line. The effects of the predictor on the two factors are represented by γ_i and γ_s (the paths from the predictor to the factors). Finally, a multivariate model is possible. Frequently in sport and exercise psychology, an attribute is measured by several variables (items). These variables may form a factor, and a multivariate LGM can describe the change of the factor over time. The quadratic and multivariate models are presented later as empirical examples.

Maximum likelihood, the method commonly used for the estimation of parameters, requires a relatively large sample size (i.e., 200) and assumes that the data come from a multivariate normal population. The estimation of parameters can be done using any one of a number of commercially available SEM programs (e.g., LISREL, EQS, MPLUS, or SEPATH). After the parameters are estimated, the goodness of a model is evaluated using a subset of the numerous goodness-of-fit indices that are reported by most SEM programs. Unless the model is evaluated as a good model, it is not worthwhile to interpret the estimated parameters. The many issues regarding estimation procedures and model evaluation are beyond the scope of this paper, and interested readers are directed to any recent SEM text for additional information (e.g., Bollen, 1989; Kline, 1998; Schumacker & Lomax, 1996).

Example 1: Univariate LGM

An artificial (computer-generated) data set was used for the following examples of LGM analyses. The generation of this data set was based on actual data of the Children's Attitude Toward Physical Activity (CATPA) scale (Schutz et al., 1985). Only one attitude dimension among the eight was used. Assume that three items have been measured from a cohort group (N = 500) once a year at grades 8, 9, 10, 11, and 12 to measure the attitude toward participation in physical activity for the purpose of health and fitness (ATPA-HF). The means and standard deviations of these three items at each time point are shown in Table 4. Table 4 also includes a predictor variable, parents' ATPA-HF, which was measured at grade 8 only. For simplicity, assume that this predictor variable is represented by a single score and measured without error (i.e., reliability = 1.0).

For an example of a univariate LGM, we will use item A only. The mean of item A decreased over time, with the change being largest between the first two time points and leveling off at subsequent time points (see Table 4). The correlation between time points ranged from .038 to .581, relatively small values, given that the same variable was measured repeatedly on the same subjects. The correlation matrix approximated a simplex pattern, with the correlation coefficients becoming smaller as a coefficient gets farther away from the main diagonal. This implies that subjects' relative positions have changed considerably over time. That is, there was a considerable between-person variation in the rate of change over time in the score of item A (i.e., considerable interindividual differences in intraindividual change). The skewness and kurtosis values of all variables were close to zero (largest absolute value was - .313), indicating only a small departure from a normal distribution. Thus, maximum likelihood estimation is the appropriate method to estimate the parameters of the LGMs.

The first step is to identify the best fitting growth model, and once that is determined, the predictor is included in the model. Thus several models may be fitted to the data and evaluated. Based on previous research and theoretical expectations, three growth models, Linear, Curve, and Quadratic, were fitted and compared in this example. The goodness-of-fit indices for these three growth models are presented in Table 5. The linear model can be accepted as a good fitting model. Although the χ^2 statistic was significant, the standardized root mean square residual (SRMR) was small, the root mean square error of approximation (RMSEA)

After the parameters are estimated, a model must be evaluated using numerous goodness-of-fit indices.

TABLE 4
Means and standard deviations of ATPA-HF measures

	Grade 8	Grade 9	Grade 10	Grade 11	Grade 12
Item A	4.50 ± .912	4.28 ± .816	4.12 ± .819	4.02 ± .980	3.98 ± 1.429
Item B	4.28 ± 1.00	4.06 ± .895	3.91 ± .919	3.81 ± 1.082	3.18 ± 1.245
Item C	4.05 ± .920	3.85 ± .840	3.71 ± .815	3.62 ± .983	2.98 ± 1.190
Parents' ATPA-HF	4.43 ± 1.12				

TABLE 5
Goodness-of-fit indices of univarite LGMs for item A

Model	χ^2 (df)	p-value	RMSEA	ECVI	SRMR	NNFI
1. Linear	28.91(10)	.001	.066	.103	.034	.97
2. Curve	26.03(7)	<.001	.078	.109	.027	.96
3. Quadratic	.683(6)	.995	≈.00	.058	.008	1.01
4. Quadratic, with predictor	2.123(8)	.997	≈.00	.080	.010	1.01

Note. df: degrees of freedom, RMSEA: root mean square error of approximation, ECVI: expected cross-validation index, SRMR: standardized root mean square residual, NNFI: non-normed fit index.

was within an acceptable range ($< .08$), and the nonnormed fit index (NNFI) was high ($> .95$). However, the χ^2 difference test between the linear and the quadratic model showed that the quadratic model was significantly better than the linear model. Other fit indices also indicated that the quadratic model fits the data better than the linear model does. The expected cross-validation index (ECVI) of the quadratic model was smallest among the three growth models, also indicating this model is the best. Thus, the quadratic model is the preferred model to explain individual change of item A over time. As indicated by the changes in mean scores, individuals change in a quadratic fashion. The goodness-of-fit of the curve model was similar to that of the linear model and showed a worse fit than that of the quadratic model.

The predictor, parents' ATPA-HF, was included in the quadratic model in the next step. The χ^2 statistic of this model was not significant, and other fit indices also indicate that this model fits the data very well (see model 4 in Table 5). This final model is presented in Figure 5 with the values for the estimated parameters included. As explained earlier, all path coefficients (factor loadings) of this model are fixed values. The numbers shown in italics are the standardized effects of the predictor on the intercept, slope, and quadratic factors. Other estimates are non-standardized values. All parameter estimates shown in Figure 5 were significant at an alpha level of .05, except the path from the predictor to the quadratic factor. The estimated mean of the intercept factor was very close to the actual mean of item A (4.499) at grade 8. The mean of the slope factor (- .25) was negative whereas the mean of the quadratic factor was positive (.03). The mean scores at each time point that are estimated by the model can be calculated as follows:

Time1: $4.50 = 4.50 + (0) \times (- .25) + (0) \times .03$
Time2: $4.28 = 4.50 + (1) \times (- .25) + (1) \times .03$
Time3: $4.12 = 4.50 + (2) \times (- .25) + (4) \times .03$
Time4: $4.02 = 4.50 + (3) \times (- .25) + (9) \times .03$
Time5: $3.98 = 4.50 + (4) \times (- .25) + (16) \times .03$

Because of the very close fit of the model to the data, these estimated mean scores showed no difference (up to two decimal places) from those of the actual data. The variance of the intercept factor was much smaller than that of the actual data (.83). This is because the variance of the intercept factor represents the variance of the true scores at grade 8 (i.e., the variance of the attitudes if they could be measured without error). The rest of the observed variance is due to the error. The variances of the slope and the quadratic factors were significant, indicating that there were considerable between-person variations in the change of item A scores. Although not shown in Figure 5, there was a significant correlation between the intercept and the slope factors (r = - .49). This indicates that the subjects who scored high at grade 8 showed a larger decline than did those who scored low at this age. The correlation between the slope and the quadratic factors was also significant (r = - .64), implying that the subjects who declined faster than others at the beginning of the time period showed a faster leveling off. The correlation between the intercept and the quadratic factors was not significant. Turning to the predictor, we can see that it has a positive effect on the intercept and a negative effect on the slope factor. The parents' ATPA-HF has a positive effect on their children's ATPA-HF (item A) at grade 8. Although parents' positive ATPA-HF leads to a faster decline in children's ATPA-HF (item A), the magnitude of this effect (- .37) was small, and it explains only 13.7% of the variation in the slope.

In summary, the quadratic model adequately explained the individual changes in the ATPA-HF (item A) over time. Children's ATPA-HF declined over a 4-year period (grades 8 through 12), and the rate of decline leveled off over time. Children showed considerable interindividual variation in the rate of change (i.e., significant variances of the slope and quadratic factors) as well as in the initial scores of ATPA-HF. The parents' ATPA-HF had a positive effect on the children's ATPA-HF at grade 8, but led to a faster decline in children's ATPA-HF over the ensuing 4 years.

Example 2: Multivariate LGM

Multivariate LGM is used to examine if the change of a latent variable (factor) shows a certain trajectory. The basic idea is the same as a univariate LGM, the only differences being that several items form a factor at each time point and higher order growth factors explain the change of the factor (see Figure 6). A multivariate LGM requires a few extra steps because before a multivariate LGM is applied to a data set, several conditions have to be satisfied. First, one has to examine if the hypothesized factor structure holds at each time point. That is, one has to examine if the measured items form a factor at each time point (in SEM terminology, this is called a *measurement model*). Second, once a factor is believed to be formed at all time points,

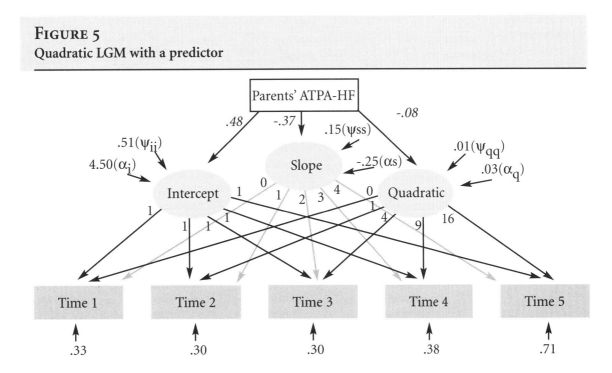

FIGURE 5
Quadratic LGM with a predictor

FIGURE 6
Multivariate LGM: Quadratic Model

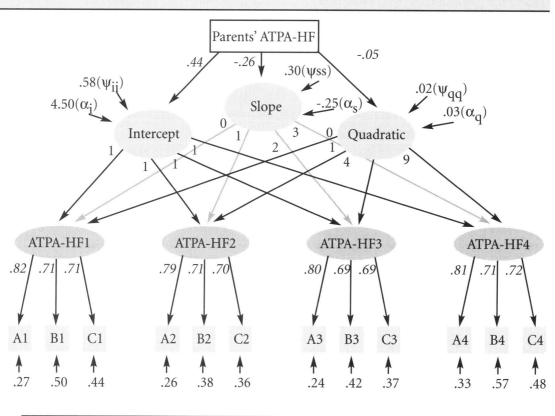

one has to examine if the factor loadings for the same item are equal over time. In other words, one should test if the same attribute (factor) is measured over time. Thus, a multivariate LGM analysis includes following steps: (a) test of a measurement model, (b) test of equality of factor loadings over time, (c) selection of the best growth model, and (d) test of predictor effects.

For the example of a multivariate LGM, all items, items A, B, and C, are used. As explained earlier, it is hypothesized that these three items form a latent variable (factor) that represents ATPA-HF. The goodness-of-fit indices of fitted models are presented in Table 6. Following the steps mentioned above, the measurement model, a 5-factor model with one factor per year, was examined first (model 1). In this model, item A was used to give a scale to the factor at each time point (i.e., the raw score factor loadings for item A were fixed at 1 — but note that the standardized loadings are given in Figure 6), and the variance of the factor was allowed to change over time. This model fits the data very well. The χ^2 statistic was not significant, and RMSEA was very low. Other fit indices also indicated that this model fit the data very well. In the next model (model 2), the equality of factor loadings over the five time points was examined. This model produced χ^2 statistic of 116.05 with 88 degrees of freedom. Because this model is nested within model 1, a χ^2 difference test is possible to compare this model to model 1. The difference in χ^2 statistic was 22.09 with 8 degrees of freedom, and this was significant at alpha level of .05. This means that model 2 is significantly worse than model 1; thus, the equality of factor loadings among the five time points was rejected. That is, the factor structure changed over the 4 years. To examine when this factor structure changed, the equality of factor loadings between first two time points, among first three time points, and among first four time points was examined in the next three additional models (models 3, 4, and 5). None of these three models was rejected (p-values for the χ^2 statistics were all greater than .10). It appears that the factor structure changed between time 4 and 5 (grades 11 and 12). This presents a problem. It would not make sense to try to interpret change from time 4 to 5 because it is a slightly different construct that is being measured at time 5. Thus for the purposes of this example, we included only the first four time points in the LGM analyses.

Models 6, 7, and 8 in Table 6 represent the three different patterns of change (linear, quadratic, curve) for the factor ATPA-HF. All three models described the data very well (see Table 6). The χ^2 statistics were not significant, and all other fit indices indicated excellent fits. Although least parsimonious, the quadratic model is selected as the best fitting model in this example because the quadratic model was significantly better than the linear model (χ^2 difference (4) = 21.1, p < .001) and also better than the curve model in terms of all fit indices (because the spline model is not nested within the quadratic model, a χ^2 difference test was not possible). In model 9, the predictor, parents' ATPA-HF, was included in the model to examine how it may explain children's change in ATPA-HF. This model also showed a good model fit, and the estimated parameters of this final model are presented in Figure 6. The estimated path coefficients (factor loadings) of observed variables at each time point as well as the path coefficients of the predictor variable (parents' ATPA-HF) are standardized values (presented in italics). All other parameter estimates are raw values. The standardized path coefficients (factor loadings) of observed variables ranged from .69 to .82, relatively high for the items of a questionnaire. These standardized path coefficients showed very similar magnitudes over time among the same item. The interpretation of the growth factors and the predictor effect is the same as that of the univariate LGM. Note that the means of the intercept, slope, and the quadratic factors are the same as in the example of a univariate LGM because the ATPA-HF factor at each time point was scaled using item A (the path coefficients for item A were fixed at 1). The variance of the intercept, slope, and quadratic factors, however, showed some differences from those of the univariate model for item A. All these estimates were significant (p < .05).

TABLE 6
Goodness-of-fit Indices of Multivariate LGMs

Model	$\chi^{2\,(df)}$	p-value	RMSEA	ECVI	SRMR	NNFI
1. 5-factor model	93.96 (80)	.136	.019	.348	.026	.99
Equal loadings over time						
2. Time 1 = 2 = 3 = 4 = 5	116.05 (88)	.024	.024	.356	.039	.99
3. Time 1 = 2	95.72 (82)	.143	.018	.342	.028	.99
4. Time 1 = 2 = 3	96.93 (84)	.158	.017	.337	.028	1.00
5. Time 1 = 2 = 3 = 4	97.32 (86)	.190	.016	.330	.028	1.00
Multivariate LGM (with only first four time points)						
6. Linear	85.33 (67)	.065	.024	.266	.045	.99
7. Quadratic	64.23 (63)	.433	.006	.237	.036	1.00
8. Curve	71.73 (65)	.265	.015	.244	.042	1.00
9. Quadratic, with predictor	69.62 (72)	.558	< .001	.220	.025	1.00

Note. df: degrees of freedom, RMSEA: root mean square error of approximation, ECVI: expected cross-validation index, SRMR: standardized root mean square residual, NNFI: nonnormed fit index.

The covariance between the intercept and slope (r = - .54) and between the slope and the quadratic factors (r = -.85) was significant and relatively high in an absolute sense. As in the univariate LGM example, there was a significant effect of the parents' ATPA-HF on the intercept (γ = .44) and slope (γ = -.26) factors, but not on the quadratic factor (γ = -.05). That is, the higher the parent's H&F attitude, the larger the child's attitude score at age 8 and the smaller the linear rate of decline from age 8 through age 12.

Summary

The LGM analyses revealed that the children's ATPA-HF declined between grades 8 and 12 in a quadratic fashion. The rate of the decline was highest between the first two time points and leveled off in subsequent time points. Unlike traditional methods, LGM identified interindividual variations in the true scores at the initial time point and in the rate of change. There was a considerable variation in the rates of change in children's ATPA-HF, and a part of this variation was explained by the parent's ATPA-HF that was measured when children were in grade 8. However, the effect of parents' ATPA-HF on the rate of change was relatively small.

Although an LGM methodology may not always be the best method of analysis, it certainly is a useful method for the analysis of change. Among the merits of the LGM, the capability of taking account of the individual level of change in a model is its most distinctive characteristic. As a result of this capability, one can estimate the variance of, and covariance between, the intercept and growth factors (i.e., the variables of interest). This further allows one to include a predictor of the intercept and change in the model. In addition, LGM is flexible, allowing one to investigate the change of a latent variable that is measured by several items. However, LGM requires a relatively large sample size and multivariate normality of the measured variables — requirements that are often difficult to satisfy in practice.

An LGM is a useful statistical model for the analysis of change.

RELIABILITY

Reliability is the degree to which individuals' scores remain relatively consistent over repeated administrations of the same measurement or alternate measurement forms (Crocker & Algina, 1986). It is sometimes represented as the consistency or reproducibility of measured scores. Ideally, a perfect measurement tool will produce the exact same scores for a group of individuals if it is repeatedly administered under identical conditions, assuming that there is no change in the subjects' attribute. However, to a certain extent, all psychological measurements are unreliable (Crocker & Algina, 1986). In other words, it is almost impossible to perfectly measure a psychological attribute—even if there exists some true level of that attribute within a person. A score resulting from the measurement (observed score) of such an attribute includes two components, a true attribute component and an unreliable component. This unreliable component is called the *measurement error*.

The relationship among the observed score, the true component, and measurement error is well explained by classical test theory. According to this theory, the observed score is a composite of two components, a true (theoretical) score and an error score. That is, x = t + e, where x is the observed score, t is the true score, and e is random error. Given a few assumptions, it can be shown that the variance of observed scores is the sum of the true and error score variances, $\sigma^2_x = \sigma^2_t + \sigma^2_e$, where σ^2_x, σ^2_t, and σ^2_e are the variance of the observed scores, true scores, and error scores, respectively. Given this, the reliability of variable x (r_x) is defined by following equation:

$$r_x = \frac{\sigma^2_t}{\sigma^2_x} = \frac{\sigma^2_t}{\sigma^2_t + \sigma^2_e}$$

Thus, reliability is represented as the amount of true score variance relative to the observed score variance. However, because the true and error scores are unobservable elements, it is difficult to estimate the reliability. Consequently, reliability is often estimated using a test-retest method (correlation), intraclass correlation, or a measure of internal consistency (Cronbach's alpha). These methods are discussed in the following section.

Many factors affect the reliability of a measure: subject characteristics (e.g., fatigue or learning), scale characteristics (e.g., length or clarity), measurement environment, measurement process, etc. The variations in these factors may result in both random and systematic errors, but standardizing the measurement procedure may reduce the error due to the variations of measurement procedures. One should also consider the motivation level of the subjects, any bias due to the test administrator, and the heterogeneity of the subjects on the measured attribute (generally, the more heterogeneous the group, the higher the calculated reliability coefficient).

> Subject characteristics, scale characteristics, measurement environment, measurement process, and many other factors affect the reliability of a measure.

Test-Retest Method

The most frequently used reliability estimation method for a single measure (variable) is the test-retest method. The same test is administered to the same subjects twice, under the same conditions, within a certain period; and the Pearson product-moment correlation (PPMC) coefficient between the two sets of scores is taken as an estimate of the test reliability. Because this coefficient is based on measurement in two time points, it is often called a stability coefficient. The idea behind this is that only true scores should be correlated between two time points because the error component is random and not correlated with any other elements. Thus, the correlated part is due to only the true score element. The important assumption that should be satisfied is that there is no change in true scores between the two time points. This assumption is questioned by many researchers (e.g., Heise, 1969; Marsh & Grayson, 1994) because there is inevitable temporal instability of measures taken at multiple points in time. Another concern is the possibility of correlated errors between two time points. More recent techniques such as structural equation modeling provide methods for accounting for these problems analytically for certain situations. This is discussed, in part, later in this chapter.

Intraclass Correlation

The intraclass correlation is used when a single item is measured repeatedly, several items are measured once, or several items are measured repeatedly (Schutz, 1998). Like all reliability coefficients, it is conceptualized as a ratio of true score variance to observed score variance, and in this case ANOVA is used to estimate various sources of variance (mean squares). Depending on what assumptions a researcher wishes to make about error variances and true score variances, different intraclass correlation coefficients can be calculated. One of the earliest attempts to use the intraclass correlation for reliability estimation can be attributed to Hoyt (1941). He derived the equation using a "Persons by Items" ANOVA design, and related it to the classical reliability definition by noting that the mean square due to the persons (MS_p) represents the variance of observed scores, and the mean square error (MS_e: the Persons × Items interaction effect) represents the variance due to the error. The following two equations are most frequently used: the intraclass correlation coefficient for the mean test score over all trials or observations:

$$r = \frac{MS_p - MS_e}{MS}$$

and that for a single item score:

$$r_i = \frac{MS_p - MS_e}{MS_p + (k-1)MS_e}$$

where MS_p is the mean square due to persons, MS_e is the mean square due to error (the Persons × Items interaction effect), and k is the number of items or repeated measurement. The latter equation yields identical results to the internal consistency reliability, Cronbach's alpha.

Internal Consistency

When several items are used to measure an attribute, the degree of agreement among these items is called internal consistency, and the most frequently used coefficient is Cronbach's alpha (Cronbach, 1951). Cronbach's alpha can be considered to be an index of reliability of the composite score that is obtained by summing item scores. On the other hand, it should not be considered equivalent to a reliability stability coefficient, and its most frequent use (and misuse) in psychological research is as an indicator of structural validity or unidimensionality of a construct. A large alpha indicates that there is small item-specific variation. However, although it suggests a strong possibility that all items represent a single factor, it is not sufficient evidence to make such a conclusion. That is, a high alpha is a necessary, but not sufficient condition for unidimensionality. One should also note that with large number of items, Cronbach's alpha could be very high, overestimating the degree of agreement among items.

Reliability Estimation for Longitudinal Data

In developmental research, one often anticipates that an attribute changes over time. The reliability of a measurement tool may also change over time, for several reasons; a change in the characteristics of the subjects (e.g., age), different measurement administrators, etc. As noted earlier, using the PPMC or intraclass r for the estimation of reliability requires the assumption that the true score does not change over time. Thus, one may not use PPMC or intraclass r directly for longitudinal data in the estimation of reliability. One simple solution for this is to measure the variable twice or more at each time point and estimate the reliability. However, this is not a very practical solution.

A few statistical models have been suggested to overcome this problem analytically. Heise (1969) was among the first to suggest using an auto-regressive model to take into account the instability (i.e., change) of true scores over time in the estimation of reliability. This basic idea has been extended and widely used by others (e.g., Joreskog, 1970; Wiley & Wiley, 1970). This model, depicted in Figure 7a, is called a quasi-simplex model. The observed score at time t is a composite of two elements, a true score (η_t) and an error score (ε_t), as in classical test theory, that is; $X_t = \eta_t + \varepsilon_t$. The successive η_t are related by the linear equation, $\eta_{t+1} = \beta_t \eta_t + \zeta_{t+1}$, and the reliability of variable X_t is calculated as follows for measures taken at times s, t and u (where; $t_s < t_t < t_u$):

$$r_{tt} = \frac{r_{st} r_{tu}}{r}$$

where r_{st} is correlation between X_s and X_t, r_{tu} is correlation between X_t and X_u, and r_{su} is correlation between X_s and X_u. Using a structural equation modeling program (e.g., LISREL), the reliability coefficient r_{tt} is reported as the R^2 of each variable. Thus, this model takes into account the change in true score over time by the regression coefficient (β, the stability coefficient), and the variance unexplained by this relationship among variables (θ_ε) is due to the error. This model, however, is not an optimal model for the estimation of reliability. First, it can be shown that the reliability coefficient of the first and the last time points cannot be obtained unless there is an additional restriction (equal error variance over time) in the model. Second, a small simulation study conducted by the current authors revealed that for certain growth data, this model systematically overestimated the true reliability (see Table 7).

Another way to estimate reliability with longitudinal data is to use a latent growth model (LGM) approach, as suggested by Tisak and Tisak (1996). In the two-factor model presented earlier in this chapter (i.e., with intercept and slope factors), the reliability of time t can be calculated using the following equation:

$$ r_t = \frac{\lambda_{ti}^2 \psi_i + \lambda_{ts}^2 \psi_s + 2\lambda_{ti}\lambda_{ts}\psi_{is}}{\lambda_{ti}^2 \psi_i + \lambda_{ts}^2 \psi_s + 2\lambda_{ti}\lambda_{ts}\psi_{is} + \theta_t} $$

where λ represents a factor loading, ψ represents a factor variance, θ represents error variance, t stands for time t, i stands for intercept factor, and s stands for slope factor (see Figure 4). This reliability coefficient is also given by R^2 in any structural equation modeling program.

When several items are used to measure an attribute, one may use several quasi-simplex models or LGMs to obtain the reliability of each item at each time point. However, the change of an individual item may not be meaningful in many cases. In this situation, a confirmatory factor analysis (CFA) model may be used. The CFA model has been widely used for reliability estimation of individual items within a scale; however, it has rarely been used for reliability estimation of multi-item, multi-occasion situations. If three items are measured at five different time points, one may have a 5-factor CFA model with one factor at each time point (see Figure 7b). Basically, this model examines how much variance among the observed item variance is due to the underlying latent trait (true score) at each time point. This CFA model has been extended (Marsh & Grayson, 1994; Raffalovich & Bohrnstedt, 1987), so that the model takes account the sources of systematic variance due to specific item as well as specific time (Figure 7c). Interestingly, it is exactly the same as the multitrait-multimethod (MTMM) model. In the situation where three items are measured at five different time points, there are five latent factors that are unique at each time point (time factors), and there are three latent factors that are unique for each item (item factors). This model can be regarded as a variance decomposition model, decomposing total variance (observed variance) into time-specific, item-specific, and residual (error) variance (Marsh & Grayson, 1994). Although Raffalovich and Bohrnstedt (1987) and others used a second-order factor model for extracting another component of the variance, the common factor variance, the existence of the second-order factor does not affect the reliability estimation of individual items.

The estimation of longitudinal reliability can be done using any SEM program such as LISREL (Joreskog & Sorbom, 1996) or EQS (Bentler, 1995). The reliability estimates are the R^2 values of the observed variables.

We now present an empirical example of these four approaches (simplex, LGM, CFA, and MTMM) to estimating reliability for longitudinal data involving multiple measures at each point in time. The data used are the same simulated CATPA data that were used in the LGM section earlier in this paper (means and standard deviations in Table 4). The first row in Table 7 shows the true reliability of each item ("true" because the value was set by us in generating the data). Internal consistency estimates measured by Cronbach's alpha for each time point were high, indicating a relatively high level of agreement among items A, B, and C. As expected, the simplex model overestimated the reliability for this data set, and the magnitudes of overestimation were large for some items (e.g., time 2, item A). On the contrary, the LGM estimates underestimated the true reliability in most cases, but not to the same absolute

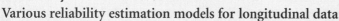

FIGURE 7
Various reliability estimation models for longitudinal data

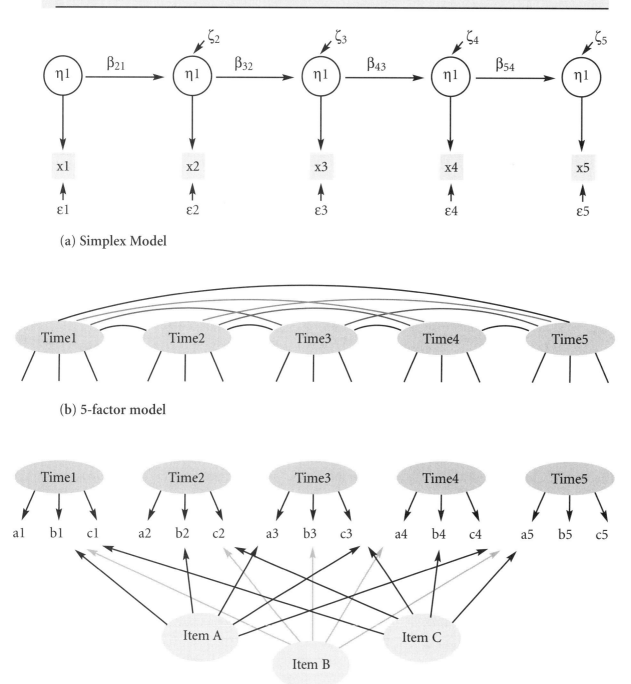

(a) Simplex Model

(b) 5-factor model

(c) Multitrait-multimethod model

Note. η = true score; β = regression (stability) coefficient; ζ = component of true score not explained by the true score of previous time points; x = observed score; ε = error component.

magnitude as the simplex model. The reliability coefficients estimated by the 5-factor CFA model and MTMM were most accurate, with all the estimated coefficients falling within +/- 0.05 of the true value, except for the MMTM model at time 2. Because the generated data are based on the model closest to the 5-factor CFA model, it is not surprising that this model yielded slightly better fits. The estimated reliability coefficients were similar between the 5-factor CFA model and MTMM, implying that item-specific variance is relatively small.

TABLE 7
Examples of Reliability Estimation Using Various Longitudinal Models

	Time 1			Time 2			Time 3			Time 4			Time 5		
Item	A	B	C	A	B	C	A	B	C	A	B	C	A	B	C
True Reliability	.64	.49	.49	.64	.49	.49	.64	.49	.49	.64	.49	.49	.64	.49	.49
Cronbach's alpha		.79			.78			.77			.78			.76	
Simplex model	.80	.77	.59	.74	.71	.51	.85	.53	.62	.79	.59	.50	.90	.69	.66
LGM	.61	.42	.50	.54	.46	.37	.55	.48	.37	.61	.39	.35	.65	.38	.53
5-factor CFA model	.69	.51	.47	.60	.53	.50	.64	.52	.44	.68	.51	.48	.66	.43	.47
MTMM	.68	.51	.48	.78	.57	.49	.63	.53	.45	.67	.52	.44	.65	.43	.49

Note. LGM: latent growth model, MTMM: multitrait-multimethod model.

Summary

In estimating the reliability of longitudinal data, there are many different methods available for computing a reliability coefficient. The decision as to which method is most appropriate depends upon the nature of the data and the specific aspect of reliability that is of primary interest. An LGM approach has the advantage that it takes into account the change in true scores, rather than just in observed scores. Different estimation methods, based on recent developments in structural equation modeling techniques, are now available to derive these LGM reliability estimates; however, a caution is needed in the application of these methods. One should choose a procedure based on hypotheses about the factor structure (when several items are measured) and/or the shape of the change of the measured variable(s).

To determine what method to use for estimating the reliability of longitudinal data, you must consider the nature of the data and the specific aspect of reliability that is of primary interest.

CHAPTER SUMMARY

In this chapter we have addressed just a few of the many methodological issues that must be considered when conducting developmental research in exercise and sport psychology. Validity and reliability are always paramount in any research endeavor; however, developmental research results in situations that require special procedures, especially with respect to reliability. Classical definitions of reliability assume no changes in mean scores over repeated assessments, whereas in developmental research we expect such changes to occur over time. Methods such as linear growth modeling are the preferred techniques to estimate reliability in this situation. LGMs are also useful in the statistical analysis of change and were shown to have certain advantages over traditional statistical techniques such as the repeated measures analysis of variance. The measurement and statistical procedures presented in this chapter are particularly appropriate for data arising from longitudinal studies. We made the argument that developmental research necessitates the measurement of change, and thus longitudinal studies are the most valid research design. Cross-sectional studies may be useful in a heuristic sense, but between-group comparisons cannot lead to valid inferences about change and development.

REFERENCES

American Psychological Association. (1985). *Standards for educational and psychological testing* (3rd ed.). Washington, DC: Author.

Bentler, P. M. (1995). *EQS structural equations program manual.* Encino, CA: Multivariate Software.

Bollen, K. A. (1989). *Structural equations with latent variables.* New York: Wiley.

Bornstein, R. F. (1996). Face validity in psychological assessment: Implications for a unified model of validity. *American Psychologist, 51,* 983-984.

Bryk, A., & Raudenbush, S. (1992). *Hierarchical linear models in social and behavioral research: Applications and data analysis methods.* Newbury Park, CA: Sage.

Collins, L. M., & Sayer, A. G. (Eds.) (2001). *New methods for the analysis of change.* Washington, D.C.: American Psychological Association.

Cortina, J. M. (1993). What is coefficient alpha? An examination of theory and applications. *Journal of Applied Psychology, 78,* 98-104.

Crocker, L., & Algina, J. (1986). *Introduction to classical and modern test theory.* New York: Holt, Rinehart and Winston.

Cronbach, L. J. (1951). Coefficient alpha and the internal structure of tests. *Psychometrika, 16,* 297-334.

Cronbach, L. J. (1971). Test validation. In R. L. Thorndike (Ed.), *Educational measurement* (pp. 443-507). Washington, DC: American Council on Education.

Duda, J. L. (1998). *Advances in sport and exercise psychology measurement.* Morgantown, WV: Fitness Information Technology Inc.

Duncan, T. E., & Duncan, S. C. (1991). A latent growth curve approach to investigating developmental dynamics and correlates of change in children's perceptions of physical competence. *Research Quarterly for Exercise and Sport, 62,* 390-398.

Duncan, T. E., Duncan, S. C., Strycker, L. A., Li, F., & Alpert, A. (1999). *An introduction to latent variable growth curve modeling.* Mahwah, NJ: Erlbaum.

Dunn, J. G. H., Bouffard, M., & Rogers, W. T. (1999). Assessing item content-relevance in sport psychology scale-construction research: Issues and recommendations. *Measurement in Physical Education and Exercise Science, 3,* 15-36.

Fabrigar, L., Wegener, D., MacCallum, R., & Strahan, E. (1999). Evaluating the use of exploratory factor analysis in psychological research. *Psychological Methods, 4,* 272-299.

Harris, C. W. (Ed.). (1963). *Problems in measuring change.* Madison: University of Wisconsin Press.

Heise, D. R. (1969). Separating reliability and stability in test-retest correlation. *American Sociological Review, 34,* 93-101.

Hoyt, C. J. (1941). Test reliability estimated by analysis of variance. *Psychometrika, 6,* 153-160.

Joreskog, K. G. (1970). Estimation and testing of simplex models. *British Journal of Mathematical and Statistical Psychology, 23,* 121-145.

Joreskog, K., & Sorbom, D. (1999). LISREL (Version 8.3). Chicago, IL: Scientific Software International.

Kane, M., & Lazarus, J. (1999). Change scores in physical education and exercise science: Revisiting the Hale and Hale method. *Measurement in Physical Education and Exercise Science, 3,* 181-193.

Kline, R. B. (1998). *Principles and practices of structural equation modeling.* New York: Guilford.

Marsh, H. W. (1994). Sport motivation orientations: Beware of jingle-jangle fallacies. *Journal of Sport & Exercise Psychology, 16,* 365-380.

Marsh, H. W. (1996). Physical self description questionnaire: Stability and discriminant validity. *Research Quarterly for Exercise and Sport, 67,* 249-264.

Marsh, H. W., & Grayson, D. (1994). Longitudinal confirmatory factor analysis: Common, time-specific, item-specific, and residual-error components of variance. *Structural Equation Modeling, 1,* 116-145.

McArdle, J. J. (1988). Dynamic but structural equation modeling of repeated measures data. In R. B. Cattel & J. Nesselroade (Eds.), *Handbook of multivariate experimental psychology* (2nd ed., pp. 561-614). New York: Plenum.

Meredith, W., & Tisak, J. (1984). *"Tuckerizing" curves.* Paper presented at the Psychometric Society Annual Meetings, Santa Barbara, CA.

Meredith, W., & Tisak, J. (1990). Latent curve analysis. *Psychometrika, 55,* 107-122.

Messick, S. (1995). Validity of psychological assessment. *American Psychologist, 50,* 741-749.

Muthen, B. (1997). Latent variable modeling of longitudinal and multilevel data. In A. E. Raftery (Ed.), *Sociological methodology* (pp. 453-480). Washington, DC: Blackwell.

Raffalovich, L. E., & Bohrnstedt, G. W. (1987). Common, specific, and error variance components of factor models: Estimation with longitudinal data. *Sociological Methods and Research, 15,* 385-405.

Reise, S., Waller, N., & Comrey, A. (2000). Factor analysis and scale revision. *Psychological Assessment, 12,* 287-297.

Roberts, B. W., & DelVecchio, W. F. (2000). The rank-order consistency of personality traits from childhood to old age: A quantitative review of longitudinal studies. *Psychological Bulletin, 126,* 3-25.

Rao, C. R. (1958). Some statistical methods for comparison of growth curves. *Biometrics, 14,* 1-17.

Rogosa, D. (1995). Myths and methods: "Myths about longitudinal research" plus supplemental questions. In J. M. Gottman (Ed.), *The analysis of change* (pp. 3-66). Mahwah, NJ: L. Erlbaum.

Schumacker, R. E., & Lomax, R. G. (1996). *A beginner's guide to structural equation modeling.* Mahwah, NJ: Lawrence Erlbaum.

Schutz, R. W. (1978). Specific problems in the measurement of change: Longitudinal studies, difference scores, and multivariate analyses. In D. Landers & R. Christina (Eds.), *Psychology of motor behavior & sport—1977* (pp. 151-175). Champaign, IL: Human Kinetics.

Schutz, R. W. (1989). Analyzing change. In J. Safrit & T. Wood, (Eds.), *Measurement concepts in physical education and exercise science* (pp. 206-228). Champaign, IL: Human Kinetics.

Schutz, R. W. (1995). The stability of individual performance in baseball: An examination of four 5-year periods, 1928-32, 1948-52, 1968-72, and 1988-92. *Proceedings of the Section on Statistics in Sports* (pp. 39-44). Alexandria, VA: American Statistical Association.

Schutz, R. W. (1998). Assessing the stability of psychological traits and measures. In J. L. Duda (Ed.), *Advances in sport and exercise psychology measurement* (pp. 393-408). Morgantown, WV: Fitness Information Technology, Inc.

Schutz, R. W., Smoll, F. L., Carre, F. A., & Mosher, R. E. (1985). Inventories and norms for children's attitudes toward physical activity. *Research Quarterly for Exercise and Sport, 56,* 256-265.

Tisak, J., & Tisak, M. S. (1996). Longitudinal models of reliability and validity: A latent curve approach. *Applied Psychological Measurement, 20,* 275-288.

Tucker, L. R. (1958). Determination of parameters of a functional relation by factor analysis. *Psychometrika, 38,* 1-10.

Weiss, M. B. (2001). Developmental sport psychology. In N. J. Smelser & P. B. Baltes (Eds.), *International encyclopedia of the social and behavioral sciences* (pp. 3620-3624). Oxford, UK: Elsevier Science Limited.

Weiss, M. B., & Bredemeier, B. J. (1983). Developmental sport psychology: A theoretical perspective for studying children in sport. *Journal of Sport Psychology, 5,* 216-230.

Wiley, D. E., & Wiley, J. A. (1970). The estimation of measurement error in panel data. *American Sociological Review, 35,* 112-117.

Zimiles, H. (1996). Rethinking the validity of psychological assessment. *American Psychologist, 51,* 980-981.

Zumbo, B. D. (1999). The simple difference score as an inherently poor measure of change: Some reality, much mythology. *Advances in Social Science Methodology, 5,* 269-304.

APPENDIX

Raw Data (Scores on "Competitiveness")

Subject	Group	Age 6	Age 7	Age 8	Age 9	Age 10	Age 11	Age 12
1	1	3	3	2	2	4	8	16
2	1	2	4	3	4	2	9	15
3	1	4	2	4	3	3	10	14
4	2	6	7	5	13	18	17	19
5	2	5	6	7	12	19	18	17
6	2	7	5	6	11	17	19	18
7	3	9	14	21	21	20	22	21
8	3	8	15	20	21	21	20	22
9	3	10	16	22	21	22	21	20

PART II
YOUTH AND
ADOLESCENCE

CHAPTER FOUR

Developmental Perspectives on Self-Perceptions in Children and Adolescents

Thelma S. Horn

There has been an increasing interest across the last several decades in children's and adolescents' perceptions of themselves and their abilities. This interest has been evidenced not only in the academic/research literature but also in the educational and sport practitioner-based literature as well as in the popular press. In educational and sport contexts, for example, there is a common belief among teachers, administrators, coaches, and parents that sport and academics can and should be used to help children "feel good" about themselves.

This interest in enhancing children's self-perceptions in sport and academic situations likely arose out of the research that has been conducted over the last several decades to show that individuals' perceptions of themselves and their skills, abilities, and competencies are related to their performance, behavior, and health. In the general and clinical psychology literatures, for example, high self-esteem (self-concept or self-worth) has been linked to such other positive constructs as low anxiety, generalized optimism, adaptability, emotional stability, happiness, life satisfaction, and the ability to cope with daily life stresses (e.g., Baumeister, 1987; Coopersmith, 1967; Diener & Diener, 1995; Sonstroem, 1984; Wylie, 1989). In the developmental psychology literature, low levels of self-esteem/self-worth among children and adolescents have been linked to depression, suicide ideation, eating disorders, antisocial behaviors, delinquency, and teen pregnancy (see reviews by Harter, 1999; Mecca, Smelser, & Vasconcellos, 1989). In regard to individuals' performance, behavior, cognitions, and affective reactions in specific achievement contexts (e.g., competitive sport or other physical activity settings), high perceptions of personal competence appear to be associated not only with higher levels of achievement but also with such positive achievement-oriented behaviors and cognitions as persistence; an intrinsic motivational orientation; an internal locus of control; and an internal, stable, and personally controllable attributional pattern as well as with higher levels of positive affect (e.g., pride, happiness) and lower levels of negative affect (e.g., anxiety, shame, boredom) (see reviews of this literature by Weiss & Ebbeck, 1996, and Weiss & Ferrer-Caja, 2002).

Given this research, it is no surprise that researchers as well as practitioners are interested in identifying techniques, strategies, and intervention programs that will enhance children's and adolescents' self-perceptions. However, before we can design intervention programs to facilitate positive self-perceptions in children and adolescents, we need to know more about

> Interest in enhancing children's self-perceptions in sport and academic situations has been stimulated by research that links individuals' perceptions of themselves with their performance, behavior, and health.

the structure of children's sense of self. That is, we need to know how they evaluate their competencies, skills, and abilities, how they assess their worth as individuals, and what personal and environmental factors affect these self-evaluative processes. In short, we need to *understand* children's sense of self before we can begin identifying ways to *enhance* their sense of self.

It is the purpose of this chapter to review the research and theory on self-perceptions in children and adolescents. This review is written from a developmental perspective because the available research and theory clearly indicate that children's and adolescents' sense of self changes both quantitatively and qualitatively as they mature. Although this chapter focuses predominantly on the theoretical models for self-concept and self-esteem, related self-perception constructs (e.g., perceived competence, perceived ability, self-confidence, self-efficacy) are also discussed in the context of the larger self-concept/self-esteem models.

This chapter begins with a discussion and explanation of the constructs that are typically considered to be under the umbrella term *self-perceptions*. In the second part of this chapter, the theoretical frameworks for both general and physical self-concept and self-esteem are presented. These frameworks are then considered, in the third part of this chapter, from a developmental perspective. That is, the research and theory on developmental progressions in children's and adolescents' sense of self are reviewed. In the fourth section of this chapter, suggestions and recommendations for future developmentally based research on self-perceptions are identified and discussed. Finally, the chapter closes with some specific guidelines that practitioners can use as they work with individual children in sport or other physical activity contexts.

DEFINITIONS AND EXPLANATIONS OF CONSTRUCTS RELATED TO SELF-PERCEPTIONS

In its most generic sense, the term *self-perceptions* can be defined as individuals' beliefs, perceptions, attitudes, thoughts, and feelings about themselves in general or about their abilities, skills, competencies, characteristics, and behaviors. Within the academic research literature, a variety of more specific terms have been used to describe particular aspects of individuals' overall perceptions of the self—especially as those terms relate to the individuals' sense of self in achievement-oriented contexts. These terms include (but are not limited to) self-concept, self-esteem, self-worth, perceived competence, perceived ability, self-efficacy, and self-confidence.

A number of theorists and researchers have attempted to describe, define, and differentiate between the various terms most commonly used in the psychological and sport psychological literatures to refer to individuals' self-perceptions (see, for example, Davis-Kean & Sandler, 2001; Feltz & Chase, 1998; Fox, 1998; Harter, 1999; McAuley & Mihalko, 1998; Weiss, 1987; Weiss & Ebbeck, 1996; Wylie, 1989). Despite some relatively minor differences in these writers' perspectives, there has been general consistency in the definitions of these constructs. To begin with, the term *self-concept* is most generally conceived to be a relatively stable assessment or description of the self in terms of personal characteristics, attributes, and abilities, whereas self-esteem (or self-worth) is conceived to be a relatively stable evaluation or judgment of the overall self. Thus, self-concept has been seen as the *descriptive* component of the self (i.e., who am I; what am I; what kind of person am I; what are my strengths and weaknesses?) whereas self-esteem (self-worth) is conceived to be the *evaluative* component of the self (i.e., how much do I value the person I am, the abilities I have, the traits and characteristics that are part of me?). Although this distinction between the two global self-perception constructs appears logical, some researchers and theorists (e.g., Harter, 1999; Shavelson, Hubner, & Stanton, 1976) have suggested that in reality the distinction may be too simplistic. Specifically, the argument has been made that individuals' evaluation of themselves, their abilities, their beliefs, and their characteristics is so much a part of their description of themselves that it is difficult to actually distinguish or differentiate between the two perceptual constructs. Moreover, as Harter (1999) notes, the labels or descriptors that individuals use to describe themselves (self-concept) are already affectively charged in that such descriptors represent what individuals perceive to be important about themselves. Thus, the psychological constructs underlying the terms *self-concept* and *self-esteem* may not really be clearly differentiated.

With regard to the terminology that is used in the research literature to describe or refer to individuals' global self-perceptions or evaluations, some individuals use the term *self-esteem* (e.g., Rosenberg, 1979), whereas others use such terms as *self-worth* (e.g., Harter, 1982, 1999) or *general self-concept* (e.g., Marsh, 1987). Given that these researchers/writers are all referring to a global self-assessment or self-perception construct and that the previously defined and differentiated constructs of self-concept and self-esteem are quite probably highly interrelated, the terminology used in this chapter to describe the global or overall self-perception construct is *self-concept/self-esteem*. In cases where an individual writer's work is being discussed, the terminology used by that individual will be employed.

The terms *perceived competence* and *perceived ability* are typically defined in the research literature as individuals' perceptions of their competencies or abilities in specific domains (e.g., academic, physical, social; Harter, 1982; Weiss, 1987; Weiss & Ebbeck, 1996). In contrast to the self-esteem and self-concept constructs, perceptions of competence or perceptions of ability are perceived to be less global (i.e., they are more typically measured in reference to specific achievement domains) and relatively less stable—especially as they fluctuate over time and across achievement domains.

The term *self-confidence* has been defined as the degree of certainty individuals possess about their ability to be successful (Feltz & Chase, 1998; Vealey, 1986). Again, this construct is most typically assessed in relation to a particular achievement domain or context (e.g., academics, sport) but can also be measured in a more generalized way (i.e., as a dispositional quality to be optimistic about one's ability to be successful across a broad array of unrelated domains). Vealey (1986) has developed and psychometrically tested scales designed to measure both state and trait levels of self-confidence in regard to sport performance.

Self-efficacy has been defined as the belief that one can successfully execute a specific activity in order to obtain a certain outcome (Bandura, 1986). As Feltz and Chase (1998) note, self-efficacy is distinguished from other self-perception constructs in that self-efficacy beliefs represent individuals' judgments concerning what they can accomplish in achievement situations. That is, although individuals' perceptions of competence are more reflective of their evaluation of their personal skills and abilities, individuals' self-efficacy beliefs reflect their judgment of whether or not such skills can be utilized in a specific achievement context to achieve a particular outcome. Recently, Maddux (1995) has distinguished between *task self-efficacy* (individuals' judgments regarding their personal ability to successfully execute a specific task) and *self-regulatory or coping efficacy* (individuals' judgment regarding their personal ability to overcome environmental or personal impediments or challenges to successful behavioral performance).

Similar to self-confidence, the construct of self-efficacy, although most typically assessed or examined in relation to task performance in a particular achievement context or situation, can also be measured or assessed in a more generalized way (i.e., as a dispositional tendency to have high or low levels of self-efficacy across a wide array of achievement contexts). However, as

McAuley and Mihalko (1998) note, individuals' judgments of personal efficacy are by definition situation specific. Thus, such beliefs are probably most profitably studied in relation to specific physical activity contexts.

As is obvious from the preceding paragraphs, the various terms that have been used in the psychological and sport psychological literatures to refer to different aspects of individuals' self-perceptions are certainly interrelated. Thus, there may be, and has been, overlap in regard to the way in which these constructs have been conceived, assessed, and examined. However, the differentiation between the terms and their underlying constructs has also been useful in that these constructs do appear to highlight different (although quite probably interrelated) aspects of individuals' sense of self. Some of the differentiation between these terms becomes more obvious as we consider the overall self-system to be hierarchical in its organization. Such a hierarchical perspective is provided in the next part of this chapter.

THEORETICAL PERSPECTIVES ON THE SELF-SYSTEM

Much of the theoretical work on the self-system has been conducted and published by researchers in the general, educational, or developmental psychology areas. More recently, however, theoretical models specific to individuals' perceptions of the self in the physical domain have been developed and published. These theoretical perspectives are explored in the following sections.

Theoretical Models From the General Psychology Literature

Early notions or perspectives on the self-system viewed self-concept or self-esteem in a simplistic and unidimensional way (e.g., Coopersmith, 1967; Piers & Harris, 1964). That is, individuals' self-concept or self-esteem was perceived to be a single unitary construct that could be measured by summing their scores on a variety of self-statements. This unidimensional model is graphically depicted in Figure 1a. As this model illustrates, the assumption underlying the unidimensional approach to global self-concept/self-esteem is that evaluations of the self across a wide variety of general and specific life situations contribute equally and completely to an overall level of self-concept (individual's assessment of who or what she or he is) and/or self-esteem (individual's evaluation of the quality, worth, or value of the self). Thus, the unidimensional perspective presumes that the individual's self-assessments in a variety of contexts can be added together to form an overall or global self-concept/self-esteem. This unidimensional perspective was certainly reflected in the early instruments that were used to assess self-concept and self-esteem (e.g., the Coopersmith Self-Esteem Inventory, Coopersmith; the Piers-Harris Children's Self-Concept Scale, Piers & Harris).

This early view of self-concept/self-esteem as a unidimensional construct was soon dispelled as researchers and theorists (e.g., Bracken, 1996; Damon & Hart, 1988; Harter, 1982; 1999; Hattie, 1992; Hattie & Marsh, 1996; Shavelson & Marsh, 1986) discovered that individuals' sense of themselves can best be described and captured in a multidimensional way. This multidimensional perspective is illustrated in Figure 1b, and it reflects the notion that individuals describe and/or evaluate themselves in a variety of different life situations or contexts and that these individual situational self-descriptions or self-evaluations contribute to an overall level of global self-concept/self-esteem. In contrast to the unidimensional perspective, however, the multidimensional approach does not assume that each individual self-evaluation contributes equally and completely to global self-concept/self-esteem, but rather that the individual self-evaluations combine in unique ways to form the global self-assessment construct. Thus, the global self-concept/self-esteem construct must be assessed or measured as an independent and distinct entity.

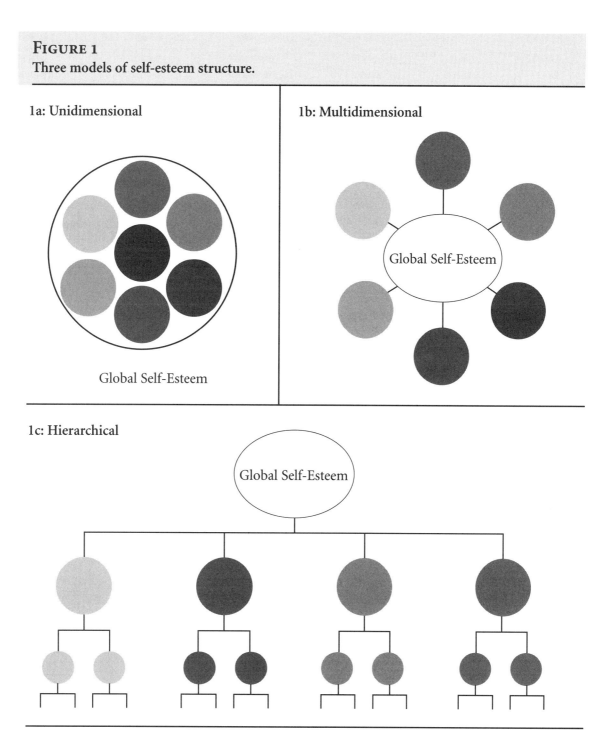

FIGURE 1
Three models of self-esteem structure.

1a: Unidimensional

Global Self-Esteem

1b: Multidimensional

Global Self-Esteem

1c: Hierarchical

Global Self-Esteem

From "The Physical Self-Perception Profile: Development and Preliminary Validation" by Kenneth R. Fox and Charles B. Corbin, 1989, *Journal of Sport and Exercise Psychology, 11* (4), p. 409. Copyright 1989 by Human Kinetics Publishers, Inc. Reprinted by permission.

More recently, this multidimensional perspective has been expanded to include a more hierarchical framework. This model, illustrated in Figure 1c, again incorporates the multidimensional perspective that there exists a global or overall self-concept/self-esteem construct that is linked to, or fed by, individuals' perceptions of themselves across a set of subdomains (e.g., academic/cognitive, social, physical). However, this framework also proposes the addition of a series of hierarchical sublevels indicating that each subdomain can be compartmentalized into more specific components. Over the last couple of decades, a number of multidimensional and hierarchical models of self-concept and self-esteem were proposed and tested using both factor-analytic procedures and other convergent and divergent statistical procedures (e.g., Bracken, 1996; Harter, 1982; Hattie, 1992; Hattie & Marsh, 1996; Marsh, 1990, 1993; Marsh, Byrne, & Shavelson, 1992). Corresponding instrumentation has been developed to measure individuals' assessments of themselves in a multidimensional and hierarchical way (e.g., Bracken 1996; Harter, 1982, 1985a, 1985b; Marsh, 1988, 1990, 1991). These instruments have recently been critically reviewed by Keith and Bracken (1996), Fox (1998), and Wylie (1989).

Although the multidimensional and hierarchical models identified in the previous paragraph do vary somewhat from each other, there are generally more similarities than differences. One of the earlier examples of these multidimensional models of self-concept is that published by Shavelson et al. (1976). Although this model is clearly linked to the examination of self-concept in educational contexts, it still serves as a good framework to understand the multidimensionality of the self-system. This model, similar to the others cited in the previous paragraph, construes self-concept to be organized in a hierarchical manner (as illustrated in Figure 1c). At the apex of this model is general or global self-concept. This, again, represents the individual's overall sense of him- or herself. At the second level, Shavelson et al. postulate domain-specific self-assessments. These include academic self-concept and nonacademic self-concept (comprised of the social, emotional, and physical domains). At the third level is individuals' sense of self within particular subdomains (e.g., English, history, math). At the fourth level are individuals' assessments of themselves in even more specific subject-matter areas. Thus, an individual's self-assessment or self-evaluation in regard to English might be broken down even further into the individual's perception of competence in regard to such specific areas as literature, grammar, basic composition, and creative writing whereas perceptions of competence in math can be assessed in such specific contexts as algebra, geometry, calculus, or even addition/subtraction, multiplication, and division. Finally, at the lowest levels, we would find individuals' assessments of themselves and their abilities/competencies in regard to very specific behavioral situations (e.g., self-efficacy or self-confidence concerning today's math test or the free throw that they are getting ready to shoot in a basketball game).

As Fox (1998) has clearly and cogently argued, in our research, and especially in our assessment of our study participants' self-assessments or self-perceptions, it is theoretically necessary for us to locate the multidimensional and hierarchical level at which we are working. That is, as individual researchers, we need to specify whether we are working at the highest (global) level, at the subdomain level (domain-specific perceptions of competence), or at one of the lower hierarchical levels where we may be assessing individuals' perceptions of their expectancies, abilities, confidence, or efficacy in relation to very specific contexts or situations. Such theoretical and empirical "location" can clear up much of the confusion that has existed in regard to research on individuals' self-perceptions in both the general and more specific physical activity areas.

Multidimmensional and hierarchical self-concept/self-esteem models propose that an individual's self-perceptual system is organized in a very individualized, complex, and multi-dimensional way.

As the multidimensional and hierarchical model of the self system (see Figure 1c) would suggest, the top or apex of the structure (i.e., general self-concept or self-esteem) is the most stable across time and thus the most resistant to external forces (Epstein, 1991; Harter, 1999; Hattie, 1992; Shavelson et al., 1976). However, at each successive level, the sense of self is less stable and thus more variable across time but also probably more open to change through external forces. From an intervention standpoint, getting an A+ on a math test or hitting a home run in a particular softball game probably will not have any impact on the individual's global self-concept/self-esteem or even on his or her academic or physical self-concept (perceived competence in specific subdomains) but certainly may have an impact on perceptions of competence, ability, efficacy, or confidence at the lower levels (i.e., in more specific situations). It may be only through repeated performance successes or mastery experiences across a wide variety of performance contexts and situations (i.e., consistently good grades on math tests or consistently successful batting performances) that the individual's sense of self at the higher levels may be affected. This notion regarding differences in stability as a function of level of self-assessment was supported in an intervention study conducted by Marsh and Peart (1988). These researchers conducted a 6-week intervention program designed to assess the effect of an aerobic training program on self-concept in adolescent girls. The results of this experimental study showed that a cooperatively oriented fitness program enhanced participants' scores on the physical ability and the physical appearance self-concept subscales but had no significant effect on other self-concept subscales. The results of this study, then, provide support for the idea that a short-term intervention program will have its most direct effect on the sublevels that are logically most related to the intervention but have relatively little or no effect on self-assessments that are unrelated to the intervention or to self-assessments at higher levels in the self-concept/self-esteem model.

Multidimensional self-concept/self-esteem theorists also maintain that there may be considerable variability not only *between* individuals in their scores on the various levels and sublevels within the hierarchical model but also *within* individuals in regard to their scores across the various domains and subdomains (Harter, 1999; Ogilvie & Clark, 1992). That is, at the lower levels in the model, an individual may perceive himself to be very competent in regard to algebra but very incompetent in geometry. At the higher levels as well, an individual's perceptions of her competence in English, history, math, and science may vary significantly from each other. Thus, assessment of individuals' self-perceptions on each of the constructs in the model will yield an individualized profile of scores that represents the individual's assessment of her- or himself across a variety of domains and subdomains. These individualized self-system or self-perception profiles appear to be much more reflective of the complexity inherent in individuals' perceptions of themselves and much more predictive of their health, well-being, and behavior than are unidimensional models (Harter, 1999).

Although the hierarchical nature of the model might suggest that individuals' overall, general, or global self-concept or self-esteem can be calculated or configured by adding up all scores at the second level, this is not the case. Rather, most multidimensional self-concept/self-esteem theorists (e.g., Bracken, 1996; Harter, 1998; Marsh, 1988, 1990, 1991; Rosenberg, 1979; Shavelson & Marsh, 1986) hypothesize that individuals' global self-concept/self-esteem exists as an independent entity that does reflect the individual's assessment of him- or herself across a number of subdomains but is not necessarily an additive function of those subdomain self-assessments. Part of this discrepancy between the subdomain self-assessment (perceived competence) scores and the overall global self-concept/self-esteem score is due to individual differences in the degree to which particular subdomains are perceived to be important to the individual. Consider an individual, for example, who has a low perception of his competence in regard to the physical domain (i.e., does not believe that he is competent in physical activities). If that individual also believes that physical competence is unimportant to him (i.e., he does not value physical competence), then such a low perception of competence in that domain may not have a negative impact on his overall or global self-concept/self-esteem. In contrast, if that individual does place importance on physical competence and he judges himself to be low in physical competence, then such a low estimate of his physical ability may contribute to a lower overall self-concept/self-esteem.

In recognition of the contribution that "importance" or "salience" of particular domains and subdomains can make to individuals' overall or global self-concept/self-esteem, some researchers have constructed an

> It is important to measure the individual's scores on each of the subdommains in the self-concept/self-esteem model.

"importance" subscale to measure this aspect of individuals' self-assessment. Harter (1990a), for example, has included this component as part of her scale to measure children's, adolescents', and adults' overall self-worth as well as their perceptions of competence across several different domains. Her research with this "importance" subscale has shown that it interacts with individuals' scores on the subdomains to predict their overall self-worth (Harter, 1990a, 1999). Furthermore, Harter provides data to show that individuals with high scores on the global self-worth scale appear able to "discount" or "devalue" the subdomains in which their self-perceptions are low, whereas individuals with low global self-worth scores appear unable to "discount" the subdomains in which they perceive low competence. These results suggest that individuals with high global self-worth scores are able to maintain or even enhance their perceptions of overall self-worth by perceiving the domains in which they know they have less competence to be unimportant. In contrast, individuals with low global self-worth scores focus their perceptions of importance on domains in which they have less competence, thus ensuring the continuation of a lower overall perception of their self-worth. As this research clearly suggests, then, it may be important not only to measure individuals' perceptions of themselves and their competencies across several domains but also to consider or assess the salience or importance they attach to each subdomain if we are to understand their overall self-concept or self-esteem.

As noted earlier, the multidimensional and hierarchical nature of these models has been supported through factor analytic and other statistical procedures (e.g. Bracken, 1996; Harter, 1982; Hattie, 1992; Hattie & Marsh, 1996; Marsh, 1990, 1993; Marsh et al., 1992). At this point, then, it appears as if these frameworks best capture the assessments that individuals make regarding themselves, their abilities, and their self-worth. However, it is important to keep in mind a few cautionary points regarding these conceptual frameworks. First, although the current multidimensional and hierarchical models of self-concept/self-esteem include a relatively large number of domains and subdomains for which statistical support has been provided, these current models may certainly not represent all of the domains and subdomains that are part of individuals' self-system. Thus, additional components or constructs may need to be, and probably will be, added as more information about the complexity with which individuals evaluate themselves is acquired. Thus, we should think of the current theoretical frameworks only as "works in progress."

Second, it also must be noted that the current self-concept/self-esteem models are normatively based. That is, these models were developed and tested for reliability and validity based on large sample studies using factor analysis and other statistical procedures to establish the multidimensional and hierarchical structure. Thus, as noted by Harter (1999), although these models may be very useful for researchers who are interested in conducting population-based research work, they may not necessarily capture or sufficiently describe an individual's sense of self. For researchers and/or practitioners, then, who are, or will be, working with individual children, adolescents, or adults, a more individualized approach to understanding their sense of self may be necessary as there may be different self-perception profiles and even different hierarchical structures for different individuals.

Third, the current multidimensional and hierarchical models of self-concept/self-esteem, along with their corresponding instrumentation, cannot and should not be automatically applied to individuals or groups who were not adequately represented in the initial validation sample. As Harter (1999) points out, her self-perception framework and accompanying instrumentation have been tested with individuals from a variety of countries and cultures (e.g., England, Germany, China, Canada, Australia, Japan). These procedures have resulted in somewhat mixed findings. That is, in some samples, the factor structure and the reliability and construct validity of the subscales have been supported whereas in other samples (countries), they were not supported. Similarly, assessment of the self-perception constructs from Harter's (1981) model with different groups of children (e.g., those with learning disabilities, medical disorders, and/or physical disabilities) has revealed both similarities and dissimilarities in the self-assessment system of these groups of children as compared to that of the "normative" sample (e.g., Harter & Silon, 1985; Renick & Harter, 1988). Thus, as Harter (1999) concludes, we need to be cautious in assuming that the current self-concept/self-esteem frameworks and their corresponding instrumentation can adequately capture the self-assessment process in all individuals. That is, we cannot presume that the multidimensional and hierarchical framework, which has been demonstrated to be reliable and valid for a particular population, will also adequately represent the self-system of individuals from different populations. Given the degree to which sociocultural and socioenvironmental influences affect individuals' sense of self (see, for example, Markus & Kitayama, 1991, for analyses concerning Eastern and Western cultural perspectives on the self), it is certainly reasonable to believe that individuals within or from different cultures may perceive the self in very different ways. Thus, different self-system "structures" may need to be constructed as we examine the self-perceptions of individuals who are "different" from the "normative" sample.

Theoretical Models Specific to the Physical Domain

Within the sport and exercise psychology literature, several researchers and theorists have also used the multidimensional and hierarchical perspective to examine individuals' self-perceptions in the physical domain only. The rationale for the need to develop a multidimensional and hierarchical framework and accompanying instrumentation that are specific to the physical domain is based on the notion that the physical self was not adequately or completely captured as just a subdomain in the broader models referred to earlier (e.g., Bracken, 1996; Harter, 1982; Shavelson et al., 1976). In the Shavelson et al. model, for example, the physical self-concept is represented by only two domains or subareas (physical ability and physical appearance). As argued by Sonstroem (1984), Marsh and his colleagues (Marsh, Richards, Johnson, Roche, & Tremayne, 1994), and Fox (1998), individuals' perceptions of their physical selves appear to be much more complex than that represented by a 2-factor/dimension subdomain model. This argument appears to be valid as subsequent models and corresponding instrumentation developed or adapted specifically to measure individuals' self-perceptions in the physical domain have been found to be more complex than the 2-item substructure postulated in the physical domain portion of the Shavelson et al. (1976) model (e.g., Fox & Corbin, 1989; Lintunen, 1987; Marsh et al., 1994; Sonstroem et al., 1994; Sonstroem, Harlow, & Salisbury, 1993; Sonstroem & Morgan, 1989).

An example of these physical domain self-perception models is the one developed and tested by Fox and Corbin (Fox, 1990; Fox & Corbin, 1989). This model, depicted in Figure 2, again employs a multidimensional and hierarchical framework. In this model, the apex or top of the model is global self-esteem. At the second level, however, is physical self-worth, defined as a higher-order construct reflecting individuals' feelings of pride, self-respect, satisfaction, and confidence in their overall physical self. At the third level are four subdomain constructs representing individuals' perceptions of their sport competence, bodily attractiveness, physical strength and muscular development, and physical conditioning and exercise. Although the instrumentation developed by Fox and Corbin to assess the model's validity includes only these three levels, Fox notes in a recent chapter (1998) that additional levels could be added to the model to represent individuals' perceptions of competence in more specific contexts. Under the sport com-

Before assessing individuals' physical self-perceptions, it's important to choose a particular hierarchical level within which to work and then use the appropriate instrumentation to assess at that level.

petence construct, for example, we could add sport-specific aspects (e.g., perceived competence in basketball, tennis, fencing, volleyball). Similarly, under the physical conditioning competence construct, we could assess individuals' perceptions of competence, ability, confidence, or efficacy in regard to such specific aspects of conditioning as aerobic conditioning, flexibility, or power. Thus, again, whatever measure we choose to use to assess individuals' physical self-perceptions, we need to consider the particular hierarchical level within which we are interested in working and then use the appropriate instrumentation to assess at that level.

Similar to theorists in the broader self-concept/self-esteem literature who have hypothesized that individuals will differ from each other in the degree of importance they assign to individual domains and subdomains, Fox (1990, 1998; Fox & Corbin, 1989) also incorporated this notion into his theoretical framework and instrumentation. Specifically, he has developed a perceived importance profile that assesses the relative centrality to the self of each subdomain construct. Fox's work with this profile scale verifies the notion that the discrepancy between individuals' perceptions of competence in a particular domain and the degree to which they consider that domain important or central to the self is a significant contributor to individuals' levels of overall self-esteem as well as their physical self-worth. Furthermore, Fox also reports that individuals with low scores on the physical self-worth or global self-esteem scales are less able to devalue or discount the subdomains in which they perceive low competence than are high self-esteem and physical self-worth individuals, who do appear able to discount their perceived inadequacies. Again, the results of this research indicate that it is not always the *number* of domains in which an individual perceives high or low competence that will affect overall self-worth or self-esteem, but rather the degree to which the individual perceives these particular domains to be important. The salience of perceived importance scores to overall self-worth was also demonstrated in a recent study conducted by Ebbeck and Stuart (1996), who found that youth sport athletes' perceptions of individual competence, combined with their perceptions of the importance of being successful (to their parents and the team), were significant predictors of their global self-worth. Thus, Fox's research, as well as that of Ebbeck and Stuart, in the physical domain is consistent with research from the general psychology literature showing the need to consider importance scores as well as competence scores in understanding individuals' overall self-concept, self-worth, or self-esteem. In a recent article, however, Fox (1998) cautions that further work on this importance construct is needed as other researchers (e.g., Marsh, 1993; Marsh & Sonstroem, 1995) have not found support for the validity of importance weightings in regard to the prediction of individuals' overall self-esteem.

As noted earlier, Fox and Corbin (1989) have developed an instrument that corresponds to their theoretical framework. This instrument, the Physical Self-Perception Profile (PSPP), has been tested for reliability and validity and has provided support for the hypothesized multidimensional and hierarchical model (see summary review provided by Fox, 1998). Similar multidimensional and hierarchical models and, in some cases, corresponding instrumentation have been developed by other researchers specifically for use in the physical domain (e.g., Lintunen, 1987; Marsh et al., 1994; Sonstroem & Morgan, 1989). These instruments are discussed in some detail by Fox (1998) in his recent chapter on the assessment of the physical self.

In summary, then, current thinking in the psychological and sport/exercise psychological literatures reflects the fact that individuals' self-perceptions, both in general and in specific life domains, are best portrayed in a multidimensional and hierarchical framework. Thus, to adequately capture an individual's assessment of him- or herself, we would need to measure self-perceptions across a wide variety of domains and at varying levels of specificity. Furthermore, we also need to recognize that individuals will differ in the degree to which they consider specific domains and subdomains to be important to their overall sense of self.

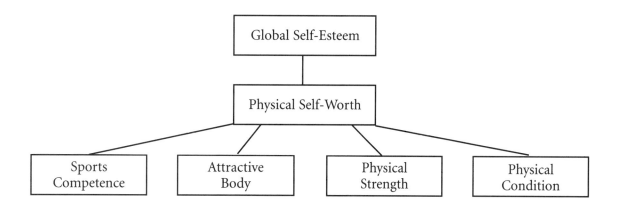

From "The Physical Self-Perception Profile: Development and Preliminary Validation" by Kenneth R. Fox and Charles B. Corbin, 1989, *Journal of Sport and Exercise Psychology, 11* (4), p. 414. Copyright 1989 by Human Kinetics Publishers, Inc. Reprinted by permission.

To add to this general picture of complexity with regard to individuals' self-systems, we also must recognize that the overall multidimensional and hierarchical framework described and depicted in this section will vary as a function of developmental level. That is, the overall structure depicted by the models portrayed in Figures 1c and 2 does not appear to be consistent across the lifespan.

Although relatively little developmentally based research on the self-system has been conducted in the physical domain, such research has been published in the broader developmental psychology literature. This research has revealed some interesting developmental themes regarding changes in children's and adolescents' perceptions of the self as they increase in age. These developmentally based changes are discussed in the next part of this chapter.

DEVELOPMENTALLY BASED CHANGES IN CHILDREN'S AND ADOLESCENTS' PERCEPTIONS OF THE SELF

Much of the research that has been conducted to examine age-related changes in children's and adolescents self-esteem, self-concept, and perceptions of competence within both the developmental psychology and sport psychology research literatures has only looked at *quantitative* changes in children's and adolescents' scores on the various constructs in the self-concept/self-esteem framework. That is, this type of research is conducted to determine if children at different chronological age levels differ in their scores on any or all of the perceived competence, self-concept, or self-esteem constructs. Such research is typically conducted using cross-sectional designs (i.e., measuring self-concept, self-esteem, or perceived competence in children of different ages and then statistically comparing the age-group scores). However, even when using longitudinal research designs (i.e., measuring the same constructs in the same group of children over time), the focus has often still been on investigating quantitative changes in children's and adolescents' self-perception scores.

At least some of the variability that occurs with age in the structure and content of children's self-perceptions can be attributed to children's cognitive maturation.

Although these quantitative research approaches do provide, and have provided, interesting information regarding age-related changes in children's and adolescents' perceptions of the self, they certainly do not, or cannot, capture the more *qualitative* changes that may occur with age. The focus of this section of the chapter will predominantly be on those research studies that have examined age-related qualitative changes that may occur in children's sense of self.

As Harter (1999) notes, the developmentally based changes that have been documented in regard to children's and adolescents' perceptions of themselves are quite probably a function of two separate but certainly interrelated factors. First, such age-related changes in self-perceptions may be due, at least in part, to cognitive-developmental maturation. That is, as children increase in age, their cognitive skills and abilities allow them to process information in increasingly more mature and sophisticated ways. Such maturation can obviously affect the way in which they view themselves and their abilities. As will be shown throughout this section of the chapter, the research conducted to date does indicate that maturational changes in children's and adolescents' cognitive abilities can be linked to changes that occur in their perceptions of the self. Thus, at least some of the variability that occurs with age in the structure and content of children's self-perceptions can be attributed to children's cognitive maturation.

However, as Harter (1996b, 1999) and others (e.g., Eccles & Midgley, 1989; Eccles, Midgley, & Adler, 1984) have noted, an additional part of the age-related changes that occur in children's self-perceptions may be caused by changes that occur in children's and adolescents' sociocultural environment as they increase in age. Particularly in regard to such achievement domains as academics and sport or physical activity, the expectations that relevant adults hold, the way in which the achievement context or learning environment is structured, the way in which children's performance is measured, and the type of feedback they receive from significant adults change as children move through the childhood and adolescent years. Such socioenvironmental changes have been detailed by Harter (1996b, 1999), Eccles and Midgley (1989), Eccles,

In the last several decades, there has been an increasing interest in children's and adolescents' perceptions of themselves and their abilities.

TABLE 1

Summary of Developmental Changes in Children's and Adolescents' Perceptions of the Self

1. Developmental Changes in the Structure and Content of the Self-Perception System
   a. Increasing proliferation of subdomains
   b. Changes in content of subdomains and in number of sublevels
   c. Changes in the global self-concept/self-esteem construct

2. Developmental Changes in the Contributions that Individual Subdomains Make to the Global Self-Concept/Self-Esteem Construct

3. Developmental Changes in the Cognitive Processes Used to Evaluate Subdomain Competence
   a. Changes in sources of competence information
   b. Cognitive changes in the conceptualization of ability

Wigfield, and Schiefele (1998), and Stipek and Mac Iver (1989) in regard to the academic domain and by Horn and Harris (2002) and Weiss and Ferrer-Caja (2002) in the physical domain. Furthermore, these socioenvironmental changes can be linked to the developmentally based changes that have been documented in regard to children's and adolescents' self-perceptions. It has been, and probably will continue to be, difficult to separate out the cognitive-maturational and socioenvironmental factors in terms of how they may or can explain the developmentally based changes in children's perceptions of themselves. In all likelihood, the two factors are not only additive but also interactive in regard to their combined effects on children's and adolescents' perceptions of the self. Thus, the review, contained in the following sections of this chapter, of the research and theory concerning developmentally based changes in children's and adolescents' self-perceptions is discussed in light of both increases in children's and adolescents' cognitive maturation as well as in light of age-related changes in the sociocultural environment.

Based on the research and theory to date, there appear to be three major developmental changes that occur in children's and adolescents' perceptions of the self. These include (a) age-related changes in the structure and content of the self-perception system, (b) age-related changes in the contributions that individual subdomains make to global self-concept/self-esteem, and (c) age-related changes in the cognitive processes used to evaluate competence and ability across the subdomains. These three major developmentally based changes are outlined in Table 1 and described and discussed in the following sections.

Developmental Changes in the Structure and Content of the Self-Perception System

As Harter (1990a) has noted, "a central theme in the developmental literature involves the extent to which psychological systems undergo ontogenetic change with regard to both differentiation and integration" (p. 70). Given that individuals' overall sense of self can be considered a psychological system, such differentiation and integration should also, and do appear to be, evident with regard to age-related changes in the basic framework of the self-concept/self-esteem model. Specifically, there appear to be three changes that occur during the childhood and adolescent years in the structure and content of the self-concept/self-esteem system. These are outlined in Table 1 and described in the following subsections.

Proliferation of Subdomains

The developmentally based research that has been conducted in the general psychology literature on children's and adolescents' perceptions of themselves clearly suggests that there is an age-related increase in the number of subdomains composing children's self-concept/self-esteem. Harter and her colleagues (as summarized in Harter, 1990a, 1999), for example, in a series of studies conducted with children, adolescents, and adults and designed to develop instrumentation to assess self-evaluations across the lifespan, have found an increasing differentiation with age in individuals' articulations regarding their sense of self. This developmentally based line of research began with several large samples of children who were currently in grades three through nine. Interviews were conducted with children in this age range. The results of these interviews, along with observations of their achievement-related behavior, were used to identify subdomain areas and items to include in an initial version of a scale to measure perceptions of competence in children. This initial scale (Harter, 1982) contained three subdomains (cognitive competence, social competence, and physical competence), along with a separate subscale to measure general self-worth. This instrument was then administered to several large samples of children in the targeted age range in order to test its reliability and validity. An updated version of the instrument (Harter, 1985a) using the same procedures as for the previous scale was developed in 1985 and was retitled the Self-Perception Profile for Children. This version of the questionnaire contains six subscales—five of which measure children's perceptions of competence in specific domains (scholastic competence, athletic competence, physical appearance, peer acceptance, and behavioral conduct) and the sixth subscale, which measures global self-worth.

Similar procedures were used by Harter and her colleagues to develop Self-Perception Profile scales for adolescents (Harter, 1988), college students (Neemann & Harter, 1987), adults in the early through middle years (Messer & Harter, 1989) as well as older adults (Harter & Kreinik, 1998). For younger children (ages 4-7), Harter and Pike (1984) have used similar but age-appropriate procedures to develop a pictorial scale to assess the self-perceptions of children in this age group. In addition, a separate instrument has been developed for use with learning disabled children (Renick & Harter, 1988).

In developing these scales, Harter and her colleagues found consistent evidence that the self-perception system becomes increasingly more diverse with age. This is reflected both in the number of subscales that are needed to capture the self-perceptions of individuals in each age group as well as factor analytic procedures that show increasing independence with age in regard to individual subscales. This age-related increase in differentiation is outlined in Table 2.

As indicated in Table 2, children in the early childhood years (ages 4-7) are able to identify and articulate five subdomain areas that constitute their sense of self. However, these five subdomains are not yet clearly differentiated. That is, factor analytic procedures show only two clear factors with perceived cognitive and physical competence loading on the first factor and the remaining three subdomain areas (peer acceptance, behavioral conduct, and physical appearance) forming a second factor (Harter, 1990a, 1998; Harter & Pike, 1984). Thus, although children in this age range are able to describe themselves in terms of five subdomain areas, these self-descriptions are not clearly differentiated from each other.

In the middle to late childhood years (ages 8-11), children do appear to differentiate the five subdomain areas (see Table 2). That is, factor analytic procedures now show that each of the five subdomains reflects its own discrete factor. These research results indicate that children at this developmental level perceive themselves in terms of a more differentiated structure than do younger children.

During the adolescent years, the number of subdomains increases again as Harter's (1988) measurement research indicates the need to add three new subdomain areas (see Table 2). This increased complexity is consistent with developmental trends suggesting increased differentiation with cognitive maturity.

As Table 2 indicates, additional subdomains appear necessary for older adolescents and young adults as Harter's Self-Perception Profile for College Students (Neemann & Harter, 1987) includes 12 subdomain areas. Further research with adults at both the early and middle adulthood years (Messer & Harter, 1989) and at late adulthood (Harter & Kreinik, 1998) shows similar numbers of subdomain areas as that found for the college students. However, some change in the content of these areas reveals continued developmental change. Given that the focus of the current chapter is on developmental changes that occur during the childhood and adolescent years, discussion concerning the developmental changes that occur during adult-

TABLE 2
Summary of Subdomains by Age Group in Harter's Self-Perception Instrumentation

Age Period	Subdomains	Age Period	Subdomains
Early Childhood[a]	Cognitive Competence Physical Competence Physical Appearance Peer Acceptance Behavioral Conduct	Early through Middle Adulthood[e]	Intelligence Job Competence Athletic Competence Physical Appearance Sociability
Middle to Late Childhood[b]	Scholastic Competence Athletic Competence Physical Appearance Peer Acceptance Behavioral Conduct Global Self-Worth		Close Friendship Intimate Relationships Morality Sense of Humor Nurturance Household Management Adequacy as a Provider Global Self-Worth
Adolescence[c]	Scholastic Competence Job Competence Athletic Competence Physical Appearance Peer Acceptance Close Friendships Romantic Relationships Conduct/Morality Global Self-Worth	Late Adulthood[f]	Cognitive Abilities Job Competence Physical Appearance Relationships with Friends Family Relationships Morality Nurturance
College Years[d]	Scholastic Competence Intellectual Ability Creativity Job Competence Athletic Competence Physical Appearance Peer Acceptance Close Friendship Romantic Relationships Relationships with Parents Morality Sense of Humor Global Self-Worth		Personal, Household Management Adequacy as a Provider Leisure Activities Health Status Life Satisfaction Reminiscence Global Self-Worth

[a] Harter & Pike, 1984
[b] Harter, 1985a
[c] Harter, 1988
[d] Neeman & Harter, 1987
[e] Messer & Harter, 1989
[f] Harter & Kreinik, 1998

hood in regard to individuals' self-evaluations and perceptions will not be provided in this chapter. However, this topic is further explored in chapter 10 of this text.

In summary, then, the research described in the previous paragraphs does show that children's and adolescents' self-evaluations or self-perceptions become more differentiated with age (i.e., there is an increasing number of subdomain areas with age). This age-related increase in the number of subscales that are needed to capture children's and adolescents' perceptions of themselves has also been demonstrated by Marsh and his colleagues in their research work on instrument development. Specifically, the Self-Description Questionnaire-I (Marsh, 1988), designed for pre-adolescents, contains 5 subscales whereas the adolescent version (the Self-Description Questionnaire-II; Marsh, 1990) contains 9 subscales, and the older adolescent/young adult version (the Self-Description Questionnaire-III; Marsh, 1991) contains 13 subscales. Thus, there is consistent evidence to show increasing differentiation with age in children's and adolescents' perceptions of themselves.

Changes in Content of Subdomains and in Number of Sublevels

In addition to the age-related changes that are seen in the *number* of subdomain areas, there also appear to be qualitative changes that take place in regard to the *content* of the subdomain areas as well as in the content of children's and adolescents' self-descriptions or evaluations. These changes are described in the following paragraphs.

Early to middle childhood. As noted earlier in this chapter, young children's (ages 3-7) self-perceptions appear to separate into five subdomain areas (see Table 2) which, in turn, coalesce into two overall factors (i.e., physical and cognitive competence load on the first factor and the remaining three subdomain areas load on a second factor). Furthermore, children's evaluations or descriptions of themselves are very much based on categorical identifications (Damon & Hart, 1988; Harter, 1996a, 1998; Rosenberg, 1979; Watson, 1990). These identifications involve statements of fact (e.g., I have long hair, I like macaroni and cheese, I have a dog named Spot, I have two sisters, I like to jump rope) that are based on very concrete behaviors, skills, abilities, and personal characteristics. In support of these self-descriptive statements, young children may often offer to demonstrate their abilities and capabilities (e.g., I can jump high. Watch me!), thus supporting the notion that their self-descriptive statements are very concrete and tied closely to actual or observable behaviors.

Children ages 3-7 tend to evaluate themselves very positively—even unrealistically.

Although the self-statements made by children in the preschool years (ages 3-5) typically tend to refer to very concrete and behaviorally based skills and abilities and to be very compartmentalized from each other (Fischer, 1980), children at the upper end of the early to middle childhood age range (ages 5-7) are beginning to be able to combine skills and behaviors to refer to more general competencies that they perceive they have (e.g., I am good at reading, I can do puzzles really fast; Case, 1985; Fischer, 1980; Harter, 1999; Harter & Pike, 1984).

In general, the self-evaluations of children in this early to middle childhood age range (ages 3-7) tend to be very positive—even unrealistically positive. Such positive self-evaluations are probably due to a combination of factors. First, children at this developmental level do not use (or maybe are unable to use) peer comparison as a source of information by which to judge their own competence (Frey & Ruble, 1990; Ruble & Frey, 1991). Thus, they can remain positive about their competence at different tasks even if their performance does not compare well with that of their peers. Second, children at this age level typically use feedback from significant adults as one of the primary ways to evaluate their competence. Because most adults (e.g., parents, teachers, coaches, caregivers) tend to be positive in their response to the performances of children at this developmental level, children's own assessment of their competencies is correspondingly high. Third, it appears that children at this developmental level are not cognitively capable of distinguishing differences between their "real" self and their "ideal" self (Fischer, 1980; Harter, 1999; Higgins, 1991). Thus, they may not have a sense of "wishing" to be smarter, stronger, or better than they currently are. This occurs because their perceptions or judgments of their actual competence are confounded with their perceptions of their desired competence. Therefore, their self-statements reflect an unrealistically high perception of competence (e.g., I can read really long books, I can run faster than anyone in the world).

As noted in the previous paragraph, most children at this developmental level tend to perceive high (even unrealistically high) levels of competence. However, there certainly are children in this age range whose self-evaluations are just the opposite (i.e., very negative or unrealistically negative, or both). These would typically be children who have already been exposed to negative life experiences (e.g., abuse, neglect, loss of "loved" ones, learning or behavioral difficulties). For these children, self-evaluations tend to be very negative (Harter, 1990c, 1999). That is, these children, similar to the positively oriented children, exhibit an "all or none" perspective on the self. Thus, each child generally concludes that she or he is either all "good" (i.e., generally all positive self-descriptions) or all "bad" (i.e., generally all negative self-descriptions).

Middle to late childhood. At the next age level, middle to late childhood (ages 8-11), children's self-perceptions reflect five differentiated subdomains (see Table 2). Each of these subdomains reflects its own factor (i.e., children can now clearly distinguish between their abilities in each of these areas). In addition, children's perceptions of themselves show increased integration. Specifically, individual children are now able to describe themselves in terms of broader traits (e.g., I am smart in school, I am not very athletic) that represent higher-order self-assessments based on information compiled from a broader array of more specific competencies (i.e., my assessment of performance in basketball, tennis, and fitness class is combined to form a higher-order judgment that I am not very athletic; Fischer, 1980; Siegler, 1991).

As the subdomains (see Table 2) suggest, although children at this developmental level continue to describe themselves in terms of their competencies in selected life subdomains (scholastic, athletic), there does seem to be an increase in the importance of relationships with others (especially peers) in terms of the self-evaluation process (Damon & Hart, 1988; Rosenberg, 1979). Thus, the subdomains of physical appearance, peer acceptance, and behavioral conduct no longer load on one factor (as occurred at the previous developmental level) but now reflect three separate and independent evaluations of the self.

In contrast to children at the earlier developmental level, children in middle to late childhood have the ability to "see" or perceive differentiation between the subdomains in regard to their relational competencies (Case, 1985, 1992; Fischer, 1980; Harter, 1986; Siegler, 1991). Thus, children at this level can begin to see differences between their abilities not only across subdomains (e.g., I am smart in school but not very athletic) but also within subdomains (e.g., I am good in English and art but not good at math). Such increasing differentiation between and within subdomains leads to more levels within the self-concept/self-esteem framework. Thus, children at the earlier level (ages 3-7) may exhibit only one level in regard to their self-concept/self-esteem framework whereas children in the middle to late childhood age range may exhibit three or more sublevels (see Figure 1c).

In contrast, again, to the earlier developmental age level, children in middle to late childhood tend to exhibit more realistic evaluations of the self (i.e., perceptions of competence are no longer highly inflated; Frey & Ruble, 1985, 1990; Harter, 1982; Harter & Pike, 1984). As noted in the previous section, this more critical self-evaluation is quite probably a reflection of increasing cognitive processing abilities (e.g., ability to use the performance of peers to evaluate one's own competence and the ability to differentiate the "real" self from the "ideal" self; Frey & Ruble, 1990; Glick & Zigler, 1985; Higgins, 1991; Ruble & Frey, 1991) as well as changes in the social environment (e.g., higher standards for student and athlete performance, greater emphasis placed on peer comparison and performance outcomes, and the creation of classrooms and competitive sport teams that are stratified by ability; see Eccles & Midgley, 1989; Eccles et al., 1984; and Horn & Harris, 2002, for further discussion on this issue).

| Children in middle to late childhood tend to evaluate themselves more realistically.

Adolescence. During the adolescent years (ages 12-18), very significant and very obvious physical, cognitive, and emotional changes occur (Eccles & Midgley, 1989; Lord, Eccles, & McCarthy, 1994). Thus, it is not surprising that significant changes might also occur with regard to adolescents' sense of self. To begin with, as noted in Table 2, the number of subdomains increases. Specifically, the five subscales from the previous age range (scholastic competence, athletic competence, physical appearance, peer acceptance, and conduct/morality) remain, but an additional three subscales appear to be necessary in order to capture adolescents' sense of self. Specifically, the addition of the job competence subscale certainly reflects the fact that many adolescents are now employed. Then, the single factor previously used to represent peer acceptance is now separated to include two other subscales that reflect social or peer relationships. These include close friendship and romantic relationships. Furthermore, as Harter's (1988) factor analytic research suggests, these three new subscales, along with the previously included five subscales, reflect independent and unique factors. Thus, again, it is apparent that with increasing age, children's/adolescents' sense of themselves becomes increasingly differentiated (i.e., more subdomains appear with each age range; Harter, 1998a). In addition, as Harter's (1998) research work indicates, there is an increase over the adolescent years in the degree to which individuals' evaluations of themselves across the different social contexts (e.g., with friends, parents, close friends, peers, as a student, on the job, as an athlete) show differentiation. Specifically, the percentage of overlap (i.e., degree of correlation) in self-ratings across the various social contexts has been found to range from 25 to 30% in the seventh and eighth grades to a low of 10% for older teenagers (Harter, Bresnick, Bouchey, & Whitesell, 1997; Harter & Monsour, 1992). Thus, adolescents become increasingly more able to distinguish their competencies and abilities across subdomains and social contexts.

It is also interesting to note that the compartmentalization of self-evaluations across subdomains that occurs during the adolescent years may have an effect on adolescents' overall self-worth. Specifically, during the early adolescent years (7th through 8th grades), it appears that although adolescents do exhibit differences in self-evaluations across subdomains (e.g., I am good at math and terrible in art, or I am not so good in sports, but I have a lot of friends), such variability in the self-evaluation process does not seem to cause major problems. That is, early adolescents exhibit few problems with regard to these different views of the self because they seem to see each "sense of the self" in an isolated and nonintegrative way (Fisher, 1980; Fischer & Ayoub, 1994; Harter & Monsour, 1992). During the middle adolescent years (9th through 10th grades), however, this increasing compartmentalization of the self-evaluation process seems to create some internal confusion. Thus, adolescents at this developmental level exhibit difficulty in reconciling the fact that they are "different" people across different domains (e.g., who am I really? what is the real me?; Fischer, 1980; Harter & Monsour, 1992; Harter et al., 1997; Higgins, 1991). During the later adolescent years (11th grade through college), such inner conflict regarding the multiple selves appears to be reconciled. That is, older adolescents are able to exhibit greater integration with regard to their evaluation of themselves across different contexts and to consider it acceptable, and even desirable, to have different competencies and abilities across subdomains. Thus, older adolescents exhibit a more sophisticated level of thinking that allows them to develop higher-order abstractions about the self that integrates previously seen "opposite" views of the self across different contexts into a whole (Case, 1985; Fischer, 1980; Fischer & Canfield, 1986; Harter & Monsaur, 1992). As an example, a younger adolescent may have difficulty reconciling her perception that she is "quiet" or "sad" with teachers and parents but "outgoing" and "talkative" with peers. In contrast, the older adolescent is able to accept such "different" views of the self across social contexts by concluding that she is "moody" (a self-assessment that provides a higher-order explanation for differences in her behavior across different social contexts).

As the information in Table 2 would suggest, the self-evaluations of adolescents reflect an increasing concern with the social self (Damon & Hart, 1988; Harter, 1999). That is, although the listing of subdomains clearly indicates that adolescents' perceptions of their competence in different contexts (e.g., school, athletics) contributes to their overall sense of self, it is also obvious that their evaluation of themselves in regard to social contexts is very salient to their overall self-esteem/self-worth. This is, of course, first of all reflected in the increasing number of social subscales, which indicates greater differentiation in regard to the social context. In addition, there is considerable research to show that children in late childhood and adolescence exhibit increasing concern with what others think of them (Harter, 1990b; Lapsley & Rice, 1988; Rosenberg, 1979, 1986). Furthermore, adolescents' increasing ability to cognitively differentiate feedback from different sources can contribute (especially during the middle adolescent years) to confusion in the self-evaluation process. As an example, parents may be giving the adolescent positive feedback about her or his academic work whereas peers may be disparaging such competence. Even more differentiation can occur, as the maturing adolescent may now be able to discern differences in the evaluation that mothers and fathers provide or that close friends versus peers may provide. Such conflicting information from different social sources concerning the value of competence in selected subdomains may create cognitive confusion for the middle-stage adolescent (Harter, 1999; Higgins, 1991). Such cognitive confusion may be resolved in the later adolescent years as the individual develops an internalized set of standards regarding personal goals, beliefs, values, and morals (Damon & Hart, 1988; Higgins, 1991). Such internalization allows the later adolescent to perceive that he or she is now "resistant" to external sources of information. Thus, he or she is able to reconcile or discount conflicting social information that is provided by different social sources.

In addition to the increase in differentiation that occurs during the adolescent years in regard to individuals' sense of self, there is also an increase in integration of adolescents' conceptions of the self. That is, their self-descriptions represent more abstract reflections about the self that are based on integration of trait labels that may, in turn, be based on more concrete, observable behaviors, skills, and abilities (Case, 1985; Fischer, 1980; Higgins, 1991). This, again, may result in an increase in the number of levels and sublevels needed to adequately capture the full framework of individuals' sense of self.

As the research cited in this section suggests, there are significant age-related changes in the content of the subdomain areas as well as in the way in which children and adolescents describe, assess, and evaluate themselves. Again, such age-related changes can be attributed to cognitive maturation as well as to changes in the sociocultural environment that occur as children increase in age.

> Adolescents' self-descriptions represent more abstract reflections, based on integration of trait labels that may, in turn, be based on more concrete, observable behaviors, skills, and abilities.

Changes in the Global Self-Worth/Self-Esteem Construct

The third developmentally based change that may occur in regard to the overall structure of the self-system relates to the apex or highest point in the self-concept/self-esteem framework (see Figure 1c). As noted in the previous section on theoretical perspectives, the apex of the self-concept/self-esteem framework is represented by a global self-worth/self-esteem construct that is typically defined as the individual's assessment, judgment, and/or evaluation of the worth or value of the self.

According to Harter (1990a), this global construct may also exhibit a developmental progression. Specifically, Harter (1990a; 1999) argues that children in the early to middle childhood years (3-7 years) do not really possess such an overall global self-esteem/self-concept. As noted earlier, children's sense of self at this early developmental level is based primarily on concrete, observable, and behavioral skills, abilities, and characteristics that are independent from one another. Thus, children at this level may not have the cognitive capabilities necessary to integrate such individualized perceptions of the self into a higher-order construct such as that defined as global self-concept/self-esteem. Harter (1990a, 1999) is careful to point out that children in this age group may exhibit a rudimentary form of overall self-concept/self-esteem, but this would be manifested in a behavioral way (Harter, 1990a). To investigate this issue, Harter and her colleagues worked with preschool and kindergarten teachers to identify behaviors that would be characteristic of children with high and low self-esteem. This behaviorally based investigation resulted in the identification of two behavioral factors that contrast children with high and low self-esteem. Specifically, the high self-esteem child exhibits curiosity, confidence, initiative, and independence in his or her play and achievement endeavors. In addition, he or she shows considerable behavioral adaptability or behavioral flexibility when exposed to environmental change or stress (i.e., ability to cope behaviorally with changing environmental conditions). In contrast, the low self-esteem child would show the opposite pattern of behaviors (e.g., dependence, lack of initiative and curiosity, and inability to adapt behaviorally to a changing environment). Thus, as Harter argues, although children in the early to middle childhood age range cannot actually verbally or cognitively articulate what would be defined as a global or overall self-concept/self-esteem, they may be able to exhibit the behaviors that would be symptomatic of such a construct.

Harter (1990a) suggests that a global self-concept/self-esteem construct becomes evident around the age of 8. That is, children in middle to late childhood exhibit differentiation across subdomains and are thus able to cognitively construct an overall self-concept/self-esteem. This cognitive ability is also enhanced by the fact that children around the age of 8 are able to differentiate between the real self and the ideal self. Thus, they are also beginning to differentiate between the subdomains in terms of importance or salience to self. This, again, probably provides them with the ability to articulate or express an overall self-concept/self-worth.

During the adolescent years, increased differentiation and integration occur. Thus, Harter and others (e.g., Demo & Savin-Williams, 1992; Leary & Downs, 1995; Rosenberg, 1986) argue that individuals at this developmental level not only exhibit a global or overall self-concept/self-esteem but that they may also exhibit a global or overall self-concept/self-esteem across multiple social contexts. That is, adolescents may possess a differentiated overall or global sense of self in each of several social contexts or domains (e.g., with their parents, in the academic classroom, in sport settings, on the job). Harter refers to these differentiated global constructs as relational self-worth (Harter, Waters, & Whitesell, 1998). Of course, this notion that adolescents and adults have multiple forms of global self-concept/self-esteem reinforces the belief earlier introduced that we may need to expand our basic self-concept/self-esteem theoretical framework (see Figure 1c) to include several such frameworks—one for each domain if we are to adequately capture individuals' sense of self.

Developmental Changes in the Contributions That Individual Subdomains Make to Global Self-Concept/Self-Esteem

A second major developmentally based change (see Table 1) in regard to children's and adolescents' perceptions of themselves concerns the antecedents of global or overall self-concept/self-esteem. In particular, some developmentally based research suggests that there are age-related differences in the contributions that particular subdomains make to individuals' global or overall self-concept/self-esteem. Harter and her colleagues (Harter, 1990a, 1999) have investigated these developmental issues with individuals ranging in age from 8 to 55. This research has been based, at least in part, on the notion earlier introduced that individuals' overall self-concept/self-esteem is differentially affected by the importance that they attach to each subdomain. If an individual sees him- or herself as low in the scholastic competence subdomain, that low perception of competence might contribute to a lower score on the overall or global self-concept/self-esteem construct only if the individual believes that scholastic competence is important or valuable. Thus, as several researchers and theorists (Harter, 1990a, 1999; Higgins, 1991; Rosenberg, 1979; Tesser & Campbell, 1983) have demonstrated, our understanding of individuals' perceptions of themselves is dependent upon our ability to obtain measures of their scores on the various subdomains as well as measures of the degree to which they perceive competence in each domain to be important or salient to themselves.

In addition to the notion that individuals' overall self-concept/self-esteem would be affected by the interaction of their scores on the individual subdomains with the importance or salience of that subdomain to the individual, Harter and her colleagues also investigated the possibility that individuals' overall self-concept/self-esteem would be affected by the support that they receive from individuals in their social environment (Harter, 1990a, 1993). Specifically, Harter and her colleagues constructed a scale to measure the degree to which individuals perceived that significant others in their social environment (e.g., parents, teachers, classmates, close friends) acknowledged their worth as a person and provided them with emotional support (Harter, 1985b). These social support scores, along with the discrepancy scores (perceived competence minus perceived importance) for each subdomain, were then correlated with individuals' scores on the overall/global self-worth scale in an effort to identify which components contributed the most to individuals' overall self-worth. The results of this developmentally based research are presented in the following paragraphs.

Because children in the early to middle childhood years (ages 3-7) may not be able to cognitively differentiate between the real self and the ideal self and are not able to articulate a sense of global self-worth (see discussion in previous two sections of this chapter), Harter's (1990a, 1999) developmental work on the antecedents of self-worth began with children in the middle to late childhood years and continued with individuals in the adolescent and adult years.

For children in the elementary and middle school grades (ages 8-15), the discrepancy score that was most related to overall self-worth was physical appearance. That is, the degree to which children perceive a discrepancy between the importance of being good-looking and their evaluation of their own attractiveness was found to be a major correlate of overall self-worth. The second highest discrepancy score contributing to overall self-worth was that corresponding to social acceptance whereas the discrepancy scores for scholastic competence, athletic competence, and behavioral conduct were less highly correlated with overall self-worth. In regard to the perceived social support scores, for children in this age range, parent and classmate support were the biggest contributors to self-worth (correlations ranging from .42 to .46) with close-friend support and teacher support being less highly correlated with self-worth.

The degree to which children perceive a discrepancy between the importance of being good-looking and their evaluation of their own attractiveness is a major correlate of overall self-worth.

Interestingly, Harter and her colleagues (Harter, 1987, 1990a) have found that for children in this middle to late childhood/early adolescence age range, the discrepancy scores as a group and the social support scores as a group appear to have an equal and additive impact on overall self-worth. That is, path-analytic procedures indicated that there were low correlations between the composite discrepancy score and the composite social support score. In addition, analysis of variance procedures indicated that the two factors, although each exhibiting a significant main effect, did not interact to affect general self-worth. Thus, the impact of the two factors on overall self-worth seems to be both equal and additive.

During the late childhood and adolescent years, Harter's (1987, 1990a) research shows that the discrepancy scores for physical appearance and peer social acceptance continue to be the primary correlates of global self-worth. In addition, parent and classmate support are significant contributors to overall self-worth. Furthermore, this strong relationship between perceived appearance and self-worth or self-esteem among children and adolescents has also been demonstrated by other researchers (e.g., Lerner & Brackney, 1978; Marsh, 1987; Simmons & Rosenberg, 1975).

Although perceived appearance seems to be a significant contributor to overall self-esteem or self-worth for both boys and girls during the childhood and adolescent years, other gender differences in the self-evaluation process surface during the adolescent years. Specifically, the results of a number of studies (e.g., Blyth, Simmons, & Carlton-Ford, 1983; Nottelmann, 1987; Simmons, Blyth, VanCleave, & Bush, 1979; Simmons & Rosenberg, 1975; Wigfield, Eccles, Mac Iver, Reuman, & Midgley, 1991) have shown that adolescent girls exhibit lower self-esteem scores than do their male adolescent peers. More recently, Block and Robins (1993) report research showing that the gender gap in overall self-esteem widens from ages 14 to 23. Some of the gender differences in self-esteem that begin in the early adolescent years may be attributed to the physical maturation process. Several sets of researchers (e.g., Brooks-Gunn, 1988; Brooks-Gunn & Peterson, 1983; Siegel, Yancey, Aneshensel, & Schuler, 1999; Simmons & Blyth, 1987; Slap, Khalid, Paikoff, Brooks-Gunn, & Warren, 1994) have found that a relationship exists between rate of maturation (especially in regard to actual or perceived pubertal changes) and adolescents' overall perceptions of themselves. In particular, children who are "off-time" in regard to the physical maturation process (i.e., those who are either early or late maturers as compared to their peers) may experience the most negative age-related changes in their overall level of self-worth and self-esteem. Because girls, on average, tend to experience pubertal changes earlier than do boys, such gender differences in the timing of the physical maturation process may be one of the causes of observed gender differences in overall self-esteem at the beginning of the adolescent period. Furthermore, it appears that the early maturing female may fare the worst in regard to self-esteem, body image, and satisfaction with her physical appearance (Siegel et al., 1999; Simmons & Blyth, 1987; Slap et al., 1994). As Simmons and Blyth argue, the early-maturing female (who is not only ahead of most of her female peers in the maturation process but also significantly advanced compared to all of the boys her age), may not be emotionally ready to cope with the social implications associated with physical maturation (e.g., dating, increased independence and responsibility).

From a related perspective, Harter and her colleagues (summarized in Harter, 1999), who have also found a consistent increase from junior high to high school in gender differences in overall self-worth (with girls showing lower scores than those of boys), suggest that such gender differences in overall self-worth may be explained by the finding that girls also show a rather consistent decline from 3rd to 11th grade in their perceptions of their physical appearance (i.e., a decrease in their perceived physical appearance scores) whereas no such age-related change is noted for boys. Correspondingly, girls also show a greater increase than do boys across the same age range in their perceptions of the importance of physical appearance. Other researchers (e.g., Maloney, McGuire, & Daniels, 1988; Mellin, 1988; Stein, 1996) have also reported that girls' dissatisfaction with their physical appearance begins in middle childhood and increases during the late childhood and adolescent years. Harter (1999) suggests that these gender differences in regard to perceived physical appearance, perceived importance of physical appearance, and overall self-worth scores are socially constructed (i.e., that girls are socialized to believe that physical appearance is a critical factor in how they will be evaluated by others and that the media portrays an "ideal" female body as so unrealistic and demanding that few females can achieve it). Furthermore, Harter points out that the gender differences in regard to these physical appearance and overall self-concept/self-worth scores may not be found, at least to the same degree, across all cultures, countries, ethnic groups, races, and subgroups of individuals. This position is reinforced by research showing that African-American girls do not show the same age-related declines in self-esteem from childhood to adolescence as do European-American girls (American Association of University Women, 1991; Orenstein, 1994; Winkler, 1990). Similarly, Harter's research work (as summarized in Harter, 1999) shows that adolescent females who exhibit a feminine gender-role orientation report more negative perceptions of their physical appearance than do females who exhibit an androgynous gender-role orientation. Furthermore, Marsh, in a recent study (1998), found that there are smaller gender differences in physical self-concept scores among elite male and female athletes than there are among male and female nonathletes. Thus, although some of the current findings may suggest an age-by-gender interaction effect with regard to the determinants or correlates of self-worth during adolescence, it is also apparent that such an effect may not be found across all cultures, groups, and individuals. Thus, further research work is needed to document how, why, and when such age-by-gender differences occur in regard to the self-evaluation process.

Developmental Changes in the Cognitive Processes Used to Evaluate Competence

The third major developmentally based change (see Table 1) that has been demonstrated in regard to children's and adolescents' perceptions of the self concerns the cognitive processes that they use to evaluate their competence or ability in each of the subdomain areas. As indicated by the theoretical framework for the self-system (see Figure 1c), individuals' perceptions or judgments of their competence either at the subdomain level (e.g., perceived scholastic competence, perceived athletic competence) or at one of the lower sublevels (e.g., perceived soccer competence, perceived math competence) are, or at least may be, important contributors to the individuals' overall self-concept/self-esteem. Thus, the developmentally based research concerning the processes that children and adolescents use to judge or evaluate their ability in each subdomain or at each sublevel is important to explore.

> Gender differences in perceived physical appearancee and overall self-concept/self-worth scores may not be found across cultures, countries, ethnic groups, races, and subgroups or individuals.

The current research shows two areas in which there appear to be developmental progressions in the cognitive processes children and adolescents use in the self-evaluation process. These two areas include (a) the sources of information used to judge competence and (b) the way in which children and adolescents conceptualize the concept of ability. The research and theory in these two areas are explored in the following sections of this chapter.

Developmental Patterns: Sources of Competence Information

Within the last two decades, a number of researchers (see recent review of this research by Horn & Amorose, 1998) have conducted research studies designed to determine what sources of information children, adolescents, college students/athletes, and adults use to evaluate or judge their competence in sport or physical activity contexts. To investigate this issue, the researchers typically compile a list (or ask the respondents to compile a list) of the possible sources of information that exist in the sport/physical activity performance environment and that individuals could use to judge how competent or capable they are at a particular sport or physical activity. Individual athletes/physical activity participants are then asked to rate how important each source of information is to them in helping them know whether they are good (competent) or not so good (incompetent) at their sport or physical activity. Although the particular sources of information that have been identified vary somewhat as a function of the context, the most typical sources include the following:

- social comparison information (i.e., comparing own performance with that of peers)

- self-comparison information (i.e., comparing own performance with that of previous own performance)

- evaluative feedback (e.g., from parents, teammates, peers, spectators, coaches, teachers, friends)

- achievement of self-set goals

- work ethic/practice effort

- attraction to sport

- physiological responses

- speed or ease of learning

- outcome-based information (e.g., win-loss records, game performance statistics, game outcome).

To date, the sources of competence information have been assessed in a variety of contexts and with children and adolescents of varying ages. The combined results of these studies have revealed some interesting developmental trends in regard to the self-evaluation process. Furthermore, these developmental trends are consistent with, or reflect, the developmental themes earlier identified in regard to the self-system. Specifically, four age-related developmental trends are evident in the research on the sources of competence information: (a) an increase in differentiation; (b) an increase in integration; (c) a shift from use of very concrete, behaviorally based sources of information to use of more abstract sources of information; and (d) an increase in the internalization of competence and performance standards. In the following paragraphs, the age-related research on sources of competence is summarized by developmental level. More specific information and discussion regarding these developmental trends and the implications of them for parents and coaches can be found in Horn and Amorose (1998) and Horn and Harris (2002). Thus, the results of this body of research are only briefly summarized in the following sections.

Early childhood (ages 4-7). Although relatively little research has been conducted in the physical domain to examine the sources of information used by children in this age group, the existing research in both the sport and general psychology literatures does provide us with some information. Specifically, children in the early childhood years base much of their perceptions of their competence on only three sources of information. First, they use simple task accomplishment. That is, children in this age range may perceive competence if they are able to complete a task that has a visually salient and intrinsically defined standard of success (e.g., hitting a tennis ball over the net, running from here to the wall, completing an obstacle course; Stipek & Mac Iver, 1989; Stipek, Recchia, & McClintic, 1992). Furthermore, children at this age range show primary interest in the "effect" of their task performance (e.g., the sound of the ball as it hits the racket or bat, how the net moves as the ball hits it).

It is important to note that children at this early childhood age level do not consistently or clearly use peer comparison to judge their own competence. Children may be interested in peers' performance (i.e., may glance over at peers while they are working or emotionally react to a peer's performance), but they do not use peer performance as a yardstick for judging their own performance (Butler, 1989; Frey & Ruble, 1990; Ruble & Frey, 1991). Rather, they use information from the peer comparison process for personal mastery reasons (i.e., to learn how to improve their own performance; Frey & Ruble, 1985; Ruble & Dweck, 1995). It is only later in the developmental process (middle childhood) that children begin to use peer comparison in order to assess their own competence.

The second source of information used by children in the early childhood years is the evaluative feedback they receive from significant adults (Stipek & Mac Iver, 1989; Stipek et al., 1992). Significant adults would include those adults with whom the child has an emotional or nurturing relationship (e.g., parents, teachers, extended family members, coaches). Furthermore, children at this developmental level accept the evaluative feedback they get from adults at "face value." That is, they do not integrate (or, more likely, are not cognitively capable of integrating) the performance information received from significant adults with that from other sources (e.g., peer performance, win/loss outcomes). Thus, the evaluative information from adults appears to be used as an independent source of information by young children.

The third source of information used by children in the preschool and early elementary years is personal effort. Specifically, the young child basically equates effort and ability, thus reasoning that "if I worked hard to finish this puzzle, then I must be good at puzzles!"

Middle to late childhood (7-12 years). During this age range, children continue to use very concrete sources of information. However, they also show greater differentiation with regard to the number of sources they use. Specifically, research by Horn and Weiss and their colleagues (Horn & Hasbrook, 1986; Horn & Weiss, 1991; Weiss, Ebbeck, & Horn, 1997) suggests that children's perceptions of the information sources that are available to them within the sport/physical activity environment increases to four to six categories including peer comparison (using performance of teammates and opponents; using game performance statistics), evaluative feedback from individuals in the sport environment (coaches, peers, spectators), internal information (perceived effort, skill improvement, speed/ease of learning), evaluative feedback from parents, game outcome (win/loss), and attraction toward the sport.

As reflected by these sources of information, children in this age range tend to be very concrete in the self-evaluation process. Thus, their primary sources of information include peer comparison (which increases in importance from the beginning to the end of this age range), evaluative feedback from peers and coaches (which increases in importance from 7 to 12 whereas feedback from parents correspondingly declines in importance), and actual performance outcomes (e.g., win/loss records, personal performance statistics; Horn & Hasbrook, 1986; Horn & Weiss, 1991; Weiss et al., 1997). There is also some evidence to suggest that children within this age range show an increasing, but probably still limited, ability to integrate the various sources of information. Specifically, in the early and middle years of this age range, children use team win-loss records as a source of individual competence information (Horn & Hasbrook). Thus, the early to middle childhood athlete may reason that "I must be bad at soccer because my team loses all of its games." However, by the end of this age range, children are beginning to be able to separate themselves and their individual abilities from that of their team. This provides perhaps indirect evidence that children can differentiate various sources of information but can also integrate them to form perceptions of their own competence.

Another example of such differentiation and integration is in regard to the evaluative feedback of significant adults. By the end of this age range, children no longer take adult feedback at face value. Rather, they evaluate that feedback in comparison to, or relative to, other sources of information. This may lead the child to reason that "if I perform worse than my teammate on a drill (using peer comparison information) and my coach gives me positive feedback anyway, then it must mean that I am really bad at this skill because my coach thinks that this is the best that I can do." Similarly, as will be discussed more fully in the next section of this chapter, children at the older end of this age range are also able to differentiate between the concepts of task difficulty, effort, and ability. Such differentiation allows them to integrate information from these various sources to form perceptions of their competence.

In general, then, children at this age range show consistent and clear developmental change in the sources of information they use to judge their competence in the physical domain. The influence or effect that such changes have on children's perceptions of competence and self-worth has been discussed by Horn and Harris (2002). In addition, Horn and Harris, as well as Stipek and MacIver (1989), provide a discussion as to how the sociocultural environment may be contributing to differences between younger and older children in the sources of information they use.

Adolescence (13-18 years). During the adolescent years, continued age-related changes occur in the sources of information adolescents use to evaluate or judge their competence. To begin with, there appears to be even greater differentiation in regard to the number of sources adolescents perceive to be available in their sport/physical environment. Specifically, Horn and her colleagues (Horn, Glenn, & Wentzell, 1993) found through factor analytic work that 10 factors were necessary to capture adolescents' perceptions regarding the sources of competence information. These include internal information (skill improvement, perceived effort, pre- or postgame feelings), competitive outcomes (game outcome, game performance statistics), evaluative feedback (parents), peer comparison (teammates and opponents), evaluative feedback (spectators), evaluative feedback (coach), speed/ease of learning, evaluative feedback (peers), achievement of self-set goals, and attraction toward sport. Comparison of this list of 10 independent information sources with the 6 identified earlier for the middle to late childhood group indicates further differentiation with regard to children's perceptions of the sources of information available to them. Specifically, for the younger age group, evaluative feedback loaded on two factors. The first included feedback from individuals directly in the sport environment (e.g., peers, coaches, and spectators) whereas the second factor included feedback from parents. For the older age group, these two factors were split into four independent sources: feedback from parents, spectators, coaches, and peers. Thus, it seems that adolescents differentiate and distinguish the evaluative feedback provided by different sources within their social environment whereas such differentiation does not occur for the younger group. Similarly, the single internal information factor found in the younger age group (comprising perceived effort, skill improvement, and speed/ease of learning) is split or differentiated into two different factors for the older age group (i.e., an internal information factor comprised of skill improvement, perceived effort, and pre- or postgame feelings as well as an additional or separate factor for speed/ease of learning).

Further examination of the sources used by younger and older adolescents indicate an age-related increase in the use of internalized or self-determined performance standards (achievement of self-set goals) and in the use of internal or more psychologically based information (e.g., self-confidence, self-motivation, enjoyment of sport; Horn et al., 1993). This age-related increase in use of internal, abstract, and psychological factors to judge athletic success has also been demonstrated by Vealey and Campbell (1988) and by Watkins and Montgomery (1989).

Other sources of information (e.g., evaluative feedback, peer comparison) continue to be used by adolescents, but there may be a change in how these are used. As has been suggested by Horn and her colleagues (Horn & Amorose, 1988; Horn et al., 1993; Horn & Harris, 2002) and by Stipek and Mac Iver (1989), children in the middle and late childhood years may use "near" peers in the peer evaluation process (i.e., they may compare their own performance with that of peers they know—teammates, friends, people in their school or neighborhood) whereas adolescents may use an "extended" peer group as their comparison sample (i.e., peer group extended to include unknown peers—all basketball players in the state, all high school seniors in the nation). The effects of such a change in the peer comparison sample on adolescents' perceptions of competence and overall self-worth have been discussed by Horn and Harris (2002).

Finally, it also appears that adolescents show evidence of the ability to integrate information obtained from the various sources in the physical domain (Horn et al., 1993). Such cognitive integration is characteristic of the older adolescent and thus reflects the developmental theories identified in the general psychology literature.

In general, then, a number of developmentally based changes occur across the childhood and adolescent years in the sources of information that individuals use to evaluate or judge their competence in the physical domain. Although these age-related changes may certainly be due to maturational changes that occur in children and adolescents' cognitive abilities, it is equally plausible that the age-related changes in children's and adolescents' sources of competence information are due to changes that occur in the social environment as children increase in age. This argument has been made by Stipek and Mac Iver (1989) in regard to the academic domain and by Horn and Harris (2002) in relation to the competitive sport domain.

Developmental Patterns: Individuals' Conceptions of Ability

The developmentally based work of Nicholls and his colleagues (e.g., Nicholls, 1989, 1990; Nicholls & Miller, 1985) as well as by Dweck and her colleagues (e.g., Dweck, 1986, 1996; Dweck, Chiu, & Hong, 1995; Dweck & Elliott, 1983; Dweck & Leggett, 1988) is predicated on the belief that a major focus of individuals in achievement contexts is to demonstrate competence. Thus, these researchers and theorists believe that perceptions of ability are a central psychological construct to consider when studying individuals' motivation, performance, behavior, and affective reactions in achievement contexts. Furthermore, both sets of researchers have postulated and found support for the notion that individuals differ in their conceptions or perceptions regarding the construct of personal ability and how it should be defined, referenced, and evaluated. Such interindividual variability in individuals' conceptions of personal ability appears to be a significant predictor of individuals' performance, behavior, motivation, cognitions, and affect in achievement contexts. Although some of the variability between individuals in their conceptions of ability can be attributed to factors in the social environment, an additional amount of variability has been found to be linked to cognitive-maturational changes. The research work of both Nicholls and his colleagues and Dweck and her colleagues is described in the following sections.

Nicholls. The developmental research work of Nicholls and his colleagues (Nicholls, 1989, 1990; Nicholls & Miller, 1985) as well as the extensions of this work into the physical domain by Duda and Fry and their colleagues (Duda & Whitehead, 1998; Fry, 2000a, 2000b; Fry & Duda, 1997) is based on the notion that children's perceptions of, or understanding regarding, the concept of ability changes in significant ways from the early childhood to the late childhood years (ages 5-12). Specifically, Nicholls' theory (1989, 1990) hypothesizes that children will reach a mature understanding of ability as they acquire the cognitive capabilities necessary to differentiate and distinguish between such constructs as luck, effort, and normative task difficulty, especially as these components variously contribute to performance in achievement contexts.

> Researchers have found support for the notion that individuals differ in their perceptions regarding personal ability and how it should be defined, referenced, and evaluated.

Nicholls' own research (1989, 1990; Nicholls & Miller, 1985) has resulted in the identification of a series of developmental stages or levels that children go through in distinguishing and differentiating between the various achievement constructs (e.g., effort, ability, luck, task difficulty). These stages suggest that with increasing age and cognitive maturation, children show an increased ability to differentiate and distinguish between the various causes of, or contributors to, performance in achievement domains. In addition, however, these successive levels of cognitive processing also suggest a pattern of increasing ability to integrate information from the various sources of information to develop or construct a perception of personal ability. Again, this pattern of increasing integration is consistent with developmental tenets.

Recently, Fry (2000a, 2000b; Fry & Duda, 1997) has conducted a series of laboratory-based experimental studies to test the applicability of these developmental patterns as they may be exhibited in the physical domain. The results of these studies have verified the developmental patterns outlined by Nicholls (1989, 1990) and have thus provided support for the notion that children's ability to distinguish and differentiate between the concepts of luck, effort, ability, and task difficulty follows a relatively clear developmental pattern.

Dweck. Similar to Nicholls' research (1989, 1990), the research work of Dweck and her colleagues (e.g. Dweck, 1986; Dweck & Elliott, 1983; Dweck & Leggett, 1988) has also focused on differences between individuals in their conceptualization of personal ability in achievement situations. In particular, Dweck's recent work (1996, 1999) has focused on individuals' beliefs concerning the malleability of personal attributes—such as intelligence, personality, or moral character. Individuals who adhere to an entity theory or belief system perceive personal attributes (e.g., intelligence, personality, morality) to be fixed or nonmalleable traits. In contrast, individuals who hold an incremental theory or belief system perceive the same personal attributes to be malleable (i.e., such personal attributes can be changed or developed).

According to Dweck (1996, 1999), these two different implicit theories (or frameworks of thinking) lead to different goals in achievement contexts. Because entity theorists perceive intelligence (or athletic ability or any other personal trait) to be fixed, their primary goal in achievement contexts is to demonstrate competence/ability. In contrast, incremental theorists who perceive that intelligence is a malleable trait would tend in achievement contexts to focus on skill development, skill learning, or task mastery. Of course, such differential goals lead to different levels of motivation, performance, affective reactions, and cognitions when individuals encounter success or failure conditions. Specifically, the research work conducted by Dweck and her colleagues (Dweck et al., 1995; Hong, Chiu, Dweck, Lin, & Wan, 1999) has demonstrated that individuals who hold an entity theory of intelligence (a) tend to focus on or choose performance-oriented goals in achievement contexts (emphasis on "proving" their ability), (b) exhibit a concern for others' judgments and evaluations of their intelligence, (c) attribute failure at an achievement task to lack of ability, and (d) exhibit learned helpless behaviors when faced with achievement setbacks. In contrast, individuals who hold an incremental theory of intelligence were found to (a) focus on learning-oriented goals in achievement contexts (emphasis on "improving" their ability), (b) exhibit a concern with developing their ability; (c) attribute failure to situational factors (e.g., lack of effort or use of inappropriate strategies); and (d) exhibit mastery-oriented behaviors under conditions of repeated failure.

Recently, Dweck's (1996, 1999) notions regarding the role of implicit theories as organizers of individuals' goals, behaviors, and reactions or responses in achievement contexts have been examined in the physical activity setting. This type of research work is necessary and important given that Dweck has repeatedly indicated that individuals' implicit theoretical frameworks are domain specific. That is, an individual might be an incremental theorist in regard to intelligence (cognitive subdomain) but an entity theorist in regard to athletic ability (physical subdomain). The initial research on individuals' conceptions of the nature of athletic ability (e.g., Biddle, Soos, & Chatzisarantis, 1999; Sarrazin et al., 1996) supports the idea that sport participants differ in their beliefs concerning athletic ability as fixed or malleable and that such beliefs are related to other achievement cognitions and beliefs.

Although Dweck (1996, 1999) has not really addressed developmental issues in regard to individuals' formation of, or adherence to, either an entity or incremental belief system, she and her colleagues have included children in their research work on implicit theories and their relationship to performance and behavior. In one study, for example, with eighth grade children (Dweck & Leggett, 1988), these researchers found that children at this age level do exhibit the two different implicit theory beliefs (entity vs. incremental) and that these beliefs affect or predict their achievement behavior (e.g., choice to engage in either a performance-based or learning-based task). In a more longitudinally-based research study, Henderson and Dweck (1990) followed a sample of junior high school students. These researchers assessed students' implicit theories of intelligence at the beginning of their seventh-grade year. They also collected measures of academic achievement (academic grades) for both students' sixth- and seventh-grade years. Analyses of this data indicated that students' implicit theories regarding intelligence were a significant predictor of their subsequent academic performance. Entity theorists who had received low grades in sixth grade continued to receive low grades in seventh grade whereas entity theorists with high sixth-grade scores tended to show significant decreases in seventh grade. In contrast, incremental theorists who had received high grades in sixth grade continued the same level of work in the seventh grade whereas incremental theorists who had previously received low grades showed significant improvement in seventh grade. In addition, entity theorists (regardless of their previous level of achievement) showed more negative affect (apprehensiveness, anxiety) about schoolwork in seventh grade and were more likely to believe that failures would reflect badly on their ability than were incremental theorists. As Dweck and her colleagues (Dweck et al., 1995) suggest, these results indicate that individuals who believe that intelligence is a fixed, nonmalleable attribute are more likely to perceive achievement outcomes (success or failure) as indicative of their level of intelligence. Even a single failure may be sufficient to persuade entity theorists to judge themselves as low in intellectual ability and to believe that this is a permanent trait. In contrast, incremental theorists who experience failure can and do perceive such failure as more unstable and subject to change with increased effort, practice, or persistence. In her 1996 chapter, Dweck provides a sociocultural context for the changes that may occur in children's development of either an entity or incremental world view.

Furthermore, in a series of studies with young children, Dweck and her colleagues (Cain & Dweck, 1995; Heyman, Dweck, & Cain, 1992; Smiley & Dweck, 1994) have found that even very young children may display the generally negative behaviors that are characteristic of individuals who hold an entity theory of intelligence. That is, these researchers have found that preschoolers and kindergartners who are exposed to repeated failure can and do display the learned helpless pattern of behavior (e.g., negative self-attributions, lowered expectancies, negative affect, decreased persistence, and failure to use constructive task strategies) when exposed to repeated failure. Of course, such learned helpless behavior is not characteristic of all children. Others display a more mastery-oriented pattern (positive affect, repeated task persistence, use of constructive strategies) in the face of failure. Thus, it appears that the origins of such a learned helpless or mastery-oriented behavioral pattern occur much earlier in the developmental process than previously thought (Dweck & Elliott, 1983; Stipek & Mac Iver, 1989). Of even more concern is that young children who exhibit the learned helpless pattern not only identify themselves as dumb when they fail, but they also label themselves as bad (Heyman et al., 1992). This overall evaluation of themselves as both dumb and bad may certainly have negative connotations with regard to their self-concept/self-esteem, especially as these children may develop an entity theory of intelligence and character that allows them to perceive their lack of intelligence and goodness as stable attributes.

As noted earlier, Dweck's (1996, 1999) notions of implicit theories about the nature of ability and the link between these theories and individuals' performance, behavior, cognitions, and affective reactions in achievement contexts have not been examined from a developmentally based perspective. Given, however, the work of Nicholls and his colleagues (1989, 1990; Nicholls & Miller, 1985) and Fry (2000a, 2000b; Fry & Duda, 1997) indicating developmental

> Some preschoolers and kindergartners who are exposed to repeated failure display a learned helpless pattern of behavior.

differences in children's ability to distinguish the concepts of ability, effort, luck, and normative task difficulty, it would seem logical that children's and adolescents' implicit beliefs regarding the malleability of intelligence as well as athletic ability would follow a developmental pattern.

In summary, the developmentally based research discussed in this section clearly indicates that children's and adolescents' perceptions of themselves, their abilities, characteristics, behaviors, and overall self-worth change qualitatively and quantitatively as they move from the early childhood years to and through the adolescent years. Thus, the hierarchical and multidimensional theoretical frameworks (see Figures 1c and 2) that have been constructed to represent the self-concept/self-esteem of older adolescents and adults may not apply (or may incompletely apply) to children and early adolescents.

> Children's and adolescent's perceptions of themselves and their abilities change qualitatively and quantitatively as they move through the childhood years.

The developmentally based research conducted to date has provided some interesting information concerning age-related changes in children's and adolescents' self-perceptions and self-evaluations. However, considerably more research is needed, especially in the physical domain, if we are to acquire a clear understanding of the self-system. Suggestions or recommendations for future research are identified and discussed in the following section of this chapter.

FUTURE RESEARCH DIRECTIONS

Given the current and general dearth of developmentally based research in the physical domain area, the field remains very open to research of any kind. However, there may be five particular areas that may be most critical and thus potentially most viable as future research directions. These are identified and discussed in the following sections.

Continued Exploration of Developmentally Based Changes in the Physical Domain

As discussed in the previous section of this chapter, the current research shows a number of developmentally based changes that occur across the childhood and adolescent years in individuals' perceptions of themselves and their competencies (as summarized in Table 1). Unfortunately, much of this developmentally based research has been conducted in the general psychology literature. Although the same developmental trends may also occur in regard to children's and adolescents' perceptions of their physical selves, we do not, at this point, have much solid empirical support for these trends. Thus, this is certainly one track for potential researchers to follow.

In exploring these developmentally based trends in regard to age-related changes in children's and adolescents' perceptions of themselves and their abilities in the physical domain, future researchers would do well to explore the full developmental range. That is, much of our current developmentally based research in the physical domain focuses on children between the ages of 8 and 14. In contrast, we have very little developmentally based research on the physical self-perceptions of children in the early and middle childhood years (ages 3-8). Furthermore, although we have some research on adolescents, these study participants (ages 14-18) are typically examined as a group (i.e., adolescents as a group are compared to younger children or to adults). As the research work by Harter and her colleagues (as summarized in Harter, 1999) on the adolescent period indicates, some very significant changes in cognitive and self-perceptual processes occur *within* the adolescent period (i.e., from early to late adolescence). We, as researchers in the physical domain, need to explore these same transitional issues.

Continued Work on Measurement and Instrumentation Issues

Although several recent instruments have been developed to assess children's self-perceptions in the physical domain (e.g., the Physical Self-Description Profile by Marsh et al., 1994; the Perceived Physical Competence Scale for Children by Lintunen, 1987; the Children's Version of the Physical Self-Perception Profile by Whitehead, 1995), continued work is needed in this area, especially from a developmental perspective. That is, as our knowledge regarding developmental changes in children's and adolescents' perceptions of themselves and their physical abilities increases, our instrumentation and our measurement systems should correspondingly change. Too many instruments designed to assess psychological constructs in children are developed solely by "adapting" adult- (or adolescent-) oriented versions. Often, this "adaptation" involves changing only the wording of items or the instructional set to make them "age appropriate." Such limited adaptation techniques certainly do not take into account the fact that children process information and make judgments or evaluations about themselves and their abilities in ways that differ significantly from that of adolescents and adults. That is, as the developmental trends cited in the earlier section of this chapter show, children's and adolescents' thoughts, perceptions, and beliefs regarding the self change both quantitatively and qualitatively with age. Thus, by simply taking instruments developed and validated for adults or adolescents and adapting them to be age appropriate only in regard to vocabulary and wording, we may certainly not be getting a true measure of their self-perceptions. This is not to say that the instruments we currently have to assess children's physical self-perceptions are worthless. In fact, they are probably quite valuable in that they provide us with the best estimate we currently have of children's self-perceptions. Nevertheless, as our knowledge base on developmental perspectives in regard to the self-system increases, our instruments will certainly have to be changed as well.

Expansion of Research Participant Groups

As noted earlier in this chapter, much of our current research on self-perceptions in children and adolescents in both the general psychology and physical domains is based on study samples that are not very diverse. Obviously, it would be important to expand our developmentally based research on the physical self-perceptions of children and adolescents to different groups (e.g., children and adolescents from different countries, ethnic, or racial groups, ability groups, and/or socioeconomic status groups) so that we are more sure that our theoretical models and instruments reflect the full range and diversity of individuals. However, in addition, such research would provide us with more knowledge regarding the role of culture, class, and other socioenvironmental influences in affecting children's and adolescents' sense of self. Therefore, we should not limit our cross-cultural or cross-group research on children and adolescents' perceptions of their physical selves to simply comparing their scores on the various domains and subdomains. Rather, we should examine whether children and adolescents from different cultures, races, classes, and countries differ in the way in which they construe or construct their self-perceptions. Whatever differences (or similarities) we find should then be discussed relative to their sociocultural/socioenvironmental context. Such research would provide us with considerably more information concerning the interrelated role that maturation and socioenvironmental factors play in the formation of children's and adolescents' self-perceptions than would research that simply compares the scores obtained by children of different groups on our current self-perception instruments.

Continued Contextually Based Developmental Research in the Physical Domain

In addition to conducting developmentally based research comparing and contrasting children and adolescents from different countries, cultures, and classes, we can also examine developmental trends in children placed in different achievement contexts. This suggestion is based on research conducted in the academic classroom that shows that changes in the achievement context as children move from one educational level to another result in corresponding changes in children's and adolescents' self-perceptions, motivational orientation, attitudes, affective reactions, and achievement behavior (e.g., Eccles & Midgley, 1989; Eccles et al., 1998; Harter, Whitesell, & Kowalski, 1992; Henderson & Dweck, 1990; Skinner, Zimmer-Gembeck, & Connell, 1998; Wigfield et al., 1991). Comparable research should be conducted in the physical activity area. This research should be comparatively easy to conduct as competitive sport settings change significantly as children increase in age. Thus, a longitudinal study that periodically assesses the self-perceptions of a large group of children as they progress from early childhood through the adolescent years should reveal some interesting information concerning the differential but interrelated effects of maturation and socioenvironmental influences on the self-perception process. Specifically, when children enter the competitive sport environment at the early ages (5-6 years), they typically all begin at a recreational level (i.e., low emphasis on win/loss outcomes, higher emphasis on skill development and fun). However, as these children move through the sport system, some choose to (and others are forced to) continue participating at a more recreational level whereas other children choose to (or are selected/recruited to) a more select/competitive level of play whereas a third group may discontinue sport participation altogether. Because this "weeding-out" process intensifies at the early adolescent level, a longitudinally based research study should result in interesting comparisons across chronological/maturational age between children who move into a progressively more competitive sport environment with those who maintain a more recreational level of play and with those who ultimately discontinue sport participation. If this type of longitudinal research project also incorporated measures of parents' and coaches' values, beliefs, and goals, a large amount of information concerning the relative contributions of cognitive-maturational and socioenvironmental influences to the formation of children's and adolescents' physical self-perceptions could be assessed. Of course, such a project would be a very ambitious one, but it is only by examining cognitive developmental changes in the self-system within a contextual model that we can begin separating out the relative contributions each makes to the developmental process.

Practical Applications

As noted in the previous section of this chapter, there are many research questions remaining to be addressed regarding children's and adolescents' perceptions of themselves and their physical abilities. However, based on the research knowledge base to date, we can identify at least some tentative recommendations regarding the facilitation of high self-concept/self-esteem in children and adolescents. These recommendations are discussed in the following sections of this chapter.

Importance of Mastery Experiences

As the current research and theory on self-concept/self-esteem in children and adolescents show, there appears to be a strong (and probably bidirectional) relationship between perceptions of competence in a variety of subdomains and children's and adolescents' overall evaluation or judgment of their worth as a person. Thus, the "formula" for raising children with high self-concept/self-esteem must include the facilitation of high perceptions of competence in such domains as the academic, the physical, and the social. As several developmental writers and theorists (e.g., Harter, 1981, 1999; Hattie, 1992; Strein, 1988; Weiss, 1987; Weiss & Ebbeck, 1996) have argued, perceptions of competence in particular achievement domains can best, or most effectively, be facilitated by providing children with mastery experiences. Mastery experiences are defined or conceptualized as opportunities children have in achievement contexts (e.g., academic classroom, competitive sport settings) to acquire, through personal effort and hard work, a skill or ability that they previously did not have. As such, mastery experiences necessarily include exposing children to an optimally challenging task (i.e., asking them to learn a skill that they currently are not able to execute but that they would have the physical and cognitive ability to acquire through practice and effort) and then encouraging them to "master" or learn the skill through repeated practice attempts.

By focusing on the provision of mastery experiences for children in specific achievement domains (as opposed to just providing children with, or guaranteeing them, successful performance outcomes), we, as adults, are also creating an achievement climate in which individual competence is referenced, evaluated, or defined in terms of skill mastery, skill improvement, or skill learning rather than in terms of successful performance outcomes (e.g., getting an "A" on all examinations and assignments; winning games and competitive events) or success at the peer comparison process (i.e., getting the highest grade on an exam; being picked for an elite team; out-performing teammates on skill drills). As the research in the goal orientation literature would suggest (Duda & Whitehead, 1998; Treasure & Roberts, 1995), a mastery- or task-oriented goal perspective is associated with, or leads to, higher intrinsic motivation and more positive affective reactions (e.g., high levels of satisfaction, pride, enjoyment, and lower levels of anxiety), than does a focus on ego- or performance-oriented ability goals. Thus, children who are provided with consistent exposure to mastery experiences should develop high perceptions of competence in that achievement domain even if their performance outcomes are not equal to, or superior to, that of their peers.

Importance of Contingent, Mastery-Oriented Feedback

In addition to the importance of mastery experiences in the facilitation of high perceptions of competence in children, the research and theory also underscore the importance and additive impact of positive feedback and approval from significant adults (e.g., Harter, 1981, 1990a, 1999). However, it is important to understand that such positive feedback from significant adults must be clearly and consistently "tied to" successful mastery attempts on the part of the child. For example, when/if my child works hard to "master" a skill or a component of a skill, I should give praise and positive feedback that is tied to her or his mastery behaviors (e.g., "I am proud of you. You worked really hard to learn to jump rope"). By providing children with positive feedback that is tied to the mastery of skills, we are not only rewarding the immediate attainment of a skill and the work effort that was needed to acquire that skill, but we are also contributing to the development of an internalized standard of performance and work effort that will ultimately allow the adolescent to develop independence from peers and adults in determining his or her own behavior in achievement contexts. As Harter (1999) notes, if the feedback from parents, teachers, and coaches during the childhood years is not provided in a contingent, clear, and consistent way, then the child cannot internalize a standard of performance and work ethic but remains dependent on other people to determine when her or his performance is "successful" and when his or her level of effort is sufficient. Such continued dependence on external sources of information to determine personal competency leads to instability in regard to the self-evaluation process and a low resistance to negative peer pressures (Damon & Hart, 1988; Higgins, 1991). From a related perspective, Greenier and colleagues (Greenier, Kernis, & Waschull, 1995) also argue that inconsistent and/or controlling feedback as given by significant adults to children during the childhood years may undermine the child's ability to develop a stable sense of self-worth (i.e., child may end up with a sense of self that varies significantly from one situational context to another).

> Current research and theory suggest that praise which is given to children for any level of performance quality is not ultimately functional in the internalization of achievement standards.

The importance of contingent, adult feedback during the childhood years suggests that current popular thinking regarding the "value" of positive adult feedback that is given without regard to the quality of the child's performance attempt is misguided. Specifically, parents, coaches, and educators are often advised to give children praise and positive feedback (irrespective of the quality of children's performance attempts) because such "positive" feedback is important in the facilitation of high self-concept/self-esteem/self-worth. Unfortunately, as the current research and theory would suggest, this advice may be misguided in that noncontingent positive adult feedback (i.e., praise that is given to children for any level of performance quality) will not facilitate children's perceptions of competence in any achievement domain and ultimately is not functional in the internalization of achievement standards. Furthermore, as Damon (1995) argues, the current overemphasis by parents, educators, and clinicians on helping children "feel good about themselves" diverts adults' attention from teaching children skills (especially mastery-based skills) that would do more to enhance children's self-perceptions than the effusive (and noncontingent) praise that parents, teachers (and maybe coaches) provide children in a misguided attempt to increase children's self-esteem.

Importance of Using an Individualized Approach

As noted earlier in this chapter, the basic theoretical framework developed to represent individuals' overall self-concept/self-esteem (see Figures 1c and 2) was formulated based on research with normative samples. Similarly, the developmental themes identified and discussed in this chapter, which outline how children's and adolescents' perceptions of the self change quantitatively and qualitatively with age, are also predominantly based on research with large samples of children and adolescents. Thus, these theoretical frameworks and developmental progressions (as well as the instrumentation corresponding to these models) are very useful for researchers. For practitioners, however, who are working with individual children in particular achievement contexts, the hierarchical and multidimensional theoretical model and the developmental progressions identified in this chapter should be used only as a basic framework for interviewing individual children to identify their self-perceptions and to determine appropriate intervention procedures. Practitioners should *not* begin such individualized work with the assumption that all children will construe or construct their perceptions of themselves in accord with the theoretical framework discussed in this chapter.

It is recommended, then, that practitioners (e.g., parents, teachers, coaches) begin by talking with the individual child in order to determine not only what her or his perceptions of the self are at both the global and the domain-specific levels (and the importance that the child attaches to competence in each domain) but also why he or she holds such self-perceptions. Specifically, practitioners should attempt to determine (a) what sources of information a child is using to make judgments concerning his or her competence in each domain, (b) what level of competence the child considers desirable for him- or herself in each domain (e.g., the "ideal" self), (c) whether or not the child considers competence in each domain to be malleable or flexible, and (d) what attributions the child ascribes to successes or failures in each domain. It is only through a complete (and very individualized) assessment of the child's thought processes in each domain that the practitioner can acquire an understanding of each child's self-perceptions and thus work with that child to enhance, maintain, or increase her or his level of self-evaluation.

Critical Periods for the Facilitation of High Self-Perceptions

As noted earlier in this chapter, an individual's sense of self at the highest or apex level of the self-perception model (e.g., self-concept/self-esteem/self-worth) may, in general, be very resistant to change and/or modification. As many theorists (e.g., Baumeister, 1993; Epstein, 1991; Hattie, 1992; Rosenberg, 1979; Swann, 1987, 1996) suggest, these higher-order self-schemas were most probably acquired early in the developmental process and are reinforced over the lifespan as individuals seek (sometimes unconsciously) information that confirms their overall sense of self and try to ignore or discount information that would contradict that overall or global self-perception. Thus, an individual's overall or global self-concept/self-esteem/self-worth may generally be very resistant to change.

Given the developmental patterns identified in this chapter, however, there may be points of time in the childhood and adolescent periods when the individual's global perception of the self (as well as her or his domain-specific self-perceptions) may be most vulnerable to change. The first of these critical periods may be the early to middle childhood years (ages 4-8). Children at this developmental time may not yet have a verbally defined global self-worth, nor do they yet appear to make cognitive distinctions between the real self and the ideal self. Thus, their self-perceptions are generally very high. Furthermore, children at this stage are very much dependent on the feedback of significant adults and on the simple mastery of skills to evaluate their personal competence. Given these developmental characteristics, it would seem as if this age period would be very important in regard to the development of high perceptions of competence in specific domains as well as the development of a positive perception of the overall self. Of course, as noted earlier in this section, such positive self-perceptions in children are best facilitated by mastery experiences and the provision of contingent, clear, and consistent feedback from significant adults in response to those mastery experiences.

The second critical period for the facilitation of positive self-perceptions may be in the early to middle adolescent years (ages 12-15), a time when fluctuations in the self-perception/self-evaluation process appear to be very common (Demo & Savin-Williams, 1992; Harter, 1990b; Rosenberg, 1986). Such fluctuations are probably due to a variety of maturational and socioenvironmental factors including (a) significant physical (pubertal) changes in regard to body size, shape, composition, and functioning; (b) significant cognitive-maturational changes in the ability to differentiate the sense of self across a variety of domains, thus resulting in confusion regarding which sense of self is "real"; (c) significant cognitive-maturational increases in both sensitivity to others' evaluation of the self and in the adolescent's increasing ability to distinguish differences in the feedback provided by important individuals (peers vs. parents; mother vs. father; best friend vs. peers); (d) significant changes in the social environment (school, sports, social situations) that present the early adolescent with increased expectations, increased performance standards, greater emphasis on peer comparison and performance outcomes, and greater social and personal responsibility.

It is probably the combination of these maturational and socioenvironmental factors that serve as causative factors for the fluctuations not only in self-concept/self-worth/self-esteem and perceived competence but also in regard to such other psychological constructs as locus of control, anxiety, and depression that occur during the early and middle adolescent years (Hankin, Abramson, Silva, McGee, Moffitt, & Angell, 1998; Kazdin, 1993; Petersen, Compas, Brooks-Gunn, Stemmler, Ey, & Grant, 1993). Given such instability in the self-perception/self-evaluation process during these years, this may be a particularly critical period for the facilitation of positive self-perceptions. That is, this period may provide significant adults (e.g., parents, teachers, coaches) with a window of opportunity (probably temporary) to have a positive impact on the individuals' global sense of self as well as on their self-perceptions in specific domains.

Intervention Approaches

In the event that a practitioner (parent, teacher, coach) determines that an individual child possesses low self-concept/self-esteem and uses an individualized approach to determine the factors that are contributing to such low overall self-concept/self-esteem, then the practitioner must determine what intervention approach to use. Assume, for example, that an individual child is low in overall self-concept/self-esteem and that such global and negative perceptions of the self appear to be caused by (or at least correlated with) a low perception of competence in the physical and social domains. Furthermore, the child perceives these domains to be very important. In this situation, the theoretical model in this chapter would suggest that the practitioner could choose one or more of three possible intervention approaches: (a) attempt to increase the child's perception of physical and social competence by providing that child with mastery experiences in those domains, (b) attempt to decrease the child's perception of the importance of competence in these two domains, or (c) attempt to change the child's evaluation or judgment of her or his competence in these domains by helping the child to change the way in which success is defined or referenced and/or modify the sources of information the child uses to evaluate personal competence.

Selection of the first intervention approach would mean that the practitioner would attempt to increase the child's perception of competence in the relevant domains by providing opportunities for the child to increase skill competence. In the academic domain, researchers have found support for the notion that intervention programs that are directed toward increasing children's academic skills, competencies, and abilities will also result in increases in children's academic self-concept/self-esteem (e.g., see Hattie, 1992, and Strein, 1988). Such skill-enhancing intervention programs have also been found to be effective in regard to the facilitation of children's and adolescents' perceptions of their physical selves as well as their overall self-esteem (see review by Gruber, 1986 as well as intervention studies by Alpert, Field, Goldstein, & Perry, 1990; Ebbeck & Gibbons, 1998; Holloway, Beuter, & Duda, 1988; Marsh & Peart, 1988). Of course, future research is needed to identify the specific factors within these intervention programs that are important for the facilitation of positive self-perceptions.

The second intervention approach may be most effective in situations where the child's perception of competence in a particular domain is very low and he or she has an inflated sense of the importance of that domain relative to life success. As an example, assume that an individual child perceives him- or herself to be low in sport competence and physical attractiveness and perceives that life would be wonderful if he or she were good at sports and more physically attractive. In response to these self-perceptions and evaluations, the practitioner might try to reduce the child's perception of the importance of competence in these two domains and also to help the child refocus his or her importance perceptions towards the domains in which the child does excel. For example, if the child does not perceive competence in the physical or the physical attractiveness domains, then perhaps he or she could be encouraged to perceive those domains as relatively unimportant to her or his overall sense of self-esteem/self-worth. Thus, the practitioner and the child might identify achievement domains where the child does perceive competence (e.g., art, music, computers, math, community service) and work to increase the child's sense of value regarding these alternate competencies. The potential value of this intervention approach was well expressed by Harter (1999) who notes that

> . . . one does not have to be a superstar in the decathlon of life in order to maintain high evaluations of one's overall worth as a person. Rather, an individual needs a certain number of domains in that there is a congruence between relatively high levels of success and the value placed upon these activities. It is hoped that the importance of those arenas in which one is less talented can be appropriately discounted. The goal, therefore, is actively opting to spend more psychological time in those life niches where favorable self-appraisals are more common and avoiding arenas in which one feels inadequate. (pp. 316-317)

The third intervention approach is based on the notion that individuals' perceptions of competence in individual subdomains can change as a function of the sources of information they use to judge that competence and/or the way in which they define success in that domain. In the physical domain, if individuals define success in relation to performance outcomes (e.g., win/loss records, performance statistics) or peer comparison (e.g., scoring the most points, getting selected for elite teams, winning Most Valuable Player awards), then perceptions of competence are dependent on being successful in these two areas. Unfortunately, not all children and adolescents can be better than their peers and/or achieve success in competitive outcomes. Thus, a large percentage of children and adolescents might have lower perceptions of competence in the physical domain. If, however, we, as adults, are able to help such children and adolescents to redefine success as personal mastery, skill improvement, achievement of self-referenced or self-set goals, then all children and adolescents will have the opportunity to perceive competence. For further detail regarding these intervention approaches, see Horn and Harris (2002), Treasure and Roberts (1995), and Weiss and Ebbeck (1996).

If adults can help children and adolescents to re-define success, they will have the opportunity to perceive competence

In summary, all of the intervention approaches described in the preceding paragraphs can be effective. The particular approach that should be used with an individual child should be selected on the basis of a complete assessment of the child's current self-perceptions. Thus, again, an individualized intervention approach is important.

Chapter Summary and Conclusions

As the research and theory reviewed in this chapter shows, individuals' sense of self can perhaps best be viewed in a multidimensional and hierarchical way. However, it is also clear that this theoretical framework does not completely apply to children and adolescents. That is, children's and adolescents' sense of self changes both quantitatively and qualitatively with increased age. It is also important to recognize that the changes in children's and adolescents' self-perceptions are due to the complex interrelationships between cognitive, physical, and socioenvironmental changes that occur as children increase in age.

Although the developmentally based research that has been conducted to date has provided us with some interesting and useful information regarding age-related changes in children's and adolescents' self-perceptions, there is still much that we do not know. Thus, further developmentally based research should not only provide us with information about developmental changes in children's and adolescents' sense of themselves and their abilities in the physical domain but should also provide us, as practitioners, with valuable information concerning the ways in which positive self-perceptions can be facilitated in children and adolescents.

Given the research that has indicated that high self-perceptions (both global and domain specific) are highly correlated with other psychological constructs (e.g., anxiety, locus of control, depression) and with positive achievement behaviors (e.g., persistence, motivation), there is certainly reason to believe that continued research to discover the processes that children and adolescents follow in their development of self-perceptions will be valuable from both a research and practical perspective.

REFERENCES

Alpert, B., Field, T., Goldstein, S., & Perry, S. (1990). Aerobics enhances cardiovascular fitness and agility in preschoolers. *Health Psychology, 9,* 48-56.

American Association of University Women. (1991). *Shortchanging girls, shortchanging America: A call to action.* Washington, DC: Author.

Bandura, A. (1986). *Social foundation of thought and action: A social cognitive theory.* Englewood Cliffs, NJ: Prentice-Hall.

Baumeister, R. F. (1987). How the self became a problem: A psychological review of historical research. *Journal of Personality and Social Psychology, 52,* 163-176.

Baumeister, R. F. (1993). Understanding the inner nature of low self-esteem: Uncertain, fragile, protective, and conflicted. In R. F. Baumeister (Ed.), *Self-esteem: The puzzle of low self-regard* (pp. 201-218). New York: Plenum.

Biddle, S., Soos, L., & Chatzisarantis, N. (1999). Predicting physical activity intentions using a goal perspectives approach: A study of Hungarian youth. *Scandinavian Journal of Medicine and Science in Sports, 9,* 353-357.

Block, J. H., & Robins, R. W. (1993). A longitudinal study of consistency and change in self-esteem from early adolescence to early adulthood. *Child Development, 64,* 909-923.

Blyth, D. A., Simmons, R. G., & Carlton-Ford, S. (1983). The adjustment of early adolescents to school transitions. *Journal of Early Adolescence, 3,* 105-120.

Bracken, B. (1996). Clinical applications of a context-dependent multidimensional model of self-concept. In B. Bracken (Ed.), *Handbook of self-concept* (pp. 463-505). New York: Wiley.

Brooks-Gunn, J. (1988). Antecedents and consequences of variations in girls' maturational timing. *Journal of Adolescent Health Care, 9,* 365-373.

Brooks-Gunn, J., & Peterson, A. (1983). *Girls at puberty: Biological and psychological perspectives.* New York: Plenum..

Butler, R. (1989). Mastery versus ability appraisal: A developmental study of children's observations of peers' work. *Child Development, 60,* 1350-1361.

Cain, K. M., & Dweck, C. S. (1995). The development of children's achievement motivation patterns and conceptions of intelligence. *Merrill-Palmer Quarterly, 41,* 25-52.

Case, R. (1985). *Intellectual development: Birth to adulthood.* New York: Academic Press.

Case, R. (1992). *The mind's staircase.* Hillsdale, NJ: Erlbaum.

Coopersmith, S. (1967). *The antecedents of self-esteem.* San Francisco: Freeman.

Damon, W. (1995). *Greater expectations: Overcoming the culture of indulgence in America's homes and schools.* New York: Free Press.

Damon, W., & Hart, D. (1988). *Self-understanding in childhood and adolescence.* New York: Cambridge University Press.

Davis-Kean, P. E., & Sandler, H. M. (2001). A meta-analysis of measures of self-esteem for young children: A framework for future measures. *Child Development, 72,* 884-906.

Demo, D. H., & Savin-Williams, R. C. (1992). Self-concept stability and change during adolescence. In R. P. Lipka & T.H. Brinthaupt (Eds.), *Self-perspectives across the lifespan* (pp. 116-150). Albany: State University of New York Press.

Diener, E., & Diener, M. (1995). Cross-cultural correlates of life satisfaction and self-esteem. *Journal of Personality and Social Psychology, 68,* 653-663.

Duda, J. L., & Whitehead, J. (1998). Measurement of goal perspectives in the physical domain. In J. L. Duda (Ed.), *Advances in sport and exercise psychology measurement* (pp. 21-48). Morgantown, WV: Fitness Information Technology.

Dweck, C. S. (1986). Motivational processes affecting learning. *American Psychologist, 41,* 1040-1048.

Dweck, C. S. (1996). Implicit theories as organizers of goals and behaviors. In P. Gollwitzer & J. Bargh (Eds.), *The psychology of action: Linking cognition and motivation to behavior* (pp. 69-90). New York: Guilford Press.

Dweck, C. S. (1999). *Self-theories: Their role in motivation, personality, and development.* Philadelphia: Taylor and Francis.

Dweck, C. S., Chiu, C., & Hong, Y. (1995). Implicit theories and their role in judgments and reactions: A world from two perspectives. *Psychological Inquiry, 6,* 267-285.

Dweck, C. S., & Elliott, E. S. (1983). Achievement motivation. In P. Musser & E. M. Hetherington (Eds.), *Handbook of child psychology:* Vol. 4. *Socialization, personality, and social development* (pp. 643-691). New York: Wiley.

Dweck, C. S., & Leggett, E. L. (1988). A social-cognitive approach to motivation and personality. *Psychological Review, 95,* 256-273.

Ebbeck, V., & Gibbons, S. L. (1998). The effect of a team building program on the self-conceptions of grade 6 and 7 physical education students. *Journal of Sport and Exercise Psychology, 20,* 300-310.

Ebbeck, V., & Stuart, M.E. (1996). Predictors of self-esteem with youth basketball players. *Pediatric Exercise Science, 8,* 368-378.

Eccles, J., & Midgley, C. (1989). Stage/environment fit: Developmentally appropriate classrooms for early adolescents. In R. Ames & C. Ames (Eds.), *Research on motivation in education* (Vol. 3, pp. 139-181). San Diego: Academic Press.

Eccles, J., Midgley, C., & Adler, T. F. (1984). Grade-related changes in the school environment: Effects on achievement motivation. In J. G. Nicholls (Ed.), *The development of achievement motivation* (pp. 283-332). Greenwich, CT: JAI Press.

Eccles, J., Wigfield, A. W., & Schiefele, U. (1998). Motivation to succeed. In W. Damon (Series Ed.) & N. Eisenberg (Vol. Ed.), *Handbook of child psychology:* Vol. 3. *Social, emotional, and personality development* (5th ed., pp. 1017-1096). New York: Wiley.

Epstein, S. (1991). Cognitive-experiential self-theory: Implications for developmental psychology. In M. R. Gunnar & L. A. Stroufe (Eds.), *Self-processes and development: The Minnesota Symposium on Child Development* (Vol. 23, pp. 111-137). Hillsdale, NJ: Erlbaum.

Feltz, D. L., & Chase, M. A. (1998). The measurement of self-efficacy and confidence in sport. In J. L. Duda (Ed.), *Advances in sport and exercise psychology measurement* (pp. 65-80). Morgantown, WV: Fitness Information Technology.

Fischer, K. W. (1980). A theory of cognitive development: The control and construction of hierarchies of skills. *Psychological Review, 87,* 477-531.

Fischer, K. W., & Ayoub, C. (1994). Affective splitting and dissociation in normal and maltreated children: Developmental pathways for self in relationships. In D. Cicchetti & S. Toth (Eds.), *Rochester Symposium on Developmental Psychopathology: Disorders and dysfunctions of the self* (Vol. 5, pp. 149-222). Rochester, NY: University of Rochester Press.

Fischer, K. W., & Canfield, R. (1986). The ambiguity of stage and structure in behavior: Person and environment in the development of psychological structure. In J. Levin (Ed.), *Stage and structure: Reopening the debate* (pp. 246-267). New York: Plenum.

Fox, K. R. (1990). *The Physical Self-Perception Profile manual.* DeKalb, IL: Office for Health Promotion, Northern Illinois University.

Fox, K. R. (1998). Advances in the measurement of the physical self. In J. L. Duda (Ed.), *Advances in sport and exercise psychology measurement* (pp. 295-310). Morgantown, WV: Fitness Information Technology.

Fox, K. R., & Corbin, C. B. (1989). The Physical Self-Perception Profile: Development and preliminary validation. *Journal of Sport and Exercise Psychology, 11,* 408-430.

Frey, K. S., & Ruble, R. N. (1985). What children say when the teacher is not around: Conflicting goals in social comparison and performance assessment in the classroom. *Journal of Personality and Social Psychology, 48,* 550-562.

Frey, K. S., & Ruble, D. N. (1990). Strategies for comparative evaluation: Maintaining a sense of competence across the lifespan. In R. J. Sternberg & J. Kolligian, Jr. (Eds.), *Competence considered* (pp. 167-189). New Haven, CT: Yale University Press.

Fry, M. D. (2000a). A developmental analysis of children's and adolescents' understanding of luck and ability in the physical domain. *Journal of Sport and Exercise Psychology, 22,* 145-166.

Fry, M. D. (2000b). A developmental examination of children's understanding of task difficulty in the physical domain. *Journal of Applied Sport Psychology, 12 (2),* 180-202.

Fry, M. D., & Duda, J. L. (1997). A developmental examination of children's understanding of effort and ability in the physical and academic domains. *Research Quarterly for Exercise and Sport, 68,* 331-344.

Glick, M., & Zigler, E. (1985). Self-image: A cognitive-developmental approach. In R. Leahy (Ed.), *The development of the self* (pp. 1-54). New York: Academic Press.

Greenier, K. D., Kernis, M. H. & Waschull, S. B. (1995). Not all high or low self-esteem people are the same: Theory and research on stability of self-concept. In M. H. Kernis (Ed.), *Efficacy, agency, and self-esteem* (pp. 51-68). New York: Plenum.

Gruber, J. J. (1986). Physical activity and self-esteem development in children: A meta-analysis. In G. A. Stull & H. M. Eckert (Eds.), *Effects of physical activity on children.* Champaign, IL: Human Kinetics.

Hankin, B. J., Abramson, L.Y., Silva, P. A., McGee, R., Moffitt, T. E., & Angell, K. E. (1998). Development of depression from preadolescence to young adulthood: Emerging gender differences in a 10-year longitudinal study. *Journal of Abnormal Psychology, 107,* 128-140.

Harter, S. (1981). A model of mastery motivation in children: Individual differences and developmental change. In A. Collins (Ed.), *Minnesota Symposium on Child Psychology* (Vol. 14, pp. 215-255). Hillsdale, NJ: Erlbaum.

Harter, S. (1982). The perceived competence scale for children. *Child Development, 53,* 87-97.

Harter, S. (1985a). *The Self-Perception Profile for Children.* Unpublished manuscript, University of Denver, Denver, CO.

Harter, S. (1985b). *The Social Support Scale for Children.* Unpublished manuscript, University of Denver, Denver, CO.

Harter, S. (1987). The determinants and mediation role of global self-worth in children. In N. Eisenberg (Ed.), *Contemporary issues in developmental psychology* (pp. 219-242). New York: Wiley.

Harter, S. (1988). *The Self-Perception Profile for Adolescents.* Unpublished manuscript, University of Denver, Denver, CO.

Harter, S. (1990a). Causes, correlates, and the functional role of global self-worth: A lifespan perspective. In R. Sternberg & J. Kolligian, Jr. (Eds.), *Competence considered* (pp. 67-98). New Haven, CT: Yale University Press.

Harter, S. (1990b). Adolescent self and identity development. In S. S. Feldman & G. R. Elliot (Eds.), *At the threshold: The developing adolescent* (pp. 352-387). Cambridge, MA: Harvard University Press.

Harter, S. (1990c). Developmental differences in the nature of self-representations: Implications for the understanding and treatment of maladaptive behaviors. *Cognitive Therapy and Research, 14,* 113-142.

Harter, S. (1993). Causes and consequences of low self-esteem in children and adolescents. In R. F. Baumeister (Ed.), *Self-esteem: The puzzle of low self-regard* (pp. 87-116). New York: Plenum.

Harter, S. (1996a). Developmental changes in self-understanding across the 5 to 7 year shift. In A. Sameroff & M. Haith (Eds.), *Reason and responsibility: The passage through childhood* (pp. 204-236). Chicago: University of Chicago Press.

Harter, S. (1996b). Teacher and classmate influences on scholastic motivation, self-esteem, and choice. In K. Wentzel & J. Juvonen (Eds.), *Social motivation: Understanding children's school adjustment* (pp. 11-42). Cambridge, UK: Cambridge University Press.

Harter, S. (1998). The development of self-representations. In W. Damon (Series Editor) & N. Eisenberg (Vol. Ed.), *Handbook of child psychology: Vol. 3. Social, emotional, and personality development* (5th ed., pp. 553-617). New York: Wiley..

Harter, S. (1999). *The construction of the self: A developmental perspective.* New York: Guilford Press.

Harter, S., Bresnick, S., Bouchey, H. A., & Whitesell, N. R. (1997). The development of multiple role-related selves during adolescence. *Development and Psychopathology, 9,* 835-854.

Harter, S., & Kreinik, P. (1998). *The Self-Perception Profile for Late Adulthood.* Unpublished manuscript, University of Denver, Denver, CO.

Harter, S., & Monsour, A. (1992). Developmental analysis of conflict caused by opposing attributes in the adolescent self-portrait. *Developmental Psychology, 28,* 251-260.

Harter, S., & Pike, R. (1984). The Perceived Pictorial Scale of Perceived Competence and Social Acceptance for young children. *Child Development, 55,* 1969-1982.

Harter, S., & Silon, E. L. (1985). The assessment of perceived competence, motivational orientation, and anxiety in segregated and mainstreamed educable mentally retarded children. *Journal of Educational Psychology, 77,* 217-230.

Harter, S., Waters, P., & Whitesell, N. R. (1998). Relational self-worth: Differences in perceived worth as a person across interpersonal contexts among adolescents. *Child Development, 69,* 756-766.

Harter, S., Whitesell, N., & Kowalski, P. (1992). Individual differences in the effects of educational transitions on young adolescents' perceptions of competence and motivational orientation. *American Educational Research Journal, 29,* 777-808.

Hattie, J. (1992). *Self-concept.* Hillsdale, NJ: Erlbaum.

Hattie, J., & Marsh, H. W. (1996). Theoretical perspectives on the structure of self-concept. In B. A. Bracken (Ed.), *Handbook of self-concept* (pp. 38-90). New York: Wiley.

Henderson, V., & Dweck, C. S. (1990). Adolescence and achievement. In S. Feldman & G. Elliott (Eds.), *At the threshold: The developing adolescent* (pp. 308-329). Cambridge, MA: Harvard University Press.

Heyman, G., Dweck, C. S., & Cain, K. (1992). Young children's vulnerability to self-blame and helplessness: Relationship to beliefs about goodness. *Child Development, 63,* 401-415.

Higgins, E. T. (1991). Development of self-regulatory and self-evaluative processes: Costs, benefits, and trade-offs. In M. R. Gunnar & L. A. Stroufe (Eds.), *Self-processes and development: The Minnesota Symposium on Child Development* (Vol. 23, pp. 125-166). Hillsdale, NJ: Erlbaum.

Holloway, J. B., Beuter, A., & Duda, J. L. (1988). Self-efficacy and training for strength in adolescent girls. *Journal of Applied Social Psychology, 18,* 699-719.

Hong, Y., Chiu, C., Dweck, C. S., Lin, D., & Wan, W. (1999). Implicit theories, attributions, and coping: A meaning system approach. *Journal of Personality and Social Psychology, 77,* 588-599.

Horn, T. S., & Amorose, A. J. (1998). Sources of competence information. In J. L. Duda (Ed.), *Advances in sport and exercise psychology measurement* (pp. 49-64). Morgantown, WV: Fitness Information Technology.

Horn, T. S., Glenn, S. D., & Wentzell, A.B. (1993). Sources of information underlying personal ability judgments in high school athletes. *Pediatric Exercise Science, 5*, 263-274.

Horn, T. S., & Harris, A. (2002). Perceived competence in young athletes: Research findings and recommendations for coaches and parents. In F. L. Smoll & R. E. Smith (Eds.), *Children and youth in sport: A biopsychosocial perspective* (2nd ed.) (pp. 435-464). Dubuque, IA: Kendall/Hunt.

Horn, T. S., & Hasbrook, C. A. (1986). Informational components influencing children's perceptions of their physical competence. In M. R. Weiss & D. Gould (Eds.), *Sport for children and youths: Proceedings of the 1984 Olympic Scientific Congress* (pp. 81-88). Champaign, IL: Human Kinetics.

Horn, T. S., & Weiss, M. R. (1991). A developmental analysis of children's self-ability judgments in the physical domain. *Pediatric Exercise Science, 3*, 310-326.

Kazdin, A. E. (1993). Adolescent mental health: Prevention and treatment programs. *American Psychologist, 48*, 127-141.

Keith, L. K., & Bracken, B. A. (1996). Self-concept instrumentation: An historical and evaluative review. In B. A. Bracken (Ed.), *Handbook of self-concept* (pp. 91-170). New York: Wiley.

Lapsley, D. K., & Rice, K. (1988). The "new look" at the imaginary audience and personal fable: Toward a general model of adolescent ego development. In D. K. Lapsley & F. C. Power (Eds.), *Self, ego, and identity: Integrative approaches* (pp. 109-129). New York: Springer-Verlag.

Leary, M. R., & Downs, D. L. (1995). Interpersonal functions of the self-esteem motive: The self-esteem system as a sociometer. In M. H. Kernis (Ed.), *Efficacy, agency, and self-esteem* (pp. 123-140). New York: Plenum.

Lerner, R. M., & Brackney, B. E. (1978). The importance of inner and outer body parts attitudes in the self-concept of late adolescents. *Sex Roles, 4*, 225-238.

Lintunen, T. (1987). Perceived Physical Competence Scale for Children. *Scandinavian Journal of Sports Science, 9*, 57-64.

Lord, S. E., Eccles, J. S., & McCarthy, K. A. (1994). Surviving the junior high school transition: Family processes and self-perceptions as protective and risk factors. *Journal of Early Adolescence, 14*, 162-199.

Maddux, J. (1995). Looking for common ground: A comment on Bandura and Kirsch. In J. Maddux (Ed.), *Self-efficacy, adaptation, and adjustment: Theory, research, and application* (pp. 377-385). New York: Plenum.

Maloney, M. J., McGuire, J. B., & Daniels, S. R. (1988). Reliability testing of a children's version of the Eating Attitude Test. *Journal of the American Academy of Children and Adolescent Psychiatry, 27*, 541-543.

Markus, H. R., & Kitayama, S. (1991). Culture and the self: Implications for cognition, emotion, and motivation. *Psychological Review, 98*, 224-253.

Marsh, H. W. (1987). The hierarchical structure of self-concept and the application of hierarchical confirmatory factor analysis. *Journal of Educational Measurement, 24*, 17-19.

Marsh, H. W. (1988). *Self-Description Questionnaire-I*. San Antonio, TX: Psychological Corporation.

Marsh, H. W. (1990). The structure of academic self-concept: The Marsh/Shavelson model. *Journal of Educational Psychology, 82*, 623-636.

Marsh, H. W. (1991). *Self-Description Questionnaire-III*. San Antonio, TX: Psychological Corporation.

Marsh, H. W. (1993). Academic self-concept: Theory, measurement, and research. In J. Suls (Ed.), *Psychological perspectives on the self* (Vol. 4, pp. 59-98). Hillsdale, NJ: Erlbaum.

Marsh, H.W. (1998). Age and gender effects in physical self-concepts for adolescent elite athletes and nonathletes: A multicohort—multioccasion design. *Journal of Sport and Exercise Psychology, 20*, 237-259.

Marsh, H. W., Byrne, B. M., & Shavelson, R. J. (1992). A multidimensional, hierarchical self-concept. In T. M. Brinthaupt & R. P. Lipka (Eds.), *The self: Definitional and methodological issues* (pp. 44-95). Albany: State University of New York Press.

Marsh, H. W., & Peart, N. (1988). Competitive and cooperative physical fitness training programs for girls: Effects on physical fitness and on multidimensional self-concepts. *Journal of Sport and Exercise Psychology, 10*, 390-407.

Marsh, H. W., Richards, G., Johnson, S., Roche, L., & Tremayne, P. (1994). Physical Self-Description Questionnaire: Psychometric properties and a multitrait-multimethod analysis of reactions to existing instruments. *Journal of Sport and Exercise Psychology, 16*, 270-305.

Marsh, H. W., & Sonstroem, R. J. (1995). Importance ratings and specific components of physical self-concept: Relevance to predicting global components of self-concept and exercise. *Journal of Sport and Exercise Psychology, 17*, 84-104.

McAuley, E., & Mihalko, S. L. (1998). Measuring exercise-related self-efficacy. In J. L. Duda (Ed.), *Advances in sport and exercise psychology measurement* (pp. 371-392). Morgantown, WV: Fitness Information Technology.

Mecca, A. M., Smelser, N. J., & Vascancellos, J. (Eds.). (1989). *The social importance of self-esteem*. Berkeley: University of California Press.

Mellin, L. M. (1988). Responding to disordered eating in children and adolescents. *Nutrition News, 51*, 5-7.

Messer, B., & Harter, S. (1989). *The Self-Perception Profile for Adults*. Unpublished manuscript, University of Denver, Denver, CO.

Neemann, J., & Harter, S. (1987). *The Self-Perception Profile for College Students.* Unpublished manuscript, University of Denver, Denver, CO.

Nicholls, J. G. (1989). *The competitive ethos and democratic education.* Cambridge, MA: Harvard University Press.

Nicholls, J. G. (1990). What is ability and why are we mindful of it? A developmental perspective. In R. J. Sternberg & J. Kolligian, Jr. (Eds.), *Competence considered* (pp. 121-148). New Haven, CT: Yale University Press.

Nicholls, J. G., & Miller, A. T. (1985). Differentiation of the concepts of luck and skill. *Developmental Psychology, 21,* 76-82.

Nottelmann, E. D. (1987). Competence and self-esteem during the transition from childhood to adolescence. *Developmental Psychology, 23,* 441-450.

Ogilvie, D. M., & Clark, M. D. (1992). The best and worst of it: Age and sex differences in self-discrepancy research. In R. P. Lipka & T. M. Brinthaupt (Eds.), *Self-perspectives across the lifespan* (pp. 186-222). Albany: State University of New York Press.

Orenstein, P. (1994). *School girls: Young women, self-esteem, and the confidence gap.* New York: Doubleday.

Petersen, A. C., Compas, B. E., & Brooks-Gunn, J., Stemmler, M., Ey, S., & Grant, K. E. (1993). Depression in adolescents. *American Psychologist, 48,* 155-168.

Piers, E. V., & Harris, D. B. (1964). Age and other correlates of self-concept in children. *Journal of Educational Psychology, 55,* 91-95.

Renick, M. J., & Harter, S. (1988). *The Self-Perception Profile for Learning Disabled Students.* Unpublished manuscript, University of Denver, Denver, CO.

Rosenberg, M. (1979). *Conceiving the self.* New York: Basic Books.

Rosenberg, M. (1986). Self-concept from middle childhood through adolescence. In J. Suls & A. G. Greenwalk (Eds.), *Psychological perspectives on the self* (Vol. 3, pp. 107-135). Hillsdale, NJ: Erlbaum.

Ruble, D. N., & Dweck, C. (1995). Self-conceptions, person conception, and their development. In N. Eisenberg (Ed.), *Review of personality and social psychology: Developmental and social psychology: The interface* (Vol. 15, pp. 109-139). Thousand Oaks, CA: Sage.

Ruble, D. N., & Frey, K. S. (1991). Changing patterns of comparative behavior as skills are acquired: A functional model of self-evaluation. In J. Suls & T.A. Wills (Eds.), *Social comparison: Contemporary theory and research* (pp. 70-112). Hillsdale, NJ: Erlbaum.

Sarrazin, P., Biddle, S., Famose, J. P., Cury, F., Fox, K., & Durand, M. (1996). Goal orientations and conceptions of the nature of sport ability in children: A social-cognitive approach. *British Journal of Social Psychology, 35,* 399-414.

Shavelson, R. J., Hubner, J. J., & Stanton, G. C. (1976). Self-concept: Validation of construct interpretations. *Review of Educational Research, 46,* 407-411.

Shavelson, R. J., & Marsh, H. W. (1986). On the structure of self-concept. In R. Schwarzer (Ed.), *Anxiety and cognition* (pp. 305-330). Hillsdale, NJ: Erlbaum.

Siegel, J. M., Yancey, A. K., Aneshensel, C. S., & Schuler, R. (1999). Body image, perceived pubertal timing and adolescent mental health. *Journal of Adolescent Health, 25 (2),* 155-165.

Siegler, R. S. (1991). *Children's thinking* (2nd ed.). Englewood Cliffs, NJ: Prentice-Hall.

Simmons, R. G., & Blyth, D. A. (1987). *Moving into adolescence: The impact of pubertal change and school context.* New York: Aldine deGruyter.

Simmons, R. G., Blyth, D. A., Van Cleave, E. F., & Bush, D. (1979). Entry into early adolescence: The impact of school structure, puberty, and early dating on self-esteem. *American Sociological Review, 44,* 948-967.

Simmons, R. G., & Rosenberg, F. (1975). Sex, sex roles, and self-image. *Journal of Youth and Adolescence, 4,* 229-258.

Skinner, E. A., Zimmer-Gembeck, M. J., & Connell, J. P. (1998). Individual differences and the development of perceived control. *Monographs of the Society for Research in Child Development, 63* (2-3, Serial No. 254).

Slap, G. B., Khalid, N., Paikoff, R., Brooks-Gunn, J., & Warren, M. (1994). Evolving self-image, pubertal manifestations, and pubertal hormones: Preliminary findings in young adolescent girls. *Journal of Adolescent Health, 15,* 327-335.

Smiley, P. A., & Dweck, C. S. (1994). Individual differences in achievement goals among young children. *Child Development, 65,* 1723-1743.

Sonstroem, R. J. (1984). Exercise and self-esteem. *Exercise and Sports Science Reviews, 12,* 123-155.

Sonstroem, R. J., Harlow, L. L., & Josephs, L. (1994). Exercise and self-esteem: Validity of model expansion and exercise associations. *Journal of Sport and Exercise Psychology, 16,* 29-42.

Sonstroem, R. J., Harlow, L. L., & Salisbury, K. S. (1993). Path analysis of a self-esteem model across a competitive swim season. *Research Quarterly for Exercise and Sport, 64,* 335-342.

Sonstroem, R. J., & Morgan, W. P. (1989). Exercise and self-esteem: Rationale and model. *Medicine and Science in Sports and Exercise, 21,* 329-337.

Stein, R. (1996). Physical self-concept. In A. Bracken (Ed.), *Handbook of self-concept* (pp. 374-394). New York: Wiley.

Stipek, D., & Mac Iver, D. (1989). Developmental change in children's assessment of intellectual competence. *Child Development, 60*, 521-538.

Stipek, D., Recchia, S., & McClintic, S. (1992). Self-evaluation in young children. *Monographs of the Society for Research in Child Development, 57*, 1-84.

Strein, W. (1988). Classroom-based elementary school affective educational programs: A critical review. *Psychology in the Schools, 25*, 288-296.

Swann, W. B., Jr. (1987). Identity negotiation: Where two roads meet. *Journal of Personality and Social Psychology, 53*, 1038-1051.

Swann, W. B., Jr. (1996). *Self-traps.* New York: Freeman.

Tesser, A., & Campbell, J. (1983). Self-definition and self-evaluation maintenance. In J. Suls & A. G. Greenwald (Eds.), *Psychological perspectives on the self* (Vol. 2, pp. 1-32). Hillsdale, NJ: Erlbaum.

Treasure, D. C., & Roberts, G. C. (1995). Applications of achievement goal theory to physical education: Implications for enhancing motivation. *Quest, 47*, 1-14.

Vealey, R. S. (1986). Conceptualization of sport-confidence and competitive orientation: Preliminary investigation and instrument development. *Journal of Sport Psychology, 8*, 221-246.

Vealey, R. S., & Campbell, J. (1988). Achievement goals in adolescent figure skaters: Impact on self-confidence, anxiety, and performance. *Journal of Adolescent Research, 3*, 227-243.

Watkins, B., & Montgomery, A. (1989). Conceptions of athletic excellence among children and adolescents. *Child Development, 60*, 1362-1372.

Watson, M. (1990). Aspects of self-development as reflected in children's role-playing. In D. Cicchetti & M. Beeghly (Eds.), *The self in transition: Infancy to childhood* (pp. 281-307). Chicago: University of Chicago Press.

Weiss, M. R. (1987). Self-esteem and achievement in children's sport and physical activity. In D. Gould & M. R. Weiss (Eds.), *Advances in pediatric sports sciences. Volume 2: Behavioral issues* (pp. 87-120). Champaign, IL: Human Kinetics.

Weiss, M. R., & Ebbeck, V. (1996). Self-esteem and perceptions of competence in youth sport: Theory, research, and enhancement strategies. In O. Bar-Or (Ed.), *The encyclopaedia of sports medicine,* Vol. VI: *The child and adolescent athlete* (pp. 364-382). Oxford: Blackwell Science Ltd.

Weiss, M. R., Ebbeck, V., & Horn, T. S. (1997). Children's self-perceptions and sources of competence information: A cluster analysis. *Journal of Sport and Exercise Psychology, 19*, 52-70.

Weiss, M. R., & Ferrer-Caja, E. (2002). Motivational orientations and sport behavior. In T. Horn (Ed.), *Advances in sport psychology* (2nd ed.) (pp. 101-184). Champaign, IL: Human Kinetics.

Whitehead, J. R. (1995). A study of children's physical self-perceptions using an adapted physical self-perception questionnaire. *Pediatric Exercise Science, 7*, 133-152.

Wigfield, A., Eccles, J. S., Mac Iver, D., Reuman, D. A., & Midgley, C. (1991). Transitions during early adolescence: Changes in children's domain-specific self-perceptions and general self-esteem across the transition to junior high school. *Developmental Psychology, 27*, 552-565.

Winkler, K. J. (1990, May 23). Scholar whose ideas of female psychology stir debate, modifies theories, extends study to young girls. *The Chronicle of Higher Education,* pp. A6, A8.

Wylie, R. C. (1989). *Measures of self-concept.* Lincoln, NE: University of Nebraska Press.

CHAPTER FIVE

Parental Influences on Youth Involvement in Sports

Jennifer A. Fredricks • *Jacquelynne S. Eccles*

After visiting any playing field or gymnasium, it is easy to observe that parents are substantially involved in their children's sports experiences. However, despite the clearly important role that parents play in youth sports, the research on family socialization in the sport context is relatively limited (Brustad, 1992; Woolger & Power, 1993). In a review of the research on sport socialization, Greendorfer (1992) argued that one of the critical areas for future work is parent socialization of sports participation. Brustad (1992) echoed this sentiment, claiming, "Everybody talks about parents in sport, but nobody does any research on them" (p. 72). Although researchers have recently responded to these claims, there are still several unanswered questions concerning parents' role in children's sport experience.

In contrast to the limited research in sports, family socialization has been well documented in a variety of other domains (e.g., academic achievement, social development, and moral development). Through their beliefs and practices, parents teach children values and provide them with opportunities that influence their choice of different activities and goals (Eccles, 1993; Maccoby & Martin, 1983). There are several reasons that the family should play a particularly important role in the athletic domain. First, a large proportion of children's time is spent in the family, especially in the early years. Second, many parents are highly involved in the athletic experience of their children. Family members play a variety of roles including coach, chauffeur, financier, spectator, and cheerleader. Third, because athletics is a highly public context, parents have several opportunities to provide immediate and specific feedback to their children (Scanlan, 1996). Through this feedback, parents can positively influence children's enjoyment of sports and self-concept development (Brustad, 1996a). However, unrealistic expectations and too much parental pressure can produce negative outcomes. Considering the potential of parents to have either a positive or negative role in children's sports experience, it is unfortunate that the research on this topic is limited.

> Because athletics is a highly public context, parents have several opportunities to provide immediate and specific feedback to their children.

This chapter has several purposes. First, we present a theoretical framework that we believe will be useful for conducting future research on parent socialization. Second, we review the existing research on parent socialization and children's sports participation. Third, we discuss some problems with previous work in this area that has limited our understanding of family socialization in the athletic context. Fourth, we describe promising directions for future research. Finally, we discuss the implications of these findings for interventions with parents in the sporting domain.

DEVELOPMENTAL ISSUES

Weiss and Bredemeier (1983) advocate taking a developmental theoretical orientation to study children's sports experience. We believe this approach is particularly appropriate to study the question of parental influences. Unfortunately, the majority of research on family socialization has not adequately considered developmental changes that occur within the child and parent-child relation (Woolger & Power, 1993). Cognitive and physical developmental changes may greatly affect parent socialization and children's athletic motivation (Brustad, 1992). Changes in children's capacity to differentiate ability and effort and increases in their capacity to incorporate social comparative information influence how they will interpret feedback from their parents. As a consequence young children rely more on adult feedback, whereas older children rely more heavily upon social comparative sources (Horn & Hasbrook, 1986). In addition, children's rate of physical development can influence the level of parental encouragement. Boys who mature earlier are likely to receive more social support from their parents for athletic participation than are boys who mature at later ages. Research that takes into account children's cognitive and physical maturity levels can help to illuminate the role that developmental factors play in parent socialization.

> Young children rely more on adult feedback, while older children rely more heavily upon social comparative sources.

The importance of parent socialization may also vary by children's developmental stage. Early research on sports socialization compared the effect of the family, peer group, and school on children's sport participation at different developmental stages (Greendorfer, 1977; Lewko & Greendorfer, 1988; Loy, McPherson, & Kenyon, 1978). Evidence from this work indicates that parents play an important role in the early athletic socialization of their children, but their influence decreases in adolescence when peers and coaches take on a more prominent role. These changes in parents' influence are likely a result of increases in the amount of time children spend with their peers and developmental changes in children's cognitive abilities. However, because this work has been primarily descriptive, it is not clear what developmental and situational factors explain differences in parent socialization over time. It is also important to remember that parents are going through their own developmental changes as children age. A critical question for future inquiry is how these concurrent changes within the child and the family influence children's sports participation.

MODEL OF PARENT SOCIALIZATION

The first purpose of this paper is to provide a conceptual framework for understanding family socialization in the athletic context. Figure 1 presents a general model developed by Eccles and her colleagues (Eccles et al., 1983; Eccles, Wigfield, & Schiefele, 1998) to explain contextual influences on the ontogeny of individual differences in motivation. The Eccles' expectancy-value model is based on the assumptions that individuals' decisions to participate in activities are made in the context of a variety of choices and it is important to understand how significant adults influence these decisions. This model was initially developed to explain the socialization of gender differences, and we believe it provides an excellent framework for understanding parent influences in the athletic domain. Using this model to explore individ-

FIGURE 1
General model of achievement choices

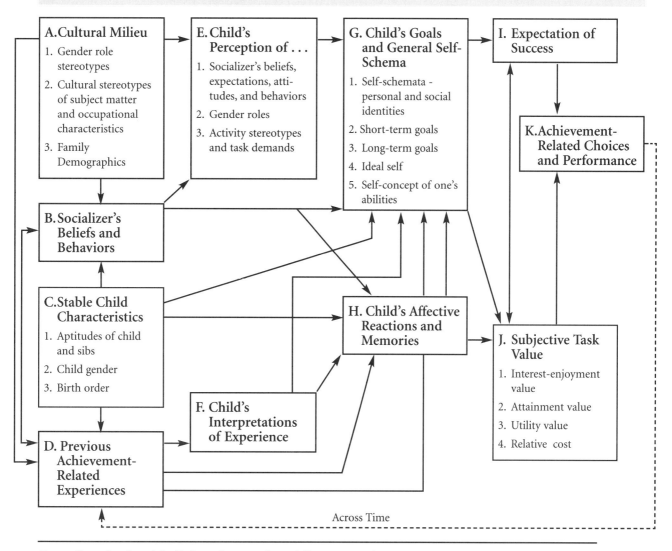

From "Motivational beliefs, values and goals" in *Annual Review of Psychology*, Vol. 53, p. 119. Reprinted by permission of the authors.

ual differences in sport participation can help address the concern that much of the existing research in sports socialization has been atheoretical (Greendorfer, 1992).

The two most important predictors of choice behaviors are children's expectations for success and task value (see Eccles et al., 1983). Expectations for success are influenced by one's self-concept of ability and one's perception of task difficulty. When this model is applied to the athletic domain, children who perceive that they have high athletic ability will be more likely to participate in athletics than will children who have less favorable beliefs about their athletic competencies. Task value comprises four components: (a) intrinsic value (enjoyment of the activity), (b) utility value (usefulness of the task in terms of future goals), (c) attainment value (personal importance of doing well at the task), and (d) costs (perceived negative aspects of engaging in the task). According to this model, individuals will have higher rates of athletic participation if they have a higher enjoyment of the activity, believe that athletics is important to both their short- and long-range goals, believe that sports participation confirms aspects of their self-schemas, and perceive low costs of involvement.

According to the expectancy-value model, socializers (parents, teachers, and peers) influence children's motivation through their beliefs and behaviors. Eccles and her colleagues

(1998) expanded their general achievement model to focus on how parents shape children's beliefs and values (see Figure 2). The two primary ways parents influence children's motivation are by being (a) interpreters of experience and (b) providers of experience (Eccles, 1993; Eccles et al., 1998). Parents help to interpret their children's experiences by providing messages about the likelihood that their children will attain success in a particular achievement domain, in combination with messages about the value of participating in that activity. Applying this model to the athletic domain, parents who have high expectations for their children's success and provide messages about the value of participating in sports will have children who have more favorable motivational outcomes.

Parents also influence their children's motivation through their behaviors. By providing experiences inside and outside of the home, parents help to structure children's exposure to

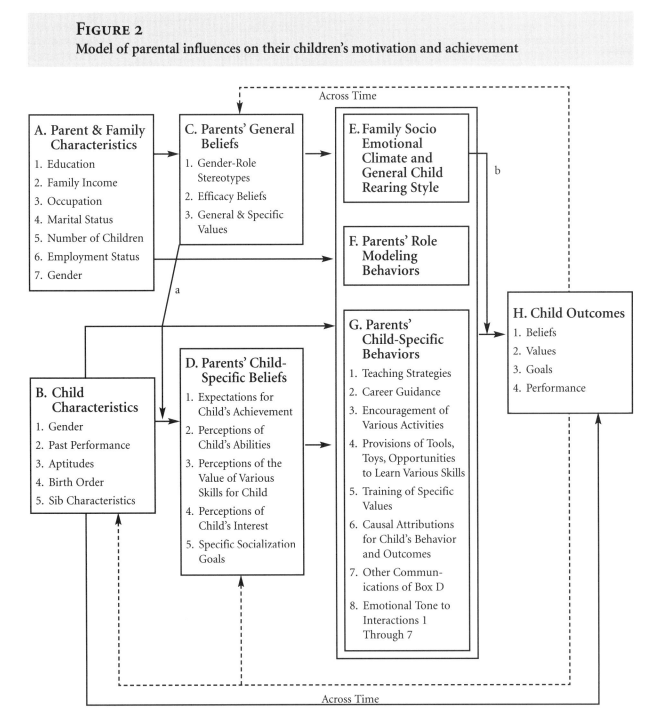

FIGURE 2
Model of parental influences on their children's motivation and achievement

athletics. For example, parents can expose their children to athletics by taking them to sporting events, buying them equipment and toys, and signing them up for special lessons. These experiences can, in turn, influence children's skills, preferences, and activity choices. Parents also influence motivation by providing differential levels of encouragement to participate in athletics. Punishment decreases the likelihood that children will engage in the activity in the future. However, it is less clear whether positive reinforcement increases children's motivation. In fact, excessive positive reinforcement that is not linked to the quality of children's performance can decrease the likelihood that they will participate in the activity in the future (Deci & Ryan, 1985). Conversely, contingent praise and appropriate feedback for performance does result in positive motivational outcomes (see Horn, 1987).

Parents adjust their beliefs and behaviors in response to characteristics of their children, including the child's gender, aptitude, interest, prior performance, and developmental level (Eccles, 1993; Eccles et al., 1983). If parents believe that boys have superior athletic competencies than do girls it is likely that they will provide different opportunities and encouragement to their children depending on their gender. As a consequence, their sons and daughters will come to have different beliefs about their athletic abilities. Similarly, parents are likely to provide more encouragement if they notice that their child has a talent in athletics, but will lower their expectations if their child loses interest in the activity.

> Parents adjust their behaviors in response to their children's gender, aptitude, interest, prior performance, and developmental level.

According to the Eccles' expectancy-value model, parents' beliefs about their children's abilities are shaped by their gender stereotypes, beliefs about their athletic ability, and knowledge of how to help their children with athletics (Eccles, 1993). For example, parents who endorse more gender stereotypic beliefs about females' competencies will likely hold lower perceptions of their daughters' athletic abilities than will parents who do not endorse traditional notions of males' and females' roles. Additionally, parents who have more knowledge of athletics will be more involved in their children's sporting pursuits than will parents who have less knowledge of appropriate teaching strategies in this domain.

Finally, this model assumes that one cannot understand the effect of the family on children's motivation unless one considers the larger social context. Parents' beliefs and behaviors are shaped by demographic factors such as education, income, marital status, employment status, cultural traditions, number of children in the family, and resources in the neighborhood (Eccles, 1993; Eccles et al., 1983). Participation in athletics requires a financial and time investment by the family. Parents who have monetary resources are in a better position to buy athletic equipment and pay for special teams and camps. The availability of athletic resources in the community also influences children's athletic participation. In some communities, children have several opportunities to be involved in sports at a variety of levels; in other neighborhoods, there are more limited opportunities for children to develop their athletic competencies.

Support for the Eccles Model

The Eccles expectancy-value model has been used extensively to study parent socialization of motivation in math and English. Several studies have documented that parents' perceptions of their children's abilities are significant predictors of children's own ability and interest in math and English, even after controlling for children's performance (Eccles, 1993; Frome & Eccles, 1998; Jacobs, 1992; Jacobs & Eccles, 1992; Parsons, Adler, & Kaczala, 1982). Further, using longitudinal data, Eccles and her colleagues have found support for the hypothesized causal relations between parents' beliefs and children's self and task beliefs (Eccles, 1993; Yoon, 1996).

The expectancy-value model has recently been applied to the athletic domain, and researchers have found some support for various aspects of the model (e.g., Dempsey, Kimiecik, & Horn, 1993; Eccles & Harold, 1991; Fredricks, 1999; Kimiecik & Horn, 1998). Because the Eccles model was designed to explain individual differences in choice behavior, it is not surprising that researchers in sport psychology have used this model. Decisions regarding math and English are relatively constrained until later in students' academic careers. In contrast, participation in athletics is voluntary. As a consequence, there should be more variation in athletic participation rates that should be more highly tied to the socialization factors outlined in the model (Eccles & Harold, 1991).

In the next section, we outline research on family socialization in the athletic context. First, we outline the existing research that has been based on the assumption that role modeling is the critical mechanism in parent socialization. We begin our review with this work because it has been a primary focus of the sport psychology literature. Next, we outline the research on the influence of parents as interpreters and providers of experiences, two central components of the Eccles model. We present the results of research that have used the expectancy-value model, as well as findings from scholars who did not explicitly test this model but whose findings fit within this theoretical framework.

Parents as Role Models

The process of observational learning has been suggested as the underlying mechanism by which the child internalizes the attitudes and behaviors of the role model (Bandura, 1977; Maccoby & Jacklin, 1974). This theory leads to the assumption that children of parents who engage in athletic activities will also be physically active. Parents can be role models by being a coach, participating in athletics on an organized team, or just doing sports for fun. Through their involvement in athletics, parents provide a model of what is considered appropriate and inappropriate behavior and help to normalize involvement in athletics. However, although modeling is often cited as theoretically important for children's acquisition of attitudes and behaviors (Bandura), the empirical support for role modeling is equivocal. In one of the few studies to empirically test the effect of role modeling on academic outcomes, Parsons (aka Eccles) and her colleagues (1982) found that parents did not influence children's achievement through role modeling. Instead, they found that the primary source of influence was parental expectations.

The findings concerning the effect of role modeling on children's athletic participation have also been mixed. A few studies have used objective measures to document a strong relation between the physical activity levels of parents and children (Freedson & Evenson, 1991; Moore et al., 1991). For example, pediatric researchers in the Framingham Children's Study (Moore et al.) used an electronic monitoring device to track the physical activity behavior of parents and their young children. Children of two active parents were six times more likely to be active than were children of two inactive parents. Freedson and Evenson used a comparable protocol to document a positive relation between the physical activity level of young children and their parents.

Parents who play sports on any level provide a model for their children and help to normalize involvement in athletics.

Studies using self-report measures of role modeling have been less conclusive; some scholars document positive associations, and others find no relation between parent and child activity levels. These discrepant findings may be function of differences in measures (objective, children's perceptions, and parents' self-reports) and differences in the age groups examined. For example, Babkes and Weiss (1999) showed that athletes who reported that their mothers and fathers were good role models had higher perceptions of competence, enjoyment, and intrinsic motivation than did athletes whose parents were not perceived as good role models. In contrast, they did not find a significant relation between mothers' and fathers' reported involvement and children's psychosocial outcomes. Several other studies have failed to document a significant relation between role modeling and children's athletic participation (Dempsey et al., 1993; Fredricks, 1999). For example, Dempsey and her colleagues reported that parents' self-reported moderate-to-vigorous physical activity (MVPA) was not related to children's MVPA behavior. Similarly, Fredricks found that parents' self-reported time involvement in athletics was not related to children's self-concept or participation in organized sports.

Parent participation in sports can be particularly important for female athletes. Across a range of sports, females who participate in sports at the college level reported that one or more of their parents also participated in sports (Greendorfer, 1983; Weiss & Knoppers, 1982). In these families, games and sports were considered normal activities and were part of the family routine. Similarly, Brown, Frankel, and Fennell (1989) found that mothers' participation in sports was a significant predictor of female adolescents' continued participation in both school and community athletic pursuits. There is also some evidence to indicate that parental participation is more important for girls' athletic involvement than for boys' involvement. For example, Greyson and Colley (1986) reported that mothers' and fathers' sport participation was significantly associated with adolescent females' sports participation, but not with males' sports participation. In a similar study, female athletes rated the influence of mothers, siblings, coaches, and friends higher than male and female nonathletes did (Weiss & Barber, 1995).

Although several studies have established an empirical link between parent participation and children's athletic involvement, there are several problems with this hypothesis. First, the role-modeling explanation focuses on the amount of participation (quantity), rather than considering the quality of parent involvement (Dempsey et al., 1993). However, more is not always better. Parents also can model affective reactions to sports participation. For example, a child would be more likely to imitate a parent who is enthusiastic about athletics than a parent who participates at the same level but does not express positive sentiments. Brustad (1993, 1996b) found empirical support for this assumption, documenting a positive relationship between parents' enjoyment of physical activity and children's attraction to athletics. A second problem is the lack of specificity in the role-modeling research. As models, parents can engage in a variety of behaviors that children can imitate. Because this research has been primarily descriptive, it is not clear what specific parenting behaviors help to explain the underlying relation between parents' and children's sport participation.

PARENTS AS INTERPRETERS OF EXPERIENCE

Another way parents influence children's ability perceptions and sports involvement is through their beliefs and values. The relation between parents' beliefs and children's motivation and achievement has been well established in the educational literature (e.g., Alexander & Entwisle, 1988; Eccles et al., 1998). There is a growing interest in how parents' beliefs may contribute to individual differences in children's athletic outcomes. We divide our review of the research on the effect of parents' beliefs on children's motivation into two sections: (a) affective outcomes and (b) self-concept development.

Research on Affective Outcomes

Several studies have examined how parents contribute to children's affective development in sport. The impact of parental pressure has been a central question in this work; the impetus behind much of this research has been a concern over the high level of stress, anxiety, and burnout experienced by some young athletes (Brustad, 1996a). In research on young wrestlers, Scanlan and Lewthwaite (1984) documented that male athletes who perceived high levels of pressure by their parents had higher state anxiety regarding wrestling competition. Similarly, Gould and his colleagues (Gould, Eklund, Petlichkoff, Peterson, & Bump, 1991) found that parental pressure to wrestle was related to young wrestlers' prematch anxiety. Weiss, Wiese, and Klint (1989) provided additional support for the potential negative effects of parental pressure. They reported that youth gymnasts' two most frequently cited worries were "what my parents will think" and "letting my parents down." Borman and Kurdek (1987) outline further evidence of the effect of parental pressure on sport participation, documenting that motivation to play soccer was significantly related to lower maternal control.

Parents can also positively influence favorable outcomes for youth in sports, though much less research has been done on this topic. Children's enjoyment of sports (amount of fun youngsters experience) has been a central component of this work. Several scholars have reported a relation between lower levels of parental pressure and greater enjoyment of athletics (Babkes & Weiss, 1999; Brustad, 1988). Additional evidence of families' influence on children's enjoyment comes from an interview study of elite figure skaters (Scanlan, Stein, & Ravizza, 1989). Results of the qualitative analysis indicated that bringing pleasure to the family was an important dimension of sports enjoyment.

Research on Self-Concept

Several studies have used the Eccles expectancy-value model to examine the effect of parents' expectations and values on children's athletic competence beliefs. For example, Eccles and Harold (1991) examined parental socialization of gender differences in sports involvement. Results from this research support the Eccles' theoretical model: Children's perceptions of the value of sports involvement to their parents were related to children's beliefs about their own physical ability. Girls reported that their parents placed lower value on sports participation than did boys. In turn, these gender differences were linked to girls' lower participation in sports (Eccles & Harold, 1991). Using longitudinal data, Fredricks and Eccles (2002) provided further evidence of the impact of parents' beliefs on the development of children's athletic competence beliefs. Parents' expectations of children's sport ability in the elementary school years helped to explain changes in children's sports competence beliefs from 1st through 12th grade. When parents had high expectations for children's sports ability, children had less dramatic declines in their self-concept over time. These findings were independent of actual ability differences.

Eccles and her colleagues found that even parents of early elementary school children report that boys have more talent in athletics and that sports is more important for their sons than for their daughters.

An important question is how gender mediates the relation between parents' beliefs and children's self-perceptions. Many parents of adolescents hold gender-stereotyped beliefs, believing that males have more athletic ability than females (Eccles, Jacobs, & Harold, 1990; Greendorfer, 1993; Jacobs & Eccles, 1992). When do these gender-stereotyped beliefs emerge? Eccles and her colleagues found that even parents of early elementary school children reported that boys had more talent in athletics and that sports was more important for their sons than for their daughters (Eccles, Wigfield, Harold, & Blumenfeld, 1993; Eccles et al., 2000).

The origin of these gender-stereotyped beliefs has been an important focus of this research. Jacobs and Eccles (1992) examined how mothers' gender-role stereotypes influence both mothers' and children's appraisals of ability in athletics. Mothers who reported that boys were more naturally gifted in sports had higher perceptions of athletic ability for their sons and lower perceptions for their daughters than did parents with less stereotyped beliefs. In accordance with the Eccles model, children's own self-perceptions of ability tended to be congruent with their mothers' appraisals of their sports ability.

The Eccles' expectancy-value model has also been applied to research on the socialization of children's MVPA, an important focus of recent public health objectives (U.S. Department of Health and Human Services, 2000). This research has contributed to our understanding of the impact of parents' beliefs on children's physical activity participation (Dempsey et al., 1993; Kimiecik & Horn, 1998; Kimiecik, Horn, & Shurin, 1996). For instance, Dempsey and colleagues reported a relation between parents' perceptions of their children's competence in MVPA and children's actual level of MVPA participation. Extending this work on the determinants of MVPA, Kimiecik and colleagues (1996) found that children who perceived that their parents valued fitness and had higher competence beliefs reported higher MVPA levels. Further, Kimiecik and Horn (1998) examined gender differences in parents' beliefs regarding children's MVPA and the relation between these beliefs and children's self-reported MVPA. In contrast to much of the other work on parent socialization, mothers and fathers did not differ in their perceptions of children's physical activity competence and the importance of MVPA for their sons and daughters. However, similar to the previous findings in this domain, parents' competence beliefs for their children were significantly related to children's MVPA (Kimiecik & Horn, 1998).

Though not explicitly testing the Eccles model, several other studies have documented a strong correspondence between parent and child appraisals of children's competence beliefs (Felson & Reed, 1986; McCullagh, Matzkanin, Shaw, & Maldonado, 1993). Related research by Scanlan and Lewthwaite (1984) provides additional support of an association between parent and children's beliefs. Young wrestlers who perceived high parental satisfaction had higher expectancies for future performance. Additionally, Babkes and Weiss (1999) found that youth soccer players who reported that their mothers and fathers had more positive beliefs about their competencies and gave more frequent positive responses to their performance were more likely to report greater enjoyment of sports and more positive beliefs about their ability. In contrast, Babkes and Weiss found no significant relation between parents' reported beliefs and behaviors and children's outcomes.

One question that arises from this work concerns how parents' beliefs are communicated to their children. Parents' extensive involvement in athletics gives them multiple opportunities to provide feedback to their children about their abilities and values. However, there has been surprisingly little research on the nature of parental feedback and the effect of these comments on children's sports beliefs and behavior. One interesting area of research categorizes parents' comments during youth sporting events (Kidman, McKenzie, & McKenzie, 1999; Randall & McKenzie, 1987). This work leads to several questions about the salience and meaning of feedback, the types of comments that are the most beneficial for young athletes, and how children integrate these comments into their developing beliefs and values.

PARENTS AS PROVIDERS OF EXPERIENCE

Parents' behaviors can influence children's sports participation in a number of ways. One way is through the pattern of reinforcement and level of encouragement parents give for engaging in athletic activities. Early encouragement of sports by the family is a critical factor in continued involvement. Most athletes acknowledge that their family stimulated their early interest and participation in sports (Brustad, 1992). Those who achieve elite status in athletics often began their participation as early as 5 or 6 years of age with the interest generated by the family. Parental encouragement is also positively associated with continued participation in athletic activities. For example, Brustad (1993) found that parental encouragement to be physically active was related to children's attraction to physical activity. Brustad (1996b) extended these findings to an urban sample, reporting that parental encouragement was positively related to both female and male children's attraction to physical activity and perceived physical competence.

Parental encouragement appears to be especially important to counteract the negative effect of gender stereotypes on girls' involvement in sport. Several studies have reported a positive correlation between parents' encouragement and current sport participation for females (Greendorfer, 1983; Higginson, 1985; Weiss & Knoppers, 1982). Social support from family members appears to be an important factor in girls' participation. For example, Lewko and Ewing (1980) found that highly involved girls identified more support from fathers, mothers, and siblings than did girls who were not as highly involved in athletics. In addition, Brown (1985) reported that social support from parents was positively related to female adolescent swimmers' participation status.

Parents also support children's sports participation by providing a variety of opportunities and athletic experiences in and outside the home. For instance, it is typically the parent (usually the mother) who enrolls children in their first sports program (Howard & Madrigal, 1990). Parents also support children's involvement by purchasing equipment and services and providing volunteer labor to help maintain children's sports programs (Green & Chalip, 1998). Spending time with children helping them to develop their skills is another way parents can bolster children's athletic involvement. Finally, parents can support children's sports involvement by becoming actively involved in coaching and/or the administration of youth sports program.

> Parental encouragement appears to be especially important to counteract the negative effect of gender stereotypes on girls' involvement in sport.

The importance of opportunities and experiences in the home for children's continued athletic participation and skill development has been illustrated in qualitative research on talent development (Alfeld-Liro, Fredricks, Hruda, Patrick, & Ryan, 1998, Bloom, 1985). In a study of elite athletes, Bloom reported that parents introduced children to the activity, provided resources and equipment to encourage their children's interest, and practiced skills with them. As children gained competence, parents played a larger role in helping them to gain access to coaches and teams to help them to improve their skills.

Gender Differences

Researchers have documented that parents are gender stereotyped in their level of encouragement and provision of opportunities in the home (Eccles, 1993; Greendorfer, 1993). Since the advent of Title IX, women have made great strides in their athletic participation. Today, young girls are much more likely to be encouraged to be involved in sports. However, despite these advances, parents continue to endorse the gender-stereotypic belief that boys are more suited for sports than girls. In addition, parents continue to encourage their daughters to try certain sports (e.g., gymnastics, skating, tennis) that may also communicate gender-stereotypic beliefs. In a recent review of the literature, Greendorfer, Lewko, and Rosengren (1996) concluded that differential treatment of play styles, toy preferences, and gender labeling of physical activities continues to exist.

Gender differences in parental encouragement of opportunities begin at a very young age. Both mothers and fathers are more likely to encourage motor activity in their sons than in their daughters (Huston, 1983; Power & Parke, 1986). Boys are also given earlier autonomy and are less restricted in their opportunities to play outside than are girls (Huston). Fathers are also more likely to play roughly with boys and teach them gross motor behavior (Huston; Power & Parke). This early exposure to rough and tumble play is likely to prepare boys for the context of many athletic teams. There is also evidence that parents reward and encourage gender-stereotyped play and discourage cross-typed play (Caldera, Huston, & O'Brien, 1989; Langlois & Downs, 1980). Boys are more likely to be given toys that are congruent with their gender such as athletic equipment, trucks, and military toys (Fisher-Thompson, 1990). This differential exposure to toys and activities gives children the opportunity to develop different competencies and values. Without the opportunity to try a particular activity, children will never get the chance to find out if they are good at it or if they enjoy it.

Parental differential treatment by gender continues in middle childhood and adolescence. Parents are more likely to encourage their sons to be physically active and participate in sports than they are to encourage their daughters (Brustad, 1993; Eccles, 1993; Greendorfer, 1993). Parents also report gender-stereotyped differences in time use with their children; they are more likely to spend time playing sports with their sons and are more likely to take their sons to sporting events (Eccles, 1993; Eccles et al., 2000). These results clearly demonstrate that parents are providing different types of athletic experiences for boys and girls. An important question is how this differential treatment within the family affects children's sports participation over time.

Extent of Overinvolvement

The amount of parental involvement in athletics activities helps to make a statement in the family about the relative importance of sports. According to Hellstedt (1987), parent involvement ranges on a continuum from under- to overinvolvement. Parents who are underinvolved do not make much of an emotional, financial, or functional investment in their children's athletics. In contrast, parents who are overinvolved emphasize winning, become angry if their children do not perform well, and make frequent attempts to help coach from the sidelines. The ideal level of involvement is between these two extremes. Parents who are moderately involved support their children's participation without being excessive, leaving ultimate decisions about participation levels up the athlete (Hellstedt, 1987). However, although the benefit of moderate involvement is an appealing idea, there is presently no empirical data to verify the relationship between over- and underinvolvement and child outcomes.

There is a growing concern about parents' excessive involvement in athletics (Williams & Lester, 2000). For some parents, their own self-esteem is tied to their child's athletic success, which results in high levels of parental involvement and an emphasis on winning at all costs (Hellstedt, 1987). This overinvolvement by parents can contribute to children's negative sports experience and can undermine even the best-intentioned youth sports program (Kamm, 1998; Smilkstein, 1980). Parents can also contribute to athlete burnout, a negative emotional outcome that is the consequence of chronic stress (Gould, Tuffey, Udry, & Loehr, 1996; Smith, 1986). In his research, Coakley (1992) reported that highly accomplished athletes whose parents made great commitments of time and energy most frequently experienced burnout. However, although there is strong anecdotal evidence of the negative effects of excessive levels of parental involvement, more systematic research is needed to document the extent of this problem and differences in the athletic experiences of children with overly involved parents and those with less involved parents.

> Healthy involvement means that parents support their children's participation in sports without being excessive and leave ultimate decisions about participation levels up to the athlete.

WHAT WE HAVE LEARNED

To help the reader synthesize our review, we developed a brief profile that summarizes the current knowledge of family socialization in the athletic context. We organize this profile around the three components of parent socialization: (a) parents as role models, (b) parents as interpreters of experiences, and (c) parents as providers of experience.

Parents as Role Models

- Active parents have active children.

- Parent participation in athletics is particularly important for girls. Female athletes are more likely to have parents who participate in athletics than are female nonathletes.

- More research is needed to understand how and why parent participation in athletics influences children's participation.

Parents as Interpreters of Experience

- Higher parental pressure is related to negative child outcomes (stress, anxiety, and burnout).

- Low to moderate levels of parental pressure is related to children's higher enjoyment of athletics.

- Parental beliefs (perceived competence, value, and enjoyment) are positively related to children's own competency beliefs, interest, and participation.

- Parents hold gender-stereotyped beliefs, believing that athletics is more important for boys than for girls and that boys have more athletic talent than girls.

- Children's perceptions of parents' beliefs are more strongly related to children's self-perceptions than are parent-reported beliefs.

Parents as Providers of Experience

- Parents support and encourage children's athletic involvement in a variety of ways, from time involvement to monetary support. There is a need for more research on how specific behaviors influence children's participation.

- Parental encouragement is positively related to children's sports involvement.

- Parents are gender-typed in their behaviors. They encourage their sons to be physically active more than they encourage their daughters. They provide more athletic opportunities to their sons than to their daughters.

- Overinvolvement by parents can contribute to children's negative emotional reactions to sports and ultimately to athlete burnout.

LIMITATIONS AND FUTURE RESEARCH

There are several gaps in the research that limit our knowledge of the sport socialization process. The majority of the research falls into two categories: (a) retrospective reports of parental behavior with college age and adult samples and (b) primary and secondary student self-reports about parental practices (Woolger & Power, 1993). In addition to assessing children's perceptions, there is a need for research that gathers information directly from parents about their beliefs, attitudes, and expectations regarding the sports involvement of their sons and daughters (Brustad, 1992). The importance of assessing both parents' and children's beliefs in the sport socialization process is illustrated in the Eccles model of parent socialization (see Figure 2).

As outlined in our review, both parents' beliefs and behaviors are important determinants of children's sports participation, and future studies should include measures of both. These parenting dimensions should not be examined in isolation, as much of the previous research has done. It is likely that parents' beliefs and behaviors interact in complex ways to influence children's motivation (Woolger & Power, 1993). For example, the effect of parental encouragement may vary as a function of parental warmth. The same level of encouragement could be viewed as either supportive or manipulative, depending on the quality of the parent-child relation.

The majority of the sport psychology research has used regression or "variable-centered" techniques to examine these questions. The usual approach in variable-centered analysis is to examine whether a factor still has an effect after accounting for its intercorrelations with other variables in the model. Although it is important to examine the effect of each socialization factor on children's sport participation after taking into account other variables in the model, it gives limited insight into the potential interactive and cumulative effect of parents' beliefs and behaviors. Supplementing variable-centered analyses with "person-centered" analyses is one approach that has been suggested to provide a more comprehensive picture of the relations among variables (Magnusson & Bergmann, 1988). In this kind of methodology, individuals are grouped together based on the patterns of their responses. Fredricks (1999) used this approach to examine the effect of different family contexts on children's athletic motivation. Families were typed based on the number of positive socialization factors in the home. Children who lived in families with a higher number of positive socialization factors had higher athletic motivation than did children living in families with less supportive factors.

Another concern is the lack of specificity in measures of parental behavior. In order to compare the influence of the family, peer group, and teachers, researchers have tended to use undifferentiated measures of "encouragement" or "involvement" (e.g., Greendorfer & Ewing, 1981; Higginson, 1985; Snyder & Spreitzer, 1973). Researchers who examine parent involvement in the achievement context have demonstrated that the type of parent involvement is more important than undifferentiated measures of the overall amount (Eccles & Harold, 1993; Grolnick, Benjet, Kurowski, & Apostoleris, 1997). Several new studies in the sports psychology literature have used specific indices of parental influences (see Babkes & Weiss, 1999; Brustad, 1993, 1996b), but it is clear that much more attention needs to focus on unpacking the constructs of parent involvement, encouragement, and support in the athletic context. Scholars who examine sport socialization might benefit by seeking relevant articles on measuring and conceptualizing these constructs.

Assessing potential differences in the effect of mothers' and fathers' beliefs on children's sports participation is another fruitful area of inquiry. There is some evidence that the same-sex parent is the most influential member of the family with regards to children's sport involvement (Lewko & Ewing, 1980; Snyder & Spreitzer, 1973). It has also been argued that fathers help to contribute to gender-stereotyped physical activity patterns because of their stricter differentiation of roles for girls and boys (Johnson, 1975; Langlois & Downs, 1980). However, the evidence that fathers are a more important figure in sport socialization is equivocal (Lewko & Greendorfer, 1988). In fact, several studies have demonstrated that mothers are more important than fathers in sport socialization (Howard & Madrigal, 1990; Kimiecik & Horn, 1998; Sallis, Patterson, Buono, Atkins, & Nader, 1988). Research that examines differences in the effect of mothers' and fathers' socialization practices on girls' and boys' sports experience can help to address this debate.

It is also important to examine parent socialization at different stages of children's involvement. The reliance on samples of children and adolescents already involved in athletics has resulted in limited information about the factors that contribute to early involvement of children in sports. As a consequence, there is information on the factors that maintain children's participation in athletics once they have become actively involved, but research "leaves unanswered the general question of how family, peers, and school shape children's socialization into sports" (Lewko & Greendorfer, 1988, p. 291). A way to help remedy this problem is for researchers to assess the socialization and motivational factors that precede children's initial sports involvement and follow these children over time (Brustad, 1992). Furthermore, understanding attrition from youth sports has been identified as a major goal of the research (Gould, 1987). Although it is likely the family plays a role in children's decision to drop out of sports, few studies have examined the impact of the family on youths' attrition from sports.

> Using the Eccles expectancy-value model, researchers can test the effect of parents' beliefs and behaviors on children's motivation.

There are several methodological problems with the previous research. First, most studies assume that parent socialization is unidirectional. However, it is very likely that sport socialization is bidirectional (Hasbrook, 1986; Snyder & Purdy, 1982). Not only do parents' beliefs and behaviors exert influence on children's behavior, but children's self-perceptions and interests also affect parent socialization in a bidirectional manner. We believe that the Eccles (1983, 1998) expectancy-value model provides a valuable theoretical framework for researchers to test bidirectional relations in the athletic domain. For example, using this model, researchers can test the effect of parents' beliefs and behaviors on children's motivation as well as testing how parents adjust their socialization in response to characteristics of the child such as the child's gender, age, interest, and ability (see Figure 2). We are encouraged that some researchers in sport psychology are beginning to use more sophisticated statistical techniques to test bidirectional influences (Green & Chalip, 1997, 1998).

A consideration of alternative research methodologies would also contribute to our understanding of the sport socialization process. Most of our current knowledge is based on cross-sectional data. Unfortunately, the dynamic and interactive nature of socialization cannot be adequately captured by data collected at a single point in time. From the current research, it is not clear how parents' beliefs and behaviors influence children's psychosocial development over time. The importance of examining socialization "across time" is illustrated in the Eccles model (see Figure 2). Assessing parent and child behaviors over time will help researchers to examine how concurrent developmental changes occurring in the child and within the parent-child relationship influence athletic participation. Qualitative research methods can also provide a greater understanding of the reciprocal nature of socialization. The reciprocal influence of sports participation on the family is eloquently articulated in the interviews with highly involved athletes (Alfeld-Liro et al., 1998; Bloom, 1985). These parents adjusted their socialization techniques in response to their child's developing talent. As their child's skills increased, the parents sought out opportunities that would facilitate their child's continued success.

To characterize the sport socialization process more effectively, research that takes a systems approach is also needed. Parents do not socialize children in isolation. They often take their cues on how to support their children from the feedback they receive from others, especially their children's coaches. Unfortunately, the majority of research has looked at parents and coaches separately, rather than considering how they jointly influence children's sports experience. Evidence from this work could be used to help improve communication between parents and coaches, a common concern of both parties (Hellstedt, 1987). Although less research has been conducted on peer influences in youth sports, it is very likely that parents and peers work together in influencing children's activity participation. For example, the quality of the parent-child rela-

The way parents interpret a child's involvement in sport significantly affects the child's experience.

tion can affect children's ability to form peer relations in the sport context (Weiss, in press). The relative influence of adults and peers on children's motivation, cognitive, and affective outcomes may also differ depending on children's developmental level.

Another application of a systems approach to the study of sports socialization concerns the role of siblings in children's sports involvement. The Eccles model includes sibling characteristics as an important aspect of the socialization process (see Figure 2). There are anecdotal accounts of how parents treat siblings differently in the athletic context, giving more or less support to one sibling depending on the needs of the other children in the family. However, there is no empirical evidence of the effect of sibling characteristics (gender, birth order, and number) on children's sports participation. We believe this represents a fruitful area of future inquiry.

Finally, there is a need for research with more diverse samples. Our current knowledge base has been generated primarily from research with white (European-American), upper-middle-class suburban families. These families have access to the time and resources necessary to support their children's sports participation. This limitation greatly affects the generalizability of these findings. In future work, it is critical that researchers consider the effect of race, ethnicity, and social class on parent socialization of children's athletic participation. Given changes in current family dynamics, it is also important to examine the impact of different family structures on children's sports experience (Babkes & Weiss, 1999). For example, it is possible that single parents may have less free time to devote to their children's sports participation than do two-parent families. By studying more diverse samples, researchers can assess the extent to which the previously identified patterns of parental influence extend to a more representative group of families.

Practical Implications

These findings have a number of practical implications. Parents can positively support children's athletic involvement through their beliefs and behaviors. Specifically, they can support children's participation by communicating positive feedback about their children's ability, giving messages to their children about the value of participation, encouraging their children's involvement, providing financial support for equipment and lessons, and attending their children's games and competitions. However, there can be too much of a good thing. Parents who put too much pressure on their children to perform, criticize their children's performance, and are too involved in their youth's sporting activities can contribute to anxiety, stress, and burnout.

Researchers have surveyed youth athletes about what they want from their parents (Stein, Raedeke, & Glenn, 1999; Wood & Abernethy, 1991). These results support the assumption that moderate levels of parental involvement are ideal. Parents need to remember that the child's enjoyment of athletics is the paramount concern. They can enhance their child's experience by providing support and encouragement, not becoming overinvolved, and not placing too much pressure on the child (Wood & Abernethy). In the end, decisions about participation should be left up to the athlete.

Although several workshops have been developed for coaches, there has been only limited intervention with parents of athletes. A few books have been written for youth sport parents (e.g., Hanlon, 1994; Rotella & Bunker, 1987; Smith, Smoll, & Smith, 1989). In addition, a few workshops have been developed that provide parents with guidelines for ways to interact with their child athlete. Parents are provided suggestions for how they can positively support their children and information on danger signs that can warn of their overinvolvement. Parents are also are given a background to the benefits of athletics and children's motives for involvement. For example, one activity is to have parents examine their own motivations for signing their child up for athletics to make sure that these motives focus on the child rather than the parent's self-interest (Kamm, 1998).

> Parent support and encouragement appears to be particularly important to female's ability to transcend traditional gender stereotypes.

Although these workshops have the best intentions, it is not clear how effective parenting education classes have been in changing parents' attitudes and behaviors. There is a need for research that evaluates the impact of these programs on parents' attitudes and behaviors and athletes' subsequent sports experiences. Studies of the effectiveness of training programs for coaches can provide a guide for these evaluations (see Smith & Smoll, 1996). Additionally, because much of the research on parental influences has used general measures of parent involvement, suggestions for parents have tended to focus on general issues. If more specific parenting behaviors and attitudes can be identified as either enhancing or interfering with children's sport experiences, researchers can make more specific suggestions regarding parental influences.

Finally, the findings have implications for family socialization of gender roles. Parent support and encouragement appear to be particularly important for females to help them transcend traditional gender stereotypes. Unfortunately, many parents still have gender-stereotyped beliefs and behaviors. Despite the inroads that females have made in athletics, many parents still believe boys are more suited for sports than girls are. It is critical that parents are given the message that both their sons and their daughters can benefit from athletic participation and that they provide equal opportunities for both sexes to enjoy these benefits.

References

Alexander, K. L., & Entwisle, D. (1988). Achievement in the first two years of school: Patterns and processes. *Monographs of the Society for Research in Child Development, 53* (2, Serial No. 218).

Alfeld-Liro, C, Fredricks, J. A., Hruda, L. Z., Patrick, H., & Ryan, A. (1998, March). Nurturing teenagers' talent: The role of parents, teachers, and coaches. In T. Scanlan (chair), *Maintaining commitment to one's talent.* Symposium conducted at the biennial meeting of the Society for Research on Adolescence, San Diego.

Babkes, M. L., & Weiss, M. R. (1999). Parental influence on cognitive and affective responses in children's competitive soccer participation. *Pediatric Exercise Science, 11,* 44-62.

Bandura, A. (1977). *Social learning theory.* Englewood Cliffs, NJ: Prentice Hall.

Bloom, B. S. (1985). *Developing talent in young people.* New York: Ballantine Books.

Borman, K. M., & Kurdek, L. A. (1987). Gender differences associated with playing high school varsity soccer. *Journal of Youth and Adolescence, 16,* 379-399.

Brown, B. A. (1985). Factors influencing the process of withdrawal by female adolescents from the role of competitive age group swimmer. *Sociology of Sport Journal, 2,* 111-129.

Brown, B. A., Frankel, B. G., & Fennell, M. P. (1989). Hugs or shrugs: Parental and peer influence on continuity of involvement in sport by female adolescents. *Sex Roles, 20,* 397-409.

Brustad, R. J. (1988). Affective outcomes in competitive youth sport: The influence of intrapersonal and socialization factors. *Journal of Sport & Exercise Psychology, 10,* 307-321.

Brustad, R. J. (1992). Integrating socialization influences into the study of children's motivation in sport. *Journal of Sport & Exercise Psychology, 14,* 59-77.

Brustad, R. J. (1993). Who will go out and play? Parental and psychological influences on children's attraction to physical activity. *Pediatric Exercise Science, 5,* 210-233.

Brustad, R. J. (1996a). Parental and peer influences on children's psychological development through sport. In F. L. Smoll & R. E. Smith (Eds.), *Children and youth sport: A biopsychosocial perspective* (pp. 112-124). Dubuque, IA: Brown & Benchmark.

Brustad, R. J. (1996b). Attraction to physical activity in urban schoolchildren: Parent socialization and gender influences. *Research Quarterly for Exercise and Sport, 67,* 316-323.

Caldera, Y. M., Huston, A. C., & O'Brien, M. (1989). Social interaction and play patterns of parents and toddlers with feminine, masculine, and neutral toys. *Child Development, 60,* 70-76.

Coakley, J. (1992). Burnout among adolescent athletes: A personal failure or social problem? *Sociology of Sport Journal, 9,* 271-285.

Deci, E. L., & Ryan, R. M. (1985). *Intrinsic motivation and self-determination in human behavior.* New York: Plenum Press.

Dempsey, J. M., Kimiecik, J. C., & Horn, T. S. (1993). Parental influences on children's moderate to vigorous physical activity participation: An expectancy-value approach. *Pediatric Exercise Science, 5,* 151-167.

Eccles, J. S. (1993). School and family effects of the ontogeny of children's interests, self- perception, and activity choice. In J. Jacobs (Ed.), *Nebraska Symposium on Motivation, 1992: Developmental perspectives on motivation* (pp. 145-208) Lincoln, NE: University of Nebraska Press.

Eccles, J. S., Adler, T. F., Futterman, R., Goff, S. B., Kaczala, C. M., Meece, J. L., & Midgley, C. (1983). Expectations, values and academic behaviors. In J. T. Spence (Ed.), *Achievement and achievement motivation* (pp. 75-146). San Francisco: W. H. Freeman.

Eccles, J. S., Freedman-Doan, C. R., Arberton, A. J., Yoon, K. S., Harold, R. D., & Wigfield, A. (2000). *Parents hold the key to the land of opportunity.* Manuscript in preparation.

Eccles, J. S., & Harold, R. D. (1991). Gender differences in sport involvement: applying the Eccles' expectancy model. *Journal of Applied Sport Psychology, 3,* 7-35.

Eccles, J. S., & Harold, R. D. (1993). Parent-school involvement during the early adolescent years. *Teachers College Record, 94,* 560-587.

Eccles, J. S., Jacobs, J. E., & Harold, R. D. (1990). Gender role stereotypes, expectancy effects, and parents' socialization of gender differences. *Journal of Social Issues, 46,* 183-201.

Eccles J. S., Wigfield, A., Harold, R. D., & Blumenfeld, P. (1993). Ontogeny of children's self-perceptions and subjective task values across activity domains during the early elementary school years. *Child Development, 64,* 830-847.

Eccles, J. S., Wigfield, A., & Schiefele, U. (1998). Motivation to succeed. In W. Damon (Series Ed.) & N. Eisenberg (Vol. Ed.), *Handbook of child psychology: Vol. 3. Social, emotional and personality development* (5th ed., pp. 1017-1094). New York: Wiley.

Felson, R. B., & Reed, M. (1986). The effect of parents on the self-appraisal of children. *Social Psychology Quarterly, 49*, 302-308.

Fisher-Thompson, D. (1990). Adult sex typing of children's toys. *Sex Roles, 23*, 291-303.

Fredricks, J. (1999). *"Girl-friendly" family contexts: Socialization into math and sports.* Unpublished doctoral dissertation, University of Michigan, Ann Arbor.

Fredricks, J., & Eccles, J. S. (2002). Children's competence and value beliefs from childhood through adolescence: Growth trajectories in two male-sex-typed domains. *Developmental Psychology, 38*, 519-533.

Freedson, P. S., & Evenson, S. (1991). Familial aggregation in physical activity. *Research Quarterly for Exercise and Sport, 62*, 384-389.

Frome, P., & Eccles, J. (1998). Parents' influence on children's achievement-related perceptions. *Journal of Personality and Social Psychology, 2*, 435-452.

Gould, D. (1987). Understanding attrition in children's sport. In D. Gould & M. R. Weiss (Eds.), *Advances in pediatric sports science: Vol. 2. Behavioral issues* (pp. 61-85). Champaign, IL: Human Kinetics.

Gould, D., Eklund, R. C., Petlichkoff, L., Peterson, K., & Bump, L. (1991). Psychological predicators of state anxiety and performance in age-group wrestlers. *Pediatric Exercise Science, 3*, 198-208.

Gould, D., Tuffey, S., Udry, E., & Loehr, J. (1996). Burnout in competitive junior tennis players: II. Qualitative analysis. *The Sport Psychologist, 10*, 341-366.

Green, C. B., & Chalip, L. (1997). Enduring involvement in youth soccer: The socialization of parent and child. *Journal of Leisure Research, 29*, 61-77.

Green, C. B., & Chalip, L. (1998). Antecedents and consequences of parental purchase decision involvement in youth sport. *Leisure Sciences, 20*, 95-109.

Greendorfer, S. L. (1977). Role of socializing agents in female sport involvement. *Research Quarterly, 48*, 304-310.

Greendorfer, S. L. (1992). Sports socialization. In T. S. Horn (Ed.), *Advances in sport psychology* (pp. 201-218). Champaign, IL: Human Kinetics.

Greendorfer, S. L. (1993). Gender role stereotypes and early childhood socialization. In G. L. Cohen (Ed.), *Women in sport: Issues and controversies* (pp. 3-14). Newbury Park, CA: Sage Publications.

Greendorfer, S. L., & Ewing, M. E. (1981). Race and gender differences in children's socialization into sport. *Research Quarterly for Exercise and Sport, 52*, 301-310.

Greendorfer, S. L., Lewko, J. H., & Rosengren, K. S. (1996). Family and gender-based influences in sport socialization of children and adolescents. In F. L. Smoll & R. E. Smith (Eds.), *Children and youth in sport: A biopsychosocial perspective* (pp. 89-111). Dubuque, IA: Brown & Benchmark.

Greyson, J. F., & Colley, A. (1986). Concomitants of sport participation in male and female adolescents. *International Journal of Sport Psychology, 61*, 311-318.

Grolnick, W. S., Benjet, C., Kurowski, C., & Apostoleris, N. H. (1997). Predictors of parent involvement in children's schooling. *Journal of Educational Psychology, 89*, 538-548.

Hanlon, T. (1994). *Sport parent.* Champaign, IL: Human Kinetics.

Hasbrook, C. A. (1986). Reciprocity and childhood socialization into sport. In L. V. Velden & J. H. Humphrey (Eds.), *Psychology and socialization of sport: Current selected research* (pp. 135-147). New York: AMS Press.

Hellstedt, J. C. (1987). The coach-parent-athlete relation. *The Sport Psychologist, 1*, 151-160.

Higginson, D. C. (1985). The influence of socializing agents in the female sport participation process. *Adolescence, 20*, 73-82.

Horn, T. S. (1987). The influence of teacher-coach behavior on the psychological development of children. In D. Gould & M. R. Weiss (Eds.), *Advances in pediatric sport sciences: Vol. 2. Behavioral issues* (pp. 121-142). Champaign, IL: Human Kinetics.

Horn, T. S., & Hasbrook, C. A. (1986). Informational components influencing children's perceptions of their physical competence. In M. R. Weiss & D. Gould (Eds.), *Sport for children and youths* (pp. 81-88). Champaign, IL: Human Kinetics.

Howard, D., & Madrigal, R. (1990). Who makes the decision: The parent or child? *Journal of Leisure Research, 22*, 244-258.

Huston, A. C. (1983). Sex typing. In P. Mussen & E. M. Hetherington (Eds.), *Handbook of child psychology* (Vol. 4, pp. 387-487). New York: Wiley.

Jacobs, J. E. (1992). The influence of gender stereotypes on parent and child ability beliefs in three domains. *Journal of Personality and Social Psychology, 63*, 932-944.

Jacobs, J. E., & Eccles, J. S. (1992). The impact of mothers' gender-role stereotypic beliefs on mothers' and children's ability perceptions. *Journal of Personality and Social Psychology, 63*, 932-944.

Johnson, M. M. (1975). Fathers, mothers, and sex typing. *Sociological Inquiry, 45*, 15-26.

Kamm, R. L. (1998). A developmental and psychoeducational approach to reducing conflict and abuse in Little League and youth sports. *Child and Adolescent Psychiatric Clinics of North America, 7*, 891-918.

Kidman, L. K., McKenzie, A., & McKenzie, B. (1999). The nature and target of parents' comments during youth sport competitions. *Journal of Sport Behavior, 22*, 54-68.

Kimiecik, J. C., & Horn, T. S. (1998). Parental beliefs and children's moderate-to-vigorous physical activity. *Research Quarterly for Exercise and Sport, 69*, 163-175.

Kimiecik, J. C., Horn, T. S., & Shurin, C. S. (1996). Relation among children's beliefs, perceptions of their parents' beliefs, and their moderate-to-vigorous physical activity. *Research Quarterly for Exercise and Sport, 67*, 324-326.

Langlois, J. H., & Downs, A. C. (1980). Mothers, fathers, and peers as socialization agents of sex-typed play behaviors in young children. *Child Development, 51*, 1217-1247.

Lewko, J. H., & Ewing, M. E. (1980). Sex differences and parental influence in sport involvement of children. *Journal of Sport Psychology, 2*, 62-68.

Lewko, J. H., & Greendorfer, S. L. (1988). Family influences in the sports socialization of children and adolescents. In F. L. Smoll, R. A. Magill, & M. J. Ash (Eds.), *Children in sport* (3rd ed., pp. 265-286). Champaign, IL: Human Kinetics.

Loy, J. W., McPherson, B. D., & Kenyon, G. S. (1978). *Sport and social systems.* Reading, MA: Addison Wesley.

Maccoby, E. E., & Jacklin, C. N. (1974). *The psychology of sex differences.* Stanford CA: Stanford University Press.

Maccoby, E. E., & Martin, J. A. (1983). Socialization in the context of the family: Parent-child interaction. In P. H. Mussen (Ed.), *Handbook of child psychology* (4th ed, pp. 1-101). New York: John Wiley & Sons.

Magnusson, D., & Bergman, L. R. (1988). Individual and variable-based approach to longitudinal research on early risk factors. In M. Rutter (Ed.), *Studies of psychosocial risk: The power of longitudinal data* (pp. 200-220). New York: Cambridge University Press.

McCullagh, P., Matzkanin, K. T., Shaw, S. D., & Maldonado, M. (1993). Motivation for participation in physical activity: A comparison of parent-child perceived competencies and participation motives. *Pediatric Exercise Science, 5*, 224-233.

Moore, L. L., & Lombardi, D. A., White, M. J., Campbell, D. L., Oliveria, S. A., & Ellison, R. C. (1991). Influence of parents' physical activity levels on activity levels of young children. *Journal of Pediatrics, 118*, 215-219.

Parsons, J., Adler, T. F., & Kaczala, C. M. (1982). Socialization of achievement attitudes and beliefs: Parental influences. *Child Development, 53,* 310-321.

Power, T. G., & Parke, R. D. (1986). Patterns of early socialization: Mother and father interactions in the home. *International Journal of Behavioral Development, 9*, 331-341.

Randall, L., & McKenzie, T. L. (1987). Spectator verbal behavior in organized youth soccer: A descriptive analysis. *Journal of Sport Behavior, 10*, 200-211.

Rotella, R. J., & Bunker, L. K. (1987). *Parenting your young superstar.* Champaign, IL: Human Kinetics.

Sallis, J. F., Patterson, T. L., Buono, M. J., Atkins, C. J., & Nader, P. R., (1988). Aggregation of physical activity habits in Mexican-American and Anglo families. *Journal of Behavioral Medicine, 11*, 31-41.

Scanlan, T. K. (1996). Social evaluation and the competitive process: A developmental perspective. In F. L. Smoll & R. E. Smith (Eds.), *Children and youth in sport: A biopsychosocial perspective* (pp. 298-308). Dubuque, IA: Brown and Benchmark.

Scanlan, T. K., & Lewthwaite, R. (1984). Social psychological aspects of competition for male youth sport participants: I: Predictors of competitive stress. *Journal of Sport Psychology, 6*, 208-226.

Scanlan, T. K., & Lewthwaite, R. (1986). Social psychological aspects of competition for male youth sport participants: IV: Predictors of enjoyment. *Journal of Sport Psychology, 8*, 25-35.

Scanlan, T. K., Stein, G. L., & Ravizza, K. (1989). An in-depth study of former elite figure skaters: II: Sources of enjoyment. *Journal of Sport & Exercise Psychology, 11*, 65-83.

Smilkstein, G. (1980). Psychological trauma in children and youth in competitive sport. *The Journal of Family Practice, 10*, 737-739.

Smith, R. E. (1986). Toward a cognitive-affective model of athletic burnout. *Journal of Sport Psychology, 8,* 36-50.

Smith, R. E., & Smoll, F. L.(1996). The coach as a focus of research and intervention in youth sports. In F. L. Smoll & R. E. Smith (Eds.), *Children and youth in sport: A biopsychosocial perspective* (pp. 125-141). Madison, WI: Brown & Benchmark.

Smith, R. E., Smoll, F. L., & Smith, N. J. (1989). *Parents' complete guide to youth sports.* Costa Mesa, CA: HDL Publishing.

Snyder, E. E., & Purdy, D. A. (1982). Socialization into sport: Parent and child reverse and reciprocal effects. *Research Quarterly for Exercise and Sport, 53*, 263-266.

Snyder, E. E., & Spreitzer, F. (1973). Family influence and involvement in sports. *Research Quarterly, 44*, 249-255.

Stein, G. L., Raedeke, T. D., & Glenn, S. D. (1999). Children's perceptions of parental sport involvement: It's not how much, but to what degree that's important. *Journal of Sport Behavior, 22*, 591-601.

U.S. Department of Health and Human Services (2000). *Healthy People 2000: National Health Promotion and Disease Prevention Objectives.* Washington, DC: Public Health Service.

Weiss, M. R. (in press). Social influences on children's psychosocial development in youth sports. In R. M. Malina (Ed.), *Youth sports in the 21st century: Organized sport in the lives of children and adolescents.* Monterey, CA: Exercise Science Publishing.

Weiss, M. R., & Barber, H. (1995). Socialization influences of collegiate female athletes: A tale of two decades. *Sex Roles, 33,* 129-140.

Weiss, M. R., & Bredemeier, B. J. (1983). Developmental sport psychology: A theoretical perspective for studying children in sport. *Journal of Sport Psychology, 5*, 216-220.

Weiss, M. R., & Knoppers, A. (1982). The influence of socializing agents on female collegiate volleyball players. *Journal of Sport Psychology, 4*, 267-279.

Weiss, M. R., Wiese, D. M., & Klint, K. A. (1989). Head over heels with success: The relationship between self-efficacy and performance in competitive youth gymnastics. *Journal of Sport and Exercise Psychology, 11*, 444-451.

Williams, W., & Lester, N. (2000). Out of control: Parents' becoming violent at youth sporting events. *Sports Illustrated, 93*, 86-95.

Wood, K., & Abernethy, B. (1991). Competitive swimmers' perceptions of parental behaviors. *Sport Coach, 14*, 19-23.

Woolger, C., & Power, T. G. (1993). Parent and sport socialization: Views from the achievement literature. *Journal of Sport Behavior, 16*, 171-189.

Yoon, K. S. (1996). Testing reciprocal causal relations among expectancy, value and academic achievement of early adolescents: A longitudinal study. *Dissertation Abstracts International, 57*, 2362.

CHAPTER SIX

A Little Friendly Competition: Peer Relationships and Psychosocial Development in Youth Sport and Physical Activity Contexts

Maureen R. Weiss • *Cheryl P. Stuntz*

If I lose, then I get mad at him. . . . Not really if he's on my team, but if he's on the other team, I'll get mad at him. I do not like to lose. . . . He doesn't like to lose either. We're both battling.

(11-year-old boy talking about his best sport friend; Weiss, Smith, & Theebom, 1996, p. 371)

In the Robbers Cave experiment, a classic social psychology study conducted over 40 years ago, Sherif and his colleagues (Sherif, Harvey, White, Hood, & Sherif, 1961) manipulated the goal-reward structure within a summer camp to emphasize either win-lose competition or intergroup cooperation. Subsequently, they observed the social and psychological consequences of these varying goal-reward structures among two groups of 12-year-old boys. To accomplish the study purposes, the naturalistic experiment consisted of three stages. The first, or *group-formation*, stage focused upon boys within each group interacting and working cooperatively to attain instrumental and social goals (i.e., problem-solving and enjoyable activities). As a result of such cooperative activities, each group developed its own unique norms, culture, and leader-follower hierarchies that fostered a sense of identity and cohesion. For example, each group adopted a group name, customs (e.g., risk taking, moral behaviors), and nicknames for each member. At this point the experimenters imposed the second, or *intergroup conflict*, stage. The two groups were introduced to one another and organized to compete against each other in sports and other activities (e.g., cabin cleanup) in which attractive rewards were distributed only to the winners. This context had a dramatic impact on enhancing intragroup relationships (i.e., cohesiveness) while escalating intergroup aggression (i.e., overt efforts to cause harm). Within-group structure and norms were transformed to maximum opportunities to beat "the enemy," whereas aggressive tactics extended beyond the playing field (e.g., food fights, cabin raids, verbal insults). In the third stage, the experimenters sought to minimize the existing win-lose goal structure and maximize intergroup cooperation. To do this, they first implemented common goals that required both groups to participate together (e.g., see a movie, use sports equipment). However, these activities required coaction, not interaction, which resulted in little change from the intergroup conflict stage. The experimenters found a solution by implementing *interdependent goals* requiring mutual cooperation by both groups over an extended period. These included problem-solving activities that were attainable only by the groups working together as a team (e.g., fixing the water system, transporting the food truck. Such goals were capable of scaling down intergroup rivalry considerably and promoting prosocial behaviors and respect for others. The take-home message of this study is clear: The social contexts of competition and cooperation exert a strong impact on the quality of peer interactions and relationships.

Sport settings contain numerous opportunities for social evaluation by peers because of the visible manner in which skills and abilities are displayed.

Sport and physical activity contexts (e.g., organized youth sport, school physical education) connote salient behavioral settings in which peer interactions and relationships abound in many forms. Moreover, peer interactions require a dynamic interplay between competition and cooperation to achieve valued individual and group goals. In fact, Hyland (1978), in a philosophical piece, points out the Latin derivation of the word *competition* meaning to strive together and contends that competition implicates an affinity with friendship. Thus, we believe physical activity contexts are unique setting in which to study peer relationships compared to school, family, and other activity contexts (e.g., socializing, music). First, sport settings contain numerous opportunities for *social evaluation* by peers because of the visible manner in which skills and abilities are displayed (Passer, 1996). Second, children usually enter organized sport programs during early to middle childhood, a time in which they acquire competitive behaviors and begin to use *social comparison* to peers as a means of judging their competence (Passer, 1996). Finally, sport is a *social institution* within Western society that is here to stay given the widespread belief that such participation has the potential to positively influence self-beliefs, emotions, social competencies, and behaviors (e.g., physical skill achievement, physical appearance).

Despite the prevalence of youth sport participation worldwide (De Knop, Engstrom, Skirstad, & Weiss, 1996), little research exists on peer group acceptance, friendships, and social competence in the physical domain. Several developmental researchers highlight the importance of studying peer relationships within specific social contexts that hold relevance to youth including sport and physical activity (e.g., Ladd & Price, 1993; Newcomb & Bagwell, 1995). Thus, our goal is to illuminate research that has been and needs to be done in the area of peer influence in the physical domain. We first overview theoretical perspectives on peer relationships, followed by a review of the robust findings from developmental psychology concerning the significance of peers during childhood and adolescence. The sport-related research on peer influence for several topical areas follows (e.g., peer acceptance and athletic ability; friendship; peer relations and moral development). Research-to-practice implications follow the review of the literature, and finally we outline directions for future research on peer relationships in an effort to inspire a much-needed expansion of the empirical database in the physical activity domain.

THEORETICAL PERSPECTIVES ON PEER RELATIONS

Definitional Hurdles

It is important to distinguish between popularity and friendship, the two most frequently studied peer variables, because they are distinct but related social constructs (Bukowski & Hoza, 1989). *Popularity* refers to how much a child is liked or accepted by members of his or her peer group. It is a *general, group-oriented, unilateral* view that entails how the peer group regards one of its members (e.g., classmate, teammate) and is often used interchangeably with such terms as *peer acceptance, social acceptance,* and *peer status.* The most common measurement of popularity has been sociometric methods that consist of asking each group member (e.g., classmate) to nominate the children (usually 3) with whom she or he would *most like* and *least like* to play (invite for a sleepover, go with to a movie, etc.). The nominations are mapped out, and children are categorized along two dimensions – social preference and social impact (see Cillessen & Bukowski, 2000). *Social preference* refers to likability by the group and is calculated by subtracting the number of negative from positive nominations. *Social impact* refers to the extent to which a child is noticed by the group and is reflected by the sum of positive and negative nominations. Subsequently, children are classified as popular (many positive, few negative nominations), average (average positive, average negative nominations), rejected (many negative, few positive nominations), neglected (few positive, few negative nominations), or controversial (many positive, many negative nominations). These groups are then compared on variables of interest (e.g., social adjustment, self-esteem). Rating scales represent an alternative means of assessing popularity where each individual in the group is asked to rate every other member and average ratings are calculated for each child.

By contrast, *friendship* refers to a close, mutual, dyadic relationship (e.g., best friendship, close friendship). Friendship represents a *specific, individual, bilateral* view of particular experiences that occur between two persons. Hartup (1996) contends that three aspects need to be considered to understand the significance of friendships on psychosocial outcomes among youth: (a) whether or not one has a friend (i.e., a reciprocated affectionate relationship), (b) the identity of one's friends (e.g., well adjusted or delinquent), and (c) the quality of one's friendships (e.g., companionship, intimacy, esteem enhancement). A variety of methods have been used to assess the existence of friendships including nomination and rating-scale procedures (Asher, Parker, & Walker, 1996; Bukowski & Hoza, 1989). As well, a number of valid and reliable friendship-quality scales now exist that assess the multidimensional nature of peer supportive functions (Furman, 1996).

Popularity and friendship are conceptually distinct dimensions of peer relations, but they may overlap in that children who are popular often have more friends, purportedly because the same social skills bode well for both types of peer relations (Bukowski & Hoza, 1989). Because group and dyadic relationships may differentially influence psychosocial and behavioral outcomes in youth, several researchers have argued that popularity and friendship should be examined simultaneously to determine their unique and relative influence on psychosocial variables (Asher et al., 1996; Bukowski & Hoza, 1989; Ladd, 1999; Newcomb, Bukowski, & Bagwell, 1999). The wisdom of differentiating among peer constructs in assessing the developmental significance of popularity and friendship also makes good sense if one takes into account prevalent theories that are relevant to the study of peer influence.

Theories Relevant to the Study of Peer Interactions and Relationships

Developmental researchers lament that most research on peer relationships is atheoretical, which is a limitation for building a case for the developmental significance of peers in children's lives (Bukowski & Hoza, 1989; Furman, 1996; Laursen, 1996; Newcomb & Bagwell, 1995). There is an effort to encourage more theory-based research on peer influence in children's psychosocial development. Several theories pose suitable and attractive candidates for examining peer relationships and children's cognitive, emotional, social, and moral development (see Bukowski & Hoza, 1989; Rubin, Bukowski, & Parker, 1998). We briefly review several of these theories in this section. Some theories were developed with the specific intention of understanding and explaining a wide array of social relationships, including parents, peers, close friends, and romantic partners (i.e., Sullivan's theory, attachment theory, social exchange theory). Other theories were developed primarily to understand and explain a specific psychological construct (e.g., self-concept, cognitive development, moral development) and not social relationships, but these theories are important to review because they identify peer influence as a critical component related to the psychological variable of interest. These theories include cognitive-developmental, symbolic interactionist, and social cognitive theories. This section is organized so theories that feature social relationships are discussed first, followed by those theories in which peer influence is a salient component of the model.

> During early childhood peer relations primarily revolve around shared activities and interests.

Sullivan's (1953) developmental theory of interpersonal relationships. Sullivan's (1953) model of interpersonal relations is the most frequently cited conceptual work outlining the developmental significance of peer relationships. According to Sullivan, the salience of peer relationships differs at various stages of the developmental cycle. During early childhood, peer relations primarily revolve around shared activities and interests. In the "juvenile period," or middle childhood (about ages 7-9 years), Sullivan stated that peer group acceptance is essential for children to feel a sense of belonging among same-age mates. Pre- and early adolescence (about ages 10-14 years) marks a time in which interpersonal intimacy needs are sought via the formation of "chumships," or close, dyadic relationships with same-sex peers. According to Sullivan, having a chumship provides youth with feelings of security, psychological well-being, and validation of worth; offers a buffer against loneliness; facilitates social adjustment; and may even compensate for negative family experiences. In later adolescence, the companionship and intimacy of romantic partners exceed the importance of same-sex friendships. Within Sullivan's theorizing, peer group acceptance and close friendships are salient at different developmental periods and serve unique functions based on developmental needs. Many studies conducted in school contexts provide support for the developmental significance of peer group acceptance and friendships according to Sullivan's model (see Bukowski, Newcomb, & Hartup, 1996; Rubin et al., 1998).

Attachment theory. Attachment theory, most notably associated with Bowlby (see Kerns, 1996; Rubin et al., 1998), addresses the quality of the parent-child relationship on a child's later ability to form friendships and effectively interact with peers. According to this perspective, a secure parent-child attachment is one in which the caregiver is characterized by availability, warmth, sensitivity, and responsiveness. The quality of the parent-child attachment is believed to help a child develop a schema or internal working model that connotes ways of thinking, feeling, and acting that translate to relationships outside the family. A secure attachment promotes children's positive social expectations, a sense of security in peer relationships, understanding of reciprocity, and feelings of self-worth. These characteristics are associated with the social skills necessary for successful formation and maintenance of peer relationships. Children who develop secure caregiver attachments, in comparison to children with insecure attachments, demonstrate superior social competence, are more accepted by their peer group, and possess greater friendship quality during the childhood years. Thus the parent-peer linkage is a significant factor to consider in understanding children's ability to develop and nurture supportive peer relationships throughout the lifespan.

Social exchange theory. Social exchange theory (Kelley & Thibaut, 1978; Thibaut & Kelley, 1959) was developed as a general theory of social behavior. The theory has been applied to understanding the initiation, maintenance, and dissolution of interpersonal relationships, including commitment to work relationships, romantic partners, and friendships. The theory emphasizes exchange between individuals in terms of the perceived rewards and costs of their relationship. For example, when individuals feel that the rewards (e.g., companionship, intimacy) of a friendship outweigh the costs of involvement (e.g., conflict), their attraction toward one another will be strong, they will be satisfied with one another, and their commitment to the relationship will remain intact. However, this will be the case only if the reward-to-cost ratio exceeds a person's minimum expectations or standards for a close friendship and potentially more attractive friendships are unavailable. An important characteristic of social exchange theory is the concept of interdependence—interactions that continue to be mutually rewarding will result in individuals' becoming more dependent on one another to obtain rewards.

Laursen (1996) observed that social exchange theory was developed primarily for understanding adult social relationships and revised exchange theory concepts to propose a social relational model of close adolescent relationships. His adaptation of exchange concepts equates closeness with rewards and conflict with costs within interpersonal relationships. That is, adolescents' satisfaction with and commitment to a friendship are determined by gauging the degree of closeness (e.g., intimacy, loyalty) with a friend to disruptions due to conflicts (e.g., fighting, arguing). In a review of literature on closeness in peer relationships, Laursen points to age-related increases in intimacy, loyalty, and companionship among peers and concomitant decreases in these characteristics with parents and siblings. Thus, closeness (i.e., rewards) with a friend during adolescence will necessarily require fulfillment of these needs. Similarly, a review of literature on conflict in peer relationships shows an increase in conflict rates among adolescents compared to younger children; that is, conflict is an important characteristic of close friendships during adolescence. However, negotiation and compromise are more frequently invoked as strategies to preserve the relationship among adolescents than among children. Because adolescents' relationships with adults and peers vary as a function of continuity and change, Laursen states, "a social relational model of development holds that interdependence in close peer relationships emerges gradually with individual maturation and social experience" (p. 190). A developmental perspective of exchange concepts acknowledges age-related changes in physical, social, and emotional needs, as well as changes in social skills and environmental constraints that affect choices in close relationships. Thus, the social relational model offers an appealing theoretical approach for understanding close friendships (same sex and opposite sex) during the important developmental epoch of adolescence.

Cognitive-developmental perspectives. Piaget (1932/1965) focused his efforts on the evolution of cognitive development in children, and peer relationships were considered a critical component contributing to this development. Piaget portrayed children's relationships with peers as being on a "level playing field" in terms of balance and equality, as opposed to children's relationships with adults, which were characterized by power imbalances. Thus children's cognitive, social, moral, and emotional growth can occur through opportunities to disagree, negotiate, and resolve conflicts with peers. In fact, Piaget believed that peer conflict was key to evoking change in children's development by instigating opportunities for friends to

Interactions that continue to be mutually rewarding will make individuals more dependent on one another to obtain rewards.

express differing points of view, problem solve by cooperating with one another in exchanging conflicting perspectives, and reach a mutually beneficial solution to the conflict. In this sense, Piaget viewed peer interactions and relationships as essential to social perspective-taking and moral development. That is, conflict, discussion, and cooperation among equals (i.e., peers) are likely to increase moral reasoning, mutual respect, and prosocial behaviors. Other constructivist theories of moral development (e.g., Haan, Gilligan; see Solomon, this volume) also emphasize reasoned dialogue and conflict resolution among peers as a means of promoting moral growth and development. The cognitive-developmental, or constructivist, perspective has garnered good support in the literature on moral development in sport (Solomon, this volume) and has shown, among other findings, that peers exert an important influence on their age mates' moral reasoning, intentions, and behaviors. Thus, this perspective offers a viable window through which to understand the association between peer relationships and moral development in the physical domain.

Symbolic interactionist perspective. The symbolic interactionist perspective, most commonly associated with James, Cooley, and Mead (see Harter, 1999; Rubin et al., 1998), is primarily concerned with self-concept development. This perspective posits that a sense of self develops as a result of how individuals perceive others view them (i.e., "looking-glass self"). The phrase "In 7th grade who you are is what other 7th graders say you are" (Kevin Arnold, Wonder Years) seems to capture this phenomenon vividly. According to this perspective, peers are an essential component in contributing toward a person's sense of self as well as the ability to understand others (i.e., social perspective taking). Thus, perceived social regard or approval support from peers is thought to be a salient source of self-concept development in youth. Harter's (1999) model of the causes, correlates, and consequences of global self-worth is premised upon the writings of James, Cooley, and Mead and views the self as both a cognitive and social construction. From a cognitive stance, global self-worth is determined by perceptions of competence or adequacy in domains valued as important to an individual. Global self-worth is also socially determined in the perceptions of regard by significant adults and peers. Youth who perceive that parents, teachers, classmates, and close friends view them favorably as people will feel self-satisfied, validated, and worthy.

Harter (1999) has examined the relative contribution of perceived social regard from parents, teachers, classmates, and close friends on global self-evaluations across the lifespan. Approval support from parents predicts self-worth in childhood through adolescence. The importance of peer-approval support in explaining global self-worth increases from childhood to adolescence. Moreover, Harter has found that perceived social regard from one's general peer group (e.g., classmates, community group peers, coworkers) is a stronger source of global self-worth during childhood, adolescence, and adulthood than are close friendships. Finally, Harter's studies show support for the additive effects of perceived competence and approval support on global self-worth among children through adults. Thus Harter's model provides a framework for empirically testing a symbolic interactionist perspective in specific achievement domains. Moreover, the developmental significance of perceived social regard from the broader peer group and close friendships can be determined because self-esteem, emotional responses, and motivational processes represent the consequences in the model.

Social cognitive theory. This theoretical perspective was developed specifically to understand children's learning of knowledge and behaviors (i.e., social, motor, self-regulation) critical for functioning within a variety of contexts. According to Bandura (1986), peers operate as behavior-change agents for one another through the processes of modeling, reinforcement, and punishment. Starting at a young age, children often use each other as a means of learning social behaviors and a variety of skills (including motor skills), as well as a source of information by which children judge their abilities in specific achievement domains. Thus, peer models serve as sources of information and motivation for similar-age observers.

Moreover, accepted behavioral norms are modeled and reinforced by peers; behaviors that go against the grain of socially accepted standards are punished. One can readily see, then, that one's peer group and close friendships may impart salient information about what behaviors are appropriate and inappropriate through the mechanisms of observational learning and social reinforcement. As well, peers serve as standards of social comparison that allow children to determine their relative rank or standing within the peer group on certain skills or abilities.

Research in the physical domain has adopted a social cognitive perspective to examine the physical skill and psychological effects of peer modeling (see McCullagh & Weiss, 2001). For example, children who are similar in personal (age, gender) and psychological (self-efficacy, fear) characteristics impart informational and motivational cues that observers use to facilitate their performance and self-efficacy. Similarly, the role of perceived team norms and approval by peers (teammates, friends) on aggressive tendencies have received considerable attention from a social cognitive perspective (see Weiss & Smith, 2002a). Sport participants who believe that their peers (i.e., teammates) approve of cheating or aggressive behavior to enhance changes of winning are more likely to endorse aggressive actions in sport.

Peer models serve as sources of information and motivation for similar-age observers.

In sum, a number of theoretical perspectives exist from which to frame studies of peer interactions and relationships in a variety of achievement domains including sport. Some of these theories are developmental in nature (Sullivan's theory, attachment theory, Laursen's social-relational model, cognitive-developmental theory). Although the symbolic interactionist and social cognitive theories are not necessarily developmentally focused, they do consider peer influence as central to children's psychosocial development and achievement behaviors. Developmental differences have emerged using the symbolic interactionist perspective regarding the influence of significant adults and peers on global self-worth (Harter, 1999) and using the social cognitive perspective on peer-modeling effects on children's observational learning of physical skills (see McCullagh & Weiss, 2001). We believe that future research adopting one or more of these theoretical perspectives will contribute to a much-needed knowledge base on the developmental significance of peer relationships in physical activity contexts.

Peer Relations Research and Contemporary Issues in Developmental Psychology

Newcomb (Newcomb & Bagwell, 1995; Newcomb, Bukowski, & Pattee, 1993) has conducted two meta-analytic reviews on studies of children's peer relations, one focused upon peer acceptance (popular, controversial, rejected, average, and neglected children) and the other on friendship. Others have relied upon more traditional literature reviews to evaluate research related to peer group acceptance and rejection (e.g., Coie, Dodge, & Kupersmidt, 1990; Ladd & Price, 1993) and friendship relations (e.g., Berndt, 1989; Hartup, 1995, 1996; see Bukowski et al., 1996). In the following section, we discuss the major findings from these reviews.

Peer Acceptance and Friendship

Extent of acceptance (or rejection) by one's peer group is a potent predictor of children's and teenagers' social adjustment, self-evaluations, emotional outcomes, and behaviors (Coie et al., 1990; Newcomb et al., 1993). Children who are well liked by their peers tend to be more socially adjusted and emotionally stable, have higher cognitive abilities and self-concepts, and possess more effective social skills that allow for positive exchanges among peers. By contrast, rejected youth are more likely to evidence adjustment problems, experience anxiety and depression, be less sociable, have lower academic skills, and be aggressive in their behaviors.

Children who fall into the controversial, average, and neglected categories exhibit cognitive abilities, emotional responses, and behaviors somewhere between those of popular and rejected youth. Thus, peer group acceptance and rejection are important antecedents of social and emotional growth, as well as later adjustment and psychopathology.

Several studies have compared characteristics of social exchanges and relationship quality with children who are friends versus those who are nonfriends or acquaintances. Children who are friends spend more time together, engage in more frequent positive interactions, display more cooperative behavior on instrumental tasks, and are more likely to pursue disagreements and arguments with conflict resolution strategies than they do with acquaintances or nonfriends (Newcomb & Bagwell, 1995, 1996). Children who have a close friendship possess better social skills and emotional stability than do children without a friend. With regard to identity of one's friends, they are likely to be similar in interests, activities, and values. Similarities among friends often depend on attributes that define a child's social reputation, a phenomenon termed reputational salience (Hartup, 1996). For example, athletically skilled boys will likely be friends with other athletic boys given that this attribute is highly valued. Finally, friendship quality refers to specific dimensions or qualitative features such as companionship, loyalty, intimacy, instrumental aid, and self-esteem support. Youth who rate their friendships higher on positive and lower on negative (e.g., conflict) qualities are associated with better psychosocial adjustment, social competence, and achievement behaviors (see Bukowski et al., 1996; Hartup & Laursen, 1999; Ladd, 1999).

> Children who have a close friendship possess better social skills and emotional stability than do children without a friend.

The findings just reviewed are rather robust and reveal several trends about children's peer relations primarily in school contexts. As a result of the extant research conducted thus far on peer acceptance and friendship in youth populations, researchers have identified several contemporary issues in the study of peer relationships that should receive more attention in future empirical inquiry. We briefly review several of these issues — ones that we feel hold special relevance for peer relations research in the physical domain. These issues include (a) developmental considerations, (b) influence of specific social contexts, (c) the distinction between peer acceptance and friendship, (d) aspects of friendship contributing to psychosocial outcomes, and (e) the negative side of friendship. We discuss each of these contemporary concerns in turn in the following paragraphs.

Contemporary Issues

Developmental variations in peer relationships and broader social networks (e.g., parents, siblings, teachers) have drawn considerable empirical interest (e.g., Aboud & Mendelson, 1996; Belle, 1989; Berndt & Perry, 1986, 1990; Epstein, 1989; Furman & Buhrmester, 1992). Younger children's friendships tend to be defined more by overt, behavioral characteristics such as shared activities and interests, whereas older children and adolescents view the psychological features of their friendships as more critical (e.g., intimate self-disclosure, loyalty, emotional support, esteem enhancement). Girls' peer groups tend to be smaller and engage in more intimate, self-disclosure activities (e.g., conversing), whereas boys' networks are quite large and tend to emphasize shared activities such as sports and games (see also Lever, 1976, 1978). Gender differences in friendship quality also abound, with girls citing esteem enhancement, emotional support, affection, and intimacy as more prevalent in their friendships, whereas boys' interactions more frequently involve conflict and competitiveness (Hartup, 1989).

The specific social context in which peer interactions occur is a crucial consideration for understanding the significance of group and dyadic relationships. The bulk of research on youths' peer relations has been conducted within school environments, prompting several researchers to recommend that peer interactions and relationships should be studied within specific social contexts that are salient to children and adolescents (Hartup, 1999; Ladd & Price, 1993; Newcomb & Bagwell, 1995; Newcomb et al., 1993). Relevant behavioral settings for youth other than academic activities include talking on the phone, playing sports, listening to or playing music, artistic activities (e.g., drawing, painting, acting), and other community activities (e.g., Patrick et al., 1999; Zarbatany, Hartmann, & Rankin, 1990). Each of these settings contains certain cultural norms and expectations that may require differential peer exchanges (e.g., competition, cooperation) or friendship supportive functions (e.g., considerateness, ego reinforcement, helping, sharing). Thus, one cannot assume that findings related to peer relations in one context necessarily generalize to relationships in other contexts.

The conceptual distinction between peer acceptance (a group-oriented construct) and friendship (a specific dyadic relationship) has elicited a call for simultaneously assessing the unique and relative influence of each social construct on adjustment, emotions, and behaviors (e.g., Aboud & Mendelson, 1996; Bukowski & Hoza, 1989; Newcomb et al., 1993). Although popular children tend to have more friends, better friendship quality, and stronger social skills than do those less popular (e.g., rejected, neglected), unpopular children often do have reciprocated friendships. For example, Parker and Asher (1993) found that all high-accepted children had reciprocated friends and most low-accepted youth did as well. Moreover, friendship quality contributed above and beyond peer acceptance to feelings of loneliness, supporting the distinct nature of these peer constructs. That is, low-accepted children who had a close friend experienced less loneliness than those who did not have a friend, suggesting that friendship may serve as a buffer against feelings of rejection from the broader peer group.

There are several aspects of friendship that may contribute to psychosocial outcomes. Hartup (1995, 1996) has argued compellingly for the need to consider three friendship aspects—having friends, the identity of one's friends, and friendship quality—as unique contributors to developmental outcomes. However, most of the research conducted to date has investigated the "having friends" aspect by comparing youth with and without a "chum" on a host of social, emotional, and behavioral variables. In response to Hartup's plea, an abundance of research has recently appeared on *who* popular and rejected youth hang out with (e.g., Mahoney & Stattin, 2000), as well as the salience of friendship quality (e.g., intimacy, companionship, conflict) on self-perceptions and socioemotional outcomes (e.g., Berndt, 1996). Others (Bukowski & Hoza, 1989; Furman, 1996; Ladd, 1999) have suggested that children's multiple friendships are worthy of study to determine whether "more is better" when it comes to social development and behaviors and whether certain friendships offer differential benefits in terms of qualitative features and fulfillment of interpersonal needs.

The negative sides of friendship such as competitiveness, aggression, and disagreement have received relatively less attention than the positive features of friendship (Berndt, 1996; Hartup & Laursen, 1999; Ladd & Price, 1993; Laursen, 1996; Newcomb & Bagwell, 1995). Yet arguing, teasing, fighting, and even betrayal are potential exchanges between friends given the amount of time spent together and the closeness achieved by disclosing thoughts and feelings. No significant differences are observed in frequency of conflict between friends and nonfriends, but friends are much more concerned with resolving disagreements and returning to harmonious interactions. However, greater conflict among friends has often been related to negative attitudes and maladaptive behaviors that are likely to threaten friendship

> Positive and negative friendship features are both essential to completely understand the developmental significance of peer relations in a variety of behavioral settings.

continuity (Newcomb & Bagwell, 1995). Certain contexts (e.g., organized sport) may be more likely to instigate conflicts such as those that promote competitiveness (Hartup, 1989). Thus, positive *and* negative friendship features are both essential to completely understand the developmental significance of peer relations in a variety of behavioral settings.

The knowledge base on peer relations within developmental psychology is particularly rich despite calls for empirical research in understudied areas such as those mentioned in this section. By contrast, research on how variations in peer acceptance and friendship influence psychosocial outcomes within physical activity contexts is much less developed. This is surprising given the salient role of peers in participation motivation, sources of enjoyment, and moral development, among others. The knowledge base on peer relations in the physical domain is presented next, with an eye toward highlighting the potential for extending the boundaries of this knowledge in future investigations.

RESEARCH ON PEER INFLUENCE IN THE PHYSICAL ACTIVITY DOMAIN

Until recently, research on peer influence in sport and physical activity contexts was primarily descriptive. For example studies established an association between popularity and athletic competence or indirectly implicated peers as a source of self-esteem enhancement. Recent inquiry has emanated more directly from concepts and issues identified in developmental psychology such as age and gender variations and distinguishing between peer group acceptance and friendship influences. Most important, this research has delved into sport and physical contexts as salient settings for forming and nurturing close peer relationships that, in turn, have the potential for promoting positive psychosocial development and achievement behaviors. In this section, we review the knowledge base on peer influence within physical activity contexts. The section is organized into five broad categories: (a) peer acceptance; (b) peers as a source of self-perceptions, affective experiences, and motivational processes; (c) friendship; (d) peer relations and moral development; and (e) interventions designed to enhance peer relationships.

Peer Acceptance

The earliest research on peer relations within sport contexts focused upon athletic ability as a salient characteristic for determining popularity among one's peer group. The following studies established this linkage.

Peer acceptance and athletic ability. Children's and adolescents' perceptions of what qualities or characteristics are important for being popular with one's peers have been the focus of many studies. Youth are asked to respond to a question such as "What would make you (or girls, boys) well liked by or popular with your classmates?" Respondents are given a choice among such qualities as being a good athlete, being handsome or pretty, getting good grades, and being a leader of activities, among others (e.g., having lots of money). Being good at sports is consistently ranked first by and for boys, but characteristics such as being pretty, getting good grades, and being an activity leader are more highly valued as social acceptance criteria for girls. These findings hold for elementary school-aged children (Buchanan, Blankenbaker, & Cotten, 1976; Chase & Dummer, 1992) and adolescents (e.g., Adler, Kless, & Adler, 1992; Feltz, 1978; Williams & White, 1983). Moreover, the gender appropriateness of the sport has been associated with higher or lower social acceptance (Holland & Andre, 1994; Kane, 1988). For example, Holland and Andre found that high school students rated their female and male peers as more popular if they participated in traditionally feminine (e.g., volleyball, gymnastics) or masculine (e.g., football, baseball) sports, respectively.

To quantify the tie between peer acceptance and athletic competence, Weiss and Duncan (1992) assessed perceived and actual (teachers' ratings) social acceptance and physical competence among 8- to 13-year-old boys and girls participating in an instructional sports program. Children who were rated as more athletically skilled and believed they were good in sports were also those who were rated as more successful in peer relations and perceived greater acceptance by their peer group. Collectively, these studies demonstrate that athletic ability (actual and perceived) and popularity with one's peer group (actual and perceived) are strongly linked for children and adolescents.

Peer acceptance, athletic ability, and leadership status. The tie between being a good athlete and acceptance by one's peer group also translates to leadership status within sport settings (i.e., team captains, central position players). Evans (cited in Evans & Roberts, 1987) studied the influence of physical competence on peer relations by observing elementary-aged boys (grades 3-6) interacting with their peers on the school playground and interviewing them about these experiences. The best athletes were afforded peer leadership status by serving as team captains, being selected for teams early in the "choosing up sides" process, playing dominant positions on offense and defense, and making decisions about who could play. These opportunities allowed the more athletic boys to further develop physically (i.e., improve skills) and socially (i.e., strengthen friendships). Low-skilled boys, by contrast, were picked much later in the "player draft," occupied peripheral positions (e.g., right field), and were often "locked out" of games by being denied entry.

> Findings suggest that high peer status is based on a combination of physical and psychological characteristics.

A few studies have explored correlates of peer leadership behavior within high school team sports. Lee, Coburn, and Partridge (1981) found that team captains within high school boys' soccer teams were among the best-skilled players and played central field positions (center backs, midfielders), which reinforces Evans and Roberts' (1987) observations of boys playing unorganized sport. Glenn and Horn (1993) studied peer leadership status within girls' high school soccer teams. In addition to skill level and field position, players' psychological characteristics were examined as predictors of peer leadership behavior. Teammates rated a player favorably on leadership ability if she was a skilled soccer player, was confident about her soccer skills, and displayed instrumental and expressive behaviors. These findings suggest that high peer status (i.e., team leader) is based on a combination of physical and psychological characteristics. Although a couple of studies exist on peer leadership within collegiate teams, the studies by Lee et al. and Glenn and Horn are the only ones located to date on peer leadership within organized youth teams. Glenn and Horn's study provides an interesting window through which to view peer group status within intact youth teams, and certainly this topic is a salient one to pursue from both theoretical and practical perspectives.

Peers as a Source of Self-Perceptions, Affective Experiences, and Motivational Processes

Sullivan (1953) contended that peer relationships are critical to developing a sense of belonging, self-validation, and psychological well-being, as well as preventing loneliness and facilitating social adjustment. Thus, it is not surprising that peers are found to be a significant influence on youths' self-perceptions, affect, and motivation in the physical domain. Peer relationships and self-perceptions, affective responses, and motivational processes related to physical activity and sport are discussed in turn in the following sections.

Self-perceptions: Perceived competence and self-esteem. A rich literature exists on sources of information children and adolescents use to judge how physically competent they are (Horn, this volume). Age-related differences are observed in judgment criteria such as adult feedback, peer evaluation and comparison, and self-referenced information (e.g., skill improvement). Across the childhood years (ages 7-12), children show a decline in use of parental feedback and performance outcome and heightened reliance upon peer comparison and evaluation as self-ability judgment sources. Peer comparison and evaluation remain salient criteria during early adolescence (ages 13-15 years) and then decline in favor of self-referenced and integrated forms of competence information (including peers) during later adolescence (ages 16-18).

Studying the interactions between players helps psychologists understand the effects of competition and cooperation.

Comparison to and evaluation by peers, then, hold special relevance for helping children and adolescents assess their ability in physical activity and sports.

Ebbeck and Stuart (1993, 1996) assessed relationships among perceived physical competence, importance of being successful (to oneself, one's parents, one's coach, and one's teammates), and global self-worth in two youth sport samples. Perceived competence was the strongest predictor of self-esteem in the first study, but perceived parent importance (ages 8-9 years) and teammate importance (ages 12-13 years) contributed beyond perceived competence to predict self-worth in the second study. These results reveal age-related differences in beliefs about who values being successful in sport and how such beliefs relate to global self-evaluations. Likewise, A. L. Smith (1999) found that perceptions of higher peer acceptance among adolescents (ages 12-15 years) were associated with greater physical self-worth that, in turn, influenced positive affect and intrinsic motivation toward physical activity.

Affective responses: Enjoyment and anxiety. Although a wide spectrum of affective responses is associated with physical achievements (e.g., "the thrill of victory and agony of defeat"), researchers frequently devote attention to feelings of enjoyment and anxiety experienced by young sport participants. During childhood and adolescence, opportunities to form and strengthen friendships, obtain social recognition for achievements, and experience positive team interactions and supportiveness are cited as important contributors to sport enjoyment (Scanlan, Carpenter, Lobel, & Simons, 1993; see Scanlan & Simons, 1992). Sport enjoyment, in turn, is one of the strongest predictors of continued involvement in sport and physical activity.

Several studies have assessed young athletes' sources of competitive anxiety and stress. Two consistent sources of stress for child and adolescent competitors are fear of performance failure and fear of negative evaluation from parents, coaches, and teammates (see Gould, 1993). Other sources of stress include problems in social relationships (e.g., no time for friends, peer pressure, missing out on activities like "hanging out") and interpersonal conflicts (Donnelly, 1993; Scanlan, Stein, & Ravizza, 1991). Taken together, these studies show that peer relationships are intimately tied to sources of sport enjoyment *and* anxiety among children and adolescents.

The influence of peer interactions on early adolescent girls' (ages 11-12 years) positive and negative affect doing physical activities was the focus of a naturalistic study by Kunesh, Hasbrook, and Lewthwaite (1992). Observations, sociometric ratings, and interviews were used to examine peer relations in varying contexts (school, neighborhood) and activity types (formal sport, physically active games, physical activity for exercise). Male classmates rated the girls in this study low in peer acceptance and treated them negatively during school physical education and sport activities. Girls reported feelings of anxiety and embarrassment as a result of the boys' teasing, criticizing, name-calling, exclusion, and subordination of physical skills, which resulted in girls' attempts to avoid these situations on future occasions. By contrast, girls reported having fun doing informal physical activity in their neighborhood and viewed the few negative peer interactions in this setting as a natural part of playing because they came from friends whom they knew liked them. Moreover, the girls remained motivated to seek and continue participating in games at home.

The Kunesh et al. (1992) study is noteworthy for its multimethod approach and sensitivity to context- and activity-specific variations in peer interactions and affective responses. The age group selected for study was also important as evidence shows that, starting at about 11-12 years, girls show a downward spiral in physical activity levels that extends throughout the adolescent years (U.S. Dept. of Health and Human Services, 1996). If negative peer interactions and concomitant anxiety and embarrassment are correlated with lower activity levels, then educational implications are apparent. It is also possible that girls in this study were similar in many respects to the low-skilled, low-accepted boys in Evans' (cited in Evans & Roberts, 1987) study of peer status and athletic ability. Interview quotes from these boys were vivid with negative affective responses and withdrawn behavior from sport activities that perpetuated the pecking order of athletic male dominance.

Motivational processes: Reasons for participating, physical activity choices, and participation levels. The extant descriptive research on participation motivation implicates social acceptance (e.g., to be part of a team) and friendship (e.g., to be with and make friends) as salient reasons for sport involvement among children and adolescents (see Weiss & Ferrer-Caja, 2002). In one of the few lifespan studies, Brodkin and Weiss (1990) assessed reasons for participating among 6- to 60+-year-old age-group swimmers. Social status reasons were highest for the 15- to 22-year-old swimmers, reasons related to significant others (parents and friends want me to participate) were highest for 6- to 9-year-olds and 10- to 14-year-olds, and affiliation reasons (be with and make friends) were salient for all age groups.

Klint and Weiss (1987) examined the theoretical linkage between social acceptance and reasons for participating among 8- to 16-year-old gymnasts. Those scoring higher on perceived peer acceptance rated affiliation motives (be with and make friends, best friends want me to participate, team atmosphere) as more important than did lower-scoring gymnasts. Thus, athletes holding stronger social acceptance beliefs may be primarily motivated to demonstrate and develop their skills in making friends and getting along with teammates. Weiss, McAuley, Ebbeck, and Wiese (1990) also reported a theoretical linkage between peer acceptance and motivational processes in the form of causal attributions. Children higher in peer acceptance reported more internal, stable, and personally controllable attributions for interpersonal success than did those lower in peer acceptance. Such attributions are hypothesized to translate to higher success expectations, positive affect, and future motivated behavior.

Coakley and White (1992) interviewed adolescents about factors related to their physical activity decisions. Two of the emergent themes were constraints related to opposite-sex friends and social support from same-sex friends. Responses varied depending on gender. For girls with a boyfriend, the relationship came first and sport interests second, meaning that they were

> Athletes holding stronger social acceptance beliefs may be primarily motivated to demonstrate and develop their skills in making friends along with teammates.

likely to sacrifice their own activity to accommodate their boyfriend's schedule. For boys with a girlfriend, their sport needs came first and the relationship was secondary such that their activity patterns were not altered in the least. Opposite-sex relationships thus had a critical impact on physical activity behavior but in differing ways for females and males. Moreover, females were more likely than males to mention the crucial importance of encouragement and support from same-sex friends in getting and staying involved in sport and physical activity. Without such support (e.g., companionship, emotional support, esteem enhancement), withdrawing from physical activity involvement was more likely. By contrast, males did not indicate that support from same-sex friends was all that important for influencing their motivation to remain physically active. Thus, peer influence on participation choices for adolescent girls and boys differed considerably, with girls particularly susceptible to variations in physical activity involvement due to their peer relationships.

Friends' (and parents') influence on physical activity behavior was the focus of a large-scale study by Anderssen and Wold (1992). They adopted a social cognitive theoretical perspective to examine the influence of parent and peer modeling, social support, and value toward physical activity on 13-year-old youths' self-reported frequency of sports and exercise participation outside of school hours. Significant but low-moderate correlations were found between best friends' and participant's physical activity level ($r = .23$ and $.31$ for boys and girls, respectively) and between friends' encouragement to exercise and participant's physical activity level ($r = .21, .30$). Correlations for friends' influence and girls' physical activity were higher than those for boys' activity. Similarly, friends' influence on physical activity levels was slightly higher than for parental influence.

Collectively, the studies reported in this section demonstrate the crucial role that peers play in youths' development of self-perceptions, enjoyable and anxiety-provoking experiences, and motivated behaviors in the physical domain. The varying perspectives employed by these studies (theoretical basis, methodology) reinforce the powerful influence of peers in this behavioral context. Given these rather robust findings, it is surprising that comparatively fewer studies have been conducted on peer influence than on that of parents and coaches. Peers have scarcely been considered as a target for intervention studies designed to change physical activity and sport behaviors.

Friendship

Studies of sport friendships have emerged over the last decade showing encouraging findings related to youths' psychological well-being and physical activity involvement. These studies have explored variations in friendship expectations, the influence of friendship quality and support on psychosocial outcomes, and friendship across activity contexts. The emergence of studies specific to the construct of friendship is consonant with a shift from peer acceptance to friendship research in mainstream developmental psychology.

Friendship expectations. A few studies have focused upon friendship expectations within sport and other peer activity contexts (Bigelow, Lewko, & Salhani, 1989; Zarbatany, Ghesquiere, & Mohr, 1992; Zarbatany et al., 1990). Bigelow et al. found that 9- to 12-year-old male ice-hockey and female ringette players viewed team sport participation as a context for forming and developing friendships in general and qualities with friends such as intimate self-disclosure (i.e., sharing feelings) and stimulation value (i.e., learning interesting things together) in particular.

Zarbatany et al. (1990, 1992) were interested in the psychological functions of peer activities among preadolescents (ages 10-12 years). Youth rated their expectations as well as liked and disliked behaviors of friends while participating in a variety of activity contexts (e.g., watching TV, studying, doing sports, conversing). In the first study (Zarbatany et al., 1990), children rated the most important activities with peers as playing noncontact sports, watching TV, listening to records, conversing, talking on the telephone, playing sports and games, going to parties, and hanging out. Subsequently, the psychological functions of peer activities were determined based on children's ratings of their most liked behaviors while doing these activities. Peer activities were seen as fulfilling three functions: (a) enhancing relationships and a sense of belonging, (b) promoting concern for achievement and integrity of the self, and (c) providing opportunities for instruction and learning. Noncompetitive activities (e.g., conversing, watching TV) were viewed as providing more opportunities for development of sociability, whereas participation in sports activities was seen as contributing more to achievement striving and opportunities for learning. The authors concluded that children should be exposed to a full range of peer activities to maximize opportunities for developing a wide range of psychosocial skills and experiences.

In a follow-up study (Zarbatany et al., 1992), friendship expectations for the most prevalent peer activities were assessed among preadolescents (ages 10-12 years). Social contexts were categorized as relationship-focused activities (talking on the telephone, watching television/listening to records), competitive activities (sports, games), and academic activities (schoolwork, library work). Children's friendship expectations varied depending on the peer context. Ego reinforcement, preferential treatment, and character and physical admiration were primary expectations when playing sports and games with friends. By contrast, inclusion, considerateness, common interests, sharing, and acceptance were prevalent expectations for TV/records and phone conversations; and helping and considerateness were paramount for academic activities. The studies of Zarbatany et al. (1990, 1992) suggest that the nature of friendships and their influence on psychosocial development should be considered within the specific social contexts in which peer interactions and relationships occur.

Friendship quality and support. Friendship quality and support on several dimensions (e.g., intimacy, loyalty, esteem enhancement, companionship) have been highlighted in the developmental psychology literature as essential aspects contributing to positive psychological growth (Furman & Buhrmester, 1992; Hartup, 1996; Newcomb & Bagwell, 1995). A number of studies exploring sport friendship quality or support have emerged in recent years (Duncan, 1993; A. L. Smith, 1999; Weiss & Smith, 1999, 2002b; Weiss et al., 1996). Duncan examined cognitive (causal attributions) and social (friendship support) contributors to early adolescents' (ages 12-14 years) emotional states and motivational processes related to physical activity. Youth who perceived greater companionship and esteem support from their friends in physical education reported greater positive affect, future success expectancies, and intrinsic interest to participate in physical activity outside of school. A. L. Smith examined the influence of close friendship on psychosocial variables and physical activity motivation among early adolescents (ages 12-15 years) based on Harter's (1978, 1987) theoretical perspective. For both boys and girls, A. L. Smith found that close friendship predicted positive affective experiences and indirectly influenced intrinsic motivation toward physical activity through affect. For girls only, close friendship also indirectly influenced physical activity behavior through positive affect and intrinsic motivation toward physical activity.

Weiss and Smith (1999, 2002b; Weiss et al., 1996) conducted a series of studies to unravel several answers about children's and teenagers' perceptions of sport friendship quality. In the first study, Weiss et al. (1996) interviewed 8- to 16-year-old children about perceptions of positive and negative aspects of their best sport friendship. An array of 12 positive friendship dimensions included companionship, pleasant play/association, self-esteem enhancement, help and guidance, prosocial behavior, intimacy, loyalty, things in common (i.e., similar

Friendship quality and support have been highlighted in the developmental psychology literature as essential contributors to positive psychological growth.

interests, beliefs, and values), attractive personal qualities, emotional support, absence of conflicts, and conflict resolution. Youth also identified some of the downsides or negative features of their best sport friendships: conflict, unattractive personal qualities, betrayal, and inaccessibility. Table 1 displays descriptions and higher-order themes for each of the positive and negative friendship features.

Age differences emerged for four of the positive friendship dimensions. The two younger groups (8-9, 10-12 years) identified prosocial behavior and loyalty more frequently than did adolescents (13-16 years), whereas the two older groups cited attractive personal qualities more often than younger children did. Intimacy was mentioned in increasingly higher percentages with age. The findings for prosocial behavior and intimacy are consistent with developmental research, but those for loyalty and attractive personal qualities are contrary. However, higher-order themes for loyalty depicted *overt* characteristics such as "he or she sticks up for me," "we pick each other to do things," and "we can depend on each other" that would align with younger children's friendship conceptions. Moreover, younger children were more likely to identify attractive *physical* qualities (e.g., "I would miss her eyes," 8-year-old girl) whereas older children and adolescents focused upon attractive *psychological* qualities (e.g., "she just watches out for people... she makes sure they don't get hurt," 11-year-old girl). These tendencies are consistent with the developmental literature. Gender differences were apparent only for the friendship dimension of emotional support, with girls citing this more frequently. Because the boys and girls in this study were voluntarily attending an instructional sport program and came from families who valued and endorsed physical activity, it was not surprising that there were more gender similarities than differences in conceptions of best friendship quality.

Based on their interview findings, Weiss and Smith (1999) developed and validated the Sport Friendship Quality Scale (SFQS) through a series of three studies using independent youth sport samples. The SFQS allows quantification of sport friendship quality and thereby can be used to answer questions related to antecedents, correlates, and outcomes of friendship quality in the physical domain. This measure consists of six friendship scales: companionship and pleasant play, loyalty and intimacy, self-esteem enhancement and supportiveness, things in common (i.e., similar interests and beliefs), conflict resolution, and conflict. Sample items for each scale are seen in Table 2.

Weiss and Smith (2002b) obtained additional support for the validity of the SFQS while concurrently investigating age and gender differences and the relationship between friendship dimensions and motivation variables among junior tennis players (ages 10-18 years). Adolescent players (ages 14-18 years) rated their best tennis friendships higher in loyalty and intimacy, things in common, and conflict than did early adolescent players (ages 10-13 years), who rated companionship and pleasant play higher. Female players rated self-esteem enhancement and supportiveness, loyalty and intimacy, and things in common as more characteristic of their best tennis friendship than did male players, who rated conflict higher. These findings are consistent with developmental psychology literature concerning age and gender variations in friendship quality. Finally, players scoring higher on friendship dimensions of companionship/pleasant play, conflict resolution, and things in common rated enjoyment of and commitment to playing tennis higher than did players scoring lower on these dimensions. Thus, young tennis players who rated their relationships with their best tennis friend as higher in positive qualities expressed greater positive affective responses and motivational intentions. These results point to the developmental significance of sport friendship quality.

Friendship and participation across activity contexts. Recent studies have investigated how participation in a variety of activity domains (e.g., socializing, sports, arts) contributes to beliefs and behaviors related to friendship characteristics, quality, and social support. Patrick et al. (1999) investigated the contribution of peer relationships to adolescents' commitment to

Table 1
Descriptions and Examples of Higher-Order Themes for Positive and Negative Friendship Features (Weiss et al., 1996)

Dimension	Description	Higher-Order Themes
Companionship	hanging out together, spending time together, doing things together	we do many things together I've known him a long time we go to each other's houses
Pleasant play/ association	a positive valence attached to being together or spending time together	we enjoy doing things together we compete in a positive way we joke around together
Self-esteem enhancement	saying or doing things to boost one's feelings of self-worth	we positively reinforce each other she is accepting of my mistakes we respect each other he makes me feel good
Intimacy	interactions or mutual feelings of a close personal nature	we disclose our feelings to each other we understand each other's feelings we trust each other we have a bond with each other
Emotional support	feelings of concern for one another	we care about each other he or she fills a void in my life
Help and guidance	instrumental assistance; tangible support	we help each other in sports we help each other to learn sport skills
Prosocial behaviors	saying or doing things that conform to social convention	he shares things we do nice things for each other she doesn't do mean things to me
Loyalty	being there for the person, a sense of obligation to another	he or she sticks up for me we pick each other to do things we can depend on each other
Absence of conflicts	refraining from arguments, fights, or judgmental attitudes	we rarely argue/fight we're accepting of each other we're agreeable with one another
Conflict resolution	getting over fights or arguments	we resolve our conflicts
Attractive personal qualities	positive personal characteristics	I like his personality his or her physical features her or his attractive personal attributes
Things in common	similarity of interests, activities, and values	similar beliefs and activities we have a similar interest in sports we have similar school interests
Conflict	negative behaviors that cause disagreement, disrespect, or dissension between friends	verbal insults argumentation negative competitiveness physical aggression
Betrayal	actions of disloyalty or insensitivity	she says she'll stop being my friend he pays more attention to another friend he'll ignore me
Unattractive personal qualities	undesirable personality or behavioral characteristics	negative characteristics different views self-centered
Inaccessible	infrequent opportunities to interact together	we don't play much together she has friends other than me he's away a lot

TABLE 2
Sample Items on the Sport Friendship Quality Scale (SFQS; Weiss & Smith, 1999)

Dimension	Sample items
Companionship and Pleasant Play	My friend and I do fun things My friend and I play well together
Self-Esteem Enhancement and Supportiveness	My friend gives me a second chance to perform a skill My friend and I praise each other for doing sports well
Loyalty and Intimacy	My friend and I can talk about anything My friend and I stick up for each other in sports
Things in Common	My friend and I have common interests My friend and I think the same way My friend and I have the same values
Conflict Resolution	My friend and I make up easily when we have a fight My friend and I try to work things out when we disagree
Conflict	My friend and I get mad at each other My friend and I fight My friend and I have arguments

their talent domains including sport, music, drama, art, and dance. A consistent theme across activity contexts, including sport, was perception of social benefits accrued from involvement such as making friends, enhancing social skills, and gaining confidence in relating to peers. Moreover, youth described their friendships as high in intimacy and fellowship, as well as having common values and attitudes.

Patrick et al. (1999) found that both female and male participants cited social benefits from their talent activity. However, girls were more likely than were boys to express dissatisfaction with amount of time spent with friends outside of their talent activity, to say that competitiveness within their activity threatened friendships, and to cite dissatisfaction and competitiveness as reasons for thinking about quitting. Finally, participants saw friendships as contributors to their enjoyment of and commitment to their talent activity. For participants who felt their intense involvement took away from precious social time with nonsport friends, commitment was undermined or negatively influenced. However, some participants addressed this dilemma by remaining involved in their talent activity *and* joining a less physically intense but more socially oriented activity in which their friends participated (e.g., school team/group). For those participants who were motivated to remain friends with members on their team, commitment was positively affected. In other words, they remained highly motivated to continue participating to sustain valued friendships that would be lost if they no longer were involved.

Zarbatany (Zarbatany, McDougall, & Hymel, 2000) pursued her line of research on context-specific variations in friendship by examining how socializing, competitive sport, and academic activities contribute to best friendship intimacy among preadolescents (ages 10-12 years). Girls were more likely than boys to participate in socializing activities with their best friends, whereas boys more frequently interacted with their best friends doing sports. However, both boys and girls engaged fairly extensively in socializing *and* competitive activities. For boys, best friendship intimacy was predicted by higher participation levels with a best friend in socializing activities, a higher proportion of opposite-sex friends, and *lower* participation in team sports. Girls' best friendship intimacy was explained only by higher participation in socializing activities with a best friend. These results point to socializing activities (conversing, going to restaurants, listening to music) as ones that promote the quality of intimacy in best friends. Interestingly, more experience in competitive team sports was associated with lower best friendship intimacy for boys. The researchers also examined contributors to boys' and girls' perceptions of intimate social support from peers, which was defined as the availability of close peers and the fulfillment of intimacy needs with peers. Again, interesting gender variations were found. For girls, only best friendship intimacy predicted perceived intimate support from peers. However, for boys, *higher* participation in team sports and studying activities contributed beyond best friendship intimacy to explain intimate peer support. These findings would appear to be at odds with those reported earlier for predictors of best friendship intimacy; the authors conjectured that while boys' higher team sport involvement was related to lower intimacy within a *dyadic* relationship, involvement was associated positively with feelings of closeness with peer *group* relationships. They went on to say that boys may fulfill their intimacy needs through team sport participation or shared activities, whereas girls are more likely to view self-disclosure activities as consonant with intimacy need fulfillment.

The structure of peer activities in relation to friendship characteristics and antisocial behavior was the focus of a study by Mahoney and Stattin (2000). The authors posited that skill-building goals, regular schedules, and adult leaders typically characterize highly structured activities (e.g., sports, girl/boy scouts). By contrast, unstructured activities are spontaneous, exclude adult guidance, and do not target skill development (e.g., watching television). Moreover, social contexts within highly structured, as compared to unstructured, activities tend to offer greater social complexity in terms of peer interactions. Girls and boys (14 years of age) who varied in structured peer activity involvement were compared on who their friends were and the propensity to engage in antisocial behaviors (e.g., gang up on others, take part in fights). Both boys and girls participating in structured activities were less likely than those in unstructured activities to have deviant friends (i.e., friends who do poorly in school, stay out late at night) and to engage in antisocial behaviors. These results suggest that organized sport may serve as a context for helping youth form and develop healthy friendships, as well as discourage antisocial behaviors.

> Some studies show that girls are more likely than boys to participate in socializing activities with their best friends, whereas boys are more likely to interact with their best friends doing sports.

The review of literature in this section demonstrates that the nature and significance of close friendship in physical activity and sport contexts have been topics of great interest over the last several years. The findings indicate that having a close friend, experiencing positive friendship quality, and perceiving social support from friends are strong predictors of positive self-evaluations, affective responses, and motivational processes in the physical domain. As such, the topic of peer influence takes on even greater meaning in an effort to promote healthy psychosocial and behavioral outcomes among youth. In the next section, we will see that peer acceptance and friendship are also important contributors to moral development in youth.

Peer Relations and Moral Development

Many theorists suggest that strong peer relationships help an individual develop moral sensitivity, enhance moral reasoning, and act in prosocial manners (e.g., Bandura, 1986; Bukowski

& Sippola, 1996; Damon, 1988; Piaget, 1932/1965; Sullivan, 1953). Moral development likely occurs through interactions that include cooperation, conflict, and negotiation with others of equal status—one's peers. Much research, in contrast, documents the negative influence peers often have on the behavior of adolescents—drugs, violence, and sexual promiscuity, among others (see Hartup, 1996). Which of these views is correct? Both points of view have been verified, suggesting that moral development occurs not only from having strong peer relations, but also from the identity and values of one's peers. In short, the values, beliefs, and behaviors of one's peer group can influence moral development in either positive or negative ways.

Friendship and moral development. Bukowski and Sippola (1996) suggested that friendship and morality are intimately linked because friendship characteristics such as generosity, loyalty, trust, commitment, and honesty are moral parameters that emphasize mutuality of relationships and responsibility towards others. Having friends often means sharing stories and moral conflicts, being responsive and committed to others, and expecting the same treatment in return. The affective ties between friends help to motivate changes in moral reasoning by allowing youth to recognize the importance of moral standards such as justice, kindness, and honesty (Damon, 1988).

The strength of these affective ties may depend on the level of friendship experienced by two individuals. Damon (1977) has outlined three levels of friendship for children. At the first level, friendships are pleasure based. Children seek friendships with others who bring them pleasure or who have concrete possessions or characteristics that make them happy. As children progress to the second level, they use psychological characteristics such as kindness and helpfulness to distinguish friends from other peers. Reciprocal trust and assisting one another are important aspects of friendship at this level. At the third level, children accept friends for who they are and are more prone to take psychological risks. Friends at this high level share their innermost thoughts, feelings, and secrets. They begin to realize the long-standing nature of friendships, emphasize loyalty, and look to maintain friendships despite temporary problems in the short run. These levels of friendship indicate the increased intimacy, assistance, and affective ties that occur as friendships reach higher levels and may parallel increases in moral reasoning (Bukowski & Sippola, 1996).

Although there exists a conceptual link between peers and moral development, little research has directly examined this tie. Research within the academic domain suggests that peer acceptance, friendship, and social behaviors are positively related to moral reasoning level. For example, Bear and Rys (1994) found that higher peer acceptance was related to higher moral reasoning among second- and third-grade boys but not among girls. Schonert-Reichel (1999) simultaneously examined the influence of a variety of peer group (acceptance, leadership status, social behaviors) and friendship (number of friends, friendship quality, friendship activities) variables on moral reasoning among fifth, sixth, and seventh graders. For girls, prosocial behavior, number of close friendships, and participation in agentic activities (e.g., sports) predicted higher moral reasoning levels. For boys, number of close friends and prosocial and antisocial behaviors positively predicted moral reasoning. Thus, both peer group and friendship relations were associated with moral reasoning among girls and boys. The finding for boys of a positive relationship between antisocial behaviors and moral reasoning ran counter to moral development research and should be pursued in future investigations.

Within the physical domain, the limited number of studies that associate peers and moral development have focused on group-level processes and perceptions rather than friendships or the influence of single individuals. The results of these studies provide insight into the growing social power of peers from childhood to adolescence. The majority of these studies emanated from social learning theory and examined the relationship between perceived social approval of aggressive actions by significant others and one's own attitudes and behaviors (see Weiss & Smith, 2002a). Aggression research taps moral development in sport because higher moral reasoning relates to lower levels of aggression. Unfortunately, the influence of *sport* friendships on moral development can only be speculated at the present time.

Peers and moral development in sport contexts. Early research by M. D. Smith (1974, 1975, 1979) focused on the influence of significant adults and peers on aggressive behavior within the sport of ice hockey. M. D. Smith (1974) found that players' perceptions of positive sanctions by nonplaying peers for engaging in aggressive behavior on the ice was related to selection of more violent role models. Moreover, peers were more influential than parents concerning these role-model selections. In turn, having more violent role models was predictive of greater assaultive behavior and penalty time. M. D. Smith (1975) found that players viewed fathers and peers (both teammates and off-ice friends) as more favorable to fighting back than were mothers or coaches. Players also perceived peers as more approving of starting fights than parents were. M. D. Smith (1979) also assessed differences in significant others' attitudes towards illegal violence. Illegal violence was viewed as increasingly commended at higher levels of competition and in older age leagues. In addition, most players perceived teammates as more approving than themselves of fighting, suggesting that individuals may act in accordance with peer norms rather than their own beliefs. Peer pressure may have played a large role in such decisions to aggress.

Mugno and Feltz (1985) replicated and extended M. D. Smith's studies of perceived social approval by significant others to playing styles among football players. Friends, followed by spectators, were viewed by the participants as most accepting of illegal violence, whereas mothers were perceived as least accepting. High school players perceived greater approval from friends than did youth league players. Comparisons between social influences on general play style and the use of aggressive acts displayed interesting trends. Although coaches were the predominant determinant of general play styles, teammates were rated as the primary influence on aggressive play of both youth league and high school football players. These results suggest that teammates have more pull in determining illegal or antisocial actions than general styles of play.

> Aggression research taps moral development in sport because higher moral reasoning relates to lower levels of aggression.

Stuart and Ebbeck (1995) also extended M. D. Smith's work by examining the influence of perceived social approval of aggressive actions on Rest's (1984) four components of moral actions (judgment, reasoning, intent, and behavior) in 9- to 15-year-old basketball players. Perceived approval from mother, father, coach and teammates was collectively predictive of moral indices. Among fourth and fifth graders, individuals who perceived less approval from all sources were less likely to judge aggressive behaviors as appropriate or to intend to engage in such behaviors. Among seventh and eighth graders, all sources were important, but teammates emerged as a stronger predictor of moral variables than mother, father, or coach. Individuals who perceived greater approval from teammates were more likely to judge aggressive behaviors as appropriate, gave lower-level reasoning responses, reported higher intentions, and engaged in those behaviors more frequently as rated by coaches. These findings stress the greater influence of peers during adolescence on moral decisions and behaviors.

Other studies have examined the relationship of prevailing team norms and beliefs with moral development indices. In a series of studies, Stephens (2000, 2001; Stephens & Bredemeier, 1996) assessed the influence of team norms on decisions to aggress among youth soccer and basketball players. Individuals who perceived that a greater number of teammates would commit aggressive acts during competition indicated a greater likelihood of aggressing against an opponent. Shields, Bredemeier, Gardner, and Bostrom (1995) examined team norms concerning cheating and aggression in relation to perceptions of group cohesion. Greater task cohesion was related to lower expectations that peers would cheat and aggress. Thus, team norms concerning aggression and cheating are influenced by the closeness of the team. Greater team cohesion is related to team norms, but does not dictate the values espoused by the group (i.e., group could either condone or not condone aggression). A recent study by Stuntz and Weiss (in press) looked at the relationship of task, ego, and social achievement goal orientations (i.e., definitions of success that include interpersonal relationships) to self-reported sportsmanlike tendencies in a variety of peer settings (e.g., best friend condones unsportsmanlike play; teammates do not condone unsportsmanlike play). The relationship between social goal orientations and sportsmanlike responses was shown to vary depending upon the views of important peers including best sport friends and teammates. These results reinforce the notion that one's peers can strongly influence participants' beliefs and behaviors regarding right and wrong actions in sport.

Unfortunately, the specific influence of sport friendships on moral development remains untested in the physical domain. However, sport friendships do entail the characteristics that are hypothesized to contribute to moral development. Weiss et al. (1996) found that prosocial behaviors, help and guidance, emotional support, loyalty, intimacy, and conflict resolution are present in best sport friendships. These qualities exemplify those cited by Bukowski and Sippola (1996) as important to developing strong affective ties between friends and show actions that typify "goodness" and "morally excellent" friendships. Conflict resolution, in particular, suggests that sport friendships may be a context in which individuals learn to reach mutually beneficial solutions within their relationships. Conflict and betrayal also emerged, suggesting that participants experience and negotiate moral dilemmas with their sport friends. With age, intimacy becomes more characteristic of close sport friendships, suggesting that affective ties between sport friends grow stronger over time. These indicators suggest that friendships occurring in sport have the potential to enhance moral development due to characteristic qualities present in such relationships.

> Conflict resolution, in particular, suggests that sport friendships may be a context where individuals learn to reach mutually beneficial solutions within their relationships.

Clearly, peers possess the power to influence moral development through observational learning, reinforcement, and conflict resolution. Strong sport friendships should enhance moral development and perhaps even counterbalance the potential negative influence of the larger peer group. Although the research is sparse, the link between peer relations and sociomoral growth is too compelling to be ignored.

Interventions Designed to Enhance Peer Relationships

The studies reported thus far implicate sport and physical activity contexts as prime settings for developing and strengthening peer relations. Improvement in peer group acceptance and/or friendship quality would naturally contribute toward positive self-evaluations, affective responses, motivational processes, and moral development in youth. Thus, sport settings hold tremendous potential as intervention sites for effecting change in the structure, content, and quality of peer interactions and relationships. However, surprisingly few experimental studies have investigated these possibilities.

Marlowe (1980) employed a games analysis intervention to target peer relationships among socially isolated children in the fifth grade. Games analysis is a process developed by Morris (1976) that is designed to empower child participants in changing parameters of a physical activity to accommodate variations in skill levels (e.g., equipment, rules). Through problem solving, shared decision making, and cooperative goals, games analysis is thought to contribute to children's physical *and* social development. After administering a sociometric questionnaire, Marlowe randomly assigned seven socially isolated children to the games analysis intervention along with seven moderately preferred classmates, whereas the five other socially isolated children participated in a traditional physical education unit with their classmates. The intervention and control groups participated daily for 5 weeks. A follow-up assessment 3 weeks after the intervention period indicated that all seven target children in the experimental group progressed in their sociometric ranking and only one still met the definition of socially isolated. By contrast, all five children in the control group were still classified as isolated. This study elucidates the physical domain as a medium for effecting change in social acceptance among socially isolated children. Unfortunately, no studies were located that replicated or extended this investigation.

Ebbeck and Gibbons (1998) implemented a Team Building through Physical Challenges (Glover & Midura, 1992) intervention with 10- to 12-year-old youth to assess changes in global and specific self-evaluations (perceived physical competence, social acceptance). The experimental group was exposed to their regular physical education curriculum and a once weekly activity that required them to strive toward instrumental goals using a problem-solving, cooperative style of interaction. A control group engaged in normal physical education activities. Group comparisons after 8 months showed a significant and meaningful effect of the team-building program on perceptions of social acceptance (also physical competence, physical appearance, and global self-worth). No doubt the success of the team-building program in improving peer acceptance beliefs was due in part to the supportive interpersonal context in which peer interactions occurred to achieve group goals. The team-building program that Ebbeck and Gibbons employed is an accessible resource that could be readily used in physical activity contexts to pursue effects on various aspects of peer relations and self-beliefs, emotions, and behaviors.

Summary

In our review of literature on peer influence in sport and physical activity contexts, we chose to "package" our discussion around five broad topics. First, peer acceptance among youth is highly related to athletic competence, and those who are skilled hold high peer status in leadership roles as well. Second, peers are a strong source of self-concept development, emotional experiences, and motivation among youth involved in physical activity. Third, the peer construct of close friendship and the positive qualities associated with friendship (e.g., intimacy, companionship, conflict resolution) are key contributors to physical-activity-related experiences. Fourth, perceptions of collective team norms and approval by peers for acting unfairly or aggressively contribute to moral reasoning and behaviors in sport. Finally, interventions designed specifically to enhance peer variables in physical activity settings have been successful. In the following section, we draw from the research just reported to offer practical implications for enhancing peer interactions and relationships among youth in sport and physical activity settings.

PRACTICAL APPLICATIONS: ENHANCING PEER RELATIONSHIPS IN THE PHYSICAL DOMAIN

Enhancing peer relations in the physical domain may not be as difficult as first appears. The first step is for practitioners to recognize that they *can* influence the quality of peer interactions and relationships by making changes in the goals and the environment in which interactions occur. Across the variety of studies reviewed, several practical implications for coaches and teachers emerged that may enhance the quality of interactions among groups of peers. These ideas highlight the development of strong peer interactions through emphasizing cooperative goals, encouraging problem solving, and sharing decision making in activities (recall the successful use of *interdependent goals* in the Robbers Cave Experiment that led off the chapter). By emphasizing group-level interactions, common goals, and respect for all, the physical domain may be transformed into an arena in which all participants feel comfortable with and accepted by their peers. These types of activities also provide individuals with opportunities to build social skills, enhance self-perceptions, and perhaps even make advances in moral reasoning.

> Practicioners must recognize that they can influence the quality of peer relationships by making changes in the environment in which interactions occur.

Cooperative goal-reward structures describe environments in which interdependent goals are emphasized and performance recognized based on *group* mastery, in contrast to competitive goal-reward structures that emphasize *normative* achievement and individualistic goal-reward structures that emphasize *personal* mastery (see C. Ames, 1984, 1986, for a discussion of these varying goal-reward structures). By having cooperative goals, individuals learn to work together, dialogue about problems and potential solutions, and share in the actual actions and decisions necessary to meet such goals. Competitive and individualistic goals, on the other hand, emphasize the types of behaviors that benefit single individuals rather than the group as a whole. An individual striving to reach a competitive or individualistic goal may work independently from others with little positive interaction with peers. Striving to attain cooperative goals, allowing all involved individuals to help reach goals, and sharing decision making among group members will help emphasize positive, productive interactions between peers.

Some specific strategies to enhance peer relationships in the physical domain may include encouraging small-group interactions through restructuring common activities (see Ebbeck & Gibbons, 1998; Gibbons, Ebbeck, & Weiss, 1995; Romance, Weiss, & Bockoven, 1986, for examples of these activities). This may be helped by running drills or games with fewer individuals and with modified rules to encourage full interaction and participation from all. Also, by providing individuals with drills and tasks that require teamwork and cooperation, students must work together and share responsibility to solve tasks or meet performance goals.

Other strategies to enhance peer relationships in the physical domain include reducing obvious displays of social status through methods of team selection. Often, coaches or physical education teachers choose the most skilled individuals as team captains. This method of selection emphasizes differences between individuals and may perpetuate the social hierarchy. Allowing for other ways of choosing peer leaders may result in individuals with personal or psychological characteristics other than athletic competence to emerge as respected leaders of choice. Sometimes physical education teachers allow the best-skilled players to "choose up sides." Individuals picked early on often occupy central roles, leaving less-skilled individuals in less important roles with fewer options for both physical improvement and social interaction with teammates. Other methods of choosing sides, including letting different individuals (e.g., less skilled or popular individuals) pick sides or using arbitrary criteria such as color of clothing or alphabetical order can help lessen obvious displays of social hierarchy and minimize perceived differences between individuals.

These methods will help groups of peers to work together productively, to minimize comparisons between individuals and worries about social status, and to enhance the overall interaction between teammates and classmates. Methods that strive for full participation encourage individuals often ignored or left out to play active roles, providing opportunities for both physical *and* social skill development. These ideas should help benefit all youth involved in sport and physical activity situations by improving their peer relationships.

FUTURE RESEARCH DIRECTIONS ON PEER RELATIONS IN THE PHYSICAL DOMAIN

Early sport research on peer relations was primarily descriptive, focused upon criteria for popularity, and established that being good in sports is highly valued for boys in our society. More recent research shows children's friendship expectations, support, and quality are different depending upon the social context. Given that physical activity represents a context in which peer relationships hold importance, considerable work is needed to understand the developmental significance of peer acceptance and friendship on psychosocial development in this behavioral setting. In the following paragraphs, we offer six suggestions for future research ideas, ones that highlight several of the concepts discussed earlier in the chapter and that we feel are especially salient for the physical domain.

First, a number of studies show that peers are a source of self-evaluations, affective responses, moral development, and motivation in physical activity. Research is needed that establishes these ties *across time*. That is, does one's standing among team peers or a best sport friendship translate to better social development, higher positive affect, lower anxiety, less aggressive behavior, and greater effort over the course of a season? Developmental psychology has employed longitudinal designs to disentangle temporal relationships among peer and psychosocial variables (e.g., Berndt & Keefe, 1995; Newcomb et al., 1999; Sabongui, Bukowski, & Newcomb, 1998). By assessing salient variables at multiple points in time, these researchers were able to determine the unique and relative contributions of intrapersonal and peer characteristics on children's school adjustment, loneliness, aggression, and popularity. Several researchers have also investigated the influence of friendship or peer acceptance *stability* on such outcomes as self-esteem, social development, and aggressive behavior (e.g., Berndt, Hawkins, & Jiao, 1999; Cillessen, Bukowski, & Haselager, 2000). Similar approaches could be adopted to determine the long-term effects of peer relations on sport-related outcomes.

Second, considerable discussion in educational psychology revolves around changes in youths' intrapersonal characteristics (e.g., self-esteem) and interpersonal relationships (e.g., friendship) in response to *environmental changes* associated with school transitions (e.g., elementary to middle school; Eccles, Wigfield, & Schiefele, 1998; Epstein, 1989). Changes in class size, organizational structure, grading emphasis, and evaluation practices as well as makeup of the peer group and friendship selection can have a dramatic impact on youths' sense of self, feelings of belonging, and behavioral inclinations (e.g., Berndt et al., 1999). Similarly, in sport children often begin in instructional leagues where program philosophy and coaching behaviors emphasize learning, improvement, camaraderie among teammates, and "love of the game." With advanced skill, youth traverse a system of tryouts for more competitive teams and semielite status (e.g., travel squad, varsity status). These higher levels usually emphasize performance outcome, norm-referenced criteria for success, and intrateam competition for coveted spots on the team and playing status (e.g., starter). It would be useful to examine the impact that transition from one level to another in sport has on peer group acceptance, friendship, and psychosocial outcomes. For instance, what becomes of a best sport friendship when one member of the dyad is successful at reaching the next level but the other one is not? What happens when a youngster who ranked high in peer status within her or his sport team is "moved up" to the next level where he or she is low girl/boy on the totem pole?

Third, several researchers have suggested that friendships are embedded within larger groups, indicating a need to *assess peer relationships at multiple levels of analysis* or social complexity (e.g., Cairns, Xie, & Leung, 1998; Rubin et al., 1998). This situation would certainly pertain to peer relationships within sport contexts, where close friendships within a team exist in the larger context of the social network of team dynamics. A participant may have a close, reciprocated friendship on the team (dyadic) and be relatively higher or lower in status within the peer group (teammates' acceptance of or regard for participant). Moreover, Cairns et al. and Rubin et al. argue for exploring peer relationships and psychosocial outcomes at the broader social group level, considering such variables as group structure, stability, and dynamics. In the sport psychology literature, group dynamics research has primarily been concerned with task and social cohesion within sport teams and the relationship of cohesion to participation behaviors (see Paskevich, Estabrooks, Brawley, & Carron, 2001). It would be interesting to integrate concepts from peer relationships at the individual level (individual characteristics, dyadic relationships) and the group level (peer acceptance, group cohesion) in an effort to understand these issues within sport teams.

Fourth, the *entire network of children's social relationships* (e.g., parents, peers, teachers, coaches) is important to consider in order to determine the relative influence of significant others on children's development of social skills, self-concept, and feelings of security. Furman and Buhrmester (Furman, 1989; Furman & Buhrmester, 1985, 1992) have systematically examined age, gender, and relationship quality differences in youths' perceptions of significant adults and peers composing their social networks. This is also an important direction for research in the sport domain because children's sport friendships do not exist in a social vacuum and include relationships with other peers (e.g., same-sex classmates, opposite-sex friends), siblings, and adults (e.g., parents, coaches, extended family members). As Furman and Buhrmester (1992) say, "future investigators should consider simultaneously examining children's relationships with various members of their social network. By taking a network perspective, we can move toward a comprehensive picture of the development of social relationships" (p. 113). Directions for inquiry may include the relative influence of social network members on children's cognitions, affect, and motivation at varying ages, for girls and boys, and in varying contexts.

> It is important to consider the entire network of children's social relationships in order to determine the influence of significant others on children's development of social skills, self-concept, and feelings of security.

Specifically, researchers suggest that the nature of the parent-child relationship has an impact on the child's ability to form and maintain close friendships, and in turn, children's peer relationships may reciprocally affect the parent-child relationship (see Rubin et al., 1998). Given the rather extensive involvement of parents in their child's sport experiences, this may be an interesting path to explore. Moreover Horn (1995) has suggested that the types of behaviors coaches exhibit in practices and games are likely to influence the quality of peer relationships children form in sport settings. Coach influence may include the type of motivational climate emphasized, the nature and quality of evaluative and informational feedback, and the degree to which coaches encourage and structure the environment for moral development and group cohesiveness. Thus, the relative influence of social network members on youths' psychosocial outcomes, as well as their influence on social relationships with other members of the network, is a crucial area of future study.

Fifth, we believe the link between *peer relationships and moral development in sport* is a key area of future study. Peer conflict, negotiation, and resolution are central to children's development of social-perspective taking, empathy, and moral reasoning. Yet research on moral development in sport has primarily investigated associations among moral reasoning, legitimacy judgments, and aggression while neglecting their sources of influence (see Weiss & Smith, 2002a). Sport contexts offer numerous opportunities for interpersonal competition and cooperation, providing a natural laboratory for investigating the ties between peer interactions and moral development. Several intervention studies (e.g., Gibbons et al., 1995; Romance et al., 1986) have employed reasoned dialogue and conflict-resolution skills among peers in physical education classes. However the experimental designs revolved around the effect of such strategies on *individual* moral indices (e.g., reasoning, intentions) and not *social relationship* variables such as social competence, friendship, and peer group acceptance. Future research should focus upon specific linkages between peer relationships and moral development as sport provides an ideal context for effecting changes in both variables.

The moral development in sport literature shows that male athletes evidence lower moral reasoning and greater aggression tendencies than do male nonathletes and female athletes and nonathletes starting at about age 11-12 years (see Weiss & Smith, 2002a). Even when a relationship between moral reasoning and aggression legitimacy is found for female athletes, the magnitude of aggression scores is minimal. However, the scenarios used in these studies focus upon verbal and physical, or more overt types, of aggression. Research by Crick (e.g., Crick, 1996; Crick, Bigbee, & Howes, 1996; Grotpeter & Crick, 1996) shows considerable gender differences in types (overt, relational) and functions (instrumental, hostile) of aggression in peer interactions. An interesting direction pertaining to peer relationships and moral development would be an examination of gender, moral reasoning, and type and function of aggression in sport. Assessment of aggression in sport could be expanded from the current focus on verbal and physical forms to include exclusion and reputational harm (i.e., relational forms) and the relationship of aggression forms with moral indices examined.

Finally, we emphasize the need for *intervention studies exploring physical activity contexts as a medium for improving peer relationships*. One natural target is a goal-reward structure or motivational climate that emphasizes cooperative mastery and performance over interpersonal competition that occurs so naturally within sport. According to researchers (e.g., Ames, 1984, 1986, 1992; Epstein, 1989), a cooperative goal-reward structure or moral motivational climate encourages interdependent learning, group problem solving and improvement, and recognition of all members as important in group functioning. To date, goal structures or motivational climate have been examined in relation to intrapersonal (e.g., perceived competence) and motivational (e.g., enjoyment) processes but not interpersonal relationships. Marlowe's (1980) intervention described earlier resembles components of a cooperative goal structure and offers a window through which to view change in peer group acceptance. Similarly, team-building activities such as those employed by Ebbeck and Gibbons (1998) offer promise in enhancing peer relationships through emphasis on interdependent goal setting, group trust, social support, and cohesiveness among group members. A host of other intervention strategies offer potential such as physical skills training (see Evans & Roberts, 1987), social skills training (see Asher et al., 1996), moral development programs (see Weiss & Smith, 2002a), and peer-assisted learning (see Cowie, 1999; Topping & Ehly, 1998).

Concluding Remarks

> [best friend says] "Good job. You did that right! . . . Others kind of say, Good job. You did it right, fine, or like, You finally did it, you finally finished, like who cares, you finally did it, finally after all these years. Like unimportant, like I didn't practice or anything. You did it finally, like lucky . . . [my best friend] says it differently, in a nice way to me." (9-year-old girl talking about her best sport friend; Weiss et al., 1996, p. 364)

Peers offer strong sources of social support during childhood and adolescence, through features such as esteem enhancement, intimate self-disclosure, loyalty, and companionship. Our review clearly shows that physical activity contexts offer excellent opportunities for positive peer interactions and relationships, as characterized in the quote above, as well as opportunities for peer conflict, negotiation, and resolution, as characterized in the opening quote. Thus, the effects of peer group acceptance and friendship quality on self-evaluations, affect, motivational processes, and moral development within physical activity settings carry significance for years to come. As Bukowski et al. (1996) aptly said, "Clearly, the company that children keep is an aspect of the developmental niche that has consequences for children's long-term development and adaptation" (p. 14). As more research delves into the significance of children's peer relationships in the *physical* domain, we will be able to confidently say the same for the company that children keep in their sport and physical activity lives.

References

Aboud, F. E., & Mendelson, M. J. (1996). Determinants of friendship selection and quality: Developmental perspectives. In W. M. Bukowski, A. F. Newcomb, & W. W. Hartup (Eds.), *The company they keep: Friendship in childhood and adolescence* (pp. 87-112). New York: Cambridge University Press.

Adler, P. A., Kless, S. J., & Adler, P. (1992). Socialization to gender roles: Popularity among elementary school boys and girls. *Sociology of Education, 65,* 169-187.

Ames, C. (1984). Competitive, cooperative, and individualistic goal structures: A cognitive-motivational analysis. In R. Ames & C. Ames (Eds.), *Research on motivation in education: Vol. 1. Student motivation* (pp. 177-207). Orlando, FL: Academic Press.

Ames, C. (1986). Conceptions of motivation within competitive and noncompetitive goal structures. In R. Schwarzer (Ed.), *Self-related cognitions in anxiety and motivation* (pp. 229-245). Hillsdale, NJ: Erlbaum.

Ames, C. A. (1992). Achievement goals, motivational climate, and motivational processes. In G. C. Roberts (Ed.), *Motivation in sport and exercise* (pp. 161-176). Champaign, IL: Human Kinetics.

Anderssen, N., & Wold, B. (1992). Parental and peer influences on leisure-time physical activity in young adolescents. *Research Quarterly for Exercise and Sport, 63,* 341-348.

Asher, S. R., Parker, J. G., & Walker, D. L. (1996). Distinguishing friendship from acceptance: Implications for intervention and assessment. In W. M. Bukowski, A. F. Newcomb, & W. W. Hartup (Eds.), *The company they keep: Friendship in childhood and adolescence* (pp. 366-405). New York: Cambridge University Press.

Bandura, A. (1986). *Social foundations of thought and action.* Englewood Cliffs, NJ: Prentice-Hall.

Bear, G. G., & Rys, G. S. (1994). Moral reasoning, classroom behavior, and sociometric status among elementary school children. *Developmental Psychology, 30,* 633-638.

Belle, D. (1989). Gender differences in children's social networks and supports. In D. Belle (Ed.), *Children's social networks and social supports* (pp. 173-190). New York: Wiley.

Berndt, T. J. (1989). Obtaining support from friends during childhood and adolescence. In D. Belle (Ed.), *Children's social networks and social supports* (pp. 308-331). New York: Wiley.

Berndt, T. J. (1996). Exploring the effects of friendship quality on social development. In W. M. Bukowski, A. F. Newcomb, & W. W. Hartup (Eds.), *The company they keep: Friendship in childhood and adolescence* (pp. 346-365). New York: Cambridge University Press.

Berndt, T. J., Hawkins, J. A., & Jiao, Z. (1999). Influences of friends and friendships on adjustment to junior high school. *Merrill-Palmer Quarterly, 45,* 13-41.

Berndt, T. J., & Keefe, K. (1995). Friends' influence on adolescents' adjustment to school. *Child Development, 66,* 1312-1329.

Berndt, T. J., & Perry, B. (1986). Children's perceptions of friendships as supportive relationships. *Developmental Psychology, 5,* 640-648.

Berndt, T. J., & Perry, B. (1990). Distinctive features and effects of early adolescent friendships. In R. Montemayor, G. R. Adams, & T.P. Gullotta (Eds.), *From childhood to adolescence: A transitional period?* (pp. 269-287). Newbury Park, CA: Sage.

Bigelow, B. J., Lewko, J. H., & Salhani, L. (1989). Sport-involved children's friendship expectations. *Journal of Sport & Exercise Psychology, 11,* 152-160.

Brodkin, P., & Weiss, M. R. (1990). Developmental differences in motivation for participating in competitive swimming. *Journal of Sport & Exercise Psychology, 12,* 248-263.

Buchanan, H. T., Blankenbaker, J., & Cotten, D. (1976). Academic and athletic ability as popularity factors in elementary school children. *Research Quarterly, 47,* 320-325.

Bukowski, W. M., & Hoza, B. (1989). Popularity and friendship: Issues in theory, measurement, and outcome. In T. J. Berndt & G. W. Ladd (Eds.), *Peer relationships in child development* (pp. 15-45). New York: Wiley.

Bukowski, W. M., Newcomb, A. F., & Hartup, W. W. (1996). Friendship and its significance in childhood and adolescence: Introduction and comment. In W. M. Bukowski, A. F. Newcomb, & W. W. Hartup (Eds.), *The company they keep: Friendship in childhood and adolescence* (pp. 1-15). New York: Cambridge University Press.

Bukowski, W. M., & Sippola, L. K. (1996). Friendship and morality: (How) are they related? In W. M. Bukowski, A. F. Newcomb, & W. W. Hartup (Eds.), *The company they keep: Friendship in childhood and adolescence* (pp. 238-261). New York: Cambridge University Press.

Cairns, R., Xie, H., & Leung, M-C. (1998). The popularity of friendship and the neglect of social networks: Toward a new balance. In W. M. Bukowski & A.H. Cillessen (Eds.), *Sociometry then and now: Building on six decades of measuring children's experiences with the peer group* (pp. 25-53). San Francisco: Jossey-Bass.

Chase, M. A., & Dummer, G. M. (1992). The role of sports as a social status determinant for children. *Research Quarterly for Exercise and Sport, 63*, 418-424.

Cillessen, A. H. N., & Bukowski, W. M. (Eds.). (2000). *Recent advances in the measurement of acceptance and rejection in the peer system*. San Francisco: Jossey-Bass.

Cillessen, A. H. N., Bukowski, W. M., & Haselager, G. J. T. (2000). Stability of sociometric categories. In A. H. N. Cillessen & W. M. Bukowski (Eds.), *Recent advances in the measurement of acceptance and rejection in the peer system* (pp. 75-93). San Francisco: Jossey-Bass.

Coakley, J. J., & White, A. (1992). Making decisions: Gender and sport participation among British adolescents. *Sociology of Sport Journal, 9*, 20-35.

Coie, J. D., Dodge, K. A., & Kupersmidt, J. B. (1990). Peer group behavior and social status. In S. R. Asher & J. D. Coie (Eds.), *Peer rejection in childhood* (pp. 17-59). New York: Cambridge University Press.

Cowie, H. (1999). Peers helping peers: Interventions, initiatives and insights. *Journal of Adolescence, 22*, 433-436.

Crick, N. R. (1996). The role of overt aggression, relational aggression, and prosocial behavior in the prediction of children's future social adjustment. *Child Development, 67*, 2317-2327.

Crick, N. R., Bigbee, M. A., & Howes, C. (1996). Gender differences in children's normative beliefs about aggression: How do I hurt thee? Let me count the ways. *Child Development, 67*, 1003-1014.

Damon, W. (1977). *The social world of the child*. San Francisco: Jossey-Bass.

Damon, W. (1988). *The moral child*. New York: The Free Press.

De Knop, P., Engstrom, L. M., Skirstad, B., & Weiss, M. R. (1996). *Worldwide trends in youth sport*. Champaign, IL: Human Kinetics.

Donnelly, P. (1993). Problems associated with youth involvement in high-performance sport. In B.R. Cahill & A. J. Pearl (Eds.), *Intensive participation in children's sports* (pp. 95-126). Champaign, IL: Human Kinetics.

Duncan, S. C. (1993). The role of cognitive appraisal and friendship provisions in adolescents' affect and motivation toward activity in physical education. *Research Quarterly for Exercise and Sport, 64*, 314-323.

Ebbeck, V., & Gibbons, S. L. (1998). The effect of a team building program on the self-conceptions of grade 6 and 7 physical education students. *Journal of Sport & Exercise Psychology, 20*, 300-310.

Ebbeck, V., & Stuart, M. E. (1993). Who determines what's important? Perceptions of competence and importance as predictors of self-esteem in youth football players. *Pediatric Exercise Science, 5*, 253-262.

Ebbeck, V., & Stuart, M. E. (1996). Predictors of self-esteem with youth basketball players. *Pediatric Exercise Science, 8*, 368-378.

Eccles, J. S., Wigfield, A. W., & Schiefele, U. (1998). Motivation to succeed. In W. Damon (Series Ed.) & N. Eisenberg (Vol. Ed.), *Handbook of child psychology*: Vol. 3. *Social, emotional, and personality development* (5th ed., pp. 1017-1095). New York: Wiley.

Epstein, J. L. (1989). The selection of friends: Changes across grades and in different school environments. In T. J. Berndt & G. W. Ladd (Eds.), *Peer relationships in child development* (pp. 158-187). New York: Wiley.

Evans, J., & Roberts, G. C. (1987). Physical competence and the development of children's peer relations. *Quest, 39*, 23-35.

Feltz, D. L. (1978). Athletics in the status system of female adolescents. *Review of Sport and Leisure, 3*, 98-108.

Furman, W. (1989). The development of children's social networks. In D. Belle (Ed.), *Children's social networks and social supports* (pp. 151-172). New York: Wiley.

Furman, W. (1996). The measurement of friendship perceptions: Conceptual and methodological issues. In W. M. Bukowski, A. F. Newcomb, & W. W. Hartup (Eds.), *The company they keep: Friendship in childhood and adolescence* (pp. 41-65). New York: Cambridge University Press.

Furman, W., & Buhrmester, D. (1985). Children's perceptions of the personal relationships in their social networks. *Developmental Psychology, 21*, 1016-1024.

Furman, W., & Buhrmester, D. (1992). Age and sex differences in perceptions of networks of personal relationships. *Child Development, 63*, 103-115.

Gibbons, S. L., Ebbeck, V., & Weiss, M. R. (1995). Fair play for kids: Effects on the moral development of children in physical education. *Research Quarterly for Exercise and Sport, 66*, 247-255.

Glenn, S. D., & Horn, T. S. (1993). Psychological and personal predictors of leadership behavior in female soccer players. *Journal of Applied Sport Psychology, 5*, 17-34.

Glover, D. R., & Midura, D. W. (1992). *Team building through physical challenges*. Champaign, IL: Human Kinetics.

Gould, D. (1993). Intensive sport participation and the prepubescent athlete: Competitive stress and burnout. In B.R. Cahill & A. J. Pearl (Eds.), *Intensive participation in children's sports* (pp. 19-38). Champaign, IL: Human Kinetics.

Grotpeter, J. K., & Crick, N. R. (1996). Relational aggression, overt aggression, and friendship. *Child Development, 67*, 2328-2338.

Harter, S. (1978). Effectance motivation reconsidered. *Human Development, 21*, 34-64.

Harter, S. (1987). The determinants and mediational role of global self-worth in children. In N. Eisenberg (Ed.), *Contemporary topics in developmental psychology* (pp. 219-242). New York: Wiley.

Harter, S. (1999). *The construction of the self: A developmental perspective.* New York: Guilford.

Hartup, W. W. (1989). Behavioral manifestations of children's friendships. In T. J. Berndt & G. W. Ladd (Eds.), *Peer relationships in child development* (pp. 46-70).New York: Wiley.

Hartup, W. W. (1995). The three faces of friendship. *Journal of Social and Personal Relationships, 12*, 569-574.

Hartup, W. W. (1996). The company they keep: Friendships and their developmental significance. *Child Development, 67*, 1-13.

Hartup, W. W. (1999). Constraints on peer socialization: Let me count the ways. *Merrill-Palmer Quarterly, 45*, 172-183.

Hartup, W. W., & Laursen, B. (1999). Relationships as developmental contexts: Retrospective themes and contemporary issues. In W. A. Collins & B. Laursen (Eds.), *Relationships as developmental contexts: The Minnesota Symposia on Child Psychology* (Vol. 30, pp. 13-35). New York: Erlbaum.

Holland, A., & Andre, T. (1994). Athletic participation and the social status of adolescent males and females. *Youth & Society, 25*, 388-407.

Horn, T. S. (1995, June). *That's what friends are for: The development of peer relationships through childhood sport participation – A reaction.* Paper presented at the annual meeting of the North American Society for the Psychology of Sport and Physical Activity, Asilomar, CA.

Horn, T.S. (2003). Developmental perspectives on self-perceptions in children and adolescents. In M.R. Weiss (Ed.), *Developmental sport and exercise psychology: A lifespan perspective.*(pp.101-143) Morgantown, WV: Fitness Information Technology.

Hyland, D. A. (1978). Competition and friendship. *Journal of the Philosophy of Sport, 5*, 27-37.

Kane, M. J. (1988). The female athletic role as a status determinant within the social system of high school adolescents. *Adolescence, 23*, 253-264.

Kelley, H. H., & Thibaut, J. W. (1978). *Interpersonal relations: A theory of interdependence.* New York: Wiley.

Kerns, K. A. (1996). Individual differences in friendship quality: Links to child-mother attachment. In W. M. Bukowski, A. F. Newcomb, & W. W. Hartup (Eds.), *The company they keep: Friendship in childhood and adolescence* (pp. 137-157). New York: Cambridge University Press.

Klint, K. A., & Weiss, M. R. (1987). Perceived competence and motives for participating in youth sports: A test of Harter's competence motivation theory. *Journal of Sport Psychology, 9*, 55-65.

Kunesh, M. A., Hasbrook, C. A., & Lewthwaite, R. (1992). Physical activity socialization: Peer interactions and affective responses among a sample of sixth grade girls. *Sociology of Sport Journal, 9*, 385-396.

Ladd, G. W. (1999). Peer relationships and social competence during early and middle childhood. *Annual Review of Psychology, 333*, 1-16.

Ladd, G. W., & Price, J. M. (1993). Playstyles of peer-accepted and peer-rejected children on the playground. In C.H. Hart (Ed.), *Children on playgrounds: Research perspectives and applications* (pp. 130-161). Albany: State University of New York Press.

Laursen, B. (1996). Closeness and conflict in adolescent peer relationships: Interdependence with friends and romantic partners. In W. M. Bukowski, A. F. Newcomb, & W. W. Hartup (Eds.), *The company they keep: Friendship in childhood and adolescence* (pp. 186-210). New York: Cambridge University Press.

Lee, M. J., Coburn, T., & Partridge, R. (1981). The influence of team structure in determining leadership function in association football. *Journal of Sport Behavior, 6*, 59-66.

Lever, J. (1976). Sex differences in the games children play. *Social Problems, 23*, 478-487.

Lever, J. (1978). Sex differences in the complexity of children's play and games. *American Sociological Review, 43*, 471-483.

Mahoney, J. L., & Stattin, H. (2000). Leisure activities and adolescent antisocial behavior: The role of structure and social context. *Journal of Adolescence, 23*, 113-127.

Marlowe, M. (1980). Games analysis intervention: A procedure to increase peer acceptance of socially isolated children. *Research Quarterly, 51*, 422-426.

McCullagh, P., & Weiss, M. R. (2001). Modeling: Considerations for motor skill performance and psychological responses. In R. N. Singer, H. A. Hausenblas, & C. M. Janelle (Eds.), *Handbook of sport psychology* (2nd ed., pp. 205-238). New York: Wiley.

Morris, G. S. D. (1976). *How to change the games children play.* Minneapolis: Burgess.

Mugno, D. A., & Feltz, D. L. (1985). The social learning of aggression in youth football in the United States. *Canadian Journal of Applied Sport Sciences, 10*, 26-35.

Newcomb, A. F., & Bagwell, C. L. (1995). Children's friendship relations: A meta-analytic review. *Psychological Bulletin, 117*, 306-347.

Newcomb, A. F., & Bagwell, C. L. (1996). The developmental significance of children's friendship relations. In W. M. Bukowski, A. F. Newcomb, & W. W. Hartup (Eds.), *The company they keep: Friendship in childhood and adolescence* (pp. 289-321). New York: Cambridge University Press.

Newcomb, A. F., Bukowski, W. M., & Bagwell, C. L. (1999). Knowing the sounds: Friendship as a developmental context. In W. A. Collins & B. Laursen (Eds.), *Relationships as developmental contexts: The Minnesota Symposia on Child Psychology* (Vol. 30, pp. 63-84). Malwah, NJ: Erlbaum.

Newcomb, A. F., Bukowski, W. M., & Pattee, L. (1993). Children's peer relations: A meta-analytic review of popular, rejected, neglected, controversial, and average sociometric status. *Psychological Bulletin, 113*, 99-128.

Parker, J. G., & Asher, S. R. (1993). Friendship and friendship quality in middle childhood: Links with peer group acceptance and feelings of loneliness and social dissatisfaction. *Developmental Psychology, 29*, 611-621.

Paskevich, D. M., Estabrooks, P. A., Brawley, L. R., & Carron, A. V. (2001). Group cohesion in sport and exercise. In R. N. Singer, H. A. Hausenblas, & C. M. Janelle (Eds.), *Handbook of sport psychology* (2nd ed., pp. 472-494). New York: Wiley.

Passer, M. W. (1996). At what age are children ready to compete? Some psychological considerations. In F. L. Smoll & R. E. Smith (Eds.), *Children and youth in sport: A biopsychosocial perspective* (pp. 73-82). Madison, WI: Brown & Benchmark.

Patrick, H., Ryan, A. M., Alfeld-Liro, C., Fredericks, J. A., Hruda, L. Z., & Eccles, J. S. (1999). Adolescents' commitment to developing talent: The role of peers in continuing motivation for sports and the arts. *Journal of Youth and Adolescence, 28*, 741-763.

Piaget, J. (1932/1965). *The moral judgment of the child.* New York: The Free Press.

Rest, J. R. (1984). The major components of morality. In W. Kurtines & J. Gerwitz (Eds.), *Morality, moral behavior, and moral development* (pp. 356-629). New York: Wiley.

Romance, T. J., Weiss, M. R., & Bockoven, J. (1986). A program to promote moral development through elementary school physical education. *Journal of Teaching in Physical Education, 5*, 126-136.

Rubin, K. H., Bukowski, W. M., & Parker, J. G. (1998). Peer interactions, relationships, and groups. In W. Damon (Series Ed.) & N. Eisenberg (Vol. Ed.), *Handbook of child psychology: Social, emotional, and personality development* (Vol. 3, pp. 619-700). New York: Wiley.

Sabongui, A. G., Bukowski, W. M., & Newcomb, A. F. (1998). The peer ecology of popularity: The network embeddedness of a child's friend predicts the child's subsequent popularity. In W. M. Bukowski & A.H. Cillessen (Eds.), *Sociometry then and now: Building on six decades of measuring children's experiences with the peer group* (pp. 83-91). San Francisco: Jossey-Bass.

Scanlan, T. K., Carpenter, P. J., Lobel, M., & Simons, J. P. (1993). Sources of enjoyment for youth sport athletes. *Pediatric Exercise Science, 5*, 275-285.

Scanlan, T. K., & Simons, J. P. (1992). The construct of sport enjoyment. In G. C. Roberts (Ed.), *Motivation in sport and exercise* (pp. 199-215). Champaign, IL: Human Kinetics.

Scanlan, T. K., Stein, G. L., & Ravizza, K. (1991). An in-depth study of former elite figure skaters: III. Sources of stress. *Journal of Sport & Exercise Psychology, 13*, 103-120.

Schonert-Reichel, K. A. (1999). Relations of peer acceptance, friendship adjustment, and social behavior to moral reasoning during early adolescence. *Journal of Early Adolescence, 19*, 249-279.

Sherif, M., Harvey, O. J., White, B. J., Hood, W. R., & Sherif, C. (1961). *Inter-group conflict and cooperation: The Robbers Cave experiment.* Norman, OK: University of Oklahoma Press.

Shields, D. L. L., Bredemeier, B. J. L., Gardner, D. E., & Bostrom, A. (1995). Leadership, cohesion, and team norms regarding cheating and aggression. *Sociology of Sport Journal, 12*, 324-336.

Smith, A. L. (1999). Perceptions of peer relationships and physical activity participation in early adolescence. *Journal of Sport & Exercise Psychology, 21*, 329-350.

Smith, M. D. (1974). Significant others' influence on the assaultive behavior of young hockey players. *International Review of Sport Sociology, 3-4*, 45-56.

Smith, M. D. (1975). The legitimation of violence: Hockey players' perceptions of their reference groups' sanctions for assault. *Canadian Review of Sociology and Anthropology, 12*, 72-80.

Smith, M. D. (1979). Towards an explanation of hockey violence: A reference other approach. *Canadian Journal of Sociology, 4*, 105-124.

Solomon, G.B. (2003). A lifespan view of moral development in physical activity. In M.R. Weiss (Ed.), *Developmental sport and exercise psychology: A lifespan perspective.* (pp. 453-474) Morgantown, WV: Fitness Information Technology.

Stephens, D. E. (2000). Predictors of likelihood to aggress in youth soccer: An examination of coed and all-girls teams. *Journal of Sport Behavior, 23*, 311-325.

Stephens, D. E. (2001). Predictors of aggressive tendencies in girls' basketball: An examination of beginning and advanced participants in a summer skills camp. *Research Quarterly for Exercise and Sport, 72*, 257-266.

Stephens, D. E., & Bredemeier, B. J. L. (1996). Moral atmosphere and judgments about aggression in girls' soccer: Relationships among moral and motivational variables. *Journal of Sport & Exercise Psychology, 18*, 158-173.

Stuart, M. E., & Ebbeck, V. (1995). The influence of perceived social approval on moral development in youth sport. *Pediatric Exercise Science, 7*, 270-280.

Stuntz, C. P., & Weiss, M. R. (in press). Influence of social goal orientations and peers on unsportsmanlike play. *Research Quarterly for Exercise and Sport.*

Sullivan, H. S. (1953). *The interpersonal theory of psychiatry.* New York: Norton.

Thibaut, J. W., & Kelley, H. H. (1959). *The social psychology of groups.* New York: Wiley.

Topping, K., & Ehly, S. (Eds.). (1998). *Peer-assisted learning.* Malwah, NJ: Erlbaum.

U. S. Department of Health and Human Services. (1996). *Physical activity and health: A report of the Surgeon General.* Atlanta, GA: U.S. Department of Health and Human Services, Centers for Disease Control and Prevention.

Weiss, M. R., & Duncan, S. C. (1992). The relationship between physical competence and peer acceptance in the context of children's sports participation. *Journal of Sport & Exercise Psychology, 14,* 177-191.

Weiss, M. R., & Ferrer-Caja, E. (2002). Motivational orientations and sport behavior. In T. S. Horn (Ed.), *Advances in sport psychology* (2nd ed., pp. 101-183). Champaign, IL: Human Kinetics.

Weiss, M. R., McAuley, E., Ebbeck, V., & Wiese, D. M. (1990). Self-esteem and causal attributions for children's physical and social competence in sport. *Journal of Sport & Exercise Psychology, 12,* 21-36.

Weiss, M. R., & Smith, A. L. (1999). Quality of youth sport friendships: Measurement development and validation. *Journal of Sport & Exercise Psychology, 21,* 145-166.

Weiss, M. R., & Smith, A. L. (2002a). Moral development in sport and physical activity: Theory, research, and intervention. In T. S. Horn (Ed.), *Advances in sport psychology* (2nd ed., pp. 243-280). Champaign, IL: Human Kinetics.

Weiss, M. R., & Smith, A. L. (2002b). Friendship quality in youth sport: Relationship to age, gender, and motivation variables. *Journal of Sport & Exercise Psychology, 24,* 420-437.

Weiss, M. R., Smith, A. L., & Theeboom, M. (1996). "That's what friends are for": Children's and teenagers' perceptions of peer relationships in the sport domain. *Journal of Sport & Exercise Psychology, 18,* 347-379.

Williams, J. M., & White, K. A. (1983). Adolescent status systems for males and females at three age levels. *Adolescence, 18,* 381-389.

Zarbatany, L., Ghesquiere, K., & Mohr, K. (1992). A context perspective on early adolescents' friendship expectations. *Journal of Early Adolescence, 12,* 111-126.

Zarbatany, L., Hartmann, D. P., & Rankin, D. B. (1990). The psychological functions of preadolescent peer activities. *Child Development, 61,* 1067-1080.

Zarbatany, L., McDougall, P., & Hymel, S. (2000). Gender-differentiated experience in the peer culture: Links to intimacy in preadolescence. *Social Development, 9,* 62-79.

AUTHOR NOTE

We are grateful to Thelma Horn for her insightful and helpful comments on an earlier draft of this manuscript.

CHAPTER SEVEN

Emotional Experience in Youth Sport

Peter R. E. Crocker • Sharleen D. Hoar
Meghan H. McDonough • Kent C. Kowalski
Cory B. Niefer

When watching a competitive sport event involving youth, one is immediately struck by the psychological involvement of the players, their parents, coaches, and significant others. Throughout the match, supporters are shouting encouragement, instructions, and criticism. Players celebrate scoring with smiles, hugs, and other "happy" expressions. The emotional experience of the losing team is often all too clear from their facial expressions. Clearly, emotional experience is a central part of youth sport. Understanding the social significance of emotional behavior and learning how to control and appropriately express emotions in various sporting cultures are challenging but critical tasks for children and adolescents. What factors generate and regulate such emotional experiences, and what impact does emotion have on children's and adolescents' psychological adjustment and motivation? Further, do the antecedents and consequences of emotional experience change with social and cognitive development? A better understanding of emotions has the potential to help parents, coaches, and other practitioners enhance sport experiences for children and adolescents.

Youth researchers in sport and exercise have recognized that emotional experiences influence social relations, performance, health, moral behavior, and motivation (Scanlan & Simons, 1992; Solomon, 2003; Treasure, 2001; Weiss & Stuntz, 2003; Weiss & Williams, 2003). Emotional experiences are entwined in many if not all facets of the sporting experience. A comprehensive understanding would require a thorough review of cognitive and social developmental issues, parental influences, peer and friendship influences, motivation, moral development, self-representations, cognitive processing, and coping. Clearly, such a wide-ranging review is beyond the scope of this chapter. The purpose of this chapter is to clarify key issues such as how emotional experiences are generated, what the consequences of emotional experience are, and how cognitive and social development might affect emotional experience in sport. A number of emotional states such as anxiety, anger, shame, joy, and pride are relevant to youth sport. We will address different emotions where relevant, but because of the quality of sport literature, special attention will be directed towards the emotional experiences of anxiety and enjoyment.

The chapter is organized into several sections. First, we present several images of children and adolescents recalling emotional experiences from sport. These cases serve two purposes:

(a) to illustrate how social and cognitive development are reflected in athletes' interpretations of emotional sport events and (b) to show how emotional experience is embedded in a personal-social world. We will use these images to illustrate key concepts discussed in the chapter. Second, we define emotions and affective feeling states, followed by an identification of key cognitive and social development factors related to emotion. Third, we review the literature on enjoyment and anxiety in youth sport. This section includes a descriptive analysis of the sources and consequences of anxiety and enjoyment. The fourth section provides a review of four cognitively based theories of emotion used by youth sport researchers. Finally, we provide suggestions for future research.

IMAGES OF EMOTIONS IN YOUTH SPORT

Susy—Age 7

I like soccer and horseback riding—is horseback riding a sport? [I enjoy soccer because] I get to be with my friends. I like my practice—I like to learn skills and stuff. It is great when we play the "cat and mouse" game. I also like the games, scoring goals, and dribbling. I also like to play defense. I didn't like it the first time I had to play goalie, and that team beat us. I had never played goalie before in a game, and I didn't like it. I got frustrated after they had scored a few goals, and our team didn't have any. I thought they were going to win, and it made me upset. I cried after that second goal. I knew I would play forward in the second half . . . that made me feel better. Rob [coach] told me that the other team was the best team we had to play, so that made me feel a bit better too. He said I had done well in the goal for my first time.

Alexander—Age 9

I enjoy soccer when everyone is trying hard. I like the exercise—you actually do a lot of running. I don't really know [why I enjoy soccer]. I like defending. You can stop a lot of goals. It makes the other team nervous. Sometimes soccer is not fun. Five days or weeks straight it rained. Everyone was frozen and nobody tried. It was too cold to play, my feet were numb, and I couldn't move. I worry when we score a goal. The other team gets madder and will get more aggressive. They will try to get the goal back. When I'm nervous I just try to play harder. I get mad when someone elbows me in the face. I feel aggressive and want my revenge. I mean, if someone pushes you down, how would that make you feel?

Nicole—Age 12

I feel passionate about soccer for several reasons. First thing is that my dad loves it too. The second thing is that it is something to look forward to at the end of the day. It is a way of getting away from reality and stress. Soccer is also fun to play. It gets me moving and fit, but it also is fun to play with my friends. Soccer is more than just a game—it's who I am, what I love. Big tournaments always get me worried because I'm afraid I'll play horribly. I remember this one time when we were about to play a really good team. I was so nervous I was shaking, my stomach hurt, and I felt we had no chance. It turned out we were playing great since we had a good warm-up and gained some confidence. Before that game, I wanted just to go back home, but I knew my team needed me. I just handled it by accepting the challenge and playing the game.

Julie—Age 17

[I feel stressed] just most of the time actually. I'm not very stressed out during training. Like I get along with my coaches, and that works out fine. Mostly, the kind of stress I get is around competition times . . . . I can compete much better than when I was younger, I freaked out at competitions. I would get so stressed out before my event; I'm so like going like this [shoulders up at her ears and demonstrating a scared facial expression]. I'm not joking. I was like the most stressed-out kid in the world when I was younger, but now it's all right. . . . [Competition] always got to be a little bit stressful because it's when you want to do your best so you are obviously going to get a little bit stressed out because you know that you have only one chance! A particular time I was very stressed was when I was coming back from an injury in the summer. I had just taken off a couple months, and I had to miss Nationals. And then I got mono, so I was really weak and getting back was really stressful because I had another major competition to go to. [In the trials for the competition] I was stressed out, but that's just how I am because I wanted to do well, but I had three weeks and I was weak. I'd never experienced anything like that, being so weak and not being able to do anything. I didn't understand. I thought that I could, like in my head, I could do it all, I knew how to do it all, and I was just so weak. It was frustrating because I would try to do stuff and couldn't and I'd get tired and then I'd have to sit down, and that was just frustrating . . . . I couldn't really put pressure on myself because this competition wasn't really the hugest deal in the world . . . . I already had a spot on the team, like it wasn't a big deal if I blew it. . . and the coaches understood that I was so weak.

These images provide an interesting picture about how children and adolescents experience and try to manage emotional experience in sport. The younger athletes' (Susy's and Alexander's) images tend to focus on concrete events and do not show the more abstract reasoning and social integration evident in Nicole's and Julie's stories. Yet all four athletes experience significant emotional events based on personal meaning of the sporting event. To further our understanding of why youth athletes experience emotions, it is necessary for us to have an understanding of basic concepts in the literature.

DEFINITIONS AND BASIC CONCEPTS

Sport scientists have wrestled with the challenge of describing and defining emotional experience (Crocker, Kowalski, Graham, & Kowalski, 2002; Vallerand & Blanchard, 2000). Sport researchers have used the terms *emotion, feeling states, affect, stress,* and *moods* interchangeably. We discussed this issue in the chapter on emotion in adulthood and will not belabor this point (see Crocker, Kowalski, Hoar, & McDonough, this volume). To help the reader, we will provide brief working definitions and illustrations of emotion and affective states.

Emotion

Many theorists argue that there are a number of discrete emotions that have distinct characteristics and motivational properties (Ekman, 1994; Izard, 1977; Lazarus, 1991). Although there is some disagreement about which emotional states are primary, the list usually includes anger, anxiety, fear, happiness/joy, sadness, and disgust. Each emotion is thought to be composed of physiological/neurological activation, subjective feeling states, an impulse to act, and facial or bodily expression (Cornelius, 1996; Lazarus, 1991). The emotional experience of the 12-year-old, Nicole, illustrates the experience of anxiety. She had a definite sense of displeasure, physiological activation, and an action tendency or impulse to escape or avoid the situation. Compare her anxiety feelings to the experience of joy, a positive emotion. Joy is characterized by intense feelings of pleasure, high activation, a desire to approach and embrace others, and a grinning expression (Jackson, 2000; Lazarus, 1991). In general, youth sport research has emphasized negative emotions, primarily anxiety (Smoll & Smith, 1996). Discrete positive emotions like joy and happiness have received scant attention (Graham, Kowalski, & Crocker, 2002) although youth research on global affective states like enjoyment is more common (Scanlan & Simons, 1992; Wankel & Kreisel, 1985; Weiss, Kimmel, & Smith, 2001).

Global affective states

Affective states have proven to be difficult to define and explain. Sport researchers have used the term to describe discrete emotional states (i.e. anxiety, happiness), ambiguous states (i.e., confidence, frustration, determination, intrinsic motivation), arousal symptoms (nervousness, distress), and global subjective emotional states (enjoyment, positive and negative affect; see Crocker, 1997; Crocker, Bouffard, & Gessaroli, 1995; Hanin, 2000; Vallerand & Blanchard, 2000; Wankel & Sefton, 1989). One reason for the varied usage of the term *affect* is the ongoing debate of whether to categorize emotional experience as a limited set of dimensions (i.e., positive and negative affect) or as discrete categories (see Lazarus, 2000a).

We will consider affect as a global subjective emotional state. Key characteristics of affect are that it is a subjective feeling state that varies in pleasantness/unpleasantness and intensity. Enjoyment is an emotional state that could be considered a global affective state. Recall the images from both Susy and Alexander. Their perceptions of enjoyment indicated a pleasant state of moderate intensity, associated with engagement in the activity. Global affective states like enjoyment do not seem to have the same strong physiological activation, facial expressions, or impulses to act as those associated with discrete emotions like anxiety or joy.

> Key characteristics of affect are that it is a subjective feeling state that varies in pleasantness/unpleasantness and intensity.

SOCIAL AND COGNITIVE DEVELOPMENT FACTORS RELATED TO EMOTION

Young athletes must learn when to experience emotions and, maybe more important, how to control and express emotions that are socially appropriate. Emotional development involves numerous skills such as awareness of their own and others' emotions, awareness of social standards of what is good and bad, the ability to form friendships that involve sharing as well as social and emotional intimacy, the development of strategies to manage emotions, and the learning of self-presentation strategies to mask internally experienced emotional states (Aldwin, 1994; Harter, 1999; Saarni, 1999). Obviously, emotional development is a complex area. Sport researchers and practitioners, however, should be aware of the ways in which specific social and cognitive changes might shape how emotions are generated, regulated, and reported in young athletes. We will briefly review three key interrelated developmental factors that influence emotional experience: (a) cognitive organization and structure, (b) information processing, and (c) social maturation.

One approach to cognitive development is to identify stages of cognitive organization and structure development (Hala, 1997). Elementary-school-aged children demonstrate concrete operational thought, or the ability to think logically about tangible events (Piaget, 1954). At this stage, children can coordinate several characteristics of an object rather than focus on just one (i.e., during soccer I can play goalie, defense, and forward), consider how characteristics interrelate, and display logical reasoning (Santrock & Yussen, 1992). Children also use concrete thought and organization when describing their sense of self, which is important because many theories hold that threats or benefits to self underlie many emotional experiences (Harter, 1999; Saarni, 1999). Part of self-representation is an internalization of social standards, which are necessary for understanding what actions and consequences are good and bad. Let's revisit the images of Susy and Alexander. First, both are aware of sport social standards and of their own emotional state. Seven-year-old Susy describes her distress when the other team scores against her but does not comment on the emotions of others. Nine-year-old Alexander is also conscious that opponents' emotions are aroused when his team scores, and that the opponent's emotions are associated with specific behaviors, subsequently increasing Alexander's anxiety level. Both Susy and Alexander, however, organize and describe their emotional experiences in concrete terms.

As athletes move through adolescence, they display increased ability to use more abstract, idealistic, and logical thought, often termed formal operations. Early adolescents begin to consider the numerous possibilities available in the world and, consequently, shift from an objective view of reality to one that is primarily subjective and idealistic (Santrock, 1998). By mid- to late adolescence, they are better able to integrate abstract thinking with concrete objective reality. The emergence of these mature thought structures enables the use of hypothetical-deductive reasoning, or the ability to consider multiple possibilities and systematically deduce the best course of action (Aldwin, 1994; Santrock, 1998). Nicole and Julie demonstrate some of the characteristics of formal operations in their discussions about important competitions. Twelve-year-old Nicole considered different coping options to manage her competitive anxiety. She recognized her social responsibility to support the team (prosocial standard) and suppressed her initial impulse to flee the stressful situation. Seventeen-year-old Julie demonstrated an advanced ability to integrate numerous factors such as the behavior and emotions of her coaches, future expectations of performance, the appropriateness of coping with injury and illness, and previous ways she had handled stress that she now considered to be inappropriate. The emotional experience descriptions provided by Nicole and Julie are cognitively more complex and demonstrate more mature organization and integration compared to those of Susy and Alexander.

Another way to consider cognitive development is to examine improvements in information-processing capabilities. These improvements are the result of changes in attention, memory, critical thinking, and problem-solving abilities (Guttentag & Ornstein, 1990; Keating, 1990; Santrock, 1998). Around age 11, children are better able to selectively attend to relevant stimuli while disregarding irrelevant information (Ross, 1976). Long-term memory improves considerably during childhood, enabling children to acquire and retain knowledge more readily (Santrock & Yussen, 1992). The maturation of attention and memory during childhood facilitates the development of decision making and, subsequently, problem-solving and critical

Challenging physical activity can do more than improve muscle tone—it can affect self-concept, motivation, and social interaction.

thinking skills in adolescence (Keating, 1990; Santrock, 1998). Adolescents are more able than children to generate options, take different perspectives, anticipate consequences, and consider the credibility of information sources. The developmental improvements in information-processing capabilities are evident in several characteristic emotional development skills. Better memory processing allows adolescents to consider multiple sources of information in determining the importance of specific sporting events and the regulation and display of emotion. Saarni (1999) has noted adolescents have the increased ability to integrate moral character and personal philosophy to manage stressful situations and to skillfully adopt self-presentation strategies for impression management.

Because so many emotional experiences occur in social settings, the ability to understand others' thoughts, emotions, and actions is important for emotional development (see Saarni, 1999). Thus, a third approach to understanding emotional development is to examine social maturation, the ability to conceptualize and reason about the interpersonal environment.

Social development is concerned with skills such as a child's ability to interpret emotional and behavioral cues in the self and others, and understand that emotional displays and behaviors influence social relationships (i.e., intimacy, social support; Banerjee, 1997; Saarni). Role taking and perspective taking are two social skills that evolve throughout childhood and early adolescence (Kurdek, 1979; Schultz, Barr, & Selman, 2001; Schultz & Selman, 2001; Selman, 1980).

Role-taking abilities emerge during mid- to late childhood. These skills allow children to understand that other people have different thoughts and feelings than they do and to comprehend the nature of those differences (Kurdek, 1979; Shantz, 1975). During early adolescence, egocentrism, the inability to distinguish one's own abstract perspectives from those of others, disrupts the integration of role-taking skills. Consequently, adult-like role taking is not demonstrated until mid- to late adolescence (Kurdek, 1979). Perspective taking is the ability to assume another person's point of view and understand his or her thoughts and feelings (Schultz & Selman, 2001; Selman, 1980). Early elementary school children are able to "put themselves in another's place." They do not, however, understand that the other person can also take that same perspective until late childhood/early adolescence (Selman). Mature perspective taking evolves during adolescence and involves (a) interpersonal understanding, or knowledge of what particular relationships should be like; (b) interpersonal action, or the ability to respond to others intimately and autonomously; and (c) personal meaning, or connecting history of social interactions to the present encounter (Schultz & Selman, 2001; Selman, 1980). Mature perspective taking is necessary to engage in reciprocal sharing of emotions and to be socially sensitive to the emotional displays and communications of others (Saarni, 1999).

In conclusion, the literature indicates that changes in cognitive organization and structure, information processing, and social maturity can affect how young people interpret and manage potentially stressful situations in sport. This literature *strongly* suggests that sport researchers need to consider developmental differences when trying to understand how emotions are generated, managed, and reported by children and adolescents. Within our review of the sport literature, we will examine whether cognitive and social developmental issues have been addressed. In the next section, we examine youth sport research for two common emotional states: anxiety and enjoyment.

> The ability to understand others' thoughts, emotions, and actions is important for emotional development.

EMOTIONAL EXPERIENCE IN SPORT: ANXIETY AND ENJOYMENT

Descriptive Analysis of Anxiety and Enjoyment

Descriptive analyses attempt to identify relationships between emotions and other intrapersonal, situational, and motivational factors. Because there is a substantial body of research on both anxiety and enjoyment in youth sport, we will highlight some of the consistent findings. More detailed reviews are available (see Gould, 1993; Gould & Eklund, 1996; Jackson, 2000; Passer, 1988; Scanlan & Simons, 1992; Smoll & Smith, 1996). For both anxiety and enjoyment, we will provide a description of how sport researchers have conceptualized the specific emotion, followed by the descriptive analysis.

Sport Anxiety

There is an extensive youth sport literature examining the causes and consequences of anxiety. In the sport literature, anxiety is often defined as an emotional response, consisting of cognitive concerns and physiological arousal to perceived threat (see Naylor, Burton, & Crocker, 2002; Smoll & Smith, 1996). Although some authors have used the terms *stress* and *anxiety* interchangeably (e.g., Passer, 1988; Scanlan, 1986), stress can produce numerous discrete emotions such anger, anxiety, fear, pride, and happiness (Crocker, Kowalski, Graham, et al., 2002; Lazarus, 2000b). Symptoms associated with anxiety include worry, apprehension, muscular tension, sweating, increased heart rate, and gastrointestinal dysfunction.

Researchers have conceptualized anxiety from both personality and situational viewpoints. *Competitive trait anxiety* refers to a relatively stable personality disposition to respond to a variety of competitive situations with increased worry and heightened physiological arousal (Martens, 1977). *Competitive state anxiety* refers to anxiety symptoms experienced in a particular sporting situation (Simon & Martens, 1979). Researchers have constructed self-report instruments to measure both trait and state anxiety in older children although measurement will be affected by both verbal ability and level of self-awareness (Raglin & Hanin, 2000).

The last decade has witnessed a move to conceptualizing anxiety as multidimensional with physiological and cognitive components. *Somatic anxiety* captures the physiological component associated with autonomic arousal whereas *cognitive anxiety* focuses on negative thoughts, worry, and negative expectations (Martens, Vealey, & Burton, 1990). Multidimensional theories of anxiety were developed primarily to account for the separate effects of each component on particular aspects of sport or motor performance.

In attempting to determine the cause of sport anxiety, researchers have concentrated on two general types of determinants: intrapersonal and situational. Heightened state anxiety is associated with the intrapersonal factors of low self-esteem, low confidence, low performance goals, low performance expectancies, and high trait anxiety (Burton & Martens, 1986; Crocker, Alderman, & Smith, 1988; Martens et al., 1990; Scanlan & Lewthwaite, 1984; Scanlan & Passer, 1978). Situational variables associated with anxiety are type of sport (individual sport is associated with higher anxiety than team sport), game outcome (losses and ties cause more anxiety than wins do), increased social evaluation, increased parental pressure, and game or situational importance (Brustad, 1988; Gould, Horn, & Spreeman, 1983; Scanlan & Lewthwaite, 1984; Scanlan & Passer, 1978; Simon & Martens, 1979).

A driving force behind research in youth sport is the belief that high anxiety is the cause of numerous negative participation, health, and performance consequences. Negative consequences include avoidance of sport, withdrawal, burnout, and reduced sport enjoyment (Gould, Feltz, Horn, & Weiss, 1982; Gould, Udry, Tuffey, & Loehr, 1996; Orlick & Botterill, 1975; Wankel & Kreisel, 1985; Weiss & Petlichkoff, 1989). High levels of anxiety can also cause gastrointestinal problems, injury, and sleep and eating disruption (see Smoll & Smith, 1996). A more controversial issue is whether anxiety impairs sporting performance. There is evidence that for some children, anxiety does disrupt performance (Burton, 1988). In contrast, some youth athletes believe that anxiety leads to better performance (Gould et al., 1983). Such findings contribute to an ongoing debate over the facilitative and debilitative effects of anxiety on performance although this issue centers mostly on older elite athletes (see Burton & Naylor, 1997; Jones, 1995).

Sport Enjoyment

Sport researchers have become increasingly interested in positive emotional experiences such as enjoyment. Sport enjoyment is more differentiated than global positive affect but is more global than specific emotions like happiness or joy (Jackson, 2000; Scanlan & Simons, 1992). In the youth sport literature, *enjoyment* and *fun* are often used as synonymous terms. Both fun and enjoyment are positive affective states although Wankel and Sefton (1989) suggest fun may have a social component. In this chapter, we will consider fun as emotionally equivalent to enjoyment. Some theorists, however, have attempted to conceptualize enjoyment beyond a mere positive affective state. Csikszentmihalyi (1990) argued that enjoyment involves an investment of attention and effort and results in psychological growth (see Jackson, 2000). However, Csikszentmihalyi's conceptualization has not been widely accepted in the sport enjoyment research with children and youth.

When children and youth enjoy sport they are more likely to continue participating, have high expectancies for continued participation, and show greater sport commitment.

Unlike anxiety, sport researchers have shown little interest in viewing enjoyment as a personality disposition. Although trait-like constructs such as *optimism* or *positive affectivity* could be considered personality dispositions closely linked to *trait enjoyment*, little research has investigated such linkage. There has also been no attempt to conceptualize enjoyment as a multidimensional construct.

Sport research on positive affective states, like enjoyment, in children and adolescents is not as comprehensive as anxiety-based research is. Intrapersonal factors associated with sport enjoyment include perceptions of competence/ability, task-oriented achievement goals, personal accomplishment, personal control, and intrinsic motivation. Sport enjoyment is also linked to involvement in challenging skills, social involvement and friendships, extrinsic rewards, high activity levels, low parental pressure, positive emotional involvement of parents, mastery-focused teaching environment, pleasing of significant adults like parents and coaches, and skill development (Brustad, 1988; Csikszentmihalyi, 1975; J. C. Harris, 1984; Ommundsen & Vaglum, 1991; Scanlan, Carpenter, Lobel, & Simons, 1993; Scanlan & Lewthwaite, 1986; Treasure, 1997; Wankel & Kreisel, 1985; Wankel & Sefton, 1989; Weiss, Smith, & Theeboom, 1996). Not surprisingly, research indicates that sport enjoyment is associated with positive consequences. When children and youth enjoy sport, they are more likely to stay in sport, have high expectancies for continued participation, and show greater sport commitment (Gill, Gross, & Huddleston, 1983; Scanlan & Lewthwaite, 1986; Weiss et al., 2001; Weiss & Petlichkoff, 1989).

Descriptive Analysis of Emotions: Limitations

Although the descriptive analyses of enjoyment and anxiety identified an extensive list of sources, there are definite limitations to such an approach. When we focus on just the sources of emotion, such analyses seldom lead to a conceptual understanding of the process, nor are we able to account for individual differences. There are so many sources of sport emotion that a purely descriptive analysis results in a fragmented and possibly simplistic understanding. Further, descriptive analyses cannot account for how cognitive and social development variables produce differences in the interpretation of events and subsequent emotional experience. Theories and models provide frameworks to assist in grouping research findings into logical conceptual frameworks and clearly defining the relationships among critical constructs (Rejeski, 1992). Any model or theory of sport emotion must also be able to explain the descriptive relationships. In the next section, we will review four specific cognitively oriented emotion models and theories used by youth sport researchers.

MODELS AND THEORIES OF EMOTION

Harter's Self-Construction and Effectance Motivation

Harter (1978) developed a model of effectance motivation that provides a developmental theoretical model through which the causes and consequences of emotional experiences can be examined in a number of contexts. Harter's theory is comprehensive and deals with a number of motivational issues that are beyond the scope of this chapter (see Weiss & Williams, 2003, for a review of these issues). In terms of emotional experience, Harter (1978) argued that children and youth are motivated to be competent, and positive feelings are experienced when mastery efforts to be competent are perceived to be successful. In contrast, lack of success leads to negative emotional states. Numerous sport studies with children and adolescents have found relationships between perceived competence and emotional experience that support Harter's basic postulation (e.g., Brustad, 1988; Wankel & Kreisel, 1985; Weiss, Bredemeier, & Shewchuk, 1986; Weiss & Horn, 1990).

Harter (1982, 1985) expanded on the idea of domain-specific competence to develop a theory on the development of global self to explain affect and motivated behavior (see Horn, this volume, for a detailed discussion). Two interrelated processes are involved in developing the self. First, self-worth is dependent upon perceptions of competence in domains or activities that the person views as important. In childhood, five domains have been identified: cognitive competence, physical competence, physical appearance, social competence, and behavioral conduct (Harter, 1985). These domains become more differentiated throughout later childhood and adolescence. Perceptions of competence in domains viewed as important are related to positive self-worth. The second process contributing to self-worth is how people perceive themselves to be socially regarded and supported. Harter (1987) found that perceived social regard and support influenced global self-worth independently of competence perceptions. Global self-worth, in turn, is thought to influence affective responses and motivational behavior.

Harter's theory is developmental in that it accounts for cognitive changes in how competence is perceived and how particular social sources influence perceptions of social regard and support. By middle to late childhood, children are able to differentiate their competencies in a number of domains, as well as to make generalized assessments of global self-worth (Harter, 1985). They are also able to internalize others' standards and use them as self-guides. This enables children to begin to use peer comparison as a means of gathering competence information (Harter, 1999). At this stage, parents and significant adults are the primary sources of social support and regard, with peers playing a minor role. In adolescence, competence perceptions are further differentiated to reflect greater cognitive capacity and the inclusion of new life experiences. Sources of social support and regard shift to include peers as well as parents and significant adults.

The nature of the relationship of the competence-importance discrepancy and perceptions of social regard and support to outcome variables, particularly affect and motivation, is the subject of considerable debate. Harter's (1987) research found that global self-worth mediated the joint effects of perceived competence and perceptions of social regard and support on emotional experience and subsequent motivation (see Figure 1). Research by Ebbeck and Weiss (1998), however, found evidence supporting two models where affect was either an antecedent or an outcome of perceived competence.

Harter's model has been adapted for use in the sport context by using perceptions of physical competence in place of competence perceptions in all five domains, restricting social regard and support to that pertaining to the sport domain, and modifying the outcomes to be sport enjoyment in place of global affect and motivation for physical activity participation in place of motivation for age-appropriate activities (see Weiss, 2000; Weiss & Ebbeck). Although the entire model has not been tested directly, there is evidence to suggest that it may not be the most appropriate representation. Sport and physical activity research seems to indicate that the specific lower-order constructs of physical competence and activity-specific social support and regard are better predictors of physical activity motivation and behavior than are higher-order, global constructs such as self-worth (Duncan, 1993; A. L. Smith, 1999).

In her most recent work, Harter (1999) has gone beyond her additive model of the causes and consequences of self-worth. She has further differentiated the links between perceptions of competence in the five domains and social support and approval from parents and peers (see Figure 2). Essentially, she has differentiated between two clusters of competence perceptions and social support/approval sources and the relationship of these clusters to emotional responses and self-worth. The first cluster comprises perceptions of physical appearance, likeability by peers, and athletic competence. These three competencies have the strongest relationship with peer support and approval, which subsequently leads to variations in self-worth, affect or mood, and hopelessness, termed the *depression/adjustment composite*. The second cluster consists of perceptions of scholastic competence and behavioral conduct, which relate most strongly to parental approval and support. This cluster also contributes to variations in the depression/adjustment composite and subsequent outcomes. Harter's research has primarily dealt with the outcome of suicidal ideation, but investigations in the sport context could examine the potential validity of this model with sport-related affective and motivational outcomes.

Harter's new model has some interesting implications for youth sport emotion and motivation research. In her previous models, social approval and support sources were one of two separate, independent antecedents. As such, social influences were often examined separately

FIGURE 1
Mediational model of self-worth.

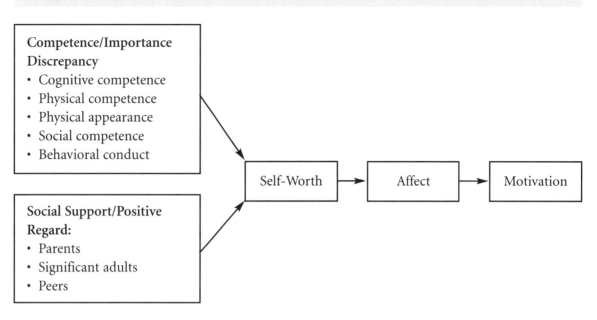

FIGURE 2
General model of the predictors of depression/adjustment.

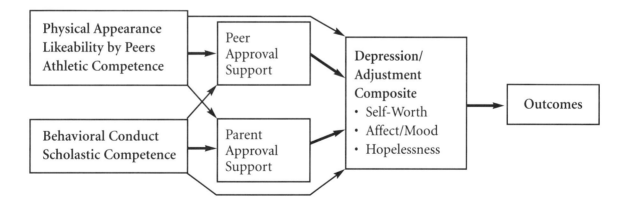

from competence perceptions or were ignored altogether in favor of examining the effects of competence perceptions in youth sport research. This has resulted in a rich literature regarding competence perceptions and a relatively weak understanding of the impact of social approval and support on affect and motivation in the youth sport context. This new model stresses the importance and integration of both competence perceptions and social regard and support. In particular, Harter's model points to the centrality of the role of peers in youth sport self-perceptions. Physical competence, likeability by peers, and physical appearance—the three competence domains most relevant to youth sport—are linked to peer approval and support in the model. This new conceptualization calls for an integration of the sport competence and peer acceptance and friendship research and will, it is hoped, lead to a better understanding of emotional experience and motivation in youth sport.

Weiner's (1985) Attribution Theory of Emotion and Motivation

Weiner's attribution theory provides a comprehensive framework for understanding emotion and motivation in achievement settings. It was a prominent theory in the investigation of sport and exercise emotional experience through the 1980s and early 1990s (Biddle & Hanrahan, 1998) although sport research with children and youth has been limited. Because we have already reviewed this theory in more detail in another chapter (see Crocker, Kowalski, Hoar, & McDonough, 2003), our treatment in this section will be more limited. Primarily we will focus on the key concepts, developmental considerations, children and youth research, and suggestions for a broader range of attribution research based on the theme of personal and social responsibility.

Weiner (1985) proposed that emotional states are the result of both achievement outcome and the reasons people attribute to the cause of the outcome. General emotional states such as happiness follow perceived success whereas sadness follows perceived failure. This process is termed *outcome-dependent attribution-independent*. A second reflective appraisal process produces more distinct emotions. This process involves the athlete's searching for reasons to explain the outcome. The most common attributions in youth sport are personal ability, effort, task difficulty, and luck although other causes may include teamwork, teammates, referee decisions, injury, and playing conditions (see Biddle & Hanrahan, 1998). This causal search process is termed *attribution dependent*. Sport enjoyment is likely to occur when achievement outcomes are perceived to be successful. Sport anxiety is more difficult to ascertain as it often occurs before and during competition. However, unsuccessful outcomes attributed to stable causes are likely to produce negative future expectancies and anxiety in similar achievement settings.

Weiner (1985) argued that the numerous specific causal attributions could be classified into three causal dimensions: locus, stability, and control. Each dimension, or combination of dimensions, was proposed to generate specific emotions. For example, a negative outcome attributed to a controllable wrongful act by another should produce anger. Joy and pride, on the other hand, are experienced when we achieve a valued goal that we attribute to personal responsibility.

An apparent challenge to the validity of attributional analysis in children's and youth's sport emotion is cognitive maturity. Children under 11 years are limited in knowledge, ability to process information, and ability to engage in hypothetical deductive reasoning (Beck, 2000). How can these children make accurate causal ascriptions when they have difficulty differentiating among ability, effort, luck, and task difficulty? Weiner and colleagues' research, however, indicates that children as young as 7 years are capable of searching for causes and making judgments about responsibility (Caprara, Pastorelli, & Weiner 1997). Recall the image of Susy trying to make sense of her soccer goalie performance. She originally relied on the outcome (goals scored against her) but then incorporated the coach's feedback of her performance to adjust her affective response. Social and cognitive development will limit the information and sources that a child or adolescent can use to search for causes for specific outcomes.

To understand how children derive specific appraisals, we need to consider their cognitive and social maturity. Because most children under the age of 11 tend to use concrete information to make sense of the world, they lack the cognitive maturity to untangle multiple factors for a sport outcome. This might lead children to focus on tangible outcomes to determine emotional experience. Young Susy understood that one object of soccer is to score more goals than the other team and that winning is good. She cried after allowing a second goal but felt better when the coach gave her information that she had played well. The emotional experience of 17-year-old Julie showed far greater cognitive-social sophistication in integrating past experience, the uncontrollability of injury and illness, and the appropriateness of the specific social support from coaches.

Sport research on attribution-emotion relationships in children and youth has produced mixed findings. There is strong evidence that outcomes are associated with the predicted general positive or negative affective states (Duncan, 1993; Graham et al., 2002; Robinson & Howe, 1989; Vallerand, 1987). The relationship between causal attributions and discrete emotions is less clear. In most studies, perception of outcome is the most influential determinant of emotional experience. Causal dimensions may be linked to specific emotions, but not always in the predicted direction (Graham et al., 2002; Robinson & Howe; Vlachpoulos, Biddle, & Fox, 1996).

> Sport is an arena to study behaviors such as friendship, conflict, and social inclusion.

Youth sport emotion research investigating Weiner's theory (1985, 1986) has generally focused on the athlete's emotional experience following an achievement situation. Sport is also an arena to study behaviors such as friendship, conflict, social inclusion, and other interpersonal behavior (Weiss et al., 1996). Social and emotional research in the education field has examined the role of attributing effort versus ability for judging personal and social responsibility (Caprara et al., 1997; Juvonen & Weiner, 1993; Weiner, 1994). Rather than focusing on self-esteem and performance, this research is directed towards understanding interpersonal behavior and emotion. It examines how children and adolescents react to others' behaviors, perceive fairness, anticipate other people's reactions, and utilize impression-management strategies (Weiner, 1994). Weiner and colleagues argue that the key dimension to understanding the emotion and behavior associated with social responsibility is controllability. A child is likely to feel angry if a negative event is attributed to a lack of effort by a teammate. Feelings of anger, in turn, are likely to lead to specific behaviors like social rejection, retaliation, and other punishment. In contrast, a child is more likely to feel sympathetic and engage in prosocial behaviors such as support and help if a failure is attributed to uncontrollable factors (see Figure 3).

Perceptions of responsibility also influence how a youth believes she or he will be treated by significant others. A player who is not succeeding due to lack of ability does not believe teammates or coaches should be angry. Recall 17-year-old Julie, who felt that her coaches' supportive behavior was justified because her performance was due to uncontrollable factors such as illness and injury, not lack of effort. If her coaches were angry, such behavior would be perceived as unfair because Julie attributed her poor performance to uncontrollable events. The perception of unjust coaching behavior is likely to increase the athlete's anxiety and reduce sport enjoyment.

A third area of emotion-behavioral research deals with the impression-management strategies of a person who believes she or he will be subjected to angry responses (Caprara et al., 1997). The youth will often feel anxious, attempt to avoid or hide out, or conceal the true cause of the negative event to reduce an anticipated angry response. In sport, impression-management strategies might include faking illness or injury and deflecting responsibility.

A number of interesting youth sport research questions can be developed from Weiner's social responsibility work. For example, given younger athletes' inability to discriminate

FIGURE 3

An attributional framework of interpersonal motivation linking events, causes, attributions, emotions, and behavioral reactions

Event	Attribution	Responsibility	Emotion	Behavior
Unable to perform a skill	Lack of effort (Controllable)	Child judged responsible	Anger	• Social rejection • Verbal criticism • Possible physical confrontation
Unable to perform a skill	Lack of ability (Uncontrollable)	Child judged not responsible	Sympathy	• Prosocial behaviors • Helping • Social support

between effort and ability (see Fry, 2001), what information are children using to form judgments of responsibility in sport, and what are the associated emotions and behaviors? How do social constructions like "obesity" influence children's and adolescents' perceptions of overweight others in sport? Other research questions include examining how athletes feel about the "fairness" of coaches' expressed emotion when the athlete is trying (or not trying) but still failing, and the emotional-behavioral strategies athletes use to avoid punishment. The area of social responsibility offers some exciting youth-sport research possibilities.

Scanlan's Model of Sport Enjoyment and Commitment

Scanlan and her colleagues (Scanlan, Carpenter, et al., 1993; Scanlan & Lewthwaite, 1986; Scanlan & Simons, 1992; Scanlan, Simons, Carpenter, Schmidt, & Keeler, 1993) have undertaken a program of research exploring the link between enjoyment and motivation in youth sport. Early research resulted in Scanlan and Lewthwaite (1986) constructing a two-dimensional model of the sources of sport enjoyment (see Figure 4). They used the two dimensions of intrinsic-extrinsic and achievement-nonachievement to create four quadrants or categories of sources of sport enjoyment. Quadrant I is the intrinsic-achievement category, and it represents personally derived perceptions of competence and control such as mastery-goal attainment and perceived ability. Quadrant II, the extrinsic-achievement category, includes perceptions of competence and control that result from social evaluation and recognition sources. Quadrant III represents intrinsic-nonachievement sources and includes movement aspects such as sensations, tension release, action, and exhilaration, as well as competition aspects including excitement. The final quadrant consists of extrinsic-nonachievement sources such as affiliation with peers and adult interactions. This framework provides a means of identifying and categorizing potential sources of sport enjoyment, and it has played a role in establishing sport enjoyment as a much broader concept than intrinsic motivation (Scanlan & Simons, 1992).

Further research on the construct of sport enjoyment resulted in the development of the Sport Commitment Model (Scanlan, Simons, et al., 1993). The model states that sport commitment is predicted by sport enjoyment, personal investments, social constraints, involvement opportunities, and involvement alternatives (see Figure 5). In studies employing the Sport Commitment Model, enjoyment has consistently emerged as the strongest predictor of commitment (Scanlan, Simons, et al., 1993; Weiss et al., 2001). This relationship between

FIGURE 4

Two-dimensional framework of the predictors of enjoyment

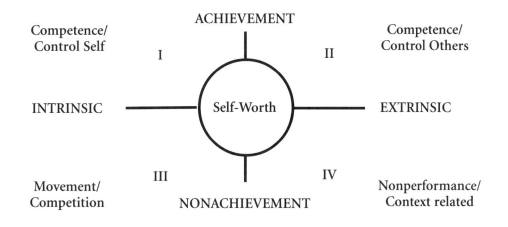

Reprinted, by permission, from T.K. Scanlan, & R. Lewthwaite, 1986, "Social psychological aspects of competition for male youth sport participants: IV. Predictors of enjoyment," *Journal of Sport Psychology, 8,* (1), 33.

affect and motivation bears a strong resemblance to that proposed in Harter's (1987) model where, regardless of the debate over the mediational nature of self-worth, most of the effects of the antecedents of motivation act via their effect on affect.

Weiss and colleagues (2001) recently explored this connection in their study testing alternative models of the Sport Commitment Model. They began by comparing two models: a modified version of the original model and a model in which enjoyment mediated the relationship between the other five predictors and commitment (see Figure 6). Modifications of the original Sport Commitment Model included the addition of social support and perceived competence (the major antecedents used in Harter's 1987 model) and the elimination of involvement opportunities. This latter construct was reasoned to conceptually overlap with social support, perceived competence, and enjoyment (Weiss et al., 2001). The alternative model was tested because (a) the strength of the relationship between sport enjoyment and commitment and (b) the moderate relationships between enjoyment and the constructs of involvement opportunities, personal investments, social support, and perceived competence rendered the possibility of the mediational role of sport enjoyment (Weiss et al., 2001). These two models fit the data equally well. In addition, a third model that combined the first two models' having both direct paths from the antecedents to commitment and a partial mediational role of enjoyment was also found to fit the data adequately. This line of research is intriguing as it links two established models of affect and motivation, and it may prove more fruitful if it is replicated in other studies with large samples.

The Sport Commitment Model was developed with children ranging in age from 10 to 19 years (Scanlan, Simons, et al., 1993), and it has been used in studies with both children and adults (Carpenter & Scanlan, 1998; VanYperen, 1998; Weiss et al., 2001). Despite its development and use with a wide range of ages and developmental stages, the Sport Commitment Model does not account for cognitive and social developmental changes. The antecedents of commitment

Children's perceptions of enjoyment, social constraints, and involvement opportunities may be tied to the support they receive from their parents, while adolescents' perceptions may be more closely tied to peer support and approval.

FIGURE 5
The sport commitment model.

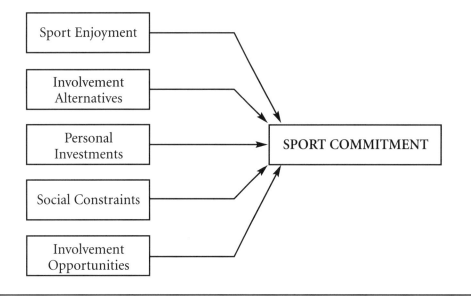

FIGURE 6
A mediational model of sport commitment.

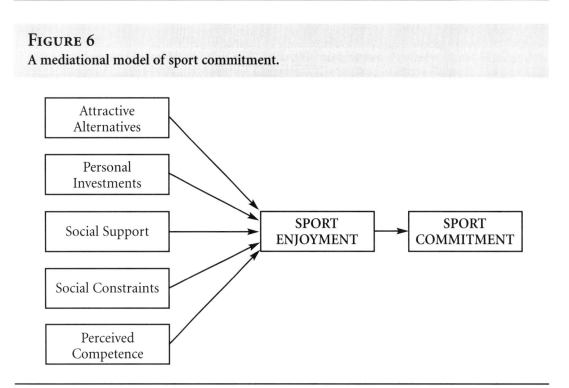

should be expected to vary with development. Because children tend to rely primarily on parents and significant adults for social support and approval, their perceptions of enjoyment, social constraints, involvement opportunities, and alternatives may be more tied to the support and approval they receive from their parents, whereas adolescents' perceptions of these constructs may be more closely tied to peer support and approval. Further, children's cognitive constructions of these abstract constructs should be different from those of older adolescents. More research is needed to examine the structure of sport enjoyment and sport commitment at different developmental stages.

Lazarus' Cognitive-Motivational-Relational Model of Emotion

Lazarus (1991, 1999) developed a transactional emotion theory that can help explain how and why children and youth experience and regulate emotion in sport. Because we have described this theory in some detail elsewhere (Crocker et al., this volume), only a brief review of this theory will be presented here. Lazarus' cognitive-motivational-relational theory of emotion attempts to integrate cognitive, motivational, and relational features. There are two key processes involved in the generation and regulation of emotions: cognitive appraisal and coping. Cognitive appraisal is theorized to have two interrelated processes: primary appraisal and secondary appraisal (Lazarus, 1991). *Primary appraisal* deals with what is at stake for the person in any person-environment encounter. It is a motivationally oriented appraisal that consists of determining whether the situation is important and whether personal goals are being attained or threatened (Lazarus, 1991). These goals can include achievement goals and social goals. *Secondary appraisal* is an evaluation of (a) coping options, (b) individual responsibility, and (c) future expectations. Essentially, it is an evaluation of what action might prevent harm, moderate it, or produce additional harm or benefit (Lazarus, 2000a). Think back to 12-year-old Nicole's image. She felt anxiety (a threat to her sense of self) in a game that she judged to be important, the opposition to be difficult, and a lack of confidence in her ability to handle the demand. She also evaluated ways of dealing with the threat, including escaping the scene or facing the challenge.

Lazarus and his colleagues (Folkman & Lazarus, 1990; Lazarus, 1999) argued that a number of environmental and person characteristics jointly contribute to individual differences in cognitive appraisal. The demands, constraints, opportunities, and cultural context may influence how an encounter is appraised. Patterns of motivation (e.g., values, commitments, and goals), beliefs about oneself and the world, and recognition of personal resources for coping (such as social support) are factors that may affect how a person-environment encounter is evaluated. Clearly, cognitive and social development will influence appraisal of the situation, what type of social support is available, and potential options to manage the stress. Lazarus (1999) states that developmental processes influence the emotion process: "There are sound reasons for giving special consideration to stress, emotion, and coping in children and adolescents. . . . Cognitive and motivational processes change over the course of development and appraisal theory suggests that stress, emotion, and coping are dependent on both cognition and motivational processes" (p. 174).

How a child or adolescent copes with stress transactions is an important feature of Lazarus's theory. *Coping* refers to thoughts and behaviors used to manage stressful demands. Cognitive and social development has a major impact on coping (Aldwin, 1994) and, thus, on how youth athletes regulate emotion. Studies indicate that with chronological age, both the structure of coping within an individual's coping repertoire (i.e., the number and types of cognitive and behavioral strategies the individual is capable of executing) and the pattern of coping strategies used during emotion-eliciting encounters change as the individual matures (Boekaerts, 1996; Compas, Malcarne, & Fondacaro, 1988; Fields & Prinz, 1997). Further, the most dramatic shifts in coping are witnessed during the adolescent years, coinciding with the cognitive and social changes characteristic of this stage of development (Boekaerts; Compas, 1998; Lazarus, 1999; Seiffge-Krenke, 1995). Seiffge-Krenke's research indicates that cognitive development and social maturity interact to influence coping:

> At about age 15 in Seiffge-Krenke's data, adolescence seems to be marked by the development of cognitive processes from simple, concrete, and more self-centered thinking to *complex, abstract*, and *relational thinking*. Early adolescents who operate at an earlier level of social cognitive maturity are, for example, unlikely to differentiate between sources of support. They are less able to recognize links between current behavior and long-range outcomes and they are possibly more motivated by self-centered needs. In contrast, late adolescents, having already reached a more mature social cognitive level, select social support strictly in accordance to the problem at hand, consider current options more often, think about the future consequences of their actions, and reflect about their position with respect to the perspectives of others (as cited in Lazarus, 1999, pp. 181-182; italics added).

Youth sport research has only recently begun to use Lazarus' (1991, 1999) theory to guide research efforts to gain a better understanding of stress and emotion. Consequently, very few studies exist and most have not considered social and development factors (e.g., Anshel, 1996; Crocker & Isaak, 1997; Graham et al., 2002; Kolt, Kirkby, & Linder, 1995; Kowalski & Crocker, 2001). Moreover, these studies vary according to the extent to which major tenets of the theory are measured. Most research has examined only the coping process with adolescent athletes. An exception is recent work by Graham et al., who examined appraisal processes and emotion in adolescent athletes. They examined how goal characteristics (goal importance and goal congruence) and causal attributions predicted discrete emotions. In a study with 174 adolescent swimming and track-and-field athletes during their regular competitions, both goal characteristics and causal attributions were important in the emotion process. However, these processes acted quite separately (as opposed to having a combined effect) to predict emotions such as joviality, self-assurance, hostility, and guilt. A limitation of this work is that it neither assessed the coping process nor considered secondary appraisal factors, and thus it provides only a partial evaluation of the emotion process as envisioned by Lazarus (1999).

> Lazarus's theory holds that we must consider how individual differences in motivation and the environment combine to produce perosnal meaning and emotion.

Lazarus's theory provides a comprehensive framework for studying emotion in youth sport. The theory holds that we must consider how individual differences in motivation and personal resources and the environment combine to produce personal meaning and emotion. Obviously, the cognitive and social maturity of the athlete will have a major role in the generation and regulation of emotion. In all of our four athletes' images of emotion, the athletes' motivational structures, cognitive evaluations, and coping reveal different levels of cognitive and social maturity. Emotion is also a constantly changing process. When we examine both Susy's and Nicole's images of negative emotions, both athletes revealed how their emotional state changed as the situation unfolded over time. This suggests that a thorough understanding of emotion in sport will require the use of appropriate designs and analyses to capture this dynamic process.

In summary, we have reviewed four cognitively based theories or models that sport researchers have used to study emotional experience in youth sport. There are other theories that could also guide youth sport emotion research including achievement goal theory (Nicholls, 1984; see Treasure, 2001), self-efficacy theory (Bandura, 1997), and self-determination theory (Deci & Ryan, 1985). In general, all these theories hold that the generation of emotional experiences is the result of differences in how youth evaluate the meaning of situations. Emotional meaning will be shaped by the interplay between ever-changing societal forces, contextual demands, and personal attributes. Cognitive maturity will constrain how youth construct the world, as well as how they evaluate their abilities to be successful in this world. Personal emotional development also requires the navigation of changing social roles and social relationships. It is a major challenge for emotional theories in sport to account for all the cognitive, social, motivational, and developmental factors connected to emotion. Nevertheless, the noted emotion-related theories can help guide researchers in investigating the complexity of emotion. Careful theoretical analysis, combined with clever and developmentally appropriate methodology, can contribute to a greater understanding of emotional experience in youth sport.

FUTURE DIRECTIONS

In this chapter we have attempted to demonstrate that emotional experience in youth sport is a complex process that involves motivational, cognitive, and behavioral processes, all affected by social and cognitive development. The images revealed by our four young athletes demonstrate that emotional experience and expression is a complex phenomenon that constantly shifts over time and integrates both personal and environmental factors. Children's and adolescents' evaluation of events, the meaning given to events, the choice of coping strategies, emotional experience, and expression will change because of development. However, our understanding of the "how" and "why" about emotion in youth sport is still very limited. Although research suggestions have been made in various sections of this chapter, we will address specific issues that can advance our understanding of emotion in children and adolescents.

As with research on emotion conducted with adults, it is important to clearly define the emotion constructs of interest at a theoretical and measurement level (see Crocker et al., this volume). Earlier in this chapter, we discussed that a construct such as enjoyment can be considered more differentiated than global affect but more global than specific emotions such as joy or happiness. However, a neat hierarchical structure of the emotion constructs has yet to be established. How discrete emotions, affective dimensions, mood states, and temperament fit together is a challenging conceptual and empirical task. It is, however, an important task that will allow us the opportunity to better understand how these emotion variables are related to other important performance, health, and developmental variables.

In this chapter, we discussed two emotional states that have primarily dominated the youth sport emotion literature: anxiety and enjoyment. Several other specific emotions are also likely to play an important adaptive role in children's and adolescents' sport experiences. Lazarus (2000b) notes the functional roles of anger, anxiety, guilt, shame, relief, and happiness in the competitive sport context; and sport researchers need to expand research to include these differing emotions. Guilt and shame, in particular, offer youth sport researchers the opportunity to gain insight into the development of emotion during childhood and adolescence, as these two emotions are theorized to develop with cognitive and social maturation (Harter, 1999; Saarni, 1999). Perhaps the most important and difficult task for researchers, though, will be to untangle the complex web of how multiple emotions interact in emotional experience.

In addition to studying a broader array of emotional experiences, youth sport researchers need to move away from descriptive studies that provide a fragmented and overly simplistic view of emotion and instead move towards more theory-driven research. Emotion constantly shifts over time and integrates both person and environmental factors (Lazarus, 1991). The social world of children and adolescents significantly affects the generation and regulation of emotion, and emotion cannot be fully understood without considering the contextual nature in which it is embedded (Lazarus, 1991). Enjoyment, for example, may not result from particular events or contexts, but rather from the transaction between environment variables and the individual's appraisal. The meaning of situations is likely to change across sports, developmental age, cultural groups, and other sociocultural contexts (Brustad, 1998; Duda & Hayashi, 1998). Instead of looking for common events that contribute to children's enjoyment of sport, we need to determine how they view particular situations and their options for coping with those situations, in addition to questions about actual emotional experience. The anxiety literature has begun to incorporate emotion theories in more recent research, but the enjoyment literature has tended to be more atheoretical with the exception of examining the relationship between affect and motivation.

The meaning of situations changes across sports, developmental age, cultural groups, and other sociocultural contexts.

From a developmental perspective, we require a better understanding of the functional and motivational role of emotions in young athletes' sporting lives. This is not an easy area to explore because although emotion theories are quite consistent in suggesting an important motivational role of emotions in our thoughts and actions, each view of emotions does differ to some degree regarding the adaptive role of the emotions in our lives (Griffin & Mascolo, 1998). These perspectives vary in emphasis from the role of emotions as a basis for directing our thoughts (i.e., a structural-developmental perspective) to an emphasis on the role of emotions in preserving social order (i.e., a social-cultural perspective). The true functional role of emotion in sport has yet to be uncovered.

It is also unclear whether the functions of emotions in sport change throughout childhood and adolescence or whether it is just the behavioral displays or expressions of those emotions that are changing. For example, we might change our responses to emotions such as anger as we mature from early childhood to adolescence, but the motivational effects and functional role of that anger emotion might remain similar over time (Izard & Ackerman, 2000). Clearly, more longitudinal studies involving youth are needed to adequately address these types of questions.

A related research question is whether changes in behavioral displays or expressions really reflect changes in our emotional experiences. Put another way: are there situations in which young athletes display certain emotions to achieve their adaptive benefits without experiencing the actual emotions? Hackfort (1993) has suggested that athletes can fake or hide emotional displays to confuse opponents and officials. Weiner (1994) also suggests that older children and adolescents learn impression-management strategies to modify how people react to them emotionally (see Saarni, 1999). Understanding the meaning of expressed emotion in sport can be a difficult task. Some coaches attempt to get a better picture of their athletes' sporting experience by asking the athletes about their emotional experience. Questions such as "Were you feeling… anxious, scared, confident, or proud?" are commonplace when coaches conduct a postanalysis of a performance. This task of information gathering is difficult, as younger athletes often find it quite difficult to accurately understand and articulate their emotional experience (P. L. Harris, 2000).

We have only touched briefly on the role of coping in the emotion process, but this area is critical to developing effective and age-appropriate emotional control interventions and to properly evaluating those interventions, in order to maximize emotional experiences in sport. Emotional-control interventions such as stress management training (SMT; R. E. Smith, 1980) and stress inoculation training (SIT; Meichenbaum, 1985) have been used with various sport populations (see Crocker, Kowalski, & Graham, 2002, for an overview of these approaches). Although there has been some research on coping-skill interventions for youth, additional studies assessing how these types of programs can be structured to achieve maximum success across various developmental age groups and different genders are still required.

Perhaps most important, there is simply a need to address developmental issues in sport more directly and thoroughly. Indeed, young athletes may have very different appraisals, perceived coping options, and resultant emotional experiences compared to older athletes in the same situation. Until these processes are examined with developmental issues in mind, the understanding of emotions in youth in sport will be incomplete. Nearly two decades ago, Weiss and Bredemeier (1983) argued that motivational and stress research in youth sport required a developmental approach. Since then, sport researchers have made significant strides in considering a cognitive developmental perspective to studying psychological dimensions in children (see Weiss & Raedeke, this volume). We believe that sport researchers need to further extend a comprehensive developmental approach to the analysis of emotional experience.

In conclusion, this article has addressed key issues such as how emotional experiences are generated, what the consequences of emotional experience are, and how cognitive and social development might affect emotional experience in sport. The stories of Susy, Alexander, Nicole, and Julie demonstrate the important role that emotions play in the lives of young athletes. However, these stories also speak to the complexities of trying to understand emotional experience and emotional expression in youth. We are limited by conceptual challenges such as how to define emotional experience and how to measure various aspects of emotion and its related processes, including appraisal and coping. We are also limited by practical concerns such as how to study emotion from a developmental perspective. It takes a great deal of time and effort (and resources!) to study the process of emotion over any significant developmental period. Harter's model of effectance motivation, Weiner's attribution theory, Scanlan's model of the sources of sport enjoyment, and Lazarus' cognitive-motivational-relational theory have been important in giving us a framework for the study of emotion in sport. In addition, research into specific emotion-related constructs such as anxiety and enjoyment have helped us to understand some of the basic relationships between emotion and sport participation and performance. Although developmental issues surrounding emotion in sport are extremely complex, it is critical we continue to explore these issues with the ultimate goal being the development of effective interventions aimed at improving the emotional lives of young athletes.

REFERENCES

Aldwin, C. M. (1994). *Stress, coping, and development*. New York: Guilford Press.

Anshel, M. (1996). Coping styles among adolescent competitive athletes. *The Journal of Social Psychology, 13*, 311-323.

Bandura, A. (1997). *Self-efficacy: The exercise of control*. New York: W.H. Freeman.

Banerjee, M. (1997). Peeling the onion: A multilayered view of children's emotional development. In S. Hala (Ed.), *The development of social cognition* (pp. 241-272). East Sussex, UK: Psychology Press.

Beck, L. E. (2000) *Child development* (5th ed.). London: Allyn and Bacon.

Biddle, S. J., & Hanrahan, S. (1998). Attributions and attributional style. In J. L. Duda (Ed.), *Advances in sport and exercise psychology measurement* (pp. 3-19). Morgantown, WV: Fitness Information Technology.

Boekaerts, M. (1996). Coping with stress in childhood and adolescence. In M. Zeidner & N. S. Endler (Eds.), *Handbook of coping* (pp. 452-484). New York: Wiley.

Brustad, R. J. (1988). Affective outcomes in competitive youth sport: The influence of intrapersonal and socialization variables. *Journal of Sport & Exercise Psychology, 10*, 307-321.

Brustad, R. J. (1998). Developmental considerations in sport and exercise psychology measurement. In J. L. Duda (Ed.), *Advances in sport and exercise psychology measurement* (pp. 461-471). Morgantown, WV: Fitness Information Technology.

Burton, D. (1988). Do anxious swimmers swim slower? Reexamining the elusive anxiety-performance relationship. *Journal of Sport & Exercise Psychology, 10*, 294-306.

Burton, D., & Martens, R. (1986). Pinned by their own goals: An exploratory investigation into why kids drop out of wrestling. *Journal of Sport Psychology, 8*, 183-197.

Burton, D., & Naylor, S. (1997). Is anxiety really facilitative? Reaction to the myth that cognitive anxiety always impairs sport performance. *Journal of Applied Sport Psychology, 9*, 295-302.

Caprara, G. V., Pastorelli, C., & Weiner, B. (1997). Linkages between causal ascriptions, emotion, and behavior. *International Journal of Behavioral Development, 20*, 153-162.

Carpenter, P. J., & Scanlan, T. K. (1998). Changes over time in the determinants of sport commitment. *Pediatric Exercise Science, 10*, 356-365.

Compas, B. E. (1998). An agenda for coping research and theory: Basic and applied developmental issues. *International Journal of Behavioral Development, 22*, 231-237.

Compas, B. E., Malcarne, V. L., & Fondacaro, K. M. (1988). Coping with stressful events in older children and young adolescents. *Journal of Consulting and Clinical Psychology, 56*, 405-411.

Cornelius, R. R. (1996). *The science of emotion: Research and tradition in the psychology of emotion.* Upper Saddle River, NJ: Prentice Hall.

Crocker, P. R. E. (1997). A confirmatory factor analysis of the positive affect negative affect schedule with a youth sport sample. *Journal of Sport & Exercise Psychology, 19*, 91-97.

Crocker, P. R. E., Alderman, R. B., & Smith, F. M. R. (1988). Cognitive-affective stress management training with high performance youth volleyball players: Effects on affect, cognition and performance. *Journal of Sport & Exercise Psychology, 10*, 448-460.

Crocker, P. R. E., Bouffard, M., & Gessaroli, M. E. (1995). Measuring enjoyment in youth sport settings. A confirmatory factor analysis of the Physical Activity Enjoyment Scale. *Journal of Sport & Exercise Psychology, 17*, 200-205.

Crocker, P. R. E., & Isaak, K. (1997). Coping during competitions and training sessions: Are youth swimmers consistent? *International Journal of Sport Psychology, 28*, 355-369.

Crocker, P. R. E., Kowalski, K., & Graham, T. R. (2002). Emotional control intervention for sport. In J. Silva & D. Stevens (Eds.), *Psychological foundations of sport* (pp. 155-176). Boston: Allyn & Bacon.

Crocker, P. R. E., Kowalski, K.C., Graham, T. R., & Kowalski, N. P. (2002). Emotion in sport. In J. Silva & D. Stevens (Eds.), *Psychological foundations of sport* (pp. 107-131). Boston: Allyn & Bacon.

Crocker, P. R. E., Kowalski, K. C., Hoar, S. D., & McDonough, M. H. (2003). Emotions in sport across adulthood. In M. R. Weiss (Ed.), *Developmental sport and exercise psychology: A lifespan perspective.* (pp. 333-355) Morgantown WV: Fitness Information Technology.

Csikszentmihalyi, M. (1975). *Beyond boredom and anxiety.* San Francisco: Josey-Bass.

Csikszentmihalyi, M. (1990). *Flow: The psychology of optimal experience.* New York: Harper & Row.

Deci, E. L., & Ryan, R. M. (1985). *Intrinsic motivation and self-determination in human behavior.* New York: Plenum Press.

Duda, J. L., & Hayashi, C. T. (1998). Measurement issues in cross-cultural research within sport and exercise psychology. In J. L. Duda (Ed.), *Advances in sport and exercise psychology measurement* (pp. 471-483). Morgantown, WV: Fitness Information Technology.

Duncan, S. C. (1993). The role of cognitive appraisal and friendship provisions in adolescents' affect and motivation towards activity in physical education. *Research Quarterly for Exercise and Sport, 64*, 314-323.

Ebbeck, V., & Weiss, M. R. (1998). Determinants of children's self-esteem: An examination of perceived competence and affect in sport. *Pediatric Exercise Science, 10*, 285-298.

Ekman, P. (1994). All emotions are basic. In P. Ekman & R. J. Davidson (Eds.), *The nature of emotion: Fundamental questions* (pp. 15-19). New York: Oxford University Press.

Fields, L., & Prinz, R. J. (1997). Coping and adjustment during childhood and adolescence. *Clinical Psychological Review, 17*, 937-976.

Folkman, S., & Lazarus, R. S. (1990). Coping and emotion. In N. L. Stein, B. Leventhal, & T. Trabasso (Eds.), *Psychological and biological approaches to emotion* (pp. 313-332). Hillsdale, NJ: Erlbaum.

Fry, M. D. (2001). The development of motivation in children. In G. C. Roberts (Ed.), *Motivation in sport and exercise* (2nd ed, pp. 51-78). Champaign, IL: Human Kinetics

Gill, D. L., Gross, J. B., & Huddleston, S. (1983). Participation motivation in youth sport. *International Journal of Sport Psychology, 14*, 1-14.

Gould, D. (1993). Intensive sport participation and the pre-pubescent athlete: Competitive stress and burnout. In B.R. Cahill & A. J. Pearl (Eds.), *Intensive participation in children's sports* (pp. 19-38). Champaign, IL: Human Kinetics.

Gould, D., & Eklund, R. C. (1996). Emotional stress and anxiety in the child and adolescent athlete. In O. Bar-Or (Ed.), *The encyclopedia of sports medicine:* Volume VI. *The child and adolescent athlete* (pp. 383-398). Oxford: Blackwell Science.

Gould, D., Feltz, D., Horn, T., & Weis, M. (1982). Reasons for discontinuing involvement in competitive youth swimming. *Journal of Sport Behavior, 5*, 155-156.

Gould, D., Horn, T., & Spreeman, J. (1983). Competitive anxiety in junior elite wrestlers. *Journal of Sport Psychology, 5*, 58-71.

Gould, D., Udry, E., Tuffey, S., & Loehr, J. (1996). Burnout in competitive junior tennis players: I. A quantitative psychological assessment. *The Sport Psychologist, 10*, 322-341.

Graham, T. R., Kowalski, K.C., & Crocker, P. R. E. (2002). The contributions of goal characteristics and causal attributions to emotional experience in youth sport participants. *Psychology of Sport and Exercise, 3, 273-291.*

Griffin, S., & Mascolo, M. F. (1998). On the nature, development, and functions of emotions. In M. F. Mascolo & S. Griffin (Eds.), *What develops in emotional development* (pp. 3-27). New York: Plenum Press.

Guttentag, R., & Ornstein, P. (1990). Attentional capacity and children's memory strategy use. In J. Ennis (Ed.), *The development of attention: Research and theory* (pp. 305-319). North Holland: Elsevier Science Publishers.

Hackfort, D. (1993). Functional attributions to emotions in sport. In J. R. Nitsch and R. Seiler, (Eds.), *Movement in sport: Psychological foundations and effects. Proceedings of the VIIIth European Congress of Sport Psychology* (Vol.1, pp.143-149). Sankt Augustin: Academia Verlag.

Hala, S. (1997). Introduction. In S. Hala (Ed.), *The development of social cognition* (pp. 3-33). East Sussex, UK: Psychology Press Ltd.

Hanin, Y. L. (2000). Individual zones of optimal functioning (IZOF) model: Emotion-performance relationships in sport. In Y. L. Hanin (Ed.), *Emotions in sport* (pp. 65-89). Champaign, IL: Human Kinetics.

Harris, J. C. (1984). Interpreting youth baseball: Players' understanding of fun and excitement, danger and boredom. *Research Quarterly for Exercise and Sport, 53,* 379-382.

Harris, P. L. (2000). Understanding emotions. In M. Lewis & J. M. Haviland-Jones (Eds.), *Handbook of emotions* (2nd ed., pp. 281-292). New York: The Guilford Press.

Harter, S. (1978). Effectance motivation reconsidered: Toward a developmental model. *Human Development, 21,* 34-64.

Harter, S. (1982). The perceived competence scale for children. *Child Development, 53,* 87-97.

Harter, S. (1985). Competence as a dimensional self-evaluation: Towards a comprehensive model of self-worth. In R. Leahy (Ed.), *The development of the self* (pp. 55-122). New York: Academic Press.

Harter, S. (1987). The determinants and mediational role of self-esteem in children. In N. Eisenberg (Ed.), *Contemporary topics in developmental psychology* (pp. 219-242). New York: John Wiley & Sons, Inc.

Harter, S. (1999). *The construction of self: A developmental perspective.* New York: Guilford Press.

Horn, T. S. (2003). Developmental perspectives on self-perceptions in children and adolescents. In M. R. Weiss (Ed.), *Developmental sport and exercise psychology: A lifespan perspective.* (pp. 101-143) Morgantown WV: Fitness Information Technology.

Izard, C. E. (1977). *Human emotions.* New York: Plenum Press.

Izard, C. E., & Ackerman, B. P. (2000). Motivational, organizational, and regulatory functions of discrete emotions. In M. Lewis & J. M. Haviland-Jones (Eds.), *Handbook of emotions* (2nd ed., pp. 252-264). New York: The Guilford Press.

Jackson, S. (2000). Joy, fun and flow states in sport. In Y.C. Hanin (Ed.), *Emotions in sport* (pp. 135-156). Champaign, IL: Human Kinetics.

Jones, J. G. (1995). More than just a game: Research developments and issues in competitive anxiety in sport. *British Journal of Psychology, 86,* 449-478.

Juvonen, J., & Weiner, B. (1993). An attributional analysis of student's interactions: The social consequences of perceived responsibility. *Educational Psychology Review, 5,* 325-345.

Juvonen, J., & Weiner, B. (1994). Social motivation in the classroom: Implications for students' achievement. *Scandinavian Journal of Educational Research, 38,* 279-289.

Keating, D. P. (1990). Adolescent thinking. In S. S. Feldman & G. R. Elliott (Eds.), *At the threshold: The developing adolescent* (pp. 54-89). Cambridge: Harvard University Press.

Kolt, G. S., Kirkby, R. J., & Linder, H. (1995). Coping processes in competitive gymnasts: Gender differences. *Perceptual and Motor Skills, 81,* 1139-1145.

Kowalski, K.C., & Crocker, P. R. E. (2001). The development and validation of the Coping Function Questionnaire for adolescents in sport. *Journal of Sport & Exercise Psychology, 23,* 136-155.

Kurdek, L. A. (1979). Perspective taking as the cognitive basis of children's moral development: A review of literature. *Merrill-Palmer Quarterly, 24,* 3-28.

Lazarus, R. S. (1991). *Emotion and adaptation.* New York: Oxford University Press.

Lazarus, R. S. (1999). *Stress and emotion: A new synthesis.* New York: Springer.

Lazarus, R. S. (2000a). Cognitive-motivational-relational theory of emotion. In Y. Hanin (Ed.), *Emotion in sport* (pp. 40-63). Champaign, IL: Human Kinetics.

Lazarus, R. S. (2000b). How emotions influence performance in competitive sports. *The Sport Psychologist, 14,* 229-252.

Martens, R. (1977). *Sport Competition Anxiety Test.* Champaign, IL: Human Kinetics

Martens, R., Vealey, R. S., & Burton, D. (1990). *Competitive anxiety in sport.* Champaign, IL: Human Kinetics.

Meichenbaum, D. (1985). *Stress inoculation training.* New York: Pergamon Press.

Naylor, S., Burton, D., & Crocker, P. R. E. (2002). Competitive anxiety and sport performance. In J. Silva & D. Stevens (Eds.), *Psychological foundations of sport* (pp. 132-154). Boston: Allyn & Bacon.

Nicholls, J. G. (1984). Achievement motivation: Conceptions of ability, subjective experience, task choice, and performance. *Psychological Review, 91,* 328-346.

Ommundsen, Y., & Vaglum, P. (1991). Soccer competition anxiety and enjoyment in young boy players: The influence of perceived competence and significant others' emotional involvement. *International Journal of Sport Psychology, 22,* 35-49.

Orlick, T. D., & Botterill, C. (1975). *Every kid can win.* Chicago: Nelson-Hall.

Passer, M. W. (1988). Determinants and consequences of children's competitive stress. In F. L. Smoll, R. A. Magill, & M. J. Ash (Eds.), *Children's sport* (3rd ed., pp. 203-227). Champaign, IL: Human Kinetics.

Piaget, J. (1954). *The construction of reality in the child.* New York: Basic Books.

Raglin, R. S., & Hanin, Y. L. (2000). Competitive anxiety. In Y. L. Hanin (Ed.), *Emotions in sport* (pp. 93-111). Champaign, IL: Human Kinetics.

Rejeski, W. J. (1992). Motivation for exercise behavior: A critique of theoretical directions. In G. C. Roberts (Ed.), *Motivation in sport and exercise* (pp.129-157). Champaign, IL: Human Kinetics.

Robinson, D. W., & Howe, B. L. (1989). Appraisal variable/affect relationships in youth sport: A test of Weiner's attributional model. *Journal of Sport & Exercise Psychology, 11,* 431-443.

Ross, A. (1976). *Psychological aspects of learning disabilities and reading disorders.* New York: McGraw-Hill.

Saarni, C. (1999). *The development of emotional competence.* New York: Guilford Press.

Santrock, J. W. (1998). *Adolescence* (5th ed.). Boston: McGraw-Hill.

Santrock, J. W., & Yussen, S. R. (1992). *Child development: An introduction* (5th ed.). Dubuque, IA: Wm C. Brown.

Scanlan, T. K. (1986). Competitive stress in children. In M. R. Weiss & D. Gould (Eds.), *Sport for children and youths* (p. 113-118). Champaign, IL: Human Kinetics.

Scanlan, T. K., Carpenter, P. J., Lobel, M., & Simons, J. P. (1993). Sources of enjoyment for youth sport athletes. *Pediatric Exercise Science, 5,* 275-285.

Scanlan, T. K., & Lewthwaite, R. (1984). Social psychological aspects of competition for male youth sport participants: I. Predictors of competitive stress. *Journal of Sport Psychology, 6,* 208-226.

Scanlan, T. K., & Lewthwaite, R. (1986). Social psychological aspects of competition for male youth sport participants: IV. Predictors of enjoyment. *Journal of Sport Psychology, 8,* 25-35.

Scanlan, T. K., & Passer, M. W. (1978). Factors related to competitive stress in young male youth sports participants. *Medicine and Science in Sports, 10,* 103-108.

Scanlan, T. K., & Simons, J. P. (1992). The construct of sport enjoyment. In G. C. Roberts (Ed.), *Motivation in sport and exercise* (pp. 199-215). Champaign, IL: Human Kinetics.

Scanlan, T. K., Simons, J. P., Carpenter, P. J., Schmidt, G. W., & Keeler, B. (1993). The sport commitment model: Measurement development for the youth-sport domain. *Journal of Sport & Exercise Psychology, 15,* 16-38.

Schultz, L. H., Barr, D. J., & Selman, R. L. (2001). The value of a developmental approach to evaluating character development programmes: An outcome study of Facing History and Ourselves. *Journal of Moral Education, 30,* 3-27.

Schultz, L. H., & Selman, R. L. (2001). *The development of social competence in children and adolescents from a developmental perspective using the relationship questionnaire.* Unpublished manuscript.

Seiffge-Krenke, I. (1995). *Stress, coping, and relationships in adolescence.* Mahwah, NJ: Lawrence Erlbaum.

Selman, R. (1980). *The growth of interpersonal understanding.* New York: Academic Press.

Shantz, C. U. (1975). The development of social cognition. In E. M. Hetherington (Ed.), *Review of child development research* (Vol. 5, pp. 257-323). Chicago: University of Chicago.

Shepp, R., Barrett, S., & Kolbert, L. (1987). The development of selective attention: Holistic perception versus resource allocation. *Journal of Experimental Child Psychology, 43,* 159-180.

Simon, J. A., & Martens, R. (1979). Children's anxiety in sport and nonsport evaluative activities. *Journal of Sport Psychology, 1,* 160-169.

Smith, A. L. (1999). Perceptions of peer relationships and physical activity participation in early adolescence. *Journal of Sport & Exercise Psychology, 21,* 329-350.

Smith, R. E. (1980). A cognitive-affective approach to stress management training for athletes. In C. Nadeau, W. Halliwell, K. Newell, & G. Roberts (Eds.), *Psychology of motor behavior and sport- 1979* (pp. 54-73). Champaign, IL: Human Kinetics.

Smoll, F. L., & Smith, R. E. (1996). Competitive anxiety: Sources, consequences, and intervention strategies. In F. L. Smoll & R. E. Smith (Eds.), *Children and youth in sport: A biopsychosocial perspective* (pp. 359-380). Toronto: Brown & Benchmark.

Solomon, G. B. (2003). A lifespan view of moral development in physical activity. In M. R. Weiss (Ed.), *Developmental sport and exercise psychology: A lifespan perspective.* (pp. 453-474) Morgantown WV: Fitness Information Technology

Treasure, D. C. (1997). Perceptions of the motivational climate and elementary school children's cognitive and affective response. *Journal of Sport & Exercise Psychology, 19,* 278-290.

Treasure, D. C. (2001). Enhancing young people's motivation in youth sport: An achievement goal approach. In G. C. Roberts (Ed.), *Motivation in sport and exercise* (2nd ed., pp. 79-100). Champaign, IL: Human Kinetics

Vallerand, R. J. (1987). Antecedents of self-rated affects in sport: Preliminary evidence on the intuitive-reflective appraisal model. *Journal of Sport Psychology, 9*, 161-182.

Vallerand, R. J., & Blanchard, C. M. (2000). The study of emotion in sport and exercise. In Y. L. Hanin (Ed.), *Emotions in sport* (pp. 3-37). Champaign, IL: Human Kinetics.

Vlachopoulos, S., Biddle, S., & Fox, K. (1996). A social-cognitive investigation into the mechanisms of affect generation in children's physical activity. *Journal of Sport & Exercise Psychology, 18*, 174-193.

VanYperen, N.W. (1998). Predicting stay/leave behavior among volleyball referees. *The Sport Psychologist, 12*, 427-439.

Wankel, L. M., & Kreisel, P. J. J. (1985). Factors underlying enjoyment of youth sport. *Journal of Sport Psychology, 7*, 51-64.

Wankel, L. M., & Sefton, J. M. (1989). A season long investigation of fun in youth sports. *Journal of Sport & Exercise Psychology, 11*, 355-366.

Weiner, B. (1985). An attribution theory of achievement motivation and emotion. *Psychological Review, 92*, 548-573.

Weiner, B. (1986). *An attributional theory of motivation and emotion.* New York: Springer-Verlag.

Weiner, B. (1994). Ability versus effort revisited: The moral determinants of achievement evaluation and achievement as a moral system. *Educational Psychologist, 29*, 163-172.

Weiss, M. R. (2000). Motivating kids in physical activity. *President's Council on Physical Fitness and Sports Research Digest, Series 3*, No. 11, 1-8.

Weiss, M. R., & Bredemeier, B. J. (1983). Developmental sport psychology: A theoretical perspective for studying children in sport. *Journal of Sport Psychology, 5*, 216-230.

Weiss, M. R., Bredemeier, B. J., & Shewchuk, R. M. (1986). The dynamics of perceived competence, perceived control, and motivational orientation in youth sports. In M. R. Weiss & D. Gould (Eds.), *Sport for children and youths* (pp. 89-101). Champaign, IL: Human Kinetics.

Weiss, M. R., & Ebbeck, V. (1996). Self-esteem and perceptions of competence in youth sports: Theory, research and enhancement strategies. In O. Bar-Or (Ed.), *The encyclopedia of sports medicine:* Volume VI. *The child and adolescent athlete* (pp. 364-382). Oxford: Blackwell Science.

Weiss, M. R., & Horn, T. S. (1990). The relation between children's accuracy estimates of their physical competence and achievement-related characteristics. *Research Quarterly for Exercise and Sport, 61*, 250-258.

Weiss, M. R., Kimmel, L. A., & Smith, A. L. (2001). Determinants of sport commitment among junior tennis players: Enjoyment as a mediating variable. *Pediatric Exercise Science, 13*, 131-144.

Weiss, M. R., & Petlichkoff, L. M. (1989). Children's motivation for participation in and withdrawal from sport: Identifying the missing links. *Pediatric Exercise Science, 1*, 195-211.

Weiss, M. R., & Raedeke, T. D. (2003). Developmental sport and exercise psychology: Research status on youth and directions toward a lifespan perspective. In M. R. Weiss (Ed.), *Developmental sport and exercise psychology: A lifespan perspective.* (pp.1-26) Morgantown WV: Fitness Information Technology

Weiss, M. R., Smith, A. L., & Theeboom, M. (1996). That's what friends are for: Children's and teenagers' perceptions of peer relationships in the sport domain. *Journal of Sport & Exercise Psychology, 18*, 347-379.

Weiss, M. R., & Stuntz, C. P. (2003). A little friendly competition: Peer relationships and psychosocial development in youth sport contexts. In M. R. Weiss (Ed.), *Developmental sport and exercise psychology: A lifespan perspective.* (pp.165-196) Morgantown WV: Fitness Information Technology.

Weiss, M. R., & Williams, L. (2003). The *why* of youth sport involvement: A developmental perspective on motivational processes. In M. R. Weiss (Ed.), *Developmental sport and exercise psychology: A lifespan perspective.* (pp. 223-268) Morgantown WV: Fitness Information Technology.

AUTHOR NOTES

The writing of this chapter was supported in part by a Social Sciences and Humanities Research Council of Canada grant to the first author. We would like to thank Robin Farrell for her helpful comments on earlier drafts or this manuscript.

CHAPTER EIGHT

The *Why* of Youth Sport Involvement: A Developmental Perspective on Motivational Processes

Maureen R. Weiss • Lavon Williams

Why individuals continue or discontinue participation in a particular achievement activity lies at the core of understanding motivation. Thus, one way of explaining motivated behavior is by answering *why* questions with *because* answers. *Why* do children choose to return each season or year to a particular sport? *Why* do some children decide *not* to return but instead try another sport or activity? *Why* do some youth try hard when provided the opportunity to show their skills, whereas others hold back on effort in similar situations? *Why* are some teenagers persistent in their efforts to learn, improve, and master challenging but realistic goals, whereas others give up before such achievements can be realized? Finally, *why* are certain children and adolescents able to attain their performance potential, whereas others fall short consistently?

The purpose of our chapter is to provide our best *because* answers to these *why* questions for the population of young children through adolescents. We attempt to do this by synthesizing the knowledge base on physical activity motivation among youth and integrating this domain-specific research with developmentally appropriate theories. Not only do we choose theories that are developmentally appropriate, but also ones that are bolstered by empirical support in the physical domain and are intuitively appealing based on the real world of competitive youth-sport involvement.

A key principle guiding our theoretical and empirical discussion is an *interactionist perspective* to understanding and explaining motivation (Gill, 2000; Weiss & Ferrer-Caja, 2002). That is, motivated behavior is understood best by considering how individual differences (e.g., self-perceptions) and social-environmental factors (e.g., significant other influence) combine interactively and dynamically. For example, a child's decision whether or not to continue competitive soccer from one year to the next is likely to be influenced by factors such as perceived competence and enjoyment (individual differences) as well as by the types of behaviors exhibited by coaches and parents (social factors). This interactionist perspective is often alluded to as a social cognitive approach to motivation, and will be our emphasis as well.

To accomplish our purposes of answering the questions posed in the opening paragraph, we have divided the chapter into several distinct sections. First, we begin with the knowledge

> Motivated behavior is best understood by examining the interactions of individual differences and social-environmental factors.

base on descriptive reasons for participation because these studies helped shape the way we conceptualize motivation today by providing the building blocks of theories of motivated behavior. Second, we delve into four theories of motivation that have been found to be suitable for the physical domain (i.e., "practical theory"; Gill, 2000), but more important, ones that consider age-related changes in the structure, content, and processes of motivation. These theories are Harter's (1978) competence motivation theory, Harter's (1987) mediational model of global self-worth, the expectancy-value model of achievement behaviors developed by Eccles et al. (1983), and Nicholls' (1978, 1989) achievement goal theory. Each of these theories and related research are synthesized and consolidated to illuminate key principles and take-home messages. Third, we pull together the common themes or threads of similarity that cut across these various theories to provide implications for practitioners. Finally, we integrate the knowledge gleaned from each of our chosen theories to suggest key areas of future research.

PARTICIPATION MOTIVATION: DESCRIPTIVE REASONS FOR YOUTH SPORT INVOLVEMENT

Early inquiry on reasons that children participate in sport and discontinue involvement was driven by a practical need to help youth agencies understand escalating and declining enrollments in their programs, as well as learn what were the most popular sports by age, gender, race, and community type (Gould, 1982; State of Michigan, 1976). Birch and Veroff's (1966) incentive motivation model in social psychology inspired some of the earliest sport-related research. They defined incentive motivation as the factors contributing toward goal-directed behaviors among human beings. Several incentive motives were named including sensory, curiosity, achievement, aggression, affiliation, power, and independence motives. Subsequently, Alderman (1978; Alderman & Wood, 1976) assessed 11- to 18-year-old athletes on a set of modified incentive motives for participating in sport. The strongest motives were (a) affiliation motives (opportunities to attain warm personal relationships), (b) excellence motives (opportunities to do something very well), (c) arousal motives (opportunities for excitement and interesting experiences), and (d) esteem motives (opportunities for social recognition and approval of achievements). Similar incentives were reported regardless of age, gender, and sport type.

Following Alderman's (1978; Alderman & Wood, 1976) lead, a number of studies taking a similar approach emerged in the 1970s and 1980s (see Weiss & Ferrer-Caja, 2002, for a review). A synthesis of study findings reveals three highly consistent reasons for participating in sport: (a) to develop or demonstrate *physical competence or adequacy* (e.g., learn and improve skills, be physically fit, get stronger, achieve goals), (b) to attain *social acceptance and approval* (e.g., make friends, feel part of a group, receive coach/parent approval), and (c) to *enjoy experiences* related to sport involvement (i.e., have fun, feel excited). It is interesting to note that these three common themes align with the strongest incentive motives in Alderman's studies: physical competence ~ excellence motives, social acceptance and approval ~ affiliation and esteem motives, and enjoy experiences ~ arousal motives. Table 1 summarizes study findings for specific participation reasons within the three motivation classifications of physical competence, social acceptance and approval, and enjoyment of experiences.

Concomitant with an empirical and practical interest in participation motivation was an equally keen interest in reasons for dropping out of youth sport (Gould, 1982, 1987). In several studies, youths were assessed on reasons for discontinuation in survey research similar to that conducted on participation motives. Among the several reasons given for decreased inter-

TABLE 1

Reasons for Participating in Youth Sport Classified by Physical Competence/Adequacy, Social Acceptance and Approval, and Enjoyment

Physical Competence/Adequacy	Social Acceptance and Approval	Enjoyment
Learn skills	Be with friends	Have fun
Improve skills	Make new friends	Excitement
Be good at something	Feel part of a group/team	Challenging
Move to a higher level	Social recognition	Movement sensations
Master difficult skills	Approval from parents	Arousal or stress seeking
Achieve goals	Approval from coach	Aesthetics
Be physically fit/get in shape	Social status	Energy release
Get stronger	Team spirit	Action
Improve attractiveness	Team atmosphere	Access to equipment

est in and subsequent withdrawal from sport were lack of fun, issues with the coach, time commitment required, lack of playing time, overemphasis on winning, and greater interest in other activities (see Weiss & Ferrer-Caja, 2002). One can infer that many of these reasons may be related in an inverse way to previously held reasons for staying involved—*not* developing or demonstrating competence, *not* feeling socially accepted, and *not* having fun.

Some researchers conducted parallel studies of participation motivation and attrition with the same population of young athletes in an effort to link reasons for participating with those for discontinuing (e.g., Gould, Feltz, Horn, & Weiss, 1982; Gould, Feltz, & Weiss, 1985). Gould et al. (1985) found that 8- to 11-year-old swimmers were more highly motivated by social status, encouragement by parents and friends, and liking the coach, whereas 12- to 19-year-olds were motivated by the developing of physical fitness and skills, and by the excitement and challenge of swimming. In the follow-up study with those swimmers who had dropped out, Gould et al. (1982) found that older swimmers (15 to 19 years old) more frequently cited "not good enough" as a reason for dropping out compared to 10- to 14-year-old swimmers. These results may signal a developmental transition as older adolescents recognize that high levels of ability are essential to "make it" in competitive sport. Moreover, older adolescents may be contemplating their "coming of age" into adulthood in terms of career goals and social relationships (Coakley & White, 1992). Specifically, Coakley and White identified five common issues among 13- to 18-year-old adolescents in how they made decisions about whether or not to engage in regular physical activity and sport. These issues were (a) considerations in making the transition to adulthood; (b) opportunities to demonstrate physical competence and autonomy; (c) social support from parents and same-sex friends; (d) social constraints imposed by finances, parents, and opposite-sex friends; and (e) recollection of experiences in physical education and sport. These reasons are reminiscent of the common themes that emerge time and again as salient—demonstrate physical competence, attain social acceptance and approval, and experience fun and enjoyment.

One of the few studies specifically designed with a developmental slant was the investigation by Brodkin and Weiss (1990) of participation motives among competitive swimmers. Age groups represented younger children (6 to 9 years), older children (10 to 14 years), adolescents (15 to 18 years), college-age (19 to 22 years), young adults (23 to 39 years), middle adults (40 to 59 years), and older adults (60 to 74 years). Results revealed that younger and older children

Younger and older children rated competition-related motives, liking the coaches, and pleasing family and friends as more important than the other age groups.

rated competition-related motives, liking the coaches, and pleasing family and friends as more important than the other age groups did. Older children, adolescents, and college-age swimmers rated social status motives higher than did other age groups. Affiliation motives (be with/make friends, feel part of a group) were rated highly by all age groups. Young and middle adults rated health and fitness reasons as most important. Finally, fun was rated as most important by older adults and younger children. These results highlight the salience of physical competence (e.g., competition aspects, health/fitness), social acceptance (i.e., significant others, status, affiliation), and fun for children and adolescents.

It is clear that more developmental research is essential to understand variations in reasons for participating in and withdrawing from sport and physical activity. However, the robust findings across studies show that developing and demonstrating physical competence/adequacy; seeking social acceptance, approval, and affiliation; and desiring fun and enjoyment are the major reasons sustaining children's and adolescents' physical activity motivation. These findings suggest that appropriate theories for explaining change in youths' perceptions and behaviors in sport settings must take into account these factors as well as recognize age-related differences in their structure and processes.

Although many motivation theories abound, we have chosen four conceptual models that adopt a developmental perspective and incorporate physical, social, and affective factors as correlates of motivation. Specifically, theories that highlight *perceptions of competence* account for children's and adolescents' motivation to develop and demonstrate athletic skills, physical fitness, and physical appearance. Theories that recognize the salience of *social influence* such as reflected appraisals, social comparison, and social support reinforce youths' desire for social recognition, peer acceptance, close friendships, and adult approval. Finally, theories that explicitly acknowledge the central role of *positive affect* such as pride, joy, happiness, and pleasure recognize that experiences that are fun and enjoyable are powerful predictors of future motivated behavior in youth sport. This made it easy for us to pinpoint theories that offer the most potential to understand youth sport motivation from a developmental perspective. We now discuss each of these four theories in turn: Harter's (1978) competence motivation theory, Harter's (1987) model of global self-worth, the expectancy-value model of Eccles et al. (1983), and Nicholls' (1978, 1989) achievement goal theory.

HARTER'S (1978) COMPETENCE MOTIVATION THEORY

Harter (1978) revitalized White's (1959) conception of *effectance motivation* articulated nearly 20 years earlier. White proposed that individuals are naturally motivated to have an *effect* on their environment and that, to do so, they engage in behaviors to develop or demonstrate mastery of certain tasks or activities. Such behaviors, according to White, are self-rewarding and are influenced by the desire for challenge, curiosity, mastery, and even playfulness; that is, intrinsic desires or motives from within the person. If the result of such challenge-seeking behavior is successful mastery or achievement of a specified task, then feelings of efficacy and inherent pleasure are experienced. Such feelings serve to maintain or enhance effectance motivation. Because empirical inquiry was constrained by an inability to operationally define effectance constructs, model testing was not implemented until Harter revived and modified White's ideas starting with her classic paper in 1978 and continued with her systematic line of research on the development of self-evaluations (see Harter, 1998, 1999).

Theoretical Concepts and Relationships

Harter (1978, 1981a) made a compelling argument for considering effectance or competence motivation as a viable conceptualization of children's achievement strivings. She portrayed competence motivation as a multidimensional construct that influences and is influenced by a number of cognitive, affective, social, and behavioral factors. A schematic of Harter's refinement of White's (1959) ideas is seen in Figure 1. Starting with the box labeled competence motivation and following the arrows, we see that a child's intrinsic desire to develop competence (i.e., urge to be *effective*) in a particular domain (e.g., school, social relationships, sport) will lead her to engage in attempts to attain mastery. The child who is high in competence motivation (i.e., intrinsically motivated) will prefer *optimally challenging* tasks, ones that are difficult but realistic given the child's capabilities and potential for improvement. If she is successful in demonstrating mastery of a task offering optimal challenge, she will experience heightened *self-perceptions* (perceived competence and control) and positive *affective responses* in the form of enjoyment, pride, and pleasure. Moreover, if *significant adults and peers* respond to her mastery attempts with contingent and appropriate approval and reinforcement, perceptions of competence and control should be positively influenced and, in turn, enjoyment and other positive emotions should also increase. Finally, these enhanced self-perceptions and affective reactions serve to maintain or enhance the child's desire to continue being effective in that particular achievement domain (i.e., competence motivation).

One can readily see that competence motivation theory is appealing because it contains the key ingredients that we know influence a child's motivation in the achievement domain of sport. Specifically, the theory accounts for developing and demonstrating competence (i.e., mastery attempts, competence at optimal challenges, perceptions of competence), attaining social acceptance (i.e., socializers' approval, modeling, and reinforcement), and enjoyment of one's experiences (i.e., positive affective responses). Moreover, Harter (1978, 1981a) cast her theoretical revision of White's (1959) ideas within a developmental worldview by specifying how motivational processes vary as a result of cognitive maturity and socialization experiences. The developmental niche of competence motivation theory is embellished in the next section.

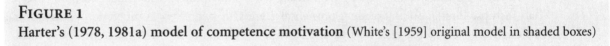

FIGURE 1
Harter's (1978, 1981a) model of competence motivation (White's [1959] original model in shaded boxes)

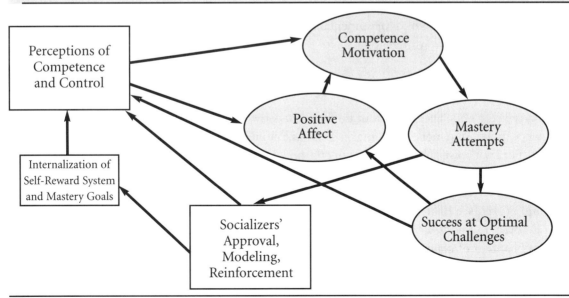

Adapted from Weiss, M.R., & Ferrer-Caja, E. (2002). Motivational orientations and sport behavior. In T.S. Horn (Ed.), *Advances in sport psychology* (2nd ed., pp. 101-183). Champaign, IL: Human Kinetics. Reprinted by permission of Human Kinetics.

Developmental Perspectives

Harter (1978, 1981a) recognized that the antecedents of competence motivation, as well as the construct of competence motivation itself, are likely to show age-related differences in their structure, content, and processes. For example, youth of varying ages are likely to differ in their desire to achieve mastery in particular achievement domains as a function of maturational changes and direct experiences in these domains. This changing desire would naturally result in variations in choosing particular domains in which to excel. For example, one 10-year-old boy may find it more important to be successful as an athlete rather than as a student to fit in with his peer group; by contrast, the same boy at age 15 may find academic achievement and social relationships more salient than demonstrating athletic competence.

A unique developmental element of Harter's (1978, 1981a) competence motivation model is the effect of a child's socialization history on development of self-regulated skills such as self-judgment, self-reinforcement, and self-set mastery goals. This idea is represented by the linkage of boxes labeled "socializers' approval, modeling, and reinforcement" with "internalization of self-reward system and mastery goals." Specifically, Harter (1978, 1981a) contends that contingent praise and informational feedback given by caregivers (especially parents) in response to children's independent mastery attempts (rather than performance outcomes) will, over time, help a child relinquish dependence upon reinforcement and goals set by others (parents, teachers, coaches). Instead, the unconditional support and encouragement for exploring one's environment will help shape a child's self-regulated learning, in which she comes to monitor her own mastery attempts, uses internal criteria for judging personal competence (e.g., improvement, effort, enjoyment), and self-reinforces successful attempts. This child sharply contrasts to one who lingers in depending upon social reinforcement and externally defined goals as criteria for determining competence or success in a domain. The successful socialization process should gradually exert its effects over the childhood years such that youth are capable of self-regulating mastery attempts and performance evaluation (see Petlichkoff, 2003).

> Unconditional support and encouragement for exploring help shape a child's self-regulated learning.

In the following sections, we systematically review key model constructs and their interrelationships. First, we explore developmental trends in perceived competence, motivational orientation (i.e., competence motivation), and social influence through conceptual and empirical viewpoints. Second, we synthesize the existing research to date, and because the bulk of this research has taken a nondevelopmental approach, we will discuss findings with an eye toward potential age-related differences.

Perceived Competence

Perceived competence is without doubt the most widely studied construct within the competence motivation model. This makes sense as a child's beliefs about his ability in a domain such as sport is a powerful determinant of emotional responses and motivational outcomes (effort, intensity, achievement). Thus, understanding the structure, content, and processes associated with perceived competence is a worthwhile endeavor. Harter (1985, 1988; Harter & Pike, 1984) and others (see Horn, 2003a) have explored the development of perceived competence among children and adolescents in primarily three interrelated ways: (a) differentiation of number and content of competence dimensions, (b) level and accuracy of perceived competence, and (c) information sources used to judge domain-specific competence. Because these topics are discussed in detail by Horn (2003a), we provide only a brief overview of these trends here.

Differentiation of Number and Content of Competence Dimensions. In middle and late childhood (ages 8 to 13), children are able to differentiate among several specific competence domains as well as a general sense of self-worth (Harter, 1982, 1985). The specific competence areas include academic, athletic, social acceptance, physical appearance, and behavioral conduct. Children and youth in this age range can further differentiate their competence *within* domains (e.g., Weiss, Bredemeier, & Shewchuk, 1986) in that ability estimates differ depending upon the specific sport.

By adolescence (ages 14 to 18 years), the number and content of competence dimensions change yet again (Harter, 1988). Beyond the five specific dimensions for middle to late childhood, three additional areas emerge as salient for teenagers: perceptions of close friendship (i.e., intimacy and loyalty), romantic relationships, and job/work competence. In her later writings, Harter (1998, 1999) highlights and poignantly articulates the sensitivity with which global self-worth develops and changes during adolescence. In a later section, we specifically address how Harter extended competence motivation ideas to derive a model of antecedents and consequences of global self-worth.

More developmental research is essential to understand variations in reasons for participating in and withdrawing from sport and physical activity.

Level and Accuracy of Perceived Competence. In the academic domain, studies have consistently shown that perceived competence declines but accuracy in assessing competence increases over the childhood years (Stipek & Mac Iver, 1989; Stipek, Recchia, & McClintic, 1992). These concomitant changes in level (i.e., low v. high) and accuracy (i.e., relation between perceived and actual) of perceived competence are believed to result from one or more age-related changes. Such changes include (a) ability to differentiate between effort and ability as causes of success, (b) shift in the relative use of task mastery and parent evaluation to peer comparison and evaluation as information sources for judging competence, and (c) changes in socioenvironmental factors that occur in the transition from elementary to middle school, such as increased emphasis on grades and normative standards for determining achievement (Harter, 1992; Nicholls, 1978; Stipek & Mac Iver, 1989; see Horn, 2003a, for a review).

Research on level of perceived *physical* competence shows equivocal findings. Some studies have found declines in perceptions of competence; others, increases; and still others, stability over the middle and late childhood years (see Weiss & Ferrer-Caja, 2002). By contrast, the few studies that have assessed accuracy of perceived physical competence show steady increases over the childhood and early adolescent years (Feltz & Brown, 1984; Horn & Weiss, 1991; McKiddie & Maynard, 1997).

There are several potential explanations for contradictory results in level of perceived competence for academic and athletic domains. First, these two domains are very different in terms of the context in which evaluation occurs. Youth obtain information about their competence in academic subjects in relatively private surrounds; by contrast, athletic competence is a public event whereby significant adults (parents, coaches) and peers (teammates, close friends) are privy to successful and unsuccessful performances. Second, studies of age-related differences in level of perceived physical competence have almost exclusively used cross-sectional designs, limiting our ability to accurately detect interindividual variability across age (see Schutz & Park, 2003). Third, in the academic domain, transitions from one level to another (e.g., elementary to middle school) are standardized in that all children move through at the same ages. However, transitions to a higher level in sport are more complex. For example, three 11-year-old boys may all play organized youth soccer but at different competitive levels (e.g., recreational, select, travel). One's peer comparison group is different at these levels and may contribute to variations in perceived competence. These three explanations suggest that future research should consider (a) directly comparing the same youths on perceived competence in academic and sport domains, (b) conducting longitudinal investigations of changes in perceived competence, and (c) examining patterns of change in perceived competence as youth transition to different levels within the structure of sport.

Information Sources Used to Judge Domain-Specific Competence. Because perceived competence is such a critical predictor of emotional experiences and motivated behavior in any achievement domain, logical questions are "How do children make judgments about how competent they are?" and "Do age differences exist in what sources children use to assess their ability?" A number of competence information sources exist in the athletic domain including parent feedback, coach evaluation, peer comparison, peer evaluation, spectator feedback, performance statistics, skill improvement, ease of learning new skills, effort exerted, attainment of goals, game-related nervousness, and event outcome. Research shows that developmental differences do exist in the frequency with which children ascribe using these varying sources (see Horn, 2003a, for a review).

In general, children under 10 years of age report greater use of parent and spectator feedback and game outcome to judge physical competence than do older children. Older children (ages 10 to 15), in contrast, use peer comparison and evaluation as well as coach evaluation relatively more than younger children do. These results align with the notion that children become more accurate in assessing competence because of greater emphasis on social comparison. Moreover, older adolescents (ages 16 to 18 years) report using self-referenced information (e.g., skill improvement, effort exerted, goal achievement, attraction toward sport) more frequently in comparison to younger adolescents, providing some support for Harter's (1978) contention that self-regulation (self-judgment, self-reinforcement, self-set goals) develops over time as a result of the socialization process. In addition, adolescents use a wider variety of information sources compared to younger children, supporting the notion of increased differentiation of perceived competence with age.

In sport, chronological age is usually confounded with competitive or skill level (i.e., as athletes grow older they participate at higher levels). For example, Horn, Glenn, and Wentzell (1993) found that older adolescent athletes used self-comparison sources more than did younger adolescents, who scored higher on using peer evaluation. However, the older group was overrepresented by varsity-level athletes whereas younger athletes played on freshmen and junior varsity teams. These age-related findings may reflect skill or competitive level differences, not necessarily age. Halliburton and Weiss (2002) were interested in how skill level may relate to sources of competence information among female gymnasts. To control for an age/skill level confound, participants represented a narrow age bandwidth (12 to 14 years) but a wide range of skill levels (levels 5 to 10). Gymnasts competing at lower skill levels (5, 6, 7) used effort and enjoyment sources (i.e., self-comparison sources) more than gymnasts competing at higher levels (8, 9, and 10), who used feelings of nervousness and spectator feedback more frequently (i.e., norm-referenced sources). These results suggest that, despite rather consistent *between-age* differences found for sources of physical competence information, *within-age* variability is an important concept to acknowledge. Skill or competitive level emerged as a viable factor explaining within-age variability in sources of competence information.

Motivational Orientation

Halliburton and Weiss (2002) also found that perceptions of a mastery climate (i.e., emphasis on learning, effort, and improvement) were associated with use of self-referenced sources of competence information, whereas perceptions of a performance climate (i.e., emphasis on outcome and normative standards of success) were associated with use of peer comparison and competition performance sources. This finding reinforces Harter's (1978, 1981a) theorizing that competence motivation (i.e., degree to which individuals are intrinsically motivated to master challenging skills) is vulnerable to socioenvironmental factors. According to Harter's model, children are naturally predisposed to be curious, playful, and excited about trying novel tasks, skills, or activities—ones that strike a balance between the degree of challenge and the child's present capabilities (i.e., optimal challenge). Because the essence of competence motivation is the need to have an effect on or master one's environment, this inherently stimulating motivational orientation is present unless certain factors influence the child to lose her emphasis on challenge, curiosity, and mastery, and to instead adopt an extrinsic motivational orientation guided by preference for easy skills and dependence upon teacher/coach approval for performing skills. To investigate the construct of competence motivation in greater detail, Harter (1981b) turned to motivational orientation in the classroom.

Structure and Content of Motivational Orientation. Based on the theoretical underpinnings of competence motivation, Harter (1981b) conceived of five distinct dimensions to characterize intrinsic and extrinsic orientations for classroom learning: (a) preference for challenge v. preference for easy work assigned, (b) curiosity/interest v. pleasing the teacher/getting grades, (c) independent mastery v. dependence on the teacher, (d) independent judgment v. reliance on the teacher's judgment, and (e) internal criteria for determining success v. external criteria for determining success. Thus, the child high in competence motivation would score high on the intrinsic side of the five scales, whereas the child low in competence motivation would score higher on the extrinsic side.

Factor analytic methods validated the distinction among these five indices of motivational orientation. However, two higher-order factors also emerged—one combining the challenge, curiosity, and mastery dimensions and the other combining the independent judgment and internal criteria dimensions. Based on the content of the items denoting each scale, Harter (1981b) labeled these two higher-order factors a motivational and cognitive-informational set of dimensions, respectively. That is, challenge, curiosity, interest, and mastery represent the classic ideas of competence motivation. By contrast, independent judgment and internal criteria are more reflective of what the child believes or how she determines whether she is competent or successful.

Developmental Trends. Harter (1981b) administered her newly developed motivation scale to students spanning grades 3 to 9 in an effort to examine age-related patterns in intrinsic and extrinsic motivation. Figure 2a depicts the mean scores across grade level for the three motivational scales—challenge, curiosity, and independent mastery. One readily sees a consistent downward trend in scores from a more intrinsic to more extrinsic orientation with increasing grade in school. Notice the marked decline in all three scales between grades 6 and 7—this represents the transition from elementary to junior high school. These results caused Harter to conjecture that the structure, grading emphasis, and teacher behavior changes associated with increasing grade levels may be stifling children's inherent interest and curiosity to learn. By contrast, youth in her study showed a linear increase on the two cognitive-informational scales—independent judgment and internal criteria. These results made good sense in light of children's increasing cognitive maturity to make decisions about schoolwork and use of self-comparison (i.e., improvement) as a means of judging ability.

Harter (1981b) expressed concern about the developmental trends for motivational orientation in the classroom. This concern seems warranted considering that a positive competence orientation is characterized by high intrinsic motivation, high perceived competence, high internal perceptions of control, and high actual achievement (Harter, 1981b; Harter & Connell,

---

FIGURE 2

(a) Harter's (1981b) findings for challenge, curiosity, and mastery motivation by grade level (grades 3 to 9). (b) Weiss et al.'s (1985) findings for challenge, curiosity, and mastery motivation by grade level (grades 3 to 6).

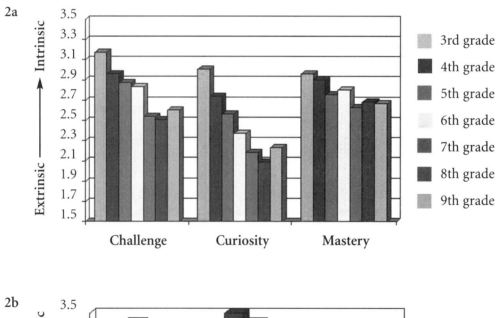

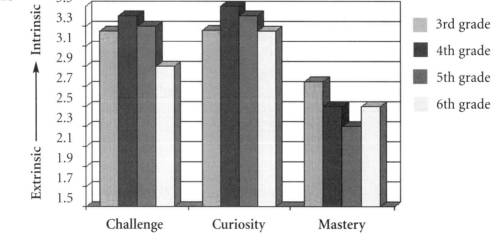

1984). Thus, her results would suggest that, over the course of a student's academic experiences in elementary and secondary school, an emerging extrinsic motivational orientation may come to be associated with lower self-perceptions and underachievement. Harter's concerns with these trends were somewhat tempered by her suggestion that an intrinsic motivational orientation may not necessarily decline in other domains such as sport or social relationships.

Weiss, Bredemeier, and Shewchuk (1985) responded to this call by modifying Harter's (1981b) scale to pertain to sports. They assessed children in grades 3 through 6 on the motivational orientation scales. Figure 2b presents graphs for the challenge, curiosity, and independent mastery scales alongside those of Harter's (1981b). Several points are noteworthy: (a) challenge and curiosity showed a slight increase from 3rd to 4th grades but then a steady decline through 6th grade; (b) independent mastery showed a steady downward trend from 3rd through 5th grades with a slight increase at 6th grade; (c) challenge and curiosity scores are higher for the sport domain compared to each corresponding grade for school scores; and (d) independent mastery scores are correspondingly lower at each grade level for sport compared to school. In sum, Weiss et al.'s (1985) findings are similar to Harter's for the academic domain—intrinsic motivation declines over the elementary years especially for independent mastery (i.e., preference for self-regulated learning). These findings hold even greater importance because an intrinsic motivational orientation is linked to higher perceived physical competence, accurate perceptions of competence, a task goal orientation, greater effort and persistence, and sport performance (Amorose, 2001; Ferrer-Caja & Weiss, 2000, 2002; Weiss et al., 1986; Weiss & Horn, 1990; Williams & Gill, 1995).

Why do declines emerge in a positive competence motivational orientation across age and grade level? Is it due to cognitive-developmental factors or socioenvironmental changes associated with higher levels in school and sport domains? Over the last 10 years, interest has surged regarding the effect of transitions and their associated changes in teacher behaviors and environmental structure on youths' perceptions of competence, social relationships, motivational orientation, and actual achievement.

Transitions. Several theorists have addressed the crucial developmental marker of transitions from elementary to middle school on youths' self-perceptions, interest, and intrinsic motivation to learn (e.g., Eccles & Midgley, 1990; Harter, 1992; Harter, Whitesell, & Kowalski, 1992; Roeser & Eccles 1998). In elementary school, teachers place an emphasis on learning, improvement, and effort, whereas students are likely to find a shift in emphasis to grades and normative standards of success when they transition to middle school. These characteristics are analogous to changes from a mastery motivational climate to one emphasizing performance outcome and favorable comparisons to other students. Moreover, teacher behaviors at the elementary school level are perceived as supportive, instructional, and positive because evaluation is based on individual improvement and positive behaviors. By contrast, at the middle-school level teachers are perceived as less supportive, and providing less responsibility, independence, and decision-making opportunities (Harter, 1992; Roeser & Eccles, 1998; Wentzel, 1998; Wentzel & Wigfield, 1998). Given these comparative findings between elementary and middle-school contexts, it is easy to infer why Harter (1981b) found a sharp decline across grades 3 to 9 in challenge seeking, curiosity, interest, and independent mastery for school learning.

Transitions also occur in competitive sport, although these transitions are aligned with advancements in skill level rather than chronological age as with school transitions. Children may "move up" from recreational to select league soccer when they are able to demonstrate the skills, strategies, and tactical knowledge to accommodate a higher level of competition. However, similar to the academic domain,

Several theorists have addressed the crucial developmental marker of transitions from elementary to middle school sport transitions can also be characterized by changes in social-contextual factors such as the psychological climate and coaching behaviors (see Ames, 1992a; Horn & Harris, 1996). Typically, recreational sport leagues offer all children the opportunity to play during practices and games, and evaluative feedback by the coach is based on effort, improvement, and learning. By contrast, more competitive levels of sport require tryouts to determine who will "make the cut"; even a child's making the team does not guarantee him playing time. Moreover, coaching behaviors are likely to be more punitive and less supportive at the higher levels because success is defined by normative standards (i.e., performance outcome, win/loss record). These changes in climate and coaching practices may be aligned with changes in youth participants' perceived competence, enjoyment, and intrinsic motivation. Thus changes in the social-contextual environment may also be a viable explanation for the progressive decline in challenge seeking and curiosity and the overall low scores for mastery found by Weiss et al. (1985).

Influence by Significant Adults and Peers

In the discussion so far, significant adults (parents, teachers, coaches) and peers (teammates, close friends, peer group) are implicated time and again as salient contributors to children's psychological (i.e., perceived competence) and motivational processes. Parents are important sources of information by which younger children judge their athletic ability, whereas peers and coaches are more prevalent sources in later childhood and adolescence. Changes in social-contextual factors such as teacher/coach behaviors and motivational climate are responsible, at least in part, for age-related changes in intrinsic and extrinsic motivational orientations. Moreover, the competence motivation model highlights a child's socialization history (reinforcement, approval, modeling) as central for shaping perceptions of competence and control that, in turn, predict variations in emotional responses and motivated behavior. Thus, in this section we accentuate the influence of significant others on children's perceived competence, affect, and motivation in the physical domain.

Parents. Parents are a ubiquitous phenomenon in youth sport. They sign their children up for initial experiences in sport, drive them to and from practices and games, offer advice and instruction, and impart expectations based on the type of comments they say after competitions (e.g., "Did you learn something new" v. "Did you win?"). Combined with the child's need for approval and acceptance, it is no wonder that mothers and fathers exert a powerful effect on children's participation experiences (see Fredricks & Eccles, 2003).

Brustad (1992), in a critical analysis integrating the socialization and youth motivation literature, pointed to competence motivation theory as one of the attractive frameworks for examining parent-child effects in the physical domain because of its developmental considerations of the linkage between significant others and motivational processes. To date, however, only a handful of studies have designed investigations specifically emanating from Harter's (1978, 1981a) model to examine the relation between parental beliefs and behaviors with children's psychological development through sport.

Felson (1989) investigated the parent-child linkage in competence beliefs with 4th- through 8th-grade youth. Children's perceptions of their parents' competency beliefs about them were strongly related to their own self-appraisals of ability. That is, children who thought their parents regarded their (the child's) abilities highly were inclined to positively judge their own abilities; by contrast, children who believed their parents held low ability expectations for them confirmed these beliefs in their own self-reports. Similarly, McCullagh, Matzkanin, Shaw, and Maldonado (1993) found a moderate relationship between parents' perceptions of their child's athletic competence with the child's own self-perceptions. According to competence motivation predictions, children may have internalized parents' beliefs as their own, and this was reflected in corresponding perceptions of competence.

Other researchers investigated a variety of parent beliefs and behaviors on children's self-perceptions, affective reactions, and motivation. Some (Brustad, 1988; Ommundsen & Vaglum, 1991) uncovered a linkage between children's (ages 9 to 13) perceptions of parental pressure and sport enjoyment (i.e., the greater the pressure, the lower the enjoyment). Weitzer (1989) found that 9- to 12-year-old children's perceptions of parent involvement, instruction, and encouragement were positively related to their perceived physical competence and activity involvement. Rose, Larkin, and Berger (1994) found that 8- to 12-year-old children demonstrating higher motor skill perceived greater parent social support than did children categorized as low in motor coordination.

The studies cited so far surveyed children that spanned a wide range of ages and competitive levels. Babkes and Weiss (1999) deliberately chose 9- to 11-year-old youth based on research that parents are especially important socializers during this age period. Children participated in a "select" soccer league where parents invested substantial time, energy, and money in their child's involvement. Thus, the parent-child relationship on competence motivation variables may be particularly relevant for these children's age and competitive sport levels. The primary research question was "Do parents' beliefs and behaviors relate to children's perceived competence, enjoyment, and motivational orientation?" Children's perceptions of mother and father influence were positively related to their perceived soccer competence, enjoyment of soccer experiences, and intrinsic motivation (see Figure 3). Parent beliefs and behaviors that were significantly related to psychosocial variables are listed in the respective boxes. Noteworthy results include (a) both parent beliefs (e.g., competence beliefs about their child) and behaviors (e.g., role modeling) were contributors to children's experiences, and (b) pressure by father only was perceived to negatively influence children's psychosocial responses. The discontinuous lines from mother- and father-reported influence to children's psychosocial

FIGURE 3

Babkes and Weiss's (1999) findings for mother and father influence on competence motivation variables among U-11 soccer players.

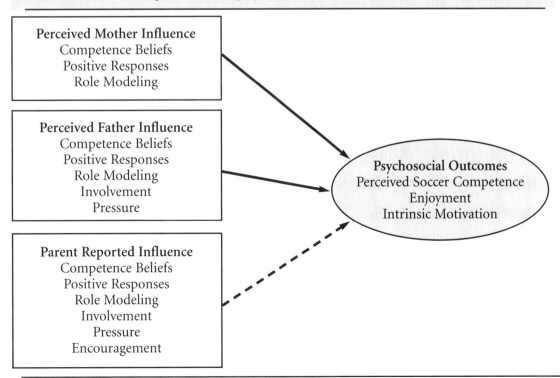

Children's perceptions of their parents' beliefs and behaviors are key to understanding variations in self-perceptions and motivational processes.

variables denote nonsignificant relationships. Thus, consistent with theorizing, children's *beliefs* about parental attitudes and behaviors are key to understanding variations in self-perceptions and motivational processes. However, less than 6% of the variance in children's psychosocial responses was explained by parent influence. Given the wide variety of sources available in sport settings and the multidimensional nature of Harter's model, more of the variance may be explained by coaches and peers, as well as other individual differences (e.g., skill improvement) and social contextual factors (e.g., climate).

Teachers/Coaches. In the academic domain, teachers' competence beliefs for students, emphasis on learning v. outcome, and structure of the classroom (i.e., ability grouping, norm- v. self-referenced criteria) are strongly related to youths' perceptions of competence and motivational orientation (e.g., Ames, 1992b; Harter, 1992: Stipek & Daniels, 1988). The analogue to the physical domain is the influence of physical education teachers and sport coaches on youths' psychological and motivational processes. Coaches' influence would be expected to exert stronger effects on participants in late childhood and adolescence, when coach or social evaluation emerges as a salient source of physical competence information (e.g., Horn et al., 1993; Horn & Hasbrook, 1987; Weiss, Ebbeck, & Horn, 1997).

A series of interrelated studies conducted by different researchers provide support for the influence of coaches on competence motivation variables. Horn (1984, 1985) assessed the relation between coaching behaviors and perceptions of competence among 13- to 15-year-old female softball players. Greater frequency of nonreinforcement (i.e., not responding positively to effort and performance) was associated with lower perceptions of competence, whereas more instances of positive reinforcement for mastery attempts and performances were also associated with *lower* perceived softball competence. Moreover, criticism for performance errors corresponded to *increases* in perceived competence. The contingency and appropriateness of coaches' feedback readily explain these latter two contradictory findings. Because lower-expectancy athletes received more positive reinforcement than higher-expectancy athletes, one may infer that praise was given for success at easy tasks or for mediocre performance rather than mastery of challenging skills. Such feedback may have easily imparted information to the athlete that she possessed low competence. By contrast, more frequent criticism that was projected toward higher-expectancy athletes may have implied that coaches expected higher levels of performance, resulting in more positive competence beliefs among these athletes. Because participants were early adolescents and probably at a beginner skill level, the contingency of the coach's evaluative feedback is key to self-perceptions and subsequent motivation.

Black and Weiss (1992) injected a developmental slant to the study of coaching feedback and competence motivation variables. Competitive swimmers represented three age groups (10-11, 12-14, 15-18) based on cognitive-developmental differences in self-ability judgments. Relationships varied by age: (a) No relationship emerged for the youngest group; (b) 12 to 14 year olds who perceived coaches as providing greater praise and instruction following mastery, and encouragement and corrective instruction following undesirable performance reported higher competence beliefs, intrinsic motivation, and enjoyment; and (c) 15- to 18-year-old athletes who perceived coaches as giving more praise and instruction following success and more encouragement/instruction and less criticism following errors, scored higher on competence motivation variables. Following Horn (1984, 1985), *contingent* praise and technical instruction in response to good swim technique and *contingent* encouragement plus corrective instruction in response to poor performance were associated with a positive competence motivation profile. The nonsignificant relationship for 10- to 11-year-old swimmers between coach feedback and motivation indices may signify an inability to differentiate effort and ability as causes of success or that other sources (e.g., parents, peers, task mastery) are more salient for judging how good a swimmer they are. Allen and Howe (1998) and Amorose and Horn (2000, 2001) replicated and extended Black and Weiss with adolescent (ages 14-18) female athletes and college athletes, respectively. Coaches giving higher frequencies of praise and instruction, and less punishment, were associated with athletes characterizing higher levels of perceived competence and interest in and enjoyment of their sport (i.e., intrinsic motivational orientation).

Peers. As seen earlier, peer comparison and evaluation are consistent means by which youth judge their ability in the physical domain, with this source becoming more widespread during the late childhood and adolescent years. Despite the obvious influence that close friends, classmates, and teammates may exert on youngsters' self-perceptions and motivation, comparatively fewer studies of peer influence exist than do those of parent and coach influence (Weiss & Stuntz, 2003). Still fewer studies have adopted a developmental theoretical perspective, preventing a full understanding of peer influence in youth sport and physical activity.

Several consistent findings strongly link peer group acceptance and sport competence during childhood and adolescence (e.g., Adler, Kless, & Adler, 1992; Chase & Dummer, 1992; Weiss & Duncan, 1992). For example, Weiss and Duncan found that children (ages 8 to 13) who believed they were pretty good in sports and were rated as athletically skilled by their teachers were also those who felt socially accepted and were identified by teachers as successful in peer interactions. These findings suggest that the physical domain is an arena in which children may come to be highly regarded by their classmates and teammates. Moreover, Klint and Weiss (1987) noted a tie between perceptions of social acceptance and participation motives among 8- to 16-year-old gymnasts. Gymnasts exhibiting more positive beliefs about social regard from peers were more motivated to participate for affiliation reasons (e.g., be with and make friends) than were gymnasts reporting lower peer acceptance. In competence motivation terms, gymnasts were motivated to demonstrate and enhance their social acceptance, approval, and support by peers.

Friendship is a specific peer construct pertaining to a mutual, reciprocated relationship between two individuals. Age differences emerge for specific dimensions of friendship quality in sport (Weiss & Smith, 2002; Weiss, Smith, & Theeboom, 1996). Adolescents (ages 13 to 18) identify intimacy, attractive personal qualities, similar interests/beliefs, and conflict as more prevalent than younger children do. Moreover, close friendship and positive friendship quality have been associated with greater enjoyment, intrinsic motivation, future success expectations, and commitment to sport among 10- to 18-year-old youths (Duncan, 1993; A. L. Smith, 1999; Weiss & Smith, 2002).

> Some youth use peer comparison and evaluation to judge their physical ability.

Competence motivation theory is a comprehensive, multidimensional view of motivation that explicitly considers age-related changes in key model constructs such as perceived competence, motivational orientation, and influence by significant others. Moreover, empirical testing shows that it is a "practical theory" when applied to the domain of sport and physical activity. Still, more developmentally related research is essential to understand how changes in competence motivation variables across age, skill or competitive level, and transitions to higher levels of involvement make an impact on achievement behaviors in the physical domain.

HARTER'S (1987) MEDIATIONAL MODEL OF GLOBAL SELF-WORTH

Harter's (1981a, 1985) finding that by age 8 children are capable of articulating a general sense of self or global self-worth led her on a quest to determine the antecedents and developmental significance of this construct from youth through adulthood (Harter, 1987, 1990, 1999). She hypothesized and tested a model of the relationships between predictors of self-worth, self-worth, and consequences of self-worth; that is, a model in which self-worth mediates the relationship between antecedents and outcomes (see Figure 4). The primary antecedents of global self-worth are perceived competence in domains valued as important, and social support, regard, and approval from important others (parents, teachers, peer group, close friends) regarding the person's worthiness. The targeted outcomes of global self-worth are positive and negative affect (e.g., mood such as depression) and motivation (interest, desire, and energy to engage in age-appropriate activities). Thus, this model integrates Harter's (1978, 1981a) earlier work in competence motivation theory (influence of perceived competence, significant others, and intrinsic pleasure on motivational orientation) with a focus on the significance of global self-worth in emotional and motivational processes. It also possesses the key ingredients for explaining motivation among youth (perceived competence/adequacy, social influence, affect) and elucidates developmental change in model constructs as well as their interrelationships.

Model Testing and Developmental Trends

Collectively, model testing has revealed several consistent findings (see Harter, 1987, 1990, 1999, for a review). First, the mediational model is strongly supported across the ages of 8 to 15 years (elementary through middle school). Second, perceptions of competence in domains deemed as important for success and social support/regard from significant others exert equally strong effects on global self-worth in both children (grades 3 to 6) and early adolescents (grades 6 to 8). Third, the effects of perceived competence and social support on global self-worth are additive; the higher one's perceived competence in important domains and the higher the perceived social acceptance by others, the higher is global self-worth.

Fourth, the competence domain that relates strongest to global self-worth in both children and adolescents is physical appearance or attractiveness. The secondary dimensions vary by age: For elementary-age youth, social acceptance by peers, scholastic competence, athletic competence, and behavioral conduct show similar magnitudes of correlations with self-worth. By contrast, peer acceptance emerges in a strong second place behind physical appearance for middle-school youth, followed by scholastic competence, behavioral conduct, and athletic

FIGURE 4
Harter's (1987) mediational model of global self-worth

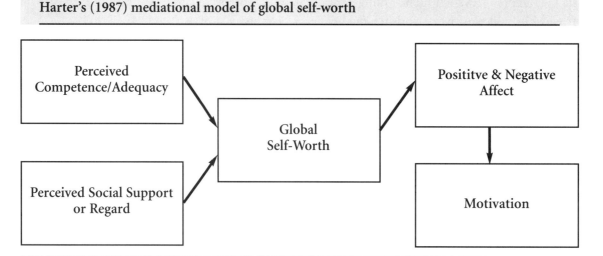

Adapted from Weiss, M.R., & Ferrer-Caja, E. (2002). Motivational orientations and sport behavior. In T.S. Horn (Ed.), *Advances in sport psychology* (2nd ed., pp. 101-183). Champaign, IL: Human Kinetics. Reprinted by permission of Human Kinetics.

competence. Fifth, the sources of social support on global self-worth are strongest for parents and classmates, although this is more pronounced in middle-school youth. The finding of significant parent influence in early adolescence is contrary to some developmental literature that suggests peers become more important than parents over the childhood years. Harter (1987) suggests that although the amount or level of parent influence does not appear to wane, the *type* of parent influence may shift from one of nurturance, help, and guidance during childhood to informational and emotional support in adolescence, especially in children's interactions with peers. Sixth, global self-worth and affect (cheerfulness, depressed) are strongly related in child and adolescent samples.

Perhaps the most important finding relative to our chapter is model testing of the role of global self-worth in motivational consequences (Harter, 1987). Assessing all model constructs simultaneously with older children (sixth grade), strong support emerged for global self-worth as a mediator of the effects of perceived competence/adequacy and social support on affect and motivational orientation. Although perceived competence, social support, and global self-worth showed modest direct relationships with motivation, the indirect effect of global self-worth via affective reactions on motivation was much stronger. Thus, we can conclude that the best model describing construct relationships is the one depicted in Figure 4, one in which global self-worth acts as a mediator of emotional responses and interest in and desire to pursue achieving one's goals.

Extension to the Physical Domain

Despite the empirical evidence and intuitive appeal of Harter's (1987) mediational model of global self-worth, few studies have tested model relationships with youth in the physical domain. Some studies investigated perceived competence and importance as antecedents of global self-worth (Ebbeck & Stuart, 1993, 1996) or global self-worth as a mediator of the relationship between perceived competence and affective reactions (Ebbeck & Weiss, 1998). We located only one study to date that tested motivational predictions of the self-worth model in the physical activity context.

A. L. Smith (1999) examined the network of relationships among perceived peer acceptance, close friendship, physical self-worth, affect, motivational orientation, and physical activity behavior among 12- to 15-year-old middle school students. This age group was selected deliberately based on the salience of peers and declines in physical activity during this period. Important to note is that Smith contextualized all constructs to physical activity, rather than retain the global nature of variables in Harter's model. Perceptions of social acceptance by classmates and having a close, intimate friendship directly predicted physical self-worth that, in turn, influenced attraction to or positive affect toward physical activity. Physical self-worth indirectly influenced both motivational orientation and frequency and intensity of physical activity (i.e., motivated behaviors) through the mediating effects of positive affect. These findings were very similar for both girls and boys and, importantly, provide support for competency antecedents and affective and motivational consequences of global self-worth specific to the physical domain.

> Researchers found that perceptions of peer acceptance and experiencing close friendship influence physical self-worth.

Based on our discussion of Harter's (1987) global self-worth model, it is clear that the model is a suitable candidate for studying the ties among self-perceptions, social influence, affect, and motivation in youth populations. For this reason, Weiss (2000) customized the mediational model of self-worth to offer practical implications for enhancing physical activity motivation in youth. Still, considerably more research is desired to validate the model's predictions for the sport and physical activity context. Horn (2003a) and Crocker et al. (2003) also reinforce the applicability of Harter's mediational model of global self-worth for the youth physical domain and suggest ideas for future research specific to self-worth and emotions, respectively.

ECCLES'S (1983) EXPECTANCY-VALUE MODEL

Eccles and colleagues (1983; Eccles, Wigfield, & Schiefele, 1998) developed a comprehensive model to explain variations in achievement choices and behaviors among youth across a variety of domains. The theory is multidimensional in specifying the social and psychological determinants of motivated behavior in specific contexts such as math, reading, sport, and music, as well as the nature of age-related changes in key model constructs and their interrelationships (see Figure 5). The developmental emphasis of this theory combined with empirical evidence of its practicality to sport and physical activity make this theory attractive for sport and exercise psychologists.

Achievement behaviors are influenced directly by two major variables—expectations of success and subjective task value. Expectations of success refer to children's beliefs about how well they think they will do in an activity; higher success expectancies are related to higher achievement behaviors. Subjective task value pertains to the importance of being successful in a particular domain and the degree to which a task fulfills an individual's goals, plans, and sense of identity. The greater one values a task, the greater his effort, persistence, and performance. As depicted in Figure 5, expectations of success and task value are influenced by a number of socioenvironmental variables and individual differences including socializers' beliefs and behaviors, children's perceptions and interpretations of socializers' behaviors and past achievement experiences, goals and perceptions of task difficulty, and self-schemas or identities.

Eccles and her colleagues have been prolific in testing model predictions, specifically investigating the determinants of success expectancies and task value, and their subsequent influence on achievement choices and performance (see Eccles & Wigfield, 1985, 1995; Eccles et al., 1998; Wigfield & Eccles, 1992, 2000). Moreover, Eccles (e.g., Eccles & Harold, 1991;

FIGURE 5
Eccles et al.'s (1983, 1998) expectancy-value model of achievement behaviors

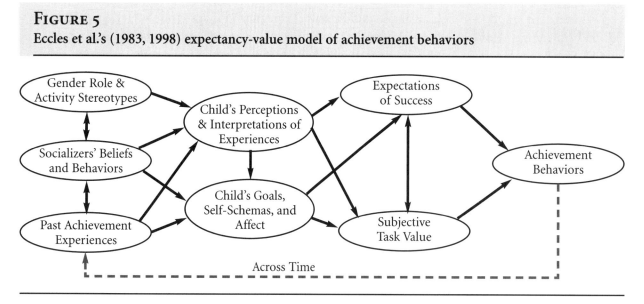

Adapted from Weiss, M.R., & Ferrer-Caja, E. (2002). Motivational orientations and sport behavior. In T.S. Horn (Ed.), *Advances in sport psychology* (2nd ed., pp. 101-183). Champaign, IL: Human Kinetics. Reprinted by permission of Human Kinetics.

Jacobs & Eccles, 1992; Wigfield et al., 1997) and sport psychology researchers (see Weiss & Ferrer-Caja, 2002, for a review) have provided support for the practicality of expectancy-value theory in understanding motivated behavior in the *physical domain*. Comparatively less research has explored the developmental structure and processes of expectancies and task value, as well as socialization and contextual influences in sport and physical activity settings. In the next sections, we elaborate upon age-related changes in key expectancy-value model constructs.

Expectations of Success

The essence of the success expectancy construct is the question "Can I do this task?" (Eccles et al., 1998). When approached from a developmental perspective, both the structure and processes of change are relevant (see Wigfield, 1994, Wigfield & Eccles, 2000). First, although self-concept of ability (i.e., domain-specific competence beliefs) and expectations of success are theoretically distinct constructs in the expectancy-value model, Eccles and Wigfield (1995; Eccles, Wigfield, Harold, & Blumenfeld, 1993) have found that 6- to 18-year-old youth do not differentiate between them (i.e., the two constructs are highly correlated and load together on one factor). Thus, whether a child expects to do well on a specific task in the future or reports high domain-specific estimates of ability results in empirically similar findings. Thus "ability beliefs" integrate the broader notion of self-judgments about competence in a domain and one's future success expectancies on a specific task in that domain.

Similar to data reported earlier, Eccles and colleagues (Eccles et al., 1993; Wigfield et al., 1997) have found that young children can differentiate their abilities across various domains (math, reading, sports, music), and this ability becomes stronger with age (e.g., responses become more strongly related to parent and teacher ratings). In addition to greater differentiation of competencies, mean levels decline for many domains (e.g., English, math, music, social activities) across the elementary school years and the transition from elementary to junior high school, and for some domains (i.e., math), declines continue across the adolescent years (e.g., Eccles & Wigfield, 1995; Wigfield, Eccles, MacIver, Reuman, & Midgley, 1991; Wigfield et al., 1997). Interestingly, Wigfield et al. (1991) found that ability beliefs in sport *increased* after the transition from elementary to junior high school. These disparate findings for the sport domain may have occurred because transitions in sport are not usually parallel with transitions in school.

Less optimistic outlooks about ability as one gets older may be due to increased understanding of ability as capacity, ability to integrate evaluative feedback and to use social comparison more frequently, and changes in the social contextual environment that emphasize normative standards and interpersonal competition. For example, Fredricks and Eccles (2002) found that declines in sport competence beliefs began during middle school and continued downwards over the high school years. A full understanding of success expectations across domains and ages is essential because research has shown that competence beliefs are the strongest predictor of academic achievement (i.e., grades).

Subjective Task Value

The value construct in Eccles' model is elaborated upon more than by most motivation theories and addresses the question "Do I want to do this task and why?" Eccles and colleagues (e.g., 1998; Wigfield & Eccles, 1992) distinguish among four task-value components. *Attainment value* pertains to the personal importance a child assigns to being good in a particular domain. The magnitude of this score is related to the relevance of the task in confirming aspects of one's self-identity (i.e., if a girl sees herself as a mathematician, then relegating high importance to doing well in math is consistent with her self-schema). *Intrinsic value* characterizes the child's enjoyment of or interest in doing an activity for its own sake, and it is analogous to intrinsic motivation as defined by Harter (1981b) and Deci and Ryan (1985). *Utility value* refers to how useful a child believes the task or activity to be relative to her long-term goals and career plans. Because this value component focuses upon doing an activity for some separable goal rather than for its own sake, Eccles aligns this component with the construct of extrinsic motivation as defined by Harter (1981b) and Deci and Ryan. Finally, cost is the negative side of value; it characterizes the risks (e.g., performance anxiety), sacrifices (e.g., effort needed to be successful), and lost opportunities (e.g., other activities) associated with choosing one activity over an alternative one. It should be noted that despite the stated importance of cost as a value component, the focus of expectancy-value research to date has been on the positive value aspects.

Eccles, Wigfield, and their colleagues have forged efforts to understand the development of subjective task value among children and adolescents in the same way as their inquiry into developmental patterns of competence beliefs (Eccles & Wigfield, 1995; Eccles et al., 1998; Wigfield, 1994; Wigfield & Eccles, 1992, 2000). Similar to ability beliefs, task value shows developmental change in both its structure and level across the childhood and adolescent years. Younger children (grades 1 to 4) differentiate two components—interest and utility/importance—and only later (grades 5 to 12) distinguish among all three as separate factors (Eccles et al., 1993; Wigfield et al., 1997). Also as with ability beliefs, task value tends to decline systematically across the elementary and middle school years. Attainment and utility values decline across a myriad of domains including sports; however, interest value declines for some domains (e.g., reading and music) but not for others such as math and sports (e.g., Fredricks & Eccles, 2002; Wigfield et al., 1991, 1997). In contrast to ability beliefs that are shown to best predict achievement performance, subjective task value is a better predictor of choice of tasks and intention to continue involvement. Eccles emphasizes the importance of distinguishing among task-value components because various dimensions may be more or less dominant for different age groups, and thus better or worse predictors of achievement-related choices, effort, persistence, and performance.

Changes in the relationship between competence beliefs and task values have also been studied as a function of age. Wigfield (1994) suggests that young children's estimates of their ability and interest value in doing an activity are unrelated; that is, children will like doing activities even if they are not very good at them. With age, youth start to develop their self-schemas or self-identities and consider future plans and goals. As a result, older youth may attach more importance and usefulness (i.e., attainment and utility values) to those tasks, activities, and domains that they are good at and thus confirm their hoped-for or ideal selves. In support of this notion, Wigfield et al. (1997) found that the correlation between expectations of success and task values in a number of domains (including sport) became stronger with age over the elementary school years. A question of increasing interest is how expectancies of success and subjective task values relate to cognitive strategies and self-regulated behavior, and subsequently, how this relationship changes with age (see Eccles & Wigfield, 1985; Eccles et al., 1998; Wigfield, 1994). The regulation of behavior to meet one's goals on valued tasks or activities deals with the question of "What do I have to do to succeed on this task?" Thus, Eccles' model is one that may be used to integrate self-beliefs, task beliefs, self-regulated learning strategies, and achievement behavior (choice of activities, effort and intensity of involvement, performance). A discussion of the self-regulation literature is beyond the scope of this chapter, but readers are directed to Schunk and Zimmerman (1994) and Petlichkoff (2003) for detailed discussion relevant to the academic and physical domains, respectively.

Social Influences

Eccles and colleagues have explored parental socialization practices as key contributors to the development of children's expectancies of success, task values, and achievement choices and behaviors in many domains including sport (see Eccles et al., 1998; Fredricks & Eccles, 2003). Eccles et al. envisioned parental influences on children's socialization of achievement motivation as an integration of family characteristics (e.g., demographics, culture), parents' general beliefs and behaviors (e.g., stereotypes, personal values, parenting styles), parents' child-specific beliefs (e.g., perceptions of child's abilities, interests, and value toward skills), parent-specific behaviors (e.g., encouragement, causal attributions), and child's psychosocial and behavioral outcomes (e.g., self-perceptions, task values, achievement). Eccles has particularly highlighted the role of parents' beliefs and behaviors in three ways—parents as role models, as providers of experience, and as interpreters of experience for their child (Fredricks & Eccles, 2003). Parents serve as models by expressing positive affect toward and engaging in daily physical activity. They provide experiences by signing children up for sport and encouraging their involvement in various activities. Finally, they interpret experiences for their child by conveying expectations or beliefs about their child's competencies and through explicit causal attributions for successful and unsuccessful performances.

Numerous studies by Eccles and colleagues and sport psychology researchers (see Fredricks & Eccles, 2003; Weiss & Ferrer-Caja, 2002, for reviews) have supported Eccles' conception of how parents' beliefs and behaviors influence children's competence beliefs, task values, and achievement motivation in the physical domain. A finding of particular interest is that parents' competency beliefs and importance of doing well in various domains (including sport) relative to their child exert a stronger effect than do past performance or actual ability on children's achievement-related beliefs (e.g., Eccles & Harold, 1991; Fredricks & Eccles, 2002; Jacobs & Eccles, 1992). Additionally, the relationship between parents' and children's competence beliefs and values becomes increasingly stronger over the elementary school years (e.g., Wigfield et al., 1997), implying a developmental trend of children's internalizing the beliefs and values of parents as their own.

> Parents interpret experiences for their child by conveying expectations or beliefs about their child's competencies.

Despite the growing knowledge base on parents' influence of children's self- and task-beliefs, motivational orientation, and domain-specific behaviors (e.g., frequency of physical activity), we know very little about the relative influence of parents and other socializers (teachers, coaches, peers) at varying ages or how the relationship between parents' and children's beliefs and behaviors changes with age. Nor do we have a complete understanding of how parental socialization experiences differ for children across (e.g., math v. sport) and within (e.g., baseball v. tennis) achievement domains. Future research that employs a developmental perspective on parent-child relationships in sport would significantly contribute to our understanding of these issues.

Although parents have been at the core of understanding the socialization of achievement motivation in children, teachers, coaches, and peers constitute significant sources for forming beliefs about one's competencies, the value attached to certain domains or activities, and achievement and non-achievement behaviors (see Eccles et al., 1998; Weiss & Ferrer-Caja, 2002). Teachers' expectancy effects were shown to predict children's future performance in various domains including sport (e.g., Madon, Jussim, & Eccles, 1997; Wigfield, Galper, Denton, & Seefeldt, 1999), and perceptions of teacher support among sixth-grade students were predictive of seventh graders' interest in school and academic achievement (Wentzel, 1998). Moreover, youths' degree of dependence upon peers in the seventh grade predicted their academic achievement and problem behaviors in later grades (Fuligni, Eccles, Barber, & Clements, 2001). Eccles and Barber (1999) examined correlates of extracurricular activity participation (school, prosocial, sports, performing arts, academic clubs) among adolescents, and found a strong linkage among type of activity involvement, peer group culture, and identity formation.

Similarly, in sport, coach and peer evaluation become more salient as competence information sources in later childhood and adolescence (Horn, 2003a). Studies have consistently shown that coach evaluative and informational feedback relates to young athletes' perceptions of competence, interest value (i.e., enjoyment), and motivational orientation (e.g., Black & Weiss, 1991; Horn, 1985). Moreover, peer influence in the form of group acceptance or rejection, close friendship, and friendship quality is related to youths' self-perceptions, valuing of activities, and physical activity behaviors (see Weiss & Stuntz, 2003). Thus, future research adopting Eccles' expectancy-value model would benefit from a developmental analysis of coach and peer socialization effects on children's self- and task-beliefs, and achievement choices and behaviors in the physical domain.

Contextual Influences

Eccles's model (1983; Eccles et al., 1998) explicitly targets contextual influences as contributors to youths' self-beliefs, task values, and achievement orientations. Such influences include social environmental factors such as classroom climate, grouping practices, evaluation techniques, and quality of teacher-student relationships (e.g., Eccles & Midgley, 1990; Roeser & Eccles, 1998; Roeser, Eccles, & Sameroff, 2000). These factors have been implicated as reasons for the declines in ability beliefs, task values, motivational orientation, and achievement choices across the elementary school years and in the transition from elementary to junior high school found in several studies mentioned earlier. Although Eccles (1998; Eccles & Midgley, 1990) acknowledges that physiological, psychological, and cognitive maturational changes that occur at the time of moving from elementary to junior high school may account for declines in self-perceptions, interest, and motivation, it is more likely these changes occur as a result of the interaction between developmental changes associated with early adolescence and social-environmental changes that emerge in the transition to middle or junior high school.

Eccles (1998; Eccles & Midgley, 1990) forwards a theory of stage-environment fit to explain transitional changes in achievement-related beliefs and behaviors during early adolescence. The stage-environment fit theory specifies that environmental and structural changes that match individuals' needs at a particular time should result in positive motivational consequences. By contrast, environments that pose a disconnect between maturational needs for competence, autonomy, and social relationships will result in negative motivational outcomes. For example, Eccles and colleagues (1998; Eccles & Midgley, 1990; Roeser & Eccles, 1998) point out that elementary schools revolve around a philosophy that emphasizes learning, effort, and interest toward subject matter. These goals are associated with teacher behaviors that recognize individual progress, provide social support, and encourage a cooperative or individualistic reward structure that evaluates success based on group or personally customized goals. As students make the transition to middle school, they find environments that emphasize norm-referenced standards, ability grouping practices, public evaluation methods, less decision making and autonomy, and less supportive teacher-student relationships (Eccles & Midgley, 1990; Eccles et al., 1998). These structural and organizational shifts and concomitant teacher behaviors that are less supportive come at a time when early adolescents experience a host of other maturational changes associated with puberty. This stage-environment misfit, then, is one explanation forwarded for the downward spiral in ability perceptions, task values, and motivation in the transition from elementary to junior high school.

A similar analogy of transitions could be made for the sport domain, where children may participate at varying levels of competitive involvement. Typically, a recreational league of play focuses upon opportunities for skill learning, positive coach-player and player-player interactions, and fun and enjoyment. This is the level at which children initiate their sport careers; if they are athletically talented and physically mature enough, they often make the transition to a "select" or higher competitive league, one that places more emphasis on social comparison standards of competence and success, a less supportive coaching style, and playing time dependent upon normative ability (Horn & Harris, 1996; Weiss & Ferrer-Caja, 2002). The transition from a skill-oriented program to one emphasizing normative standards and competitive outcomes should conceivably influence participants' success expectations, task values, motivational orientation, and performance. However, at the present time we can only speculate on such outcomes based on the transition research in the educational domain.

As mentioned earlier, Wigfield et al. (1991, 1997) found that ability beliefs and interest value for sport *increased* in the transition from elementary to junior high school, which contrasts to the declines in self-beliefs and task beliefs for other domains (math, English, reading, music). We would contend that the transition in the sport domain has already occurred (e.g., recreational to select league soccer), and only those youths exhibiting the best athletic potential have survived the tryouts required to reach the next level. Because transitions in sport are a function of skill ability and not chronological age, it would make sense that those youths still involved in sport during the *academic transition* from sixth to seventh grade maintain high self-perceptions of competence and attraction toward their sport (i.e., they made an *athletic transition* earlier). They are the players who, by virtue of being selected for their athletic talents, have obtained considerable information that they do possess high ability. Moreover, because the relation between perceptions of competence and task value become stronger with age, their interest value should match their high levels of competence beliefs in sport.

Even though considerable theorizing exists about differences in league philosophy, organizational structure, and coaching behaviors at lower and higher levels of sport involvement (Horn & Harris, 1996; Weiss & Ferrer-Caja, 2002), no empirical studies were located that investigated the effects of sport transitions on participants' psychosocial outcomes (e.g., from recreational to select league). Moreover, no studies exist to determine whether changes in expectations of success, subjective task values, and motivational orientation occur as a function of sport transitions and, if so, whether they are associated with changes in motivational climate and coaching behaviors. Although Wigfield et al. (1991, 1997) found changes in the opposite direction for sport compared to school subjects, we believe that tapping youths' self-perceptions, task values, and motivation commensurate with moving from a lower to a higher competitive level would show similar declines. Several reasons are offered for such a trend. First, the transition from lower to higher competitive levels occurs at a time when youth start using peer comparison and evaluation more frequently (about ages 9 to 11 years). Second, the nature of competitive youth sport is one that slowly but surely emphasizes the importance of demonstrating superior ability relative to that of others (teammates, opponents). Third, because the pool of players in which to compare ability is now smaller, perceptions of physical competence should decline except for the star players; moreover, such downward trends in perceived competence combined with the increased emphasis on competitive outcomes should result in lower interest value for most players. It is possible that those youths who did not "make the cut" to higher sport levels either stayed at a recreational level or perhaps dropped out.

> When the pool of players becomes smaller, perceptions of physical competence usually decline except for star players.

Despite the tremendous numbers of youth participating in both agency and school sports (De Knop, Engstrom, Skirstad, & Weiss, 1996), we know little about *when* children and adolescents discontinue organized sport and exactly for *what* reasons. Longitudinal studies of youth sport participants, from initiation of involvement to transitions to higher levels and eventually to discontinuation, would reveal a wealth of information related to achievement-related beliefs and behaviors such as self-perceptions, task values, and motivational orientation. Eccles' model would appear to be an excellent framework from which to explore such questions in the sport domain.

Nicholls's (1989) Achievement Goal Theory

Most of us feel good when we accomplish something; often the more difficult the task, the more successful we feel. Likewise, we feel bad when we fail to accomplish a task. In this case, failing on easy tasks often feels worse than failing on tasks that are more difficult. Although we may experience similar feelings associated with success and failure, there are differences in our approach toward success and failure. Several theorists (Ames, 1984; Dweck, 1999; Maehr & Nicholls, 1980; Nicholls, 1989) have forwarded their own unique ideas concerning success and failure in achievement situations, but would agree that ability and goals are important to the understanding of achievement-related cognitions, affect, and behaviors.

Of these theorists, Maehr and Nicholls (1980) posit that individuals in achievement settings are motivated to demonstrate high ability and avoid demonstrating low ability. Building on this, Nicholls (1984, 1989) developed his achievement goal theory. According to Nicholls, individuals feel successful when they demonstrate high ability and unsuccessful when they demonstrate low ability. However, what people think it takes to demonstrate ability is not necessarily common to all. Individuals' goals are intimately linked to their thoughts about what is required to demonstrate ability. Nicholls' (1990) key question was "What is ability?"

According to Nicholls (1989, 1990), individuals can be concerned with the goals of learning and improving. In cases like this, individuals believe they are demonstrating ability and, thus feel successful when experiencing personal mastery. Individuals are considered to be *task involved* when they are concerned with performing their best, defined in terms of personal mastery. Individuals can also be concerned with how their performances compare to those of others. In cases like this, individuals believe they are demonstrating ability when they outperform others with equal effort or perform equally as well with less effort. Individuals are considered to be *ego involved* when they are concerned with superior performances relative to the performance of others. Whether an individual is task or ego involved in any given situation is influenced by dispositional, environmental, and developmental factors. Each of these factors is discussed in turn in the following paragraphs.

Goal orientations are the dispositional "relative" of goal involvement. Goal orientations indicate one's proneness to be task or ego involved across different situations and domains. Task orientation reflects a tendency, across situations, to be concerned with performing one's best or with learning, whereas ego orientation reflects a tendency to be concerned about performing better than others. The majority of research in the physical domain has examined the relationship between goal orientations and motivation. This research has shown that individuals higher in task goal orientation show more adaptive motivational patterns than do those lower in task orientation. In contrast, those higher in ego orientation demonstrate more maladaptive patterns. An adaptive motivational pattern is characterized by greater effort, perceived competence, positive affect, and intrinsic motivation, whereas a maladaptive pattern is characterized by lower effort, perceived competence, positive affect, and intrinsic motivation (see Duda & Hall, 2001, for a review).

Environmental factors such as the objective (reward structure) and subjective (motivational climate) nature of a situation can also influence goal involvement (Nicholls, 1989, 1990). Specifically, situations that highlight interpersonal competition and social comparison tend to evoke a state of ego involvement, whereas situations emphasizing individual improvement are thought to induce a state of task involvement. This may be particularly true when the nature of the situation matches one's goal orientation. Thus, individuals in situations, or who perceive they are in situations, where winning is valued and rewarded (competitive reward structure or performance climate) are more likely to be ego involved, particularly if they are predominantly ego oriented. Conversely, individuals in situations where personal improvement is or is perceived to be valued and rewarded (individualistic reward structure or mastery climate) are more likely to be task involved, particularly if they are predominantly task oriented. Several researchers have examined the influence of competitive and mastery situational factors on goal involvement in academic (Ames & Ames, 1981; Ames & Archer, 1988) and physical activity settings (Cury, Biddle, Sarrazin, & Famose, 1997, Harwood & Swain, 1998; Swain & Harwood, 1996; Williams, 1998). In general, this research supports Nicholls' contentions regarding the influence of the environment on goal involvement.

Developmental factors related to goal involvement will be the focus of the remainder of this section of the chapter. In environmen , that do not emphasize either competition or mastery, children are thou, ht to be task involved until they develop a mature or adult-like understanding of ability. This is because they do not yet differentiate the concept of ability from other achievement-related concepts such as task difficulty, luck, and effort (Nicholls, 1989, 1990, 1992; Nicholls, Jagacinski, & Miller, 1986). As noted by earlier researchers (e.g., Veroff, 1969), children think of ability differently than adults do, and Nicholls set out to understand how youth come to view ability (Nicholls, 1978, 1984; Nicholls & Miller, 1983, 1984). Nicholls contended that individuals with a mature understanding of ability can differentiate between task difficulty and effort, and between ability and luck and effort, whereas those with an immature conception cannot differentiate among these concepts. Therefore, he was interested in how children come to differentiate these constructs.

As an educational psychologist, Nicholls conducted his research in the academic setting. Through this research Nicholls (1990) identified three levels of understanding related to the differentiation between task difficulty and ability and four levels of differentiation between ability and luck and ability and effort (see Table 2). Only recently have sport psychologists begun to examine the developmental aspects of Nicholls' theory, and the majority of this research has followed the research protocol he used in the academic setting. In the two sections that follow, we overview the developmental tenets of Nicholls' theory and review the related research, with particular emphasis on research conducted in the physical activity domain.

Developing a Mature Understanding of Ability: An Overview of Nicholls' Theory

In the process of developing a mature understanding of ability, children come to differentiate between task difficulty and ability (Nicholls, 1978, 1980, 1990; Nicholls et al., 1986). Young children (about 5 years) have a self-referenced view of task difficulty. They use personal task completion or a combination of completion and task complexity as an indicator of task difficulty. At this most immature or *egocentric* level of task difficulty, children consider tasks that they believe they can complete successfully as easy and tasks they think they cannot complete as difficult. For children at the egocentric level, hard means hard *for me*. At the next level, the *objective* level, children around 6 years of age begin to understand that task difficulty is independent of their personal expectancies for success and is determined, in part, by the complexity of the task. Yet they still believe that personally challenging tasks are an indicator of their ability. Around the age of 7, children typically have a norm-referenced view of task difficulty and understand that tasks few children can do are difficult, and those who can do these tasks have high ability. This is referred to as the *normative* level. Despite this mature understanding of the relationship between task difficulty and ability, children at this level are unlikely to hold a completely mature conception of ability as they have yet to differentiate ability from luck or effort.

Children are not fully able to differentiate between ability and luck or ability and effort until early adolescence (Nicholls, 1989, 1992; Nicholls et al., 1986; Nicholls & Miller, 1984). At 5 to

> In environments that do not emphasize either competition or mastery, children are thought to be task-involved until they develop a mature or adult-like understanding of ability.

TABLE 2

Developmental Levels for Luck-Ability, Effort-Ability, and Task Difficulty-Ability Conceptions

Level 1:	Undifferentiated Conception of Ability
Luck	The outcome on luck and skill tasks can improve with effort.
Effort	Effort or outcome indicates ability.
Difficulty	Task difficulty is based on one's own expectations for success.

Level 2:	Early Stages of Partially Differentiated Conception of Ability
Luck	The outcome of luck and skill task can improve with greater effort, but children cannot explain why. Nonetheless, skill tasks benefit more from effort.
Effort	Effort causes outcomes. Equal effort will produce equal outcome.
Task Difficulty	Task difficulty is independent of one's own expectations for success, but children cannot determine if failure was due to low ability or high task difficulty

Level 3:	Later Stages of Partially Differentiated Conception of Ability
Luck	The outcome of luck and skill task can improve with greater effort, and children can explain why. Nonetheless, skill tasks benefit more from effort.
Effort	Effort is not the only cause of outcomes. Children imply that ability limits effort.
Task Difficulty	Task difficulty is judged relative to others' performances. Tasks that few can do are seen as difficult and individuals who can do tasks that few can do are seen as able.

Level 4:	Completely Differentiated Conception of Ability
Luck	The outcome on luck skills cannot be improved with effort.
Effort	The impact of effort on outcome is limited by one's ability.

6 years of age, children cannot differentiate ability from luck or effort (Level 1). For them, more diligent workers are more able, and they believe that effort will improve the outcome of both luck and skill tasks. At this level, children believe that those who work harder have greater ability. Children aged 7 to about 11 years begin to differentiate between these constructs (Levels 2 & 3). During this time, children believe that performance on both luck and skill tasks can be improved with effort, but acknowledge that performance on skill tasks benefits more from effort. Although they are beginning to understand that unequal outcomes from equal effort can be explained by differences in ability, they still believe that effort is the cause of ability. Thus, children at these levels can only partially differentiate ability from luck or effort. By the age of 12 years, children are thought to hold a mature understanding of ability because they can completely differentiate between ability and luck and between ability and effort (Level 4). At this time they understand that (a) effort cannot alter the outcome on luck tasks, (b) the impact that effort has on performance is limited by one's ability, and (c) individuals who perform better with less effort are more able. Thus, children have a fully mature understanding of ability when they are able to differentiate ability from task difficulty, effort, and luck.

According to Nicholls (1989, 1990), when children no longer equate ability with task difficulty, luck or effort, they understand that ability is influenced by personal limitations and that it is these personal limitations or their capacity that limits the impact of effort. Said another way, they now view ability as finite rather than infinite and realize that the quality of their performance is limited by their ability, which is now seen as capacity. Once individuals view ability as capacity, they may use self-referenced (e.g., personal improvement) or norm-referenced (e.g., out-performing others) criteria when evaluating their ability and success. Because of this, whether individuals who are capable of conceiving ability in the "differentiated sense" will be ego involved or task involved will depend on their goal orientations and environmental cues.

This is not to say that those with an undifferentiated conception of ability cannot be ego involved. In fact, Nicholls (1989, 1990) acknowledges that this is plausible, particularly when the social comparison cues in the environment are strong (e.g., rivalry). Nicholls (1990) interpreted results by Heckhausen (1984, cited in Nicholls, 1990) as evidence that in situations promoting interpersonal rivalry, young children can adopt another person's performance as a standard of adequacy even though they may not conceive of ability as capacity. In his book, Nicholls (1989) also reasons that, although

> no comparable studies appear to have been done with young children. . . the studies reviewed above are consistent with the notion that when we draw a young child's attention to the standards of competence implicit in the work of others, the quality of the child's involvement is likely to change from a focus on the requirements of the task. . . to a state of ego involvement wherein the child evaluates herself in terms of another's performance. (p. 17)

Research by Butler (1989a, 1989b) has shown support for the notion that young children become more ego involved in competitive as compared to personal mastery situations. In these studies, she asked children ages 4-10 to create a picture using stickers. Children in the competitive group were told to see who could create the best picture whereas those in the noncompetitive condition were told that their picture would be part of a collection of all the students' work. Children in the competitive group looked at their peers' work more often than did children in the noncompetitive group. When asked why they looked at their peers' work, younger children (5 year olds) gave more mastery-related explanations such as to learn how to do the task, whereas older children (10 year olds) gave more ability-related explanations such as how well they were doing (Butler, 1989b). Butler (1989b) concluded that children presumably too young to hold a differentiated conception of ability observe others primarily to develop mastery, whereas older children who are capable of holding at least a partially differentiated conception of ability observe others to evaluate relative ability.

Butler (1989a) also demonstrated that although children do tend to be more ego involved in situations that emphasize competition, only the older children (ages 9-11) seemed to suffer the negative motivational effects of ego involvement. After experiencing the competitive or mastery conditions, children were provided with the opportunity to play with the stickers in their free time. Only the 9 and 10 year olds in the competitive group demonstrated less interest in playing with the stickers in their free time. Thus, it appears that observing others' performance in competitive situations does not undermine the motivation of very young children, who likely hold an undifferentiated conception of ability, but it does undermine the motivation of those children that likely hold a partially differentiated or fully differentiated conception of ability.

Nicholls' observations and Butler's research provide evidence that prior to attaining a mature conception of ability and in situations promoting interpersonal competition, young children are capable of being ego involved in that they socially compare, understand that only one person can win, can evaluate their performance relative to others, and can experience neg-

In noncompetitive situations, young children are more likely to watch others so they can learn and improve rather than compare abilities.

ative affect when they do not measure up to others. Nonetheless, when working in situations that do not promote rivalry, these young children are more likely to observe others for the purpose of learning and improving rather than for ability comparison.

We may interpret Nicholls to mean that because young children cannot differentiate ability, task difficulty, luck, and effort, they tend to be task oriented and task involved when performing in the presence of others who are performing similar tasks. However, as shown by Butler (1989a, 1989b), it is possible that environmental cues may induce even young children to be ego involved. When in a state of ego involvement, they are still inclined to believe that they could perform better relative to others if they tried harder, even on luck tasks. In contrast, because individuals with a differentiated conception of ability are capable of being task and/or ego oriented, they are likely to be ego involved when performing in the presence of others doing similar tasks because they understand that their ability level is defined relative to the performance of others. Thus, prior to viewing ability as capacity, being task or ego oriented/involved should not undermine one's motivation. In contrast, once one understands ability as capacity, being high ego and low task oriented, or ego involved, should reduce one's motivation, unless one feels one has the ability to compare favorably to others (i.e., possesses high perceived competence).

We are aware of only one study that has examined the relationships among conceptions of ability, goal involvement, and performance. Butler (1999) examined whether age differences in goal preference (involvement), improvement, and expectancies for improvement were a function of conceptions of ability. Fifty-four percent of the fifth and sixth graders in the study had a completely differentiated and 46% had a partially differentiated conception of ability (Levels 2 & 3). Children were placed in either a task- or ego-involving condition and asked to complete a novel cognitive task. In the ego-involving condition, children with the most mature conceptions of ability were more ego involved, did not expect to improve, and performed more poorly over time if they had low perceptions of ability, whereas those in the task-involving condition were more task involved, expected to improve, and actually improved. Interestingly, regardless of condition, more children with a partially differentiated conception of ability were more ego involved, expected to improve, and did not improve than those who were completely differentiated. These results support Nicholls' contention of the disadvantages of ego-involving situations in combination with a mature conception of ability, particularly when individuals are low in perceived competence. The results also highlight the potential "costs" of such conditions in combination with a partially differentiated conception of ability.

Relationships among conceptions of ability, goal orientation, goal involvement, and motivation processes have not been explored in the physical domain. Recently, however, physical activity researchers have examined the relationship between conceptions of ability and goal orientations among 4th-, 8th-, and 11th-grade students (Xiang & Lee, 1998; Xiang, Lee, & Shen, 2001). Students with a differentiated conception of ability were more likely to be high in ego orientation (~ 67%) compared to those with an undifferentiated conception (~ 37%). Although these results lend support for a correspondence between conceptions of ability and goal orientations, about one fourth (~ 22%) of the students with an undifferentiated conception of ability were high in task and ego orientation, and 15% of undifferentiated individuals were high in ego and low in task orientation. These results give credence to the suggestion that a differentiated conception of ability is *not* necessary for youngsters to be ego oriented.

In sum, regardless of whether children have the cognitive maturity to understand ability in the differentiated sense, situations promoting interpersonal competition will likely heighten their concern for how they perform relative to others (i.e., ego involvement/orientation). The difference is that without a mature conception of ability, it is unclear whether children interpret their performance outcome in terms of effort, luck, or task difficulty (Nicholls, 1990). For children with a mature conception of ability, it is clear that performance reflects one's normative ability and that ability is evaluated in light of task difficulty, luck, and effort. This, however, does not necessarily mean they do not value effort; rather, they have "less faith in the power of effort to raise our performance relative to that of others" (Nicholls, 1989, p. 60). Understanding ability in the differentiated sense affords individuals the option of being task and/or ego oriented/ involved. It is this "flexibility" that allows them to understand that effortful people are not necessarily more able, but it does not deny them the capability of valuing effort and feeling successful even when they are not the best in the class. For example, physical education students in the 4th, 8th, and 11th grades who were identified as holding a differentiated conception of ability acknowledged the value of hard work and viewed effort as a means of improvement (Xiang, Lee, & Williamson, 2001). It is clear that more research is needed to better understand developmental changes in children's conceptions of ability, effort, luck, and task difficulty in the physical domain and how such conceptions relate to goal orientations/involvement and motivational processes (cognitions, affect, behavior).

Developing a Mature Understanding of Physical Ability

Although Duda first discussed the utility of Nicholls' achievement goal theory from a developmental perspective in 1987, other researchers have only recently begun to explore children's understanding of ability in the physical domain from a developmental perspective. The majority of these studies focused on the differentiation of ability and effort (Fry & Duda, 1997; Lee, Carter, & Xiang, 1995; Whitehead & Smith, 1996; Xiang & Lee, 1998; Xiang, Lee, & Shen, 2001; Xiang, Lee, & Williamson, 2001). Only one study has examined children's understanding of luck and ability (Fry, 2000a) and task difficulty (Fry, 2000b). The remainder of this section highlights the current research investigating the developmental tenets of Nicholls' theory as they apply to physical task achievement.

Differentiating Effort and Ability. One of the initial studies of children's understanding of ability examined the criteria children use for determining one's ability (Lee et al., 1995). Children in kindergarten, 1st, 4th, and 5th grades were asked to explain how they knew whether someone was high or low in ability (i.e., good or not good in physical education). Younger children's explanations were self-referenced in that they used examples of mastering tasks and that others would do better if they were willing to work and actually worked harder. In contrast, older children (4th and 5th graders) referred to natural ability when explaining how someone would know she was an outstanding student in physical education. For example, one student said, "My Dad was an athlete, and he went pro football, so I have a lot of these skills" (Lee et al., p. 389). Concomitant with these shifts in effort to ability criteria was an increase in the number of social comparison comments. That is, more of the older students described their ability by comparing performance relative to that of their peers. Similar trends regarding criteria for determining ability were found for 4th, 8th, and 11th graders by Xiang, Lee, and Williamson (2001). Interestingly, more 11th than 4th and 8th graders indicated that others would do better if they were willing to try harder, and students regardless of grade level were equally likely to use social comparison as a criterion for determining one's ability. Although neither study directly tested Nicholls' theory, the authors concluded that results support Nicholls' (1984, 1989) contention that young children assume effort and task mastery will lead to greater ability/success, whereas older children were more apt to view ability as a more stable construct. Findings were also congruent with those of Watkins and Montgomery (1989), who interviewed elementary, middle, and high school students about their beliefs concerning determinants of athletic excellence. They found that the tendency for individuals to think that ability comes from effort decreased and the belief that it stems from natural ability increased with age.

To accurately investigate children's understanding of ability as capacity, researchers need to assess whether they can recognize that a person who must try harder to accomplish what another can accomplish is less able (Nicholls, 1989). To this end, Whitehead and Smith (1996) interviewed 8- to 13-year-old boys after they had watched two split-screen video clips depicting two performers shooting at off-screen baskets with unequal effort. In one clip, participants were informed that the high-effort performer scored fewer baskets. In the second clip, they

> As students get older, they
> are more likely to describe
> their ability by comparing
> their performance to that
> of their peers.

were told that both performers scored the same number of baskets. Results revealed that most (57%) of the 8 to 9 year olds engaged in immature levels of reasoning regarding effort and ability, whereas most (56%) of the 10 to 13 year olds demonstrated reasoning at more mature levels. A closer look reveals that the trend toward a more mature understanding of ability resides primarily among children between 8 and 11 years. Specifically, 8 year olds either failed to distinguish between effort and ability (Level 1) or displayed a partially differentiated conception of ability (Level 2). With each increasing year children demonstrated more mature levels of reasoning (Levels 3 & 4) until the ages of 12 to 13 years. Interestingly, most of the 12 to 13 year olds (~ 55%) reasoned similarly to the 8 to 9 year olds (i.e., partially differentiated conception of ability). The levels found by Whitehead and Smith parallel those Nicholls found in the academic realm, thereby providing support for his developmental levels. Nonetheless, the variability in levels of conception of ability, particularly within the 12 to 13 age group, suggests that the tie between age and conceptions of ability may be different depending on the achievement domain studied.

The findings by Whitehead and Smith (1996) bring to light the amount of within-age group variability relative to children's understanding of effort and ability. Theoretically, 12 to 13 year olds should be functioning at Level 4; however, only 33% of these children actually differentiated between effort and ability, whereas 67% still held a partially differentiated view of ability (Levels 2 & 3). This is particularly interesting given that all of the 10 to 11 year olds were at Level 2 and 3 as expected. In our attempt to explain why some children in the 12- to 13- age group did not demonstrate an understanding of ability in the differentiated sense, we suggest they may have lacked the cognitive maturity to understand ability as capacity. Assessment of cognitive maturity in future research may help shed light on the variability in conceptions of ability among different age groups, particularly because chronological age and cognitive maturity are not equivalent (Amorose & Weiss, 1998).

Fry (2001) discusses the results by Whitehead and Smith (1996) from a methodological perspective. She notes that the number of basket attempts made by the high-effort performer was at least 4 times greater than that of the low-effort performer. Fry speculates that the imbalance in the number of shooting attempts may have resulted in children's focusing on the number of attempts rather than the degree of effort exerted by the performers. Some confirmation for this criticism is evidenced by the fact that several participants (~ 19%) could not be categorized on levels of differentiation because they acknowledged that the low-effort performer did not take as many shots as the high-effort performer took.

The potential confound regarding the number of shots taken was addressed by Xiang and colleagues (Xiang & Lee, 1998; Xiang, Lee, & Shen, 2001). Instead of using filmed actors to examine individuals' understanding of ability, they used written basketball-shooting scenarios to assess conceptions of ability. In the scenarios, two students made the same number of baskets while displaying unequal effort. The results, based on interview responses from 4th, 8th, and 11th grade American physical education students, revealed a developmental trend from an undifferentiated to a differentiated understanding of the effort-ability relationship. Specifically, the majority (~ 60%) of 4th graders and only about 6% of the 11th graders viewed ability and effort equivalently (Level 1), whereas about 50% of 11th graders and only about 5% of the 4th graders understood the notion of ability as capacity (Level 4). Similar to Whitehead and Smith (1996), Xiang and Lee discovered great variability within age groups. Only 38% of the 8th graders and 50% of the 11th graders held a differentiated view of ability and effort. A similar developmental pattern was found among Chinese 4th, 8th, and 11th graders. These results raise questions that by 12 years most children will hold a differentiated view of ability.

Collectively, the research reviewed thus far provides only partial support for Nicholls' (1978, 1990; Nicholls et al., 1986) views concerning the developmental progression of children's conceptions of ability and his (1992) contention that children's reasoning about ability is consistent across achievement domains. To adequately examine the nature of children's understanding of ability and effort, research directly comparing achievement domains is needed. To test Nicholls' assertions more directly, Fry and Duda (1997) replicated and extended developmental research conducted by Nicholls and his colleagues (Nicholls, 1978, 1984; Nicholls & Miller, 1984) by investigating children's understanding of effort and ability in the academic and physical achievement domains simultaneously.

Using methods similar to those of Nicholls and his colleagues (Nicholls, 1978; Nicholls & Miller, 1984), Fry and Duda (1997) had 144 boys and girls ranging in age from 5 to 13 years view four films. Two of the films showed two children working on math problems (academic domain) and two showed children throwing beanbags through a hula hoop (physical domain). Both types of films depicted two children working with unequal effort (a diligent and an intermittent worker). In one film, both children performed equally. In the other film, the intermittent worker outperformed the diligent or hard worker. The number of performance attempts was controlled addressing concerns with Whitehead and Smith's (1996) study. Participants were asked to explain why variations in performance occurred given that the children's effort at the tasks differed.

Four primary findings emerged. First, inductive content analysis revealed four levels of reasoning similar to those found by Nicholls (1978). Second, a fifth level (Level 0) emerged in which children were unable to identify the harder worker or gave responses unrelated to the effort-ability relationship (e.g., "I don't know"). Third, the strong correlation between age and reasoning level in both the academic ($r = .70$) and physical ($r = .67$) domains revealed that children's level of reasoning regarding ability increases with age. Fourth, there was consistency in children's reasoning about ability and effort across domains ($r = .70$), indicating a general conception of ability. Fry and Duda's (1997) results replicate the work by Nicholls in the academic domain and provide evidence supporting Nicholls' (1989) contention that conceptions of ability are consistent across domains. Still there was variability within age groups, and participants who we might expect to have a mature understanding of ability and effort did not. Only 63% and 56% of 13 year olds held a mature understanding of the relationship between effort and ability in the physical and academic domains, respectively. This variability among individuals within age groups illustrates again that children mature cognitively at different rates and that chronological age may not be the best marker when testing developmental hypotheses.

> Because children mature cognitively at different rates, chronological age may not be reliable when testing developmental hypotheses.

Differentiating Luck and Ability. Fry (2000a) continued investigating the developmental tenets of Nicholls' (1984, 1989) theory within the physical domain by examining 5- to 13-year-old children's differentiation between luck and ability. Using methods and procedures similar to those of Nicholls and Miller (1985), Fry explained two games to each study participant. One game required skill to win, whereas the other required luck. In the "skill"-game scenario the child drew a card with a colored star and then attempted to throw the beanbag into the basket that corresponded in color to the star on the card. In the "luck"-game scenario the child guessed which color he would draw and tried to throw the beanbag into the appropriate basket; then the child drew the card to see if he guessed correctly. Participants were told of two children who both failed at each of these games. The child playing the skill game drew a green card, but threw the beanbag it into the yellow basket, whereas the child playing the luck game threw the beanbag into the pink basket, but then drew an orange card. Each participant was then interviewed to determine their level of understanding of luck and ability. After the interview, participants were given the opportunity to play either game or switch between games. During this time, the child's time engaged in each task was recorded.

Four levels of reasoning parallel to those found by Nicholls and Miller (1985) emerged (see Table 2). Interview results along with a strong correlation between age and level of reasoning (r = .73) revealed that children increasingly differentiate ability and luck from age 5 to 13 years. They move from believing that effort can improve performance on both luck and ability tasks to recognizing that the luck game was more difficult but that greater effort would result in a better outcome to realizing that performance on luck tasks cannot be improved with effort. Specifically, the majority of younger children (5 and 6 year olds) explained that both performers could have done better if they had tried harder and were more careful. Most of the 7 to 11 year olds explained that the luck game was harder than the skill game because the performer did not know which basket to aim to, but they were convinced that both players could have done better if they had tried harder. The majority of the older children (12 and 13 year olds) explained that trying harder on the luck game would not have resulted in a different outcome. For some of these older children, their reasoning was inconsistent (Level 3), but for others it was very consistent (Level 4).

Further validity of the developmental levels was evident when children were given the opportunity to play either game or a combination of each game. Older students preferred the skill game to the luck game, whereas younger children did not demonstrate a preference. This makes sense given younger children did not understand the difference between ability and luck. Overall, these results provide partial support for the developmental nature of Nicholls' theory by demonstrating that as children age, there is a progressively greater differentiation between luck and ability. As with children's understanding of ability and effort, there was substantial within-age variability. In fact, only 62% of 12- to 13-year-old children held a Level 4 luck-ability reasoning level.

Differentiating Task Difficulty and Ability. With the same sample as her 2000a study, Fry (2000b) also examined children's understanding of task difficulty. Using methods and procedures similar to those used by Nicholls and colleagues (Nicholls, 1978, 1980; Nicholls & Miller, 1983), Fry showed participants two photographs of brightly colored targets. In one picture, targets of different sizes were hanging on a fence. In the other picture, targets of the same size were placed 10 yards behind and to the side of each other. When viewing these pictures children were told that some children liked to throw balls to different-size targets or to kick balls to targets at different distances. This information required children to make judgments about the difficulty of the tasks based on their size or distance relative to each other (i.e., a smaller target is more difficult to hit than a larger one or a close target is easier to hit than one farther away). She also showed the children four boxes with smiley faces on them. The boxes were filled with equipment. The participants were told that the equipment in the boxes was needed to play a new game and that the different colored smiley faces represented how many children who tried a new game were unsuccessful or successful. The information presented about the boxes required children to make task-difficulty judgments based on the performance of others. All students experienced each condition and were asked questions about the skill required to hit the targets or to play the game, and they were asked which target/game they would prefer to play.

Three levels of reasoning emerged that paralleled those found by Nicholls (1978, 1980; Nicholls & Miller, 1983; see Table 2). Interview results in combination with the correlation between age and level of reasoning ($r = .73$) revealed a developmental progression in children's understanding of task difficulty from an egocentric to objective to normative conception of ability. Specifically, 95% of 5 year olds and 50% of 6 year olds held an egocentric conception in which task difficulty was determined relative to their personal expectations. A task, regardless of its objective (relative to other targets) or normative (few can do it) difficulty, was difficult if it was deemed difficult *for them*. On average, about one fourth (19-31%) of children between the ages of 7 and 11 years demonstrated objective reasoning regarding task difficulty by acknowledging that the smallest and farthest targets were the most difficult. About 97% of 12 to 13 year olds held a normative view of task difficulty in that their judgments were based on how many others had been successful or unsuccessful. It is noteworthy that 50% of 7 year olds, 75% of 8 year olds, and 80% of 9 to 13 year olds held a normative view of task difficulty. These results are similar to Nicholls (1978), who found that 62% of 7 year olds, 80% of 8 year olds, and 92% of children over 9 years held a normative understanding of task difficulty. These results provide evidence to suggest that developmental trends regarding children's understanding of ability and task difficulty are consistent across academic and physical domains.

Collectively, the research examining the development of children's concept of ability in the physical domain supports those found in the academic domain. Moreover, this research illustrates that children move from an undifferentiated view of ability when ability, effort, task difficulty, and luck are indistinguishable to a differentiated view when ability is viewed as separate from task difficulty, luck, and effort. Once ability is conceived in the differentiated sense, individuals may use self- and/or norm-referenced criteria when evaluating ability. Whether one is ego involved or task involved will depend on one's goal orientation and environmental cues. We feel confident in our interpretation that a mature conception of ability is not required for ego involvement, particularly in competitive environments, but that a mature conception of ability does increase the chance of being ego involved in competitive and non-competitive environments. There is little doubt that more sport-related research within Nicholls' (1984, 1989) framework is needed, particularly from a developmental standpoint.

Conceptions of Ability, Goal Involvement, and Motivated Behaviors

The quest for knowledge concerning developmental aspects of achievement motivation and the relationships among developmental, dispositional, and environmental factors relative to motivational processes is far from over. Despite the number of studies discussed in this section, only one attempted to examine the link between conceptions of ability and motivated outcomes (Butler, 1999). One reason for this may be the lack of clarity regarding the relationship between conceptions of ability and goal involvement. For example, Nicholls (1984) applies the terms task and ego involvement to states in which individuals seek to demonstrate ability in the undifferentiated and differentiated sense, respectively. From a developmental perspective, it seems unlikely that once children understand that ability is not equivalent to effort they would lose this understanding. That is, once it is understood that ability *is not* effort, it is doubtful that anyone would truly conceive of ability as effort. We argue instead that once individuals have a mature conception of ability, they can choose to define success relative to personal improvement and mastery (task goal orientation) or to the performance of others (ego goal orientation). Whether individuals are task or ego involved, then, will depend upon developmental (conceptions of ability), dispositional (task and ego goal orientations), *and* environmental (task- or ego-involving climate) factors, which in turn should affect motivational processes such as effort, persistence, and actual achievement (see also Butler, 1999; Harwood, Hardy, & Swain, 2000).

Once individuals have a mature conception of ability, they define success relative to personal improvement and mastery or to the performance of others.

We depict the relationships among the key components of Nicholls' (1989) theory in Figure 8. This model shows that individuals' developmental level relative to conceptions of ability is linked to dispositional factors of goal orientations and perceived competence. Although there are exceptions (Xiang & Lee, 1998), individuals with an undifferentiated conception of ability will be predominantly task oriented, whereas those with a differentiated conception of ability will be some combination of task and ego oriented.

The model also depicts goal involvement as a function of dispositional factors (e.g., goal orientations) and environmental conditions (Butler, 1989a, 1989b). Sport and exercise researchers have just recently begun to investigate the interactive effects of goal orientations and environmental factors, especially the nature of the achievement situation as task or ego involving, on goal involvement (e.g., Newton & Duda, 1999). In general, this research has provided some evidence that competitive situations elicit a state of ego involvement among individuals who are predominantly high in ego orientation and that mastery situations elicit task involvement among predominantly task-oriented individuals.

The relationships among developmental level, dispositional characteristics, environmental factors, and motivational processes are mediated by goal involvement. Despite this contention, much of the research grounded in Nicholls' (1989) theory has been conducted on the relationship between goal *orientations* and motivation processes (see Duda & Hall, 2001). In contrast, research examining the relationship between goal involvement and motivational processes is more limited (Cury et al., 1997, Harwood & Swain, 1998; Swain & Harwood, 1996; Williams, 1998). These two areas of research show that task orientation/involvement is associated with

FIGURE 6
Schematic of relationships among developmental level, dispositional factors, environmental conditions, goal involvement, and motivational processes (based on Nicholls, 1989)

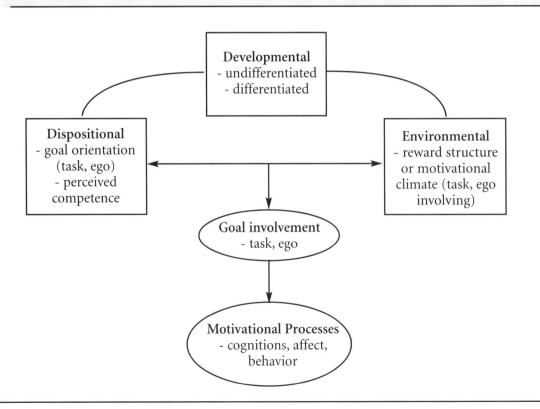

adaptive motivation indices such as effort, persistence, and positive affect. In contrast, ego orientation/involvement is related to lower effort and persistence and negative affect.

Central to Nicholls' (1989) theory is the interaction between dispositional and environmental factors on motivational processes from a developmental perspective. This is a neglected area of study. The information we have regarding these relationships is from research conducted in the academic domain. Butler's (1989a, 1989b, 1999) research provides evidence of the utility of investigating Nicholls' theory from a developmental perspective. Her research suggests that (a) children who do not have a mature conception of ability can be ego involved in competitive situations; (b) among children who hold a mature conception of ability, competitive environments can negatively affect their intrinsic interest, performance expectancies, and task performance; and (c) children at the greatest risk for maladaptive motivation are those who have a mature conception of ability and low perceived competence.

One potentially undesirable motivational outcome is children's discontinuation from sport programs. Perhaps children's conception of ability in combination with the interpersonal competitive nature of sport programs is one reason for the drop in participation during early adolescence (see also Butler, 1999; Digelidis & Papaioannou, 1999). That is, as sport participants begin to understand the concept of ability as capacity they become more inclined to evaluate their ability relative to others, and some begin to realize that they do not measure up. A better understanding of conceptions of ability, and how they interact with environmental conditions, in the sport context may help researchers and practitioners design interventions to keep children involved in sport and physical activity at various levels of participation.

FROM THEORY TO PRACTICE: ENHANCING PHYSICAL ACTIVITY MOTIVATION AMONG YOUTH

Several common threads emerge to offer practical applications stemming from the four theories of motivation we identified as developmentally appropriate for children and adolescents. First, *self-perceptions* including perceived competence, expectations of success, and global self-worth are key determinants of motivated behavior. Intervention strategies should focus upon maintaining or enhancing youths' physical competence beliefs to ensure an intrinsic motivational orientation to learn and perform skills. Second, *positive affective experiences* including enjoyment, interest value, and fun associated with physical activity maintain or enhance positive achievement behaviors including choice, effort, persistence, and performance. Thus, contexts and teaching strategies that maximize positive emotional feelings in physical activity will enhance motivation. Third, a *task goal orientation and involvement*, or intrinsic motivational orientation, that focuses upon defining competence and success in self-referenced terms such as improvement, effort, and learning will ensure optimal challenge-seeking, curiosity, and preference for independent mastery. Teaching environments and coach behaviors that emphasize self-referenced criteria for defining success, rather than the usual emphasis on competitive outcomes, will increase the probability that children adopt a task-involved perspective to participation. Finally, *social support* and regard by parents, teachers, coaches, and peers (teammates, close friends) is essential to ensuring heightened interest in and commitment toward continued participation. We recommend five strategies for enhancing perceptions of competence, enjoyment, task orientation, and social support that, in turn, should foster an intrinsic motivational orientation and positive behaviors such as choice, effort, and persistence (see also Weiss, 1991, 1995, 2000, for discussion of positive motivation strategies with youth).

Provide Optimal Challenges

An optimally challenging activity or skill is one that matches task difficulty with the child's present skill capabilities. Thus, children's successful mastery of skills is within reach, but they need to exert necessary effort and persistence to attain the goal. We think of optimal challenges as "matching the activity to the child, and not the child to the activity." Skills that are too easy are boring and do not allow for attaining hard but realistic goals. Skills that are too difficult invoke anxiety and frustration because they exceed the child's current developmental level. Unsuccessful performance is the probable result that may induce even more anxiety and stress when the child is asked to try the task again. Because children use mastery of skills, effort, and improvement as means of determining how physically competent they are, optimal challenges offer children a prime opportunity for developing and demonstrating competence that is at the cutting edge of their capabilities. Teachers, coaches, and parents should ensure developmental progressions in skills and physical activities, collaborate with children in setting realistic goals, and modify activities to optimize task difficulty in relation to the child's skill level. Success at optimal challenges will be within reach, and such outcomes will enhance perceptions of competence and subsequent intrinsic motivation.

Make Sure that Sport and Physical Activity Experiences Are Fun

Intrinsic task value and positive affective responses such as enjoyment consistently emerge as strong predictors of motivated behavior. When youth enjoy doing certain activities, they are motivated to do them again in the future. What makes activities fun? Children and adolescents indicate that opportunities for high levels of action, personal involvement in the action, close games, and affirming friendships are key to activity enjoyment (Coakley, 1993). Change-of-pace activities (e.g., varying activity type and doing so relatively often) and allowing children some choices in activity selection and game strategies are also key to maximizing intrinsically pleasing experiences (Weiss, 1991). Unfortunately, in many competitive environments we see adults controlling the action and choices more and more frequently. Although such practices may maximize the probability of winning, it does not provide children and youths what they desire in terms of personal autonomy and competence. Providing opportunities for youth to make decisions and control their own experiences translates to greater fun and enjoyment.

> Skills that exceed a child's developmental level invoke anxiety and frustration.

Create a Mastery Motivational Climate

Coaches may influence children's competence beliefs, goal involvement, affective responses, and motivated behaviors by shaping the learning environment or motivational climate in which activities take place (Ames, 1992a, 1992b). Motivational climate refers to contextual and teacher-behavior influences that convey how success is defined, how children are evaluated, what is recognized and valued, and how mistakes are viewed. A *mastery motivational climate* is one that promotes learning, effort, and self-improvement, and mistakes are viewed as part of the learning process. Success is self-referenced, and personal improvements are recognized, praised, and emphasized. In contrast, a *performance climate* emphasizes defining success in norm-referenced terms and invokes evaluation practices and criteria for recognition that focus upon favorable comparison to peers. Children's perceptions of the motivational climate make a strong impact on their perceptions of ability, task or ego orientation, attraction toward physical activity, and motivation.

The acronym TARGET has been used to identify effective strategies for structuring a mastery motivational climate (see Ames, 1992a, 1992b; Eccles et al., 1998; Epstein, 1988). TARGET stands for dimensions of Task, Authority, Recognition, Grouping, Evaluation, and Time. The

Task dimension refers to the use of task variety and optimal challenges, whereas Authority refers to the locus of decision making (i.e., teacher or student centered?). Some opportunities for choice and shared decision making are key to developing self-regulation and enhancing motivation toward the activity. Recognition focused upon effort and self-improvement, rather than peer comparison and competitive outcomes, fosters positive competence beliefs, task orientation, enjoyment, and increased effort and persistence. As far as the Grouping dimension, heterogeneous partner and small-group problem-solving tasks, rather than ability grouping, emphasizes cooperative learning and success and de-emphasizes interpersonal competition and rivalry. Evaluation criteria that emphasizes self-referenced standards such as learning, effort, and individual progress reinforces an intrinsic motivational orientation, and adequate Time for learning and mastering skills increases the probability of being successful at optimal challenges and ensuing feelings of competence, pleasure, and desire to continue mastery attempts in the future. In sum, these six elements define the ingredients for maximizing a mastery motivational climate.

Maximize Social Support

Positive social regard by parents, coaches, and peers strongly influences youths' perceptions of competence, goal orientations, affect, and motivational orientation and behaviors. We will focus our comments on coaching behaviors because parents (Fredricks & Eccles, 2003) and peers (Weiss & Stuntz, 2003) are detailed in other chapters. Horn (1987; Horn, Lox, & Labrador, 1998) recommends three major guiding principles for developing positive self-perceptions, enjoyment, and motivation in young participants through coaching feedback and reinforcement: (a) contingency and quality of praise and criticism, (b) frequency and contingency of skill-relevant feedback, and (c) appropriate attributional feedback for performance outcomes. Contingent praise provides children with information about their competence, the performance standard they are expected to reach, and the criteria (i.e., winning or skill mastery) by which their competence will be evaluated. Appropriate use of praise means providing reinforcement relative to the difficulty of the skill attained. If children succeed at a simple task or demonstrate mediocre performance, praise for these behaviors may convey negative information and expectations to this athlete. According to Horn (1987), it is the *quality*, not quantity, of reinforcement that is key to desirable psychological and motivational processes.

The second principle of providing appropriate skill-relevant feedback is crucial for influencing children's perceptions of competence and motivational orientation. In competitive sport, opportunities for committing skill errors are numerous and have the potential for conveying low ability information to youth. However, when skill errors are viewed as temporary setbacks or a natural part of the learning process, competence perceptions and motivation are not negatively affected. When coaches and parents respond to children's skill errors with encouragement and corrective instruction, self-perceptions of ability and control are enhanced, and effort and persistence increase. By contrast, punitive behaviors are likely to arouse fear of failure and worries about making mistakes that, unfortunately, may result in a self-fulfilling prophecy because the child may be more focused inwards than to the environment in which play is taking place.

Punitive behaviors are likely to arouse fear of failure and may result in a self-fulfilling prophecy if the child is more focused inwards than on the play environment.

Finally, attributional feedback plays a role in level of self-perceptions and motivation. When effort attributions are made for performance errors, they are likely to enhance motivated behavior because effort is under the control of the young athlete. That is, she may try harder, use a different strategy, or increase attention (all indices of increased effort) on subsequent mastery attempts. It is important to note that children must perceive they have the requisite skills to eventually achieve success; otherwise, greater effort will not be perceived as effective. To do this, coaches can make effort attributions for unsuccessful performance combined with instruction on how to modify the skill technique or strategy on the next attempt. Age differences in the ability to distinguish ability and effort as causes of performance outcomes must also be considered. Young children who hold an undifferentiated view of the concept of ability should definitely benefit from effort attributions made for skill errors. Older children and adolescents who view ability as capacity may not perceive an effort attribution as credible if they believe that increased effort will not make an impact on future performance. However, effort attributions are the most common causes given for unsuccessful performance in sport (e.g., poor choice of skill or strategy, inadequate preparation for game, lackadaisical play). The key is the participant's perception that she or he can control future mastery attempts and that using alternative amounts of effort or decision-making strategies can alter performance.

Help Children Help Themselves

Mastering skills, achieving goals, and improving on a progressive basis are salient means by which children judge their competence and remain motivated in a specific domain. Thus, teaching children self-regulated learning strategies will allow them to adopt self-reliant standards for monitoring and evaluating their performance. Self-regulated learning consists of three processes: self-observation, self-judgment, and self-reaction (see Petlichkoff, 2003). Self-observation entails monitoring one's behaviors regularly through some means of self-recording (e.g., training logs or diaries). Self-observation serves an informational function by showing progression toward one's goals and a motivational function by encouraging behavior change through increased awareness of skills and strategies. Self-judgment is a process whereby learners compare present performance level with desired goals, and is influenced by the types of goals adopted (e.g., task v. ego), task difficulty, the importance of goal attainment, and attributions for performance outcomes. Finally, self-reaction refers to positive or negative evaluations concerning progress toward goal attainment. Positive evaluations raise self-perceptions and motivation, although negative evaluations need not deter motivation if the individual believes that he or she is capable of making improvements in the future. Self-reaction can include evaluations based on self-reinforcement or external sources such as rewards and feedback. Children who are effective in using self-regulation strategies to guide behavior are characterized by favorable self-perceptions, high perceived performance control, high levels of motivation, and attainment of goals (see Petlichkoff, 2003, for detailed discussion of self-regulation skills).

FUTURE RESEARCH DIRECTIONS

Early research findings on *why* children participate in sport were *because* they wanted to develop physical competence, attain social acceptance, and experience positive affect. These consistent findings led to studies using motivational frameworks that considered competence, social, and affective factors. We reviewed four theories that considered not only these major reasons why children participate in sport, but also ones that explicitly address developmental change and individual differences within developmental level. Based on these theories and related research, we offer five recommendations for future inquiry that would bolster the developmental knowledge base in the physical domain.

    First, more developmental research on motivation needs to be conducted in sport and exercise psychology! Despite early conceptual papers that encouraged such a perspective (e.g.,

Weiss & Bredemeier, 1983), relatively few true developmental studies have been conducted in the sport psychology literature. That is, few studies have specifically chosen age groups based on cognitive or physical criteria, compared specific age groups believed to differ on cognitive or other variables, or adopted longitudinal designs to investigate change in psychological constructs over time as a function of maturity or environmental changes (see Horn, 2003b; Schutz & Park, 2003; Weiss & Raedeke, 2003). The sparse developmental knowledge in sport psychology contrasts that in mainstream developmental psychology conducted in academic contexts. In fact, many of the developmentally oriented findings pertaining to sport motivation constructs have been conducted by nonsport researchers (see Eccles et al., 1998; Fredricks & Eccles, 2003; Harter, 1999). The most appropriate theories (Horn, in p2003b), research templates (Weiss & Raedeke, 2003), and methodologies (Schutz & Park, 2003) are all in place for researchers to pursue important developmental questions that we highlighted in this chapter. We hope that some readers will tackle the challenge and enhance our knowledge of developmental differences in motivation among youth.

A common research finding that cuts across motivation theories is age-related differences in competence beliefs, social influence, and motivational orientation. These included variations in level, accuracy, and sources of perceived competence; conceptions of ability and goal orientation/involvement; sources and types of influence by significant others; and intrinsic v. extrinsic perspectives of learning. Thus, a second future research direction is uncovering the individual difference and social contextual factors that explain these age variations as they occur in the physical domain. Are they due to cognitive or physical maturity changes, environmental changes in how success is defined and what criteria are used to recognize and evaluate performance, or some combination of the two? This direction is intricately related to the previous one, which suggests studies must be designed specifically to tease out contributors to age differences in self-perceptions, affective reactions, and motivated behavior. The systematic work by Harter, Eccles, Nicholls, and their colleagues paves the way for translating similar questions and research designs to the physical domain.

A third area in dire need of attention is intervention studies that would allow us to better understand how to maintain or enhance a positive motivational orientation among youth in sport and physical activity. The most logical targets of intervention are significant others and the motivational climate. Effectiveness of parent and peer intervention studies is virtually nonexistent (see Fredricks & Eccles, 2003; Weiss & Stuntz, 2003), and only the R. E. Smith and Smoll (1996) studies constitute interventions designed to induce coach behavior change. Given the accumulated knowledge of the powerful role of socializing agents on children's motivational processes (e.g., perceived competence, goal orientations, affect, effort, and persistence) at varying ages and competitive levels, intervention studies and associated evaluation research are imperative to advance the field. Similarly, motivational climate has become a hot topic in youth sport psychology over the last decade (see Weiss & Ferrer-Caja, 2002). We know that a mastery climate is associated with positive, and a performance climate with negative, motivational processes, yet only a handful of studies have been designed to alter the situation or climate and observe concomitant change in beliefs, affect, and behavior among participants (e.g., Solmon, 1996; Swain, 1996; Theeboom, De Knop, & Weiss, 1995). We urge readers to consider existing theory and research and to translate these into sound field experimental studies that demonstrate the effectiveness of social and contextual factors on competence beliefs, goal orientations, affect, and achievement motivation among youth of varying ages in the physical domain.

The effect of transitions emerged time and again as a major contributor to age-related changes in self-perceptions, social relationships, intrinsic interest, and achievement motivation in the academic domain. A fourth area of future research, then, is investigating the effect of transitions within competitive sport on youths' motivational processes. Transitions in sport do not occur simultaneously with academic transitions such as elementary to middle school or middle to high school (see also Wylleman & Lavallee, 2003). This may partially explain the relative stability of sport-related competence beliefs and intrinsic value across the childhood and adolescent years compared to declines in these constructs for many academic subjects (Fredricks & Eccles, 2002; Wigfield et al., 1997). However, without any hard data of differences between lower and higher competitive levels in behaviors by coaches and parents and the structure of the climate, we can only speculate as to what occurs as youth transition and why this happens. Being able to follow children longitudinally from the time they initiate involvement in a sport program through transitions to higher levels to the time they cease participation would provide invaluable information on the processes affecting choices, intensity of behavior, and actual achievement levels.

Finally, we believe that theoretical predictions need to be tested more fully in the physical domain including multivariate relationships among constructs and how these relationships vary over time. For example, many studies have adopted competence motivation theory as a guiding framework and have examined relationships among social influences, perceptions of competence, affect, and motivational orientation. What is missing is a developmental approach that considers how the patterns and magnitudes of these relationships vary with age, as well as the relationship of these psychological constructs with actual motivated *behavior* such as choice, effort, persistence, and performance. Another example is how conceptions of ability (undifferentiated, differentiated) relate to goal orientations/involvement and subsequent achievement motivation in sport. Can undifferentiated youth be ego involved, and if so, what factors contribute to this perspective despite their inability to view ability as capacity? Are children who hold a differentiated view vulnerable to higher levels of ego orientation/involvement, and is this accentuated in sport where norm-referenced standards of defining success are paramount? How do conceptions of ability, goal orientation, and perceived competence interact to predict variations in motivation, especially actual *behavior*? A final example comes from Eccles' model, whereby socializers' beliefs and behaviors need to be studied in relation to children's expectancies for success and subjective task value and subsequent achievement *behaviors*. By examining developmental motivation theories more comprehensively, we will be more likely to achieve a greater understanding of motivational processes among youth in sport and physical activity.

CONCLUDING REMARKS

We began this chapter by suggesting one way of explaining motivated behavior is by answering *why* questions with *because* answers. The early descriptive work pointed to physical competence, social affiliation, and enjoyable experiences as reasons why children and youth maintain sport involvement. Our chosen theories frame these reasons within comprehensive models that specify the relationships among social, psychological, and behavioral motivational constructs, as well as address age-related variations in these relationships as a function of cognitive maturity and social contextual factors. Thus, we are at an optimal time to move the youth-motivation knowledge base forward by adopting one or more of these theories, customizing constructs for the physical domain, and conducting research that goes beyond correlational designs and snapshots of motivation at a single point in time. Adopting developmental research designs, methodologies, and analyses; testing theoretical models more comprehensively; conducting intervention studies targeting significant adults and peers and the motivational climate; and observing changes in participants' beliefs and behaviors as a result of transitions in sport are critical steps to advancing our knowledge of *developmental sport and exercise psychology*.

REFERENCES

Adler, P.A., Kless, S.J., & Adler, P. (1992). Socialization to gender roles: Popularity among elementary school boys and girls. *Sociology of Education, 65*, 169-187.

Alderman, R.B. (1978). Strategies for motivating young athletes. In W.F. Straub (Ed.), *Sport psychology: An analysis of athlete behavior* (pp. 49-61). Ithaca, NY: Mouvement Publications.

Alderman, R.B., & Wood, N.L. (1976). An analysis of incentive motivation in young Canadian athletes. *Canadian Journal of Applied Sport Sciences, 1*, 169-175.

Allen, J.B., & Howe, B. (1998). Player ability, coach feedback, and female adolescent athletes' perceived competence and satisfaction. *Journal of Sport & Exercise Psychology, 20*, 280-299.

Ames, C. (1984). Competitive, cooperative and individualistic goal structures: A cognitive motivational analysis. In R. Ames & C. Ames (Eds.), *Research on motivation in education: Student motivation* (pp. 177-207). New York: Academic Press.

Ames, C. (1992a). Achievement goals, motivational climate, and motivational processes. In G.C. Roberts (Ed.), *Motivation in sport and exercise* (pp. 161-176). Champaign, IL: Human Kinetics.

Ames, C. (1992b). Classrooms: Goals, structures, and student motivation. *Journal of Educational Psychology, 84*, 261-271.

Ames, C., & Ames, R. (1981). Competitive versus cooperative reward structures: The salience of past performance information for causal attributions and affect. *Journal of Educational Psychology, 73*, 411-418.

Ames, C., & Archer, J. (1988). Achievement goals in the classroom: Students' learning strategies and motivation processes. *Journal of Educational Psychology, 80*, 260-267.

Amorose, A.J. (2001). Intraindividual variability of self-evaluations in the physical domain: Prevalence, consequences, and antecedents. *Journal of Sport & Exercise Psychology, 23*, 222-244.

Amorose, A.J., & Horn, T.S. (2000). Intrinsic motivation: Relationships with collegiate athletes' gender, scholarship status, and perceptions of their coaches' behavior. *Journal of Sport & Exercise Psychology, 22*, 63-84.

Amorose, A.J., & Horn, T.S. (2001). Pre- to post-season changes in the intrinsic motivation of first year college athletes: Relationships with coaching behavior and scholarship status. *Journal of Applied Sport Psychology, 13*, 355-373.

Amorose, A.J., & Weiss, M.R. (1998). Coaching feedback as a source of information about perceptions of ability: A developmental examination. *Journal of Sport & Exercise Psychology, 20*, 395-420.

Babkes, M.L., & Weiss, M.R. (1999). Parental influence on cognitive and affective responses in children's competitive soccer participation. *Pediatric Exercise Science, 11*, 44-62.

Birch, D., & Veroff, J. (1966). *Motivation: A study of action.* Belmont, CA: Brooks/Cole.

Black, S.J., & Weiss, M.R. (1992). The relationship among perceived coaching behaviors, perceptions of ability, and motivation in competitive age-group swimmers. *Journal of Sport & Exercise Psychology, 14*, 309-325.

Brodkin, P., & Weiss, M. R. (1990). Developmental differences in motivation for participating in competitive swimming. *Journal of Sport & Exercise Psychology, 12*, 248-263.

Brustad, R.J. (1988). Affective outcomes in competitive youth sport: The influence of intrapersonal and socialization factors. *Journal of Sport & Exercise Psychology, 10*, 307-321.

Brustad, R.J. (1992). Integrating socialization influences into the study of children's motivation in sport. *Journal of Sport & Exercise Psychology, 14*, 59-77.

Butler, R. (1989a). Interest in the task and interest in peers' work in competitive and noncompetitive conditions: A developmental study. *Child Development, 60*, 562-570.

Butler, R. (1989b). Mastery versus ability appraisal: A developmental study of children's observations of peers' work. *Child Development, 60*, 1350-1361.

Butler, R. (1999). Information seeking and achievement motivation in middle childhood and adolescence: The role of conceptions of ability. *Developmental Psychology, 35*, 146-163.

Chase, M.A., & Dummer, G.M. (1992). The role of sports as a social status determinant for children. *Research Quarterly for Exercise and Sport, 63*, 418-424.

Coakley, J.J. (1993). Social dimensions of intensive training and participation in youth sports. In B.R. Cahill & A.J. Pearl (Eds.), *Intensive participation in children's sports* (pp. 77-94). Champaign, IL: Human Kinetics.

Coakley, J.J., & White, A. (1992). Making decisions: Gender and sport participation among British adolescents. *Sociology of Sport Journal, 9*, 20-35.

Crocker, P.R.E., Hoar, S.D., McDonough, M.H., Kowalski, K.C., & Niefer, C.B. (2003). Emotional experience in youth sport. In M.R. Weiss (Ed.), *Developmental sport and exercise psychology: A lifespan perspective* (pp. 197-221). Morgantown, WV: Fitness Information Technology.

Cury, F., Biddle, S., Sarrazin, P., & Famose, J.P. (1997). Achievement goals and perceived ability predicts investment in learning a sport task. *British Journal of Educational Psychology, 67*, 293-309.

De Knop, P., Engstrom, L.M., Skirstad, B., & Weiss, M.R. (1996). *Worldwide trends in youth sport*. Champaign, IL: Human Kinetics.

Deci, E.L., & Ryan, R.M. (1985). *Intrinsic motivation and self-determination in human behavior*. New York: Plenum.

Digelidis, N., & Papaioannou, A. (1999). Age-group differences in intrinsic motivation, goal orientations and perceptions of athletic competence, physical appearance and motivational climate in Greek physical education. *Scandinavian Journal of Medicine and Science in Sport, 9*, 375-382.

Duda, J.L. (1987). Toward a developmental theory of children's motivation in sport. *Journal of Sport Psychology, 9*, 130-145.

Duda, J.L., & Hall, H.K. (2001). Achievement goal theory in sport. In R.N. Singer, H.A. Hausenblas, & C.M. Janelle (Eds.), *Handbook of sport psychology* (2nd ed., pp. 417-443). New York: Wiley.

Duncan, S.C. (1993). The role of cognitive appraisal and friendship provisions in adolescents' affect and motivation toward activity in physical education. *Research Quarterly for Exercise and Sport, 64*, 314-323.

Dweck, C.S. (1999). *Self-theories: Their role in motivation, personality, and development*. Philadelphia: Psychology Press.

Ebbeck, V., & Stuart, M.E. (1993). Who determines what's important? Perceptions of competence and importance as predictors of self-esteem in youth football players. *Pediatric Exercise Science, 5*, 253-262.

Ebbeck, V., & Stuart, M.E. (1996). Predictors of self-esteem with youth basketball players. *Pediatric Exercise Science, 8*, 368-378.

Ebbeck, V., & Weiss, M.R. (1998). Determinants of children's self-esteem: An examination of perceived competence and affect in sport. *Pediatric Exercise Science, 10*, 285-298.

Eccles, J.S., Adler, T.E., Futterman, R., Goff, S.B., Kaczala, C.M., Meece, J.L., & Midgley, C. (1983). Expectancies, values, and academic behaviors. In J.T. Spence (Ed.), *Achievement and achievement motivation* (pp. 75-146). San Francisco: W.H. Freeman.

Eccles, J.S., & Barber, B.L. (1999). Student council, volunteering, basketball, or marching band: What kind of extracurricular involvement matters? *Journal of Adolescent Research, 14,* 10-43.

Eccles, J.S., & Harold, R.D. (1991). Gender differences in sport involvement: Applying the Eccles' expectancy-value model. *Journal of Applied Sport Psychology, 3*, 7-35.

Eccles, J.S., & Midgley, C. (1990). Changes in academic motivation and self-perception during early adolescence. In R. Montemayor, G.R. Adams, & T.P. Gullotta (Eds.), *From childhood to adolescence: A transitional period?* (pp. 134-155). Newbury Park: CA: Sage.

Eccles, J., & Wigfield, A. (1985). Teacher expectations and student motivation. In J.B. Dusek (Ed.), *Teacher expectations* (pp. 185-226). Hillsdale, NJ: Erlbaum.

Eccles, J.S., & Wigfield, A. (1995). In the mind of the actor: The structure of adolescents' achievement task values and expectancy-related beliefs. *Personality and Social Psychology Bulletin, 21*, 215-225.

Eccles, J.S., Wigfield, A., Harold, R., & Blumenfeld, P. (1993). Age and gender differences in children's self- and task perceptions during elementary school. *Child Development, 64*, 830-847.

Eccles, J.S., Wigfield, A.W., & Schiefele, U. (1998). Motivation to succeed. In W. Damon (Series Ed.) & N. Eisenberg (Vol. Ed.), *Handbook of child psychology: Social, emotional, and personality development* (5th ed., Vol. 3, pp. 1017-1095). New York: Wiley.

Epstein, J.L. (1988). Effective schools or effective students? Dealing with diversity. In R.H. Haskins & D. MacRae (Eds.), *Policies for America's public schools: Teachers, equity, and indicators* (pp. 89-126). Norwood, NJ: Ablex.

Felson, R.B. (1989). Parents and the reflected appraisal process: A longitudinal analysis. *Journal of Personality and Social Psychology, 56*, 965-971.

Feltz, D.L., & Brown, E.W. (1984). Perceived competence in soccer skills among youth soccer players. *Journal of Sport Psychology, 6*, 385-394.

Ferrer-Caja, E., & Weiss, M.R. (2000). Predictors of intrinsic motivation among adolescent students in physical education. *Research Quarterly for Exercise and Sport, 71*, 267-279.

Ferrer-Caja, E., & Weiss, M.R. (2002). Cross-validation of a model of intrinsic motivation with students enrolled in high school elective courses. *Journal of Experimental Education, 71*, 41-65.

Fredricks, J.A., & Eccles, J.S. (2002). Children's competence and value beliefs from childhood through adolescence: Growth trajectories in two male-sex-typed domains. *Developmental Psychology, 38*, 519-533.

Fredricks, J.A., & Eccles, J.S. (2003). Parental influences on youth involvement in sports. In M.R. Weiss (Ed.), *Developmental sport and exercise psychology: A lifespan perspective.* (pp. 145-164) Morgantown, WV: Fitness Information Technology.

Fry, M.D. (2000a). A developmental analysis of children's and adolescents' understanding of luck and ability in the physical domain. *Journal of Sport & Exercise Psychology, 22*, 145-166.

Fry, M.D. (2000b). A developmental examination of children's understanding of task difficulty in the physical domain. *Journal of Applied Social Psychology, 12*, 180-202.

Fry, M.D. (2001). The development of motivation in children. In G. C. Roberts (Ed.), *Advances in motivation in sport and exercise* (2nd ed., pp. 51-78). Champaign, IL: Human Kinetics.

Fry, M.D., & Duda, J.L. (1997). A developmental examination of children's understanding of effort and ability in the physical and academic domains. *Research Quarterly for Exercise and Sport, 68*, 331-344.

Fuligni, A.J., Eccles, J.S., Barber, B.L., & Clements, P. (2001). Early adolescent peer orientation and adjustment during high school. *Developmental Psychology, 17*, 28-36.

Gill, D.L. (2000). *Psychological dynamics of sport and exercise*. Champaign, IL: Human Kinetics.

Gould, D. (1982). Sport psychology in the 1980's: Status, direction and challenge in youth sports research. *Journal of Sport Psychology, 4*, 203-218.

Gould, D. (1987). Understanding attrition in youth sport. In D. Gould & M.R. Weiss (Eds.), *Advances in pediatric sport sciences: Vol. 2. Behavioral issues* (pp. 61-85). Champaign, IL: Human Kinetics.

Gould, D., Feltz, D., Horn, T., & Weiss, M. (1982). Reasons for attrition in competitive youth swimming. *Journal of Sport Behavior, 5*, 155-165.

Gould, D., Feltz, D., & Weiss, M. (1985). Motives for participating in competitive youth swimming. *International Journal of Sport Psychology, 6*, 126-140.

Halliburton, A.L., & Weiss, M.R. (2002). Sources of competence information and perceived motivational climate among adolescent female gymnasts varying in skill level. *Journal of Sport & Exercise Psychology, 24*. 396-419.

Harter, S. (1978). Effectance motivation reconsidered. *Human Development, 21*, 34-64.

Harter, S. (1981a). A model of intrinsic mastery motivation in children: Individual differences and developmental change. In W.A. Collins (Ed.), *Minnesota Symposium on Child Psychology* (Vol. 14, pp. 215-255). Hillsdale, NJ: Erlbaum.

Harter, S. (1981b). A new self-report scale of intrinsic versus extrinsic orientation in the classroom: Motivational and informational components. *Developmental Psychology, 17*, 300-312.

Harter, S. (1982). The perceived competence scale for children. *Child Development, 53*, 87-97.

Harter, S. (1985). *Manual for the self-perception profile for children*. Denver: University of Denver.

Harter, S. (1987). The determinants and mediational role of global self-worth in children. In N. Eisenberg (Ed.), *Contemporary topics in developmental psychology* (pp. 219-242). New York: Wiley.

Harter, S. (1988). *Manual for the self-perception profile for adolescents*. Denver: University of Denver.

Harter, S. (1990). Causes, correlates, and the functional role of global self-worth: A life-span perspective. In R.J. Sternberg & J. Kolligian, Jr. (Eds.), *Competence considered* (pp. 67-97). New Haven, CT: Yale University Press.

Harter, S. (1992). The relationship between perceived competence, affect, and motivational orientation within the classroom: Processes and patterns of change. In A.K. Boggiano & T.S. Pittman (Eds.), *Achievement and motivation: A social developmental perspective*. New York: Cambridge University Press.

Harter, S. (1998). The development of self-representations. In W. Damon (Series Ed.) & N. Eisenberg (Vol. Ed.), *Handbook of child psychology: Social, emotional, and personality development* (5th ed., Vol. 3, pp. 553-618). New York: Wiley.

Harter, S. (1999). *The construction of the self: A developmental perspective*. New York: Guilford.

Harter, S., & Connell, J.P. (1984). A comparison of alternative models of the relationships between academic achievement and children's perceptions of competence, control, and motivational orientation. In J.G. Nicholls (Ed.), *The development of achievement-related cognitions and behaviors* (pp. 219-250). Greenwich, CT: JAI Press.

Harter, S., & Pike, R. (1984). The pictorial scale of perceived competence and social acceptance for young children. *Child Development, 55*, 1962-1982.

Harter, S., Whitesell, N., & Kowalski, P. (1992). Individual differences in the effects of educational transitions on young adolescents' perceptions of competence and motivational orientation. *American Educational Research Journal, 29,* 777-808.

Harwood, C.G., Hardy, L., & Swain, A. (2000). Achievement goals in sport: A critique of conceptual and measurement issues. *Journal of Sport and Exercise Psychology, 22*, 235-255.

Harwood, C.G., & Swain, A. B. J. (1998). An interactionist examination of the antecedents of pre-competitive achievement goals within national junior tennis players. *Journal of Sports Sciences, 16*, 357-371.

Horn, T.S. (1984). Expectancy effects in the interscholastic athletic setting: Methodological considerations. *Journal of Sport Psychology, 6,* 60-76.

Horn, T.S. (1985). Coaches' feedback and changes in children's perceptions of their physical competence. *Journal of Educational Psychology, 77*, 174-186.

Horn, T. S. (1987). The influence of teacher-coach behavior on the psychological development of children. In D. Gould & M. R. Weiss (Eds.), *Advances in pediatric sport sciences,* Vol. 2: *Behavioral issues* (pp. 121-142). Champaign, IL: Human Kinetics.

Horn, T.S. (2003a). Developmental perspectives on self-perceptions in children and adolescents. In M.R. Weiss (Ed.), *Developmental sport and exercise psychology: A lifespan perspective*. (pp. 101-143) Morgantown, WV: Fitness Information Technology.

Horn, T.S. (2003b). Lifespan development in sport and exercise psychology: Theoretical Perspectives. In M.R. Weiss (Ed.), *Developmental sport and exercise psychology: A lifespan perspective*. (pp. 27-71) Morgantown, WV: Fitness Information Technology.

Horn, T.S., Glenn, S.D., & Wentzell, A.B. (1993). Sources of information underlying personal ability judgments in high school athletes. *Pediatric Exercise Science, 5,* 263-274.

Horn, T.S., & Harris, A. (1996). Perceived competence in young athletes: Research findings and recommendations for coaches and parents. In F.L. Smoll & R.E. Smith (Eds.), *Children and youth in sport: A biopsychosocial perspective* (pp. 309-329). Madison, WI: Brown & Benchmark.

Horn, T.S., & Hasbrook, C.A. (1987). Psychological characteristics and the criteria children use for self-evaluation. *Journal of Sport Psychology, 9,* 208-221.

Horn, T.S., Lox, C.L., & Labrador, F. (1998). The self-fulfilling prophecy theory: When coaches' expectations become reality. In J.M. Williams (Ed.), *Applied sport psychology: Personal growth to peak performance* (3rd ed., pp. 74-91). Palo Alto, CA: Mayfield.

Horn, T.S., & Weiss, M.R. (1991). A developmental analysis of children's self-ability judgments. *Pediatric Exercise Science, 3,* 312-328.

Jacobs, J.E., & Eccles, J.S. (1992). The impact of mothers' gender-role stereotypic beliefs on mothers' and children's ability perceptions. *Journal of Personality and Social Psychology, 63,* 932-944.

Klint, K.A., & Weiss, M.R. (1987). Perceived competence and motives for participating in youth sports: A test of Harter's competence motivation theory. *Journal of Sport Psychology, 9,* 55-65.

Lee, A.M., Carter, J. A., & Xiang, P. (1995). Children's conceptions of ability in physical education. *Journal of Teaching in Physical Education, 14,* 384-393.

Madon, S., Jussim, L., & Eccles, J. (1997). In search of the powerful self-fulfilling prophecy. *Journal of Personality and Social Psychology, 72,* 791-809.

Maehr, M.L., & Nicholls, J.G. (1980). Culture and achievement motivation: A second look. In N. Warren (Ed.), *Studies in cross-cultural psychology* (Vol. 3, pp. 221-267). New York: Academic Press.

McCullagh. P., Matzkanin, K.T., Shaw, S.D., & Maldonado, M. (1993). Motivation for participation in physical activity: A comparison of parent child perceived competencies and participation motives. *Pediatric Exercise Science, 5,* 224-233.

McKiddie, B., & Maynard, I.W. (1997). Perceived competence of school children in physical education. *Journal of Teaching in Physical Education, 16,* 324-339.

Newton, M., & Duda, J.L. (1999). The interaction of motivational climate, dispositional goal orientations, and perceived ability in predicting indices of motivation. *International Journal of Sport Psychology, 30,* 63-82.

Nicholls, J.G. (1978). The development of the concepts of effort and ability, perception of own attainment, and the understanding that difficult tasks require more ability. *Child Development, 49,* 800-814.

Nicholls, J.G. (1980). The development of the concept of difficulty. *Merrill-Palmer Quarterly, 26,* 271-281.

Nicholls, J.G. (1984). Achievement motivation: Conceptions of ability, subjective experience, task choice, and performance. *Psychological Review, 91,* 328-346.

Nicholls, J.G. (1989). *The competitive ethos and democratic education.* Cambridge, MA: Harvard University Press.

Nicholls, J.G. (1990). What is ability and why are we mindful of it? A developmental perspective. In R.J. Sternberg & J. Kolligian (Eds.), *Competence considered* (pp. 11-40). New Haven, CT: Yale University Press.

Nicholls, J.G. (1992). The general and the specific in the development and expression of achievement motivation. In G.C. Roberts (Ed.), *Motivation in sport and exercise* (pp. 31-56). Champaign, IL: Human Kinetics.

Nicholls, J.G., Jagacinski, C.M., & Miller, A.T. (1986). Conceptions of ability in children and adults. In R. Schwarzer (Ed.), *Self-related cognitions in anxiety and motivation* (pp. 265-284). Hillsdale, NJ: Erlbaum.

Nicholls, J.G., & Miller, A.T. (1983). The differentiation of the concepts of difficulty and ability. *Child Development, 54,* 951-959.

Nicholls, J.G., & Miller, A.T. (1984). Reasoning about the ability of self and others: A developmental study. *Child Development, 55,* 1990-1999.

Nicholls, J.G., & Miller, A.T. (1985). Differentiation of the concepts of luck and skill. *Developmental Psychology, 21,* 76-82.

Ommundsen, Y., & Vaglum, P. (1991). Soccer competition anxiety and enjoyment in young boy players: The influence of perceived competence and significant others' emotional involvement. *International Journal of Sport Psychology, 22,* 35-49.

Petlichkoff, L.M. (2003). Self-regulation skills for children and adolescents. In M.R. Weiss (Ed.), *Developmental sport and exercise psychology: A lifespan perspective* (pp. 269-288). Morgantown, WV: Fitness Information Technology.

Roeser, R.W., & Eccles J. (1998). Adolescents' perceptions of middle school: Relation to longitudinal changes in academic and psychological adjustment. *Journal of Research on Adolescence, 8,* 123-158.

Roeser, R.W., Eccles, J.S., & Sameroff, A.J. (2000). School as a context of early adolescents' academic and social-emotional development: A summary of research findings. *The Elementary School Journal, 100,* 443-471.

Rose, B., Larkin, D., & Berger, B.G. (1994). Perceptions of social support in children of low, moderate and high levels of coordination. *ACHPER Healthy Lifestyles Journal, 41*(4), 18-21.

Schunk, D.H., & Zimmerman, B.J. (1994). *Self-regulation of learning and performance: Issues and educational applications.* Hillsdale, NJ: Erlbaum.

Schutz, R.W., & Park, I. (2003). Some methodological considerations in developmental sport and exercise psychology. In M.R. Weiss (Ed.), *Developmental sport and exercise psychology: A lifespan perspective* (pp. 73-99). Morgantown, WV: Fitness Information Technology.

Smith, A.L. (1999). Perceptions of peer relationships and physical activity participation in early adolescence. *Journal of Sport & Exercise Psychology, 21*, 329-350.

Smith, R.E., & Smoll, F.L.(1996). The coach as a focus of research and intervention in youth sports. In F.L. Smoll & R.E. Smith (Eds.), *Children and youth in sport: A biopsychosocial perspective* (pp. 125-141). Madison, WI: Brown & Benchmark.

Solmon, M.A. (1996). Impact of motivational climate on students' behaviors and perceptions in a physical education setting. *Journal of Educational Psychology, 88*, 731-738.

State of Michigan (1976). *Joint legislative study on youth sports programs, Phase I.* East Lansing: Michigan State University.

Stipek, D.J., Daniels, D.H. (1988). Declining perceptions of competence: A consequence of changes in the child or in the educational environment? *Journal of Educational Psychology, 80*, 352-356.

Stipek, D., & Mac Iver, D. (1989). Developmental change in children's assessment of intellectual competence. *Child Development, 60*, 521-538.

Stipek, D.J., & Recchia, S., & McClintic, S. (1992). Self-evaluation in young children. *Monographs of the Society for Research in Child Development, 5*, 71-84.

Swain, A. (1996). Social loafing and identifiability: The mediating role of achievement goal orientations. *Research Quarterly for Exercise and Sport, 67*, 337-344.

Swain, A.B.J., & Harwood, C.G. (1996). Antecedents of state goals in age-group swimmers: An interactionist perspective. *Journal of Sports Sciences, 14*, 111-124.

Theeboom, M., De Knop, P., & Weiss, M.R. (1995). Motivational climate, psychosocial responses, and motor skill development in children's sport: A field based-intervention study. *Journal of Sport & Exercise Psychology, 17*, 294-311.

Veroff, J. (1969). Social comparison and the development of achievement motivation. In C. Smith (Ed.), *Achievement related motives in children* (pp. 46-110). New York: Russell Sage Foundation.

Watkins, B., & Montgomery, A.B. (1989). Conceptions of athletic excellence among children and adolescents. *Child Development, 60*, 1362-1372.

Weiss, M.R. (1991). Psychological skill development in children and adolescents. *The Sport Psychologist, 5*, 335-354.

Weiss, M.R. (1995). Children in sport: An educational model. In S. Murphy (Ed.), *Sport psychology interventions* (pp. 39-69). Champaign, IL: Human Kinetics.

Weiss, M.R. (2000). Motivating kids in physical activity. *President's Council on Physical Fitness and Sports Research Digest, 3* (11), 1-8.

Weiss, M.R., & Bredemeier, B.J. (1983). Developmental sport psychology: A theoretical perspective for studying children in sport. *Journal of Sport Psychology, 5*, 216-230.

Weiss, M.R., Bredemeier, B.J., & Shewchuk, R.M. (1985). An intrinsic/extrinsic motivation scale for the youth sport setting: A confirmatory factor analysis. *Journal of Sport Psychology, 7*, 75-91.

Weiss, M.R., Bredemeier, B.J., & Shewchuk, R.M. (1986). The dynamics of perceived competence, perceived control, and motivational orientation in youth sports. In M.R. Weiss & D. Gould (Eds.), *Sport for children and youths* (pp. 89-101). Champaign, IL: Human Kinetics.

Weiss, M.R., & Duncan, S.C. (1992). The relation between physical competence and peer acceptance in the context of children's sport participation. *Journal of Sport and Exercise Psychology, 14*, 177-191.

Weiss, M.R., Ebbeck, V., & Horn, T.S. (1997). Children's self-perceptions and sources of competence information: A cluster analysis. *Journal of Sport & Exercise Psychology, 19*, 52-70.

Weiss, M.R., & Ferrer-Caja, E. (2002). Motivational orientations and sport behavior. In T.S. Horn (Ed.), *Advances in sport psychology* (2nd ed., pp. 101-183). Champaign, IL: Human Kinetics.

Weiss, M.R., & Horn, T.S. (1990). The relation between children's accuracy estimates of their physical competence and achievement-related characteristics. *Research Quarterly for Exercise and Sport, 61*, 250-258.

Weiss, M.R., & Raedeke, T.D. (2003). Developmental sport and exercise psychology: Research status on youth and directions toward a lifespan perspective. In M.R. Weiss (Ed.), *Developmental sport and exercise psychology: A lifespan perspective* (pp. 1-26). Morgantown, WV: Fitness Information Technology.

Weiss, M.R., & Smith, A.L. (2002). Friendship quality in youth sport: Relationship to age, gender, and motivation variables. *Journal of Sport & Exercise Psychology, 24*, 420-437.

Weiss, M.R., Smith, A.L., & Theeboom, M. (1996). "That's what friends are for": Children's and teenagers' perceptions of peer relationships in the sport domain. *Journal of Sport & Exercise Psychology, 18*, 347-379.

Weiss, M.R., & Stuntz, C.P. (2003). A little friendly competition: Peer relationships and psychosocial development in youth sport contexts. In M.R. Weiss (Ed.), *Developmental sport and exercise psychology: A lifespan perspective* (pp. 165-196). Morgantown, WV: Fitness Information Technology.

Weitzer, J.E. (1989). *Childhood socialization into physical activity: Parental roles in perceptions of competence and goal orientations.* Unpublished master's thesis, University of Wisconsin-Milwaukee.

Wentzel, K.R. (1998). Social relationships and motivation in middle school: The role of parents, teachers, and peers. *Journal of Educational Psychology, 90,* 202-209.

Wentzel, K.R., & Wigfield, A. (1998). Academic and social motivational influences on students' academic performance. *Educational Psychology Review, 10,* 155-175.

White, R.W. (1959). Motivation reconsidered: The concept of competence. *Psychological Review, 66,* 297-330.

Whitehead, J., & Smith, A.G. (1996). Issues in development of a protocol to evaluate children's reasoning about ability and effort in sport. *Perceptual and Motor Skills, 83,* 355-364.

Wigfield, A. (1994). Expectancy-value theory of achievement motivation: A developmental perspective. *Educational Psychology, 6,* 49-78.

Wigfield, A., & Eccles, J.S. (1992). The development of achievement task values: A theoretical analysis. *Developmental Review, 12,* 265-310.

Wigfield, A., & Eccles, J.S. (2000). Expectancy-value theory of achievement motivation. *Contemporary Educational Psychology, 25,* 68-81.

Wigfield, A., Eccles, J.S., Mac Iver, D., Reuman, D.A., & Midgley, C. (1991). Transitions during early adolescence: Changes in children's domain-specific self-perceptions and general self-esteem across the transition to junior high school. *Developmental Psychology, 27,* 552-565.

Wigfield, A., Eccles, J.S., Yoon, K.S., Harold, R.D., Arbreton, A.J., Freedman-Doan, C., & Blumenfeld, P.C. (1997). Change in children's competence beliefs and subjective task values across the elementary school years: A 3-year study. *Journal of Educational Psychology, 89,* 451-469.

Wigfield, A., Galper, A., Denton, K., & Seefeldt, C. (1999). Teachers' beliefs about former Head Start and non-Head Start first-grade children's motivation, performance, and future educational prospects. *Journal of Educational Psychology, 91,* 98-104.

Williams, L. (1998). Contextual influences on goal perspectives among female youth sport participants. *Research Quarterly for Sport and Exercise, 69,* 47-57.

Williams, L., & Gill, D.L. (1995). The role of perceived competence in the motivation of physical activity. *Journal of Sport and Exercise Psychology, 17,* 363-378.

Wylleman, P., & Lavallee, D. (2003). A developmental perspective on transitions faced by athletes. In M.R. Weiss (Ed.), *Developmental sport and exercise psychology: A lifespan perspective* (pp. 503-523). Morgantown, WV: Fitness Information Technology.

Xiang, P., & Lee, A.M. (1998). The development of self-perceptions of ability and achievement goals and their relations in physical education. *Research Quarterly for Exercise and Sport, 69,* 231-24.

Xiang, P., Lee, A., & Shen, J. (2001). Conceptions of ability and achievement goals in physical education: Comparisons of American and Chinese students. *Contemporary Educational Psychology, 26,* 348-365.

Xiang, P., Lee, A., & Williamson, L. (2001). Conceptions of ability in physical education: Children and adolescents. *Journal of Teaching in Physical Education, 20,* 282-294.

CHAPTER NINE

Self-Regulation Skills for Children and Adolescents

Linda M. Petlichkoff, Ph.D.

Sally and Melissa, two 10-year-old golfers, signed up to play junior golf at a local course. Both girls showed promise with their physical skills and were having fun learning golf with their friends. After a number of lessons, Lynne, the teaching professional, encouraged Sally and Melissa to participate in a junior golf tournament scheduled at the end of the summer. The girls, then, took two very different paths to get ready for the tournament:

- Sally practiced three days per week to improve her golf skills. Over the next few weeks, Sally set daily goals and monitored her progress in all aspects of the game to see how she improved. When she needed help with her short game, Sally asked Lynne for help and took lessons. She began watching LPGA tournaments on television with her mom, who also took Sally to the driving range and practice green to work on her skills. Sally watched her mom—a former collegiate player—practice her swing; then, she tried to imitate many of her mom's swing mechanics. As the tournament approached, Sally looked forward to competing with her friends, focusing on her own game and playing strategies. After the tournament, Sally was motivated to learn more about the game of golf, and she looked forward to playing in future golf tournaments.

- Melissa decided just to play golf every day. She was pleased with her game only when she scored better than the other youngsters she played against or how her score compared to "par." She did not like setting goals because she had a hard time keeping track or evaluating those goals. Melissa did not like spending time on the practice range; she cared only about how her performance compared to that of other children in her group. On the day of the tournament, Melissa was paired with Judy, who had been playing golf for several years and had won the tournament last year. Moreover, it was very windy, and Melissa disliked playing in the wind. In fact, she avoided practicing or playing when it was windy. After the tournament, Melissa was very discouraged about her game because she did not score well, and she played less frequently with friends.

What is different about these two children? Why do they think, feel, and behave differently in the same situation? The contrasting methods of preparation tend to identify Sally as a self-regulated learner. That is, she has the skills to self-monitor progress, manage her emotions, focus on self-improvement, and seek help from others. In contrast, Melissa assumes a more passive role in managing her play, relies heavily on external feedback to evaluate performance, blames her lack of success on factors out of her control, and fails to take responsibility for her own actions. As a self-regulated learner, Sally focuses on self-directed thoughts, feelings, and actions to play golf successfully. More important, Sally defines success as achieving her goals and taking responsibility for learning and developing strategies to accomplish those goals.

This chapter will review the research on how children and adolescents become self-regulated learners. Specifically, I will discuss (a) the nature of self-regulation and the processes involved in self-regulation, (b) children and adolescents as *learners* versus *performers*, (c) self-regulation research with children and adolescents, (d) recommendations to enhance self-regulation, and (e) future research directions. Particular emphasis will be placed on the developmental levels of self-regulatory skills.

UNDERSTANDING SELF-REGULATION SKILLS

The majority of research on how children and adolescents use self-regulation skills to improve learning and performance evolved from research on student learning and academic achievement (for reviews, see Bronson, 2000; Schunk & Zimmerman, 1994; Zimmerman & Schunk, 1989). Zimmerman (1989a) conducted a critical review of the major theoretical perspectives on self-regulated learning. Specifically, his review examined the development of self-regulation from six theoretical perspectives: (a) operant learning, (b) phenomenological, (c) social cognitive, (d) volitional, (e) Vygotskian, and (f) cognitive constructivist. Zimmerman determined that all six perspectives converge on three common elements characteristic of self-regulatory learning, but suggested age-related differences may exist that limit an individual's ability to use specific self-regulation skills (e.g., Bronson, 2000; Schunk, 1994).

The majority of research on how children and adolescents use self-regulation skills to improve learning and performance evolved from research on student learning and academic achievement.

The first element necessary for self-regulated learning is that children and adolescents assume responsibility for their own learning. That is, self-regulated learners believe they play an instrumental role in whether they achieve their goals (i.e., self-directed behavior) because they have the ability to initiate and successfully use a number of strategies to improve skills. For younger children, self-directed behavior may be limited because they lack either the necessary skills to process information effectively or the requisite physical skills to be successful (Schunk, 1994; Zimmerman, 1990).

The second characteristic self-regulatory learning theorists emphasize is the importance of self-oriented feedback. Zimmerman (1989a) stresses that feedback is a cyclical process. It relies not only on what children and adolescents learn from employing various strategies or methods (i.e., perceptions about how effective those strategies were), but also how they utilize feedback to change behaviors (i.e., what strategy or strategies they may use next time). Self-regulated learners receive feedback from internal standards of competence (i.e., what they think is correct) that is based primarily on past experiences and what they observe (i.e., modeling), as well as how their performance is reinforced or rewarded by significant others (Bronson, 2000; Zimmerman, 1989a).

The third aspect of self-regulated learning focuses on the motivational dimension—the *how* and *why* students use one strategy or process over others. Zimmerman (1989a) suggests, however, the theoretical perspectives tend to differ greatly on this element of self-regulated learning. Whether children and adolescents are motivated to become self-regulated learners may depend on perceived choice of activities, outcomes, or the importance they place on the activity. Therefore, to further address developmental issues related to self-regulation skills, it is best to limit my discussion to one theoretical perspective.

I will use a social cognitive perspective to understanding self-regulation processes and the impact these processes have on learning and performance in sport and physical activity. This theoretical perspective is particularly appealing for understanding self-regulation skill development with children and adolescents because it considers the collective impact of personal, behavioral, and environmental influences on self-regulated learning (Bandura, 1986; Schunk, 1989; Zimmerman, 1989a).

From a social cognitive perspective, self-regulation is a process whereby children and adolescents exercise control over how they think, act, and feel as they attempt to attain their goals (Schunk, 1989; Zimmerman, 1990). The key characteristic of self-regulation focuses on an individual's ability to execute a sense of choice (i.e., recognize the personal value) and control (i.e., self-initiate) when employing various self-regulatory strategies (Zimmerman, 1994). These strategies emerge via feedback children and adolescents receive from self-monitoring and self-evaluating their progress (i.e., covert processes), as well as feedback they receive from their environment (Zimmerman, 1989b).

Zimmerman (1989b, 2000) identified three feedback loops: (a) *behavioral self-regulation* uses self-observing performances and making adjustments in strategies; (b) *environmental self-regulation* requires self-observations and then adjustments to different situations and social feedback; and (c) *covert self-regulation* involves self-monitoring strategies and adjustments of how one thinks and feels about the process (see Figure 1). These feedback loops parallel Bandura's (1986) contention that "behavior is . . . a product of both self-generated [what children and adolescents think and do] and external sources of influence [reactions to that behavior by significant others, peers, as well as rewards and punishments]" (p. 454). This cyclic process (see Figure 1—solid lines) suggests that children and adolescents develop strategies based on their beliefs (e.g., "I know I can do this") that influence what they do (i.e., behaviors) and that these strategies may be reinforced by external sources (i.e., the environment) as they progress toward their goals. Then, based on the feedback received from their behaviors and the environment, as well as their own self-monitoring (i.e., see Figure 1—dotted lines), children

FIGURE 1
Triadic forms of self-regulation

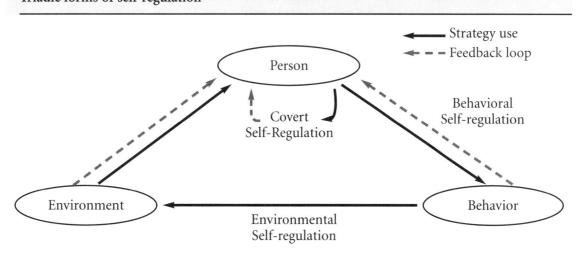

From "Attaining self-regulation: A social cognitive perspective," by B.J. Zimmerman, 2000, *Handbook on self-regulation* (p. 15). Copyright 2000 American Psychologoical Association. Reproduced by permission.

and adolescents may persist in an activity, try a different strategy, or learn new skills to achieve their goals.

Zimmerman (2000) further explains self-regulation as a cyclical process because the experiences (i.e., prior performances) of children and adolescents elicit adjustments in their current performance. These adjustments allow children and adolescents to take a proactive approach to alter goals (i.e., increase task difficulty) and behaviors when they receive favorable feedback for their efforts. They may also choose to adjust strategies, goals, or expectations when they receive less favorable feedback from their behaviors. Hence, children and adolescents may experience more inherent success because they either possess or develop the necessary strategies to effectively deal with what they do and think in relation to their ever-changing environment. If their performance demonstrates a lack of skills, teachers or coaches can alter teaching strategies. This approach may elicit a different response from the learner. Each of these feedback loops plays a different role in how children and adolescents become self-regulated learners and relies heavily on age-related differences in cognitive, affective, and behavioral factors.

A deeper understanding of the feedback loops within a social cognitive perspective provides researchers and practitioners with explanations as to why some children and adolescents fail to use self-regulation processes to initiate, maintain, or achieve their goals. For example, Melissa's decision to withdraw from junior golf illustrates how relying on one source of feedback (i.e., social comparison) can be detrimental while learning skills. It appears that Melissa relied heavily on feedback from the environment; that is, her success in golf was based on performance (i.e., outcome) rather than on how she improved her golf skills (i.e., covert self-regulation). When her performance failed to measure up to that of others in the junior golf program, her thoughts and feelings limited her ability to shift her attention to other strategies or processes to initiate change (i.e., self-directed behaviors).

Children and adolescents may experience more inherent success because they either possess or develop the necessary strategies to effectively deal with what they do and think in relation to their ever-changing environment.

Zimmerman (1989b, 1990) suggests that self-regulated learners possess certain *attributes* to be self-starters and continue to pursue their goals in the absence of external or augmented feedback. In addition to identifying attributes of self-regulated learners, social cognitive theorists in the academic domain strive to understand the *process* of self-regulation (Bandura, 1986; Schunk, 1989, 1994). Self-regulated learning consists of three processes: self-observation, self-judgment, and self-reaction (Bandura; Schunk, 1989).

Self-observation provides individuals with the necessary information to set realistic goals and to evaluate whether changes in behavior are achieved (Bandura, 1986). Self-observation can be accomplished through a number of strategies such as self-monitoring, self-recording, and goal setting. It is important, however, to develop self-awareness about how performance relates to target behaviors (i.e., quality, quantity, frequency; see Mace, Belfiore, & Shea, 1989; Schunk, 1989, for reviews). Before learners can self-regulate, they need to know what they are doing compared to what they are supposed to be doing (i.e., Schunk, 1990, 1994). Hence, self-observation provides the learner with the necessary information to set and later evaluate goals.

In addition to providing information about what the learner wants to accomplish, self-observation plays a key role in motivating learners to change behavior (Schunk, 1990, 1994). As children and adolescents observe and record what they are doing, this process should increase their self-efficacy when they see how they can effect change in their own behaviors (Zimmerman, 1989b). For example, Sally's ability to self-monitor her progress motivated her to ask for help to improve her golf skills, which helped her to achieve her goals. Hence, Sally's desire to continue her involvement in junior golf was enhanced because of her self-regulatory activities (i.e., setting goals, asking for help). It appears, then, that self-monitoring or self-recording is essential when making self-observations (Schunk, 1989).

The second self-regulation process is *self-judgment*, which refers to the personal standards children and adolescents use to evaluate their performance (Bandura, 1986). Bandura (1986) and Schunk (1989) suggest these personal standards are not simply related to reaching goals (i.e., self-comparison), but may include comparisons made to normative and social standards, as well as what the learner attributes his or her success to. In sport, social comparison is the most frequently used standard of achievement—how one's individual performance compares to that of others. For children and adolescents with low perceptions of their ability, this standard of achievement may be detrimental to overall development.

As alluded to earlier, Melissa's performance suffered from just such a comparison (i.e., how her score compared to that of others). She was not provided with feedback or encouragement to play her own game; rather, she believed that scoring better than others scored or close to par was the only measure of success. When children and adolescents are encouraged to set goals and self-record their progress against their own past performance (i.e., self-comparison), self-regulated learning may develop through this type of self-judgment process. Hence, setting goals and structuring the environment for skill improvement (cf. Sally's preparation) are two distinguishing characteristics of a self-regulatory learner (Zimmerman & Martinez-Pons, 1992). Self-comparison encourages children and adolescents to focus attention on personal development, whereas normative comparisons force them to focus on how their development compares with standards that may not be attainable given their present skill level or experience. Bandura (1986) also suggests that young children or inexperienced learners tend to lack the ability to differentiate the degree of task difficulty in order to effectively self-judge or compare their efforts to normative standards.

The third self-regulation process, *self-reaction*, determines whether performance evaluation or goal attainment is viewed as favorable or unfavorable. Zimmerman (1989b) suggests self-reactions are not limited to evaluations associated with goal attainment or reestablishing goals, but also include behaviors such as receiving overt praise or criticism for a performance and altering one's perception of the environment to attain favorable outcomes. Hence, self-regulated learners who have high perceptions of ability and rely on a variety of strategies to regulate their behavior tend to evaluate their performance favorably. When evaluations are negative and individuals perceive that improvement is possible, self-regulation helps maintain motivation and persistence (Schunk, 1990). In contrast, individuals who have lower perceptions of ability and/or who lack sufficient skills or strategies to evaluate their performance tend to react unfavorably to their performance. These individuals may withdraw when they fail to achieve or maintain a level of personal accomplishment (cf. Melissa).

Social cognitive theorists believe individuals who develop into self-regulated learners rely on some aspect of each of these three interdependent processes of self-observation, self-judgment, and self-reaction (Bandura, 1986; Zimmerman, 1989b). Children and adolescents learn to self-monitor and record their performances in an effort to determine ways to master their environment and improve skills and eventually enhance their self-regulation strategies to achieve success. These three self-regulation processes will now be further examined to determine how each contributes to self-regulation learning in sport.

> According to social cognitive theorists, self-regulated learners rely on self-observation, self-judgment, and self-reaction.

Children and Adolescents as Learners versus Performers

Before key self-regulation strategies can be identified, along with their impact on skill development in sport, it is necessary to differentiate between learning and performance (Schunk, 1989). Magill (1999) defines learning as a relatively permanent change in one's ability to perform a skill that typically results from practice or experience. In contrast, performance refers to "performing a skill at a specific time and in a specific situation" (Magill, 1999, p. 169). One may conclude from these two definitions that *learning* is what children and adolescents do at practice as they attempt to acquire and improve physical skills. *Performing* is what children and adolescents are asked to do when they engage in competitive situations and is not contingent on whether they have successfully learned the skills necessary to achieve desired outcomes.

Teachers and coaches, as well as children and adolescents, can determine whether learning has occurred by examining four performance characteristics of skill learning: improvement, consistency, persistence, and adaptability (Magill, 1999). If participants are given sufficient practice and feedback, their skills tend to improve and become more consistent, and they are capable of adapting to a variety of situations (i.e., self-regulated learners), but learning is not limited to "doing."

Bandura (1986) suggests that learning can also occur when children and adolescents perform skills (i.e., enactive learning) or observe models (i.e., vicarious learning). *Enactive learning* requires individuals to make adjustments based on the feedback they receive from their own actions. Hence, if we expect enactive learning to occur, children and adolescents must be active participants in the process of acquiring skills. When their actions result in successful outcomes, the skills they used will be retained, whereas actions resulting in unsuccessful attempts are altered or discarded (Schunk, 1989). *Vicarious learning* (i.e., modeling) can serve to expedite the learning process when learners are exposed to skills and strategies that exceed their present abilities. Modeling also may remove some of the negative consequences of learning new skills (Schunk, 1989). Hence, when children and adolescents are provided opportunities to observe models performing skills they are striving to master, learning occurs. Both experiences (i.e., enactive and vicarious learning) encourage children and adolescents to persist longer at skill mastery, thus serving to increase motivation.

Carver and Scheier (1998) indicate learners suffer fewer negative consequences as a skill becomes routine. At that point, children and adolescents can shift their thoughts to the outcome of their performance. If learners focus on outcomes prior to mastering the skill, they may impair their ability to actually learn the skill. Bouffard and Dunn (1993) state "what a learner does during learning time [i.e., skill acquisition] is also a major determinant of learning and performance" (p. 393). That is, the strategies employed while learning a skill may differ from those used once the skill has been learned (i.e., performing).

Research indicates that until the age of 12, children have less mature cognitive abilities such as coding processes, rehearsal strategies, and attentional and decision-making skills, all of which influence the ability to learn—verbally and visually—from models (Gallagher, French, Thomas, & Thomas, 1996). Developmental differences are reflected also in the degree of learners' expertise. Novice performers possess less sport-specific knowledge than do comparably aged experts, and both are less sophisticated in their cognitive representations than are adult experts (e.g., see French & McPherson, 2003; McPherson, 1999; Nevett & French, 1997). These developmental differences, then, are likely to influence children's ability to use self-regulation strategies when performing physical skills. It is also important to consider self-regulation as a process that helps children and adolescents incorporate skill mastery through observation of models and feedback from the environment so they become self-regulatory learners (Zimmerman, 2000).

Zimmerman (2000) indicates that self-regulatory skills are acquired through four developmental levels: observation, emulation, self-control, and self-regulation. In the *observation level* of self-regulatory skill development, children and adolescents initially learn how to self-regulate as they watch (i.e., observe) competent models. This level of self-regulatory skill development relies heavily on "social guidance" through observation. Children and adolescents are provided with a "picture" of the skill—its components, verbal descriptions, necessary actions, and consequences of those actions (i.e., rewards and punishments). Essentially, learners observe the "target" behavior—what they are trying to do.

McCullagh and Weiss (2002) and Weiss (1991) regard observational learning or modeling as the "forgotten" method for teaching psychological (i.e., self-regulation) skills to help children and adolescents regulate their thoughts, feelings, and behaviors. As a method to teach self-regulatory skills, observational learning fits nicely into Zimmerman's (2000) developmental levels of self-regulatory skills because it "shows" the observer what to do or how to do it—a less frustrating path to learning self-regulation skills for young inexperienced learners than trial-and-error learning.

A self-regulated child has different ways of thinking about her performance, her emotions, and her goals.

The majority of research on observational learning in sport psychology has focused on skill acquisition and thus is consistent with development of self-regulatory skills. Weiss and Klint (1987), for example, demonstrated that young children (ages 5-6 years), as compared to older children (ages 9-11 years), benefited from "show-and-tell" models. The models integrated verbal rehearsal strategies such as repetitions, labeling, and self-instruction into their demonstrations. The more learners used these different strategies, the more it can be inferred they became self-regulatory learners. Weiss, Ebbeck, and Rose (1992) also found developmental differences in skill acquisition based on the type of model children observed and whether the learner was actually performing or learning a motor skill. Their findings suggest that younger children learn and perform better when they observe a model who verbalizes rehearsal strategies in the process. Bouffard and Dunn (1993) also found that verbalization and language skills play a key role in enhancing self-regulatory skills in children and that these skills increase with age. That is, 9-year-olds as compared to 6-year-olds talked to themselves to learn the skill components or self-regulate learning. Hence, children benefit from observing competent models who verbalize task-relevant cues. It is this verbalization along with the demonstration of the skill that plays a key role in self-regulatory learning (Schunk, 1986).

McCullagh and Weiss (2002) and Zimmerman (2000) suggest that similarity between the model and observer, as well as the observer's desire to learn and perform various skills and strategies, plays a significant role in the level of motivation of the observers. Specifically, learning or coping models—individuals who are learning a skill and receiving feedback—are better than someone who performs the skill flawlessly (i.e., mastery model). These findings suggest that when children and adolescents are learning skills, they benefit from observing models who are processing information related to their own performance (i.e., how to perform better). Hence, children and adolescents can learn acceptable and unacceptable performance standards when they watch the model's reaction to his or her performance (Zimmerman, 2000). Schunk (1987) suggests that the age of the model is less important when the model is competent than when the observer has self-doubts. In the latter case, a peer-coping model is more appropriate because children learn different strategies to alter how they think, feel, and act when learning and performing skills.

It is when children and adolescents begin to imitate the model that they move to the second level—the *emulation level.* At this level, self-regulatory skills are achieved as the learner's performance, or use of strategies, begin to look more like the model he or she is trying to emulate. Zimmerman (2000) suggests, however, the learner's behavioral outcomes are not expected to be exact replications of the model's behavior. Rather, the learner is acquiring skills to reproduce the performance and will make closer approximations with practice and feedback. Zimmerman and his colleagues (Zimmerman, 2000; Zimmerman & Kitsantas, 1997, 1999) suggest that social feedback serves primarily a motivational role for the learner at this developmental level. Modeling will be particularly effective if the model demonstrates coping strategies or other self-regulatory skills when successful (e.g., Weiss, McCullagh, Smith, & Berlant, 1998).

Weiss and colleagues (1998) examined the role of peer modeling (coping and mastery models) as a self-regulatory learning method to enhance physical and psychological responses. On the basis of their present swimming abilities, children (age 6 years) were matched to one of three model type conditions: (a) peer mastery—a technically correct demonstration of swimming skills; (b) peer coping—models initially engaged in high task difficulty, low self-efficacy, and negative statements, then demonstrating the swimming skills partially correctly; and (c) control—a group who watched cartoons that contained no information about swimming skills. Results suggested that both peer-model groups consistently scored better than the control group at the postintervention and follow-up assessments on all swimming skills and self-efficacy measures. Moreover, both peer-model groups experienced a greater reduction in fear of swimming than did the control group at the postintervention assessment. These modeling effects suggest that children who lack physical skills or beliefs about what they can "do" may acquire skills or enhance their beliefs by observing similar skilled peer models (mastery or coping).

In one of the few studies to separate observation (Level 1) from emulation (Level 2), Kitsantas, Zimmerman, and Cleary (2000) examined the effects of two different model types (i.e., coping vs. mastery) and social feedback (i.e., present or not) on performing a novice task of dart throwing. As indicated earlier, Level 1—observation—requires learners to watch a proficient model, whereas Level 2—emulation—indicates learners "imitate" the model's behavior but do so with the assistance of social feedback. One group of learners (i.e., female high school physical education students) was taught to identify errors in the coping models' performance prior to trying to reproduce the skill; then, they were compared to learners who simply observed a mastery model (i.e., no errors). When learners were exposed to a coping model and asked to attend to how to get better, they experienced superior forms of

Observation requires learners to watch a proficient model, while emulation is when learners imitate a model with the assistance of social feedback.

self-regulation, learned the skill better, and had higher intrinsic motivation than did learners who observed a mastery model. Kitsantas and colleagues concluded that coping models during early stages of skill acquisition (i.e., observation) enhance the learners' ability to acquire self-regulatory skills. This study needs to be replicated with a younger group of learners to determine whether they have the cognitive ability to differentiate errors in the model's performance or whether they just imitate the mistakes.

At the *self-control level* of self-regulation skill development, the learner begins self-directed practice to refine skills in an attempt to achieve consistency across performances. The learner's level of proficiency should be a personal standard of performance but representative of the model's actions and verbal descriptions. Zimmerman (2000) suggests skills will be more "covert images" or verbal representations of what the model did than simple emulations of the model. Hence, it is the process of the skill (i.e., technique) rather than the outcome that individual learners try to achieve during this level—the internal picture they will use to evaluate whether they performed the skill correctly. The closer the approximation to that internal image (i.e., personal standard), the more positive self-reaction the learner will experience. Hence, at this level, learners rely on self-monitoring and process goals to evaluate their progress rather than on social feedback as in the emulation level (Zimmerman & Kitsantas, 1996).

Zimmerman and Kitsantas (1996) examined the effects of setting process versus product goals with the added strategy of self-monitoring (i.e., self-recording) to determine whether these self-regulation strategies would enhance skill acquisition, self-efficacy, and intrinsic interest. Fifty girls between 14 and 16 years of age learned the novice task of dart throwing while participating in physical education classes. Two groups were taught to set process goals that focused on executing the skill correctly (i.e., sighting, throwing, and follow-through), whereas two other groups were taught to set product (i.e., outcome) goals that focused on hitting the bull's eye on the target. In addition, a group from each condition (i.e., process and product goal-setters) was asked to self-record some aspect of their practice. Process goal-setters were asked to record any component of the skill missed while they practiced; product goal-setters were asked to record their scores after each trial. Results revealed process goals were more effective than product goals during dart-throwing practice, and self-recording enhanced performance across both conditions. When learners are instructed to pay attention to specific components of a skill and then monitor their practice, skill development is enhanced. At the self-control level, learners must practice independently and with little direct feedback from the model, thus relying heavily on their internal picture to make adjustments in their process goals.

Finally, as children and adolescents progress to the *self-regulation level*, they can adapt to different situations and use various strategies to cope with environmental and personal demands. Zimmerman (2000) indicates it is during this phase that learners shift their attention from process to outcomes. Unlike those at the self-control level, this shift does not negatively influence performance; hence, it appears that some level of "automaticity" in skill execution must be achieved before learners fully develop self-regulation skills. Zimmerman and Kitsantas (1997) designed a study to differentiate between the *self-control* and *self-regulation* levels. Following their (Zimmerman & Kitsantas, 1996) earlier protocol, which examined process-product goals and self-monitoring with 14- to 16-year-old participants, Zimmerman and Kitsantas (1997) added two more conditions. A transform-goal group was one in which the girls assessed the outcome of their dart throwing (i.e., hit the bull's-eye) and used various strategies to make corrections in their throws. A shifting-goal group was one in which girls were instructed to focus on execution of the last two steps of dart throwing (i.e., throwing and follow-through). After they had practiced for a set time period, the group shifted their goal to scoring the highest number of points for the remaining practice time (i.e., outcome). Results revealed that girls who focused on self-directed process goals and then shifted to outcome goals (i.e., score) had a higher dart-throwing proficiency score, as well as self-efficacy beliefs, self-reaction, and intrinsic interest, than did all other groups. These findings appear to hold true not only for learning and performing physical skills, but also for writing skills (i.e., rewriting problem sentences as a single nonrepetitive sentence; Zimmerman & Kitsantas, 1999).

Zimmerman and Kitsantas (1997) contend that self-regulation skills can be achieved through developmentally appropriate goal-setting strategies, but it is not simply the act of setting goals that is important. It is imperative that learners acquire the ability to set both process and product goals and then self-monitor their progress until these skills become automatic. More importantly, Zimmerman and Kitsantas found that "students who shifted goals from processes to outcomes after reaching Level 4 surpassed classmates who adhered only to process goals or only to outcome goals" (p. 32). This finding has important implications for sport psychology consultants, coaches, and parents on how to interact with children and adolescents when setting goals. That is, children and adolescents who are encouraged to focus on outcome goals before they have adequate physical or self-regulatory skills to perform proficiently may hinder the learning process. The four developmental levels of self-regulatory skills identified above are best acquired when learners master the skills sequentially—observe, emulate, make adjustments, and perform. There is no guarantee, however, that participants who acquire self-regulatory skills sequentially will employ such skills because their personal interests, motivation, and the activity itself may affect their ability to self-regulate.

> These four self-regulatory skills are best acquired when learners master them sequentially— observe, emulate, make adjustments, and perform.

SELF-REGULATION RESEARCH WITH CHILDREN AND ADOLESCENTS

Self-regulation research in sport and exercise psychology emerged almost two decades ago. Kirschenbaum (1984, 1987) and Kirschenbaum and Wittrock (1984) summarized self-regulation as a five-stage process: (a) problem identification, (b) commitment, (c) execution, (d) environmental management, and (e) generalization (for explanations see Gould & Chung, 2003). This model of self-regulation established a process to examine self-regulated behavior in sport that recognizes not only what the individual can do, but also the influence of the environment. Kirschenbaum (1984) further indicated an overlap exists between sport performance and self-regulation that goes beyond simply the process of setting goals. Specifically, elite adult athletes pursue their goals over long periods with a strong reliance on self-judgment and self-evaluation to improve performance. Unfortunately, self-regulation research in sport and exercise psychology has focused primarily on elite adult athletes with little attention paid to how these principles apply to children and adolescents in organized sports. The scant research conducted on self-regulation skills training with children and adolescents involved in sport will be examined in the following sections.

Differentiating Self-Regulation and Psychological Skills Training

There is a need to differentiate between self-regulation and psychological skills training. It also is important to distinguish between self-regulated learning *processes* and the *strategies* used to enhance skills and to differentiate between *skills* and *methods* as they relate to psychological skills training (Vealey, 1988, 1994; Weiss, 1991). At times, these terms are used interchangeably, which may lead to some confusion. Reconsidering psychological skills training within sport and exercise psychology as self-regulated-learning skills may make it possible to intervene more appropriately with younger, inexperienced athletes. This approach is congruent with contemporary social cognitive theory.

Zimmerman (1990) indicates that self-regulated learners use the processes of self-observation, self-judgment, and self-reaction when they are gaining knowledge and skills. Once they obtain the knowledge and skills, self-regulated learners implement strategies (i.e., self-recording, asking for help, rehearsing, or memorizing) to achieve their goals. Hence, until children and adolescents acquire the necessary knowledge and skills (cf. become experienced performers), they must be taught—through observational learning or social feedback—to effectively use strategies to self-monitor performance to achieve their goals and attribute their success to the use of such strategies.

In sport, Vealey (1988, 1994) and Weiss (1991) make a similar argument with regard to psychological *skills* and *methods*. Specifically, psychological *skills* refer to characteristics or qualities children and adolescents may gain by participating in sport that tend to influence their personal and psychological well-being. Weiss (1991) suggests it is important for children and adolescents to gain skills that enhance self-perceptions (i.e., self-efficacy, perceived competence), intrinsic motivation, and learning to cope with the pressures associated with sport participation. These skills are not necessarily automatic byproducts of sport participation; rather, they are skills learned through personal experience or observing models who use such skills.

The processes and/or strategies that bring about such changes in psychological skills are best referred to as psychological *methods* (Weiss, 1991). Weiss suggests psychological methods include both environmental (e.g., coach education, effective communication) and self-control strategies (e.g., goal setting, self-talk, problem solving). This notion fits nicely with Zimmerman's (2000) "triadic forms of self-regulation" identified earlier (see Figure 1). That is, learners should be encouraged to acquire skills and strategies to learn "how" to self-regulate from observing behaviors, as well as their internal reactions to the outcomes of those behaviors. At times, these strategies can be both a method and skill (e.g., goal setting, communication) and based on the role they play, they can effect change on skill acquisition and psychological responses.

For a number of years, sport psychology consultants have assisted athletes in developing psychological skills training programs to regulate behavior and enhance performance. These programs are designed to teach athletes strategies to cope with the demands of competition, enhance self-confidence, manage emotions, and assist with attentional control (Vealey, 1994). The majority of athletes who use psychological skills training are amateur and elite adult performers (i.e., national, elite, international; Vealey, 1988; Weiss, 1991). These athletes have well-developed physical skills, and they are looking to gain a competitive edge through mental skills training (i.e., Level 4—Self-Regulation; Vealey, 1994; Zimmerman & Kitsantas, 1997).

At the heart of these psychological skills programs is performance enhancement, rather than focusing on the total development (i.e., psychological, social, physical, and emotional) of the athlete. Some sport psychology consultants, however, suggest that a performance-enhancement model may be inappropriate for children and adolescents involved in youth sports. In fact, as early as 1982, Orlick recommended that sport psychology consultants utilize a personal development model to develop psychological skills with children and adolescents. That is, a psychological skills program for young inexperienced athletes should include learning strategies to improve their self-directed learning and psychological well-being (Gould, 1982, 1983; Orlick, 1982; Weiss, 1991).

Orlick's (1982) recommendations fit nicely into the social cognitive perspective that children can learn and acquire the necessary skills to be *self-regulatory learners* (Bandura, 1986; Schunk, 1989; Zimmerman, 1989b). More importantly, it appears there is a connection between acquiring psychological skills typically designed to improve sport performance and teaching children and adolescents how to become self-regulated learners. A self-regulated learning perspective encourages students to develop strategies (i.e., learning strategies) to

> It appears there is a connection between psychological skills typically designed to improve sport performance and teaching children and adolescents how to become self-regulated learners.

improve on past performance and interact more effectively with their environment (Schunk, 1990; Zimmerman, 1989a, 1989b). As indicated earlier, it is through self-observation, self-evaluation, and self-reaction processes that these strategies are acquired.

Sport-Related Research With Children and Adolescents

Although few sport-related studies have been conducted that specifically address self-regulation skills training with children and adolescents, those that have tend to reinforce the notion that children and adolescents can learn and effectively employ the three self-regulation processes (i.e., self-observation, self-evaluation, self-reaction). Blais and Vallerand (1986), for example, assessed the effects of electromyographic (EMG) biofeedback with children who were taught how to regulate precompetitive anxiety levels. Twenty boys, ranging in age from 10 to 13 years and identified as high trait anxious, were told they had been selected to compete in a competition contrived to simulate game-like conditions. The boys were assigned to either a biofeedback or placebo group. The task consisted of determining how long the boys could balance on a stabilometer. The results supported the notion that children can be taught muscle relaxation through biofeedback training (i.e., self-monitoring). Furthermore, participants successfully transferred these skills to precompetitive situations without the aid of the biofeedback equipment. Hence, it appears young athletes can be taught self-regulatory skills (e.g., emotional control) through biofeedback training, which promotes self-awareness as they monitor their behaviors.

Wrisberg and Anshel (1989) examined the impact of relaxation and imagery on free-throw shooting with young basketball players. Boys (ages 10 to 12 years) participated in a 6-week sports camp where they learned a variety of sports skills in a competitive environment, and they were selected because they were "skilled" in basketball free-throw shooting. The boys were assigned to one of four groups: (a) imagery-only group, (b) arousal-regulation group, (c) combination group, and (d) control group. The results indicated that the combination group (i.e., imagery-arousal regulation) performed better on the free-throw skills test than did either the arousal-regulation or control groups. The authors concluded that cognitive strategies (i.e., covert processes) could be learned and effectively employed by younger athletes. They also suggested that further developmental considerations must be addressed to determine whether there is a minimum age at which these strategies can be learned and employed.

Zhang, Ma, Orlick, and Zitzelsberger (1992) examined whether a mental-imagery training program would enhance the performance of young children ($M = 8.3$ yrs.) attending a sport school for promising table-tennis players. The children were divided into one of three groups: (a) relaxation training, followed by video observation of the best table tennis players in the world and mental imagery of selected skills demonstrated by a "preferred" player; (b) observation of the video introduced to Group 1; and (c) control group. Early in the study, children in Group 1 were introduced to relaxation training to develop self-awareness of their activation level prior to playing table tennis. The participants in the two intervention groups then observed a video of table-tennis skills (i.e., forehand attack) by elite players who made technically correct shots. They also received technical cues on what to watch for during the observation session, and then they were encouraged to practice these skills during their training sessions. The results indicated that Group 1 (relaxation-video combination) was the only group to enhance performance on all measures (i.e., accuracy, technical quality) assessed from pre- to postintervention. Of particular interest to self-regulation skill development was the active role children played in mentally rehearsing their skills after observing a competent model.

Zhang et al.'s (1992) intervention protocol aligns with Zimmerman's (2000) developmental self-regulation levels of *observation* and *emulation*. That is, table-tennis players observed competent models who performed skills they were trying to acquire and then were encouraged to attempt those skills during practice. These findings suggest that children are capable of using mental skills (i.e., relaxation, imagery) to gain control over their personal potential (i.e., self-directed behavior). Furthermore, it illustrates how "mental skills"—a "covert" self-regulation strategy—provide feedback to participants to enhance their performance. These mental skills may lay the foundation for children and adolescents to self-direct their practice in sport, as well as introduce them to strategies to help them become self-regulated learners.

Self-efficacy and personal goals are two major sources of self-regulated learning (Schunk, 1989). Self-efficacy represents the belief a person has about his or her ability, whereas goal setting serves a self-motivation role. Kane, Marks, Zaccaro, and Blair (1996) conducted a study to examine the relationship between self-efficacy, personal goals, and wrestling performance in high school athletes. Results indicated self-efficacy did not directly influence performance; rather, personal goals were found to mediate the effects of self-efficacy on performance. The authors concluded that goal setting is a key strategy for self-regulation because it helps focus athletes' attention on what they need to do to experience success (i.e., self-judgment). These authors also suggest that it is more than simply "setting" goals; rather, athletes must develop self-regulation strategies to achieve both training and performing goals for their sport. Children and adolescents should be encouraged to set learning goals to enhance self-efficacy and motivation and to gauge their progress.

Research conducted in academic (Schunk, 1989; Zimmerman, 1986, 2000) and sport settings (Kitsantas & Zimmerman, 1998; Zimmerman & Kitsantas, 1996) suggests self-observation (i.e., the first processes of self-regulation) is aided by self-recording, especially when it is done with some degree of regularity. Zimmerman and Kitsantas (1996) also argue that self-monitoring and goal setting naturally complement each other because goal setting directs the learner's attention to what needs to be observed and recorded. In addition to goal setting, self-regulated learners are capable of using other strategies to regulate their behavior, and these strategies play an important role in children's and adolescents' skill learning and performance. Individuals who become active participants while they acquire and employ a variety of self-regulatory strategies may learn to deal more effectively with their situation. That is, they learn to make adjustments in their performance based on feedback they receive from internal sources (covert feedback) and how their performance measures up to their internal standards of success (behavioral feedback), as well as the feedback they receive from the environment (see Figure 1).

Self-regulatory learners use and interpret feedback from the environment to effect changes in their behavior. For younger, inexperienced participants, this feedback loop may have the most influential impact on self-perceptions, motivation, and standards for success (Bandura, 1986; Weiss, 1995; Zimmerman, 1990). Weiss, for example, suggests that younger children (e.g., under 10 years of age) tend to be more reliant on adult feedback and reinforcement to assess their competency, whereas older children (i.e., over 10 years of age) are more dependent on peer evaluations. This reliance on different sources of feedback is associated with age-related changes that occur as children learn to differentiate concepts of ability (Nicholls, 1989). When children and adolescents participate in sports, they typically get involved to learn and improve skills (i.e., physical and psychological); thus, the more coaches and parents know about how to enhance participants' experience as learners, the better chance they have of developing self-regulated learners. Weiss (1991) indicates, "Educating coaches and parents about children's perceptions of instructional feedback and reinforcement,

> Individuals who become active participants while they acquire and employ a variety of self-regulatory strategies may learn to deal more effectively with their situation.

and providing strategies for bringing about change in self-perceptions, motivation, sportsmanship, and anxiety, is the most powerful way of developing psychological skills [i.e., self-regulatory skills]" (p. 342). Hence, if children and adolescents are to benefit from environmental feedback, they must also acquire strategies to use the information appropriately.

The sport-related research reviewed here supports the notion that children and adolescents can learn skills to self-monitor their progress (i.e., setting goals), control their emotions, imagine success, and emulate proficient models. That is, with sufficient instruction, practice, and feedback, children and adolescents can acquire a variety of strategies to enhance self-perceptions and performance. The simple process of being taught strategies does not infer they will become self-regulated learners; rather, children and adolescents must learn to initiate the use of these strategies in the absence of social feedback and rewards (Zimmerman, 2000). Self-regulated learners develop strategies to improve on past performances and set internal standards to determine whether they experience success. They also develop the ability to utilize different strategies to alter their thoughts, feelings, and behaviors when their performance is viewed as less successful.

RECOMMENDATIONS FOR ENHANCING SELF-REGULATION IN CHILDREN AND ADOLESCENTS

The social cognitive perspective adopted in this review serves as a suitable framework to understand how to develop self-regulation skills with children and adolescents in sport. This theoretical perspective identifies self-regulated learners as active participants who initiate, maintain, or achieve self-directed goals. Self-regulated learners rely on three feedback loops that reciprocally influence goal-directed behavior: (a) *behavioral self-regulation*, (b) *covert self-regulation*, and (c) *environmental self-regulation* (see Figure 1). The theory also posits that three self-regulatory processes—self-observation, self-judgment, and self-reaction—are instrumental in self-regulation skill development. This section focuses on the practical implications of these feedback loops and self-regulatory processes to enhance self-regulation in children and adolescents and offers recommendations to assist in the development of self-regulatory learners in the sport domain.

Weiss (1995) indicates that self-observation requires children to self-monitor behavior with some degree of regularity and proximity. For younger children, self-recording progress from one performance (i.e., practice and/or competition) to another tends to enhance self-efficacy and increase the time they are willing to spend on learning a task (Schunk, 1989). Self-observation is not limited, however, to self-recording but also includes such skills as goal setting, self-talk, relaxation, and visualization, which enhance self-perceptions, increase motivation, and reduce anxiety (Weiss, 1991). Children and adolescents must be encouraged to self-monitor behavioral outcomes and processes (i.e., cognitive strategies) as well as the strategies they observe from external sources (i.e., observational learning). Hence, self-observation not only informs them of their progress, but it also may motivate them to determine how to get better at the skill.

Zimmerman and Kitsantas (1996) recommend that children and adolescents set *process goals* before setting *product goals*. Process goals first help children master the task by concentrating their efforts on the necessary elements of the skill, whereas product goals specify the outcomes of their efforts. To illustrate this point, consider the two 10-year-old golfers introduced at the beginning of this chapter. Although both girls were new to golf, Sally set daily goals and monitored her progress on skill improvement rather than performance outcomes. In contrast, Melissa measured her success as playing better than others—her performance outcome. Process goals tend to enhance skill acquisition as well as self-perceptions, beliefs about success, and motivation.

Zimmerman and Kitsantas (1997) also recommend the importance of learning to *shift* goals from process to product when skills become more automatic and back again when efforts do not reach expectations. Children and adolescents should be guided to set goals that are within their control. They need to stay focused on what they can do to take control of their own learning (i.e., self-directed goals) and then set process goals to accomplish desired outcomes. Children and adolescents may need help to set goals that reflect their current capabilities, future potential, and skill acquisition. Thus, feedback from significant others—coaches, parents, peers—will play an important role for younger, inexperienced children.

Self-judgment refers to the personal standards children and adolescents use to evaluate their performance (Zimmerman, 2000). They base their judgments on normative standards, social comparisons, and self-comparisons. Normative standards, at times, require children and adolescents to judge their performance based on how they compare to the model or peer they just observed (Schunk, 1989). Children and adolescents who are inexperienced with and express doubts about a skill may benefit from observing a peer learning or coping model rather than a mastery model. Coping models initially demonstrate some degree of difficulty in their performance, but then gradually gain confidence as they improve on their performance. When children and adolescents observe a coping model, they learn different strategies—decision-making, verbalizations—to correct errors and experience positive outcomes. Researchers (Schunk, 1989; Weiss et al., 1998) specifically recommend that younger, inexperienced children observe peer coping models rather than rely on mastery models.

At other times, self-judgment involves comparing one's current performance to past performances (i.e., self-comparison). Self-comparison goes hand-in-hand with setting process goals. When children and adolescents are encouraged to set process goals that are based on past performances, they may observe incremental changes in behavior that tend to increase the intrinsic value of their performance. Social comparisons become more meaningful with age because they require a higher level of cognitive development and experience (Schunk, 1989). Specifically, Schunk indicates that children younger than 5 or 6 years of age cannot use information from their performance to evaluate performance. They rely on amount of effort to determine the cause of their performance—the harder they try, the more favorably they evaluate their performance. By early childhood, they show some interest in self-evaluation but rely on similarities and differences to make those comparisons, not necessarily whether the performance was successful. It is not until about 8 or 9 years of age that children use peer comparisons regularly to make self-evaluations about their competencies. It is recommended that children and adolescents make every effort to judge current performances based on their past performances. Given these developmental differences, children and adolescents will benefit from setting process, rather than product, goals to make self-evaluations of ability.

The third process, self-reaction, refers to the positive or negative evaluation children and adolescents make related to goal attainment. If children and adolescents achieve their goals or perceive there is room for improvement based on past performances, they will tend to evaluate the outcome as favorable. More than likely, this approach enhances their self-perceptions and motivation to continue. Again, there is a link between how the performance is evaluated and the types of goals the learner sets. The more children and adolescents are encouraged to set goals related to mastery and learning of skills, rather than to performing better than others, the more likely thcy will become self-regulated learners. This evaluation process does not rely solely on the individual's interpretation, but is greatly influenced by external sources of feedback.

As alluded to earlier, the social cognitive perspective emphasizes the importance of socializing agents such as parents, teachers, coaches, and peers in the development of self-regulation

(Zimmerman, 2000). Children and adolescents initially learn or pick up cues from the environment (i.e., significant others) regarding self-evaluative standards. That is, participants who receive positive feedback only when they do better than others on similar tasks eventually learn that social comparison is considered an important component in measuring success. Likewise, a model's self-reaction greatly influences whether children and adolescents view their performance as favorable or unfavorable (for reviews, see McCullagh & Weiss, 2002; Weiss, 1995). This notion has important ramifications on early stages of self-regulated learning. For example, younger children who observe and emulate a proficient model are more likely to view the performance favorably and try harder to acquire these skills if they observe the model being rewarded or self-rewarding performance. Hence, it is recommended that children and adolescents not only progress through each level of self-regulatory learning sequentially, but also that they learn strategies (i.e., verbalizations, self-instructions) to make adjustments in their performance when they are less successful.

The role of the three self-regulatory processes is demonstrated by the actions of Sally and Melissa. Sally used a number of the strategies introduced in this chapter to improve her golf skills. She relied on competent models (i.e., her coach and mom), seeking their help when she needed more instruction to develop her golf skills. Conversely, Melissa relied solely on social comparison and performance outcomes to evaluate her success and failure. These self-judgments were viewed unfavorably, which prompted her to withdraw from the sport. Unfortunately, every time Melissa signs up for an organized sport, she relies on performance outcomes because it is what her dad models as an important component to her success in sport. Melissa, and others like her, can certainly benefit from observing different models (i.e., teachers, coaches, peers) who demonstrate more appropriate self-regulatory skills.

Given the impact of environmental feedback on self-regulation skills with children and adolescents, organizers of youth programs must create programs that promote self-regulatory skills through their curriculum and support staff. One such program is reflected in the efforts of The First Tee (www.thefirsttee.org). The goal of The First Tee is to introduce children and adolescents to the inherent values of the game of golf while exposing them to life skills designed to enhance their ability to set goals and self-evaluate their progress. Through three program levels—Par, Birdie, and Eagle—children and adolescents learn how to set goals to evaluate their performance as they engage in age-appropriate activities. Participants receive a *Yardage Book* to record and monitor their progress against internal standards (i.e., Personal "Par"—a personal "can do") rather than compare their efforts with others.

Instructors at each site are encouraged to model and reinforce appropriate strategies (i.e., manage emotions, goal setting, decision making) while they teach golf to The First Tee participants. Zimmerman (2000) indicates it is difficult for some children and adolescents to learn some self-regulation strategies if such strategies are not taught, modeled, and rewarded in their community or homes. Hence, The First Tee site leaders and volunteers play key roles in whether participants acquire sufficient self-regulatory skills to deal with personal problems or achieve higher standards in school. Instructors are provided opportunities to attend regional training workshops that demonstrate various aspects of the life and golf skills curriculum and to learn self-regulatory strategies to assist in their teaching. To date, little evaluative research has been conducted on the program's effectiveness in guiding the development of self-regulation skills in children and adolescents. The efforts of The First Tee, however, support the notion that self-regulatory skills can be taught across different domains (i.e., Gould & Chung, 2003; Zimmerman, 2000; Zimmerman & Kitsantas, 1996, 1997).

FUTURE RESEARCH DIRECTIONS

Although self-regulated learning continues to receive much attention in the academic literature, developmental sport psychologists have not systematically studied self-regulation skills with children and adolescents in sport. In an environment that relies so heavily on social comparisons, children and adolescents must be taught and encouraged to initiate, maintain, and achieve self-directed goals to become self-regulated learners. To examine this issue, I forward several challenges for future research endeavors. The first challenge deals with targeting children and adolescents as participants in our research. All too often, we adopt a performance-enhancement approach, which focuses on elite adult athletes with little attention paid to the development of self-regulation strategies in children and adolescents. This challenge may also force us to shift our attention from performers to learners. Children and adolescents are in the process of acquiring skills and strategies to self-direct their behaviors and ultimately develop the necessary skills to perform successfully in their sport. Adopting such a focus will align our efforts with the work being conducted in academic settings. Furthermore, we may find that we cannot simply assume what works—self-observation, self-judgment, and self-reaction—for "performers" (i.e., elite, highly skilled athletes) will work also for "learners" (i.e., children who are developing their skills).

A second challenge relates to examining the impact of setting process versus product goals to assist with enhancing self-directed behaviors and self-control strategies with children and adolescents. Although Zimmerman and Kitsantas (1996, 1997, 1999) have incorporated process and product goals with writing skills and dart throwing (a novel task), further work is needed to assess developmental issues related to these types of goals in "real-world" sport settings. Specifically, can younger, inexperienced children learn to "shift" from process to product goals and back again, when appropriate to adjust performance? Can children and adolescents independently set these goals, or do they need help from external sources (i.e., significant others) to assist with this process?

The third challenge is to systematically examine the different levels of self-regulation skill development (i.e., observation, emulation, self-control, self-regulation) forwarded by Zimmerman (2000) with younger, inexperienced learners involved in sport. If children and adolescents rely on observing models to initiate their self-regulatory skill learning, then research needs to be conducted that focuses on strategies used by the model and the impact these strategies have on self-regulation skill learning. It is important also to determine whether children and adolescents who sequentially progress through these levels develop into self-regulatory learners. Developmental sport psychologists will benefit from Zimmerman and colleagues' protocol that attempts to differentiate between observation and emulation and emulation and self-control, as well as self-control and self-regulation (Kitsantas et al., 2000; Zimmerman & Kitsantas, 1997). This line of research has the potential to enhance our understanding of how children and adolescents become self-regulated learners.

Similarly, there is a need to conduct longitudinal assessments of community-based programs that employ strategies such as self-monitoring, goal setting, and peer mentoring (e.g., Danish & Nellen, 1997). These programs claim to teach life skills to children and adolescents, but little, if any, evaluative research exists to determine their effectiveness.

CONCLUDING REMARKS

Self-regulation plays a key role in how children and adolescents react to behavioral outcomes and environment feedback. The behaviors of Sally and Melissa demonstrate how different interpretations—how they feel, think, and behave—about the same situation result in either positive or negative outcomes. Children and adolescents initially gain these skills through observation, and they need to observe models who demonstrate strategies and skills that will encourage them to become self-regulatory learners. Sally had those positive models, who focused on learning skills and strategies to improve her golf skills. Melissa learned from observing her dad's behavior that winning and being better than others was important to him. After observing the interaction between Melissa and her dad, Lynne (the coach) helped her set daily goals and monitored her progress based on skill improvement and rewarded her efforts rather than the outcome. Melissa began to enjoy golf again and expressed a desire to return to the youth program for more lessons. There is a need, then, to educate teachers, coaches, and parents about their role in the development of self-regulation skills.

This review also illustrates that children and adolescents benefit from participating in a mastery-oriented environment, an environment that encourages skill improvement and self-referent measures of success until skills become more automatic. Social feedback must reward improvement and teach children and adolescents to value the little things they do to get better rather than focus upon social comparison as a standard of success. These notions challenge the very structure and organization of youth sports. Hence, adult leaders should make every effort to encourage the development of not only physical skills but also self-regulation skills and strategies with children and adolescents involved in their programs.

REFERENCES

Bandura, A. (1986). *Social foundations of thought and action*. Englewood Cliffs, NJ: Prentice-Hall, Inc.

Blais, M. R., & Vallerand, R. J. (1986). Multimodal effects of electromyographic biofeedback: Looking at children's ability to control precompetitive anxiety. *Journal of Sport Psychology, 8*, 283-303.

Bronson, M. B. (2000). *Self-regulation in early childhood*. New York: Guilford.

Bouffard, M., & Dunn, J. G. H. (1993). Children's self-regulated learning of movement sequences. *Research Quarterly for Exercise and Sport, 64*, 393-403.

Carver, C. S., & Scheier, M. F. (1998). *On the self-regulation of behavior*. Cambridge, UK: Cambridge University Press.

Danish, S. J., & Nellen, V. C. (1997). New role for the sport psychologist: Teaching life skills through sport to at risk youth. *Quest, 49*, 100-113.

French, K. E., & McPherson, S. L. (2003). Development of expertise in sport. In M. R. Weiss (Ed.), *Developmental sport and exercise psychology: A lifespan perspective*. (pp. 403-423) Morgantown, WV: Fitness Information Technology, Inc.

Gallagher, J. D., French, K. E., Thomas, K. T., & Thomas, J. R. (1996). Expertise in youth sport: Relations between knowledge and skill. In F. L. Smoll & R. E. Smith (Eds.), *Children and youth in sport: A biopsychosocial perspective* (pp. 338-358). Madison, WI: Brown & Benchmark.

Gould, D. (1982). Sport psychology in the 1980s: Status, direction, and challenge in youth sports research. *Journal of Sport Psychology, 4*, 203-218.

Gould, D. (1983). Developing psychological skills in young athletes. In N. Wood (Ed.), *Coaching science update* (pp. 4-10). Ottawa, Canada: Coaching Association of Canada.

Gould, D., & Chung, Y. (2003). Self-regulation skills in young, middle, and older adulthood. In M. R. Weiss (Ed.), *Developmental sport and exercise psychology: A lifespan perspective*. (pp. 383-402) Morgantown, WV: Fitness Information Technology, Inc.

Kane, T. D., Marks, M. A., Zaccaro, S. J., & Blair, V. (1996). Self-efficacy, personal goals, and wrestlers' self-regulation. *Journal of Sport & Exercise Psychology, 18*, 36-48.

Kirschenbaum, D. S. (1984). Self-regulation and sport psychology: Nurturing an emerging symbiosis. *Journal of Sport Psychology, 6*, 159-183.

Kirschenbaum, D. S. (1987). Self-regulation and sport performance. *Medicine and Science in Sports and Exercise, 19*, S106-S113.

Kirschenbaum, D. S., & Wittrock, D. A. (1984). Cognitive-behavioral interventions in sport: A self-regulatory perspective. In J. M. Silva & R. S. Weinberg (Eds.), *Psychological foundations of sport* (pp. 81-90). Champaign, IL: Human Kinetics.

Kitsantas, A., & Zimmerman, B. J. (1998). Self-regulation of motoric learning: A strategic cycle view. *Journal of Applied Sport Psychology, 10*, 220-239.

Kitsantas, A., Zimmerman, B. J., & Cleary, T. (2000). The role of observation and emulation in the development of athletic self-regulation. *Journal of Educational Psychology, 92*, 811-817.

Mace, F. C., Belfiore, P. J., & Shea, M. C. (1989). Operant theory and research on self-regulation. In B. J. Zimmerman & D. H. Schunk (Eds.), *Self-regulated learning and academic performance* (pp. 27-50). New York: Springer-Verlag.

Magill, R. A. (1999). *Motor learning: Concepts and applications* (6th ed.). Dubuque, IA: McGraw Hill.

McCullagh, P., & Weiss, M. R. (2002). Observational learning: The forgotten psychological method in sport psychology. In J. L. Van Raalte & B. W. Brewer (Eds.), *Exploring sport and exercise psychology* (2nd ed., pp. 131-149). Washington, DC: American Psychological Association.

McPherson, S. L. (1999). Expert-novice differences in performance skills and problem representations of youth and adults during tennis competition. *Research Quarterly for Exercise and Sport, 70,* 233-251.

Nevett, M. E., & French, K. E. (1997). The development of sport-specific planning, rehearsal, and updating of plans during defensive youth baseball game performance. *Research Quarterly for Exercise and Sport, 68,* 203-214.

Nicholls, J. G. (1989). *The competitive ethos and democratic education.* Cambridge, MA: Harvard University Press.

Orlick, T. (1982). Beyond excellence. In T. Orlick, J. T. Partington, & J. H. Salmela (Eds.), *Mental training for coaches and athletes* (pp. 1-7). Ottawa, Canada: Coaching Association of Canada.

Schunk, D. H. (1986). Verbalization and children's self-regulated learning. *Contemporary Educational Psychology, 11,* 347-369.

Schunk, D. H. (1987). Peer models and children's behavioral change. *Review of Educational Research, 57,* 149-174.

Schunk, D. H. (1989). Social cognitive theory and self-regulated learning. In B. J. Zimmerman & D. H. Schunk (Eds.), *Self-regulated learning and academic performance* (pp. 83-110). New York: Springer-Verlag.

Schunk, D. H. (1990). Goal setting and self-efficacy during self-regulated learning. *Educational Psychologist, 25,* 71-86.

Schunk, D. H. (1994). Self-regulation of self-efficacy and attributions in academic settings. In D. H. Schunk & B. J. Zimmerman (Eds.), *Self-regulation of learning and performance: Issues and educational applications* (pp. 3-21). Hillsdale, NJ: Erlbaum.

Schunk, D. H., & Zimmerman, B. J. (1994). *Self-regulation of learning and performance: Issues and educational applications.* Hillsdale, NJ: Erlbaum.

Vealey, R. S. (1988). Future directions in psychological skills training. *The Sport Psychologist, 2,* 318-336.

Vealey, R. S. (1994). Current status and prominent issues in sport psychology interventions. *Medicine and Science in Sports and Exercise, 26,* 495-502.

Weiss, M. R. (1991). Psychological skill development in children and adolescents. *The Sport Psychologist, 5,* 335-354.

Weiss, M. R. (1995). Children in sport: An educational model. In S. M. Murphy (Ed.), *Sport psychology interventions* (pp. 39-69). Champaign, IL: Human Kinetics.

Weiss, M. R., Ebbeck, V., & Rose, D. J. (1992). "Show and tell" in the gymnasium revisited: Developmental differences in modeling and verbal rehearsal effects on motor skill learning and performance. *Research Quarterly for Exercise and Sport, 63,* 292-301.

Weiss, M. R., & Klint, K. A. (1987). "Show and tell" in the gymnasium: An investigation of developmental differences in modeling and verbal rehearsal of motor skills. *Research Quarterly for Exercise and Sport, 58,* 234-241.

Weiss, M. R., McCullagh, P., Smith, A. L., & Berlant, A. R. (1998). Observational learning and the fearful child: Influence of peer models on swimming skill performance and psychological responses. *Research Quarterly for Exercise and Sport, 69,* 380-394.

Wrisberg, C. A., & Anshel, M. H. (1989). The effect of cognitive strategies on the free throw shooting performance of young athletes. *The Sport Psychologist, 3,* 95-104.

Zhang, L., Ma, Q., Orlick, T., & Zitzelsberger, L. (1992). The effect of mental-imagery training on performance enhancement with 7- to 10-year-old children. *The Sport Psychologist, 6,* 230-241.

Zimmerman, B. J. (1986). Development of self-regulated learning: Which are the key subprocesses? *Contemporary Educational Psychology, 16,* 307-313.

Zimmerman, B. J. (1989a). Models of self-regulated learning and academic achievement. In B. J. Zimmerman, & D. H. Schunk (Eds.), *Self-regulated learning and academic achievement: Theory, research, and practice* (pp. 1-25). New York: Springer-Verlag.

Zimmerman, B. J. (1989b). A social cognitive view of self-regulated academic learning. *Journal of Educational Psychology, 81,* 329-339.

Zimmerman, B. J. (1990). Self-regulating academic learning and achievement: The emergence of a social cognitive perspective. *Educational Psychology Review, 2,* 173-201.

Zimmerman, B. J. (1994). Dimensions of academic self-regulation: A conceptual framework for education. In D. H. Schunk & B. J. Zimmerman (Eds.), *Self-regulation of learning and performance: Issues and educational applications* (pp. 3-21). Hillsdale, NJ: Erlbaum.

Zimmerman, B. J. (2000). Attaining self-regulation: A social cognitive perspective. In M. Boekaerts, P. R. Pintrich, & M. Zeidner (Eds.), *Handbook of self-regulation* (pp. 13-39). San Diego, CA: Academic Press.

Zimmerman, B. J., & Kitsantas, A. (1996). Self-regulated learning of a motoric skill: The role of goal setting and self-monitoring. *Journal of Applied Sport Psychology, 10,* 60-75.

Zimmerman, B. J., & Kitsantas, A. (1997). Developmental phases in self-regulation: Shifting from process goals to outcome goals. *Journal of Educational Psychology, 89,* 26-36.

Zimmerman, B. J., & Kitsantas, A. (1999). Acquiring writing revision skill: Shifting from process to outcome self-regulatory goals. *Journal of Educational Psychology, 91,* 241-250.

Zimmerman, B. J., & Martinez-Pons, M. (1992). Perceptions of efficacy and strategy use in the self-regulation of learning. In D. H. Schunk & J. L. Meece (Eds.), *Student perceptions in the classroom* (pp. 185-207). Hillsdale, NJ: Erlbaum.

Zimmerman, B. J., & Schunk, D. H. (1989). *Self-regulated learning and academic achievement: Theory, research, and practice.* New York: Springer-Verlag.

ACKNOWLEDGMENT

I thank Donna Ehrenreich for her helpful comments and suggestions on an earlier draft of this chapter.

PART III
YOUNG, MIDDLE, AND OLDER ADULTHOOD

Chapter Ten

Seeing Isn't Always Believing: Self-Perceptions and Physical Activity Behaviors in Adults

Diane E. Whaley

How we see or think about ourselves as persons—who we are, who we want to be, what we believe we are capable of doing or not doing—is intimately tied to what we actually do. Self-perceptions, the most general term for these thoughts and feelings, are guided by our past and present experiences, as well as our hopes and dreams for what we would like to happen (or avoid happening) in the future. The evaluative component of the self-concept, referred to as self-esteem, has been implicated in an individual's ability to change behavior, as well as her or his resistance to change (Stein & Markus, 1996). As we age, how we think about ourselves and our abilities may not match our actual ability; that is, we may believe we are more or less capable than we really are. Maintaining a positive sense of self may require discounting our faults or comparing ourselves favorably to others "worse off" than we are. Thus, with regard to how we perceive ourselves, it is often the case that seeing is not *always* believing.

Physical activity is consistently related to increases in perceptions of the self and global measures of satisfaction such as quality of life (Alfermann & Stoll, 2000; Berger, 1996). Unfortunately, research has shown an inverse relationship between physical activity and age (Talbot, Metter, & Fleg, 2000). Although we know levels of physical activity decline with age, our understanding of this phenomenon remains elusive. Interestingly, research indicates that the most precipitous declines occur in adolescence, with a less steep but significant decline through young adulthood (18-29 years). In middle adulthood (30-64 years), patterns are relatively stable; then they begin to decline once again in older adulthood (Caspersen, Pereira, & Curran, 2000). For middle-aged and older persons, declines in health make physical activity even more imperative. Accumulating evidence suggests that early physical activity experience tracks into adult physical activity participation (Pate, Heath, Dowda, & Trost, 1996). Given the linkage between self-perceptions and physical activity behavior, understanding the self is essential to understanding variations among individuals in choosing an active lifestyle and exerting effort to maintain this lifestyle. The purpose of this chapter is to explore what we know about self-perceptions in the lives of young, middle-aged, and older adults. How do self-perceptions influence physical activity behavior? How do self-perceptions related to physical

Understanding the self is essential to understanding physical activity behavior.

activity change over the lifespan? Does the relationship between self-perceptions and physical activity change with increasing age? These questions will be addressed, reviewing selected theories and empirical research specific to or applicable to the physical domain. The chapter will conclude with a proposed model specific to adult physical activity behavior that integrates the theories and concepts highlighted throughout the chapter. In addition, future research directions will be offered and take-home messages discussed.

THE ISSUE OF TERMINOLOGY

Terms related to the self flourish in the psychology literature. Some of these are viewed as interchangeable, although Harter (1990a) points out that "constructs such as self-esteem, perceived competence, perceptions of control, self-efficacy, ego strength, (and) working model of self, are *not* interchangeable" (pp. 135). Thus, conceptual clarity is needed in addition to operational definitions. The following section is designed to help clarify the myriad of terms associated with research relating to the self. A table is included as a quick reference guide for readers (see Table 1).

Fox (1997) provides definitions for several of the most commonly used self-related terms. The most general term is *self-perceptions*, denoting all terms relating to statements about the self, from global to specific. Another umbrella term is the *self-system* (Markus, Cross, & Wurf, 1990), referring to the interrelated knowledge structures related to the self. Individuals participate in a lifelong project of maintaining and validating the integrity of their self-system (Fox, 1997). The *self-concept* (or self-conceptions) can be defined as the individual as known to the individual. It is the totality of the self, serving as an interpretive framework for an individual's experiences and providing meaning to events across time (Markus & Herzog, 1992). Self-conceptions have both cognitive and evaluative components (Rosenberg, 1979). The cognitive component is multidimensional, so that one can have multiple beliefs about the self, such as "I am a daughter," "I am a golfer," and "I am healthy." These beliefs can focus on aspects of the self such as values, abilities, and traits (McCrae & Costa, 1988).

Self-esteem is the evaluative component of the self-concept. It has been described as the degree to which an individual perceives him or herself to be an "OK" person (Gergen, 1971). Also referred to as *self-worth* (Harter, 1990a) or *self-evaluations*, these perceptions of the self can be positive or negative. Self-esteem is generally considered a global construct, referring to one's perceived overall worth as a person (Harter, 1990a; Rosenberg, 1986). It has also been studied at the domain level such as the social, academic and, important for this discussion, the physical domain.

Perceived competence is described by Fox (1997) as an assessment of ability that generalizes across a particular domain. Research by Harter and her colleagues (Harter & Pike, 1984; Messer & Harter, 1986; Neeman & Harter, 1986) has indicated that the number of domains articulated and differentiated increase with age. For example, Messer and Harter found 11 distinct domains in an adult's life, including 2 domains directly related to physical activity, athletic abilities, and physical appearance. *Physical self-worth* has been further subdivided by Fox (1990) into components of physical attributes (physical appearance, strength, conditioning) and athletic competence. Others (Harter, 1990a; Weiss & Ebbeck, 1996) recognize that assessments of one's ability can be made at the domain (e.g., physical) or subdomain (e.g., strength) level. Perceptions of competence are considered critical to individual functioning throughout life (H. Markus et al., 1990). A closely associated construct is *sport-confidence*, defined by Vealey (1986) as "the degree of certainty individuals possess about their ability to be successful in sport" (p. 55). Perceived competence will be discussed in more detail throughout this chapter.

Identity is "the integration of beliefs, values, self-perceptions, and behaviors into a consistent, coherent, and recognizable self-package" (Fox, 1997, p. xii). In adult development, identity refers to an individual's sense of self over time, incorporating the domains of physical, psychological, and social functioning (Whitbourne & Collins, 1998). In turn, one's sense of self is influenced by the social context (Paoletti, 1998). In the physical domain, having an identity as an exerciser has been shown to promote future exercise behavior (Kendzierski, Furr, & Schiavoni, 1998; Whaley & Ebbeck, 2002), although having an exclusive identity as an athlete may put those individuals at risk for impaired decision making (Murphy, Petitpas, & Brewer, 1996). Identity has been an important area of aging research in psychology, but has not been extensively explored in sport and particularly in exercise contexts. In this chapter, we will discuss the potential for research on identity to help us better understand how individuals can use exercise as a coping strategy for dealing with the deficits often confronted in old age.

With all the cognitive information available to individuals, mechanisms are needed that help individuals decipher, code, and organize that information. Schemata, conceptualized by Markus (1977), are internal cognitive structures that allow individuals to encode and represent that information. Self-schemata are cognitive structures specific to the self, derived from past experiences that are regarded as important to the individual. Self-schemata can be general representations of the self ("I am an exerciser") or deal with a specific event ("last week I felt comfortable joining the exercise class"). Self-schemas help an individual predict his or her future behavior in a given domain (Cross & Markus, 1994). In this way, they serve as a foundation for future-oriented cognitive representations, or what Markus and Nurius (1986) call "possible selves." Self-schemata and possible selves will be explored in detail in the sections that

TABLE 1
Glossary of Self-Relevant Terms

Term (similar terms)	Key references	Brief definition
Self-Perceptions (Self-System)	Fox (1997); Markus et al. (1990)	General term for all statements about the self; interrelated knowledge about the self.
Self-Concept	Rosenberg (1979); Markus & Herzog (1992)	Individual as known to the individual; totality of the self.
Self-Esteem (Self-Worth)	Gergen (1971); Harter (1990)	Evaluative component of the self; can be global or domain specific.
Perceived competence (Sport-Confidence)	Fox (1997); Harter (1990)	Assessment of abilities; can be made at domain or subdomain level.
Identity	Fox (1997); Whitbourne & Collins (1998)	Integration of values, beliefs, and behaviors into a coherent sense of self.
Self-Schemata	Markus (1977)	Internal cognitive structures that allow individual to code and organize information about the self.
Possible selves	Markus & Nurius (1986)	Future-oriented self-conceptions.
Self-Efficacy	Bandura (1997)	Belief in one's ability to accomplish a task successfully.

follow as theoretical constructs applicable to the study of adult self-perceptions in the physical domain.

At the most specific level, *self-efficacy* is defined as beliefs in one's ability to successfully accomplish a specific task (Bandura, 1997). Given its specificity, this construct is the most amenable to change. Its utility in research of adult exercise behavior is recognized here as influential in the study of adult self-perceptions (McAuley & Rudolph, 1995).

Many other self-terms abound in the literature. Clearly, the multiplicity of terms can create confusion. However, a few issues are almost universal. First, the self is multidimensional, being composed of multiple components, or domains (Harter, 1999; Shavelson & Bolus, 1982). These domains contribute toward an overall or global sense of self, although not in a simple additive fashion. Associated with this is the issue of specificity. *Global self-esteem* is considered to be a distinct construct, measured not by combining domains but with its own set of questions pertinent to an overall judgment of one's worth (Harter, 1990b; Rosenberg, 1979). Although this is empirically important, it can make the job of assessing how or why an intervention is successful difficult. Thus, measuring domain-specific judgments of ability or adequacy (e.g., perceived physical ability, perceived appearance) allows the researcher to measure change in a specific context of one's life and to measure the influence of that same intervention on global self-esteem as well.

There is also general acceptance of the notion of the self as both stable and dynamic (Baltes, Lindenberger, & Staudinger, 1998; McCrae & Costa, 1988; Ruvolo & Markus, 1992). That is, although an individual may have a stable "core self," aspects of the self are subject to change, depending on the presence or absence of a variety of mediating factors such as social support or a significant life event (Ruvolo & Markus). The component of the self more likely to exhibit change is referred to as the *working self*. Thus, although the self is partly a social product shaped by societal expectations and norms, the issue of choice enables an individual to take a number of different roads. It is only fitting that the self be studied over the course of the lifespan, so that we might see how changes in individuals' lived experience and context influence the views people have of themselves. First, though, it is important to more explicitly state why the study of self-perceptions in the physical domain is warranted.

> Aspects of the self are subject to change according to environmental factors like social support or a significant life event.

WHY STUDY SELF-PERCEPTIONS?

Over the past decade, research on the self has proliferated, although the focus of this research has been more descriptive than explanatory. Harter (1990b) addressed this issue when she pondered why the zeal that researchers display in studying the self had not been matched by an equally aggressive program to discover the precise role the self may play. The importance of studying the self becomes clear when the relationship between self-related constructs and various behavioral and affective outcomes are explored. Theoretical assumptions for the role of self-esteem, self-concept, and self-schema have more recently been forwarded, and empirical evidence gathered with regard to the importance of the self in the functioning of adults. These issues have centered on the relationship of the self with performance, successful aging, affect, and health behaviors.

The relationship between self-perceptions and physical activity performance has been extensively explored in adult populations. Studies have examined how self-related constructs such as perceived physical competence (e.g., Sonstroem, Speliotis, & Fava, 1992), self-efficacy (e.g., Garcia & King, 1991), and self-schemata (Kendzierski, 1990) increase participation in physical activity behavior. These studies consistently show that higher perceptions of one's

Studies show that exercise habits remain consistent through middle age and begin to decline in later years.

ability in the physical domain, as well as a stronger, more defined schemata for physical activity behavior, are related to higher actual participation rates.

There is also considerable evidence that self-perceptions directly and indirectly affect successful aging (Markus & Herzog, 1992). Successful aging is positively related to the ability of the individual to plan and develop friendships, to select age-friendly environments, and to optimize the use of certain skills while compensating for the loss of others. These processes can be directly linked to a view of oneself in the past, present, and future. For example, a middle-aged tennis player who has had success in his sport and views himself as a tennis player is likely to do things that increase the possibility that his participation will continue. He may join appropriate clubs where he can meet others who share his interest. He is also likely to do or say things that support his positive view of himself such as "I'm pretty good for my age." This perspective is supported by Whitbourne and Collins (1998), who found that the ability of adults to create positive self-referential statements contributed to an individual's emotional well-being. This type of adaptive behavior is also highlighted by Baltes et al. (1998), who state that although biological functioning decreases with age, this negative trajectory is less debilitating to the sense of self than it is to cognitive functioning (e.g., memory). The self and personality serve a "lifelong orchestrating function" (Baltes et al., p. 1112), monitoring gains and losses and allocating resources as needed to optimize functioning. Critical to this process is the availability of self-regulatory mechanisms, or strategies employed by the individual to meet the challenges of experience that might threaten his or her sense of self.

In addition to actual performance and successful aging, a number of findings have highlighted the impact of the self on affective reactions, both negative and positive. Harter (1992) points out that level of self-esteem is implicated in one's mood, ranging from cheerful to depressed. Negative self-evaluations have been implicated in depressive symptoms in children and adolescents (Renouf & Harter, 1990), and Higgins (1987) believes that the *discrepancy* between one's actual self and one's ideal self produces dejection-related emotions such as depression or agitation-related emotions such as fear. In college students, Sonstroem and Potts (1996) found that physical self-concept was positively related to life adjustment. In adults and older adults, positive affect is generally conceptualized as well-being, quality of life, and enhanced mood. Much of this research has related the effects of exercise on these positive affective variables, with a number of studies showing positive relationships (Alfermann & Stoll, 2000; for reviews see Berger, 1996; Biddle, 1995: Fox, 2000; McAuley & Rudolph, 1995). In all, empirical research points to a robust and positive relationship between self-perceptions and affective reactions.

Finally, across domains, studies have consistently implicated the role of self-perceptions in the initiation and maintenance of a wide variety of health behaviors, from cessation of smoking and alcohol use to weight control and exercise (Markus & Herzog, 1992; Prochaska & Velicer, 1997; Stein & Markus, 1996). Stein and Markus explored in detail how the self is involved in the process of behavioral change, as well as an individual's resistance to change. Thus, there is ample reason to pursue the role of self-perceptions in physical activity behavior.

DOES THE SELF INFLUENCE BEHAVIOR OR VICE VERSA?

Various models have attempted to explain the relationship between self-perceptions and physical activity behavior. Sonstroem and Morgan (1989) created one of the first models specifically linking self-esteem with exercise involvement. Their exercise and self-esteem model posits that the effects of physical training generalize to global self-esteem (Sonstroem, 1997). In this view, the actual process of participation in exercise (or conceivably, other forms of physical activity) influences self-perceptions in a hierarchical manner, beginning at the specific level of efficacy beliefs and eventually generalizing to physical self-perceptions and global self-esteem. Because improvement in self-esteem is attributed to the learning of skills and abilities as a result of participation in physical activity, this perspective is referred to as a *skill development* view. A number of studies have supported the exercise and self-esteem model (Sonstroem, Harlow, & Josephs, 1994; Sonstroem, Harlow, & Salisbury, 1993).

An alternative view is represented in the *self-enhancement* perspective, favored by Harter (1985) and Fox (1990, 1997). This view maintains that individuals are motivated to maintain or enhance their sense of self and that they will participate in activities where they can display their competencies. More specifically, Harter (1985) posited that the discrepancy between perceptions of competence in a given domain and the *importance* the individual attaches to that domain, in combination with the level and quality of social support received from others, affects one's level of self-worth. Levels of self-worth then directly impact affective reactions and indirectly influence motivated behavior. Although there is considerable support for the relationships among perceived competence, the role of significant others, self-worth, and behavior (see Weiss & Ferrer-Caja, 2002), the impact of importance attached to domains is less well defined. In fact, Marsh (1994; Marsh & Sonstroem, 1995) found no support for the "importance of importance" (p. 306). However, Harter (1986) maintains that if a domain *is* deemed important, and individuals perceive themselves to have *low* competence in that domain, then it will negatively affect their self-esteem and, ultimately, their behavior. For instance, an adult participating in a recreational tennis league with low perceived athletic competence may be unaffected with regard to his or her overall sense of self if this domain is considered of low importance. In this case, the individual is able to discount this domain and replace it with perceptions of competence in other domains (occupation, social). However, if the same individual has low perceived competence in sport and that domain is deemed important, it is likely to influence his or her sense of self, affect, and ultimately behavior.

Intuitively, the discrepancy between domain-specific importance and perceptions of competence seems applicable to exercise behavior in adults, but rarely has this issue been examined in the physical domain. Often, older adults acknowledge the importance of exercise, but because of little prior experience with structured exercise settings, they have low perceived competence for those activities. Thus, this framework may aid our understanding of why an adult may be inclined to exercise but fail to follow through and importantly how practitioners might facilitate the transition from intention to behavior. For example, interventions might directly target perceptions of competence in the physical domain as a preliminary step in encouraging adults with limited prior experience to exercise. It is also important to recognize that psychological well-being and physical activity behaviors, as consequences of self-conceptions, are not isolated entities (Markus & Herzog, 1992). Thus, research is needed that not only looks at relationships among these constructs, but that also takes into account the social context and the impact of activity choice on self-conceptions in adult populations.

THEORIES APPLICABLE TO ADULT PHYSICAL ACTIVITY BEHAVIOR

A number of theories have been forwarded in an effort to describe, explain, and predict physical activity behavior in adults. Some of these, such as social cognitive theory (Bandura, 1986), the theories of reasoned action and planned behavior (Ajzen, 1985; Ajzen & Fishbein, 1980), and, more recently, the transtheoretical model (Prochaska & DiClemente, 1986) applied specifically to the exercise domain (e.g., Marcus, Eaton, Rossi, & Harlow, 1994) have received empirical support and have helped researchers and practitioners *begin* to understand the complex process of physical activity behavior. Texts by Dishman (1994), Fox (1997), and O'Brien Cousins (1998) review these theories with regard to physical activity behavior in a variety of populations and age groups.

Instead of focusing on those theoretical constructs, in the spirit of Berger (1996), who encouraged researchers to "pursue new approaches to old questions. . ." (p. 344), I have chosen to focus on a few underused theories and concepts that afford an alternative view. The theories to be described directly address the role of the self in behavior and how the self-system is involved in the development, maintenance, and breakdown of competence (H. Markus et al., 1990). These theories address the specific representations of the self that characterize and give rise to feelings of efficacy, competence, and control and provide a mechanism through which they affect behavior (Ruvolo & Markus, 1992). Recognizing the need for consistency and change in beliefs and behaviors across time, each theory is developmentally appropriate to adults and older adults. Although not widely studied in the physical activity context, they have expanded our understanding of other health-related behaviors. One reason these theories may be underused is a lack of understanding regarding their applicability to physical activity behavior and in interventions designed to increase physical activity. These three distinct yet interrelated topics are self-schema theory (H. Markus, 1977), the construct of possible selves (Markus & Nurius, 1986), and self-discrepancy theory (Higgins, 1987).

Self-Schema Theory

Given the enormous amount of information available to individuals at any given time, there must be mechanisms that help people decipher, code, and organize that information. Because individuals attend to specific portions of the information available to them, this selection process is assumed to be deliberate. Markus (1977) hypothesized internal cognitive structures, or schemata, that allow individuals to encode and represent information. Information that deals specifically with the self (rather than others) is referred to as *self-schemata*. According to Markus, self-schemata incorporate patterns of behavior recognized by the individual. That information is processed and then used as a basis for future decisions or predictions about the self.

| Schemas are the basis for cognitive representations of oneself in the future. | To be "schematic" for a particular attribute, the individual must view the behavior as *descriptive* of her or him and consider the attribute to be *important* to her or his self-image (Kendzierski, 1994). Measurement is accomplished through the use of a questionnaire first developed by |

Markus (1977) and extended to the physical domain by Kendzierski (1988). Participants are asked to indicate on an 11-point scale whether key phrases about the behavior in question are descriptive of them and then whether this same phrase is important to the image they have of themselves. In the case of exercise, the typical phrases would be "someone who is physically active," "someone who keeps in shape," and "physically active." An individual who indicates that at least 2 of the 3 descriptors are extremely descriptive and extremely important (at least an 8 on the 11-point scale) would be categorized as schematic for exercise. Nonschematic individuals are those who classify 2 of the 3 descriptors as extremely nondescriptive but extremely important, and aschematic individuals include those who rate 2 of the 3 descriptors as moderately descriptive and not important to their sense of self. In this way, individuals can be classified and their behaviors compared across classifications.

Several studies have supported the existence of self-schemata in a variety of domains such as body weight (Markus, Hamill, & Sentis, 1987), Type A and Type B behavior patterns (Strube et al., 1986), and exercise (Yin & Boyd, 2000). In the case of exercise, individuals schematic for exercise see themselves as exercisers, and nonschematic individuals see themselves as nonexercisers. Aschematic individuals differ from both in that they are likely exercising but do not view that behavior as important to their sense of self. Although Markus believed that self-schemata had an effect on behavior, there was little empirical evidence for that connection until recently (Kendzierski, 1994). For example, in a series of investigations with college-aged men and women, Kendzierski (1988, 1990) found significant differences between individuals' schematic for exercise and those nonschematic and aschematic for exercise with regard to actual physical activity levels and intentions to exercise in the future. Specifically, individuals with an exerciser self-schema exercised more than nonschematics or aschematics did and predicted they were more likely to engage in future behaviors that encouraged exercise.

As a follow-up to Kendzierski's studies, Estabrooks and Courneya (1997) further explored the relationship between self-schema, intention, and exercise behavior. They found support for the contention that exerciser schematics intended to exercise and exercised more often than either nonschematics or aschematics did. Further, partial evidence was found for the moderating effect of exercise self-schema on the exercise intention-behavior relationship. That is, correlations between intention to exercise and exercise behavior were higher for exerciser schematics than for nonschematics, but not higher than for aschematics, as would be hypothesized. Recently Yin and Boyd (2000) found support for the link between having an exercise schema and exercise behavior in a college-aged population and further showed that schematics differed from other groups on the cognitive-motivational determinants of self-efficacy and perceptions of physical fitness. Sheeran and Orbell (2000), using a longitudinal design, found that self-schemas moderated the intention-behavior relationship in college exercisers. Exerciser schematics were more likely to enact their intentions to exercise compared to non- and aschematics, and the importance dimension of self-schema was responsible for the moderator effect.

Although this discussion of self-schema theory has focused on cognitive processes, it is a social cognitive approach. Markus (1990) states that attention to the context is critical, acknowledging that "while hypothesized to reside inside one individual's head or heart, self-schemas are in large measure interpersonal achievements" (p. 249). By this, she means that what we deem important and descriptive of us is often influenced by the perceptions and opinions of others. The influence of the social context on older adults' schemas for exercise was investigated by Whaley and Ebbeck (2002). Among 13 older adults who had been exercising for an average of 28 months, only 6 were schematic for exercise. Of the remaining 7, all but one rated their exercise behavior as very important to their sense of self, but only moderately descriptive (i.e., did not fall into any of the three exercise self-schemata classifications). When asked why they did not consider themselves exercisers, they responded that exercisers "were younger than they" or "exercised all the time." For these individuals, their exercise behavior did not necessarily subscribe to societal perceptions of what an exerciser looks like, so they preferred to use other terms such as "I am physically inclined." Further research is needed to clarify the role of schemas in physical activity contexts across the lifespan, with particular attention to cognitive processes and social contexts.

The Concept of Possible Selves

According to Cross and Markus (1994), being schematic for exercise best predicts future behavior in that domain. In this way, schemata serve as the foundation for cognitive representations of oneself in the future. These future-oriented self-conceptions have been termed possible selves (Markus & Nurius, 1986). Possible selves can be either positive images of oneself in the future, called hoped-for selves, or negative, feared selves that the individual works actively to avoid becoming. Nurius (1991) states that "the ability to construct, invoke, and sustain possible selves may be one critical determinant of actual goal achievement" (p. 243). If this is true, then possible selves are clearly applicable to sport and exercise behavior.

Because possible selves represent what an individual would like to become or avoid becoming, they are particularly pertinent to health-related behaviors. Hooker (1992; Hooker & Kaus, 1992, 1994) examined possible selves across the lifespan and found that adults were more likely to have possible selves related to health than were college students, and these health-related selves were positively related to health-enhancing behaviors (i.e., exercising, having regular medical checkups, practicing good nutrition). In the physical domain, Whaley (2003) investigated the possible selves of middle-aged women across a range of exercise behaviors, from inactive to long-term exercisers. Results indicated that exercisers and nonexercisers differed in the content of their possible selves. For example, nonexercisers cited hoped-for and feared possible selves related to body image (e.g., "to be trimmer," "become very overweight") more often than their exercising counterparts did. Exercisers were more likely to cite possible selves related to the physical self (e.g., "to be active," "to lose mobility"). This is intriguing because one might expect that an individual with a possible feared self such as "myself as overweight, unhealthy, or dependent on others" would be more likely to exercise to avoid this self's coming to fruition. However, we can begin to understand this contradiction by examining the statements made with regard to these possible selves. Findings indicated that the possible selves of exercisers were considered more important, and the individuals felt more capable (self-efficacy) and more likely of achieving those possible selves (outcome expectancy) than did nonexercisers. This finding illustrates an important issue related to the construct of possible selves. Although the presence of a possible self is necessary for behavior, it is not sufficient. The possible self must be associated with self-regulatory strategies (i.e., an action plan) in order for that self to be realized.

Research indicates that well-conceived and complex possible selves are most conducive to behavior (Stein & Markus, 1996), and these selves must be accessible to the individual. Imagery manipulations can increase the accessibility of specific possible selves, thereby changing behavior (Ruvolo & Markus, 1992). In addition, possible selves are most likely to be realized when they are tied to established current self-schemata (Stein & Markus, 1996). In the case of the exercisers in Whaley (2003), in addition to having strong self-regulatory behaviors (i.e., self-efficacy, outcome expectancy), it is likely that their possible selves were consistent with existing schemata for exercise. Together, these findings suggest an important role for possible selves in exercise behavior change.

A large body of research supports the utility of possible selves in changing behavior such as delinquency (Oyserman & Saltz, 1993), academic achievement (Leondari, Syngollitou, & Kiosseoglou, 1998), career counseling (Meara, Day, Chalk, & Phelps, 1998), and completion of a unique writing task (Ruvolo & Markus, 1992). Findings show that individuals can be guided through the process of developing or expanding possible selves to encourage a particular behavior. For example, it is appropriate to expect that an individual who desires to maintain a possible self of "independent" in old age can be taught self-regulatory strategies that make attainment of this self more likely to occur in the future. In the shorter term, eliciting well-defined and fully developed possible selves may help an elite athlete find a more structured path toward achieving a goal. Specifically, a possible self of "me winning an Olympic medal" can be made more attainable by developing specific actions and pathways toward realization of that possible self. Thus, possible selves provide a means of *achieving* goals and contain the emotional weight and value necessary to convert a "want to" to a "can do."

Self-Discrepancy Theory

To this point, I have discussed various aspects of the self, highlighting the temporal component of selves (past, present, and future) as well as various domains of the self (actual, hoped for, feared). What happens when various aspects of the self conflict; that is, when there is a discrepancy between what an individual would like to do and what the individual believes a significant other desires that person to do? Many theorists have proposed the need for consistency within the self to create a unified self-concept (Harter, 1986; Markus & Nurius, 1987; Scheier & Carver, 1982). Self-discrepancy theory (Higgins, 1987) is a candidate for understanding the emotional consequences of incompatible self-beliefs with adults in the physical domain.

According to Higgins (1987), there are three basic domains of the self: (a) the actual self, (b) the ideal self, and (c) the ought self. The actual self represents the self either you or someone else believes you actually possess. The ideal self is your representation of attributes that either you or someone else would *like* you to possess (i.e., goals, aspirations, or wishes). The ought self are representations of what you or others believe you *should*, or ought, to possess (i.e., duties, expectations, and responsibilities). The three domains of the self can be judged from two different points of view, known as standpoints: your own or that of a significant other (parent, spouse, closest friend, coach). Combining the domains of the self with the standpoints yields six basic types of self-state representations: actual/own, actual/other, ideal/own, ideal/other, ought/own, and ought/other. The first two constitute what we typically mean by the self-concept (actual self with own standpoint and actual self with other standpoint), and the remaining four represent self-guides. These self-guides can be thought of as either self-directed standards or acquired guides for behavior. For instance, an athlete may be motivated to achieve an ideal self as an Olympic performer she has imposed on herself (an ideal/own self-guide). People are assumed to differ in which self-guide they are most motivated to achieve, so that some individuals may focus on an ideal self, whereas others may possess only ought self-guides (Higgins, 1987).

Regardless of individuals' self-guides, we are all motivated to strive for congruence between our self-concept (who we are) and our personally relevant self-guides (who we or others would like or think we are). An inability to achieve this congruence is believed to result in specific types of negative emotional and motivational problems, or vulnerabilities. To illustrate the need for congruence, consider an exerciser whose actual self (as judged by himself) is one of a busy but sedentary individual. The self-guide deemed important to this individual is of the ought/own variety, in this case represented by a self-guide of himself as physically active. The lack of congruence between who he is and who he feels he ought to be with regard to physical activity is sure to raise negative feelings. Self-discrepancy theory goes the next step to predict the *nature* of these negative feelings.

Negative emotional states come in two varieties: (a) the absence of positive outcomes, associated with dejection-related emotions (e.g., disappointment, sadness), and (b) the presence of negative outcomes, associated with agitation-related emotions (e.g., fear, aggression). Dejection-related emotions are likely to result from discrepancies between actual and ideal self-structures, where as agitation-related emotions emanate from actual-ought discrepancies. In the exerciser described above, the actual/ought discrepancy should result in agitation-related emotions. He may be frustrated at not being able to find the time or motivation to begin exercising. A second example highlights the usefulness of this theory in a therapeutic setting. Perhaps one is counseling a college athlete who presents with dejection-related emotions such as dissatisfaction with current level of play. These emotions are likely the result of a discrepancy of the actual/own: ideal/own variety. This could occur when the athlete's current level of play (as judged by herself) does not match her own ideal aspirations. Thus, disappointment and dissatisfaction are a likely result. Compare this with the same athlete, whose discrepancy is between her actual level of play and that which she perceives a significant other (e.g., the coach, parents) has. In this case, the individual is vulnerable to feelings of shame or embarrassment. Similarly, discrepancies in other self-states are likely to result in agitation-related emotions such as fear, guilt, or self-contempt. Thus, for the skilled professional working with this athlete, knowledge of the types of discrepancies available may afford a window for understanding emotions and subsequent behaviors.

There is considerable evidence for the utility of self-discrepancy theory. A number of studies have examined the influence of discrepancies on depression and other indicators of emotional distress (e.g., Bruch, Rivet, & Laurenti, 2000; Gonnerman, Parker, Lavine, & Huff, 2000). Other studies have examined the role of discrepant self-views on body image and eating disorders in college women (Snyder, 1997); the prediction of anxiety and guilt in college students from ought, ideal, and feared self-discrepancies (Carver, Lawrence, & Scheier, 1999); and the impact of self-discrepancies in appearance on peer relationships in children (Cobb, Cohen, Houston, & Rubin, 1998). In all of these studies, discrepancies were found to influence affective reactions and subsequent behavior. In a recent review of discrepancy theory research, Higgins (1999) underscored the importance of examining not only the discrepancy itself but also its magnitude, accessibility, relevance to the context, and importance to the individual.

The framework of self-discrepancy theory allows for a further examination of the role of emotion in sport. Lazarus (2000) has called for renewed interest and clarification of the role that emotions play in competitive athletic performance. He urges sport psychologists to consider stress and emotion as a single topic and advises us to use discrete emotion categories in order to improve our understanding of the role emotion plays in sport performance. Emotion is involved in exercise participation and adherence as well, and this framework could be used to further examine how we might design more effective interventions that optimize affective reactions to exercise participation. In addition, Higgins (1987) called for investigations to examine how the theory might predict *positive* emotions (i.e., the absence of discrepancies) and how our beliefs regarding the likelihood of ever meeting our self-guides influence our behavior. These questions are similar to those posed by researchers examining possible selves. The discrepancy between hoped-for and feared selves, or between current and hoped-for selves, is also believed to result in motivational problems (see, for example, Oyserman, Gant, & Ager, 1995). To date, little research has addressed these issues, particularly in the physical domain. As in many other areas of self-perception research, there is a dearth of information for populations past college-aged individuals. These theories could be helpful for practitioners and researchers in the area of lifespan sport and exercise psychology, a point to be addressed later in this chapter.

Maintaining a Positive Sense of Self over the Adult Lifespan

Now that theoretical models of the self applicable to adults in the physical activity context have been examined, it is time to discuss perhaps the most significant challenge to adults engaged in physical activity. Lifespan developmentalists and gerontologists have explored in depth how people maintain a sense of competence over the lifespan, in the face of actual and perceived declines in abilities. This issue will be addressed in the following section, focusing on how the self adapts to changing life conditions that can threaten one's current sense of self and, ultimately, one's level of physical activity.

Developmental Tasks

Over the years, a number of theories have been forwarded that look at the life course as a series of developmental tasks. In young adulthood, these tasks include such issues as completing one's education, committing to a career, marriage, and parenthood (H. Markus et al., 1990). Successfully meeting these tasks requires the development and maintenance of a sense of competence in those tasks. Although the tasks of young adulthood are monumental and require major shifts in priorities, they are by and large positive transitions. Throughout middle age, changes are less dramatic and competencies, fairly stable. Even in the face of a major life event (e.g., losing one's job or having a health problem), competence can be maintained by the existence of a stable core of friends, family, work colleagues, or social structures.

Neugarten (1977, 1979) has described the existence of age norms, or a social clock, superimposed on a biological clock, that regulates changes in behavior and self-perceptions over time. Developmental tasks take into consideration physical maturation, cultural beliefs and norms, and individual differences. Whether one is "on time" or "off time" determines any changes in self-evaluations. This framework has been tested in order to examine long-term motivation in adult women (Helson & McCabe, 1994; Helson, Mitchell, & Moane, 1984). Helson and her colleagues have taken into account multiple positive trajectories for development, going beyond the gender-stereotyped tasks described in the original conceptualization (i.e., graduate from college, get married, raise children). This longitudinal project is intriguing in that it has provided a plethora of information regarding the types of tasks deemed important for individuals in their 20s, 30s, 40s, and beyond, and how these tasks affect identity and behavior.

> Successfully accomplishing life's tasks requires the development and maintenance of a sense of competence at those tasks.

The idea of the social clock has potential to inform researchers about changing attitudes regarding physical activity involvement over the life course. For example, Helson and McCabe (1994) believe that the social-clock concept may be most important for young adulthood, when the transition from family and school to independent adulthood, with all of the responsibilities inherent in that transition, takes place. This transition clearly affects physical activity behavior, when priorities shift and previously active young adults choose to use their time to work and raise families. Recognition of these changes may facilitate interventions by portraying physical activity behavior as a way to take responsibility and become an independent, healthy adult. It also suggests that life tasks change as we mature and that these life transitions require us to change, adapt, or perhaps abandon aspects of ourselves once considered to be critical to a sense of self. For instance, an athlete who completes her competitive college career will need to change the priority of sport when she enters the workforce. This should not mean that physical activity behavior ends. Instead, the transition signals a move to other activities consistent with the individual's sense of self but reflective of the new priorities and time constraints of this new life task.

In older adulthood, changing life tasks and major life events can pose a considerable threat to one's sense of self and perceptions of control. Retirement, loss of family members, changing dynamics of power, and diminishment of physical abilities all have the potential to negatively affect the older adult's self-concept. How, then, do older adults maintain a positive sense of self? Why is it that most older adults rate their health as good or excellent, even to the point of distorting or denying reality (Coleman, 1996)? Gerontologists have addressed these questions under the framework of successful aging (Baltes & Baltes, 1990; Coleman, 1996). That is, how do individuals maximize the gains or desirable goals or outcomes of aging, while minimizing the losses or undesirable goals or outcomes? Various adaptive strategies have been discussed, including maintaining previous patterns of behavior, purposefully selecting behaviors that the individual can successfully complete, or changing personal perspectives regarding what is desirable or undesirable for that individual. These adaptive strategies will be reviewed next.

Continuity Theory

Atchley (1989, 1994) assumes that adult development is continuous and that older adults are resilient to physical, mental, and social losses. Continuity theory states that individuals adapt to aging by maintaining patterns of ideas and actions that were constructive for them in the past. For example, an individual may deal with retirement from work by remaining active in that field through volunteer activities or as a member of a board. It concentrates the individual's energies in familiar domains where practice can offset declines or minimize the effects of aging. Whereas *internal continuity* refers to the persistence of a personal structure of ideas based on memory, *external continuity* relates to living in familiar environments and interacting with familiar people. Developing, maintaining, and preserving adaptive capacity are principal goals in this theory (Atchley, 1994). In the physical domain, we might see this theory in action with professional athletes who "retire" from their sport only to begin a new career as a coach or television announcer. At the recreational level, continuity theory would hypothesize that an individual who has been successful in sport might look for opportunities to display his or her competence in similar environments as the individual ages. The individual's participation in a recreational and then a senior league allows for the maintenance of both internal and external continuity. Research is needed that examines the relative contribution of internal and external continuity in maintaining positive perceptions of the self, as well as examining what constitutes legitimate forms of transitional activity for various populations (e.g., college sport participants, masters athletes).

Selective Optimization With Compensation

The model of selective optimization with compensation (Baltes & Baltes, 1990) follows nicely from continuity theory, postulating a process to explain how individuals deal with the inevitable losses in competence and objective abilities with age. It is a general approach that can be tailored to domains of functioning, from work competence to physical skills. The model recognizes that various antecedent conditions, both biological and cultural, affect development and attainment of goals. It further postulates that a process of goal *selection* occurs whereby the individual, either consciously or unconsciously, selects a limited number of goals from a population of possibilities. From here, a process of *optimization* occurs. Optimization focuses on the goal-related strategies needed to achieve the goal. *Compensation* involves the acquisition of new goals, priorities, or strategies to replace those that have been lost. An example will help illustrate this model. Take the case of a master's track athlete. This individual may have as her goal to remain competitive in road races. Strategies she may use to help her attain this goal may include optimizing the context (i.e., only running when the weather is favorable, running shorter rather than longer races) or her goal structure (i.e., being competitive in her age group rather than an overall finish). Compensation is a natural outcome of selection. As one puts more energy and resources into a goal, other goals become less likely to be achieved. In the case of our master's athlete, allocating more time to training and being more selective in which races to run may necessitate a compensation in the overall number of races to be tackled over the course of a race season. Compensation can also apply directly to decrements in an individual's level of functioning. For example, different shoes or orthotics may compensate for physical changes.

Langley and Knight (1999) used a narrative approach to examine how one older adult athlete maintained a positive sense of self through his participation in sport over the life course. They concluded that the participant's sport participation could best be understood within the framework of continuity theory and eloquently described the process of selective optimization with compensation that occurred as a natural part of the aging process. For example, changes across sport (switching from baseball to tennis) and within sport (singles play to doubles) were made in order to adapt to changing abilities. This study represents a model for examining self-perceptions and sport over the lifespan, using a research strategy (i.e., narrative case study) underemployed in the field of sport and exercise psychology.

Identity Assimilation and Accommodation

Similar to the selective optimization with compensation model but specific to physical identity and aging are the processes of identity assimilation and accommodation forwarded by Whitbourne (1996; Whitbourne & Collins, 1998). In this view, individuals are believed to view changes in their bodies according to their current view of themselves with regard to appearance, competence, and health. Here the adage "you're only as old as you feel" is very fitting. For example, an individual with a youthful self-image accompanied by positive attributes about that image will be able to discount or undervalue experiences that threaten the self. For example, an individual who "feels young" may experience a good deal of pain following an exercise bout, but if he has a well-developed schema as "young" (or "not-old"; see Whaley & Ebbeck, 2002), then he is likely to discount the pain as a pulled muscle or some other transitory condition rather than a reflection of an age-related decline. Heidrich and Ryff (1993) found evidence for individuals being able to sustain a youthful view of themselves for many years, even in the face of declining health.

Eventually, it becomes increasingly difficult to maintain this youthful self-image. At this point, the process of identity accommodation occurs, as the individual incorporates age-related changes into his self-conceptions. Taking our exerciser example into accommodation, he may now attribute the pain from exercise as "earned" from years of activity. A balance between the processes of assimilation and accommodation is most effective in maintaining a stable sense of self. Too much assimilation can lead to serious health risks, as in the case when an individual ignores pain. Too much accommodation can lead to a premature assessment of oneself as "old," taking on all of the societal baggage attached to this label. For example, an otherwise healthy but sedentary older adult may fear beginning an exercise program, because "old people" can get hurt exercising.

Rescaling Goals

Another way older adults maintain a successful view of themselves as competent and in control is by rescaling goals (Brandtstädter & Rothermund, 1994). This view capitalizes on the interplay between perceptions of control in particular domains of life and the importance associated with that domain. Traditionally, developmental and gerontological research assumed that this accommodation to change brings with it a decrease in a sense of control over one's life. On the contrary, Brandtstädter and others (Baltes & Baltes, 1990; Markus & Herzog, 1992) have found that adjusting goals to a feasible range is an adaptive strategy and that these processes help to maintain a sense of personal efficacy and well-being in the transition to older adulthood.

Sources of Competence Information

Up to now, I have discussed adaptive strategies that are internal to the individual and criteria for judging one's abilities that are primarily self-referenced (e.g., improvement, effort). Flexibility in the use of sources of information used to judge competence may be the key to successful aging (Frey & Ruble, 1990). One potent source of information regarding one's abilities comes from social comparison. The use of appropriate comparison groups can empower the adult to manage gains and losses associated with aging (Baltes et al., 1998). For example, Markus and Herzog (1992) underscore the importance of using *selective* social comparisons to enhance the chances that the self will be viewed as superior to others. Heidrich and Ryff (1993) found that effective use of social comparisons, both upward and downward, mediated the effects of physical health on psychological distress, well-being, and developmental outcomes in older women. *Upward comparison* involves comparing oneself to those better off who can serve as a model for learning, whereas *downward comparison* involves comparing oneself with someone worse off in order to allow yourself to feel better about one's situation.

The use of upward or downward comparison groups likely relates to individuals' goals. Baltes et al. (1998) indicate that "better functioning groups are selected for comparison, that is upward comparison, if the goal is to maintain and to improve, while more poorly functioning group referents, that is downward comparisons, tend to be selected if the goal is to deal with losses" (p. 1108). Thus, upward comparison would be a logical strategy if a person was recovering from an injury or illness and looking to a similar other as a role model. In the exercise context, upward comparison could also be a logical choice for fit middle-aged participants whose goal (or possible self) was to improve fitness, get better in their leisure or competitive activity (golf, tennis, bowling, tai chi), or maintain their current level of functioning relative to their peers. On the other hand, downward comparisons are adaptive for the less fit individual at any age or for the adult exerciser or master's athlete dealing with performance decrements.

There is some evidence that social comparison becomes a more important source of competence information with increasing age during adulthood. Frey and Ruble (1990) found that runners with declining performance were more likely than improving or stable runners to mention how they compared to others in the competition and less likely to mention finish times as a goal. Thus, with declining performance, temporal (past performance) comparisons were not used in favor of social comparison (less adept but similar aged others). The research in this area, however, is far from conclusive. As intuitively appealing as the contention that downward comparisons are protective is, Baltes et al. (1998) warn that many reasons can account for this such as who constitutes the downward comparison group and the use of clinical populations in the research. This is an area deserving of future research using healthy populations in externally valid settings.

FUTURE RESEARCH DIRECTIONS

The pace of our research on the psychology of adult and older adult physical activity behavior has not kept up with the demand, particularly with regard to controlled intervention studies. A quick glance at the *Journal of Aging and Physical Activity* for the year 2000 indicates a lack of any studies designed to measure the effectiveness of physical activity programs on self-perceptions. Thus, a plea for intervention studies, particularly longitudinal designs, is in order. In addition, instrumentation appropriate to these populations is a necessity, as is the continued use of expanded theoretical approaches and methodologies appropriate to the research question. What follows are specific suggestions for research that uses some of the theories discussed in this chapter.

With regard to self-schema theory and the concept of possible selves, we should continue to investigate the utility of these constructs in sport and exercise contexts. With the exception of Whaley and Ebbeck (2002), the majority of research in the physical domain using self-schema theory has focused on college-aged populations. We need to know more about the schemata of middle-aged and older populations, as well as of diverse populations. Researchers have established a strong connection between self-schema, intentions, and behavior, where behavior is generally measured as time spent on task (e.g., frequency and duration of exercise). We know far less about issues related to the influence of self-schemata on activity choice and persistence, or precisely how schemata influence (or are influenced by) other psychological and social variables such as anxiety or significant others. Other areas for future research include the best way to help individuals develop an existing schema for desirable behaviors. For example, many adults know they should exercise but do not. It may be that these individuals would benefit from developing schemata and associated possible selves consistent with exerciser schemata. Psychological tools to encourage the development of these schemata might include appropriate modeling of behaviors, imagery, and self-talk.

The surface has only been scratched with regard to research relating specifically to the possible-selves construct. More information is needed regarding the possible selves of active and sedentary individuals. Other potential areas applicable to possible-selves research include career transitions (e.g., What are the possible selves of retiring athletes, and how can this information aid in this transition?) and injury rehabilitation (e.g., Are the possible selves of injured sport participants consistent with their rehabilitation process?). Given the link between possible selves and behavior, this is a construct with great potential for a variety of applied settings.

Self-discrepancy theory also holds the potential to describe, predict, and explain why individuals may be motivated to participate in physical activity but choose not to. Research should begin to examine the discrepancies described in the theory and to investigate the consequences of these discrepancies on sport and exercise behavior. For example, are discrepancies related to burnout in athletes or coaches? Further, we do not know where discrepancies come from. That is, specific to the physical domain, what are the antecedents that result in these discrepancies? What role does a coach, parent, or physical education teacher play in the development of discrepancies in the physical domain? These are but a few of the potential research questions emanating from these theories. Of course, from a lifespan perspective, it would be important to examine how schemata, possible selves, and discrepancies change over the life course, as well as how these constructs can facilitate the developmental process.

Measurement is another area in need of continuing research. Lately, a few promising measures specific to adult and older adult populations have been forwarded. For example, the Multidimensional Scale for Assessing Positive and Negative Social Influences on Physical Activity (containing a self-esteem subscale) has recently been developed by Chogahara (1999). Sorensen's Self-Perception in Exercise Questionnaire (1997) also has the potential to contribute to our understanding of this topic, but both need further testing to establish their reliability and validity in various adult contexts. These measures complement existing scales such as Messer and Harter's (1986) Adult Self-Perception Profile and Fox and Corbin's (1989) Physical Self-Perception Profile. Although we can achieve high internal consistencies with some existing measures, we cannot assume that measures designed for younger groups are *meaningful* for older populations. Thus, continued emphasis must be on the creation and use of measures that are pertinent to the values, beliefs, and self-conceptions of adults and older adults.

Finally, we must continue to expand our methodologies for studying adults and older adults in ways that best answer our research questions. Quantitative methods such as multidimensional scaling and preference mapping (Patrick & Dzewaltowski, 2000) and the use of within-person variability, or intraindividual change (Eizenman, Nesselroade, Featherman, & Rowe, 1997) show promise for further developing our knowledge base with these groups. In the qualitative arena, the life history approach of Langley and Knight (1999) and Paoletti's (1998) phenomenological study of the social production of identity in older women are exemplary models of time-intensive but incredibly rich forms of research. These alternative methods are simply additional tools to add to our toolbox to best explore questions particular to the lives of adults and older adults in the physical domain.

> It is essential to use measures and methodologies that best suit adult and older adult populations and associated research questions.

IMPLICATIONS FOR PRACTICE

The compatibility between the theories discussed in this chapter (e.g., possible selves, discrepancy theory) and the methods employed by adults to maintain positive self-perceptions (e.g., selective optimization with compensation, assimilation and accommodation) should be evident. For instance, a likely mechanism by which someone with declining physical capacities adapts to his condition is through adjustments and changes to his self-perceptions. Possible selves are elements of the self-system that can most easily assume a new form (Cross & Markus, 1991). In fact, Stein and Markus (1996) describe how self-schemata and possible selves function at the recognition, initiation, and maintenance stages of the behavioral change process. Thus, one way to cope with changes in ability is by reconfiguring possible selves so that the discrepancy between what one is presently doing and who one would like to become in the future is diminished, thereby leading to goal-directed behaviors consistent with that view of self.

A logical question emanating from this statement is, how might that be accomplished? A model for this process, based on Markus et al.'s (1990) work, can be found in Figure 1. Beginning from the left-hand side and following the bold boxes, the model predicts that individuals with the physical ability to exercise who also have a self-schema (or identity) for exercise will develop future-oriented conceptions of themselves consistent with that identity. In an exerciser, an example would be to have a possible self as "a healthy older adult." When that possible self is combined with self-regulatory strategies, effective performance (physical activity behavior) will result.

Below the main row, competence in the physical domain is believed to develop as a result of the process of refining one's possible selves and their associated self-regulatory strategies. The circle below the competence box represents strategies that can be used to support and encourage perceptions of and actual competence. For example, interventions could provide sources of social support and positive feedback and encouragement. Such interventions could also teach the individual how to set appropriate and sensible goals and to use positive self-talk and imagery. These strategies facilitate the development of competence and action plans designed to help the individual achieve his or her possible selves. The skills and techniques listed above have been found to effectively influence behavior in sport contexts. There is ample reason to believe that they would be equally helpful in the exercise context. Imagery has been shown to be very useful in clinical psychology practice, from helping clients rehearse different strategies to dealing with guilt-inducing interactions to helping healthy adults deal with stress (Suinn, 1996). The idea behind using imagery is to enable the individual to construct and/or to retrieve richly detailed but focused and task-relevant possible selves (Markus et al., 1990). Imagery manipulations have been used to increase the accessibility of specific possible selves (Ruvolo & Markus, 1992) and thus represent a realistic intervention approach for physical contexts.

However, the process just described is subject to short-circuiting if discrepancies between a hoped-for and feared self, or between an actual self and an ideal self exist (top box in the model). Thus, any application of the theory designed to change or adapt possible selves must take into account the content of possible selves relevant to the individual at that point in time. In this way, the researcher or practitioner will have a better picture of the true nature of the self. This process has potential application for another area of vital interest to adults: body image or perceptions of physical appearance.

Harter (1990a) has found that the relationship between perceived physical appearance and global self-worth is robust. In fact, across the life span, Harter has discovered that perceived physical appearance is the most significant contributor to global self-worth. Wilcox (1997), in a study of 20 to 80 year olds, found that attitudes regarding the body remained high across age groups, and did not differ by gender. However, when the specific relationship between participation in regular exercise and body satisfaction was examined, with increasing age, women exercisers had greater body satisfaction, whereas among women nonexercisers, increasing age

FIGURE 1
A proposed model for the role of self-schema and possible selves in physical activity behavior

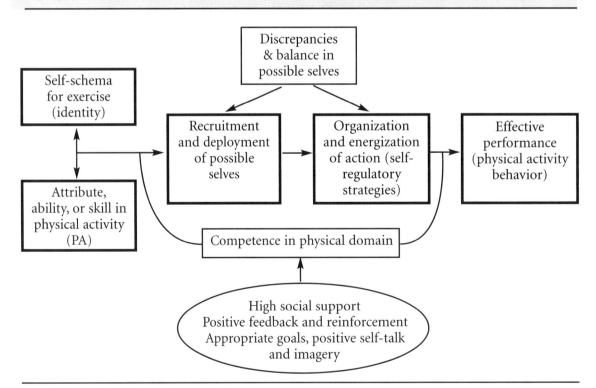

Adapted from "The Role of The Self-System in Competence," by H. Markus, S. Cross, and E. Wurf, 1990, Competence Considered, ed. R. J. Sternberg and J. Kolligan, Jr. (New Haven, CT: Yale University Press), p. 208.

was associated with less body satisfaction. Consistent with these findings, Loland (2000) found that satisfaction with appearance increased with age among moderate and high active individuals, whereas it decreased among inactive individuals. Across age groups, men were generally more satisfied with their appearance than women were. Thus, although all groups (men, women, active and sedentary) seem to be concerned about issues related to the body, nonexercisers (particularly women) appear to be especially vulnerable. It may be that these individuals have not *developed* or *accessed* the possible selves and associated self-regulatory mechanisms necessary to achieve a hoped-for or avoid a feared self. On the other hand, active individuals likely think about their bodies but have translated that self-perception into an action plan that enables them to be more satisfied with their appearance. Clearly, the next step in this line of investigation is to see if individuals can be "taught" to access or develop more appropriate and fully refined possible selves, and if in turn their associated self-regulatory mechanisms can prompt appropriate exercise behaviors. There is enough evidence from Markus and her colleagues (1990) to suggest that this is indeed the case.

There are other practical applications for the models described in this chapter. For example, we have seen how appropriate use of selective optimization with compensation can benefit older athletes and exercisers. It is important to remember, however, that adults as young as 40 are sensitive to age-related changes in competence (Whitbourne & Collins, 1998). Baltes et al. (1998) provide an example that is illustrative of how selective optimization with compensation works. They describe how Arthur Rubinstein, as an 80-year-old, managed to maintain his high level of expert piano playing by playing fewer pieces (selection), practicing those pieces more often (optimization), and playing the slower parts more slowly so the faster parts were still perceived to be faster (compensation). The adult tennis player can do similar selection, optimization, and compensation, as described by Langley and Knight (1999). In this case, the individual switched from singles to doubles play (selection), changed to a larger racket (optimization), and chose partners who he knew covered more of the court than he was now able to (compensation). In this way, individuals are able to hold onto the view they have of themselves (expert pianist, capable tennis player) even though abilities are declining.

Finally, it is important to keep in mind the variety of sources of information that adults can use to assess their competence and how these may differ from the sources used by younger individuals. Recall that Heidrich and Ryff (1993) advocate the use of selective social comparison for adults whose goal is to improve (upward comparison) or if the goal is to deal with losses (downward comparison). In the exercise context, my observations are that using age norms for tests of functional ability can be motivating if the individual has scored at or above norms for their age. Naturally, we must be careful with such information, particularly for individuals who may fall below age norms. However, if we remember that individuals are striving for ways to maintain a positive sense of self, then a logical beginning for most physical activity programs would be to have individuals verbalize what that sense of self is. From there, the individuals and their fitness specialist, consultant, coach, or other significant person can develop a plan designed to maximize their chances for maintaining or enhancing those self-perceptions.

FINAL THOUGHTS

This chapter has ventured to describe the role of self-perceptions in adult physical activity behavior. It should be evident how views of oneself in the past, present, and future play an enormous role in adult development. Models and theoretical constructs have been described, some with considerable research in the physical domain, others with promise but little empirical support. These conceptual models and theories hold the potential not only to expand our understanding of adult physical activity behavior, but also to translate that knowledge into practical settings. As we enter the new millennium, the importance of an emphasis on adult and older adult populations was never more evident. The percentage of older adults will continue to rise well into this century, so that by 2030, when the last of the baby boomers turns 65, more Americans will be seniors than ever before (U.S. Department of Health and Human Services, 1999). The critical issue then becomes one of living better, rather than simply living longer. I know I share the hope of many authors of this volume that future research will not only target a particular age group, but also will compare individuals across time and *across* age groups so that we might discover how changing self-perceptions relate to physical activity over the life course. Only then will we truly understand in all its complexity why, for example, older adults may not *believe* what they *see*.

REFERENCES

Ajzen, I. (1985). From intentions to actions: A theory of planned behavior. In J. Kuhl & J. Beckman (Eds.), *Action-control: From cognition to behavior* (pp. 11-39). Heidelberg: Springer.

Ajzen, I., & Fishbein, M. (1980). *Understanding attitudes and predicting social behavior.* Englewood Cliffs, NJ: Prentice-Hall.

Alfermann, D., & Stoll, O. (2000). Effects of physical exercise on self-concept and well-being. *International Journal of Sport Psychology, 30,* 47-65.

Atchley, R. C. (1989). A continuity theory of normal aging. *The Gerontologist, 29,* 183-190.

Atchley, R. C. (1994). *Social forces and aging* (7th ed.). Belmont, CA: Wadsworth.

Baltes, P. B., & Baltes, M. M. (1990). Psychological perspectives on successful aging: The model of selective optimization with compensation. In P. B. Baltes & M. M. Baltes (Eds.), *Successful aging: Perspectives from the behavioral sciences* (pp. 1-34). New York: Cambridge University Press.

Baltes, P. B., Lindenberger, U., & Staudinger, U. M. (1998). Life-span theory in developmental psychology. In R. M. Lerner (Vol. Ed.), *Handbook of child psychology: Vol. 1. Theoretical models of human development* (5th ed., pp. 1029-1143). New York: Wiley.

Bandura, A. (1986). *Social foundations of thought and action.* Engelwood Cliffs, NJ: Prentice Hall.

Bandura, A. (1997). *Self-efficacy: The exercise of control.* New York: W.H. Freeman and Company.

Berger, B. G. (1996). Psychological benefits of an active lifestyle: What we know and what we need to know. *Quest, 48,* 330-353.

Biddle, S. (1995). Exercise and psychosocial health. *Research Quarterly for Exercise and Sport, 66,* 292-297.

Brandtstädter, J., & Rothermund, K. (1994). Self-percepts of control in middle and later adulthood: Buffering losses by rescaling goals. *Psychology and Aging, 9,* 265-273.

Bruch, M. A., Rivet, K. M., & Laurenti, H.J. (2000). Type of self-discrepancy and relationships to components of the tripartite model of emotional distress. *Personality & Individual Differences, 29,* 37-44.

Carver, C. S., Lawrence, J. W., & Scheier, M. F. (1999). Self-discrepancies and affect: Incorporating the role of feared selves. *Personality & Social Psychology Bulletin, 25,* 783-792.

Caspersen, C. J., Pereira, M. A., & Curran, K. M. (2000). Changes in physical activity patterns in the United States, by sex and cross-sectional age. *Medicine & Science in Sports & Exercise, 32,* 1601-1609.

Chogahara, M. (1999). A multidimensional scale for assessing positive and negative social influences on physical activity in older adults. *Journal of Gerontology Series B: Psychological Sciences and Social Sciences, 54B,* S356-S367.

Cobb, J. C., Cohen, R., Houston, D. A., & Rubin, E. C. (1998). Children's self-concepts and peer relationships: Relating appearance self-discrepancies and peer perceptions of social behaviors. *Child Study Journal, 28,* 291-308.

Coleman, P. G. (1996). Identity management in later life. In R.T. Woods (Ed.), *Handbook of the clinical psychology of aging* (pp. 93-113). New York: Wiley.

Cross, S., & Markus, H. (1991). Possible selves across the life span. *Human Development, 34,* 230-255.

Cross, S. E., & Markus, H. R. (1994). Self-schemas, possible selves, and competent performance. *Journal of Educational Psychology, 86,* 423-438.

Dishman, R. K. (1994). *Advances in exercise adherence.* Champaign, IL: Human Kinetics.

Eizenman, D. R., Nesselroade, J. R., Featherman, D. L., & Rowe, J. W. (1997). Intraindividual variability in perceived control in an older sample: The MacArthur successful aging studies. *Psychology and Aging, 12,* 489-502.

Estabrooks, P., & Courneya, K. S. (1997). Relationships among self-schema, intention, and exercise behavior. *Journal of Sport & Exercise Psychology, 19,* 156-168.

Fox, K. R. (1990). *The Physical Self-perception Profile manual.* DeKalb, IL: Office for Health Promotion, Northern Illinois University.

Fox, K. R. (1997). Let's get physical. In K. R. Fox (Ed.), *The physical self: From motivation to well being* (pp. vii - xiii). Champaign, IL: Human Kinetics.

Fox, K. R. (2000). Self-esteem, self-perceptions, and exercise. *International Journal of Sport Psychology, 31,* 228-240.

Fox, K. R., & Corbin, C. B. (1989). The Physical Self-perception Profile: Development and preliminary validation. *Journal of Sport & Exercise Psychology, 11,* 408-430.

Frey, K. S., & Ruble, D. N. (1990). Strategies for comparative evaluation: Maintaining a sense of competence across the life span. In R. Sternberg & J. Kolligian (Eds.), *Competence considered* (pp. 167-189). New Haven: Yale University Press.

Garcia, A. W., & King, A. C. (1991). Predicting long-term adherence to aerobic exercise: A comparison of two models. *Journal of Sport & Exercise Psychology, 13,* 394-409.

Gergen, K. (1971). *The concept of the self.* New York: Holt, Rinehart, & Winston.

Gonnerman, M. E., Parker, C. P., Lavine, H., & Huff, J. (2000). The relationship between self-discrepancies and affective states: The moderating roles of self-monitoring and standpoints of the self. *Personality & Social Psychology Bulletin, 26,* 810-819.

Harter, S. (1985). Competence as a dimension of self-evaluation: Toward a comprehensive model of self-worth. In R. Leahy (Ed.), *The development of the self* (pp. 55-118). New York: Academic Press.

Harter, S. (1986). Processes underlying the construction, maintenance, and enhancement of the self-concept in children. In J. Suls & A. Greenwald (Eds.), *Psychological perspectives on the self* (Vol. 3, pp. 137-181). Hillsdale, NJ: Erlbaum.

Harter, S. (1990a). Developmental differences in the nature of self-representations: Implications for the understanding, assessment, and treatment of maladaptive behavior. *Cognitive Therapy and Research, 14,* 113-142.

Harter, S. (1990b). Causes, correlates, and the functional role of global self-worth: A life-span perspective. In R. J. Sternberg & J. Kolligan Jr. (Eds.), *Competence considered* (pp. 67-97). New Haven, CT: Yale University Press.

Harter, S. (1992). Visions of self: Beyond the me in the mirror. In J. E. Jacobs (Vol. Ed.), *Nebraska Symposium on Motivation* (Vol. 40, pp. 99-144). Lincoln, NE: University of Nebraska Press.

Harter, S. (1999). *The construction of the self: A developmental perspective.* New York: Guilford.

Harter, S., & Pike, R. (1984). The pictorial scale of perceived competence and social acceptance in young children. *Child Development, 55,* 1969-1982.

Heidrich, S. M., & Ryff, C. D. (1993). Physical and mental health in later life: The self-system as mediator. *Psychology and Aging, 8,* 327-338.

Helson, R., & McCabe, L. (1994). The social clock project in middle age. In B.F. Turner and L. E. Troll (Eds.), *Women growing older: Psychological perspectives* (pp. 68-93). Thousand Oaks, CA: Sage.

Helson, R., Mitchell, V., & Moane, G. (1984). Personality and patterns of adherence and non-adherence to the social clock. *Journal of Personality and Social Psychology, 46,* 1079-1096.

Higgins, E. T. (1987). Self-discrepancy: A theory relating self and affect. *Psychological Review, 3,* 319-340.

Higgins, E. T. (1999). When do self-discrepancies have specific relations to emotions? The second-generation question of Tangney, Niedenthal, Covert, and Barlow. *Journal of Personality & Social Psychology, 77,* 1313-1317.

Hooker, K. (1992). Possible selves and perceived health in older adults and college students. *Journal of Gerontology: Psychological Sciences, 47,* pp. 85-95.

Hooker, K., & Kaus, C. R. (1992). Possible selves and health behaviors in later life. *Journal of Aging and Health, 4,* 390-411.

Hooker, K., & Kaus, C. R. (1994). Health-related possible selves in young and middle adulthood. *Psychology and Aging, 9,* 126-133.

Kendzierski, D. (1988). Self-schemata and exercise. *Basic and Applied Social Psychology, 9,* 45-59.

Kendzierski, D. (1990). Exercise self-schemata: Cognitive and behavioral correlates. *Health Psychology, 9,* 69-82.

Kendzierski, D. (1994). Schema theory: An information processing focus. In R. Dishman (Ed.), *Advances in exercise adherence* (2nd ed., pp. 137-159). Champaign, IL: Human Kinetics.

Kendzierski, D., Furr, M., & Schiavoni, J. (1998). Physical activity self-definitions: Correlates and perceived criteria. *Journal of Sport & Exercise Psychology, 20,* 176-193.

Langley, D. J., & Knight, S. M. (1999). Continuity in sport participation as an adaptive strategy in the aging process: A lifespan narrative. *Journal of Aging and Physical Activity, 7,* 32-54.

Lazarus, R.S. (2000). How emotions influence performance in competitive sports. *The Sport Psychologist, 14,* 229-252.

Leondari, A., Syngollitou, E., & Kiosseoglou, G. (1998). Academic achievement, motivation and possible selves. *Journal of Adolescence, 21,* 219-222.

Loland, N.W. (2000). The aging body: Attitudes toward bodily appearance among physically active and inactive women and men of different ages. *Journal of Aging and Physical Activity, 8*, 197-213.

Marcus, B. H., Eaton, C. A., Rossi, J. S., & Harlow, L. L. (1994). Self-efficacy, decision-making, and stages of change: An integrative model of physical exercise. *Journal of Applied Social Psychology, 24*, 489-508.

Markus, H. (1977). Self-schemata and processing information about the self. *Journal of Personality and Social Psychology, 35*, 63-78.

Markus, H. (1990). Unresolved issues of self-representation. *Cognitive Therapy and Research, 14*, 241-253.

Markus, H., Cross, S., & Wurf, E. (1990). The role of the self-system in competence. In R. J. Sternberg & J. Kolligan Jr. (Eds.), *Competence considered* (pp. 205-225). New Haven, CT: Yale University Press.

Markus, H., Hamill, R., & Sentis, K.P. (1987). Thinking fat: Self-schemas for body weight and the processing of weight relevant information. *Journal of Applied Social Psychology, 17*, 50-71.

Markus, H., & Nurius, P. (1986). Possible selves. *American Psychologist, 41*, 954-969.

Markus, H. R., & Herzog, A. R. (1992). The role of the self-concept in aging. In K. W. Shaie & M. P. Lawton (Eds.). *Annual review of gerontology and geriatrics* (Vol. 11, pp. 110-143). New York: Springer.

Marsh, H. W. (1994). The importance of being important: Theoretical models of relations between specific and global components of physical fitness. *Journal of Sport & Exercise Psychology, 16*, 306-325.

Marsh, H. W., & Sonstroem, R. J. (1995). Importance ratings and specific components of the physical self-concept: Relevance to predicting global components of self-concept and exercise. *Journal of Sport & Exercise Psychology, 17*, 84-104.

McAuley, E., & Rudolph, D. (1995). Physical activity, aging, and psychological well-being. *Journal of Aging and Physical Activity, 3*, 67-96.

McCrae, R. R., & Costa, P.T., Jr. (1988). Age, personality, and the spontaneous self-concept. *Journal of Gerontology: Social Sciences, 43*, S177-S185.

Meara, N.M., Day, J. D., Chalk, L. M., & Phelps, R. E. (1998). Possible selves: Applications to career counseling. *Journal of Career Assessment, 3*, 259-277.

Messer, B., & Harter, S. (1986). *Manual for the Adult Self-Perception Profile.* Denver, CO: University of Denver.

Murphy, G. M., Petitpas, A. J., & Brewer, B. W. (1996). Identity foreclosure, athletic identity, and career maturity in intercollegiate athletes. *The Sport Psychologist, 10*, 239-246.

Neeman, J., & Harter, S. (1986). *Manual for the Self-Perception Profile for College Students.* Denver, CO: University of Denver.

Neugarten, B. L. (1977). Personality and aging. In J. E. Birren & K. W. Shaie (Eds.), *Handbook of the psychology of aging* (pp. 626-649). New York: Van Nostrand Reinhold.

Neugarten, B. L. (1979). Time, age, and the life cycle. *American Journal of Psychiatry, 136*, 887-894.

Nurius, P. (1991). Possible selves and social support: social cognitive resources for coping and striving. In J. Howard & P. Callero (Eds.), *The self-society dynamic: Cognition, emotion, and action* (pp. 239-258). Cambridge, MA: Cambridge University Press.

O'Brien Cousins, S. (1998). *Exercise, aging, and health.* Philadelphia: Taylor & Francis.

Oyserman, D., Gant, L., & Ager, J. (1995). A socially contextualized model of African American identity: Possible selves and school persistence. *Journal of Personality and Social Psychology, 69*, 1216-1232.

Oyserman, D., & Saltz, E. (1993). Competence, delinquency, and attempts to attain possible selves. *Journal of Personality and Social Psychology, 65*, 360-374.

Paoletti, I. (1998). *Being an older woman: A study in the social production of identity.* Mahway, NJ: Erlbaum.

Pate, R. P., Heath, G. W., Dowda, M., & Trost, S.G. (1996). Associations between physical activity and other health behaviors in a representative sample of US adolescents. *American Journal of Public Health, 86*, 1577-1581.

Patrick, L. E., & Dzewaltowski, D. A. (2000). Multidimensional scaling and preference mapping: Promising methods for investigating older adults' physical activity perceptions and preferences. *Journal of Aging and Physical Activity, 8*, 343-362.

Prochaska, J. O., & DiClemente, C. C. (1986). Toward a comprehensive model of change. In W. R. Miller & N. Heather (Eds.), *Treating addictive behaviors: Processes of change* (pp. 3-27). New York: Plenum Press.

Prochaska, J. O., & Velicer, W. F. (1997). The transtheoretical model of health behavior change. *American Journal of Health Promotion, 12*, 38-48.

Renouf, A. G., & Harter, S. (1990). Low self-worth and anger as components of the depressive experience in young adolescents. *Development and Psychopathology, 2*, 293-310.

Rosenberg, M. (1979). *Conceiving the self.* New York: Basic Books.

Rosenberg, M. (1986). Self-concept from middle childhood through adolescence. In J. Suls & A. G. Greenwald (Eds.), *Psychological perspectives on the self* (Vol. 3, pp. 107-136). Hillsdale, NJ: Erlbaum.

Ruvolo, A. P., & Markus, H. R. (1992). Possible selves and performance: The power of self-relevant imagery. *Social Cognition, 10*, 95-124.

Scheier, M. F., & Carver, C. S. (1982). Cognition, affect, and self-regulation. In M. S. Clark & T. Fiske (Eds.), *Affect and cognition: The seventeenth annual Carnegie symposium on cognition* (pp. 157-183). Hillsdale, NJ: Erlbaum.

Shavelson, R. J., & Bolus, R. (1982). Self-concept: The interplay of theory and methods. *Journal of Educational Psychology, 74,* 3-17.

Sheeran, P., & Orbell, S. (2000). Self-schemas and the theory of planned behaviour. *European Journal of Social Psychology, 30,* 533-550.

Snyder, R. (1997). Self-discrepancy theory, standards for body evaluation, and eating disorder symptomatology among college women. *Women & Health, 26,* 69-84.

Sonstroem, R. J. (1997). The physical self-system: A mediator of exercise and self-esteem. In K. R. Fox (Ed.), *The physical self: From motivation to well being* (pp. 3-26). Champaign, IL: Human Kinetics.

Sonstroem, R. J., Harlow, L. L., & Josephs, L. (1994). Exercise and self-esteem: Validity of model expansion and exercise associations. *Journal of Sport & Exercise Psychology, 16,* 29-42.

Sonstroem, R. J., Harlow, L. L., & Salisbury, K. S. (1993). Path analysis of a self-esteem model across a competitive swim season. *Research Quarterly for Exercise and Sport, 64,* 335-342.

Sonstroem, R. J., & Morgan, W.P. (1989). Exercise and self-esteem: Rationale and model. *Medicine and Science in Sports and Exercise, 21,* 329-337.

Sonstroem, R. J., & Potts, S. A. (1996). Life adjustment correlates of physical self-concepts. *Medicine and Science in Sports and Exercise, 28,* 619-625.

Sonstroem, R. J., Speliotis, E. D., & Fava, J. L. (1992). Perceived physical competence in adults: An examination of the Physical Self-perception Scale. *Journal of Sport & Exercise Psychology, 10,* 207-221.

Sorensen, M. (1997). Self-referent thoughts in exercise: The Self-perception in Exercise Questionnaire. *European Journal of Psychological Assessment, 13,* 195-205.

Stein, K. F., & Markus, H. R. (1996). The role of the self in behavioral change. *Journal of Psychotherapy Integration, 6,* 349-384.

Strube, M. J., Berry, J. M., Lott, C. L., Fogelman, R., Steinhart, G., Moergen, S., & Davison, L. (1986). Self-schematic representation of the Type A and B behavior patterns. *Journal of Personality and Social Psychology, 51,* 170-180.

Suinn, R. M. (1996). Imagery rehearsal: A tool for clinical practice. *Psychotherapy in Private Practice, 15,* 27-31.

Talbot, L. A., Metter, E. J., & Fleg, J. L. (2000). Leisure-time physical activities and their relationship to cardiorespiratory fitness in healthy men and women 18-95 years old. *Medicine & Science in Sports and Exercise, 32,* 417-425.

U.S. Department of Health and Human Services (1999). Preventing the diseases of aging. *Chronic Disease Notes & Reports, 12*(3), 1-12.

Vealey, R. S. (1986). Conceptualization of sport-confidence and competitive orientation: Preliminary investigation and instrument development. *Journal of Sport Psychology, 8,* 221-246.

Weiss, M. R., & Ebbeck, V. (1996). Self-esteem and perceptions of competence in youth sport: Theory, research, and enhancement strategies. In O. Bar-Or (Ed.), *The encyclopedia of sports medicine: Vol. V. The child and adolescent athlete* (pp. 364-382). Oxford: Blackwell Scientific Publications, Ltd.

Weiss, M. R., & Ferrer-Caja, E. (2002). Motivational orientations and sport behavior. In T. S. Horn (Ed.), *Advances in sport psychology* (2nd ed., pp. 101-183). Champaign, IL: Human Kinetics.

Whaley, D. E. (2003). Future-oriented self-perceptions and exercise behavior in middle-aged women. *Journal of Aging and Physical Activity, 11,* 1-17.

Whaley, D. E., & Ebbeck, V. (2002). Self-schemata and exercise identity in older adults. *Journal of Aging and Physical Activity, 10,* 245-259.

Whitbourne, S. K. (1996). *The aging individual: Physical and psychological perspectives.* New York: Springer.

Whitbourne, S. K., & Collins, K. J. (1998). Identity processes and perceptions of physical functioning in adults: Theoretical and clinical implications. *Psychotherapy, 35,* 519-530.

Wilcox, S. (1997). Age and gender in relation to body attitudes. *Psychology of Women Quarterly, 21,* 549-565.

Yin, Z., & Boyd, M. P. (2000). Behavioral and cognitive correlates of exercise self-schemata. *The Journal of Psychology, 134,* 269-282.

CHAPTER ELEVEN

Social Influence on the Psychological Dimensions of Adult Physical Activity Involvement

Robert J. Brustad • *Megan L. Babkes*

A lifespan developmental perspective directs our attention to individual change processes that occur as a consequence of maturation and experience. However, these change processes do not occur in isolation but within a social context. As Cialdini and Trost (1998) commented, "Those who wish to understand fully the process of personal change must understand just as fully the process of interpersonal influence" (p. 151). In our examination of physical activity across the lifespan, we will attempt to integrate knowledge from developmental and social psychology because the two disciplines are closely linked. In fact, many theorists argue that the study of developmental psychology is fundamentally grounded in social psychology because an important source of developmental change occurs as a consequence of social interaction (Durkin, 1995; Ruble & Goodnow, 1998; Taylor, 1998).

This chapter is dedicated to the examination of social influence upon physical activity and sport behavior throughout adulthood. Our specific focus is upon the interaction between social influences and developmental change processes so that we may better understand psychosocial outcomes of sport and physical activity involvement throughout the life cycle. Relevant groups of interest include college-aged and young adult athletes, older athletes, and adult exercise populations. There is a growing body of knowledge related to adult populations in physical activity contexts although a limited amount of this research has focused extensively on developmental influences on physical activity throughout the life cycle (Langley & Knight, 1999; O'Brien Cousins & Keating, 1995).

An important characteristic of sport and physical activity involvement at any point in the life cycle is that such involvement almost invariably occurs within a social milieu. Thus, although it is important to keep in mind personal factors such as individual motives and self-perception characteristics, it is essential to simultaneously consider social factors as such factors may influence physical activity behavior. In this chapter, we will use the term *social* to refer to those aspects of our lives that involve, or are influenced by, past, current, or anticipated relationships with others (Ruble & Goodnow, 1998). Given the importance of both personal and social forms of influence, we will adhere to the classic "interactionist" (Lewin, 1951) social psychological perspective that requires that we attend to the interactive effects of the personal and the social realms. This focus extends to individuals' efforts to develop the interpersonal skills that enable them to develop and maintain interpersonal relationships with others and to fit into, and function effectively within, various social groups. Relevant social groups include the family, peer groups, work groups, athletic teams, and groups specific to particular social settings such as exercise classes.

This chapter will focus on four fundamental forms of social influence as each may affect participatory involvement and psychosocial outcomes for individuals engaged in sport and physical activity. First, we discuss the role of cultural influences in shaping the framework of participation surrounding physical activity for individuals of any age. We will also discuss how culture can affect individuals' participatory motives and how cultural stereotypes can shape participatory involvement in physical activity and sport. Second, group membership influences will be considered. Specifically, we will discuss how group membership may affect cognitive, behavioral, and affective outcomes for individuals and how these outcomes are shaped in accordance with particular characteristics of the group such as its norms, level of cohesion, status arrangements, and the role characteristics of group members. Third, we will consider social support as a form of influence that has particular relevance for a lifespan perspective. The provision of social support can facilitate the learning of new skills, contribute to physical activity participation and adherence, reduce stress and anxiety during involvement, and generally enhance psychosocial outcomes of participation for individuals. Finally, we will concentrate on leadership processes in sport and exercise, specifically, the influence of coaches and exercise leaders in the physical activity and sport context. Prior to discussing each of these forms of social influence, we will present a general conceptual framework from which to consider the psychological aspects of sport and physical activity across the lifespan.

UNDERSTANDING SOCIAL INFLUENCE: A CONCEPTUAL FRAMEWORK

Because this chapter is focused upon social influence during adulthood, we will try to provide a general frame of reference for examining developmental change during the adult years. However, applying a developmental perspective during adulthood is a substantially different undertaking than doing so in the study of childhood and adolescence. Growth and development during childhood and adolescence tend to be fairly rapid and relatively predictable. For example, children's ability to engage in abstract reasoning processes can be anticipated to occur in relation to some well-established maturational and chronological age markers and typically manifests in a sequential manner. However, adult social and psychological development is neither nearly as rapid nor as predictable. We cannot anticipate that adults will necessarily pass through identical developmental stages in a similar manner within a given chronological era. For example, adults' motives for involvement in physical activity may increasingly reflect health-related concerns with age. Whereas this general trend may occur, it is not possible to identify a specific chronological age range that corresponds with this tendency. Thus, we can only anticipate that commonalities will exist for many adults across broad age-related phases.

One major reason for differences between patterns of developmental change for children and adolescents in comparison to adults involves fundamental differences in the underlying contributors to change in each developmental era. During childhood and adolescence, development is primarily attributable to biological and cognitive maturation. Because this maturation usually occurs in a given direction and within a fairly predictable time frame, it is relatively easy to anticipate when children will pass through particular stages of cognitive, physical, and emotional development. Developmental change during adulthood, however, is rarely considered to be the consequence of maturational processes because individuals have typically reached full maturity by late adolescence or early adulthood. Change during adulthood is much more commonly linked to important life events and experiences (Ruble & Goodnow, 1998). Key life events and experiences may include career changes, change in marital status, adoption of a caregiver role to children and parents, illnesses, and the salience of one's own mortality. Each of these life experiences reflects directly on social forms of influence upon the individual. In Ruble and Goodnow's words, "the social timetable is now likely to matter more than the biological clock" (p. 774). Thus, developmental change during adulthood is less predictable than it is during childhood and is much more dependent upon social, as opposed to maturational, influences. Consequently, we will structure our discussion in terms of general tendencies toward change with development during adulthood, particularly they are shaped by social factors.

An appropriate conceptual framework for the study of physical activity involvement across the lifespan is a systems perspective (Hellstedt, 1995; Wylleman, 2000). A systems viewpoint is relevant for our discussion of social influence in sport and physical activity for at least three reasons. First, a systems perspective places principal focus upon the influence of interpersonal relationships in social settings such as sport and physical activity. These interpersonal relationships shape the social structure within which individual participation occurs and provide additional meaning to the experience (Wylleman, 2000). We should conceive of the social system in sport as being composed of those individuals who have immediate involvement in the sport experience, such as teammates and coaches, as well as those individuals who may be indirectly involved through their roles as parents and friends. Thus, the social system surrounding involvement is extensive and involves people with unique roles and contributions to the human context of participation.

Second, a systems perspective keeps a broad focus on the functioning of an overall system, or set of interrelationships, rather than on the various parts in isolation. In this case, our focus is on the relationships that exist within a social system such as a family, exercise group, or athletic team where the individual group members share common bonds and in which the actions of one member directly or indirectly have influence upon other members. Within a systems view, we consider forms of mutual influence in our broader focus. Given this perspective, influence is not unidirectional but multidirectional in that all parts of the system may influence other parts and each component can influence the functioning of the system as a whole. Most important for our purposes is the bidirectional relationship that exists between the social system and the individual. In this regard, individual behavior is not considered to be determined or "caused by" the social system. Rather, the individual and the social system function in relation to each other and in interaction with each other. For example, if an individual joins a group (e.g., athletic team, exercise class), the person is likely to be influenced by the group, but the group is also changed by the individual's presence, which reflects a reciprocal form of influence. Thus, in our discussions, the individual is not to be regarded as passively influenced by social forces but rather as someone who is active and influential within the social system of interest.

A third core concept of a systems perspective is that the system is regarded as highly dynamic in nature. From this viewpoint, change is a given. We anticipate change over time and place a high priority on understanding why and how things change. Within an athletic team, for example, change can occur in relation to leadership of the group, the individual roles and responsibilities of team members, and the relative status of group members as a consequence of the team's history over time. Individuals can also change with regard to their appraisals of their sport and exercise experiences in relation to their own life experiences and developmental status. The dynamic nature of a systems perspective is highly appropriate to the study of developmental processes because developmental researchers have a primary interest in the nature of change across the lifespan.

A systems perspective has been widely used in family therapy and organizational settings (e.g., Imber-Black, 1988; Katz & Kahn, 1978). For example, in counseling psychology a family systems approach developed as a means of addressing individual issues and problems as they are related to the overall structure and dynamics of the family. In this case, the focus is on attempting to understand and address individual issues through an enhanced understanding of family dynamics. A similar approach has been recommended for applied work with athletic teams (Brustad & Ritter-Taylor, 1997; Hellstedt, 1995; Zimmerman, Protinsky, & Zimmerman, 1994) in which efforts are made to understand how leadership characteristics, family influences, the social network of the group, individual roles, norms, and status arrangements may influence the overall functioning of the team as well as the individual members within the team. While maintaining the dynamic perspective offered by a systems viewpoint, we will now turn our attention to the discussion of four principal forms of social influence.

CULTURAL INFLUENCES

Culture consists of the shared belief systems that exist within a given society or social group. We can think of culture as a collective view of reality that exists among people and that shapes the norms, rules, cognitions, social practices, and behaviors of individuals and the "ways of life" of a society (Coakley, 2001; Fiske, Kitayama, Markus, & Nisbett, 1998; McPherson, 1994). Culture exerts a pervasive influence upon all forms of human behavior, and the extent of this influence is no less in sport and physical activity than in other domains because sport is itself a cultural product. In fact, sport and physical activity forms are highly important in reaffirming basic cultural values and, at least occasionally, in transforming the culture of which they are a part (Coakley, 2001). Like any other social activity, there exist various culturally specific values, beliefs, and expectations that are present that structure physical activity and provide it with meaning (McPherson, 1994). The types of sport and games that people play, and the inherent value that is perceived to result from these activities, correspond with principal cultural beliefs. For example, changing cultural values about the importance of physical activity involvement for positive health outcomes has influenced exercise-related beliefs and behaviors in North America (McPherson, 1994)

The nature of our personal psychological development is also strongly influenced by culture. As Fiske et al. (1998) commented, "Humans are born with the capacity to function in any culture, but as they mature they develop psyches that are organized to function in one specific culture" (p. 916). Thus, our self-perceptions as well as our beliefs about how and why others behave in the way that they do are strongly shaped by cultural belief systems. In this way, culture affects our psychological development. In addition, in order to function effectively in any culture or social setting, one must have effectively internalized cultural values about appropriate behavior. Much of the power of culture rests in the fact that what we learn in our social world becomes a form of "taken-for-granted" knowledge that we rarely consider or question (Coakley, 2001; McPherson, 1994; Vertinsky, 1995).

With regard to physical activity and sport forms, we can consider culture to constitute the framework that defines what are "appropriate" forms of physical activity and sport for individuals, and the activities that are considered to be "appropriate" may vary according to the gender, age, race, or socioeconomic status of the individual (McPherson, 1994). Cultural influences are particularly identifiable when we consider the nature of gender-related stereotypes and expectations. Historically, females have had many fewer opportunities to participate in sport, and female participation in team and contact sports, in particular, has only recently been possible in many cultures. These constraints to female participation have not come from formal rules and strictures but rather from culturally accepted beliefs about the "appropriateness" of various sport forms for females (Coakley, 2001; Vertinsky, 1991). Currently, we see many notable gender differences in participation levels in various types of sport and physical activities (e.g., aerobics classes, football, figure skating) that reflect an underlying "gender-logic" that is grounded in gender-related stereotypes that are infrequently considered or challenged (Coakley, 2001).

> Our own self-perceptions and our beliefs about others' behavior are strongly shaped by cultural belief systems.

If we substitute age-related stereotypes for gender-related stereotypes in our analysis, we can appreciate some of the influence that culture has on physical activity participation across the lifespan. As McPherson (1994) commented, "Aging is a social as well as a biological process wherein individuals interact with, and are influenced by, the particular social, physical and cultural environments in which they age" (p. 330). For example, during many historical eras, the participation of older adults in exercise and sport was discouraged because of perceptions that it was unhealthy (Vertinsky, 1995). Vertinsky reviewed North American historical trends in cultural perceptions of aging and concluded that popular perceptions have been primarily responsible for shaping social expectations about aging, the nature of professional exercise prescriptions, and public policies with regard to the exercise and physical activity behavior of older adults.

As a means of assessing stereotypical beliefs of older adults about physical activity and sport, Ostrow and Dzewaltowski (1986) examined older adults' perceptions of the appropriateness of various forms of sport and physical activity in relation to the age of hypothetical participants. In this case, adults 60 years of age and older assessed age-appropriateness of involvement in various strenuous (marathon running, racquetball) and less strenuous (archery) activities for individuals in varying age groups (20 through 80 years in 20-year age increments). Their findings indicated that the study participants viewed participation in each type of physical activity as less appropriate as the age of the referent person increased. Furthermore, these older individuals viewed participation in all physical activities as more appropriate for males than for females, with the exception of ballet involvement.

Vertinsky (1991, 1995) has argued that gender- and age-related stereotypes interact in such a way as to inhibit the physical activity involvement of many older women. Her analysis suggests that many older women "accept persistent stereotypes that link aging with physical decline and remain or become sedentary because they believe that it is inappropriate or dangerous to be physically active" (1995, p. 224). She argued that many health care practitioners who adhere to antiquated stereotypes about female aging all too frequently reinforce this stereotype. "The result is an image of female old age that can be a seriously unbalanced version of the realities of later life, propelling a self-fulfilling prophecy where health is compromised and physical decline is hastened rather than slowed by chronic inactivity" (Vertinsky, 1995, p. 232). As McPherson (1994) noted, ageism and sexism thus interact to increase barriers to physical activity for many older women, and this is especially true for poor women and women of minority groups.

As a consequence of changing social attitudes and knowledge advances related to the benefits of physical activity for individuals of all ages, cultural beliefs about physical activity by older people now represent less of a barrier to the physical activity involvement of older individuals in North America than in the past (McPherson, 1994; Vertinsky, 1995). Furthermore, as health promotion efforts have become influential in reshaping cultural beliefs about the relationship between physical activity and health, the idea that older adults should be passive during their later years is much less widely accepted than in the past, which reflects upon the dynamic nature of social and cultural change. However, this is not to suggest that stereotypes no longer exist that impede the physical activity involvement of older people in our society because cultural attitudes related to age (and gender) still affect physical activity involvement (Vertinsky, 1995). In sum, culture represents the broadest form of social influence and without consideration for cultural influences we miss a large part of the "big picture" related to social influences upon physical activity. We will now direct our attention to more context-specific forms of social influence upon physical activity, beginning with a consideration for the nature of group-involvement effects upon physical activity participation.

Group Involvement

Identification with others as a member of a common social group can be a primary form of social influence at any point in the lifespan. Baumeister and Leary (1995) have provided compelling evidence that attaining a sense of "belonging" is a fundamental human motive that explains a considerable amount of human social behavior and that results in numerous, important psychological and affective consequences for individuals. Research on group processes and group-involvement effects is extensive, of course, and we will constrain our discussion to some of the most important behavioral, psychological, and affective outcomes that can occur through group involvement in sport and exercise settings. We will begin this section with a general discussion of social relational and affiliative needs in sport and physical activity from a lifespan perspective and then shift our focus to the general knowledge base on group-involvement effects.

One of the primary motives for individuals to become involved, and to stay involved, in groups in sport and physical activity settings is the desire for affiliation with others in these contexts. The importance of this motive has consistently been recognized in the youth sport research (Weiss & Petlichkoff, 1989), but studies examining participation motives at later stages of the lifespan also point to the role of affiliation motivation as a principal motive for involvement in both sport and exercise contexts (Ashford, Biddle, & Goudas, 1993; Brodkin & Weiss, 1990; Ebbeck, Gibbons, & Lokendahle, 1995; Gill, Williams, Dowd, Beaudoin, & Martin, 1996; Wankel, 1985; Whaley & Ebbeck, 1997).

Although establishing and maintaining friendships with others are important to individuals throughout the lifespan, the number and quality of these relationships can change considerably over the years because of differences in the nature of the social systems with which individuals are involved. For example, early adulthood is a developmental phase during which individuals become highly interested in establishing an extensive network of friendships as they form associations with individuals in the workplace, in new neighborhoods, with their partner's friends, and in other social contexts (Ruble & Goodnow, 1998). However, at later stages of adulthood, friendship quality, as opposed to friendship quantity, typically becomes of greater concern, and older individuals tend to have fewer friends but expect each friendship to be emotionally rewarding (Ruble & Goodnow). Thus, many older adults have less extensive networks of social interaction, but this is due to selectivity rather than as a consequence of a lack of interest in being involved with others. During later adulthood, many individuals have lost close friends through death or retirement, thus further shrinking their social networks. Many times, the smaller social circle of the older adult can convey the impression that the individual is in the process of disengaging from social roles. However, developmental researchers do not necessarily agree that older individuals choose to disengage from society but rather that the decline in social activity occurs as a natural consequence of the loss of members of individuals' most important social networks (Demo, 1992; Palmore, Fillenbaum, & George, 1984). Thus, we may conclude that establishing and maintaining social relationships with others are of great importance to individuals throughout the lifespan but that the nature of these affiliative goals may change in relation to development and that the maintenance of strong social ties during later adulthood is compromised by the loss of important social relationships.

With regard to adult participatory involvement in any activity, sharing a common identity with others as a group member can be an important stimulus for initiating and maintaining involvement in group activities (Baumeister & Leary, 1995). Psychologically, group membership can provide the individual with a desired identity through association with the group and can foster a positive sense of self (Baumeister & Leary, 1995; Tajfel & Turner, 1986). From an emotional standpoint, group membership should contribute to the enjoyment one experiences in sport and exercise contexts, particularly given the recognition that affiliative goals represent a principal motive for many individuals to engage in sport and physical activity in the first place (Wankel, 1985) and that favorable social interactions constitute an important reason to maintain involvement in these contexts (Gauvin & Rejeski, 1993). The benefits of group involvement in physical activity were highlighted in research conducted by Carron, Hausenblas, and Mack (1996). In their meta-analysis of exercise behavior research, these investigators concluded that individuals exercising in a group setting receive greater psychological and behavioral benefits than do individuals exercising alone, with an average effect size of .32 for exercising in a group setting.

Sport and physical activity involvement at any point in the lifecycle almost invariably occurs within a social milieu.

It is helpful to attempt to understand group influence in reference to specific group process dimensions to better understand how group involvement can affect the individual. Important dimensions include the group's norms, status system, role characteristics, and cohesion levels. In sport and exercise research, considerable attention has been devoted to certain dimensions of group involvement, but other dimensions have received little or no attention. Specifically, group cohesion has received extensive scholarly interest in both sport and exercise contexts. The influence of group norms has attracted some attention, but the nature of status systems and role characteristics within groups have been largely ignored. This has been unfortunate because our knowledge base on group processes in nonsport contexts reflects a much broader and more balanced understanding of group-involvement effects upon individual behavior (see Cialdini & Trost, 1998).

Group Norms

Group norms are the shared expectations that exist about how group members ought to behave. Group norms can be powerful forces for compliance and conformity, particularly under competitive situations, when threat to the group is perceived, and in situations where in-group and out-group differences are considered to be large (Tajfel & Turner, 1986). Furthermore, group norms can exert substantial influence upon the individual when people are members of highly cohesive, task-oriented groups that emphasize uniform behavior and in situations in which outcome uncertainty is a prominent feature (Cialdini & Trost, 1998). In tightly knit groups, group members have frequent opportunities to communicate expectations to others, to direct attention toward agreed-upon task outcomes, and in accordance with these standards, have criteria by which to sanction members who do not adhere to these norms. One motivation for adhering to group norms is that doing so aids individuals in affiliating with others. Specifically, by conforming to the practices of important reference groups, we can become more likable and desirable to these important others (Cialdini & Trost, 1998; Levine & Moreland, 1998).

In sport contexts, group norms have been linked to a variety of motivational, behavioral, and performance outcomes; and normative influence can affect individuals' behavior away from the sport setting as well (Donnelly & Young, 1988). Group norms can result in many favorable sport performance outcomes by contributing to group members' desires to conform to the expectations of other members of the team. For example, positive group norms in sport can affect individuals' promptness to practice and the intensity of effort that they put forth while practicing and competing with the team. In a study conducted by Munroe, Estabrooks, Dennis, and Carron (1999) with adolescent and young adult athletes, norms related to productivity, punctuality, and preparedness were consistently cited by group members as normative influences upon behavior. However, social norms do not necessarily always yield favorable outcomes. For example, group norms about desirable appearance have been linked to unhealthy weight-control behaviors in women's gymnastics and other sports (Chopak & Taylor-Nicholson, 1991; Noden, 1994). Similarly, Adler and Adler (1991) found that normative beliefs within a university athletic subculture adversely affected the academic motivation and performance of male college basketball players.

In adult exercise settings, favorable group norms should enhance group members' motivation and adherence to exercise involvement, thus serving to assist individuals in achieving their physical activity goals. For example, if a group norm exists that group members will regularly attend classes and will provide assistance and emotional support to other members of the group, this norm should strengthen motivation and contribute to beneficial outcomes for each of the individual group members. However, although we can assume that highly cohesive groups generate a positive normative influence (Carron, Hausenblas, & Estabrooks, 1999), we do not yet have much direct evidence about the relationship between cohesion and norms in exercise groups.

In general, researchers interested in studying normative influence in exercise have employed either the theory of reasoned action (Ajzen & Fishbein 1980; Fishbein & Ajzen, 1975) or the theory of planned behavior (Ajzen, 1991) as the conceptual framework for their investigations. In each theory, normative influence is a core component, but norms have been operationalized as subjective norms, which are considered to be an individual's perception of the normative beliefs held by significant others in general. However, norms measured in this way do not tap one's perceptions about those sets of beliefs held by members of an intact group (e.g., exercise class) but rather only people's perceptions about how other important individuals in their lives (e.g., spouse, friends) feel. As a consequence of a rather narrow approach to measuring normative influence in exercise, our understanding of the potential benefits of social norms on exercise behavior in intact exercise groups is limited (Biddle & Mutrie, 2001). Potentially, however, the examination of group norms in exercise settings will prove to be a fruitful area for both scholarship and intervention.

> The effects of group involvement upon the individual will be influenced by his or her status within the group.

Status Systems

Power and decision-making opportunities are generally not distributed equally within groups, which reflects the presence of status arrangements. The effects of group involvement upon the individual will be, to a certain extent, influenced by one's relative status within the group. Individuals with greater status generally have higher satisfaction with their involvement and are more resistant to change than are those with lesser status (Levine & Moreland, 1998).

Status as a group member can be attained in a variety of different ways. Individuals may be accorded status because they are heavily involved in group decision making or because other group members perceive that they have great potential to contribute to the realization of group goals. Furthermore, gender, race, and the perceived attractiveness of the individual also can play a role in status attainment (Levine & Moreland, 1998). Irrespective of the origins of the status arrangements within any particular group, it appears that groups generally develop status systems fairly rapidly, and these arrangements are often quite stable and difficult to change (Levine & Moreland, 1998).

Within sport and exercise groups, we might presume that individuals with higher ability are typically accorded greater status. As a consequence of this greater status, these individuals will likely have more input into group goals and norms and have higher relative influence upon the participatory climate. Greater status is also likely to affect the psychological and affective characteristics of involvement. On athletic teams, starters and substitutes are likely to experience differing levels of satisfaction with their involvement, and they would logically have differing levels of commitment to group goals because starters have more direct influence in shaping group outcomes. Consequently, if we are interested in understanding the psychological, social, and emotional consequences of involvement within an athletic team or exercise group, it is important to consider the individual's relative status within the group, as status can exert a fundamental influence upon how individuals perceive their involvement and the opportunities present for them as a group member.

Role Characteristics

For a group to function effectively, there must be considerable interdependence among the group members. In order to facilitate group functioning, group members typically adopt unique roles within the group. Roles reflect the shared expectations of group members about the specific duties that a given member should perform for the benefit of the group as a whole (Levine & Moreland, 1998). The assignment of roles to group members is known as *role differentiation*. The extent to which role differentiation benefits the group depends upon considerations related to role assignment and role acceptance. *Role assignment* refers to the group's decisions about who should assume which roles whereas *role acceptance* refers to an individual's willingness to accept assigned roles and his or her subsequent level of commitment to those roles. More effective groups provide role assignments for members that most effectively utilize individuals' unique capacities and maximize each person's potential contribution to the group while minimizing their involvement in tasks at which they have limited potential to make a contribution. Potential problems are inherent in any group with regard to role differentiation. Such problems can be caused, for example, by poor assignment of roles, a lack of acceptance of assigned roles, ambiguity about one's role(s), or lack of ability to perform a role. The psychological, social, and emotional consequences of group membership will also depend substantially upon the extent to which people are satisfied with the roles that they are expected to perform within the group and the degree to which they fulfill those roles to the satisfaction of others (Levine & Moreland, 1998).

As status systems and role characteristics become clearly defined, the group functions within a more formalized structure, or social system. Nixon (1992) described such structures within athletic teams as "social networks" in which a web of interaction connects team members and formalizes their communication patterns within the constraints of well-established group norms.

Cohesion

Group cohesion has been the dimension of group processes that has received the most extensive attention within sport and exercise psychology. Cohesion literally refers to a group's desire to stick together. Carron, Brawley, and Widmeyer (1998, p. 213) defined *cohesion* more formally as "a dynamic process that is reflected in the tendency of the group to stick together and to remain united in the pursuit of its instrumental objectives and/or for the satisfaction of member affective needs." This definition is important to the current conceptualization of cohesion because it highlights the role of both instrumental and affective outcomes for group members. *Instrumental outcomes* refer to the task-related outcomes that individuals collectively seek to achieve whereas *affective outcomes* pertain to favorable social dimensions of involvement such as feelings of satisfaction, affiliation, and enjoyment that can result from group membership (Paskevich, Estabrooks, Brawley, & Carron, 2001).

A growing body of research on group cohesion has addressed the role of cohesion in shaping adult physical activity and exercise involvement. Carron, Widmeyer, and Brawley (1988) conducted the first in a series of studies on the relationship between group cohesion and exercise participation levels. These researchers found that young adult exercise participants who were better adherers to exercise classes generally perceived higher levels of cohesiveness within the class than did those individuals with poorer adherence rates. These findings were replicated in subsequent research by Spink and Carron (1992, 1993), also with young adult participants, and suggested that individuals who perceived that they were members of a cohesive group were more motivated to maintain their involvement with the group.

Subsequent research by Carron and Spink (1993) was directed toward the proactive development of cohesion during adult exercise classes to determine if such efforts resulted in favorable behavioral outcomes for participants. In this study, the researchers attempted to enhance cohesion in university exercise classes by augmenting feelings of distinctiveness of the group members, enhancing positive group norms, developing fitness-based subgroups (positions within the group), facilitating intragroup interaction and communication, and encouraging small individual sacrifices for the group. At the end of a 13-week intervention, groups that had experienced the group cohesion treatment had higher cohesion and had higher levels of individual satisfaction with the class than did those in the control condition.

In order to foster feelings of group cohesion, Estabrooks and Carron (1999) conducted a team-building exercise with exercise classes composed of older adults. In this study of first-time exercise class attendees, individuals who were members of the team-building groups had higher rates of attendance than did members of control and placebo conditions and had a higher return rate to the exercise class after a 10-week break than did the control-group members.

Practical suggestions for the enhancement of group cohesion were provided by Carron et al. (1999). They highlighted the fact that exercise classes are populated by individuals with limited previous interaction and that, consequently, these classes typically lack the common group goals, normative and role expectations for group members, and stable social structures that characterize more naturally occurring groups such as athletic teams or work groups. Carron et al. (1999) recommended that fitness instructors could enhance group cohesion by facilitating group goal-setting practices. For example, group members could identify a collective group goal (total weight loss, exercise attendance levels) toward which each group member can make a contribution. A second suggestion was to enhance distinctiveness of the group through clothing, names, or slogans. Distinctiveness serves to highlight individuals' sense of attachment to the group as well as their identity as a group member. A third suggestion was directed toward the enhancement of positive group norms related, for example, toward promptness in arriving to class or toward exercising at appropriate intensities. Increased social interaction outside of the class setting should further contribute to feelings of cohesion as would greater opportunities for interpersonal communication during the class.

The potential benefits of group cohesion to favorable exercise outcomes for adult participants were highlighted by the findings of a meta-analysis conducted by Carron et al. (1996). These researchers found a significant effect for task cohesion upon adherence behavior with an average effect size of .62 across studies.

The role of group membership in shaping psychosocial and participatory aspects of exercise involvement is increasingly recognized as a fundamental form of social influence upon adult physical activity behavior. Proactive efforts to facilitate favorable group norms and group cohesion seem to be highly appropriate strategies for intervention in this area, and a growing body of empirical research provides support for such approaches. A highly aligned form of social influence is social support, and the influence of social support upon adult physical activity behavior has been extensively studied.

SOCIAL SUPPORT

Social support is an important form of social influence when we consider physical activity involvement from a lifespan developmental perspective. Theory and research on social support emerged principally from health-based research on the study of individual response patterns to stress and individual differences in coping capacity (Lazarus & Folkman, 1984; Thoits, 1986). Social support has been considered to be the exchange of resources between at least two individuals in which either the provider or the recipient perceives the exchange to be intended for the recipient's benefit (Shumaker & Brownell, 1984; Udry, 1997). For our purposes, we will consider social support to reflect the intentions of individuals to provide emotional, informational, and tangible assistance to others. This characterization of social support is also consistent with the perspective of most current sport and exercise psychology researchers, who consider social support to be a multidimensional, rather than a global, construct (Rosenfeld & Richman, 1997; Udry, 1997).

In line with this multidimensional view, Cutrona and Russell (1990) identified four different types of social support. In their terminology, *emotional support* is considered to be the form of assistance provided that helps individuals to feel cared for by others under situations of stress or insecurity. A second type of support, *esteem support*, is provided with the intent of bolstering an individual's sense of competence or self-esteem through the provision of favorable competence-based feedback. *Tangible support* consists of concrete assistance in which the supportive individual provides needed resources such as financial or physical assistance. Finally, *informational support* is a matter of providing the individual with advice or guidance in such a way as to provide a possible solution to a problem.

The construct of social support has been frequently employed in the adult sport and exercise psychology literature, most notably in stress and coping research (Andersen & Williams, 1988; Smith, 1986), investigations of the psychological consequences of injury and injury rehabilitation (Hardy, Richman, & Rosenfeld, 1991; Udry, 1997; Udry, Gould, Bridges, & Tuffey, 1997), and more recently in understanding high-level athletic performance (Rees & Hardy, 2000). Social support may benefit the individual in a number of different ways. For example, social support may reduce an individual's perception of events as being stressful (Lazarus & Folkman, 1984), and because social relationships are more amenable to change than is exposure to stress, the provision of social support should be a primary focus in stress and coping interventions (Thoits, 1986). Social support may also increase the likelihood that individuals will engage in appropriate problem-solving behaviors, or it may enhance an individual's self-perceptions so that he or she approaches a given task with greater self-efficacy and motivation to resolve the problem.

Chogahara, O'Brien Cousins, and Wankel (1998) provided a comprehensive review of research on the influence of social support upon physical activity outcomes for older adults. In their review, studies were included that examined the relationship between social support and exercise behavior outcome variables (e.g., exercise class attendance, change in level of exercise) as well as studies examining social support and outcome variables that were psychosocial in nature (self-efficacy, intention to exercise). Twenty-nine published research articles met these criteria and were included in their evaluation. Across all studies, social support characteristics were measured on 85 occasions because many studies assessed multiple forms of social support. Overall, the researchers found that roughly half (42 of 85) of the social support characteristics were significantly related to desirable behavioral outcomes for adult exercise participants. The most important sources of social support for adults as identified in these studies were spouses, children, other family members, peers, exercise instructors, and physicians. In their review, Chogahara et al. also examined research from seven studies that included participants 65 years of age and older. The findings from this research suggested that social support was even more important in affecting physical activity outcomes for older individuals than for the general adult population. In these studies, the researchers found that 11 of the 15 social support variables were significantly associated with positive physical activity outcomes for older adults. Particularly noteworthy investigations from this sample were Sallis et al.'s (1989) study that demonstrated the greater importance of peer support for women over 50 years than for women under 50 years and O'Brien Cousins' (1995) research that indicated that social support was as important as self-efficacy for exercise involvement for women over 70 years of age.

> Research suggests that social support is even more important in affecting physical activity outcomes for older individuals than for the general adult population.

In their meta-analysis, Carron et al. (1996) found moderate to large effect sizes (*ES* .50 - .80) for various social support influences upon psychological and behavioral dimensions of exercise behavior. These larger effect sizes were associated with family support toward attitudes about exercise, important others' (including physicians and work colleagues) influence on attitudes toward exercise, and family support with compliance behavior. In sum, it seems evident that family members and important others represent important forms of influence upon individuals' attitudes toward, and compliance to, exercise.

Chogahara et al. (1998) expressed two major concerns about the social support research conducted to date in physical activity contexts. First, they commented that the overwhelming majority of studies in the physical activity literature focus upon *sources* of social support rather than upon *type* of social support. The concern for social support sources has directed attention toward the role of particular individuals (e.g., spouses, physicians) rather than to the functional or behavioral characteristics of support such as emotional support or esteem support. The tendency within the physical activity literature to focus upon sources of support is misguided, according to Chogahara et al., because it fails to adequately address the question of *how* others provide support in physical activity contexts. In other words, the more important issue is to identify how others can enhance physical activity outcomes for individuals as opposed to who affects these outcomes. A second concern expressed by these authors was that the measurement of social influence in physical activity, and specifically social support, has often been simplistic. In this regard, these authors noted that many researchers have ignored the separate dimensions of social support (tangible support, esteem support, etc.) most widely used in health-related literature and also have tended to collapse many social support types into one overall index of social support.

LEADERSHIP INFLUENCES

The leadership behavior of coaches and instructors constitutes a fundamentally important form of social influence in sport and exercise settings. Leadership practices can certainly affect motivational outcomes for groups and individuals including the extent of motivation, as well as the intrinsic or extrinsic nature of this motivation. Similarly, leadership behaviors can influence a variety of affective outcomes for individuals in the physical domain, including levels of satisfaction, anxiety, enjoyment, and burnout. Leadership behaviors can also be anticipated to shape performance outcomes, specifically success levels in sport, as well as participatory outcomes in exercise classes such as class attendance and adherence levels. Although leadership is an essential form of social influence in physical activity settings, it is helpful to examine leadership practices separately in sport and exercise settings, given fundamental differences between these two contexts, and in accordance with differing research traditions and types of research questions in the two areas of study.

Sport Leadership

The study of sport leadership has a long history, and theoretical approaches to this topic have undergone substantial change and evolution. Initial research on sport leadership reflected orientations popular in the general leadership research literature that typically focused on trait or behaviorally based approaches. The trait perspective reflected an underlying belief that leadership effectiveness depended primarily on the personality characteristics, or traits, of the leader whereas behaviorally based approaches directed primary attention to specific behavioral characteristics of coaches such as their decision-making styles (e.g., autocratic or democratic). Neither trait nor behaviorally based approaches have endured because each represented a narrow, relatively simplistic approach to the study of coach influence (Horn, 1992).

Chelladurai (1980) developed a multidimensional model of leadership that is specific to the sport context. In Chelladurai's model, leadership practices are considered in relation to both team performance and athlete satisfaction. In order to maximize performance and satisfaction outcomes, Chelladurai contends that there must be a good match between required coach behavior, preferred coach behavior, and actual coach behavior. *Required coach behavior* is the behavior most appropriate given the demands of the sport, the situation, and the unique characteristics of the group such as their age and level of experience. *Preferred coach behavior* is the pattern of coach behavior desired by group members whereas *actual coach behavior* consists of coaches' behavioral responses. In Chelladurai's model, coaching behaviors are also considered in relation to five specific dimensions of leadership. These dimensions include training and instruction behaviors, democratic and autocratic leadership styles, social support behaviors, and positive feedback. Chelladurai's model has been widely used in the sport domain because it was developed for use in this context, avoids the oversimplifications inherent in other models, and addresses both performance and psychosocial outcomes for participants.

Given the scope of Chelladurai's (1980) model, it is difficult for researchers to conduct a complete test of his theory in any given study. Consequently, researchers have directed their attention to examining certain components of the model such as the relationship between coaching behaviors and athlete satisfaction levels (e.g., Chelladurai, 1984; Chelladurai, 1993; Horne & Carron, 1985; Schliesman, 1987; Weiss & Friedrichs, 1986). Two types of research questions have emerged in this line of research. The first question has addressed the issue of whether athlete satisfaction results from a high level of congruence between athletes' preferred coaching behaviors and coaches' actual behaviors whereas the second research question has examined the specific types of coaching behaviors (e.g., social support, democratic decision-making style) that are most strongly associated with athlete satisfaction.

In an initial test of his model, Chelladurai (1984) found that greater congruence between perceived and preferred coaching behaviors was related to higher levels of satisfaction for university-level athletes. Training and instruction were the dimensions of coaching behavior that contributed most strongly to satisfaction. In a follow-up study, Horne and Carron (1985) found that training and instruction, social support, and positive feedback were the coaching behaviors that were most strongly associated with athlete satisfaction, whereas Schliesman (1987) also found these same three coaching behaviors to be predictors of athlete satisfaction. In a similar line of research, Gordon (1988) found that greater discrepancies between actual and preferred coach decision-making styles (in this case, autocratic, democratic, consultative, and delegative styles) were associated with lower satisfaction for male collegiate soccer players. Weiss and Friedrichs (1986) found that athletes' perceptions of greater frequencies of positive feedback, social support, and a democratic decision-making style were associated with higher levels of player satisfaction for male collegiate basketball players.

> Several separate groups of researchers found that training and instruction, social support, and positive feedback were the coaching behaviors most strongly associated with athlete satisfaction.

Additional research has investigated the influence of coaching behaviors on affective and motivational outcomes for athletes, although not strictly from Chelladurai's (1980) framework. Vealey, Armstrong, Comar, and Greenleaf (1998) examined the relationship between female college athletes' perceptions of their coach's behavior and communication style with athletes' burnout and anxiety. In this case, athletes who reported higher levels of burnout perceived that their coaches were higher in autocratic style, were less empathic, used less praise, and emphasized winning more in comparison to athletes who reported lower levels of burnout.

Research on coach influence supports the belief that coaches' leadership practices also affect motivational outcomes for athletes. Amorose and Horn (2000) conducted a study with 386 male and female college athletes participating at the NCAA Division 1 level. Using Deci and Ryan's (1985) cognitive evaluation theory as their theoretical framework, these researchers found that athletes with higher levels of intrinsic motivation to participate in sport perceived that their coaches emphasized greater training and instruction, used democratic style, and were lower in the use of an autocratic style. Furthermore, athletes with higher levels of intrinsic motivation perceived that their coaches provided a greater frequency of positive, informationally grounded feedback and a lower frequency of punishment-oriented and ignoring behaviors.

Exercise Leadership

The exercise leader, or class instructor, should also constitute an important form of social influence within the adult physical activity environment. Nonetheless, remarkably little research attention has been dedicated to understanding the role of the exercise leader in shaping psychosocial and participatory outcomes for individuals in structured physical activity programs (Biddle & Mutrie, 2001). Research to date has primarily focused on exercise leaders' roles in shaping participants' involvement and adherence in physical activity classes (McAuley & Jacobson, 1991), participants' exercise self-efficacy and motivation (McAuley & Jacobson, 1991; Turner, Rejeski, & Brawley, 1997), and individuals' affective responses to the exercise experience (Fox, Rejeski, & Gauvin, 2000; Turner et al., 1997).

McAuley and Jacobson (1991) conducted a study with previously sedentary adult females, ages 45 to 64 years, who volunteered to participate in an 8-week aerobic exercise program. At the end of the program, the researchers classified individuals into high- and low-attendance groups. Baseline self-motivation was not a significant predictor of subsequent attendance, but individuals who maintained higher levels of involvement throughout the program felt that the instructor was more important to their continued participation than did those who had poorer attendance. Furthermore, good attendees had a more favorable evaluation of the program and perceived a higher level of personal success than did poorer attendees. The researchers credited these favorable perceptions to the influence of the exercise leaders in enhancing the exercise self-efficacy beliefs of those individuals who were more regularly present in the class.

Turner et al. (1997) investigated the effects of leader influence in shaping the social context of exercise and subsequent affective and psychological outcomes for participants. In this study, participants were college-aged women who engaged in a single exercise session in which the physical activity leader was responsible for creating either a socially enriched or socially bland environment. In the socially enriched leadership condition, the exercise leaders addressed participants by name, engaged in general conversation with the participants, provided encouragement and positive comments during the performance of the skills while ignoring mistakes, provided specific instructions, and verbally rewarded effort and ability immediately following the exercise. In contrast, these favorable forms of interpersonal interaction were not present in the socially bland environment in which the instructor noted mistakes and generally provided negative comments throughout the session. This setting might have been more accurately characterized as a "negative" or "unsupportive" environment, as opposed to a bland environment, because of the prevalence of negativity in the instructor's comments. Participants in the socially enriched exercise environment reported stronger feelings of revitalization during exercise and greater exercise self-efficacy than did the individuals in the contrasting environment. Furthermore, a substantial portion of the variance in postexercise affective states was attributable to enjoyment of the leadership approach employed by the instructor in the socially enriched condition.

In a follow-up study, Fox et al. (2000) contrasted socially enriched and bland leadership styles and environments upon participants' enjoyment and self-reported probability of future exercise involvement. Participants were involved in only a single exercise session consisting of a step aerobics class. In the socially enriched leadership condition, the exercise leaders engaged in the same pattern of behaviors as in the Turner et al. (1997) study. With regard to the exercise environment, eight students served as confederates for the researchers and were trained to behave in such a way so as to contribute to a socially supportive, or socially bland, group environment. Participants in the socially enriched leadership condition who also experienced the enriched social environment had higher enjoyment levels and reported a higher probability of future involvement in step aerobics than did those in the other conditions.

Overall, research conducted to date clearly supports the important role of exercise leaders in contributing to favorable affective, psychological, and participatory outcomes for individuals in structured exercise settings. However, further research can contribute greatly to the depth of our knowledge in this area. Future research exploring leadership behavior in naturally occurring, as opposed to contrived settings, and across periods of greater duration is particularly warranted.

SUMMARY AND FUTURE DIRECTIONS

Social influences can have a profound effect upon the nature and quality of people's sport and physical activity experiences. As presented in this chapter, social influence can be manifested in at least four principal ways, including through cultural values and beliefs, as a consequence of group membership, in relation to social support opportunities, and in response to leadership influences. The study of social influence is particularly relevant to a lifespan developmental view on physical activity because adult psychosocial development occurs, in large part, in response to social forms of influence such as life events and changing social relationships (Durkin, 1995; Ruble & Goodnow, 1998).

Of the four forms of social influence discussed in this chapter, cultural influence has received the least amount of research attention. However, theory and research on cultural influences in sport and physical activity point to the importance of cultural belief systems and values in shaping physical activity patterns, particularly in relation to age- and gender-related stereotypes (McPherson, 1994; Ostrow & Dzewaltowski, 1986; Vertinsky, 1995). A particularly fruitful area for future research would address the impact of physical activity promotion efforts upon changes in cultural stereotypes about physical activity among the aging population. Such a line of research could help us to determine to what extent more favorable culturally held images about the physical activity participation of older adults contributes to increased participatory motivation within this population.

Group membership constitutes a second fundamental form of social influence. As humans, we are highly motivated to affiliate with others and to belong to social groups (Baumeister & Leary, 1995). However, membership in sport and exercise groups carries with it a variety of psychosocial and behavioral effects in relation to the group's norms (Chopak & Taylor-Nicholson, 1991; Donnelly & Young, 1988), status system and role characteristics (Nixon, 1992), and cohesion levels (Carron et al., 1996; Paskevich et al., 2001). Consequently, we cannot effectively understand physical activity behavior without considering the human social context within which it occurs. Research conducted to date on group-membership effects in sport and physical activity has focused principally on group cohesion and consistently demonstrates the influence of group cohesion on various psychological and behavioral consequences of participation (Paskevich et al., 2001). Although our knowledge base on group cohesion effects is relatively well developed, knowledge about other forms of group influence has lagged substantially behind. Consequently, we need to develop a much more extensive knowledge base relating to other characteristics of group involvement. For example, empirical work is needed to understand the relative importance of role assignment and role acceptance on athlete satisfaction, the means by which group norms are developed and maintained in sport and exercise groups, and the influence of status characteristics on individuals' motivation and satisfaction in sport and exercise groups. Greater attention to group process characteristics would yield important new insight into the psychological and emotional dimensions of group involvement in sport and exercise.

Social support has emerged as a key form of social influence in sport and physical activity contexts. Social support constitutes an exchange of resources between individuals in which the intention is to provide benefits to the recipient such as reducing anxiety, enhancing the person's sense of competence or worth, or providing essential information. Current perspectives on the role of social support are grounded in the concept that distinct types of social support exist (e.g., emotional support, informational support) and that the effectiveness of social support depends upon a matching between the specific needs of the individual and the particular type of social support provided. The research literature clearly indicates that social support makes an important, and beneficial, contribution in sport and exercise (Carron et al., 1997). However, as Chogahara et al. (1998) have noted, our research has been rather narrowly focused on examining sources of social support, as opposed to types of social support, which would be more helpful in addressing theoretically based research questions. Consequently, future researchers are encouraged to dedicate attention to understanding the influence of social support in relation to contextual and personal needs. For example, better understanding of the benefits of type of social support in relation to the age, gender, or experience level (novice, intermediate, advanced) of the individual and the effects of type of social support upon context-specific self-efficacy, stress perceptions, adherence motivation, and other outcomes would provide additional depth of understanding about the role of social support.

Leadership practices constitute a fourth important form of social influence. In sport, leadership has received extensive theoretical and empirical attention. This knowledge base indicates that coaching behaviors are linked to a variety of psychological outcomes such as athlete satisfaction (Chelladurai, 1984; Horne & Carron, 1985), burnout (Vealey et al., 1998), and motivation (Amorose & Horn, 2000). However, exercise leadership research is woefully lacking (Biddle & Mutrie, 2001). Future researchers in this area are encouraged to consider developing theoretical approaches that are specific to the unique characteristics of leadership in the exercise setting because exercise groups commonly differ from sport groups with regard to group members' familiarity with other members, their level of identification with the group, the extent to which common group goals are present, and the stability of the group's composition.

An important general goal for future adult-based research is to conduct a greater proportion of research with middle-aged and older adults. A large proportion of the adult-based research has actually been conducted with young adults, typically university-level athletes and exercisers. Consequently, our knowledge base in the area is overrepresented by research on this young adult population that makes generalizations to older populations difficult. Furthermore, we need extensive research on middle-aged and older adults to capture many of the unique, developmentally related factors that can influence physical activity participation and the psychosocial consequences of this participation.

Finally, and in accordance with a lifespan developmental perspective, greater attention should be dedicated to understanding the influence of key life events in shaping adult physical activity behavior. Theoretical approaches to the study of adult developmental change point to the importance of life events and transitions in shaping behavioral opportunities and choices (Durkin, 1995; Ruble & Goodnow, 1998; Taylor, 1998). However, we could benefit from further physical activity-related research that examines the influence of life events and transitions on adult physical activity behavior. For example, research examining the role of career changes, changes in family responsibilities, retirement, and the loss of close social relationships could shed considerable light on the influence of life events in shaping physical activity behavior across the life cycle.

References

Adler, P. A., & Adler, P. (1991). *Backboards and blackboards: College athletes and role engulfment.* New York: Columbia University Press.

Ajzen, I. (1991). The theory of planned behavior. *Organizational Behavior and Human Decision Processes, 50*, 179-211.

Ajzen, I., & Fishbein, M. (1980). *Understanding attitudes and predicting social behavior*. Englewood Cliffs, NJ: Prentice-Hall.

Amorose, A. J., & Horn, T. S. (2000). Intrinsic motivation: Relationships with collegiate athletes' gender, scholarship status, and perceptions of their coaches' behavior. *Journal of Sport & Exercise Psychology, 22*, 63-84.

Andersen, M. B., & Williams, J. M. (1988). A model of stress and athletic injury: Prediction and prevention. *Journal of Sport & Exercise Psychology, 10*, 294-306.

Ashford, B., Biddle, S., & Goudas, M. (1993). Participation in community sports centers: Motives and predictors of enjoyment. *Journal of Sports Sciences, 11*, 249-256.

Baumeister, R. F., & Leary, M. R. (1995). The need to belong: Desire for interpersonal attachments as fundamental human motivation. *Psychological Bulletin, 117*, 497-529.

Biddle, S. J. H., & Mutrie, N. (2001). *Psychology of physical activity: Determinants, well-being, and interventions*. New York: Routledge.

Brodkin, P., & Weiss, M. R. (1990). Developmental differences in motivation for participating in competitive swimming. *Journal of Sport & Exercise Psychology, 12*, 248-263.

Brustad, R. J., & Ritter-Taylor, M. (1997). Applying social psychological perspectives to the sport psychology consulting process. *The Sport Psychologist, 11*, 107-119.

Carron, A. V., Brawley, L. R., & Widmeyer, W.N. (1998). The measurement of cohesiveness in sport groups. In J. L. Duda (Ed.), *Advances in sport and exercise psychology measurement* (pp. 213-226). Morgantown, WV: Fitness Information Technology.

Carron, A. V., Hausenblas, H. A., & Estabrooks, P. A. (1999). Social influence and exercise involvement. In S. J. Bull (Ed.), *Adherence issues in sport and exercise* (pp. 1-17). New York: John Wiley & Sons.

Carron, A. V., Hausenblas, H. A., & Mack, D. (1996). Social influence and exercise: A meta-analysis. *Journal of Sport & Exercise Psychology, 18*, 1-16.

Carron, A. V. & Spink, K. S. (1993). Team building in an exercise setting. *The Sport Psychologist, 7*, 8-18.

Carron, A. V., Widmeyer, W.N., & Brawley, L. R. (1988). Group cohesion and individual adherence to physical activity. *Journal of Sport & Exercise Psychology, 10*, 127-138.

Chelladurai, P. (1980). Leadership in sport organizations. *Canadian Journal of Applied Sport Sciences, 5*, 226-231.

Chelladurai, P. (1984). Discrepancy between preferences and perceptions of leadership behaviors and satisfaction of athletes in varying sports. *Journal of Sport Psychology, 6*, 27-41.

Chelladurai, P. (1993). Leadership. In R. N. Singer, M. Murphey, & L. K. Tennant (Eds.), *Handbook of research on sport psychology* (pp. 647-671). New York: Macmillan.

Chogahara, M., O'Brien Cousins, S., & Wankel, L. M. (1998). Social influences on physical activity in older adults: A review. *Journal of Aging and Physical Activity, 6*, 1-17.

Chopak, J. S., & Taylor-Nicholson, M. (1991). Do female college athletes develop eating disorders as a result of the athletic environment? In D. Black (Ed.), *Eating disorders among athletes* (pp. 87-109). Reston, VA: American Alliance for Health, Physical Education, Recreation, and Dance.

Cialdini, R. B., & Trost, M. R. (1998). Social influence: Social norms, conformity, and compliance. In D. T. Gilbert, S. T. Fiske, & G. Lindzey (Eds.), *The handbook of social psychology* (4th ed., pp. 151-192). New York: Oxford University Press.

Coakley, J. (2001). *Sport in society: Issues & controversies* (7th ed.). Dubuque, IA: McGraw-Hill.

Cutrona, C. E., & Russell, D. W. (1990). Type of social support and specific stress: Toward a theory of optimal matching. In B.R. Sarason, I.G. Sarason & G. R. Pierce (Eds.), *Social support: An interactional view* (pp. 319-366). New York: Wiley.

Deci, E. L., & Ryan, R. M. (1985). *Intrinsic motivation and self-determination in human behavior*. New York: Plenum Press.

Demo, D. H. (1992). The self-concept over time: Research issues and directions. *Annual Review of Sociology, 18*, 303-326.

Donnelly, P., & Young, K. (1988). The construction and confirmation of identity in sport subcultures. *Sociology of Sport Journal, 5*, 223-240.

Durkin, K. (1995). *Developmental social psychology: From infancy to old age*. Cambridge, MA: Blackwell.

Ebbeck, V., Gibbons, S. L., & Lokendahle, L. J. (1995). Reasons for adult physical activity: An interactional approach. *International Journal of Sport Psychology, 26*, 262-275.

Estabrooks, P. A., & Carron, A. V. (1999). The role of the group with elderly exercisers. *Small Group Research, 30*, 438-452.

Fishbein, M., & Ajzen, I. (1975). *Belief, attitude, intention, and behavior*. New York: Addison-Wesley.

Fiske, A. P., Kitayama, S., Markus, H. R., & Nisbett, R. E. (1998). The cultural matrix of social psychology. In D. T. Gilbert, S. T. Fiske, & G. Lindzey (Eds.), *The handbook of social psychology* (4th ed., pp. 915-981). New York: Oxford University Press.

Fox, L.D., Rejeski, W. J., & Gauvin, L. (2000). Effects of leadership style and group dynamics on enjoyment of physical activity. *American Journal of Health Promotion, 15*, 277-283.

Gauvin, L., & Rejeski, W. J. (1993). The exercise induced feeling inventory: Development and initial validation. *Journal of Sport & Exercise Psychology, 5*, 141-157.

Gill, D. L., Williams, L., Dowd, D. A., Beaudoin, C. M., & Martin, J. J. (1996). Competitive orientations and motives of adult sport and exercise participants. *Journal of Sport Behavior, 19*, 307-318.

Gordon, S. (1988). Decision styles and coaching effectiveness in university soccer. *Canadian Journal of Sport Sciences, 13*, 56-65.

Hardy, C. J., Richman, J. M., & Rosenfeld, L. B. (1991). The role of social support in the life stress/injury relationship. *The Sport Psychologist, 5*, 128-139.

Hellstedt, J. (1995). Invisible players: A family systems model. In S. M. Murphy (Ed.), *Sport psychology interventions* (pp. 117-146). Champaign, IL: Human Kinetics.

Horn, T. S. (1992). Leadership effectiveness in the sport domain. In T. S. Horn (Ed.), *Advances in Sport Psychology* (pp. 181-199). Champaign: IL: Human Kinetics.

Horne, T., & Carron, A. (1985). Compatibility in coach-athlete relationships. *Journal of Sport Psychology, 7*, 137-149.

Imber-Black, E. (1988). *Families and larger systems: A family therapist's guide through the labyrinth.* New York: The Guilford Press.

Katz, D., & Kahn, R. L. (1978). *The social psychology of organizations* (2nd ed.) New York: Wiley.

Langley, D. J., & Knight, S. M. (1999). Continuity in sport participation as an adaptive strategy in the aging process: A lifespan narrative. *Journal of Aging and Physical Activity, 7*, 32-54.

Lazarus, R. S., & Folkman, S. (1984). *Stress, appraisal, and coping.* New York: Springer.

Levine, J. M., & Moreland, R. L. (1998). Small groups. In D. T. Gilbert, S. T. Fiske, & G. Lindzey (Ed.), *The handbook of social psychology* (4th ed., pp. 415-469). New York: Oxford University Press.

Lewin, K. (1951). *Field theory in social science.* New York: Harper.

McAuley, E., & Jacobson, L. (1991). Self-efficacy and exercise participation in sedentary adult females. *American Journal of Health Promotion, 5*, 185-191.

McPherson, B. (1994). Sociocultural perspectives on aging and physical activity. *Journal of Aging and Physical Activity, 2*, 329-353.

Munroe, K., Estabrooks, P., Dennis, P., & Carron, A. (1999). A phenomenological analysis of group norms in sport teams. *The Sport Psychologist, 13*, 171-182.

Nixon, H.L. (1992). A social network analysis of influences on athletes with pain and injuries. *Journal of Sport and Social Issues, 16*, 127-135.

Noden, M. (1994). Dying to win. *Sports Illustrated, 81*, 52-60.

O'Brien Cousins, S. (1995). Social support for exercise among elderly women in Canada. *Health Promotion International, 10*, 273-282.

O'Brien Cousins, S., & Keating, N. (1995). Life cycle patterns of physical activity among sedentary and active older women. *Journal of Aging and Physical Activity, 3*, 340-359.

Ostrow, A. C., & Dzewaltowski, D. A. (1986). Older adults' perceptions of physical activity participation based on age-role and sex-role appropriateness. *Research Quarterly for Exercise and Sport, 57*, 167-169.

Palmore, E. B., Fillenbaum, G. G., & George, L. K. (1984). Consequences of retirement. *Journal of Gerontology, 3*, 109-116.

Paskevich, D. M., Estabrooks, P. A., Brawley, L. R., & Carron, A. V. (2001). Group cohesion in sport and exercise. In R. N. Singer, H. A. Hausenblas, & C. M. Janelle (Eds.), *Handbook of sport psychology* (2nd ed., pp. 472-494). New York: John Wiley & Sons.

Rees, T., & Hardy, L. (2000). An investigation of the social support experiences of high-level sports performers. *The Sport Psychologist, 14*, 327-347.

Rosenfeld, L. B., & Richman, J. M. (1997). Developing effective social support: Team building and the social support process. *Journal of Applied Sport Psychology, 9*, 133-153.

Ruble, D. N., & Goodnow, J. J. (1998). Social development in childhood and adulthood. In D. T. Gilbert, S. T. Fiske, & G. Lindzey (Eds.), *The handbook of social psychology* (4th ed., pp. 741-787). New York: Oxford University Press.

Sallis, J. F., Hovell, M. F., Hofstetter, C. R., Faucher, P., Elder, J. P., Blanchard, J., et al. (1989). A multivariate study of determinants of vigorous exercise in a community sample. *Preventive Medicine, 18*, 20-34.

Schliesman, E. (1987). Relationship between the congruence of preferred and actual leader behavior and subordinate satisfaction with leadership. *Journal of Sport Behavior, 10*, 157-166.

Shumaker, S. A., & Brownell, A. (1984). Toward a theory of social support: Closing conceptual gaps. *Journal of Social Issues, 40*, 11-36.

Smith, R. E. (1986). Toward a cognitive-affective model of athletic burnout. *Journal of Sport Psychology, 8*, 36-50.

Spink, K. S., & Carron, A. V. (1992). Group cohesion and adherence in exercise classes. *Journal of Sport & Exercise Psychology, 14*, 78-86.

Spink, K. S., & Carron, A. V. (1993). The effects of team building on the adherence patterns of female exercise participants. *Journal of Sport & Exercise Psychology, 15*, 39-49.

Tajfel, H., & Turner, J. C. (1986). The social identity theory of intergroup behavior. In S. Worchel and W. G. Austin (Eds.), *Psychology of intergroup relations* (pp. 7-24). Chicago: Nelson-Hall.

Taylor, S. E. (1998). The social being in social psychology. In D. T. Gilbert, S. T., Fiske, & G. Lindzey (Eds.), *The handbook of social psychology* (4th ed., pp. 58-95). New York: Oxford University Press.

Thoits, P. A. (1986). Social support as coping assistance. *Journal of Consulting and Clinical Psychology, 54,* 416-423.

Turner, E. E., Rejeski, W. J., & Brawley, L. R. (1997). Psychological benefits of physical activity are influenced by the social environment. *Journal of Sport & Exercise Psychology, 19,* 119-130.

Udry, E. (1997). Coping and social support in injured athletes following surgery. *Journal of Sport & Exercise Psychology, 19,* 71-90.

Udry, E., Gould, D., Bridges, D., & Tuffey, S. (1997). People helping people? Examining the social ties of athletes coping with burnout and injury stress. *Journal of Sport & Exercise Psychology, 19,* 368-395.

Vealey, R. S., Armstrong, L., Comar, W., & Greenleaf, C. A. (1998). Influence of perceived coaching behaviors on burnout and competitive anxiety in female college athletes. *Journal of Applied Sport Psychology, 10,* 297-318.

Vertinsky, P. (1991). Old age, gender, and physical activity: The biomedicalization of aging. *Journal of Sport History, 18,* 64-80.

Vertinsky, P. (1995). Stereotypes of aging women and exercise: A historical perspective. *Journal of Aging and Physical Activity, 3,* 223-237.

Wankel, L. M. (1985). Personal and situational factors affecting exercise involvement: The importance of enjoyment. *Research Quarterly for Exercise and Sport, 56,* 275-282.

Weiss, M. R., & Friedrichs, W. (1986). The influence of leader behaviors, coach attributes, and institutional variables on performance and satisfaction of collegiate basketball teams. *Journal of Sport Psychology, 8,* 332-346.

Weiss, M. R., & Petlichkoff, L. M. (1989). Children's motivation for participation in and withdrawal from sport: Identifying the missing links. *Pediatric Exercise Science, 1,* 195-211.

Whaley, D. E., & Ebbeck, V. (1997). Older adults' constraints to participation in structured exercise classes. *Journal of Aging and Physical Activity, 5,* 190-212.

Wylleman, P. (2000). Interpersonal relationships in sport: Uncharted territory in sport psychology research. *International Journal of Sport Psychology, 31,* 555-572.

Zimmerman, T. S., Protinsky, H. O., & Zimmerman, C. S. (1994). Family systems consultation with an athletic team: A case study of themes. *Journal of Applied Sport Psychology, 6,* 101-115.

Chapter Twelve

Emotion in Sport Across Adulthood

Peter R. E. Crocker • Kent C. Kowalski
Sharleen D. Hoar • Meghan H. McDonough

> Anyone can become angry. That is easy. But to be angry with the right person,
> to the right degree, at the right time, for the right purpose and in the right
> way—that is not easy. (Aristotle)

Emotions make life worth living. They are essential to sporting life, whether experienced as a child or adult, player or spectator. Our sporting memories are dominated by strong emotional events. In the 2000 Olympics, many in the world rejoiced with Australia's Cathy Freeman as she captured gold in the 400 meters. At the other extreme, many Major League Baseball fans reacted with disgust to Roberto Alomar's spitting into the face of an umpire during an angry exchange. Emotions can also rapidly transform as sporting situations unfold. Joy turns to despair as certain victory turns to defeat, as when the U.S. men's basketball team lost in the 1972 Olympic gold medal game against the Soviet Union. Strong emotions are not just limited to elite athletes; they occur at all levels and all ages. Moreover, emotions are not just mere reactions: Scientists argue they are a key component in motivated behavior (Malatesta & Izard, 1984; Vallerand & Blanchard, 2000).

Sport and exercise scientists have recognized that emotions have personal and social consequences (Hackfort, 1999; Hanin, 2000a; Hardy, Jones, & Gould 1996; Vallerand & Blanchard, 2000). Emotions can both facilitate and impair performance (Hanin, 2000b; Jones, 1995; Naylor, Burton, & Crocker, 2002) and can influence choices about continued participation and other motivated behavior in sport and exercise (Berger & Motl, 2000; Biddle, 2000; Vallerand & Blanchard, 2000). Emotional expressions also play an important social function. Showing anger, sadness, and joy conveys information about what situations people within cultures deem to be important and conveys social expectations about appropriate behavior. Obviously, emotional expressions can influence the thoughts, emotions, and behaviors of others including teammates, opponents, coaches, and fans (Hackfort, 1999). Consider the comments of Vancouver hockey player Jarkko Ruutu after scoring a goal against rival Colorado: "I was pretty happy when I scored and even happier when I saw (team-mate) Jason Strudwick's face because I realized how big a goal it was. . . . It was probably the most pumped I've been. It was an unbelievable experience"(MacIntyre, 2001).

Understanding the causes and consequences of emotional responses has been a central focus of sport psychology for over three decades. There are already a number of good reviews of research on emotion, moods, and affective feeling states in sport. Most reviews have focused

Sport and exercise scientists have recognized that emotions have personal and social consequences.

on emotionality–performance relationships in sport (e.g., Gould & Tuffey, 1996; Hanin, 2000a; Landers & Boutcher, 1998; Prapavessis, 2000; Terry, 1995), although some reviews have focused on exercise (Berger & Motl, 2000; Gauvin & Spence, 1998) and health-related behavior (Biddle, 2000; Heil, 2000). However, there have been few attempts to consider "how" emotional responses in sport might change over adulthood. This chapter will provide knowledge about the emotion process in adult development. Over time, there are changes in physiological and cognitive functioning, social norms and expectations, social status, and experience given the changes. What differences can we expect in adults' emotional experience and expression in physical activity settings? We will primarily limit our focus to sport settings, although exercise and other physical activity settings will be considered where appropriate to demonstrate important points. Information is based on both theory and research and is designed to help the reader understand the social and psychological complexities that underlie emotion in sport across adulthood.

The chapter is organized into several sections. First, we present three images of adults recalling strong emotional experiences from sport. These cases serve two purposes: (a) to illustrate how emotions are embedded in a person-social context and (b) to highlight key processes that are critical to emotion such as cognitive evaluation, felt impulses, coping, expression, and subjective experiences. Next, we discuss differences between emotions, moods, and affective feeling states. Third, we briefly review different perspectives on studying emotion including physiological, social constructivist, cognitive appraisal, and cognitive-motivational approach. Last, we engage in a discussion of changes in emotional experience and expression in sport settings across adulthood. We will argue that individual differences within and across age groups can be best understood by examining personal and social changes that influence processes underlying the components of emotion.

Millie—23-Year-Old Female Flat-Water Kayaker[1]

Last spring I participated in my first Olympic team trials. I have been a kayaker for the last 10 years of my life, and the opportunity to compete for a spot on the Olympic team sounded kind of thrilling in the months and years leading up to trials. But the previous summer's competitive season had been pretty sub par, with poor performances at national team trials, and leaving early from national championships when I got word that my mother was dying. This was my first national-level regatta since then, and I felt a bit anxious about racing and seeing everyone again. I had decided to stay home in the fall to finish my undergraduate degree even though it meant not being able to do much sport-specific training during that period. When I came to race, I felt that I was not prepared enough. So it was with a fair amount of negative thoughts and emotions that I went into my races. I tried to use positive self-talk and to focus on my own race and do my best, but I just couldn't shake the pervading feeling that maybe I wasn't good enough to be there, at least not then. In the semifinal, I drew a lane next to a girl who had a much faster start than me. I got behind and had to contend with interference from the waves of her boat for most of the race. By the end of the race I was significantly behind, and my boat got turned a bit so it was pointing to go through the finish lane on the wrong side of my lane buoy. We were at the end of a more-than-2-minute all-out sprint, and the spacing of the lane markers is such that if you get turned at the right angle, it is possible to think that you are going down your lane when you are really crossing it at an angle. I got confused and, thinking I was going the right way, finished the race just outside my lane and was disqualified. I wasn't aware that I was disqualified during my cooldown and was feeling pretty badly about my poor placing in the semifinal. When I got back to the dock, I learned that I had been disqualified. I felt humiliated! Not only was I slow but despite all my years of racing experience I was disqualified by a stupid, avoidable error. I felt ashamed for failing to complete the simple task of staying in my lane, let alone compete well, at such a high-level competition. I kept replaying the finish of the race in my mind. I could see my mistake very vividly. Part of me wished I could go back and do it again, but mostly I wanted to hide. I didn't want to talk to anyone and feel like I was making excuses for myself. I wanted to go home. However, trials are 2 days long and I had to come back and do it all over again the next day. I think I relaxed a little that day since I thought that it couldn't possibly be worse. I raced better the second day, making it to the B final and not getting as far behind the pack, but I still left the competition with an overriding feeling of having failed, of having shown the effects of my sometimes substandard training over the past year, and of showing myself to not be the motivated, disciplined, hard-working athlete that I like to think I am.

Ronald—43-Year-Old Male Soccer Player

I can recall the incident vividly. I was attacking the defense when this defender chopped me down right across the knees. It hurt like hell – I thought my leg was broken. I was instantaneously mad. I looked at the referee, who simply yelled, "Play on." I was furious! If the referee wouldn't take care of it, I would. I chased the player (who now had the ball) down the field – it was probably the fastest I had run in 10 years! I took him down with a clumsy tackle. Several thoughts immediately came to me. The referee might red card (expel) me, the player might punch me out, and what would my teammates and others think. I helped the player up and

---

[1]The athletic situations described are real but the athletes' names are pseudonyms.

made like I was sorry, which I was at one level. The referee gave me a stern lecture and a yellow card – I had to suppress telling him what I thought of him. My anger slowly transformed into shame as I realized how I had lost control for such a meaningless event – I mean, this is master-level soccer – not the World Cup! Reflecting upon the incident, I realize I was so angry for two reasons. First, I'm afraid of serious injury at this stage of my life, and I felt the player's tackle was dangerous and stupid. Second, the referee didn't make the call. It is funny how stupid beliefs like "taking care of matters and not allowing others to intimidate you" suddenly influence your actions when you are stressed out.

Jocko—60-Year-Old Male Masters Swimmer

The Canadian National Masters Swimming Championships were a very significant event in my competitive career. I had been active in master's swimming for 20 years and had always managed to establish world records each time I moved into a new age category (every 5 years) and was wondering how I would do at the 60-year-old level. The meet in Ottawa was very competitive, with swimmers from several foreign countries, including the U.S.A., Japan, Mexico, and Germany. My goals were to set world records in my specialty, the individual medley; and as there were three of these events in the program, I felt I had a fairly good chance in all three. The first day, I was to swim the 200 Individual Medley as my first event. This was an event in which I had always had considerable success – I had established a world best time in the event in 1961 when I won the NCAA 200 Individual Medley and had continued to set world standards in the event all through my masters career. I was quite sure, barring any unforeseen errors, that I could quite comfortably erase that mark. I vividly remember becoming adrenaline charged, vis-à-vis the usual nervousness, and was very emotionally high for start of the race. There was a large crowd in the stands, with many of them expecting me to set a world record. I was quite excited about the race knowing that I had trained well, had prepared my race strategy well, and had shaved down for the races to come. All I had to do was concentrate on the task at hand and not be concerned about the other swimmers in the race. I can vividly remember getting a very fast start and feeling very strong and loose in the first length of the butterfly and thinking that I knew that I was ready for a fast race. At the end of the first 50 meters, I was already well ahead of the field and continuing to gain distance with every stroke. I had to concentrate on my stroke mechanics, my breathing, and setting up for the all-important backstroke turns; and then I was into my favorite part of the race, the breast-stroke section. I had always been a strong breaststroker and knew that, if I was relaxed going into this third section, I would finish strong. By this time, the crowd was into the race as they knew by the times appearing on the electronic timing board that I was on the way to a new world record. I was able to really press hard on the breaststroke and increase my lead going into the final 50 meters of freestyle. Fatigue was beginning to raise its ugly head by the time I had turned but I said to myself, "Well, only two lengths to go, and no problem. Just keep each pull long and strong, and don't forget to kick hard to the finish." I did just that and won the race quite handily, and as I looked up at the timing clock I heard the roar of the crowd and knew that my time was a new world record. I had gone almost 10 full seconds faster than the old record, and I was delighted by the time of 2:35.89, which was only a half-second slower than my current world record in the 55- to 59-year bracket I had set 5 years previously. I was very pleased and relieved that I had been able to meet my expectations and the crowd's. When I climbed out of the pool, I was met with a lot of cheering and congratulations all around the deck accompanied by handshakes and backslaps from my close friends on the team. It was a moment I will always remember and one in which I find great delight and satisfaction. It was good to know that I could still compete at a world level and continue to establish records that would be difficult to beat. It was very satisfactory to know that I am the best in the world in these individual medley swims. My confidence was enhanced by this first race, and I went on to establish world records in the two other individual medley events, as well as an unexpected world record in the 100 meters breaststroke. It was well worth the training and the race preparation to swim this well, and I was personally very happy with my performances. I always am amazed at one's ability to repeat competitive experiences over such a long time span. I still get a very emotional-high charge from racing and wonder how long this will go on? Each time I "age up," I look forward to setting new standards, and the thrill is always there to race and put myself in the high-pressure zone of tough competition. I don't really know why I do this, but perhaps it is only to gain the recognition of peers and the self-satisfaction of accomplishment of difficult goals.

DEFINITIONS AND BASIC CONCEPTS

The three athletes' stories provide dramatic pictures of emotional experience in sport. Quite clearly, sport is a setting in which adults across a wide range of ages experience strong emotions. We certainly cannot assume that as we progress through our adult years, sport and physical activity become devoid of emotion. However, there is much yet to be learned. General emotion theory provides a good starting point for understanding the development of emotions as they relate to sport and physical activity settings throughout adulthood, and it all starts with the question "What is an emotion?"

A perplexing challenge is developing a definition of emotion that is acceptable to all emotion theorists (Vallerand & Blanchard, 2000). Yet, it is difficult to develop a coherent understanding of the causes and consequences of emotion in sport and exercise without some sort of working definition. Researchers have contributed to the conceptual confusion by using the terms *emotion, feeling states, affect, and moods* interchangeably (see Crocker, Kowalski, Graham, & Kowalski, 2002; Vallerand, 1984). One way to disentangle these terms is to describe the involvement of key components involved in each type of "emotional state." The key components include physiological changes, action tendencies, subjective experience, and behavioral expression (Cornelius, 1996).

Emotion

Discrete emotions have the following common characteristics: quick onset, common cognitive appraisal antecedents, distinctive physiological or neurological patterns, distinctive subjective feeling states, and distinctive facial or bodily expression (Cornelius, 1996; Ekman, 1994; Lazarus, 1991). The emotion process is distinct for each individual emotion. Recall the image of the middle-aged soccer player. Anger involves a strong sense of displeasure (subjective state), high physiological arousal, an impulse to strike at a target (but not necessarily acted upon), and a facial expression involving furrowed eyebrows and baring of teeth. On the other hand, happiness involves feelings of pleasure, impulse to approach others in an outgoing manner, and a grinning expression with raised eyebrows. Although there is disagreement about the exact number of basic emotions, the following are often accepted as discrete emotions: happiness, surprise, sadness, disgust, anger, anxiety, shame, guilt, and fear. Sport research has emphasized negative emotions like anxiety (see Gould & Tuffey, 1996; Jones, 1995; Martens, Vealey, & Burton, 1990; Naylor et al., 2002) although positive emotions like joy and the related affect of enjoyment have received attention (Jackson, 2000; Scanlan & Simons, 1992; Wankel & Kreisel, 1985).

> The emotion process is distinct for each individual emotion.

Mood

Unlike emotions, mood involves more durable global subjective feeling states. In moods there is an absence of emotion-defining attributes like facial expressions, specific physiological patterns, and specific cognitive appraisals (Davidson, 1994; Frijda, 1994). Frijda argued that moods do not involve relationships between a person and a particular object. For example, when Ronald, the soccer player was angry, he was angry with both the offending player and referee. When in a bad mood, however, the emotional state is not directed towards or activated by a particular person or thing (although we all know it is best to avoid someone in a bad mood).

Mood has been a favorite topic when examining "emotional states" in sport and exercise (Biddle, 2000; LeUnes & Burger, 2000). The majority of research looking at mood and sport performance relationships has been conducted using the Profile of Mood States (POMS; McNair, Lorr, & Droppleman, 1971). The POMS assesses six dimensions of mood including tension, depression, anger, vigor, fatigue, and confusion. The POMS has been so prevalent in the study of mood and performance that an entire issue of the *Journal of Applied Sport Psychology* was recently (2000) devoted to conceptual and empirical issues and findings involving the instrument. Much work has also been conducted to look at the relationship between mood and sport performance. Early work in the area focused on using the POMS to discriminate between successful and unsuccessful athletes by a typical mood profile (the "iceberg" profile; Morgan, 1979). The result of this work was the contention that athletes who are less anxious, angry, depressed, confused, and fatigued, as well as more vigorous, are more successful than are athletes who do not demonstrate this iceberg profile. However, there has been a great deal of debate regarding the appropriateness of this conclusion due to methodological concerns (see Prapavessis, 2000).

Affect and Feeling States

One of the most difficult emotional terms to define is *affect*. In sport research, it has often been used interchangeably with emotion (i.e., Hanin, 1997). Affect has several key characteristics in that it is a subjective feeling state that varies in hedonic tone (pleasant or unpleasant), as well as intensity, and is often associated with thoughts and actions (Weiner, 1986). Affect is typically described as more generalized and primitive in nature than either moods or emotions (Gauvin & Spence, 1998; Vallerand & Blanchard, 2000) and does not include physiological arousal or facial/bodily expression (Weiner, 1986). However, affect has also often been used interchangeably with mood and emotion in sport research. Terms used to describe affective states in sport settings include basic emotions (i.e., anger, anxiety, happiness), mood states (i.e., vigorous, calm, pleased, annoyed), and more cognitive-behavioral states (i.e., competence, confidence, motivated) (see Hanin, 2000a; Hanin & Syrja, 1995; Vallerand, 1987).

The term *feeling state* has also been used to describe diverse affective states. Feeling states are probably the most vague of the emotional terms, with feeling states referring to experiences that describe bodily reactions, instrumental responses, cognitive appraisals, or some combination of the three (Gauvin & Spence, 1998). Despite both conceptual and theoretical elusiveness, feeling-state research continues to flourish in the exercise domain. Several instruments such as the Exercise-Induced Feeling Inventory (EFI; Gauvin & Rejeski, 1993) and the Subjective Exercise Experience Scale (SEES; McAuley & Courneya, 1994) have been developed to assess such states as tranquility, revitalization, positive engagement, psychological distress, and fatigue. Gauvin and Spence (1998) have provided an excellent review of the potential pitfalls and benefits of assessing moods, affect, and feeling states in exercise settings.

In summary, sport and exercise researchers have used *emotion* to describe different types of cognitive, motivational, behavioral, and affective states. In this paper, our discussion of emotion in sport will focus on the classic description involving the key components of physiological changes, action tendencies, subjective experience, and behavioral expression. Emotion will include such terms as happiness, sadness, anxiety, fright, anger, shame, and pride. However, because sport and exercise researchers have sometimes mixed emotions with other cognitive-affective states, we will clarify how researchers have defined emotion in their research.

Conceptual Views of Emotion: A Brief Review

How researchers assess and study the causes and consequences of emotions and other affective states in sport is driven by various conceptual viewpoints. Historically, the study of emotion has been dominated by physiological explanations that focus on bodily and brain processes (Cannon, 1927; LeDoux, 1995). Sport psychology research emphasizing physiological systems has primarily concentrated on arousal mechanisms. Researchers have attempted to determine how physiological activation affects performance though impairment of underlying mechanisms such as attention, decision making, memory, and neuromuscular control (see Hardy et al., 1996; Landers & Boutcher, 1998). However, theorists have argued that arousal states, although part of many emotions, are only part of the story (Lazarus, 1991). Contemporary theorists have placed far greater emphasis on information processing, motivation, and social and cultural processes (Averill, 1993; Lazarus, 1999; Vallerand, 1987; Weiner, 1985). In this section, we will consider how social, cognitive, and cognitive-motivational views have shaped the study of emotion.

Social constructivist theorists argue that emotional development revolves around learning social norms and rules about when and how to express emotions (Averill, 1984). Instead of focusing on specific components such as physiological changes or subjective feeling, social constructionists are more interested in how emotions become part of the culture's social practices (Averill, 1980, 1993; Ellsworth, 1994). The social construction perspective looks at how societal rules "help constitute (not simply regulate) the way we think, feel, and act during an emotional episode [and maintains that]. . . a primary goal of research should be to specify such rules for a variety of different emotions, both within and across cultures" (Averill, 1995, p. 205).

Let's revisit the stories of Ronald (the soccer player) and Jocko (the swimmer). Ronald had a very angry experience. He believed the opponent had committed a wrongful act to gain an unfair advantage and also had inflicted unnecessary pain. The belief that this was an appropriate situation in which to experience and express anger had become internalized through reinforcement (and other learning processes like modeling) by a socialization process directed by authority figures (parents, teachers, coaches, other significant players). The athlete's expression of anger was also guided by social convention. A retaliatory tackle is common and, if within certain physical constraints, an accepted practice within soccer. This is especially true if the referee has not punished the original offending player. The shame expression was based on the athlete's belief that the overt expression had crossed the line of expected behavior of a senior player within the context of the specific competition. Similarly, Jocko experienced a great deal of pride when he achieved a standard that was quite unexpected for someone of his age. Achieving results beyond the societal norm for someone of his age resulted in positive emotional experience.

A key implication of the social construction position is that cultural differences will lead to differences in the experience and expression of emotion. Differences in the patterns of behavior taught within various sport subcultures will lead to differences in how athletes evaluate when certain emotional states should be experienced and the acceptable ways to express such emotions. Although the social constructivist view has a strong following in many life domains (see M. M. Gergen & Gergen, 1995; Harre, 1986), this viewpoint has not had a strong impact on sport or exercise emotion research. This is somewhat unexpected because sporting events are experienced in a social context. There has been some recognition such as M. Smith's (1983) work on the learning of aggressive behavior in Canadian ice-hockey players that social processes are a strong contributor to violence and aggression in sport. However, most sport- and exercise-related research has been more directed towards psychological factors such as the role of cognition.

The three images of adult emotion revealed that the athletes' evaluation of the sporting situation was intimately linked to the perception of specific emotional experiences within a social context. Millie experienced shame because of what she deemed a stupid, avoidable error. Ronald's anger was based on his perception that the opponent's tackle was inappropriate and that the referee was, to some degree, incompetent. Jocko's happiness and pride were in part due to his belief he was able to meet, even exceed, his and the crowd's expectations of him. Cognitively oriented theorists hold that either automatic or reflective cognitive processes are necessary for emotion (Vallerand & Blanchard, 2000). These cognitive processes activate internalized values and beliefs, which provide personal meaning to a sporting context. These cognitive processes also activate emotions and protective behaviors. For example, why would a gymnast easily perform a double-back walkover on a 10-cm high beam with little sign of fear or anxiety but then completely freeze with fear when the beam is raised to regulation height? Her physical skills and the actual movement demands have not changed, but clearly her appraisal of danger has shifted dramatically.

Numerous emotion and affective models utilized in sport and exercise research follow a cognitive perspective. These models include Vallerand's (1987) intuitive-reflective appraisal model, multidimensional sport anxiety theory (Martens et al., 1990), R. E. Smith's (1996) sport anxiety model, Hanin's (2000a) zones of optimal functioning model, and Hackfort's (1999) extension of action theory to sport emotion. There are two theories of emotion and motivation that have had a major impact on sport and exercise research and theory construction involving stress, emotion, and coping. We will briefly review Weiner's (1985) attribution theory of emotion and motivation and Lazarus's (1991) cognitive-motivational-relational theory of emotion to demonstrate how cognitive and behavioral processes are thought to influence the generation, regulation, and expression of emotion in achievement settings like sport.

Weiner's (1985) Attribution Theory of Emotion and Motivation

Emotion theorists recognized that how a person evaluates a situation determines the specific types of emotion he or she experiences. Following in the footsteps of Arnold (1960), who postulated the existence of both automatic and reflective appraisal processes, Weiner (1985) proposed a comprehensive theory of motivation and emotion in achievement settings. He argued that emotional states are the result of both achievement outcome and the reasons people attribute to the cause of the outcome. In outcome appraisal, performance is evaluated automatically in terms of subjective success or failure. This appraisal produces general emotional states such as happiness following success and sadness following failure. Recall the image of Millie, the flat-water kayaker. Immediately after the competition, she experienced a general negative affective state. These general emotions occur independent of the reflective appraisal of causes such as ability, luck, or effort; thus, this process is termed *outcome-dependent-attribution independent* emotional responses.

> How a person evaluates a situation determines the specific types of emotion he or she experiences.

The causal attribution process, however, leads to more distinct emotions that give rise to a variety of actions. This reflective appraisal process involves the athlete's searching for reasons to explain the outcome. Common attributions in sport include personal ability, teamwork, teammates, short- and long-term effort, opponent's ability, luck, referee decisions, injury, playing conditions, and task difficulty (see Biddle & Hanrahan, 1998; Hardy et al., 1996). Searching for specific causes is more likely to occur in important achievement settings and when there are unexpected or negative outcomes (McAuley & Duncan, 1989; Weiner, 1986). Again, recall the dilemma of Millie. Not only was she distressed by a poor performance at Olympic trials, but she also then learned, unexpectedly, that she had been disqualified. The reflective attribution process that identified physical and mental incompetence as a cause fuelled her experience of shame. This causal search process is termed *attribution-dependent* emotional responses.

Weiner (1985) argued that the numerous specific causal attributions could be classified into three causal dimensions: locus, stability, and control. *Locus* refers to the cause being attributed to oneself or to external factors. The *stability* dimension captures causes that vary from permanent to constantly changing. *Control* refers to whether the cause is under intentional control. Each dimension, or combination of dimensions, was proposed to generate specific emotions. A failure attributed to a wrongful act by an external person (locus-external) who had intentional control over one's actions produces anger. Failure subscribed to one's own action (locus-internal) and that was controllable produces shame. A successful outcome attributed to one's ability (locus-internal) produces pride. The stories about Ronald (anger), Millie (shame), and Jocko (pride) showed clearly the role of these attributions in action. The complete appraisal-emotion process is outlined in Figure 1.

Weiner's (1985) theory has generated a wealth of sport and exercise research over the last two decades, but as Vallerand and Blanchard (2000) noted, the research support has been mixed. First, attributions explain only a small portion of emotions. Second, many emotions seemed to be predicted better by intuitive appraisals (i.e., performance assessment) than by attribution processes. One reason for this latter result is that it is impossible to clearly separate outcome and attribution appraisals in research settings. Athletes are asked to recall these processes after both have occurred, effectively confounding their effects. Overall, the sport

FIGURE 1
Weiner's model of the appraisal – emotion process.

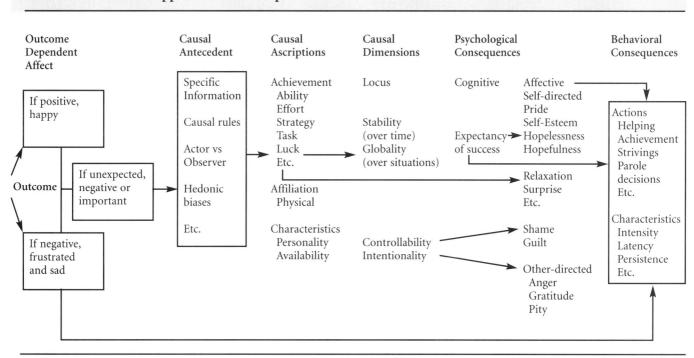

From Weiner, B. (1986). *An attributional theory of motivation and emotion.* New York: Springer-Verlag, 16. Copyright by Springer-Verlag. Reprinted with permission.

research has demonstrated that appraisal processes, whether outcome or attribution, do seem to influence the emotion experience. Nevertheless, sport and exercise researchers have not considered age-related differences in attributions and their influence on emotions and behavioral consequences.

Lazarus's (1991) Cognitive-Motivational-Relational Theory

Lazarus has been a prominent stress and emotion theorist whose work has had a major impact on stress, coping, and emotion research in sport (e.g., Crocker & Graham, 1995; Crocker, Kowalski, & Graham, 1998; Gould, Finch, & Jackson, 1993; Graham, Kowalski, & Crocker, 2002; Hanin, 1997). Lazarus argued that emotions arise as a joint product of personality and environment and reflect cognitive, motivational, and relational features (Lazarus, 1991, 1999, 2000a, 2000b). Independently, neither the person nor the environment is inherently emotional. Rather, Lazarus (1991) contends that it is the ongoing transaction or relationship between the two that produces emotion. This relationship is the basic unit of analysis for emotion and is referred to as *the person-environment relationship*.

In the sport literature, a considerable amount of research has examined the sources of stress that are experienced (e.g., Dale, 2000; Gould et al., 1993; Gould & Weinberg, 1985; Rainey, 1995; Scanlan, Ravizza, & Stein, 1989; Scanlan, Stein, & Ravizza, 1991). These stressors include media pressure, performance expectations, unforeseen events, preparatory training, life directions, interpersonal conflicts financial costs, and other demands. Although such descriptive research is important for identifying specific environmental encounters that athletes commonly experience as stressful, it does little to advance why and how emotions are created during such encounters. Lazarus (1991, 2000a) argues that to understand why specific environmental encounters are associated with emotion such as stress, it is also critical to identify the personal meanings athletes attach to such encounters.

Motives and cognition are important because a person evaluates the significance of the encounter in terms of his or her motives and beliefs. In other words, motives and cognition are critical for establishing personal meaning or the personal significance of the person-environment relationship. In the absence of a goal or a personal stake, an encounter will not generate an emotion (Lazarus, 2000a). That is, a person will experience emotion within a specific environmental encounter only when the encounter is evaluated or judged by the individual to be personally relevant. The evaluation or appraisal process involves making a number of decisions, many of which occur automatically, about how the encounter will maintain, enhance, or harm one's well-being. During sport transactions such as Millie's Olympic trials experience, many emotions are likely to emerge because performers approach such complex transactions with a variety of different goals, objectives, expectations, and desired outcomes (for example, to perform a personal best score, to perform well in front of important others, to achieve an Olympic standard).

> In the absence of a goal or a personal stake, an encounter will not generate an emotion.

Lazarus (1991) applies two levels of analysis, molar and molecular, to delineate the specific emotion(s) that are experienced. At the molar level, summary statements, or *core-relational themes,* describe patterns of appraisal regarding the person-environment relationship (Lazarus, 1991). The purpose of a core-relational theme is to summarize the personal harms and/or benefits that are inherent to person-environment relationships (Lazarus, 1991). In other words, a core-relational theme is a generalized evaluative statement an individual derives about a specific environmental encounter in terms of the degree of harm or benefit to a person's well-being. Athletes might experience different types of physical and psychological harms (i.e., injury, loss of status and self-esteem) during person-environment transactions, which lead to a discrete relational theme (i.e., evaluative statement) that describes a particular negative emotion. Athletes also experience different types of benefits (i.e., enhanced self-esteem, change of a potentially unpleasant situation into a pleasant experience through one's performance), leading to a discrete relational theme that describes a particular positive emotion. Thus, each emotion (or emotion family) has its own core-relational theme (Lazarus, 1991, 2000a). Table 1 lists core-relational themes conceptualized for emotions commonly experienced during sport.

In addition to core-relational themes, Lazarus (1991) delineates emotion through the specific components of the *appraisal and coping processes* during person-environment encounters, or a molecular analysis. Lazarus and his colleagues (C. A. Smith, Haynes, Lazarus, & Pope, 1993; C. A. Smith & Lazarus, 1993) contend that two distinct but related types of cognition are involved in the generation of appraisal. Knowledge, a construct similar to attributions, is a nonevaluative, fact-oriented "cold" belief about how things work in general and during specific encounters (C. A. Smith et al., 1993). Knowledge alone is not sufficient to evoke emotion. A "hot" appraisal regarding the personal meaning about what is known is required to generate an emotion. Recall Millie's experience of "being disqualified" during the Olympic trials in

TABLE 1.
Core-Relational Themes, Appraisal Components, and Action Tendencies of Specific Emotions Experienced in Sport

Emotion	Core-Relational Theme	Primary Appraisal	Secondary Appraisal	Action Tendency
ANGER	Demeaning against me and mine	- Goal relevance - Goal incongruence - Ego involvement including preserve or enhance self- or social-esteem	- Blame to self (internalized anger) or to another (externalized anger) - Attack considered as coping potential - Positive future expectancy about environment responding to attack	To attack
ANXIETY	Uncertain, existential threat	- Goal relevance - Goal incongruence - Ego involvement including protection of personal meaning or ego identity against existential threats	- Uncertain coping potential but tendency to objectify - Uncertain future expectancy	To avoid or escape – no concrete goal of what to avoid or escape from
FRIGHT	Concrete and sudden danger of imminent physical harm	- Goal relevance - Goal incongruence (threat to bodily integrity by sudden harm)	- Uncertain coping potential - Uncertain future expectancy	To avoid or escape – concrete goal of what to avoid or escape from
SHAME	Failure to live up to an ego ideal	- Goal relevance - Goal incongruence	- Type of ego involvement including the failure to live up to an ego ideal - Blame to oneself - Coping potential to direct efforts to live up to an ego ideal - Positive future expectancies to reduce and possible mitigate shame	To hide or avoid having one's personal failures observed by anyone
HAPPY	Reasonable progress toward the realization of our goals	- Goal relevance - Goal congruence	- Positive future expectancy for good fortune to continue	Psychological and motor expressions of pleasure and security
PRIDE	Enhancement of ego identity by taking credit for a valued object or achievement	- Goal relevance - Goal congruence	- Ego involvement includes enhancement of self- or social-esteem - Credit to self	Expansiveness and an urge to draw attention to accomplishments

kayaking. Millie stated that the disqualification occurred as a result of poor performance and confusion in the race. The "cold" fact of being disqualified became emotional for Millie when she judged or appraised this encounter to be personally meaningful or a relevant means (i.e., through physical accomplishment, positive peer comparison) to establishing personal well-being.

Lazarus (1991) contends that personal meanings or appraisals are important in determining the emotional experience of individuals during person-environment transactions. Appraisal is theorized to have two interrelated processes, primary and secondary appraisal. *Primary appraisal* is a motivationally oriented appraisal that consists of determining whether the situation is important, whether personal goals are being attained or threatened, and the type of ego involvement (Lazarus, 1991, 1993). During all or most emotions, diverse aspects of self-identity or personal commitments such as self-esteem and social esteem, moral values, ego ideals, meanings and ideas, and other persons and their well-being are the focus of personal goals. Primary appraisal, on the one hand, evaluates "What do I have at stake in this encounter?" On the other hand, *secondary appraisal* assesses "What can I do?" (Folkman, 1992). It is an evaluation of whether any given action might prevent harm, moderate it, or produce additional harm or benefit. Secondary appraisal includes an evaluation of blame and credit of who is responsible, coping options available to deal with the situation, and whether for any reason things are likely to change for the better or worse (Lazarus, 1991, 2000a). Table 1 lists the molecular appraisal pattern for specific emotions (i.e., primary appraisal, secondary appraisal).

Coping, together with appraisal, influences the type of emotion(s) that is experienced as well as the shift of emotion over the course of the person-environment transaction (Lazarus, 1999). Coping is conceptualized to be the psychological analogue to action tendencies (Lazarus, 2000a). Action tendencies are thought to be automatic, nondeliberate, and primitive acts engendered when a person is in danger. Coping involves both behavioral and cognitive efforts in a dynamic, complex, deliberate, and planful process that is heavily influenced by appraisal of what is (a) possible, (b) likely to be effective in a specific context, and (c) compatible with social and personal standards of conduct (Lazarus, 1991). Thus, an important component of the coping process is to augment or inhibit action tendencies. The initial impulse of Ronald, the soccer player, was to attack the offending opponent; however, in response to his goals (i.e., to get the referee's attention, to remain injury free, to not receive a red card, to not offend teammates), he chose to cope by executing a "clumsy" tackle that (somewhat) inhibited his intention to physically attack the opponent.

Coping efforts act to change the appraisal of a person-environment relation through two broad-based functions (Lazarus & Folkman, 1984). *Problem-focused coping* reflects efforts to obtain information about what to do and mobilize actions for the purpose of changing the reality of the troubled person-environment encounter (Lazarus, 1991). For example, an athlete who feels unprepared for a competitive event may sit down with his or her coach and plan the best course of action for the competitive event and/or change the desired outcome goal based upon the current ability of the athlete. *Emotion-focused coping*, on the other hand, reflects efforts to regulate emotions without changing the realities of the encounter. This may be accomplished through attention deployment (i.e., avoidance) or through reinterpretation of the troubled transaction (Lazarus, 2000a). Lazarus (1996) noted that any thought or action could serve a problem-focused or emotion-focused function. Further, often times, a particular effort may serve both. For example, Ronald chose to tackle the offending player in the attempt to manage the distressful encounter (i.e., the ill actions of an opponent and poor referee calls). The tackle, in fact, served both problem- and emotion-focused functions. That is, the tackle served to change the situation in that it prompted the referee to be more aware of the actions of the players on the field, as well as to regulate the emotional response in creating a cathartic release that was (somewhat) socially acceptable. Coping actions are viewed as an integral component of the emotion process in that changes to the meaning of the person-environment relationship produce a change in the emotion experienced. Ronald stated that after the tackle, his anger shifted to shame as he realized a new meaning of the person-environment encounter.

In summary, Lazarus' (1991) cognitive-motivational-relational theory of emotion is a prominent model that could guide emotion research in sport. With respect to sport-related stress and coping research, Lazarus' (1991) theory has become the most dominant model guiding research efforts during the past decade (Crocker et al., 1998; Hardy et al., 1996). Where other theories, such as Weiner's (1985) attribution theory, conceptualize the person or individual to be primarily responsible for the development of an emotional experience, the transactional nature of Lazarus' (1991) theory is an important advance in understanding emotion experienced during sport. There has, however, been little research that has examined the efficacy of the theory to predict emotion in sport with adult populations.

EMOTION ACROSS ADULTHOOD

This chapter has provided persuasive evidence that emotions are pervasive and are an essential motivating force in sport. As Vallerand and Blanchard (2000) noted, emotions have profound influence on cognition, health, performance, and interpersonal relationships. However, much of what we know about emotion in sport and exercise is based on research and theory that focuses on adolescents and young adults. What about middle-aged and older adults? We do know that as one progresses through adulthood the sport and exercise settings do not become domains absent of emotions for participants, as was clearly demonstrated in Ronald's and Jocko's stories. Emotional experiences exist at all ages. However, a related question is "Do the processes that generate and regulate emotion change over the course of adulthood?" There is scant research on adult developmental processes involving emotion in sport and exercise. Most of the existing research is descriptive, reporting simple relationships between physical activity and general dispositional affective states, self-efficacy, and psychological well-being (Berger, 1988, 1996; Chogahara, O'Brien Cousins, & Wankel, 1998; McPherson, 1986; O'Brien Cousins, 1996). Involvement in physical activity is associated with increased physical functioning, reduced anxiety and depression, increased physical self-efficacy, and a better quality of life. Unfortunately, this research tells us little about how and why emotional life in physical activity might change across adult development.

To understand how emotions change in sport and exercise contexts across adult development, we can examine theory and empirical research in other domains. Studying change in emotional experience and expression is extremely challenging. Are there similarities or differences within or across age groups? Are differences due to inevitable biological changes or to sociocultural experiences? Are there experiences unique to individual cohorts, like World War II and the baby boom, that create social expectations that shape individuals' perceptions about involvement and appropriate emotional experience and expression in sport? As Bee (2000) suggests, understanding the process of adulthood is extremely complex because it involves genetics, cognitive and social development, social psychology, sociology, and economics. Obviously, we cannot cover all the various theoretical approaches that can explain how emotions change across adulthood. Instead, we will cover viewpoints that emphasize either an individual difference method or an age-based change theory. Both viewpoints will accentuate social and cognitive processes.

Before we begin, we must decide, however, if the term adult *"development"* is appropriate. Unlike changes in childhood that involve biological, cognitive, and social processes (see Harter, 1999), there is no clear consensus about development across adulthood (Bee, 2000; Malatesta & Izard, 1984). Averill (1984) suggests emotional development involves learning social norms and rules. Malatesta and Izard (1984) suggest development implies differentiation and hierarchical integration. Differentiation would be reflected by emotional maturity, characterized by the more rational control and better use of coping skills. Hierarchical integration implies that people develop flexible personalities that would react and regulate emotions in a socially accepted manner. Changes in emotions based on differentiation have also been examined using Erikson's (1959/1980) stage theory of self-identity and personality development (Stewart & Healey, 1984; Whitbourne, 1996). On the other hand, Lazarus (1999) feels that it is a major error to assume change in emotions across adulthood is developmental. There is little evidence

> The components of emotion are neural/physiological, subjective feelings, action tendencies, and expressive behaviors.

of change in structure and function of the mind. He advocates an individual difference approach that seeks to identify personal and environmental factors, which create meaningful transactions. Given these divergent views on adult development, we prefer to simply talk about potential changes.

Individual Differences

A general approach, consistent with emphasizing individual differences, is to investigate how the components of emotion change over adulthood and to identify changes in the physiological, cognitive, and social factors that influence appraisal and coping processes. Recall the components of emotion are neural/physiological, subjective feelings, action tendencies, and expressive behaviors. How would changes associated with biological and social aging affect each of these emotion components? The emotion process, illustrated in Figure 2, consists of numerous factors that might change or stay stable over time. Consistent with Lazarus' cognitive-motivational-relational model, sport participants bring to the situation person-related characteristics including values, commitments, social-role expectations, and physical, technical, and mental capabilities. These person factors transact with environmental demands and resources. This person-environmental transaction is appraised in terms of its personal signifi-

FIGURE 2
Simple schematic diagram of emotion process based on Lazarus's (1999) cognitive-motivational-relational theory.

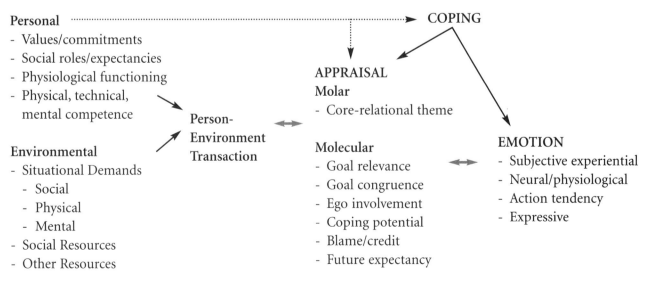

cance to the individual. Problem and emotion-focused coping strategies can moderate the appraisal process, the resulting emotional state, and the ongoing person-environment relationship.

There is a consensus that the core aspects of emotional experience do not change over adulthood (Dougherty, Abe, & Izard, 1996; Lazarus, 1999). Emotional experiences are still strong and influence cognitions and actions. People still experience physiological changes, subjective feeling states, and action tendencies associated with discrete emotions, whether they are 20 or 70 years of age. What do change are the personal and environmental antecedent conditions and regulatory mechanisms that result in relational meaning (the appraisal of the personal significance of the person-environment transaction) and control the production, regulation, and expression of emotion. Changes in social roles, social expectations, individual goals, physical and mental competencies, and coping skills combined with different environmental demands have a profound impact on when and how people experience and express emotion (Aldwin, 1994; Averill, 1984; Lazarus, 1996, 1999; Malatesta & Izard, 1984).

How people experience and express emotions is strongly influenced by sociocultural forces (Aldwin, 1994; Averill, 1984; Ellsworth, 1994). Cultures are not a single unified force that shape behaviors; instead, they consist of multiple mazes that create different pathways for different subcultural groups such as males and females, ethnic groups, and maybe even across different sports (Aldwin, 1994). Based on Lazarus (1999) and Aldwin, there are at least five ways sociocultural forces affect changes in the elicitors of and expression of emotion in sport across adulthood: (a) They influence the types of sporting situations a person chooses to encounter; (b) they provide different institutional and social mechanisms to help the person; (c) they influence the meaning attached to the person-environment transaction; (d) they influence the selection of coping strategies to regulate emotion; and (e) they influence the expression of emotion.

Lazarus (1999) argued that the experience of discrete emotions is governed primarily by the appraisal of personal significance. To a large extent, a person's internalized beliefs, values, and commitments will determine what is at stake. Sixty-year-old golfing legend Jack Nicklaus had a terrible time controlling his emotions on the 18th green in the 2000 U.S. Open. In subsequent interviews, Nicklaus commented on how important the U.S. Open was to him and that he realized that this was probably the last time he would play. Nicklaus also felt he could no longer compete at this level (an appraisal of his physical competence and environmental demands). Nicklaus' comments, along with those of the two older athletes featured in our emotional images, clearly indicate that older athletes do not have impoverished emotional lives and these strong emotions are linked to values, beliefs, and commitments.

Changes in what sporting situations trigger emotions and their intensity are also due to ever-changing social and physical demands. Within Western cultures, responsible adults are expected to manage increasing demands related to interpersonal relationships, family, employment, and other community responsibilities. Changing social demands are often associated with the value societal groups attach to participation in sport and exercise. Further, there is general deterioration in physiological functioning and physical competence associated with aging. Previously managed and valued sporting activities are now beyond achievement. To handle increasing social and physical demands, people may slowly divest themselves of commitments and identification of sporting roles (see Greendorfer, 1992; Grove, Lavallee, & Gordon, 1997). This process will cause people to choose different sport and exercise settings and to create different relational meanings within these settings.

Successful adaptation to changing social demands and reduced physical prowess requires people to modify or learn new coping strategies (Aldwin, 1994; Lazarus, 1996). These strategies allow people to anticipate the flow of stressful events, control arousal and action tendencies, transform the personal significance of transactions, and thus, influence emotion

(Lazarus, 1999). With age, people not only acquire new strategies but they also become more skilled in understanding societal rules governing the regulation and expression of experienced emotions (Averill, 1984). Emotional expression becomes more sophisticated and is influenced by status and role within sport. Basketball great Michael Jordan became highly skilled in his later career in containing both his pride and his anger. Demonstrating a refined social-emotional skill, sorely missing in many young professional athletes, Jordan was able to express pride without appearing conceited and attributed victory to the action of teammates and coaches. Effective self-presentation skills related to emotions are not easily acquired. Changing social roles and demands require people to understand and continually internalize the values and expectations of one's peer or reference groups (Hansson, Hogan, & Jones, 1984).

Can we predict how and when coping changes over time? Most research has been normative comparative, using cross-sectional methods to determine age differences in the relative use of different types of coping (see Aldwin, 1994). The most striking finding from this program of research is not the normative differences in coping, but rather the normative differences in the *sources of stress* experienced by adults at different ages (Lazarus, 1996). Young adults are most concerned with developing their families and careers, whereas older retired adults experience the loss of occupation and social roles as well as suffer medical problems (Aldwin, 1994; Lazarus, 1996). It is possible that differences observed in the coping process with changes in chronological age may be simply due to what younger and older adults have to cope with rather than to normative developmental changes (Lazarus, 1996, 1999).

Lazarus (1999) has been extremely critical of studies examining normative developmental trends in coping from a biological aging perspective. He stated,

> . . . as people grow old, the probability of important losses of function increases, but the aging process remains highly *individual*. Cross-sectional research, which dominates the field, reveals only very modest differences among people. . . . This research almost never gives as much attention to individual variations as it does to trying to identify normative or average patterns, which turns out to be all but useless as descriptions of the way it is for individuals. (pp. 165-166)

Differences in coping observed with changes in chronological age may be due to what younger and older adults have to cope with rather than normative developmental changes.

There are researchers who do not ascribe to Lazarus's view and who believe that studying variables that change in a predictive manner over time can provide information to help understand the emotion process. There are many examples of such theories including Erikson's (1959/1980) identity development theory, Levinson's (1990) seasons of adulthood theory, and Charles and Carstensen's (1999) socioemotional selectivity theory. We will briefly review socioemotional selectivity theory to highlight how such theories attempt to explain how and why emotions may change in a predictable manner over time.

Socioemotional Selectivity Theory

General theories of emotion provide a strong basis for our understanding of adults' emotional experiences in sport and exercise. However, theories developed specifically to understand emotions in adulthood can add significantly to our understanding of the emotion process throughout the adult years. One such theory is the socioemotional selectivity theory (Carstensen, Gross, & Fung, 1997; Carstensen, Isaacowitz, & Charles, 1999; Charles & Carstensen, 1999). Socioemotional selectivity theory emphasizes the role of time as being a critical factor in understanding emotional experience in adulthood. According to the theory, time is fundamental to human motivation, as it influences the selection and pursuit of social goals across adulthood. These social goals encompass a wide range of goals an individual might have including physical goals such as physical protection or psychological goals such as regulation of emotions or seeking information about the social world (Carstensen et al., 1997). Information regarding our perceptions of time is provided by one's age (Charles & Carstensen, 1999). Older adults typically experience time as being limited, whereas younger adults tend to envision time as expansive. However, according to the theory, it is the concept of time that is more important than chronological age (Carstensen et al., 1999). Off-time events such as a terminal illness or improved medical procedures can also alter our experience of time by making it either more limited (as in the former) or more expansive (as in the latter). Thus, although age is important because of the tendency to view time as limited as we grow older, events can occur at any age to make our perception of time more or less limited or expansive.

There are two main classes of psychological goals towards which an individual will strive: the pursuit of knowledge and the pursuit of positive emotional experience. Our perception of time becomes critically important in both the selection and pursuit of these psychological goals (Carstensen et al., 1999; Charles & Carstensen, 1999). When time is perceived as limited, our psychological goal is to enhance our positive emotions in the social context. When time is perceived as expansive, we tend to select preparatory goals (i.e., gaining knowledge) that will give us a larger repertoire of skills that we can use for later success.

One of the primary reasons for the development of socioemotional selectivity theory was to better explain why, despite decreased social interactions throughout adulthood, older adults do not have dampened emotional experiences in social interactions (Charles & Carstensen, 1999). Persons who view time as limited will primarily engage in social interactions with individuals who maximize emotional benefits, and they will discard less emotionally meaningful social interactions because of the emotional costs. Older individuals especially learn to arrange their social environment to maximize optimal emotional experience, and the decreased social interaction reflects changes in psychological goals as a function of time.

There are many implications that socioemotional selectivity theory has for understanding the experience of emotion in sport and exercise settings throughout adulthood. First, it predicts that our psychological goals change throughout adulthood. As one ages, the pursuit of positive emotional experiences takes precedence over other psychological goals we might have (such as seeking information that will allow us to advance in sport). Second, depending on the perceived time status of the participant, the psychological goals we try to reach might be quite different. For example, a young adult who views time as limited (e.g., because of terminal illness) would likely attempt to maximize positive emotional experience in sport and exercise, whereas another individual who views time as expansive would likely forgo positive emotions at times to achieve preparatory goals (i.e., competes on a team he or she does not like because skills are improving). Also, when we see time as limited, we will simply not engage in as many activities that are unpleasant or devoid of meaning (Carstensen et al., 1999). Third, whom we participate with in sport and exercise will depend upon our perceptions of time. If time is perceived as limited, we will likely choose to participate only with people who are close to us in order to gain the maximal positive emotional benefits, whereas, if we view time as expansive, we will be more willing to participate with more diverse groups of individuals because of the potential information that can be gained in such an environment.

There is evidence in studies that have examined socioemotional selectivity theory that emotional control increases throughout adulthood and that older people experience fewer negative emotions (Carstensen, Gottman, & Levenson, 1995; Carstensen et al., 1999; Gross et al., 1997; McConatha & Huba, 1999). For example, McConatha and Huba found, with adults from 19 to 92 years of age, that emotional control over aggression, impulsiveness, and inhibition increased with age; and McConatha and Huba concluded these findings supported the theory of emotional selectivity. Also, individuals who value positive emotional experiences will use strategies to help them maximize interactions in important social relationships (Charles & Carstensen, 1999). Therefore, in the sport and exercise setting, we might expect older adults (or individuals with limited perceptions of time) to have more positive emotional experiences and be more adept at controlling their emotions compared to individuals who value other psychological goals (such as gathering information). This is because (a) they will use more strategies and put more effort into trying to regulate their emotions and (b) their social setting has been constructed in a way to better facilitate positive emotions (i.e., only emotionally close social relationships are maintained).

FUTURE RESEARCH RECOMMENDATIONS

This chapter has discussed many issues regarding the experience of emotions in sport; however, it is clear that there is much yet to be learned about emotions. Most of what we know about emotions in adulthood is based on research with young adults, primarily from high-performance sport. Clearly, we must diversify our research populations and contexts to give us a comprehensive understanding of emotion from early adulthood to old age. We would like to provide a few suggestions that should enhance our understanding of this critical process underlying motivated behavior.

An important first step in understanding emotional experience in sport and exercise is to be clear whether we are looking at emotion, mood, affect, feeling states, or other emotion-related constructs. It is imperative to know how these various emotion constructs are related and whether or not we can distinguish among them at both theoretical and measurement levels. Without a clear theoretical framework and careful consideration of which emotion dimension is of interest prior to a research study, a thorough understanding of the nature of the relationship between emotion and other important variables (such as sport withdrawal or performance) will be very difficult. Relevant theories of emotion (such as the ones discussed in this chapter) should serve as a basis for this distinction among emotion dimensions.

Several conceptual models exist within the emotion literatures that offer insight into the potential mechanisms through which emotion develops. Testing the basic tenets of a model within the sport and exercise domain offers further support to the validity of the model under interest. The most promising models appear to be those that consider the person, the environment, and the ongoing transaction between the person and environment (Crocker et al., 2002; Hardy et al., 1996). A challenge, however, is deciding on a research methodology that allows the researcher to determine the causal pathways among critical variables. It is likely that research programs will need to incorporate both qualitative and quantitative research methods because no research method will be without limitations.

Like many issues in psychological science, there are many viewpoints on how best to examine emotion (Lazarus, 1999). One approach involves traditional analytic processes in which we identify key variables and processes in the emotion system and try to identify causal linkages. Researchers could test the basic tenets of any theoretical model with adult sport samples. For example, Lazarus' (1991) cognitive-motivational-relational theory makes specific predictions about what primary and secondary appraisals lead to the experience of specific emotions (see Table 1). It is important that these links be tested through well-designed research studies. However, given the comprehensiveness of the theory, measurement of all relevant variables will be a daunting task. Ensuring the appropriateness of existing measures or developing reliable and valid measures for each of the relevant appraisals (i.e., goal relevance, ego involvement, coping resources and potential, future expectancies, etc.) and specific emotions is an important step. This type of research strategy will provide information about how "emotion" variables change over time and contexts and how they are related to emotion. However, given the complexity of the emotion process, researchers will likely be able to examine only parts of the emotion process. The researcher will still need to synthesize the parts back together into some meaningful whole (Lazarus, 1999). The utility of such a systems approach may be limited in studying a phenomenon like emotion that can change rapidly from moment to moment.

Lazarus (1999) has suggested that an alternative to the reductionism approach is to use a narrative or storied approach to each emotion. This requires combining "the narratives of many individuals to see in what ways the stories are shared and reflect the collective experience of people in each of the emotions, and in what ways they diverge" (Lazarus, 1999, p. 205). The narrative approach would require researchers to develop a prototypical narrative for each emotion. A prototype for an emotion like happiness would describe the conditions required when a sport or exercise participant typically experiences happiness. Theoretical models would guide the development of the prototype. Think back to the happiness narrative described by Jocko, the master swimmer. A greater understanding of the emotion experienced by Jocko was gained from not only knowing about the swim meet, but also knowing how the swimming event fit into his life history of achievement in swimming and the personal meaning the event represented. One could use Lazarus' theory to construct a prototype of the transactional conditions necessary for happiness and examine if Jocko's story fit the prototype. This could be repeated across athletes in different contexts and ages. Obviously, narrative methods are more complex than can be described here (see K. J. Gergen & Gergen, 1986; M. M. Gergen & Gergen, 1995; Lazarus, 1999; McAdams, 1997), but they do offer a promising alternative to understanding both the antecedents and consequences of emotions across the lifespan in sport and exercise.

> Emotion plays an important role in our choice of activities and our experiences in those settings throughout the lifespan.

CONCLUSION

Emotion plays an important role in our choice of activities and our experiences in those settings throughout the lifespan. One of the limitations to understanding the role emotion plays in our lives is the lack of a clear conceptual and empirical distinction among the terms *emotion*, *feeling states*, *affect*, and *mood*. Emotions are generally considered the most discrete type of emotional experience, whereas terms such as moods, affect, and feeling states are more general in nature. Regardless of the term used, sport researchers have shown that emotions can both facilitate and impair performance. Nevertheless, to understand the antecedents and consequences of emotion in sport and exercise, researchers need to carefully define the scientific construct "emotion."

Although much work has been done to understand the link between emotion and performance, little research has been devoted to understanding how the emotion processes involved in sport and exercise change throughout the adult years. Cognitively oriented theories of emotion (such as attributional theory, cognitive-motivational-relational theory, and socioemotional selectivity theory) offer insight into how the potential emotion mechanisms develop or change over time. Conceptually, factors such as the choice of activities, the resources perceived to be available, meanings attached to the person-environment encounter, the coping strategies used to regulate emotions, and the ways emotion is expressed all change over time. Moreover, time is required to learn the social rules and norms surrounding how and when emotion is expressed within a particular culture.

When examining developmental shifts or changes in emotion, researchers are advised to explore individual differences rather than establish normative patterns of change in emotion in sport and physical activity environments. Simple descriptive studies that report age differences in either the emotions experienced or those factors involved in emotion regulation and expression provide only a superficial glimpse into this complex process. Instead, we need to investigate the relationship in the linkages among components in the emotion process and how these relationships change. Research from the psychological and sociological literature suggests a number of potential variables for the study of emotional development across adulthood within the sport and exercise environment, including social rules, social roles, expectations, social resources, physical and mental competence, and coping. Recall that the emotional images of the three athletes (Millie, Ronald, and Jocko) were each embedded in a complex socio-personal context. These images, combined with the theoretical perspectives we have reviewed in this chapter, tell us that any clear understanding of emotion in sport will require facing many exciting research challenges.

REFERENCES

Aldwin, C. M. (1994). *Stress, coping, and development.* New York: Guilford Press.

Arnold, M. B. (1960). *Emotion and personality* (Vols. 1 & 2). New York: Columbia University Press.

Averill, J. R. (1980). A construction view of emotion. In R. Plutchik & H. Kellerman (Eds.), *Emotion: theory, research, and experience* (Vol. 1, pp. 23-43). New York: Academic Press.

Averill, J. R. (1984). The acquisition of emotions during adulthood. In C.Z. Malatesta & C. E. Izard (Eds.), *Emotion in adult development* (pp. 23-43). Beverly Hills, CA: Sage

Averill, J. R. (1993). Illusions of anger. In R. B. Felson & J. T. Tedeschi (Eds.), *Aggression and violence: Social interactionist perspectives* (pp. 171-192). Washington, DC: American Psychological Association.

Averill, J. R. (1995). Passersby [a commentary on Lazarus, 1995]. *Psychological Inquiry, 6,* 204-208.

Bee, H. C. (2000). *The journey of adulthood.* (4th ed.). Upper Saddle River, NJ: Prentice Hall.

Berger, B. G. (1988). The role of physical activity in the life quality of older adults. *American Academy of Physical Education Papers, 22,* 42-58.

Berger, B. G. (1996). Psychological benefits of an active lifestyle: What we know and what we need to know. *Quest, 48,* 330-353.

Berger, B. G., & Motl, R. W. (2000). Exercise and mood: A selective review and synthesis of research employing the Profile of Mood States. *Journal of Applied Sport Psychology, 12,* 69-92.

Biddle, S. J. (2000). Exercise, emotions, and mental health. In Y. L. Hanin (Ed.), *Emotions in sport* (pp. 267-291). Champaign, IL: Human Kinetics.

Biddle, S. J., & Hanrahan, S. (1998). Attributions and attributional style. In J. Duda (Ed.), *Advances in sport and exercise psychology measurement* (pp. 3-19). Morgantown, WV: Fitness Information Technology.

Cannon, W. B. (1927). The James Lange theory of emotions: A critical examination and an alternative theory. *American Journal of Psychology, 39,* 106-124.

Carstensen, L. L., Gottman, J. M., & Levenson, R. W. (1995). Emotional behavior in long-term marriage. *Psychology of Aging, 10,* 140-149.

Carstensen, L. L., Gross, J. J., & Fung, H. H. (1997). The social context of emotional experience. In K. W. Schaie & M. P. Lawton (Eds.), *Annual review of gerontology and geriatrics* (pp. 325-352). New York: Springer.

Carstensen, L. L., Isaacowitz, D. M., & Charles, S. T. (1999). Taking time seriously: A theory of socioemotional selectivity. *American Psychologist, 54,* 165-181.

Charles, S. T., & Carstensen, L. L. (1999). The role of time in the setting of social goals across the life span. In T. M. Hess & F. Blanchard-Fields (Eds.), *Social cognition and aging* (pp. 319-342). San Diego, CA: Academic Press.

Chogahara, M., O'Brien Cousins, S., & Wankel, L. L. (1998). Social influences on physical activity in older adults: A review. *Journal of Aging and Physical Activity, 6,* 1-17.

Cornelius, R. R. (1996). *The science of emotion: Research and tradition in the psychology of emotion.* Upper Saddle River, NJ: Prentice Hall.

Crocker, P. R. E., & Graham, T. R. (1995). Coping by competitive athletes with performance stress: Gender differences and relationships with affect. *The Sport Psychologist, 9,* 325-338.

Crocker, P. R. E., Kowalski, K.C., & Graham, T. R. (1998). Measurement of coping strategies in sport. In J. Duda (Ed.), *Advances in sport and exercise psychology measurement* (pp. 149-161). Morgantown, WV: Fitness Information Technology.

Crocker, P. R. E., Kowalski, K.C., Graham, T. R., & Kowalski, N. P. (2002). Emotion in sport. In J. Silva & D. Stevens (Eds.), *Psychological foundations of sport* (pp. 107-131). Boston: Allyn & Bacon.

Dale, G. A. (2000). Distractions and coping strategies of elite decathletes during their most memorable performances. *The Sport Psychologist, 14,* 17-41.

Davidson, R. J. (1994). On emotion, mood, and related constructs. In P. Ekman & R. J. Davidson (Eds.), *The nature of emotion: Fundamental questions* (pp. 51-55). New York: Oxford University Press.

Dougherty, L. M., Abe, J. A., & Izard, C. E. (1996). Differential emotion theory and emotional development in adulthood and later life. In C. Magai & S.H. McFadden (Eds.), *Handbook of emotion, adult development and aging* (pp. 27-41). New York: Academic Press.

Ekman, P. (1994). All emotions are basic. In P. Ekman & R. J. Davidson (Eds.), *The nature of emotion: Fundamental questions* (pp. 15-19). New York: Oxford University Press.

Ellsworth, P. C. (1994). Sense, culture, and sensibility. In S. Kitayama & H. R. Markus (Eds.), *Emotion and culture: Empirical studies of mutual influence* (pp. 23-50). Washington, DC: American Psychological Association.

Erikson, E. H. (1959). *Identity and the life cycle*. New York: Norton. (Reissued 1980)

Folkman, S. (1992). Making the case for coping. In B.N. Carpenter (Ed.), *Personal coping: Theory, research, and application* (pp.31-46). Westport, CT: Praeger.

Frijda, N.H. (1994). Varieties of affect: Emotions and episodes, moods, and sentiments. In P. Ekman & R. J. Davidson (Eds.), *The nature of emotion: Fundamental questions* (pp. 59-67). New York: Oxford University Press.

Gauvin, L., & Rejeski, W. J. (1993). The Exercise-induced Feeling Inventory: Development and initial validation. *Journal of Sport & Exercise Psychology, 15*, 403-423.

Gauvin, L., & Spence, J. C. (1998). Measurement of exercise-induced changes in feeling states, affect, mood, and emotions. In J. L. Duda (Ed.), *Advances in sport and exercise psychology measurement* (pp. 325-336). Morgantown, WV: Fitness Information Technology.

Gergen, K. J., & Gergen, M. M. (1986). Narrative form and the construction of psychological science. In T. R. Sarbin (Ed.), *Narrative psychology: The storied nature of human conduct* (pp. 22-44). New York: Praeger.

Gergen, M. M., & Gergen, K. J. (1995). What is this thing called love? Emotional scenarios in historical perspective. *Journal of Narrative Life History, 5*, 221-237.

Gould, D., Finch, L. M., & Jackson, S. A. (1993). Coping strategies used by national figure skaters. *Research Quarterly for Exercise and Sport, 64*, 453-468.

Gould, D., & Tuffey, S. (1996). Zones of optimal functioning research: A review and critique. *Anxiety, Stress, and Coping, 9*, 53-68.

Gould, D., & Weinberg, R. (1985). Sources of worry in successful and less successful intercollegiate wrestlers. *Journal of Sport Behavior, 8*, 115-127.

Graham, T. R., Kowalski, K.C., & Crocker, P. R. E. (2002). The contributions of goal characteristics and causal attributions to emotional experience in youth sport participants. *Psychology of Sport and Exercise, 3*, 273-291.

Greendorfer, S. L. (1992). Sport socialization. In T. S. Horn (Ed.), *Advances in sport psychology* (pp. 201-218). Champaign, IL: Human Kinetics.

Gross, J. J., Carstensen, L. L., Pasupathi, M., Tsai, J., Skorpen, K., & Hsu, A. Y. C. (1997). Emotion and aging: Experience, expression, and control. *Psychology of Aging, 12*, 590-599.

Grove, J. R., Lavallee, D., & Gordon, S. (1997). Coping with retirement from sport: The influence of athletic identity. *Journal of Applied Sport Psychology, 9*, 191-203.

Hackfort, D., (1999). The presentation and modulation of emotions. In R. Lidor & M. Bar-Eli (Eds.), *Sport psychology: Linking theory and practice* (pp. 231-244). Morgantown, WV.: Fitness Information Technology.

Hanin, Y. L. (1997). Emotions and athletic performance: Individual zones of optimal functioning model. In R. Seiler (Ed.), *European yearbook of sport psychology* (pp. 29-72). Sankl Augustin, Germany: Academia Verlag.

Hanin, Y. L. (2000a). Individual zones of optimal functioning (IZOF) model. In Y. L. Hanin (Ed.), *Emotions in sport* (pp. 65-89). Champaign, IL: Human Kinetics.

Hanin, Y. L. (2000b). Individual Zones of Optimal Functioning (IZOF) model: Emotion-performance relationships in sport. In Y. L. Hanin (Ed.), *Emotions in sport* (pp. 65-89). Champaign, IL: Human Kinetics.

Hanin, Y. L., & Syrja, P. (1995). Performance affect in junior ice hockey players: An application of the individual zones of optimal functioning model. *The Sport Psychologist, 9*, 169-187.

Hansson, R.O., Hogan, R., & Jones, W.H. (1984). In C.Z. Malatesta & C. E. Izard (Eds.), *Emotion in adult development* (pp. 195-209). Beverly Hills, CA: Sage.

Hardy, L., Jones, G., & Gould, D. (1996). *Understanding psychological preparation for sport: Theory and practice of elite performers*. New York: John Wiley & Sons.

Harre, R. (Ed.). (1986). *The social construction of emotion*. Oxford: Blackwell.

Harter, S. (1999). *The construction of self: A developmental perspective*. New York: Guilford Press.

Heil, J. (2000). The injured athlete. In Y. L. Hanin (Ed.), *Emotions in sport* (pp. 245-265). Champaign, IL: Human Kinetics.

Jackson, S. (2000). Joy, fun and flow states in sport. In Y.L. Hanin (Ed.), *Emotions in sport* (pp. 135-156). Champaign, IL: Human Kinetics.

Jones, J. G. (1995). More than just a game: Research developments and issues in competitive anxiety in sport. *British Journal of Psychology, 86*, 449-478.

Landers, D. M., & Boutcher, S.H. (1998). Arousal-performance relationships. In J. M. Williams (Ed.), *Applied sport psychology* (3rd ed., pp.197-218). Mountain View, CA: Mayfield.

Lazarus, R. S. (1991). *Emotion and adaptation*. New York: Oxford University Press.

Lazarus, R. S. (1993). From psychological stress to the emotions: A history of changing outlooks. *Annual Reviews of Psychology, 44*, 1-21.

Lazarus, R. S. (1996). The role of coping in the emotions and how coping changes over the life course. In C. Magai & S.H. McFadden (Eds.), *Handbook of emotion, adult development and aging* (pp. 289-306). New York: Academic Press.

Lazarus, R. S. (1999). *Stress and emotion: A new synthesis*. New York: Springer.

Lazarus, R. S. (2000a). Cognitive-motivational-relational theory of emotion. In Y. L. Hanin (Ed.), *Emotions in sport* (pp. 40-63). Champaign, IL: Human Kinetics.

Lazarus, R. S. (2000b). How emotions influence performance in competitive sports. *The Sport Psychologist, 14*, 229-252.

Lazarus, R. S., & Folkman, S. (1984). *Stress, appraisal, and coping*. New York: Springer.

LeDoux, J. E. (1995). Emotion: Clues from the brain. *Annual Review of Psychology, 46*, 209-235.

LeUnes, A., & Burger, J. (2000). Profile of Mood States research in sport and exercise psychology: Past, present, and future. *Journal of Applied Sport Psychology, 12*, 5-15.

Levinson, D. J. (1990). A theory of life structure development in adulthood. In C.N. Alexander & E. J. Langer (Eds.), *Higher stages of human development* (pp. 35-54). New York: Oxford University Press.

MacIntyre, I. (2001). *Essensa sparks Canucks rally*. Vancouver Sun Newspaper, Feburary 2, 2001, F2.

Malatesta, C.Z., & Izard, C. E. (1984). Introduction: Conceptualizing emotional development in adults. In C.Z. Malatesta & C. E. Izard (Eds.), *Emotion in adult development* (pp. 13-21). Beverly Hills, CA: Sage

Martens, R., Vealey, R. S., & Burton, D. (1990). *Competitive anxiety in sport*. Champaign, IL: Human Kinetics.

McAdams, D. P. (1997). *The stories we live by: Personal myths and the making of the self*. New York: Guilford.

McAuley, E., & Courneya, K. A. (1994). The Subjective Exercise Experience Scale (SEES): Development and preliminary validation. *Journal of Sport & Exercise Psychology, 16*, 163-177.

McAuley, E., & Duncan, T. E. (1989). Causal attributions and affective reactions to disconfirming outcomes in motor performance. *Journal of Sport & Exercise Psychology, 11*, 187-200.

McConatha, J. T., & Huba, H. M. (1999). Primary, secondary, and emotional control across adulthood. *Current Psychology: Developmental, Learning, Personality, Social, 18*, 164-170.

McNair, D. M., Lorr, M., & Droppleman, L. F. (1971). *Manual for the Profile of Mood States*. San Diego, CA: Educational and Industrial Testing Service.

McPherson, B. D. (1986). *Sport and aging*. Champaign, IL: Human Kinetics.

Morgan, W.P. (1979). Prediction of performance in athletics. In P. Klavora & J. F. Daniel (Eds.), *Coach, athlete, and the sport psychologist* (pp. 173-186). Champaign, IL: Human Kinetics.

Naylor, S., Burton, D., & Crocker, P. R. E. (2002). Competitive anxiety and sport performance. In J. Silva & D. Stevens (Eds.), *Psychological foundations of sport* (pp. 132-154). Boston: Allyn & Bacon.

O'Brien Cousins, S. (1996). Exercise cognition among elderly women. *Journal of Applied Sport Psychology, 8*, 131-145.

Prapavessis, H. (2000). The POMS and sports performance: A review. *Journal of Applied Sport Psychology, 12*, 34-48.

Rainey, D. (1995). Sources of stress among baseball and softball umpires. *Journal of Applied Sport Psychology, 7*, 1-10.

Scanlan, T. K., Ravizza, K., & Stein, G. L. (1989). An in-depth study of former elite figure skaters: I. Introduction to the project. *Journal of Sport & Exercise Psychology, 11*, 54-64.

Scanlan, T. K., & Simons, J. P. (1992). The construct of sport enjoyment. In G. C. Roberts (Ed.), *Motivation in sport and exercise* (pp. 199-216). Champaign, IL: Human Kinetics.

Scanlan, T. K., Stein, G. L., & Ravizza, K. (1991). An in-depth study of former elite skaters: III. Sources of stress. *Journal of Sport & Exercise Psychology, 13*, 102-120.

Smith, C. A., Haynes, K. N., Lazarus, R. S., & Pope, L. K. (1993). In search of the "hot" cognitions: Attributions, appraisals, and their relation to emotion. *Journal of Personality and Social Psychology, 65*, 916-929.

Smith, C. A., & Lazarus, R. S. (1993). Appraisal components, core relational themes, and the emotions. *Cognition and Emotion, 7*, 233-269.

Smith, M. (1983). *Violence and sport*. Toronto: Butterworths.

Smith, R. E. (1996). Performance anxiety, cognitive interference, and concentration enhancement strategies in sports. In I.G. Sarason, G. R. Pierce, & B.R. Sarason (Eds.), *Cognitive interference: Theories, methods, and findings* (pp. 261-284). Hillsdale, NJ: Erlbaum.

Stewart, A. J., & Healy, J. M. (1984). Processing affective responses to life experiences: The development of adult self. In C.Z. Malatesta & C. E. Izard (Eds.), *Emotion in adult development* (pp. 277-295). Beverly Hills, CA: Sage.

Terry, P. (1995). The efficacy of mood state profiling with elite performers: A review and synthesis. *The Sport Psychologist, 9*, 309-324.

Vallerand, R. J. (1984). Emotion in sport: Definitional, historical, and social psychological perspectives. In W. F. Straub & J. M. Williams (Eds.), *Cognitive sport psychology* (pp. 65-78). Lansing, NY: Sport Science Associates.

Vallerand, R. J. (1987). Antecedents of self-rated affects in sport: Preliminary evidence on the intuitive-reflective appraisal model. *Journal of Sport Psychology, 9*, 161-182.

Vallerand, R. J., & Blanchard, C. M. (2000). The study of emotion in sport and exercise. In Y. L. Hanin (Ed.), *Emotions in sport* (pp. 3-37). Champaign, IL: Human Kinetics.

Wankel, L. L., & Kreisel, P. J. J. (1985). Factors underlying enjoyment of youth sport. *Journal of Sport Psychology, 7*, 51-64.

Weiner, B. (1985). An attribution theory of achievement motivation and emotion. *Psychological Review, 92*, 548-573.

Weiner, B. (1986). *An attributional theory of motivation and emotion.* New York: Springer-Verlag.

Whitbourne, S. K. (1996). Psychosocial perspectives on emotions: The role of identity in the aging process. In C. Magai & S.H. McFadden (Eds.), *Handbook of emotion, adult development and aging* (pp. 83-98). New York: Academic Press.

CHAPTER THIRTEEN

Motivational Processes Among Older Adults in Sport and Exercise Settings

Martyn Standage • Joan L. Duda

A consistent and compelling body of literature now exists that documents the many positive physiological and psychological benefits associated with habitual physical activity (cf. American College of Sports Medicine [ACSM], 2000; Bouchard, Shephard, & Stephens, 1994; McAuley & Rudolph, 1995; Pate et al., 1995; Shephard, 1997; U.S. Department of Health and Human Services [USDHHS], 1996). Research has also shown that such derived benefits extend across the lifespan (cf. Bouchard et al., 1994). On the other hand, physical inactivity has also been recognized as a major risk factor for disease in child, adult, and elderly populations (ACSM, 2000; Pate et al., 1995). Taken collectively, such findings underscore the importance from a public health perspective of the need to understand and enhance individuals' motivation to become and remain physically active throughout the years of their lives. Although a plethora of studies have addressed the motivational processes that underpin the affective, behavioral, and consequential effects of physical activity participation with children, youth, and adult populations (cf. Roberts, 2001a; Weiss & Williams, 2003), a paucity of research has addressed motivational factors as they relate to the older adult. This represents a significant void in the current literature.

Statistical reports, in recent years, have documented increases in elderly populations (over 65 years) worldwide (Kalache & Kickbusch, 1997; Rapid Reports, 1993; Tourt, 1989). Demographically, the most striking increments have been witnessed in western societies such as Australia (Australian Bureau of Statistics, 1999), the United Kingdom (Office of National Statistics, 1996), and the United States (U.S. Bureau of Census, 1996), where in addition to a rapid growth in those 65 years and over, notable population increases for those 80 years and over have been reported. In the United States, for example, the older segment of society (65 years or over) is growing at such a vast rate that projections forecast that this subgroup will almost double to represent around 20% of the total population between 1996 and 2020 (U.S. Bureau of Census, 1996). It has been predicted, too, that, by the year 2040, the number of individuals 80 years or over in the United Kingdom will grow by approximately 1.5 million, when compared to 1990 (Organisation for Economic Cooperation and Development [OECD], 1994). Such marked increases in the so-called graying of modern societies, via reductions in infant mortality, improvements in health care, and lifestyle modifications (Stuart-Hamilton, 2000), have provided further justification for examining the determinants of successful aging.

Despite such striking enlargements in the number of older adults in contemporary societies, the elderly population has received little attention in sport and exercise texts. Thus, the purpose of the present chapter is to outline the various implications that physical activity may have for the older adult and to present various models of motivation to engage in physical activity settings with this population. Specifically, we begin by outlining the various benefits that physical activity has for the older adult and the importance of promoting adherence to such activity for this population. We then present the motives and barriers that the elderly give for their participation or nonparticipation in exercise, respectively. Next, we advocate the application of social cognitive models of motivation to further provide insight into the motivational processes that underlie the affective, behavioral, and cognitive responses of older adults participating in the physical activity domain. Subsequently, three prominent social cognitive theories of motivation are presented and discussed: (a) self-efficacy theory (Bandura, 1986, 1997), (b) self-determination theory (Deci & Ryan, 1985, 1991), and (c) achievement goal theory (Dweck, 1999; Nicholls, 1984, 1989). Finally, we conclude with some theoretical comments and suggest several directions for future research in this area of inquiry.

PHYSICAL ACTIVITY AND OLDER ADULTS

Maintaining an active, healthy, happy, and independent lifestyle represents an important component of physical and psychological well-being in humans, regardless of age. For the older individual, in particular, concerns regarding actual or potential decrements in personal well-being and one's capacity to function independently can be cause for apprehension and distress (Buchner & Wagner, 1992). These fears would appear to be substantiated when one considers that the elderly population in the United States accounts for the largest percentage of chronic disease (Hoffman, Rice, & Sung, 1996), with approximately 80% of individuals over the age of 65 years suffering from at least one health ailment (Pescatello & DiPietro, 1993).[1] Stimulated by such increased demands on health care systems, coupled with the known and inescapable repercussions of aging (i.e., lower functional ability, poorer cardiovascular health, etc.), medical, sport, and exercise scientists have turned their attention towards examining the impact that physical activity may have on older adults' functional, physiological, psychological, and social status (cf. Shephard, 1997; Spirduso, 1995). Likewise, and aligned with the old adage "prevention is the finest cure," a second line of inquiry has focused on the role that physical activity may play in the maintenance of an independent lifestyle (i.e., sustaining of activities of daily living; ADL; Katz, 1983; Schroeder, Naum, Osness, & Potteiger, 1998). Specifically, this behavioral medicine approach to the study of physical activity in elderly populations has been influenced by the functional decline of some older individuals to carry out ADLs. It epitomizes the principle that the role of physical activity is to "add quality to one's years, as opposed to years to one's life." Such a philosophy is nicely illustrated by Ashley Montague, who stated that "the goal of life is to die young, as late as possible" (cited in Pu & Nelson, 1999).

Despite findings pertaining to the benefits of maintaining an active lifestyle across the lifespan, physical activity and age have been shown to share an inverse relationship (Dishman, 1994a; Stephens & Caspersen, 1994). In their recent study, Goggin and Morrow (2001) found

---

[1]It should be noted that the prevalence of chronic disability among older adults in the United States declined from 24.9 % to 21.3% during 1982 to 1994 as a result of improved medical care and lifestyle changes (Manton, Corder, & Stallard, 1997). Despite these promising findings, the marked increases in population growth among older adults from 1982 to 1994 and future projections (U.S. Bureau of Census, 1996) confound the actual figures regarding the number of age-related ailments that place demands of the health care systems each year.

that although most older adults (89%) acknowledged the importance of physical activity for obtaining health benefits, 69% of older adults were not participating in sufficient levels of physical activity to obtain any positive consequences. Their results also showed that this trend increased with age and that older men tended to be more physically active than older women. The significance of this decrease in physical activity, coupled with the biological consequences of aging (cf. Shephard, 1997) is alarming, especially when one considers that in excess of 250,000 Americans are predicted to die each year as a result of a sedentary lifestyle (Powell & Blair, 1994).

> There is an inverse relationship between physical activity and age.

Besides those older adults who do exercise in order to stay physically capable (i.e., maintain control and competence in terms of ADLs), thousands of elderly individuals worldwide engage in intense exercise and participate in high levels of competitive sport (e.g., the Masters Games, Senior Olympics). Symbolic of older adults' capacity to continue to perform admirably within the physical activity domain are the recent track-and-field performances of athletes in the over-80-year category. For example, male and female competitors have completed the 100 meters in 14.35 and 18.4 seconds, respectively. Further, in the same age group, a result of 44 minutes and 29 seconds for men and 58 minutes 40 seconds for women have been posted for the 10,000 meters (World Association of Veteran Athletes [WAVA], 2000).

In addition to the physiological benefits associated with regular exercise and sporting involvement for elderly individuals, psychological advantages have also been reported. Contemporary research involving older adults has shown physical activity to be related to enhanced levels of life satisfaction (Mihalko & McAuley, 1996; Morgan et al., 1991), positive mood states (Arent, Landers, & Etnier, 2000), self-efficacy (Deforche & Bourdeaudhuij, 2000; Grembowski et al., 1993; Hogan & Santomier, 1984), subjective well-being (McAuley, Blissmer, Katula, & Duncan, 2000), lower levels of depression (P.S. O'Connor, Aenchbacher, & Dishman, 1993; Ruuskanen & Ruoppila, 1995) and decreased negative mood (Arent et al., 2000; Engels, Drouin, Ahu, & Kazmierski, 1998; King, Taylor, & Haskell, 1993).

The positive physiological and psychological health consequences associated with physical activity for older adults are dependent on regular engagement. Given the potential impact that the adoption of an inactive lifestyle may have on older people's quality of life, independence, and mortality, a fundamental question arises: How do we encourage older adults to regularly participate in physical activity? Answering this question becomes especially salient and challenging when one considers that older individuals already represent the most sedentary segment of society (Dishman, 1994a) and exercise programs, in general, have high attrition rates (ACSM, 2000; Dishman, 1994b). With such matters in mind, it is important to account for varying levels of investment and adherence in this population if we are to facilitate public health and quality of life in this expanding population commensurate with recent position statements and guidelines (e.g., ACSM, 2000; Pate et al., 1995; World Health Organization [WHO], 1997).

PHYSICAL ACTIVITY MOTIVATION IN OLDER ADULTS

To date, a major limitation of previous work addressing the reasons (motives) for and against physical activity within most populations, including older adults, has been the descriptive and atheoretical nature of these investigations (Biddle, 1995; Biddle & Nigg, 2000). That is, although descriptive information pertaining to lifespan differences in the motives for being active such as health, appearance, psychological, and social reasons (Hirvensalo, Lampinen, & Rantanen, 1998; Lehr, 1992) represent a foundation for study, they neither offer explanation nor enhance our knowledge of the motivational processes associated with physical activity engagement (Biddle & Nigg, 2000). In a similar vein, descriptive and atheoretical research does not provide much insight into the determinants of perceived barriers (such as lack of health and lack of interest) that the elderly give for poor activity levels (Hirvensalo et al., 1998). As with all facets of society, the likelihood of the older individual's adhering to a fitness program relies largely on their perceiving more positive opposed to negative consequences associated with physical activity (*cost* versus *benefit* approach; ACSM, 2000). Figure 1 illustrates this principle using the motivating factors versus physical activity barriers, as identified by the World Health Organization (WHO, 1997) in their recent guidelines aimed at promoting physical activity among older populations.

As can be seen in Figure 1, there are numerous disincentives pertinent to the older adult that may encourage a sedentary lifestyle. In addition to conventional barriers associated with physical activity participation, older adults confront numerous and unique obstacles. Comparable to most populations, for older adults, perceptions of competence are a central variable in determining the likely adoption and adherence to exercise participation (this point will be expanded on in the self-efficacy section of this chapter). Unlike younger populations, however, older adults find perceptions of inadequate competence (i.e., "I cannot exercise because I am too old") to be supported by societal beliefs that physical activity participation for older adults is not "expected behavior" and perhaps even a health risk. Because such stereotypes have been shown to develop during childhood (McTavish, 1971), Behlendorf, MacRae, and Vos Strache (1999) examined the perceptions of children towards competence and appropriateness of physical activity based on the age and gender of the targeted group. Results supported the presence of age-based bias, with the children perceiving that the possession of necessary competence and acceptability of physical activity participation decrease as individuals become older. Clearly, if such attitudes are to change, there is a need to (a) encourage a greater appreciation of physical activity among policy makers at the community, regional, and national

FIGURE 1
Motives and barriers that affect the older adults' adherence to physical activity: A cost/benefit approach.

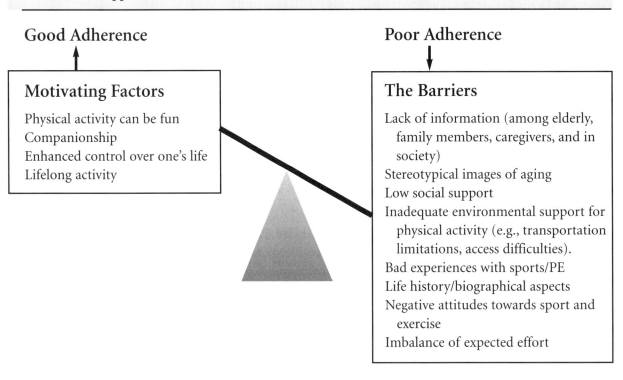

Good Adherence

Poor Adherence

Motivating Factors

Physical activity can be fun
Companionship
Enhanced control over one's life
Lifelong activity

The Barriers

Lack of information (among elderly, family members, caregivers, and in society)
Stereotypical images of aging
Low social support
Inadequate environmental support for physical activity (e.g., transportation limitations, access difficulties).
Bad experiences with sports/PE
Life history/biographical aspects
Negative attitudes towards sport and exercise
Imbalance of expected effort

levels and (b) encourage an increased foci on education, with the resultant information regarding healthy aging being distributed to a wide variety of societal sectors (i.e., the media, peer support groups, etc.; WHO, 1997).

> Older adults' perceptions of inadequate competence are supported by societal beliefs that physical activity participation for older adults is not expected and may be a health risk.

SOCIAL COGNITIVE MODELS OF MOTIVATION

As mentioned earlier, much of the research to date addressing exercise and sport motivation in older adult populations has been void of a theoretical base. To delineate the motivational processes that potentially account for age-related changes in physical activity patterns among older men and women, we aim to emphasize and illustrate the benefits of employing social cognitive approaches to the study of motivation within this population. Social cognitive models have evolved from traditional approaches pertaining to motivation (Atkinson, 1958; McClelland, 1961). The emphasis of the social cognitive paradigm is on the dynamics between a set of social cognitive antecedents and consequences of behavior. As Roberts (2001b) notes, social cognitive theoretical frameworks that are evident within contemporary physical activity research include, among others, (a) self-efficacy theory (Bandura, 1986, 1997), (b) self-determination theory (Deci & Ryan, 1985, 1991), and (c) achievement goal theory (Dweck, 1999; Nicholls, 1984, 1989).

There are numerous reasons and merits for selecting these theoretical frameworks for inclusion in the current chapter. First, perceived competence or one's belief in one's own capabilities is one of the most frequently cited psychosocial determinants of both the adoption and continued participation in physical activity. All three models of motivation encompass such perceptions and beliefs albeit in distinct ways, thus each adding a unique contribution to our understanding of motivation. Second, all three frameworks have shown to be informative when applied to younger populations (cf. Feltz & Lirgg, 2001; Roberts, 2001a; Vallerand & Rousseau, 2001; Weiss & Ferrer-Caja, 2002; Weiss & Williams., 2003). Between the three frameworks, self-efficacy theory in particular has been consistently shown to be tenable when applied to older populations (cf. McAuley, Pena, & Jerome, 2001). We suggest, though, that the other two theories have great promise for investigating the motivational striving of older adults in physical activity settings. Indeed, an aim of this chapter is to promote further work on the motivational patterns of older adults that is grounded in the self-determination and achievement-goal frameworks. Finally, each of the selected conceptualizations discussed in this chapter embraces antecedents that are modifiable. As a result, all three frameworks offer potential theoretical backdrops for intervention studies with older populations.

SELF-EFFICACY THEORY

Originally conceptualized to foster understanding of clinical interventions for the treatment of symptoms of anxiety, self-efficacy theory (Bandura, 1986, 1997) has emerged as a prominent framework in contemporary sport and physical activity research (c.f. Feltz & Lirgg, 2001; McAuley & Mihalko, 1998; McAuley et al., 2001). Indeed, many studies in the physical activity domain have ascertained self-efficacy to be a determinant of both acute and long-term physical activity behaviors, a response to participation, and a construct related to other cognitive and affective responses in physical activity settings. Although the early work grounded in this framework focused on self-efficacy of younger samples or middle-aged populations, recent research has shown self-efficacy theory relevant to gerontology research (e.g., Clark & Northwehr, 1999; Estabrooks & Carron, 2000; Li, McAuley, Harmer, Duncan, & Chaumeton, 2001; McAuley, 1993a; McAuley et al., 1999; McAuley, Lox, & Duncan, 1993).

Reflecting a form of "situational specific self-confidence," self-efficacy refers to "beliefs in one's capabilities to organize and execute the courses of action required to produce given attainments" (Bandura, 1997, p. 3). These efficacy judgments relate to the level of performance expected and the strength or certainty of those attainment beliefs. It is important to note, however, that self-efficacy does not relate to capacity beliefs (amount of ability), but rather to the judgment that one *can* achieve attainments with the skills one possesses (Bandura, 1986).

Also embraced by self-efficacy theory are *outcome expectations* that relate to the "judgement of the likely consequence a behavior will produce" (Bandura, 1986, p. 391). For example, an older adult's belief that a regular exercise routine will bring about improvements in functional capability would represent an outcome expectation, not an efficacy judgment. Bandura (1997) proposes that outcome expectations are contingent upon self-efficacy judgments and are not predictive beyond these judgments.

According to the self-efficacy framework (Bandura, 1986, 1997), older individuals who possess high levels of self-efficacy towards physical activity tasks are more likely to readily participate, work harder, perform at a higher level, and persist in the face of difficulty or failure. Research with older adults has supported these tenets by displaying self-efficacy to be an important construct in predicting physical activity adoption (McAuley, 1993a), exercise adherence (McAuley, 1993a; McAuley et al., 1993), program attendance (Estabrooks & Carron, 1998; Li et al., 2001), health status and other health-related behaviors (Grembowski et al., 1993; McAuley et al., 1993).

Research has also shown that older adults exposed to various modes of physical activity including tai chi (Li et al., 2001), resistance training (McAuley et al., 1999), and most commonly aerobic training (McAuley et al., 1993; McAuley et al., 1999), have reported increases in self-efficacy as a function of participation. These improvements have, however, been shown to decline at the cessation of participation, thus suggesting a curvilinear pattern in efficacy enhancement before, during, and following structured exercise programs (McAuley et al., 1999). McAuley and colleagues (1999) supported this proposed pattern in a multimode (aerobic and a stretching/ toning condition) randomized controlled study. Specifically, their results revealed that efficacy of the formerly sedentary older adults increased during a 6-month exercise trial but decreased at a follow-up assessment 6 months subsequent to the experiment. This curvilinear pattern suggests a need for more intervention studies addressing not only how to encourage participation, but also how to maintain it beyond structured experimental protocols in *real-life settings*.

In line with theoretical predictions of self-efficacy theory (Bandura, 1997), research has found older adults who have low self-efficacy beliefs to be prime candidates to withdraw from physical activity programs. Previous work has also shown older women to be less physical efficacious than older men (McAuley et al., 1993). Both males and females, as they grow older, need to overcome barriers to physical activity that impede their relative efficacy levels (e.g., societal beliefs, medical cautions, lack of experience with physical activity in recent years). Perhaps among the principal factors hindering self-efficacy in this population is the recorded increase in the number of ailments associated with advancing age (Pescatello & DiPietro, 1993). Such increases in physical problems are likely to lead older adults to the faulty conclusion that physical activity is indeed adverse to their health (e.g., "Since I have angina I should not exercise. It may be dangerous"). In essence, we can have a vicious circle occurring, where existing ailments support the elderly individuals' perception that they possess low efficacy towards physical activity tasks. In turn, this resultant lack of physical activity will contribute to additional medical conditions and further declines in physiological and psychological well-being. Moreover, such declines coupled with the "social norms" pertaining to older adults and physical activity participation may nurture older individuals' perceptions of low physical efficacy. This, in turn, can support a self-fulfilling prophecy and may contribute to the societal conception that the elderly are physically incapable.

Older adults who begin an exercise program after being inactive for many years may have low efficacy levels.

In view of the reciprocal relationship that self-efficacy shares with many aspects of physical activity participation, it is fortunate from a health perspective that judgments regarding older adults' personal efficacy are modifiable and can be altered via intervention programs targeting one or more of the known sources of efficacy information (McAuley, 1993b; McAuley et al., 1993). Moreover, because research suggests that self-efficacy about physical tasks may generalize to other ADL-related tasks (e.g., walking, household chores; Hogan & Santomier, 1984), a fundamental question arises: How can we increase physical activity self-efficacy in older adults? As Figure 2 shows, self-efficacy theory proposes four main antecedents to task-specific confidence judgments. Implications for increasing self-efficacy in older adults aligned with the proposed sources of self-efficacy are elaborated on below.

Enactive mastery accomplishments represent the strongest source of efficacy (Bandura, 1997). Past performance accomplishments are most influential when one successfully completes a difficult as opposed to an easy task, completes it without external assistance, and experiences infrequent failure. Empirical work in the physical activity domain has shown mastery experiences to enhance self-efficacy in younger adult populations (Feltz, 1982; Weinberg, Gould, & Jackson, 1979; Weinberg, Gould, Yukelson, & Jackson, 1981; Weinberg, Yukelson, & Jackson, 1980). In essence, this antecedent to self-efficacy instills the belief of "I have done it before, so I can do it again." Because older adults who are initiating an exercise program may not have been exposed to physical activity for many years, their efficacy levels may be low. Thus, it may be appropriate to introduce them to exercise-related tasks gradually, ensuring a

FIGURE 2
The relationships among sources of efficacy, self-efficacy judgments, and consequences.

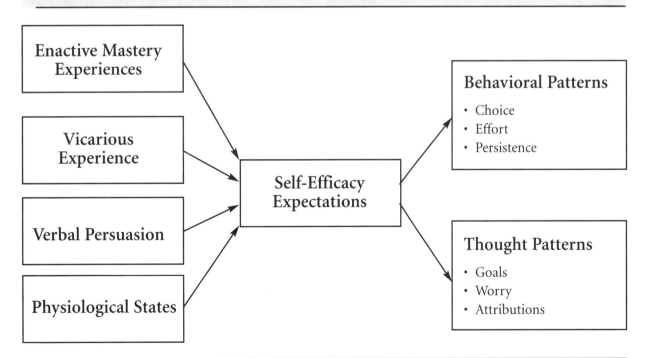

Feltz, D.L., & Chase, M.A. (1998). The measurement of self-efficacy and confidence in sport. In J.L. Duda (Ed.), Advances in Sport and Exercise Psychology Measurement (Morgantown, WV: Fitness Information Technology) pp. 65-80. Reprinted with permission.

degree of success in order to foster efficacy levels. Subsequent task progression should be commensurate with obtained success.

Comparing oneself with others represents another antecedent to older adults' self-efficacy. Bandura (1986, 1997) proposes that the vicarious experience of viewing others successfully accomplish tasks (especially if the model is similar to the person in question) enhances self-efficacy judgments. The utility of watching others has been demonstrated with younger populations in the physical activity domain (c.f., McCullagh & Weiss, 2001). Specifically, studies have shown self-efficacy and performance to be enhanced as a result of modeling (Feltz, Landers, & Raeder, 1979; George, Feltz, & Chase, 1992; Gould & Weiss, 1981; see McCullagh & Weiss, 2001, for a comprehensive review). Clark (1999) argues that older adults who belong to community organizations/programs (e.g., senior citizens' centers) greatly enhance their chances of observing a similar model. However, as Clark further stresses, it is typical for those most in need of the informational and motivating effects of modeling (i.e., inactive seniors) to decline participation in such programs. Examples of seniors successfully engaging in exercise activities (from the beginner to Senior Olympian) are needed as they may increase perceptions of self-efficacy and act as a precursor to successful aging.

Verbal persuasion is another source of self-efficacy that has yielded support with younger populations doing sport and physical activity tasks (e.g., Feltz & Riessinger, 1990; Weinberg, Grove, & Jackson, 1992). In the case of the older adults, verbal information is likely to derive from sources such as doctors, family members, peers, and exercise leaders. Verbal persuasion can take the form of feedback ("This is how you do this") or motivational ("You can do it!") statements. The impact of verbal persuasion is influenced by the credibility, expertise, and assumed knowledge of the persuader (e.g., a doctor prescribing exercise). Exercise leaders, therefore, play an influential role in gerontology exercise programs as their feedback can aid or thwart older adults' perceptions of self-efficacy. That is, although words of encouragement can augment self-efficacy, messages that the older adult receives can also serve to diminish their task-related confidence. For example, warning statements regarding the dangers of exercising with advancing age may curtail the older exerciser's self-efficacy (Dzewaltowski, 1989). Therefore, if we are to encourage the appropriateness of, and the efficacy to partake in, physical activity in older adult populations, medical and exercise professionals must be careful to emphasize suitable cues and stress efficacy-enhancing messages.

The final source of efficacy judgments is physiological states, which represent the individual's views about his or her physiological condition when in the activity setting. Although links between this source of efficacy information and various affective and performance variables have been reported in younger populations (Feltz & Riessinger, 1990; Treasure, Monson, & Lox, 1996), Clark (1999) suggests that in older adults, physiological states may have a more powerful influence on self-efficacy given the inverse relationship between age and physical health status. For example, with advancing age, movements and mobility may become more painful. This can potentially lead to lower self-efficacy beliefs when individuals are assessing their physiological state to determine the likelihood that they can successfully complete the task. Given that physical activity participation does not elicit instantaneous benefits (e.g., weight loss or strength gains require many weeks of regular workouts) and instead may evoke negative repercussions (e.g., fatigue, muscle soreness, breathlessness), exercising for older adults may be largely weighted in favor of re-adopting their inactive lifestyle. As a result, we should aim to foster efficacy beliefs via encouraging a more positive interpretation of the messages received from physiological cues (e.g., "This doesn't feel too bad, I can do this" or "I am just starting to exercise, so it's normal to feel a little soreness" as opposed to "I can't do this at my age, it hurts too much"). To do this, it is important to encourage older adults to start "easy" and gradually increase activity intensity. Also, it is essential to make sure the older person (particularly if sedentary for many years) has a reasonable understanding of the sensations she or he will experience when engaged in exercise.

Numerous intervention studies have successfully manipulated the various sources of efficacy in the physical activity domain and observed ensuing influences on self-efficacy with younger populations (see Feltz & Lirgg, 2001, for a review). Similar investigations conducted with older adults engaged in various modes of physical activity would certainly be of great benefit. Also, as McAuley et al. (2001) highlight, intervention studies embracing a longitudinal design would be beneficial and informative regarding developmental patterns of efficacy-behavior relationships in physical activity involvement.

Recommendations pertaining to promoting exercise among older populations may be similar to Ewart's (1989) work with cardiac rehabilitation patients. Specifically, strategies for encouraging older adults to engage in physical activity for which they lack self-efficacy may include (a) exposure to recommended activities in gradually increasing doses (performance accomplishments); (b) providing similar models so that they may see others similar to themselves performing the activity (vicarious experience); (c) recruiting qualified and respected exercise leaders to provide encouragement, reassurance, and emphasizing older adults' accomplishments (verbal persuasion); and (d) providing for a relaxed, yet upbeat exercise environment (physiological states).

More research is necessary to fully understand what motivates certain individuals to maintain exercise habits while others abandon them.

SELF-DETERMINATION THEORY

Self-determination theory (Deci & Ryan, 1985, 1991; R. M. Ryan & Deci, 2000; Vallerand, 1997) is another framework that may potentially enhance our understanding of older adults' motivation to engage in physical activity. Initial attempts to employ self-determination theory with older adults in various life domains have supported its tenability with this population (e.g., Kasser & Ryan, 1999; Vallerand, O'Connor, & Blais, 1989; Vallerand, O'Connor, & Hamel, 1995). Further, applications of the self-determination framework to the study of motivation-

The sequential pattern of motivation proposed by self-determination theory (Deci & Ryan, 1985, 1991; Vallerand, 1997). Reprinted with permission

Social Factors	Psychological Mediators	Motivation	Consequences
• Perceptions of choice in exercise environment • Feedback that enhances/thwarts competence(ies) • Perceptions of support (e.g., spousal, family, friends)	Perceptions of • Autonomy • Competence • Relatedness	• Intrinsic motivation • Integrated regulation • Identified regulation • Introjected regulation • External regulation • Amotivation	• Enhanced well-being • Enjoyment • Behavioral persistence • Enhanced efficacy • Increased effort • Improved mood

Vallerand, R. J., & Losier, G. F. (1999). An integrative analysis of intrinsic and extrinsic motivation in sport. Journal of Applied Sport Psychology, 11, 142-169. Reprinted with permission.

al process among younger participants in sport and physical education settings have provided evidence for the utility of this theory (cf. Vallerand, 2001; Vallerand & Rousseau, 2001).

Self-determination theory proposes that an individual's motivation is not a direct function of social environmental factors (e.g., degree of autonomy supported in the exercise class). Rather, it is assumed that the impact of social situational variables is mediated by the psychological needs for autonomy (the belief that one is the origin and regulator of one's actions), competence (the belief that one can efficaciously interact with the environment), and relatedness (the seeking and development of secure and connected relationships with others). This theoretical approach makes certain assumptions about the nature of social contexts that will satisfy or thwart the needs for autonomy, competence, and relatedness. For example, based on the theorizing of Deci and Ryan (1985, 1991), autonomy-supportive environments, as opposed to controlling situations, are assumed to facilitate self-determined motivation. Support for this assumption has been provided in educational contexts (e.g., Deci, Nezlek, & Sheinman, 1981; Deci, Schwartz, Sheinman, & Ryan, 1981; R. M. Ryan & Grolnick, 1986). Additionally, lab-based work in the physical activity domain has shown various social factors such as rewards (Orlick & Mosher, 1978; E. D. Ryan, 1977, 1980), competition (Vallerand, Gauvin, & Halliwell, 1986), and feedback (Vallerand & Reid, 1984), when perceived as controlling, to have negative effects on intrinsic motivation. When competitive environments focus on imparting information (Duda, Chi, Newton, Walling, & Catley, 1995; Reeve & Deci, 1996), task-related feedback is positive (Vallerand & Reid), and positive competitive outcomes emerge (Chi, 1993; McAuley & Tammen, 1989; Weinberg & Jackson, 1979), intrinsic motivation is enhanced. Figure 3 depicts the sequence of relationships, from the social environment to motivational consequences, hypothesized via self-determination theory (Deci & Ryan, 1985, 1991).

Self-determination theory (Deci & Ryan, 1985, 1991) highlights three broad types of motivation. These motivation types consist of intrinsic motivation[2] (self-determined behavior),

[2]Vallerand and his colleagues (see Vallerand, 1997) have suggested that there are three types of intrinsic motivation: to accomplish things, to experience stimulation, and to know. For the sake of brevity, we have chosen to discuss intrinsic motivation as the overriding construct aligned with the writings of Deci and Ryan (1985, 1991).

extrinsic motivation (controlled behavior), and amotivation (nonintentional behavior). Going beyond the dichotomized conceptualization of intrinsic versus extrinsic motivation that has marked past work (e.g., deCharms, 1968), Deci and Ryan (1985, 1991) have proposed that several different types of regulatory styles underpin these types of motivation and that they can be conceptualized along a self-determination continuum (see Figure 4). Figure 4 illustrates this motivational continuum together with assumed associated processes.

According to the tenets of self-determination theory, when older adults are motivated to participate in exercise for the inherent satisfactions that they gain from taking part in the chosen activity, they are said to be intrinsically motivated (R. M. Ryan & Deci, 2000). Intrinsically motivated behaviors and actions are self-directed and are performed for the fun, pleasure, challenge, and satisfaction that are embedded within activities. When an older person participates in exercise "for its own sake," rather than because of some constraints or external reinforcement, she or he is intrinsically motivated.

In contrast to intrinsic motivation, extrinsic motivation incorporates a range of regulations that are characterized by an individual's goals being directed by some separable consequence (i.e., reward, threat, and punishment). Deci and Ryan (1985, 1991) have reconceptualized and extended traditional views of extrinsic motivation, proposing that the various types of extrinsic motivation can be located along the self-determination continuum ranging from lower (i.e., external regulation) to higher levels of self-determined motivation (i.e., integrated regulation).

External regulation represents the least self-determined extrinsic regulation and refers to actions that are carried out to gain an external reward or avoid punishment (i.e., the action is a vehicle to reach some end). For example, an older man who feels pressured by significant others (e.g., his spousal partner) to partake in a leisure activity would be considered externally regulated. That is, his motivation is controlled by feelings of coercion towards participating in the activity to avoid confrontation or comply with the wishes of his wife. Such motivation is, therefore, directed by separable outcomes (in this case, the pleasing of another).

Next on the continuum is *introjected regulation*. With introjected regulation, engagement in the activity is still externally controlled, yet the source of control is internalized. That is, actions arise from the feeling that one "should" partake in an activity as opposed to the feeling that one "must" participate. Older adults who take part in an aerobics class, not because they like the class, but rather because they would feel a sense of personal guilt if they were not to attend would be directed by such a motive.

The third type of extrinsic motivation is referred to as *identified regulation*, and it relates to behaviors that stem from the value an individual places on an activity. When identified regulation is manifested, physical activity is deemed important to the individual and is freely performed. Yet being active still represents a means to an end in this instance (e.g., fitness gains, weight loss). Physical activity is not considered enjoyable or pleasurable in and of itself. For example, older adults may willingly partake in jogging because they see the activity as an important means to weight control. These individuals may not enjoy the feelings that derive from running per se, but have identified the activity as important to the self (i.e., personal appearance).

The most self-determined extrinsic motivation is *integrated regulation*, which occurs when separable goals have been incorporated within the self, meaning they have been assessed and brought into congruence with individuals' other values and needs (R. M. Ryan & Deci, 2000). For example, an individual who says, "I participate in physical activity because it is important to me" illustrates the principle underlying integrated regulation. It is important to note, though, that although integrated regulation shares many of the same attributes of intrinsic motivation (i.e., it is autonomous; R. M. Ryan & Deci, 2000), it is still considered extrinsic as instrumental actions are performed to achieve a personal goal, rather than for inherent joy, the principle that characterizes intrinsic motivation (Deci & Ryan, 1991).

The final type of motivation embraced by self-determination theory (Deci & Ryan, 1985, 1991) is termed *amotivation*. Representing the absence of intrinsic and extrinsic motivation, amotivation occurs when an individual lacks the intent to act, does not perceive contingencies between his or her behaviors and subsequent outcomes, sees no value in the activity, and/or feels incompetent to engage in the activity at hand (R. M. Ryan & Deci, 2000). For example, an elderly man who has been attending a tennis class for several weeks and is generally unsuccessful at the sport may perceive that he is incompetent and believe that his actions and effort have no bearing on performance outcomes. As a result, the individual may become amotivated and believe that there is no reason to participate ("I am participating in tennis, but am not sure that it is worth it") and will probably drop out.

Self-determination theory also embraces a concept termed *internalization*. The notion of internalization encompasses a progressive process in which interactions with social and cultural norms convey the meaning of activities to the individual so he or she accepts and internalizes these norms as important to self-representation. It is through this process that external regulations are transformed into internal regulations that the person "takes in" the value of the activity so that actions are believed to originate from a sense of self (R. M. Ryan & Deci, 2000). As a result of this assimilation, these regulations become increasingly self-determined in nature. To this end, some older adults may start participating in physical activity for external reasons (e.g., weight loss, appearance), but after time start to value the activity (identified regulation) and/or start to participate out of inherent pleasure (intrinsic motivation). That is, self-determination theory assumes that it is possible for an individual to have multiple motives for participation in physical activities. Indeed, an individual can possess both intrinsic and extrinsic reasons for engaging in physical activity.

> Internalization encompasses a progressive process in which interactions with social and cultural norms convey the meaning of activities to the individual so they accept and internalize these norms as important to self-representation.

As shown in Figure 4, these regulatory styles are hypothesized to be linked to different motivational processes and outcomes. Intrinsic motivation and self-determined extrinsic motivation (identified and integrated regulations), as opposed to amotivation and less self-determined forms of extrinsic motivation (external and introjected regulation), relate to enhanced psychological functioning and well-being (see R. M. Ryan & Deci, 2000; Vallerand, 1997, for reviews). Likewise, motivation types characterized by low levels of self-determination (e.g., external regulation and, in particular, amotivation) have been associated with maladaptive responses (Vallerand, 1997).

Recently, researchers have begun to apply the self-determination framework to examine motivation in older populations (Kasser & Ryan, 1999; B. P. O'Connor & Vallerand, 1994; Vallerand & O'Connor, 1989; Vallerand, O'Connor, & Blais, 1989). Much of this research has been conducted in nursing home settings and has supported many of the theoretical postulations offered by Deci and Ryan (1985, 1991). First, it has been shown that environments that foster autonomy enhance life satisfaction, psychological adjustment, and positive well-being among older adults (Vallerand & O'Connor, 1991; Vallerand et al., 1989). Second, personal autonomy has been shown to be associated with increases in vitality (Kasser & Ryan, 1999). Third, perceived high-quality relationships with relatives and friends have been positively linked with life satisfaction and well-being (Kasser & Ryan, 1999). Fourth, self-determined motivational regulations (intrinsic motivation and self-determined extrinsic motivations), rather than controlling types (i.e., external and introjected regulation), are positively associated with indices of quality of life (B.P. O'Connor, Vallerand, & Hamel, 1992, cited in Losier, Bourque, & Vallerand, 1993; Vallerand & O'Connor, 1989).

Collectively, findings support the tenability of the self-determination framework to understanding the motivational strivings of older populations in physical activity settings. Limited work has applied self-determination theory to older adults in the physical activity domain. One exception is work by Losier and colleagues (1993), who developed a motivational model of leisure participation aligned with the tenets of self-determination theory (Deci & Ryan, 1985, 1991). Losier et al. proposed that (a) social factors (leisure opportunities/leisure constraints) affect leisure motivation, (b) leisure motivation influences leisure satisfaction, and (c) leisure satisfaction predicts leisure participation. Results supported the proposed model with leisure opportunities rather than constraints facilitating leisure motivation. Also aligned with self-determination theory (Deci & Ryan, 1985, 1991), leisure motivation predicted both leisure satisfaction and leisure participation.

The findings of Losier and associates (1993) suggest that research grounded in this framework may provide insight into many issues relating to older adults' physical activity participation and adherence. Drawing from the tenets of self-determination theory (Deci & Ryan, 1985, 1991) and previous research with younger populations (cf. Vallerand & Rousseau, 2001), several suggestions concerning how to promote prolonged physical activity participation in older adults can be generated. We will address these strategies in accordance with the sequential pattern proposed in Figure 3. Thus, we will start with the social factors aspect and proceed through the needs and motivational regulation components of the model.

Consistent with sport and exercise research with younger populations, physical activity leaders/managers should aim to foster environments in which choice is offered (i.e., *autonomy-supportive* rather than *controlling*). In addition to the direct physical activity context, local authorities should aim to make activities accessible to all older adults, as perceptions of inac-

FIGURE 4

The self-determination continuum outlining types of motivation, and their regulatory styles, behavior, and associated processes.

Motivation	Amotivation		Extrinsic Motivation			Intrinsic Motivation
Regulatory Style	Non-Regulation	External Regulation	Introjected Regulation	Identified Regulation	Integrated Regulation	Intrinsic Regulation
Behavior	Non-Intentional/ Non-Self-determined					Autonomous/ Self-determined
Associated Processes	Lack of • competence • contingency • intention • activity relevance	Presence of external constraints • rewards • compliance • punishments	Ego directed • desire to gain approval from others or self	Acceptance of/ valuing of activity • self-endorsed goals	Hierarchical synthesis of goals • congruity of values and needs	Inherent • enjoyment • fun • satisfaction • pleasure

Ryan, R. M., & Deci, E. L. (2000). Self-determination and the facilitation of intrinsic motivation, social development, and well-being. American Psychologist, 55, 68-78. Reprinted with permission.

cessibility (constraints) to leisure and physical activity have been shown to undermine motivation within this population (Losier et al., 1993; Whaley & Ebbeck, 1997). Likewise, because there are no medicines that can safely and efficiently result in the same benefits as exercise (Shephard, 1997), medical organizations, bodies, and practitioners should be more forthcoming to publicly recognize and encourage the adoption of physical activity within this population. Because physicians are the primary factor in prompting patients to participate in physical activity (Ades et al., 1992, cited in ACSM, 2000), endorsement by one's medical doctor may well facilitate perceptions of choice (e.g., the beliefs that the person has some control over her or his health and behaviors) and subsequently enhance older adults' desire to become/remain physically active. Efforts may facilitate perceptions of competence (i.e., belief that older adults can capably exercise) and autonomy (i.e., perceptions of choice in regard to participation in physical activity) and may go some way in eradicating the stereotypical perceptions that engaging in physical activity is inappropriate for older populations (Behlendorf et al., 1999).

The constructs of relatedness, perceived competence, and perceived autonomy have been studied independently in previous research with older adults (Chogahara, O'Brien Cousins, & Wankel, 1998; Greendale, Hirsch, & Hahn, 1993; McAuley et al., 1999). All seem pertinent to older persons' physical and psychological well-being. Deci and Ryan (1985, 1991) propose that these three constructs represent the nutriments that facilitate self-determined motivation and are central to enhanced personal growth, social development, and quality of life (e.g., see Reis, Sheldon, Gable, Roscoe, & Ryan, 2000). Thus, practitioners should look towards cultivating physical activity sessions so that competence (e.g., by providing positive feedback and exercises that are optimally challenging), relatedness (e.g., by having an "exercise buddy" and caring and supportive exercise leaders), and autonomy (e.g., by allowing some choice in exercises and music) are supported.

As with all populations, there are a myriad of motives for why older adults participate in physical activity. Research based on self-determination theory (Deci & Ryan, 1985, 1991) has shown that intrinsic motivation and self-determined extrinsic motivation foster positive affective, cognitive, and behavioral responses (cf. Vallerand, 1997; Vallerand & Rousseau, 2001). With such findings in mind, those interested in advancing physical activity in older populations should aim to promote activities and develop environments that are intrinsically motivating (i.e., climates that emphasize and support the personal satisfaction and enjoyment facets of physical activity). We would argue that the importance of enhancing intrinsic motivation in this population is important for numerous reasons, yet none more so than the potential role that intrinsic motivation may play in fostering adherence among older adults. For example, R. M. Ryan, Frederick, Lepes, Rubio, and Sheldon (1997) examined the motives underlying exercise adherence in a sample of university students and employees. Results revealed that motives underscoring intrinsic aspects of motivation (competence, social interaction, and enjoyment) were related to continued exercise participation. In contrast, motives that revolved around the extrinsic facets of motivation (fitness and appearance) were unrelated to maintenance of involvement in the exercise program.

Other research has shown that external motives may facilitate the initiation of exercise (Frederick & Ryan, 1993), but not continued involvement. Commenting on these findings as well as their own, R. M. Ryan and colleagues (1997) proposed that although external factors (e.g., exercising to improve appearance) may be important motives to prompt initial participation in exercise, motives and processes that are more closely tied with intrinsic motivation (i.e., having fun while engaging in physical activity) are linked with exercise participation (R. M. Ryan et al., 1997). Such findings support the theoretical tenets of self-determination theory (Deci & Ryan, 1985, 1991) and suggest that those advancing physical activity among older adults (as with any population) should be cautious of offering extrinsic incentives and/or reinforcements to promote adherence to physical activity. Offering rewards, especially when they become expected, can become controlling and eventually debilitative to intrinsic interest (Lepper & Greene, 1978).

Based on self-determination theory, we would argue that if the exercise leaders working with older adults are adequately qualified and experienced (cf. ACSM, 2000), they should aim to minimize the use of rewards and aim to facilitate intrinsic motivation should they wish to foster optimum and long-lasting motivation (cf. Deci & Ryan, 1985, 1991). This can be accomplished through their enthusiasm, professionalism, knowledge of the proper principles of exercise training, awareness of the benefits of regular exercise, and ability to maintain interest in the activity.

ACHIEVEMENT GOAL THEORY

Perceptions of competence, a construct central to the two theories previously reviewed, are also prominent in another contemporary theory of motivation, namely achievement-goal theory (AGT; Dweck, 1999; Nicholls, 1984, 1989). This framework also assumes that individuals' level of perceived ability helps to explain variations in motivational processes. However, AGT places emphasis on how people judge or construe their level of competence (Nicholls, 1984, 1989).

In this last major section of the chapter, we propose that achievement-goal theory also holds promise with respect to understanding the motivational patterns of older persons in the physical activity domain. In this case, however, we face a more striking paucity of research on older adults in the physical activity domain than with self-efficacy and self-determination theories. As a result, an aim of this chapter is to encourage further investigations on older adults and exercise engagement that is couched in this theoretical framework. To facilitate this objective, we briefly present the central constructs and assumptions embedded in AGT and draw attention to relevant findings in the achievement-goal literature.

A major tenet of AGT is that, while engaging in competence-related activities, there is variability in the goal perspectives operating. The two major goal perspectives, namely task and ego involvement, entail different bases for deciding whether high or low ability has been demonstrated at the task at hand (Nicholls, 1989). These conceptions of ability, then, are presumed to underlie individuals' definitions of subjective success.

When task-involved, perceptions of competence are self-referenced with respect to performance and exerted effort (Nicholls, 1989). When the individual feels that he or she has tried one's best and has experienced personal performance improvement or task mastery, the person feels competent and successful. In contrast, when in a state of ego involvement, perceptions of demonstrated competence are dependent on comparisons with the performance and exerted effort of relevant others (Nicholls, 1989). Ego-involved individuals feel that they exhibited high competence when they have shown that they are more able than those in a comparison group. When superior ability is revealed, the ego-involved person perceives that she or he has been successful. People vary with respect to the tendency to approach situations in a task- and/or ego-involving manner. In other words, we differ in terms of our degree of task and ego orientation (Duda, 2001).

The goal perspectives deemed to be emphasized by significant others in particular situations are also assumed to influence whether task and/or ego involvement prevails (Ames, 1992; Ames & Archer, 1988). That is, perceived social environments (or motivational climates) can be distinguished with regard to their task- and ego-involving features (Ames, 1992). Research in sport (e.g., Newton, Duda, & Yin, 2000; Seifriz, Duda, & Chi, 1992), physical education (e.g., Papaiaonnou,

> Ego-involved individuals feel that they exhibited high competence when they have shown that they are more able than those in a comparison group.

1994), and exercise (e.g., Lloyd & Fox, 1992) settings with younger populations has supported this contention. Situational dimensions such as type of goals emphasized by coaches/PE teachers/exercise leaders, the nature of and criteria underlying evaluation and recognition, responses to mistakes, the manner in which participants are encouraged to view other participants (e.g., as someone to cooperate with or someone to outdo), and the degree to which participants of differing abilities receive differential treatment contribute to perceptions of the motivational climate. In short, various aspects of the psychological environments that others create make it more or less likely that individuals focus on improvement at the task at hand (i.e., a task-involved conception of ability) *or* the adequacy of their competence in relation to others (i.e., an ego-involved conception of ability or success).

So, what may be the implications of achievement goals for older adults' participation in the physical activity domain? At the heart of AGT is the proposition that task involvement can foster long-term quality engagement (Duda, 2001; Nicholls, 1989). Another key tenet revolves around the assumed maladaptive implications of ego involvement, particularly when there is not a parallel emphasis on task goals *and* there are questions about how good one really is in the activity at hand. These propositions are based on an appreciation of several motivational processes that are reviewed below. In the description of each, we highlight potential implications for the exercise involvement of older persons.

Achievement Goals and Perceived Competence

Older people should be more likely to participate and perform acceptably in physical activities when they think they possess adequate competence for doing so. When task involved, such perceptions tend to be self-referenced, and as a result, it is less likely for a person to feel incompetent (Dweck, 1999; Nicholls, 1989). Further, in a state of task involvement, "How good am I?" is *not* the central concern. Thus, if an older adult is exhibiting low confidence in her or his capabilities (perhaps due to years of sedentary behavior, some physical ailments, societal stereotypes, etc.), such doubts about competence should not be so debilitating when the individual is task involved.

On the other hand, a state of ego involvement "shines the light" on the adequacy of personal levels of competence. The concern here is "How do I measure up?" with respect to other people. Because such a comparative, other-referenced conception of ability is of central import when an older person is ego involved, there is a greater chance for that person to believe himself or herself to be deficient. Coupled with the tendency for individuals to doubt their ability as they grow older (McAuley, 1993a), we might suggest that entering into a state of ego involvement could be even more costly (with respect to optimal motivation) among older adults.

Studies in physical activity contexts have provided evidence for the hypothesized links between task and ego achievement goals and perceived competence. For example, in a laboratory experiment, Hall (1990) found that college students with low perceived ability who received ego-involving instructions reported lower performance expectations than did their low-perceived-ability counterparts who were assigned to a task-involving condition. Moreover, even high-perceived-ability students in the ego-involving condition started to doubt their competence toward the latter performance trials. In another laboratory study involving college students (Chi, 1993), high task-oriented/low ego-oriented participants exhibited higher perceived competence before two competitive cycle ergometer races (against an opponent) than did high ego-oriented/low task-oriented participants. Among students enrolled in beginning tennis classes, a positive relationship emerged between task orientation and self-efficacy judgments regarding tennis strokes (Kavussanu & Roberts, 1996). More research is needed to discern whether the observed relationship between achievement goals and perceptions of competence hold for older adults in the physical activity domain.

Achievement Goals and Self-Determination

A second, albeit related, mechanism by which the achievement goals adopted by older individuals can differentially lead to positive or negative participation patterns revolves around the concept of self-determination (Deci & Ryan, 1985, 1991). Positive motivational outcomes are held to be a result of behavioral regulations that are more self-determined in nature (e.g., intrinsic motivation, integrated regulation). In contrast, if older adults are engaging in physical activity because of extrinsic reasons that are less self-determined (e.g., external regulation, introjected regulation), maladaptive motivational patterns may ensue. If individuals are task involved when engaged in exercise or sport, the activity is an end in itself (Nicholls, 1989). The focus is on the task per se and doing the activity as well as one can. Such an approach to physical activity engagement should thus be more self-determined and correspond with greater enjoyment of the activity.

What if an older participant manifests an ego-involved perspective during participation in physical activities? The activity, in this instance, is interpreted as a means to an end (Nicholls, 1989). In other words, when ego involved, the individual is *less* likely to "be in the moment" and centered on the inherent qualities of the exercise experience in and of itself. Rather, the older adult is paying attention to whether high or low comparative competence is being exhibited. As a result, she or he tends to be more "outside" of the activity, and the participation is governed by such self- and/or other-imposed constraints.

Previous research in sport and physical education contexts has repeatedly revealed a positive relationship between task orientation (and a perceived task-involving environment) and enjoyment of the activities among younger populations (e.g., Duda, Fox, Biddle, & Armstrong, 1992; Seifriz et al., 1992). Moreover, studies have supported the hypothesized association between an emphasis on task goals and self-determined motivation (e.g., Brunel, 1996; Duda et al., 1995; Ferrer-Caja & Weiss, 2000, 2002). In contrast, ego orientation or perceptions of an ego-involving climate are generally unrelated to enjoyment and intrinsic motivation in sport or physical education (Duda & Hall, 2001). It should be noted that in some cases when perceived competence is high, ego orientation has been linked with positive affect (Hom, Duda, & Miller, 1993) and to more externally regulated forms of motivation (e.g., Petherick & Weigand, 2002).

As reviewed earlier in this chapter, Deci and Ryan's (1991) self-determination theory assumes that intrinsically motivated behavior is more often realized when individuals feel competence, autonomy, and a sense of relatedness. We have already touched on the interplay between achievement goals and perceptions of competence, but what of the other two needs? What is it about a task versus ego "interpretive lens" (Duda, 2001) that should promote feelings of personal control and connection with other people?

One of the most consistent findings in the achievement-goal literature is the interdependence between task and ego goals in sport and individuals' beliefs about the causes of success in that context (e.g., Biddle, Akande, Vlachopoulos, & Fox, 1996; Duda, 1989; Duda & Nicholls, 1992; Seifriz et al., 1992; Treasure & Roberts, 1998). Drawing from samples of young recreational, junior elite, and college-level athletes, the results pertinent to this question have generalized across sports as well as cultural backgrounds. In brief, task orientation and perceptions of a task-involving climate have been coupled with the view that sport success stems from more personally controllable causes such as one's own hard work. Ego orientation and perceptions of an ego-involving atmosphere, on the other hand, have been associated with less self-determined reasons for achievement such as the possession of superior ability and external factors (such as clothing and equipment). Thus, it seems that when individuals emphasize task goals, there is greater autonomy in terms of what are deemed the keys to accomplishment.

Task-involving environments are marked by the salience of cooperation and a sense that all members of the team have something to contribute.

One could surmise, too, that task goals might "set the stage" for a greater sense of connection between people. Past studies (e.g., Duda & Nicholls, 1992) have found strong associations between task orientation and the emphasis placed on cooperative goals. Task orientation and a perceived task-involving motivational climate have been tied to the belief that individuals within a physical activity setting need to cooperate if success is to be realized (e.g., Duda & White, 1992). Task-involving environments are marked by the salience of cooperation and a sense that all members of the team have something to contribute (Newton et al., 2000). On the other hand, intrateam member rivalry has been found to be one dimension underlying a perceived ego-involving motivational climate (Newton et al., 2000).

Sarrazin and colleagues (Sarrazin, Vallerand, Guillet, Cury, & Pelletier, 2002) tested the mediating role of perceived competence, autonomy, and relatedness with regard to the influence of the motivational climate on self-determined motivation. Adolescent handball players who perceived a greater task-involving environment scored higher on perceived competence, autonomy, and relatedness than those who perceived their team environment to be less task-involving. Perceptions of a greater ego-involving climate predicted lower perceived autonomy only. In turn, higher perceptions of autonomy, competence, and relatedness were associated with greater self-determined motivation. Further, self-determined motivation negatively related to intentions to discontinue involvement in one's sport. Behavioral intentions predicted dropping out of handball 21 months later. Replicating such a study in the case of senior sport participants or older adult exercisers would be an intriguing direction for subsequent research.

Compatibility Between Personal Goals and the Motivational Climate

Finally, there is another plausible mechanism through which achievement goals can influence older peoples' motivation in the physical activity realm. Previous research (e.g., Duda & Tappe, 1989) has found the elderly to be more task oriented and centered on personal health benefits when engaged in exercise programs as compared to their younger counterparts. If older adults are prone to adopt a task goal perspective and other more intrinsic exercise goals, then they should be *less* likely to experience motivational difficulties in the physical activity domain. As discussed at the onset of this chapter, this unfortunately does not tend to be the case. Thus, what we might have among older individuals involved in exercise programs is a case of a striking motivational "mismatch" (Duda, 1997). This might be operating if exercise settings are structured to emphasize competition, comparison, and norm-based evaluations (i.e., ego-involving climate). In essence, this type of context is not giving people what they want (experience the joy of moving, personal mastery, friendly and supportive context, well-being, [Heitmann, 1986]), and as a result, they may be more likely to drop out. This premise has been tested in terms of the health benefit goals associated with exercise among middle-aged and older exercise program participants (Duda & Tappe, 1988). Duda and Tappe (1988) stated, "The greater congruence between the importance placed on the health benefits of exercise and the perceived opportunity to obtain health benefits through the present exercise program . . . corresponded to more positive expectations of future physical activity engagement" (p. 548).

Research on older populations. With respect to studies involving children through young adult participants in sport and physical education settings, the predicted links between achievement goals and indices of motivation have been supported (see Duda, 2001; Duda & Hall, 2001; Roberts, 2001b, for recent reviews). The hypothesized mechanisms by which achievement goals are assumed to influence motivational patterns also seem relevant to the understanding of older people's investment in the physical domain. Much more work is needed to address such possibilities. Although the past decade has seen an abundance of studies grounded in AGT (Duda, 2001), to our knowledge only two investigations have specifically tested the tenets of this theory in the case of older adults (Newton & Fry, 1998; Sorensen, 1998).

Newton and Fry (1998) examined goal orientations, views regarding perceived purposes of sport participation, beliefs about the causes of success, and intrinsic motivation of senior athletes (M Age = 64.5 years; Range = 49-83 years). Participants were involved in a variety of sports including tennis and track and field. On average, they had been participating in sport for 24 years, competing for slightly over 3 years, and training for approximately 5 hours per week. Newton and Fry found that these senior athletes generally viewed more intrinsic consequences as the preferred purposes of sport engagement (e.g., increase one's personal fitness level, improve personal mastery). Not surprisingly, therefore, they reported high intrinsic motivation for their participation in athletic activities. Consonant with theoretical tenets and previous work on younger sport participants (e.g., Duda, 1989; Duda & White, 1992), task orientation positively related to the belief that hard work leads to success among these senior athletes. Ego orientation was aligned with the belief that external elements and high ability are prerequisites for sport achievement. Finally, consistent with predictions emanating from AGT and past studies involving adolescent and college-aged athletes (e.g., Duda et al., 1995; Seifriz et al., 1992), task orientation was positively associated with the enjoyment of one's sport, intrinsic motivation, interest, and the importance placed on one's athletic participation.

Sorensen (1998) was interested in investigating how achievement goals affect the participation and experience of older Norwegian exercisers. Middle-aged sedentary adults (between 40 and 50 years of age; M = 44.9 years) completed a one-year intervention. The study participants were assigned to one of four groups: diet, exercise, diet and exercise, or a no-intervention control group. All exhibited several risk factors for cardiovascular disease (e.g., elevated cholesterol), and their major reason for engaging in the study was to improve their health status. The participants in Sorensen's study were involved in a follow-up investigation 3 years following the onset of the intervention. Seventy percent of the initial 209 study participants responded to a questionnaire assessing their goal orientations and perceptions of the motivational climate specific to exercise activities. In total, 94 of the 146 respondents were active exercisers. Sorensen found current exercisers to be higher in task orientation than their sedentary counterparts were. Sorensen suggested that although expected health benefits were important to the initiation of exercise among these middle-aged adults, achievement goals were more relevant to the maintenance of exercise behavior. Participants who were able to center on self-referenced goals were more likely to adhere to their exercise regime. There was also evidence (based on interviews) that ego-related concerns (e.g., feeling pressured to achieve, feeling that one could keep up with the others) contributed to dropping out. Further, being highly ego oriented corresponded to exercise engagement among those who were highly fit. All in all, Sorensen's findings are in accordance with the tenets of AGT.

In sum, achievement-goal theory has proved to be a valuable framework for the investigation of motivation-related patterns in the physical domain among children, adolescents, university sport competitors, and elite athletes (Duda, 2001; Roberts, 2001b). We would suggest that this model of motivation has considerable potential for fostering insight into physical activity engagement in more senior populations.

CONCLUSION

When we consider engagement in physical activity among older adults, we are faced with an unfortunate and often unnecessary Catch-22. As people grow older, there is a tendency for exercise participation to curtail. The psychological and physical costs of doing everyday activities as a result of such physical activity withdrawal among older persons are appreciable. The benefits of regular physical activity, however, among our "graying" populations have not tarnished with the passing years. Therefore, whether we focus on what can be done to contribute to the quality of life among a sample of older adults and implications of a sedentary lifestyle among middle-aged and elderly individuals from a public health (and health-cost) perspective, the conclusion is clear. For older persons who are active, we need to keep them moving. Among those who no longer engage in any form of physical activity on a regular basis (and/or at a sufficient intensity) to accrue the positive mental and physical health consequences, the goal should be to get them moving.

To accomplish both aims, we need to better comprehend the motivational processes operating in the case of the older adult exerciser and nonexerciser. To best contribute to our knowledge in this area and lay the basis for sound interventions, it is important for the research conducted to be theoretically based. In this chapter, three major theoretical frameworks were reviewed that have (and can) provide insight into what motivates older individuals to participate in physical activity and what may lead them to become or stay inactive. The amount of sport/exercise research that has been grounded in each of these different models of motivation and has involved middle-aged and elderly people is not consistent. What is constant, though, is the promise that these theoretical frameworks hold (independently and, perhaps, collectively; Duda & Hall, 2001) for subsequent investigation. It is our hope that this chapter has played a small role in encouraging such needed and meaningful lines of inquiry.

REFERENCES

American College of Sports Medicine. (2000). *ACSM's guidelines for exercise testing and prescription* (6th Ed.). Baltimore: Williams & Wilkins.

Ames, C. (1992). Classrooms: Goals, structures and student motivation. *Journal of Educational Psychology, 84*, 261-271.

Ames, C., & Archer, J. (1988). Achievement goals in the classroom: Students' learning strategies and motivation processes. *Journal of Educational Psychology, 80*, 260-267.

Arent, S. M., Landers, D. M., & Etnier, J. L. (2000). The effects of exercise on mood in older adults: A meta-analytic review. *Journal of Aging and Physical Activity, 8*, 407-430.

Atkinson, J. W. (1964). *An introduction to motivation.* Princeton, NJ: Van Nostrand.

Australian Bureau of Statistics. (1999). *Older people, Australia: A social report.* Commonwealth of Australia: Canberra.

Bandura, A. (1986). *Social foundations of thought and action: A social cognitive theory.* Englewood Cliffs, NJ: Prentice Hall.

Bandura, A. (1997). *Self-efficacy: The exercise of control.* New York: Freeman.

Behlendorf, B, MacRae, P. G., & Vos Strache, C. (1999). Children's perceptions of physical activity for adults: Competence and appropriateness. *Journal of Aging and Physical Activity, 7*, 354-373.

Biddle, S. J. H. (1995). Exercise motivation across the life span. In S. J. H. Biddle (Ed.), *European perspectives on exercise and sport psychology* (pp. 3-25). Champaign, IL: Human Kinetics.

Biddle, S. J. H., Akande, A., Vlachopoulus, S., & Fox, K. (1996). Towards an understanding of children's motivation for physical activity: Achievement goal orientations, beliefs about sport success, and sport emotion in Zimbabwean children. *Psychology and Health, 12*, 49-55.

Biddle, S. J. H., & Nigg, C. R. (2000). Theories of exercise behavior. *International Journal of Sport Psychology, 31*, 290-304.

Bouchard, C., Shephard, R. J., & Stephens, T. (Eds.). (1994). *Physical activity, fitness, and health: International proceedings and consensus statement.* Champaign, IL: Human Kinetics.

Brunel, P. (1996). The relationship of task and ego orientation to intrinsic and extrinsic motivation. *Journal of Sport & Exercise Psychology, 18* (Supplement), S59.

Buchner, D. M., & Wagner, E. H. (1992). Preventing frail health. *Clinics in Geriatric Medicine, 8*, 1-17.

Chogahara, M., O'Brien Cousins, S., & Wankel, L. M. (1998). Influences on physical activity in older adults: A review. *Journal of Aging and Physical Activity, 6*, 1-17.

Chi, L. (1993). *Prediction of achievement-related cognitions and behaviors in the physical domain: A test of the theories of goal perspectives and self-efficacy*. Unpublished doctoral dissertation, Purdue University, West Lafayette, IN.

Clark, D.O. (1996). Age, socioeconomic status, and exercise self-efficacy. *The Gerontologist, 36*, 157-164.

Clark, D. O., & Nothwehr, F. (1999). Exerciser self-efficacy and its correlates among socioeconomically disadvantaged older adults. *Health Education & Behavior, 26*, 535-546.

deCharms, R. C. (1968). *Personal causation: The internal affective determinants of behavior*. New York: Academic Press.

Deci, E. L., Nezlek, J., & Sheinman, L. (1981). Characteristics of the rewarder and intrinsic motivation of the rewardee. *Journal of Personality and Social Psychology, 40*, 1-10.

Deci, E. L., & Ryan, R. M. (1985). *Intrinsic motivation and self-determination in human behavior*. New York: Plenum.

Deci, E. L., & Ryan, R. M. (1991). A motivational approach to self: Integration in personality. In R. A. Dienstbier (Ed.), *Nebraska Symposium on Motivation: Perspectives on motivation* (Vol. 38, pp. 237-288). Lincoln, NE: University of Nebraska.

Deci, E. L., Schwartz, A. J., Sheinman, L., & Ryan, R. M. (1981). An instrument to assess adults' orientations toward control versus autonomy with children: Reflections on intrinsic motivation and perceived competence. *Journal of Educational Psychology, 73*, 642-650.

Deforche, B., & Bourdeaudhuij, I. (2000). Differences in psychological determinants of physical activity in older adults participating in organized versus non-organized activities. *Journal of Sports Medicine and Physical Fitness, 40*, 362-372.

Dishman, R. K. (1994a). Motivating older adults to exercise. *Southern Medical Journal, 87*, S79-S82.

Dishman, R. K. (Ed.). (1994b). *Advances in exercise adherence*. Champaign IL: Human Kinetics.

Duda, J. L. (1989). The relationship between task and ego orientation and the perceived purposes of sport among male and female high school athletes. *Journal of Sport & Exercise Psychology, 11*, 318-335.

Duda, J. L. (1997). Goal perspectives and their implications for an active and healthy life style among girls and women. *Women in Sport and Physical Activity Journal*, 6, 239-253.

Duda, J. L. (2001). Goal perspectives research in sport: Pushing the boundaries and clarifying some misunderstandings. In G. C. Roberts (Ed.), *Advances in motivation in sport and exercise* (pp. 129-182). Champaign, IL: Human Kinetics.

Duda, J. L., Chi, L., Newton, M. L., Walling, M. D., & Catley, D. (1995). Task and ego orientation and intrinsic motivation in sport. *International Journal of Sport Psychology, 26*, 40-63.

Duda, J. L., Fox, K. R., Biddle, S. J. H., & Armstrong, N. (1992). Children's achievement goals and beliefs about success in sport. *British Journal of Educational Psychology, 62*, 313-323.

Duda, J. L., & Hall, H. (2001). Achievement goal theory in sport: Recent extensions and future directions. In R. N. Singer, H. A. Hausenblas, & C. M. Janelle (Eds.), *Handbook of sport psychology* (2nd ed., pp. 417-443). New York: Wiley.

Duda, J. L., & Nicholls, J. G. (1992). Dimensions of achievement motivation in schoolwork and sport. *Journal of Educational Psychology, 84*, 290-299.

Duda, J. L., & Tappe, M.K. (1988). Predictors of personal investment in physical activity among middle-aged and older adults. *Perceptual and Motor Skills, 66*, 543-549.

Duda, J. L., & Tappe, M.K. (1989). Personal investment in exercise among adults: The examination of age and gender-related differences in motivational orientation. In A. Ostrow (Ed.), *Aging and motor behavior* (pp. 239-256). Indianapolis: Benchmark Press.

Duda, J. L., & White, S. A. (1992). The relationship of goal perspectives to beliefs about success among elite skiers. *The Sport Psychologist, 6*, 334-343.

Dweck, C. S. (1999). *Self-theories and goals: Their role in motivation, personality, and development*. Philadelphia: Taylor and Francis.

Dzewaltowski, D. A. (1989). A social cognitive theory of older adult exercise motivation. In A. C. Ostrow (Ed.), *Aging and motor behavior* (pp. 257-281). Indianapolis: Benchmark Press.

Engels, H., Drouin, J., Zhu, W., & Kazmierski, J. F. (1998). Effects of low-impact moderate-intensity exercise training with and without wrist weights on functional capacities and mood states in older adults. *Gerontology, 44*, 239-244.

Estabrooks, P. A., & Carron, A. V. (2000). Predicting scheduling self-efficacy in older adult exercisers: The role of task cohesion. *Journal of Aging and Physical Activity, 8*, 41-50.

Ewart, C. E. (1989). Psychological effects of resistive weight training: Implications for cardiac patients. *Medicine and Science in Sports and Exercise, 21*, 683-688.

Feltz, D. L. (1982). Path analysis of the causal elements in Bandura's theory of self-efficacy and an anxiety-based model of avoidance behavior. *Journal of Personality and Social Psychology, 42*, 764-781.

Feltz, D.L., & Chase, M.A. (1998). The measurement of self-efficacy and confidence in sport. In J.L. Duda (Ed.), *Advances in sport and exercise psychology measurement* (pp. 65-80). Morgantown, WV: Fitness Information Technology.

Feltz, D.L., Landers, D.M., & Raeder, U. (1979). Enhancing self-efficacy in high-avoidance motor tasks: A comparison of modeling techniques. *Journal of Sport Psychology, 1*, 112-122.

Feltz, D. L., & Lirgg, C. D. (2001). Self-efficacy beliefs of athletes, teams, and coaches. In R. N. Singer, H. A. Hausenblas, & C. M. Janelle (Eds.), *Handbook of sport psychology* (2nd ed., pp. 340-361). New York: Wiley.

Feltz, D. L., & Riessinger, C. A. (1990). Effects of in vivo emotive imagery and performance feedback on self-efficacy and muscular endurance. *Journal of Sport & Exercise Psychology, 12*, 132-143.

Ferrer-Caja, E., & Weiss, M. R. (2000). Predictors of intrinsic motivation among adolescent students in physical education. *Research Quarterly for Exercise and Sport, 71*, 267-279.

Ferrer-Caja, E., & Weiss, M. R. (2002). Cross-validation of a model of intrinsic motivation with students enrolled in high school elective courses. *Journal of Experimental Education. 71*, 41-68.

Frederick, C. M., & Ryan, R. M. (1993). Differences in motivation for sport and exercise and their relations with participation and mental health. *Journal of Sport Behavior, 16*, 124-146.

George, T. R., Feltz, D. L., & Chase, M. A. (1992). The effects of model similarity on self-efficacy and muscular endurance: A second look. *Journal of Sport & Exercise Psychology, 14*, 237-248.

Goggin, N. L., & Morrow, J. R., Jr. (2001). Physical activity behaviors of older adults. *Journal of Aging and Physical Activity, 9*, 58-66.

Gould, D., & Weiss, M.R. (1981). The effects of model similarity and model talk on self-efficacy and muscular endurance. *Journal of Sport Psychology, 3*, 17-29.

Greendale, G. A., Hirsch, S.H., & Hahn, T. J. (1993). The effects of a weighted vest on perceived health status and bone density in older persons. *Quality of Life Research, 2*, 141-152.

Grembowski, D., Patrick, D. L., Diehr, P., Durham, M., Beresford, S., Kay, E., et al. (1993). Self-efficacy and health behavior among older adults. *Journal of Health and Social Behavior, 34*, 89-104.

Hall, H.K. (1990). *A social-cognitive approach to goal setting: The mediating effects of achievement goals and perceived ability*. Unpublished doctoral dissertation, University of Illinois at Urbana-Champaign.

Heitmann, H. H. (1986). Motives of older adults for participating in physical activity programs. In B. D. McPherson (Ed.), *Sport and aging* (pp. 199-204). Champaign, IL: Human Kinetics.

Hirvensalo, M., Lampinen, P., & Rantanen, T. (1998). Physical exercise in old age: An eight-year follow-up study on involvement, motives, and obstacles among persons age 65-84. *Journal of Aging and Physical Activity, 6*, 157-168.

Hoffman, C., Rice, & Sung, H. (1996). Persons with chronic conditions: Their prevalence and costs. *The Journal of the American Medical Association, 276*, 1473-1479.

Hogan, P.I., & Santomier, J. P. (1984). Effects of mastering swim skills on older adults' self-efficacy. *Research Quarterly for Exercise and Sport, 56*, 284-296.

Hom, H., Jr., Duda, J. L., & Miller, A. (1993). Correlates of goal orientations among young athletes. *Pediatric Exercise Science, 5*, 168-176.

Kalache, A., & Kickbusch, I. (1997). A global strategy for healthy aging. *World Health, 50*, 4-5.

Kasser, V.G., & Ryan, R. M. (1999). The relation of psychological needs for autonomy and relatedness to vitality, well-being, and mortality in a nursing home. *Journal of Applied Social Psychology, 29*, 935-954.

Katz, S. (1983). Assessing self-maintenance: Activities of daily living, mobility, and instrumental activities of daily living. *Journal of the American Geriatric Association, 31*, 721-727.

Kavussanu, M., & Roberts, G. C. (1996). Motivation in physical activity contexts: The relationship of perceived motivational climate to intrinsic motivation and self-efficacy. *Journal of Sport & Exercise Psychology, 18*, 264-280.

King, A., Taylor, C. B., & Haskell, W.L. (1993). The effects of differing intensities of formats of 12 months of exercise training on psychological outcomes in older adults. *Health Psychology, 12*, 292-300.

Lehr, U. M. (1992). Physical activities in old age: Motivation and barriers. In S. Harris, R. Harris, & W.S. Harris (Eds.), *Physical activity, aging, and sports* (Vol. 2, pp. 51-62). Albany, NY: Center for the Study of Aging.

Lepper, M. R., & Greene, D. (1978). Overjustification research and beyond: Toward a means-end analysis of intrinsic motivation and extrinsic motivation. In M. R. Lepper & D. Greene (Eds.), *The hidden costs of reward* (pp. 109-148). Hillside, NJ: Erlbaum.

Li, F., McAuley, E., Harmer, P., Duncan, T. E., & Chaumeton, N. R. (2001). Tai chi enhances self-efficacy and exercise behavior in older adults. *Journal of Aging and Physical Activity, 9*, 161-171.

Lloyd, J., & Fox, K. (1992). Achievement goals and motivation to exercise in adolescent girls: A preliminary intervention study. *British Journal of Physical Education Research Supplement, 11*, 12-16.

Losier, G.F., Bourque, P. E., & Vallerand, R. J. (1993). A motivational model of leisure motivation in the elderly. *Journal of Psychology, 127*, 153-170.

Manton, K.G., Corder, L.S., & Stallard, E. (1997). Chronic Disability Trends in Elderly United States Populations: 1982-1994. *Proceedings of the National Academy of Sciences, 94*, 2593-2598.

McAuley, E. (1993a). Self-efficacy and the maintenance of exercise participation in older adults. *Journal of Behavioral Medicine, 16*, 103-113.

McAuley, E. (1993b). Self-efficacy, physical activity, and aging. In R. Kelly (Ed.), *Activity and aging: Staying involved in later life* (pp. 187-206). Newbury Park, CA: Sage.

McAuley, E., Blissmer, B., Katula, J. A., & Duncan, T. E. (2000). Exercise environment, self-efficacy, and affective responses to acute exercise in older adults. *Psychology and Health, 15*, 341-355.

McAuley, E., Katula, J., Mihalko, S. L., Blissmer, B., Duncan, T., Pena, M., et al. (1999). Mode of physical activity and self-efficacy in older adults: A latent growth curve analysis. *Journal of Gerontology: Psychological Sciences, 54B*, 283-292.

McAuley, E., Lox, C. L., & Duncan, T. (1993). Long-term maintenance of exercise, self-efficacy, and physiological change in older adults. *Journal of Gerontology, 48*, 218-223.

McAuley, E., Pena, M. M., & Jerome, G. J. (2001). Self-efficacy as a determinant and an outcome of exercise. In G. C. Roberts (Ed.), *Advances in motivation in sport and exercise* (pp. 235-261). Champaign, IL: Human Kinetics.

McAuley, E., & Rudolph, D. (1995). Physical activity, aging, and psychological well-being. *Journal of Aging and Physical Activity, 3*, 67-96.

McAuley, E., & Tammen, V.V. (1989). The effects of subjective and objective competitive outcomes on intrinsic motivation. *Journal of Sport & Exercise Psychology, 11*, 84-93.

McClelland, D. C. (1961). *The achieving society.* New York: Free Press.

McCullagh, P., & Weiss, M. R. (2001). Modeling: Considerations for motor skill performance and psychological responses. In R. N. Singer, H. A. Hausenblas, & C. M. Janelle (Eds.), *Handbook of sport psychology* (2nd ed., pp. 205-238). New York: Wiley.

McTavish, D.G. (1971). Perceptions of old people: A review of research methodologies and findings. *The Gerontologist, 11*, 90-101.

Mihalko, S. L., & McAuley, E. (1996). Strength training and effects on subjective well-being and physical function in the elderly. *Journal of Aging and Physical Activity, 4*, 56-68.

Morgan, K., Dallosso, H., Bassey, E.J., Ebrahim, S., Fentem, O.H., & Arie, T.H. (1991). Customary physical activity, psychological well-being and successful aging. *Aging and Society, 11*, 399-415.

Newton, M., Duda, J. L., & Yin, Z. (2000). Examination of the psychometric properties of the Perceived Motivational Climate in Sport Questionnaire-2 in a sample of female athletes. *Journal of Sports Sciences, 18*, 275-290.

Newton, M. L., & Fry, M. D. (1998). Senior Olympians' achievement goals and motivational responses. *Journal of Aging and Physical Activity, 6*, 256-270.

Nicholls, J. G. (1984). Achievement motivation: Conceptions of ability, subjective experience, task choice, and performance. *Psychological Review, 91*, 328-346.

Nicholls, J. G. (1989). *The competitive ethos and democratic education.* Cambridge, MA: Harvard University Press.

O'Connor, B.P., & Vallerand, R. J. (1994). Motivation, self-determination, and person environment fit as predictors of psychological adjustment among nursing-home residents. *Psychology and Aging, 9*, 189-194.

O'Connor, P.S., Aenchbacjer, L. E. III, & Dishman, R. K. (1993). Physical activity and depression in the elderly. *Journal of Aging and Physical Activity, 1*, 34-58.

Office of National Statistics. (1996). *1994 national based population projections* (Series PP2, No. 20). London: The Stationary Office.

Organisation for Economic Cooperation and Development. (1994). *New orientations for social policy.* Paris: Author.

Orlick, T., & Mosher, R. (1978). Extrinsic awards and participation motivation in a sport-related task. *International Journal of Sport Psychology, 9*, 27-39.

Papaioannou, A. (1994). Development of a questionnaire to measure achievement orientations in physical education. *Research Quarterly for Exercise and Sport, 65*, 11-20.

Pate, R. R., Pratt, M., Blair, S. N., Haskell, W. L., Macera, C. A., Bouchard, C., et al. (1995). Physical activity and public health: A recommendation from the Centers for Disease Control and Prevention and the American College of Sports Medicine. *Journal of the American Medical Association, 273*, 402-407.

Pescatello, L.S., & DiPietrio, L. (1993). Physical activity in older adults: An overview of health benefits. *Sports Medicine, 16*, 353-364.

Petherick, D., & Weigand, D. A. (2002). The relationship of dispositional goal orientations and perceived motivational climates on indices of motivation in male and female swimmers. *International Journal of Sport Psychology, 33*, 218-237.

Powell, K. E., & Blair, S.N. (1994). The public health burdens of sedentary living habits: Theoretical but realistic estimates. *Medicine and Science in Sports and Exercise, 26*, 851-856.

Pu, C. T., & Nelson, M. E. (1999). Aging, function, and exercise. In W. R. Frontera, D. M. Dawson, & D. M. Slovik (Eds.), *Exercise in rehabilitation medicine* (pp. 391-424). Champaign, IL: Human Kinetics.

Rapid Reports. (1993). *Older people in the European community: Population and employment.* Luxembourg: B. Knauth.

Reeve, J., & Deci, E. L. (1996). Elements of the competitive situation that affect intrinsic motivation. *Personality and Social Psychology Bulletin, 22*, 24-33.

Reis, H. T., Sheldon, K. M., Gable, S. L., Roscoe, J., & Ryan, R. M. (2000). Daily well-being: The role of autonomy, competence, and relatedness. *Personality and Social Psychology Bulletin, 26*, 419-435.

Roberts, G. C. (Ed.). (2001a). *Advances in motivation in sport and exercise.* Champaign, IL: Human Kinetics.

Roberts, G. C. (2001b). Understanding the dynamics of motivation in physical activity: The influence of achievement goals on motivational processes. In G. C. Roberts (Ed.), *Advances in motivation in sport and exercise* (pp. 1-50). Champaign, IL: Human Kinetics.

Ruuskanen, J. M., & Ruoppila, I. (1995). Physical activity and psychological well-being among people aged 65 to 84 years. *Age and Aging, 24,* 292-296.

Ryan, E. D. (1977). Attribution, intrinsic motivation, and athletes. In L.I. Gedvilas & M.E. Kneer (Eds.), *Proceedings of the National College of Physical Education Association for Men/National Association for Physical of College Women, National Conference* (pp. 346-353). Chicago, IL: University of Illinois at Chicago Circle.

Ryan, E. D. (1980). Attribution, intrinsic motivation, and athletics: A replication and extension. In C.H. Nadeau, W. R. Halliwell, K. M. Newell, & G. C. Roberts (Eds.), *Psychology of motor behavior and sport-1979* (pp. 19-26). Champaign, IL: Human Kinetics.

Ryan, R. M., & Deci, E. L. (2000). Self-determination and the facilitation of intrinsic motivation, social development, and well-being. *American Psychologist, 55,* 68-78.

Ryan, R. M., Frederick, C. M., Lepes, D., Rubio, N., Sheldon, K. M. (1997). Intrinsic motivation and exercise adherence. *International Journal of Sport Psychology, 28,* 335-354.

Ryan, R. M., & Grolnick, W.S. (1986). Origins and pawns in the classroom: Self-report and projective assessments of individual differences in children's perceptions. *Journal of Personality and Social Psychology, 50,* 550-558.

Sarrazin, P., Vallerand, R., Guillett, E., Pelletier, L., & Cury, F. (2002). Motivation and drop-out in female handballers: A 21-month prospective study. *European Journal of Social Psychology, 32,* 395-418.

Schroeder, J. M., Nau, K. L., Osness, W.H., & Potteiger, J. A. (1998). A comparison of life satisfaction, functional ability, physical characteristics, and activity level among older adults in various living settings. *Journal of Aging and Physical Activity, 6,* 340-349.

Seifriz, J., Duda, J. L., & Chi, L. (1992). The relationship of perceived motivational climate to intrinsic motivation and beliefs about success in basketball. *Journal of Sport & Exercise Psychology, 14,* 375-391.

Shephard, R. J. (1997). *Aging, physical activity, and health.* Champaign, IL: Human Kinetics.

Sorensen, M. (1998, August). *Achievement goals in health-related exercise.* Paper presented at the 24th International Congress of Applied Psychology, San Francisco, CA.

Spirduso, W. W. (1995). *Physical dimensions of aging.* Champaign, IL: Human Kinetics.

Stephens, T., & Caspersen, C. J. (1994). The demography of physical activity. In C. Bouchard, R. J. Shephard, & T. Stephens (Eds.), *Physical activity, fitness, and health: International proceedings and consensus statement* (pp. 204-213). Champaign, IL: Human Kinetics.

Stuart-Hamilton, I. (2000). *The psychology of aging: An introduction* (3rd ed.). London: Jessica Kingsley Publishers.

Tourt, K. (1989). *Aging in developing countries.* Oxford: Oxford University Press.

Treasure, D. C., Monson, J. W., & Lox, C. L. (1996). Relationship between self-efficacy, wrestling performance, and affect prior to competition. *The Sport Psychologist, 10,* 73-83.

Treasure, D. C., & Roberts, G. C. (1998). Relationship between female adolescents' achievement goal orientations, perceptions of the motivational climate, beliefs about success, and sources of satisfaction in basketball. *International Journal of Sport Psychology, 29,* 211-230.

U.S. Bureau of Census (1996). *65+ in the United States.* Washington DC: Author.

U.S. Department of Health and Human Services. (1996). *A report of the surgeon general: Physical activity and health.* Atlanta, GA: Centers for Disease Control and Prevention.

Vallerand, R. J. (1997). Toward a hierarchical model of intrinsic and extrinsic motivation. In M. P. Zanna (Ed.), *Advances in experimental social psychology* (Vol. 29, pp. 271-360). New York: Academic Press.

Vallerand, R. J. (2001). A hierarchical model of intrinsic and motivation in sport and exercise. In G. C. Roberts (Ed.), *Advances in motivation in sport and exercise* (pp. 263-319). Champaign, IL: Human Kinetics.

Vallerand, R. J., Gauvin, L., & Halliwell, W. R. (1986). Negative effects of competition on children's intrinsic motivation. *Journal of Social Psychology, 126,* 649-657.

Vallerand, R. J., & Losier, G.F. (1999). An integrative analysis of intrinsic and extrinsic motivation in sport. *Journal of Applied Sport Psychology, 11,* 142-169.

Vallerand, R. J., & O'Connor, B.P. (1989). Motivation in the elderly: A theoretical framework and some promising findings. *Canadian Psychology, 30,* 538-550.

Vallerand, R.J., & O'Connor, B.P. (1991). Construction et validation de l'Échelle de Motivation pour les Personnes Agées (EMPA). *International Journal of Psychology, 26,* 219-240.

Vallerand, R. J., O'Connor, B.P., & Blais, M. R. (1989). Life satisfaction of elderly individuals in regular community housing, in low-cost community housing, and high and low self-determination nursing homes. *International Journal of Aging and Human Development, 28,* 277-283.

Vallerand, R. J., O'Connor, B.P., & Hamel, M. A. (1995). Motivation in later life: Theory and assessment. *International Journal of Aging and Human Development, 41,* 221-238.

Vallerand, R. J., & Reid, G. A. (1984). On the causal effects of positive and negative verbal feedback on males' and females' intrinsic motivation. *Canadian Journal of Behavioural Sciences, 20*, 239-250.

Vallerand, R. J., & Rousseau, F. L. (2001). Intrinsic and extrinsic motivation in sport and exercise: A review using the hierarchical model of intrinsic and extrinsic motivation. In R. N. Singer, H. A. Hausenblas, & C. M. Janelle (Eds.), *Handbook of sport psychology* (2nd ed., pp.389-416). New York: Wiley.

Weinberg, R. S., Gould, D., & Jackson, A. (1979). Expectations and performance: An empirical test of Bandura's self-efficacy theory. *Journal of Sport Psychology, 1*, 320-331.

Weinberg, R. S., Gould, D., Yukelson, D., & Jackson, A. (1981). The effect of preexisting and manipulated self-efficacy on a competitive muscular endurance task. *Journal of Sport Psychology, 4*, 345-354.

Weinberg, R. S., Grove, R., & Jackson, A. (1992). Strategies for building self-efficacy in tennis players: A comparative analysis of Australian and American coaches. *The Sport Psychologist, 6*, 3-13.

Weinberg, R. S., & Jackson, A. (1979). Competition and extrinsic rewards: Effect on intrinsic motivation and attribution. *Research Quarterly, 50*, 494-502.

Weinberg, R. S., Yukelson, D., & Jackson, A. (1980). Effects of public and private efficacy expectations on competitive performance. *Journal of Sport Psychology, 2*, 340-349.

Weiss, M. R., & Ferrer-Caja, E. (2002). Motivational orientations and sport behavior. In T. S. Horn (Ed.), *Advances in sport psychology* (2nd ed., pp. 101-183). Champaign, IL: Human Kinetics.

Weiss, M. R., & Williams, L. (2003). The *why* of youth sport involvement: A developmental perspective on motivational processes. In M. R. Weiss (Ed.), *Developmental sport and exercise psychology: A lifespan perspective.* (pp. 223-268) Morgantown WV: Fitness Information Technology.

Whaley, D. E., & Ebbeck, V. (1997). Older adults' constraints to participation in structured exercise classes. *Journal of Aging and Physical Activity, 5*, 190-212.

World Association of Veteran Athletes. (2001). *Promoting veteran athletics throughout the world in co-operation with the IAAF Handbook, 1991-2001.* Monaco: IAAF.

World Health Organization. (1997). The Heidelberg guidelines for promoting physical activity among older persons. *Journal of Aging and Physical Activity, 5*, 2-8.

CHAPTER FOURTEEN

Self-Regulation Skills in Young, Middle, and Older Adulthood

Daniel Gould • Yongchul Chung

Bob loves golf, and now that he is retired, he is looking forward to improving his game. He begins by talking to his club pro, Nicole, and engages in considerable self-reflection relative to the strengths and weaknesses of his game. Bob then outlines a practice plan for improving his weaknesses and maximizing his strengths. This involves taking lessons, going to the driving range, and playing practice rounds. With Nicole's help, he sets some specific goals, develops practice strategies, and monitors his progress. He also learns some mental skills to deal with the frustration he encounters when he makes mistakes or plays poorly.

Jennifer is a collegiate gymnast. She was injured at the start of last season, had major surgery, and entered long-term rehabilitation while she was at the university. She returned home in the summer, continued her rehabilitation, and began some initial practice by herself. Scared that she would not be fully recovered and be able to rejoin the team, she continually overdid her rehabilitation and tried to do too much too soon in practice. Jennifer re-injured herself and will miss her senior year.

It has been 3 years since A.J. graduated from college. A.J. played basketball for most of his life and had great success as a player. For him, the key for success as an athlete was to follow his coaches' guidance. He ran when his coach yelled at him, took the classes he was told to take, and rested whenever he was told to do so. The biggest challenge that he had to face after graduation was to deal with his increased autonomy and the fact that there was no coach around to tell him what to do and when to do it. Unfortunately, he had a hard time keeping up with his own exercise schedule and has struggled to keep pace at work. For the first time in his life, A.J. has had to direct his own behavior and motivate himself.

Morella's doctor's orders were clear: "Start to regularly exercise, lose some weight, and take better care of yourself physically." If she does not, her health is likely to continue to deteriorate, and she will have to give up her home and enter the assisted living units. However, there are problems: For the better part of her 68 years, Morella never exercised; she is embarrassed to show her overweight frame in public and generally does not like physical activity.

Self-regulation involves the ability to work towards one's short- and long-term goals by effectively monitoring and managing one's thoughts, feelings, and behaviors. All of the above case stories, then, focus on the problem of self-regulating behavior in sport and exercise. Whether trying to improve performance, recover from injury, make the transition from elite competitive sport to recreational physical activity and nonsport achievement striving, or beginning an exercise program after years of inactivity, self-regulation is critical for making behavioral changes. In fact, self-regulation forms the foundation for almost everything we do in applied sport psychology.

Self-regulation involves the ability to work towards goals by managing thoughts, feelings, and behaviors.

Similarly, regardless of where one falls in the adult lifespan, one needs self-regulation skills. Both elite and recreational athletes must successfully self-regulate to improve performance and maintain involvement, but so too must middle and older adults initiating exercise programs to physically rehabilitate after major injuries and illnesses in efforts to resume daily living tasks such as stair climbing, gardening, and carrying groceries. It is no surprise, then, that psychologists and sport psychologists have been interested in studying athlete and exerciser self-regulation.

This chapter will review and synthesize the research and theory on self-regulation in sport and physical activity in young, middle, and older adults. In it, we will discuss (a) what self-regulation is and the self-regulation process, (b) sport psychology self-regulation research, (c) key self-regulation skills, (d) future research and theory directions, and (e) implications for guiding practice. Particular focus will be placed on the self-regulation skills of self-monitoring, self-talk, imagery, and goal setting. Finally, throughout the chapter, developmental considerations will be addressed.

UNDERSTANDING SELF-REGULATION AND THE SELF-REGULATION PROCESS

Within the psychology literature in general and sport psychology specifically, self-regulation has been defined in various ways and used interchangeably with similar or associated terms. In general psychology literature, for example, Karoly (1993) lists more than 20 different terms that have been interchangeably used to denote self-regulation. In sport psychology, Crews, Lochbaum, and Karoly (2000, p. 566) indicate that self-regulation is often used interchangeably with associated terms such as *volition*, *self-discipline*, and *intrinsic motivation*. However, the interchangeable use of these terms is not clear or systematic. Therefore, the definition of *self-regulation* varies depending on the context and individual author.

Various theoretical approaches have also been applied to understand and explain self-regulation processes over the years. These approaches to self-regulatory change include (but are not limited to) social cognitive (e.g., Bandura, 1986); cognitive affective (e.g., Lazarus, 1991); and cognitive behavioral (e.g., Meichenbaum, 1977). In essence, all of the above theories look at changes in human behavior with a slightly different emphasis on key forces that evoke such changes. For example, one of the best-known self-referent theories, Bandura's self-efficacy theory, places primary emphasis on the role that one's self-efficacy or confidence plays in behavior change. For instance, a high-efficacy individual successfully regulates action to achieve goals because the individual believes that he or she will improve and therefore seeks out instruction, is motivated to practice, and sustains effort over time. In contrast, a low-efficacy individual may have more difficulty self-regulating because when faced with stressful situations, this individual experiences greater anxiety or depression and has more difficulty sustaining involvement. The low-efficacy individual is also less likely to approach challenging situations.

Lazarus' (1991) cognitive-affective approach contends that behavior change is driven by cognitive appraisals and the personal and environmental antecedents of these appraisals. Primary appraisal focuses on one's perception of the meaning (i.e., positive or negative) of an event whereas secondary appraisal focuses on one's perception of one's ability to cope with the event. Behavior change, then, is mediated by primary and secondary appraisals that lead to immediate effects like positive and negative feelings.

Finally, for Meichenbaum (1977), "behavior change occurs through a sequence of mediating processes involving the interaction of inner speech, cognitive restructuring, behavior and then resultant outcomes" (p. 219). Phases in this process include self-observation, incompatible thoughts and behaviors, and cognitions concerning change.

In sum, the plausible explanations of the self-regulation processes offered by various (although somewhat overlapping) theoretical approaches have also made it difficult to derive one universally accepted definition of self-regulation. Thus, the plethora of associated terms as well as the different emphases from various theoretical perspectives makes the task of defining self-regulation difficult. In the following section, we will present several proposed definitions of self-regulation in an effort to identify key components involved and derive a general definition to use in this review.

Defining Self-Regulation

Karoly (1993) provides a definition that is concise but includes key aspects of self-regulation. His definition is "voluntary action management" (Karoly, 1993, p. 24). Later in his article, however, he elaborates and actually broadens his definition by stating:

> processes that enable an individual to guide goal-directed activities over time and context. Regulation implies modulation of thought, affect, behavior, or attention via deliberate or automated use of specific mechanisms and supportive metaskills. (Karoly, 1993, p. 25)

Supportive metaskills are skills that coordinate complex action or sequences of action such as the ability to keep focus, emotionally regulate oneself, and the capability to learn vicariously. They are conscious, reasoning centered, and potentially trainable (Karoly, 1993).

Within the sport-specific setting, self-regulation is often defined relative to athletic performance. Kane, Marks, Zaccaro, and Blair (1996) define self-regulation as "changes in behavior and cognition that occur as people try to reach their performance goals" (p. 36). Kirschenbaum (1984), one of the first sport psychology researchers to study self-regulation, defined self-regulation as "the processes by which people manage their own goal-directed behaviors in the relative absence of immediate external constraints" (p. 161). Moreover, for Kirschenbaum, improving performance is the major goal-directed behavior athletes self-regulate. A more recent and concise definition of self-regulation has been suggested by Crews et al. (2000), who define self-regulation as "psychological mechanisms underlying goal-directed movement" (p. 566). Further, "complex, time-dependent, and multi-level" characteristics of self-regulation are recognized by considering the dynamic interaction of planning and decision making, the idea that future directed action is modifiable, and the distinction between process and outcome (i.e., failure to attain goals should not be considered as failure; Crews et al., 2000, p. 568).

Self-regulation is a set of processes.

Based on the numerous definitions of self-regulation, a composite definition will be used in this chapter. Specifically, for our purposes, *self-regulation* is defined as a complex process whereby athletes or exercisers engage in voluntary goal-directed behaviors over time and context by initiating, monitoring, sustaining, and achieving certain thoughts, feelings, and behaviors. There are a number of salient points to remember about this definition. First, self-regulation involves "voluntary goal-directed behaviors" where individuals attempt to improve performance or maintain task involvement over time and context as a result of their own choice or free will. Second, self-regulation is a "process," or in many ways, a set of processes. It involves an ongoing general sequence of steps such as problem identification, commitment, execution, and generalization that interact with one another to help a person work towards and achieve his or her goals, and although specific self-regulation skills and strategies will vary across athletes and exercisers, the same general process or sequence of steps will be involved. Finally, self-regulation is "multifaceted and complex." It is typically thought of as involving mental skills, strategies, and characteristics such as self-awareness, self-monitoring, problem solving, thought management, goal setting, intrinsic motivation and self-reward, self-efficacy, and imaginal strategies.

The Self-Regulation Process

Based on work of Kanfer and Karoly (1972), Karoly (1977), and Mahoney and Thoresen (1974), Kirschenbaum (1984) developed a model describing the general stages in the self-regulation process. This model is contained in Figure 1 and shows that self-regulation involves identifying a problem such as Bob's need to improve his golf game or Morella's need to exercise (both described at the outset of this chapter). Recognizing the problem, however, is not enough. The athlete or exerciser must make a commitment to change (Stage 2) and deal with those sacrifices that will arise during the change process. Bob seems committed to improve his game, but commitment seems to be a major challenge for Morella.

Execution is the workhorse stage of self-regulation in which the athlete or exerciser will need to self-evaluate, self-monitor, develop expectancies, and self-reinforce. Morella, for

FIGURE 1
Kirschenbaum's (1984, 1987) 5-stage model of self-regulation.

Stage 1: Problem Identification
- the ability to identify a problem, determine that change is possible and desirable, and take responsibility for its solution.

↓

Stage 2: Commitment
- actually deciding to change and make the sacrifices needed to change.

↓

Stage 3: Execution
- the active process of behavioral change involving self-monitoring, self-evaluation, developing expectancies for success, and self-reinforcement and punishment. It also involves sustaining efforts despite setbacks.

↓

Stage 4: Environmental Management
- planning and deriving strategies to manage the social and physical environment (e.g., coaches, spectators, teammates) that affect the athlete or exerciser.

↓

Stage 5: Generalization
- sustaining efforts over long time periods and extending behaviors to new conditions and settings.

instance, might set a goal of walking 5 days a week for 20 minutes whereas Bob would focus on driving longer and improving accuracy in his short game. Each might self-monitor by keeping an activity or practice log, and Bob might chart his scores when he plays competitively. Both might reward themselves for meeting their goals. Morella, for example, might buy herself a new dress if she achieves her goal of exercising regularly whereas Bob might buy a new putter he wants if he meets his goals. The fourth, environmental management stage involves planning and deriving strategies for managing the physical and social environment. Morella, for example, might plan on walking with friends at the mall (maximize social support) where she will not be affected by inclement weather (maximize environmental support). Bob might schedule regular lessons and purposefully practice shots with less than perfect lies. Finally, the generalization stage would involve sustaining efforts over time and extending behaviors to new conditions and settings. Bob, for example, might use the same self-regulation strategies he used in golf to improve his muscular strength by engaging in a weight-training program whereas Morella might begin to manage her weight by employing many of the same mental and affective skills she used to increase her physical activity.

In addition to the five stages contained in the model, Kirschenbaum (1984) emphasizes several additional principles of self-regulation. These include the recognition that self-monitoring is necessary for self-regulation; that individual's personality dispositions and styles such as self-esteem, optimism, or hardiness will influence self-regulation; and that self-regulation is influenced by one's emotional state. For example, studies by Gottman and McFall (1971) and Kirschenbaum and Tomarken (1982) have shown that self-regulated behavior change occurred only when self-monitoring was activated whereas Waschall and Kernis (1996) have found that individuals with low and unstable self-esteem focus more on aversive interpersonal events and are more affected by everyday events than are individuals with high and stable self-esteem. Finally, it is emphasized the all five of the self-regulation stages interact in a complex fashion and should not be viewed as fixed or invariant.

Sport Psychology Self-Regulation Research

Sport and exercise psychology researchers have been studying self-regulation for several decades. Kirschenbaum (1984, 1987), for example, has reviewed much of the early research and theorizing on the topic, whereas Crews and her associates (2000) have recently conducted a comprehensive review of the latest research in the area. Although a comprehensive review of this literature is beyond the scope of this chapter, general trends in the area will be identified, and example studies, discussed.

Most of the self-regulation sport psychology work can be classified in two categories: micro (focused short-term) versus macro (broad long-term) self-regulation efforts.[1] Micro-level self-regulation effort studies report results examining the voluntary goal-management process of improving performance on specific athletic or physical activity tasks (e.g., golf putting, dart throwing, shooting free throws) of relatively short duration (50 trials) using specific performance-enhancing strategies (e.g., imagery, self-talk, self-monitoring, and stress management technique). This level of self-regulation heavily overlaps with topics of mental skills training (see Gould & Damarjian, 1998 for a review). Traditionally, the majority of self-regulation athletic-performance research studies conducted in exercise and sport science fall into this category.

---

[1]The micro and macro level categorization is a general way to organize the literature. However, it should be noted that a few studies seem to fall somewhere between these two general categories.

On the other hand, macro-level self-regulation studies denote voluntary goal-management processes aimed at achieving more general goals (e.g., winning a tournament, being successful in sport, graduating from high school) over an extended period. The focus of the programs in this research is on using behavioral strategies to overcome the barriers to the attainment of goals not so much on specific tasks, but in broader domains. There are far fewer research examples in this category, but several life-skills educational programs fall within it.

Finally, few efforts have been made to examine developmental differences between early, middle, and late adults in the uses and abilities to use self-regulation. The majority of studies have used traditional college-aged individuals as participants. More developmentally diverse samples are needed, as well as more developmentally based studies.

Micro-Level Self-Regulation Studies

To reiterate, micro-level self-regulation studies focus on examining the voluntary goal-management process of improving or maintaining performance on specific tasks of relatively short duration using specific performance-enhancing strategies. These studies typically focus on examining the effects of having athletes employ various mental strategies such as goal setting (e.g., Kane et al., 1996), attentional cueing (e.g., Hill & Borden, 1985), self-monitoring (e.g., Martin & Anshel, 1995), self-reinforcement (e.g., Simek, O'Brien & Figlerski, 1994), biofeedback (e.g., Kavussanu, Crews, & Gill, 1998), and anxiety management (e.g., Prapavessis, Grove, McNair, & Cable, 1992), or the interaction effects of these variables on performance (e.g., Zimmerman & Kitsantas, 1996). Although the bulk of these studies have employed convenience samples of college-aged participants, a few investigations have studied individuals in middle adulthood. Examples of these studies will now be examined, moving from studies of young adults to those examining individuals in other stages of adulthood.

In an example of a study looking at the interaction of two self-regulatory variables, goal setting and self-monitoring, Zimmerman and Kitsantas (1996) studied novice adolescent dart throwers. The 50 female physical education students (M age = 16 years) were randomly assigned to one of five conditions: those who set a (1) product goal and did not self-monitor; (2) product goal and self-monitored; (3) process goal and did not self-monitor; and (4) process goal and self-monitored; and those who composed a (5) control, no goal and self-monitoring condition. Product-goal participants were told to try to get the highest score possible whereas process-goal groups were instructed to focus on three performance steps: sighting, throwing, and follow-through. Self-monitoring involved writing one's scores down in a logbook. Findings revealed that both goal setting and self-recording significantly improved performance, but did not interact with one another. Moreover, additional analyses showed that goal setting had a larger performance impact than self-recording did, but that self-recording had a stronger influence on self-efficacy.

Using a case study approach, Prapavessis et al. (1992) had a 20-year-old rifle shooter who suffered from high anxiety in competition take part in a 6-week anxiety-management program. The anxiety-management program included instruction in relaxation, thought stopping, refocusing, coping, and biofeedback. Dependent variables included self-report, physiological and behavioral measures of anxiety in an actual competition taken after the 6-week training period. Results revealed that the shooter's self-confidence and performance increased from a baseline to treatment condition and that self-report and physiological anxiety decreased. Hence, using these techniques, the shooter was able to self-regulate anxiety, increase confidence, and improve performance.

> Researchers found that goal setting had a larger performance effect than self-recording, but self-recording had a greater influence on self-efficacy.

Not all results have been positive. Kavussanu et al. (1998) studied the effects of single versus multiple measures of biofeedback on basketball free-throw performance of 36 intermediate college-aged basketball players. Participants took part in biofeedback training focusing either on single (EMG) or multiple methods (EEG, EMG, HR) or to a control no-biofeedback group. All participants completed 60 free throws pre-and post biofeedback training, as well as after each of six treatment sessions. Results revealed that biofeedback training did not significantly improve performance.

Finally, using a slightly older sample, Hill and Borden (1995) examined the effect that attentional cueing had on the performance of 31 male competitive bowlers (*M* age = 32 years). Using a pretest-posttest randomized group design, the attentional cueing group was given a script that consisted of images, cue words, and focus points that they employed before delivering their first ball of each frame during three games. Specifically, attentional cueing participants were instructed to "look at the pins and relax," visualize the path of the ball, think "loose and oily body," image an optimal arm swing, and think "shake hands with the pin." Their performance was compared to a group of control subjects who did not employ

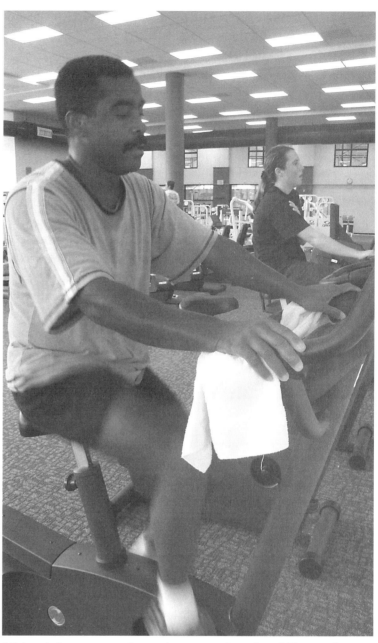

Maintaining an exercise regimen requires the ability to formulate and stick to both short- and long-term goals.

this attentional cueing script before bowling each ball. Results revealed that the attentional cueing group had significantly higher first-ball score improvements than did the control participants. Hence, it was concluded that using attentional cueing scripts was associated with improved performance.

So what can be concluded from these and other self-regulation studies? Luckily, Crews et al. (2000) recently conducted a comprehensive review of this literature. Specifically, these investigators identified over 30 data-based sport psychological self-regulation studies, the majority falling into what we have labeled the micro-effort category. Dependent variables included performance and sustained task involvement. The majority of studies were conducted in the field, with almost half employing some sort of control condition. Although not always supportive, the majority of the studies that examined if various self-regulation strategies improve performance have found that these strategies do indeed help performance and facilitate positive cognitions and affective states. As evidenced by the age ranges of individuals studied in the example investigations presented here, self-regulation effects have also been demonstrated for early and middle adult participants.

Macro-Level Self-Regulation Studies

Macro self-regulation studies are long-term and focus on assessing or helping athletes and exercisers develop a wide variety of mental skills. An especially encouraging aspect of these studies is, as a group, that they have employed a wider range of samples, with a number examining older adults. Comparisons across adult developmental stages have not been made, however.

Kane, Baltes, and Moss (2001) for example, recently conducted an important and innovative global self-regulation study using young adults. Specifically, these investigators examined the influence that free-set goals (goals athletes set on their own accord) had on athlete performance. Two hundred sixteen high school wrestlers reported their naturally set preseason, season, and long-term personal goals. The investigators then coded these goals relative to their specificity and difficulty. Results revealed that prior performance experiences were related to free-set season goals and that free-set goals influence wrestling performance. Both free-set goal difficulty and specificity strongly influenced performance. This study is important because the bulk of previous sport psychology goal-setting research has examined goals prescribed or suggested by others to athletes and exercisers. However, in much of normal human functioning, people set goals on their own, and setting such free set goals is a cornerstone of self-regulation. This study showed, then, athletes' free-set goals play an important role in the self-regulation of their performance.

Anshel and Porter (1996) conducted a study to determine the extent to which elite young adult (*M* age = 20.4 years) and nonelite young adult (*M* age = 17.6 years) competitive swimmers used various components of Kirschenbaum's (1984) self-regulation theoretical model. Survey results found support (relative to use) of four of the five model components: problem identification, commitment, execution, and environmental management. Moreover, more skilled swimmers more often used problem identification, displayed commitment, and executed performance strategies. A follow-up manuscript (Anshel & Porter, 1995) using the same data set also showed that the elite versus nonelite swimmers more often engaged in regulatory thoughts and behaviors before and during competition. Hence, Kirschenbaum's (1984) theoretical model received support, and components were also found to discriminate between more and less successful athletes.

An especially important study was conducted by Kirschenbaum, Owens, and O'Connor (1998), who examined the effectiveness of Smart Golf, a self-regulation training program based on Kirschenbaum's (1984) theoretical model, on the performance of five experienced golfers, ranging in age from 38 to 57 years. Specifically, an 8-hour seminar was conducted where golfers learned mental preparation, positive focusing (self-monitoring), and planning self-regulation principles. However, these principles were implemented via very practical means of an expanded golf scorecard that assessed not only normal performance scores, but also critical self-regulation information such as planning and positive self-focusing. Similarly, participants were taught the acronym PAR to remember three critical self-regulation components: P for plan, A for apply, and R for react. The authors, then, did an excellent job of making self-regulation both understandable and practical. As predicted, results revealed that all five golfers improved their emotional control and positive self-talk, as well as their golf performance relative to average score and handicap.

In an early exercise psychology study with 40 older adults (mean age of 74), Rodin (1983) examined whether self-regulation and coping-skills training enhanced feelings and expectations of choice. A pretest (assessing current and desired expectations of choice and control, depression, and perceived stress) and several postintervention tests (using the same assessments) were conducted comparing four randomly assigned groups: (a) a no-treatment control group, (b) a group that received communication to enhance feeling states, (c) a group that received six sessions of self-regulating/coping-skills training, and (d) an attention-control group. Results showed that the self-regulation and coping-skills training group felt more in control and engaged in more active exercise behavior than the other three groups. Thus, self-regulation and coping-skills training enhanced the feeling states and physical activity levels of these older adults.

More recently, in another study with middle and older adults (ages 50-65), Gorely and Gordon (1995) examined the relationship between transtheoretical model stages of change (precomtemplation, contemplation, preparation, action, and maintenance) and process-of-change factors such as seeking new information about exercise, emotional and cognitive reappraisal of values with respect to inactivity, reinforcement management and social support, as well as self-efficacy and decision balance. Findings revealed that a variety of cognitive self-regulation factors such as self-reevaluation and consciousness ratings were found within the various stages of change. It was also found that people at the different stages of change differed relative to 5 of the 10 process-of-change factors, self-efficacy, and decision balance. For example, participants at the maintenance stage of exercise demonstrated higher self-efficacy than did those at the precontemplation stage (thinking about exercise), and the balance between exercise pros and cons changed in the expected manner (pros outweigh cons) from precontemplation to maintenance stages. These results, then, demonstrated that exercise behavior is self-regulated and that the transtheoretical model is a useful way to better understand the process. Most important relative to the focus of this chapter, the authors concluded their results with middle and older adults were similar to previous literature with adults of other ages. Hence, the process of behavior change seemed to hold for adults of different ages.

Finally, in a related area of scholarly writing, sport psychologists have become increasingly interested in teaching life skills (social, psychological, emotional, and behavioral skills such as the ability to set goals, control emotions, and communicate that can be taught through sport and then transferred to other life endeavors such as in one's work or family life) to athletes (Danish, Nellen, & Owens, 1996). Danish and Nellen (1997), for instance, have described their Sports United to Promote Education and Recreation (SUPER) program, a life-skills program in which college-aged student-athletes teach children life skills. Specifically, this program involves a 30-hour, 10-session sport-based life skills clinic that aims at developing goal-setting and goal-achieving strategies not only in sport but also in life. Thus, although the program teaches sports skills, its main focus is on having the student-athletes teach life skills (e.g., goal setting, emotional control) related to sports. It is assumed that these self-regulatory life skills can then be used by the participants to facilitate personal growth in nonsport areas. Interestingly, although the program is aimed at children, the authors have noted that by teaching others how to succeed, the student-athlete mentors' ability to succeed is enhanced as well, and new leadership skills, developed. Hence, teaching the program may be a powerful technique for life-skill development.

In a similar vein, the National Collegiate Athletic Association also sponsors a life-skills program for student athletes, the goal of which is to help the athletes self-regulate behavior off the field by developing nonsport academic life skills. To achieve this objective the CHAMPS (Challenging Athletes' Minds for Personal Success)/Life Skills Program involves instructing and supporting student-athletes in other areas such as personal development (i.e., promoting well-balanced lifestyle and emotional well-being), career development (i.e., developing career and life goals), and community service (i.e., engaging actively campus and community service activities). Unfortunately, little research exists to support its effectiveness. That is, studies are needed that assess whether these life skills are actually learned by the student-athletes and if learning these skills successfully leads to off-the-field self-regulation.

Self-regulation skills include self-monitoring, goal setting, self-talk, and imagery.

Although self-regulatory life-skills programs like SUPER and CHAMPS are increasing in popularity, the effectiveness of such programs needs to be more formally assessed. It is especially important to examine the effectiveness and transferability of life skills from sport to other general life situations.

Looking across both the micro and macro self-regulation research, it is clear that more research is needed, and results are not always supportive. However, the majority of studies conducted to date are encouraging and show that self-regulation and self-regulation strategies improve performance and enhance long-term persistence in physical activity and sport. These results have also been found in young, middle, and late adult participants. Hence, self-regulation and self-regulation strategies should be used by sport psychology specialists and coaches across the adult lifespan.

KEY SELF-REGULATION SKILLS

Although self-regulation research can involve any number of variables, some of the more frequently used ones include self-monitoring, goal setting, self-talk, and imagery. In many ways, these are the fundamental components of self-regulation. It is extremely difficult to regulate one's behavior, for example, unless goals are identified, visualized, set, and executed. We also need to self-monitor progress made toward goal achievement and any type of behavior change. Moreover, we constantly engage in self-talk, and our self-talk influences almost everything we do. Finally, imagery is a skill that not only helps athletes and exercisers improve performance, but it also helps control emotions—a key process in self-regulation. To help athletes and exercisers self-regulate, then, requires a basic understanding of these strategies.

Self-Monitoring

Self-monitoring focuses on the manner in which one observes and examines one's behaviors (Kirschenbaum, 1987). Therefore, it is considered a key component of the self-regulatory process. Sport and exercise psychology self-monitoring studies typically focus on having athletes or exercisers use tally systems to record behaviors, log performance, make self-observations, and increase awareness of situation and task variables. Increasing awareness of these factors is considered a critical step in the self-regulation process, and after reviewing the literature, Crews et al. (2000) concluded that self-monitoring influences performance and other affective states such as anxiety and confidence. For example, Kirschenbaum, Ordman, Tomarken, and Holtbauer (1982) compared relatively low-skilled versus moderately skilled adult women bowlers (no participant age listed in article) who participated in one of several conditions. Treatment-condition participants received either basic instruction on the components of effective bowling (foot position, stance, grip, spot, approach, push away, finish position) and positive self-monitoring or basic instruction and negative self-monitoring. Positive self-monitoring required participants to record if they executed one of the basic instruction components well, whereas negative self-monitoring recorded if one of the basic components was poorly executed. Results revealed that the low-skilled bowlers improved performance more than the other groups did. Only positive self-monitoring facilitated performance. Thus, in addition to demonstrating the importance of self-regulation, these results demonstrate that self-monitoring may not be as simple as it first appears.

TABLE 1

- Awareness of the need to change is a critical initial self-regulatory step. Start with activities that help individuals recognize the need to change.
- Use teachable moments (e.g., immediately after an important, good, or bad match) to reinforce self-monitoring.
- Focus on successes when regulating difficult tasks.
- Focus on failures/mistakes when regulating easy tasks.
- Be specific on what you are intending to monitor (i.e., performance, emotion, thought).
- Be specific on when you are monitoring (e.g., practice vs. competition and pre-, during, postperformance).
- Set a standard (e.g., performance goal) when monitoring your performance.
- Provide consistent reinforcement for self-monitoring.
- Practice self-monitoring using a tangible item (e.g., take paper clip out of your pocket every time you monitor a negative thought).
- Implement self-monitoring combined with other self-regulatory skills.
- Use different strategies to evaluate self-monitoring.

The finding that positive self-monitoring facilitated performance on a relatively easy task is consistent with other self-monitoring research. Specifically, it has also been found that positive self-monitoring (keeping track of one's successes) enhances expectancies and increases performance, but only for difficult or poorly mastered tasks. Recording instances of ineffective behaviors can improve self-regulated performance on well-learned tasks (Tomarken & Kirschenbaum, 1982). Finally, a number of important guidelines are available for those who desire to teach self-regulation strategies. Table 1 contains some of these guidelines.

Goal Setting

Goal setting is a key self-regulation strategy. A *goal* is usually defined as "attaining a specific standard of proficiency on a task, usually within a specified time limit" (Locke, Shaw, Saari, & Latham, 1981, p. 145). In recent reviews of the sport psychology goal-setting research, Weinberg (1994, 2001) and Gould (2001) have identified different types of goals (outcome goals such as win-loss, performance goals such as running a personal best time in track, and process goals such as maintaining good form) athletes and exercisers set. They also indicate that goals influence performance by directing attention to important elements of the skill being performed, mobilizing performer efforts, prolonging performer persistence, fostering the development of new learning strategies, and influencing psychological characteristics like confidence and anxiety. Goal setting, then, is an effective technique for facilitating self-regulation. Based on this research, key goal-setting principles have been identified to guide practice (see Table 2). Researchers and practitioners interested in self-regulation must understand these principles and effectively employ them.

Self-Talk

Another psychological skill that is used in many self-regulatory efforts is self-talk management. This makes complete sense when we consider how much internal dialogue athletes and exercisers engage in each day. Just think about it: Athletes and exercisers say things to themselves all the time (e.g., "Easy does it," " I can do this, just relax," "I stink"). Managing self-talk helps

TABLE 2
Key Goal-Setting Principles (Weinberg & Gould, 1999)

- Set specific versus general "do best" goals.
- Set moderately difficult but realistic goals.
- Set long- and short-term goals.
- Set performance, process, and outcome goals.
- Set goals for both practice and competition.
- Record goals.
- Develop specific strategies for goal achievement,
- When helping athletes and exercisers set goals, consider participant personality and motivation.
- Foster goal commitment in athletes and exercisers.
- Provide support for goal achievement.
- Provide evaluation and feedback about goals.

individuals manage their internal thoughts and focus on productive versus unproductive thinking. Williams and Leffingwell (1996) for instance, indicate that self-talk serves a variety of uses in sport such as guiding bad-habit corrections, focusing attention, arousing or activating oneself, building and maintaining confidence, and facilitating motivation. They also indicate that techniques for managing self-talk include becoming aware of one's internal dialogue and its effects on behavior via observation, imagery, or logs and then modifying it by stopping negative thoughts, purposefully changing negative to positive thoughts, countering negative statements, and reframing unproductive thoughts. Although sport psychology research on self-talk is limited, initial research efforts are encouraging (Van Raalte, Brewer, Rivera, & Petitpas, 1994; Weinberg, 1985; Weinberg, Smith, Jackson, & Gould, 1984; Wrisberg & Anshel, 1996) and general psychological research shows that it is a critical component of self-regulation (Van Raalte, 2001). Table 3 also contains key self-talk principles that should be used when guiding practice.

Imagery

Imaginal experiences are a powerful self-regulation component (Kirschenbaum, 1987) and a key psychological skill emphasized in the sport psychology literature (Gould & Damarjian, 1996). *Imagery* is defined as the process by which sensory experiences are stored in memory and later internally recalled and performed in the absence of external stimuli (Murphy, 1996). Imagery training is hypothesized to enhance self-regulation by facilitating positive expectancies; promoting the maintenance of self-monitoring, self-evaluation, and self-reinforcement;

> Imagery is defined as a process by which sensory experiences are stored in memory and later internally recalled and performed in the absence of external stimuli.

and directing attention to aspects of oneself and performance that can sustain effective self-regulation (Kirschenbaum, 1987). Research has also shown that imagery is an important mental skill associated with enhanced learning and performance (Vealey & Greenleaf, 2001; Weinberg & Gould, 1999). Studies like the one conducted by Woolfolk, Parrish, and Murphy (1985) have also shown that imagery influences self-regulation. Finally, guidelines suggested for using imagery to enhance physical activity performance and sustained effort have been derived (Gould & Damarjian; see Table 4).

TABLE 3
Self-Talk Principles for Guiding Practice (Williams & Leffingwell, 1996; Zinsser, Bunker, & Williams, 2000)

- Athletes and exercisers need to develop the ability to control their self-talk and inner dialogue.
- Self-talk can be used to enhance performance and skill acquisition, adopt or maintain exercise behavior, change bad habits, enhance attention, create or change certain moods and affect control effort, and build self-confidence.
- Awareness of one's self-talk patterns is needed before self-talk can be changed.
- Observation, retrospection, imagery, and logs can be used to increase awareness of self-talk.
- It is especially important to identify negative, irrational, and distorted thinking.
- Strategies for controlling self-talk include thought stopping, changing negative to positive thoughts, countering (using internal debate and reasoning to counter negative thoughts), and reframing (changing one's general perspective about how one views situations).

TABLE 4
Key Imagery Principles for Guiding Practice (Gould & Damarjian, 1996)

- Practice imagery on a regular basis.
- Use all the senses to enhance image vividness.
- Develop control of one's images.
- Use both internal and external imagery perspectives.
- Use relaxation to facilitate imagery use and ability.
- Develop coping strategies through imagery.
- Use imagery in practice as well as for competition.
- Use audio- and videotapes to enhance imagery.
- Use triggers to or cues to facilitate imagery quality.
- Emphasize dynamic kinesthetic imagery.
- Imagine in real time.
- Use logs to enhance imagery use.

FUTURE RESEARCH AND THEORY DIRECTIONS

Although our knowledge of self-regulation and the self-regulation process has increased, much more needs to be known about the topic, especially in the sport and exercise domain. More theory-directed studies like those conducted by Anshel and Porter (1996) and Kirschenbaum et al. (1998, 1999) are needed. Such studies will allow us to determine if self-regulation model components and predictions hold up to empirical testing. It is especially important to study the planning process relative to the problem identification and execution stages of Kirschenbaum's (1984) model. We know little about how athletes and coaches identify performance problems and set out to solve them. Most likely, this involves goal setting, but the vast majority of current sport psychology goal-setting research focuses on how goals relate to performance, not on how athletes and exercisers go about identifying goals or selecting certain goals over others. The free-set goal research by Kane et al. (2001) is a nice exception in this regard, and more studies like it are needed. Similarly, little is known about how athletes and exercisers develop goal-achievement strategies. Finally, Kirschenbaum and his associates (1999) have recently shown that golfers are often unrealistic in their planning (demonstrating positive illusions) and that a more deliberate and realistic approach facilitates performance. Understanding this process is critical for successful self-regulation, so additional studies along these lines are needed.

It is also important to note that the Kirschenbaum model is only one of many self-regulation models. As we described earlier in this chapter, many other models taken from social-cognitive, cognitive-affective, and cognitive-behavioral approaches can be applied to understand and explain self-regulation. Efforts to examine the utility of additional self-regulation theoretical frameworks are needed, as well as a comparison of those frameworks to the one proposed by Kirschenbaum (1984).

Relative to studies that could be categorized into the micro self-regulation classification, we concur with many of the recommendations made by Crews et al. (2000). Specifically, self-regulation investigations should employ multiple outcome measures (e.g., performance, affect, cognition), use more experimental designs (randomization of participants, control groups), employ more sophisticated statistical techniques, and examine effects on varying tasks and with participants who differ in skill level. Making these methodological improvements will produce better studies and, in turn, facilitate knowledge development in the area.

We also believe that although micro self-regulation studies certainly contribute to our knowledge in the area, some of the greatest gains will come from examining macro efforts at self-regulation. Such studies have great potential because they focus on how athletes and exercisers regulate behavior in naturally occurring settings, focus heavily on free-set goals, and allow investigators to examine the often overlooked generalization stage of self-regulation. Most needed are longitudinal examinations of programs such as the NCAA CHAMPS/Life Skills Program and SUPER as these efforts are based on the notion that participants develop self-regulation skills that transfer across time and context. To date, however, little evidence exists to support these assumptions.

The issue of generalizability or transferability is one of the most important needing study in the self-regulation area. Little if any sport and exercise psychology research has been conducted on the issue. However, as A.J.'s (struggle to guide his own behavior after basketball) and Morella's (efforts to self-regulate her exercise) case examples at the opening of this chapter revealed, individuals need self-regulation skills across the lifespan and in all phases of their lives. We need to know whether athletes who use self-regulation strategies to learn and maintain performance in some skill areas (e.g., basketball free-throw shooting) will on their own transfer these skills to other problem areas (e.g., boxing out on defense)? Similarly, if college athletes are taught goal-setting self-regulation skills in their sport do they transfer and use these same skills in nonathletic settings such as in the classroom? Finally, do self-regulation life skills taught through youth sport carry over time and context into adulthood?

It is important to recognize that self-regulated efforts will not always work. When confronting roadblocks to their goals, athletes have two options: keep trying or quit. In sport psychology, we tend to emphasize how to keep trying by continuing to exert effort to overcome adversities, and coaches continually stress the importance of not quitting in the face of adversity. Hence, we see reference to mental toughness and sustained motivation quite often in the applied literature (e.g., Loehr, 1994). Less is said about quitting or disengaging. Traditionally in sport psychology literature, the term *disengagement* has been used in negative connotation, often coupled with such adjectives as *forced* (e.g., Hallinan & Snyder, 1987) or *involuntary* (e.g., Boydell & Lothian, 1993) and related to issues like burnout, career termination, dropping out (e.g., Koukouris, 1991), and maladaptive coping (e.g., Finch, 1994). However, giving up is absolutely necessary in some cases (e.g., seeking an unattainable goal thereby limiting alternative goals) and the most logical course of action. In fact, disengagement is an indispensable part of self-regulation (Carver & Scheier, 1998), and it oftentimes induces positive affect. In a recent interview study with 12 first-year university female athletes (*M* age = 18.5) who had failed to make the final selection for a varsity team, for example, Munroe, Albinson, and Hall (1999) found that positive changes such as fewer uncertainties, fewer feelings of disappointment, and more alternatives occurred as a result of disengagement from sport. The athletes' general perception was negative immediately after disengagement, but became more positive 4 months later. A key area of future study, then, is to examine the positive aspects of disengagement, the conditions under which disengagement occurs, and how disengagement fits into the self-regulation process.

Researchers might also find it useful to examine the role of optimism in self-regulation because optimistic individuals focus more on positive environmental information and have higher expectancies than their pessimistic counterparts do. Such an orientation, then, might lead athletes and exercisers to set more goals and be more positive in their self-regulation efforts. Not only has the personality disposition of optimism been associated with success in a number of areas (Buchanan & Seligman, 1995; Gigerenzer, 2000; Scheier & Carver, 1992, 1993; Seligman, 1991; Snyder, 2000), but Schneider (2001) has recently discussed the importance of developing realistic optimism that combines a positive focus with the ability to accurately perceive environmental information and possibilities. Would realistic optimists be better self-regulators, and is realistic optimism developed over a lifetime and, hence, developmentally focused?

Last, and most ironically given the focus of this book and chapter, a need exists to study self-regulation from a developmental perspective. In this review, no studies were identified that examined self-regulation across early, middle, and late adulthood. In fact, almost all the sport studies have been conducted with college-aged samples. Yet from a developmental perspective, one could argue that the older an athlete became, the better he or she could self-regulate because of increased life and sport experiences. However, we know that for most sports, physical talents peak around the age of 30, so older athletes might find it difficult to deal with declining physical abilities and the need to readjust expectations. Interestingly, Burton (1989) reported that collegiate swimmers had no trouble adjusting goals upward (working for faster times), but experienced difficulty lowering goals after missing training due to injury or illness. Finally, in the youth and young adult sport psychology literature, transferring psychological skills learned through sport to other endeavors is often emphasized. With middle and later stage adults, however, it is quite possible that individuals learned life skills through their jobs and other nonsport endeavors and that these skills could be transferred to help them perform better in sport or begin exercise programs. This developmental issue needs to be explored.

IMPLICATIONS FOR GUIDING PRACTICE

Sport psychological self-regulation research has a number of implications for guiding practice. Chief among these is the importance of understanding general stages of self-regulation and using these to guide practice. Too often, we focus our attention on teaching athletes particular psychological skills like goal setting or imagery, but do not teach athletes how to fit these into a long-term process for behavioral change that can be used across time and situations.

Kirschenbaum's (1984) 5-stage model of self-regulation can be used to do this. Using the first stage, problem identification, not only can practitioners help athletes identify particular problems of immediate importance, but they can also help athletes learn how to develop a system for ongoing problem identification. For example, Orlick (1986) has developed postcompetition evaluations that can be used to help athletes routinely monitor performance strengths and areas needing improvement. Helping athletes learn how to monitor their performance and focus on the most important performance problems is a critical skill needed for development. It is important, however, to do this away from competition in an objective environment as recent self-monitoring research has shown that negative self-monitoring during performance can cause performance declines (Martin & Anshel, 1995). Also, helping athletes identify the most important aspects of performance (from many) to focus on is important.

Commitment is the second stage of the model, and strategies for facilitating commitment to change can be devised, much as been the case in the stages-of-change exercise research conducted by Marcus and colleagues (Marcus, Bock, Pinto, & Clark, 1996). It might be particularly useful to help athletes identify potential roadblocks to performance change and then work with them to devise strategies for dealing with such obstacles.

In the execution stage, we would focus on solving the identified performance problems by adhering to many of the principles outlined in the mental skills training literature (Gould & Damarjian, 1998). For instance, Martens' (1987) three-stage (education, acquisition, practice) approach to psychological skills training might be employed. Similarly, Gould and Damarjian have discussed the importance of identifying and devising ways to overcome barriers to mental training, cultivating coach support and follow-up, and not trying to do too much mental training too soon with athletes.

The fourth, environmental management stage, is often overlooked in psychological skills training, but is critical for success. That is, how does the athlete engineer and manage the physical and social environment (e.g., organizational, coach, teammate support) needed for athletic success? Interestingly, Woodman and Hardy (1998) have identified social, political, and organizational stressors (lack of funding, pressure from administrators, sport organization politics) as critical influences on elite athletes. Hence, sport psychology consultants and coaches must help athletes anticipate such influences and develop strategies for managing them. Along these lines, the Sport Science and Technology Division of the U.S. Olympic Committee (2000) developed a video titled *Achieving the Dream: Performing Your Best at the Olympics* in which, among other things, elite athletes are urged to talk to their families and significant others and instruct them as to the best ways they can help facilitate performance. Similarly, Gould, Udry, Bridges, and Beck (1997) and Peterson (2001) have offered suggestions for how injured athletes can orchestrate their own social support systems when recovering from serious athletic injuries, whereas Wankel (1984) has identified the importance of fostering spouse support in the exercise-adherence process.

Finally, the fifth generalization stage is critical to emphasize as it is often ignored. Too often, we assume athletes will automatically transfer the psychological skills and strategies we teach to other situations and contexts. However, it is our experience that this does not occur. We must teach for transfer. Thus, time must be spent talking to athletes and showing them how they might use their mental skills in new situations or take what they have learned through sport and apply it outside the sport environment.

Although using self-regulation research and theory to guide practice, we must remember that self-regulation is a complex process that involves many interacting factors. For example, self-monitoring has been found to interact with task difficulty (Martin & Anshel, 1995). Positive self-monitoring (recording what one does correctly) is most effective on difficult tasks whereas negative self-monitoring (recording what one does not execute correctly) is more effective on easy tasks. Although specific research findings like this will not always be available to guide practice, we must be keenly aware and monitor our practical efforts for the presence of such interactions.

Last, it is also critical to recognize that self-regulation is used throughout one's life and certainly through all stages of development. It is not just a performance-enhancement technique. Therefore, it is critical that we focus on better understanding the self-regulation process. Especially important is the need to use it at all stages of adult development and begin to learn how stages of adult development might influence the self-regulation process.

CONCLUSION

Self-regulation and self-regulation skills are critical for athletic success and sustained involvement in physical activity. In this chapter, self-regulation was defined, and evidence, presented to show that self-regulation is an important means of influencing performance and sustaining task involvement. The key self-regulation skills of self-monitoring, goal setting, self-talk, and imagery were also discussed. However, it was concluded that more research on both the self-regulation process and key self-regulation skills is needed. Implications for practice were also forwarded and emphasized, using the five stages of Kirschenbaum's (1984) model to guide applied efforts in the area.

With this knowledge in hand, it is now possible to return to the four case examples that began this chapter and see how self-regulation knowledge can be used to help individuals better function in the sport and exercise environment. In the first case (involving Bob, the retiree who wants to improve his golf game), Bob has done a good job of monitoring the general strengths and weaknesses of his game and developing a self-regulated plan for improvement. He could further improve by setting more specific goals for improvement. It would also be helpful if, with his instructor Nicole, Bob developed a specific practice and competition plan (like the SMART golf program) and a strategy for self-monitoring his progress (above and beyond round scores). His plan for learning some mental skills to deal with the frustration he encounters when he makes mistakes or plays poorly is a good idea and should be more specifically identified.

For Jennifer, the injured collegiate gymnast, developing a self-regulation program seems critical. In conjunction with her physical therapist/athletic trainer, Jennifer needs to identify specific short-term rehabilitation goals (most likely relative to strength, flexibility, and endurance) that will lead to her long-term goal of returning to competition, as well as exercises that need to be performed. She then needs to self-monitor her progress as she executes her program. Strategies for staying committed seem to be of little importance as she seems highly committed (her problem seems to be over- versus undertraining). However, a plan for providing social support and self-monitoring checks to make sure she is not overtraining would be essential. Finally, providing Jennifer with some positive self-talk instruction and ways to use imagery to facilitate recovery and deal with her anxiety over recovering in time for the season would be very useful A.J.'s case is one of the toughest because during his college days he did not develop many self-regulation strategies or skills (recall his coach made all the decisions), and he is now trying to learn them on his own. It would be best if he could see a counselor who could advise him as to ways to develop self-regulation skills. Help with goal setting, self-motivation, and commitment would be essential to his development.

In our fourth case (Morella's lack of motivation for exercise), Morella might be best helped by a personal trainer with a background in sport and exercise psychology and especially self-regulation. She needs to understand the benefits of exercise and find a form of exercise that will not be perceived as distasteful to her. Realistic goals should then be set, and a clear exercise plan, initiated. A support system for building and maintaining commitment (exercise with friends) must be initiated. Developing a self-monitoring and reward system and cognitive strategies for dealing with her negative thoughts about exercise (e.g., thought stopping, reframing) should also be developed.

Finally, it is ironic that the focus of this chapter was on developmental differences in stages of adulthood relative to self-regulation in sport and physical activity because little, if any, of this research was developmental in theory, design, or methodology. A critical need exists, then, to examine differences in self-regulation across the adult lifespan. It is hoped that some of the developmentally based ideas fostered in this chapter will facilitate this process.

REFERENCES

Anshel, M. H., & Porter, A. (1995). Self-regulatory characteristics of competitive swimmers as a function of skill level and gender. *Journal of Sport Behavior, 19,* 91-110.

Anshel, M. H., & Porter, A. (1996). Efficacy of a model for examining self-regulation with elite and non-elite male and female and competitive swimmers. *International Journal of Sport Psychology, 27,* 321-336.

Bandura, A. (1986). *Social foundations of thought and action: A social cognitive theory.* Englewood Cliffs, NJ: Prentice Hall.

Boydell, C., & Lothian, S. (1993). *Adjustment to involuntary disengagement from organized athletics.* London, Ontario: University of Western Ontario.

Buchanan, G. M., & Seligman, M. E. P. (1995). *Explanatory style.* Hillsdale, NJ: Erlbaum.

Burton, D. (1989). Winning isn't everything: Examining the impact of performance goals on collegiate swimmers' cognitions and performance. *The Sport Psychologist, 2,* 105-132.

Carver, C. S., & Scheier, M. F. (1998). *On the self-regulation of behavior.* New York: Cambridge University Press.

Crews, D. J., Lochbaum, M. R., & Karoly, P. (2000). Self-regulation: Concepts, methods and strategies in sport and exercise. In R. N. Singer, H. A. Hausenblas, & C. M. Janelle (Eds.), *Handbook of sport psychology* (2nd ed., pp. 566-581). New York: John Wiley & Sons, Inc.

Danish, S., & Nellen, V. C. (1997). New role for the sport psychologist: Teaching life skills through sport to at-risk youth. *Quest, 49,* 100-113.

Danish, S., Nellen, V. C., & Owens, S. S. (1996). Teaching life skills through sport: Community-based program for adolescents. In J. L. Van Raalte & B. W. Brewer (Eds.), *Exploring sport and exercise psychology* (pp. 205-225). Washington, DC: American Psychological Association.

Finch, L. (1994). *The relationships among coping strategies, trait anxiety, and performance in collegiate softball players.* Unpublished doctoral dissertation, University of North Carolina, Greensboro.

Gigerenzer, G. (2000). *Adaptive thinking.* New York: Oxford University Press.

Gorely, T., & Gordon, S. (1995). An examination of the transtheoretical model of exercise behavior in older adults. *Journal of Sport & Exercise Psychology, 17,* 312-324.

Gottman, J. M., & McFall, R. M. (1971). Self-monitoring effects in a program of potential high school dropouts: A time series analysis. *Journal of Consulting and Clinical Psychology, 39,* 273-281.

Gould, D. (2001). Goal setting for peak performance. In J. M. Williams (Ed.), *Applied sport psychology: Personal growth to peak performance* (4th ed., pp. 190-205). Mountain View, CA: Mayfield.

Gould, D., & Damarjian, N. (1996). Imagery training for peak performance. In J. L. Van Raalte & B. W. Brewer (Eds.), *Exploring sport and exercise psychology* (pp. 25-50). Washington, DC: American Psychological Association.

Gould, D., & Damarjian, N. (1998). *Mental skills training for sport.* In B. Elliott (Ed.), *Training in sport: Applying sport science* (pp. 70-116). London, UK: Wiley.

Gould, D., Udry, E., Bridges, D., & Beck, L. (1997). Coping with season-ending injuries. *The Sport Psychologist, 11,* 379-399.

Hallinan, C., & Snyder, E. (1987). Forced disengagement and the collegiate athlete. *Arena Review, 11*(2), 28-34.

Hill, K. L., & Borden, F. (1995). The effect of attentional cueing scripts on competitive bowling performance. *International Journal of Sport Psychology, 26,* 503-512.

Kane, T. D., Baltes, T. R., & Moss, M. C. (2001). Causes and consequences of free-set goals: An investigation of athletic self-regulation. *Journal of Sport & Exercise Psychology, 23,* 55-75.

Kane, T. D., Marks, M. A., Zaccaro, S. J., & Blair, V. (1996). Self-efficacy, personal goals, and wrestlers' self-regulation. *Journal of Sport & Exercise Psychology, 18,* 36-48.

Kanfer, F. H., & Karoly, P. (1972). Self-control: A behavioristic excursion into the lion's den. *Behavior Therapy, 3,* 398-416.

Karoly, P. (1977). Behavioral self-management in children: Concepts, methods, issues, and directions. In M. Hersen, R. M. Eisler, & P. M. Miller (Eds.), *Progress in behavior modification* (Vol. 5, pp. 197-262). New York: Academic Press.

Karoly, P. (1993). Mechanisms of self-regulation: A systems view. *Annual Review of Psychology, 44*, 23-52.

Kavussanu, M., Crews, D. J., & Gill, D. L. (1998). The effects of single versus multiple measures of biofeedback on basketball free throw shooting performance. *International Journal of Sport Psychology, 29*, 132-144.

Kirschenbaum, D. S. (1984). Self-regulation and sport psychology: Nurturing and emerging symbiosis. *Journal of Sport Psychology, 6*, 159-183.

Kirschenbaum, D. S. (1987). Self-regulation of sport performance. *Medicine and Science in Sports and Exercise, 19*, S106-S113.

Kirschenbaum, D. S., O'Connor, E. A., & Owens, D. (1999). Positive illusions in golf: Empirical and conceptual analyses. *Journal of Applied Sport Psychology, 11*, 1-27.

Kirschenbaum, D. S., Ordman, A. M., Tomarken, A. J., (1982). Effects of differential self-monitoring and level of mastery on sports performance: Brain power golf. *Cognitive Therapy & Research, 6*, 335-342.

Kirschenbaum, D. S., Owens, D., & O'Connor, E. A. (1998). Smart golf: Preliminary evaluation of a simple, yet comprehensive, approach to improving and scoring the mental game. *The Sport Psychologist, 12*, 271-282.

Kirschenbaum, D. S., & Tomarken, A. J. (1982). On facing the generalization problem: The study of self-regulatory failure. In P. C. Kendall (Ed.), *Advances in cognitive-behavioral research and therapy* (Vol. 1, pp. 121-200). New York: Academic Press.

Koukouris, K. (1991). Quantitative aspects of the disengagement process of advanced and elite Greek male athletes from organized competitive sport. *Journal of Sport Behavior, 14*, 227-246.

Lazarus, R. S. (1991). *Emotions and adaptation.* New York: Oxford University Press.

Locke, E. A., Shaw, K. N., Saari, L. M., & Latham, G. P. (1981). Goal setting and task performance. *Psychological Bulletin, 90*, 125-152.

Loehr, J. E. (1994). *The new toughness training for sports.* New York: Plume.

Mahoney, M. J., & Thoresen, C. E. (1974). *Self-control: Power to the person.* Monterey, CA: Brooks/Cole.

Marcus. B. H., Bock, B. C., Pinto, B. M., & Clark, M. M. (1996). Exercise initiation, adoption, and maintenance. In J. L. Van Raalte & B. W. Brewer (Eds.), *Exploring sport and exercise psychology* (pp. 153-158). Washington, DC: American Psychological Association.

Martens, R. (1987). *Coaches is guide to sport psychology.* Champaign, IL: Human Kinetics.

Martin, M. B., & Anshel, M. H. (1995). Effect of self-monitoring strategies and task complexity on motor performance and affect. *Journal of Sport & Exercise Psychology, 17*, 453-470.

Meichenbaum, D. (1977). *Cognitive behavioral modification.* New York: Plenum.

Munroe, K., Albinson, J., & Hall, C. (1999). The effect of first year female varsity athletes. *Avante, 5*(3), 63-81.

Murphy, S. M. (1996). Imagery interventions in sport. *Medicine and Science in Sports and Exercise, 26*, 486-494.

Orlick, T. (1986). *Psyching for sport: Mental training for athletes.* Champaign, IL: Human Kinetics.

Peterson, K. (2001). Supporting athletes during injury rehab. *Olympic Coach, 11*(2), 7-9.

Prapavessis, H., Grove, J. R., McNair, P. J., & Cable, N.T. (1992). Self-regulation training, state anxiety, and sport performance: A psychophysiological case study. *The Sport Psychologist, 6*, 213-229.

Rodin, J. (1983). Behavioral medicine: Beneficial effects of self control training in aging [Electronic version]. *International Review of Applied Psychology, 32*, 153-181. [Abstract from: PsycINFO Item: 1984-02213-001]

Scheier, M. F., & Carver, C. S. (1992). On the power of positive thinking: The benefits of being optimistic. *Current Directions of Psychological Science, 2*, 26-30.

Scheier, M. F., & Carver, C. S. (1993). Effects of optimism on psychological and physical well-being: Theoretical overview and empirical update. *Cognitive Therapy and Research, 16*, 201-228.

Schneider, S. L. (2001). In search of realistic optimism: Meaning, knowledge, and warm fuzziness. *American Psychologist, 56*, 250-263.

Seligman, M. E. P. (1991). *Learned optimism.* New York: Knopf.

Simek, T.C., O'Brien, R.M., & Figlerski, L.B. (1994). Contracting and chaining to improve the performance of a college golf team: Improvement and deterioration. *Perceptual and Motor Skills, 78*, 1099-1105.

Snyder, C. R. (2000). The past and possible futures of hope. *Journal of Social and Clinical Psychology, 19*, 11-28.

Tomarken, A. J., & Kirschenbaum, D. S. (1982). Self-regulatory failure: Accentuate the positive? *Journal of Personality and Social Psychology, 43*, 584-597.

United States Olympic Committee. (2000). *Achieving the dream: Performing your best at the Olympic Games* [Videotape]. Colorado Springs, CO: Author.

Van Raalte, J. L. (2001). Self-talk and sport performance: Some theoretical possibilities. In A. Papaioannou, M. Goudas, & Y. Theodorakis (Eds.), *10th World Congress of Sport Psychology: Proceedings* (Vol. 3, pp. 1-3). Skiathos, Greece: International Society of Sport Psychology.

Van Raalte, J. L., Brewer, B. W., Rivera, P. M., & Petitpas, A. J. (1994). The relationship between observable self-talk and competitive junior tennis players' match performances. *Journal of Sport & Exercise Psychology, 16*, 400-115.

Vealey, R. S., & Greenleaf, C. A. (2001). Seeing is believing: Understanding and using imagery in sport. In J. M. Williams (Ed.), *Applied sport psychology: Personal growth to peak performance.* (4th ed., pp. 247-281). Mountain View, CA: Mayfield.

Wankel, L. M. (1984). Decision making and social support structures for increasing exercise adherence. *Journal of Cardiac Rehabilitation, 4,* 124-128.

Waschall, S. B., & Kernis, M. H., (1996). Level and stability of self-esteem as predictors of children's intrinsic motivation and reactions to anger. *Personality and Social Psychology Bulletin, 22,* 4-13.

Weinberg, R. S. (1985). Relationship between self-efficacy and cognitive strategies in enhancing endurance performance. *International Journal of Sport Psychology, 17,* 280-292.

Weinberg, R. S. (1994). Goal setting in sport and exercise settings: A synthesis and critique. *Medicine and Science in Sports and Exercise, 26,* 469-477.

Weinberg, R. S. (2001). Motivation in sport & exercise: The special case of goal-setting. In A. Papaioannou, M. Goudas, & Y. Theodorakis (Eds.), *10th World Congress of Sport Psychology: Proceedings* (Vol. 3, pp. 247-260). Skiathos, Greece: International Society of Sport Psychology.

Weinberg, R. S., & Gould, D. (1999). *Foundations of sport and exercise psychology* (2nd ed.). Champaign, IL: Human Kinetics.

Weinberg, R. S., & Grove, R., & Jackson, A. (1992). Strategies for building self-efficacy in tennis players: A comparative analysis of Australian and American coaches. *The Sport Psychologist, 6,* 3-13.

Weinberg, R.S., Smith, J., Jackson, A., & Gould, D. (1984). Effect of association, dissociation and positive selftalk strategies on endurance performance. *Canadian Journal of Applied Sport Sciences, 9,* 25-32.

Williams, J. M., & Leffingwell, T. R. (1996). Cognitive strategies in sport and exercise psychology. In J. L. Van Raalte & B. W. Brewer (Eds.), *Exploring sport and exercise psychology* (pp. 51-73). Washington, DC: American Psychological Association.

Woodman, T., & Hardy, L. (1998). Le stress organisationnel: une étude de cas. [Organizational stress: A study of one case]. Paper presented at the Journées nationales d'études de la société française de psychologie du sport. Poitiers, France.

Woolfolk, R. L., Parrish, M. W., & Murphy, S. M. (1985). The effects of positive and negative imagery on motor performance. *Cognitive Therapy and Research, 9,* 335-342.

Wrisberg, C. A., & Anshel, M. H. (1996). The use of self-talk on a warming-up activity. *Journal of Applied Sport Psychology, 8,* S136.

Zimmerman, B. J., & Kitsantas, A. (1996). Self-regulated learning of a motoric skill: The role of goal setting and self-monitoring. *Journal of Applied Sport Psychology, 8,* 60-75.

Zinsser, N., Bunker, L. K., & Williams, J. M. (2001). Cognitive techniques for building confidence and enhancing performance. In J. M. Williams (Ed.), *Applied sport psychology: Personal growth to peak performance.* (4th ed., pp. 284-311). Mountain View, CA: Mayfield.

PART IV
LIFESPAN
TOPICS

CHAPTER FIFTEEN

Development of Expertise in Sport

Karen E. French • *Sue L. McPherson*

Every year, millions of children participate in a variety of youth sports. Many choose to continue participation into adolescence and early adulthood. During this time frame, children are developing the knowledge and skills that underlie adult sport performance. During the past 20 years, researchers have attempted to discover mechanisms that describe or explain how individuals acquire high levels of sport performance in childhood and adolescence. In this chapter, we will present some of the theories, research paradigms, and information that represent our present understanding regarding how adult sport performance develops. Our intent is to dispel myths and misconceptions about the experiences in childhood and adolescence that provide the foundation for adult performance. In addition, we present challenges for future research that may lead to a better understanding of how youth sport programs can provide a rich experience for all children, not just those who reach elite levels of performance in adulthood.

CHARACTERISTICS OF ADULT SPORT EXPERTS

Extensive research has shown that adult sport experts exhibit superior response-selection performance (tactical decision making) as well as superior motor-skill execution. Abernethy, Burgess-Limerick, and Parks (1994) briefly summarized a list of characteristics that distinguish the performance of sport experts from those of novices. In motor execution, sport experts (a) perform motor skills in a less effortful, more automatic way, (b) produce movement patterns of greater consistency and adaptability, (c) are superior perceivers of kinesthetic information, and (d) possess superior self-monitoring of motor skills. In response selection processes, adult sport experts, when compared to novices, are known to (a) be faster and more accurate in recognizing patterns, (b) have superior knowledge of both factual and procedural matters, (c) possess knowledge organized in a deeper, more structural form, (d) have superior knowledge of situational probabilities, (e) plan their own actions in advance, (f) anticipate the actions of an opponent, and (g) possess superior self-monitoring of tactical decision-making processes (for more extensive reviews, see Abernethy, Thomas, & Thomas, 1993; Starkes & Allard, 1993; Tenenbaum, 1999). Studies comparing child experts with similarly aged child novices reveal many of the differences in response selection and motor execution characteristics listed above, but seldom does the performance of child experts reach the level of sophistication exhibited by adult sport experts (see French & McPherson, 1999; Nielsen & McPherson, 2001; McPherson, 1999a).

In recent years, research has begun to shift from describing the characteristics of elite performers to trying to discover mechanisms that underlie the development of sport expertise. In the next section, we present information on the window of time across the lifespan in which elite sport performance develops. In addition, biological and experiential factors that facilitate or constrain improvement in performance during this time frame are presented. The emphasis in this section is on motor skill acquisition.

DEVELOPMENT OF SPORT EXPERTISE ACROSS THE LIFESPAN: NATURE-NURTURE ISSUES

Age at Peak Performance

The most common way to identify the window of opportunity for the development of expertise in a given domain is to document the age or age range in which elite performers commonly reach peak performance. Several authors have identified the age of peak performance in a variety of domains (chess, music, scholarship, sports; Haywood, 1993; Lehman, 1953; Malina, Bouchard, Shoup, Lariviere, 1982). Lehman provided age ranges for the individuals who had won championships in a variety of sports. For tennis and baseball, the age of individuals who won major championships in tennis ranged from 22 to 26. The age range for individuals who produced the highest runs batted in or stolen bases in baseball was 25 to 30. Champions in bowling (age 32.7), golf (32.1), and billards (35.7) tended to be older. Malina et al. studied the age range of participants in the 1976 and 1968 Olympics. The male participants ranged from 14 to 49 years in age. Average age of male participants tended to be younger in swimmers (19.2 and 19.8 years) and divers (21.3) whereas the average age of weight lifters (26.7 and 27.8) and wrestlers (25.8) tended to be the oldest. Female participants ranged in age from 12 to 38 years. The youngest participants tended to be gymnasts and swimmers whereas the oldest participants were divers and rowers.

The age of peak performance is likely influenced by biology. For example, underlying physical proficiency abilities such as strength tend to peak in the twenties (Haywood, 1993). In sports that require speed, strength, and power, the age at peak performance is likely younger than in the less physically demanding activities such as bowling, golf, or rifle shooting.

The age of peak performance may also be skill specific in a given sport. The age for peak performance of stealing bases in baseball occurs in the early twenties whereas the age at peak performance in batting and pitching occurs in the late twenties to early thirties (Schultz, Musa, Staszewski, & Siegler, 1994). Schultz and Curnow (1988) and Schultz et al. (1994) suggest that the age of peak performance is related to the optimal developmental time in which the systems underlying performance (basic perceptual motor abilities and physical proficiencies; Fleishman, 1972) are functioning at the most efficient levels. Thus, the age at which peak performance typically occurs for a given sport or sport skill within a sport is at least partially determined or constrained by biological factors (physical proficiencies such as strength, power, speed, and perceptual motor abilities).

Recent studies suggest that a minimum of 10 years of practice and experience in a domain is necessary to develop elite performance (Ericsson, 1996). Performance in most of the sports mentioned above peak in the twenties or early thirties. Thus, the window of developmental time for individuals to establish and acquire elite performance in most sports requires that participation and practice in the sport begin in childhood or early adolescence.

Biological Factors That Influence Selection for Advanced Competition

Biological factors also serve to facilitate or limit motor skill performance during childhood and adolescence. For example, world-class performers in specific sports possess similar physiques (Malina, 1994, 1996; Spurgeon & Giese, 1980; Spurgeon, Spurgeon, & Giese, 1984). Optimal body size or somatotype for a given set of task requirements in a specific sport or position within a given sport probably facilitates reaching more elite levels of performance.

Biological factors also interact with practice and training at specific times during development to influence performance and selection for more advanced competition or preparation. Early or late maturation influences the selection of individuals for more advanced levels of competition. Young male athletes who possess larger body size and are early maturers tend, on average, to be selected for more advanced competition in baseball, basketball, and football. Young male elite athletes in gymnastics and figure skating tend, on average, to be shorter and lighter than reference medians (see Malina, 1996, for extensive review). Thus, the biological advantage of early or late maturation is sport specific and related to the requirements of task-specific motor skills. This body of literature suggests that biology interacts with selection during early adolescence or near puberty.

Body size, physique, and maturation appear to influence selection for more advanced preparation very early in participation as well. A relative age effect has been found in a number of sports, including baseball (Thompson, Barnsley, & Stelbelsky, 1991), ice hockey (Barnsley & Thompson, 1988; Boucher & Mutimer, 1994), soccer (Dudink, 1994), and tennis (Dudink). A higher proportion of elite adult performers in these sports were born in the months of the year that would have made them chronologically older than peers during their participation in age-group competition during childhood. This suggests that the biological advantage of being chronologically older and more mature may influence performance positively and indirectly influence selection for more advanced preparation and competition at very young ages. French, Spurgeon, and Nevett (2002) found more highly skilled baseball players ages 7 to 12 years old had larger body size than that of less skilled players. Thus, biological advantages may influence skill performance and selection processes at very young ages, not just at puberty.

ROLE OF DELIBERATE PRACTICE IN DEVELOPMENT OF EXPERTISE

Extensive research has shown that without intensive practice and physical training over a long period of time, world-class performance of sport skills is not possible. Ericsson, Krampe, and Tesch-Romer (1993) presented a theoretical framework that provides the strongest case that accumulation of thousands of hours of intensive practice and training over at least 10 years is necessary to achieve elite performance. *Deliberate practice* was the term used to describe the practice activities that lead to greatest improvement in performance. Deliberate practice was further defined as being effortful, not inherently enjoyable, engaged in by the individual for the specific purpose of improving performance, and activities that were often selected by a coach or teacher to facilitate learning. Since the introduction of the theory of deliberate practice, many studies (see Ericsson, 1996, for review) have documented that elite performers in a variety of domains, including sport, have accumulated thousands of hours of deliberate practice in the domain over at least a 10-year period.

Many of the studies have compared elite, intermediate, and recreational players in retrospective reports of their own practice experiences across their entire career. In a variety of domains, expert performers had accumulated thousands of hours of practice more than had intermediate or recreational participants by 13 to 15 years into their career (see Ericcson, 1996, for review in all domains; Starkes, Deakin, Allard, Hodges, & Hayes, 1996, for sport). The individuals who had reached higher levels of performance in their respective domain also had accumulated the greatest amount of deliberate practice in the domain.

Age- or Skill-Level Appropriate Amounts of Deliberate Practice

In sports, accumulation of deliberate practice and the 10 years of preparation for elite performance often begin in childhood or early adolescence and continue into early adulthood. It would be tempting to just generalize that *more practice is better*. Ericsson et al. (1993) clearly document data that suggest individuals require periods of rest after engaging in deliberate practice. Individuals must recuperate from intense activities, avoid overuse injuries, and sustain motivation to continue to engage in effortful practice over a period of years.

Some research suggests that the amount of deliberate practice gradually increases from lower levels during childhood to larger amounts during adolescence and early adulthood. One of the earliest and most comprehensive studies of elite performers (Bloom, 1985) identified at least three important stages in the development of expertise in a variety of domains, including tennis and swimming. The amount and intensity of practice increased in each stage. The first stage was termed *play and romance*. During this phase, often in childhood, the individual was introduced to the domain by a parent. The focus of early teachers was to make the activity enjoyable and fun. The description of this stage by Bloom emphasizes development of intrinsic motivation to engage in the activity. The second stage began near 11 or 12 years of age. The focus of practice was on developing and refining skills and technique in this stage. Usually, a more advanced teacher was found, and the demands for focused, effortful practice activities intensified. The third stage, in early adulthood, focused on individualizing performance in the domain.

> The individuals who had reached higher levels of performance in their respective sport had also practiced the most.

Another study reports a gradual increase in the amount of deliberate practice based upon current *skill level* rather than age. Starkes et al. (1996) report the ranges of hours of deliberate practice per week engaged in by elite performers (wrestling, figure skating, piano, and violin) at various years into their career. At the beginning of their career, individuals engaged in 5 to 7 hours per week; at 10 years into their career, from 17 to 20 hours per week; and at 15 years into career, 20-25 hours per week. Despite the different starting ages in each of these activities (5 to 13) and the different activities included, the hours engaged in deliberate practice per week increased linearly as the *skill* level increased. The authors suggested that the number of hours spent in deliberate practice is driven by the skill level, not age-related changes in the ability to sustain concentration. Thus, a gradual increase in intense deliberate practice activities, regardless of age, may be necessary to provide a foundation for motivation to sustain practice of the activity for longer, more intense practice as skill progresses.

Individual or Team Practice

Recently, Helsen, Starkes, and Hodges (1998) conducted retrospective interviews of international-, national-, and provincial-level participants in soccer and field hockey. The authors found that international-level players in these team sports engaged in more practice of the individual motor skills of the sport before the age of 15 or 16 than did national- or provincial-level participants. Furthermore, the practice of the individual skills was conducted outside of team practices. By 15 or 16 years of age, the international-level players began to engage in more hours of practice with a team than did national- or provincial-level players.

Other studies comparing highly skilled child team sport performers in baseball (French, Spurgeon, & Nevett, 1995) and basketball (French & Thomas, 1987) suggest that highly skilled children practiced more hours per week outside team practices than did less skilled children. Practice of individual skills outside of team practices may be very important to establish high motor-skill performance at young ages. Those who engage in more practice of the individual motor skills prior to early adolescence may have a higher probability of being selected for more advanced competition or advanced teams during adolescence.

The number of hours of practice of individual skills outside of team practices per week reported by experts early in their careers in the studies listed above was remarkably similar in the team sports. For example, child expert basketball players in French and Thomas (1987) practiced about 3.5 hours per week outside of team practice. Youth baseball experts reported practicing approximately 4.4 hours per week outside of team practices (French et al., 1995). International soccer players at the beginning of their career engaged in approximately 4.2 hours of practice a week at age 5 and slightly under 5 hours per week at age 8 (Helsen et al., 1998). International field-hockey players engaged in approximately 3.5 hours per week at age 9 and slightly more than about 4 hours per week at age 12.

Recent studies suggest that a minimum of 10 years of practice and experience in a domain is necessary to develop elite performance.

The hours of practice engaged in per week in individual activities were slightly higher than those in the team sports. Experts in piano, violin, figure skating, and wrestling tended to practice approximately 5 to 7 hours per week at the beginning of their career (Starkes et al., 1996). Starkes et al. suggested the similarities in the hours practiced per week may represent a maximum number of hours of effective deliberate practice that could be performed in a week. Further research is needed to establish clearer guidelines for the appropriate amount of practice at a given age or skill level. These studies do provide useful information to parents and coaches regarding reasonable expectations for time spent practicing skills that prevent overuse injuries and burnout.

Development of Response Selection Processes

Biological and Experiential Influences

Clearly, biological and experiential factors directly facilitate or limit the development of motor skills during acquisition of elite performance. The impact of biology on response selection processes is largely indirect through biology's influence on developing motor skills. The one exception is speed of processing (reaction time), which is clearly age related (see Salthouse, 1996, for more extensive review). We believe response selection processes are largely learned and do not improve without extensive practice that focuses explicitly on their development and improvement.

Definition of the Knowledge Base and Problem Representation

Early research in sport expertise attributed the superior performance of experts in a variety of experimental cognitive tasks to more sophisticated problem representations (or knowledge bases). Traditionally, the knowledge base has been conceptualized as propositional networks of declarative knowledge or as procedural knowledge in the form of productions or condition-action procedures that are stored in long-term memory. In propositional networks (node-link networks), concepts are represented by nodes, features are words that define or clarify the concept, and links represent associations between or among concepts. Knowing more in propositional networks would entail having more concepts, more features, and more associations between and among concepts.

Production systems refer to another way that knowledge may be represented. Productions are generalized stimulus-response pairs (i.e., if-then links). Anderson (1982) describes learning mechanisms associated with converting knowledge from propositional networks into the form of productions (i.e., goal, condition, action linkages). The advantages of creating and building productions are an increase in processing speed and a reduction in errors in performance. In sports, tactical sport knowledge has been modeled successfully by propositional networks and as productions (condition-action-goal linkages, see McPherson, 1993a). For example, if these game conditions exist (runner at first; no outs; count 2 balls, 2 strikes; ball hit to shortstop), then execute these actions (i.e., shortstop throws to second baseman, who tags second and then throws to first for a double play). In this example, the game conditions listed above could be represented as condition concepts linked to the actions (throw to second, tag, throw to first) and the overall goal (make a double play).

Based on our research, we view the knowledge base for sport to include all the traditional propositional networks of declarative knowledge (both tactical and skill related) and procedures for response selection and execution. In addition, we believe the knowledge base also includes other sport-specific memory adaptations and structures such as action-plan profiles, current-event profiles, game-situation prototypes, scripts for competition, and sport-specific strategies that are stored in and accessible from long-term memory. A more detailed description of these additional knowledge structures will be presented later in the chapter.

When individuals perform a sport-related task (solve a static tactical problem or choose a response during actual competition), only a portion of the knowledge base specifically related to the task may be accessed from long-term memory. We (French, Nevett, et al. 1996; Nevett & French, 1997; McPherson, 1993a, 1993b, 1999a, 1999b, 2000) and others (Chi, 1997; Chi, Feltovich, & Glaser, 1981) refer to the process of accessing (to the level of working memory) the portion of the entire knowledge base (stored in long-term memory) that will be used to perform a specific task as representation of the problem or problem representation. This is a critical issue for two reasons. First, only a portion of the knowledge base can be uncovered through performance on a specific sport task. Performance in a variety of sport situations is necessary to elicit a more accurate picture of the entire knowledge base. Second, many participants, especially beginners and novices, display great difficulty representing the problem. The novice or beginner may access much sport-related knowledge; however, it is often not the relevant knowledge needed for successful performance of the specific sport task.

Techniques and Approaches to Study Sport Problem Representations

One of the techniques we have found most useful to study problem representations in sport has been verbal reports of thought processes during problem solving of static sport tactical situations (situation interviews) and verbal reports of participants' thoughts during actual competition. Because many readers may not be familiar with the theoretical frameworks that underlie the collection, interpretation, and analysis of verbal protocols during performance, we will briefly present some of the critical ideas regarding verbal protocols and refer the reader to the most important papers that provide thorough theoretical presentations.

Verbal reports of participants' thoughts during performance is a common paradigm in cognitive psychology to reveal the content and cognitive processes that are used to solve problems. Verbal reports of thoughts are *overt behaviors* and must be interpreted through a theoretical model for how verbalizations are generated. Ericsson and Simon (1993) provide the most extensive theoretical framework for collecting and interpreting verbal reports of thoughts during performance. Ericsson and Simon describe the processing activities involved in a variety of performances that may be verbalizable and those that are not. The thoughts that are verbalizable are the information that is accessed to the level of working memory. Some processes are not directly verbalizable (recognition process) or must be translated into a verbal code in order to be verbalizable (perceptual, visual processing including visual search). Although these processes are not directly verbalizable, the output of the process (visual search, cue selected, or recognized) may be accessed to the level of working memory and can be verbalized.

Two types of verbal report techniques are common. In a think-aloud (talk-aloud) protocol, an individual verbalizes aloud his or her thoughts during performance. Think-aloud protocols provide the most accurate representation of the actual thought processes used during performance. When performance involves very fast perceptual motor types of activities, retrospective reports of thoughts immediately following the performance can provide valid indicators of an individual's thoughts during performance. Ericsson and Simon (1993) suggest that retrospective reports may be the preferred way to accurately trace an individual's thoughts during perceptual motor performance.

Analysis of Verbal Reports

We have used think-aloud protocols to elicit sport participants' thoughts while the participants solved static game situations (French et al., 1996; McPherson, 1999a; McPherson & Thomas, 1989). These situation interviews provide insight into *what knowledge content and response selection processes may be part of the participants' knowledge base*. We have also conducted think-aloud or retrospective protocols with sport participants during actual competition (French, Werner, & Rink, Taylor, et al., 1996; McPherson, 1993a, 1999b, 2000; McPherson & Thomas, 1989; Nevett, 1996, Nevett & French, 1997). Verbal protocols during competition provide insight into *what knowledge is accessed during competition and how the knowledge is used to mediate performance.* In these studies, we have audiotaped participants' verbal utterances verbatim. We used principles from Chi's (1997) verbal analysis method to develop sport-specific methods to analyze the verbal reports (see French et al., 1996; Nevett & French, 1997; McPherson, 1993a, 1994, 1999a, 1999b, 2000).

The verbal transcripts in each study were segmented into units of information for analysis based on the question being addressed and the natural tactics of the sport under investigation. In the following sections, we present more detail concerning the analysis of verbal reports during sport competition, memory adaptations that have been discovered, and changes in the knowledge base that seem to underlie improvement in response-selection processes during competition. Although we have conducted studies in other sports, we chose to present data from studies that elicit players' thoughts during competition in baseball and tennis because we have the best representation of data across increasing levels of age and expertise in these sports.

DEVELOPMENTAL TRENDS IN KNOWLEDGE ACCESSED DURING COMPETITION

Knowledge Content

Verbal reports can be segmented at a micro level of analysis. Segmenting the reports at a micro level of analysis provides an understanding of what knowledge is attended to during performance and accessed to the level of working memory. Micro-level analysis identifies words accessed by participants in terms of sport concepts (i.e., conditions, actions, goals, do, regulatory). Concepts are defined as a unit of information (word or proposition) about response selection in the context of a game. To date, five major concepts have been used to examine knowledge content: goal, condition, action, do, and regulatory concepts. See Table 1 for examples of goal, condition, and action concepts commonly reported in tennis. Several exemplars of verbatim concepts accessed by youth and adult (college varsity women and professional) experts and novices during tennis competition are included as well. The concepts presented in Table 1 are labeled according to the age and expertise of the participant who generated the concept. For example, a concept labeled ME was generated by an adult male professional (expert), WE by a female college varsity player, YE by a youth expert, WN by an adult female novice, and YN by a youth novice.

> Five major concepts have been used to examine knowledge content: goal, condition, action, do, and regulatory.

Goal concepts are units of information that refer to the game's goal structure such as winning the game or keeping the ball in play. *Condition concepts* are units of information that specify when or under what circumstances to apply the action or pattern of actions usually to achieve a goal. Conditions may be explicit cues available in the game environment (i.e., in tennis, wind conditions, prior shot, opponent's position on the court) or implicit cues available through tactical analysis and/or retrieval from long-term memory (i.e., in tennis, opponent strength or weakness, player's own strength or weakness, opponent tendencies). In baseball, condition concepts might include explicit environmental cues such as the base runner's position or implicit conditions such as a pitcher's or batter's tendencies. *Actions* are units of information that refer to the action selected or patterns of actions that may produce goal-related changes in the context of a game. Action statements might refer to a motor execution statement such as hitting a forehand in tennis down the line or a perceptual response statement such as watching a pitcher's release point or racket contact point (see Table 1 for other examples in tennis).

Individuals may generate regulatory or do concepts regarding an action concept. *Regulation statements* refer to the player's ability to carry out an action. For example, I was trying to hit a

TABLE 1
Some Possible Subconcept Categories and Sample Verbal Reports for Immediate Recall Interviews Between Points

Goal Concepts	Condition Concepts	Action Concepts	Regulatory Concepts
Execution of the skill Get first serve in ME Get the first return in ME To practice my net game WE Go for a winner YE Keep it simple—don't try to hit a winner MN To get it over net MN Hitting it MN To try and return it WN To run faster WN Get my ball in YN **Keeping the ball in play** Keep the balls in play here WE Getting the ball back WN **Preventing opponent's aggressive shots** Keep him deep ME Keep him in a rally ME Keep him on the defensive ME Get him to move ME Not let him attack ME So it doesn't give her a chance to come in WE To pull him out of the court YE Keep him back MN Make him move MN Move him around MN **Win the point or game** Win two in a row WE Winning this point WE To get that point WN Win this game YE	**Their weakness** feel a little slow out here ME I'm starting to get tired MN **Their strength** I'm just better YN but I hit the ball harder WN I still have the edge on him ME I'm anticipating where this guy's gonna serve that's what is good for me ME **Their prior shot** hit an unforced error off the forehand side ME tried to come up on a stupid shot ME **Their position** caught me up short on the court ME while I was at the net YE I wasn't in a position to hit it back MN we were both at the net MN **Their tendencies** don't take those first serves for granted MN I'm trying to hit too many winners MN another good first serve to the backhand ME I lost my serves again MN **Opponent's weakness** make him run around it he'll over hit it ME his lobs have not been too accurate today MN **Their weakness** three balls in play and he is making a lot of mistakes ME **Opponent's strength** Boy, that ball comes in pretty fast WN she is serving well WE **Opponent's prior shot** he hit a short return to me MN he hit a good serve MN he hit an unforced error ME **Opponent's position** He played up at the net MN **Opponent's tendencies** He usually goes to my backhand ME He can surprise me sometimes MN I know he attacks and loves to play the net ME he's been serving and volleying a lot ME **Shot type** if we have a really long rally WE until I get the short shot WE keep my shots deep WE hit lobs and hit them high because he can't swing around them MN **Game status** I'm one up on him ME I'm down a point MN I guess the games tied up WN **Environment** since the wind is blowing to the right WE how cold it is right now WN wind is still blowing WN	**Serve** second serve him a little more pace ME I'm going to serve it to her backhand WE get the serve to her forehand side WE get the serve wide to his forehand YE **Ground stroke** hit it with more pace and get it deep to the baseline WE hit it over his head YN **Return of serve** hit a nice solid return just down, more down the middle towards the left side of the net WE **Lob** I lobbed him YE to lob her WE **Approach Shot** played smart chip to his backhand ME **Drop shot** tried a drop shot ME hit a couple of drop shots YE **Passing shot** try to pass her WE **Visual act** watch the ball WE **Position move** start coming in ME maybe to charge the net YE	**Serve** got the first serve in ME good aggressive serve but to the wrong place ME I kept it real low at his feet ME I did serve successfully WM **Ground stroke** I didn't hit it WN how I swung and missed that next ball WN **Position move** I think I moved my feet well there ME moved in ME **Do Concepts** **Serve** Keeping my body down WE continuing to follow through on my serves WN trying to slow down my serve MN got to bend my knees MN **Ground stroke** extending my arms WE stepping into the ball WN I have to step forward more WN I didn't hold my racket right MN **Volley** snapping my wrist back and stepping into it YE

Note: YE = youth experts; YN = youth novices; WE = women collegiate varsity; WN = women collegiate beginners; ME = male professionals; MN = male collegiate beginners volley cross-court, but hit it in the net. Regulatory concepts involve monitoring whether an action was successful or not. *Do concepts* refer to units of information that describe how to perform the action. For example, in tennis, I am going to brush up on the ball to put more top spin on my serve. Do and regulatory concepts would be classified as similar to the possible sub-concept categories for actions in Table 1.

Developmental Trends in Knowledge Content Accessed During Tennis Competition

In a series of studies (McPherson, 1999b, 2000; McPherson, French, & Kernodle, 2002; McPherson & Thomas, 1989), McPherson and colleagues compared retrospective verbal reports of three age levels (10-11 years old, 12-13 years old, adults) of experts and novices between points in tennis. Youth experts of both ages were highly skilled with tournament experience. Adult experts were members of a university varsity team or professionals. In each study, participants played a set or modified set (Nielsen & McPherson, 2001) versus an opponent of equal ability. After each point during play, participants immediately walked to the end of the court and verbalized their responses into an audiotape recorder. The prompt for the verbal reports was consistent in each study: "What were you thinking about while playing that point?" Transcripts were analyzed for differences in knowledge content. Table 2 provides a very brief description of the differences in condition, action, regulatory, and do concepts accessed by youth and adult experts and novices during tennis competition.

There were large differences in the conditions and actions accessed during competition. Youth and adult novices often attended to irrelevant conditions in the current environment. Most of the conditions attended to by youth and women novices were related to some characteristic of their own play. Rarely did novices attend to their opponent, environmental conditions, and player position on the court. In addition, these novices did not use encoding and retrieval strategies to diagnose opponents' strengths, weaknesses, or tendencies as competition progressed. In contrast, some male novices were using rudimentary strategies to monitor conditions such as their own and opponents' prior shots, tendencies, or weaknesses. However, their diagnoses were inappropriate or weak. Adult experts accessed a variety of conditions including the current context regarding themselves and their opponent (i.e., player positions on court, prior shots) and profiles about their performance as the competition progressed (strengths, weaknesses, specific shot or serve types, and certain environmental conditions). Furthermore, adult experts built condition profiles of opponent strengths, weaknesses, and tendencies that were checked for accuracy and modified when appropriate. Among adult experts, male professionals with more years of competitive experience generated more conditions than female varsity players did. Youth experts accessed a greater variety and more detailed conditions than novices. However, youth experts, unlike adult experts, did not build profiles of opponents' strengths, weaknesses, or tendencies.

Youth and women novices accessed limited actions, primarily serves and ground strokes. Youth experts accessed a frequency of actions similar to that of women experts, and both groups generated fewer actions than male professionals did. However, women varsity and male professional experts' actions were much more specific and detailed (i.e., included features such as topspin, slice, location on court, speed). As the variety of skill options increases with age and expertise, the actions that may be used by the player and/or the opponent may increase as well and facilitate the development of detail of actions within the knowledge base. Youth experts also accessed actions within the context of current play. Adult experts often accessed potential future actions in addition to current actions.

Youth novices rarely mentioned the success or failure (i.e., regulatory concepts) of response selection or motor execution. Women novices did produce some regulation of skill execution,

TABLE 2
Developmental Trends in Concept Content and Structure for Verbal Reports During Tennis Competition.

KNOWLEDGE CONTENT	YOUTH AND ADULT NOVICES	YOUTH EXPERTS	ADULT EXPERTS
Goal Concepts	Male novices more total than youth or women, goals regarding themselves and execution generated most often, variety similar for all novices	Similar total to women experts, variety similar for all experts, goals regarding themselves and execution generated most often	Males generated more than women, goals regarding themselves and execution generated most often, variety similar for all experts
Condition Concepts	Limited diagnosis, unrelated or inappropriate environmental features or game events, males more appropriate conditions with one feature than women or youth	Few attempts to diagnosis or build condition profiles, rarely elaborated on conditions that produced their action, less variety and total than adult experts, most conditions about the current context	Attended to and interpreted pertinent conditions and formed profiles; conditions were updated, checked, and modified continuously; specific environmental features and long-term memory conditions accessed
Action Concepts	Limited and weak (Youth more than collegiate), actions consisted primarily of ground strokes and serves	Similar total and variety of actions for all experts; most actions with one feature; actions and based on current context	Males more total actions than women, variety of actions similar for all experts; actions with two or more features; planned actions based on current context and long-term memory condition profiles such as shot tactics, own, and opponent's characteristics
Regulatory Concepts	Minimal for youth; women some regulation but poor labels or corrections	Some monitoring of motor executions; less than adult experts	Regulated response selections and response executions; more regulations than youth experts
Do Concepts	Limited, weak error detection about failed motor execution	Youth generated more than male experts, used to enhance current or failed motor executions	Women used do concepts to enhance planned or failed motor executions and/or to overcome an environmental constraint
Profiles	Action plan profiles nonexistent or weak	Action plan profiles	Action plan and current event profiles
Reactive statements	When reactive, did not employ profiles	When reactive, employed action plan profiles	When reactive, adult experts employed action plan and current event profiles

but did not access verbal labels for correction of the error (i.e., do concepts). Adult experts often regulated both response selection and motor execution and had verbal labels for correction (i.e., do). Youth experts did regulate some motor actions but not to the same extent as adult experts.

Interestingly, only one male professional stated a do concept. Professionals seemed to diagnose events for future reference via condition profiles by interpreting why failed or successful actions occurred and modifying their plans according to their strengths, weaknesses, and tendencies. Professionals may consider motor execution problems as temporary and view the need to access do or "how to do the skill" statements only when motor problems are consistent or when modifying some aspect of their motor execution.

Developmental Trends in Knowledge Content Accessed in Baseball

Nevett (1996) and Nevett and French (1997) conducted think-aloud verbal protocols with skilled shortstops ages 8, 10, 12, and 15-16. Players were asked to verbalize thoughts between pitches to batters as the individual played defense during a regularly scheduled game. Players wore a small fanny pack attached at the waist that carried a microcassette audiorecorder. This arrangement allowed players to have freedom of movement during the games. Games were also videotaped so that the game context for protocols could be determined. Table 3 provides a brief description of the developmental trends in knowledge content. As in tennis, the very young (more novice) players accessed a very high percentage of irrelevant concepts. Many of these concepts were baseball related; however, they were irrelevant to the game situation. Eight-year-old players seemed to access different patterns of irrelevant information. To illustrate the point, examples of two 8-year-old players are provided below:

Game situation—Leadoff batter of the game, no runners on base, 6 pitches to the batter, who hits the ball to the player, who makes a fielding error. Prompt to player prior to pitch– What are you thinking? "*He is going to hit it real far.*" Second pitch and prompt repeated. "*Oh, I will probably get him out.*" Third pitch, prompt repeated. "*Um, and then I will keep going and try and get the other runners out. But mostly I am concerned about this batter.*" Fourth pitch and prompt repeated. "*He is a good hitter.*" Fifth pitch and prompt repeated. "*He is going to knock, knock somebody in.*" Sixth pitch. "*Oh, I guess he'll probably get out somehow.*" The ball was hit to the player, who made a fielding error. When asked retrospectively what he was thinking during the play, he said, "*Uh, I was a little confused.*"

Throughout this 8-year-old's protocols, not just this example, he talked about (accessed to working memory) runners on base when there were no runners on base at all. He seemed to just access baseball terms and language that had nothing to do with the actual circumstances in the game situation. Thus, he had baseball knowledge but did not access the knowledge critical to the current game situation. This is an example of a poor representation of the problem that seems to be characteristic of beginners in general.

Game situation—One out, no runners on base. Four pitches to batter, who is safe at first. Prior to first pitch, prompt, What are you thinking? "*Um, he's my worst enemy. My Mom doesn't like him, he's mean. Hey, batter, swing.*" Second pitch and prompt repeated. "*Hey, batter, hey batter, swing.*" Third pitch and prompt repeated. "*Oh my God, I hope he strikes out. Hey batter, hey batter, swing.*" Fourth pitch and prompt repeated. "*I hope he strikes out, and if he doesn't, then get him out. Hey batter, hey batter, swing.*"

This 8-year-old focused most of his thought on chatter statements and his dislike of the other player. Notice that at no time did he keep track of critical game conditions such as the number of balls and strikes or the number of outs, nor did he plan what he might execute if the ball were hit to his area of responsibilities. As a group, most 8 year olds seemed to be learn-

TABLE 3
Developmental Trends in Knowledge Content Accessed by 8-, 10-, 12-, and 15- to 16-Year-Old Highly Skilled Shortstops.

	Age of experts			
	8	9	12	15-16 YEAR OLDS
All concepts	Many irrelevant concepts	Less irrelevant concepts	Few irrelevant concepts	Few irrelevant concepts
Conditions	Mostly egocentric; if the ball is hit to me. Ignored base runners. Occasionally monitored pitch count. Occasionally monitored outs	Mostly egocentric. Beginning to monitor base runners. Monitored pitch count and outs	Egocentric and specific location of potential hit. Monitored base runners. Monitored pitch count and outs	More specific and detailed related to locations of potential hits. Consistently monitored base runners. Monitored pitch count and outs
Actions	One simple plan	One simple plan	More than one action plan	More than one plan, detailed chunks of special plays and alternatives actions when ball hit in play
Special plays (bunts, steals, pick off plays)	Did not access	Very few, bunts and steals	Bunt and steal plays	Many more bunt, steal, and pickoff plays
Motivational statements	Almost none	Accessed a few	20% of all concepts motivational to teammates	25% of all concepts motivational to teammates

TABLE 4
Developmental Trends for Sport-Specific Strategies Accessed During Defensive Baseball Performance.

	Age of experts			
	8	10	12	15-16 YEAR OLDS
Planning	Rarely planned what to do if the ball was hit to them	Fifty percent of players planned a response if the ball was hit to them.	Plans for special plays, did not consistently plan for specific actions once was ball hit in play	Plans for special plays and more than one specific action once ball was hit in play
Rehearsal	Rehearsed one plan	Content rehearsed was more advanced	More advanced content and plans, more mature rehearsal	More advanced content and plans, mature rehearsal
Modifying plans based on new information	No modification, did not plan most of time	Few modifications of their first plan	Beginning to modify plans	More consistently modified and updated plans
Predictions	Some predictions, all irrelevant	Both low-level and high-level predictions	High-level predictions	Greater number of high-level predictions

ing baseball terms and "what the game was about," but they could not translate this knowledge into meaningful action plans during competition.

The conditions accessed by younger shortstops (8 and 10) were mostly egocentric (i.e., if the ball comes to me, if it is hit to me). By 12 years old, players were beginning to build more specific conditions related to different locations on the field (i.e., if it is hit to my right, if it is hit up the middle, if it is hit to the left side). These conditions were often linked to specific action sequences for specific locations of hits. Interestingly, the younger shortstops (8 and 10) rarely attended to base runners. Older players consistently monitored base runners. All shortstops monitored the pitch count and outs on occasion; however, older players did so much more consistently during each at bat. The 15- and 16-year-old shortstops were the only age group who used encoding and retrieval strategies to remember the prior location of a batter's previous hit or to assess the pitcher's effectiveness in the game or used foul balls as a cue to modify player position on the field during an at bat.

The actions accessed by younger shortstops were simple, one alternative (throw to first, second, or third base; tag a base). With increasing age and expertise, more action-plan alternatives were accessed for a given game situation. At 10 years of age, bunts and steals were introduced in game play. Few 10-year-olds accessed plans for bunts and steals (special plays). Frequently, the 12-year-old shortstops accessed only these special plays as plans and did not access other plans for what to do should the ball be hit in their vicinity. Only the 15- to 16-year-old shortstops accessed both special plays and more than one alternative action plan should the ball be hit in play in their area.

Other Aspects of Knowledge Content

One other trend in the content of the verbal reports merits attention. In McPherson's studies, emotional statements, both positive and negative, were coded as reactive statements (see Table 2). Novices of both age groups in tennis verbalized many more reactive statements. A similar trend was found for novices in badminton (French, Werner, Rink, et al., 1996). Youth and collegiate experts uttered fewer reactive statements than novices did and seemed to focus their attention and cognitive resources on the task at hand. Furthermore, adult male novices and professionals generated similar amounts of reactive statements; however, they also remained focused on events related to successful performance (McPherson et. al. 2002).

In Nevett (1996), the older shortstops (12 and 15-16 years) frequently verbalized aloud or talked to teammates regularly during game play. Most of the discussion between teammates was focused on tactical plans, position moves, and motivational comments to teammates. In many cases, the motivational statements were linked to cues for concentration or to statements concerning how to perform the skill. Taken together, these studies suggest that highly skilled players learn to access the thoughts that most benefit performance. In tennis, these thoughts centered on knowledge content related to response selection and execution. In baseball, a team game, the thoughts included knowledge content and communication among teammates that facilitated team performance.

The adult male novices and professionals studied generated similar amounts of reactive statements.

Sport-Specific Processes

A number of sport-specific processes have been also been documented in the verbal reports of sport performers during competition by segmenting the verbal reports to identify specific processes. Among these sport-specific processes include planning, rehearsal, specialized encoding and retrieval strategies used to modify or update plans, self-regulation strategies to monitor ongoing response execution and response selection. Table 4 provides a brief summary of changes in sport-specific strategies used by 8-, 10-, 12-, and 15- to 16-year-old highly skilled shortstops during defensive performance in baseball games (Nevett & French, 1987). For readers to understand how we determined these processes from the verbal protocols, an example of the protocol for a 15- to 16-year-old shortstop is presented and coded below.

- 15-year-old. Game situation – double play, runner on first, no outs, 3 pitches to batter. Prompt. What are you thinking? *"Ok, right-handed batter. Second (baseman) is going to cover second, if he steals. If it's up the middle, we'll do a double play."* First pitch, foul ball. Prompt repeated. *"He tried to bunt, move up some, John (third baseman), in case he tries again."* Second pitch. Prompt. *"We'll do a double play, up the middle, and if it's in the outfield, they'll throw it to cut off at third."* (third pitch pop up to first base).

In this protocol, we coded the total number of solutions accessed if the ball was hit to the player. In this case, there were two, a double play prior to the first and third pitch. We counted the total number of action plans (solutions plus special plays such as bunts or steals). In this case there were two solutions for the double play and three special plays, one steal before the first pitch, one bunt before the second pitch, and one outfield play before the third pitch. He repeated the plan for the double play (rehearsal) prior to the third pitch, so we coded 1 for rehearsed solution. He updated or accessed new or different special plays or solutions after the first pitch, so we coded the total number of updated action sequences as 2, 1 for concern for a bunt and 1 for the outfield play. These codings of the protocols allowed us to generate dependent variables for the total number of solutions (plans), total number of rehearsal of plans after the first pitch, and total number of updated or new plans after the first pitch. From these dependent variables, we could track the developmental trends.

Younger baseball experts did not generate a plan in most baseball situations. With increasing age, years of competition, and expertise, players more consistently generated multiple action plans and either rehearsed the plans or modified and updated plans based on changing environmental conditions. In many cases, younger baseball experts may have used a strategy such as rehearsal; however, the knowledge content rehearsed was very poor in comparison to older experts. For example, several younger players continuously rehearsed the same plan prior to every pitch, (i.e., "throw to third, throw to third"). In the same game situation, an older expert might access and rehearse plans for a bunt, steal, and what to do if the ball was hit to a variety of locations. In other cases, even 8-year-old experts generated predictions; however, almost all of these predictions were irrelevant to the current game situation. The accuracy and sophistication of predictions improved with increasing age and expertise.

Similar developmental trends in sport-specific strategies are reported for tennis (McPherson, 1994, 1999b, 2000). For example, novices of both age groups rarely exhibited any sport-specific strategy. Like baseball players, if a strategy was accessed, the knowledge content contained within the strategy was poor. Older experts in tennis used much more sophisticated strategies than did younger experts.

Action Plan and Current Event Profiles

At a macro level of analysis of verbal transcripts, larger memory profiles become apparent. Adult experts exhibited two types of larger memory profiles that are used during competition to mediate response selection. McPherson (1999a, 1999b) suggested that the *action plan profile* consisted of rule-governed prototypes stored in long-term memory that consisted of matching certain current conditions with their appropriate actions or position moves. Action plan profiles may reflect experts' current skill level (younger experts generated fewer total tactical actions compared to adult experts), style of play (in tennis, some experts said they were a baseline player rather than a net player), and/or desires (in tennis, some experts said they preferred net play). Younger baseball players and novice tennis players (youth and adult) exhibited weak or less advanced action plan profiles. Both adult tennis experts and older baseball experts were more consistent in terms of solutions regarding the best possible tactics. Most tennis and baseball motor-skill drills promote action plan profiles as these drills are designed to promote decision making based exclusively on current environmental conditions.

Current event profiles are structures used to keep active relevant information with potential past, current, and possible future events. McPherson (1999a, 1999b) suggests that current event profiles consist of tactical scripts that guide the constant building and modifying of pertinent concepts to monitor during the competitive event. Building the current event profile is much like weaving together a story composed of your opponent, yourself, the game events, environmental advantages or disadvantages, etc. to form a current representation of competition (McPherson, 1999a, 1999b).

The current event profile is built from past competition or previous experiences prior to the immediate competition and from specialized monitoring, encoding, and retrieval processes used to collect information throughout the current competition. These specialized encoding and retrieval processes are used to "fill in the blanks" to build a profile to assess their opponents strengths, weaknesses, and tendencies as well as their own. Below are some examples of protocols from adult experts that illustrate the building of current event profiles.

- "It's so shaky, that passing shot of his, an easy one. I should have made it. God, should have just done the same thing. I want to try and keep the ball deeper, so that he doesn't come in and I know he attacks and loves to play at the net, so I'm going to try and keep him behind." Male adult expert

This example shows that this adult expert was interpreting and monitoring shot selections of himself and his opponent, past accounts of his own behavior and that of his opponent, as well as shot-and-serve tactics. From monitoring these conditions across competition, he could build a profile of his opponent's tendencies as well as a profile to assess his own tactics and skill execution to counter his opponent's tendencies.

- "Um, I'm just rallying cross-courts, and so, just kind of getting the feel for the wind because it's pretty windy, so I am just kind of playing with it in this first game and then I'll probably have my game plan." Woman college varsity player

This protocol provides an example of developing a game plan by depending on her interpretation of the wind conditions. She was monitoring the effects of the wind on her own performance and that of her opponent during the first game. She suggests that she will make adjustments in her game plan based on her own assessment of how the wind is affecting play.

- "Uh, I was thinking about getting the ball to his forehand, I did that. Got another cheap point. I think his forehand is a little looser on the return of serve." Male adult expert

These examples show that adult experts were basing some actions on assessments of their opponent's weaknesses that had been monitored early in the match and/or point to form a profile of opponent weaknesses.

Novices and younger experts seemed to be "in the moment" and did not access past events or information from previous competitions. Seldom did novices use encoding and retrieval strategies to gather information to form profiles of opponent strengths, weaknesses, or tendencies. Below are some quotes from novices and youth experts:

- "I was thinking that she ran awfully hard up there to get that ball" Woman novice.

- "The wind is blowing really hard" Woman novice.

- "I was trying to get the serve wide to his forehand to pull him out of the court" Youth expert.

- "I was just going to play out the point and maybe charge the net" Youth expert.

The novices and youth experts reported thoughts that were related to immediate performance and did not exhibit characteristics of gathering information during competition to develop profiles of opponents and/or interpretation of events during competition.

Novices (both adult and youth) did not show evidence of current event profiles. From a developmental perspective, the youth experts in tennis and younger players in baseball (8, 10, 12) also were not building current event profiles. Only the older experts in tennis and baseball were building current event profiles during competition and using these profiles to modify and adjust responses to changing conditions as competition progressed.

Situation Interviews

Differences among levels of expertise are also evident in verbal protocols of participants' solutions to static game situations (situation interviews; see French, Nevett, et al., 1996 for baseball; McPherson, 1993a, 1999b for tennis). McPherson (1999b) and McPherson and Thomas (1989) conducted interviews to elicit problem representations of experts and novices of various ages and levels of expertise in six tennis-game scenarios. The more highly skilled the participant, the more highly developed the knowledge content, sport-specific strategies, action plans, and current event profiles. Furthermore, verbal reports were also collected during competition for these same subjects (McPherson, 1999b, McPherson & Thomas, 1989). McPherson (1999b) suggests that if individuals are not able to access sophisticated knowledge representations in static problem-solving tasks, they do not access sophisticated knowledge representations during competition that has added demands of time and motor execution constraints. Thus, individuals cannot talk a good game in static problems if they are not somehow trained during competition to create adaptations in memory structures that facilitate performance during competition.

IMPLICATIONS FOR INSTRUCTION

Much more research is needed to understand how to facilitate learning of response-selection processes and practice activities that facilitate development of the knowledge base. Most motor learning texts superficially cover knowledge or tactical elements of sport performance. Most instructional texts or approaches emphasize activities to teach tactics that facilitate development of action plan profiles. Very few individuals have even thought about how we might practice or teach skills related to current event profiles. We are only beginning to understand the various memory structures that more elite performers use to mediate performance. Many questions remain unanswered and await further research.

> The more highly skilled the participant, the more highly developed the knowledge content, sport- specific strategies, action plans, and current event profiles.

In our earlier work, we used observational instruments to study motor skill execution and decision making during performance (French & Thomas, 1987; McPherson & French, 1991; McPherson & Thomas, 1989). Based on this preliminary observational data with young subjects, we suggested that knowledge and decision making processes may develop faster than motor skills. These statements are clearly wrong. Knowledge development and response-selection processes develop much more slowly. If one reviews Tables 2-4, it is apparent that some children have participated in sport for 5 to 7 years yet still exhibit very poor knowledge representations. In fact, we have been surprised that adult novices and youth experts exhibit such poor knowledge representations. Many teachers and coaches assume that students, of any age, can be instructed in the rules of the game and basic tactics and immediately be able to translate this knowledge into effective tactical performance. Our studies clearly show this just does not happen without much practice of the tactics over a period of time, longer than typical units of instruction in physical education.

Preliminary evidence suggests that the focus of practice activities may influence *what outcomes are learned*. For example, French and Thomas (1987, Exp. 2) found that child expert and novice basketball players improved basketball knowledge (paper pencil test) and decision making during games, but did not improve basketball skills, when team practices primarily focused practice on tactics and organization for competitive play. In baseball (French, Spurgeon, & Nevett, 1995; French, Nevett et al. 1996), just the reverse was found. Players were primarily developing motor skills and exhibited poor knowledge structures. Team practice sessions in baseball were focused on skill execution, and players rarely had the opportunity to practice decisions.

Short-term instructional studies (badminton: French, Werner, Rink et al. 1996; French, Werner, Taylor, Hussey, & Jones, 1996; tennis: McPherson, 1994; McPherson & French, 1991) provide some preliminary evidence that the focus of practice and instruction affects what aspects of performance are acquired. Furthermore, these studies indicate that different instructional approaches produce different knowledge representations that affect how performers view and interpret game events. All of these studies were relatively short-term (3 weeks, 6 weeks, one semester of instruction), and the actual knowledge representations exhibited by the learners were not highly developed. The participants still exhibited a novice knowledge representation. The following are a few suggestions for coaches and teachers that may elicit the types of cognitive processing necessary to facilitate development of both the action plan and current event profiles. At the moment, these represent some of our "best guess approaches."

- Reward and reinforce good decision making, not just good skill execution. Stop play and point out good decision making when it occurs during games and practices.

- Design practice activities that force individuals to make decisions in the context of game play. Often in youth baseball, we have observed infield practice to consist of the coach's hitting balls to different players who are told which base to throw to. Unless players practice with runners on base and different pitch counts and number of outs, they are unlikely to develop visual search strategies to monitor runners and develop encoding and retrieval strategies to keep track of pertinent information to use in planning future responses, anticipating actions, and modifying plans based on changing game conditions. In tennis, practice of skill technique often becomes hitting back and forth to a partner. To develop tactics, individuals need to hit away from the opponent, monitor where the opponent is on the court, and select different shots based on opponent strengths and weaknesses.

- Repeat practice of decision choices hundreds of times. Be patient and say the same thing over and over again. We have observed adult coaches displaying anger at children for children's not remembering a tactic during games, yet the coach never really had the child practice the tactic during team practice.

- During practice ask players what they are thinking. Stop play at various points to ask what players are thinking. Just asking questions can focus attention toward thinking about tactics. Listen to what information they are attending to. What environmental cues do they attend to? Do they plan? Are they paying attention and remembering what tactics their opponent may be using during play? A coach can gain useful information about what individuals are processing and what they are not processing and can give feedback.

- Have players develop profiles of their opponents after a period of play or after watching a videotape of an opponent. What were their opponent's strengths and weaknesses? How could players capitalize on "my game" to counter the opponents' strengths? How could players protect "my own weaknesses" against this opponent?

- Establish a mentoring program to pair players who use more advanced tactics with players who use less advanced tactics to work on diagnosing an opponent and/or team.

FUTURE RESEARCH

Three areas for future research seem salient. First, more research is needed to access the amount of deliberate practice that is appropriate at a given age or skill level. To date, some studies have suggested that the amount of deliberate practice engaged in by participants increases with age whereas other studies suggest that the amount of deliberate practice is related to skill level. Additional retrospective studies of the practice histories of adult performers may provide additional insight into the amount of deliberate practice at given ages that is conducive to long-term motivation and that reduces the risk of overuse injury. Other studies need to be conducted that tap into the motivation and social support systems at given ages that influence the decision to practice and the intensity of the practice. Research in these areas would provide a better understanding of how much practice is appropriate and the environment and/or social support systems that are necessary for sustained motivation to practice.

A second area for future research involves continuing to describe changes in the development or learning of cognitive and motor processes that underlie performance in a variety of sports. Over the past 20 years, much research has focused on the mechanisms that underlie adult performance; however, there are fewer studies involving children or adolescents. Much more work is needed to examine how these mechanisms (knowledge base, cognitive processes, motor patterns) change across extended periods of practice during childhood and adolescence.

The previous suggestions for future research largely involve description and can be conducted in a cross-sectional manner or using retrospective reports from adults. The third area for future research involves the much more challenging task of attempting to uncover *what types of practice activities* produce *what types of improvement in response selection and execution.* Longitudinal studies and instructional/learning studies seem necessary to begin to understand how different types of practice produce certain types of improvement in response selection and motor execution at different ages. Describing practice activities and documenting the current state of response selection and motor execution performance at given ages may provide some useful clues into what types of practice produce certain response-selection and motor-execution outcomes. Short-term and long-term experimental studies that manipulate practice activities and monitor cognitive and motor outcomes are needed to fully understand developmental and learning mechanisms that underlie changes in performance associated with specific types of practice.

The primary purpose of youth sport programs is not to produce elite athletes. Just as in other domains, understanding the gifted and talented individuals in the athletic domain provides a window into the constraints, obstacles, and activities that are necessary for elite performance. Many of the problems and controversial issues in youth sport are in some way related to an overemphasis by adults on winning, unrealistic performance expectations of children, and practice activities that undermine motivation or do not produce the desired learning outcome. Thus, research that informs the public about the conditions and constraints that are related to the development of elite performance in adulthood can provide practical information that parents and coaches can use to guide the choices of all children, regardless of the level of competence.

References

Abernethy, B., Burgess-Limerick, R., & Parks, S. (1994). Contrasting approaches to the study of motor expertise. *Quest, 46,* 186-198.

Abernethy, B., Thomas, J. R., & Thomas, K. T. (1993). Strategies for improving understanding of motor expertise (or mistakes we have made and things we have learned!!). In J. L. Starkes & F. Allard (Eds.), *Cognitive issues in motor expertise* (pp. 317-356). Amsterdam: Elsevier Science Publishers.

Anderson, J. R. (1982). Acquisition of cognitive skill. *Psychological Review, 89,* 369-406.

Barnsley, R. H., & Thompson, A. H. (1988). Birthdate and success in minor hockey: The key to the NHL. *Canadian Journal of Behavioral Science, 20,* 167-176.

Bloom, B. S. (Ed.). (1985). *Developing talent in young people.* New York: Ballantine.

Boucher, J. L., & Mutimer, B. T. P. (1994). The relative age phenomenon in sport: A replication and extension with ice-hockey players. *Research Quarterly for Exercise and Sport, 65,* 377-381.

Chi, M. T. H. (1997). Quantifying qualitative analyses of verbal data: A practical guide. *The Journal of the Learning Sciences, 6,* 271-315.

Chi, M. T. H., Feltovich, P. J., & Glaser, R. (1981). Categorization and representation of physics problems by experts and novices. *Cognitive Science, 4,* 121-152.

Dudink, A. (1994). Birth date and sporting success. *Nature, 368,* 592.

Ericsson, K. A. (Ed.). (1996). *The road to excellence: The acquisition of expert performance in the arts and sciences, sports, and games.* Mahwah, NJ: Erlbaum.

Ericsson, K. A., Krampe, R. T., & Tesche-Romer, C. (1993). The role of deliberate practice in the acquisition of expert performance. *Psychological Review, 100,* 363-406.

Ericsson, K. A., & Simon, H. A. (1993). *Protocol analysis: Verbal reports as data.* Cambridge, MA: The MIT Press.

Fleishman, E. A. (1972). On the relation between abilities, learning, and human performance. *American Psychologist, 27,* 1017-1032.

French, K. E., & McPherson, S. L. (1999). Adaptations in response selection processes used during sport competition with increasing age and expertise. *International Journal of Sport Psychology, 30,* 173-193.

French, K. E., Nevett, M. E., Spurgeon, J. H., Graham, K. G., Rink, J. E., & McPherson, S. L. (1996). Knowledge representation and problem solution in expert and novice youth baseball players. *Research Quarterly for Exercise and Sport, 67,* 386-395.

French, K. E., Spurgeon, J. H., & Nevett, M. E. (1995). Expert-novice differences in cognitive and skill execution components in youth baseball performance. *Research Quarterly for Exercise and Sport, 66,* 194-201.

French, K. E., Spurgeon, J. H., & Nevett, M. E. (2002). *Body size and form of highly and low skilled youth baseball players ages 7-12 years.* Manuscript in preparation [Data currently available upon request].

French, K. E., & Thomas, J. R. (1987). The relation of knowledge development to children's basketball performance. *Journal of Sport Psychology, 9,* 15-32,

French, K. E., Werner, P. H., Rink, J. E., Taylor, K., Hussey, K. (1996). The effects of a 3-week unit of tactical, skill, or combined tactical and skill instruction on badminton performance of ninth-grade students. *Journal of Teaching in Physical Education, 15,* 418-438.

French, K. E., Werner, P. H., Taylor, K., Hussey, K., & Jones, J. (1996). The effects of a 6-week unit of tactical, skill, or combined tactical and skill instruction on badminton performance of ninth-grade students. *Journal of Teaching in Physical Education, 15,* 439-463.

Haywood, K. M. (1993). *Life span motor development.* Champaign, IL: Human Kinetics.

Helsen, W. F., Starkes, J. L., & Hodges, N. J. (1998). Team sports and the theory of deliberate practice. *Journal of Sport & Exercise Psychology, 20,* 12-34.

Lehman, H. C. (1953). *Age and achievement.* Princeton, NJ: Princeton University Press.

Malina, R. M. (1994). Physical growth and biological maturation of young athletes. *Exercise and sport science reviews, 22,* 389-433.

Malina, R. M. (1996). The young athlete: Biological growth and maturation in a biocultural context. In F. L. Smoll & R. E. Smith (Eds.), *Children and youth in sport* (pp. 161-186). Dubuque, IA: Brown & Benchmark.

Malina, R. M., Bouchard, C., Shoup, R. F., & Lariviere, G. (1982). Age, family size and birth order in Montreal Olympic athletes. In J. E. L. Carter (Ed.), *Physical structure of Olympic athletes, Part I* (pp.13-24). Basel, Switzerland: S Karger.

McPherson, S. L. (1993a). Knowledge representation and decision making in sport. In J. L. Starkes & F. Allard (Eds.), *Cognitive issues in motor expertise* (pp. 159-188). Amsterdam: Elsevier Science Publishers.

McPherson, S. L. (1993b). The influence of player experience on problem solving during batting preparation in baseball. *Journal of Sport & Exercise Psychology, 15,* 304-325.

McPherson, S. L. (1994). The development of sport expertise: Mapping the tactical domain. *Quest, 46,* 223-240.

McPherson, S. L. (1999a). Expert-novice differences in performance skills and problem representations of youth and adults during tennis competition. *Research Quarterly for Exercise and Sport, 70,* 233-251.

McPherson, S. L. (1999b). Tactical differences in problem representations and solutions in collegiate varsity and beginner women tennis players. *Research Quarterly for Exercise and Sport, 70,* 369-384.

McPherson, S. L. (2000). Expert-novice differences in planning strategies during collegiate singles tennis competition. *Journal of Sport & Exercise Psychology, 22,* 39-62.

McPherson, S. L., & French, K. E. (1991). Changes in cognitive strategy and motor skill in tennis. *Journal of Sport & Exercise Psychology, 13,* 26-41.

McPherson, S. L., French, K. E., & Kernodle, M. W. (2002, April). *Problem representation of male entry-level professionals and novices during singles tennis competition.* Paper presented at the annual conference of the American Alliance for Health, Physical Education, Recreation, and Dance, San Diego, CA.

McPherson, S. L., & Thomas, J. R. (1989). Relation of knowledge and performance in boys' tennis: Age and expertise. *Journal of Experimental Child Psychology, 48,* 190-211.

Nevett, M. E. (1996). *Knowledge content, sport-specific strategies, and other self-talk accesed by shortstops of different ages during defensive game play.* Unpublished doctoral dissertation, University of South Carolina, Columbia.

Nevett, M. E., & French, K. E. (1997). The development of sport-specific planning, rehearsal, and updating of plans during defensive youth baseball game performance. *Research Quarterly for Exercise and Sport, 68,* 203-214.

Nielson, T. M., & McPherson, S. L. (2001). Response selection and execution skills of professional and beginners during singles tennis competition. *Perceptual and Motor Skills, 93,* 541-555.

Salthouse, T. (1996). The processing-speed theory of adult age differences in cognition. *Psychological Review, 103,* 403-428.

Schultz, R., & Curnow, C. (1988). Peak performance and age among superathletes: Track and field, swimming, baseball, tennis, and golf. *Journal of Gerontology: Psychological Sciences, 43,* 113-120.

Schultz, R., Musa, D., Staszewski, J., & Siegler, R. S. (1994). The relationship between age and Major League Baseball performance: Implications for development. *Psychology of Aging, 9,* 274-286.

Spurgeon, J. H., & Giese, W. K. (1980). Physique of world-class female basketball players. *Scandinavian Journal of Sport Science, 2,* 63-69.

Spurgeon, J. H., Spurgeon, N. L., & Giese, W. K. (1984). Physique of world-class female swimmers. *Scandinavian Journal of Sport Sciences, 1,* 11-14.

Starkes, J. L., & Allard, F. (1993). *Cognitive issues in motor expertise.* Amsterdam: Elsevier Science.

Starkes, J. L., Deakin, J. M., Allard, F., Hodges, N. J., Hayes, A. (1996). Deliberate practice in sports: What is it anyway? In K. A. Ericsson (Ed.), *The road to excellence: The acquisition of oc expert performance in the arts and sciences, sports and games.* (pp 81-106). Mahwah, NJ: Lawrence Erlbaum Associates.

Tenenbaum, G. (Ed.) (1999). The development of expertise in sport: Nature and nurture [Special issue]. *International Journal of Sport Psychology, 30,* 2.

Thompson, A. H., Barnsley, R. H., & Stebelsky, G. (1991). Born to play ball: The relative age effect and Major League Baseball. *Sociology of Sport Journal, 8,* 146-151.

CHAPTER SIXTEEN

Psychosocial Factors and Disability: Effects of Physical Activity and Sport

Martin E. Block • Liza-Marie Griebenauw • Shirley Brodeur

An ever-increasing number of children have some sort of disability. For example, a recent report from the U.S. Department of Education's National Center for Educational Statistics (1999) showed that about 13% of public school children from birth through age 21 were enrolled in special education programs, a 3% increase compared to statistics compiled in 1981. Most public school children with disabilities were born with their disability (congenital, such as learning disabilities or mental retardation) or acquired their disability very early in their life (such as a traumatic brain injury).

> Unlike children, the vast majority of adults with disabilities acquired their disability or later in life.

There has been a similar increase in the number of adults who have disabilities (Ostir, Carlson, Black, Rudkin, Goodwin, & Markides, 1999). Disability data compiled by the U.S. Bureau of the Census (McNeil, 1997) found that 20.6% of the general population, or about 54 million people, live with some level of disability, with about half that number (26 million) experiencing severe disability that significantly affects one or more activities of daily living. Unlike children, the majority of adults with disabilities acquired their disability or later in life (e.g., heart disease, back problems, arthritis, adult-onset diabetes, spinal cord injuries).

Whether one is born with a disability or acquires one later in life, the actual disability is only one small part of the problems one faces. Many suggest that social and psychological problems associated with having a disability can be just as important as how an individual deals with the disability itself (Best, Carpignano, Sirvis, & Bigge, 1991; J. M. Dunn, 1997; Groce, 1999; Henderson & Bryan, 1997; Marks, 1999; Sherrill, 1998). For example, Storey and Horner (1991) showed that attitudes toward a person with a disability determined types of treatment and, in turn, that treatment helped shape the person's personality (i.e., positive or negative reaction to disability). In addition, negative societal attitudes including avoidance, pity, segregation, stereotyping, prejudice, discrimination, and overprotection often produced devastating effects for the person with disabilities such as negative self-perceptions and poor educational and rehabilitation outcomes (Blinde & McClung, 1997; Henderson & Bryan, 1997; Sherrill, 1986). In addition to these external factors, internal factors such as how well the individual adapts, copes, masters, and adjusts to the disability will affect the success of education and rehabilitation (J. M. Dunn, 1997; Sherrill, 1998). As Best et al. (1991) noted:

Each person with a disability has two major psychological tasks: to understand the nature of his/her disability and become as independent as possible . . . Those who learn healthy, adaptive attitudes at an early age are more likely to have the necessary skills to meet conflicts and stresses with confidence and self-assurance. (p. 105)

One thing that is clear from the literature is that physical activity and sport can have a positive effect on how society views an individual with disabilities and how that individual views him- or herself (Blinde & McClung, 1997; P. R. E. Crocker, 1993; Hutzler & Bar-Eli, 1993; Sherrill, 1986). As noted by Hutzler and Bar-Eli in their review of the extant literature,

in general, the studies reviewed reveal significant positive changes. . . in the self-concept of disabled populations after sports participation sessions. In addition, significantly higher values of self-concept were observed among disabled people regularly participating in sports compared with sedentary, inactive individuals. (p. 221)

What is not as clear is how or why physical activity and sport positively affect self-concept (P. R. E. Crocker, 1993; Sherrill, 1997). Specifically, much of the research on the psychological impact of physical activity and sport participation on individuals with disabilities has been descriptive and atheoretical (P. R. E. Crocker; Porretta & Moore, 1997; Sherrill, 1986). Although we have learned that physical activity and sport can help individuals with disabilities develop greater self-esteem (Blinde & McClung, 1997; Campbell & Jones, 1994; Patrick, 1986), perceived competence (S. L. Gibbons & Bushakra, 1989; Greenwood, Dzewaltowski, & French, 1990; Riggen & Ulrich, 1993), and social acceptance and competence (Dykens & Cohen, 1996; S. L. Gibbons & Bushakra, 1989; Williams & Kolkka, 1998), the underlying mechanisms that contribute to these positive changes have yet to be fully explored.

Noting this limitation in the research, Sherrill (1996, 1998) applied various theories (e.g. competence motivation and social learning theory) to the study of psychological aspects of physical activity and sport in individuals with disabilities. Similarly, P. R. E. Crocker (1993) applied transactional stress, attribution theory, and the theory of planned behavior to existing literature. The purpose of this chapter is to expand on this application of theory to the research on psychological aspects of physical activity and sport for individuals with disabilities and to apply these theories to implications for practice and future research. First, we will present a definition of disability and discuss how this definition itself affects the psychology of individuals with disabilities. This will be followed by a review of psychosocial factors related to physical activity participation among individuals with disabilities. This will be followed by an examination of how social factors influence self-perception in individuals with disabilities. Finally, we will conclude this chapter with recommendations for future research regarding how psychosocial factors interact with physical activity to affect self-esteem in individuals with disabilities as well as implications for practitioners who work with individuals with disabilities in physical activity settings.

Definition of Disability

There have been many definitions of the term *disability*. Although a definition itself seems rather unimportant, many suggest that the definition of disability and the subsequent attitudes attached to the definition affect how a person with a disability perceives him- or herself as well as how society perceives this individual (Marks, 1999; Sherrill, 1997, 1998; World Health Organization [WHO], 2000). As Sherrill (1998) noted, "of the many variables that might affect self-esteem of individuals with disabilities, terminology is among the most powerful" (p. 258).

Some have suggested that labeling and the subsequent placement in a special education classroom can lead to stigma and lower self-esteem (Karagiannis, Stainback, & Stainback, 1996; Lipsky & Gartner, 1997; Reynolds, 1991). Although research does not directly associate stigma with labeling (Reynolds), there is enough anecdotal evidence to suggest that many children and parents perceive that labeling has negative consequences. Labeling has become such an issue that some parents avoid having their children tested altogether so as to prevent them from receiving a label. Other parents lobby against certain labels they feel have greater stigma (e.g., mental retardation) over other labels that they feel have less stigma (e.g., learning disability). Several years ago, Hobbs (1975) suggested that schools de-emphasize labeling children and focus more on services children require to reach their maximum development. This concept has been echoed in the recent inclusion movement (Karagiannis et al., 1996; Lipsky & Gartner, 1997).

Definition of the World Health Organization

Several years ago, the World Health Organization (WHO) attempted to create a standardized definition for disability and other commonly used words related to disability (Wood, 1981; see Table 1). In 1981, the organization's definition had three separate classifications and definitions: impairment, disability, and handicap. Note that each term and associated definition conveys subtly different meanings. The term *impairment* was simply a descriptor relating the fact that a person has a particular limitation, challenge, disadvantage, or inconvenience. For example, a person who is missing a leg clearly has an impairment as defined above. However, if this impairment does not affect this person's ability to work, live, take care of him- or herself, and play, then the person does not have a disability. As defined by WHO, a person with an

TABLE 1
World Heath Organization Definition of a Disability (1981 v. 2000 definitions)

Term	Definition
Impairment (1981)	Any loss or abnormality of psychological, physiological, or anatomical structure or function.
Impairment (2000)	Same as above.
Disability (1981)	Any restriction or lack of ability to perform an activity in the manner or within the range considered normal for a human being as a result of an impairment.
Activity (2000)	Nature and extent of functioning at the level of the person (e.g., taking care of oneself, maintaining a job). Activities may be limited in nature, duration, and/or quality.
Handicap (1981)	Any disadvantage to an individual resulting from an impairment or disability that limited or prevented the fulfillment of a role that was normal (depending on age, sex, social and cultural factors) for that individual.
Participation (2000)	Nature and extent of a person's involvement in life situations in relation to impairment, activities, health conditions, and contextual factors (e.g., participating in community activities, obtaining a driver's license).

impairment would have a disability only if the impairment led to loss or reduction of functional ability. Continuing with the example, if the person with one leg was unable to work or take care of him- or herself because of complications related to the impairment, then the person would be considered disabled. Still, with certain accommodations (e.g., adapted equipment, assistance), this person could find work, live in the community, and lead a relatively normal life. Now, if this person with a disability cannot be accommodated and is unable to lead a relatively normal life, then the person would be considered *handicapped*. The person might be considered handicapped due to the severity of the impairment (e.g., Lou Gehrig's Disease, which prevents the person from doing almost anything, even with accommodations and assistance). However, what if the person has limitations (impairment) that lead to functional limitations (disability), yet the impairment and disability could be accommodated so that the person could lead a relatively normal life? What if this person is nevertheless denied the right to work, to live in the community, or to participate in sports and recreational activities because of prejudice and stereotyping? This person, not due to the impairment but due to society's reactions to the impairment, is now handicapped. This is what WHO was trying to convey in their definition (Marks, 1999; Wood, 1981; WHO, 2000).

WHO recently proposed modifications to their original classification system (WHO, 2000; see Table 1). Although still in draft form, the definition of impairment is the same as in the previous edition. However, the term *disability* has been replaced with the term *activity*, and the term *handicap* has been replaced with the term *participation*. These new terms more clearly convey the notion that a person can be restricted from participation in typical activities by social and environmental factors (e.g., social attitudes, architectural characteristics, legal and social structures), which in turn affect the quality of one's life.

Social Construct of Disability

As noted above, WHO emphasized the influence of society on the construct of disability. Some have argued that societal influences are the most important factor in defining disability (Asch, 1984; Marks, 1999). As Marks proposed: "The social model . . . locates disability not in an impaired or malfunctioning body, but in an excluding and oppressive social environment" (p. 79). Restrictions in participation due to disability such as a person in a wheelchair not being able to enter a building, a person who is deaf being unable to understand a movie, or a qualified person who is blind being unable to gain employment are a product of social and environmental barriers rather than the disability itself. Clearly, in these examples, individuals would not be restricted if the building were accessible, if the movie had closed-captioning, or if the employer were not prejudiced.

Sherrill (1997) noted that societal influences shape how individuals construct their disability and, in turn, how they perceive themselves. In other words, self-esteem of individuals with disabilities is shaped by attitudes, beliefs, practices, and policies of society. She further noted that these social influences can occur at the macro (governmental, societal, cultural) and micro (individual interactions) levels. For example, Casey Martin, the golfer who sued and recently won a ruling against the PGA tour so that he can ride a golf cart to accommodate his disability (Lane, 2001), has to deal with social influences at the macro level (federal law, how the law is interpreted, the PGA tour, how society feels about the issue) and the micro level (how players whom he interacts with daily feel about him, what they say to him, and how they treat him).

Many specific social factors can affect whether or not individuals with disabilities are included or excluded from participation in various activities, which, in turn, will affect development of self-esteem. These factors often begin with simple ambivalence towards a person with a disability, but ambivalence can lead to stereotyping, stigmatization, and even prejudice and discrimination (Sherrill, 1997). We review each of these social factors that can affect self-esteem.

Ambivalence. Many people simply do not know what to make of individuals with disabilities. They immediately see differences, and these differences make them feel uncomfortable. Some have argued that most people without disabilities are not necessarily prejudiced against people with disabilities; rather, they just feel uncomfortable and even fearful when they are around someone who is so different from themselves (Henderson & Bryan, 1997; Katz, 1981). The lack of factual information about a particular disability leads to further anxiety and withdrawal. Thus, people without disabilities have mixed feelings when they encounter a person with disabilities. On the one hand, they are probably curious about the person and wonder what is the exact nature of their disability, when did it happen, how did it happen, do they need help doing things, do they work, etc. On the other hand, there is a sense of uneasiness and even fear. Is the person's condition contagious, is the person in pain, is the person depressed with his or her condition, what if I was in a wheelchair someday, should I offer to help the person, should I stare at the person or look away, should I talk to the person, etc.? Because of this ambivalence, individuals with disabilities are often ignored and disregarded; that, in turn, can affect how an individual feels about him- or herself (Sherrill, 1997). If, for example, peers never ask a teenager with a disability to go to watch a ball game or go the park to toss a ball around, then this teenager may begin to develop a lower self-esteem.

Stereotyping. Part of ambivalence is not knowing much about a person with a disability. With more direct interactions, persons without disabilities usually begin to see the person with a disability as an individual with many unique characteristics. On the other hand, without direct contact, some persons without disabilities may begin to form their own opinions about a person with a disability. These opinions may be based on a global view of disability. Unfortunately, one of the most prominent social factors that affects an individual's self-esteem is that many people simply lump all people with disabilities into one category (Sherrill, 1997). Rather than looking at each person's unique characteristics, abilities, and disabilities, many people simply focus on one prominent attribute—a person's disability (Asch, 1984). This stereotyping or generalization is often an unfair characterization of the person with a disability. Not all people in wheelchairs are alike, not all people with developmental disabilities are alike, and not all people who are blind are alike.

> Just like racial, ethnic, and gender minorities, self-concepts of people with disabilities may be shaped by their minority status.

Some stereotyping goes further and casts all people with disabilities into a single minority category. For example, some people without disabilities assume that Special Olympics serves all people with disabilities. The fact is that Special Olympics is for individuals with mental retardation whereas other sports organizations serve other disability groups (e.g., United States Association for Blind Athletes, United States Cerebral Palsy Athletic Association, American Athletic Association of the Deaf). Sherrill (1997) noted that this type of stereotyping is an antecedent to the development of social minority status. Uniqueness is devalued, and one shared attribute (i.e., having a disability) is accentuated. Just as with racial, ethnic, and gender minorities, the self-concept of people with disabilities may be shaped by their minority status (Marks, 1999).

Stigmatization. Stereotyping a person with a disability can lead to stigmatization. *Stigmatization* can be defined as discriminatory or unfair treatment towards a person or group of persons believed to be different (J. Crocker & Major, 1989; Sherrill, 1997). Stigmatization results when the focus is on one attribute of an individual or group of individuals that is perceived to be different or undesirable, with a shortcoming or a handicap. For example, stigmatization may result if the owner of a bowling alley does not allow a group of adults with developmental disabilities to join a local bowling league simply because they have mental retardation. The owner focused on the single attribute of mental retardation and viewed this attribute (and the adults with this attribute) negatively, resulting in their stigmatization. Sherrill (1997) noted that three factors contribute to stigmatization: (a) fear of the person who is different, (b) association of differences with inferiority and/or danger, and (c) belief that the person is not quite human and thus does not require the same level of respect given to others. Sherrill (1986) reported that most athletes with disabilities whom she interviewed described examples of stigmatization that led to discrimination such as different treatment, being ignored and subjected to lower expectations. Similarly, Blinde and McCallister (1998) found that children with physical disabilities were stigmatized by their general physical education teachers, which resulted in the children's being excused from physical education, sitting out and watching, keeping score, and being given lesser roles in activities. Interestingly, Taub, Blinde, and Greer (1999) found that selected male college students believed that participation in sport and physical activity, demonstration of physical skill, and a fit, healthy body may be effective ways of dispelling stigmatization and creating an alternative, positive view of individuals with disabilities.

Prejudice and discrimination. Stigmatization of persons with disabilities can lead to prejudice and discrimination. Prejudice (inaccurate beliefs or attitudes) and discrimination (acting on these inaccurate beliefs or attitudes) can prevent individuals with disabilities from participating in sports (Sherrill, 1997). For example, a 9-year-old with cerebral palsy (he used a walker) was not allowed to play in his community soccer program (discrimination) because the commissioner of the league felt that he would be a danger to others (prejudice). The courts determined that under the Americans with Disabilities Act, the league had to make reasonable accommodations for this child (Boyd, 1999). Similarly, the National Collegiate Athletic Association (NCAA) was forced to change its policies (discrimination) towards athletes with learning disabilities. The NCAA had not accepted high school coursework that was specifically designed for students with learning disabilities because the NCAA thought those courses were not rigorous enough (prejudice) (U. S. Department of Justice [USDOJ], 2000).

In summary, it appears that persons with disabilities often face ambivalence, stereotyping, stigmatization, and discrimination. These negative reactions to disability are directed more towards misconceptions and misinformation about disability rather than a true reflection of any one individual's abilities and attributes. Fortunately, positive examples of people with disabilities such as the actor Christopher Reeve and favorable images of Special Olympians and Paralympians are slowly changing these misconceptions. In addition, federal laws such as the Americans with Disabilities Act are preventing wholesale discrimination. Nevertheless, stereotyping and discrimination still exist, and these negative reactions towards an individual with a disability affect how that person feels about him- or herself.

PSYCHOSOCIAL FACTORS RELATED TO PHYSICAL ACTIVITY PARTICIPATION AMONG INDIVIDUALS WITH DISABILITIES

Although it is clear that many individuals with disabilities are victims of negative reactions such as stereotyping and discrimination, what is less clear is how psychosocial factors affect their physical activity and participation. We address several topics on which research has examined psychosocial factors and physical activity participation including attitudes towards individuals with disabilities, attributional patterns, affective responses to stress, and self-perceptions. Note that the effects these psychosocial factors have on physical activity involvement are affected by several personal factors related to individuals with disabilities such as physical appearance; type of disability; when the disability occurred (congenital or acquired); gender; cognitive functioning of the individual; individual temperament; parent, peer, and teacher reactions to the disability; support systems; and goals and aspirations of the individual

At this point, only some of the effects of exercise on adults with disabilities are understood.

(Best et al., 1991; J. M. Dunn, 1997; Sherrill, 1997, 1998). Space does not permit a review of these personal factors, but see Sherrill for an excellent review.

Motivation to Participate

Several studies considered issues such as motivation to participate, encouragement to participate, attitudes to try, and the impact of stigmatization on participation by individuals with disabilities (e.g., Cooper, 1984; Cooper, Sherrill, & Marshall, 1985; P. R. E. Crocker & Bouffard, 1992; Rose, Larkin, & Berger, 1997). For example, Cooper found elite adult athletes with cerebral palsy cited the following reasons for choosing to participate in sport: challenge of competition, fun and enjoyment, love of sport, fitness and health, knowledge and skill about sport, contribution to the team, and team sport atmosphere. P. R. E. Crocker and Bouffard found the evaluation of such benefits of learning and demonstrating skill, seeking social approval, and health and fitness improvements as being important in physical activity by adults with various physical disabilities. Cooper et al. found that rankings of the six attitude subdomains were similar in that adult athletes are considerably more positive toward aesthetic, social, fitness, and catharsis subdomains than toward thrill and long, hard training subdomains. Findings of these studies are consistent with research using nondisabled populations.

On the other hand, Hopper (1986) suggested that athletes with disabilities are less influenced by socializing agents and actually follow a different pattern of sport socialization compared to athletes without disabilities. Hopper attempted to explain four variables that represented socialization via sport (athletic aspiration, educational aspiration, occupational aspiration, and self-esteem) through general demographics such as age, age of onset of disability, severity of disability, and socializing demographics such as personnel commitment, duration of participation, sport-role socialization, and financial outlay. Subjects included 87 athletes aged 16 to 60 with disabilities ranging from partial quadriplegia (limited upper body movement, no leg movement) to bilateral lower limb amputations. Results showed that younger athletes with disabilities who had participated in sport for a long time and who spent a great deal of money on their sport participation had higher athletic and educational aspirations. Interestingly, none of the demographic variables were found to significantly influence occupational aspirations. Finally, different variables influenced self-esteem. Athletes with disabilities who had participated the longest in sport, acquired their disability later in life, and had a less severe disability had greater self-esteem. It appears then that younger athletes who are less disabled and who have participated in sport for a long time are more motivated to continue to participate in sport, but unlike athletes without disabilities, typical socializing factors such as personnel commitment and sport-role socialization have less of an influence on sport participation.

Attitudes Toward Individuals With Disabilities

As noted earlier in this chapter, many have argued that individuals with disabilities face negative perceptions by others including stigmatization, stereotyping, and prejudice (Hedrick, 1985; Sherrill, 1986). Some recent research suggests negative perceptions of physical education teachers can have extremely negative effects on participation in and attitudes toward physical activity among individuals with disabilities (Blinde & McCallister, 1998; Goodwin & Watkinson, 2000). As reported earlier, Blinde and McCallister's interviews revealed that many children with physical disabilities had severe restrictions placed on their participation (e.g., retrieving balls, keeping score) whereas others were excluded from physical education altogether by their physical education teacher. Although their findings were not as bleak, Goodwin and Watkinson similarly found the children with physical disabilities they interviewed often had "bad days" in physical education in which they faced restricted participation, felt socially isolated, and questioned their competence. Clearly, stigmatization, stereotyping, and prejudice can have devastating consequences for children with disabilities in both their ability to develop motor and sport competence and the effect such restricted practices have on self-esteem. It is important that further research be conducted to determine if such prejudice exists in recreation and sport contexts and whether or not such prejudice limits an individual's attempts to engage in sport and exercise.

There is quite a large body of work which has examined physical education teachers' attitudes (Block & Rizzo, 1995; Rizzo & Vispoel, 1991; Rizzo & Wright, 1988; Theodorakis, Bagiatis, & Goudas, 1995), youth coaches' attitudes (Kozub & Porretta, 1998; Rizzo, Bishop, & Tobar, 1997), and aquatics instructors' attitudes (Conatser, Block, & Lepore, 2000) towards working with children with disabilities in general physical education and sport settings. The vast majority of these studies used Ajzen and Fishbein's (1980) theory of reasoned action, which suggests that attitudes and social norms predict intentions and, in turn, that intentions predict actual behaviors. In these studies above, attitudes and intentions towards working with students with disabilities were measured, which then allowed the prediction of actual behavior (i.e., whether or not a teacher or coach would actually work with a child with a disability).

Physical educators and coaches who receive training and gain experience working with individuals with disabilities have more favorable attitudes.

Results showed that attitudes of physical educators and coaches varied based on a number of student and personal characteristics. For example, more favorable attitudes were related to student characteristics such as type of disability (more favorable attitudes towards including a child with a learning disability v. a child with a behavior disorder) and degree of disability (more favorable towards children with mild to moderate disabilities v. students with severe disabilities). Teacher or coach characteristics that appeared to improve attitudes towards working with children with disabilities included perceived competence, training, and experience.

It appears then that physical educators and coaches may have stereotypical and stigmatizing views of their students and athletes with disabilities. These views can lead to prejudice such as limiting and even excluding participation. However, it appears that physical educators and coaches who receive training, gain experience, and perceive that they have the skills necessary to successfully work with individuals with disabilities have more favorable attitudes towards working with these individuals. In turn, people with disabilities exposed to coaches with more favorable attitudes will have greater opportunities to participate in physical education, develop competence, and improve self-esteem.

Attributional Patterns

Some research suggests that individuals with disabilities are more likely to attribute their success in a given activity to luck or ease of an activity. Moreover, this research suggests individuals with disabilities often perceive failure as due to lack of ability (Cooley & Ayres, 1988; Rogers & Saklofske, 1985). Attribution theory holds that causal attributions used to explain success or failure outcomes influence future achievement-oriented experiences. It focuses on the relationship between event outcomes (winning/losing, success/failure), beliefs about causes of these outcomes, and emotions and behaviors that follow (Horn, 1987; Sherrill, 1986).

There are generally four major causes that people use for explaining success and failure outcomes: (a) ability, (b) effort, (c) task difficulty, and (d) luck (P. R. E. Crocker, 1993; Weiner, 1972). These causes and others can be classified into the three dimensions of stability (stable v. unstable), controllability (control or lack of control), and locus of control (internal v. external), the latter two dimensions primarily affecting emotional experiences. Internal attributions (e.g., ability, effort) following success lead to positive emotions such as joy, accomplishment, and pride as well as positive future success expectations. External attributions (e.g., luck, poor facilities) may lead to negative emotions and low success expectancies. According to P. R. E. Crocker (1993) and Sherrill (1998), attributions have important consequences for individuals with disabilities. Persons with a severe disability or low skills, or both, tend to use different attributions than do able-bodied peers and thus need different motivational approaches. Persons with severe disabilities tend to explain their success and failure more by luck and task difficulty than by ability and effort, indicating external locus of control. Low-skilled children with disabilities often attribute poor performance to a lack of innate ability (Cooley & Ayres, 1988; Hedrick, 1985; Rogers & Saklofske, 1985), possibly because of feeling inferior. In their study with adults with cerebral palsy, Dummer, Ewing, Habeck, and Overton (1987) reported that winners were more likely than losers to use internal attributions, but interestingly, winners also used external attributions. Dummer et al. also found differences between the characteristics of athletes with cerebral palsy and their level of disability—the greater the level of disability, the more the athlete used external, unstable attributions to explain performing well.

Among students with cognitive disabilities, the ability to understand and use attributions to improve their performance may be delayed or stagnated. Sherrill (1998) recommended attributional training to ameliorate the problem. Attributional training encourages students to talk through tasks and provide stories, mottos, and poems about effort and self-control; and it encourages visualization of the self expending effort and succeeding. Judgments that teachers and other significant others make about characteristics are as important as self-judgments because they influence the way students are subsequently treated (see section on self-fulfilling prophecy).

Affective and Coping Responses to Stress

Lazarus and Folkman (1984) and Sherrill (1986) hold that stress occurs as a result of a dynamic transaction between the person and the environment and that coping is generated in response to the evaluation of environment and/or internal demands plus the evaluation of coping options (P. R. E. Crocker, 1993). Termed the *transactional model* (Lazarus & Folkman, 1984), stressful appraisals of harm/loss (already done), threat (the potential for harm/loss), and challenge (referring to the opportunity for growth, mastery, or gain) may arise. One would speculate that individuals with disabilities would have greater levels of stress in their lives; however, sport participation could be a positive way for these individuals to cope with their stress and, in turn. enhance self-regard. For example, in their study of individuals with physical disabilities, P. R. E. Crocker and Bouffard (1992) found that perceived challenge was characterized by high levels of positive affect and low levels of negative affect. In addition, positive affect was positively associated with task value and opportunity to learn skills and demonstrate competence, improve fitness and health, and seek social approval. These findings are consistent with Sherrill's (1986) investigation of participation motives for athletes with cerebral palsy. The important feature is that individuals with physical disabilities perceive appraisals and use coping strategies similar to those reported in studies of nondisabled individuals (P. R. E. Crocker, 1993; P. R. E. Crocker & Bouffard, 1992).

There are many ways an individual with disabilities can deal with the social factors of stereotyping, stigmatization, and prejudice that often accompany having a disability and that can cause stress. Some ways of dealing with these social factors can be negative themselves such as denial, anger, perception of oneself as a victim, inner self-contempt, or simply giving up. These types of negative reactions to a disability are more common in individuals with acquired disabilities (e.g., spinal cord injury or macular degeneration), especially in the first several months after the person acquires the disability (Best et al., 1991). Negative feelings also can occur in children born with disabilities such as children with mental retardation, cerebral

TABLE 2

Reynell's (1973) Developmental Model for Psychological Reaction to a Disability

Age	Reaction and Probable Causes
Preschool	Confusion, fear, loss of typical childhood play due to parental attitudes, early hospitalizations, separation from parents during treatment, and limitations on physical activity (e.g., "Why can't I play at home?" "Why can't I run around and play?" "Why can't my mommy stay with me?")
Childhood	Entrance into school that presents lower perceived competence as the child with disabilities compares him- or herself to peers and begins to be more aware of differences (e.g., "I cannot keep up with my peers on the playground").
Early adolescence	Presents social isolation as social relationships, peer acceptance, and friendship become important (e.g., "No one calls me to come over and play"; "I can't play on sports teams with my friends").
Late adolescence	Brings new reactions as the adolescent with disabilities sees limitations young adulthood affecting independence (e.g., "I can't drive a car." "Will I be able to go to college?" "Will I be able to live on my own?").
Adulthood	New reactions that continue to focus on independence but with a greater focus on the need for assistance ("Who will take care of me?" "How much will it cost me to have someone take care of me?" "What living arrangements must I make to ensure support?").

palsy, and learning disabilities, particularly at critical stages in development when these children realize that they cannot do certain things (Sherrill, 1998).

Reynell (1973) detailed a developmental model outlining when psychological reactions to a disability are most prominent at various points throughout a person's lifespan (see Table 2). Reynell hypothesized that reactions of individuals with disabilities would vary depending on the person's age and what is important to the individual at that particular age. For example, preschoolers focus on family interactions and play, both of which may be limited or altered due to hospitalizations and therapy sessions, whereas adults focus on independent living issues such as getting a job and living on their own. It is easy to see how a person with a disability could easily form negative reactions at various stages of life.

Fortunately, negative reactions are often replaced with more positive reactions through the course of habilitation (those with congenital disabilities) or rehabilitation (those with acquired disabilities). As Best et al. (1991) noted, individuals with disabilities have to learn how to (a) accept their limitations, (b) learn how to make accurate appraisals of their strengths and abilities, and (c) apply as much effort as possible to what can rather than what cannot be achieved. In addition, individuals with disabilities should not punish themselves or use their disability as an excuse. Most individuals with disabilities eventually are able to face the reality of their disability, yet focus on their abilities and achievable goals.

Self-Perceptions

Competence motivation theory (Harter, 1978) holds that the more competent individuals feel with regard to a specific activity, the more their interest will be sustained and the more likely they will persist in the activity. This, then, leads to higher achievement in that particular domain (academic, social, physical). Perceived competence is defined as a person's judgment of his or her ability or adequacy in specific domains such as academic competence, athletic competence, physical appearance, social acceptance, and behavioral conduct (Weiss & Ebbeck, 1996). Harter stated that individuals' need to feel competent is fulfilled through mastery, which results in positive feelings and subsequent motivation toward further achievement. Therefore, an individual will likely participate in those activities in which he or she feels competent.

> The more competent individuals feel about a specific activity, the more it will hold their interest over a period of time.

This theory has been implemented in several studies of perceived competence with children and adolescents with mental and physical disabilities. Although results are mixed, results tend to show children with disabilities who perform poorly in physical education or sport settings have lower perceived athletic and physical competence compared to peers without disabilities. For example, Van Rossum and Vermeer (1990) compared a motor remedial teaching (MRT) group with a non-motor remedial teaching (non MRT) group in children, ages 8 to 12 years. They found that the MRT group was less successful in motor skills, and they also scored lower in perceived physical competence. Similarly, Rose et al. (1997) showed that children (ages 8-12 years) with poor motor coordination generally have lower perceived competence in the athletic, social, physical appearance, and scholastic domains. Also, Lintunen, Heikinaro-Johansson, and Sherrill (1995) compared perceived competence of adolescents (13-18 years) with orthopedic and various health impairments to that of nondisabled children and nondisabled athletes. Students with disabilities perceived fitness levels similar to that of nondisabled peers, but significantly lower than that of athletes without disabilities.

J. L. K. Dunn and Watkinson (1994) examined affects of awkwardness on the perceived competence of children in grades 3 through 6 with particular emphasis on the relationship between severity of awkwardness and perceived competence. They found children in grade 3 demonstrated decreasing perceptions of physical competence as awkwardness increased, whereas those in grades 5 and 6 demonstrated an increase in perceptions of physical competence as degree of awkwardness increased. It was thus concluded that the presence of difficulties do not necessarily lead to perceptions of incompetence. Older awkward children may implement other strategies to maintain positive perceptions of competence and motivation.

Other studies showed no relationship between perceived competence and disability. For example, Silon and Harter (1985) found no difference between self-evaluations of children (ages 9-12 years) attending mainstream classes and those attending self-contained classes. This could be due to the children's using their own classmates as a reference group rather than children without disabilities (see later section on social comparisons). When studying a group of children with mild mental retardation, Yun and Ulrich (1997) reported a weak correlation between perceived and actual competence in young children aged 7 to 10 years and only moderate relationships in youth aged 11 to 12 years. They suggested that children with mental retardation may not be cognitively mature enough to adequately evaluate their competence in a particular domain.

On the positive side, there is growing evidence for increased perceived competence in children and adults with disabilities as a result of successful participation in sport and physical activity. For example, S. L. Gibbons and Bushakra (1989) investigated the effects of physical activity on perceived competence in children with mental retardation aged 9-13 years participating in Special Olympics. Participation in physical activities had a positive effect on and improved perceived competence of these participants. Similarly, Hedrick (1985) found adolescents with physical disabilities (age 10-18 years) who participated in wheelchair tennis showed improved perceived competence.

Although perceived competence refers to domain-specific self-judgment, self-esteem refers to a more global self-perception—the extent to which one believes that one is worthy, capable, and satisfied with oneself as a person. Several studies have examined a wide variety of physical activities and their effect on the self-esteem of diverse groups of individuals with disabilities. Studies include wheelchair sport (Campbell & Jones, 1994; Greenwood et al., 1990; Hedrick, 1985; Henschen, Horvat, & French, 1984; Monnazzi, 1982; Patrick, 1986), outdoor adventure sports activities (MacKinnon et al., 1995; McAvoy, Schatz, Stuts, Schleien, & Lais, 1989; Shiraishi, Tanaka, Goto, Kami, & Hiraoka, 1999), and multiple sports (Hanrahan, Grove, & Lockwood, 1990). Other studies focused on specific disabilities such as persons with cerebral palsy (Dummer et al., 1987; Sherrill, Hinson, Gench, & Low, 1990), persons with mental retardation (Lawrence & Winscel, 1973; White & Zientek, 1991; Wright & Cowden, 1986), athletes with visual impairment (Gilstrap & Sherrill, 1989; Hanrahan et al., 1990), as well as a combination of persons with disabilities (Craft & Hogan, 1986; King, Shultz, Steel, Gilpin, & Cathers,1993; Valliant, Bezzubyh, Daley, & Asu, 1985). In general, these studies reveal significant positive changes in self-concept of individuals with disabilities after sports participation sessions. The intensity and duration of these changes in self-concept varied from study to study based on the type of disability, initial level of self-concept, duration of study, and whether or not the participants continued to participate in physical activities.

How Social Factors Influence Self-Perceptions

One of the best ways individuals with disabilities can begin to accept their disability and in turn enhance their self-esteem is through successful participation in physical activity and sport (Hutzler & Bar-Eli, 1993; Sherrill, 1998). The relationship between physical activity or sport participation and self-esteem is well established in the literature (see Fox, 1997). What is less clear are underlying mechanisms that result in such positive changes in self-esteem. In other words, what is it about physical activity and sport participation that seems to have such a positive effect on the self-esteem of individuals with disabilities? We suggest that there are at least three possible explanations for the positive effects of physical activity on self-esteem of individuals with disabilities: reflected appraisals, social comparisons, and self-fulfilling prophecies.

Reflected Appraisals

One possible explanation of the relationship between social factors, physical activity, and self-esteem is the phenomenon known as *reflected appraisal* or *looking-glass self* in the development of self-esteem (Weiss & Ebbeck, 1996). In this view, one's self-concept is based on how one thinks that others view one. If a person believes that others view him or her in high regard, then this view posits that the person should have a higher self-concept. In contrast, if a person believes that others view him or her in low regard, then the person should have a lower self-concept (J. Crocker & Major, 1989). Because individuals with disabilities are often stigmatized and discriminated against (held in negative regard; e.g., Blinde & McCallister, 1998; Goodwin & Watkinson, 2000), their self-concept is likely to be lower than that of individuals without disabilities who are not stigmatized. Note that reflected appraisals can come from immediate interactions with significant others (e.g., peers, parents, teachers, employers) or from the larger cultural environment (e.g., seeing negative images of peoples with disabilities on television, in movies, or in books). For example, several studies showed that children who were labeled as clumsy or poorly coordinated had negative experiences in physical activity programs and, in turn, had lower self-esteem (Cantell, Smyth, & Ahonen, 1994; J. L.K. Dunn & Watkinson, 1994; Rose et al., 1997; Shaw, Levine, & Belfer, 1982). Reported negative experiences in physical activity could have been influenced by teachers and peers treating these students differently. In fact, some research has shown people with disabilities are aware that they are often viewed negatively (Avillion, 1986, F. X. Gibbons, 1981; Scott, 1969).

Fortunately, the looking-glass self phenomenon can also have a positive effect on individuals with disabilities. Research shows that positive experiences in physical activity allow individuals with disabilities to show others (and themselves) that they are competent in activities such as camping (Briery & Rabian, 1999), wheelchair sports (Campbell & Jones, 1994; Patrick, 1986; Taub et al., 1999), and Special Olympics (Dykens & Cohen, 1986; S. L. Gibbons & Bushakra, 1989; Wright & Cowden, 1986) had a positive effect on self-esteem in individuals with disabilities. For example, Taub and her colleagues determined whether college students with physical disabilities felt that sport participation affected how others perceived them. Results showed that college males with physical disabilities believed that participation in sport and the appearance of a physically fit body countered stereotyping and stigmatization associated with a physical disability. In other words, respondents felt they were less stigmatized by able-bodied observers and friends as a result of participation in sport and physical activity (note that Taub et al. did not interview able-bodied observers to confirm attitude change towards individuals with disabilities).

Social Comparisons

One of the most common ways people determine their self-worth is through comparisons with peers. Social comparison is particularly prominent in sport and physical education settings where one is apt to compare motor, fitness, and sport skills to others in the same physical education class or in the same sport program (Weiss, 1987). Social comparison theory (Festinger, 1954) provides a two-part model for examining how individuals use social comparisons: (a) normative evaluation and (b) self-comparison. *Normative evaluation* refers to how significant others behave and act, whereas *self-comparison* involves comparison of all aspects of self

One of the most common ways people determine their self-worth is through comparisons with peers.

(actions, opinions, beliefs) with those of significant others. This two-part social comparison process results in either psychological comfort or discomfort. Comfort results when one believes one thinks and acts similarly to others in one's immediate social group. On the other hand, discomfort results when one perceives that one is a minority or outcast compared to one's social group. Discomfort motivates the individual to become more like the group, make the group become more like the individual, or reject the group norm as irrelevant and compare oneself to another social group.

According to the theory, people tend to compare their own abilities to those of others who possess similar attributes. For example, fifth-grade children would compare their results on a physical fitness test to those of other fifth graders in their class and perhaps in their school. Similarly, high school softball players would likely use teammates and other high school softball players as their referent for softball abilities. An interesting question regarding individuals with disabilities is whom do they use as a referent group when making social comparisons. In other words, do individuals with disabilities use peers with similar disabilities when determining their physical competence or do they use an able-bodied reference group? According to social comparison theory, children with mental retardation would use other children with mental retardation as their referent group, children who use wheelchairs would use other children who use wheelchairs as their referent group, and so on. To do otherwise (i.e., compare oneself to able-bodied peers) could be devastating to one's self-evaluation of competence and self-worth.

Research in the area of social comparison consistently shows that children with learning disabilities use peers with similar disabilities as their social comparison groups for estimating their academic competence. For example, Coleman (1983), Meisel and Shaeffer (1985), and Renick and Harter (1989) found that children with learning disabilities who used peers with similar disabilities as a comparison group had higher levels of perceived academic competence (in some cases equal to peers without disabilities) compared to children with learning disabilities who used peers without disabilities as a source of social comparison. This is in line with social comparison theory in that students with learning disabilities who seek out a social comparison group consisting of children with similar abilities have higher levels of perceived competence.

The previous studies focused upon perceived academic competence, which is clearly different from perceived competence in other domains. That is, who do children with learning disabilities use as a comparison group when judging perceived physical competence, an area in which children with learning disabilities are not necessarily delayed compared to peers without disabilities? A recent study examined the reference group used by children (ages 10-13) with and without learning disabilities, all of whom were placed in general education settings (Shapiro & Ulrich, 2001). Results showed that children with learning disabilities used peers without disabilities as a reference group for judging their athletic competence and perceived themselves to be equally competent to peers without disabilities. Subjects with learning disabilities in this study received physical education in the general setting; thus, comparisons to children without disabilities were more likely. As noted by Kistner, Haskett, White, and Robbins (1987), students with learning disabilities who spend more time in general education classes may be more likely to compare themselves to peers in these classes (i.e., children without disabilities). However, many children with learning disabilities do not have motor or fitness problems, so comparison to peers without disabilities would not necessarily negatively affect perceived physical competence. However, general physical education placement and subsequent comparison to peers without disabilities may negatively affect perceived competence in children who have disabilities that affect motor and fitness abilities (e.g., children with cerebral palsy or children with mental retardation).

Unfortunately, studies on perceived physical competence have not examined social comparisons across different ages. Research on children without disabilities would suggest that there would be developmental differences in what information one uses to determine physical competence (e.g., Horn & Hasbrook, 1986; Horn & Weiss, 1991; see Weiss & Ebbeck, 1996). Children 10 to 14 years of age are more likely to focus on peer comparisons, whereas younger children tend to focus more on parent and teacher feedback. Such developmental comparisons are needed in future research. In addition, it would be interesting to determine whom children with physical or sensory disabilities use as their social comparison group, especially given that most children with these types of disabilities are placed in general education classes.

Self-Fulfilling Prophecies

As noted earlier, it is not unusual for physical education teachers, coaches, and even sport directors to stereotype individuals with disabilities. For example, a physical educator might assume that all children with mental retardation will have difficulty understanding and playing team sports. Yet, this is not true because many children and adults with mental retardation compete in team sports in their community and through Special Olympics. Similarly, a Little League coach might assume that a child who is missing an arm is probably not going to be a very good baseball player. However, former professional baseball player Jim Abbott, who had one functioning arm yet pitched a no-hitter for the New York Yankees in the early 1990s, proved this stereotype wrong. Once a teacher or coach has an opportunity to work with a child with a disability, stereotypes are often replaced by an appreciation of the individual's unique abilities and strengths.

Unfortunately, although stereotyping itself may not be a problem, stereotyping can lead teachers and coaches to act in inequitable ways towards individuals with disabilities. As noted earlier, stereotyping has led to discrimination by physical education teachers (Goodwin & Watkinson, 2000; Blinde & McCallister, 1998), and even worse in the inequitable way directors of large sports organizations such as the NCAA (USDOJ, 2000) and PGA Tour (Lane, 2001) have treated athletes with disabilities. Beside the obvious problems of not being allowed to try out or play, there can be serious psychological problems to children who are treated differently based on one characteristic (i.e., having a particular disability).

According to self-fulfilling prophecy theory, a teacher's or coach's expectations about the abilities and behaviors of a student can serve as a prophecy that determines the level of achievement that student will eventually reach (Horn, 1987; Horn, Lox, & Labrador, 1998). In other words, the person begins to act in a way that is consistent with the leader's or coach's beliefs. Others' beliefs may be false, but the person perceives these beliefs to be fact and behaves accordingly. For example, if the teacher thinks that children who are blind are fragile and should not be in general physical education classes and if the teacher behaves in such a way as to convey this message to a new child in his class who is blind (does not allow the child to participate in many activities, praises child for being careful, tells others to always watch out for this child), then this child will begin to behave as if he or she were fragile and not wanted in general physical education.

> The self-fulfilling prophecy theory holds that a teacher's or coach's expectations of a student can determine the level of achievement that student will reach.

Horn and her colleagues (1998) outlined a four-step model showing how the self-fulfilling prophecy phenomenon works in the physical domain. This model can be applied to individuals with disabilities (see Table 3). Note how this is a sequential model in which an individual with a disability may in fact have some very good sport skills and appropriate behaviors at the beginning of the season. However, as this person is faced with differential treatment by his or her coach (e.g., less praise, less instruction, inappropriate attributions), the athlete begins to conform to the coach's expectations. For example, a child with mental retardation is placed on a Little League baseball team. In actuality, he is one of the better players on the team (he has three older sisters who all play softball, and his dad was a former minor league baseball player). However, because peers and coaches believe and treat this child as if he is not very good at baseball (e.g., given fewer opportunities, less prescriptive feedback for errors), the child's skills begin to match his coach's and teammate's expectations.

Horn et al. (1998) noted that there are several things teachers and coaches can do to prevent the self-fulfilling prophecies. These ideas are applicable to teachers and coaches who work with individuals with disabilities. For example, coaches and teachers should realize that their initial appraisal of a child with a disability may be based on preconceived and inaccurate stereotypes and not on the individual's actual abilities. Coaches and teachers need to make sure they objectively evaluate the individual to determine his or her true abilities rather than rely on preconceived notions. Coaches and teachers also should monitor the number and type of interactions they have with their students with disabilities. The number of interactions should be at least the same as the number they have with peers without disabilities, and the type of interactions should focus more on instructional and corrective feedback rather than nonspecific feedback and praise. Coaches and teachers also need to monitor the time students with disabilities spend in noninstructional activities such as shagging balls and keeping score. Students with disabilities should not be assigned to these type of activities any more frequently than should their typically developing peers. Finally, coaches and teachers should focus on and reinforce students for skill improvement rather than some outcome measure such as number of baskets made or how fast one gets from point A to point B. For example, a coach could

TABLE 3
Self-Fulfilling Prophecy Model With Application to Individuals With Disabilities

1. Coach or teacher develops an expectation for each athlete that predicts level of performance and type of behavior that athlete will exhibit.	Coach or teacher has certain expectations for an individual with a disability based on the coach or teacher's limited knowledge of people with that disability. Label (i.e., stereotype).
2. Coach or teacher's expectations influence his/her treatment of individual student/athlete.	Coach/teacher begins to treat individual with disability differently than peers, in accordance with his or her expectations for this individual.
3. The way the coach or teacher treats each person on the team or in the class affects the self-concept of the individuals with disabilities, their achievement motivation, and their level of aspiration.	Because the coach or teacher treats person with disabilities differently than other people in the program, the person with a disability is affected in terms of how he/she feels about him/herself and how motivated he/she is toward the activity.
4. The athlete's/student's performance and behaviors mirror the expectations conveyed by the coach/teacher. The coach/teacher mentally confirms the original stereotype (i.e., the person is not able to do the skills).	Individual's poor physical skills and behavior conform to the coach's/teacher's expectations, which reinforces the coach/teacher's initial expectations.

praise a child who uses a wheelchair for improving her shooting form rather than focusing on the fact that she has made only 2 of 10 baskets.

FUTURE RESEARCH DIRECTIONS

Although there has been increasing interest in research on the effects of physical activity on self-esteem of individuals with disabilities, those who have conducted extensive reviews of the literature agree that much more research is needed (Hutzler & Bar-Eli, 1993; P. R. E. Crocker, 1993; Sherrill, 1996, 1997; 1997; Porretta & Moore, 1997). Given the theory and research discussed previously, there are several implications for researchers interested in expanding the knowledge base regarding the psychosocial factors and physical activity participation in individuals with disabilities. The following highlights some implications and suggestions for researchers based on research and theory discussed earlier.

Effects of Stigmatization and Discrimination

There has been a great deal of speculation as to the effects of stereotyping, stigmatization, and discrimination on the physical activity and sport participation of individuals with disabilities (Asch, 1984; J. Crocker & Major, 1989; Sherrill, 1997). However, to date, there has been very little empirical evidence to support (a) the fact that individuals with disabilities typically experience stigmatization or discrimination in physical activity contexts and (b) whether or not such stigmatization and discrimination actually affect self-esteem. Additionally, there has been no effort to determine whether or not stigmatization and discrimination are more prevalent in children or adult programs, and there has been no effort to determine whether or not stigmatization and discrimination have a greater effect on the self-esteem of children or adults with disabilities. Clearly, there are examples of stigmatization and discrimination towards children with disabilities (e.g., Blinde & McCallister, 1998; Boyd, 1999; Goodwin & Watkinson, 2000) and adults with disabilities (USDOJ, 2000; Lane, 2001), but it is less clear whether or not stigmatization and discrimination are commonplace with relation to physical activity and sport. Furthermore, although stigma theory suggests that stigmatized persons (including individuals with disabilities) should have lower self-esteem, research does not provide such support (J. Crocker & Major, 1989). Interestingly, Sherrill (1997) suggested that some individuals with disabilities may develop stronger self-esteem when forced to deal with adversity. Again, taken from a developmental perspective, does adversity improve self-esteem in younger children v. older children and children v. adults, or are certain age groups better able to use adversity in a positive way?

Unfortunately, there has been no real concerted effort to examine the effects of stigma on self-esteem in children or adults with disabilities. As noted earlier, Taub and her colleagues (1999) examined the relationship between stigma and college students with disabilities who participate in sport. However, Taub et al. did not measure self-esteem changes in her subjects, so it is impossible to determine if self-esteem was enhanced as perceived stigma was reduced. Similarly, Blinde and McCallister (1998) did not measure self-esteem in the children they interviewed who were clearly discriminated against in physical education. These types of research questions need to be asked and answered within the framework of stigma theory (J. Crocker & Major, 1989; Sherrill, 1997).

Related to the question of stigma is an examination of the underlying motives for stigmatization and discrimination. Why do some physical educators, coaches, administrators, and others associated with physical activity and sport stigmatize and discriminate against individuals with disabilities? This type of question, although difficult to ask and even more difficult

> Research suggests one reason physical activity professionals stigmatize students with disabilities is because they feel incompetent when working with them.

to get a truthful answer for, needs to be asked and studied. As noted earlier, research on attitudes of physical educators (Block & Rizzo, 1995), coaches (Kozub & Porretta, 1998), and aquatics instructors (Conatser et al., 2000) suggests that many physical activity professionals feel incompetent when working with individuals who have disabilities. Perhaps these feelings of incompetence lead to discrimination as a means of self-protection ("If I do not allow this individual to participate in my program, then I will not feel incompetent"), but such underlying feelings as to why teachers, coaches, and others associated with physical activity and sport programs stigmatize individuals with disabilities have not been examined.

Perceived Competence

Some researchers have suggested that motor skill improvement is related to increased perceived competence and is one of the best approaches to increasing self-esteem and enjoyment in physical activity in children and adults without disabilities (Weiss, 2000; Weiss & Ebbeck, 1996). Sherrill (1997) noted that many adapted physical education teachers similarly view skill improvement as the key to improving self-esteem. Some evidence suggests that this may be true (e.g., Blinde & McClung, 1997; Dykens & Cohen, 1996; S. L. Gibbons & Bushakra, 1989). Others have found no such relationship between improved perceived physical competence and more general self-perceptions and self-worth (e.g., Riggen & Ulrich, 1993). Unfortunately, the majority of studies simply measured perceived competence and then assumed that increased perceived competence would enhance self-esteem and motivation to participate (e.g., Hedrick, 1985; Ulrich & Collier, 1990; Yun & Ulrich, 1997). As noted by S. L. Gibbons and Bushakra (1989) when referring to their study, "A logical follow-up to the present study would be to continue investigation of the subsequent step in the competence motivation cycle . . . . [W]ill increased perceived competence lead to increased participation?" (p. 49). Clearly, unless follow-up research is conducted, there is no way of knowing the answer to this question or whether or not self-esteem is enhanced as perceived competence increases.

Additionally, there has been no effort to determine whether or not developmental trends found in children without disabilities hold true for children with disabilities. For example, Horn and Hasbrook (1986) found that younger children (ages 8 to 11) rated parent feedback as a more important source of competence whereas older children (ages 12-14) tended to rate social comparison as more important. Similarly, Weiss (2000) summarized research that showed that children aged 5 to 9 tend to judge physical competence based on the mastery of simple tasks, their difficulty, and the enjoyment level. Children aged 10 to 15 relied more on peer comparison and teacher or coach feedback, and children aged 16 to 18 focused more on self-set goals and attraction towards physical activity. Do these developmental patterns hold true for children and adolescents with disabilities? It would seem that children with physical, health, and/or sensory disabilities would follow the developmental pattern noted above. However, Sherrill (1998) noted that children with mental retardation (cognitive delays) may behave more like younger children when it comes to using sources to determine competence. Unfortunately, there has been no research to date that has examined such developmental issues in children with disabilities.

Class Placement

An area of research that seemed to be more prevalent in the late 1970s and early 1980s was the impact class placement had on self-esteem. Scholars who favored regular class placement suggested that pulling children with disabilities out of their regular class setting and placing them into a self-contained setting with other children with disabilities would have a negative effect on self-esteem. This notion was based on the *Brown v. Board of Education* case (segregating African Americans from whites in public schools) in which Chief Justice Earl Warren stated that separateness generated feelings of inferiority, and such feelings of inferiority may affect a child's motivation to learn and even retard educational and mental development (Stainback, Stainback, & Bunch, 1989). On the other hand, empirical research suggests that placing students with certain types of disabilities (e.g., children with learning disabilities) into homogenous groups creates a more appropriate social comparison group, which, in turn, fosters self-esteem (e.g., Bear, Clever, & Proctor, 1991; Coleman, 1983; Renick & Harter, 1989; Ribner, 1978).

With a renewed push towards including children with disabilities into general education classes including general physical education, it seems appropriate that research refocus on issues related to placement. For example, following a model similar to Bear et al. (1991), a comparison of perceived physical competence, as well as choice of social comparison group could be made between children with similar disabilities who are placed full-time in general physical education, part-time in general and part-time in adapted, and full-time in adapted physical education. Similar research could be conducted in a sport setting, for example, taking children with mental retardation and randomly placing some in a regular community soccer league and others in a Special Olympics soccer program.

In fact, one such study was conducted recently in France (Ninot, Bilard, Delignieres, & Sokolowski, 2000). These researchers conducted an 8-month longitudinal study examining integrated v. segregated sport placement (basketball and swimming) on sport skill improvement and perceived athletic competence of adolescents with mental retardation. Both the integrated and segregated groups showed significant improvement in skill development. Moreover, there were no significant differences between the integrated and segregated groups on perceived athletic competence, social acceptance, physical appearance, and general self-worth. Interestingly, results did show the integrated basketball group had significantly lower perceived athletic competence compared to a sedentary control group. Nevertheless, this type of comparison between integrated and segregated settings is critical to determine the effects of placement on perceived athletic competence. Such comparisons could begin to determine the effects of placement on perceived physical and athletic competence as well as the effects placement has on whom one chooses for one's social comparison group.

From a developmental perspective, Shapiro and Ulrich (2001) have created a nice start for determining if age and disability influence whom one chooses for social comparison and how such comparisons affect perceived physical competence in children with disabilities. Unfortunately, these authors used a limited age sample (ages 10-13), which may have affected their nonsignificant results. In addition, these authors did not have the ability to examine children with learning disabilities who were placed in different settings (all of the subjects were in a general physical education class). However, extending this general design to younger and older children with learning disabilities as well as to children with learning disabilities placed in different settings would begin to determine if, in fact, there is an interaction between age, social comparison choices, class placement, and perceived physical competence. Interestingly, there seems to be a subtle shift away from inclusion towards more specialty programs, particularly for children with learning disabilities or behavior disorders who have not done well in inclusive classrooms. Thus, it is conceivable that a researcher could take an intact group of students of different ages from a special school for children with learning disabilities and compare these students to children of similar ages with learning disabilities who are placed in a general education school.

Psychological Skills and Methods

Asken and Goodling (1986) and Porretta and Moore (1997) suggested an applied line of research that focuses on program effectiveness with direct implication to elite athletes with disabilities and their coaches. In particular, they suggested exploring psychological skill training such as goal setting, visual rehearsal, and relaxation training with individuals with disabilities. Some research suggests that athletes with disabilities are more similar than different to athletes without disabilities in the use of psychological skills (e.g., Henschen et al., 1984; Mastro & French, 1986). However, Asken and Goodling and P. R. E. Crocker (1993) warned that service providers should not assume performance-enhancement techniques that have been used by nondisabled athletes would work with individuals with disabilities and that the unique problems faced by this population may interact with the psychological technique to produce an unexpected outcome. For example, many adult athletes with acquired disabilities have to deal with serious trauma and loss that require major adjustment, whereas children who were born with their disability often have to deal with overprotecting parents and stereotyping and ridicule by peers and even teachers. Yet, there is virtually no research on how such factors affect the choices and implementation of traditional sport psychology techniques.

Also, one has to consider the unique characteristics of the individual. For example, how does one do whole-body, progressive relaxation training with an athlete who is paralyzed and cannot feel his or her leg muscles? How does one teach cognitive strategies such as visual imagery and goal setting to individuals with mental retardation? Porretta and Moore (1997)

> It may help to determine why an individual with disabilities has chosen a specific sport or program.

noted that such issues and even attempts at providing sport psychological training to athletes with disabilities have received little attention in the literature. Clearly, much more research is needed to determine if traditional sport psychology techniques are effective with athletes who have disabilities, and, if so, how such techniques interact with age and type of disability.

IMPLICATIONS FOR PRACTITIONERS

The body of knowledge previously presented in this chapter has many implications for practitioners interested in helping individuals with disabilities have more successful physical activity and sport experiences. Whether creating a new physical activity or sport program or assisting others in the implementation of existing programs that include individuals with disabilities, it is critical that protection and development of self-esteem are important considerations in the planning and implementation of the program. Too often, physical activity and sport programs focus on competition at the expense of success, enjoyment, and self-fulfillment. The following are some suggestions for practitioners working with individuals with disabilities in physical activity and recreational settings based on research and theory discussed earlier.

1. Determine each participant's physical education and sport background, and identify what the participant would like to learn, has difficulty learning, avoids, or fears. According to Craft and Hogan (1985), such factors could affect which activity one targets and the interest and motivation of the person. As noted by Hutzler and Bar-Eli (1993), the type of activity introduced should be important to the individual with disabilities. Something as simple as determining why an individual with disabilities has chosen a specific sport or program may reveal his or her motivation to participate (e.g., Brasile, 1988; Brasile & Hedrick, 1991). This is particularly important for adolescents and young adults, who may have different motives for participating in sport and physical activity (friendship, aspira-

tions to compete at state and national competitions) compared to those of young children (have fun) and older adults (maintain health).

2. Make sure individuals with disabilities experience success, particularly in the early stages of learning and rehabilitation. Failure can lead to perceptions of incompetence (Craft & Hogan, 1985; Hutzler & Bar-Eli, 1993). On the other hand, successful experiences can lead to increased perceived competence. This is particularly true for adolescents and young adults who may have recently acquired a new disability and who may be having trouble adjusting to their new limitations (e.g., spinal cord injury) as well as young children, who become easily frustrated. To facilitate success, task-analyze skills into smaller steps; then, focus early instruction on helping the individual with disabilities master these smaller steps (Craft & Hogan, 1985: Sherrill, 1998; Wessel & Kelly, 1986).

3. Gradually reduce the amount of support provided to the individual with a disability so that eventually he or she is performing the activity independently (Craft & Hogan, 1985; Hutzler & Bar-Eli, 1993). Although support early on may be critical to ensure success, self-efficacy also can be increased when an individual who is dependent on others begins to gain independence. As noted by Bandura (1981), success achieved with external support provides less self-efficacy because the individual may credit some of the success to external factors. According to Reynell's (1973) model, adolescents and young adults in particular are concerned about independence and will want to test their ability to do things on their own as soon as possible.

4. Set realistic but challenging goals for individuals with disabilities (Craft & Hogan, 1985). If one succeeds in a task that is perceived to be optimally challenging, then perceived competence should increase. However, creating goals that are challenging but realistic has to be done on a case-by-case basis. For example, some adolescents and young adults who have acquired a disability will feel as if they cannot do anything, so asking them to do almost anything physical may be perceived as unrealistic. This could have a negative effect on self-esteem. On the other hand, some individuals with acquired disabilities want to show themselves and their families that they are not "handicapped." These individuals will want greater challenges. This is particularly important for adults who have acquired disabilities who want to show their spouses and families that they will not be a burden. With reference to individuals with more severe disabilities, Sherrill (1998) suggested that teachers, coaches, and therapists make the individual with disabilities "feel safe, loved, and appropriately challenged so that they see themselves as competent before trying the task" (p. 200). In other words, success may be judged differently for each person. Although an able-bodied person might be judged on competencies related to dribbling, shooting, and passing a basketball as well as playing the game, an adult with a severe anxiety disorder would be judged competent and successful by simply walking out on the court. Similarly, a child with cerebral palsy might be judged on competency in a gymnastics unit for getting out of the

wheelchair and onto a mat independently whereas a child without disabilities would be judged on the quality of a cartwheel.

5. Verbally reinforce the individual with disabilities in an attempt to convince the person that he or she is capable of being successful in the targeted activity (Craft & Hogan, 1985). Some individuals with disabilities have an "I can't" attitude. This is particularly true for children with disabilities who have experienced failure in physical education, recreation, and sports. This also is true for adults who have acquired their injury later in life and who suddenly have to deal with new limitations. Sometimes these individuals need a little verbal persuasion to even try a physical activity. However, Sherrill (1998) noted that teachers and therapists have to be careful not to provide false information. Teachers and therapists should accept mistakes and errors in performance ("good try" or "that throw went farther than the last one"), but should not falsely praise attempts that are obviously incorrect. This is particularly true for older children and adults who can quickly determine what is false praise.

6. Use peer models that match the age, abilities, disabilities, and general characteristics of the individual with disabilities (Hutzler & Bar-Eli, 1993). Observing and talking to others who have similar disabilities but who lead an active life may lead the observer to feel that he or she too can succeed in a similar task. Using peer models can be something as simple as showing a Special Olympics video of people with mental retardation being successful in various sports or introducing an older adult who has recently lost his or her vision to macular degeneration to another adult with the same disability but who is active in physical activity.

7. When working in an integrated setting, create an environment that is accepting of individual differences, focuses on individual accomplishments rather than competitive comparisons, and is nonthreatening and success oriented (Craft & Hogan, 1985; Sherrill, 1998). This is particularly important in the early stages of the program when individuals with disabilities may be prone to give up quickly if they are not successful and not having fun. Upper-elementary- through high-school-aged children will be particularly influenced by peer comparisons. Creating a program in which multiple activities are offered as well as multiple ways to measure success may avoid peer comparisons. For example, a high school physical education program could offer three choices to their students (who include students with disabilities): aerobics/yoga, soccer, and tennis. A student with cerebral palsy who uses a wheelchair could choose aerobics/yoga, an activity at which he or she would have greater success.

8. Include individual and small-group counseling as part of the physical activity and sport experience (Sherrill, 1998). This is particularly important for adolescents and young adults who are worried about personal relationships and independence (Reynell, 1973). Offer individuals with disabilities opportunities to talk about their feelings, fears, and aspirations in a safe, nonjudgmental fashion. Try to draw out these individuals while being a good, empathetic listener. For example, a physical educator might

create a group for children who have movement difficulties and problems in physical education. Talking about such topics as how they can become more successful, how the educator is interested in students' improvement and effort and not necessarily their mastering a skill or winning games, and how the educator will listen to their ideas on how he or she can make the setting even more accepting and rewarding for them.

9. In integrated settings, teach peers without disabilities how to be more accepting of peers with disabilities. Simply placing an individual with a disability into a regular physical education class or physical activity/sport program will not ensure a successful, rewarding integration experience that increases self-esteem and the feeling of belonging. Block (2000) suggested several ways in which peers with disabilities can learn more about, and in turn become more accepting of, peers without disabilities including role playing, talking about the concept of handicapping in sports such as golf and bowling, showing videos of successful athletes with disabilities, brainstorming about ways to make fair modifications, and talking about specific students with disabilities who will be in the program and how to help them. These and other activities that teach students to be more understanding and caring of each other can have positive influences on self-esteem for individuals with and without disabilities (Sherrill, 1998).

CONCLUDING COMMENTS

Labeling someone as disabled can have a tremendous impact on his or her self-esteem, perhaps more than having a disability itself. Furthermore, how others close to the individual as well as society as a whole treat an individual with disabilities can further affect self-esteem. The ugly cycle of stereotyping, stigmatization, prejudice, and finally discrimination clearly wears on individuals with disabilities and limits opportunities for sport and physical activity participation. Even with antidiscrimination laws such as the Americans with Disabilities Act, too many children with disabilities never have the chance to play Little League baseball or soccer, and too many adults with disabilities never have the chance to work out at their local fitness center or join an adult golf league.

What is particularly distressing about the limited opportunities for participation in sport and physical activity is the research that suggests physical activity and sport can change how an individual with a disability feels about him- or herself and how society feels about the individual with a disability. As highlighted in this chapter, participation in sport and physical activity can increase perceived competence, self-esteem, and social acceptance and competence in individuals of all ages with a variety of disabilities. Furthermore, it is heartening to see more researchers examining the effects of participation in physical activity on the psychology of individuals with disabilities. Nevertheless, so much more research is needed, particularly research that uses contemporary theories such as those discussed throughout this book. Perhaps as more research shows the positive impact physical activity and sport have on the psychology of individuals with disabilities, society as a whole will begin to open doors and create more opportunities so all individuals with disabilities will be able to reap the benefits of physical activity and sport.

REFERENCES

Ajzen, I., & Fishbein, M. (1980). *Understanding attitudes and predicting social behaviors.* Englewood Cliffs, NJ: Prentice-Hall.

Asch, A. (1984). The experience of disability. *American Psychologist, 39,* 529-536.

Asken, M. J., & Goodling, M. D. (1986). Sport psychology: An underdeveloped discipline from among the sport sciences for disabled athletes. *Adapted Physical Activity Quarterly, 3,* 312-319.

Avillion, A. E. (1986). Barrier perceptions and its influence on self-esteem. *Rehabilitation Nursing, 11,* 11-14.

Bandura, A. (1981). Self-referent thought: The development of self-efficacy. In J. H. Flavell & L.D. Ross (Eds.), *Development of social cognition: Frontiers and possible futures* (pp. 1-21). New York: Cambridge University Press.

Bear, G. G., Clever, A., & Proctor, W. A. (1991). Self-perceptions of nonhandicapped children and children with learning disabilities in integrated classrooms. *The Journal of Special Education, 24,* 409-426.

Best, S., Carpignano, J., Sirvis, B., & Bigge, J. (1991). Psychological aspects of physical disability. In J. Bigge (Ed.), *Teaching individuals with physical and multiple disabilities* (3rd ed.). New York: Macmillan Publishing.

Blinde, E. M., & McCallister, S.G. (1998). Listening to the voices of students with physical disabilities. *Journal of Physical Education, Recreation, and Dance, 69*(6), 64-68.

Blinde, E. M., & McClung, L. R. (1997). Enhancing the physical and social self through recreational activity: Accounts of individuals with physical disabilities. *Adapted Physical Activity Quarterly, 14,* 327-344.

Block, M. E. (2000). *A teacher's guide to including students with disabilities into general physical education* (2nd ed.). Baltimore: Paul H. Brookes.

Block, M. E., & Rizzo, T. L. (1995). Attitudes and attributes of physical education teachers towards including students with severe and profound disabilities into regular physical education. *Journal of the Association for Persons with Severe Handicaps, 20,* 80-87.

Boyd, D. (1999, November 12). Judge grants boy permission to play. *Associated Press State and Local Wire.* News Section, p. 8.

Brasile, F. (1988). Psychological factors that influence participation in wheelchair basketball. *Palaestra, 4*(3), 16-19, 25-27.

Brasile, F., & Hedrick, B. (1991). A comparison of participation incentives between adult and youth wheelchair basketball players. *Palaestra, 7*(4), 40-46.

Briery, B. G., & Rabian, B. (1999). Psychological changes associated with participation in a pediatric summer camp. *Journal of Pediatric Psychology, 24,* 183-190.

Campbell, E., & Jones, G. (1994). Psychological well-being in wheelchair sport participants and nonparticipants. *Adapted Physical Activity Quarterly, 11,* 404-415.

Cantell, M. H., Smyth, M. M., & Ahonen, T.P. (1994). Clumsiness in adolescence: Educational, motor and social outcomes. *Adapted Physical Activity Quarterly, 11,* 115-129.

Coleman, J. M. (1983). Self-concept and the mildly handicapped: The role of social comparisons. *The Journal of Special Education, 17,* 38-45.

Cooley, E. J., & Ayres, R. R. (1988). Self-concept and success-failure attributions of nonhandicapped students and students with learning disabilities. *Journal of Learning Disabilities, 21,* 174-178.

Conatser, P. K., Block, M. E., & Lepore, M. (2000). Aquatic instructors' attitudes toward teaching students with disabilities. *Adapted Physical Activity Quarterly, 17,* 173-183.

Cooper, M. (1984). *Attitudes toward physical activity and sources of attraction to sport of cerebral palsied athletes.* Unpublished doctoral dissertation, Texas Woman's University, Denton.

Cooper, M., Sherrill, C., & Marshall, D. (1985). Attitudes toward physical activity of elite cerebral palsy athletes. *Adapted Physical Activity Quarterly, 3,* 14-21.

Craft, D. H., & Hogan, P. I. (1986). Development of self-concept and self-efficacy: Considerations for mainstreaming. *Adapted Physical Activity Quarterly, 2,* 320-327.

Crocker, J., & Major, B. (1989). Social stigma and self-esteem: The self-protective properties of stigma. *Psychological Review, 96,* 608-630.

Crocker, P. R. E. (1993). Sport and exercise psychology and research with individuals with physical disabilities: Using theory to advance knowledge. *Adapted Physical Activity Quarterly, 10,* 324-335.

Crocker, P. R. E., & Bouffard, M. (1992). Ways of coping by individuals with physical disabilities to perceived barriers to physical activity. *Canadian Association for Health, Physical Education and Recreation Journal, 56,* 28-33.

Dummer, G. M., Ewing, M. E., Habeck, R.V., & Overton, S. R. (1987). Attributions of athletes with cerebral palsy. *Adapted Physical Activity Quarterly, 4,* 278-292.

Dunn, J. L. K., & Watkinson, E. J. (1994). A study of the relationship between physical awkwardness and children's perceptions of physical competence. *Adapted Physical Activity Quarterly, 11,* 275-283.

Dunn. J. M. (1997). *Special physical education* (7th ed.). Madison, WI: McGraw-Hill.

Dykens, E. M., & Cohen, D. J. (1996). Effects of Special Olympics International on social competence in persons with mental retardation. *Journal of the American Academy of Child and Adolescent Psychiatry, 35,* 223-229.

Festinger, L. (1954). A theory of social comparison processes. *Human Relations: Studies Towards the Integration of the Social Sciences, 7,* 117-140.

Fox, K. R. (Ed.). (1997). *The physical self: From motivation to well-being.* Champaign, IL: Human Kinetics.

Gibbons, F. X. (1981). The social psychology of mental retardation: What's in a label? In S. S. Brehm, S. M. Kassin, & F. X. Gibbons (Eds.), *Developmental social psychology* (pp. 249-270). New York: Oxford University Press.

Gibbons, S. L., & Bushakra, F. B. (1989). Effects of Special Olympics participation on the perceived competence and social acceptance of mentally retarded children. *Adapted Physical Activity Quarterly, 6,* 40-51.

Gilstrap, T., & Sherrill, C. (1989). Personality profiles of elite blind female athletes. *Palaestra, 6*(1), 21-23, 31-34.

Goodwin, D. L., & Watkinson, E. J. (2000). Inclusive physical education from the perspective of students with physical disabilities. *Adapted Physical Activity Quarterly, 17,* 144-160.

Greenwood, C. M., Dzewaltowski, D. A., & French, R. (1990). Self-efficacy and psychological well-being of wheelchair tennis participants and wheelchair non-tennis participants. *Adapted Physical Activity Quarterly, 7,* 12-21.

Groce, N. E. (1999). Disabilities in cross-cultural perspective: Rethinking disability. *Lancet, 354,* 756-757.

Hanrahan, S. J., Grove, J. R., & Lockwood, R. J. (1990). Psychological skills training for the blind athlete: A pilot program. *Adapted Physical Activity Quarterly, 7,* 143-155.

Harter, S. (1978). Effectance motivation reconsidered: Toward a developmental model. *Human Development, 21,* 34-64.

Hedrick, B.N. (1985). The effects of wheelchair tennis participation and mainstreaming upon the perceptions of competence of physically disabled adolescents. *Therapeutic Recreation Journal, 19*(2), 34-46.

Henderson, G., & Bryan, W.V. (1997). *Psychological aspects of disability.* Springfield, IL: Charles C. Thomas.

Henschen, K., Horvat, M., & French, R. (1984). A visual comparison of psychological profiles between able-bodied and wheelchair athletes. *Adapted Physical Activity Quarterly, 1,* 118-124.

Hobbs, N. (1975). *The future of children.* San Francisco: Jossey-Bass.

Hopper, C. A. (1986). Socialization of wheelchair athletes. In C. Sherrill (Ed.), *Sport and the disabled athlete* (pp. 197-202). Champaign, IL: Human Kinetics.

Horn, T. S. (1987). The influence of teacher-coach behavior on the psychological development of children. In D. Gould & M. R. Weiss (Eds.), *Advances in pediatric sport sciences:* Vol. 2. *Behavioral issues* (pp. 121-142). Champaign, IL: Human Kinetics.

Horn, T. S., & Hasbrook, C. (1986). Informational components influencing children's perceptions of their physical competence. In M. R. Weiss & D. Gould (Eds.), *Sport for children and youths* (pp. 81-88). Champaign, IL: Human Kinetics.

Horn, T. S., Lox, C., & Labrador, F. (1998). The self-fulfilling prophecy theory: When coaches' expectations become reality. In J. M. Williams (Ed.), *Applied sport psychology: Personal growth to peak performance* (3rd ed., pp. 74-91). Mountain View, CA: Mayfield.

Horn, T. S., & Weiss, M. R. (1991). A developmental analysis of children's self-ability judgments in the physical domain. *Pediatric Exercise Science, 3,* 310-326

Hutzler, Y., & Bar-Eli, M. (1993). Psychological benefits of sports for disabled people: A review. *Scandinavian Journal of Medical Science and Sports, 3,* 217-228.

Karagiannis, A., Stainback, S., & Stainback, W. (1996). Rationale for inclusive schooling. In S. Stainback & W. Stainback (Eds.), *Inclusion: A guide for educators* (pp. 3-16). Baltimore: Paul H. Brookes.

Katz, I. (1981). *Stigma: A social psychological analysis.* Hillsdale, NJ: Erlbaum.

King, G. A., Shultz, K. S., Steel, K., Gilpin, M., & Cathers, T. (1993). Self-evaluation and self-concept of adolescents with physical disabilities. *The American Journal of Occupational Therapy, 47,* 132-140.

Kistner, J., Haskett, M., White, K., & Robbins, F. (1987). Perceived competence and self-worth of LD and normally achieving students. *Learning Disabilities Quarterly, 10,* 37-44.

Kozub, F. M., & Porretta, D. L. (1998). Interscholastic coaches' attitudes toward integration of adolescents with disabilities. *Adapted Physical Activity Quarterly, 15,* 328-344.

Lane, C. (2001, May 30). Disabled pro golfer wins right to use cart. *The Washington Post,* p. A01.

Lawrence, E. A., & Winscel, J. F. (1973). Self-concept and the retarded: Research and issues. *Exceptional Children, 39,* 310-318.

Lazarus, R. S., & Folkman, S. (1984). *Stress, appraisal, and coping.* New York: Springer.

Lintunen, T., Heikinaro-Johansson, P., & Sherrill, C. (1995). Use of perceived competence with adolescents with disabilities. *Perceptual and Motor Skills, 80,* 571-577.

Lipsky, D. K., & Gartner, A. (1997). *Inclusion and school reform: Transforming America's classrooms.* Baltimore: Paul II. Brookes.

MacKinnon, J. R., Noh, S., Lariviere, J., MacPhail, A., Allan, D. E., & Laliberte, D. (1995). A study of therapeutic effects of horseback riding for children with cerebral palsy. *Physical and Occupational Therapy in Pediatrics, 15* (1), 17-34.

Marks, D. (1999). *Disability: Controversial debates and psychological perspectives.* London: Rutledge.

Mastro, J., & French, R. (1986). Sport anxiety and blind athletes. In C. Sherrill (Ed.), *Sport and disabled athletes* (pp. 203-208). Champaign, IL: Human Kinetics.

McAvoy, L. H., Schatz, E. C., Stuts, M. E., Schleien, S. J., & Lais, G. (1989). Integrated wilderness adventure: Effects on personal lifestyle traits of persons with and without disabilities *Therapeutic Recreation Journal, 23*(3), 50-64.

McNeil, J. M. (1997). *Americans with disabilities: 1994-95, U.S. Bureau of the Census. current population reports.* Washington, DC: U.S. Government Printing Office.

Meisel, C. J., & Shaeffer, B. (1985). Social comparison choices of mainstreamed academically handicapped children. *Journal of Special Education, 19,* 345-357.

Monnazzi, G. (1982). Paraplegics and sports: A psychological survey. *International Journal of Sports Psychology, 13,* 85-95.

National Center for Educational Statistics. (1999). *Digest of educational statistics.* Washington, DC: U.S. Department of Education.

Ninot, G., Bilard, J., Delignieres, D., & Sokolowski, M. (2000). Effects of integrated sport participation on perceived competence for adolescents with mental retardation. *Adapted Physical Activity Quarterly, 17,* 208-221.

Ostir G. V., Carlson J. E., Black S. A., Rudkin L., Goodwin J. S., & Markides, K. S. (1999). Disability in older adults 1: Prevalence, causes, and consequences. *Behavioral Medicine, 24*(4), 147-156.

Patrick, G.D. (1986). The effects of wheelchair competition on self-concept and acceptance of disability in novice athletes. *Therapeutic Recreational Journal, 20*(4), 61-71.

Porretta, D. L., & Moore, W. (1997). A review of sport psychology research for individuals with disabilities: Implications for future inquiry. *Clinical Kinesiology, 50*(4), 83-93.

Renick, M. J., & Harter, S. (1989). Impact of social comparison on the developing self-perceptions of learning disabled students. *Journal of Educational Psychology, 81,* 631-638.

Reynell, J. (1973). Children with physical handicaps. In N. P. Varma (Ed.), *Stresses in children* (pp. 145-168). London: University of London.

Reynolds, M. C. (1991). Classification and labeling. In J. W. Lloyd, N. N. Singh, & A. C. Repp (Eds.), *The regular education initiative: Alternative perspectives on concepts, issues, and models* (pp. 22-42). Sycamore, IL: Sycamore Publishing Co.

Ribner, S. (1978). The effects of special class placement on the self-concept of exceptional children. *Journal of Learning Disabilities, 11,* 60-64.

Riggen, K., & Ulrich, D. (1993). The effects of sport participation on individuals with mental retardation. *Adapted Physical Activity Quarterly, 10,* 42-51.

Rizzo, T. L., Bishop, P., & Tobar, D. (1997). Attitudes of soccer coaches toward youth players with mild mental retardation: A pilot study. *Adapted Physical Activity Quarterly, 14,* 238-251.

Rizzo, T. L., & Vispoel, W. H. P. (1991). Physical educators' attributes and attitudes toward teaching students with handicaps. *Adapted Physical Activity Quarterly, 8,* 4-11.

Rizzo, T. L., & Wright, R. G. (1988). Selected attributes related to physical educators' attitudes toward teaching students with handicaps. *Mental Retardation, 26,* 307-309.

Rogers, H., & Saklofske, D. H. (1985). Self-concepts, locus of control and performance expectations of learning disabled children. *Journal of Learning Disabilities, 18,* 273-277.

Rose, B., Larkin, D., & Berger, B. G. (1997). Coordination and gender influences on the perceived competence of children. *Adapted Physical Activity Quarterly, 14,* 210-221.

Scott, R. A. (1969) *The making of blind men: A study of adult socialization.* New York: Russell Sage Foundation.

Shapiro, D. R., & Ulrich, D. A. (2001). Social comparisons of children with and without learning disabilities when evaluating physical competence. *Adapted Physical Activity Quarterly, 18,* 273-288.

Shaw, L., Levine, M. D., & Belfer, M. (1982). Developmental double jeopardy: A study of clumsiness and self-esteem in children with learning problems. *Developmental and Behavioral Pediatrics, 3,* 191-196.

Sherrill, C. (1986). Social and psychological dimensions of sports for disabled athletes. In C. Sherrill (Ed.), *Sports and the disabled athlete* (pp. 21-33). Champaign, IL: Human Kinetics.

Sherrill, C. (1997). Disability, identity, and involvement in sport and exercise. In K. R. Fox (Ed.), *The physical self: From motivation to well-being* (pp. 257-285). Champaign, IL: Human Kinetics.

Sherrill, C. (1998). *Adapted physical activity, recreation, and sport* (5th ed.). Madison, WI: WCB McGraw-Hill.

Sherrill, C., Hinson, M., Gensch, B., & Low, S.O. (1990). Self-concepts of disabled youth athletes. *Perceptual and Motor Skills, 70,* 1093-1098.

Shiraishi, T., Tanaka, T., Goto, Y., Kami, Y., & Hiraoka, A. (1999). Outdoor sports camps for persons with disabilities. In H. Nakata (Ed.), *Adapted physical activity: Self-actualization through physical activities* (pp. 211-215). Fujisawa, Japan: Shonan Shuppansha.

Silon, E. L., & Harter, S. (1985). Assessment of perceived competence, motivational orientation, and anxiety in segregated and mainstreamed educable mentally retarded children. *Journal of Educational Psychology, 77*, 217-230.

Stainback, W., Stainback, S., & Bunch, G. (1989). Introduction and historical background. In S. Stainback, W. Stainback, & M. Forest (Eds.), *Educating all students in the mainstream of regular education* (pp. 3-14). Baltimore: Paul H. Brookes.

Storey, K., & Horner, R. H. (1991). An evaluative review of social validation research involving persons with handicaps. *Journal of Special Education, 25*, 352-401.

Taub, D. E., Blinde, E. M., & Greer, K. R. (1999). Stigma management through participation in sport and physical activity: Experiences of male college students with physical disabilities. *Human Relations, 52*, 1469-1483.

Theodorakis, Y., Bagiatis, K., & Goudas, M. (1995). Attitudes toward teaching individuals with disabilities: Application of the planned behavior theory. *Adapted Physical Activity Quarterly, 12*, 151-160.

Ulrich, D. A., & Collier, D. H. (1990). Perceived physical competence in children with mental retardation: Modification of a pictorial scale. *Adapted Physical Activity Quarterly, 7*, 338-354.

U. S. Department of Justice. (2000). *NCAA settlement with the Justice Department: Fact sheet.* Retrieved July 25, 2002, from *www.usdoJ. Gov/crt/ada/ncaafact/htm.*

Valliant, P. M., Bezzubyh, I., Daley, L., & Asu, M. E. (1985). Psychological impact of sport on disabled athletes. *Psychological Reports, 56,* 923-929.

Van Rossum, J. H. A., & Vermeer, A. (1990). Perceived competence: A validation study in the field of motoric remedial teaching. *International Journal of Disability, Development and Education, 37*(1), 71-81.

Weiner, B. (1972). *Theories of motivation from mechanisms to cognition.* Chicago: Markham.

Weiss, M. R. (1987). Self-esteem and achievement in children's sport and physical activity. In D. Gould & M. R. Weiss (Eds.), *Advances in pediatric sport sciences* (Vol. 2, pp. 87-119). Champaign, IL: Human Kinetics.

Weiss, M. R. (2000). Motivating kids in physical activity. *President's Council on Physical Fitness and Sports Research Digest, Series 3,*(11), 1-8.

Weiss, M. R., & Ebbeck, V. (1996). Self-esteem and perceptions of competence in youth sports: Theory, research, and enhancement strategies. In O. Bar-Or (Ed.), *The encyclopedia of sports medicine: The child and adolescent athlete* (Vol. 6, pp. 364-382). Oxford: Blackwell Scientific Publications.

Wessel, J. A., & Kelly, L. (1986). *Achievement-based curriculum development in physical education.* Philadelphia: Lea & Febiger.

White, S. A., & Zientek, C. (1991). Verbal persuasion and self-concept: An exploratory analysis in Special Olympians. *Clinical Kinesiology, 45*, 9-13.

Williams, T., & Kolkka, T. (1998). Socialization into wheelchair basketball in the United Kingdom: A structural functionalist perspective. *Adapted Physical Activity Quarterly, 15*, 357-369.

Wood, P. (1981). *International classification of impairment, disabilities, and handicaps.* Geneva: World Heath Organization.

World Health Organization. (2000). *International classification of functioning, disability, and health* [draft]. Geneva: Author.

Wright, J., & Cowden, J. E. (1986). Changes in self-concept and cardiovascular endurance of mentally retarded youths in a Special Olympics swim training program. *Adapted Physical Activity Quarterly, 3*, 177-183.

Yun, J., & Ulrich, D. A. (1997). Perceived and actual physical competence in children with mental retardation. *Adapted Physical Activity Quarterly, 14*, 285-297.

CHAPTER SEVENTEEN

A Lifespan View of Moral Development in Physical Activity

Gloria B. Solomon

There has been a surge of interest and concern about the moral values of our culture. Many decry the mainstream media content pervading newspapers, magazines, radio, television, and now the Internet. Unfortunately, most of these concerns are about the destructive composition of these sources—concerns that the media are undermining moral and ethical values in American society.

Lickona (1991a) delineates 10 examples depicting the moral decline of our society including increases in youth violence, bigotry, and cheating. Certainly, sport is not immune from this cultural critique as "sport is a moral practice, grounded as it is in the concepts of fairness and freedom" (Miller, Bredemeier, & Shields, 1997, p. 115). In fact, sport often represents diametrically opposed ends of the moral decay issue. On one end, there is the perception that sport is a location for character building. Athletic programs often tout this "fact" in their mission statement, imparting the notion that sport participation builds character (Stoll & Beller, 1998). On the opposite pole, sport is perceived as contributing to the moral decline of our society. This position was bluntly articulated by Leonard (1972) when he stated that "if sport builds character, it's character fit for a criminal" (p. 77). Both of these extreme positions can be argued, and it is likely that they both hold some truth. However, other activity contexts such as physical education may offer a different perspective on the contribution of physical activity to character development. For example, according to Shields and Bredemeier (1995), "physical education is probably the most significant physical activity context for developing moral character" (p. 199). They offer several sagacious points to elucidate their position, specifically contrasting physical education and sport.

> There is some debate over whether sport is beneficial or detrimental to society.

Twenty years ago, Weiss and Bredemeier (1983) made a plea for the consideration of a developmental approach to research in sport psychology. More recently, Weiss (2001) acknowledged that moral development is one of the few topics that systematically include a developmental perspective. Moral development by definition implies a developmental emphasis or lifespan approach. The purpose of this chapter is to illuminate the progression of inquiry on the topic of moral development in sport and physical education. To set the stage, I will highlight the major theoretical perspectives and models followed by the current state of moral development research in the parent discipline of psychology. Further, I will address moral development research in physical activity, moral intervention and character education programs, and directions the next generation of inquiry must tackle.

Major Theoretical Perspectives and Models

There exists an array of guiding frameworks created to explore the construct of moral development. It appears that although most of these approaches are still used, there is a shift away from internalization approaches toward constructivist approaches. Because there exists vast discourse on all of the theories presented here, the focus will be on a brief glimpse of the developmental components proffered by these varied positions.

Internalization Approaches

One of the earliest means for understanding moral development, internalization approaches stem from the 20th century. Beginning with psychodynamic perspectives, the major premise of internalization approaches to the study of moral development is that moral learning occurs through the internalization of socially appropriate behaviors. Moral growth occurs as part of the socialization process. Children thus learn to understand and accept societal standards for moral behavior. They then internalize those standards and become a part of the moral fabric of society.

Social learning theory. On the heels of the psychodynamic approaches, social learning theory offered an alternative internalization approach to the study of moral development. Popularized by Bandura (1969, 1977), social learning theory suggests that children learn to internalize appropriate cultural norms and behaviors, including morally relevant issues. When significant others model and reinforce moral behavior, children become aware of what is acceptable by societal standards and subsequently internalize those standards. Therefore, moral behaviors, like all behaviors, are actions that conform to social norms. Morality is perceived as residing in society, and socialization processes allow for the development of moral behavior. Other theorists have purported that morality does not exist solely in the environment but also involves cognitions that serve to process moral content and facilitate moral behavior.

Structural Developmental Approaches

A more recent approach to conceptualizing the psychological construct of moral development is guided by structural developmentalists. These theorists acknowledge both the impact of the environment and the structure of psychological growth as influences on moral development. Furthermore, they distinguish between moral content, what a person believes is right at a given point in time, and moral structure, how a person cognitively organizes moral contents. Two categories of structural developmental theorists emerged: constructivists and interactionists.

Constructivists. Piaget (1965) believed that there was more to children's moral development than simply internalizing contextual cues in the environment. A major leader in the creation of this approach, Piaget construed that there is a mental dialogue that takes place as children encounter moral issues in their environment. In his puissant research that explored children playing marbles, Piaget determined that developmentally, children progress in their moral behaviors through a two-stage sequence of cognitive steps. In brief, the morality of constraint evidenced in preschool children portrays adult authority as all-powerful, and the child is completely submissive to this unilateral authority. School-aged children demonstrate the morality of cooperation where the child is now able to engage in reciprocal social interactions with peers. At this stage, children are cognizant that rules are adaptable and mutual respect directs the adaptation of rules.

Building on Piaget's important contributions, Kohlberg (1969, 1976) created the most widely used psychological model of moral development. Beginning with the study of male Harvard college students, Kohlberg (1969) determined that individuals develop through a six-stage invariant sequence of moral growth. Divided into three broader categories, the preconventional level, demonstrated by children younger than age 9, is distinguishable by the consequences of a given action defining its moral appropriateness. At the conventional level, moral maturity is expressed through judgments based on shared agreements; maintenance of positive social approval is sought. Most adolescents reason at this level, and many adults do not move beyond it. The postconventional level is the most sophisticated mode of moral operations and is exhibited by adults. Those operating at this level follow a code of universal values, also referred to as principles of justice, that guide their responses to moral situations. Because Kohlberg (1969) believed in the idea of moral principles or universally recognized moral issues, the level of justice reasoning is one that, when reached, is exercised impartially. Although six stages exist, Kohlberg and others found that not all adults, and fewer women than men, reach the postconventional stages (Colby & Kohlberg, 1984; Gilligan, 1982).

In a critique of the finding that more men than women reach the highest level of moral reasoning according to Kohlberg's model, Gilligan (1977, 1982) created a developmental model of morality. Gilligan's framework was evoked from the personal moral dilemmas of young women considering abortion. Results of her study detected that although corresponding levels were found comparable to Kohlberg's preconventional and conventional stages, Gilligan noted that at the postconventional level, women's moral reasoning is reflected in an ethic of caring rather than an ethic of justice. Both Kohlberg's and Gilligan's models have undergone scrutiny from their peers. See Shields and Bredemeier (1995) and Turiel (1998) for detailed critiques of these stage models.

Interactional morality. Although the messages of social learning theorists and the constructivists remain active frameworks in sport research, more recently scholars have used Haan's interactionist model of morality (Haan, 1977; Haan, Aerts, & Cooper, 1985). The basic premise of Haan's five-stage model is that because morality is socially constructed, individuals must engage in moral dialogue and obtain moral balance to become morally mature. Thus, the principles of moral dialogue and balance lay the groundwork for constructing morality. These five stages are housed into three broader categorizations: assimilation, accommodation, and equilibration. In short, people prioritize their own needs in the assimilation phase; in the accommodation phase, people subordinate their own needs to those of others; the equilibration phase allows for the consideration of one's own needs and those of others simultaneously. Like the other structural developmental models discussed here, this model of morality assumes that as individuals mature, they will progress through the stages. However similar to Kohlberg's scheme, not all adults will ultimately reason at the highest level. Several scholars have compared and contrasted the contributions of Kohlberg and Haan (see Shields & Bredemeier, 1995, and Weiss & Smith, 2002). Another perspective on psychological morality goes beyond the identification of moral reasoning development.

Models of Moral Action

The work of Rest and his colleagues (Rest, 1986; Rest, Narvaez, Bebeau, & Thoma, 1999) attempts to go beyond the basic identification of moral reasoning schemata and bridge the gap between moral thought and subsequent behaviors. Rest's model is based on the simple question "When a person is behaving morally, what must we suppose has happened psychologically to produce that behavior?" (Rest, p. 3). The answers to this question led Rest to create a multi-dimensional four-component model of morality. Recently, J. Rest et al. refined the components. Component one is labeled *moral sensitivity*; one must first interpret the situation and identify that a dilemma is in fact a moral issue. Component two is called *moral judgment*; one must then reason about a course of action. Component three is identified as *moral motivation*; one must demonstrate the intention to act based on the chosen course. Component four is *moral character*; one must act informed by one's reasoning and intent. Note that most of the previous constructivist models are basically testing component two. Rest's model is particularly useful in that it allows the simplification and categorization of the complexities of moral development to be separated and studied. Its utility also resides in the fact that Rest is interested in moral intentions and actions, not just the reasoning processes.

The team of Bredemeier and Shields has contributed to the knowledge base of moral development, particularly in the context of sport and physical education for over 20 years. With an affinity toward Rest's model, they expanded the four components by adding three major sources of influence that affect each component: contextual factors, personal competencies, and ego-processing variables. This 12-component model reiterates the strengths of Rest's original conceptualization; each category of moral behavior can be extracted and studied independent of the others. Because of the complexities associated with the study of psychological variables and processes, this expanded model holds potential for the future of moral development inquiry both in and out of sport (see Table 1).

This brief journey through the models of moral development now leads us to examine the current state of knowledge on moral development in psychology. The following section will be organized by theoretical perspective, and again, it will focus on the developmental findings and implications of empirical research.

TABLE 1
12-Component Model of Moral Action

Influences	Processes			
	Moral Interpretation	Moral Judgment	Moral Choice	Moral Action
Personal	social perspective taking; role taking	moral reasoning	moral judgment	problem-solving skills
Contextual	goal structure situational ambiguity	moral atmosphere	domain cues	power structure
Ego Processing	intraceptive processes	ego processes	affective processes	attentional processes

Adapted from *Character Development and Physical Activity*, by D. L. L. Shields and B. J. L. Bredemeier, 1995 (Champaign, IL: Human Kinetics), p. 92. Permission granted by the authors.

MORAL DEVELOPMENT RESEARCH IN PSYCHOLOGY

Child and developmental psychologists have long explored various components of moral maturation as is evidenced by the preceding theoretical overview. Those who adopt the social learning view focus primarily on prosocial behavior (Arsenio, 1988). Proponents of the structural developmental approach explore positive justice, moral reasoning and judgments, and the role of perspective taking in the moral maturation process. The purpose of this section is to probe these two prominent perspectives focusing on the current state of knowledge over the lifespan.

Prosocial Behavior Development: Infancy Through Adulthood

In order to decipher the etiology of moral understanding, researchers often study expressions of prosocial behavior (Hay, Castle, Stimson, & Davies, 1995). Simply stated, prosocial behaviors are those that benefit another person such as helping, sharing, and cooperating (Bar-Tal, 1982). Numerous perspectives exist on how prosocial behaviors develop (see Crain, 1987; Zahn-Waxler & Radke-Yarrow, 1990).

Evidence of prosocial activity is expressed in infancy. In a series of studies, sharing behaviors were demonstrated in 100% of the 18-month-old infants in both the United States and Britain (Hay et al., 1995; Rheingold, Hay, & West, 1976). Other prosocial forms discernible in infancy include empathy (Poresky, 1990), helping behaviors (Jennings, Fitch, & Suwansky, 1987), comforting and empathic demonstrations (Dunn & Munn, 1986), and cooperation (Rheingold & Emery, 1986). Although Damon (1983) suggests that prosocial behavior is relatively rare among preschool children, infants as young as 9 months to those near age 3 are capable of and appear to be motivated to express prosocial behavior.

> As adolescence approaches, prosocial expressions continue to increase in complexity.

In childhood, the elicitation of prosocial activity from ages 4 to 12 shows varying patterns. Although sharing continues to be a common expression in early childhood (ages 4-6), it increases with age (10-11 years) and becomes more equitable (Knight, Bohlmeyer, Schneider, & Harris, 1993). Although the number of helping acts did not differ with age among 4- to 13-year-old children, the strategies implemented were more varied among older children, and girls were more helpful than boys (Strayer & Schroeder, 1989). Conversely, Stockdale, Hegland, and Chianomonte (1989) found few spontaneous helping behaviors among children aged 4 to 6 and no gender differences.

As adolescence approaches, prosocial expressions continue to increase in complexity. Prosocial behavior is more typically examined via intervention studies designed to promote some aspect of prosocial behavior. For example, when children in third grade were exposed to a specialized curriculum aiming to facilitate positive social skills, they did increase along with reductions in off-task behaviors (Sharpe, Brown, & Crider, 1995). In a similar vein, Grant and Roberts (1982) created a program to increase prosocial interactions and self-concept among academically at-risk (low IQ) adolescents and reported positive results. Even less attention is paid to prosocial behavior among adults. However, Naparstek (1990) found that adults are comparable to adolescents in their expressions of prosocial behaviors.

The psychological literature is replete with research on the demonstration of prosocial behaviors. From infancy through childhood, there are numerous studies documenting the prosocial engagement of children. In later years, these descriptive data become less explanatory, and researchers acknowledge that other factors, both personal and psychological, influence prosocial activity.

Positive Justice: Infancy Through Adulthood

Based on the theoretical guidance provided by structural developmental thinkers, an extensive body of literature exists on positive justice, moral reasoning and judgment, and the role of perspective taking. A major concept driving the psychological inquiry in moral development is that of positive justice. Generally, *justice* can be defined as "the awareness of the degree of fairness associated with the disposition of resources in social situations" (Charlesworth, 1991, p. 352). Positive justice is that aspect of justice concerned with prosocial interactions including the fair distribution of property, or distributive justice. There appear to be some developmental features that distinguish the distributive justice reasoning of infants, children, adolescents, and adults.

Although assessing distributive justice among infants is indeed difficult, Charlesworth (1991) postulates that a child's earliest sense of justice is expressed via emotional responses to resource distribution situations. Although the child may be unable to verbalize, expressions of anger are good indicators of injustice, and expressions of delight can indicate positive justice. As Damon's (1975, 1980) model suggests, children progress through various stages of distributive justice development. Prior to age 5, children's distributive justice reasoning focuses on self-interest, progresses to entitlement by physical status, equality, effort, need, and finally an integration of effort and need. Numerous studies support this developmental progression among children aged 5 through 10 in North America (Damon 1983; Lerner & Grant, 1990) and abroad (Enright et al. 1984; Watanabe, 1986).

The study of distributive justice among adolescents is scant. College-aged students were tested on equity and equality distributions (Boldizar, Perry, & Perry, 1988). Contrary to their hypothesis, females consistently judged equity distributions more favorably than males did. Authors concluded that because equity is a more mature distributive justice response, women are more advanced than men are, and this counters the position that women are morally inferior to men.

A void exists in the distributive justice literature when a lifespan approach is advocated. This might be explained by the preference for the examination of more sophisticated elements of moral reasoning maturity among older children and adults. Now we will convene to the psychological research on moral reasoning, judgment, and perspective taking.

Moral Reasoning, Judgment, and Perspective Taking: Childhood Through Adulthood

Although no research exists on infant moral reasoning, probably due to vast difficulties in comprehending structure of cognitions prior to speech acquisition, the psychological literature is replete with studies conducted on school-aged children (see Killen & Hart, 1995, and Turiel, 1998, for thorough reviews). Glover and Steele (1990), in a particularly clever study, attempted to examine moral reasoning processes of children aged 4 through 12 years. By identifying the developmental patterns of skills that underlie a moral dilemma, they concluded that children are able to determine the consequences of disobeying a rule or moral principle prior to being able to define the concept itself.

In the presentation of their 20-year longitudinal study of moral reasoning, Colby and Kohlberg (1984) documented a clear relationship between age and moral judgment. The sample consisted of 53 boys beginning at age 10, 13, and 16. This study offers support for Kohlberg's theory of morality as well as provides some of the minimal research on adult populations. In fact, scant research has been conducted on the moral reasoning of individuals older than 25. Certainly, the stage models, although inclusive of adult development, do not consider changes that may occur later in adulthood.

Using the framework provided by Gilligan, researchers determined that younger children emphasized the morality of care, regardless of gender, and older children were more justice oriented (Donenberg & Hoffman, 1988; Garrod, Beal, & Shin, 1990). Specifically, 1st-, 3rd-, and 5th-grade children and 5th and 6th graders all emphasized a care orientation. The latter groups did so significantly more often than did 10th- and 11th-grade students, who adopted a justice response.

What are the cognitive processes that children develop that allow for this maturational progression to occur? Several researchers have claimed that perspective taking provides the cognitive footing for mature moral judgment (Kurdek, 1980; Selman, 1976). Cognitive perspective-taking occurs when one can infer another person's cognitions, in essence the other's thoughts, intentions, and motives. In order to do so, one must be able to coordinate two viewpoints. Kurdek (1978) surmises that "cognitive perspective-taking [is] a prerequisite cognitive ability for mature intention-based moral judgments" (pp. 7-8). Testing a sample of 1st- and 3rd-grade children over a 10-month period, Kurdek (1980) determined that the period of middle childhood is one of rapid development in children's cognitive perspective-taking and moral judgment abilities.

In summation, there is evidence that supports the stage model of moral reasoning development, that this maturation is related to cognitive perspective-taking, and that during the transition from childhood to adolescence, a care orientation gives way to a justice orientation. What we do not know is how malleable adult moral reasoning becomes; a lifespan approach to this developmental question is still ripe for investigation.

MORAL DEVELOPMENT RESEARCH IN PHYSICAL EDUCATION AND SPORT

In the past 25 years, sport scholars and pedagogues have conducted an abundance of research on moral development in the physical activity context. In an attempt to operationalize the abstract concept of morality, specifically in a sporting context, Shields and Bredemeier (1995) created a threefold definition. They proposed that morality in sport is related to character, fair play, and sportspersonship.[1] These three elements are studied in various modes from both theoretical perspectives. They allow us to clearly connect the famous adage "sport builds character" to discussions of moral development. A common assumption, framed in the historical tomes, is that simply by participating in sport, positive character qualities will develop. By using the definition posited by Shields and Bredemeier, sport can then be considered a morally relevant context. Broun (1941) expressed a different connection between sport participation and character development when he posited that sports do not build character, they reveal it. What does the empiricism on this topic suggest? Does sport build or reveal character? I will attempt to decipher this question in the following section.

Promoting Prosocial Behavior: Childhood Through Adulthood

Some of the earliest work performed by sport scholars in the assessment of moral development examined the potential for physical activity to impact prosocial behavior. In his classic studies using cooperative games as the venue for prosocial development, Orlick (1981) and his colleagues (Orlick & Foley, 1978) found increases in prosocial behaviors among children. Specifically, an experimental group of preschool children, ages 2 to 4 years, engaged in more spontaneous cooperative behaviors during free play than did a control group. Among 5-year-

---

[1]Due to the exclusive nature of the term *sportsmanship* and the awkwardness of the alternative, *sportspersonship*, the terms *sportship* and *sporting behavior* will be used.

old children, one of two experimental groups demonstrated increases in sharing whereas children in a control group actually decreased in sharing episodes. The researchers concluded that preschool children are fully capable of enacting unsolicited cooperating and sharing behaviors.

Several studies have targeted late elementary school-aged children. Bovyer (1963) believed that a purpose of education was to facilitate children's prosocial development, including sportship. Content-analyzed data from 213 fourth- through sixth-grade children showed a developmental trend in that the sixth graders generated more ideas regarding sportship than the fourth graders did, and children rated as "good sports" by self and teachers offered more ideas of sportship than did those identified as "poor sports." These ideas included such sentiments as play by the rules, exhibit fair play, and respect others. A similar recent study found parallel expressions among elementary school children (Entzion, 1991). Clearly, these ideas generated by children denote some common themes with moral implications.

In a field experiment designed to add a competitive element, Kleiber and Roberts (1981) assessed reward distribution prosocial behaviors. Children aged 10-11 participated in a 2-week kickball tournament, and data were collected over 10 trials. Results demonstrated that exposure to competition did not affect children's giving patterns; the only difference emerged in the final trial when the generosity of boys decreased.

In middle childhood, children can and do show prosocial behaviors in physical activity settings. Children are cognizant of sportship behaviors and define them in the form of prosociability. However, there exists a limited amount of research on prosocial development through sport, particularly in adolescence and adulthood. More empiricism exists on efforts to reduce problematic behaviors.

Reducing Behavioral Problems: Childhood Through Adulthood

Although the above studies explored expressions and perceptions of prosocial behavior, another series of works examined methods of reducing behavioral problems such as asocial or antisocial behaviors. A prosocial physical education curriculum was implemented among third-grade academically and economically at-risk children (Sharpe et al., 1995). The team sport curriculum targeted leadership and problem-solving skills using multiple methods including peer respect, helping, and conflict resolution. In addition, teachers evaluated these social behaviors and allowed for student leadership opportunities. The two experimental classes improved in both target skills at the completion of the intervention; the control class did not. These behavioral improvements also translated to the classroom. This prosocial curriculum was also implemented with younger (first grade) and older (sixth grade) children and was found to be equally effective (Sharpe, Crider, Vyhlidal, & Brown, 1996).

Through modeling and reinforcement, prosocial behaviors can be taught and problematic behaviors reduced.

Targeting four boys (mean age of 12.3) identified as "poor sports," Giebink and McKenzie (1985) implemented a prosocial intervention to increase sport-like behaviors. Set in team sport contexts (softball class and recreational basketball), the boys were exposed to the social learning strategies of modeling and reinforcement to increase sportship and decrease unsporting behaviors. In softball class, the intervention proved effective; it was not effective in recreational basketball. Although able to reduce unsporting behaviors in the educational setting, the recreational environment was not conducive to increasing sportship.

Smith (1978, 1988) conducted a series of studies including a vast age group (children, adolescents, and adults) of male ice-hockey players. Although Smith was not attempting to reduce behavioral problems, he was able to identify and describe the expression of problematic behaviors using the social learning paradigm. In a large-scale study of individuals aged 12-21, Smith (1978) found that 64% advocated the use of illegal tactics. Mugno and Feltz (1985) conducted a similar study among 12- to 18-year-old male American football players. They too found a link between illegal tactics learned through observation and number employed during their own play. Although descriptive and not causal, these studies provide some support that problematic behaviors can be learned by observing models. An important next step might be to determine how these behavioral problems could be minimized.

From the social learning perspective, evidence suggests that through modeling and reinforcement, prosocial behaviors can be taught and problematic behaviors, reduced. However, we know little about the prosocial, asocial, and antisocial tendencies of adult sporting populations. Fortunately, there is a larger theoretical and empirical database examining sport and moral development from a structural developmental perspective.

Moral Reasoning and Judgment: Childhood

Although the social learning research has a longer history, a surge in structural developmental thinking in the study of moral development in sport has occurred. In an attempt to test Piaget's two-stage theory developed in a game context (marbles), Jantz (1975) made application to a sport setting by asking elementary school boys (ages 7-12) to dialogue about the rules of basketball. In doing so, he found support for Piaget's theory; specifically, the younger children voiced a perspective in line with the morality of constraint whereas the older children espoused the morality of cooperation.

Using the setting of a summer sport camp, Bredemeier (1995) tested children's (ages 9-13) moral reasoning levels in sport and in daily life contexts using hypothetical moral dilemmas. Although the younger children's scores across dilemma type were parallel, older children diverged in their moral reasoning. Specifically, older children (ages 12-13) reasoned at a higher level in daily life contexts than in sport. This disparity in moral reasoning is not unique to young adolescent children. In fact, Bredemeier and Shields (1984, 1986a) initially found this divergence in older adolescents and adults. The next section will present these results.

Moral Reasoning and Judgment: Athletes and Nonathletes

Two basic lines of inquiry have emerged in this classification (Shields & Bredemeier, 1995, 2002, for detailed reviews). One, adolescent and adult athletes have been assessed on their moral reasoning levels in sport and daily life. Two, adolescent and adult athletes and nonathletes have been contrasted in their moral reasoning usage. The following studies described all derive from a structural developmental grounding.

Bredemeier and Shields were the forerunners in developing a line of research to assess moral development among athletes. When they compared athletes to their nonathletic counterparts, findings indicated that high school athletes and nonathletes did not differ in moral reasoning (Bredemeier & Shields, 1986a). More recently, Beller and Stoll (1995) evaluated moral reasoning among high school students and concluded that nonathletes scored significantly higher in sport moral reasoning than high school athletes did. The different sources of measurement might explain these disparate findings.

College athletes scored significantly lower than their nonathletic peers on sport and daily life moral reasoning (Bredemeier & Shields, 1986a, 1986b). In contrast, Hall (1986) found that college basketball players exhibited higher levels of moral reasoning than nonathletes did. These contrary findings may be rationalized through the use of two types of dilemmas. Hall's dilemmas were contextualized in sport but outside of the action (i.e., coach requesting time-keeper to tamper with game clock) whereas Bredemeier and Shield's dilemmas were set within the competitive complexity of the game.

There appears to be a developmental process evidenced in late childhood and early adolescence whereby divergence in moral reasoning patterns exists when comparing sport to other aspects of life. This is true for athletes and nonathletes (Bredemeier & Shields, 1984, 1986a). Young adult athletes exhibit lower levels of moral reasoning than those of their nonathletic peers whereas adolescents do not differ based on athletic status. This begs the question "Does level of competition (high school, college, recreational) influence these patterns?" This will be the focus of the next section.

Young adult athletes exhibit lower levels of moral reasoning than those of their nonathletic peers whereas adolescents do not differ based on athletic status.

Moral Reasoning and Judgment: Competitive Level and Type of Sport

When Bredemeier and Shields (1984, 1986a) conducted the series of studies on moral reasoning divergence and distinctions between athletes and nonathletes, they also inquired as to whether competitive level might help to explain variations in moral decisions. Participants in college basketball exhibited lower levels of moral reasoning in both sport and daily life than their younger high school peers did (Bredemeier & Shields, 1984). However, this was not replicated when comparing high school and college swimmers. Does type of sport play a role in moral reasoning processes?

Another way to compare competitive levels is not by grade but by level of intensity. Priest and his colleagues (Priest, Krause, & Beach, 1999) found that in a 4-year longitudinal study conducted at the United States Military Academy, intercollegiate athletes scored significantly lower in sport moral reasoning than did intramural athletes. The authors documented a decline in reasoning scores across the 4 years of college for both athletic groups; however, intercollegiate athletes' scores were lower than intramural athletes' scores at the outset and conclusion of their education.

In the first iteration of this series of studies, Bredemeier and Shields (1984) determined that basketball players and swimmers, representing both high school and college levels, did not differ in their sport or daily life reasoning. Furthermore, Bredemeier and Shields (1986a) found that the sport moral reasoning of college basketball players was significantly lower than college swimmers. Beller and Stoll (1995) also found no differences in sport moral reasoning among high school team and individual sport athletes. However among college athletes, individual sport participants scored significantly higher on sport moral reasoning than team sport participants (Priest et al., 1999). Again it appears that another critical developmental period occurs between high school and college.

Bredemeier and Shields (1986b) coined the term game reasoning to explain the divergence between life and sport dilemmas among athletes and nonathletes and among various competitive levels. Specifically, individuals engage in a process whereby their moral reasoning in sport reverts back to a lower or more egocentric level than their moral reasoning outside of sport. Hence in sport, a form of bracketed morality occurs; the form of morality exhibited in sport is set apart from the morality exhibited in every other context. One explanation for this occurrence is that athletes' moral obligation in sport is given over to coaches and referees who assume their moral judgments and behaviors.

Legitimacy Judgments and Aggression: Childhood

Many who have invested in the study of moral development also examine the manifestation of poor moral choices. One of these consequent behaviors is that of aggression. This is a ripe topic for the context of sport where various forms of aggression are oftentimes justified. Bredemeier (1985) found that among 40 high school and college basketball players, many acknowledged that hurting an opponent is a legitimate part of competition. Moral theorists are particularly intent on the moral processes whereby individuals judge aggressive acts as legitimate or illegitimate.

Studies examining legitimacy judgments made by children depict a moderate negative relationship between moral reasoning level and the legitimization of potentially injurious acts (Bredemeier, 1994; Bredemeier, Weiss, Shields, & Cooper, 1986; Stuart & Ebbeck, 1995). Furthermore, children aged 9 to 13 years with lower levels of moral reasoning validated greater legitimacy of aggressive acts (Bredemeier, 1994; Bredemeier, Weiss, Shields, & Cooper, 1986). Level of sport contact appeared to mediate responses. Specifically, boys in high-contact sports and girls in medium-contact sports reported lower levels of moral reasoning and higher incidences of aggressive behaviors. As children grow older and continue to participate in sport, competition also typically becomes fiercer. Would this likely be replicated when assessing adolescent and adult legitimacy judgments regarding aggression?

Legitimacy Judgments and Aggression: High School and College

Few investigations have examined legitimacy judgments in high school and college athletics. Twenty high school and 20 college athletes were interviewed regarding legitimacy judgments of their own and a hypothetical athlete's aggressive behaviors (Bredemeier, 1985). Basketball players who reported lower sport moral reasoning scores accepted more aggressive acts, particularly those performed by the fictional athlete. In a study of female high school basketball players, Ryan and her colleagues (Ryan, Williams, & Wimer, 1990) were interested in the association between legitimacy judgments and actual aggressive behaviors. A relationship was uncovered: Those athletes who legitimized injurious acts prior to the season also performed more aggressive acts. Overall, however, legitimacy judgments of aggressive acts and actual acts of aggression were low. What other poor moral choices are legitimized in the context of sport? Recently, Fisher and Bredemeier (2000) found that intentionally injurious acts could be self-inflicted, such as professional athletes choosing to use steroids.

What factors might influence an athlete's acceptability of intentionally injurious acts in an activity espousing sportship, fair play, and character building? Reflecting on the 12-component model of moral action (Shields & Bredemeier, 1995), we might benefit from examining contextual factors and gain insight into these cognitive processes. Specifically, do the context of sport and the moral atmosphere surrounding competition play a role in moral reasoning responses?

Moral Atmosphere

Examining the context of sport as an influencing factor in predicting moral development has received sparse attention. One contextual factor that has been studied is that of moral atmosphere, which refers to the influence of group norms on moral behavior (Higgins, Power, & Kohlberg, 1984). Clearly, there are multiple factors within the sport environment that may affect moral decision making. Examining the team norm toward proaggressive acts, Stephens and Bredemeier (1996) found that among female youth soccer players, the major predictor of likelihood to enact aggressive behaviors was the team's proaggressive norms. A replication study performed among age-group female and male soccer players showed parallel results (Stephens, 2000). Thus, Stephens (2000) was able to conclude that among youth sport participants, team norms served to predict aggressive acts for both girls and boys.

Although Stephens (2000) explored team norms as predictors of moral behavior, Duquin and Shroeder-Braun (1996) examined coaches' behavior as the contextual factor potentially affecting moral behavior. Presented with scenarios illustrating coach-athlete conflicts, three groups (ages 12-14, 15-17, 18+) of past and current sport participants were asked to judge the propriety of coach behavior. Results showed that males rated coach improprieties as less problematic than females did, and the 15- to 17-year-olds judged the acts portrayed by the coaches as less problematic than did the other age groups. There appear to be some developmental implications in this study. Specifically, younger and older male participants viewed the scenarios as morally inappropriate; the adolescent participants were not as troubled by the hypothetical coaches' behaviors.

> Evidence suggests that athletes and non-athletes differ in their moral reasoning maturity.

From the research presented here, some trends have emerged. First, prosocial behaviors are recognized by children and demonstrated in the sport context oftentimes via sporting behaviors. Second, evidence suggests that athletes and nonathletes differ in their moral reasoning maturity; athletes exhibit lower levels of moral maturation than their nonathletic peers do. Third, level of competition may mediate the moral development of athletes. Fourth, children, youth, and adolescents exhibiting lower levels of moral reasoning legitimize acts of aggression in sport. Finally, contextual factors might serve to explain moral behaviors in the sport setting; team norms and coach behaviors explained moral responses. As stated earlier, many support the notion that sport builds character, yet much of the research shows that sport participants may be espousing less mature moral responses. Can moral development be enhanced in the context of sport? To answer this question, a review of moral education and character development programs in schools and in sport is warranted.

MORAL EDUCATION AND CHARACTER DEVELOPMENT

Moral education and character development programs have existed in the educational setting since the origins of formal public education in colonial America (Mulkey, 1997). Initially aligned with Christian principles, moral education programs became more secular in the early 1800s. Subsequently, numerous educators created programs to address the teaching of morals and values in school settings. In the past 30 years, the efficacy of various school and community character-education programs has been tested.

Moral education refers to the "deliberate and intentional activity of cultivating both moral growth and moral judgment" (Stoll & Beller, 1998, p. 22). In contrast to *moral training*, which emphasizes rule conformity among children, moral education involves the process of teaching children about moral principles and autonomous decision making (Arnold, 1994). Through this process, children are exposed to differentiating good and bad behavior by exposure to environmental and social stimuli that require increasingly more morally mature reasoning patterns. Goals of moral education vary depending on the specific program. For example, Lickona (1991b) delineates three goals in his model of moral education: to move from egocentrism toward cooperation, to lay the foundation of good character, and to develop moral community.

Lickona (1991a) sums up the need for character education by delineating 10 reasons why schools should address moral education and character development. These reasons range from the view that literally millions of children are not receiving moral education in other settings such as at home or in religious institutions to the supposition that a values-free education is a myth. He notes that there is increasing support for values education in schools among agencies and individuals including the government, business, and parents. Educational companies that sell character education tools illustrate the availability of resources for including character education in school settings. For example, the At-Risk Resources winter 2001 catalog (Bureau for At-Risk Resources, 2001) offers 12 pages of "Character Education" resources that teachers can use to teach character development. With a growing consensus that schools are an important location for character development, it is essential to explore the types of programs that currently exist in educational settings, physical education classes, and sport contexts. Character education programs have been implemented in elementary and secondary school classrooms. Evidence suggests that the programs appear to affect moral development among children and adolescents (Battistich, Watson, Solomon, Schaps, & Solomon, 1991; Mulkey, 1997; Power, Higgins, & Kohlberg, 1989). In addition, several scholars have integrated character education programs in physical education and sport settings. These programs have been implemented at the elementary, secondary, and college levels.

Moral Development Interventions in Physical Education

Over the past 20 years, several researchers have explored the potential for physical education curricula to enhance moral development among children and adolescents. Some of these programs derive from detailed theoretically grounded programs (i.e., Hellison's Self and Social Responsibility Model and Canada's Fair Play for Kids curriculum). Other studies represent specific intervention programs that are theoretically grounded but not replicated (i.e., Bredemeier, Weiss, Shields, & Shewchuk, 1986; Romance, Weiss, & Bockoven, 1986; Solomon, 1997).

Moral Development Interventions in Physical Education: Elementary School

With the intent of exploring whether social learning or structural developmental teaching strategies were more salient in enhancing children's moral reasoning, Bredemeier, Weiss, Shields, and Shewchuk (1986) assessed children (ages 5-7) who were participants at a summer sport camp. The children were assigned to one of three conditions: social learning, structural developmental, or control. Two instructors trained in that particular instructional strategy led each group for the 6-week program. Results of two moral reasoning assessments (Piagetian Intentionality Task and Distributive Justice Scale) showed that children in both experimental conditions improved in moral reasoning significantly more than did the control group. More recently, Solomon (1997) created a curricular model to enhance moral development in second graders. The 13-week intervention included one intact second-grade class as the structural developmental experimental group and another intact second-grade class as the control group. Children in the experimental group showed significant gains in distributive justice reasoning when compared to their counterparts. Overall, these studies show that specialized teaching strategies can facilitate moral growth.

Solomon (1999) expanded the components of her previous work with second graders and created a structural developmental curricular model for children (grades 1-4) identified as academically at risk due to learning disabilities. This model was developed to address both moral and motor skills. Early results indicate that children exposed to this model increased in distributive justice reasoning and motor skill development. A common concern among physical educators is that focusing on affective development delimits the motor skill improvements that are often the basis of accountability in physical education. This study begins to assuage that concern.

Several programs target middle elementary school children in the promotion of moral development via theoretical instructional strategies. Similar to the purpose of Solomon's work, the research of Romance et al. (1986) assessed the theoretical veracity of instruction on moral development while assessing motor skill improvements. Specifically, two intact fifth-grade classrooms were used: an experimental group that was taught via structural developmental principles and a control group. The experimental group scored significantly higher in moral reasoning and gymnastics ability than did the control group. In contrast, the control group showed greater improvements in basketball performance. No group differences were reported in fitness activities. These two studies present two issues. One, structural developmental interventions are effective for enhancing moral development of children; and two, motor skill performance is not compromised. However, it is important to note that the control group did outperform the experimental group in basketball; this warrants further investigation as to the potential impact of moral development interventions on motor skill curricular goals.

Whereas Solomon (1999) is in the process of creating a comprehensive physical education curriculum for moral and motor skill development, Canada boasts a widespread educational program developed by the Commission for Fair Play called Fair Play for Kids. Gibbons and her colleagues (Gibbons & Ebbeck, 1997; Gibbons, Ebbeck, & Weiss, 1995) were instrumental in evaluating the efficacy of this program among 4th- through 6th-grade students. The first study was designed to test the impact of the Fair Play program over a 7-month period. Eighteen classrooms, six at each grade level were assigned to one of three conditions: fair play in physical education and classroom subjects, fair play in physical education only, and no fair-play curriculum (control group). Both experimental groups reported significantly higher scores on four measures of moral development than did control group participants; no differences were documented between the two experimental groups.

Gibbons and Ebbeck (1997) extended the previous study in two major ways. One, can the improvements shown in the first study occur earlier than 7 months, and two, do different instructional strategies affect moral maturational gains? Nine intact classes of children in grades 4 through 6 were assigned to one of three conditions: social learning group, structural developmental group, and control group. Both experimental groups scored significantly higher in three of the four moral development components (moral judgment, moral intention, prosocial behaviors) at the midpoint and at the end of the 7-month intervention. Those children in the structural developmental group scored significantly higher in moral reasoning than did the other two groups at the midpoint and at the end of the intervention. Overall, both theoretical instructional strategies provide effective means for promoting moral development, and these improvements are evidenced as early as 4 months into the intervention. The utility of this program appears to be scientifically supported and is also endorsed by the teachers exposed to this curriculum.

Moral Development Interventions in Physical Education: High School

Hellison is a major leader in the promotion of moral maturation among adolescents, specifically at-risk and delinquent adolescents. A noted physical educator and academician, Hellison (1985, 1995) has worked on a model for the integration of social and motor skill development for over 20 years. His model of self and social responsibility has been adopted by physical educators throughout the country. Based on his work with inner-city at-risk youth, the main premise of this model is to empower students (self responsibility) and teach specific values (social responsibility). He has proposed five hierarchical levels of responsibility: irresponsibility, respect, participation, self-direction, and caring. Numerous evaluative studies have been conducted and demonstrate the utility of this model for high school-aged youth (Hellison & Georgiadis, 1992; Hellison, Martinek, & Cutforth, 1996). Recently, Hellison's model of personal and social responsibility was combined with Siedentop's (1994) sport education model for a group of sixth-grade boys (Hastie & Buchanan, 2000). The outcome of their 26-lesson curriculum was a "hybrid model" called Empowering Sport, which demonstrated the utility of Hellison's model among middle school children.

Another physical education curriculum, Sport for Peace, also was created for adolescents in urban high schools (Ennis et al., 1999). Sport for Peace was modeled after the sport education model (Siedentop) using roles and responsibilities such as team membership and leadership to teach curricular strategies such as conflict resolution and full participation. Testing of this curriculum, which focused on enhancing positive social interactions, was conducted in six high schools with 10 physical educators. A traditional unit of soccer was followed by Sport for Peace training, then implementation of Sport for Peace strategies in a basketball unit. Results from observation and interview data suggest that students, regardless of skill level, experienced greater engagement in activity and more positive social dialogues involving trust, responsibility, and respect.

Successful programming in physical education contexts has been initiated at various educational levels from early elementary through high school. Comparatively, research in moral development programming in competitive sport is sparse. Although previous research documents serious concerns underlying competitive sport participation, such as divergent reasoning patterns and legitimization of aggressive acts, programming designed to build character in sport is lacking.

MORAL DEVELOPMENT INTERVENTIONS IN SPORT

The popular belief, which extends back several hundred years, that sport builds character is predominantly refuted in contemporary scientific inquiry. However Shields and Bredemeier (1995) note: "The main difference between sport and everyday life is that moral experience is condensed and exposed in sport. We believe this makes it a valuable context for moral education" (p. 2). Although Shields and Bredemeier offer 10 recommendations for coaches to positively affect moral character, moral-development intervention programs are rare in sport settings. Two programs have been identified that specifically address moral education as part of the sport experience.

Moral Development Interventions in Sport: Middle School

In 1985, Wandzilak created a values education model designed to facilitate reasoning development, sportship, and positive behaviors. This model served as the intervention for a season-long study of two junior high school boys' basketball teams (Wandzilak, Carroll, & Ansorge, 1988). One team served as the control group, and the other was exposed to the values intervention. The latter spent time during practice sessions discussing morally relevant issues such as sportship and basketball-specific dilemmas. End-of-season analyses indicated no significant between-group differences on the two aforementioned variables. However, within-group analyses showed trends of improvement for moral reasoning and sportship in the experimental group. The short intervention (9 weeks) and the small number of participants (10 per team) may have posed some limitations.

Moral Development Interventions in Sport: College

A longitudinal atheoretical moral development intervention is being implemented among intramural athletes at the United States Military Academy (Butler, 2000). This program, called the West Point Fair Play Project, emerged from observations of positive and negative behaviors occurring during intramural basketball games. All personnel involved in the program attend a fair-play workshop targeting issues of respect and using actual observed scenarios to generate discussion. Along with actual win-loss record, points are allocated for fair play behaviors: 10 points for good behavior, 5 points for below-average behavior, and 2 points for unacceptable behavior. A final end of the season tally includes a win-loss score and a fair play score that together add up to a total score. Thus, the team with the best win record does not necessarily win the league championship. Results from this 4-year program showed improved sporting behaviors in competitive basketball. Butler acknowledges that this type of program is likely to be most successful in middle and high school settings as well as recreational college settings.

It is disappointing to note that few educators and researchers have approached the sport setting to affect moral development. Although many cite the ripe context for sport to affect moral development, programs and interventions are lacking. The good news is that several centers have been created to provide resources and services to those attempting to enhance moral development through sport and other forms of physical activity. See Table 2 for a listing of centers.

DIRECTIONS FOR FUTURE RESEARCH

A substantial number of theoretical and empirical contributions on moral development in physical activity settings have emerged in the past 20 years. Based on the theoretical wisdom, research testing various intervention strategies was undertaken particularly in physical education contexts. Although the study of moral development is by definition developmental, there

TABLE 2
Centers for Moral Education Through Sport and Physical Activity

Center Name	Affiliation	Web Site Address
Character and Sport Initiative Program	Boston University	www.bu.edu/education/csi
Mendelson Center for Sport, Character and Culture	University of Notre Dame	www.nd.edu/~cscc
Center for Sport, Spirituality and Character Development	Neumann College	www.neumann.edu

is a paucity of research on adult populations. Furthermore, much of the research to date is descriptive. At this juncture, the knowledge base is clearly mature enough to move from a descriptive understanding of moral maturation to that of explaining and predicting moral growth. These two points set the stage for the next generation of research in moral development.

To begin to decipher the "whys" and "whats" of moral decision making, longitudinal research designs need to be employed. For example, we know that athletes in different sports (team, individual) and at different competitive levels (high school, college) show varied patterns of moral maturity (Beller & Stoll, 1995; Bredemeier & Shields, 1984, 1986a). What we do not know is "why" there are differences among athletes in these various classifications. Furthermore, we know that children are responsive to moral intervention programs in elementary school physical education (Bredemeier, Weiss, Shields, & Shewchuk, 1986; Romance, et al., 1986; Solomon, 1997). What we do not know is "what" becomes of their moral-maturity gains once the intervention has ceased. Longitudinal designs will allow researchers to answer questions on moral development patterns across sport participants and long-term effects of moral education.

The majority of literature in sport moral development queries children, youth, and adolescents. Another void in the literature is the study of adult moral-maturation qualities including young adults, those entering middle age, and older adult populations. Levels of sport and exercise involvement among adults are increasing. In fact, many adults are competing in sports for the first time. Participation in master's competitive events has increased dramatically over the past 10 years. Also, knowledge regarding health benefits of exercise has entered the mainstream consciousness. There is a large pool of active adults who could lend the topic of moral development additional insight. Let us truly examine moral development as a developmental topic by insisting on a lifespan approach to fully comprehend its parameters.

Much of the research to date has situated the sport participant as an individual, disregarding the potential impact of the social context of sport. The problem with this premise is that one cannot take the individual out of the social context, study his or her intentions, and predict future behaviors. Social learning theory has demonstrated the significance of modeling and reinforcement by significant others on moral behavior (Mugno & Feltz, 1985; Sharpe et al., 1995). Researchers would benefit from including contextual factors in their designs as both antecedents and mediators of moral development. The moral action model posited by Shields and Bredemeier (1995) might serve as the starting point for asking, "What contextual variables might be influential in understanding the complexity of this group's moral development processes?" Furthermore, what other factors are parts of the moral fabric of sport? For example, Solomon and Bredemeier (1999) queried whether children identify gender inequality in sport as a moral issue. The recent research on moral atmosphere and group norms begins to address the inclusion of contextual factors affecting moral development (Duquin & Shroeder-Braun, 1996; Stephens, 2000; Stephens & Bredemeier, 1996). We might also ask, "How do significant others such as officials, opponents, and parents influence the moral maturation process in sport?" Weiss and her colleagues (Weiss & Smith, 1999; Weiss & Stuntz, 2003) call for the consideration of peer relations in the understanding of the youth sport experience.

Intervention research in physical education has benefited from extensive model generation over many years by Hellison (1985, 1995) and more recently by Gibbons and her colleagues (Gibbons & Ebbeck, 1997; Gibbons et al., 1995). A void exists in the application and testing of moral intervention models in sport settings (Stephens, 1997). Moral development scholars could make a huge contribution by creating and testing the efficacy of moral intervention models in sport settings at all ages and levels of competition. Although easier said than done, there are many youth sport agencies that are yearning to find ways to promote a healthier learning environment for children. Clearly, the more intense the level of competition, the more difficult this intervention plan becomes (Butler, 2000). However, the Citizenship Through Sports Alliance, an organization of 10 members including major professional leagues (i.e., Major League Baseball, National Basketball Association, National Hockey League, National Football Association, Women's National Basketball Association) and amateur associations (National Collegiate Athletic Association, United States Olympic Committee) was recently formed. The purpose is to address the breakdown in sporting behavior by focusing on six principles including ethical conduct and nonviolence. A 3-year program, the alliance intends to minimize or eradicate the problematic features associated with sport and improve the positive values of sport including sportship.

Finally, in order to adequately and accurately perform the above-mentioned research, appropriate measurement devices must be available. Although there exist several measures of moral reasoning and judgment, the quality of some of these tools is suspect (B. J. L. Bredemeier & Shields, 1998). For example, some instruments are not situated in a sport or physical activity context (i.e., the Distributive Justice Scale, or DJS). Solomon worked to remedy this problem by adapting the DJS (Adapted Distributive Justice Scale; Solomon, 1997, 1999) for use in physical activity settings. Considering the complexity of assessing moral reasoning and judgment, it may be helpful to seek out and determine the adequacy of alternative methods of measurement. Those interested in measurement issues might consider developing quasi-quantitative approaches such as direct observation and coach or teacher ratings and inductive and deductive qualitative methods.

In addition, instrument selection may need refining. Some researchers choose instruments for convenience, which do not accurately assess the target variable. For example, if one chooses to assess the process of moral judgment and considers the 12-component model of moral action, one would have to ascertain whether one was actually assessing moral reasoning, a personal competency, or moral atmosphere, a contextual influence. Finally, some existing moral development tools might benefit from further psychometric examination. Additional psychometric evaluation is warranted to document reliability and validity based on the purported purpose of this instrument. See Bredemeier and Shields (1998) for a comprehensive overview of measurement issues in sport moral development.

Although we have learned so much in the past few decades, the previous inquiry in moral development has served the purpose of providing theoretical guidance and testing basic descriptive level questions about moral development in physical activity. Good research always leads to more questions than it answers. This is true for the current state of knowledge in sport moral development.

SUMMARY

Most would agree that moral development is a maturational goal for all people. Through continual and complex human interactions, we learn how to affiliate in our social world. The context of physical activity is but one of the social settings where moral maturation can be targeted. As educators and scientists, we have the responsibility to provide sound principles and effective educational programs for practitioners. In effect, one does not really have the choice to address moral issues in physical activity. These issues arise, and ignoring them, at best, wastes a teachable moment; at worst, as Leonard (1972) decried, we could be teaching character fit for a criminal. For sport and physical activity not only to reveal character, but also to build it, concepts of sportship and fair play must be promoted. With additional theoretically derived empirical inquiry, we can move closer toward promoting moral development in physical education and sport contexts throughout the lifespan.

References

Arnold, P. J. (1994). Sport and moral education. *Journal of Moral Education, 23*, 75-89.

Arsenio, W. F. (1988). Children's conceptions of the situational affective consequences of sociomoral events. *Child Development, 59*, 1611-1622.

Bandura, A. (1969). *The principles of behavior modification.* New York: Holt, Rinehart, & Winston.

Bandura, A. (1977). *Social learning theory.* Englewood Cliffs, NJ: Prentice-Hall.

Bar-Tal, D. (1982). Sequential development of helping behavior: A cognitive-learning approach. *Developmental Review, 2*, 101-124.

Battistich, V., Watson, M., Solomon, D., Schaps, E., & Solomon, J. (1991). The Child Development Project: A comprehensive program for the development of prosocial character. In W. M. Kurtines & J. L. Gewirtz (Eds.), *Handbook of moral behavior and development:* Vol. 3. *Application* (pp. 1-34). Hillsdale, NJ: Erlbaum.

Beller, J. M., & Stoll, S. K. (1995). Moral reasoning of high school student athletes and general students: An empirical study versus personal testimony. *Pediatric Exercise Science, 7*, 352-363.

Boldizar, J. P., Perry, D.G., & Perry, L.C. (1988). Gender and reward distribution: A test of two hypotheses. *Sex Roles, 9/10*, 569-579.

Bovyer, G. (1963). Children's concepts of sportsmanship in the fourth, fifth, and sixth grades. *Research Quarterly, 34*, 282-287.

Bredemeier, B. J. (1985). Moral reasoning and the perceived legitimacy of intentionally injurious sport acts. *Journal of Sport Psychology, 7*, 110-124.

Bredemeier, B. J. L. (1994). Children's moral reasoning and their assertive, aggressive, and submissive tendencies in sport and daily life. *Journal of Sport & Exercise Psychology, 16*, 1-14.

Bredemeier, B. J. L. (1995). Divergence in children's moral reasoning in daily life and sport specific contexts. *International Journal of Sport Psychology, 26*, 453-463.

Bredemeier, B. J., & Shields, D. L. (1984). Divergence in moral reasoning about sport and everyday life. *Sociology of Sport Journal, 1*, 348-357.

Bredemeier, B. J., & Shields, D. L. (1986a). Moral growth among athletes and nonathletes: A comparative analysis. *Journal of Genetic Psychology, 147*, 7-18

Bredemeier, B. J., & Shields, D. L. (1986b). Game reasoning and interactional morality. *Journal of Genetic Psychology, 147*, 257-275.

Bredemeier, B. J., Weiss, M. R., Shields, D. L., & Cooper, B. A. B. (1986). The relationship between children's legitimacy judgments and their moral reasoning, aggression, tendencies, and sport involvement. *Sociology of Sport Journal, 4*, 48-60.

Bredemeier, B. J., Weiss, M. R., Shields, D. L., & Shewchuck, R. M. (1986). Promoting moral growth in a summer sport camp: The implementation of theoretically grounded instructional strategies. *Journal of Moral Education, 15*, 212-220.

Bredemeier, B. J. L., & Shields, D. L. L. (1998). Moral assessment in sport psychology. In J. Duda (Ed.), *Advances in sport and exercise psychology measurement* (pp. 257-276). Morgantown, WV: Fitness Information Technology.

Broun, H. (1941). *Collected edition of Heywood Broun.* New York: Harcourt, Brace and Company.

Bureau for At-Risk Resources. (Winter, 2001). *At-risk resources.* Plainview, NY: The Guidance Channel.

Butler, L.F. (2000). Fair play: Respect for all. *Journal of Physical Education, Recreation, and Dance, 71*(2), 32-35.

Charlesworth, W. R. (1991). The development of the sense of justice. *American Behavioral Scientist, 34*, 350-370.

Colby, A., & Kohlberg, L. (1984). Invariant sequence and internal consistency in moral judgment stages. In W. M. Kurtines & J. L. Gewirtz (Eds.), *Morality, moral behavior, and moral development* (pp. 41-51). New York: John Wiley & Sons.

Crain, W. C. (1987). Widespread disturbance in children's leisure. *Leisure Information Quarterly, 13*, 11-12.

Damon, W. (1975). Early conceptions of positive justice as related to the development of logical operations. *Child Development, 46*, 301-312.

Damon, W. (1980). Patterns of change in children's social reasoning: A two-year longitudinal study. *Child Development, 51*, 1010-1017.

Damon, W. (1983). *Social and personality development: Infancy through adolescence.* New York: W. W. Norton & Company.

Donenberg, G. R., & Hoffman, L. W. (1988). Gender differences in moral development. *Sex Roles, 11/12*, 701-717.

Dunn, J., & Munn, P. (1986). Siblings and the development of prosocial behavior. *International Journal of Behavioral Development, 9*, 265-284.

Duquin, M. E., & Schroeder-Braun, K. (1996). Power, empathy, and moral conflict in sport. *Peace and Conflict: Journal of Peace Psychology, 2*, 351-367.

Ennis, C. D., Solmon, M. A., Satina, B., Loftus, S. J., Mensch, J., & McCauley, M. T. (1999). Creating a sense of family in urban schools using the "Sport for Peace" curriculum. *Research Quarterly for Exercise and Sport, 70*, 273-285.

Enright, R. D., Bjerstedt, A., Enright, W. F., Levy, V. M., Lapsley, D. K., Buss, R. R., Harwell, M., & Zindler, M. (1984). Distributive justice development: Cross-cultural, contextual, and longitudinal evaluations. *Child Development, 55*, 1737-1751.

Entzion, B. J. (1991). A child's view of fairplay. *Strategies, 4*, 16-19.

Fisher, L. A., & Bredemeier, B. J. L. (2000). Caring about injustice: The moral self-perceptions of professional female bodybuilders. *Journal of Sport & Exercise Psychology, 22*, 327-344.

Garrod, A., Beal, C., & Shin, P. (1990). The development of moral orientation in elementary school children. *Sex Roles, 22*, 13-27.

Gibbons, S. L., & Ebbeck, V. (1997). The effect of different teaching strategies on the moral development of physical education students. *Journal of Teaching in Physical Education, 17*, 85-98.

Gibbons, S. L., Ebbeck, V., & Weiss, M. R. (1995). Fair Play for Kids: Effects on the moral development of children in physical education. *Research Quarterly for Exercise and Sport, 66*, 247-255.

Giebink, M. P., & McKenzie, T. C. (1985). Teaching sportsmanship in physical education and recreation: An analysis of intervention and generalization effects. *Journal of Teaching in Physical Education, 4*, 167-177.

Gilligan, C. (1977). In a different voice: Women's conceptions of the self and of morality. *Harvard Educational Review, 47*, 481-517.

Gilligan, C. (1982). *In a different voice; Psychological theory and women's development.* Cambridge, MA: Harvard University Press.

Glover, R. J., & Steele, C. (1990). Applying Neopiagetian theory to the moral reasoning process. *Psychological Reports, 66*, 1259-1272.

Grant, B. C., & Roberts, K. D. (1982). The development of self-concept through a physical activity programme. *New Zealand Journal of Health, Physical Education, and Recreation, 15*, 15-18.

Haan, N. (1977). *Coping and defending: Processes of self-environment organization.* New York: Academic Press.

Haan, N., Aerts, E., & Cooper, B. (1985). *On moral grounds: The search for practical morality.* New York: New York University Press.

Hall, E. (1986). Moral development levels of athletes in sport-specific and general social situations. In L. Vander Velden & J. H. Humphrey (Eds.), *Psychology and sociology of sport: Current selected research* (pp. 191-204). New York: AMS Press.

Hastie, P. A., & Buchanan, A. M. (2000). Teaching responsibility through sport education: Prospects of a coalition. *Research Quarterly for Exercise and Sport, 71*, 25-35.

Hay, D. F., Castle, J., Stimson, C. A., & Davies, L. (1995). The social construction of character in toddlerhood. In M. Killen & D. Hart (Eds.), *Morality in everyday life: Developmental perspectives* (pp. 23-51). Cambridge: Cambridge University Press.

Hellison, D. R. (1985). *Goals and strategies for teaching physical education.* Champaign, IL: Human Kinetics.

Hellison, D. R. (1995). *Teaching personal and social responsibility through physical activity.* Champaign, IL: Human Kinetics.

Hellison, D. R., & Georgiadis, N. (1992). Teaching values through basketball. *Strategies, 5*, 5-8.

Hellison, D. R., Martinek, T. J., & Cutforth, N. J. (1996). Beyond violence prevention in inner city physical activity programs. *Peace and Conflict: Journal of Peace Psychology, 2*, 321-337.

Higgins, A., Power, C., & Kohlberg, L. (1984). The relationship of moral judgment to judgments of responsibility. In J. L. Gewirtz & W. M. Kurtines (Eds.), *Morality, moral development, and moral behavior: Basic issues in theory and research* (pp. 74-106). New York: Wiley Interscience.

Jantz, R. K. (1975). Moral thinking in male elementary pupils as reflected by perception of basketball rules. *Research Quarterly, 46*, 414-421.

Jennings, K. D., Fitch, D., & Suwansky, J. T. D. (1987). Social cognition and social interaction in three-year-olds: Is social cognition truly social? *Child Study Journal, 17*, 1-14.

Killen, M., & Hart, D. (Eds.). (1995). *Morality in everyday life.* Cambridge: Cambridge University Press.

Kleiber, D. A., & Roberts, G. C. (1981). The effects of sport experience on the development of social character. An exploratory investigation. *Journal of Sport Psychology, 3*, 114-122.

Knight, G. P., Bohlmeyer, E. M., Schneider, H., & Harris, J. D. (1993). Age difference in temporal monitoring and equal sharing in a fixed-duration sharing task. *British Journal of Developmental Psychology, 11*, 143-158.

Kohlberg, L. (1969). Stage and sequence: The cognitive-developmental approach to socialization. In D. A. Goslin (Ed.), *Handbook of socialization theory and research* (pp. 347-480). Chicago, IL; Rand McNally.

Kohlberg, L. (1976). Moral stages and moralization: The cognitive-developmental approach. In T. Lickona (Ed.), *Moral development and behavior: Theory, research, and social issues* (pp. 31-53). New York: Holt, Rinehart & Winston.

Kurdek, L. A. (1978). Perspective taking as the cognitive basis of children's moral development: A review of the literature. *Merrill-Palmer Quarterly, 24*, 3-28.

Kurdek, L. A. (1980) Developmental relations among children's perspective taking, moral judgment, and parent-rated behaviors. *Merrill-Palmer Quarterly, 26,* 103-121.

Leonard, G. B. (1972). *The transformation: A guide to the inevitable changes in humankind.* New York: Delacorte, Press.

Lerner, M. J., & Grant, P. R. (1990). The influences of commitment to justice and ethnocentrism on children's allocations of pay. *Social Psychology Quarterly, 53,* 229-238.

Lickona, T. (1991a). *Educating for character: How our schools can teach respect and responsibility.* New York: Bantam Books.

Lickona, T. (1991b). Moral development in the elementary school classroom. In W. M. Kurtines & J. L. Gewirtz (Eds.), *Handbook of moral behavior and development: Vol. 3. Application* (pp. 143-161). Hillsdale, NJ: Erlbaum.

Miller, S. C., Bredemeier, B. J. L., & Shields, D. L. L. (1997). Sociomoral education through physical education with at-risk children. *Quest, 49,* 114-129.

Mugno, D. A., & Feltz, D. L. (1985). The social learning of aggression in youth football in the United States. *Canadian Journal of Applied Sport Sciences, 10,* 26-35.

Mulkey, Y.J. (1997). The history of character education. *Journal of Physical Education, Recreation, and Dance, 68*(9), 35-37.

Naparstek, N. (1990). Children's conceptions of prosocial behavior. *Child Study Journal, 20,* 207-220.

Orlick, T., & Foley, C. (1978). Pre-school cooperative games: A preliminary perspective. In B. A. Kerr (Ed.) *Human performance and behavior* (pp. 129-138). Banff: University of Calgary Press.

Orlick, T. D. (1981). Positive socialization via cooperative games. *Developmental Psychology, 17,* 426-429.

Piaget, J. (1965). *The moral judgment of the child.* New York: The Free Press. (Original work published 1932).

Poresky, R. H. (1990). The young children's empathy measure: Reliability, validity and effects of companion animal bonding. *Psychological Reports, 66,* 931-936.

Power, C., Higgins, A., & Kohlberg, L. (1989). *Lawrence Kohlberg's approach to moral education.* New York: Columbia University Press.

Priest, R. F., Krause, J.V., & Beach, J. (1999). Four-year changes in college athletes' ethical value choices in sports situations. *Research Quarterly for Exercise and Sport, 70,* 170-178.

Rest, J., Narvaez, D., Bebeau, M. J., & Thoma, S. J. (1999). *Postconventional moral thinking: A neo-Kohlbergian approach.* Mahwah, NJ: Erlbaum.

Rest, J. R. (1986). *Moral development: Advances in research and theory.* New York: Praeger Press.

Rheingold, H.L., & Emery, G.N. (1986). The nurturant acts of very young children. In D. Olweus, J. Block, & M. Radke-Yarrow (Eds.), *Development of antisocial and prosocial behavior: Research, theories, and issues* (pp. 75-96). New York: Academic Press.

Rheingold, H.L., Hay, D. F., & West, M. J. (1976). Sharing in the second year of life. *Child Development, 47,* 1148-1158.

Romance T. J., Weiss, M. R., & Bockoven, J. (1986). A program to promote moral development through elementary school physical education. *Journal of Teaching in Physical Education, 5,* 126-136.

Ryan, M.K., Williams, J. M., & Wimer, B. (1990). Athletic aggression: Perceived legitimacy and behavioral intentions in girls' high school basketball. *Journal of Sport & Exercise Psychology, 12,* 48-55.

Selman, R. L. (1976). The relation of role taking to the development of moral judgment in children. *Child Development, 42,* 79-91.

Sharpe, T., Brown, M., & Crider, K. (1995). The effects of sportsmanship curriculum intervention on generalized positive social behavior of urban elementary school students. *Journal of Applied Behavior Analysis, 28,* 401-416.

Sharpe, T., Crider, K., Vyhlidal, T., & Brown, M. (1996). Description and effects of prosocial instruction in an elementary physical education setting. *Education and Treatment of Children, 19,* 435-457.

Shields, D. L. L., & Bredemeier, B. J. L. (1995). *Character development and physical activity.* Champaign, IL: Human Kinetics.

Shields, D. L., & Bredemeier, B. L. (2002). Moral development and behavior in sport. In R. N. Singer, Hausenblas, H. A., & Janelle, C. M. (Eds.) Handbook of sport psychology (2nd Ed. pp. 585-603). New York, Wiley.

Siedentop, D. (1994). *Sport education: Quality PE through positive sport experiences.* Champaign, IL: Human Kinetics.

Smith, M. D. (1978). Social learning of violence in minor hockey. In F. L. Smoll & R. E. Smith (Eds.), *Psychological perspectives in youth sports* (pp. 91-106). Washington, DC: Hemisphere Publishing.

Smith, M. D. (1988). Interpersonal sources of violence in hockey: The influence of parents, coaches, and teammates. In F. L. Smoll, R. A. Magill, & M. J. Ash (Eds.), *Children in sport* (pp. 301-313). Champaign, IL: Human Kinetics.

Solomon, G. B. (1997). Fair play in the gymnasium: Improving social skills among elementary school students. *Journal of Physical Education, Recreation, and Dance, 68*(5), 22-25.

Solomon, G. B. (1999). Sociomoral enrichment through physical activity: Lab testing of a curricular model. *Association for the Advancement of Applied Sport Psychology, Conference Abstracts,* 45-46.

Solomon, G. B., & Bredemeier, B. J. L. (1999). Children's moral conceptions of gender stratification in sport. *International Journal of Sport Psychology, 30*, 350-368.

Stephens, D. E. (1997). Sportspersonship in youth sport: Issues in the application of psychological models. *Journal of Applied Sport Psychology, 9*, S11.

Stephens, D. E. (2000). Predictors of likelihood to aggress in youth sport: An examination of coed and all-girls teams. *Journal of Sport Behavior, 23*, 311-325.

Stephens, D. E., & Bredemeier, B. J. L. (1996). Moral atmosphere and judgments about aggression in girls' soccer: Relationships among moral and motivational variables. *Journal of Sport & Exercise Psychology, 18*, 158-173.

Stockdale, D. F., Hegland, S. M., & Chianomonte, T. (1989). Helping behaviors: An observational study of preschool children. *Early Childhood Research Quarterly, 4*, 533-543.

Stoll, S. K., & Beller, J. M. (1998). Can character be measured? *Journal of Physical Education, Recreation, and Dance, 69*(1), 19-24.

Strayer, J., & Schroeder, M. (1989). Children's helping strategies: Influences of emotion, empathy, and age. *New Directions for Child Development, 44*, 85-105.

Stuart, M. E., & Ebbeck, V. (1995). The influence of perceived social approval on moral development in youth sport. *Pediatric Exercise Science, 7*, 270-280.

Turiel, E. (1998). The development of morality. In N. Eisenberg (Ed.), *Handbook of child psychology:* Vol. 3. *Social, emotional, and personality development* (pp. 863-932). New York: John Wiley & Sons.

Wandzilak, T. (1985). Values development through physical education and athletics. *Quest, 37*, 176-185.

Wandzilak, T., Carroll, T., & Ansorge, C. J. (1988). Values development through physical activity: Promoting sportsmanlike behaviors, perceptions, and moral reasoning. *Journal of Teaching in Physical Education, 8*, 13-23.

Watanabe, Y. (1986). Distributive justice development. *Japanese Journal of Educational Psychology, 34*, 84-90.

Weiss, M. R. (2001). Developmental sport psychology. In N. J. Smelser & P. B. Baltes (Eds.), *International encyclopedia of the social and behavioral sciences* (pp. 3620-3624). Oxford, UK: Elsevier Science Limited.

Weiss, M. R., & Bredemeier, B. J. (1983). Developmental sport psychology: A theoretical perspective for studying children in sport. *Journal of Sport Psychology, 5*, 216-230.

Weiss, M. R., & Smith, A. L. (1999). Quality of friendships in youth sport: Measurement development and validation. *Journal of Sport & Exercise Psychology, 21*, 145-166.

Weiss, M. R., & Smith, A. L. (2002). Moral development in sport and physical activity: Theory, research, and intervention. In T. S. Horn (Ed.), *Advances in sport psychology* (2nd ed., pp. 243-280). Champaign, IL: Human Kinetics.

Weiss, M.R., & Stuntz, C.P. (2003). A little friendly competition: Peer relationships and psychosocial development in youth sport and physical activity contexts. In M.R. Weiss (Ed.), Developmental sport and exercise psychology: A lifespan perspective. (pp. 165-196) Morgantown, WV: Fitness Information Technology.

Zahn-Waxler, C., & Radke-Yarrow, M. (1990). The origins of empathic concern. *Motivation and Emotion, 14*, 107-130.

CHAPTER EIGHTEEN

Gender and Cultural Diversity Across the Lifespan

Diane L. Gill

In this chapter, I have taken on the challenging task of covering gender and cultural diversity in developmental sport and exercise psychology. We have a substantial body of sport and exercise psychology work on gender (e.g., Gill, 2002), but almost none of that literature takes a developmental perspective. Furthermore, we have almost nothing on any cultural diversity issues other than gender in sport and exercise psychology, let alone any research or theoretical work with a developmental perspective. To add further challenge, I will take a feminist, gender-relations perspective and assume that gender and multiple cultural identities are interrelated and dynamic. Everything interacts and changes with the time and context. When we try to look at gender and culture in developmental sport and exercise psychology, we find no research or theoretical work that fits such a perspective.

I might end the chapter here with the standard call for more research to address the issues, but that would not be at all helpful in advancing our understanding and practice. We can never find a definitive endpoint with a relational, dynamic system, but we can progress. Gender and cultural relations continue to change and develop with the times, just as they change across an individual lifespan. In this chapter, I will focus on the limited literature related to gender and culture in sport and exercise, draw upon related psychology and sport studies works, and try to find patterns and connections to bring the diverse works together in a developmental framework.

In the first section, I will use the theoretical work of the feminist sport-studies scholars and growing work on feminist psychology to provide a guiding framework for the chapter. Just as gender scholarship has expanded to incorporate cultural diversity, the framework for this chapter extends to include multiple, intersecting cultural identities and relations. Next, we will turn to research in psychology and in sport and exercise psychology, focusing on the gender scholarship and then extending to other cultural diversity issues, particularly sexuality and race/ethnicity. The bulk of the research involves college and young adults, but in this chapter, we will pay particular attention to the research on children and youth sport, as well as the work with older adults.

Research with youth and older adults brings us closer to development, but age comparisons also reflect changing times and the social-historical context. Age comparisons may not show pure development, but incorporating age illustrates the dynamic complexities of cultural relations. We cannot separate age from gender and cultural relations, and everything changes with the times and context. This chapter will not provide definitive conclusions, but we have a truer picture of developmental sport and exercise psychology when we incorporate gender and culture relations.

GENDER AND CULTURAL DIVERSITY IN DEVELOPMENTAL SPORT AND EXERCISE PSYCHOLOGY

Why do we include gender and cultural diversity in a developmental sport and exercise psychology text? We include this chapter because gender and cultural diversity is an integral part of sport and exercise. We cannot take gender and diversity out of the real world of sport and exercise, and if we are to understand sport and exercise behavior, we must include gender and diversity.

Before considering the theory and research, let us see if gender and culture do make a difference. Consider how gender, race, class, or sexual orientation might affect interpretations, responses, and possible approaches to the following:

- A college basketball player lacks control, is prone to angry outbursts, and explains by stating, "I really get up for the game, and sometimes I just lose it."

- A 16-year-old figure skater may have an eating disorder, but the skater explains, "I'm working to keep that 'line,' make it to nationals, and get endorsements."

- A 70-year-old in the cardiac rehab program has never played sports and is hesitant to participate in any physical activity.

- A professional tennis player criticizes officials and ignores waiting spectators after losing the final match in a major tournament.

Sport is socially-charged by race, ethnicity, class, and sexuality.

Does gender influence your responses? Did you identify athletes as male or female? Do you think a coach, sport psychology consultant, friend, or family member would behave the same with a female and a male? If you try to be nonsexist, treat everyone the same, and assume that gender does not matter, you will have difficulty. Gender does matter.

Try to imagine the scenarios with athletes of different racial/ethnic identities. What if the tennis players were Venus Williams and Andre Agassi? If your reactions differ, do they differ because of gender, race, or something else? What if the athletes were gay? Trying to treat everyone the same does a disservice to participants. Furthermore, when we try to treat everyone the same, we invariably treat everyone like the dominant cultural group (male, white, etc.), and we clearly do a disservice to those in minority groups.

Sport is gendered, and sport is socially charged by race/ethnicity, class, and sexuality. Biological sex is related to gender, but biology does not explain gendered sport, and biology does not explain race, sexuality, or class in sport and exercise. All the meanings, social roles, expectations, standards of appropriate behavior, beauty, power, and status associated with gender and culture are socially constructed. We are not born to wear high heels or high-top sneakers, but from the time we are born, our parents, teachers, peers, and coaches react to us as girls or boys. Gender is so pervasive in society that we often do not recognize the influence. Race and ethnicity are nearly as pervasive, but the increasing multiracial identities and cultures force us beyond dichotomous male/female or black/white categories. Sexuality is closely linked to gender, and sexual orientation and gender identity are powerful, albeit less visible, influences in sport and exercise. Gender (and race/ethnicity, sexuality, class) makes a difference in the real world; we must consider people in context to understand their behavior and the development of that behavior.

Theory and research on gender, particularly from a feminist perspective, incorporate multiple cultural identities and address intersecting cultural relations. That is, we all have gender, and we all also have racial/ethnic identity, sexual orientation, and so on. Moreover, those multiple identities intersect in unique ways in each of us. Feminist theory is prominent within the sport studies scholarship, and psychology has begun to address gender and culture from a feminist perspective. Thus, an understanding of feminist theory and gender relations may provide a framework for exploring gender and culture relations in developmental sport and exercise psychology.

A Feminist Sport and Exercise Psychology Framework

Feminism

As we develop a feminist sport and exercise psychology framework, we might clarify some terms. In particular, the term *feminist* carries many meanings, and no single feminist perspective is shared by all. Feminist sport and exercise psychology, as presented here, reflects my interpretations of scholarship that guides my work.

I find hooks' 1984 (pp. 17, 31) definition of feminism as "a movement to end sexist oppression" useful, and an appropriate guide for this chapter. In her more recent book, hooks (2000) invites everybody to read and understand that "feminism is a movement to end sexism, sexist exploitation, and oppression" (p. viii). The definition is inclusive rather than exclusive, and it focuses on action to end oppression. Clearly, men have the power in a sexist system, but men are also restricted by sexism, and men can be part of the movement. hooks has written extensively, in very accessible language, on feminist theory, and she has always emphasized the need to incorporate race and class into a true feminist perspective. The feminist perspectives that I find most helpful for sport and exercise psychology share those inclusive, action-oriented characteristics.

Feminist Sport Studies

Sport and exercise psychology does not have well-developed feminist theories or models, and we must look to other areas for feminist guides. Feminist theory and scholarship in the humanities, such as hooks' work, inform scholarship in social and behavioral sciences, but "hard" science and medical models dominate and present challenges. Psychology has only begun to adopt true feminist approaches, and sport and exercise psychology lags farther behind. Those of us with stronger ties to exercise and sport science also have the work of feminist sport-studies scholars as a guide.

I recommend Hall's (1996) book for any sport and exercise psychologists interested in gender. Hall has been a leading sport studies scholar and clear voice for feminism throughout her career. Hall's stated purpose is to "speak feminism"—to communicate the knowledge and understanding of the substantial feminist theory and research to exercise and sport studies scholars and participants. Hall's book moves the reader from the earlier feminist models to cultural studies and a gender-relations perspective.

Hall's (1996) presentation is clear and concise, and even research-oriented sport and exercise psychologists will recognize the limits of our biologic and categorical models and the need to take a relational perspective. Gender relations acknowledges the pervasive, dynamic role of gender in all our interactions and behaviors. Moreover, a cultural studies view extends that relational analysis to multiple power relations. That is, gender relations involve power—males have a more dominant, privileged status in gender relations; and race, class, and other power relations operate in society and interact with gender in varying, complex ways. Finally, Hall moves from theory into action, as she discusses feminist research as praxis (moving from our theories to real-world action) and social-political action.

> Gender relations acknowledges the pervasive, dynamic role of gender in all our interactions and behaviors.

Listed below are the key themes from the feminist theory and sport studies scholarship that form my sport and exercise psychology perspective on gender and cultural diversity:

- Gender is relational, not categorical. Gender influences everyone, and gender relations are complex and dynamic. Research and theory that assume simple, dichotomous categories cannot explain real-world behavior.

- Gender is inextricably intertwined with race/ethnicity, sexuality, social class, and other cultural identities, including age. We all have multiple, intersecting identities. It is probably impossible to sort out how much any one aspect of our identity (e.g., gender, race) influences any given behavior.

- Power, privilege, and oppression are relational and dynamic. Most people are both in positions of privilege and targets of oppression. The salience of our varying identities and power relations varies with time and context. Certainly, our cultural identities mix, and power relations vary developmentally.

- Feminist theory must move to action. Feminism demands action to end oppression, through our professional work and political/social action.

Feminist Psychology and Cultural Relations

The themes cited in the previous section are evident in the growing feminist psychology work with its calls for social analysis and action. The gender scholarship in psychology has moved away from categorical research to an emphasis on social context and relations. That shift is evident in the research reviewed in the next major section. Recent feminist works cite isolated women scholars in the early days of psychology, but the more feminist and social analyses did not emerge until the women's movement of the 1970s.

Sport and exercise psychologists can look to these early feminist psychologists, and in particular, to Carolyn Sherif. Sherif often contributed to sport and exercise psychology, and she challenged our thinking about many issues, including competition, group processes, and gender. Sherif posed an early, feminist challenge that helped turn psychology toward a more social and woman-oriented perspective. Sherif (1982) likened the term *sex roles*, which dominated sport psychology as well as psychology gender research, to a "boxcar carrying an assortment of sociological and psychological data along with an explosive mixture of myth and untested assumptions" (p. 392). Sherif's early and persistent advocacy of *social* psychology, which helped psychologists advance gender scholarship, has had considerable influence on several of us in sport and exercise psychology.

Several other psychology scholars who have taken a feminist approach have influenced sport and exercise psychology research on gender, and that work is covered in the section on research. One of the clearest feminist trends in current psychology is the call for feminist practice. Sport and exercise psychology has not yet embraced this key feminist psychology contribution.

Toward feminist psychology practice. Moving from feminist theory to feminist practice is a challenge for sport and exercise psychology—to understate the obvious—but the expanding literature on feminist practice in psychology provides some guidance. Feminist practice (Worell & Remer, 1992) incorporates gender scholarship, emphasizes neglected women's experiences (e.g., sexual harassment), and takes a more nonhierarchical, empowering, process-oriented approach that shifts emphasis from personal change to social change.

Recently, calls for feminist practice have been broadened. Worell and Johnson (1997) note that feminist practice is widely defined to include activities related to all areas of psychology—research, teaching, clinical practice and supervision, scholarly writing, leadership, and any other activities in which psychologists participate. All of the chapters in Worell and Johnson's edited volume can provide guidelines for sport and exercise psychologists who wish to be more inclusive, empowering, and effective in their research and practice. In the afterword, Johnson and Worell (1997) list common themes of feminist practice (see Table 1).

The views of the feminist psychologists and the common themes reflect many of the calls for relational analyses and attention to power relations by the feminist sport-studies scholars, but the psychologists also retain concern for the individual. The combined focus on the individual and social relations may seem paradoxical at first glance, but that combination is the essence of a useful feminist sport and exercise psychology. Our goal is to understand behavior and then to apply our understanding to help individuals in the real world. From a feminist perspective, we not only put our theories and research into action for individuals, but we also can work for social change. To meet the challenge of a feminist sport and exercise psychology, we must incorporate gender relations and value diversity in all areas of our professional practice.

TABLE 1
Common Themes of Feminist Practice (Johnson & Worell, 1997)

- Includes therapy/intervention, teaching, political action, consultation, writing, scholarship, research, supervision, assessment and diagnosis, administration, and public service
- Promotes transformation and social change
- Assumes the personal is political
- Embraces diversity as a requirement and foundation for practice
- Includes an analysis of power and the multiple ways in which people can be oppressed and oppressing
- Promotes empowerment and the individual woman's voice
- Promotes collaboration
- Promotes the value of diverse methodologies
- Promotes feminist consciousness
- Promotes self-reflection on personal, discipline, and other levels as a lifelong process
- Promotes continued evaluation and reflection of our values, ethics, and process, which is an active and reflective feminist process
- Asserts that misogyny and other inequities are damaging
- Encourages demystification of theory and practice
- Views theory and practice as evolving and emerging

Psychology and cultural diversity. Feminist cultural analyses are rare, but psychology is beginning to incorporate feminist theory and multicultural perspectives. For example, the American Psychological Association's recent National Multicultural Conference and Summit-II (NMCS-II) included keynote addresses on gender, race/ethnicity, sexual orientation, and physical disabilities; and the overall program highlighted intersections and overlapping of these cultural identities. Garnets (2001) in her address at the NMCS-II, noted that sexual minorities share common elements with other minority groups, including

- Stereotypes—Individuals from these groups all confront stereotypes.

- Discrimination—All groups face discrimination and confront barriers to equal opportunity.

- Hostility and violence—Individuals in minority groups are vulnerable to hostile acts ranging from jokes and name-calling to violence and hate crimes.

- Identity development—Individuals from minority groups confront and reject the devalued identity reinforced by society and transform it into a positive identity.

- Group solidarity—Minorities develop group solidarity based on shared experiences and commitment to ending prejudice and discrimination.

Of course, we also find divergences, with minority groups differing from each other in some ways. For example, racial and ethnic minorities typically develop in families and communities with shared identity, whereas sexual minorities and people with disabilities typically grow up without such community. Also, as Garnets (2001) and most scholars who address multicultural diversity emphasize, cultural identities intersect in many ways. We all have gender, racial/ethnic and sexual identities, as well as many other social identities, and all our identities interact and influence our behavior.

By definition, psychology focuses on individual behavior, thoughts, and feelings, but we cannot fully understand the individual without considering the larger world. Trickett, Watts, and Birman (1994) note that diversity has challenged the foundations of psychology by suggesting that traditional psychology is particularistic rather than universal and that its theories reflect views, limits, and social contexts of those who created them. Trickett et al. further suggest that psychology's biggest challenge is paradigmatic. We need new ways of thinking to understand diversity. They advocate moving from the dominant psychology view, which emphasizes biology, isolating basic processes, rigorous experimental designs, and a critical-realist philosophy of science, to an emphasis on *people in context.*

Adopting a feminist gender-relations perspective in sport and exercise psychology fits the framework of Trickett et al. (1994). Sport and exercise psychology is explicitly context dependent, and the context encompasses diverse participants in all forms of physical activities, in varied exercise and sport settings. Gender makes a difference, and we must consider people in context to understand their behavior.

Gender Relations and Feminist Theory in Sport and Exercise Psychology

Clearly, sport and exercise psychology has not taken a feminist path. We have addressed some gender issues, and we have no lack of gender and culture issues that could benefit from feminist approaches. Sport and exercise psychology reflects the larger discipline of psychology, which has been slow to move beyond isolated studies of sex differences to more complex issues of gender relations, but our neglect of gender also reflects the place of women in sport.

The social context of gender and sport. To move toward feminist sport and exercise psychology, we must recognize our unique social and historical context. Although early feminist psychologists such as Sherif (1982) provide guidance, our physical education roots give sport and exercise psychology a unique gender context. In psychology, isolated women pioneers faced discriminatory practices and attitudes but persisted to make a place in the academic discipline of psychology, much as women have made a place in many scholarly fields. In physical education, we have a legacy of strong women leaders who developed *women's* physical education as an alternative, separate from men's physical education programs. Women's physical education provided a women-oriented environment long before the women's movement of the 1970s began to encourage such programs.

Despite the active participation of women in early sport and exercise, some of the early practices seem at odds with today's women's sport. At a 1923 conference, which is a benchmark for this anticompetition movement, key physical education leaders set guidelines that included putting athletes first, preventing exploitation, downplaying competition while emphasizing enjoyment and sportsmanship, promoting activity for all rather than an elite few, and developing women as leaders for girls and women's sports. A related clarifying statement (National Amateur Athletic Federation [NAAF], 1930, p. 41) concluded with the classic "*A game for every girl and every girl in a game.*"

> Despite the active participation of women in early sport and exercise, some of the early practices seem at odds with today's women's sport.

These sentiments dominated women's physical education and sports programs through the social movements of the 1960s and 1970s and the 1972 passage of Title IX of the Educational Amendments Act. Discrimination persists, and Title IX challenges continue today, but women and girls have taken giant steps into the competitive sport world. In the United States, women now constitute about one third of the high school, college and Olympic athletes in the United States. However, one third is not one half, and in other ways, women have lost a place. Sport remains male dominated with a clear hierarchical structure that is widely accepted and communicated in so many ways that we seldom notice.

Our research follows our sport model and lacks a feminist perspective. Despite the pervasiveness and power of gender in sport and the infinite number of psychological questions we could ask, sport and exercise psychology research on gender is limited in all ways. Our research questions and methods focus on differences, while neglecting complex gender issues and relations, and we lack guiding conceptual frameworks to help us understand the complexities of gender in sport and exercise contexts. We are making moves toward more feminist perspectives on gender and cultural relations, and continued moves in that direction will enhance our developmental scholarship. The next section covers, briefly (see Gill, 2002, for extended discussion), gender scholarship in sport and exercise psychology.

GENDER SCHOLARSHIP IN SPORT AND EXERCISE PSYCHOLOGY

Gender scholarship in sport and exercise psychology follows psychology. That scholarship has progressed from sex differences (males and females are opposites) to an emphasis on gender role as personality (males = females, if treated alike), to more current social psychology models that emphasize social context and processes. As Basow and Rubin (1999) explain in their chapter on gender influences in adolescence, *gender* refers to the meaning attached to being female or male in a particular culture, and gender role expectations also vary with ethnicity, social class, and sexual orientation.

Sex Differences

Although current gender scholarship has moved beyond sex differences, that work still captures public attention. Maccoby and Jacklin's (1974) review of the literature on sex differences exemplifies the psychology research. Their main finding, which often is ignored, was that few conclusions could be drawn from the diverse literature on sex differences. They did note (and this was definitely not ignored) possible sex differences in four areas: math ability, visual-spatial ability, verbal ability, and aggressive behavior. Subsequent research, particularly meta-analyses, casts doubt even on these differences.

Ashmore (1990) summarized that continuing sex differences research in a more recent review. He concluded that sex differences are relatively large for certain physical abilities (i.e., throwing velocity) and body use/posturing, more modest for other abilities and social behaviors (e.g., math, aggression), and negligible for all other domains (e.g., leadership, attitudes, some physical abilities such as reaction time and balance). Even the larger sex differences are confounded with nonbiological influences. Ashmore, as well as Maccoby (1990) and Jacklin (1989), advocates abandoning sex differences approaches for more multifaceted and social approaches. Most biological factors are not dichotomously divided, but normally distributed within both females and males. For example, the average male basketball center is taller than the average female center, but the average female center is taller than most men. For social psychological characteristics such as aggressiveness or confidence, even average differences are elusive, and the evidence does not support biological dichotomous sex-linked connections.

Personality and Gender Role Orientation

With criticisms of the sex differences approach and its failure to shed light on gender-related behavior, psychologists turned to personality. Specifically, psychologists focused on gender-role orientation, following Bem's (1974, 1978) lead and using the Bem Sex Role Inventory (BSRI). According to Bem, personality is *not* a function of biology. Instead, both males and females can have masculine or feminine personalities, and androgyny (high levels of both) is best. More recently, the masculine and feminine categories and measures have been widely criticized, and even Bem has progressed to a more encompassing gender perspective. Bem (1993) suggests that the gender lenses of gender polarization (male-female difference as basic organizing principle), androcentrism (male is norm), and biological essentialism (differences are inevitable) interact and perpetuate our gendered social structure. Still, most sport and exercise psychology gender research is based on that early work.

> Research suggests that female athletes have more masculine personality characteristics than females who aren't athletes.

Helmreich and Spence (1977), who developed their own gender-role model and measure (Personality Attributes Questionnaire or PAQ), sampled intercollegiate athletes and reported that most female athletes were either androgynous or masculine, in contrast to nonathlete college female samples, who were most often classified as feminine. Several subsequent studies with female athletes yielded similar findings. Harris and Jennings (1977) surveyed female distance runners and reported that most were androgynous or masculine. Both Del Rey and Sheppard (1981) and Colker and Widom (1980) found that most intercollegiate athletes were classified as androgynous or masculine. Myers and Lips (1978) reported that most female racquetball players were androgynous whereas most males were masculine. Many more studies have surveyed women athletes using the BSRI or PAQ, but listing more findings would not enlighten us about gender and sport.

Overall, this research suggests that female athletes possess more masculine personality characteristics than do female nonathletes (Gill, 1995). This is not particularly enlightening. Sport and physical activity, especially competitive athletics, demands instrumental, assertive (certainly competitive) behaviors. Both the BSRI and PAQ include "competitive" as a masculine item, and the higher masculine scores of female athletes probably reflect an overlap with competitiveness. Competitive orientation can be measured directly (e.g., Gill & Deeter, 1988; Gill & Dzewaltowski, 1988), and we do not need to invoke more indirect, controversial measures that do not add any information.

More important, athlete/nonathlete status is an indirect and nonspecific measure of behavior. If instrumental and expressive personality characteristics predict instrumental and expressive behaviors, we should examine those instrumental *and* expressive behaviors. Even within highly competitive sports, expressive behaviors may be advantageous. Creative, expressive actions may be the key to success for a gymnast. Supportive behaviors of teammates may be critical on a soccer team, and sensitivity to others may help an Olympic coach (or a sport psychology consultant) communicate with each athlete. Today, most psychologists recognize the limits of earlier sex differences and gender role approaches, and look beyond the male-female and masculine-feminine dichotomies to social development and social cognitive models for explanations.

Social Perspectives

In the 1980s, gender research moved away from sex differences and personality to emphasize gender beliefs and stereotypes. How people *think* males and females differ is more important than how they actually differ. Although actual differences between females and males on such characteristics as independence or competitiveness are small and inconsistent, we maintain our stereotypes (e.g., Bem, 1985; Deaux, 1984; Deaux & Kite, 1987, 1993; Deaux & Major, 1987; Spence & Helmreich, 1978). These gender stereotypes are pervasive. We exaggerate minimal differences into larger perceived differences, and these perceptions exert a strong influence that may elicit further gender differences. This cycle reflects the feminist position that gender is socially constructed.

Gender stereotypes certainly exist within sport. Metheny (1965) identified gender stereotypes in her classic analysis of the social acceptability of various sports. Metheny concluded that it is *not appropriate* for women to engage in contests in which

- the resistance of the *opponent* is overcome by bodily contact,

- the resistance of a *heavy object* is overcome by direct application of bodily force, or

- the body is projected into or through space over long distances or for extended periods of time.

In contrast, acceptable sports for women (e.g., gymnastics, swimming, tennis) emphasize aesthetic qualities and often are individual activities without direct competition. Although Metheny offered her analysis nearly 40 years ago, our gender stereotypes did not fade away with the implementation of Title IX. For example, Kane and Snyder (1989) confirmed gender stereotyping of sports, as suggested by Metheny, and more explicitly identified physicality and the emphasis on male's physical muscularity, strength, and power as the key feature.

Gender and Competitive Achievement Orientation

The topic of competitive achievement illustrates the move from sex differences and gender roles to more complex social models. The early achievement research (McClelland, Atkinson, Clark, & Lowell, 1953) took male behavior as the norm until Horner's (1972) doctoral work on fear of success (FOS) focused attention on gender. Horner's work was widely publicized, but quickly dismissed by critics (e.g., Condry & Dyer, 1976; Tresemer, 1977). McElroy and Willis (1979), who specifically considered women's achievement conflicts in sport contexts, concluded that no evidence supports a FOS in female athletes and that achievement attitudes of female athletes are similar to those of male athletes.

In order to analyze exercise patterns across the lifespan, it is necessary to consider the effects of gender.

We have replaced global achievement motives with multidimensional constructs and an emphasis on achievement cognitions. My work (Gill, 1988, 1993) on competitive sport orientation also suggests that gender influences vary across dimensions. We developed a sport-specific, multidimensional measure (Sport Orientation Questionnaire, SOQ; Gill & Deeter, 1988) that assesses three dimensions: competitiveness (desire to strive for success in competitive sport), win orientation (a desire to win and avoid losing), and goal orientation (an emphasis on achieving personal goals). With several samples, athletes were higher on all SOQ measures, and the competitiveness score was the primary discriminator between athletes and nonathletes (Gill, 1993).

We considered gender throughout our research and found that males consistently scored higher than females on SOQ competitiveness and win orientation, and males also reported more competitive sport activity and experience. However, females were just as high as males, and sometimes higher, on SOQ goal orientation and general achievement. Also, females were just as likely as males to participate in noncompetitive sport and nonsport achievement activities (Gill, 1993).

When using the SOQ with several athlete samples, we found differences among athlete groups on competitive orientations, but the variation was not simply a gender difference. With international and university athletes and nonathletes from Taiwan (Kang, Gill, Acevedo, & Deeter, 1990), we found strong differences between athletes and nonathletes, but minimal gender differences. With one unique sample of ultramarathoners, we found low win orientations, but very high goal orientations and no gender differences (Gill, 1993).

An overview of our competitiveness research helps put the gender "differences" into perspective. Generally, males are more competitive than females, but overlap and similarity are the rule. Moreover, differences between athletes and nonathletes, and within athlete samples, typically are stronger than gender differences. Overall, gender differences in competitiveness are limited and do not seem to reflect either general achievement orientation or interest in sport and exercise activities per se. Instead, competitiveness seems to reflect opportunity and experience in competitive sport, and gender influence is most evident when there is an emphasis on social comparison and winning within sport.

Other researchers report similar gender influences on reactions to competitive sport. When McNally and Orlick (1975) introduced a cooperative broomball game to children in urban Canada and in the northern territories, they found girls were more receptive to the cooperative rules than were boys. They also noted cultural differences with northern children more receptive, but the gender influence held in both cultures. Duda (1986) similarly reported both gender and cultural influences on competitiveness with Anglo and Navajo children in the southwestern United States. Male Anglo children were the most win oriented and placed the most emphasis on athletic ability. Weinberg and Jackson (1979) found that males were more affected by success/failure than were females, and in a related study, Weinberg and Ragan (1979) reported that males were more interested in a competitive activity whereas females preferred a noncompetitive activity.

Recently, Weinberg collaborated with colleagues in Australia and New Zealand to investigate gender and cultural variations in sport and physical activity motivation (Weinberg et al., 2000). Using participation motivation measures similar to those used in early studies with youth sport, they found similar factor structures across the three countries, but gender differences similar to those reported in other studies. Gender differences were similar across the three cultures, with males higher on competitive, extrinsic, and social recognition motives and females higher on fitness, fun, and teamwork motives.

Eccles' (1985, 1987; Eccles et al., 1983) model incorporates sociocultural factors along with achievement cognitions. Eccles recognizes that both expectations and importance or value determine achievement choices and behaviors. Gender differences in expectations are common, and gender also influences the value of achievement. Eccles further notes that gender differences in expectations and value develop over time and are influenced by gender role socialization, stereotyped expectations of others, and sociocultural norms, as well as individual characteristics and experiences. Eccles and Harold (1991) summarized existing work and provided evidence showing that her model holds for sport achievement, that gender influences children's sport-achievement perceptions and behaviors at a very young age, and that these gender differences seem to be the product of gender-role socialization.

Physical Activity and Self-Perceptions

As research, popular media, and our observations suggest, females often lack confidence in their sport and exercise capabilities. As noted in the previous section, Eccles has conducted considerable research on the development of expectations, competence, and self-esteem. In a recent chapter (Eccles, Barber, Jozefowicz, Malenchuk, & Vida, 1999), she noted that gender differences in self-perceptions are usually much larger than one would expect given objective measures of actual performance and competence. Eccles is one of the few developmental psychologists to include sport competence in her work, and she consistently finds larger gender differences in perceptions of sport competence than in other domains. Moreover, even in sport, the gender differences in perceptions are much larger than the gender differences in actual sport-related skills.

With the gender differences in perceived sport competence, physical activity has a tremendous potential to enhance women's sense of competence and control. Physical activity offers the opportunity to develop physical strength and confidence, to strive for excellence, to accomplish a goal through effort and training, and to test oneself in competition.

Many women who begin activity programs report enhanced self-esteem and a sense of physical competence that often carries over into other aspects of their lives. A few studies add some support to these testimonials. Holloway, Beuter, and Duda (1988), Brown and Harrison

Females often lack confidence in their sport and exercise capabilities.

(1986), and Trujillo (1983) all report that exercise programs, particularly weight and strength training, enhance the self-concepts of women participants. Tiggemann and Williamson (2000), in one of the few studies including both women and men, also sampled a wide age range (16-60 years) to examine the effects of exercise on body satisfaction and self-esteem. They found a negative relationship between exercise and self-perceptions for the younger women, but found a positive relationship for mature women and both young and mature men. The results suggest developmental changes and also different social processes operating for the young women.

Physical activity and body image. Self-perceptions of the body are highlighted within sport and exercise settings, and we should note the work on gender and body image (Melpomene Institute, 1990; Rodin, Silberstein, & Striegel-Moore, 1985). Our images of the ideal body, and particularly the ideal female body, have changed through history and across social contexts. Certainly, today's ideal is a slender, lean female body. Just as clearly, most women recognize and strive for that ideal, which is much less than ideal in terms of physical and mental health. Boys and men also have concerns about body image, but the literature indicates that girls and women are much more negative about their bodies. Moreover, the concerns are gender related. Girls are particularly concerned with physical beauty and maintaining the ideal thin shape, whereas boys are more concerned with size, strength, and power. Society shapes body image, and this societal pressure for a body image that is neither particularly healthy nor attainable for many women likely has a negative influence on self-esteem and psychological well-being, as well as on physical health and well-being.

Concerns about body image affect all women, and athletes are just as susceptible as other women to societal pressures toward unrealistic, unhealthy thinness and eating disorders. Such pressures are of particular concern in the "thin-body" sports such as gymnastics, dance, and running. For example, one athlete reported, "At age 14 my cycling coach told me I was 'fat' in front of my entire team . . . At 5'5", 124 pounds, I was not fat, but my self-esteem was so low that I simply believed him. After all, he was the coach" (Melpomene, 1990, p. 36). Pressuring an athlete, who already has tremendous societal pressure to lose weight, is not a desirable approach. Most enlightened coaches and instructors follow nutritional guidelines and emphasize healthy eating and exercise behaviors rather than weight standards.

Physical Activity and Adolescent Development

Recently, researchers and community service professionals have turned attention to adolescent girls. Some of that work emphasizes the role of sport and activity in adolescent development, and the most recent work takes a cultural relations perspective to explore intersections of gender, race, and class. No doubt we have seen the ads with young women proclaiming that they will be more confident, avoid pregnancy and other adolescent risks, and generally be healthier and better off "if you let me play sports." The ad is based on and does have some research support. The President's Council on Physical Fitness and Sport (1997) report *Physical Activity and Sport in the Lives of Girls: Physical and Mental Health Dimensions From an Interdisciplinary Approach* summarizes that research with a call for activity programs for girls. Specifically, the report notes the physical benefits of sport and physical activity (motor skill development, fitness, reproductive function, body density, immune function) and also gives special attention to the psychosocial benefits (self-concept, emotional well-being, social competence). Psychosocial benefits, our focus here, are less well documented, and interpretations are more cautious, but growing evidence does support developmental benefits.

Richman and Shaffer (2000) add some support for the "if you let me sports" view. They sampled college females to obtain retrospective reports of their precollege sport participation, as well as body image, physical competencies, gender identity, and self-esteem. The results supported the positive relationship between sport participation and self-esteem, but also indicated that the positive relationship was accounted for by the intervening variables. That is, sport participation led to more positive body image, physical competencies, and gender flexibility; and those intervening variables led to greater self-esteem. This study is retrospective, and the sample is limited to predominantly white college students (not representative of all adolescents). Some other recent work does sample adolescents from a wider population and also incorporates cultural analyses.

Miller, Sabo, Farrell, Barnes, and Melnick (1999) used data from the CDC national 1995 *Youth Risk Behavior Survey* of high school students to examine the relationship between sport participation and sexual behavior, contraceptive use, and pregnancy. Miller and colleagues used cultural resource theory to explore the intersection of gender and sexuality in the sport context and to address the practical question—does sport reduce the risk of teen pregnancy? The survey sample is purposely culturally diverse, with similar numbers of black/African-American, Hispanic/Latino, and white youth. Miller and colleagues controlled for race/ethnicity, age, and mother's education (a class indicant) in their analyses. The results indicated that girls who participated in sport were indeed at less risk for teen pregnancy. Girls in sport (compared to those not in sport) reported lower rates of sexual experience, fewer partners, later age of first intercourse, higher rates of contraception use, and lower rates of past pregnancies. Boys in sport also reported higher contraceptive use, but on other measures reported more sexual experience. Miller and colleagues, following cultural resource theory, suggested that athletic participation for girls leads to less adherence to conventional cultural scripts and more social/personal resources in sexual bargaining. Sport for boys provides similar resources, while strengthening their commitment to traditional masculine scripts.

In addition to the main results, this study is notable for including both males and females, as well as a racially/ethnically diverse sample. Miller and colleagues (1999) noted that males had higher sport participation rates than did females, and whites had the highest participation of the three race/ethnic groups, with Hispanic youth reporting the lowest rates. Few studies within sport and exercise psychology have incorporated diverse samples or taken a cultural relations approach. However, some growing work on adolescent development, often focused on underserved youth, brings that perspective and often provides insights into the role of physical activity for these adolescents.

Urban youth: Intersections of gender, race, and class. In one particularly exciting report, Erkut, Fields, Sing, and Marx (1996) describe their study of experiences (including sport experiences) that influence diverse urban girls. In introducing the study, Erkut and colleagues took a feminist, cultural relations approach. They noted that gender is a risk factor for eating disorders, depression, and suicide for adolescents. They further noted that most of the research involves white, privileged girls and that risk and resilience are typically described in white, middle-class models. Erkut and colleagues focused on the intersections of gender, race/ethnicity, and social class to explore differences within as well as across groups.

Erkut et al. (1996) sampled girls from across the United States representing five ethnic backgrounds (Native American, African American, Anglo-European American, Asian Pacific Islander, Latina) and asked the girls "what activities make you feel good about yourself?" Athletics was the most common response, mentioned by nearly half (46%) of the girls. When asked what about the activity made them feel good, the most common response was related to mastery or competence (e.g., "I'm good at it") followed by enjoyment. Erkut et al. purposely sampled to consider ethnic and SES influences, and they found variations in patterns illustrating the power of the social context background. Of most relevance for sport and exercise psychology, Native American and Asian Pacific Islander girls were most likely to cite athletics as the activity that made them feel good. Also, high SES girls were less likely to cite athletics and more likely to cite art activities. In discussing the results, Erkut et al. expressed surprise at the prominence of athletics. They suggested the findings called attention to the importance of historical context (post-Title IX for these girls). They also noted that sport as a source of mastery and enjoyment is not part of the traditional or contemporary female role. Erkut et al.'s large, diverse sample and the many variations in findings highlight the importance of social contexts in the lives of these girls. Although Erkut et al. offer more questions than answers, they suggest exciting directions for sport and exercise psychology.

Several others are working from feminist, cultural relations perspectives and converging on adolescent development issues. Much of that work focuses on underserved urban youth, and intersections of race/ethnicity and class are inevitable. Weis and Fine have been engaged in this work for some time, and their recent collaborative effort (Weis & Fine, 2000) focuses on the intersections of gender, race, and class in urban youth, with contributions from scholars and community activists in varied areas. Weis and Fine take a feminist, action-oriented approach and recognize the role of community and nonschool spaces on youth development. Two of the chapters in their edited book specifically address sport and exercise in the lives of adolescent girls.

Carney (2000) notes the role of race and class in the public discourse and scholarly work on adolescent bodies. She notes that crime, pregnancy, and drug abuse reports typically feature girls of color, but eating disorders, self-esteem, and suicide reports feature white, middle/upper class, heterosexual girls—despite similar incidence of all issues across race and class boundaries. Carney draws on her experience as a figure-skating coach and data from focus groups and interviews to investigate sport as a site that enables girls to rework their physical selves as functioning, beautiful, and strong. Her results suggest that traditional femininity, emphasizing thin, feminine, delicate, is unquestioned by these girls. The girls do see some possibilities for skating as empowerment, but they also see the limits and constraints. The girls expressed dissatisfaction with their bodies, but also appreciation for their physical-ness.

In the same volume, Webster (2000) explores girls' identity development through sport and the arts. Citing the President's Council report and similar claims of benefits, she used interviews to see if girls participating in sport teams and the arts programs recognize such benefits. Sport participants discussed individual success and the excitement of sport, recognized that they were resisting stereotypes, and reported athletic success carried into academics. Girls in the arts discussed opportunity for reflection, freedom, and release from stress through the arts. They also reported success, recognition, and carryover to academics. The girls did recognize that the arts discriminate against men, and they cited gay stereotypes and homophobia. Overall, Webster reported the arts and sports provide space for diverse expressions of gender, and these spaces are important for overall identity development and academic work.

We have few sport and exercise psychology scholars working on these important issues. Clearly, the role of physical activity in adolescent development is a major issue for us. Some physical educators have developed important programs with underserved youth. The work of Hellison and colleagues around the country is particularly notable (Hellison et al., 2000). All authors are working with physical activity programs for underserved youth that focus on adolescent development and promote resiliency and responsibility. Clearly gender, race, and class issues enter these programs, and the feminist, cultural relations perspectives of the scholars from nonsport areas are particularly relevant. Sport and exercise psychologists could contribute to this work with feminist, cultural relations analyses and research. We could also gain greatly from collaboration in these action-oriented, real-life programs.

Gender affects men as well as women in sport and exercise.

Gender Relations and Cultural Diversity—Promising Directions

Feminist and cultural studies perspectives call for consideration of gender within the wider context of cultural diversity. Sport is not only male, but white, young, middle-class, heterosexual male; and gender affects men as well as women in sport and exercise. Sport and exercise psychology has progressed from the limited sex-differences and gender-role approaches, but we have not incorporated diversity or adopted relational analyses that might help us develop a useful feminist sport and exercise psychology. As Hall (1996) notes, sport psychologists have relied on categorical research to study gender. We focus on differences, whether we rely on biological or socialization explanations. We focus on individuals and fail to analyze the powerful ways in which gender and race relations are socially and historically constructed. Smith (1992), in her review of the research (or lack of) on women of color, called for "more relational analyses of and by diverse women of color and to understand how collective personal experiences and processes are informed by race, gender, and class power relations." (p. 224). To move toward feminist sport psychology we must heed the call of the sport studies scholars and consider the many intersections of gender, race, class, and other power relations.

In this major section, we will first consider extensions of gender analyses to sexuality and sexual orientation. Then, in the following subsection, we will consider cultural diversity and the emerging scholarship on the intersections of race/ethnicity, social class, and gender.

Gender and Sexuality

Messner, a sport studies scholar who gave a wonderful keynote address at the 1999 AAASP conference, describes sport as a powerful force that socializes boys and men into a restricted masculine identity. Messner (1992) cites the major forces in sport as

- competitive hierarchical structure with conditional self-worth that enforces the "must-win" style and
- homophobia.

Heterosexism and homophobia. Like Hall (1996) and other feminist sport-studies scholars, Messner (1992) emphasizes the social context and relational analyses as he describes the intersecting influences of gender and homophobia on sport behavior. Messner describes the extent of homophobia in sport as staggering and states that homophobia leads all boys and men (gay or straight) to conform to a narrow definition of masculinity. Real men compete and avoid anything feminine that might lead them to be branded a sissy. One successful elite athlete interviewed by Messner noted that he was interested in dance as a child, but instead threw himself into athletics as a football and track jock. He reflected that he probably would have been a dancer but wanted the macho image of the athlete. Clearly, we have gender and heterosexist stereotypes operating in youth sport and school settings, with certain developmental implications.

Messner (1992) notes that homophobia in athletics is closely linked with misogyny; sport bonds men together as superior to women. Messner's analysis reflects Lenskyj's (1987, 1991) citing of compulsory heterosexuality as the root of sexist sport practices and Bem's (1993) contention that sexism, heterosexism, and homophobia are all related consequences of the same gender lenses in society. We expect to see men dominate women, and we are uncomfortable with bigger, stronger women who take active, dominant roles expected of athletes.

Homophobia in sport has been discussed most often as a problem for lesbians, with good reason. Nelson (1991) illustrated restrictions and barriers for lesbians by describing one LPGA tour player who remains closeted to protect her status with friends, family, sponsors, tour personnel, and the general public (prior to Muffin Spencer-Devlin's public and relatively accepted coming-out statement in 1997). Not surprisingly, those involved with women's athletics often go out of the way to avoid any appearance of lesbianism. Griffin (1992, 1998), who has written extensively on homophobia in sport and physical education, notes lesbians are not the problem; homophobia is the problem. Homophobia manifests itself in women's sports as

silence,

denial,

apology,

promotion of a heterosexy image,

attacks on lesbians, and

preference for male coaches.

We stereotypically assume that sport attracts lesbians (of course, not gay men), but there is no inherent relationship between sexual orientation and sport (no gay gene will turn an individual into a softball player or figure skater). No doubt, homophobia has kept more heterosexual women than lesbians out of sports, and homophobia restricts the behavior of all women in sport. Moreover, as Messner (1992) and Ponger (1990) suggest, homophobia probably restricts men in sport even more than it restricts women. Men who deviate from the heterosexual norm within the homophobic athletic culture often face ridicule, harassment, or physical violence. Few men, particularly adolescents who are concerned about fitting in, step outside the boundaries.

Sexual harassment and sexual assault. Sexual harassment is an issue with clear gender connotations and relevance to sport and exercise psychology. Given the prevalence of sexual harassment and sexual assault, especially for college women, female athletes are much more likely to present problems related to these issues than eating disorders or any other potentially clinical issues. Yet, I have seen virtually nothing in the sport psychology research or professional literature on this topic.

Considerable research and public attention demonstrate the prevalence of sexual harassment and assault. Koss (1990; Koss, Gidycz, & Wisniewiski, 1987) finds that 38 of 1000 college women experience rape or attempted rape in one year, that 85% of sexual assaults are by acquaintances, and that men and women interpret sexual situations and behaviors differently. All women are at risk, and no particular psychological pattern characterizes victims, although college students are at risk and alcohol is often involved. Given that most sport psychology consultants work with college athletes, we should be familiar with this work. Sexual harassment can be a tremendous barrier to educational and athletic achievement, and rape can be a devastating experience. Many victims remain anxious and depressed months later, and some experience severe substance abuse, eating disorders, major depression, or other symptoms years later (e.g., Gordon & Riger, 1989; Koss, 1990; Murphy et al., 1988).

Although sport and exercise psychology research is limited and just beginning, the issues have been raised. Nelson (1991) noted that harassment is almost routine and expected by women runners; women cannot run any time, any place. Lenskyj (1992) discussed sexual harassment in sport, drawing ties to power relations and ideology of male sports, and she noted some unique concerns for female athletes. Sport (as a nonfeminine activity) may elicit derisive comments; clothes are revealing; male coaches are often fit and conventionally attractive; female athletes spend much time training and less in general social activity; coaches are authoritarian; and for some sports, merit is equated with heterosexual attractiveness.

> Female coaches may be so worried about charges of lesbianism that they refrain from complaining about harassment or seeking equity for their programs.

Interestingly, sexual harassment and abuse are receiving considerable attention at the international level. At the 2001 International Society of Sport Psychology Congress, Fasting of Norway and Brackenridge of the United Kingdom (2001) organized a symposium on sexual harassment and abuse with colleagues who had been working on these issues around the world. These scholars came from varying perspectives as well as from different countries, but their work converged on common feminist themes and clearly showed the prevalence of sexual harassment and abuse throughout the sport world. This work provides data and offers feminist analyses that emphasize social context and power relations, particularly with coaches and athletes, in the sport world. The work of these scholars indicates that the sport climate fosters sexual harassment and abuse; that young, elite female athletes are particularly vulnerable; that neither athletes nor coaches have education or training about the issues; and that we clearly need both research and professional development in sport psychology to address issues of sexual harassment and abuse (Brackenridge, 1997; Brackenridge & Kirby, 1999; Bringer, Brackenridge, & Johnston, 2001; Kirby & Wintrup, 2001; Leahy, Pretty, & Tenenbaum, 2001; Volkwein, 2001; Volkwein, Schnell, Sherwood, & Livezey, 1997).

Overwhelmingly, sexual harassment is males harassing females, even in less gender-structured settings than sports, and lesbians and gay men are more likely to be the targets than perpetrators of sexual harassment. Still, stereotypes persist, and as Lenskyj (1992) notes, allegations of lesbianism may deter female athletes (regardless of sexual orientation) from rejecting male advances or complaining about harassment. Given the sport climate, female coaches may be so worried about charges of lesbianism that they refrain from complaining about harassment or seeking equity for their programs. Sexual harassment (heterosexual or homophobic harassment) intimidates women and maintains traditional power structures.

Sexual harassment and assault are a concern for male athletes, as well as female athletes. The international work cited earlier indicates that even though young female athletes are particularly at risk, young male athletes are not immune from sexual harassment and abuse. Some accounts (e.g., Neimark, 1993) suggest that male athletes are particularly prone to sexual assault. These popular media reports, as well as more theoretical work (e.g., Lenskyj, 1992; Messner, 1992), suggest that male bonding, the privileged status of athletes, and the macho image of sport are contributing factors.

Sexual harassment and assault probably occur much more often than we recognize, and many athletes would not discuss the problem with a sport psychology consultant or anyone else. Consultants who are aware of gender dynamics might be quicker to recognize such issues and help athletes deal with the situation. Both female and male athletes must be aware of issues, and we can solicit cooperation of male and female administrators to support educational efforts and promote social action.

Russell and Fraser's (1999) chapter on lessons learned from self-defense training illustrates a feminist approach for optimizing women's educational experiences and, specifically, for helping women deal with fears of sexual assault and move from victim status to an empowered position. They studied participants in the Model Mugging (MM) program, which includes female instructors, male "model muggers" in pads, and participants practicing using full force to "knock out" muggers. Russell and Fraser drew lessons from the MM program and results to suggest guidelines for optimizing women's educational environments. They cited the importance of a safe environment, female instructors as competent models, inclusion of men as allies but not protectors, and allowing participants to demonstrate competence in relation to men. They concluded that programs are most effective if they are structured to ensure success and focus on competencies rather than vulnerabilities.

Gender and sexuality are part of a complex, dynamic, ever-changing social context and a particularly salient, powerful part within sport and exercise settings. Moreover, consideration of gender relations and recognition of diversity are critical to effective sport and exercise psychology practice. We will now turn to race and ethnicity and explore the intersections of race/ethnicity with gender, as well as look for guidance for sport and exercise psychology work on racial/ethnic diversity.

Race and Ethnicity

Ten years ago, Duda and Allison (1990) pointed out the striking void in sport psychology on race and ethnicity—and the void persists. Most of the issues raised for gender have parallels in race and ethnicity. That is, racial or ethnic stereotypes are pervasive; socialization, self-perceptions, and social context influence sport and exercise behavior; and a cultural relations perspective would enhance our understanding. Although parallel issues arise, race and ethnicity are qualitatively different from gender, and we do not even have the limited work on stereotypes and individual characteristics to parallel the gender research.

Intersections of race/ethnicity, class, and gender. Marable, a noted historian and African-American studies scholar, called for a new and critical study of race and ethnicity in a February 2000 article. Marable drew attention to the changing nature of race/ethnicity relations and cited immigration as a key source of change. We have incredible diversity within racial/ethnic groups, and the scholarly models of just 10 years ago no longer serve us well. Marable (2000) cited significant class, nationality, language, and religion variations within racial/ethnic groups and stated, "A new racial formation is evolving rapidly in the United States, with a new configuration of racialized ethnicity, class and gender stratification and divisions" (p. B7). The color-based categories are being reconfigured, and we need a critical study that recognizes the intersections of gender and cultural identity within a dynamic social context.

As Marable (2000) eloquently states, and as we have emphasized throughout this chapter, gender, race/ethnicity, and other diversity characteristics interact in complex ways within varying social contexts. For example, the experiences of a black, female tennis player are not simply a combination of the experiences of white female and black male players. Gibson's (1979) personal account highlights some of the complex interactions of race and gender and illustrates influences of social history and the immediate social situation in her development as a tennis player and as a person. Venus and Serena Williams grew up in a different world. Society has changed, and gender and race relations have changed from Gibson's day.

Social class often is combined with race/ethnicity in public discussion and professional work, but social class is qualitatively different from race/ethnicity. As Marable (2000) and other scholars report, class operates within all racial/ethnic groups and also interacts with gender. We have little research or analyses of social class in relation to gender, and certainly none within sport and exercise psychology. Race/ethnicity does overlap with social class in many practical settings and research issues. Power relations operate to discriminate against racial/ethnic minorities, as well as against the poor and working class, and more minorities are in the poor and working classes. It is logical to recognize the overlap, but it is time to consider the intersecting relations in our continuing theory and research.

Most of the limited research covered in this section focuses on race/ethnicity, and almost none incorporates class. As the work with youth discussed in an earlier section suggests, intersections of gender, race, and class are inevitable in sport and exercise and have psychological implications. As work continues, we may add to our understanding of class, as well as race/ethnicity in sport and exercise. Psychology has begun to address race/ethnicity, and increasingly from a welcome multicultural perspective. We have little in sport and exercise psychology, but we can turn to the sport studies scholars for some directions.

Sport studies scholarship on race/ethnicity. Sport studies scholars note that significant numbers of athletes are not white and middle class, yet power remains solidly white and middle/upper class. The popular media and some scholars have discussed such practices as "stacking" (e.g., assigning African Americans to positions such as football running back or baseball outfield but not in central quarterback or pitching roles) and the white male dominance of coaching and management positions. To date, few of these reports have included in-depth or critical analysis of race or class within sport.

Majors (1990) added more critical analysis with his discussion of the "cool pose" (i.e., a set of expressive lifestyle behaviors) used by black males to counter racism. Majors noted that although a few black males escape limits and express pride, power, and control, the emphasis on the cool pose is self-defeating for the majority because it comes at the expense of education and other opportunities for advancement. Moreover, Majors notes that the cool pose uses sexist oppression to counter racist oppression rather than encouraging more empowering strategies. Majors' analysis reflects intersections of race and gender, but few others have done so. In her review, Smith (1992) reached the primary conclusion that we have a deafening silence on diverse ethnic women in sport.

Brooks and Althouse (1993) edited a volume on racism in college athletics, including a welcome section on gender and race. Corbett and Johnson (1993) drew upon the limited research and their own insights to focus on African-American women in college sport. They noted that African-American women have a social-historical context of sexual exploitation, low wages, substandard education, and that they are stereotyped as independent, loud, and dominating. They also debunked our popular myth that African-American women gravitate to track. African-American women have had more opportunities in track than some other activities, and talented athletes from Wilma Rudolph to Jackie Joyner-Kersee are widely recognized, but survey data indicate that track is *not* a particularly popular activity for African-American students, and opportunities likely are limited by social stereotypes and constraints. In another chapter, Green (1993) optimistically discussed such opportunities as Girls Clubs, YWCA, PGM golf, and the NCAA's national Youth Sport Program as strategies to help overcome barriers and encourage more young African-American women to participate and develop their full potential in sports and athletics.

Psychology scholarship on race/ethnicity. Sport studies scholarship on race/ethnicity is not as well developed as the gender scholarship, and it provides more questions than answers for sport and exercise psychology. We also have some psychology scholarship on race/ethnicity, and psychologists are beginning to make noticeable efforts to take a multicultural perspective in their research and practice. For example, Claude Steele and John Dovidio, both of whom have done extensive research on racial/ethnic stereotypes and their psychological effects, presented the opening keynotes at the National Multicultural Conference and Summit-II, which also included the Garnets (2001) keynote cited earlier. Like the gender scholarship discussed earlier, the psychology research on race/ethnicity emphasizes stereotypes and social cognition and the effects of social perceptions on individual behavior and social relations.

> Research shows that discrimination, stereotypes, and conformity pressures on racial/ethnic minorities affect their health and well-being.

Contrada et al. (2000) summarized research on ethnicity-related stress. They noted that evidence indicates racial/ethnic minorities face stress based on discrimination, stereotypes, and conformity pressures within groups and that these stresses affect health and well-being. Steele (1997) has done extensive research on gender and racial/ethnic stereotypes and their effects on behavior. Steele's research indicates that stereotypes affect all of us, and the most devastating effects are on those minority group members who have abilities and are motivated to succeed. Steele's research also suggests that even simple manipulations that take away the stereotype threat (e.g., telling students the test does not show race differences) negate the stereotype effects. Sport and exercise psychologists might note that Steele describes one study in which black and white athletes performed a golf task. Some were told the task reflected "natural" ability (invoking the stereotype) whereas others were told the task was not related to athletic ability. Black athletes performed better in the stereotype condition, but not in the other condition.

Contrada et al. (2000) cite five forces of ethnic discrimination: (a) verbal rejection (insults), (b) avoidance, (c) disvaluation (negative evaluation), (d) inequality – exclusion (unequal access), and (e) threat-aggression (actual harm). The research of Steele (1997), Contrada et al. and others suggests that stereotypes are common and influential, that social cognitive processes are important, and that minority group members are active agents in the process. Generally, the social psychology research invokes frameworks similar to the relational analyses of feminist sport-studies scholars. Sport and exercise psychologists can take direction from the psychology research on race/ethnicity. Clearly racial/ethnic minorities face similar stresses in sport and exercise settings, and stereotypes influence behaviors and relations in our settings.

Although I cannot cite any sport and exercise psychology research on race/ethnicity that reflects the gender relations and cultural analysis perspectives, Barnes, Zieff, and Anderson (1999) adopted such an approach in their critical analysis of the motor development research on black and white infants. In reviewing the research from the 1930s through 1992, Barnes et al. noted social power relations and historical context operating to influence our presumably "objective" science. They noted that the dominant views on racial relations influence research methods and interpretations. McGraw's (1931) classic research reflects the prevailing societal views with biology-based notions of racial superiority. Motor development research in the 1940s began to give greater attention to environmental explanations. As with gender research, motor development research on race favored biological explanations and categorical analyses until the 1980s. More current motor development research follows more complex, dynamical systems models.

Extending multicultural perspectives. Sport and exercise psychology can adopt similar complex, dynamic models of gender and cultural relations to advance our work on race/ethnicity. We can extend further to incorporate diverse racial/ethnic groups, social class, and other social categories such as physical attributes. At this point, we lack sport and exercise psychology research on any category other than gender, and we have little research from psychology or other areas to help. Some work on youth development is beginning to address social class, and sport and exercise psychologists may join that effort. The NMCS-II cited earlier specifically included physical disabilities, as well as gender, race/ethnicity, class, and sexuality, as multicultural issues.

As sport and exercise psychologists, we deal with physical activities, and certainly, physical abilities and characteristics are relevant issues. We do address physical disabilities and adapted activity, but we seldom address psychosocial issues and are even less likely to address gender and cultural diversity issues. DePauw (1997a, 1997b) has been doing research on individuals with physical disabilities in sport and exercise for some time, and she has addressed the intersections of gender and disability from a cultural relations perspective. Henderson and Bedini (1995) also explored gender and disability issues in physical activity, recreation, and leisure. They noted that women with disabilities report leisure, therapeutic, and health values, but some see little value for physical activity in their lives. Blinde and McCallister (1999) explored the intersections of gender and disability with women aged 19-54 who had varied physical disabilities. Results of their interview analyses indicated that these women participated in more fitness than sport activities, that they participated to maintain functional capabilities, that they valued intrinsic gains (perceived competence, enhanced body image, control), and that the women perceived differences in the activity experiences of men and women with disabilities.

ADVANCING ALONG THE LIFESPAN: OLDER ADULTS

Very little of the sport and exercise psychology work on gender and the more limited work on race, class, sexuality, and other areas of cultural diversity is developmental. The work that does take a developmental perspective focuses on adolescents, as discussed in the earlier section on physical activity and self-perceptions. Almost none of that research involves adults older than typical college students. However, the rapidly growing research on older adults and physical activity (as covered in other chapters of this text) has expanded the sport and exercise psychology lifespan. That growing literature with its focus on health-oriented exercise has begun to incorporate gender and cultural issues, as well as extend that work across the entire lifespan.

We have almost no research on developmental trends across the adult lifespan in such common sport and exercise psychology topics as motivation and self-perceptions. Clearly, we continue to develop our sport and exercise perceptions and behaviors after age 20. Adults develop in many ways as they move through the young adult years into middle age and into their senior years. No doubt our motives, behaviors, and reactions to sport and physical activity change from age 20 to 40, 60, 80, and even 100. Just as clearly, the social context, including gender and cultural relations, affects that development.

Physical Activity Patterns

As all epidemiological surveys and analyses indicate, the older age groups are the fastest growing segment of the population, and the oldest groups are growing the most. Gerontologists, researchers in all areas of health and social sciences, and the aging public itself are focusing attention on maintaining health and well-being, and all recognize that physical activity is critical. Rowe and Kahn (1998), in their report of the MacArthur Study of Aging in America, present a model of successful aging with three components: avoiding disease (prevention), maintaining cognitive and physical function (promotion), and maintaining engagement with life (key to overall well-being). Physical activity is the key to these overlapping components, and scholars from all fields recognize the role of physical activity. Sport and exercise psychology focuses on behavior, and we can take the lead in developing the knowledge base and helping practitioners develop effective programs for older adults.

National databases and research reports indicate that physical activity generally decreases across the adult lifespan. Moreover, the decreases (and increasing rates of physical inactivity) interact with gender, race, and class. Generally, men are more active and women more likely to be inactive. Also, racial/ethnic minorities are less active across all age groups; older, minority women are particularly likely to be inactive and, therefore, at greater risk for varied health problems.

Crespo, Ainsworth, Keteyian, Heath, and Smit (1999) used the data from the third National Health and Nutrition Examination Survey to examine social class. They also noted the gender differences in physical inactivity, but theirs is one of the few studies from any area to specifically look at social class. Using a multiple measure of social class (education, income, employment status), they found inactivity more common in less privileged social classes. They also noted females were more inactive in all social class groups.

Crespo (2000) calls for physicians to recognize these patterns and consider unique needs and constraints of minority groups when giving professional advice on exercise. Sport and exercise psychology should be providing information and guidelines on this behavioral issue, but we have little research in psychology or sport and exercise psychology to draw upon.

Motives and Self-Perceptions

My colleagues and I (Gill, Williams, Dowd, Beaudoin, & Martin, 1996) surveyed different adult activity groups to obtain initial information about motives and goals for physical activity. We first surveyed participants in a community running club, exercise classes, and a cardiac rehab program, and then surveyed participants in a state senior games event. We used the SOQ measure of competitive orientation as well as a measure of specific motives for participating. The runners and exercise-class members were primarily young to middle-aged adults (average age mid-30s), whereas the cardiac rehab group (average age mid-60s) was closer to the senior group in age. All of the groups in this study were less competitive and less win oriented, but more goal oriented, than were the college athletes surveyed in most research with the SOQ (as discussed in an earlier section). Also, the seniors were more competitive than the other three groups, suggesting the importance of context, and reminding us that even older adults can be active and competitive. Within the senior group, men were more competitive than were women, and younger seniors were more competitive than older seniors, but we also found an interesting gender by age interaction. Senior men were less competitive with increasing age, but women were more competitive with age. This pattern likely reflects comparisons to similar age/gender cohorts and also suggests developmental changes even in the senior years.

We also found similar developmental changes within an older sample as part of a larger project on motor and psychological correlates of falls within older adults. In this study (Gill, Williams, Williams, Butki, & Kim, 1997), we had motor/mobility measures as well as measures of physical activity and perceived health and well-being for our main sample of older women, ranging from age 65 to 95, and a 20- to 30-year-old comparison sample. We examined age differences within the older sample as well as comparisons with the younger group. We found declines in mobility with age, but no age differences in perceived well-being. Older women engaged in less intense activity, but they were just as active as younger women. When we examined the relationships of physical activity and age to well-being, we found that physical activity was the stronger predictor. Even the oldest women maintained activity and a sense of well-being.

> Researchers found that older women engage in less intense activity but are just as active as younger women.

Gender and Culture in the Physical Activity Context

O'Brien Cousins (1998) has done considerable research on physical activity and older adults from a social psychological perspective. Her composite model provides a nice framework for sport and exercise psychology researchers in this area, and her model recalls the cultural relations and feminist models presented earlier. O'Brien Cousins includes the situational environment in her model, noting not only the role of childhood experiences, but also the importance of the adult situational context. The environmental context interacts with cognitive beliefs and physical activity behavior in a complex, dynamic model. As a side note, O'Brien Cousins reports that social support, often incorporated in research on health-related exercise, is particularly important for older adults. She also reports that a low percentage of older adults receive social support for activity and that support decreases with age, probably when that support is most needed.

O'Brien Cousins' (1998) model and research clearly take a social perspective and call for relational analyses. We have a growing body of research on physical activity with older adults, but most takes a traditional approach and fails to incorporate gender and cultural analyses. In one of the few studies to look at gender and race/ethnicity, Heesch, Brown, and Blanton (2000) examined the exercise barriers in relation to exercise adoption state with adult women over age 40. Their large sample (nearly 3000) included similar numbers of African-American, Hispanic,

Native American, and white women. They compared perceived barriers for the four racial/ethnic groups and across the stages of precontemplators, contemplators, and preparers/actives. They found several common barriers across racial/ethnic groups within stages. For example, being tired was a barrier for all precontemplators, and lack of time was a barrier for most contemplators. However, they also reported differences between stages that varied by racial/ethnic group. In offering suggestions for targeting barriers in interventions, the authors noted some consistent barriers, but cautioned that their reported differences and specific community needs preclude definitive guidelines. They called for continued qualitative as well as quantitative research to more appropriately design interventions to increase exercise.

CONCLUDING REMARKS

These calls for multiple methods and consideration of gender and cultural relations in physical activity research and interventions for older adults apply to all of our sport and exercise psychology research and practice. We have research issues and findings on gender and useful feminist and cultural relations theory to provide a framework for that work. Sport and exercise psychology can extend those perspectives to larger cultural diversity issues involving the intersections of gender, race/ethnicity, class, sexuality, and physical abilities. Moreover, we can put our theories and methods into motion as we incorporate age and take a dynamic, developmental perspective. We can see developmental trends in some of our work. The research on physical activity and adolescent development comes from multiple perspectives, and the most useful and applicable work explores intersections of gender, race, and class in work on the role of physical activity in the development of psychological well-being. The growing research on activity in older adults also comes from varied perspectives and suggests continuing and changing developmental processes as adults move through the lifespan. Although much of that work comes from health and traditional sciences, we see recognition of gender and culture in that work. Sport and exercise psychologists could contribute to this important work, and to the larger issues related to sport and exercise behavior across the lifespan. Many other chapters in this text offer empirical evidence of our contribution to developmental issues. In this chapter, I have tried to convince you that we can only make important contributions to the real world of developing sport and exercise participants when we incorporate gender and cultural analyses.

REFERENCES

Ashmore, R. D. (1990). Sex, gender, and the individual. In L. A. Pervin (Ed.), *Handbook of personality theory and research* (pp. 486-526). New York: Guilford.

Barnes, B. A., Zieff, S. G., & Anderson, D. (1999). Racial differences and social meanings: Research on "Black" and "White" infants' motor development, c. 1931-1992. *Quest, 51*, 328-345.

Basow, S. A., & Rubin, L. R. (1999). Gender influences and adolescent development. In N.G. Johnson, M. C. Roberts, & J. Worell (Eds.), *Beyond appearance: A new look at adolescent girls* (pp. 25-52). Washington, DC: American Psychological Association.

Bem, S. L. (1974). The measurement of psychological androgyny. *Journal of Consulting and Clinical Psychology, 42*, 155-162.

Bem, S. L. (1978). Beyond androgyny: Some presumptuous prescriptions for a liberated sexual identity. In J. Sherman & F. Denmark (Eds.), *Psychology of women: Future directions for research* (pp. 1-23). New York: Psychological Dimensions.

Bem, S. L. (1985). Androgyny and gender schema theory: A conceptual and empirical integration. In T.B. Sonderegger (Ed.), *Nebraska Symposium on Motivation, 1984: Psychology and gender* (pp. 179-226). Lincoln: University of Nebraska Press.

Bem, S. L. (1993). *The lenses of gender*. New Haven: Yale University Press.

Blinde, E. M., & McCallister, S. G. (1999). Women, disability, and sport and physical fitness activity: The intersection of gender and disability dynamics. *Research Quarterly for Exercise and Sport, 70*, 303-312.

Brackenridge, C. (1997). Playing safe: Assessing the risk of sexual abuse to elite child athletes. *International Review for the Sociology of Sport, 32*, 407-418.

Brackenridge, C., & Kirby, S. (1997). "He owned me basically. . ." : Women's experience of sexual abuse in sport. *International Review for the Sociology of Sport, 32*, 115-130.

Bringer, J. D., Brackenridge, C.H., & Johnston, L. H. (2001). A qualitative study of swimming coaches' attitudes towards sexual relationships in sport. In A. Papaioannou, M. Goudas, & Y. Theodorkis (Eds.), *International Society of Sport Psychology 10th World Congress of Sport Psychology: Programme & Proceeding* (Vol. 4, pp. 187-189) Thessaloniki, Greece: Christodoulidi Publications.

Brooks, D., & Althouse, R. (1993). *Racism in college athletics: The African-American athlete's experience.* Morgantown, WV: Fitness Information Technology.

Brown, R. D., & Harrison, J. M. (1986). The effects of a strength training program on the strength and self-concept of two female age groups. *Research Quarterly for Exercise and Sport, 57*, 315-320.

Carney, S. K. (2000). Body work on ice: The ironies of femininity and sport. In L. Weis & M. Fine (Eds.), *Construction sites: Excavating race, class, and gender among urban youth.* (pp. 121-139). Teachers College, Columbia University.

Colker, R., & Widom, C. S. (1980). Correlates of female athletic participation. *Sex Roles, 6*, 47-53.

Condry, J., & Dyer, S. (1976). Fear of success: Attribution of cause to the victim. *Journal of Social Issues, 32*, 63-83.

Contrada, R. J., Ashmore, R. D., Gary, M. L., Coups, E., Egeth, J. D., Sewell, A., Ewell, K., Goyal, T., & Chasse, V. (2000). Ethnicity-related sources of stress and their effects on well-being. *Current Directions in Psychological Science, 9*, 136-139.

Corbett, D., & Johnson, W. (1993). The African-American female in collegiate sport: Sexism and racism. In D. Brooks & R. Althouse (Eds.), *Racism in college athletics: The African-American athlete's experience* (pp. 179-204). Morgantown, WV: Fitness Information Technology.

Crespo, C. J. (2000). Encouraging physical activity in minorities: Eliminating disparities by 2010. *The Physician and SportsMedicine, 28*, 36-51.

Crespo, C. J., Ainsworth, B. E., Keteyian, S. J., Heath, G. W., & Smit, E. (1999). Prevalence of physical inactivity and its relations to social class in U.S. adults: Results from the Third National Health and Nutrition Examination Survey, 1988-1994. *Medicine & Science in Sports & Exercise, 31*, 1821-1827.

Deaux, K. (1984). From individual differences to social categories: Analysis of a decade's research on gender. *American Psychologist, 39*, 105-116.

Deaux, K., & Kite, M. E. (1987). Thinking about gender. In B. B. Hess & M. M. Ferree (Eds.), *Analyzing gender* (pp. 92-117). Beverly Hills, CA: Sage.

Deaux, K., & Kite, M. (1993). Gender stereotypes. In F. L. Denmark & M. A. Paludi (Eds.), *Psychology of women: A handbook of issues and theories* (pp. 107-139). Westport, CT: Greenwood Press.

Deaux, K., & Major, B. (1987). Putting gender into context: An interactive model of gender-related behavior. *Psychological Review, 94*, 369-389.

Del Rey, P., & Sheppard, S. (1981). Relationship of psychological androgyny in female athletes to self-esteem. *International Journal of Sport Psychology, 12*, 165-175.

DePauw, K. P. (1997a). Sport and physical activity in the lifecycle of girls and women with disabilities. *Women in Sport and Physical Activity Journal, 6*, 225-237.

DePauw, K.P. (1997b). The (in)visibility of disability: Cultural context and "sporting bodies." *Quest, 49*, 416-430.

Duda, J. L. (1986). A cross-cultural analysis of achievement motivation in sport and the classroom. In L. VanderVelden & J. Humphrey (Eds.), *Current selected research in the psychology and sociology of sport* (pp. 115-132). New York: AMS Press.

Duda, J. L., & Allison, M. T. (1990). Cross-cultural analysis in exercise and sport psychology: A void in the field. *Journal of Sport & Exercise Psychology, 12*, 114-131.

Eccles, J. S. (1985). Sex differences in achievement patterns. In T. Sonderegger (Ed.), *Nebraska Symposium of Motivation, 1984: Psychology and Gender* (pp. 97-132). Lincoln, NE: University of Nebraska Press.

Eccles, J. S. (1987). Gender roles and women's achievement-related decisions. *Psychology of Women Quarterly, 11*, 135-172.

Eccles, J. S., Adler, T. F., Futterman, R., Goff, S. B., Kaczala, C. M., Meece, J. L., & Midgley, C. (1983). Expectations, values and academic behaviors. In J. Spence (Ed.), *Achievement and achievement motives* (pp. 75-146). San Francisco: Freeman.

Eccles, J. S., Barber, B., Jozefowicz, D., Malenchuk, O., & Vida, M. (1999). Self-evaluation of competence, task values and self-esteem. In N.G. Johnson, M. C. Roberts, & J. Worell (Ed.), *Beyond appearance: A new look at adolescent girls* (pp. 53-84). Washington, DC: American Psychological Association.

Eccles, J. S., & Harold, R. D. (1991). Gender differences in sport involvement: Applying the Eccles expectancy-value model. *Journal of Applied Sport Psychology, 3*, 7-35.

Erkut, S., Fields, J. P., Sing, R., & Marx, F. (1996). Diversity in girls' experiences: Feeling good about who you are. In B. J. Ross Leadbeater & N. Way (Eds.), *Urban girls: Resisting stereotypes, creating identities.* (pp. 53-64). New York: New York University Press.

Fasting, K., & Brackenridge, C. (2001, June). *Sexual harassment and abuse in sport—Challenges for sport psychology in the new millennium.* Symposium presented at the International Society of Sport Psychology 10th World Congress of Sport Psychology, Skiathos, Greece.

Garnets, L. (2001, January). *Sexual orientations in perspective.* Keynote address presented at the National Multicultural Conference and Summit-II. Santa Barbara, CA.

Gibson, A. (1979). I always wanted to be somebody. In S. L. Twin (Ed.), *Out of the bleachers* (pp. 130-142). Old Westbury, NY: Feminist Press.

Gill, D. L. (1988). Gender differences in competitive orientation and sport participation. *International Journal of Sport Psychology, 19,* 145-159.

Gill, D. L. (1993). Competitiveness and competitive orientation in sport. In R. N. Singer, M. Murphey, & L. K. Tennant (Eds.), *Handbook on research in sport psychology* (pp. 314-327). New York: Macmillan.

Gill, D. L. (1995). Gender issues: A social-educational perspective. In S. M. Murphy (Ed.), *Sport psychology interventions* (pp. 205-234). Champaign, IL: Human Kinetics.

Gill, D. L. (2002). Gender and sport behavior. In T. S. Horn (Ed.), *Advances in sport psychology* (2nd ed., pp. 355-375). Champaign, IL: Human Kinetics.

Gill, D. L., & Deeter, T. E. (1988). Development of the Sport Orientation Questionnaire. *Research Quarterly for Exercise and Sport, 59,* 191-202.

Gill, D. L., & Dzewaltowski, D. A. (1988). Competitive orientations among intercollegiate athletes: Is winning the only thing? *The Sport Psychologist, 2,* 212-221.

Gill, D. L., Williams, L. Dowd, D. A., Beaudoin, C. M., & Martin, J. J. (1996). Competitive orientations and motives of adults sport and exercise participants. *Journal of Sport Behavior, 19,* 307-318.

Gill, D. L., Williams, K., Williams, L., Butki, B. D., & Kim, B. J. (1997). Physical activity and psychological well-being in older women. *Women's Health Issues, 7,* 3-9.

Gordon, M. T., & Riger, S. (1989). *The female fear: The social cost of rape.* New York: Free Press.

Green, T. S. (1993). The future of African-American female athletes. In D. Brooks & R. Althouse (Eds.), *Racism in college athletics: The African-American athlete's experience* (pp. 205-223). Morgantown, WV: Fitness Information Technology.

Griffin, P. (1992). Changing the game: Homophobia, sexism, and lesbians in sport. *Quest, 44,* 251-265.

Griffin, P. (1998). *Strong women, deep closets: Lesbians and homophobia in sport.* Champaign, IL: Human Kinetics.

Hall, M. A. (1996). *Feminism and sporting bodies.* Champaign, IL: Human Kinetics.

Harris, D.V., & Jennings, S. E. (1977). Self-perceptions of female distance runners. *Annals of the New York Academy of Sciences, 301,* 808-815.

Heesch, K.C., Brown, D. R., & Blanton, C. J. (2000). Perceived barriers to exercise and stage of exercise adoption in older women of different racial/ethnic groups. *Women and Health, 30,* 61-76.

Hellison, D., Cutforth, N., Kallusky, J., Martinek, T., Parker, M., & Stiehl, J. (2000). *Youth development and physical activity.* Champaign, IL: Human Kinetics.

Helmreich, R. L., & Spence, J. T. (1977). Sex roles and achievement. In R. W. Christina & D. M. Landers (Eds.), *Psychology of motor behavior and sport—1976* (Vol. 2, pp. 33-46). Champaign, IL: Human Kinetics.

Henderson, K. A., & Bedini, L. A. (1995). "I have a soul that dances like Tina Turner, but my body can't": Physical activity and women with disability impairments. *Research Quarterly for Exercise and Sport, 66,* 151-161.

Holloway, J. B., Beuter, A., & Duda, J. L. (1988). Self-efficacy and training for strength in adolescent girls. *Journal of Applied Social Psychology, 18,* 699-719.

hooks, b. (1984). *Feminist theory: From margin to center.* Boston: South End Press.

hooks, b. (2000). *Feminism is for everybody: Passionate politics.* Cambridge, MA: South End Press.

Horner, M. S. (1972). Toward an understanding of achievement-related conflicts in women. *Journal of Social Issues, 28,* 157-176.

Jacklin, C.N. (1989). Female and male: Issues of gender. *American Psychologist, 44,* 127-133.

Johnson, N.G., & Worell, J. (1997). Afterword. In J. Worell & N.G. Johnson (Eds.), *Shaping the future of feminist psychology* (pp. 245-249). Washington, DC: American Psychological Association.

Kane, M. J., & Snyder, E. (1989). Sport typing: The social "containment" of women. *Arena Review, 13,* 77-96.

Kang, L., Gill, D. L., Acevedo, E. D., & Deeter, T. E. (1990). Competitive orientations among athletes and nonathletes in Taiwan. *International Journal of Sport Psychology, 21,* 146-152.

Kirby, S. L., & Wintrup. G. (2001). Running the gauntlet: An examination of initiation/hazing and sexual abuse in sport. In A. Papaioannou, M. Goudas, & Y. Theodorkis (Eds.), *International Society of Sport Psychology 10th World Congress of Sport Psychology: Programme & Proceedings,* (Vol. 4, pp. 186). Thessaloniki, Greece: Christodoulidi Publications.

Koss, M. P. (1990). The women's mental health research agenda. *American Psychologist, 45,* 374-380.

Koss, M. P., Gidycz, C. A., & Wisniewski, N. (1987). The scope of rape: Incidence and prevalence of sexual aggression and victimization in a national sample of higher education students. *Journal of Consulting and Clinical Psychology, 55,* 162-170.

Leahy, T., Pretty, G., & Tenenbaum, G. (2001). "Once I got into the elite squad, it was a lot easier for him to get me" Sexual abuse in organised sport, a comparison of elite and club athletes' experiences. In A. Papaioannou, M. Goudas, & Y. Theodorkis (Eds.), *International Society of Sport Psychology 10th World Congress of Sport Psychology: Programme & Proceedings* (Vol. 4, pp. 190-192). Thessaloniki, Greece: Christodoulidi Publications.

Lenskyj, H. (1987). *Out of bounds: Women, sport and sexuality*. Toronto: Women's Press.

Lenskyj, H. (1991). Combating homophobia in sport and physical education. *Sociology of Sport Journal, 8*, 61-69.

Lenskyj, H. (1992). Unsafe at home base: Women's experiences of sexual harassment in university sport and physical education. *Women in Sport & Physical Activity Journal, 1*, 19-33.

Maccoby, E. E. (1990). Gender and relationships. *American Psychologist, 45*, 513-520.

Maccoby, E., & Jacklin, C. (1974). *The psychology of sex differences*. Stanford, CA: Stanford University Press.

Majors, R. (1990). Cool pose: Black masculinity and sports. In M. A. Messner & D. F. Sabo (Eds.), *Sport, men, and the gender order* (pp. 109-114). Champaign, IL: Human Kinetics.

Marable, M. (2000, February 25). We need new and critical study of race and ethnicity. *The Chronicle of Higher Education*, B4-B7.

McClelland, D. C., Atkinson, J. W., Clark, R. A., & Lowell, E. C. (1953). *The achievement motive*. New York: Appleton-Century-Crofts.

McElroy, M. A., & Willis, J. D. (1979). Women and the achievement conflict in sport: A preliminary study. *Journal of Sport Psychology, 1*, 241-247.

McGraw, M. B. (1931). A comparative study of a group of southern white and Negro infants. *Genetic Psychology Monographs, 10*, 5-105.

McNally, J., & Orlick, T. (1975). Cooperative sport structures: A preliminary analysis. *Mouvement, 7*, 267-271.

Melpomene Institute (1990). *The bodywise woman*. Champaign, IL: Human Kinetics.

Messner, M. A. (1992). *Power at play: Sports and the problem of masculinity*. Boston: Beacon Press.

Metheny, E. (1965). Symbolic forms of movement: The feminine image in sports. In E. Metheny, *Connotations of movement in sport and dance* (pp. 43-56). Dubuque, IA: W.C. Brown.

Miller, K. E., Sabo, D. F., Farrell, M. P., Barnes, G. M., & Melnick, M. J. (1999). Sports, sexual behavior, contraceptive use, and pregnancy among female and male high school students: Testing cultural resource theory. *Sociology of Sport Journal, 16*, 366-387.

Murphy, S. M., Kilpatrick, D.G., Amick-McMullen, A., Veronen, L., Best, C. L., Villeponteanx, L. A., & Saunders, B. E. (1988). Current psychological functioning of child sexual assault survivors: A community study. *Journal of Interpersonal Violence, 3*, 55-79.

Myers, A. E., & Lips, H. M. (1978). Participation in competitive amateur sports as a function of psychological androgyny. *Sex Roles, 4*, 571-578.

National Amateur Athletic Federation. Women's Division. (1930). *Women and athletics. Compiled and edited by the Women's Division, National Amateur Athletic Federation*. New York: A. S. Barnes.

Neimark, J. (1993). Out of bounds: The truth about athletes and rape. In D. S. Eitzen (Ed.), *Sport in contemporary society: An anthology* (4th ed., pp. 130-137). New York: St. Martin's Press.

Nelson, M. B. (1991). *Are we winning yet: How women are changing sports and sports are changing women*. New York: Random House.

O'Brien Cousins, S. (1998). *Exercise, aging, and health*. Philadelphia: Taylor & Francis.

Ponger, B. (1990). Gay jocks: A phenomenology of gay men in athletics. In M. A. Messner & D. F. Sabo (Eds.), *Sport, men and the gender order* (pp. 141-152). Champaign, IL: Human Kinetics.

President's Council on Physical Fitness and Sports. (1997). *Physical activity and sport in the lives of girls: Physical and mental health dimensions from an interdisciplinary approach*. Washington, DC: Department of Health and Human Services.

Richman, E. L., & Shaffer, D. R. (2000). "If you let me play sports": How might sport participation influence the self-esteem of adolescent females? *Psychology of Women Quarterly, 24*, 189-199.

Rodin, J., Silberstein, L., & Streigel-Moore, R. (1985). Women and weight: A normative discontent. In T.B. Sonderegger (Eds.), *Psychology and gender: Nebraska Symposium on Motivation, 1984* (Vol. 32, pp. 267-307).

Rowe, J. W., & Kahn, R. L. (1998). *Successful aging*. New York: Pantheon Books.

Russell, G. M., & Fraser, K. L. (1999). Lessons learned from self-defense training. In S.N. Davis, M. Crawford, & J. Sebrechts (Eds.), *Coming into her own: Educational success in girls and women* (pp. 260-274). San Francisco: Jossey-Bass.

Sherif, C. W. (1982). Needed concepts in the study of gender identity. *Psychology of Women Quarterly, 6*, 375-398.

Smith, Y.R. (1992). Women of color in society and sport. *Quest, 44*, 228-250.

Spence, J. T., & Helmreich, R. L. (1978). *Masculinity and femininity*. Austin, TX: University of Texas Press.

Spence, J. T., & Helmreich, R. L. (1983). Achievement-related motives and behaviors. In J. T. Spence (Ed.), *Achievement and achievement motives: Psychological and sociological approaches* (pp. 7-74). San Francisco: W.H. Freeman.

Steele, C. M. (1997). A threat in the air: How stereotypes shape intellectual identity and performance. *American Psychologist. 52*, 613-629.

Tiggemann, M., & Williamson, S. (2000). The effect of exercise on body satisfaction and self-esteem as a function of gender and age. *Sex Roles, 43*, 119-127.

Tresemer, D. W. (1977). *Fear of success.* New York: Plenum.

Trickett, E. J., Watts, R. J., & Birman, D. (Eds.). (1994). *Human diversity: Perspectives on people in context.* San Francisco: Jossey-Bass.

Trujillo, C. (1983). The effect of weight training and running exercise intervention on the self-esteem of college women. *International Journal of Sport Psychology, 14*, 162-173.

Volkwein, K. A. E. (2001). Sexual harassment of women in athletics vs academia. In A. Papaioannou, M. Goudas, & Y. Theodorkis (Eds.), *International Society of Sport Psychology 10th World Congress of Sport Psychology: Programme & Proceedings* (Vol. 4, p. 183). Thessaloniki, Greece: Christodoulidi Publications.

Volkwein, K. A. E., Schnell, F.I., Sherwood, D., & Livezey, A. (1997). Sexual harassment in sports: Perceptions and experiences of female student athletes. *International Review for the Sociology of Sport, 32*, 283-296.

Webster C. (2000). Pitching, dancing and budget cuts. In L. Weis & M. Fine (Eds.). *Construction sites: Excavating race, class, and gender among urban youth* (pp. 235-248). Teachers College, Columbia University.

Weinberg, R. S., & Jackson, A. (1979). Competition and extrinsic rewards: Effect on intrinsic motivation. *Research Quarterly, 50*, 494-502.

Weinberg, R. S., & Ragan, J. (1979). Effects of competition, success/failure, and sex on intrinsic motivation. *Research Quarterly, 50*, 503-510.

Weinberg, R., Tennenbaum, G., McKenzie, A., Jackson, S. J., Anshel, M., Grove, R., & Fogarty, G. (2000). Motivation for sport and physical activity: Relationships to culture, self-reported activity levels, and gender. *International Journal of Sport Psychology, 31*, 321-346.

Weis, L., & Fine, M. (2000). *Construction sites: Excavating race, class, and gender among urban youth.* New York: Teachers College Press, Columbia University.

Worell, J., & Johnson, N.G. (Eds.). (1997). *Shaping the future of feminist psychology.* Washington, DC: American Psychological Association.

Worell, J., & Remer, P. (1992). *Feminist perspectives in therapy: An empowerment model for women.* Chichester: Wiley.

CHAPTER NINETEEN

A Developmental Perspective on Transitions Faced by Athletes

Paul Wylleman • David Lavallee

To reach and to remain at the elite level in competitive sport require athletes—and those around them—to "invest" at different levels (e.g., physical, social, financial) during a long period of time. The termination of such a high-level athletic career can, therefore, be an emotional experience, not only for the athletes themselves but also for those in their close environment (e.g., parents, children, friends). Such a career end will also generate attention from the press, as reflected in these press clippings:

> Next Sunday, the all-time greatest pole vaulter, and for some the greatest athlete ever, will announce his official retirement from track and field . . . His record of achievements includes among others 35 World records set between 1984 and 1994. . . . Only an Olympic medal seemed to be out of reach of Sergeï Bubka (Het Volk, 2000).

> Those who look at women's tennis should think about Steffi Graf. This German player has been at the forefront in the world of tennis since she made her entry in the professional tennis circuit . . . Her farewell in 1999 exceeded the expectations of the 22-fold Grand Slam winner: "I've been very lucky. I've left sports with a feeling of happiness and fulfillment . . . I haven't looked back. I've reached everything in tennis." (Topsport eist, 2000).

Although the end of a sport career is a clearly identifiable moment to all, it is not the only moment that athletes find crucial. Annelies, 34 years of age, silver medallist at the 1992 Olympic Games at Barcelona, reflects on some of the moments she found – retrospectively – important throughout her elite rowing career. One of these moments include her initial involvement in rowing:

> I first played one and a half years of volleyball at regional level – the lowest of the lowest. I then started rowing when I was 16. I learned it at school where we went rowing instead of doing gymnastics and actually some of us stuck with

it. . . . Looking back I feel that I landed in a very good sport in view of my capabilities. Rowing means endurance, technique, strength.

Not qualifying for a World championship and breaking through at world level were two other moments that clearly stuck in her memory as she perceived them to influence the quality and level of her involvement in competitive rowing:

> Once I got very disappointed because I failed to make the selection for a World championship. I quit my job and I tried to break through at elite level. . . .

> I rowed some 6 years at sub-elite level since I was 18 years of age, in-between 7th and 10th at world level. Since 1991, I consistently trained twice a day. Since then, I remained at the top until Atlanta 1996.

Naturally, she remembers vividly the moment she decided to discontinue her competitive career:

> I knew that I wanted to quit after the [Olympic] Games in Atlanta. A couple parties were thrown in my honor . . . I ended my career voluntarily. I wanted to start a family. Age was important, although not as if I wouldn't be able to compete anymore, but now I'm 32, and if I wanted to go on for another 4 years, I would have been 36 at the Games in Sydney . . . Once you've been to the Olympic Games, you start to think in Olympic years, and those 4 years seemed too much to me.

These moments or events that Annelies describes can be viewed as turning points or "transitions." The most visible transitions include the moment that Annelies started with rowing, which reflects her transition *into* sport, whereas the moment she decided to end her competitive rowing career characterizes her transition *out* of sport.

Since the 1970s, sport psychologists have focused their attention on these two clearly identifiable transitions in organized sport—transition into and out of sport. Youth sport researchers have not only studied why and how children start participating in organized sport, but have also looked at the process of attrition among young athletes (see Brustad, Babkes, & Smith, 2001). Other researchers also examined the process of terminating involvement in competitive sport among elite athletes (for an overview, see Lavallee, 2000). Although the transition out of (elite) sport has become a well-delineated topic of study among the sport psychology community as reflected in the growing number of publications, conference symposia and workshops, position statements and even a special interest group (Lavallee, Sinclair, & Wylleman, 1998; Lavallee, Wylleman, & Sinclair, 1998), relatively little attention has been paid to the broad range of transitions that athletes face during their sport career and that athletes perceive to influence the quality of their athletic involvement (Wylleman, Lavallee, & Alfermann, 1999).

This chapter aims to provide a view on the relevance and occurrence of the different transitions that athletes may face during their sport career. First, a description is given of the nature and types of transitions that athletes may face throughout their athletic lifespan. Ensuing sections will include those transitions that are not only related to the athletic context, but also those that occur in the athlete's psychological, social, academic, vocational, financial, and legal course of development. Next, a developmental model on the transitions faced by athletes will be presented. Finally, the model will be used to illustrate how to approach a case study from a developmental and holistic perspective.

Nature and Types of Transitions Faced by Athletes

A transition generally results from one or a combination of events (Lavallee, 2000; Taylor & Ogilvie, 2001) that are perceived by the athlete to bring about personal and social disequilibria (Wapner & Craig-Bay, 1992). These disequilibria are presumed to be beyond the ongoing changes of everyday life (Sharf, 1997) and cause "a change in assumptions about oneself" (Schlossberg, 1981, p. 5). These transitions are, among others, developmental in nature (Alfermann, 1995; Pearson & Petitpas, 1990; Wylleman, De Knop, Ewing, & Cumming, 2000), and they can be characterized by predictability and developmental context of occurrence.

Two types of transitions can be discerned: normative and nonnormative transitions. During a normative transition, the athlete exits one stage and enters another stage, which makes these normative transitions generally predictable and anticipated (Schlossberg, 1984; Sharf, 1997). Normative transitions are part of a definite sequence of age-related biological, social,

> There are two types of transitions: normative and nonnormative.

and emotional events or changes (Baltes, 1987) and are generally related to the socialization process (Wapner & Craig-Bay, 1992) and the organizational nature of the setting in which the individual is involved (e.g., school, family). In the athletic domain, normative transitions include, for example, the transition from junior to senior level, from regional to national-level competitions, from amateur to professional status, or from active participation to discontinuation from competitive sport.

Nonnormative transitions, on the other hand, do not occur in a set plan or schedule but are the result of important events that take place in an individual's life. For athletes, these transitions may include a season-ending injury, the loss of a personal coach, or an unanticipated "cut" or termination from the team. These idiosyncratic transitions are generally unpredicted, unanticipated, and involuntary (Schlossberg, 1984). These transitions also include those that are expected or hoped for, but that did not happen – labeled *nonevents* (Schlossberg, 1984). Not making the first team although making the final preselection, and not being able to participate in a major championship (e.g., the 1980 Olympic Games) after years of preparation are two examples of nonevents. Although athletes will certainly face a combination of both types of transitions, this chapter will focus on the normative transitions because they are fairly voluntary, anticipated, and predictable.

Transitions are also related to the developmental context in which they occur. For an athlete, these will include those transitions inherent to the athlete's involvement in the athletic context (i.e., athletic transitions), as well as those transitions related to her or his development at psychological, psychosocial, academic, and vocational levels (i.e., general or nonathletic transitions; Wylleman et al., 1999).

Transitions Related to Athletic Contexts

Although competitive sport is unpredictable at moments, it actually is characterized by normative athletic transitions that are also referred to as normal (Petitpas, Champagne, Chartrand, Danish, & Murphy, 1997) or planned (Sinclair & Orlick, 1994) transitions. A first type of transition is determined by age, for example, going from junior to senior level. Although being at the top end in their age group, a junior elite athlete will become part of a larger group of senior athletes at the bottom end in level of athletic achievement. This is also a transition in which a number of athletes do not progress to the next age category. For example, in their study of female track-and-field athletes, Bussmann and Alfermann (1994) found that only 14 out of the 51 national elite junior athletes made it to the national senior level.

A second type of transition is determined by the structural or organizational characteristics of competitive sport, which may differ worldwide. In the United States, where organized sport is firmly embedded in the educational system, an athlete will be confronted with the transition from high school to collegiate athletics (Leonard, 1996). On the European continent, however, athletes will transit organized sport by making the transition from the local sports clubs to regional and national teams (De Knop, Wylleman, Van Houcke, & Bollaert, 1999).

Finally, athletic proficiency also confronts athletes with specific transitions. As the level of athletic achievements increases, an athlete will go from regional to national to continental competitions and finally to competitions at world level (e.g., World championships, World Games, Olympic Games). For example, making the Olympic Games had a long-lasting effect on the participation, personal satisfaction and fulfillment, and future success of Olympic athletes (Gould, Guinan, Greenleaf, Medbery, & Peterson, 1999). Moreover, Bussmann and Alfermann's (1994) study of female track-and-field athletes showed that junior athletes who were among the very best in the world in their age category were more likely to remain in elite sports as a senior athlete than were junior athletes who ranked lower in level of performance. Making a transition successfully is thus also related to the athlete's level of sporting achievements.

Bloom (1985) identified three stages of talent development (within the fields of science, art, and sport) that are delineated by specific transitions. These include (a) the *initiation* stage in which young athletes are introduced to organized sports and during which they are identified as talented athletes; (b) transition into the *development* stage during which athletes become more dedicated to their sport and the amount of training and level of specialization are increased; and (c) transition into the *mastery or perfection* stage in which athletes reach their highest level of athletic proficiency. Using retrospective qualitative data, Wylleman, De Knop, Menkehorst, Theeboom, and Annerel (1993) related these stages to the ages at which former Olympic athletes made the relevant transitions. They transited into the initiation stage at the average age of 14.3 years, into the development stage at age 15, and into the mastery stage at 18.5 years of age. Although normative in nature, the age at which these transitions occur as well as the age range between transitions may vary. For example, female gymnasts tend to end their competitive career between 15 and 19 years of age (Kerr & Dacyshyn, 2000), the age at which male rowers make the transition from the development into the mastery stage (Wylleman et al., 1993). Although the average tenure in major league baseball, football, basketball, and ice hockey in the United States is between 4 and 7 years (Leonard, 1996), the mastery stage of Belgian Olympic athletes spans on average 10 years (Wylleman et al., 1993) and that of German Olympic athletes almost 15 years (Conzelmann, Gabler, & Nagel, 2001).

Côté (1999), similar to Bloom (1985), identified normative transitions occurring between the stages of sampling, specializing, investment, and mastery in the development of deliberate practice. Finally, Stambulova (1994, 2000) considered the athletic career as consisting of predictable stages and transitions, including (a) the beginning of the sports specialization, (b) transition to intensive training in the chosen sport, (c) transition to high-achievement sports and adult sports, (d) transition from amateur sports to professional sports, (e) transition from culmination to the end of the sports career, and (f) end of the sports career. The occurrence of these normative transitions underlines the developmental nature of the athletic career.

Nonathletic transitions generally include those faced by athletes in their development at psychological, psychosocial, academic, and vocational levels (Wylleman et al., 1999). Recently, research has shown that athletes also make specific transitions at financial and legal levels when transiting from one athletic stage to another. These specific developmental transitions are addressed in the following sections.

Transitions in Psychological Development

Different conceptual frameworks have been developed that describe the stages and transitions relevant to the athlete's psychological development, such as Erikson's (1963) developmental stages, Piaget's (1971) stages of cognitive development, and Havighurst's (1973) developmental tasks over the lifespan. Major developmental stages include childhood, adolescence, and adulthood. Each of these stages is related to a specific pattern of participation in competitive sport. For example, 70.5% of (former West) German track-and-field athletes who started competitive sport participation during childhood discontinued involvement by the time they reached adolescence, 89.6% terminated their sports career when transiting to adulthood; and 61.8% of athletes who started during adolescence quit competitive sport at adulthood (Bussmann & Alfermann, 1994). The applicability of these conceptual frameworks to the entire athletic career may be limited (Lavallee & Andersen, 2000); thus, attention will be directed to the developmental stages of childhood and adolescence.

An important developmental task relevant to young athletes during childhood includes their readiness for structured sport competition (see Passer, 1996). From a motivational point of view, *readiness* refers to the extent to which a child is motivated to participate in sport because of his or her own interest in and attraction to the activity. Because a child's initial participation in organized sport may reflect a parental decision, the young athlete may not necessarily be motivationally ready to participate. Motivational readiness also relates to a child's interest in comparing his or her skills with those of other children, which is not likely to be present for youngsters prior to age 7 or 8 years (Passer, 1996). From a cognitive point of view, readiness refers to the child's capacity for abstract reasoning and an understanding of roles, responsibilities, and relational characteristics that are relevant to the athletic setting. For example, a child's role-taking abilities are not fully developed until 8 to 10 years of age (van der Meulen & Menkehorst, 1992). Children who are expected (e.g., by the parents) to participate in sport earlier than their cognitive maturational level may experience considerable frustration and could lose interest in subsequent sport participation because they do not have the cognitive capacities to handle the demands placed on them.

A young athlete also needs to understand the causes of performance outcomes. Because children do not effectively distinguish among the various contributors to achievement outcomes until around age 10 to 12 years, it may be that young athletes cannot estimate accurately their own ability and therefore need to rely on adults for information about their competence (Fry & Duda, 1997). As 10- to 14-year-old athletes start to rely more on comparison with peers, they could have a higher chance of dropping out if they are strongly ability oriented and if they perceive themselves to have less ability than do other athletes (Roberts, 1993). Young athletes thus need to be cognitively and motivationally mature to be able to progress in competitive sport.

Adolescence is a period during which individuals are confronted with a number of developmental tasks. These include achieving new and more mature relations with peers of both sexes, identifying with a masculine or feminine role in society, accepting one's physique and using the body effectively, and attaining emotional independence from parents and other adults (Rice, 1998). Developing a self-identity is, therefore, a crucial developmental task for adolescents. This is especially relevant for an athlete as it has been shown that participation and continued involvement in competitive sport can have a significant influence on the way self-identity develops (Brewer, Van Raalte, & Petitpas, 2000). The degree to which an individual will develop an athletic identity can have both positive and negative consequences for the athlete. As young athletes become and remain involved in high-level competitive sport through adolescence, their self-identity may become strongly and exclusively based on athletic performance (Coakley, 1993). Individuals who strongly commit to the athlete role may be less likely to explore other career, education, and lifestyle options (Baillie & Danish, 1992; Werthner & Orlick, 1986). *Identity foreclosure*, which is the process by which individuals make commitments to roles without engaging in exploratory behavior (Petitpas, 1978), also plays an important role as it may negatively influence the use of coping strategies that are essential during career transitions (Crook & Robertson, 1991; Gordon, 1995; Pearson & Petitpas, 1990). Both athletic identity and identity foreclosure have been found to be inversely related to career maturity among intercollegiate athletes (Murphy, Petitpas, & Brewer, 1996). Both play a crucial role in the way adolescents seek and establish continuity of the self in search of an identity (Rice, 1998). Adolescents' search for a self-identity will lead them to strive toward more autonomy from their parents by developing their own lifestyles or by identifying their own place within their psychosocial environment (Dusek, 1987). For example, as the onset of puberty and associated biopsychosocial changes may be delayed for female gymnasts until their retirement from sport, their transition of identity exploration may also be delayed (Kerr & Dacyshyn, 2000).

> Both athletic identity and identity foreclosure are inversely related to career maturity among intercollegiate athletes.

An athlete's self-identity has also been found to play a significant role in successfully making a transition. Athletes with a strong athletic identity, and those with a strong identity foreclosure, may lack coping strategies essential during career transitions (Crook & Robertson, 1991; Gordon, 1995; Pearson & Petitpas, 1990) and, consequently, may experience a more difficult adjustment to psychological transitions than do those athletes who committed themselves to nonsport participatory roles (e.g., Chamalidis, 1995; Grove, Lavallee, & Gordon, 1997; Werthner & Orlick, 1986). For example, Chamalidis showed that former Greek and French athletes who placed great importance on their athletic role were more likely to experience problems when ending their sport career than were those athletes who placed less value on the athletic component of their self-identity. Adolescence is important for an athlete to navigate the developmental task of developing a self-identity that is not only defined in terms of his or her athletic role, but that also allows effective coping with transitions essential to an athletic career.

The empirical data on the relationship between the athlete's psychological and athletic development is still relatively limited. The available findings, however, do suggest that the way in which athletes cope with developmental tasks such as cognitive and motivational readiness for competitive sport participation, and successfully develop a multidimensional self-identity, influences if and when they are able to progress from one athletic stage to the next.

Transitions in Social Development

As relationships with other people are the most important part of an individual's life (Hinde, 1997), it should not be surprising that social development can be characterized in terms of specific stages and transitions (e.g., Trickett & Buchanan, 1997). During childhood, young children need to learn how to get along with their peers; adolescents need to achieve new and more mature relations with their peers, as well as establish emotional independence from parents and other adults; and adults need to establish stable and permanent family and social relationships (Rice, 1998).

Relevant in the athlete's psychosocial development is her or his role within the social environment and the role other relationships play in the quality of athletes' sport involvement throughout the athletic lifespan. The role of relationships is significant throughout the sport career in view of the support they can provide to athletes. For example, in a recent study on the importance of social support perceived by high-level sports performers, Rees and Hardy (2000) concluded that there was a need to recognize "that important others can play a crucial role in the life of the performer, and that the consequences of performers being isolated from support are damaging" (p. 344). Research has also shown that the athlete's social network is strongly determined by the stage of the athletic career. Bona (1998) asked two 18-year-old former elite athletes to indicate the persons they perceived to be significant to them during the mastery and discontinuation stages. After making the transition out of sport, both athletes perceived they lost contact with almost all individuals who were significant to them during their active sport career (e.g., coach, teammates), and their interactions especially with friends and family were rekindled.

The athlete's social network generally consists of coaches, parents, and peers. The importance of parents and coaches to athletes is illustrated in the fact that the athlete-parents, athlete-coach, and coach-parents relationships have become known as a network, namely as *the athletic triangle* (Smith, Smoll, & Smith, 1989), or as the *primary family of sport* (Scanlan, 1988). The relevance of this triangle was shown by Carlsson (1988) in a study of Swedish tennis players, which revealed that the quality of the interpersonal relationships in the athletic triangle was one of the major factors that determined whether young talented tennis players made it to world level or not. Although peer relationships can also play a significant role, the focus of attention will be centered on the role played by parents and coaches.

Parents

Although the role of parents has generally been situated during the initiation stage (e.g., Kirk et al., 1997; Régnier, Salmela, & Russell, 1993), research has shown more and more that athletes perceive parental involvement to be salient throughout the athletic lifespan. For example, Hellstedt (1987, 1990) found that 12- and 13-year-old elite ski racers perceived their parents to have a strong influence on their athletic development. Additionally, Ewing and Wiesner (1996) interviewed parents of regionally ranked 12- to 15-year-old tennis players and found that parents consistently reported a direct involvement with their children's development as competitive tennis players, even though each child had a coach from one of the local clubs. In a study in which 8- to 21-year-old athletes were studied over a 2-year period, Würth (2001) found that athletes who perceived they had a successful transition from one stage to another reported that their parents provided more sport-related advice and emotional support than did athletes who did not make the transition. These findings confirmed earlier results by Carlsson (1988) that parents of successful Swedish elite tennis players had, in comparison to parents of players who did not make it to world level, been supportive by not putting their children under too much pressure to achieve.

Wylleman and colleagues have conducted several studies pertaining to parental involvement throughout athletes' career stages. Wylleman, Vanden Auweele, De Knop, Sloore, and Martelaer (1995) assessed 13- to 21-year-old talented athletes competing in one of 14 different sports at national (66.4%) or international (33.6%) levels. They discovered that athletes perceived parental involvement as important throughout the development and mastery stages of their athletic career, even though the quality of interactions with both parents changed. For example, as athletes reached the mastery stage, they perceived themselves to expect less emotional support from their mother but more emotional support from their fathers. This finding was related to a decrease in mothers' involvement, which started in the initiation stage, in favor of fathers' surging interest in their children's athletic achievements when they reached a higher level of proficiency. In a related study with 20-year-old talented swimmers and their parents, Wylleman, De Knop, and Van Kerckhoven (2000) found that swimmers perceived that their parents played an emotional-supportive role during their childhood participation, underlining the need for discipline and motivation in order to enhance the athlete's level of athletic achievements. During adolescence, parental influence was perceived to evolve from an active,

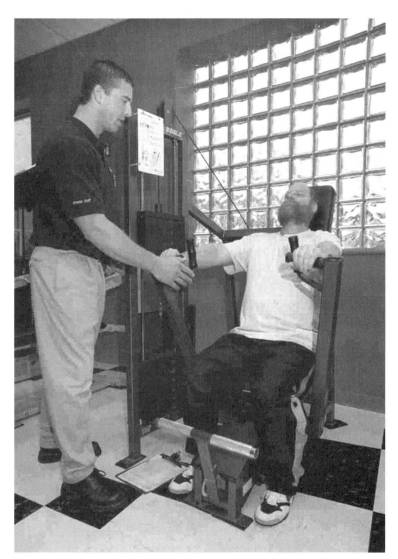

More research must be done to understand the psychological effects of sport injury on older participants.

participation-inducing role, advocating the need for hard work to develop their athletic abilities. During young adulthood, swimmers perceived that their parents acknowledged swimmers' need for more freedom and personal space, and the athletes felt that their parents would accept and support their son's or daughter's decision to discontinue their athletic career.

Côté (1999) presented empirical data suggesting that the role of parents changes over the different stages of athletic development. During the sampling years, parents assume a leadership role by initially getting their children interested in sport and allowing them to sample a wide range of enjoyable sporting activities. During the specializing years, parents are committed supporters of their child-athlete's decision to be involved in a limited number of sports. During the investment years, parents respond to the various demands and expectations put on their child-athlete by fostering an optimal learning environment rather than creating new demands or pressure. Finally, parental involvement remains relevant, even as young adult athletes make the transition into the mastery stage. Moreover, Wylleman and De Knop (1998) investigated 15- to 22-year-old competitive swimmers and track-and-field athletes who were coached by one of their own parents. Results revealed that although the majority of "parent-coaches" (67%) started to coach their child during the initiation stage of the athlete's sport career, another 20% initiated their cooperation during the development stage, and even 13% still during the mastery stage.

Coaches

Research shows that, similar to parents' influence, the quality and content of the coach-athlete relationship change during the different athletic stages. For example, the aforementioned study by Bloom (1985) revealed that during the initiation stage, coaches generally rewarded the young children for the effort they put in, rather than for the result itself. This positive reinforcement encouraged the children to remain in sport. These findings are confirmed by the coach effectiveness training studies conducted by Smith and Smoll (1996), which revealed that dropout rates were lower during the initiation stage for young athletes who played for coaches trained to use more praise following desirable performances and more instruction and encouragement following skill errors than they were for athletes who played for untrained coaches (Barnett, Smoll, & Smith, 1992). Black and Weiss (1992) also found that among 12- to 18-year-old swimmers, a relationship existed between their perceptions of the coach's behaviors and their own self-perceptions, enjoyment, and intrinsic motivation.

During the development stage, Bloom (1985) contends that coaches become more personally involved, emphasize the technical proficiency of the young athletes, and expect progress through discipline and hard work. In the mastery stage, athletes became more responsible for their training and competitions, whereas coaches placed greater demands upon these elite-level athletes. Serpa and Damasio (2001) reinforced this evolution in the way coaches interact with their athletes throughout the athletic career in a study of 13- to 30- year-old trampoline athletes. Although the coach was perceived by athletes to remain friendly toward them, the coach's dominating role was perceived to diminish during the latter stages of the athlete's sport career in favor of a more equal partnership. Martin, Jackson, Richardson, and Weiller (1999) found that 10- to 13- and 14-to-18-year-old athletes reported they preferred similar coaching behaviors, including possibilities for greater participation in making decisions pertaining to group goals, practice methods, and game tactics. They also preferred the coach to develop warm interpersonal relations with team members and create a positive group atmosphere.

The role of the coach-athlete relationship has also been underlined in instances where the coach is also the athlete's marital partner. For example, Jowett and Meek (2000) found among coach-athlete relationships in married couples that coaches were seen as good friends by their elite-level athlete-partner, that their common goals promoted a common direction, and that feelings were augmented while working together to tackle the perceived demands of top-level sport.

Research reveals that the quality and content of the coach-athlete relationship are influenced by the athlete's transition to the next athletic stage. Alfermann and Würth (2001) conducted a 2-year study of 11- to 15-year-old handball, basketball, and hockey players and found that players who perceived their coaches gave them more instruction and feedback made a more successful transition into the next athletic stage compared to players coached by less attentive coaches. However, the quality of the coach's behaviors can also be negatively related to athletes' responses such as higher anxiety and burnout, contributing to an unsuccessful transition to the next athletic stage. At the high school level, athlete burnout was related to lower social support, positive feedback, training and instruction, and democratic decision making (Price & Weiss, 2000), whereas at the collegiate level, athlete burnout was primarily due to a lack of coach empathy and praise and a greater emphasis on winning (Vealey, Armstrong, Comar, & Greenleaf, 1998). Other coach-related factors that contribute to career termination among athletes include a conflicting or problematic athlete-coach relationship and psychological abuse by the coach (Kerr & Dacyshyn, 2000; Werthner & Orlick, 1986).

Although the parents-coach relationship has largely been neglected as a topic of study (Wylleman, 2000), some research has shed light on the way in which parent-coach interactions evolve during the athlete's sport career. For example, Wylleman and colleagues (1995) found that athletes in the mastery stage perceived, in contrast to those in the development stage, their parents and coaches to interact in a less consultative and more independent way. The quality of the parents-coach relationship also influenced athletes' progress toward the next athletic stage. Vanden Auweele, Van Mele, and Wylleman (1994) found that coaches and parents perceived themselves to have a good relationship if coaches worked with their athletes toward reaching a higher level of athletic achievement.

Few studies have actually studied the direct relationship between the athlete's psychosocial and athletic development. However, the existing research reveals that the quality of athletes' relationships not only changes during each of the athletic stages, but that it also influences the way in which athletes are able to transit to the next athletic stage.

Transitions in Academic and Vocational Development

Formal education and development of a professional occupation compose a process that will be pursued by a majority of individuals (Newman, Lohman, Newman, Myers, & Smith, 2000). This process consists of (a) transition into primary education/elementary school at 6 or 7 years of age, (b) transition into secondary education/high school at the age of 12 or 13, (c) transition into higher education (college or university) at 18 or 19 years old, (d) transition into vocational training and a professional occupation, and (e) transition into a postgraduate, life-long learning phase. Research shows that this lifespan process challenges individuals to adapt to shifts in role definitions, expected behaviors, membership within social networks, personal and social support resources, and coping with stressors resulting from uncertainty about the ability to accomplish transition tasks (Elias, Gara, & Ubriaco, 1985).

Because most countries have compulsory education up until the age of 16 or 17 years, most athletes will be confronted with a major overlap between their academic and athletic development (De Knop et al., 1999). For example, the normative transitions in the sport life-cycle of a basketball player in the United States will run parallel to transitions at academic levels—from youth sport to high school junior varsity to high school varsity to college and, finally. professional level (Petitpas et al., 1997). In nonprofessional sports, Beamish (1992) found that 6 in 10 Canadian Olympians were students at the time of participating in the Olympic Games, whereas during the 2000 Olympic Games in Sydney, 1 Belgian athlete in 10 was a current or recently graduated university student-athlete. This dual role of student and athlete puts individuals in a situation where they need to invest their available time and energy into developing potential in two areas of achievement (De Knop et al., 1999). This is reflected in the fact that academic or vocational training, or developing a professional occupation, has been an important reason for talented athletes to terminate their sport career (Bussmann & Alfermann, 1994; Greendorfer & Blinde, 1985; Koukouris, 1991; Petitpas, Brewer, & Van Raalte, 1996; Wylleman et al., 1993).

Transition Into Secondary Education/High School

Many developmental tasks and challenges must be negotiated by adolescents during the transition into secondary education or high school, including physical maturation, cognitive advancements, emotional development (e.g., becoming more self-reliant, more autonomous from parents), expanding relationships with peers, and gaining the ability to have intimate friendships (Newman & Newman, 1999). The intensity and level of classes and studying for subjects change. For incoming high school freshmen, this transition is accompanied by increased choices, changes, and responsibilities in the adolescent's academic and social worlds (Newman et al., 2000). Newman and colleagues found that the transition to high school was a significant stressor to youngsters as it couples maturational changes with family system changes and changes in the nature of peer relations. This transition may even become more important when athletic achievements are given a prominent role through participation in high school athletics. The transition into high school is a pivotal point for most talented athletes in North America, because failing to make the high school team means that their sports participation will largely be limited to recreational opportunities. Athletes who are selected are provided with another 3 to 4 years to learn and develop physically, and they may experience even greater opportunities to make the transition into intercollegiate sports, which is the steppingstone to most Olympic and professional sport opportunities (Ewing & Seefeldt, 1996).

With the establishment of schools focused on talented athletes, secondary education has also been awarded a prominent role in the development of talented athletes in European countries (De Knop et al., 1999). For example, talented Belgian athletes are given the opportunity to complete their secondary education in a "topsport" school that provides "pupil-athletes" with a weekly 20-hour academic program similar, albeit in compressed form, to that of their nonathletic peers. Specialized coaches in local or nearby sporting facilities provide this academic program. Similar schools exist, for example, in France and in the Netherlands (De Knop et al., 1999). For athletes who do not attend such schools, problems arise ranging from compulsory school attendance, which restricts the athlete's training, to lack of time and a lack of notes or tutoring due to absenteeism for participating in training camps and competitions (De Knop et al., 1999). Athletes in secondary education have also shown underdeveloped peer group relationships and a lack of academic skills (De Knop et al., 1999). Athletes and parents have also "fought battles" with school administrators over timetables, deferring tests and exams, and allowing athletes to stay at home to study for tests or to complete required assignments that were neglected due to athletic activities (Donnelly, 1993).

The transition out of secondary education may entail a diversification in career paths among talented athletes. Some may choose to end their academic pursuits and go for a professional sport career. The probability that an athlete will be able to make this type of transition successfully is very small as reflected in the fact that only two tenths of 1% of high school athletes attain a professional sports career (Leonard, 1996)! Of those athletes who discontinued their academic career at this point in favor of a professional sports career, some regretted not pursuing their academic endeavors after retiring from a professional or elite-level sport career (Donnelly, 1993). However, a majority of athletes have little perspective on a full-time professional athletic career and will probably discontinue participation in high-level competitive sport altogether to look for or engage in a part- or full-time professional occupation. This decision may also be brought about by the lack of a structured and organized level of professional sports, which is generally the case for female athletes. For example, Wylleman et al. (2001) found that talented young female basketball players chose not to continue in competitive basketball after graduating from secondary education due to the lack of professional-level possibilities.

> Research has shown that coaches are more personally involved and expect progress during the athletes' development stage.

Transition Into Higher Education

Athletes may further their academic career by transiting into higher education (college or university). This is an important stage in a long-term process whereby the risks and disadvantages of high-performance sport gain more and more significance, while the need for educational and vocational training becomes apparent. Parents play an important role in this transition. They have been shown to "gently" pressure their children into continued formal education on the way to a professional future (Koukouris, 1991), although their guidance, support, and involvement have been related to the amount of reported transition distress among student-athletes (Zaichkowsky, King, & McCarthy, 1997). Moreover, because only 5% of high school athletes play in 1 of the 4 major U.S. team sports (football, baseball, basketball, ice hockey) at the collegiate level (Leonard, 1996), most student-athletes will need to learn to cope with not making the team or the next athletic career level. This may affect the incoming student-athlete's athletic identity that was strongly reinforced at the high school level based on successful performances (Danish, Petitpas, & Hale, 1993; Finch & Gould, 1996).

In contrast to secondary education, student-athletes need to be more personally involved in developing their academic career. The relatively high degree of freedom in college or university requires a stronger personal investment from student-athletes to attend academic activities, systematically plan their course of study, and commit enough time to academic activities (De Knop et al., 1999; Donnelly, 1993). De Knop et al. compared student-athletes' adherence to academic activities with that of students involved in nonacademic activities (e.g., fraternities) and found that although both groups of students invested a similar amount of time to academic activities, student-athletes reported more academic problems caused by lack of time and physical fatigue related to their sports involvement. Student-athletes are required to cope with changes within the social environment of higher education, which strongly differs from that at the secondary level. Although student-athletes rated the support provided by their academic institute, coaches, and parents as influential to their success in their academic and athletic careers, the role of their peers was perceived to be crucial in sustaining their efforts in furthering both careers (De Knop et al., 1999).

The way in which athletes conclude their college or university career is largely determined by the choices made when entering higher education (e.g., selection of a specific subject of study or a major) as well as by the status of their sport career. Athletes who were not able to pursue a professional athletic career elected to further their academic endeavors (De Knop et al., 1999). Maintaining the status of student-athlete allows them to not have to focus on looking for a professional occupation, of being able to enjoy the support provided to student-athletes (e.g., financial, logistic, coaching), and of bridging one or more years in preparation for a major competition (e.g., Olympic Games).

TRANSITION FROM ACADEMIC TO VOCATIONAL DEVELOPMENT

The transition out of an academic career is often accompanied by an athlete's increased efforts to secure greater financial and personal security (e.g., by entering the job market). This is necessary for those athletes who cannot rely on a revenue-income via their athletic achievements. Because only 3% of collegiate athletes and a mere two tenths of 1% of high school athletes will play football, baseball, basketball, and ice hockey at the professional level in the United States (Leonard, 1996), it should not be surprising that a large majority of athletes will try to enter the job market. Although sports-governing bodies such as the International Olympic Committee emphasize that elite athletes be provided with opportunities to develop a professional career (Olympic News, 1994), obtaining vocational training and finding a job to earn a living are among the top reasons athletes give for terminating their sport career (Bussmann & Alfermann, 1994).

Those athletes who are actually able to start a professional occupation may be confronted with the process of "occupational delay" (Naul, 1994). As most athletes have been busy with the development of their athletic career, few will have had the opportunity to participate in summer jobs or vocational or in-service training. Therefore, these athletes may, in comparison to their nonathletic peers, lack the relevant professional skills, experience, and networking necessary for vocational success.

The athlete's academic career is in view not only because of its duration, but also because of its concurrence with at least two (or possibly three) consecutive athletic stages – the initiation, development, and the mastery stages. The combination of a compulsory law requiring education and the value attributed to an academic background by society at large results in talented athletes' going through a multiyear process of academic development within structured schools, colleges, and universities. From this perspective, one could argue that the educational system could act as the "backbone" for the development of talented athletes. Although this may be the case in North America, where organized competitive sport is greatly embedded in the educational system, it is only relatively recently that national sport-governing bodies in Europe have started to cooperate with academia at local (e.g., schools) or central levels (e.g., Ministry of Education) to further the development of talent athletes (De Knop et al., 1999). The successful progress of student-athletes from one academic transition to the next has consequently become a crucial factor in athletic talent development. The importance of the relationship between academic and athletic development was confirmed in a survey on participation in and attrition from organized sport in a sample of Flemish 11- to 18-year-olds (Van Reusel et al., 1992). Results showed that a majority of these youngsters quit participating in organized sport on average at 12.1 years of age, the age at which pupils transit from their primary school and disperse to new schools at the secondary level. This geographical dispersion reduced the possibilities for former school friends to keep up their initial frequency and quality of interactions, causing one of their major participation motives, namely "being together with friends," to dwindle and thus increasing the chances for youths to drop out.

TRANSITIONS AT FINANCIAL AND LEGAL LEVELS

Finally, two types of transitions have become more visible during the last 5 years (Wylleman, De Knop, Maeschalck, & Taks, 2002) and include those faced by athletes at financial and legal levels. At the financial level, athletes at the initiation and development stages (or their family) will need to spend money and endure costs (e.g., renting the skating rink during extra hours, hiring a top-level coach, buying sports equipment) to promote their athletic career. However, except for a minority, some athletes will be able to reduce costs or earn money (e.g., sponsorship, starting money) once in the pinnacle of the mastery stage. In fact, some of the former world-level athletes are still able to earn money via long-running sponsorship contracts. Although little research has been conducted on the psychosocial ramifications of these economic transitions, it could be assumed that, for young athletes, the large amount of financial investment made by their families and, for adult athletes, the need to earn a good living for themselves and their families can be a heavy burden on their sport involvement.

The legal transitions occur simultaneously with those at the financial level and refer to the athlete's status of being an "amateur" or a "professional." In Belgium, for example, an athlete's legal status will change from "amateur" or "nonprofessional athlete" to that of "paid" or "professional" athlete when he or she receives financial rewards for athletic achievements. Although the status of nonprofessional athlete is legally under the control of local or state government, the professional athlete is considered to be a "laborer" and will, therefore, come under the control of the federal or national government. This generally occurs when the athlete is in the mastery stage. Although the relevant empirical data are still lacking on this issue, it could be hypothesized that this transition could bring about changes in the quality of an athlete's participation in competitive sport.

A DEVELOPMENTAL MODEL ON TRANSITIONS FACED BY ATHLETES

Although the stages and transitions that athletes may face at different levels of development were described independently in the previous sections, one should take into account that they will generally occur in an interacting way. Because sport psychologists should take a "holistic" approach to the study of transitions faced by athletes (Wylleman et al., 1999), a developmental model is proposed that (a) takes a "beginning-to-end" perspective and (b) reflects the developmental, as well as the interactive, nature of normative transitions at athletic, psychological, social, academic, and vocational levels (see Figure 1).

This developmental model consists of four layers. The top layer represents the stages and transitions athletes face in their athletic development including the three stages identified by Bloom (1985) and a discontinuation stage. This latter stage was added in line with research reflecting that former elite athletes describe their transition out of competitive sport as a process that could have a relatively long duration (e.g., Lavallee, 2000; Taylor & Ogilvie, 2001; Wylleman et al., 1993, 2000). The ages at which transitions occur and the age range of the four athletic stages are tentatively based upon empirical data gathered with former Olympic athletes (Wylleman et al., 1993), elite student-athletes (Wylleman & De Knop, 1997; Wylleman et al., 2000) and talented young athletes (Wylleman et al., 1995; Wylleman & De Knop, 1998). The athletic transitions include (a) transition into organized competitive sports at about 6 to 7 years of age, (b) transition to an intensive level of training and competitions at age 12 or 13, (c) transition into the highest or elite level at about 18 or 19 years of age, and (d) transition out of competitive sports between 28 and 30 years of age. Of course, one should take into account that these age ranges are averaged over many athletes and several different sports, and therefore may not be sport specific. For example, female gymnasts discontinue their sport between 15 and 19 years of age (Kerr & Dacyshyn, 2000).

The second layer of the developmental model of transitions reflects the normative stages and transitions occurring at a psychological level. It consists of the developmental stages of childhood (up until 12 years of age), adolescence (13 to 18 years), and adulthood (from 19 years of age onward; Rice, 1998). Although not represented in the model itself, the developmental task of being psychologically ready for competition is related to childhood, whereas developing a self-identity is a developmental task during adolescence.

The third layer is representative of the changes that can occur in the athlete's social development relative to her or his athletic involvement. It is based upon conceptual frameworks related to the development of the athletic family (Hellstedt, 1995) and marital relationships (e.g., Coppel, 1995), as well as empirical data on athletes' interpersonal relationships described earlier (e.g., Alfermann & Würth, 2001; Bloom, 1985; Price & Weiss, 2000; Vealey et al., 1998; Wylleman & De Knop, 1998; Wylleman et al., 1993, 1995).

The final layer contains the specific stages and transitions at academic and vocational levels. It reflects the transition into primary education/elementary school at 6 or 7 years of age, the stage of secondary education/high school at ages 12-13 (including junior high, middle

FIGURE 1

A developmental perspective on transitions faced by athletes at athletic, individual, psychosocial, and academic/vocational levels.

AGE	10	15	20	25	30	35
Athletic Level	Initiation	Development		Mastery		Discontinuation
Psycho-logical Level	Childhood	Adolescence		Adulthood		
Psycho-social Level	Parents Siblings Peers	Peers Coach Parents		Partner Coach		Family (Coach)
Academic Vocational Level	Primary education	Secondary education	Higher education		Vocational training Professional occupation	

Note. A dotted line indicates that the age at which the transition occurs is an approximation.

school, and senior high), and at 18 or 19 years of age, the transition into higher education (college/university). Although the transition into vocational training or a professional occupation may occur at an earlier age (e.g., after high school), it was included after the stage of higher education. This not only reflects the "predictable" sports career in North America, where college/university sport bridges high school varsity and professional sport (Petitpas et al., 1997), but also mirrors the current developments in Europe, where many talented athletes continue their education up to the level of higher education (De Knop, et al., 1999). For elite athletes, this professional occupation may also be in the field of professional sports and, thus, may concur with the athletic mastery stage.

> The successful progress of student-athletes from one academic transition to the next has become a crucial factor in athletic talent development.

It should be noted that some of these normative transitions may not occur, and thus, they become nonevents. For example, due to a stagnating level of athletic achievement, an athlete may not make the transition to the next athletic developmental stage; or due to a lack of support, an athlete may discontinue her academic career and not make the transition into college. Although athletes will also face nonnormative transitions that may affect the quality of their participation in competitive sport, these are not included in this model.

This developmental model is intended to provide sport psychologists with a conceptual model or framework on the transitions athletes may face throughout their athletic career. However, it should also enable sport psychologists to situate and reflect upon the developmental, interactive, and interdependent nature of transitions and stages faced by individual athletes. This approach is illustrated with a brief analysis of a case study in the following section. Some of the basic questions that remain are also formulated and used to construct a follow-up interview with the athlete.

Case Study

Tim is 16 years old, and he has recently taken his school examinations, producing results that exceeded his expectations. As an international swimmer, he has been training for about 18 hours per week, getting up at 5:30 a.m. four mornings a week and training after school on each of the five weekdays with his teammates. This year has been especially demanding because additional training was required in order to gain selection for a major championship. Tim was selected and performed creditably. Tim is very mature for his age and has a desire to do everything perfectly as evidenced by his acute frustration when he does not meet his personal standards. On the other hand, he sometimes disagrees with what he considers to be an unrealistic training load that the coach imposes upon him that disregards other demands upon his time. It is clear that he is talented both academically and athletically, with the capacity for hard work and a strong desire to be organized. He says he is especially "stressed out" when hard physical demands are placed upon him in training, and he is currently considering whether he should continue to focus on his swimming as much as he previously has or dedicate more time to his academic studies. His parents are very supportive and have not pressured him either way, although Tim sometimes perceives pressure to focus more on his swimming from his coach.

Questions

The first step will consist of situating Tim's athletic career stage in the developmental model by using his chronological age and various levels of development. In a second step, Tim's current profile will be described briefly by analyzing (a) the people who are significant in Tim's life and

(b) the principal issues that Tim faces. The third step will involve describing in more detail Tim's development by answering a number of questions that are summarized below.

With regard to Tim's athletic development:

- Is Tim in the stage of athletic development identified in the model based on his chronological age, his athletic experience, or his level of athletic achievements?

- To what extent are the people who are significant in Tim's life (parents, coach) influential in his athletic development?

- What does Tim's coach need to take into account for Tim to successfully develop in his athletic development?

- How can the coach cooperate with Tim's parents in maximizing positive developments in Tim's athletic development?

With regard to Tim's psychological development:

- In what way does Tim's athletic identity influence the quality of his athletic involvement?

- Is Tim psychologically ready to cope with the requirements of competitive sport?

- What does Tim's coach need to take into account with regard to Tim's psychological development for him to successfully develop as an athlete?

- How can the coach cooperate with Tim's parents in this?

With regard to Tim's social development:

- What is the quality of Tim's relationships with significant persons in his life?

- In what way do these relationships influence Tim's athletic development?

- What does Tim's coach need to take into account with regard to his social development for him to successfully develop as an athlete?

- How can the coach cooperate with Tim's parents in this?

With regard to Tim's academic development:

- To what degree is Tim able to combine his academic and athletic careers?

- How does the combination of academic and athletic activities influence Tim's athletic development?

- What does Tim's coach need to take into account with regard to his academic development for him to successfully develop as an athlete?

- How can the coach cooperate with Tim's parents in this?

Brief Report

Step 1. Using his chronological age on the developmental model to present a profile across each level of development reveals that (a) Tim has reached the mastery level in terms of his athletic development; (b) Tim is psychologically at the adolescent level; (c) the key people in his life should be peers, coach, and parents; and (d) Tim is at the secondary education level.

Step 2. Tim's coach and parents play important roles in his current situation. (Could we not expect that his peers such as swimming teammates should also be an important part of Tim's life?) The principal issues reflected in the case description involves Tim's desire to perform perfectly, his coach's unrealistic expectations and pressure to focus more on his swimming, and Tim's being "stressed out" as a result of self-imposed and coach-imposed expectations and standards.

Step 3. Tim has performed exceptionally well as a swimmer to date. His athletic development reflects that he has reached the mastery level at a relatively early age. (Was the development stage too brief?) Tim has shown a high level of commitment to his sport, including his capacity for hard work and organization. (Does this cause him to be "stressed out"?) Tim perceives his coach as imposing too heavy a burden upon him. (Has he always worked with his current coach? If not, why and since when did he switch coaches?) His parents have influenced his development as a swimmer to a great extent and are not perceived as putting pressure on him to perform. (In what way are his parents actually involved in his swimming: emotionally, logistically, financially?) Tim's coach could look at the way in which the mastery stage could be planned over a period of 3 to 5 years. (Can we expect that Tim's mastery stage could end earlier than expected for an average elite swimmer if his development stage was relatively short?) What are the expectations of Tim's parents with regard to their son's future swimming career?

In terms of his psychological development, the degree to which Tim identifies with his role as a swimmer has significantly influenced the quality of his involvement. Before reaching this transition in his career, he has coped reasonably well with the requirements of competitive sport. (Does he feel "stressed out" due to a lack of readiness to cope at the mastery level?) In order for Tim to continue to develop as an elite-level swimmer, his coach will need to take into account his athletic identity and work with Tim's parents in developing a balanced plan for his future. On a social level, the quality of Tim's relationship with his coach and parents appears reasonably sound (see earlier question about the actual involvement of Tim's parents in his swimming career). These particular relationships have influenced his athletic development in significant ways, although we know little about his teammates and peers. (Does Tim have any intimate same- or opposite-sex relationships?) The coach could envisage that Tim may need and want to relate more with his peers from within as well as from outside the world of swimming. The coach could consult with Tim's parents in finding more quality time for him to interact with his peers.

Finally, Tim has been able to combine his academic and sporting careers quite successfully up until this point, having achieved better grades in school than expected (for someone who has already achieved elite level). Tim's capacity to work hard and his strong desire for organization help him in combining athletic and academic requirements. (To what extent do the physical training demands leave him enough rest to do work for school and to recuperate?) The coach should take into account that Tim is a good student, so he will probably want to continue into higher education. The coach and Tim's parents could inform him of the possibilities available for Tim to select a university or college that will allow him to develop fully at both academic and athletic levels.

CONCLUSION

If we want to have a better understanding of how an athlete's sport career develops, then it is essential to focus on her or his athletic, psychological, social, academic, and vocational development. If we want to know the *whole* athlete, however, then the reciprocal and interactive nature of these different developmental contexts needs to be taken into account. The model presented in this chapter provides an overview of the stages and transitions that athletes may face and represents a step toward a more holistic and developmental perspective on the athletic lifespan. It is aimed at facilitating an understanding of the role of developmental factors by linking them to the demands of a particular stage and transition. However, more empirical research is required to investigate the sport-, gender- and cultural-specific variations required of the developmental model (e.g., Seiler, Anders, & Irlinger, 1998). There is also a need to link the demands of the particular stages and transitions described in this developmental model with the resources available to athletes to make each transition successfully. In this way, professionals working with athletes could assist athletes at all developmental levels, stages, or transitions in structuring optimal experiences throughout their sport career.

REFERENCES

Alfermann, D. (1995). Career transitions of elite athletes: Drop-out and retirement. In R. Vanfraechem-Raway & Y. Vanden Auweele (Eds.), *Proceedings of the 9th European Congress of Sport Psychology* (pp. 828-833). Brussels: European Federation of Sports Psychology.

Alfermann, D., & Würth, S. (2001). Coach-athlete interaction in youth sport. In A. Papaioannou, M. Goudas, & Y. Theodorakis (Eds.), *In the dawn of the new millennium. Programme and proceedings of the 10th World Congress of Sport Psychology* (Vol. 3, pp. 165-166). Thessaloniki, Greece: Christodoulidi Publ.

Baillie, P. H. F., & Danish, S. J. (1992). Understanding the career transition of athletes. *The Sport Psychologist, 6,* 7798.

Baltes, P. (1987). Theoretical propositions of life span developmental psychology: On the dynamics between growth and decline. *Developmental Psychology, 23,* 611-626.

Barnett, N. P., Smoll, F. L., & Smith, R. E. (1992). Effects of enhancing coach-athlete relationships on youth sport attrition. *The Sport Psychologist, 6,* 111-127.

Beamish, R. (1992). Towards a sociocultural profile of Canada's high performance athletes. *International Review for the Sociology of Sport, 27,* 279-292.

Black, S. J., & Weiss, M. R. (1992). The relationship among perceived coaching behaviors, perceptions of ability, and motivation in competitive age-group swimmers. *Journal of Sport & Exercise Psychology, 14,* 309-325.

Bloom, B.S. (Ed.). (1985). *Developing talent in young people.* New York: Ballantine.

Bona, I. (1998). Soziale netzwerke ehemaliger jugendlicher leistungssportler. In R. Seiler, G. Anders, & P. Irlinger (Eds.), *Das leben nach dem spitzensport. La vie après le sport de haut niveau* [Life after high-level sport] (pp. 221-231). Magglingen, Switzerland: Bundesamt für Sport Magglingen.

Brewer, B. W., Van Raalte, J. L., & Petitpas, A. J. (2000). Self-identity issues in sport career transitions. In D. Lavallee & P. Wylleman (Eds.), *Career transitions in sport: International perspectives* (pp. 29-43). Morgantown, WV: Fitness Information Technology.

Brustad, R. J., Babkes, M. L., & Smith, A. L. (2001). Youth in sport: Psychological considerations. In R. N. Singer, H.A. Hausenblas, & C. M. Janelle (Eds.), *Handbook of sport psychology* (pp. 604-635). New York: Wiley.

Bussmann, G., & Alfermann, D. (1994). Drop-out and the female athlete: A study with track-and-field athletes. In D. Hackfort (Ed.), *Psycho-social issues and interventions in elite sport* (pp. 89-128). Frankfurt: Lang.

Carlsson, R. (1988). The socialization of elite tennis players in Sweden: An analysis of the players' backgrounds and development. *Sociology of Sport Journal, 5,* 241-256.

Chamalidis, P. (1995). Career transitions of male champions. In R. Vanfraechem-Raway & Y. Vanden Auweele (Eds.), *Proceedings of the 9th European Congress of Sport Psychology* (pp. 841-848). Brussels: European Federation of Sports Psychology.

Coakley, J. (1993). Social dimensions of intensive training and participation in youth sports. In B.R. Cahill & A. J. Pearl (Eds.), *Intensive participation in children's sports* (pp. 77-94). Champaign, IL: Human Kinetics.

Conzelmann, A., Gabler, H., & Nagel, S. (2001). *Hochleistungssport: Persönlicher gewinn oder Verlust. Lebenslaufe van Olympioniken [Elite-level sport: Personal success or loss. Life of Olympians].* Tubingen: Attempto.

Coppel, D. B. (1995). Relationship issues in sport: A marital therapy model. In S. M. Murphy (Ed.), *Sport psychology interventions* (pp. 193-204). Champaign, IL: Human Kinetics.

Côté, J. (1999). The influence of the family in the development of talent in sport. *The Sport Psychologist, 13,* 395-417.

Crook, J. M., & Robertson, S. E. (1991). Transitions out of elite sport. *International Journal of Sport Psychology, 22,* 115127.

Danish, S. J., Petitpas, A. J., & Hale, B. D. (1993). Life development intervention for athletes: Life skills through sports. *The Counseling Psychologist, 21,* 352385.

De Knop, P., Wylleman, P., Van Houcke, J., & Bollaert, L. (1999). Sports management—A European approach to the management of the combination of academics and elite-level sport. In S. Bailey (Ed.), *Perspectives – The interdisciplinary series of Physical Education and Sport Science. Vol. 1. School sport and competition* (pp. 49-62). Oxford: Meyer & Meyer Sport.

Donnelly, P. (1993). Problems associated with youth involvement in high-performance sport. In B.R. Cahill & A. J. Pearl (Eds.), *Intensive participation in children's sports* (pp. 95-126). Champaign, IL: Human Kinetics.

Dusek, J. B. (1987). *Adolescent development and behavior*. Englewood Cliffs, NJ: Prentice-Hall.

Elias, M. J., Gara, M., & Ubriaco, M. (1985). Sources of stress and support in children's transition to middle school. *Journal of Clinical Child Psychology, 14*, 112-118.

Erikson, E. H. (1963). *Childhood and society*. New York: Stonton.

Ewing, M. E., & Seefeldt, V. (1996). Patterns of participation and attrition in American agency-sponsored youth sports. In F. L. Smoll & R. E. Smith (Eds.), *Children and youth in sport. A biopsychosocial perspective* (pp. 31-45). Madison, WI: Brown & Benchmark.

Ewing, M. E., & Wiesner, A.R. (1996). Parents' perceptions of the role of sport programs in the development of youth. *Journal of Applied Sport Psychology, 8* (Supplement), S25.

Finch, L. M., & Gould, D. (1996). Understanding and intervening with the student-athlete-to-be. In E. F. Etzel, A. P. Ferrante, & Pinkney, J. W. (Eds.), *Counseling college student-athletes: Issues and interventions* (pp. 223-245). Morgantown, WV: Fitness Information Technology.

Fry, M. D., & Duda, J. L. (1997). A developmental examination of children's understanding of effort and ability in the physical and academic domains. *Research Quarterly for Exercise and Sport, 68*, 331-344.

Gordon, S. (1995). Career transitions in competitive sport. In T. Morris & J. Summers (Eds.), *Sport psychology: Theory, applications and issues* (pp. 474-501). Brisbane: Jacaranda Wiley.

Gould, D., Guinan, D., Greenleaf, C., Medbery, R., & Peterson, K. (1999). Factors affecting Olympic performance: Perceptions of athletes and coaches from more and less successful teams. *The Sport Psychologist, 13*, 371-394.

Greendorfer, S. L, & Blinde, E. M. (1985). "Retirement" from intercollegiate sport: Theoretical and empirical considerations. *Sociology of Sport Journal, 2*, 101110.

Grove, J. R., Lavallee, D., & Gordon, S. (1997). Coping with retirement from sport: The influence of athletic identity. *Journal of Applied Sport Psychology, 9*, 191-203.

Havighurst, R. J. (1973). History of developmental psychology: Socialization and personality development through the life span. In P. B. Baltes & K. W. Schaie (Eds.), *Life-span developmental psychology: Personality and socialization* (pp. 3-24). New York, NY: Academic Press.

Hellstedt, J. C. (1987). The coach/parent/athlete relationship. *The Sport Psychologist, 1*, 151-160.

Hellstedt, J. C. (1990). Early adolescent perceptions of parental pressure in the sport environment. *Journal of Sport Behavior, 13*, 135-144.

Hellstedt, J. C. (1995). Invisible players: A family systems model. In S. M. Murphy (Ed.), *Sport psychology interventions* (pp. 117-146). Champaign, IL: Human Kinetics.

Het Volk (2000, February 1). Bubka's laatste [Bubka's last].

Hinde, R. A. (1997). *Relationships. A dialectical perspective*. Hove, UK: Psychology Press.

Jowett, S., & Meek, G. A. (2000). The coach-athlete relationship in married couples: An exploratory content analysis. *The Sport Psychologist, 14*, 157-175.

Kerr, G., & Dacyshyn, A. (2000). The retirement experiences of elite, female gymnasts. *Journal of Applied Sport Psychology, 12*, 115-133.

Kirk, D., O'Connor, A., Carlson, T., Burke, P., Davis, K., & Glover, S. (1997). Time commitments in junior sport: Social consequences for participants and their families. *European Journal of Physical Education, 2*, 51-73.

Koukouris, K. (1991). Disengagement of advanced and elite Greek male athletes from organized competitive sport. *International Review for the Sociology of Sport, 26*, 289-306.

Lavallee, D. (2000). Theoretical perspectives on career transitions in sport. In D. Lavallee & P. Wylleman (Eds.), *Career transitions in sport: International perspectives* (pp. 1-27). Morgantown, WV: Fitness Information Technology.

Lavallee, D., & Andersen, M. (2000). Leaving sport: Easing career transitions. In M. B. Andersen (Ed.), *Doing sport psychology* (pp. 249-260). Champaign, IL: Human Kinetics.

Lavallee, D., Sinclair, D. A., & Wylleman, P. (1998). An annotated bibliography on career transitions in sport: I. Counselling-based references. *Australian Journal of Career Development, 2*, 34-42.

Lavallee, D., Wylleman, P., & Sinclair, D. A. (1998). An annotated bibliography on career transitions in sport: II. Empirical references. *Australian Journal of Career Development, 3*, 32-44.

Leonard, W. M. (1996). The odds of transiting from one level of sports participation to another. *Sociology of Sport Journal, 13*, 288-299.

Martin, S. B., Jackson, A. W., Richardson, P. A., & Weiller, K. H. (1999). Coaching preferences of adolescent youths and their parents. *Journal of Applied Sport Psychology, 11*, 247-262.

Murphy, S. M., Petitpas, A. J., & Brewer, B. W. (1996). Identity foreclosure, athletic identity, and career maturity in intercollegiate athletes. *The Sport Psychologist, 10*, 239-246.

Naul, R. (1994). The elite athlete career: Sport pedagogy must counsel social and professional problems in life development. In D. Hackfort (Ed.), *Psycho-social issues and interventions in elite sport* (pp. 237-258). Frankfurt: Lang.

Newman, B. M., Lohman, B. J., Newman, P. R., Myers, M. C., & Smith, V. L. (2000). Experiences of urban youth navigating the transition to ninth grade. *Youth & Society, 31*, 387-416.

Newman, B. M., & Newman, P. R. (1999). *Development through life: A psychosocial approach*. Pacific Grove, CA: Brooks/Cole.

Olympic News (1994, December). *De 61 aanbevelingen en conclusies van het IOC Conges [The 61 recommendations and conclusions of the IOC Congress]*, pp. 11-12.

Passer, M. W. (1996). At what age are children ready to compete? In F. L. Smoll & R. E. Smith (Eds.), *Children and youth in sport. A biopsychosocial perspective* (pp. 73-86). Madison, WI: Brown & Benchmark.

Pearson, R. E., & Petitpas, A. J. (1990). Transitions of athletes: Developmental and preventive perspectives. *Journal of Counseling and Development, 69*, 710.

Petitpas, A. (1978). Identity foreclosure: A unique challenge. *Personnel and Guidance Journal, 56*, 558-561.

Petitpas, A. J., Brewer, B. W., & Van Raalte, J. L. (1996). Transitions of the student-athlete: Theoretical, empirical, and practical perspectives. In E. F. Etzel, A. P. Ferrante, & J. W. Pinkney (Eds.), *Counseling college student-athletes: Issues and interventions* (pp. 137-156). Morgantown, WV: Fitness Information Technology.

Petitpas, A. J., Champagne, D., Chartrand, J., Danish, S. J., & Murphy, S. M. (1997). *Athlete's guide to career planning. Keys to success from the playing field to professional life*. Champaign, IL: Human Kinetics.

Piaget, J. (1971). *Biology and knowledge: An essay on the relations between organic regulations and cognitive processes*. Chicago: University of Chicago Press.

Price, M. S., & Weiss, M. R. (2000). Relationships among coach burnout, coach behaviours, and athletes' psychological responses. *The Sport Psychologist, 14*, 391-409.

Rees, T., & Hardy, L. (2000). An investigation of the social support experiences of high-level sports performers. *The Sport Psychologist, 14*, 327-347.

Régnier, G., Salmela, J., & Russell, S. J. (1993). Talent detection and development in sport. In R. N. Singer, M. M. Murphey, & L. K. Tennant (Eds), *Handbook on research in sport psychology* (pp. 290-313). New York: MacMillan.

Rice, P.F. (1998). *Human development: A life-span approach*. Upper Saddle River, NJ: Prentice Hall.

Roberts, G. C. (1993). Motivation in sport: Understanding and enhancing the motivation and achievement of children. In R. N. Singer, M. M. Murphey, & L. K. Tennant (Eds), *Handbook on research in sport psychology* (pp. 405-420). New York: MacMillan.

Scanlan, T. K. (1988). Social evaluation and the competition process: A developmental perspective. In F. L. Smoll, R. A. Magill, & M. J. Ash (Eds.), *Children in sport* (pp. 135-148). Champaign, IL: Human Kinetics.

Schlossberg, N. K. (1981). A model for analyzing human adaptation to transition. *The Counseling Psychologist, 9*, 218.

Schlossberg, N. K. (1984). *Counseling adults in transition: Linking practice with theory*. New York: Springer.

Seiler, R., Anders, G., & Irlinger, P. (Eds.) (1998). *Das leben nach dem spitzensport. La vie après le sport de haut niveau* [Life after elit-level sport]. Paris: INSEP.

Serpa, S., & Damasio, L. (2001). Relationship coach-athlete during the athletes' career. In J. Mester, G. King, H. Strüder, E. Tsolakidis, & A. Osterburg (Eds.), *Perspectives and profiles. Book of abstracts of the 6th Annual Congress of the European College of Sport Science* (p. 57). Cologne, Germany: Sport und Buch Strauss.

Sharf, R. S. (1997). *Applying career development theory to counseling*. Pacific Grove, CA: Brooks/Cole Publ. Cy.

Sinclair, D. A., & Orlick, T. (1994). The effects of transition on high performance sport. In D. Hackfort (Ed.), *Psychosocial issues and interventions in elite sports* (pp. 29-55). Frankfurt: Lang.

Smith, R. E., & Smoll, F. L. (1996). The coach as focus of research and intervention in youth sports. In F. L. Smoll & R. E. Smith (Eds.), *Children and youth in sport: A biopsychosocial perspective* (pp. 125-141). Dubuque, IA: McGraw-Hill.

Smith, R. E., Smoll, F. L., & Smith, N. J. (1989). *Parents' complete guide to youth sports*. Costa Mesa, CA: HDL Publishing.

Stambulova, N.B. (1994). Developmental sports career investigations in Russia: A post-perestroika analysis. *The Sport Psychologist, 8*, 221-237.

Stambulova, N.B. (2000). Athletes' crises: A developmental perspective. *International Journal of Sport Psychology, 31*, 584-601.

Taylor, J., & Ogilvie, B. (2001). Career termination among athletes. In R. N. Singer, H.A. Hausenblas, & C. M. Janelle (Eds.), *Handbook of sport psychology* (pp. 672-691). New York: John Wiley & Sons.

Topsport eist tol bij Steffi Graf [High-level sport takes its toll with Steffi Graf] (2000, December 20). De Morgen.

Trickett, E. J., & Buchanan, R. M. (1997). The role of personal relationships in transitions: Contributions of an ecological perspective. In S. Duck (Ed.), *Handbook of personal relationships. Theory, research and interventions* (pp. 575-593). New York: Wiley.

van der Meulen, M., & Menkehorst, H. (1992). Intensieve sportbeoefening in ontwikkelingspsychologisch perspectief [Intensive sports participation in developmental psychological perspective]. In M. van der Meulen, H. A.B. M. Menkehorst, & F. C. Bakker (Red.), *Jeugdig sporttalent: Psychologische aspecten van intensieve sportbeoefening* [Talented young athletes: Psychological aspects of intensive sport participation] (pp. 93-114). Amsterdam: Vereniging Sportpsychologie Nederland.

Van Reusel, B., De Knop, P., De Martelaer, K., Impens, G., Roelandt, F., Teirlynck, P., et al. (1992). *Fysieke fitheid en sportbeoefening van de Vlaamse jeugd: Volumen 4. Participatie en drop out: een onderzoek naar jongeren van 12 tot 18 jaar in sportverenigingen* [Physical fitness and sports participation of Flemish youth: Vol. 4. Participation and drop out: a study on 12-18 year-old youths in sports clubs]. Brussels: Interuniversitair Onderzoekscentrum voor Sportbeleid.

Vanden Auweele, Y., Van Mele, V., & Wylleman, P. (1994). La relation entraîneur-athlète [The relationship coach-athlete]. *Enfance, 2-3*, 187-202.

Vealey, R. S., Armstrong, L., Comar, W., & Greenleaf, C. A. (1998). Influence of perceived coaching behaviours on burnout and competitive anxiety in female college athletes. *Journal of Applied Sport Psychology, 10*, 297-318.

Wapner, S., & Craig-Brey, L. (1992). Person-in-environment transitions: Theoretical and methodological approaches. *Environment and Behavior, 24*, 161-188.

Werthner, P., & Orlick, T. (1986). Retirement experiences of successful Olympic athletes. *International Journal of Sport Psychology, 17,* 337363.

Würth, S. (2001). Parental influences on career development. In A. Papaioannou, M. Goudas, & Y. Theodorakis (Eds.), *Proceedings 10th World Congress of Sport Psychology* (Vol. 3, pp. 21-23). Thessaloniki, Greece: Christodoulidi Publ.

Wylleman, P. (2000). Interpersonal relationships in sport: Uncharted territory. *International Journal of Sport Psychology, 31*, 1-18.

Wylleman, P., & De Knop, P. (1997). The role and influence of the psycho-social environment on the career transitions of student-athletes. In J. Bangsbo, B. Saltin, H. Bonde, Y. Hellsten, B. Ibsen, M. Kjaer, & G. Sjogaard (Eds.), *Book of abstracts I. 2nd Annual Congress of the European College of Sports Science* (pp. 90-91). Copenhagen, Denmark: University of Copenhagen.

Wylleman, P., & De Knop, P. (1998, August). *Athletes' interpersonal perceptions of the "parent-coach" in competitive youth sport*. Paper presented at the 28th Congress of the International Association of Applied Psychology, San Francisco, CA.

Wylleman, P., De Knop, P., Anseeuw, L., De Clercq, D., Bouckaert, J., Bassez, P., et al. (2001). *Evaluatie van de opzet en de werking van de topsportscholen in Vlaanderen. Globaal rapport.* [Evaluation of the aim and functioning of the topsportschools in Flanders. Global report.]. Brussels: IOS-Bloso.

Wylleman, P., De Knop, P., Ewing, M., & Cumming, S. (2000). Transitions in youth sport: A developmental perspective on parental involvement. In D. Lavallee & P. Wylleman (Eds.), *Career transitions in sport: International perspectives* (pp. 143-160). Morgantown, WV: Fitness Information Technology.

Wylleman, P., De Knop, P., Maeschalck, J., & Taks, M. (2002). Sport en carrière-ontwikkeling [Sport and career development]. In P. De Knop, B. Vanreusel, & J. Scheerder (Eds.), *Sportsociologie. Het spel en de spellers.* [Sport Sociology. The game and the players] (pp. 384-391). Maarssen, the Netherlands: Elsevier gezondheidszorg.

Wylleman, P., De Knop, P., Menkehorst, H., Theeboom, M., & Annerel, J. (1993). Career termination and social integration among elite athletes. In S. Serpa, J. Alves, V. Ferreira, & A. Paula-Brito (Eds.), *Proceedings of the VIII World Congress of Sport Psychology* (pp. 902-906). Lisbon, Portugal: International Society of Sport Psychology.

Wylleman, P., De Knop, P., & Van Kerckhoven, C. (2000, October). *The development of the athlete family as perceived by talented swimmers and their parents*. Paper presented at the AAASP Conference, Nashville, TN.

Wylleman, P., Lavallee, D., & Alfermann, D. (Eds.). (1999). *Transitions in the career of competitive athletes*. Lund, Sweden: FEPSAC.

Wylleman, P., Vanden Auweele, Y., De Knop, P., Sloore, H., & De Martelaer, K. (1995). Elite young athletes, parents and coaches: relationships in competitive sports. In F.J. Ring (Ed.), *The 1st Bath Sports Medicine Conference* (pp. 124-133). Bath, United Kingdom: University of Bath - Centre for Continuing Education.

Zaichkowsky, L., King, E., & McCarthy, J. (2000). The end of an era: The case of forced transition involving Boston University football. In D. Lavallee & P. Wylleman (Eds.), *Career transitions in sport: International perspectives* (pp. 195-205). Morgantown, WV: Fitness Information Technology.

CHAPTER TWENTY

From Skinned Knees and Peewees to Menisci and Masters: Developmental Sport Injury Psychology

Diane M. Wiese-Bjornstal

The last 10 years has seen an explosion of research related to psychological factors in the sport injury process. Drawing from medicine, psychology, and sport science literatures, researchers have identified a number of psychological and social factors that affect both vulnerability and response to sport injury. The majority of this research, however, has focused on a very narrow window in the developmental continuum of sport and physical activity participation: the late adolescent and early adulthood period. Little attention has been paid either to younger or older sport participants even though influential factors in sport injury vary with age and developmental level.

If one examines participation motivation, for example, the reasons that people play sport vary on many dimensions, including age. Among younger athletes, playing for fun is an important motivator. Yet one can see how the intensity and demands of sport participation that increase with increasing age and skill level not only reduce the fun but can also increase perceptions of stress—a factor commonly linked to increased sport injury vulnerability. Young athletes are also socialized with increasing age into accepting the sport normative expectations of playing with pain and injury, which, in turn, increases injury vulnerability and disrupts psychological management of injury once it occurs.

By the same token reasons for dropping out of sport also vary by age, and often relate to injury. Among younger athletes, injury is commonly cited as a reason for dropping out. Amid athletes in the peak of their careers, perhaps the most common reason for early career termination is injury and its consequences, which often negatively affect an optimal transition out of sporting life. Among older athletes and exercisers, pain and injury are often experienced with exercise initiation following a hiatus from physical activity and can lead to premature dropout and psychological distress.

> Injury is a common reason for younger athletes to drop out.

Developmental factors do affect the occurrence of and response to sport injury, and these factors are worthy of further examination than has been given them to date. This chapter first outlines the conceptual bases underlying the study of developmental sport injury psychology and second describes several of the influential psychological and social factors in sport injury at three stages of athlete development—childhood and adolescence, early adulthood, and middle-to-late adulthood—using the conceptual models as organizers of these influential factors. The chapter framework relies largely on insight and data from North American, European, British, and Australian populations and literature. This is acknowledged as a limitation in understanding possible cross-cultural differences.

Conceptual Bases of Sport Injury

Deductively derived models of pre-injury vulnerability (Andersen & Williams, 1988; Williams & Andersen, 1998) and post-injury response (Wiese-Bjornstal, Smith, & LaMott, 1995; Wiese-Bjornstal, Smith, Shaffer, & Morrey, 1998) have provided conceptual bases upon which much of the sport injury research to date has relied. These operational models have not yet progressed to the level of theory, but nonetheless have served as stimuli for conceptual and empirical development in sport injury psychology. Recently, practitioners and researchers have contributed experientially (e.g., Heil, 2000) and inductively (e.g., Mainwaring, 1999; Rose & Jevne, 1993) derived explanatory models as well.

Figure 1
Factors affecting sport injury vulnerability.

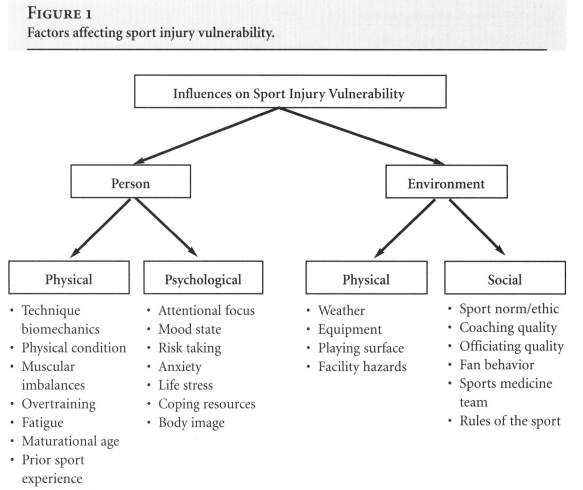

Pre-Injury

Before injury occurs, psychological and social factors have been implicated as affecting injury vulnerability. First, an overall view of the factors affecting sport injury vulnerability is identified, and then a description is given as to how psychological and social factors operate within this overall view. Subsequently, the conceptual model of Williams and Andersen (1998) is used to identify specific ways in which psychological and social factors affect pre-injury vulnerability.

Vulnerability to Sport Injury

Many factors in combination create a situation in which sport injury is more or less likely to occur. These factors cluster into the four major areas identified in Figure 1; although injuries may occur as a function of one area, they are more often a consequence of two or more areas in combination. *Personal-physical* factors represent the physical characteristics of individual athletes and include such items as their physical condition, age, and existing muscular imbalances. *Personal-psychological* factors represent psychological characteristics of the individual athlete, including mood state, life stress, and risk taking. *Environmental-physical* factors encompass the physical environment surrounding participation. Situations precipitating injury occurrence might include uneven surfaces, slippery conditions, and unsafe equipment. *Environmental-social* factors included might be such influences as the quality of officiating (e.g., Do the officials allow more contact than they should?) and the quality and style of coaching (e.g., Does the coach teach unsafe techniques?).

Among all four categories, the role of developmental level is apparent. For example, personal-physical factors encompass developmental factors such as the physical vulnerability associated with growth (e.g., incomplete epiphyseal closure and risk of growth-plate injuries in young athletes; deterioration of joints in older athletes). Examples of personal-psychological factors related to growth and development across the lifespan are the more limited coping skills and capabilities of children and the increased mental distress associated with chronic health conditions in the elderly. Developmental level-related environmental-physical factors examples would be the often ill-fitting, hand-me-down equipment provided to young athletes and the reduced balance abilities of older athletes leading to increased risk of a fall on slippery surfaces. Environmental-social factors and age-related influences might be the often less knowledgeable volunteer coaches assigned to work with young athletes and the reduction in social interaction and support experienced by many older persons.

The theoretical model of stress and athletic injury (Andersen & Williams, 1988; Williams & Andersen, 1998) encompasses some of the personal-psychological and environmental-social factors in explaining the role of psychological and social factors in vulnerability to sport injury and thus is next described.

Model of Stress and Athletic Injury

Andersen and Williams (1988; Williams & Andersen, 1998) proposed that the central psychological mechanism influencing the occurrence of athletic injury is the stress response (see an outline of the basic components in Figure 2). In their model of stress and athletic injury, they identified three major contributors to pre-injury stress response: personality, history of stressors, and coping resources. *Personality* encompassed such factors as psychological hardiness, locus of control, and sense of coherence, whereas *history of stressors* included major life events, chronic daily hassles, and previous injuries. *Coping resources* included a wide variety of behaviors and social networks that help individuals manage life's challenges by relying on personal and social resources. They also identified psychological interventions such as cognitive restructuring, thought stoppage, relaxation skills, and imagery as methods to moderate perceptions and consequences of stress. These clusters of contributors were predicted to relate to the actual stress response—that is, changes in attentional/cognitive and physiological

FIGURE 2
Model of Stress and Athletic Injury.

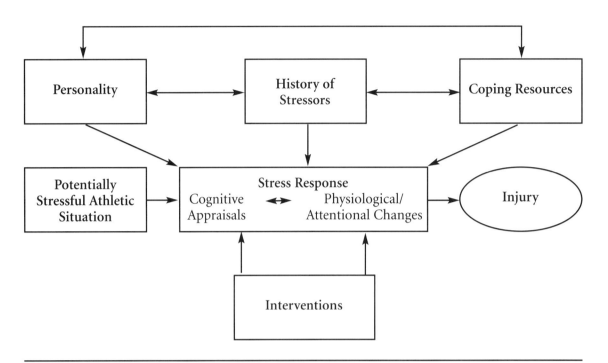

FIGURE 3
Types of Injury in Sport.

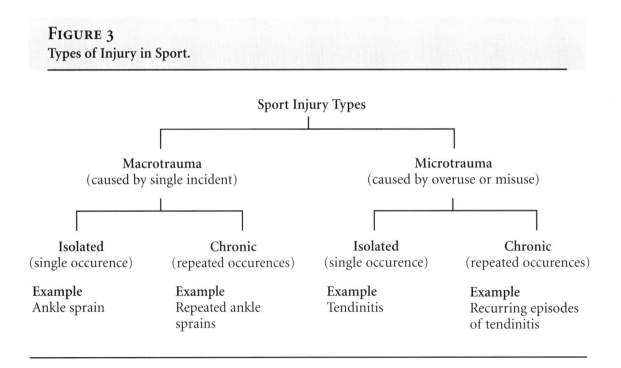

factors—exhibited by athletes, and in turn, the level of stress response was thought to affect injury vulnerability. Readers are referred to the original paper by Andersen and Williams (1988) and their update (Williams & Andersen, 1998) for more specific information on their pre-injury model of stress and athletic injury.

Injury Types
An understanding of the general typology of sport injuries provides the grounding for understanding both potential causal factors in their occurrence as well as variability in cognitive, emotional, and behavioral responses to injury. Figure 3 presents a schematic of an injury typology tree, intuitively derived from Flint (1998) and DiFiori (1999). Macrotrauma, or acute, injuries typically have a defined specific incident in which the injury was incurred. Subsequent to the initial injury, repeated incidences of the macrotrauma can lead to the injury's becoming a chronic or recurring phenomenon. Microtrauma, or overuse, injuries occur with repetitive, cumulative submaximal loading of a body tissue without adequate recovery (DiFiori, 1999). Overuse injuries can also occur with "misuse" (e.g., improper mechanics; Whiteside, Andrews, & Fleisig, 1999). With recurrence, these injuries often lead to chronic degradation, accompanied by weakness, chronic pain, and loss of flexibility (DiFiori, 1999).

What has not yet been examined to any great extent in the sport injury psychology literature are variations in causal factors affecting the occurrence of injury types nor how injury type relates to psychosocial response. Yet intuitively, one might speculate, for example, that chronic, overuse injuries might be causally associated with an ego orientation and a compulsive, perfectionist personality that sees winning and outcome as supremely important, someone who "must" compulsively continue to train even when the early symptoms of overuse injuries are beginning to manifest themselves (thus not allowing adequate recovery time to the tissue). Post-injury responses for this same chronic overuse-injured athlete might be predicted to be cognitively and behaviorally denying the injury by ignoring the advice of medical professionals in order to continue the intensity of training.

By the same token, one might speculate that an athlete sustaining an isolated acute injury might have been one whose life-event stress interfered with her or his ability to concentrate on the task at hand and read the environmental cues of an impending collision. Post-injury, we might predict that this isolated acute-injured athlete might be one who—failing to address the life-event stress and subsequent heightened stress response—might become discouraged and frustrated with interrupted sport goals and post-injury rehabilitation. Although these relationships are purely speculative at this point, they serve to illustrate the importance of examining injury causality and type in understanding the psychology of sport injury.

Post-Injury

Post-injury, researchers have found that psychological and social factors affect both the physical and mental recovery status of athletes. The post-injury response model of Wiese-Bjornstal and colleagues (see an outline of the basic components in Figure 4) is next used to provide a conceptual understanding of what is thought to transpire post-sport injury.

Dynamic Model of Psychological Response to Sport Injury and Rehabilitation
The dynamic model of psychological response to sport injury and rehabilitation (Wiese & Weiss, 1987; Wiese-Bjornstal et al., 1995; Wiese-Bjornstal et al., 1998) represents a comprehensive attempt to organize both clinical experience and research evidence in a way that explains some of the interrelationships among post-injury responses, relying on classic stress-response process models such as that of Lazarus and Folkman (1984).

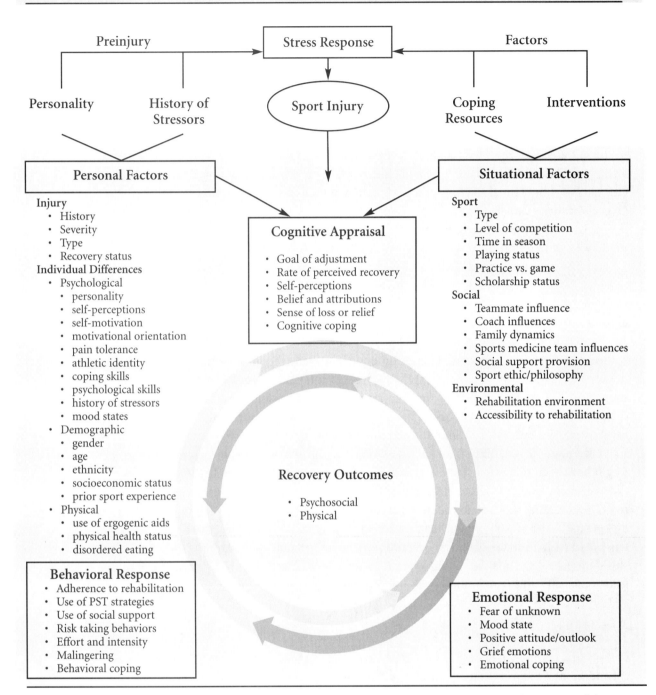

From "An Integrated Model of Response to Sport Injury: Psychological and Sociological Dynamics," by D. M. Wiese-Bjornstal, A. M. Smith, S. M. Shaffer, and M. A. Morrey, 1998, *Journal of Applied Sport Psychology, 10,* 46-69. Reprinted with permission.

Factors just described as affecting the pre-injury stress responses of athletes may be amplified post-injury. For example, when an athlete experiences the breakdown of an important personal relationship and then sustains an injury, the stress of dealing with the broken relationship is compounded by the stress of dealing with the injury. Thus, the first part of the dynamic model of psychological response to sport injury and rehabilitation reflects the moderating impact of these factors both pre- and post-injury.

Moderating Factors

An interactional approach, which specifies that resultant responses and behaviors are functions of both personal and situational factors, provides the broad conceptual framework for these moderating factors. This is consistent with the broader psychological literature on stress and coping. These moderators certainly do not operate in isolation, however, but interact to influence the dynamic responses of athletes to injury throughout the injury and rehabilitation process.

From a temporal standpoint, there are two major groups of moderators: those preexisting the injury and those that arise subsequent to injury and during the recovery process. The first category, pre-injury moderators, includes major factors identified by Andersen and Williams (1988) in their model of stress and athletic injury as well as additional factors not included in their model. These primarily include personal individual difference factors such as demographic (e.g., age), psychological (e.g., motivational orientation), and physical (e.g., overall health status) factors, but also tap into other categories such as injury (e.g., injury history), sport (e.g., sport type), and social (e.g., coaching quality) factors.

The second temporal category, post-injury moderators, includes those that arise subsequent to injury, many of which likely will change dynamically throughout the injury recovery process. Personal factors in this category might include more transient individual difference (e.g., self-perceptions), physical (e.g., disordered eating), and injury (e.g., actual recovery status) variables. Many situational factors encompassing the social situation and physical environment such as sport (e.g., time in season), social (e.g., sports medicine team interactions), and environmental (e.g., rehabilitation environment) factors also fluctuate throughout the recovery process.

For a discussion of research supporting the role of these moderators, see Wiese-Bjornstal et al. (1995). Understanding these moderators is important because of their influence on the thoughts, feelings, and behaviors of injured athletes, which are next described.

Responses to Sport Injury

Once injury occurs, it typically becomes an additional stressor to the athlete (Bianco, Malo, & Orlick, 1999; Heniff, 1998). At the heart of the model is the cyclic stress response process, with recovery at the core. Cognitive, emotional, and behavioral responses continuously interact to influence recovery throughout the rehabilitation process and operate in an environment of changing moderators that influence these responses. The responses described in this portion of the model are thought to be a direct result of the injury experience. Although the continuum of ultimate physical recovery may range from limited recovery such as with a permanent spinal cord injury to a complete return to pre-injury physical status, the potential exists for a complete psychological recovery. In fact, many athletes come back from injury physically and mentally stronger than they were before the injury.

Cognitive appraisal and response. The first component, cognitive appraisal and response, encompasses the thoughts of injured athletes, both immediately post-injury and dynamically throughout the rehabilitation and recovery cycle. Many things are "appraised" by athletes post-injury. For example, athletes think about the perceived cause of injury, their perceived recovery status, the availability of social support, and their perceived ability to cope with injury. Athletes can also appraise that they have "lost" something due to the injury (e.g., loss of starting position, loss of status afforded athletes, financial loss, scholarship loss). The key element of appraisal consists of an assessment of the demands of the injury situation and one's perceived resources to meet these demands (i.e., ability to cope; Lazarus & Folkman, 1984). These thoughts affect both subsequent emotions and behaviors.

Emotional response. Emotional responses of athletes to injury often stem directly from their thoughts. The post-injury affective responses of athletes change dynamically throughout the injury and recovery process. The most commonly used means of assessing athlete affect post-injury has been to evaluate their mood state. Some of the most commonly noted mood states post-injury include anxiety or tension, depression, and frustration (see reviews by A. M. Smith, 1996, and Wiese-Bjornstal et al., 1998). Other emotions commonly observed include boredom (particularly during long rehabilitative periods), anger, and fatigue (e.g., Bianco et al., 1999). Many athletes, however, also respond to injury with more positive emotions such as optimism, vigor, and relief (e.g., Udry, Gould, Bridges, & Tuffey, 1997). Some authors (e.g., Evans & Hardy, 1995) have written about grief as a response to sport injury; the emotions of grief in response to a cognitively perceived sense of loss are certainly a reality for many athletes.

Behavioral response. Behavioral responses include such overt actions as adherence or compliance to treatment regimens (Duda, Smart, & Tappe, 1989; Fisher, Domm, & Wuest, 1988), use of psychological skills (Ievleva & Orlick, 1991; Rotella & Heyman, 1993), use of social networks (Duda et al., 1989; Pearson & Jones, 1992), risk-taking behaviors (Rose & Jevne, 1993), and the effort and intensity with which the athlete pursues rehabilitation. The model predictions suggest that the cognitive appraisals and emotional responses of the athletes will influence their actual behaviors. Overall, the research indicates that athletes who adhere to rehabilitation, utilize psychological skills to manage pain and direct energies, effectively use available social support, reduce risk-taking behaviors that inhibit rehabilitation, and pursue rehabilitation goals with maximum effort and intensity are more likely to recover from injury and return to previous athletic levels than are those who do not engage in these actions.

Recovery

The exit point of this model can be thought of as helix or vortex either in an upward or positive direction from the dynamic core or in a downward or negative direction. Figure 5 depicts these positive and negative exit points. Given the varying temporal dimension of sport injury and the dynamic nature of the process, it is likely that during the rehabilitation and recovery process the vortex action resembles that of a Slinky® toy with athletes spiraling both upward and downward throughout the duration of the process based on setbacks, plateaus, and other psychological challenges as well as breakthroughs and improvements. The overall general progression, however, is likely in either a positive (recovery) or negative (failure to recover) progression. The target, or core, of the conceptual model is physical and psychological recovery, but these two often do not occur simultaneously, nor are they necessarily complete recoveries.

Childhood and Adolescence

Children's playing sport involves the risk of injury. More than three fourths of a million children under the age of 15 are treated each year in hospital emergency rooms for injuries sustained in sports, making sports injuries the number one reason for childhood emergency department visits (Centers for Disease Control and Prevention [CDC], 2001). Approximately 80% of these injuries occur in the sports of basketball, football, baseball, and soccer (CDC), and primarily involve strains and sprains, although about 5% involve broken bones. Pedal cycling, ice or roller skating and skateboarding, gymnastics, and cheerleading also frequently result in emergency room visits (CDC). Overall about one third of all injuries among children and youth are related to sports and recreation participation, with sports and recreation injury

FIGURE 5

Positive and negative recovery outcomes vortex as exit points in the model of psychological response to sport injury and rehabilitation.

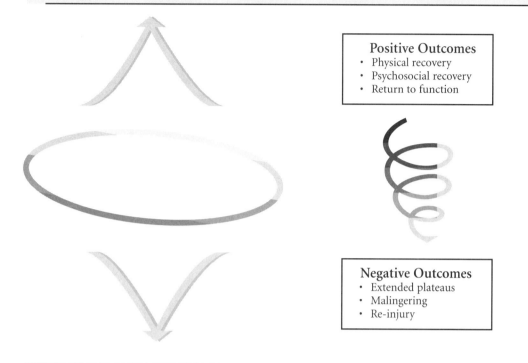

Positive Outcomes
- Physical recovery
- Psychosocial recovery
- Return to function

Negative Outcomes
- Extended plateaus
- Malingering
- Re-injury

rates increasing with age (Bijur et al., 1995). Boys are almost twice as likely to have a sports-related injury as girls are (Bijur et al.), although when comparable high school sport-injury patterns are examined—such as girls' softball and boys' baseball or boys' and girls' soccer—injury rates for girls are slightly higher than those for boys (Powell & Barber-Foss, 2000).

Pre-Injury Research and Application

Based on the conceptual outline of Williams and Andersen's (1998) model, the subsequent sections explore some of the factors affecting young sport participants during the childhood and early adolescent years and explain how these factors might affect sport injury vulnerability. Figure 6 depicts some hypothesized young athlete factors in the context of the model of stress and athletic injury.

Individual Differences

Personality

One component of personality that seems common among elite young performers is that of perfectionism. Perfectionism involves self-imposed high standards of performance that often stem from adult expectations, and it is a pattern that commonly begins by early adulthood. Perfectionism in young athletes has been found related to a variety of constructs in the sport context such as anxiety (Hall, Kerr, & Matthews, 1998), burnout (Gould, Udry, Tuffey, & Loehr, 1996), body image/social physique anxiety (Haase, Prapavessis, & Owens, 1999), and disordered eating (Lindeman, 1999). Perfectionism has also been found to have a relationship—albeit a complex one—with injury vulnerability in young elite dancers and gymnasts (Krasnow, Mainwaring, & Kerr, 1999). Young ballet dancers, modern dancers, and artistic gymnasts all demonstrated high incidence of injuries; however, different relationships between injury and

FIGURE 6

Young athlete version of the model of stress and athletic injury.

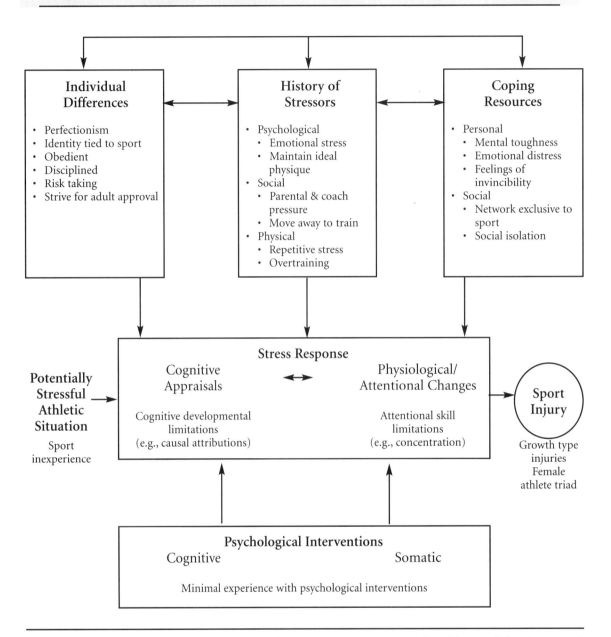

Adapted from "Psychosocial Antecedents of Sport Injury: Review and Critique of the Stress and Injury Model," by J. M. Williams and M. B. Andersen, 1998, *Journal of Applied Sport Psychology, 10,* 5-25.

stress and injury and perfectionism were found by group. A study of adolescent gymnasts, swimmers, and tennis players, however, failed to find a relationship between perfectionism scores and sport injury (Bringer, 1998). Recent research in sport has led to the conclusion that future studies involving perfectionism need to distinguish between positive and negative perfectionism, as the consequences of each may be different (Owens & Haase, 1999).

Emotions

Although emotional dispositions such as trait anxiety have been examined relative to injury vulnerability, inconsistent findings have resulted. The anxiety and fear associated with performing new and possibly even dangerous sport skills, however, seem intuitively to affect confidence and, in turn, actual attempts at performing these skills. Having sustained a previous injury can also be a source of fear for young athletes as they consider the risks and consequences of incurring future injury. Developmental studies of children and adolescents have revealed that normal fear (defined as a normal reaction to a real or imagined threat) decreases in frequency and strength with age and that specific fears are temporary in nature (Gullone, 2000). It has also been found that higher levels of fear and anxiety are associated with lesser quality of life among youth (Gullone & Cummins, 1999). Among adolescents, the most common fears are related to death and danger (Lane & Gullone, 1999), which has implications for the sport injury situation.

Participation Motives

As mentioned in the introduction, the reasons young athletes play sport are somewhat different from the reasons that older athletes play sport. With younger athletes, many are playing for fun and exercise, but increasingly so adolescent athletes are also motivated by pursuit of elite status and opportunities for financial reward (e.g., college scholarships, professional contracts, endorsements). It is apparent how the reasons athletes' play sports can affect their perceptions of stress. The latter depiction of elite young athletes' motives might render them particularly vulnerable to heightened stress responses (such as burnout-related attention-concentration difficulties) that, in turn, increase their risks of injury.

Perceptions of competence and perceived ability are major contributors to participation motivation (Koester, 2000), and such perceptions represent individual differences that might also be related to injury vulnerability. For example, athletes high in perceived competence and ability would appraise their skill level and their ability to meet sport challenges also as high, which, in turn, might render them less susceptible to perceptions of stress (defined as perceiving that one does not have the ability to meet the demands in an important arena) because they perceive their ability as equal to the challenge. Also, because younger children tend to rely more on adult feedback for ascertaining their level of ability than do older athletes—who rely more on internal assessments and more standardized measures of actual performance—one can see how younger children might be more strongly affected by negative coaching styles that belittle their abilities and competencies, thus either pushing themselves too hard to "please the coach" or dropping out of sport altogether.

Risk Taking

There are a number of behavioral, cognitive, and social factors that have been implicated in the age and gender differences that exist in injury risk among young children. Some of these differences are highlighted in Table 1. This literature suggests that boys and girls differ with respect to their beliefs about and their actions related to risk of physical injury, which, in turn, culminates in the greater actual occurrence of injury among young boys. Boys are more likely to minimize the possibility of injury, be physically active, take risks, and suffer injury than are girls.

The explanation for these differences likely arises from a combination of biologically, socially, and cognitively based contributors. Biologically based sex differences in such factors as hormonal levels likely influence differences in the physical risk-taking behaviors of boys and girls. Socially based factors such as parents' viewing risk taking as more desirable for boys than girls and treating children differently throughout the early childhood years also influence the gender differences in physical injury among children. Cognitively based factors such as children's ratings of risk in various play situations, beliefs about injury vulnerability in comparison to their peers, and attributions for injury causality also contribute to gender differences in injury risk behavior (e.g., Morrongiello & Rennie, 1998).

TABLE 1

Gender Differences in Behavioral, Cognitive, and Social Factors That Affect Physical Injury Risk in Children

Factor	Girls	Boys
Physical activity levels	Lower	Higher
Injury rate	Lower	Higher
Risk-taking behavior	Lower	Higher
Attributions for cause of injury	Own behavior	Bad luck
Perceived vulnerability to injury	More vulnerable	Less vulnerable
Rating of potential injury severity	Rate as higher	Rate as lower
Parents' reactions to risk taking	More cautious	Less cautious

Note: From "Child's Play" ("Counseling Your Athletes" column) by D. M. Wiese-Bjornstal, 2001, *Athletic Therapy Today, 6*(4), 38-39. Table contents derived from "Mother's Responses to Sons and Daughters Engaging in Injury-risk Behaviors on a Playground: Implications for Sex Differences in Injury Rates," by B. A. Morrongiello and T. Dawber, 2000, *Journal of Experimental Child Psychology, 76*, 89-103.

Additional work by Morrongiello and colleagues has consistently documented age as well as gender differences in children's perspectives on injury risk. For example, Hillier and Morrongiello (1998) found that 6-year-old children appraising injury risk in play activities identified fewer risk factors and were slower to identify the risk factors than were 10-year-old children. Already by the age of six, children have differential beliefs about injury vulnerability for boys and girls and perceive girls to be at greater risk of injury than boys are even though the opposite is true (Morrongiello, Midgett, & Stanton, 2000). A study of adolescents confirmed that both risk taking and injury are higher in boys that in girls (Jelalian et al., 1997) and boys are also more likely than girls to repeat injurious risk-taking behaviors (Morrongiello, 1997), thus experiencing recurring injuries. The majority of adolescents derive many positive benefits from sport participation, however, and in fact adolescents who participate in sports have been found to have lower overall risk scores (a score reflecting their risk of negative consequences from a wide variety of life risks) but greater chance of one specific type of risk: risk of physical injury (Steiner, McQuivey, Pavelski, Pitts, & Kraemer, 2000). For some adolescents, excessive risk taking in sport can be detrimental to normal health and development in that the risk taking becomes an obsession with participating in very high-risk or "extreme" sporting activities (Patel & Luckstead, 2000).

> Boys are more likely to minimize the possibility of injury, be physically active, take risks, and suffer injury than are girls.

Because injury prevention is one of the most important roles of sport professionals and because large numbers of children participate in sport activities, knowing about these differences in behaviors and perceptions can help in the design of risk-education and injury-prevention programs, both for parents and children. For example, positive changes in knowledge, attitudes, and behaviors relative to injury vulnerability were found among children who participated in an elementary school program aimed at preventing spinal cord and brain injuries (Morrongiello, Miron, & Reutz, 1998). Reid and Losek (1999) examined intervention strategies with youth ice-hockey players, specifically their compliance with protective equipment guidelines and their attitudes toward risk taking. The role of moral development entered into their results in that they found that approximately a third of the children injured in ice hockey stated that they would check illegally in order to win, and 6% of young athletes said that they would purposely injure another player. They suggested that injured youth-hockey players are not as well informed as they should be about the hazards of their sport and that their attitudes represent a dangerous willingness to engage in potentially injurious activities in the name of winning. Roberts, Brust, Leonard, and Hebert (1996) found in a study of adolescent male ice-hockey players in tournament play that fair play rules (i.e., earning points for playing without excessive penalties) reduced injury rates and rules infractions compared with traditional rules. Considering that tournament play in ice hockey typically results in injury rates significantly higher than regular season play (Roberts, Brust, & Leonard, 1999), this is an important finding with implications for injury prevention efforts.

Behavior Problems

There is some indication in the medical literature that children who have behavior problems may overtly behave in ways that render them vulnerable or predisposed to injuries (Bradbury, Janicke, Riley, & Finney, 1999; Jaquess & Finney, 1994). Cataldo et al. (1992) found that children injured in unstructured play situations among other things were more disruptive and more active, whereas the uninjured children were described as exhibiting more "appropriate" behavior. An emotion related to behavior problems, outward directed anger, was found by Thompson and Morris (1994) to be predictive of injury among male high school football players. Childhood aggression has also been found to be a predictor of adolescent injury and "close calls" (i.e., near accidents) including sport injury (Cobb, Cairns, Miles, & Cairns, 1995; Levy, 1995).

Female Athlete Triad

The *female athlete triad* is a term used to describe an interrelated set of health risks among females: eating disorders, amenorrhea, and osteoporosis (A. D. Smith, 1996). There are several psychological and social components within these physical health risks that are related to injury and other health risks. As depicted in Figure 7, for example, a certain set of personality and emotional characteristics (Kostanski & Gullone, 1998) and family dynamics can create a situation in which inaccurate or poor body images are common. In turn, excessive exercise can become one way in which girls choose to control their weight and thus manage their physical image (Lindeman, 1999). Another often interrelated way of doing this is by engaging in disordered eating habits and patterns, which begin among young girls as early as age seven (Kostanski & Gullone, 1999). In turn, these poor nutritional habits and excessive wear and tear on the body can lead to reductions in bone density, sequentially increasing vulnerability to certain types of injuries such as stress fractures (DiFiori, 1999). These triad-affected athletes are also more vulnerable to a wide variety of other negative physical and mental health conditions such as anemia, hypothermia, and depression. Given that the root problem of poor body image is often not changed, however, many female athletes continue to exercise excessively even when injured because of their fear of gaining weight. Sport injury itself has also been found to be a trigger factor associated with the onset of eating disorders (Sundgot-Borgen, 1994).

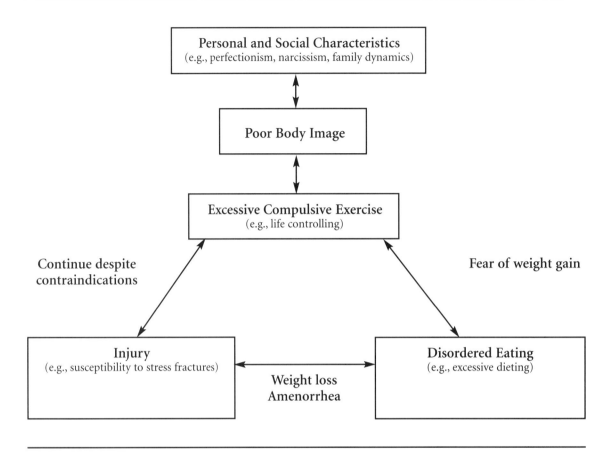

History of Stressors

Life Stress

Children in today's North American society more than ever before live in a climate where intact, supportive family structures are often the exception rather than the rule. Many of the major life-event stressors such as separation or divorce of parents, moving to a new town, changing schools, and illness or death of loved ones are experienced—and often repeatedly—by young athletes. It would be remiss to think that these major life-event stressors did not lead to increased stress responses among young athletes, in turn leading to injury vulnerability. Indeed, R. E. Smith, Smoll, and Ptacek (1990) found that life event stress in high school athletes was related to injury vulnerability and was moderated by coping resources. R. E. Smith, Ptacek, and Smoll's (1992) study of high school athletes found a significant relationship between negative major life-event stress and injury time loss, but only among athletes low in the personality characteristic of sensation seeking. A study of adolescent football players, for example, found that higher levels of stressful life events elevated sport injury risk by reducing attentional vigilance (Thompson & Morris, 1994), a finding in line with the theoretical predictions of Andersen and Williams (1988).

Minor life-event stressors are also commonplace and may accumulate to negatively affect injury vulnerability. Young people perceive that on a day-to-day basis, they have many hassles such as disagreements with parents and teachers, homework expectations, lack of transportation, and limited finances. Although research to date on minor life-event stress is limited, evidence from the general medical literature would suggest that the cumulative effects would be detrimental to health in the same way as is major life-event stress.

Socialization and Role Modeling

Athletes train and perform within a social system that emphasizes physical and mental sacrifice, toughness, endurance, and fortitude. The negative effect of these expectations is that many athletes are unwilling to stop participating regardless of the pain or injury experienced. The socialization experiences of many competitors' careers illustrate aspects of the "sport ethic" (Hughes & Coakley, 1991). As athletes are socialized into sport, this normative ethic provides the framework within which athletes learn to define sacrifice, risk, pain, and injury as the prices that must be paid to be competitive athletes. Figure 8 depicts the conflict athletes often feel when confronted with making a decision about whether or not to play with pain and injury. One only need look at chronicles of life in elite-level sport such as the National Football League (Huizenga, 1994), gymnastics and figure skating (Ryan, 1995) to realize the extraordinary risks being taken with young athlete's health, and even lives, in the name of sport.

Curry's (1993) case study of a wrestler's competitive career illustrates the process through which athletes are socialized to cope with pain and injury. As a young athlete, his early observations of other wrestlers taught him to adopt pain and injury as the sport norm. Progressing to higher levels of competition demonstrated that endurance of injury was mandatory. To be successful as a wrestler, one had to adopt the following beliefs, attitudes, and actions:

> "(1) to 'shake off' minor injuries; (2) to see special treatment for minor injuries as a form of coddling; (3) to express desire and motivation by playing

FIGURE 8
To play or not to play, that is the question.

From Wiese-Bjornstal, D.M. (2000, March). Playing with injury. In D.M. Wiese-Bjornstal (Ed.), "Counseling Your Athletes" column, *Athletic Therapy Today,* 5(2), 60-61.

while injured or in pain; (4) to avoid using injury or pain as excuses for not practicing or competing; (5) to use physicians and trainers as experts whose roles were to keep him competing when not healthy; (6) to see pain-killing anti-inflammatory drugs as necessary performance-enhancing aids; (7) to commit himself to the idea that all athletes must pay a price as they strive for excellence, and; (8) to define any athlete (including himself) unwilling to pay the price or to strive for excellence as morally deficient" (as summarized by Coakley, 1996, p. 358).

> **Some sports medicine professionals treating competitors may unknowingly promote playing with pain.**

The socialization cycle was completed when this athlete in turn became a role model for a new generation of wrestlers (Curry, 1993).

Some sports medicine professionals treating competitors may unknowingly promote playing with pain (Wiese-Bjornstal & Shaffer, 1999). For example, as attending physicians at a wrestling tournament, Strauss and Lanese (1982) noted that 9- to 14-year-old wrestlers "over-reported" their injuries because they sought medical attention for muscle strains and contusions – injuries that would have been ignored by older wrestlers. "The children seemed to have less tolerance for discomfort" and reported their pain "more readily" than did the older competitors (Strauss & Lanese, p. 2018). This view of young athletes as "over-reporting" their injuries—therefore implicitly not being tough enough to compete with injury—and for failing to model the behavior of the older, more experienced wrestlers is one of the very reasons that many young athletes are at risk for incurring permanent physical damage. The lesson they gradually learn over their years of participation in sport is that to report injuries and seek out treatment is a sign of weakness and lack of courage. Because their natural desire is to emulate the more physically and psychologically mature high school and college athletes, this learned failure to report renders them vulnerable to ignoring injuries, particularly those with a gradual onset that could be effectively dealt with if caught early.

Social Vulnerability

Coaching, parent, and officiating-related factors also affect the social vulnerability of young athletes to injury. For example, the expertise and teaching ability of the coach play an important role in proper technique instruction and injury prevention. Failing to teach young athletes about proper conditioning methods and skill performance and succumbing to traditional but erroneous sport training beliefs such as "more is always better" can create a vulnerable climate for young athletes (Koester, 2000). Koester also suggested that inexpert communication between athlete and coach can both affect the ability of the young athletes to glean the relevant information from instruction and lead to low perceptions of ability, which, in turn, leaves them lacking in understanding about performance risks and safe techniques as well as vulnerable to performance-related anxiety.

Two published reports of the experiences of young gymnasts illustrate another aspect of the social vulnerability of young athletes to their coaches: motivational climate. Ryan (1995) elucidated the role that elite gymnastics coach Bela Karolyi played in creating a climate in which vulnerability to serious injury was apparent. By calling athletes "bloody imbeciles" and "fat cows," by creating a climate in which fevers, chicken pox, sprains, and broken bones were unacceptable excuses for missing practice, by creating a "code of silence" among athletes when injured, and by convincing parents not to question his coaching methods, he established a very dangerous and even deadly sport environment. One of his young protégés in the 1980s, Julissa Gomez, was among those destroyed by this offensive climate. Her untimely death was the result of a chain of events that began prior to her injury when she was training within this injury-normative climate. No one protected her from the unhealthy demands placed upon her; her own mother—who had relinquished control over her daughter to Coach Karolyi—reported that "as a parent. . . you only see what you want to see" (Ryan, 1995, p. 43). Overly controlling parents who place an unhealthy emphasis on winning and who live vicariously through their children endanger the physical and mental health of their own children (DiFiori, 1999).

Krane, Greenleaf and Snow (1997) referred to this type of gymnastics climate as an ego-involved motivational climate in which mental and physical health are sacrificed in the quest of winning. In an insightful paper, Krane et al. reported the following example of this climate in their own interview of a young female gymnast relative to the "cause" of her injury according to her coach:

> "[Coach 1] would get mad if I got an injury. He would be so pissed off. He'd be like, 'oh no, not again,' and then he'd want me in the gym working out and everything. . . [He] thought that [an injury] was a lack of concentration. So, he was mad at me because if I was concentrating better, I wouldn't have [gotten injured]." (p. 59)

Sport officials also relate to young-athlete injury vulnerability. This might include the decisions of officials of a governing body such as a youth sport board, state high school league, or national governing body as well as the decisions of officials such as referees and judges. Both of these groups of officials make very important decisions about the rules and conduct of sport that affect the health and safety of athletes. For example, relative to the first type of officials, prior to governing-body rule changes about numbers and types of pitches that could be thrown, young baseball pitchers were vulnerable to serious, permanent growth-related arm injury (Whiteside et al., 1999); fortunately, such rules now exist in such youth organizations as Little League Baseball. Relative to the second type of officials, it has been found, for example, that with the addition of protective devices in youth ice hockey, there has been an alteration in officials' being more lenient in administering penalties, resulting in an increase of different types of injuries (Murray & Livingston, 1995).

Training Intensity

With the increasing expectation of year-round, specialized training for even young athletes has come an increase in overuse types of injuries, injuries uncommonly seen in free-play situations. Overuse injuries in pediatric athletes have been estimated to be as high as 50% of total sport injuries (DiFiori, 1999) sustained by a substantial proportion of athletes (e.g., an injury incidence of over 40% among young baseball pitchers, as reported by Whiteside et al., 1999). The etiology of these injuries includes not only physical factors—such as improper mechanics—but also psychosocial factors such as pressure from coaches to train excessively and to allow inadequate rest and recovery. Hollander, Meyers, and LeUnes (1995) describe the final stage in the overtraining of young athletes as injury/withdrawal from sport.

A. M. Smith, Stuart, Wiese-Bjornstal, and Gunnon (1997), for example, found that self-reported fatigue and low vigor were the predominant psychological predictors of injury among male high school ice-hockey players. It was not possible to determine from this investigation whether this fatigue consisted of physical or mental fatigue, or both. Both forms of fatigue are problematic in terms of injury risk, however, in that mental fatigue can lead to reductions in the ability to tolerate or manage stress perceptions (a factor in acute sport injury vulnerability), and physical fatigue plays a role in the etiology of overuse injuries. Young gymnasts have also been found to exhibit this relationship between fatigue and injury (Kolt & Kirkby, 1994).

Coping Resources

Coping Skills and Mechanisms

In general, evidence from young-athlete sport populations indicates that social support as a coping resource can directly affect injury outcome and/or moderate the relationship between life stress and sport injury (Williams & Andersen, 1998). For example, one study of high school athletes found that those reporting high life-event stress and both low social coping mechanisms (e.g., social support) and personal coping skills (e.g., ability to concentrate, keep a positive attitude, and control arousal levels) were at greatest risk for sport injuries (R. E. Smith et al., 1990). R. E. Smith et al. (1992) found the personality characteristic of sensation seeking to be a stress resiliency factor. Cogan and Brown (1999), however, found that athletes participating in risk sports scored higher on paratelic dominance (somewhat akin to sensation seeking) but also sustained more frequent and more serious injuries.

Medical and social science research has in general found that social support contributes to health and well-being both by reducing exposure to stressors (i.e., a preventive or direct effect) and enhancing coping efforts (i.e., a palliative or buffering effect). Social support as a construct comprises structural (e.g., support networks), functional (e.g., development and nurturing of interactive support exchanges), and perceptual (e.g., appraisal of quantity and quality of support) characteristics. Structurally, social support networks—especially those not linked to the sport network—may be lacking among young elite athletes whose lives revolve around sport, and thus they may perceive themselves to be socially isolated. They may be training away from home, family, friends, and teachers and may lack opportunities for social development in contexts outside of sport.

Family Dynamics

Among younger athletes, family plays a particularly important role in helping children cope with health conditions, perhaps including sport injury. Although there is little direct evidence of this role in sport, the evidence exists in the general medical literature. For example, in reviewing research studies on family dynamics related to the psychological adjustment of children with chronic health conditions, Drotar (1997) found more adaptive family relationships as well as parental psychological adjustment to be associated with more positive psychological adjustment among children.

Post-Injury Research and Application

Figure 9 depicts a young athlete view of the Wiese-Bjornstal et al. (1998) model of response to sport injury and rehabilitation. The factors identified represent but a few of the many possible psychosocial developmental factors playing a role in cognitive, emotional, and behavioral sport injury responses.

Cognitions

Compliance With Medical Advice

Adolescents' sense of immortality (Thornton, 1990), coupled with pertinent developmental issues, significantly relates to their frequent unwillingness to comply with medical advice (Cromer & Tarnowski, 1989). For example, level of cognitive ability represents one of the most important developmental differences between adolescents and adults (Ginsberg & Opper, 1979). The age at which formal thinking abilities develop differs from child to child; thus, a normal adolescent may lack the ability to foresee the potentially negative implications of his or her behavior (Friedman & Litt, 1986). Young athletes functioning at a lower reasoning level, therefore, would have greater difficulties complying with preventive health or medical treatment recommendations than would their teammates who have well-developed abstraction abilities (Cromer & Tarnowski, 1989).

An example of this sense of invincibility is illustrated in the following quote from a young female basketball player:

The first time my injury occurred, I ignored it as I assumed it would go away, as did my previous aches and pains. Bruising, swelling, and muscle pain are integral aspects of basketball. Once the pain persisted, it became annoying. It never occurred to me at the age of 14 that my body was breaking down and needed a rest. I simply pushed harder because my injury was causing me to fall behind in my progress. (Young & White, 1995, p. 51)

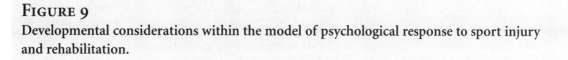

FIGURE 9
Developmental considerations within the model of psychological response to sport injury and rehabilitation.

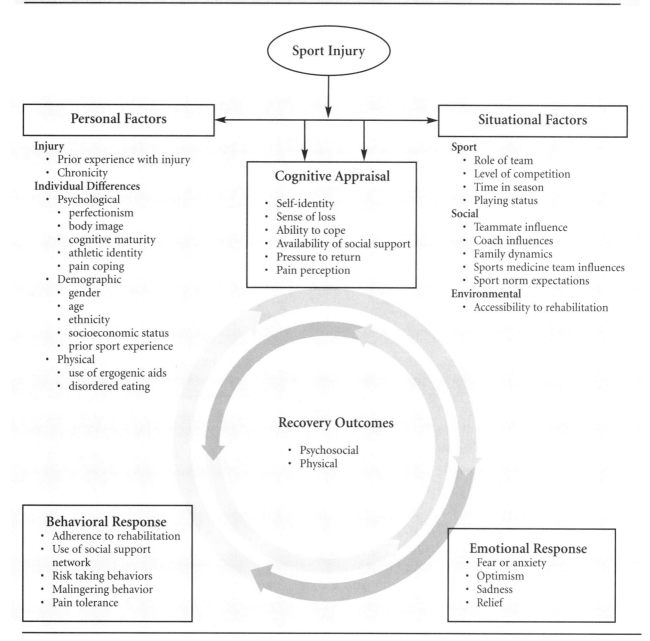

Adapted from "An Integrated Model of Response to Sport Injury: Psychological and Sociological Dynamics," by D. M. Wiese-Bjornstal, A. M. Smith, S. M., Shaffer, and M. A. Morrey, 1998, *Journal of Applied Sport Psychology, 10*, 46-69.

Cognitive Preparation for Receiving Medical Treatment

Preparing younger children for receiving medical treatment relative to sport injury requires knowledge of developmental factors affecting cognitive understanding. Children's conceptions of illness, for example, are not necessarily simpler versions of adult conceptions (Kalish, 1996), and they may develop in a manner consistent with a Piagetian framework (Hansdottir & Malcarne, 1998).

Brannon and Feist (2000) outlined several areas that affect children's ability to cope with their fears of health treatment. First, the understanding of illness or injury and the associated treatments and tests possessed by young children is not typically as comprehensive as that of adults. Second, children's early, unpleasant experiences with medical treatment may be cognitively and emotionally generalized to future interactions with the medical system (Dahlquist et al., 1986). Third, parents can either help or hinder their child's preparation for stressful medical procedures depending on what techniques they employ. For example, using such techniques as giving children some control over the medical procedures they must endure and employing attentional distraction in helping children cope with distressing medical procedures have been found to be helpful in some cases (Brannon & Feist). On the other hand, continual parental reassurance, for example, may tend to increase the child's feeling of distress. Preparing parents for the psychological demands accompanying their support roles for their children during stressful medical procedures can result in less anxiety and better coping among the children (Brannon & Feist).

Psychosocial predictors such as anxiety and distress have been found to influence the pain perceptions of children (Palermo & Drotar, 1996). For example, greater anticipatory surgical distress was associated with higher postoperative pain among children ages 7 to 17 years (Palermo, Drotar, & Lambert, 1999). Research attempts to use psychological interventions such as mental preparation and parental involvement procedures to minimize the distress of children faced with medical procedures, however, have met with minimal success (Palermo, Drotar, & Tripi, 2000).

Emotions

Mood State

A recent study examined whether age and greater involvement in sport were related to mood state (Johnston & Carroll, 2000b). The results showed that younger (late adolescent), more time-involved athletes displayed greater confusion during the middle and end of rehabilitation as well as perceiving that their recovery was less at the end of rehabilitation than did older, less time-involved athletes. Johnston and Carroll (2000b) concluded that these more time-involved athletes may not have had their needs for information about injury and rehabilitation met, thus resulting in confusion about their return to full recovery status. Overall, however, the results demonstrated increases in self-rated energy and recovery and decreases in anxiety, depression, confusion, anger, and fatigue across the time course of recovery as has been found in previous research.

Elite athletes with chronic injury have been found to have levels of intrusive and avoidance thoughts that mimic those of persons traumatized by natural disaster.

Schwenz (2001), in a qualitative study of adolescent female athletes recovering from anterior cruciate reconstruction, found high levels of agitation and low levels of positive thoughts after surgery, but found a gradual reduction in negative thinking and agitation and an improvement in positive thoughts over the time course of recovery. Particularly salient in influencing emotions among these adolescent females was the role of social support.

Posttraumatic Stress

Nearly one fourth of children hospitalized for physical trauma have been found to be experiencing posttraumatic stress disorder (Aaron, Zaglul, & Emery, 1999), experiencing symptoms such as thought suppression, fear responses, and internalizing behaviors. Although no studies were located on children with sport injuries and posttraumatic stress disorder, elite athletes with chronic injury have been found to have levels of intrusive thoughts and avoidance thoughts that mimic those of persons traumatized by natural disaster (Shuer & Dietrich, 1997).

Attributions and Emotions

Gable and Peterson (1998) interviewed 8- and 9-year-old children about their attributions for injury causality and their emotional responses to naturally occurring minor injuries. Children most frequently reported that "fate" was the primary cause of their injury; however, their attributions varied by pre-injury behavior and post-injury feelings.

Behaviors

Attrition Motives and Behaviors

Many young athletes are "motivated" to leave sport because of injury. Weiss, Amorose, and Allen (2000) described a series of elite young gymnast studies that identified participation motivation issues related to sport injury. Among this series of studies was that of Klint and Weiss (1986) in which they found that among young male and female competitive gymnasts, "being injured" was the most important reason for dropping out of gymnastics. DuRant, Pendergast, Donner, Seymore, and Gaillard (1991) found that over one fourth of high school athletes dropped off a team in a given year. The most frequent reason for attrition was injury, with attrition being higher among students reporting sport injuries, those injured playing football, and those sustaining knee injuries.

EARLY ADULTHOOD

Sports injuries are also common among athletes in their early adulthood years. The overall incidence and risk factors for sport and physical activity related injury, however, have been poorly assessed. An average of 2.6 million sport-related emergency room visits per year are made by those 5 to 24 years of age, with over 3.7 million emergency room visits due to sport injuries by persons of all ages (Burt & Overpeck, 2001). According to Gilchrist, Jones, Sleet and Kimsey (2000), injury risks increase in a dose-response manner as a result of the same exercise parameters that enhance physical fitness (i.e., frequency, intensity, and duration). Severity and chronicity of injury tend to increase with increasing age and the concomitant increase in level of participation and intensity of training, and injuries range in severity from mild to career ending and even life ending.

Pre-Injury Research and Application

The Williams and Andersen (1998) model of stress and athletic injury is again used to organize developmental factors affecting the injury vulnerability of athletes in early adulthood and often the elite phases of their competitive careers (refer back to Figure 2).

Individual Differences

Personality

Several dimensions of personality have been explored relative to injury risk among early adulthood athletes. For example, Ford, Eklund, and Gordon (2000) found high-level athletes with more optimism, hardiness or global self-esteem to be less vulnerable to sport injury; the researchers speculated that it was because these athletes dealt more effectively with life event stress. Type A behavior patterns and exercise dependency have been associated with injuries in running (Ekenman, Hassmen, Koivula, Rolf, & Fellander-Tsai, 2001).

Individual differences in cognitive strategies such as attentional style have also been examined relative to sport injury vulnerability. Masters and Ogles (1998) reported in a compilation of research on cognitive strategies in running and exercise that the attentional strategy of association is related to faster performance as well as greater risk of injury

Anxiety and Competitive Worry

Competitive trait anxiety has been found as a possible factor affecting injury vulnerability (Hanson, McCullagh, & Tonymon, 1992; Lavallee & Flint, 1996), although results have been mixed. Garcia and Aragues (1998) found that the presence of an "optimum" trait-anxiety score (i.e., not too high or low) was related to the lowest injury risk among male soccer players. In exploring the content of competitive worries in ice hockey, Dunn (1999) has outlined four content domains, one of which is injury or physical danger. One might speculate that such "worry" or anxiety would lead to increased perceptions of stress and heightened stress response, in the absence of coping strategies to modulate the worry.

History of Stressors

Life Stress

Findings of a relationship between stressful life events and sport injury vulnerability have been relatively consistent among athletes in early adulthood. Williams and Andersen (1998) reported that, in general, higher levels of perceived negative life-event stress prior to the season are predictive of increased sport injury vulnerability during that season, particularly in cases where concomitantly athlete coping skills are low. It has also been found in several studies (e.g., Luo, 1994) that positive life-event stress is related to increased vulnerability to injury. Recent work has attempted to look at the role of in-season major life-event stress as well. For example, a study of National Collegiate Athletic Association Division I female athletes revealed that athletes uninjured during the competitive season reported lower total life-event stress during the season that did those sustaining injury (Heniff, 1998).

Recent investigations have also attempted to look at whether levels of minor life-event stress (also known as daily hassles or everyday problems) are related to injury vulnerability. Two studies have found indication that minor life-event stress is also related to injury vulnerability (Heniff, 1998; Luo, 1994) although more work remains to be done examining these findings.

Overtraining

Overtraining is the label given to the physical and mental condition that results when an athlete is training excessively, and yet performance deteriorates. The cytokine hypothesis has recently been offered as an explanatory paradigm for overtraining syndrome (OTS; L. L. Smith, 2000). This hypothesis suggests that overtraining syndrome is representative of the third stage of Selye's (1950) general adaptation syndrome, the stage that focuses on a protective response to excessive physical and/or psychological stress. As typically defined, part of the overtraining syndrome consists of a set of mood and behavior changes (e.g., "sickness behaviors" such as increased depression, apathy, and attentional disruption) and physical changes (e.g., elevated cortisol levels, headaches, compromised immune system) that occur concomitant with a decrease in physical performance. L. L. Smith suggested that excessive exercise and lack of recovery time, in fact, lead to repetitive microtrauma injury, which, in turn, is the causal factor in the psychological and physical changes. In making her case, L. L. Smith (2000) expressed the following beliefs about the cytokine hypothesis of overtraining:

> The cytokine hypothesis of overtraining will propose that repetitive trauma to the musculoskeletal system, due to high intensity/high volume training, associated with insufficient rest/recovery time, is the predominant cause of overtraining. It will be suggested that many of the physiological, behavioral, and psychological signs and symptoms associated with OTS could emerge from the presence of an injury. Additionally, the cytokine hypothesis will attempt to accommodate alternate stressors that may be causal or may contribute in an additive sense, such as psychological stress or acute viral infection. (p. 320)

Injury History

Athletes' record of prior injury has been found related to future injury vulnerability. Van Mechelen et al. (1996) found in a prospective multivariate approach that previous injury was an independent predictor of sport injury. Decisions made by coaches relative to the participation of injured athletes in competition have been found related to the coaches' own personal experiences with competing when injured (Vergeer & Hogg, 1999).

Sport Context

The circumstances surrounding the sport participation relate to risk of injury. In general, for example, incidence and severity of injury increase with intensity and level of play. The social and competitive context affecting play contributes to risk of injury, as mentioned earlier. Among collegiate intramural sport participants, for example, the factor rated the highest relative to the causality of their injury was "intensity and/or level of play," with rates of injury among intramural participants noticeably increasing during play-off competitions (Haines, 1997).

Coping Resources

Social Support

Because social support is a multidimensional construct (Udry, 1996), there are not only many possible providers of support but also many forms. These include such forms as emotional, informational, and tangible support. Emotional support, for exam-

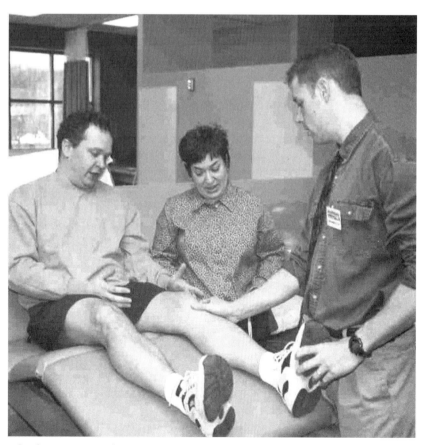

The last 10 years has seen an explosion of research related to psychological factors in the sport injury process.

ple, could best be provided by other members of the athlete's social network such as teammates, friends and family (e.g., Udry et al., 1997). Informational support falls well within the purview of sports medicine professionals; in fact, patient education is among their primary responsibilities. Providing information about the injury prevention as well as about the nature of the injury and rehabilitation program worded in a way that athletes can understand is a very basic, yet often overlooked form of support. Tangible support can also be provided by sports medicine personnel, in such forms as providing pre-injury preventative bracing or taping, icing, or assistance with stretching.

Consistent with the predictions of the Wiese-Bjornstal et al. (1998) post-injury model, research has found that availability and use of social support is associated with more positive mood states. Green and Weinberg (2001), for example, found among adult recreational sport participants recovering from injury that those more satisfied with their social network reported less total mood disturbance.

Stress Management

Davis (1991) explored the role of stress intervention on injury rates for university swimmers and football players. He reported a 52% reduction in injuries among swimmers and a 33% reduction in serious injuries among football players during the year in which the psychological intervention was conducted relative to the previous-year injury statistics. Kerr and Goss (1996) examined the effects of a stress management program on injuries and stress levels of male and female gymnasts. Athletes in the stress management program reported significantly less negative athletic stress than did the control group, but there were no differences in time injured.

Post-Injury Research and Application

The Wiese-Bjornstal et al. (1998) model for understanding post-injury responses is again used as the organizing framework for understanding the responses of early-adulthood-aged athletes (refer back to Figure 4).

Cognitions

Appraisal

The general cognitive appraisals of athletes post-injury have been examined. Quinn and Fallon (1999) examined appraisals at four phases during the injury rehabilitation through the return-to-sport process. Increased confidence was noted across the recovery period, and confidence of adhering to rehabilitation remained stable over time. Shelley (1998) found cognitive appraisal and emotional response changes over the course of recovery among four intercollegiate athletes. In the no-participation phase, cognitive appraisals involved perceptions of isolation and abandonment and concern as to how coaches perceived the injury whereas emotional responses included bitterness and jealousy as well as a sense of hope. During the limited-participation phase, athletes reported cognitive appraisals of increased confidence and perceptions of being unsupported and misunderstood; emotional response included caution and a continued fear of re-injury. In the return-to-play phase, cognitive appraisals included increased confidence and satisfaction, and emotional responses were typified both by a positive attitude and fear of re-injury and return.

Self-Perceptions

Perhaps most examined among the post-injury cognitions has been athlete self-perception. This category includes empirical studies on athletes' self-perceived worth, value, general abilities, and specific capabilities. Recall that the core of the integrated model—as is consistent with the psychology literature on the stress process—posits that cognitions such as self-perceptions are important because they in turn influence the emotional and behavioral responses of athletes to injury.

The use of global measures of self-perception has revealed somewhat mixed results. For example, when Chan and Grossman (1988) used a global measurement tool to quantify self-esteem changes in runners, self-esteem was significantly lower in injured runners than in noninjured runners. Conversely, a prospective study of 13 high school, Junior A hockey and National Collegiate Athletic Association (NCAA) Division I university teams in basketball, volleyball, baseball, and hockey did not demonstrate pre-injury to post-injury differences in global self-esteem scores (A. M. Smith et al., 1993).

Using a more domain-specific measure, Brewer (1993) employed a physical self-worth subscale with injured athletes at a sports medicine clinic and found that it predicted post-injury depression. In a prospective, controlled investigation of NCAA Division I male university athletes from 10 sports, Leddy, Lambert, and Ogles (1994) identified pre-injury to post-injury reductions in total and physical self-esteem among injury groups. Both self-confidence (a generalized belief in oneself) and self-efficacy (a belief in oneself as competent and effective in specific situations) were found to be improved following a peer-modeling intervention among female athletes who had anterior cruciate ligament (ACL) reconstruction (Flint, 1991). Other investigations involving the more situation-specific construct of self-efficacy also found it to vary as a function of sport injury. Shaffer (1991), for example, found history of previous injury related to improved efficacy for rehabilitating a current injury.

Goal Orientations and Motivation

The goal orientation of the athlete appears to also be an important factor in rehabilitation (Duda, 1993). For example, athletes who demonstrated greater treatment adherence were found to place more emphasis on mastery or task-involved goals in sport (Duda et al., 1989). Linking self-perception and goal focus, Lampton and Lambert (1993) noted that patients low in self-esteem and high in ego involvement tended to miss the most treatment appointments. Fisher et al. (1988) and Duda et al. (1989) both found greater self-motivation among athletes who demonstrated greater treatment adherence.

Athletic Identity

Brewer (1993) has identified the psychological construct of athletic identity—defined as the degree to which a person identifies with the athletic role to the exclusion of other important roles—and has hypothesized that the more strongly sport identified athletes are, the more vulnerable they are to negative post-injury consequences such as negative mood states. Some gender and developmental level changes have been noted in athletic identity. For example, college-aged male athletes have been found to report higher athletic identity than females report (Brewer, VanRaalte, & Linder, 1993). Research with high school athletes has found gender, race/ethnicity, and developmental differences in athletic identity (Wiechman & Williams, 1997). Males reported a stronger athletic identity than did females, whereas Mexican Americans reported greater athletic identity than did whites and African Americans. Although not significant, there was a trend toward a strengthening of athletic identity from freshman to junior varsity to varsity participants.

Athletes also see tolerating injury as part of their identity as athletes (Coakley, 1998). Coakley (1998) suggested that those athletes whose "identities or future chances for success and significance are completely tied to their sport" (p. 156) are most likely to overconform to the sport ethic described earlier. Relative to sport injury risk and response, such

Recent work with female athletes has shown that females are also accepting of the normative pain and injury expectations associated with sport.

overconformity or positive deviance (Coakley, 1998) can take several forms such as self-injurious overtraining and continuing to compete when injured.

Sport Ethic

Some gender differences have been found among endorsement of the sport ethic. Nixon (1996) found males more likely than females to express a tough attitude, agree that "winning is everything," and buy into the notion of "no pain, no gain," indicating that playing with pain demonstrates character. Males were also found to feel more pressed to play hurt, including feeling "pressured by coaches and fans to play hurt" and "feeling guilty if not willing to play hurt" (Nixon, 1996). Recent work with female athletes, however, has found that females are also accepting of the normative pain and injury expectations associated with sport (Young & White, 1995).

Data from a variety of sports such as cycling (Albert, 1999), soccer (Roderick, Waddington, & Parker, 2000), wrestling (Shaffer, 1996), and surfing (Stranger, 1999) support the existence of these normative expectations for accepting the risks and consequences of physical danger and injury, embracing the ascetic value of discipline and sacrifice (Shaffer, 1996), and celebrating the aesthetic quality of searching for thrills and risk taking in sport (Stranger). The recent death of auto-racing legend Dale Earnhardt illustrates the inherent life-threatening danger of sport that is not only tolerated but also celebrated by many. Earnhardt, among other athletes, went so far as to shun basic safety innovations implemented by NASCAR, suggesting that they were for "sissies" (Bechtel, M., 2001).

Cognitive Function

Impairments in attention, concentration and memory have been reported as negative consequences of injury to the head. These cognitive consequences range on a continuum from temporary to chronic to permanent. Mild traumatic brain injury occurs among high school athletes, with football (63.4%), wrestling (10.5%), girls' soccer (6.2%), and boys' soccer (5.7%) accounting for the highest percentages of cases (Powell & Barber-Foss, 1999). Among elite soccer players, for example, concussions occurred primarily as consequences of player-to-player contact or heading the ball, and they resulted in headaches, being "dazed", and dizziness (Barnes et al., 1998). Among boxers, permanent cognitive impairment has even been given a name: *dementia pugilistica*. A study of 42 professional boxers (average age of 25.6 years) involved completing a history of boxing exposure as well as neuropsychological testing (Jordan, Matser, Zimmerman, & Zazula, 1996). It was found that sparring—which involved repetitive blows to the head—was the aspect of boxing most related to reductions in cognitive performance (attention, concentration, memory). Chronic traumatic brain injury and the associated neuropsychological impairment have also been noted in current (Kirkendall, Jordan, & Garrett, 2001; Matser, Kessels, Lezak, Jordan, & Troost, 1999) and former (Baroff, 1998) soccer players.

Recently, many professional, collegiate, and even high school teams competing in sport in which traumatic brain injuries are common have established baseline neurological testing (e.g., memory, attention, mental processing speed, motor speed) as measures of cognitive status before the season ("Baseline," 1998). These baseline data are used to assess the cognitive effects of head injuries that occur during the season. Although other physical symptoms (such as headaches, fatigue, and difficulty sleeping) are also considered as indicators of concussion status, the advantage of neuropsychological testing (Echemendia, Putukian, Mackin, Julian, & Schoss, 2001) includes the ability to detect those athletes who might be hiding symptoms and to determine the long-term impact of multiple concussions. However, return to baseline assessments of cognitive function alone may be insufficient, especially with adolescents, who would be expected to undergo normal changes in cognitive function over time due to the developmental process (Daniel et al., 1999).

Emotions

Mood State

In the research literature, studies that have explored the mood responses of athletes to injury have shown mood states to fluctuate across the time course from injury through recovery and return to sport. Initial studies saw reductions in mood disturbance that paralleled athletes' perceptions of recovery. More recent investigations, however, have shown the pattern of mood changes to be more dynamic. Doctoral dissertation studies by LaMott (1994) and Morrey (1997)—examining 3-month and 6-month post-injury intervals respectively—documented elevated negative mood scores of surgically repaired anterior cruciate ligament (ACL)-injured athletes at the first interval, improvements in mood state during the second and third intervals, and increases in overall mood disturbance again during the fourth time-period evaluations. Data from the total mood-disturbance scores showed changes in mood responses across the recovery time course resembling a clipped U-shaped patterning in both studies. Data from a University of Minnesota master's thesis by Heniff (1998) demonstrated that those intercollegiate athletes sustaining an injury displayed more negatively disturbed moods before, during, and after injury than did their uninjured counterparts on the same team (Wiese-Bjornstal, 2001).

It is also apparent from the research literature that looking only at measures of total mood disturbance masks the subtleties of individual mood-state changes. Individual mood state data (LaMott, 1994; Morrey, Stuart, Smith, & Wiese-Bjornstal, 1999) illustrate that certain negative moods predominate at different points in the ACL rehabilitation cycle. For example, in the data of Morrey et al., one negative mood state—boredom—showed a linear decline across 6 months' time whereas another—frustrated—demonstrated a U-shaped patterning. A positive mood state—optimistic—showed an inverted U of positive emotion across the 6-month post-surgery period. Morrey et al. also found that competitive athletes given the okay to return to sport at 6 months reported significant negative mood disturbances, thus implying that they perhaps lacked confidence in the health of their injured body parts as well as in their ability to meet game demands.

Recent work by Udry, Gould, Bridges, and Beck (1997) has elaborated on the cognitive, emotional, and behavioral responses of elite skiers to season-ending injuries. Athlete cognitions regarding the nature and extent of the injury and the associated negative consequences were common. Emotionally, athletes in this investigation described such feelings as being emotionally agitated (e.g., angry, panicky, worried) and emotionally depleted (e.g., disappointed, depressed). Quinn and Fallon (1999) reported, in general, that there were decreased negative emotional responses and increased vigor over recovery, but found that changes over time were not at a constant rate.

Pain

Pain might be thought of as having interrelated physiological (e.g., pain sensation or threshold), perceptual (e.g., pain perception or intensity), cognitive (e.g., pain attitudes and coping), and behavioral (e.g., pain tolerance) components. The attitudes that athletes hold toward pain as well as the cognitive strategies they use to cope with pain may be reflected in their actual actions toward pain (e.g., performance with pain, adherence to sport injury rehabilitation).

Athletes have been found to have higher pain tolerance thresholds (Tajet-Foxell & Rose, 1995) and to report less pain (Sullivan, Tripp, Rodgers, & Stanish, 2000) than do their sedentary counterparts. Following exercise, both pain threshold and pain tolerance have been found to increase (Koltyn, 2000; Sternberg, Bailin, Grant, & Gracely, 1998), supporting the existence of a phenomenon of exercise-induced analgesia. Higher pain report has been related to slower speed of recovery in intercollegiate athletes (Berlin, 2001).

Cognitive strategies used by athletes such as association have also been found related to increased pain tolerance (Pen & Fisher, 1994). On the other hand, an "exaggerated negative appraisal of pain sensations" has been labeled "catastrophizing" (Sullivan et al., 2000, p. 152), the interrelated dimensions of which are the tendency toward excessive focus on pain sensations, amplification of the threat of pain sensations, and a perceived inability to control one's pain intensity (Sullivan et al., 2000). Catastrophizing has been found to be predictive of pain perception and emotional distress. It is possible that individuals who adopt a catastrophizing appraisal of pain might also differ in their preferred ways of coping with stressful situations .

Illness/Injury Emotions and Behaviors

The illness attitudes and beliefs of elite runners have been found to differ from those of nonathlete populations (Currie, Potts, Donovan, & Blackwood, 1999). Middle- and long-distance runners in this study were found to be more somatically focused, have higher levels of hypochondriacal concerns, and to be more likely to deny the impact of stresses in their life. These results were likened to those of Little (1969), who reported on anxiety neuroses exhibited by athletic individuals under his observation. As with the Currie et al. study, Little's athletes also displayed evidence of hypochondriasis and somatisation, forms of abnormal illness behavior in which "subjective symptomatology is present in a degree disproportionate to objective signs and pathology" (Currie et al., p. 19). These evidences of abnormal illness behavior are often associated with the presence of clinically significant levels of depression and anxiety. In protracted injury-recovery experiences, for example, where negative mood states have frequently been documented (e.g., LaMott, 1994; Morrey et al., 1999), one might expect that these mood states influence health beliefs and behaviors.

Behaviors

Behavioral responses such as use of coping mechanisms and adherence to rehabilitation stem from the thoughts and feelings of athletes about the injury.

Coping Behavior

In line with thinking of injury rehabilitation as a dynamic process, for example, the types of coping mechanisms employed may change over the course of rehabilitation (Henert, 2000; Johnston & Carroll, 2000a; Udry, 1997). Recent investigations with elite skiers have noted that athletes employ a wide variety of coping mechanisms (Gould, Udry, Bridges & Beck, 1997a). On the other hand, Quinn and Fallon (1999) found among elite injured athletes that passive and emotion-focused coping remained stable over time.

Also worthy of further attention is the possibility that the types of coping strategies employed might vary not only by time but also by type of injury. Both Henert (2000) and Wasley and Lox (1998) found differences in coping strategies based on microtrauma versus macrotrauma injuries. Differences in the use of coping strategies have also been found based on sport type (i.e., team sport versus individual sport) (Henert, 2000; Johnson, 1997) and on gender (Henert, 2000; Johnston, 1999; Johnston & Carroll, 2000b), although the nature of these differences was not consistent across studies.

Adherence Behavior

One specific type of behavior essential for successful rehabilitation is adherence behavior. Several factors have been suggested as influencing adherence behavior, including personal factors (e.g., anxiety, confidence), social factors (e.g., training-room climate, social support), and physical factors (e.g., pain, recovery progress) (Fisher, Mullins, & Frye, 1993; Fisher, Scriber,

Matheny, Alderman, & Bitting; 1993). Heil (1993) has suggested that poor adherers may be more somatically anxious, having psychological adjustment problems, less confident about treatment, lacking a sense of social support, less self-motivated, and less goal oriented. Factors predicting successful adherence, according to Heil, include athlete perception of need for particular intervention, expectation for a positive outcome, belief that benefits of rehabilitation outweigh the costs, and a sense of active involvement in treatment.

Malingering Behavior

Another behavioral response consideration involves malingering behavior. Malingering behavior is an adjustment to negative circumstances requiring an external incentive for being injured (Rotella, Ogilvie, & Perrin, 1993). In their opinion, malingering athletes are those who intentionally deceive sports medicine professionals and coaches about their injury—by consciously faking symptoms of discomfort or physical distress—in order to avoid practice or competition. Most athletes who have a repeated habit of malingering do so primarily as a result of fears and/or a need for attention (Rotella et al.). Sports medicine professionals certainly need to believe athletes' claims of injury, but must also recognize that there are many reasons for malingering behavior related to the moderating factors, cognitions, and emotions described earlier. These reasons include (Rotella et al.): rationalizing the loss of starting status, playing time reduction, or poor performance; personally realizing limited ability; attracting needed attention not elsewhere received; using injury as an escape from sport pressures; and avoiding rigors of practice to save oneself for game day.

> Malingering behavior is an adjustment to negative circumstances requiring an external incentive for being injured.

Social Support-Seeking Behavior

Injured athletes' seeking and receiving social support can have positive effects on athlete morale and behavior. For example, research has demonstrated that social support is positively related to rehabilitation adherence (Duda et al., 1989; Fisher et al., 1988). Henert (2000) found that NCAA Division I male and female athletes felt that all types of social support were important to their overall well-being when injured; this was particularly true for microtrauma-injured athletes. Other investigations of social support, however, have not always found all of the relationships between social support and injury to be positive (e.g., Luo, 1994; Quinn & Fallon, 2000). It is possible that certain types of support—such as task challenge or emotional challenge—might be perceived as pressure rather than as helpful as intended.

MIDDLE AND OLDER ADULTHOOD

Although athletes of increasing age are participating in competitive sport at a "physically elite" level (Spiriduso, 1995), virtually no research has been conducted examining the role of psychological and social factors in sport injury occurrence in middle and older adulthood. Yet master's-level athletes often report sport injuries in levels similar to their younger, more intensely participating counterparts. A study of shoulder injuries in swimmers, for example, found that although collegiate-level swimmers were involved with more workouts and higher yardage than were their master's-level counterparts, both groups reported similar levels of shoulder pain (Stocker, Pink, & Jobe, 1995). With proper treatment and care, however, older athletes can achieve medical outcomes comparable to those of their younger counterparts (c.f., Novak, Bach, & Hager, 1996).

Substantial numbers (over 60%) of older Americans are physically active in their leisure time even if they might not be competitive athletes (United States Public Health Service, 1992). Scott and Couzens (1996) reported their belief that injured master's-level athletes and active seniors should receive injury prevention and rehabilitation treatment comparable to that of their younger counterparts. Scott and Couzens suggested that senior-level athletes recover just as rapidly as younger patients when following similar protocols for rehabilitation and treatment, and the researchers dispelled the myth that older sports medicine patients will be significantly set back by a sport injury.

Given, then, that older athletes and exercisers also experience sport injuries, the following represent some possible areas for exploration drawn from the broader literature on psychology and physical health in older adults.

Pre-Injury Research and Application

Possible pre-injury factors affecting sport injury vulnerability in older adults are identified organized around the unifying model of Williams and Andersen (1998).

Individual Differences

Psychological Differences in Motivational Approach to Sport

Older adults may have different motives for sport participation than those of their younger counterparts (Gill, Williams, Dowd, Beaudoin, & Martin, 1996). The social and health benefits attained through sport participation may be valued more highly than the competitive, ego-oriented aspects (Ashford, Biddle, & Goudas, 1993; Brodkin & Weiss, 1990). These differences in motives might be a factor reducing their vulnerability to the stress response because sport participation may not impose the same pressures and expectations that it does on younger athletes. The motives of many older persons for physical activity participation involve an appreciation that the benefits achieved will be to their overall health and functional capacity rather than to winning contests and beating others (McMurdo, 1999).

Sense of Control

A sense of control over one's life is very important to overall well-being. As many older adults face losses of control—such as losing their independent living status or ability to be mobile (e.g., driving a vehicle)—they may also face reductions in self-perceptions and in a sense of control over their health. Adults who do feel a sense of control may be "more likely to take health-enhancing actions, such as gathering health information, engaging in good health habits, interacting with medical providers, and adhering to medical, health, and fitness regimens" (Spiriduso, 1995, p. 318). These actions, in turn, might serve as buffers to injury vulnerability. On the other hand, when health deteriorates, individuals lose confidence in their ability to maintain control and, in turn, may feel vulnerable and anxious (Spiriduso).

Health Attitudes

Spiriduso (1995) suggested the following:

> Although many factors are modifiers of health, people's views of the importance of health, their ability to control their lives, and their self-awareness, self-esteem, and perceived health status have a direct bearing on the likelihood that they will take action to maintain health and prevent disease. (p. 307)

Finding a way to remain physically competent and maintain health status might be very important to older adults, in turn affecting their actual participation in sport and vulnerability to injury.

History of Stressors

Losses of Physical Competence

A routine part of aging is a loss of physical competence. With increasing age, increasing numbers of persons, including about 80% of those over age 70, suffer from chronic diseases (Guralnik, LaCroix, Everett, & Kovar, 1989). These actual losses of ability affect older adults both psychologically and physically. Minimizing these losses of physical competence and experiencing enjoyment of physical activity would likely have both physical and psychological benefits that might reduce risk of injury. Recent studies of exercise in elderly populations have found positive benefits of physical activity participation including preservation of existing physical function, restoration of lost function, and an absence of serious adverse physical consequences (McMurdo, 1999). Progressive exercise training has also been used to the benefit both of physical performance and emotional performance of older adults recovering from an injurious fall (Hauer et al., 2001).

Perceived Vulnerability and Anxiety

The perceptions of vulnerability and anxiety that occur with reductions in perceptions of control can have a negative effect on disease resistance. Immune systems become less efficient with age, and because of this immune system suppression, older adults are more vulnerable to the effects of stressors (Spiriduso, 1995). Both the psychological loss of control and the physiological aging interact to impair the body's ability to ward off disease (Spiriduso).

Self-Presentation and Impression Management

Martin, Leary, and Rejeski (2000) speculated on several ways in which the self-presentation motives of older adults might render them more vulnerable to injury. For example, they suggested that older persons might engage in more strenuous physical activity behaviors than they should based on their physical and health condition (e.g., walking too fast, lifting too much weight) in the interest of demonstrating that they are still capable. These self-presentation motives might put their health at risk.

Coping Resources

Religious Faith

In sport there is much talk about development of the whole athlete: spirit, mind, and body. One manifestation of the athletic spirit is religious faith. Many athletes believe religious faith helps them conquer such sport challenges as fear, performance slumps, injury, and anger. On the basis of some of the latest evidence from the medical field, faith and religious factors influence the physical and mental health of athletes.

A number of investigations have found that religious faith can make people healthier, and older adults are more likely to be actively involved in their religious faith. From a preventive standpoint, studies have found that individuals derive both physical and mental health benefits from behaviors associated with religious beliefs. Koenig's (1997) review of studies on the relationship between religion and health found that religion can positively affect health by enhancing social support, alleviating stress, and promoting healthy practices. Older athletes who hold an active religious faith may be less vulnerable to the deleterious psychological and social effects of life stress on the stress response—a factor consistently linked to increased risk of sport injury.

Post-Injury Research and Application

Although no research has been conducted with older adults to verify its utility, in the absence of competing explanations at present, the post-injury response model of Wiese-Bjornstal et al.

(1998) is used as a framework to examine possible cognitive, emotional, and behavioral responses of older adults to sport injury.

Cognitions and Emotions

Well-Being and Life Satisfaction

Feelings of emotional balance, happiness, and optimism about life constitute well-being and life satisfaction. These cognitions and emotions are highly personal and relatively transitory; subjective well-being is related to individuals' feelings about themselves. Actual health status is strongly related to subjective well-being in older adults (Spiriduso, 1995). "Older athletes who consider exercise and physical competition to be a high priority in their lives, that is, masters athletes or age-group sports competitors, report that they experience a high quality of life" (Spiriduso, 1995, p. 307). In addition to competitive sport participation, community-based exercise programs for older adults have also been found to improve both functional and well-being outcomes (King et al., 2000; Rejeski et al., 2001). One important question in future research is to ask how loss of health—such as sport injury—affects well-being and feelings of life satisfaction.

> Community-based exercise programs for older adults improve both functional and well-being outcomes.

Subjective Health Status

"Much of the way people view their health depends on their life experiences, their goals, and the coping mechanisms that they use to deal with failure and disappointments" (Spirduso, 1995, p. 304). Subjective health status typically has been found as related to feelings of well-being and life satisfaction. Health becomes increasingly important in life moving from middle age into older age, and in one study, physical changes and health events were reported by both middle-aged and older-aged groups as the most negative of changes and events in their lives (Ryff, 1989). Loss of health can contribute to a decline in the sense of well-being of older athletes.

Optimism and Pessimism

The benefit of maintaining a positive attitude and outlook has been predicted to improve recovery from physical illness. Indeed, dispositional optimism (the tendency to expect positive life outcomes) has been linked to fewer physical illness symptoms and quicker recoveries (Mahler & Kulik, 2000). Recent work has suggested that the role of both optimism and pessimism (expectation of negative life outcomes) be explored relative to recovery from illness and that they be considered not as functional opposites but as separate constructs. In a study of older coronary bypass surgery patients, for example, it was found that lack of pessimism was more predictive of positive affect, pain, and functional status over time than was optimism (Mahler & Kulik, 2000); these authors also implied a dynamic nature to this relationship in finding that the role of optimism and pessimism may be different at different points during the recovery process.

One might predict these constructs to operate in similar ways in recovery from sport injury. For example, a study by Grove (1993) noted a relationship between personality and post-injury mood states. He examined three personality variable: pessimistic explanatory style, dispositional optimism, and hardiness. Among 21 anterior cruciate ligament (ACL)-injured sport patients, depression and anger were greatest in the first month of rehabilitation for athletes with a pessimistic explanatory style. Athletes high in dispositional optimism had less depression and less confusion, whereas those high in total hardiness reported less overall mood disturbance than did those low in hardiness. Ford et al. (2000) found that athletes with more optimism cope more effectively with life change stress, thus affecting their recovery rates.

Emotional Consequences

Very limited evidence about potential long-term consequences of physical activity-related injury exists among older participants. One study of the long-term effects of injuries due to bicycle accidents found that psychological effects were present even 3 years after the reported accident (Kingma, Duursma, & ten Duis, 1997). It is worth further study to explore not only the short-term emotional responses to injury but also longer term emotional consequences.

Behaviors

Social Support

Social support networks have been found invaluable in helping older adults manage health problems such as myocardial infarction. Social interaction is one of the major correlates of well-being in older adults (Spiriduso, 1995). One study of patients at a sports medicine clinic found, among other things, that perceived social support for rehabilitation was correlated with post-injury depression (Brewer, Linder, & Phelps, 1995). Udry's (1996) review of social support in the context of athletic injuries found that social support during the rehabilitation process was positively associated with adherence to various regimens of exercise and rehabilitation.

Religious Faith

From a rehabilitative standpoint, religion and faith likely play a role in recovery. Psychological variables such as stress and anxiety delay surgical wound healing through their effects on

FIGURE 10

Possible interconnections between spirit, mind, and body in the sport injury context.

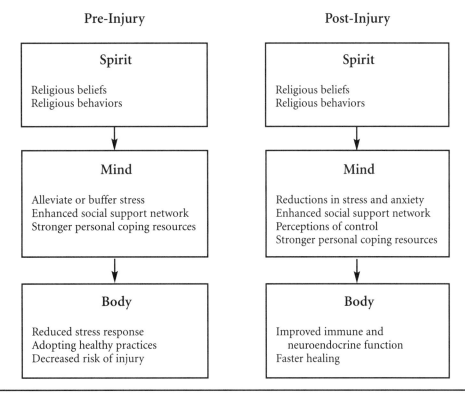

From Wiese-Bjornstal, D.M. (2000, January). Spirit, mind, and body. In D.M. Wiese-Bjornstal (Ed.), "Counseling Your Athletes" column, *Athletic Therapy Today, 5*(1), 41-42.

immune and neuroendocrine functions (Kiecolt-Glaser, Page, Marucha, MacCallum, & Glaser, 1998). Individuals under psychological stress—even relatively minor stress—heal more slowly (Marucha, Kiecolt-Glaser, & Favengehi, 1998). Psychological interventions lessen the effects of stress and improve physical recovery. If the intervention of religious faith can aid in the reduction of stress and anxiety, one would expect similar physical and mental health benefits. There is also strong evidence that social support can moderate the effects of psychological stress, and one of the primary benefits of religious affiliation and activity is the maintenance of a social support network. On the basis of these findings, Figure 10 depicts the possible interconnections between spirit, mind, and body during both the pre-injury and post-injury periods, recognizing that these relationships are speculative at present (Sloan, Bagiella, & Powell, 1999).

PRACTICAL APPLICATIONS

Pre-Injury Interventions

From a pre-injury standpoint, there are a number of interventions that might be engaged in by sport professionals to reduce the vulnerability of athletes to sport injury (Shaffer & Wiese-Bjornstal, 1999).

Stress Management
Enhancing the personal and social coping networks of athletes can aid in the management of life stress. For young athletes, this social network should involve maintaining a broad and diverse support network of family, friends, school, and religious community members. For collegiate athletes, enhancing the social network involves the establishment of new support networks both inside and outside of sport at a time when they have moved to a new community. For elite athletes, pre-injury stress management might involve such factors as financial and career planning in advance of injury so that if the worst should happen, the athlete is prepared for it. For older adults, pre-injury stress management might involve seeing exercise as a lifestyle, not an intervention, and such a strategy would, it is hoped, include a social network of friends who also engage in physical activity and sport for health and exercise. Certainly, personal stress management strategies such as relaxation skills would be important components of injury prevention efforts as well.

Risk Management
Sports medicine professionals could work with both boys and girls to enhance their ability to make more realistic assessments of their risk of physical injury. Discussions could be held at parent meetings about reinforcing to their children the importance of protective equipment and behavioral guidelines as established by the league and coach to reduce the risk of injury. The potential severity of injury could be more carefully explained to athletes, especially to boys who appear less cognizant of injury risk than girls do. Explaining why certain rules are in place rather than just giving the rules might help children recognize the good reasons behind the rules. Actions such as putting the "stop" sign on the back of youth ice-hockey player jerseys provide an example of an intervention intended to serve as a visual reminder of the seriousness of the injury risk posed by illegally checking from behind.

The sports professional has a role to play in helping achieve the balance between stretching the physical limits of children in order to improve physical skill and taking unnecessary and dangerous physical risks. As sports professionals help parents increase their awareness of their differential tolerances for risk taking among boys and girls, they can also help them find a middle ground that best advantages both sexes. Finally, sports professionals can help parents recognize when it is best to intervene in the physical risk-taking behaviors of both boys and girls.

Post-Injury Interventions

Once injury occurs, there are also a number of ways in which professionals and friends might intervene to benefit the athlete. A review of the effects of psychological interventions on medical outcomes (Kiecolt-Glaser et al., 1998) clearly demonstrates the positive effects of these interventions on both mental and physical outcomes. Similarly, an overview of psychological interventions employed in sport injury settings (Durso-Cupal, 1998) found that, in general, the use of these interventions demonstrated positive physical and psychological outcomes.

Psychological Skills Training Interventions
Ford and Gordon (1998) suggested that injured athletes use the same mental skills that benefit their sport performance to benefit their recovery from sport injury. These strategies can range from assertiveness training to arousal control and goal setting. As an example, the use of a task-focused approach to goal setting was recommended by Magyar and Duda (2000) as a way of restoring confidence post-injury. Evans, Hardy, and Fleming (2000) had success across the recovery time span with a variety of intervention strategies such as goal setting, social support, and imagery. Ross and Berger (1996) reported that a stress-inoculation training program for injured athletes resulted in less post-surgical pain and anxiety and a faster return to physical functioning. Injured athletes have reported imagery use—particularly motivational imagery—to be beneficial in their recovery process (Sordoni, Hall, & Forwell, 2000; White, 2001).

Communication
Wiese-Bjornstal, Gardetto, and Shaffer (1999) outlined a variety of ways in which attention to communication elements can enhance post-injury recovery. These strategies range from the use of effective listening skills on the part of the athletic trainer to the careful dissemination of injury education information. Thus, both the content and quality of communication should be of concern to coaches, athletic trainers, and sport psychology professionals working with injured athletes. Communication skills have been found to be among the most important aspects of effective rehabilitation, in the opinion of sports medicine professionals (Francis, Andersen, & Maley, 2000; Ninedek & Kolt, 2000; Wiese, Weiss, & Yukelson, 1991).

Coping Strategies

Philosophical Change in Mindset About Role of Pain and Injury in Sport
It is paramount that coaches and athletic trainers involved in youth and adolescent sport programs pay close attention to the training habits of young athletes, especially in light of the fact that younger athletes do not always make the wisest long-term health decisions. For every young performer who is lucky enough to succeed with injury and escape more serious consequences (e.g., gymnast Kerry Strug, Atlanta Summer Olympic Games 1996), there are many more lost to injury along the way (e.g., the death of gymnast Julissa Gomez, as described in Ryan, 1995). As Coakley (1998) suggested, perhaps athletic courage should be defined as "the ability to accept the discipline necessary to become well, not the willingness to disregard the consequences of injuries" (p. 153).

Pain Management
Given the role that pain plays in speed and quality of recovery from sport injury, strategies for coping with pain would be of benefit to injured athletes. Taylor and Taylor (1998) outlined a variety of pain education and management issues relative to an athletic population. For exam-

ple, teaching athletes to use pain as information, assessing pain perceptions, and managing pain through pharmacological and nonpharmacological techniques can all benefit both injury prevention and recovery.

Referrals

Treating the whole athlete and not just the medical case encompasses addressing physical, psychological, and spiritual needs (Wiese-Bjornstal, 2000, January). Psychological needs that cannot be met by athletes' existing personal and social coping resources may require referrals to a wide variety of mental health professionals including sport psychologists, counselors, psychologists, and psychiatrists. Referrals to religious experts (such as ministers, priests, chaplains, or rabbis) make sense in enhancing physical and psychological recovery of some athletic patients who desire such support. Sports professionals should also recognize how religious views may affect the actual medical decisions that athletes make.

FUTURE RESEARCH DIRECTIONS

Based on the findings of this review, the following recommendations for future research on developmental sport injury psychology are made. First, clearly more inclusiveness is needed in sport injury research. Little is known about the factors either increasing injury vulnerability or affecting injury response among athletes at the younger and older ages of the sport participation spectrum. Linked to chronological age is the level of participation at which the athlete competes; again, research is needed with athletes outside of the intercollegiate and elite populations. We know very little about the psychology of injury relative to participation in physical activity other than competitive sport; future studies might consider factors related to exercise and recreational sport participation as well. Possible gender differences also have received little attention in this literature, and even less attention has been paid to possible ethnic or cultural differences in sport injury psychology.

Second, it is important to continue examining the psychology of sport injury process as a dynamic process, both in its injury vulnerability factors and in the response of athletes to injury. Using prospective, repeated assessments as well as a variety of methodologies (e.g., quantitative and qualitative approaches) and designs (e.g., time series) would benefit the study of such dynamic phenomenon.

Third, intervention research is limited. Given that we are beginning to have a better understanding of some of the predisposing factors to, as well as some of the consequences of, sport injury, it is time to better explore the benefit that interventions might offer to reducing risks of injury as well as lessening the negative impact of injury once it occurs.

Fourth, the members of the sports network vary across the developmental lifespan. At each phase of the lifespan, however, those in the sports network of athletes have a shared responsibility to work together in the best interest of the athlete relative to sport injury prevention and response. Identifying the influence and roles of these various members of the sports network through research would help these team members better know how to fulfill their responsibilities to athletes.

CONCLUSIONS

Based on the research data reviewed in this chapter, it is apparent that a wide variety of developmental factors across the lifespan affect both risk of and response to sport injury. Cognitive-developmental level and physical maturational age, as well as athlete level of participation, appear strongly related to injury vulnerability as well as to the cognitive, emotional, and behavioral responses of athletes to injury. Psychological interventions can be of benefit in reducing injury vulnerability as well as improving both physical and psychological recovery from injury. These interventions can be used across the lifespan to enhance perceptions of confidence, competence, and control.

The practical messages from this chapter reinforce that it takes a collaborative effort involving sport professionals (e.g., coaches, teachers, officials, administrators), sports medicine professionals (e.g., athletic trainers, physical therapists, physicians), athletes themselves, and their nonsport social networks to proactively reduce injury vulnerability. This can be achieved through an understanding of the developmental factors affecting risk of sport injury and the consequent modification of expectations to match the motives and capabilities of the athletes. The needs, interests, and abilities of the athletes should supersede the externally imposed demands and expectations of the sport in order to find the balance between physically and psychologically challenging athletes and allowing them safe and beneficial physical and psychological environments in which to learn and perform. When injuries do occur, the use of a variety of ethical, psychological, and structural interventions by these same individuals can help athletes' recovery foci stay on positive cognitive, emotional, and behavioral tracks to the benefit of all.

References

Aaron, J., Zaglul, H., & Emery, R. E. (1999). Posttraumatic stress in children following acute physical injury. *Journal of Pediatric Psychology, 24*, 335-343.

Albert, E. (1999). Dealing with danger: The normalization of risk in cycling. *International Review for the Sociology of Sport, 34*, 157-171.

Andersen, M. B., & Williams, J. M. (1988). A model of stress and athletic injury: Prediction and prevention. *Journal of Sport and Exercise Psychology, 10*, 294-306.

Ashford, B., Biddle, S., & Goudas, M. (1993). Participation in community sport centers: Motives and predictors of enjoyment. *Journal of Sport Sciences, 11*, 249-256.

Barnes, B. C., Cooper, L., Kirkendall, D. T., McDermott, T. P., Jordan, B. D., & Garrett, W. E. Jr. (1998). Concussion history in elite male and female soccer players. *American Journal of Sports Medicine, 26*, 433-438.

Baroff, G. S. (1998). Is heading a soccer ball injurious to brain function? *Journal of Head Trauma Rehabilitation, 13(2)*, 45-52.

Baseline neurologic testing grows: Pro teams lead the way. (1998). *The Physician and Sportsmedicine, 26(7)*, 13-16.

Berlin, T. (2001). *The relationships among pain perception, pain coping, and speed of recovery in male intercollegiate athletes.* Unpublished master's thesis, University of Minnesota, Minneapolis.

Bechtel, M. (2001, February 26). Crushing. *Sports Illustrated, 94(9)*, 36-44.

Bianco, T., Malo, S., & Orlick, T. (1999). Sport injury and illness: Elite skiers describe their experiences. *Research Quarterly for Exercise and Sport, 70*, 157-172.

Bijur, P. E., Trumble, A., Harel, Y., Overpeck, M. D., Jones, D., & Scheidt, P. C. (1995). Sports and recreation injuries in U.S. children and adolescents. *Archives of Pediatrics and Adolescent Medicine, 149*, 1009-1016.

Bradbury, K., Janicke, D. M., Riley, A. W., & Finney, J. W. (1999). Predictors of unintentional injuries to school-age children seen in pediatric primary care. *Journal of Pediatric Psychology, 24*, 423-433.

Brannon, L., & Feist, J. (2000). *Health psychology: An introduction to behavior and health* (4th ed.). Belmont, CA: Wadsworth.

Brewer, B. W. (1993). Self-identity and specific vulnerability to depressed mood. *Journal of Personality, 61*, 343-364.

Brewer, B. W., Linder, D. E., & Phelps, C. M. (1995). Situational correlates of emotional adjustment to athletic injury. *Clinical Journal of Sports Medicine, 5*, 241-245.

Brewer, B. W., Van Raalte, J. L., & Linder, D. E. (1993). Athletic identity: Hercules' muscle or Achilles' heel? *International Journal of Sport Psychology, 24*, 237-254.

Bringer, J. D. (1998). *Psychosocial precursors to athletic injury in adolescent competitive athletes.* Microform Publications: University of Oregon, Eugene, OR.

Brodkin, P., & Weiss, M. R. (1990). Developmental differences in motivation for participating in competitive swimming. *Journal of Sport and Exercise Psychology, 12*, 248-263.

Burt, C. W., & Overpeck, M. D. (2001). Emergency visits for sports-related injuries. *Annals of Emergency Medicine, 37,* 301-308.

Cataldo, M. F., Finney, J. W., Richman, G. S., Riley, A. W., Hook, R. J., Brophy, C. J., & Nau, P. A. (1992). Behavior of injured and uninjured children and their parents in a simulated hazardous setting. *Journal of Pediatric Psychology, 17,* 73-80.

Centers for Disease Control and Prevention (2001). *SAFE USA: Sport injury prevention-Children and adolescents.* Retrieved March 7, 2002 from http://www.cdc.gov/safeusa/sports/child.htm.

Chan, C.S., & Grossman, H.Y. (1988). Psychological effects of running loss on consistent runners. *Perceptual and Motor Skills, 66,* 875-883.

Coakley, J. J. (1996). Socialization through sports. In O. Bar-Or (Ed.), *The child and adolescent athlete* (pp. 353-363). Oxford, England: Blackwell Science.

Coakley, J. J. (1998). *Sport in society: Issues and controversies* (6th ed.). Boston: McGraw-Hill.

Cobb, B. K., Cairns, B. D., Miles, M. S., & Cairns, R. B. (1995). A longitudinal study of the role of sociodemographic factors and childhood aggression on adolescent injury and "close calls." *Journal of Adolescent Health, 17,* 381-388.

Cogan, N., & Brown, R. I. F. (1999). Metamotivational dominance, states, and injuries in risk and safe sports. *Personality and Individual Differences, 27,* 503-518.

Cromer, B. A., & Tarnowski, K. J. (1989). Noncompliance in adolescents: A review. *Journal of Developmental and Behavioral Pediatrics, 10,* 207-215.

Currie, A., Potts, G., Donovan, W., & Blackwood, D. (1999). Illness behaviour in elite middle and long distance runners. *British Journal of Sports Medicine, 33,* 19-21.

Curry, T. (1993). A little pain never hurt anyone: Athletic career socialization and the normalization of sports injury. *Symbolic Interaction, 16,* 273-90.

Dahlquist, L. N., Gil, K. M., Armstrong, D., DeLawyer, D. D., Green, P., & Wvori, D. (1986). Preparing children for medical examinations: The importance of previous medical experience. *Health Psychology, 5,* 249-259.

Daniel, J. C., Olesniewicz, M. H., Reeves, D. L., Tam, D., Bleiberg, J., Thatcher, R., et al. (1999). Repeated measures of cognitive processing efficiency in adolescent athletes: Implications for monitoring recovery from concussion. *Neuropsychiatry, Neuropsychology, and Behavioral Neurology, 12,* 167-169.

Davis, J. O. (1991). Sports injuries and stress management: An opportunity for research. *The Sport Psychologist, 5,* 175-182.

DiFiori, J. P. (1999). Overuse injuries in children and adolescents. *The Physician and Sportsmedicine, 27(1),* 75-87.

Drotar, D. (1997). Relating parent and family function to the psychological adjustment of children with chronic health conditions: What have we learned? What do we need to know? *Journal of Pediatric Psychology, 22,* 149-165.

Duda, J. L. (1993). Goals: A social-cognitive approach to the study of achievement motivation in sport. In R. N. Singer, M. Murphey, & D. L. Tennant (Eds.), *Handbook of research in sport psychology* (pp. 421-436). New York: Macmillan.

Duda, J. L., Smart, A. E., & Tappe, M. K. (1989). Predictors of adherence in the rehabilitation of athletic injuries: An application of personal investment theory. *Journal of Sport and Exercise Psychology, 11,* 367-381.

Dunn, J. G.H. (1999). A theoretical framework for structuring the content of competitive worry in ice hockey. *Journal of Sport and Exercise Psychology, 21,* 259-279.

DuRant, R. H., Pendergrast, R. A., Donner, J., Seymore, C., & Gaillard, G. (1991). Adolescents' attrition from school-sponsored sports. *American Journal of Diseases in Children, 145,* 1119-1123.

Durso-Cupal, D. (1998). Psychological interventions in sport injury prevention and rehabilitation. *Journal of Applied Sport Psychology, 10,* 103-123.

Echemendia, R. J., Putukian, M., Mackin, R. S., Julian, L., & Schoss, N. (2001). Neuropsychological test performance prior to and following sports-related mild traumatic brain injury. *Clinical Journal of Sports Medicine, 11,* 23-31.

Ekenman, I., Hassmen, P., Koivula, N., Rolf, C., & Fellander-Tsai, L. (2001). Stress fractures of the tibia: Can personality traits help us detect the injury-prone athlete? *Scandinavian Journal of Medicine and Science in Sports, 11(2),* 87-95.

Evans, L., & Hardy, L. (1995). Sport injury and grief responses: A review. *Journal of Sport and Exercise Psychology, 17,* 227-245.

Evans, L., Hardy, L., & Fleming, S. (2000). Intervention strategies with injured athletes: An action research study. *The Sport Psychologist, 14,* 188-206.

Fisher, A.C., Domm, M. A., & Wuest, D. A. (1988). Adherence to sports-related rehabilitation programs. *The Physician and Sportsmedicine, 16,* 47-52.

Fisher, A.C., Mullins, S.A., & Frye, P.A. (1993) Athletic trainers' attitudes and judgments of injured athletes' rehabilitation adherence. *Journal of Athletic Training, 28,* 43-47.

Fisher, A.C., Scriber, K.C., Matheny, M.I., Alderman, M.H., & Bitting, L.A. (1993). Enhancing athletic injury rehabilitation adherence. *Journal of Athletic Training, 28*, 312-318.

Flint, F.A. (1991). *The psychological effects of modeling in athletic injury rehabilitation.* Unpublished doctoral dissertation, University of Oregon, Eugene.

Flint, F.A. (1998). Integrating sport psychology and sports medicine in research: The dilemmas. *Journal of Applied Sport Psychology, 10*, 83-102.

Ford, I.W., Eklund, R. C., & Gordon, S. (2000). An examination of psychosocial variables moderating the relationship between life stress and injury time-loss among athletes of high standard. *Journal of Sport Science, 18*, 301-312.

Ford, I.W., & Gordon, S. (1998). Guidelines for using sport psychology in rehabilitation. *Athletic Therapy Today, 2*, 41-44.

Francis, S. R., Andersen, M. B., & Maley, P. (2000). Physiotherapists' and male professional athletes' views on psychological skills for rehabilitation. *Journal of Science and Medicine in Sport, 3*, 17-29,

Friedman, I. M., & Litt, I. F. (1986). Promoting adolescents' compliance with therapeutic regimens. *Pediatric Clinics of North America, 33*, 955-973.

Gable, S., & Peterson, L. (1998). School-age children's attributions about their own naturally occurring minor injuries: A process analysis. *Journal of Pediatric Psychology, 23*, 323-332.

Garcia, A. P., & Aragues, G. M. (1998). Sport injuries and level of anxiety in soccer players. *Medicina Clinica, 111*(2), 45-48.

Gilchrist, J., Jones, B. H., Sleet, D. A., & Kimsey, C. D. (2000). *Exercise-related injuries among women: Strategies for prevention from civilian and military studies.* Centers for Disease Control, National Center for Injury Prevention and Control. Retrieved May 29, 2001 from http:/www.cdc.gov/mmwr/preview/mmwrhtml/rr4902a3.htm.

Gill, D. L., Williams, L., Dowd, D. A., Beaudoin, C., & Martin, J. J. (1996). Competitive orientations and motives of adult sport and exercise participants. *Journal of Sport Behavior, 19*, 307-318.

Ginsberg, H., & Opper, S. (1979). *Piaget's theory of intellectual development.* Englewood Cliffs, NJ: Prentice-Hall.

Gould, D., Udry, E., Bridges, D., & Beck, L. (1997a). Coping with season-ending injuries. *The Sport Psychologist, 11*, 379-399.

Gould, D., Udry, E., Bridges, D., & Beck, L. (1997b). Stress sources encountered when rehabilitating from season-ending injuries. *The Sport Psychologist, 11*, 361-378.

Gould, D., Udry, E., Tuffey, S., & Loehr, J. (1996). Burnout in competitive junior tennis players: I. A quantitative psychological assessment. *The Sport Psychologist, 10*, 322-340.

Green, S. L., & Weinberg, R. S. (2001). Relationships among athletic identity, coping skills, social support, and the psychological impact of injury in recreational participants. *Journal of Applied Sport Psychology, 13*, 40-59.

Grove, J. R. (1993). Personality and injury rehabilitation among sport performers. In D. Pargman (Ed.), *Psychological bases of sport injuries* (pp. 99-120). Morgantown, WV: Fitness Information Technology.

Gullone, E. (2000). The development of normal fear: A century of research. *Clinical Psychology Review, 20*, 429-451.

Gullone, E., & Cummins, R. A. (1999). The Comprehensive Quality of Life Scale: A psychometric evaluation with an adolescent sample. *Behaviour Change, 16*, 127-139.

Guralnik, J. M., LaCroix, A.Z., Everett, D. F., & Kovar, M.G. (1989). Aging in the eighties: The prevalence of comorbidity and its association with disability. *Advance Data* [Vital and Health Statistics of the National Center for Health Statistics], *170*, 1-8.

Haase, A. M., Prapavessis, H., & Owens, R. G. (1999). Perfectionism, social physique anxiety and disturbed eating attitudes among female Australian athletes. Abstract retrieved July 2, 2001 from SPORT Discus, Access Number S-502483.

Hall, H.K., Kerr, A., & Matthews, J. (1998). Precompetitive anxiety in sport: The contribution of achievement goals and perfectionism. *Journal of Sport and Exercise Psychology, 20*, 194-217.

Haines, D. J. (1997). Injury contextual factors in university recreation. *National Intramural and Recreational Sport Association Journal, 21*(2), 27-33.

Hansdottir, I., & Malcarne, V. (1998). Concepts of illness in Icelandic children. *Journal of Pediatric Psychology, 23*, 187-195.

Hanson, S. J., McCullagh, P. M., & Tonymon, P. (1992). The relationship of personality characteristics, life stress, and coping resources to athletic injury. *Journal of Sport and Exercise Psychology, 14*, 262-272.

Hauer, K., Rost, B., Rutschle, K., Opitz, H., Sprecht, N., Bartsch, P., et al. (2001). Exercise training for rehabilitation and secondary prevention of falls in geriatric patients with a history of injurious falls. *Journal of the American Geriatric Society, 49*, 10-20.

Heil, J. (1993). *Psychology of sport injury.* Champaign, IL: Human Kinetics.

Heil, J. (2000). The injured athlete. In Y. L. Hanin (Ed.), *Emotions in sport* (pp. 245-265). Champaign, IL: Human Kinetics.

Henert, S. (2000). *Exploring injured athletes' perceptions of social support and use of coping strategies as a function of injury type and gender over the course of rehabilitation.* Unpublished doctoral dissertation, University of Minnesota, Minneapolis.

Heniff, C. D. (1998). *A comparison of life event stress, weekly hassles, and mood disturbance between injured and uninjured female university athletes.* Unpublished master's thesis, University of Minnesota, Minneapolis.

Hillier, L. M., & Morrongiello, B. A. (1998). Age and gender differences in school-age children's appraisals of injury risk. *Journal of Pediatric Psychology, 23,* 229-238.

Hollander, D. B., Meyers, M. C., & LeUnes, A. (1995). Psychological factors associated with overtraining: Implications for youth sport coaches. *Journal of Sport Behavior, 18,* 3-20.

Hughes, R. H., & Coakley, J. (1991). Positive deviance among athletes: The implications of over conformity to the sport ethic. *Sociology of Sport Journal, 8,* 307-325.

Huizenga, R. (1994). *You're okay, it's just a bruise.* New York: St. Martin's Press.

Ievleva, L., & Orlick, T. (1991). Mental links to enhanced healing: An exploratory study. *The Sport Psychologist, 5,* 25-40.

Jaquess, D. L., & Finney, J. W. (1994). Previous injuries and behavior problems predict children's injuries. *Journal of Pediatric Psychology, 19,* 79-89.

Jelalian, E., Spirito, A., Rasile, D., Vinnick, L., Rohrbeck, C., & Arrigan, M. (1997). Risk taking, reported injury, and perception of future injury among adolescents. *Journal of Pediatric Psychology, 22,* 513-531.

Johnson, U. (1997). Coping strategies among long-term injured competitive athletes: A study of 81 men and women in team and individual sports. *Scandinavian Journal of Medicine and Science in Sports, 7,* 367-372.

Johnston, L. H., & Carroll, D. (2000a). Coping, social support, and injury: Changes over time and the effects of level of sports involvement. *Journal of Sport Rehabilitation, 9,* 290-301.

Johnston, L. H., & Carroll, D. (2000b). The psychological impact of injury: Effects of prior sport and exercise involvement. *British Journal of Sports Medicine, 34,* 436-439.

Jordan, B. D., Matser, E. J. T., Zimmerman, R. D., & Zazula, T. (1996). Sparring and cognitive function in professional boxers. *The Physician and Sportsmedicine, 24*(5), 87-95.

Kalish, C. (1996). Causes and symptoms in preschoolers' conceptions of illness. *Child Development, 67,* 1647-1670.

Kerr, G., & Goss, J. (1996). The effects of a stress management program on injuries and stress levels. *Journal of Applied Sport Psychology, 8,* 109-117.

Kiecolt-Glaser, J. K., Page, G. G., Marucha, P.T., MacCallum, R. C., & Glaser, R. (1998). Psychological influences on surgical recovery: Perspectives from psychoneuroimmunology. *American Psychologist, 53,* 1209-1218.

King, A. C., Pruitt, L. A., Phillips, W., Oka, R., Rodenburg, A., & Haskell, W.L. (2000). Comparative effects of two physical activity programs on measured and perceived physical functioning and other health-related quality of life outcomes in older adults. *The Journals of Gerontology: Series A, Biological Sciences and Medical Sciences, 55*(2), M74-83.

Kingma, J., Duursma, N., & ten Duis, H.J. (1997). The aetiology and long-term effects of injuries due to bicycle accidents in persons aged fifty years and older. *Perceptual and Motor Skills, 85,* 1035-1041.

Kirkendall, D. T., Jordan, S. E., & Garrett, W.E. (2001). Heading and head injuries in soccer. *Sports Medicine, 31,* 369-386.

Koenig, H.G. (1997). *Is religion good for your health?* Binghamton, NY: Haworth Pastoral Press.

Koester, M. C. (2000). Youth sports: A pediatrician's perspective on coaching and injury prevention. *Journal of Athletic Training, 35,* 466-470.

Kolt, G. S., & Kirkby, R. J. (1994). Injury, anxiety, and mood in competitive gymnasts. *Perceptual and Motor Skills, 78,* 955-962.

Koltyn, K. F. (2000). Analgesia following exercise: A review. *Sports Medicine, 29,* 85-98.

Kostanski, M., & Gullone, E. (1998). Adolescent body image dissatisfaction: Relationships with self-esteem, anxiety, and depression controlling for body mass. *Journal of Child Psychology and Psychiatry and Allied Disciplines, 39,* 255-262.

Kostanski, M., & Gullone, E. (1999). Dieting and body image in the child's world: Conceptualization and behavior. *Journal of Genetic Psychology, 160,* 488-499.

Krane, V., Greenleaf, A., & Snow, J. (1997). Reaching for gold and the price of glory: A motivational case study of an elite gymnast. *The Sport Psychologist, 11,* 53-71.

Krasnow, D., Mainwaring, L., & Kerr, G. (1999). Injury, stress, and perfectionism in young dancers and gymnasts. *Journal of Dance Medicine and Science, 3,* 51-58.

LaMott, E. E. (1994). *The anterior cruciate ligament injured athlete: The psychological process.* Unpublished doctoral dissertation, University of Minnesota, Minneapolis.

Lampton, C., & Lambert, M. (1993). The effects of psychological factors in sports medicine rehabilitation adherence. *Journal of Sports Medicine and Physical Fitness, 33,* 292-299.

Lane, B., & Gullone, E. (1999). Common fears: A comparison of adolescents' self-generated and fear survey schedule generated fears. *Journal of Genetic Psychology, 160,* 194-204.

Lavallee, L., & Flint, F. (1996). The relationship of stress, competitive anxiety, mood state, and social support to athletic injury. *Journal of Athletic Training, 31*, 296-299.

Lazarus, R. S., & Folkman, S. (1984). *Stress, appraisal, and coping.* New York: Springer.

Leddy, M.H., Lambert, M.J., & Ogles, B.M. (1994). Psychological consequences of athletic injury among high level competition. *Research Quarterly for Exercise and Sport, 65*, 349-354.

Levy, A. M. (1995). A longitudinal study of the role of sociodemographic factors and childhood aggression on adolescent injury and "close calls." *Journal of Adolescent Health, 17*, 381-388.

Lindeman, A. K. (1999). Quest for ideal weight: Cost and consequences. *Medicine and Science in Sports and Exercise, 31*, 1135-1140.

Little, J. C. (1969). The athlete's neurosis: A deprivation crisis. *Acta Psychiatrica Scandinavica, 45*, 187-197.

Luo, Yi. (1994). *The relationship of daily hassles, major life events, and social support to athletic injury in football.* Unpublished doctoral dissertation, University of Minnesota, Minneapolis.

Magyar, T. M., & Duda, J. L. (2000). Confidence restoration following athletic injury. *The Sport Psychologist, 14*, 372-390.

Mahler, H.I.M., & Kulik, J. A. (2000). Optimism, pessimism and recovery from coronary bypass surgery: Prediction of affect, pain and functional status. *Psychology, Health and Medicine, 5*, 347-358.

Mainwaring, L. M. (1999). Restoration of self: A model for the psychological response of athletes to severe knee injuries. *Canadian Journal of Rehabilitation, 12*, 145-154.

Martin, K. A., Leary, M. R., & Rejeski, W. J. (2000). Self-presentational concerns in older adults: Implications for health and well-being. *Basic and Applied Social Psychology, 22*, 169-179.

Marucha, P.T., Kiecolt-Glaser, J. K., & Favengehi, M. (1998). Mucosal wound healing is impaired by examination stress. *Psychosomatic Medicine, 60*, 362-365.

Masters, K. S., & Ogles, B. M. (1998). Associative and dissociative cognitive strategies in exercise and running: 20 years later, what do we know? *The Sport Psychologist, 12*, 253-270.

Matser, E. J., Kessels, A. G., Lezak, M. D., Jordan, B. D., & Troost, J. (1999). Neuropsychological impairment in amateur soccer players. *Journal of the American Medical Association, 282*, 971-973.

McMurdo, M. E. T. (1999). Exercise in old age: Time to unwrap the cotton wool. *British Journal of Sports Medicine, 33*, 295-296.

Morrey, M. A. (1997). *A longitudinal examination of emotional response, cognitive coping, and physical recovery among athletes undergoing anterior cruciate ligament reconstructive surgery.* Unpublished doctoral dissertation, University of Minnesota, Minneapolis.

Morrey, M. A., Stuart, M. J., Smith, A. M., & Wiese-Bjornstal, D. M. (1999). A longitudinal examination of athletes' emotional and cognitive response to anterior cruciate ligament injury. *Clinical Journal of Sports Medicine, 9*, 63-69.

Morrongiello, B. A. (1997). Children's perspectives on injury and close-call experiences: Sex differences in injury-outcome processes. *Journal of Pediatric Psychology, 22*, 499-512.

Morrongiello, B. A., & Dawber, T. (2000). Mother's responses to sons and daughters engaging in injury-risk behaviors on a playground: Implications for sex differences in injury rates. *Journal of Experimental Child Psychology, 76*, 89-103.

Morrongiello, B. A., Midgett, C., & Stanton, K. L. (2000). Gender biases in children's appraisals of injury risk and other children's risk taking behaviors. *Journal of Experimental Child Psychology, 77*, 317-336.

Morrongiello, B. A., Miron, J., & Reutz, R. (1998). Prevention of paediatric acquired brain injury: An interactive, elementary-school program. *Canadian Journal of Public Health, 89*, 391-396.

Morrongiello, B. A., & Rennie, H. (1998). Why do boys engage in more risk taking than girls? The role of attributions, beliefs, and risk appraisals. *Journal of Pediatric Psychology, 23*, 33-43.

Murray, T. M., & Livingston, L. A. (1995). Hockey helmets, face masks, and injurious behavior. *Pediatrics, 95*, 419-421.

Ninedek, A., & Kolt, G. S. (2000). Sport physiotherapists' perceptions of psychological strategies in sport injury rehabilitation. *Journal of Sport Rehabilitation, 9*, 191-199.

Nixon, H.L. (1996). Explaining pain and injury attitudes and experiences in sport in terms of gender, race, and sports status factors. *Journal of Sport and Social Issues, 20*, 33-44.

Novak, P. J., Bach, B.R., Jr., & Hager, C. A. (1996). Clinical and functional outcome of anterior cruciate ligament reconstruction in the recreational athlete over the age of 35. *American Journal of Knee Surgery, 9*, 111-116.

Owens, R. G., & Haase, A. M. (1999). Reinforcement theory and the study of perfectionism: Lessons for problems in sport psychology. Abstract retrieved July 2, 2001 from SPORT Discus, Access Number S-502501.

Palermo, T. M., & Drotar, D. (1996). Predictions of children's postoperative pain: The role of presurgical expectations and anticipatory emotions. *Journal of Pediatric Psychology, 21*, 683-698.

Palermo, T. M., Drotar, D., & Lambert, S. (1999). Psychosocial predictors of children's postoperative pain. *Clinical Nursing Research, 7*, 275-291.

Palermo, T. M., Drotar, D., & Tripi, P. A. (2000). Current status of psychosocial intervention research for pediatric outpatient surgery. *Journal of Clinical Psychology in Medical Settings, 6*, 405-426.

Patel, D. R., & Luckstead, E. F. (2000). Sport participation, risk taking, and health risk behaviors. *Adolescent Medicine, 11*, 141-155.

Pearson, L., & Jones, G. (1992). Emotional effects of sports injuries: Implications for physiotherapists. *Physiotherapy, 78*, 762-770.

Pen, L. J., & Fisher, A.C. (1994). Athletes and pain tolerance. *Sports Medicine, 18*, 319-329.

Powell, J. W., & Barber-Foss, K. D. (1999). Traumatic brain injury in high school athletes. *Journal of the American Medical Association, 282*, 989-991.

Powell, J. W., & Barber-Foss, K. D. (2000). Sex-related injury patterns among selected high school sports. *American Journal of Sports Medicine, 28*, 385-391.

Quinn, A. M., & Fallon, B. J. (1999). The changes in psychological characteristics and reactions of elite athletes from injury onset until full recovery. *Journal of Applied Sport Psychology, 11*, 210-229.

Quinn, A. M., & Fallon, B. J. (2000). Predictors of recovery time. *Journal of Sport Rehabilitation, 9*, 62-73.

Reid, S. R., & Losek, J. D. (1999). Factors associated with significant injuries in youth ice hockey players. *Pediatric Emergency Care, 15*, 310-313.

Rejeski, W., Shelton, B., Miller, M., Dunn, A. L., King, A. C., & Sallis, J. F. (2001). Mediators of increased physical activity and change in subjective well-being: Results from the Activity Counseling Trial (ACT). *Journal of Health Psychology, 6*(2), 163-170.

Roberts, W. O., Brust, J. D., & Leonard, B. (1999). Youth ice hockey tournament injuries: Rates and patterns compared to season play. *Medicine and Science in Sports and Exercise, 31*, 46-51.

Roberts, W. O., Brust, J. D., Leonard, B., & Hebert, B. J. (1996). Fair-play rules and injury reduction in ice hockey. *Archives of Pediatric and Adolescent Medicine, 150*, 140-145.

Roderick, M., Waddington, I., & Parker, G. (2000). Playing hurt: Managing injuries in English professional football. *International Review of Sport Sociology, 35*, 165-180.

Rose, J., & Jevne, R. F. J. (1993). Psychosocial processes associated with athletic injuries. *The Sport Psychologist, 7*, 309-328.

Ross, M. J., & Berger, R. S. (1996). Effects of stress inoculation training on athlete's postsurgical pain and rehabilitation after orthopedic injury. *Journal of Consulting and Clinical Psychology, 64*, 406-410.

Rotella, R.J., & Heyman, S.R. (1993). Stress, injury, and the psychological rehabilitation of athletes. In J. Williams (Ed.), *Applied sport psychology: Personal growth to peak performance* (pp. 338-355). Mountain View, CA: Mayfield.

Rotella, R. J., Ogilvie, B. C., & Perrin, D. H. (1993). The malingering athlete: Psychological considerations. In D. Pargman (Ed.), *Psychological bases of sport injuries* (pp. 85-97). Morgantown, WV: Fitness Information Technology.

Ryan, J. (1995). *Little girls in pretty boxes.* New York: Doubleday.

Ryff, C. D. (1989). In the eye of the beholder: Views of psychological well-being among middle-aged and older adults. *Psychology and Aging, 4*, 195-210.

Schwenz, S. (2001). *Athletes' perceptions of rehabilitation and the use of biofeedback to enhance psychological recovery following anterior cruciate ligament reconstruction.* Unpublished doctoral dissertation, University of Minnesota, Minneapolis.

Scott, W. A., & Couzens, G. S. (1996). Treating injuries in active seniors. *The Physician and Sportsmedicine, 24*, 63-68.

Selye, H. (1950). *The stress of life.* London: Longmans, Green, and Co.

Shaffer, S. M. (1991). *Attributions and self-efficacy as predictors of rehabilitative success.* Unpublished master's thesis, University of Illinois, Champaign-Urbana.

Shaffer, S. M. (1996). *Grappling with injury: What motivates young athletes to wrestle with pain?* Unpublished doctoral dissertation, University of Minnesota, Minneapolis.

Shaffer, S. M., & Wiese-Bjornstal, D. M. (1999). Psychosocial intervention strategies in sports medicine. In R. Ray & D. M. Wiese-Bjornstal (Eds.), *Counseling in sports medicine* (pp. 41-54). Champaign, IL: Human Kinetics.

Shelley, G. A. (1998). *The lived experience of the injured athlete: A phenomenological study.* Unpublished doctoral dissertation, University of Utah-Logan.

Shuer, M. L., & Dietrich, M. S. (1997). Psychological effects of chronic injury in elite athletes. *Western Journal of Medicine, 166*, 104-109.

Sloan, R. P., Bagiella, E., & Powell, T. (1999). Religion, spirituality, and medicine. *The Lancet, 353*, 664-667.

Smith, A. D. (1996). The female athlete triad: Causes, diagnosis, and treatment. *The Physician and Sportsmedicine, 24*(7), 67-75.

Smith, A. M. (1996). Psychological impact of injuries in athletes. *Sports Medicine, 22*, 391-405.

Smith, A. M., Stuart, M. J., Wiese-Bjornstal, D. M., & Gunnon, C. (1997). Predictors of injury in ice hockey players: A multivariate, multidisciplinary approach. *American Journal of Sportsmedicine, 25*, 500-507.

Smith, A. M., Stuart, M. J., Wiese-Bjornstal, D. M., Milliner, E. K., O'Fallon, W. M., & Crowson, C. S. (1993). Competitive athletes: Pre-injury and post-injury mood state and self-esteem. *Mayo Clinic Proceedings, 68*, 939-947.

Smith, L. L. (2000). Cytokine hypothesis of overtraining: A physiological adaptation to excessive stress? *Medicine and Science in Sports and Exercise, 32*, 317-331.

Smith, R. E., Ptacek, J. T., & Smoll, F. L. (1992). Sensation seeking, stress, and adolescent injuries: A test of stress-buffering, risk-taking, and coping skills hypotheses. *Journal of Personality and Social Psychology, 62*, 1016-1025.

Smith, R. E., Smoll, F. L., & Ptacek, J. T. (1990). Conjunctive moderator variables in vulnerability and resiliency: Life stress, social support and coping skills, and adolescent sport injuries. *Journal of Personality and Social Psychology, 58*, 360-370.

Sordoni, C., Hall, C., & Forwell, L. (2000). The use of imagery by athletes during injury rehabilitation. *Journal of Sport Rehabilitation, 9*, 329-335.

Spiriduso, W. W. (1995). *Physical dimensions of aging.* Champaign, IL: Human Kinetics.

Steiner, H., McQuivey, R. W., Pavelski, R., Pitts, T., & Kraemer, H. (2000). Adolescents and sports: Risk or benefit? *Clinics in Pediatrics, 39*, 161-166.

Sternberg, W. F., Bailin, D., Grant, M., & Gracely, R. H. (1998). Competition alters the perception of noxious stimuli in male and female athletes. *Pain, 76*, 231-238.

Stocker, D., Pink, M., & Jobe, F. W. (1995). Comparison of shoulder injury in collegiate- and master's-level swimmers. *Clinical Journal of Sports Medicine, 5*, 4-8.

Stranger, M. (1999). The aesthetics of risk: A study of surfing. *International Review for the Sociology of Sport, 34*, 265-276.

Strauss, R. H., & Lanese, R. R. (1982). Injuries among wrestlers in school and college tournaments. *Journal of the American Medical Association, 284*, 2016-2019.

Sullivan, M. J. L., Tripp, D. A., Rodgers, W. M., & Stanish, W. (2000). Catastrophizing and pain perception in sport participants. *Journal of Applied Sport Psychology, 12*, 151-167.

Sundgot-Borgen, J. (1994). Risk and trigger factors for the development of eating disorders in female elite athletes. *Medicine and Science in Sports and Exercise, 26*, 414-419.

Tajet-Foxell, B., & Rose, F. D. (1995). Pain and pain tolerance in professional ballet dancers. B*ritish Journal of Sports Medicine, 29*, 31-34.

Taylor, J., & Taylor, S. (1998). Pain education and management in the rehabilitation from sports injury. *The Sport Psychologist, 12*, 68-88.

Thompson, N. J., & Morris, R. D. (1994). Predicting injury risk in adolescent football players: The importance of psychological variables. *Journal of Pediatric Psychology, 19*, 415-429.

Thornton, J. S. (1990). Playing in pain: When should an athlete stop? *The Physician and Sportsmedicine, 18(9)*, 138-142.

Udry, E. M. (1996). Social support: Exploring its role in the context of athletic injuries. *Journal of Sport Rehabilitation, 5*, 151-163.

Udry, E. M. (1997). Coping and social support among injured athletes following surgery. *Journal of Sport and Exercise Psychology, 19*, 71-90.

Udry, E. M., Gould, D., Bridges, D., & Beck, L. (1997). Down but not out: Athlete responses to season-ending injuries. *Journal of Sport and Exercise Psychology, 19*, 229-248.

Udry, E.M., Gould, D., Bridges, D., & Tuffey, S. (1997). People helping people? Examining the social ties of athletes coping with burnout and injury stress. *Journal of Sport and Exercise Psychology, 19*, 368-395.

United States Public Health Service (1992). *Healthy people 2000: Public Health service action.* Washington, DC: Department of Health and Human Services.

Van Mechelen, W., Twisk, J., Molendijk, A., Blom, B., Snel, J., & Kemper, H. C. (1996). Subject-related risk factors for sports injuries: A 1-yr prospective study in young adults. *Medicine and Science in Sports and Exercise, 28*, 1171-1179.

Vergeer, I., & Hogg, J. M. (1999). Coaches' decision policies about the participation of injured athletes in competition. *The Sport Psychologist, 13*, 42-56.

Wasley, D., & Lox, C. L. (1998). Self-esteem and coping resources of athletes with acute versus chronic injuries. *Perceptual and Motor Skills, 86*, 1402.

Weiss, M. R., Amorose, A. J., & Allen, J. B. (2000). The young elite athlete: The good, the bad, and the ugly. In B. Drinkwater (Ed.), *Women in sport: Volume VIII of the Olympic encyclopaedia of sports medicine* (pp. 409-440). Oxford, UK: Blackwell Scientific, Ltd.

White, S. (2001). *Imagery use and speed of recovery in female intercollegiate athletes.* Unpublished master's thesis, University of Minnesota, Minneapolis.

Whiteside, J. A., Andrews, J. R., & Fleisig, G. S. (1999). Elbow injuries in young baseball players. *The Physician and Sportsmedicine, 27(6)*, 87-95.

Wiechman, S. A., & Williams, J. M. (1997). Relation of athletic identity to injury and mood disturbance. *Journal of Sport Behavior, 20*, 199-210.

Wiese, D. M., & Weiss, M. R. (1987). Psychological rehabilitation and physical injury: Implications for the sportsmedicine team. *The Sport Psychologist, 1*, 318-330.

Wiese, D. M., Weiss, M. R., & Yukelson, D. P. (1991). Sport psychology in the training room: A survey of athletic trainers. *The Sport Psychologist, 5*, 15-24.

Wiese-Bjornstal, D. M. (2000, January). Spirit, mind, and body ["Counseling Your Athletes" column]. *Athletic Therapy Today, 5*(1), 41-42.

Wiese-Bjornstal, D. M. (2000, March). Playing with injury ["Counseling Your Athletes" column]. *Athletic Therapy Today, 5*(2), 60-61.

Wiese-Bjornstal, D. M. (2001, May). In the mood ["Counseling Your Athletes" column]. *Athletic Therapy Today, 6*(3), 38-39.

Wiese-Bjornstal, D. M. (2001, July). Child's play. ["Counseling Your Athletes" column]. *Athletic Therapy Today, 6*(4), 38-39.

Wiese-Bjornstal, D. M., Gardetto, D. M., & Shaffer, S. M. (1999). Effective interaction skills for sports medicine professionals. In R. Ray & D. M. Wiese-Bjornstal (Eds.), *Counseling in sports medicine* (pp. 55-74). Champaign, IL: Human Kinetics.

Wiese-Bjornstal, D. M., & Shaffer, S. M. (1999). Psychosocial dimensions of sport injury. In R. Ray & D. M. Wiese-Bjornstal (Eds.), *Counseling in sports medicine* (pp. 23-40). Champaign, IL: Human Kinetics.

Wiese-Bjornstal, D. M., & Smith, A. M. (1999). Counseling strategies for enhanced recovery of injured athletes within a team approach. In D. Pargman (Ed.), *Psychological bases of sport injuries* (2nd ed., pp. 125-156). Morgantown, WV: Fitness Information Technologies.

Wiese-Bjornstal, D. M., Smith, A. M., & LaMott, E. E. (1995). A model of psychologic response to athletic injury and rehabilitation. *Athletic Training: Sports Health Care Perspectives, 1*, 16-30.

Wiese-Bjornstal, D. M., Smith, A. M., Shaffer, S. M., & Morrey, M. A. (1998). An integrated model of response to sport injury: Psychological and sociological dynamics. *Journal of Applied Sport Psychology, 10*, 46-69.

Williams, J. M., & Andersen, M. B. (1998). Psychosocial antecedents of sport injury: Review and critique of the stress and injury model. *Journal of Applied Sport Psychology, 10*, 5-25.

Young, K., & White, P. (1995). Sport, physical danger, and injury: The experiences of elite women athletes. *Journal of Sport and Social Issues, 19*, 45-61.

Index

Bubka, Sergeï, 503

Buhrmester, D., 190

Bukowski, W. M., 184, 186, 192

Burgess-Limerick, R., 403

burnout, 155, 511

Burton, D., 397

Bushakra, F. B., 436, 442

Bussmann, G., 505, 506

Butler, L. F., 468

Butler, R., 249, 250, 257

C

Cairns, R., 190

Campbell, J., 126

Carlsson, R., 509

Carney, S. K., 488

Carroll, D., 544

Carron, A. V., 319, 320, 322, 323, 324, 326

Carstensen, L. L., 348

Carver, C. S., 274

Cass, V., 61

Cataldo, M. F., 537

Chamalidis, P., 508

CHAMPS (Challenging Athletes' Minds for Personal Success)/Life Skills program, 391-392, 396

Chan, C. S., 549

Charles, S. T., 348

Charlesworth, W. R., 458

Chase, M. A., 103

Chelladurai, P., 11, 325-326

Chi, M. T. H., 409

Chianomonte, T., 457

Children's Attitude Toward Physical Activity (CATPA) scale, 75, 87

Children's Version of the Physical Self-Perception Profile, 131

Chodzko-Zajko, W. J., 5

Chogahara, M. 304, 324-325, 329

Cialdini, R. B., 313

Citizenship Through Sports Alliance, 470

Clark, D. O., 364

Cleary, T., 276-277

coaches, 236-237, 259-260, 510-511; actual coach behavior, 325; attitudes toward disabilities, 432-433; effect on social vulnerability, 540-541; guidelines for conducting practice, 420-421; preferred coach behavior, 325; required coach behavior, 325; white males as, 493

Coakley, J., 155, 178, 225, 550, 559

Coburn, T., 175

Cogan, N., 542

cognitive-developmental theory, 45-47, 169-170, 201; approaches in the sport and exercise psychology literature, 47-48; evaluation of, 48-50; summary of, 39. *See also* information-processing theory

cognitive evaluation theory, 18, 48

cognitive-motivational-relational theory, 20, 342-345, 350, 384-385; core-relational themes, appraisal components, and action tendencies, 343

cognitive social learning theory, 37

Colby, A., 458

Coleman, E., 61

Coleman, J. M., 438

Colker, R., 482

Colley, A., 151

Collins, K. J., 293

Comar, W., 326

competence, 366, 370, 371; developmental changes in the cognitive processes used to evaluate, 123; domains of competence, 206; sources of information on, 123-127, 303

competence motivation theory, 4, 7, 18, 47, 48, 226, 227, 262, 439; developmental perspectives, 228; and influence of significant adults and peers, 234-237; and motivational orientation, 231-234; and perceived competence, 228-231; theoretical concepts and relationships, 227 competition, 166

Comrey, A., 77

concepts, 410; action concepts, 410; condition concepts, 410; do concepts, 412; example subconcept categories and verbal reports, 411; goal concepts, 410; regulatory concepts, 410, 412

confirmatory factor analysis (CFA) model, 95

contextual theory, 55-58; approaches in the sport and exercise psychology literature, 58; evaluation of, 58-59; summary of, 42

continuity theory, 301

Contrada, R. J., 493, 494

Cooper, M., 431

Coopersmith Self-Esteem Inventory, 104

coping, 214, 217, 344-345, 348; emotion-focused coping, 344; problem-focused coping, 344

Corbett, D., 493

Corbin, C. B., 109, 110

Coté, J. 506, 510

Cortina, J. M., 76

Courneya, K. S., 296

Couzens, G. S., 553-554

Craft, D. H., 444

Crespo, C. J., 495

Crews, D. J., 384, 385, 387, 389, 392, 396

Crick, N. R., 191

Crocker, P. R. E., 240, 426, 431, 433, 434, 444

Cross, S. E., 297

Csikszentmihali, M., 204

cultural diversity. *See* gender; race and ethnicity

culture, 316-318, 328, 347; cultural identities, 480

Curnow, C., 404

Currie, A., 552

Curry, T., 539-540

Cutrona, C. E., 323

D

Damarjian, N., 398

Damasio, L., 511

Damon, W., 47, 134, 184, 457, 458

Danish, S., 17, 391

Darwin, C., 53

Davis, J. O., 548

Deci, E. L., 48, 242, 326, 366, 366n, 368, 370. *See also* self-determination theory

De Koop, P., 506, 509, 510, 513-514

Del Rey, P., 482

Dempsey, J. M., 151, 153

Dennis, P., 320

De Pauw, K. P., 494

development, 1, 30-31; adult development, 345-346; compared with change, 30-31; continuity perspective on, 34-35; discontinuity perspective on, 34-35; domains of, 31-32; idiopathic, 32; normative, 32; qualitative view of, 34; quantitative view of, 34-35

developmental domains, 31-32

developmental patterns, 123-124; adolescence (ages 13-18), 126-127; early childhood (ages 4-7), 124-125; and individuals' conceptions of ability, 127-130; middle childhood (ages 7-12), 125-126

developmental psychology, 4; lifespan developmental psychology, 4-5

developmental tasks, 300-301

DiFiori, J. P., 529

disabilities, 425-426; and ambivalence, 429; and the Americans with Disabilities Act, 430; and class placement, 442-443; definition of disability, 426-429; future research directions, 441-444; implications for practitioners, 444-447; and the inclusion movement, 427; and labeling, 427; and perceived competence, 442; and prejudice and discrimination, 432, 441-442; psychosocial factors related to physical activity participation, 430-435; self-perceptions of individuals with disabilities, 435-441; and sports

feminism, 477; common themes of feminist practice, 479; feminist psychology and cultural relations, 478-480; feminist sport studies, 477-478; feminist theories, 60, 63; gender relations and feminist theory in sport and exercise psychology, 480-481

Fennell, M. P., 151

Ferrer-Caja, E., 113

Fields, J. P., 487-488

Fine, M., 488

Fishbein, M., 432

Fisher, A. C., 549

Fisher, L. A., 463

Fiske, A. P., 316

Fleming, S., 559

Flint, F. A., 529

Folkman, S., 433, 529

Ford, I. W., 546, 556, 559

Fox, K. R., 105, 106, 109-110, 290, 294, 295, 327

Framingham Children's Study, 150

Frankel, B. G., 151

Fraser, K. L., 491

Frederichs, W., 326

Frederick, C. M., 370

Fredricks, J., 151, 152, 157, 241

Freedson, P. S., 150

French, K. E., 11, 405, 407, 414, 420

Freud, S., 33, 35-36, 50-53

Frey, K. S., 303

friendship, 167, 237; distinction from popularity, 167; friendship expectations, 179; friendship quality and support, 179-180, 182; and gender, 172-173, 174-175, 178, 183; and moral development, 184-185; and participation across activity contexts, 182-184

Frijda, N. H., 338

Fry, M. D., 12-13, 127, 128, 130, 252, 253, 254-255, 375

Furman, W., 190

G

Gable, S., 545

Gaillard, G., 545

game reasoning, 463

games analysis, 187

Garcia, A. P., 546

Garcia Bengoechea, E., 58

Garcia Coll, C., 60

Gardetto, D. M., 559

Gardner, D. E., 186

Garfinkel, I., 60

Garnets, L., 479

Gauvin, L., 338

gender, 476-477; and competitive achievement orientation, 483-485; and friendships, 172-173, 174-175, 178, 183; gender differences in adolescence, 122-123; gender stereotyping, 152, 154-155, 156, 158, 160-161, 316-31, 483; personality and gender role orientation, 482-483; and physical activity's effect on self-perceptions, 485-486; sex differences, 481-482; and sexuality, 489-492; and social perspectives, 483. *See also* feminism

general self-concept, 103

Gibbons, S. L., 9, 187, 191, 436, 442, 466, 469

Gibson, A., 492

Giebink, M. P., 460

Gilchrist, J., 545

Gill, D. L., 14-15, 16, 63, 484-485, 495-496

Gilligan, C., 33, 48, 455, 459

Glenn, S. D., 175, 230

Glover, R. J., 458

goal-reward structures, 188, 191

goal setting, 281, 392, 393; goal-setting principles, 394; outcome goals, 393; performance goals, 393; process goals, 282, 283, 393; product goals, 282; shifting goals, 283

Goggin, N. L., 358-359

Gomez, Julissa, 540

Goodling, M. D., 444

Goodnow, J. J., 315

Goodwin, D. L., 432

Gordon, S., 326, 391, 546, 559

Gorely, T., 391

Goss, J., 548

Gottman, J. M., 79, 387

Gould, D., 6-7, 8, 9, 11, 152, 225, 393, 398, 551

Graf, Steffi, 503

Graham, T. R., 214

Grant, B. C., 457

Green, S. L., 548

Green, T. S., 493

Greendorfer, S. L., 145, 154

Greenier, K. D., 134

Greenleaf, A., 541

Greenleaf, C. A., 326

Greer, K. R., 430

Greyson, J. F., 151

Griffin, N. S., 9-10

Griffin, P., 63, 490

Grossman, H. Y., 549

group involvement, 318-319, 328; group cohesion, 322-323; group norms, 320-321; group roles, 321-322; status systems, 321

Grove, J. R., 556

Gunnon, C., 541

H
Haan, N., 33, 455

Habeck, R. V., 433

Hackfort, D., 216, 336

Hall, C., 397

Hall, E., 461

Hall, H. K., 372

Hall, M. A., 477-478, 489

Hall, R., 63

Halliburton, A. L., 230-231

Hanin, Y. L., 340

Hardy, L., 398, 508-509, 559

Harold, R. D., 152, 485

Harris, A., 113, 124, 126, 127, 137

Harris, D. V., 482

Harrison, J. M., 485-486

Harter, S., 3, 4, 7, 11, 33, 47, 48, 103, 107, 112, 113, 114, 118, 120, 121-123, 131, 134, 137, 170, 179, 205-208, 211, 224, 290, 292, 293, 294, 306, 435, 436, 438. *See also* competence motivation theory; mediational model of global self-worth

Hartup, W. W., 167, 173

Hasbrook, C. A., 177, 442

Haskett, M., 438

Hausenblas, H. A., 319

Havighurst, R. J., 507

Hayashi, C. T., 19

Heath, G. W., 485

Hebert, B. J., 537

Hedrick, B. N., 436

Heesch, K. C., 496

Hegland, S. M., 457

Heidrich, S. M., 302, 303, 307

Heikinaro-Johansson, P., 435

Heil, J., 553

Heise, D. R., 94

Hellison, D. R., 17, 467, 469, 488

Hellstedt, J. C., 155, 509

Helmreich, R. L., 482

Helms, J. E., 60

Helsen, W. F., 406

Helson, R., 300

Henderson, K. A., 494

Henderson, V., 129

Henert, S., 552, 553

Heniff, C. D., 551

Herzog, A. R., 303

Higgins, E. T., 293. *See also* self-discrepancy theory

Hill, K. L., 389

Hillier, L. M., 536

Hobbs, N., 427

Hodges, N. J., 406

Hogan, P. I., 444

Hollander, D. B., 541

Holloway, J. B., 485-486

Holtbauer, R., 392

homophobia, 489-490

homosexuality, 489-490

Hooker, K., 297

hooks, b., 477

Hopper, C. A., 431

Horn, T. S., 11-12, 113, 124, 125, 126-127, 137, 153, 175, 190, 230, 236, 237, 240, 259, 326, 439-440, 442

Horne, T., 326

Horner, M. S., 483

Horner, R. H., 425

Howe, B., 237

Hoyt, C. J., 93

Huba, H. M., 349

human development theories: criteria for comparing and contrasting (summary), 31; and definition and direction of development, 33-34; and mechanisms of developmental change, 32-33; overlapping-waves theory, 35; and patterns of developmental change, 34-35; philosophical assumptions and investigational methods of, 35-36; scope or range of, 31-32; stage-based theories, 33, 35, 49, 50

Hutzler, Y., 426, 444

Hyland, D. A., 166

I

identity, 291; identity assimilation and accommodation, 302

identity foreclosure, 508

imagery, 392, 394; principles for using imagery, 395

imprinting, 53

information-processing theory, 46, 47, 49, 50, 202

intelligence theory: entity theory, 128-130; incremental theory, 128-130

internalization, 368

International Olympics Committee, 514

Iversen, G. E., 9

Izard, C. E., 346

J

Jacklin, C., 481, 482

Jackson, A., 485, 511

Jacobs, J. E., 152-153

Jacobson, L., 327

Jantz, R. K., 47, 461

Jennings, S. E., 482

jingle-jangle fallacy, 77-78

Johnson, N. G., 479

Johnson, W., 493

Johnston, L. H., 544

Jones, B. H., 545

Jordan, Michael, 348

Journal of Aging and Physical Activity, 304

Journal of Sport and Exercise Psychology, 74

Jowett, S., 511

K

Kahn, R. L., 495

Kane, M. J., 483

Kane, T. D., 281, 385, 390, 395

Kanfer, F. H., 386

Karoly, P., 384, 385, 386

Karolyi, Bela, 540-541

Kavussanu, M., 389

Keith, L. K., 105

Kendzierski, D., 296

Keogh, J. F., 9-10

overtraining syndrome (OTS), 546-547

Owens, D., 390

P

pain, 551-552; and "catastrophizing," 552

pain management, 559-560

Paoletti, I., 305

paradigm, 29

parents, influence of on youth involvement in sports, 145-146, 160-161, 234-236, 509-510, 513; and developmental issues, 146; gender differences, 154-155; model of parent socialization, 146-150; overinvolvement, 155; parents as interpreters of experience, 151-153, 156; parents as providers of experience, 153-155, 156-157; parents as role models, 150-151, 156; research on, 157-160

Parker, J. G., 173

Parks, S., 403

Parrish, M. W., 394

Partridge, R., 175

Passer, M. W., 7, 9

Patrick, H., 182-183

Patterson, P., 16

Peart, N., 106

peer relations, 165-167, 208, 237; contemporary issues, 172-174; definitional hurdles, 167; future research directions, 189-191; interventions to enhance peer relations, 180-189; and moral development, 184-186; peer acceptance and friendship, 171-172, 174-175; peers as a source of self-perceptions, affective experiences, and motivational processes, 175-178; and popularity, 167; and social impact, 167; and social preferences, 167. *See also* friendship; peer relations theories

peer relations theories: attachment theory, 168-169; cognitive-developmental perspectives, 169-170; social-cognitive theory, 170-171; social exchange theory, 169; Sullivan's model, 168; symbolic interactionist perspective, 170

Pendergast, R. A., 545

perceived ability, 103

perceived autonomy, 370

perceived competence, 103, 228, 290, 291, 370, 372, 435, 436, 442; differentiation of number and content of competence dimensions, 228-229; information sources used to judge domain-specific competence, 230-231; level and accuracy of, 229-230

Perceived Physical Competence Scale for Children, 131

performance, 274; distinction from learning, 274-278; performance enhancement, 279

Personality Attributes Questionnaire (PAQ), 482

person-centered analysis, 157

perspective taking, 203

Peterson, K., 398

Peterson, L., 545

Physical Activity and Sport in the Lives of Girls report, 486

Physical Self-Perception Profile (PSPP), 110, 131, 305

Piaget, J., 45-46, 49, 50, 169-170, 454-455, 507

Piers-Harris Children's Self-Concept Scale, 104

Pike, R., 114

Ponger, B., 490

Porretta, D. L., 444

Porter, A., 390, 395

possible selves concept, 291, 297-298

Potts, S. A., 293

practice, 405-406; appropriate amounts, 406; coaching guidelines for, 420-421; individual or team practice, 406-407

praise. *See* feedback

Prapavessis, H., 388

Priest, R. F., 462

primary family of sport, 509

Profile of Mood States (POMS), 338

Sabo, D. F., 487

Sallis, J. F., 324

Santilli, N. R., 47

Sarrazin, P., 374

Scanlan, T. K., 7, 11, 15, 152, 153, 211, 213. *See also* sport commitment model

Scheier, M. F., 274

Schiefele, U., 113

Schliesman, E., 326

Schneider, S. L., 397

Schonert-Reichel, K. A., 184

Schunk, D. H., 242, 273, 276, 283

Schultz, R., 404

Schutz, R. W., 79

Schwenz, S., 544

Scott, W. A., 553-554

Sefton, J. M., 204

Seiffge-Krenke, I., 214

Seitz, V., 2, 7

selective optimization with compensation model, 301-302

self and social responsibility model, 465

self-concept, 102-103, 104, 290, 291, 298

self-concept/self-esteem construct, 103, 104; changes in the construct, 119-123; and minority status, 429; and subdomains, 114-119

self-confidence, 103, 549

Self-Description Questionnaires, 116

self-determination theory, 48, 215, 365-371, 373; self-determination continuum, 369; sequential pattern of motivation, 366

self-discrepancy theory, 298-300

self-efficacy, 103-104, 281, 291, 292, 362, 384, 549; self-regulatory or coping efficacy, 103; task self-efficacy, 103

self-efficacy theory, 215, 361-365, 445

self-enhancement, 294

self-esteem, 102-103, 104, 289, 290, 291, 436; effect of exercise on, 291, 294; global self-esteem, 292

self-evaluations, 290

self-fulfilling prophecies, 439-441

self-judgment, 260, 273, 283

self-monitoring, 392-393, 398; self-monitoring principles, 393

self-observation, 260, 272-273, 281, 282

self-perception, 101-102, 257, 289-290, 291; critical periods for the facilitation of high self-perceptions, 135-136; developmentally based changes in children's and adolescents' perceptions, 110-113; future research directions, 304-305; and influence of the self on behavior, 294-295; reasons for studying self-perception, 292-294, 113-119; self-perception constructs, 102-104. *See also* continuity theory; developmental tasks; identity, identity assimilation and accommodation; possible selves concept; self-discrepancy theory; selective optimization with compensation model; self-schema theory

Self-Perception in Exercise Questionnaire, 304

Self-Perception Profiles, 114; summary of subdomains by age group, 115

self-perception theory, 3

self-reaction, 260, 273, 283, 284

self-regulation, 385-387; behavioral self-regulation, 271, 282; covert self-regulation, 271, 282; environmental self-regulation, 271, 282. *See also* self-regulation skills in adulthood; self-regulation skills in childhood and adolescence

self-regulation skills in adulthood, 383-385; future research directions, 395-402; practice guidelines and, 397-399; research on, 387-392. *See also* goal setting; imagery; self-monitoring; self-talk

self-regulation skills in childhood and adolescence, 269-274; children and adolescents as learners versus performers, 274-278; emulation level, 276-277; enhancing self-regulation in children and adolescents, 282-285; future research directions, 285; observation level, 275-276; psychological skills compared to

social-movement-based theory, 59-61; approaches in the sport and exercise psychology literature, 61; evaluation of, 61-63; summary of, 43

social support, 323-325, 328-329, 542, 547-548, 553, 557; emotional support, 323, 547-548; esteem support, 323; informational support, 324, 548; tangible support, 323, 548

sociocultural bias, 32

socioeconomic status (SES), 487-488

socioemotional selectivity theory, 348-350

sociological systems model, 32

Solomon, G. B., 465-466, 469, 470

Sonstroem, R. J., 109, 293, 294

Sorensen, M., 375

Spence, J. C., 338

Spence, J. T., 482

Spencer-Devlin, Muffin, 489-490

Spink, K. S., 322

Spiriduso, W. W., 554

sport commitment model, 15, 211, 212, 213

sport-confidence, 290

sport ethic, 550

sport/exercise psychology, 28

sport expertise: and action plans, 417-419; age at peak performance, 404-405; biological factors, 405; characteristics of adult sport experts, 403-404; and current event profiles, 417-419; future research directions, 421-424; implications for instruction, 419-421; knowledge accessed during competition, 410-417; and the role of practice, 405-407

Sport for Peace curriculum, 469

Sport Friendship Quality Scale (SFQS), 180, 182; sample items, 182

sport injury, 525-526, 560-561; behavioral response to, 532; cognitive appraisal and response to, 531; and communication skills, 559; dynamic model of psychological response to sport injury and rehabilitation, 529-530; emotional response to, 532; and family dynamics, 542; future research directions, 560; injury types, 528, 529; model of stress and athletic injury, 527, 528, 529; moderating factors, 531; need for change in mindset concerning, 559; psychological skills training interventions and, 559; recovery from, 532; and referrals, 560; vulnerability to, 526, 527. *See also* sport injury, in children and adolescents; sport injury, in early adulthood; sport injury, in middle and older adulthood

sport injury, in children and adolescents, 532-533; attrition motives and behaviors and, 545; behavior problems and, 537; cognitive preparation for receiving medical treatment, 544; and compliance with medical advice, 542-543; and coping skills and mechanisms, 541-542; emotions and, 535, 544-545; participation motives and, 535; perfectionism and, 533-534; risk taking and, 535-537; role modeling and, 539-540; social vulnerability and, 540-541; and training intensity, 541

sport injury, in early adulthood, 545; adherence behavior and, 552-553; anxiety and competitive worry and, 546; appraisal and, 548; and cognitive function, 550-551; coping behavior and, 552; illness/injury emotions and behaviors and, 552; injury history and, 547; and mood state, 551; personality and, 546; self-perceptions and, 548-549; sport context and, 547; stress management and, 548

sport injury, in middle and older adulthood, 553-554; emotional consequences, 557; health attitudes and, 554; losses of physical competence and, 555; optimism and, 556; perceived vulnerability and anxiety and, 555; and psychological differences in motivational approach to sport, 554; religious faith and, 555, 557-558; self-presentation motives and, 555; and sense of control, 554; and subjective health status, 556; well-being and life satisfaction and, 556

About the Editor

Maureen R. Weiss, Ph.D., is the Linda K. Bunker Professor of Education at the University of Virginia. Her research has focused on the psychological and social development of children and adolescents through participation in sport and physical activity, with particular interests in the areas of self-perceptions, motivation, observational learning, moral development, and the influence of significant others (parents, peers, coaches). Research and its applications were implemented frequently through Weiss' role as Director of the Children's Summer Sports Program at the University of Oregon from 1982-1997, a developmental skills program serving youth 5 to 13 years of age.

Weiss has published over 100 refereed articles and book chapters in her areas of expertise revolving around children's physical activity. In addition to the current book, she has co-edited 3 books on youth sport and physical activity: *Competitive Sport for Children and Youths* (with Daniel Gould), *Advances in Pediatric Sport Sciences, Vol. 2: Behavioral Issues* (with Daniel Gould), and *Worldwide Trends in Youth Sport* (with De Knop, Engstrom, and Skirstad). Weiss has mentored 17 doctoral students who hold faculty positions in higher education or research programs, and advised over 85 master's students who contribute to the field as coaches, teachers, athletic trainers, and exercise specialists.

Weiss served as President of the Association for the Advancement of Applied Sport Psychology (1995-1998), and President of the Research Consortium of AAHPERD (2001-2004). She was Editor of *Research Quarterly for Exercise and Sport* (1993-1996), Associate Editor of *Journal of Sport and Exercise Psychology* (1998-present), and Associate Editor of *Research Quarterly for Exercise and Sport* (1990-1993). She is a Fellow of the American Academy of Kinesiology and Physical Education, AAASP, and the Research Consortium.

About the Contributors

Megan L. Babkes, Ed.D., is an assistant professor in sport and exercise science at University of Northern Colorado. Her research focuses on the influence that significant others have on youths' self-perceptions, motivation, and affective responses, as well as physical activity participation among individuals with mental retardation. A former elite and intercollegiate gymnast, Megan enjoys the outdoors and teaching skiing for the National Sport Center for the Disabled.

Martin E. Block, Ph.D., is an associate professor in kinesiology at the University of Virginia. He teaches in the area of adapted physical education, and his research interests focus on including children with disabilities in general physical education. Dr. Block is the author of *A Teacher's Guide to Including Students with Disabilities in General Physical Education.*

Shirley Brodeur is a doctoral student in adapted physical education at the University of Virginia. She served as an adapted physical education specialist for Jefferson County Schools in Birmingham, Alabama, and currently is the adapted physical education specialist for the University of Virginia Children's Medical Center.

Robert J. Brustad, Ph.D., is a professor of sport and exercise science at University of Northern Colorado. His research focuses on the social psychology of sport and physical activity with particular attention devoted to socialization and developmental influences on youngsters' participation, as well as on cultural influences on involvement. He is a former editor and associate editor for the *Journal of Sport & Exercise Psychology* and served as social psychology section chair for the Association for the Advancement of Applied Sport Psychology.

Yongchul Chung, Ph.D., is an adjunct assistant professor at North Carolina A&T State University where he teaches sport psychology and research methods. He is interested in the psychology of injury, life skills development through sport, women in sport, and psychological skills training in tennis and golf. Yong is a former competitive swimmer and enjoys playing tennis and golf.

Peter R. E. Crocker, Ph.D., is Director of the School of Human Kinetics at the University of British Columbia. A professor in sport and exercise psychology, he is a former editor of *The Sport Psychologist* and President (2002) of the Canadian Society for Psychomotor Learning and Sport Psychology (SCAPPS). His research interests include stress, coping, and emotion; physical self; determinants of physical activity.

Joan L. Duda, Ph.D., is a professor of sport and exercise sciences at University of Birmingham (UK) and an adjunct professor of psychological sciences at Purdue University. Dr. Duda has been on executive boards of several sport psychology organizations including AAASP, NASPSPA, ISSP, and Division 47 of APA. She has written over 130 scientific publications and book chapters on motivation and the psychological dimensions of sport and exercise behavior.

Jacquelynne S. Eccles, Ph.D., is the Wilbert McKeachie Collegiate Professor of Psychology, Women's Studies and Education at the University of Michigan, a research scientist at the Institute for Social Research, and chair of the MacArthur Foundation Network for Successful Pathways Through Middle Childhood. Over the last 30 years, she has conducted research on a wide variety of topics including gender-role socialization, teacher expectancies, classroom influences on student motivation, and social development in the school and family context.

Jennifer A. Fredricks, Ph.D., received her doctoral degree from the Combined Program in Education and Psychology at the University of Michigan. She is an assistant professor in human development at Connecticut College. Her research focuses on motivation and school engagement, parental influences and sports, extracurricular participation, and gender-role socialization.

Karen E. French, Ph.D., is professor and chair of physical education at the University of South Carolina, Columbia. Her research focuses on development of expertise in sport, the role of cognition in sport performance, and acquisition of motor skills in children.

Diane L. Gill, Ph.D., is a professor in exercise and sport science at the University of North Carolina at Greensboro. She is past-president of Division 47 (Exercise and Sport Psychology) of the American Psychological Association, former president of NASPSPA and of the Research Consortium of AAHPERD, and former editor of the *Journal of Sport and Exercise Psychology*. Her research interests focus on physical activity and well-being across the lifespan, with an emphasis on gender and cultural diversity.

Daniel Gould, Ph.D., is the Bank of America Excellence Professor in exercise and sport science at the University of North Carolina at Greensboro. Dr. Gould's teaching efforts over the last 20 years have focused on applied sport psychology, psychology of coaching, and children in sport. His research has centered on issues such as the stress-performance relationship, burnout in young athletes, sources of athletic stress, mental preparation for peak performance, talent development, and psychological skills training. Dan has co-edited several books on children's sports and written numerous articles on the topic.

Liza Griebenauw, originally from Capetown, South Africa, is a doctoral student in kinesiology with a concentration in adapted physical education at the University of Virginia. She formerly was a lecturer at the University of the North in Pietersburg, South Africa.

Sharleen D. Hoar, Ph.D., is an assistant professor at York University in Toronto, Canada. A former competitive figure skater, Sharleen's dissertation at the University of British Columbia is an investigation of social support processes and coping with interpersonal stress in young adolescent athletes.

Thelma S. Horn, Ph.D., is an associate professor in physical education, health, and sport studies at Miami University. Her research focuses on how children's and adolescents' self-perceptions are affected by behaviors of significant adults. Dr. Horn is the former editor of the *Journal of Sport and Exercise Psychology*, a current section editor for the *Journal of Applied Sport Psychology*, and has recently edited the second edition of the text, *Advances in Sport Psychology*.

Kent C. Kowalski, Ph.D., is an assistant professor in kinesiology at the University of Saskatchewan. Winner of the SCAPPS Young Scientist Award, Kent's research focuses on the function of coping, coping with social physique anxiety, and the measurement of physical activity in children.

David Lavallee, Ph.D., is a Reader of Psychology at University of Strathclyde, Scotland. An Associated Fellow and Chartered Psychologist with the British Psychological Society, he has research and applied interests in counseling in sport and exercise settings. Dr. Lavallee serves on the editorial board of *The Sport Psychologist* and *Journal of Loss and Trauma.*

Meghan H. McDonough is a Ph.D. student in kinesiology at the University of British Columbia. A competitive flat-water kayaker and dragon-boat paddler, Meghan's research has focused upon friendship qualities and perception of competence in predicting enjoyment and commitment in young adolescent female athletes.

Sue L. McPherson, Ph.D., is a professor of physical therapy at Western Carolina University, Cullowhee, NC. Her research interests focus on cognitive factors in children's and adults' motor skill acquisition in sport and rehabilitation contexts.

Cory B. Neifer is a master's student in kinesiology at the University of Saskatchewan. A national level air-rifle competitor, Cory's research focuses on emotion and stress in competitive athletes.

Ilhyeok Park, Ph.D., specializes in measurement and applied statistics. His interests include validity and reliability issues in questionnaire development, analysis of change, structural equation modeling, and biostatistics. Currently, he is a post-doctoral fellow and research statistician at the Institute of Health Promotion Research, University of British Columbia, where he is involved in several epidemiological research projects.

Linda M. Petlichkoff, Ph.D., is a professor of kinesiology at Boise State University. She is on the National Faculty for the American Sport Education Program and a consultant for The First Tee™ Life Skills Curriculum. She has provided psychological skills training for the US Yacht Racing Union, National Guard Biathlon teams, and Boise State Women's Gymnastics and Tennis teams. Dr. Petlichkoff is President of the Association for the Advancement of Applied Sport Psychology (2002-2003). Her research interests are youth sport participation and withdrawal, competitive anxiety, goal setting techniques, and self-regulation skills.

Thomas D. Raedeke, Ph.D., is an assistant professor in sport and exercise psychology at East Carolina University. He taught at the University of Colorado for 3 years prior to his current appointment, as well as one year each as a research assistant at the Olympic Training Center in Colorado Springs and the American Sport Education Program. His interests include motivation, stress, performance psychology, and most recently, athlete and coach burnout where he has taken a motivational perspective to complement the popular view of burnout as a consequence of chronic stress.

Robert W. Schutz, Ph.D., is Professor/Director Emeritus of the School of Human Kinetics at the University of British Columbia. His research deals with statistical and measurement issues, with a specific focus on measurement and analysis of change (stochastic models, repeated measures ANOVA/MANOVA, structural equation modeling). Questionnaire and survey design is another area of interest, where he collaborated in developing three commonly used psychological scales. A third interest area, mathematical analyses of sport phenomena, involved projects such as the validity of scoring systems and tournament structures, and the prediction of ultimate performance in track and field events. He is a past president of NASPSPA and of the Canadian Association of Sport Sciences, and served on the editorial boards of numerous journals.

Gloria B. Solomon, Ph.D., is an assistant professor of kinesiology and health science at California State University, Sacramento. Dr. Solomon's research interests include the study of sociomoral development in physical activity settings and expectancy effects in competitive sport. She is a Certified Consultant and AAASP Fellow.

Martyn Standage, Ph.D., holds the position of Lecturer in sport and exercise psychology in the School of Sport and Exercise Science at the University of Bath, United Kingdom. His research interests focus on the motivational processes of individuals engaged in various physical activity contexts.

Cheryl P. Stuntz is a doctoral student in sport and exercise psychology at the University of Virginia. A former competitive swimmer, her research interests include peer relationships, aggression, character development, and motivation.

Diane E. Whaley, Ph.D., is an assistant professor of kinesiology at the University of Virginia. Her research examines the relationship between self-perceptions and physical activity behavior in adults and older adults, with a particular interest in developing effective interventions that encourage at-risk groups to become more physically active.

Diane M. Wiese-Bjornstal, Ph.D., is an associate professor and Director of Graduate Studies in the School of Kinesiology at the University of Minnesota. Her research focusing primarily on psychological responses to sport injury has been published in a wide variety of sport psychology and sports medicine journals; she also has co-edited a textbook entitled *Counseling in Sports Medicine.* Dr. Wiese-Bjornstal is a Certified Consultant and Fellow in AAASP, and has served on the editorial boards of several sport psychology journals including *JASP, TSP,* and *JSEP.*

Lavon Williams, Ph.D., is an assistant professor of kinesiology at Purdue University. Her research focuses on self-perceptions and motivational processes among adolescent and adult physical activity participants. She is a Fellow of the Research Consortium of AAHPERD, an executive board member of Research Consortium and National Association for Girls and Women in Sport, and on the editorial boards for *Women in Sport and Physical Activity Journal* and *The Sport Psychologist.* She served as an associate editor of the *AAASP Newsletter* and *Research Quarterly for Exercise and Sport.*

Paul Wylleman, Ph.D., is an associate professor at Vrije Universiteit Brussel, Belgium. His research interests include career development and interpersonal relationships of young elite athletes. He is coordinator of the "Topsport and Study" program at Vrije Universiteit Brussel where he assists student-athletes in combining academic and elite athletic careers. He is a mental consultant to the Belgian Olympic and Interfederal Committee, as well as to different elite athletes and national teams. Dr. Wylleman currently serves as member of the managing council of the European Federation of Sport Psychology (FEPSAC) and has been coordinator of FEPSAC's Special Interest Group on Career Transitions since 1993. He serves on the editorial board of *The Sport Psychologist.*

Photo List

p. 17 "The way children judge their ability changes over the elementary and middle school years." (Photo reprinted by permission of Eyewire.)

p. 62 "Recent work based on feminist theory has been a welcome addition to the literature in sport and exercise psychology." (Photo reprinted by permission of Eyewire.)

p. 84 No caption. (Photo reprinted by permission of Bright Images.)

p. 112 "In the last several decades, there has been an increasing interest in children's and adolescents' perceptions of themselves and their abilities." (Photo reprinted by permission of Eyewire.)

p. 159 "The way parents interpret a child's involvement in sport significantly affects the child's experience." (Photo reprinted by permission of Eyewire.)

p. 176 "Studying the interactions between players helps psychologists understand the effects of competition and cooperation." (Photo reprinted by permission of Bright Images.)

p. 202 "Challenging physical activity can do more than improve muscle tone—it can affect self-conception, motivation, and social interaction." (Photo reprinted by permission of The University of British Columbia Athletics Department.)

p. 229 "More developmental research is essential to understand variations in reasons for participating and withdrawing from sport and physical activity." (Photo reprinted by permission of Eyewire.)

p. 275 "A self-regulated child has different ways of thinking about her performance, her emotions, and her goals." (Photo reprinted by permission of Bright Images.)

p. 293 "Studies show that exercise habits remain consistent through middle age and begin to decline in later years." (Photo reprinted by permission of HealthWorks.)

p. 319 "Sport and physical activity involvement at any point in the lifecycle almost invariably occurs within a social milieu." (Photo reprinted by permission of Eyewire.)

p. 334 "Sport and exercise scientists have recognized that emotions have personal and social consequences." (Photo reprinted with the permission of The University of British Columbia Athletics Department.)

p. 365 "More research is necessary to fully understand what motivates certain individuals to maintain exercise habits while others abandon them." (Photo reprinted by permission of Bright Images.)

p. 389 "Maintaining an exercise regimen requires the ability to formulate and stick to both short- and long-term goals." (Photo reprinted by permission of Bright Images.)

p. 407 "Recent studies suggest that a minimum of 10 years practice and experience in a domain is necessary to develop elite performance." (Photo reprinted by permission of Eyewire.)

p. 431 "At this point, only some of the effects of exercise on adults with disabilities are understood." (Photo reprinted with permission of Martin Block.)

p. 462 "Young adult athletes exhibit lower levels of moral reasoning than those of their nonathletic peers whereas adolescents do not differ based on athletic status." (Photo reprinted by permission of Eyewire.)

p. 484 "In order to analyze exercise patterns across the lifespan, it is necessary to consider the effects of gender." (Photo reprinted with permission of HealthWorks.)

p. 510 "More research must be done to understand the psychological effects of sport injury on older participants." (Photo reprinted with permission of HealthWorks.)

p. 547 "The last 10 years has seen an explosion of research related to psychological factors in the sport injury process." (Photo reprinted with permission of HealthWorks.)